Britain

THE ROUGH GUIDE

There are more than eighty Rough Guide titles covering
destinations from Amsterdam to Zimbabwe

Forthcoming titles include
China • Corfu • Jamaica • New Zealand • South Africa
Southwest USA • Vienna

Rough Guide Reference Series
Classical Music • The Internet • Jazz • Opera • Rock Music • World Music

Rough Guide Phrasebooks
Czech • French • German • Greek • Indonesian • Italian • Mandarin Chinese
Mexican Spanish • Polish • Portuguese • Spanish • Thai • Turkish • Vietnamese

Rough Guides on the Internet
http://www.roughguides.com/
http://www.hotwired.com/rough

Rough Guide Credits

Edited by:	Rob Humphreys, Jonathan Buckley, Amanda Tomlin, Catherine McHale and Graham Parker
Series Editor:	Mark Ellingham
Editorial:	Martin Dunford, Jo Mead, Samantha Cook, Alison Cowan, Annie Shaw, Lemisse Al-Hafidh, Paul Gray, Vivienne Heller
Online Editors:	Alan Spicer (UK), Andrew Rosenberg (US)
Production:	Susanne Hillen, Andy Hilliard, Judy Pang, Link Hall, Nicola Williamson, Helen Ostick
Cartography:	Melissa Flack, David Callier
Marketing & Publicity:	Richard Trillo, Simon Carloss (UK), Jean-Marie Kelly, Jeffrey Kaye (US)
Finance:	John Fisher, Celia Crowley, Catherine Gillespie
Administration:	Tania Hummel

Thanks to the following for their help in the preparation of this guide:
Dave Reed; Lucy Ridout; Geoffrey Young; Doug Baird; Mr and Mrs Edwards at Pickett Howe; Mr and Mrs Johnson at Longlands; Celia Deeley; Gary Shaeffer and John Brown; Mr and Mrs Watson at the Falcon Hotel; Diana Ward in Malvern; Mr and Mrs Buck at Spark Bridge; Lorna Jones; Howard Nash and Leicestershire Tourism; Kate Feenan; Vicky Hunsworth; Alison Patrick; Vikki Fear; Agatha Scamporrino; Kristan Sanderson; Philip Krynsky; André Klein; Ewen Denney; Mrs A Cameron, Michael Lavelle and Chrissy Boyd; Mr & Mrs M Haycox; Polyanna Chapman; Brian Smith; Tracy Bonham; George Hay; Kevin Bruce; Janet McLaren and Fiona Martin; Toni MacPherson; Dan Smith; Ian Drum; Emma Clarke, Buzz magazine; Don Jones; Sion Brynach, at the Plaid Cymru office in Cardiff; Mel and Mary Ford; Simon Bolton; Jim Coe; Simon Lynch; Gruffudd Roland Williams; the Cox family in Brecon; Jo Griffin and Claire Hobbs; James Adam, J.A. Cragg, Sarah Price and Lorna Rotbart; Liz Porter and Robert Pickstone; Annie Surtees; Andy Moorhouse and Jelly Clarke; Chris Sharratt and Mick Tems; Jonathan Tucker; Stuart Render at National Express; the Youth Hostels Association; the National Trust; English Heritage; the Isle of Man Steam Packet Company; Caledonian MacBrayne ferries; Historic Scotland; the National Trust for Scotland; the Scottish Tourist Board; the Scottish Youth Hostel Association; and the regional tourist boards of England, Wales and Scotland.

Thanks also to Gareth Nash for proofreading; to Helen Ostick for typesetting; to Mick Bohoslawec and Melissa Flack for the maps.

The publishers and authors have done their best to ensure the accuracy and currency of all information in *The Rough Guide to Britain*; however, they can accept no responsibility for any loss, injury, or inconvenience sustained by any traveller as a result of information or advice contained in the guide.

This first edition published June 1996 by Rough Guides Ltd, 1 Mercer Street, London WC2H 9QJ.
Reprinted in 1997.

Distributed by the Penguin Group:
Penguin Books Ltd, 27 Wrights Lane, London W8 5TZ
Penguin Books USA Inc., 375 Hudson Street, New York 10014, USA
Penguin Books Australia Ltd, 487 Maroondah Highway, PO Box 257, Ringwood, Victoria 3134, Australia
Penguin Books Canada Ltd, 10 Alcorn Avenue, Toronto, Ontario, Canada M4V 1E4
Penguin Books (NZ) Ltd, 182–190 Wairau Road, Auckland 10, New Zealand

Typeset in Linotron Univers and Century Old Style to an original design by Andrew Oliver.
Printed in the United Kingdom by Cox and Wyman Ltd (Reading).
Illustrations in Part One and Part Three by Edward Briant; illustrations on p.1 and p.981 by Henry Iles.

Mapping is based upon the Ordnance Survey maps with the permission of the Controller of Her Majesty's Stationery Office, © Crown copyright

LRT Registered User No.96/2417, London Underground Map.

1040pp. Includes index.

A catalogue record for this book is available from the British Library.

ISBN 1-85828-208-X

Britain

THE ROUGH GUIDE

Written and researched by

**Robert Andrews, Jules Brown,
Samantha Cook, Emily Hatchwell,
Rob Humphreys, Tim Jepson, Phil Lee,
Mike Parker, Harriet Podger, Paul Whitfield,
Lindsay Hunt, Chris Scott, Dave Abram,
Donald Greig, Alastair Hamilton,
Gordon McLachlan, Sophie Pragnell,
Helena Smith, Tania Smith and Julian Ward**

Additional contributions by
Hamish Brown, Colin Irwin, Alan McIntosh, Sally Roy,
James D Scarlett and Mark Whatmore

THE ROUGH GUIDES

CONTENTS

LIST OF MAPS

MAP SYMBOLS

	Motorway	Λ	Campsite
	Main road		Cave
	Minor road		Public Gardens
	Railway	✕	Battlefield
	Ferry route		Motor racing circuit
	Waterway	▲	Mountain peak
	National border		Waterfall
	County border		Marshland
	Chapter division boundary	(i)	Tourist office
	Wall	⊠	Post office
✕	Airport	⊖	London Underground Station
🏛	Stately home	⊠	Gate
♙	Castle		Building
⌂	Abbey		Church
∴	Ruins	+₊+	Cemetery
♦	Museum		Park
△	Youth hostel		National Park

INTRODUCTION

I n so many ways **Britain** is a declining country. Furthermore, it has a less than brilliant climate, a laughable indigenous cuisine, and an attitude to social class that is ingrained with the habits of feudalism. Yet it is a fabulous place to travel. The capital ranks among the most characterful and multi-ethnic cities in Europe; there's a panoply of ancient towns to explore; and the countryside yields all manner of delights, from walkers' trails around the hills and lakes, through prehistoric stone circles, to traditional villages and their pubs.

The monuments of the past are a major part of the attraction, especially in **England**, the dominant and most urbanized member of the British partnership. Virtually every town bears a mark of former wealth and power, whether it be a Gothic cathedral financed from a monarch's treasury, a parish church funded by the tycoons of medieval trade, or a triumphalist Victorian civic building, raised on the income of the British Empire. In the south of England you'll find old dockyards from which the navy patrolled the oceans, while in the north there are mills that employed whole town populations. Britain's museums and galleries – several of them ranking among the world's finest – are full of treasures trawled from Europe and farther afield. And in their grandiose stuccoed terraces and wide esplanades the old resorts bear testimony to the heyday of the British holiday towns, when Brighton, Bath and diverse other towns were as fashionable and elegant as any European spa.

The English in particular tend to dwell on former glories, which is perhaps not surprising: in 1950 London was the capital of the sixth wealthiest nation on earth, but by 1980 Britain had slipped out of the top twenty. However, if London is no longer the dynamo of an empire, the dynamism of British culture is not extinct: punk rock was one of the great exports of the 1970s, and the Britpop wave is headline news in the 1990s; the art schools of London and Glasgow continue to produce major-league players on the world art scene; and when Jean-Paul Gaultier runs short of new ideas he comes to London's markets, outlets for Europe's riskiest street fashion. This is a large part of Britain's fascination, this tension between a deeply conservative tendency and a strain of individualism that often verges on the anarchic.

No less marked are the contrasts between England and its neighbours. As soon as you cross the border into predominantly rural **Wales**, you are immediately aware that you have entered a Celtic land; in **Scotland** – a land whose absorption into Britain was a rather more recent event – the presence of a profoundly non-English worldview is just as striking. In both countries there are areas in which the ancient language predominates, and in both there's an active nationalist movement striving to convert a cultural identity into political terms. Although they retain a separate legal and educational system, the Scots have no regional assembly, few autonomous powers, and are effectively governed from London, at the moment by a Conservative party that has virtually no representation north of the border. And for the Welsh the future seems to hold nothing but continuing subservience to a country that's been in control for some seven hundred years.*

Where to go

To get to grips with England, **London** is the place to start. Nowhere else in the country can match the scope and innovation of the metropolis, a colossal, frenetic city, perhaps not as immediately attractive as its European counterparts, but with so much variety

---

*Northern Ireland, constitutionally part of Great Britain, is a region to explore in conjunction with the rest of the island of Ireland. If that's your destination, you'll want a copy of the *Rough Guide to Ireland*, the most comprehensive guidebook to the Republic and the North.

that lack of cash is the only obstacle to a great time. It's here that you'll find England's best spread of nightlife, cultural events, museums, galleries, pubs and restaurants. The other large cities, such as **Birmingham**, **Newcastle**, **Leeds**, **Manchester** and **Liverpool**, lack the capital's glamour, but each of these regional cities has its strengths – for example, a resurgent arts scene in Birmingham, or the brilliant clubs in Manchester.

To be honest, though, the regional centres don't rank among the most alluring of destinations, and for many people they come a long way behind ancient cities such as **Lincoln**, **York**, **Salisbury**, **Durham** and **Winchester**, to name just those with the most celebrated of England's cathedrals. Left adrift by the industrialization of the last century and spared the worst of postwar urban development, these cities remain small-scale and manageable, more hospitable than the big commercial and industrial centres. Most beguiling of all are the long-established villages of England, hundreds of which amount to nothing more than a pub, a shop, a gaggle of cottages and a farmhouse offering bed and breakfast – **Devon**, **Cornwall**, the **Cotswolds** and the **Yorkshire Dales** harbour some especially picturesque specimens, but every county can boast a decent showing of photogenic hamlets.

Evidence of England's pedigree is scattered between its settlements as well. Wherever you're based, you're never more than a few miles from a ruined castle, a majestic country house, a secluded chapel or a monastery, and in some parts of the country you'll come across the sites of civilizations that thrived here before England existed as a nation. In the southwest there are remnants of a Celtic culture that elsewhere was all but eradicated by the Romans, and from the south coast to the northern border you can find traces of prehistoric settlers – the most famous being the megalithic circles of **Stonehenge** and **Avebury**.

Then, of course, there's the English countryside, an extraordinarily diverse terrain from which Constable, Turner, Wordsworth, Emily Brontë and a host of other native luminaries took inspiration. Most dramatic and best known are the moors and uplands – **Exmoor**, **Dartmoor**, **Bodmin Moor**, the **North York Moors** and the **Lake District** – each of which, especially the Lakes, has its over-visited spots, though a brisk walk will usually take you out of the throng.

Although the Welsh capital, **Cardiff**, boasts most of the national institutions, including the National Museum and St Fagan's Folk Museum, the essence of Wales' appeal lies outside the towns, where there is ample evidence of the warmongering which has shaped the country's development. Castles are everywhere, from hard little stone keeps of the early Welsh princes to Edward I's incomparable fortresses such as **Conwy**, **Beaumaris**, **Caernarfon** and **Harlech**. Passage graves and stone circles offer a link to the pre-Roman era when the priestly order of Druids ruled over early Celtic peoples, and great medieval monastic houses – like ruined **Tintern Abbey** – are not that difficult to find. All these attractions are enhanced by the beauty of the wild Welsh countryside. The backbone of the Cambrian Mountains terminates in the soaring peaks of **Snowdonia National Park** and the angular ridges of the Brecon Beacons, both superb walking country and both national parks. A third national park follows the **Pembrokeshire Coast**, and much of the rest of the coast remains unspoilt, though long sweeps of sand are often backed by traditional British seaside resorts: the **north Wales coast**, the **Cambrian coast** and the **Gower Peninsula** are home to many.

The majority of visitors begin their tour of Scotland in the capital, **Edinburgh**, a handsome and ancient town famous for its magnificent castle and the Palace of Holyroodhouse, as well as for the excellence of its museums – not to mention the **Edinburgh International Festival**, a world-acclaimed arts shindig held for three weeks in August and early September. From here it's just a short journey west to the capital's rival, **Glasgow**, a sprawling industrial metropolis that was once the second city of the British Empire. In recent years, though its industrial base remains in decline,

Glasgow has done much to improve its image, making the most of the impressive architectural legacy of its late eighteenth- and nineteenth-century heyday.

Southern Scotland, often underrated, features some gorgeous scenery, but nothing quite to compare to the shadowy glens and well-walked hills of the **Trossachs**, nor to the **Highlands**, whose multitude of mountains, sea cliffs, glens and lochs cover the northern two-thirds of the country. **Inverness** is an obvious base for exploring the region, although Fort William, at the opposite end of the Great Glen close by **Ben Nevis**, Scotland's highest peak, is a possible alternative. Britain's most thrilling wilderness experiences are to be had here and on the Scottish **islands**, the most accessible of which extend in a long rocky chain off Scotland's Atlantic coast, from **Arran**, through **Skye** (the most visited of the Hebrides) to the Western Isles, where the remarkably hostile terrain harbours some of the last bastions of the Gaelic language. At Britain's northern extreme lie the sea- and wind-buffeted **Orkney** and **Shetland** islands, whose rich Norse heritage makes them distinct in dialect and culture from mainland Scotland, while their wild scenery offers some of Britain's finest birdwatching and some stunning archeological remains.

When to go

Considering the temperateness of the British climate, it's amazing how much mileage the locals get out of the subject – a two-day cold snap is discussed as if it were the onset of a new Ice Age, and a week in the upper 70s starts rumours of a heatwave. The fact is that summers rarely get hot and the winters don't get very cold, except in the north of Scotland and on the highest points of the Welsh and Scottish uplands. Rainfall is fairly even, though again the mountainous areas of Wales and Scotland get higher rainfall throughout the year (the west coast of Scotland is especially damp, and Llanberis, at the foot of Snowdon, gets more than twice as much rainfall as Caernarfon, seven miles away), and in general the south of the country gets more hours of sunshine than the north.

The bottom line is that it's impossible to say with any degree of certainty what the weather will be like. May might be wet and grey one year and gloriously sunny the next, and the same goes for the autumnal months – November stands an equal chance of being crisp and clear or foggy and grim. Obviously, if you're planning to lie on a beach, or camp in the dry, you'll want to go between June and September – a period when you shouldn't go anywhere without booking your accommodation in advance. Elsewhere, if you're balancing the likely fairness of the weather against the density of the crowds, the best months to explore Britain are April, May, September and October.

AVERAGE TEMPERATURES

	Jan	Feb	March	April	May	June	July	Aug	Sept	Oct	Nov	Dec
Birmingham	42	43	48	54	60	66	68	68	63	55	48	44
	5	6	9	12	16	19	20	20	17	13	9	6
London	42	43	50	56	62	69	71	71	65	58	48	44
	5	6	10	14	17	21	22	22	19	14	9	6
Plymouth	47	47	50	54	59	64	66	68	64	58	52	49
	8	8	10	12	15	18	19	20	18	15	11	9
York	43	44	50	55	61	67	70	69	64	57	49	45
	6	7	10	13	16	19	21	21	18	14	10	7
Edinburgh	43	43	48	51	56	62	65	65	61	55	48	45
	6	6	9	11	14	17	18	18	16	13	9	7
Fort William	43	44	48	51	59	62	62	62	59	55	48	45
	6	7	9	11	15	17	17	17	15	13	9	7
Lerwick	42	42	43	46	50	55	56	56	55	50	45	43
	5	5	6	8	10	13	14	14	13	10	7	6

The figures above represent average daily maximum temperatures in°F/°C

AVERAGE RAINFALL

	Jan	Feb	March	April	May	June	July	Aug	Sept	Oct	Nov	Dec
Birmingham	3	2.1	2	2.1	2.5	2	2.7	2.7	2.4	2.7	3.3	2.6
	74	54	50	53	64	50	69	69	61	69	84	67
London	2.1	1.6	1.5	1.5	1.8	1.8	2.2	2.3	1.9	2.2	2.5	1.9
	54	40	37	37	46	45	57	59	49	57	64	48
Plymouth	3.9	2.9	2.7	2.1	2.5	2.1	2.8	3	3.1	3.6	4.5	4.3
	99	74	69	53	63	53	70	77	78	91	113	110
York	2.3	1.8	1.5	1.6	2	2	2.4	2.7	2.2	2.2	2.6	2
	59	46	37	41	50	50	62	68	55	55	65	50
Edinburgh	1.8	1.6	1.6	1.6	1.9	1.8	2.7	2.9	2.2	2.2	2.3	2.2
	47	39	39	38	49	45	69	73	57	56	58	56
Fort William	7.9	5.2	6	4.4	4.1	4.9	5.4	5.9	7.8	8.5	8.7	9.4
	200	132	152	111	103	124	137	150	199	215	220	238
Lerwick	5	3.7	3.7	2.8	2.5	2.5	2.6	3	4.4	4.7	5.5	5.8
	127	93	93	72	64	64	67	78	113	119	140	147

The figures above represent average monthly rainfall in inches/millimetres

PART ONE

THE
BASICS

TRAVELLING FROM NORTH AMERICA

For visitors from the US and Canada, the range of options will always be greatest – and the fares will usually be lowest – flying into London, Britain's busiest gateway city. Two of London's airports – Heathrow and Gatwick – handle transatlantic flights, and in terms of convenience they are about equal (see p.62). If you're planning to tour the north of England, Scotland or Wales, you might consider one of the growing number of direct flights into Manchester or Birmingham, or Glasgow in Scotland (there are no transatlantic flights into Wales). Birmingham airport is the one best equipped to get you on your way around England or Wales quickly, since it's directly linked to the rail network. It's also possible to connect in London to several other regional airports, such as Newcastle or Aberdeen, on one of Britain's domestic carriers. Domestic services to Cardiff are minimal and you are better off reaching Wales overland. See p.21 for full details on domestic flights.

SHOPPING FOR TICKETS

Given the enormous volume of air traffic crossing the Atlantic, you should have no problem finding a seat – the problem will be sifting through all the possibilities. Basic fares, especially to London, are kept very reasonable by intense competition, and discounts by bulk agents and periodic special offers from the airlines themselves can drive prices still lower. Any local **travel agent** should be able to access airlines' up-to-the-minute fares, although in practice they may not have time to research all the possibilities – you might want to call a few **airlines** direct (see p.5).

The cheapest tickets widely available from the airlines are **Apex** (Advance Purchase Excursion) tickets, which carry certain restrictions: you have to book – and pay – at least 21 days before departure, spend at least seven days abroad (maximum stay three months), and you tend to get penalized if you change your schedule. There are also winter **Super Apex** tickets, sometimes known as "Eurosavers" – slightly less expensive than an ordinary Apex, but limiting your stay to between 7 and 21 days. Some airlines also issue **Special Apex** tickets to those under 24, often extending the maximum stay to a year.

Whatever the airlines are offering, however, any number of specialist travel companies should be able to beat it. These are the outfits you'll see advertising in the Sunday newspaper travel sections, and they come in several forms. **Consolidators** buy up large blocks of tickets which airlines don't think they'll be able to sell at their published fares, and sell them at a discount. Many advertise fares on a one-way basis, enabling you to fly into one city and out from another without penalty. Besides being cheap, consolidators normally don't impose advance purchase requirements (although in busy times you'll want to book ahead just to be sure of getting a ticket), but they often charge very stiff fees for date changes; note also that airlines generally won't alter tickets after they've gone to a consolidator, forcing you to make changes only through the consolidator. Also, these companies' margins are pretty tiny, so they make their money by dealing in volume – don't expect them to entertain lots of questions.

Discount agents also wheel and deal in blocks of tickets off-loaded by the airlines, but they tend to be most worthwhile to students and under-26s, who can often benefit from their special fares and deals. Agents can also offer a range of other travel-related services such as travel insurance, rail passes, youth and student ID cards, car rentals, tours and the like. Some agencies specialize in **charter flights**, which may be even cheaper than any available scheduled flight, but again there's a trade-off: departure dates are fixed and cancellation penalties are high. **Discount travel clubs** are another option for those who travel a lot – most charge an annual membership fee, which may be worth it for discounts on air tickets, car rental and the like.

Incidentally, don't automatically assume that tickets purchased through a travel specialist will be the least expensive on offer – once you get a quote, check with the airlines and you may turn up an even cheaper promotional fare. Be advised also that the pool of travel companies is swimming with sharks – exercise caution with any outfit that sounds shifty or impermanent, and *never* deal with a company that demands cash up front or refuses to accept payment by credit card.

Regardless of where you buy your ticket, the **fare** will depend on when you travel. Fares to Britain are highest from around early June to

mid-September; they drop during the shoulder seasons, mid-September to early November and mid-April to early June, and you'll get the best deals during the low season, November through to April (excluding Christmas). The Christmas–New Year holiday period is a thing unto itself – if you want to travel at this time, book at least two or three months ahead, and be prepared for fares even higher than those in summer.

A further possibility is to see if you can arrange a **courier flight**, although the hit-or-miss nature of these makes them most suitable for the single traveller who travels light and has a very flexible schedule. In return for shepherding a parcel through customs and possibly giving up your baggage allowance, you can expect to get a highly discounted ticket. A couple of courier brokers are listed in the box below; for more options, consult *A Simple Guide to Courier Travel* (Pacific Data Sales Publishing).

DISCOUNT AGENTS, CONSOLIDATORS, TRAVEL CLUBS AND COURIER BROKERS

Air Brokers International, 323 Geary St, Suite 411, San Francisco, CA 94102 (☎1-800/883-3273). Consolidator.

Air Courier Association, 191 University Blvd, Suite 300, Denver, CO 80206 (☎303/278-8810). Courier flight broker.

Airtech, 584 Broadway, Suite 1007, New York, NY 10012 (☎1-800/575-TECH). Standby seat broker (mainly from Northeastern US cities).

Council Travel, 205 E 42nd St, New York, NY 10017 (☎1-800/743-1823) plus branches in many other US cities. Youth/student travel organization. A sister company, *Council Charter* (☎1-800/223-7402), specializes in charter flights.

Educational Travel Center, 438 N Frances St, Madison, WI 53703 (☎1-800/747-5551). Student/youth discount agent.

Last Minute Travel Club, 132 Brookline Ave, Boston, MA 02215 (☎1-800/LAST-MIN). Travel club specializing in standby deals.

Moment's Notice, 425 Madison Ave, New York, NY 10017 (☎212/486-0500). Discount travel club.

New Frontiers/Nouvelles Frontières, 12 E 33rd St, New York, NY 10016 (☎1-800/366-6387); 1001 Sherbrook East, Suite 720, Montréal, H2L 1L3 (☎514/526-8444); plus other branches in Los Angeles, San Francisco and Québec City. French discount travel firm.

Now Voyager, 74 Varick St, Suite 307, New York, NY 10013 (☎212/431-1616). Courier flight broker.

Preferred Traveler's Club, 4501 Forbes Blvd, Lanham, MD 20706 (☎1-800/444-9800). Discount travel club.

STA Travel, 48 E 11th St, New York, NY 10003 (☎1-800/777-0112) and other branches in the Los Angeles, San Francisco and Boston areas. Worldwide specialist in independent travel.

TFI Tours International, 34 W 32nd St, New York, NY 10001 (☎1-800/745-8000) plus other offices in Las Vegas and Miami. Consolidator.

Travac, 989 6th Ave, New York, NY 10018 (☎1-800/872-8800). Consolidator and charter broker.

Travel Avenue, 10 S Riverside, Suite 1404, Chicago, IL 60606 (☎1-800/333-3335). Discount travel agent.

Travel CUTS, 187 College St, Toronto, ON M5T 1P7 (☎416/979-2406) plus other branches all over Canada. Student/youth travel organization.

Travelers Advantage, 3033 S Parker Rd, Suite 900, Aurora, CO 80014 (☎1-800/548-1116). Discount travel club.

UniTravel, 1177 N Warson Rd, St Louis, MO 63132 (☎1-800/32-2222). Consolidator.

Worldtek Travel, 111 Water St, New Haven, CT 06511 (☎1-800/243-1723). Discount travel agency.

If Britain is only part of a longer journey, you might want to consider buying a **round-the-world (RTW) ticket**. Some travel agents can sell you an "off-the-shelf" RTW ticket that will stop in about half a dozen cities, in which London is very easily included; connections to other parts of Britain will probably have to be added on separately. Others will assemble a route for you, which can be tailored to your needs but is apt to be more expensive. Prices start at around $1400 ($1600 if travelling in summer) for a simple RTW ticket stopping in London.

Prices quoted in the sections below are based on the lowest typical Apex fares, exclusive of tax (which is around $40–60). Youth/student and consolidator tickets will usually be cheaper on high-volume routes, but not necessarily on the more obscure ones. Flying at weekends ordinarily adds $20–60.

FLIGHTS FROM THE US

Dozens of airlines fly from New York to London, and a few fly direct from other **East Coast** and Midwestern cities. The best low-season fares

from New York to London hover around $420 round-trip. Low-season fares to London can also start as low as $420 from Boston, $520 from Washington DC or $550 from Chicago; *Delta* flies from Atlanta for about $530; *Virgin* from Miami or Orlando for $580; *TWA* from St Louis for $600; and *Continental* from Houston for about $600. For high-season fares, add $150–250.

Don't assume you'll have to change planes when flying from the **West Coast** – *American*, *BA*, *Delta*, *United* and *Virgin* all fly nonstop to LA. Several carriers connect with flights to London from Los Angeles or San Francisco, with low-season midweek fares from both cities starting at around $600. From Seattle the price will be more in the region of $650. High-season fares will be at least $200 higher.

Several airlines fly direct to a few of Britain's **regional airports**, notably **Manchester** (from New York with *American Airlines* and *British Airways*, from Chicago with *British Airways*, from Newark with *Continental*, and from Atlanta with *Delta*), **Birmingham** (*British Airways* from New York and *American* from Chicago), **Glasgow** and **Edinburgh**. Flying direct to

---

MAJOR NORTH AMERICAN AIRLINES AND ROUTES

Only direct routes are listed below; many other routings are possible through these "gateway" cities.

Aer Lingus (☎1-800/223-6537). New York and Boston to Dublin or Shannon with connections to many major British airports.

Air Canada (Canada ☎1-800/555 1212 for local toll-free number; US ☎1-800/776-3000). Halifax, Montréal, Toronto and Vancouver to London; Toronto to Manchester; Montréal and Toronto to Glasgow.

Air India (☎212/751-6200). New York and Toronto to London.

American Airlines (☎1-800/433-7300). Boston, Chicago, Dallas-Fort Worth, Los Angeles, Miami, Nashville, New York and Raleigh-Durham to London; Chicago and New York to Manchester; Chicago to Birmingham and Glasgow.

British Airways (☎1-800/247-9297). Atlanta, Baltimore, Boston, Charlotte, Chicago, Dallas-Fort Worth, Detroit, Houston, Los Angeles, Miami, Montréal, New York, Orlando, Philadelphia, Pittsburgh, San Francisco, Seattle, Toronto, Vancouver and Washington DC to London (with extensive connections on to other UK destinations); also New York to Manchester, Birmingham and Glasgow.

Canadian Airlines (Canada ☎1-800/665-1177; US ☎1-800/426-7000). Calgary and Toronto to London.

Continental Airlines (☎1-800/231-0856). Newark and Houston to London; Newark to Manchester.

Delta Airlines (☎1-800/221-1212). Atlanta, Boston, Cincinnatti, Los Angeles, Miami, Newark, New York, Orlando and San Francisco to London; Atlanta to Manchester.

Kuwait Airways (☎1-800/458-9248). New York to London.

Northwest Airlines (☎1-800/447-4747). Boston, Detroit and Minneapolis to London.

TWA (☎1-800/221-2000). St Louis to London.

United Airlines (☎1-800/538-2929). Chicago, Los Angeles, Newark, New York, San Francisco and Washington DC to London (with many other onward connections possible through a co-operative agreement with *British Midland*).

Virgin Atlantic Airways (☎1-800/862-8621). Boston, Los Angeles, Miami, Newark, New York, Orlando and San Francisco to London; onward connections to Edinburgh with *British Midland*.

Scotland, **Glasgow** is your most likely destination, served by *American Airlines* from Chicago and *British Airways* from New York. *British Airways* offers the greatest selection of onward connections to Scotland: from Glasgow, or **Edinburgh** (via London), you can pick up connections to Aberdeen, Inverness and the islands. *Aer Lingus* also serves Edinburgh via Dublin, and *United* can ticket you straight through to a number of Scottish destinations through an agreement with *British Midland*. These airports are "common rated" with London, which means that the Apex fare should be the same. However, it's much harder to find discounted fares (consolidators and discount agents tend to deal only in high-volume destinations), and there are far fewer direct flights to these destinations than there are to London. If you fly to London on a discounted ticket, expect to pay $100–150 each way for an onward connection within Britain.

FLIGHTS FROM CANADA

In Canada, you'll get the best deal flying to London from the big gateway cities of **Toronto** and **Montréal**, where low-season midweek fares start at around CDN$650 round-trip; direct flights from Ottawa and Halifax will probably cost only slightly more. From **Edmonton** and **Calgary**, London flights start at CDN$950, from **Vancouver** around CDN$900. High-season travel will add a premium of $300–400 to all these fares.

Only *Air Canada* flies nonstop to **Manchester** (from Toronto) and **Glasgow** (Toronto and Montréal), but you can pick up direct flights from many Canadian cities to Manchester, Birmingham and Newcastle (usually via London), and to Glasgow from Vancouver, often at no extra cost over the fare to London. Again, *British Airways* is the best source for onward connections.

NORTH AMERICAN TOURS TO BRITAIN

Bargain Boating (☎1-800/637-0782). Specializes in canal trips.

BCT Scenic Walking (☎1-800/473-1210). Extensive line-up of walking trips (6–16 days) in regions including the Cotswolds, Cornwall, Devon, Dorset, the Lake District, the Scottish Borders and Highlands, and Snowdonia; also canal trips.

British Travel International (☎1-800/327-6097). Agent for all independent arrangements: air tickets, rail and bus passes, and hotels, with a comprehensive vacation home and B&B reservation service.

Dullien River and Canal Cruises (☎1-800/925-0444). Canal boat rentals.

English Lakeland Ramblers (☎1-800/724-8801). Walking tours (usually 7 or 8 days) in the Lake District, the Cotswolds and the Scottish Highlands.

English Experience ☎1-800/892-9317). Homestays with English families.

Especially Britain (☎1-800/869-0538). Fly-drives and independent rail tours built around accommodation in B&Bs, country houses and castles.

Hostelling International (US ☎202/783-6161; Canada ☎613/237 7884 or ☎800/663 5777).

Affiliated with the Youth Hostels Association and the Scottish Youth Hostels Association; organizes walking, cycling and general youth tours.

Journeys Through Scotland (☎1-800/828-7583).
Customized sightseeing and golf tours.

Le Boat (☎1-800/922-0291).
Specializes in canal trips.

Lynott Tours (☎1-800/221-2474).
Special-interest tours, hotel and castle stays, and self-drives. Agent for Ireland–Wales ferries.

Mountain Travel/Sobek (☎1-800/227-2384).
Hiking and cycling tours.

Renaissance Travel (☎1-800/43-SCOTS).
Scottish travel specialist.

Scottish Connections (☎617/770-4172).
Tours of Scotland.

Sterling Tours (☎1-800/727-4359).
Offers a variety of independent itineraries and some packages.

Select Travel Service (☎1-800/752-6787).
Customized history, literature, theatre and horticulture tours.

Travel Bound (☎1-800/456-8656).
Virgin Atlantic's tour arm.

All these companies' tours can be booked through a travel agent at no extra cost.

PACKAGES AND ORGANIZED TOURS

Although you'll want to see Britain at your own speed, you shouldn't dismiss out of hand the idea of a **package deal**. Many agents and airlines put together very flexible deals, sometimes amounting to nothing more restrictive than a flight plus accommodation and car or rail pass, and these can actually work out cheaper than the same arrangements made on arrival – especially car rental, which is expensive in Britain. A package can also be great for your peace of mind, if only to ensure a worry-free first week while you're finding your feet for a longer tour.

There are hundreds of **tour operators** specializing in travel to the British Isles. Most can do packages of the standard highlights, but of greater interest are the outfits that help you explore Britain's unique points: many organize walking or cycling trips through the countryside, boat trips along canals, and any number of theme tours based around Britain's literary heritage, history, pubs, gardens, theatre, golf – you name it. A few of the possibilities are listed in the box below, and a travel agent will be able to point out others. For a full listing, contact the *British Tourist Authority* or *Scottish Tourist Board* (see p.18).

Be sure to examine the fine print of any deal, and bear in mind that everything in brochures always *sounds* great. Choose only an operator that is a member of the *United States Tour Operator Association* (*USTOA*) or has been approved by the *American Society of Travel Agents* (*ASTA*).

TRAVELLING FROM AUSTRALIA AND NEW ZEALAND

The route from Australia and New Zealand to London is a highly competitive one, with flights via Asia generally being the cheapest option; *Philippine Airlines, Garuda, Aeroflot, Britannia, MAS* and *KLM* all offer good deals. More expensive, but worth considering for the extras – such as fly-drive, accommodation packages and free onward travel to Ireland and Europe – are *Thai Airways, Singapore Airlines, Qantas, British Airways* and *Air New Zealand*. There are few direct flights to Scotland or England's regional airports – and none to Wales – and you will generally have to route through London. **Fares** obviously depend on the time of the year: low season is from October to mid-November and mid-January to February; shoulder season is March to mid-May, September, mid-November to December 11 and December 24 to mid-January; and high season is mid-May to August and December 11–23. Students and under-26s are usually able to get a further ten percent off published prices. Travel agents such as *STA* and *Topdeck* (see below) can often get a further ten percent reduction on the airline's quoted fares.

FLIGHTS FROM AUSTRALIA

Most of the major airlines quote the same fare from all the eastern cities, with flights from Perth via Asia and Africa costing around $100 less and via the Americas about $200 more. Many of the airlines offer **stopovers** in their main cities for no extra cost.

The cheapest direct **scheduled** flight from Sydney to London Heathrow is with *Philippine Airlines*, which flies twice weekly via Manilla and Frankfurt for $1499 in low season and $1810 in high season. *Garuda* flies weekly from Sydney and Brisbane to London Gatwick via Denpasar or Jakarta for $1550–2030, and from Perth and Darwin for $1459–1750. *MAS* offers a good deal

once a week from Cairns to Heathrow via Kuala
Lumpur for $1975–2510, while *Aeroflot's* lowest
fare from Sydney to Heathrow via Moscow starts
at $1870. At the pricier end of the scale, both
British Airways and *Qantas* fly daily from
Brisbane, Sydney and Melbourne to Heathrow via
Bangkok or Singapore, and *Singapore Airlines*
flies daily from Sydney, Melbourne and Perth via
Singapore; all quote fares from $2299 in low
season up to $3099 in high season.

Via North America *United* offers the cheapest
deal: to Heathrow from Sydney or Melbourne via
LA and either New York, Washington or Chicago
for $2299 in low season, $2899 high season. *Air
New Zealand* also flies from Sydney, Melbourne
and Perth to Heathrow via Auckland and LA
several times a week for $2499–3099 ($2699–
3299 from Perth), while *Canadian Airlines* departs
daily from Sydney and Melbourne for Heathrow
via Toronto or Vancouver for $2499–3099.

Currently the best fare of all is the *Britannia
Airways* direct **charter** flight to Gatwick and
Manchester, via Singapore and Abu Dhabi, which
operates from Cairns, Brisbane, Sydney,
Melbourne, Adelaide and Perth several times a
month between November and March. Fares start
at $1199 in low season and range up to $1799 in
high season.

JAL is the only carrier to fly to **Edinburgh**, with a
daily service from Sydney and several flights a
week from Brisbane and Cairns, including an
overnight stopover in either Tokyo or Osaka and a
connecting flight from London Heathrow with
British Midland. The low-season fare is $2800.
Otherwise, the cost of an add-on flight from
London to Glasgow or Edinburgh will be anything
from $200 to $300, depending on the season; if
you're intending to visit the rest of Britain, you
may prefer to travel overland (see p.22).

VIA NEW ZEALAND

Both *British Airways* and *Qantas* fly daily from
Auckland to London Heathrow, with *Qantas* going
via Asia and *BA* via Los Angeles. *Air New
Zealand* flies four times a week from Auckland to
Heathrow via Los Angeles. Several airlines have
a stopover or a change of plane at their main city
– *Thai Airways*, for example, flies three times a
week from Auckland via Bangkok; *Korean Air* flies
four times a week from Auckland and once a
week from Christchurch via Seoul; and *JAL* flies
several times a week from Auckland with an
overnight stop in Tokyo or Osaka. There is very
little difference in price between airlines, with all
the major carriers quoting fares of NZ$2399 in

AIRLINES IN AUSTRALIA AND NEW ZEALAND

Aeroflot, 388 George St, Sydney (☎02/9233
7911); 142 Great North Road, Auckland (☎09/378
0157).

Air New Zealand, 5 Elizabeth St, Sydney (☎02/
9223 4666); corner of Customs and Queen streets,
Auckland (☎09/366 2424).

Britannia Airways, 263 Alfred St, North Sydney
(☎02/9251 1299).

British Airways, 64 Castlereagh St, Sydney
(☎02/9258 3300); Dilworth Building, corner of
Queen and Customs streets, Auckland (☎09/367
7500).

Canadian Airlines, 30 Clarence St, Sydney
(☎02/9299 7843); Floor 15, Jetset Centre, 44 Emily
Place, Auckland (☎09/309 3620).

Garuda, 175 Clarence Street, Sydney (☎02/334
9900); 120 Albert St, Auckland (☎09/366 1855).

Japanese Airlines (JAL), 17 Bligh St, Sydney
(☎02/9233 4500).

KLM, 5 Elizabeth St, Sydney (☎02/9231 6333 or 1-
800/222 747).

Korean Air, 36 Carrington St, Sydney (☎02/9262
6000); 7–9 Falcon St, Parnell, Auckland (☎09/307
3687).

Malaysian Airways (MAS), 388 George St,
Sydney (☎02/9231 5066 or 1-800/269 998); Floor
12, Swanson Centre, 12–26 Swanson St, Auckland
(☎09/373 2741).

Philippine Airlines, 49 York St, Sydney (☎1-800/
112458).

Qantas, International Square, Jamison St,
Sydney (☎02/957 0111 or 9236 3636); Qantas
House, 154 Queen St, Auckland (☎09/303 2506).

Singapore Airlines, 17 Bridge St, Sydney (☎02/
9236 0111); Lower Ground Floor, West Plaza
Building, corner of Customs and Albert streets,
Auckland (☎09/379 3209).

Thai Airways, 75–77 Pitt St, Sydney (☎02/9844
0999 or 1-800/221 320); Kensington Swan Building,
22 Fanshawe St, Auckland (☎09/377 3886).

United Airlines, 10 Barrack St, Sydney (☎02/
9237 8888); 7 City Road, Auckland (☎09/307 9500).

low season, NZ$2599 shoulder season and NZ$3199 high season, though booking through a travel agent can get you discounts of up to twenty percent.

United offers the best-value scheduled fares, with a weekly flight to Heathrow from Auckland stopping in LA and Chicago for NZ$2170 in low season and NZ$2970 high season.

The very cheapest fare is *Britannia Airways'* **charter** flight from Auckland to Gatwick and Manchester (several times a month Nov–March). Low-season fares are NZ$1415, shoulder-season

NZ$1835 and high-season NZ$2119. The only direct flight from Auckland to **Edinburgh** is the *JAL* service, which connects with *British Midland* at Heathrow for a low-season fare of NZ$3100. Arranging your own connecting flight to Scotland will cost you around NZ$250–350, depending on season.

ROUND THE WORLD FARES

If you're planning a long trip, a **round-the-world** (RTW) ticket that includes London can work out at very good value. Currently the best deals on offer

DISCOUNT TRAVEL AGENTS

Accent on Travel, 545 Queen St, Brisbane (☎07/3832 1777).

Adventure World, 73 Walker St, North Sydney (☎02/956 7766); 8 Victoria Ave, Perth (☎09/221 2300; ☎08/9221 2300 from Sept 1997).

Anywhere Travel, 345 Anzac Parade, Kingsford, Sydney (☎02/663 0411).

Brisbane Discount Travel, 360 Queen St, Brisbane (☎07/3229 9211).

Budget Travel, PO Box 505, Auckland (☎09/309 4313).

Discount Travel Specialists, Shop 53, Forrest Chase, Perth (☎09/221 1400; ☎08/9221 1400 from Sept 1997).

Flight Centres *Australia*: Circular Quay, Sydney (☎02/9241 2422); Bourke St, Melbourne (☎03/9650 2899); plus other branches nationwide. *New Zealand*: National Bank Towers, 205–225 Queen St, Auckland (☎09/309 6171); Shop 1M, National

Mutual Arcade, 152 Hereford St, Christchurch (☎09/379 7145); 50–52 Willis St, Wellington (☎04/472 8101); plus other branches nationwide.

Passport Travel, 320b Glenferrie Rd, Malvern, Melbourne (☎03/9824 7183).

STA Travel *Australia*: 732 Harris St, Ultimo, Sydney (☎02/9212 1255 or 9281 9866); 256 Flinders St, Melbourne (☎03/9347 4711); plus other offices in Townsville, Cairns and state capitals. *New Zealand*: Traveller's Centre, 10 High St, Auckland (☎09/309 4058); 233 Cuba St, Wellington (☎04/385 0561); 223 High St, Christchurch (☎03/379 9098); plus other offices in Dunedin, Palmerston North and Hamilton.

Topdeck Travel, 45 Grenfell St, Adelaide (☎08/8410 1110).

Tymtro Travel, Suite G12, Wallaceway Shopping Centre, Chatswood, Sydney (☎02/413 1219).

SPECIALIST AGENTS

Adventure Specialists, 1st Floor, 69 Liverpool St, Sydney (☎02/9261 2927). A selection of walking and cycling holidays throughout Britain.

Adventure World *Australia*: 73 Walker St Sydney (☎1-800/221 931), plus branches in Melbourne, Brisbane, Adelaide and Perth. *New Zealand*: 101 Great South Rd, Auckland (☎09/524 5118). A wide variety of tours around England and based in London.

Explore Holidays, corner of Marsden and Pennet Hills roads, Carlingford (☎02/9872 6222). Organizes guest house, farm, country inn and hotel accommodation throughout Britain, as well as special interest and rambling trips.

Destination Adventure, 2nd Floor, Premier Building, corner of Queen and Durham streets,

East Auckland (☎09/309 0464). New Zealand agents for *Peregrine Adventures*.

Peregrine Adventures, 258 Lonsdale St, Melbourne (☎03/9663 8611). Specializes in small-group walking, cycling and canoeing trips, with travel between main points by minibus.

Wiltrans/Maupintour, Level 10, 189 Kent St, Sydney (☎02/9225 0899). Fully escorted tours around Britain's historic homes and gardens, staying in upmarket accommodation.

YHA Travel Centre *Australia*: 205 King St, Melbourne (☎03/9670 9611). *New Zealand*: 36 Customs House, Auckland (☎09/379 4224). Organizes budget accommodation throughout Britain for *HI* members.

are *Cathay Pacific/United's* "Globetrotter" ticket and *Air New Zealand/KLM/Northwest's* "World Navigator", both of which offer six stopovers worldwide with limited backtracking for $2349–2899 (NZ$2999–3449). *Qantas/BA's* "Global Explorer" ticket is slightly more restrictive, allowing six stopovers but no backtracking within the US, for $2499–3099 (NZ$2399–2999). For more

flexibility, but at a higher price, *Singapore Airlines/TWA's* "Easyworld" fare (only available in Australia) allows unlimited stopovers worldwide with limited backtracking for a flat rate of $3023. Note that while it's easy enough to include London on your itinerary, a stop in Scotland may involve backtracking and can be harder to arrange.

TRAVELLING FROM IRELAND AND THE CONTINENT

If you're a student, under 26 or over 60, you'll find the ferry the most cost-effective way of getting to Britain **from Ireland**: a crossing to one of the Welsh ports plus a combined onward rail ticket costs as little as IR£40–50 return. If you're not in any of these categories, return fares start at around IR£60 – in which case, it might be worth paying a little extra for the added convenience of flying. A Super Apex return flight with *Aer Lingus*, *Ryanair* or *British Midland* from **Dublin to London** should cost in the region of IR£75, plus IR£5 tax. An *Aer Lingus* Super Apex from **Dublin to Manchester** can cost as little as IR£60 return, which is virtually identical to the train plus ferry option. *Aer Lingus* also flies direct from Dublin to **Glasgow and Edinburgh** for an Apex fare of IR£80. You can also get to either city direct from **Belfast** with both *Aer Lingus* and *British Airways* for around £60.

With the Channel Tunnel finally operational, **drivers from Europe** now have the option of taking *Le Shuttle*, as the freight trains carrying coaches, cars and motorbikes are known. *Le Shuttle* runs every fifteen minutes at peak periods – there are no advance booking facilities because in theory there's no queue – and takes 35 minutes to cover the distance between the loading terminals at Folkestone and Calais. **Fares** on *Le Shuttle* are comparable to those on the shortest ferry routes; a five-day return in low season travelling off-peak starts at £75 for a car and passengers and ranges up to £308 for a trip of more than five days, travelling on a bank holiday in peak hours. Travel between 6pm and 6am is always less expensive and you should keep an eye out for the frequent promotional fares; call ☎0990/353535 for up-to-the-minute information.

For foot passengers there are frequent through **trains** between Paris, Brussels, Lille and London run by *Eurostar*. The least expensive return fare (which must be booked 14 days in advance and include a Saturday night) is the equivalent of £87 from Paris, £79 from Brussels and £72 from Lille. Full fares with no restrictions are £155 from Paris and Brussels and £132 from Lille. Youth tickets (for under-26s) have no restrictions attached and cost £87 from Paris, £77 from Brussels and £70 from Lille. *Eurostar* also has frequent promotional fares; call ☎01233/617575 for information and reservations.

Tariffs on the **ferries** are bewilderingly complex: prices vary with the month, day or even hour at certain times of the year, not to mention how long you're staying and the size of your car. Another thing to bear in mind is that some kind of sleeping accommodation is often obligatory on the longer night crossings, pushing the price way above the basic rate. As an indication of cost, two people driving in a small car from Calais,

AIRLINES, FERRIES AND AGENTS IN IRELAND

AIRLINES

Aer Lingus, 46 Castle St, Belfast (☎01232/245151); 40 O'Connell St, Dublin 1 (☎01/844 4777).

British Airways, 9 Fountain Centre, College St, Belfast (☎0345/222111); through *Aer Lingus* in Dublin (reservations ☎1800/626747).

British Midland, Nutley, Merrion Road, Dublin (☎01/283 8833).

Ryanair, 3 Dawson St, Dublin (☎01/677 4422).

FERRIES

Irish Ferries, 16 Westmoreland St, Dublin 2 (☎01/661 0511); St Patrick's Buildings, Cork (☎021/504333); 24-hr information ☎01/661 0715.

P&O European Ferries, Rosslare (☎053/33115); c/o Tourist Office, Grand Parade, Cork (☎021/272 965).

Stena Line, Adelaide House, Haddington Terrace, Dun Laoghaire (☎01/280 7777).

Sea Cat, Sea Cat Terminal, Donegall Quay, Belfast (☎01232/312002).

Swansea Cork Ferries, 52 South Mall, Cork (☎021/276000).

AGENTS

USIT, Fountain Centre, Belfast (☎01232/324073); 10–11 Market Parade, Patrick St, Cork (☎021/270900); 33 Ferryquay St, Derry (☎01504/371888); Aston Quay, Dublin (☎01/679 8833); Victoria Place, Eyre Square, Galway (☎091/565177); Central Buildings, O'Connell St, Limerick (☎061/415064); 36–37 Georges St, Waterford (☎051/72601).

Boulogne, Dieppe, Zeebrugge or Ostend to one of the English Channel ports could expect to pay anything from £80 to £160 (the return fares are usually just twice the price), whereas the Newcastle–Gothenburg route, one of the longest crossings, would cost over £300 even at the least expensive time of the year. All the current crossings to Britain, including foot-passenger, hovercraft and catamaran services, are listed in the box above.

FERRY CONNECTIONS

	Company	Frequency	Duration
From Belgium			
Ostend–Dover	*P&O* Jetfoil	6 daily	1hr 40min
Ostend–Ramsgate	*Sally Ferries*	6 daily	4hr–4hr 30min
Zeebrugge–Hull	*North Sea*	1 daily	14hr 30min
From Denmark			
Esbjerg–Harwich	*Scandinavian*	3–7 weekly	20hr
Esbjerg–Newcastle	*Scandinavian*	Easter–Oct 6–7 weekly	20hr
From France			
Boulogne–Folkestone	*Hoverspeed* SeaCat	4–6 daily	55min
Caen–Portsmouth	*Brittany*	2–3 daily	6hr
Calais–Dover	*Hoverspeed* Hovercraft	6–14 daily	35 min
Calais–Dover	*P&O*	20–25 daily	1hr 15min
Calais–Dover	*Stena Line*	25 daily	1hr 30min
Cherbourg–Poole	*Brittany*	1–2 daily	4hr 15min
Cherbourg–Portsmouth	*P&O*	1–4 daily	5hr
Cherbourg–Southampton	*Stena Line*	1–2 daily	6–8hr
Dieppe–Newhaven	*Stena Line*	4 daily	4hr
Dieppe–Newhaven	*Stena Line*/Sea Lynx	4 daily	2hr 15min
Dunkerque–Ramsgate	*Sally Ferries*	5 daily	2hr 30min
Le Havre–Portsmouth	*P&O*	3 daily	5hr 30min
Roscoff–Plymouth	*Brittany*	1–3 daily	6hr
St Malo–Poole	*Brittany*	April–Sept 2–4 weekly	8hr
St Malo–Portsmouth	*Brittany*	1–7 weekly	8hr 45min
From Germany			
Hamburg–Harwich	*Scandinavian*	3–7 daily	21hr
Hamburg–Newcastle	*Scandinavian*	4–7 weekly	23hr 30min
From Holland			
Amsterdam–Newcastle	*Scandinavian*	mid-May to mid-Sept 3–7 weekly	15hr
Hook of Holland–Harwich	*Stena Line*	2 daily	7hr
Rotterdam–Hull	*North Sea*	1 daily	14hr
Vlissingen–Sheerness	*Eurolink*	2 daily	7hr
From Ireland.			
Cork–Swansea	*Swansea–Cork Ferries*	1 daily	10hr
Dun Laoghaire–Holyhead	*Irish Ferries*	2 daily	3hr 45min
Dun Laoghaire–Holyhead	*Stena Line*	2–4 daily	3hr 30min
Dun Laoghaire–Holyhead	*Stena Line*/Sea Lynx	4 daily	1hr 50min
Dun Laoghaire–Holyhead	*Stena Line*/Stena HSS	4 daily	1hr 40min
Rosslare–Fishguard	*Stena Line*	1–2 daily	3hr 30min
Rosslare–Fishguard	*Stena Line*/Sea Lynx	3–4 daily	1hr 40min
Rosslare–Pembroke	*Irish Ferries*	2 daily	4hr 15min
From Norway			
Stavanger/Bergen–Newcastle	*Color Line*	1–3 weekly	20hr/27hr

FERRY CONNECTIONS (cont.)			
	Company	**Frequency**	**Duration**
Bergen–Lerwick–Aberdeen	*P&O Scottish Ferries*	June–Aug 3 weekly	14hr/26hr
From Spain			
Bilbao–Portsmouth	*P&O*	1–2 weekly	30hr
Santander–Plymouth	*Brittany*	March–Nov 1–2 weekly	24hr
Santander–Portsmouth	*Brittany*	Nov–March 1 weekly	30–33hr
From Sweden			
Gothenburg–Harwich	*Scandinavian*	3–4 weekly	24hr
Gothenburg–Newcastle	*Scandinavian*	June to mid-Sept 1 weekly	24hr

VISAS, CUSTOMS, REGULATIONS AND TAX

Citizens of all the countries of Europe – other than Albania, Romania, Bulgaria and the republics of the former Soviet Union (with the exception of the Baltic States) – can enter Britain with just a passport, generally for up to three months. US, Canadian, Australian and New Zealand citizens can enter the country for up to six months with just a passport. All other nationalities require a visa, obtainable from the British Consular office in the country of application.

For stays of longer than six months, **US**, **Canadian**, **Australian** and **New Zealand** citizens should apply to the British Embassy or High Commission (see box overleaf). In the US, full-time, bona fide college students can get temporary work or study permits through the *Council on International Education Exchange (CIEE)*, 205 E 42nd St, New York, NY 10017 (☎212/661-1414).

Work permits cost $200 to arrange and are good for six months. Australian and New Zealand citizens need an Entry Clearance Certificate for stays of longer than six months; those between the ages of 17 and 26 can stay for up to two years with a Working Holiday Entry Certificate. Extended stays are also possible for those with British grandparents. Applications must be made to the High Commission in person or by post, which takes around four weeks.

Since the inauguration of the EU Single Market, travellers coming into Britain directly from another EU country do not have to make a declaration to **Customs** at their place of entry. This means you can bring almost as much French wine or German beer across the Channel as you like – the limits are 90 litres of wine and 110 of beer, which should suffice for anyone's requirements. However, there are still restrictions on the volume of **tax- or duty-free** goods you can bring into the country, so you can't invest in a stockpile of cheap cigarettes on your flight, whether you're coming from Paris or New York. The duty-free allowances are as follows:

• **Tobacco**: 200 cigarettes, or 100 cigarillos, or 50 cigars, or 250 grammes of loose tobacco.

• **Alcohol**: Two litres of still wine **plus** one litre of drink over 22 percent alcohol, or two litres of alcoholic drink not over 22 percent, or another two litres of still wine.

• **Perfumes**: 60ml of perfume plus 250ml of toilet water.

Plus **other goods** to the value of £136.

BRITISH EMBASSIES AND HIGH COMMISSIONS ABROAD

Australia British High Commission, Commonwealth Ave, Yarralumla, Canberra, ACT 2600 (☎06/257 1982).

Canada British High Commission, 80 Elgin St, Ottawa, ON K1P 5K7 (☎613/237-1530).

Ireland 31–33 Merrion Rd, Dublin 4 (☎01/295 5211).

New Zealand British High Commission, 44 Hill St, Wellington (☎04/726-049).

USA 3100 Massachusetts Ave, NW, Washington, DC 20008 (☎202/462-1340).

OVERSEAS REPRESENTATION IN BRITAIN

Australia High Commission, Australia House, The Strand, London WC2 (☎0171/379 4334).

Consulate, 80 Hanover St, Edinburgh (☎0131/226 6271).

Canada High Commission, 1 Grosvenor Square, London W1 (☎0171/258 6600).

Consulate, 151 St Vincent St, Glasgow (☎0141/221 4415).

Ireland Embassy, 17 Grosvenor Place, London SW1 (☎0171/235 2171).

New Zealand High Commission, New Zealand House, 80 Haymarket, London SW1 (☎0171/930 8422).

USA Embassy, 5 Upper Grosvenor St, London W1 (☎0171/499 9000).

Consulate, 3 Regent Terrace, Edinburgh (☎0131/556 8315).

There are **import restrictions** on a variety of articles and substances, from firearms to furs derived from endangered species, none of which should bother the normal tourist. However, if you need any clarification on British import regulations, contact HM Customs and Excise, Dorset House, Stanford Street, London SE1 9PJ (☎0171/928 3344). You are not allowed to bring **pets** into Britain.

Most goods in Britain, with the chief exceptions of books and food, are subject to **Value Added Tax** (VAT), which increases the cost of an item by 17.5 percent and is usually included in the quoted price. Visitors from non-EU countries can save a lot of money through the Retail Export Scheme, which allows a refund of VAT on goods to be taken out of the country. (Savings will usually be minimal for EU nationals, because of the rates at which the goods will be taxed upon import to the home country.) Note that not all shops participate in this scheme (those doing so will display a sign to that effect) and that you cannot reclaim VAT charged on hotel bills or other services.

MONEY, BANKS AND COSTS

The easiest and safest way to carry your money is in travellers' cheques, available for a small commission (normally one percent) from any major bank. The most commonly accepted travellers' cheques are American Express, followed by Visa and Thomas Cook – most cheques issued by banks will be one of these three brands. You'll usually pay commission again when you cash each cheque, normally another one percent or so, or a flat rate – though no commission is payable on Amex cheques exchanged at Amex branches. Keep a record of the cheques as you cash them, and

you can get the value of all uncashed cheques refunded immediately if you lose them.

You'll find that most hotels, shops and restaurants in Britain accept the major **credit cards** – *Access/MasterCard*, *Visa/Barclaycard*, *American Express* and *Diners Club* – although they're less useful in the most rural areas, and smaller establishments all over the country, such as B&B accommodation, will often accept cash only. Your card will also enable you to get cash advances from certain ATMs – call the issuing bank or credit company to get a list of British locations. In addition, you may be able to make withdrawals using your **ATM cash card** – your bank's international banking department should be able to advise on this. Make sure you have a personal identification number (PIN) that's designed to work overseas.

There are no exchange controls in Britain, so you can bring in as much cash as you like and change travellers' cheques up to any amount.

BANKS AND BUREAUX DE CHANGE

Banks are almost always the best places to **change money and cheques**, and every sizeable town in England and Wales has a branch of at least one of the big four high-street banks: *National Westminster*, *Barclays*, *Lloyds* and *Midland* (listed in descending order of the number of branches). Basic **opening hours** are Mon–Fri 9.30am–3.30pm, though many branches in larger towns stay open an hour later in the afternoons and also open on Saturday morning. In Scotland the big high-street names are *Bank of Scotland*, *Royal Bank of Scotland*, *Clydesdale* and *TSB Scotland*, all open Monday to Friday 9.15am to 4 or 4.45pm, until 5.45pm on Thursdays. In remoter parts of Scotland, however, there may be only a mobile bank that runs to a timetable, usually available from the local post office.

Outside banking hours you're best advised to go to a **bureau de change**, which are to be found in most city centres, often at train stations or airports; try to avoid changing money or cheques in hotels, where the rates are normally the poorest on offer.

If, as a foreign visitor, you run out of money or there is some kind of emergency, the quickest way to get **money sent out** is to contact your bank at home and have them wire the cash to the nearest bank. You can do the same thing through *Thomas Cook* or *American Express* if there is a branch nearby. Americans and Canadians can have cash sent out through *Western Union* (☎1-800/325 6000) or *American Express MoneyGram* (☎1-800/543 4080). Both companies' fees depend on the destination and the amount being transferred, but as an example, wiring $1000 to England will cost around $75. The funds should be available for collection at *Amex*'s or *Western Union*'s local office within minutes of being sent.

CURRENCY

The British **pound sterling** (£; *punt* in Welsh) is a decimal currency, divided into 100 pence (p; in Wales, c for *ceiniogau*). Coins come in denominations of 1p, 2p, 5p, 10p, 20p, 50p and £1. Notes come in denominations of £5, £10, £20 and £50; shopkeepers will carefully scrutinize any £20 or £50 notes, as forgeries are widespread, and you'd be well advised to do the same. The quickest test is to hold the note up to the light to make sure there's a thin wire filament running through the note from top to bottom; this is by no means foolproof, but it will catch most fakes.

Bank of England and *Northern Ireland* banknotes are accepted **in Scotland**, where the *Bank of Scotland*, the *Royal Bank of Scotland* and the *Clydesdale Bank* also issue their own banknotes in denominations of £1, £5, £10, £20, £50 and £100. Although these Scottish banknotes are legal tender in the rest of Britain, some traders south of the border may be unwilling to accept them.

COSTS

Britain has become an expensive place to visit. The **minimum expenditure**, if you're camping, hitching a lot of the time and preparing most of your own food, would be in the region of £15 a day, rising to around £20–25 a day using the hostelling network, some public transport and grabbing the odd takeaway meal. Couples staying at budget B&Bs, eating at unpretentious restaurants and visiting a fair number of tourist attractions are looking at around £30–40 each per day, and if you're renting a car, staying in comfortable B&Bs or hotels and eating well, budget on at least £50 each per day. Single travellers should count on spending around 60 percent of what a couple would spend (single rooms cost more than half a double), and on any visit to London, work on the basis that you'll need at least an extra £10 per day to get any pleasure out of the place. On the other hand, costs are often lower in rural areas, and average costs in Scotland and Wales can be marginally lower than in the equivalent areas of England. For more detail on the cost of accommodation, transport and eating, see the relevant sections below.

Youth and Student Discounts

Various official and quasi-official youth/student ID cards are widely available and most will pay for themselves in savings pretty soon. Full-time students over the age of sixteen are eligible for the **International Student ID Card (ISIC)**, which entitles the bearer to special fares on local transport, and discounts at museums, theatres and other attractions; for Americans and Canadians there's also a health benefit (see below). The card costs $16 for Americans, CDN$15 for Canadians, AUS$10 for Australians, and £5 in the UK, and is available from branches of *Council Travel, STA* and *Travel CUTS* around the world (see p.4 and p.9).

The only requirement for the **Go-25 Card** is that you are aged 25 or younger; it costs the same as the ISIC and carries the same benefits. It can be purchased through *Council Travel* in the US, *Hostelling International* in Canada and *STA* in Australia.

STA also sells its own ID card that's good for some discounts, as do various other travel organizations. A university photo ID might open some doors, too.

INSURANCE, HEALTH AND EMERGENCIES

Wherever you're travelling from, it's a very good idea to have some kind of **travel insurance**, since with this you're covered for loss of possessions and money, as well as the cost of all medical and dental treatment. Among **British** insurers, *Endsleigh* are about the cheapest, offering a month's cover for around £12. Their policies are available from most youth/student travel specialists or direct from their offices (see box opposite). Whatever your policy, if you have anything stolen, get a copy of the police report of the incident, as this is essential to substantiate your claim.

In the **US** and **Canada** you should carefully check the insurance policies you already have before taking out a new one. You may discover that you're covered already for medical and other losses while abroad. Canadians especially are usually covered by their provincial health plans. Holders of an official student/teacher/youth card, such as ISIC (see above), are entitled (outside the USA) to be reimbursed for accident coverage and hospital in-patient benefits, with up to $3000 in emergency medical coverage and $100 a day for up to 60 days in hospital, plus a 24-hour hotline to call in the event of a medical, legal or financial emergency. Students may also find their health coverage extends during vacations, and many bank and charge accounts include some form of travel cover; a certain level of insurance may be included if you pay for your trip with a credit card. Premiums vary, so shop around. The best deals are usually to be had through student/youth travel agencies – *ISIS* policies, for example, cost $48–69 for fifteen days (depending on coverage), $80–105 for a month, $149–207 for two months, and up to $510–700 for a year. If you're planning to do any dangerous sports, be sure to ask whether these activities are covered: some policies add a hefty surcharge.

Note that most North American travel policies apply only to items lost, stolen or damaged while in the custody of an identifiable, responsible third party – hotel porter, airline, luggage consignment, etc – and very few insurers will arrange on-the-spot payments in the event of a major expense or loss; you will usually be reimbursed only after going home.

TRAVEL INSURANCE COMPANIES

In Britain

Columbus (☎0171/375 0011).

Endsleigh (☎0171/436 4451).

Frizzell (☎01202/292 333)

In North America

Access America (☎1-800/284-8300).

Carefree Travel Insurance (☎1-800/323-3149).

Desjardins Travel Insurance (Canada; ☎1-800/463 7830).

International Student Insurance Service (ISIS) – sold by STA Travel (head office ☎1-800/777- 0112).

Travel Assistance International (☎1-800/821-2828).

Travel Guard (☎1-800/826-1300).

Travel Insurance Services (☎1-800/937-1387).

In Australia and New Zealand

AFTA (☎02/956 4800).

Cover-More Insurance Services (☎02/9202 8000).

Ready Plan (☎1-800/337462).

UTAG (☎02/819 6855).

Travel insurance policies in **Australia** and **New Zealand** tend to be put together by the airlines and travel agent groups, such as *UTAG*, *AFTA* and *Ready Plan*, which are all fairly similar in terms of coverage and price. A typical policy for the UK, covering medical costs, lost baggage and personal liability, will cost around $161 (NZ$180) for a month and $226 (NZ$254) for two months. *CIC Insurance*, offered by *Cover-More Insurance Services*, has some of the widest cover available and can be arranged through most travel agents.

MEDICAL MATTERS

No vaccinations are required for entry into Britain. Citizens of all EU countries are entitled to free medical treatment at National Health Service hospitals and Britain also has a reciprocal arrangement with Australian Medicare, but citizens of other countries will be charged for all medical services except those administered by accident and emergency units at NHS hospitals.

Thus a US citizen who has been hit by a car would not be charged if the injuries simply require stitching and setting in the emergency unit, but would have to pay if admission to a hospital ward were necessary. Health insurance is therefore extremely advisable for all non-EU nationals.

There are no particular health risks in Britain, though if you're visiting Scotland you should be prepared to encounter the **midge** (*culicoides*) – a tiny biting fly prevalent in the highlands and islands. To most people these insects are merely a nuisance; others have a violent allergic reaction when bitten. Unless you visit in the winter, midges are hard to avoid: they love still, damp, shady conditions and are at their most vicious around sunrise and sunset. You'll soon notice if they're near; cover up arms and legs and try to avoid wearing dark colours, which attract them. Various repellents, widely available from pharmacists, are worth a try.

Pharmacists can dispense only a limited range of drugs without a doctor's prescription. Most pharmacies are open standard shop hours, though in large towns some may stay open as late as 10pm – local newspapers carry lists of late-opening pharmacies. Doctor's surgeries tend to be open from about 9am to noon and then for a couple of hours in the evenings; outside surgery hours, you can turn up at the casualty department of the local hospital for complaints that require immediate attention – unless it's an emergency, in which case ring ☎999 for an ambulance.

POLICE

Although the traditional image of the friendly British "Bobby" has become increasingly tarnished by stories of corruption, racism and crooked dealings, the **police** continue to be approachable and helpful. If you're lost in a major town, asking a police officer is generally the quickest way to pinpoint your destination; alternatively, you could ask a **traffic warden**, a much-maligned species of law-enforcer responsible for reporting parking offences and other vehicle-related matters. Most traffic wardens are distinguishable by their flat caps with a yellow band (though uniforms do vary), and by the fact that they are generally armed with a book of parking-fine tickets; police officers on street duty wear a distinctive domed hat with a silver tip, or a peaked flat hat with a black and white chequered band, and are generally armed with just a truncheon.

As in any country, the major towns of Britain have their dangerous spots, but these tend to be inner-city housing estates where no tourist has any reason to be. The chief risk on the streets is pickpocketing, and there are some virtuoso villains at work in London, especially on the big shopping streets and the Underground. Carry only as much money as you need, and keep all bags and pockets fastened. Should you have anything stolen or be involved in some incident that requires reporting, go to the local police station; the ☎999 number should only be used in emergencies.

EMERGENCIES

For **Police**, **Fire Brigade**, **Ambulance** and, in certain areas, **Mountain Rescue** or **Coastguard**, dial ☎**999**.

INFORMATION AND MAPS

If you want to do a bit of research before arriving in Britain, you could contact the **British Tourist Authority** (BTA) in your country — the addresses are given in the box below. The BTA will send you a wealth of free literature, some of it just rosy-tinted advertising copy, but much of it extremely useful — especially the maps, city guides and event calendars. If you want more hard facts on a particular area, you should approach the **regional tourist offices** in Britain, which are also listed below. Some are extremely helpful, others give the impression of being harassed to breaking point by years of understaffing, but all of them will have a few leaflets worth scanning before you set out.

Tourist offices (usually called Tourist Information Centres) exist in virtually every British town — you'll find their phone numbers and opening hours in the relevant sections of the guide. The average opening hours are much the same as standard shop hours, with the difference that in summer they'll often be open on a Sunday and for a couple of hours after the shops have closed on weekdays; opening hours are generally shorter in winter, and in more remote areas the office may even be closed. All centres offer information on accommodation (which they can often book — see p.29), local public transport, attractions and restaurants, as well as town and regional maps. In many cases this is free, but a growing number of offices make a small charge for an accommodation list or a town guide with an accompanying street

---

BRITISH TOURIST AUTHORITY HEAD OFFICES

Australia: 210 Clarence St, 4th Floor, Sydney, NSW 2000 (☎02/267 4555).

Canada: 111 Avenue Rd, Toronto, Ontario M5R 3J8 (☎416/961-8124).

Ireland: 18–19 College Green, Dublin 2 (☎01/670 8000).

New Zealand: Suite 305, 3rd Floor, Dilworth Building, corner of Customs and Queen streets, Auckland (☎09/303 1805).

USA: 2580 Cumberland Pkwy, Suite 470, Atlanta, GA (☎404/432-9641);

625 N Michigan Ave, Suite 1510, Chicago, IL (no telephone enquiries);

World Trade Center, Suite 450, 350 S Figueroa St, Los Angeles, CA (☎213/628-3525);

551 5th Ave, Suite 701, New York, NY 10176 (☎1-800/GO BRITAIN).

ENGLISH TOURIST BOARD OFFICES

British Travel Centre, 12 Regent St, London SW1Y 4PQ (no telephone enquiries).

Cumbria Tourist Board, Ashleigh, Holly Rd, Windermere, Cumbria LA23 2AQ (☎01539/444 444).

East Anglia Tourist Board, Toppesfield Hall, Hadleigh, Suffolk IP7 5DN (☎01473/822 922).

East Midlands Tourist Board, Exchequergate, Lincoln LN2 1PZ (☎01522/531521).

Heart of England Tourist Board, Woodside, Larkhill Road, Worcester WR5 2EF (☎01905/763 436).

London Tourist Board, 26 Grosvenor Gdns, Victoria, London SW1W 0DU (no telephone enquiries).

North West England Tourist Board, Swan House, Swan Meadow Road, Wigan Pier, Wigan WN3 5BB (☎01942/821 222).

Northumbria Tourist Board, Northumbria Tourist Board, Aykley Heads, Durham DH1 5UX (☎091/384 6905).

South East England Tourist Board, The Old Brew House, Warwick Park, Tunbridge Wells, Kent TN2 5TU (☎01892/540 766).

Southern Tourist Board, 40 Chamberlayne Rd, Eastleigh, Hampshire SO50 5JH (☎01703/620 006).

West Country Tourist Board, 60 St David's Hill, Exeter, Devon EX4 4SY (☎01392/76351).

Yorkshire & Humberside Tourist Board, 312 Tadcaster Rd, York YO2 2HF (☎01904/707 961).

SCOTTISH TOURIST BOARD OFFICES

Scotland's 31 regional tourist boards have recently been merged into just 14. At the time of going to press, the exact location of each regional office had yet to be decided, so the addresses and phone numbers given below are liable to change.

Scottish Tourist Board, 23 Ravelston Terrace, Edinburgh EH4 3EU (☎0131/332 2433); 19 Cockspur St, London SW1 5BL (☎0171/930 8661 or 8662 or 8663).

Aberdeen & Grampian Tourist Board, Migvie House, North Silver St, Aberdeen AB1 1RJ (☎01224/632727).

Angus & City of Dundee Tourist Board, 4 City Square, Dundee DD1 3BA (☎01382/227723).

Argyll, the Isles, Loch Lomond, Stirling & Trossachs Tourist Board, 41 Dumbarton Rd, Stirling FK8 2QQ (☎01786/475019).

Ayrshire & Arran Tourist Board, Burns House, Burns Statue Square, Ayr KA7 1UT (☎01292/288688).

Dumfries and Galloway Tourist Board, Campbell House, Bankend Rd, Dumfries DG1 4TH (☎01387/253862).

Edinburgh & Lothians Tourist Board, 4 Rothesay Terrace, Edinburgh EH3 7RY (☎0131/557 1700).

Glasgow & Clyde Valley Tourist Board, 39 St Vincent Place, Glasgow G1 2ER (☎0141/204 4400).

Highlands of Scotland Tourist Board, Beechwood Park North, Inverness IV2 3ED (☎01463/223512).

Kingdom of Fife Tourist Board, Huntsman's House, 33 Cadham Centre, Glenrothes KY7 6RU (☎01334/472021).

Orkney Tourist Board, 6 Broad St, Kirkwall, Orkney KW15 1DH (☎01856/872856).

Perthshire Tourist Board, 45 High St, Perth PH1 5TJ (☎01738/627958).

Scottish Borders Tourist Board, 70 High St, Selkirk TD7 4DD (☎01835/863435).

Shetland Island Tourism, Market Cross, Lerwick, Shetland ZE1 0LU (☎01595/693434).

Western Isles Tourist Board, 26 Cromwell St, Stornoway, Isle of Lewis HS1 2DD (☎01851/703088).

WELSH TOURIST BOARD OFFICES

Wales Tourist Board, Head Office, Brunel House, 2 Fitzalan Rd, Cardiff CF2 1UY (☎01222/499909); write to: WTB, Dept RJ3, PO Box 1, Cardiff CF1 2XN.

Wales Information Bureau, British Travel Centre, 12 Regent St, London SW1Y 4PQ (☎0171/409 0969).

North Wales Tourism Ltd, 77 Conway Rd, Colwyn Bay, LL29 7LN (☎01492/531731).

Mid-Wales Tourism Ltd, Canolfan Owain Glynd r, Machynlleth, SY20 8EE (☎01654/702653).

Tourism South Wales Ltd, Pembroke House, Phoenix Way Enterprise Park, Swansea SA7 9DB (☎01792/781212).

plan. Areas designated as **National Parks** (such as the Lake District, Dartmoor or Snowdonia) also have a fair sprinkling of National Park Information Centres, which are generally more expert in giving guidance on local walks and outdoor pursuits.

MAPS

The most comprehensive series of **maps**, renowned for their accuracy and clarity, are produced by the **Ordnance Survey**. The 204 maps in its 1:50,000 (a little over one inch to one mile) *Landranger Series* cover the whole of Britain and show enough detail to be useful for most walkers. The more detailed 1:25,000 *OS Pathfinder Series* is invaluable for serious hiking and covers the entire country; the same-scale *OS Outdoor Leisure* series takes in the most popular walking regions, with each map covering a specific area. Less well known is the *Goldeneye* series, a range of fairly ordinary road touring maps for various English counties, but made interesting with the addition of historical and recreational details on the back. Scotland's official tourist map series, published by Estate Publications, is perfect if you're driving or cycling round one particular region since it marks all the major tourist sights as well as

MAP OUTLETS

London *Daunt Books*, 83 Marylebone High St, W1 (☎0171/224 2295); *National Map Centre*, 22–24 Caxton St, SW1 (☎0171/222 4945); *Stanfords*, 12–14 Long Acre, WC2 (☎0171/836 1321) and 156 Regent St, London W1R 5TA; *The Travel Bookshop*, 13–15 Blenheim Crescent, London W11 2EE (☎0171/229 5260); *The Travellers Bookshop*, 25 Cecil Court, WC2 (☎0171/836 9132).

Edinburgh, *HMSO Books*, 71 Lothian Rd, EH3 9AZ (☎0131/228 4181).

Glasgow, *John Smith and Sons*, 57–61 St Vincent St, G2 5TB (☎0141/221 7472).

Maps are available by **mail order** from *Stanfords* (☎0171/836 1321).

NORTH AMERICA

Chicago *Rand McNally*, 444 N Michigan Ave, IL 60611 (☎312/321-1751).

Los Angeles *Map Link Inc*, 25 E Mason St, Santa Barbara, CA 93101 (☎805/965-4402).

Montréal *Ulysses Travel Bookshop*, 4176 St-Denis (☎514/289-0993).

New York *British Travel Bookshop*, 551 5th Ave, NY (☎800/448-3039 or ☎212/490-6688); *The Complete Traveler Bookstore*, 199 Madison Ave, NY 10016 (☎212/685 9007); *Rand McNally*, 150 E 52nd St, NY 10022 (☎212/758-7488); *Traveler's Bookstore*, 22 W 52nd St, NY 10019 (☎212/664-0995).

San Francisco *The Complete Traveler Bookstore*, 3207 Filmore St, CA 92123 (☎415/923-1511); *Rand McNally*, 595 Market St, CA 94105 (☎415/777-

3131); *Phileas Fogg's Books & Maps*, #87 Stanford Shopping Center, Palo Alto, CA 94304 (☎1-800/233-FOGG in California; ☎1-800/533-FOGG elsewhere in US).

Seattle *Elliot Bay Book Company*, 101 S Main St, WA 98104 (☎206/624 6600).

Toronto *Open Air Books and Maps*, 25 Toronto St, M5R 2C1 (☎416/363 0719).

Vancouver *World Wide Books and Maps*, 1247 Granville St (☎604/687-3320).

Washington DC *Rand McNally*, 1201 Connecticut Ave NW, Washington, DC 2003 (☎202/223-6751).

Rand McNally now have 24 stores nationwide. For details of your local branch and direct-mail maps call ☎1-800/333-0136 ext 2111.

AUSTRALIA

Adelaide *The Map Shop*, 16a Peel St, Adelaide, SA 5000 (☎08/231 2033).

Brisbane *Hema*, 239 George St, Brisbane, QLD 4000 (☎07/ 221 4330).

Melbourne *Bowyangs*, 372 Little Bourke St, Melbourne, VIC 3000 (☎03/670 4383).

Sydney *Travel Bookshop*, 20 Bridge St, Sydney, NSW 2000 (☎02/241 3554).

Perth *Perth Map Centre*, 891 Hay St, Perth, WA 6000 (☎09/322 5733).

youth hostels and campsites. The best **road atlases** are the large-format items produced by the *AA*, *RAC*, *Collins* and *Ordnance Survey*, which cover all of Britain at around three miles to one inch and include larger-scale plans of major towns.

The full range of Ordnance Survey maps is only available at a few big-city stores (see box above), but in any walking district of Britain you'll find the relevant maps in local shops or information offices. Virtually every service station stocks one or more of the big road atlases.

GETTING AROUND

As you'd expect, just about every place in Britain is accessible by train or bus. However, **Britain's public transport** has to a large extent fallen victim to Conservative economics, and costs are among the highest in Europe – London's commuters spend more on getting to work than any of their European counterparts. Government policies in recent years have been biased towards car owners, with new roads being carved through the countryside regardless of the environmental costs; and despite this never-ending programme of road-building, congestion around the main cities can be bad. Even the motorways (especially the notorious M25 London orbital road) are liable to sporadic gridlocks.

While England's southeast, the central belt of Scotland and the South Wales valleys support comprehensive public transport networks, in more remote and thinly populated areas services can be few and far between, although with careful planning practically everywhere is reachable and you'll have no trouble getting to the main tourist destinations.

As a basic rule, if you're using public transport make sure you're aware of all the passes and special deals on offer. If you're driving, take the more scenic backroads unless you're in a real hurry.

FLIGHTS

Since the distances involved are so small, internal **flights** are not the most obvious choice for getting around Britain. The domestic traffic handled by the main regional airports of Birmingham, Manchester, Glasgow and Edinburgh is generally aimed at commuters and saves little time over the equivalent train journey. The only flight you might seriously consider taking is one from England to Scotland.

You can fly to **Scotland's main airports** – Edinburgh, Glasgow and Aberdeen – in an hour or so from all three London airports (Heathrow, Gatwick and Stansted), as well as from various provincial airports. There's usually a confusingly wide range of fares, the **best deals** being special-offer tickets sold within seven days of departure; the next cheapest seats are **Apex** tickets, available for about half the price of a full-price scheduled ticket, with the usual booking and cancellation restrictions. For the best prices, it's worth checking fares through a specialist travel agency such as *Campus Travel* or *STA Travel* – see the box below.

There are flights almost hourly to **Edinburgh and Glasgow** from London, and about eight or so daily to **Aberdeen**. As a broad guide to what you're likely to pay, reckon on around £80 for the cheapest fares from London to Edinburgh or Glasgow with *British Airways*, *British Midland* or *Air UK;* around £100 for an Apex. Flights from other parts of Britain are less frequent: about seven flights a day leave Birmingham for Edinburgh, Glasgow and Aberdeen – the cheapest return fares with *British Airways* are around £100. From the south of England, *Manx Airlines* fly from Southampton to Edinburgh or Glasgow for an Apex fare of around £150.

AIRLINES, AIRPORTS AND TRAVEL AGENTS

Air UK
☎0345/666 777
London to Edinburgh, Glasgow and Aberdeen;
Norwich to Edinburgh.

British Airways
☎0345/222 111
London, Birmingham and Bristol to Edinburgh,
Glasgow and Aberdeen; Manchester to Aberdeen.

British Airways Express (Loganair)
☎0141/889 1311
Flights within Scotland only.

British Midland
☎0345/554 554
London and East Midlands to Edinburgh and
Glasgow.

Business Air
☎0500/340 146
East Midlands to Edinburgh and Aberdeen;
Manchester to Edinburgh, Glasgow, Aberdeen and
Dundee.

Manx Airlines
☎0345/256 256
Isle of Man to Glasgow; Southampton to Glasgow
and Edinburgh.

FLIGHT AGENTS IN BRITAIN

Campus Travel
52 Grosvenor Gdns, London SW1
☎0171/730 3402
Also many branches around the country.

Council Travel
28A Poland St, London W1
☎0171/287 3337

Destination Group
41–45 Goswell Rd, London EC1
☎0171/253 9000

STA Travel
86 Old Brompton Rd, London SW7
☎0171/937 9921
Offices nationwide.

Trailfinders
42–50 Earls Court Rd, London W8 6FT
☎0171/938 3366
Many branches nationwide.

Travel Bug
597 Cheetham Hill Rd, Manchester M8 5EJ
☎0161/721 4000

Union Travel
93 Piccadilly, London W1
☎0171/493 4343

If you're short of time, Scotland's seventeen internal airports, many of them on the islands, can be useful. **Inter-island flights** are mainly operated by *British Airways Express* (also known as *Loganair*, ☎0141/889 1311), with *British Airways* (☎01345/222111) flying between Edinburgh, Glasgow, Aberdeen and Inverness and to some of the main islands. Call the airports listed above for further details.

RAIL TRAVEL

Due to a lack of investment and the government's obsession with privatization, **rail** travel in Britain has been in decline over the past decade. The privatization process is causing great uncertainty and confusion on the railways, with the track and stations now being owned by *Railtrack*, and the trains and services being run by a tangle of private companies. The logo and name of the rump state company, **British Rail** (BR), is rarely seen these days except on tickets, which at the time of going to press were still issued by BR. In Scotland, where some lines are rated among the world's great scenic routes, the national network is called **ScotRail**. Few lines and services have been axed so far, and there are not many major towns that cannot be reached by rail, although travelling across Britain – rather than out from London – can involve a certain amount of changing. In addition to the national networks, there still survive a number of scenic steam railways, particularly in Snowdonia in Wales, which are nowadays mostly run as private tourist attractions; we've detailed the best in the relevant parts of the guide.

You can buy **tickets** for most trains at stations or from major travel agents. For busy long-distance routes, generally known as *InterCity* services, it's advisable to **reserve** a seat – especially if you're travelling between London and Manchester, Liverpool, Leeds, Newcastle, Glasgow or Edinburgh.

A seat reservation costs £2, and on most trains a group of up to four people can reserve seats for the same £2 charge; reservations are often included in the price if you book in advance. Ordinary second-class **fares** are high, and first-class cost an extra 33 percent. At the time of going to press, there were five types of reduced-fare ticket – *Leisure First, Saver, SuperSaver, Apex* and *SuperApex* – but whether these will all survive the privatization process is anybody's guess.

Savers are return tickets that can be used on all trains on Saturdays, Sundays and Bank Holidays, on most weekday trains outside rush hour for the outward journey and on all trains for the return leg. If you buy a return ticket at any station outside the rush hour, you'll routinely be issued with a *Saver*. **SuperSavers**, which are cheaper, cannot be used on Fridays nor on half a dozen other specified days of the year, and are not valid for any peak-hour service to, from or through London. *Saver* and *SuperSaver* tickets are valid for one month (outward travel has to be within two days of the date on the ticket), and can be used on London Underground if your journey involves crossing from one London station to another.

Apex tickets are issued in limited numbers on certain *InterCity* journeys of 150 miles or more, and have to be booked at least seven days before travelling; a seat reservation is included with the ticket. The rock-bottom **SuperApex** tickets have to be booked fourteen days in advance, and are available in limited numbers on *InterCity* services between London and selected towns and cities. To take the London–York service as an example, an ordinary single fare costs £49, which is more than some of the available reduced return fares: a *Leisure First* ticket is £72, a *Saver* £56, a *SuperSaver* £46 and an *Apex* £35; there's no *SuperApex* ticket on this route. For all special-offer tickets you should book as far in advance as you possibly can – many *Apex* and *SuperApex* tickets are sold out weeks before travel date.

Children aged 5 to 15 pay half the adult fare on most journeys – but there are no discounts on *Apex* and *SuperApex* tickets. Under-5s travel free.

On Sundays, many long-distance services have a special deal whereby you can convert your second-class ticket to a first-class one by buying a *First-Class Supplement*, which costs £5 and is well worth paying if you're facing a five-hour journey on a popular route – every other Brit has a horror story about having to stand all the way from London to Newcastle in a smelly second-class carriage.

The ticket offices at many rural and commuter stations are closed at weekends; in these instances there's sometimes a vending machine on the platform. If there isn't a functioning machine, you can buy your ticket on board – but if you've embarked at a station that does have a machine and you've got on the train without buying a ticket, there's an on-the-spot fine of £10.

ROUTES INTO SCOTLAND AND WALES

Glasgow and **Edinburgh** are both served by frequent direct *InterCity* services **from London**, and are easily reached from other main English towns and cities, though you may have to change trains en route. **Journey times** from London can be as little as 4hr 30min to Edinburgh and 5hr to Glasgow; from Manchester reckon on around 2hr 30min to Edinburgh and 3hr to Glasgow. From either of these two points allow another 2hr 30min to Aberdeen and 3hr 30min to Inverness. All these destinations are served by overnight **sleeper trains**, for which reservations cost an additional £25 and can be made at any mainline train station.

Wales has just two major rail lines, both providing frequent services to and from England. Along the south coast, Newport, Cardiff and Swansea are linked by a fairly fast route via Bristol **to London**; the **north Wales** line follows the coast from the ferry port at Holyhead through to Chester in England and on to London. You can also travel directly into **mid-Wales** from Birmingham, but from other cities you'll probably need to change trains en route. Journey times are remarkably short: London to Cardiff takes less than 2hr and London to Holyhead just over 4hr.

RAIL PASSES

For foreign visitors who anticipate covering a lot of ground around Britain, a rail pass is a wise

RAIL OFFICES AND AGENCIES IN NORTH AMERICA

BritRail Travel International, 1500 Broadway, New York, NY 10036 (☎1-800/677-8585). Sells all British rail passes, rail-drive and multi-country passes, and Channel Tunnel tickets. Also sells ferry tickets across the Channel.

Canadian Reservations Centre, 2087 Dundas East, Suite 105, Mississauga, ON L4X 1M2 (☎1-800/361-7245. Specializes in Eurail and other rail passes.

CIE Tours International, 108 Ridgedale Ave, PO Box 2355, Morristown, NJ 07962 (☎1-800/243-7687). Sells rail passes valid for Britain and Ireland.

CIT Tours, 342 Madison Ave, Suite 207, New York, NY 10173 (☎800/223-7987). Eurail passes on sale.

Rail Europe, 226–230 Westchester Ave, White Plains, NY 10604 (☎800/438-7245). Specializes in Eurail and also sells the widest range of regional passes.

RAIL INFORMATION AND BOOKING IN BRITAIN

Where two phone numbers are given, the first is the one to ring for information, the second for credit-card bookings (*Access, Amex, Visa, Diner's Club* and *Switch*). All *Apex* and *SuperApex* tickets can be booked by credit card on ☎0800/450 450 – the call is free.

INTERCITY SERVICES FROM LONDON

All numbers should be preceded by ☎0171 if dialling from outside the ☎0171 code area.

West Midlands, north Wales & northwest England (from Euston): ☎387 7070; ☎387 8541.

Northeast England (from King's Cross): ☎278 2477; ☎278 9431.

East Anglia (from Liverpool Street): ☎928 5100; ☎620 2032.

South Wales, west England & south Midlands (from Paddington): ☎262 6767; ☎922 4372.

East Midlands and south Yorkshire (from St Pancras): ☎387 7070; ☎837 5483.

SERVICES IN SCOTLAND

The following numbers handle both information and credit-card bookings. Local and mainline information is also available from all manned Scottish stations (see Yellow Pages for telephone numbers).

Edinburgh: ☎0131/556 2451.
Glasgow: ☎0141/204 2844.

Aberdeen: ☎01224/594222.
Inverness: ☎01463/238924.

SERVICES IN WALES

Cardiff: ☎01222/228000; ☎01222/499811.
Haverford West: ☎01437/764361.
Holyhead: ☎01407/769222.
Llandrindod Wells: ☎01597/822053.
Llandudno: ☎01492/585151.

Machynlleth: ☎01654/702311.
Newport: ☎01633/842222; ☎01633/257271.
Pembroke Dock: ☎01646/684896.
Swansea: ☎01792/467777; ☎01792/632410.

investment. The standard **BritRail Pass**, which must be bought before you enter the country, is available from *BritRail Travel International* (see box above) and many specialist tour operators outside Britain (see pp.6 & 9) It gives unlimited travel in England, Scotland and Wales for 8 days ($230), 15 days ($355), 22 days ($445) or a month ($520). The **BritRail Flexipass** is good for travel on 4 days out of a month ($195), 8 days out of a month ($275), or 15 days out of a month ($405).

Note that with both these passes there are discounts for those under 26 (*BritRail Youth* passes) or over 60 (*BritRail Senior* passes), and the *Flexipass* has a special 15 days out of two months rate for under-26s ($319). *BritRail* also sells an **England/Wales Flexipass**, costing $155 for 4 days out of one month; a **London Visitor Travelcard**, for unlimited bus and Tube travel in the capital ($25 for 3 days, $32 for 4 days, $49 for a week); and the **London Extra**, which throws in Oxford, Canterbury and Brighton ($85 for 3 days, $115 for 4 days, $175 for a week). **Australians** and **New Zealanders** can buy *BritRail* passes from branches of *Thomas Cook*: the 8-day version costs A$280/NZ$310, 15 days A$395/NZ$440, 22 days A$525/NZ$590, and a month A$575/NZ640; the *BritRail Flexipass* is A$240/NZ$265 for 4 days out of a month, A$345/NZ$385 for 8 days and A$500/NZ$555 for 15 days.

If you are planning to travel widely around Europe by train, then it may be worth while buying a **Eurail Pass**. The pass, which must be purchased before arrival in Europe, allows unlimited free train travel in the UK and sixteen other countries. The **Eurail Youthpass** (for under-26s) osts $398 for 15 days, $578 for one month or 768 for two months; if you're 26 or over you'll ave to buy a first-class pass, available in 15-day 498), 21-day ($648), one-month ($798), two-month ($1098) and three-month ($1398) increments. You stand a better chance of getting your money's worth out of a **Eurail Flexipass**, which is valid for a certain number of travel days in a two-month period. This, too, comes in under-26/first-class versions: 5 days cost $255/$348, 10 days $398/$560 and 15 days $540/$740.

There are a number of passes and discount cards available only in Britain itself, to foreign visitors and British nationals alike, from main train stations and some travel agents. The **All-Line Rail Rover** gives unlimited travel on the entire network throughout England, Scotland and Wales for 7 (£230) or 14 consecutive days (£375). If your trip is limited to Scotland, the **ScotRail Rover** is a more economical option, allowing unlimited travel on *ScotRail* for varying periods; prices range from £60 for 4 days' travel out of 8 to £115 for 12 out of 15 days. There are also three regional *Rover* passes: the **West Highland Rover** (covering the area from Glasgow to Fort William), which costs £39 for 4 out of 8 days; the **North Highland Rover**, which costs the same and is valid on all lines from Thurso to Aberdeen; and the **Festival Cities Rover**, which includes routes from Glasgow to Edinburgh and Stirling, and costs £21 for 3 out of 7 days. The **Freedom of Scotland Travelpass** gives unlimited train travel and is also valid on all *CalMac* west coast ferry links (for ferry information see p.28), as well as offering 33 percent reductions on many buses and on some *P&O* Orkney and Shetland ferries. It costs £99 for 8 days, £139 for 15 days or £110 for

8 out of 15 days, and comes complete with time-tables and a card allowing discounts at tourist attractions, shops and restaurants throughout Scotland.

Three passes cover the Welsh lines specifically, the most comprehensive being the **Freedom of Wales** pass, which allows travel throughout Wales (and the connecting lines through England) for a period of 7 days (£47); additional benefits are reduced fares on some long-distance bus routes. The **North and Mid-Wales Rail Rover**, available for 7 days (£36) or 3 days out of 7 (£23), covers the Welsh and connecting English lines north of Aberystwyth. Most regions also have their own local **Day Ranger** tickets, which may be worthwhile if you're not straying far.

If a rail pass doesn't seem economical, you may be eligible for one of *BR*'s discount cards: the **Young Person's Railcard** costs £16 and gives 33 percent reductions on all standard, *Saver* and *SuperSaver* fares to full-time students and those aged 16 to 25. A **Senior Citizens' Rail Card**, also £16 and offering 33 percent reductions, is available to those aged 60 or over. The **Family Railcard** costs £20, and gives a variety of discounts from 20 to 33 percent for up to four adults travelling with children. Even more enticingly, it allows up to four children aged 5–15 to travel anywhere in the country for a flat fare of £2 each (which includes a seat reservation). Another pass worth mentioning is the **Network Card**, which costs £14 (or just £17 for two) and gives a 33 percent discount on off-peak services throughout London and the southeast (including Oxford, Cambridge and all the Home Counties).

BUSES AND COACHES

Inter-town **bus** services (known as **coaches** in Britain) duplicate many rail routes, very often at half the price of the train or less. The frequency of service is often comparable to rail, and in some instances the difference in journey time isn't great enough to be a deciding factor; coaches are comfortable, and the ones on longer routes often have drinks and sandwiches available on board. There's a plethora of regional companies operating buses and coaches, but by far the biggest national operator is **National Express** (☎0990/808080) and its subsidiary **Scottish Citylink Coaches** (☎0990/898989), whose network extends to every corner of

England and Scotland and the main centres in Wales. With rail prices becoming exorbitant, these coach services are so popular that for busy routes and on any route at weekends and during holidays it's a very good idea to buy a "reserved journey ticket", which guarantees you a seat.

One of the longest journeys you may wish to make, the twelve-hour trip from London to Inverness, costs about £47 return. However, UK residents under 25, in full-time education or of retirement age can buy a *National Express* **Discount Coach Card**, which costs £7, is valid for one year and entitles the holder to a thirty percent discount on all journeys. Foreign travellers can purchase a **Tourist Trail Pass**, which offers unlimited travel on the *National Express* and *Citylink* network: unlimited travel on any 8 days within 16 costs £90 for students and under-23s, £119 for others; unlimited travel on any 15 days within 30 costs £145 and £179 respectively. In Britain you can obtain both from major travel agents, at Gatwick and Heathrow airports, at the British Travel Centre in London (see p.19), or at the main *National Express* office in Victoria Coach Station, Buckingham Palace Rd, London SW1 (☎0990/808 080). Scottish outlets include the main bus stations in Glasgow and Edinburgh. In North America these passes are available for the dollar equivalent through specialist tour operators (see box on p.6), or direct from *British Travel Associates*, PO Box 299, Elkton, VA 22827 (☎1-800/327-6097); in Australia and New Zealand you can get them from *Thomas Cook*.

Local bus services are run by a bewildering array of companies, most private, a few not. In many cases, timetables and routes are well integrated, but it's increasingly the case that private companies duplicate the busiest routes in an attempt to undercut the commercial opposition, leaving the remoter spots neglected. Thus if you want to get from one end of a big city to another, you'll probably have a choice of buses all offering cut-price fares and cheap day passes, but to get out into the suburbs or to a satellite village, you may have to wait several hours; services are even less frequent in the evenings and at weekends. As a rule, the further away from urban areas you get, the less frequent and more expensive bus services become; however, there are very few rural areas that aren't served by at least the occasional privately owned minibus or **postbus**, which also collects and delivers mail. The postbus network is especially useful in Scotland, where it's the only way to reach many far-flung spots (routes and timetables from the *Royal Mail Public Relations Unit*, 102 West Port, Edinburgh EH3 9HS; ☎0131/228 7407). All rural bus services in Britain can be excruciatingly slow, however, and if you want to cover a lot of the countryside in a short time you'll need your own transport.

DRIVING

In order to **drive** in Britain you need a current **driving licence** supplemented by an **international driving permit** available from national motoring organizations for a small fee. If you're bringing your own vehicle you should also carry your **vehicle registration or ownership document** at all times. Furthermore, you must be adequately **insured**, so be sure to check your existing policy.

In Britain you **drive on the left**, a situation which can lead to a few tense days of acclimatization for overseas drivers. **Speed limits** are 30–40mph (50–65kph) in built-up areas, 70mph (110kph) on motorways (freeways) and dual carriageways and 50mph (80kph) on most other roads. As a rule, assume that in any area with street lighting the speed limit is 30mph (50kph) unless stated otherwise. Out in the remoter regions, particularly in Wales and Scotland, many roads are steep, **single-track** lanes, with passing places – these are used to enable cars to overtake. In the Highlands of Scotland, the roads are littered with sheep which are entirely oblivious to cars, so slow down and edge your way past – should you kill one, it is your duty to inform the local farmer; in Wales you may have to stop to open gates designed to keep sheep from straying.

Fuel is expensive compared to North American prices – leaded 4-star petrol (gasoline) costs in the region of £2.80 per English gallon (4.56 litres), unleaded and diesel slightly less. The lowest prices of all are charged at out-of-town supermarkets; suburban service stations are usually fairly reasonable (special offers are quite common); and the highest prices are charged by motorway stations.

The *Automobile Association*, the *Royal Automobile Club* and *National Breakdown* all operate 24-hour emergency **breakdown** services. The *AA* and *RAC* provide many other motoring services and operate a reciprocal arrangement for free assistance with many overseas motoring organizations – check the situation with your association before setting out. On motorways the *AA* and *RAC* can be called from roadside booths; elsewhere ring ☎0800/887 766 for the *AA*, ☎0800/828 282 for the *RAC* and ☎0800/400 600 for *National Breakdown*; in remote areas you may have to wait a considerable time for help to arrive. You can use these emergency numbers even if you are not a member of the respective organization, although a substantial fee will be charged.

CAR AND MOTORBIKE RENTAL

Compared to rates in North America, **car rental** in Britain is expensive, and you'll probably find it cheaper to arrange things in advance through one of the multinational chains, or by opting for a fly-drive deal. If you do rent a car from a company in Britain, the least you can expect to pay is around £130 a week, which is the rate for a small hatchback from *Holiday Autos*, the most competitive company; reckon on paying £40 a day direct from one of the multinationals, £5 or so less with a local firm. Rental agencies prefer you to pay with credit card, otherwise you may have to leave a deposit of at least £100, on top of the rental charge. There are very few automatics at the lower end of the price scale – if you want one, you should book well ahead. To rent a car you need to show your driving licence; few companies will rent to drivers with less than one year's experience and most will only rent to people between 21 and 70 years of age.

Motorbike rental is ludicrously expensive, at around £45 a day/£200 a week for a 500cc machine, and around £80/£300 for a one-litre tourer, including everything from insurance to helmets and luggage. In the capital it may be worth trying some of the rental companies who rent out well-used ex-despatch bikes; for addresses, check out the weekly newspaper *Motor Cycle News*, which can also be useful for locating spare parts.

MOTORING ORGANIZATIONS

Automobile Association, Fanum House, Basingstoke, Hants RG21 2EA (☎01256/20123).

Royal Automobile Club, PO Box 100, RAC House, 7 Brighton Rd, South Croydon CR2 6XW (☎0181/686 0088).

American Automobile Association (AAA), 4100 E Arkansas Ave, Denver, CO 80222 (☎1-800/222-4357).

Canadian Automobile Association, 2 Carlton St, Toronto, ON M4B 1K4 (☎416/964-3002).

Australian Automobile Association, 212 Northbourne Ave, Canberra, ACT 2601 (☎61/6247 7311).

New Zealand Automobile Association, PO Box 1794, Wellington (☎64/4738738).

CAR RENTAL FIRMS

IN THE UK

Avis, Hayes Gate House, Uxbridge Rd, Hayes, Middlesex (☎0181/848 8733).

Eurodollar, Swan National House, Warwick Place, Uxbridge, Middlesex (☎01895/233 300).

Europcar, InterRent House, Aldenham Rd, Watford WD2 2LX (☎0345/222 525).

Hertz, 1272 London Rd, London SW16 4XW (☎0181/679 1799).

Holiday Autos, 25 Savile Row, Mayfair, London W1X 1AA (☎0171/491 1111).

IN AUSTRALIA
Avis ☎1800/22 5533
Budget ☎13 2848
Hertz ☎13 1918
Renault Eurodrive ☎02/9299 3344

IN THE USA
Alamo ☎1-800/522-9696
Avis ☎1-800/331-1084
Budget ☎1-800/527-0700
Europe By Car ☎1-800/223-1516
Hertz ☎1-800/654-3001
Holiday Autos ☎1-800/422-7737
National Car Rental ☎1-800/CAR-RENT

IN NEW ZEALAND
Avis ☎09/525 1982
Budget ☎09/309 6737
Fly and Drive Holidays ☎09/366 0759
Hertz ☎09/309 0989

HITCHING AND LIFT-SHARING

It's inadvisable for anyone, alone or not, to **hitch** in Britain. Only in exceptionally remote areas, such as parts of the Scottish Highlands, is there a tradition of giving lifts, but even there locals clearly have priority and you may have to wait a long time before you're picked up. However, this decrease in the popularity of hitching has led to the appearance of a number of **lift-sharing services** which offer a cheap and safe way of getting around the country. The small-ads paper *Loot*, available daily in London, Bristol and Manchester, has a section in which private individuals offer and seek lifts around the country, while *Freewheelers* (☎0191/222 0090) is an established, Newcastle-based lift-share agency. Potential passengers pay a £5 annual registration fee, plus a £2 fee for each journey and 3.5p per mile as a contribution to the driver's costs – a fraction of the cost of any public transport service.

SCOTLAND'S FERRIES

Scotland has 130 inhabited islands, and **ferries** play an important part in travelling around the country. Most ferries carry cars and vans, for which advance reservations can be made – highly advisable, particularly during the busy summer season (April–Oct). Of the major operators, **Caledonian MacBrayne** (known as *CalMac*) covers the majority of routes.

CalMac has a virtual monopoly on services on the River Clyde and those to the Inner and Outer Hebrides, sailing to 23 islands altogether. Fares aren't cheap, but two **reduced-fare passes** are available, the *Island Hopscotch* and the *Island Rover*. The *Hopscotch* covers a range of economy fares for cars and passengers on 23 pre-planned routes and is valid for three months from the date of the first journey. The *Island Rover* pass entitles you to either 8 or 15 consecutive days' unlimited travel on *CalMac* ferries: you need to provide an exact itinerary and the price is calculated accordingly. Schedules vary and are highly complicated; get details from the address below.

The other main operators are *P&O Scottish Ferries*, which sails to Orkney and Shetland from Aberdeen and Scrabster (Thurso); *Western Ferries*, which operates between Gourock and Dunoon on the mainland between the islands of Islay and Jura; and the *Orkney Islands Shipping Co Ltd*, linking the various Orkney islands. To give an idea of fares, the trip from Aberdeen to Shetland takes 14hr and costs about £50 for a foot passenger, plus £120 or so for a car; no reduced-fare passes are available. There are also numerous small operators running day trips round the Scottish coast; their phone numbers are listed in the guide.

It is possible to book ferry tickets in **North America**, if you're organized enough to know exactly when you'll be making the crossing. In **Australia** and **New Zealand**, you can book ferry tickets at branches of *Thomas Cook*.

FERRY OFFICES AND INFORMATION IN SCOTLAND

Caledonian MacBrayne Ltd, The Ferry Terminal, Gourock, Renfrewshire PA19 1QP (☎01475/650100).

Orkney Islands Shipping Co Ltd, Head Office, 4 Ayre Rd, Kirkwall KW15 1QX (☎01856/872044).

P&O Scottish Ferries, PO Box 5, Jamieson's Quay, Aberdeen AB9 8DL (☎01224/572615).

Western Ferries (Clyde) Ltd, 16 Woodside Crescent, Glasgow G3 7UT (☎0141/332 9766).

ACCOMMODATION

Britain has scores of upmarket hotels, ranging from bland business-oriented places to plush country mansions and ancient castles, as well as budget accommodation in the form of hundreds of bed and breakfast places (B&Bs) and youth hostels. Nearly all tourist offices will book rooms for you, although the fee for this service varies considerably. In some areas you will pay a deposit that's deducted from your first night's bill (usually ten percent), in others the office will take a percentage or flat-rate commission – on average around £2, but twice that amount in tourist centres like London and Oxford. Another useful service operated by the majority of tourist offices is the *Book-a-bed-ahead* service, which locates accommodation in your next port of call for a charge of £2–3. For a full explanation of the price-coding system used in this book see the box below.

HOTELS AND B&Bs

There is no formalized system for grading **hotel** accommodation in Britain as a whole, but the tourist authorities and various private organizations classify hotels, B&Bs and guest houses on a system of stars, crowns, rosettes or similar badges, with five stars typically the top rank.

The national **tourist boards** of England, Scotland and Wales each use two ratings systems: facilities such as en-suite bathrooms, TVs and phones are denoted by one to five crowns, while badges such as Highly Commended or Deluxe give a better reflection of the kind of service and general comfort you can expect. It can be easier to use the grades supplied by the **AA** and **RAC**, which combine evaluation of facilities with a degree of subjective judgement – thus a hotel offering a whirlpool in each room will not earn its five stars if the management is unhelpful or the hotel food atrocious.

Though there's no hard-and-fast correlation between standards and price, you'll probably be paying in the region of £50–60 per night for a double room at a one-star hotel (breakfast included), rising to around £100 in a three-star and from around £200 for a five-star – in Scotland and Wales you might pay around twenty percent less, in London the price doubles. In some towns and cities you'll find that the larger hotels often offer cut-price deals on Saturdays and Sundays to fill the rooms vacated by the week's business trade, but these places tend to be soulless multinational chain operations. If you have money to throw around, stay in a nicely refurbished old building – the historic towns of Britain are chock-full of top-quality old coaching inns and similar ancient hostelries, while out in the countryside there are numerous converted mansions, manor houses and castles, often with brilliant restaurants attached.

ACCOMMODATION PRICES

Throughout this guide, hotel and B&B accommodation is priced on a scale of ① to ⑨, the number indicating the **lowest price** you could expect to pay per night in that establishment for a **double room** in high season. The prices indicated by the codes are as follows:

① under £20/$30	④ £40–50/$60–75	⑦ £70–80/$105–120
② £20–30/$30–45	⑤ £50–60/$75–90	⑧ £80–100/$120–150
③ £30–40/$45–60	⑥ £60–70/$90–105	⑨ over £100/$150

At the lower end of the scale, it's sometimes difficult to differentiate between a hotel and a **Bed and Breakfast** (B&B) establishment. At their most basic, these typically British places – often known also as **guest houses** in resorts and other tourist towns – are ordinary private houses with a couple of bedrooms set aside for paying guests and a dining room for the consumption of a rudimentary breakfast. At their best, however, B&Bs offer rooms as well furnished as those in hotels costing twice as much, with delicious home-prepared breakfasts, and an informal hospitality that a larger place can't match. B&Bs are graded in the same way as hotels, but using slightly different conventions – for example, the *AA* awards "Q"s (for quality) rather than stars. As a guideline on costs, it's easy to find a one-Q place for under £40 per night for a double B&B, and right at the top end of the scale there are some four-Qs for as little as £70 – farmhouse B&Bs are especially good value. Since many B&Bs, even the pricier ones, have a very small number of rooms, you should book as far in advance as possible. An important point to remember is that some hotels and B&Bs in rural areas, particularly in Scotland, are only open between Easter and October; where this is the case, we've said so in the guide.

Finally, don't assume that a B&B is no good if it's ungraded. There are so many B&Bs in Britain that the grading inspectors can't possibly keep track of them all, and in the rural backwaters some of the most enjoyable accommodation is to be found in welcoming and beautifully set houses whose facilities may technically fall short of official standards.

HOSTELS

The **Youth Hostels Association** network consists of some 240 properties in **England and Wales**, with the **Scottish Youth Hostels Association** responsible for around 80 properties in Scotland, all offering bunk-bed accommodation in single-sex dormitories or smaller rooms. A few of these places are spartan establishments of the sort traditionally associated with the wholesome, fresh-air ethic of the first hostels, but most have moved well away from the old-fashioned, institutional ambience.

Membership of the YHA is open only to residents of England and Wales and costs £3 per year for under-18s, £9.30 for others; Scottish nationals can join the SYHA for £6 a year, £2.50 for under-18s. You can join by either writing to the associations (see box opposite for addresses) or in person at any YHA and most SYHA hostels. The membership fee also gives you membership of the hostelling associations of the 60 countries affiliated to *Hostelling International* (*HI*); visitors who belong to any *HI* association have automatic membership of the YHA and SYHA; if you aren't a member of such an organization, you can join the HI at any English or Welsh and most Scottish hostels for a £9 fee.

Throughout most of Britain, **prices** for under-18s range from £3.40 per night to £7.60, while for over-18s the range is £5.10 to £11.40 (London hostels are more expensive). Students aged 18–25 can get a £1 reduction on production of a valid student card. Length of stay is normally unlimited, and the hostel warden will provide a linen sleeping bag for a small charge. The cost of hostel **meals** is similarly low: breakfast is around £2.80, a packed lunch is about £3, and evening meals start at just £4.15. Nearly all hostels have kitchen facilities for those who prefer self-catering.

At any time of year it's best to **reserve your place** well in advance, and it's essential at Easter, Christmas and from May to August. Most hostels accept payment by *Mastercard* or *Visa*; with those that don't, you should confirm your reservation in writing, with payment, at least seven days before arrival. Reservations made less than seven days in advance will be held only until 6pm on the day of arrival. If you're tempted to turn up on the spur of the moment, bear in mind that very few hostels are open year-round, many are closed at least one day a week even in high season, and several have periods during which they accept reservations from groups only. To give the full details of opening times within this guide would be impossibly unwieldy, so **always phone** – we've given the number for every hostel mentioned. Most hostels are closed from 10am to 5pm, with an 11.30pm curfew, although six of the London hostels offer 24-hour access. If you're planning to make full use of the system, it's worth getting hold of the annual *Hostelling International* handbook for Europe and the Mediterranean, free to members, which includes a listing for every property with copious details of opening hours and facilities.

At best, **independent hostels** offer facilities commensurate with those of YHA/SYHA places

YOUTH HOSTEL ASSOCIATIONS

Australia *Australian Youth Hostels Association*, Level 3, 10 Mallett St, Camperdown, NSW (☎02/5651699).

Canada *Hostelling International-Canadian Hostelling Association*, Room 400, 205 Catherine St, Ottawa, ON K2P 1C3 (☎613/237-7884 or ☎800/663-5777).

England *Youth Hostels Association* (*YHA*), Trevelyan House, 8 St Stephen's Hill, St Alban's, Herts AL1 2DY (☎01727/855 215). London information office: 14 Southampton St, London WC2E 7HY (☎0171/836 1036). There are fifteen other YHA city locations throughout England.

Ireland *An Oige*, 61 Mountjoy St, Dublin 7 (☎01/830 4555).

New Zealand *Youth Hostels Association of New Zealand*, PO Box 436, Christchurch 1 (☎03/799970).

Northern Ireland *Youth Hostel Association of Northern Ireland*, 22 Donegal Rd, Belfast BT12 5JN (☎01232/324733).

Scotland *Scottish Youth Hostels Association*, 7 Glebe Crescent, Stirling FK8 2JA (☎01786/451 181).

USA *Hostelling International-American Youth Hostels* (HI-AYH), 733 15th St NW, Suite 840, PO Box 37613, Washington, DC 20005 (☎202/783-6161).

at a lower price and in a less constricted atmosphere. However, many of these hostels make their money by over-cramming their rooms with beds; kitchens are often inadequate or non-existent and washing facilities can be similarly poor. That said, a lot of people find the freedom to smoke, drink and chat to fellow travellers ample compensation for the less than salubrious environment. In Scotland 37 hostels, mainly situated in the Highlands and islands, have banded together to form the **Independent Backpackers Hostels Association**. Most are family-run places, with no membership or curfew, and open all year, charging around £7 per person per night. Housed in buildings ranging from croft-houses to converted churches, they all have decent facilities and kitchens, while many organize outdoor activities. A brochure listing all the properties is available from *The Independent Backpackers Hostels Scotland*, c/o The Loch Ness Backpackers Lodge, Leiston, Drumnadrochit, Inverness-shire IV3 6UT (☎01456/450807). Some cities throughout Britain use **YMCA** and **YWCA** hostels, though these are only attractive if you're staying for at least a week, in which case you can get discounts on rates that are otherwise no better than budget B&Bs.

In British university towns you can usually find out-of-term accommodation in the **student halls**, though in many instances this gives you the frugality of hostel dorms at the cost of a more comfortable B&B. In some instances, however, this may be the only budget accommodation on offer in the centre of town – for example, if you

were to arrive in Durham in high summer with nothing booked in advance. All the useful **university addresses** are given in the guide, but if you want a list of everything that's on offer, write to the *British Universities Accommodation Consortium*, PO Box 1274, University Park, Nottingham NG7 2RD (☎0115/950 4571).

In the wilder parts of England and Wales, such as the north Pennines, north Yorkshire, Dartmoor, Exmoor and Snowdonia, the YHA administers basic accommodation for walkers in **camping barns**. Holding up to twenty people, these agricultural outbuildings are often unheated and are very sparsely furnished, with wooden sleeping platforms, a couple of tables, a toilet and a cold water supply; but they are weatherproof, extremely inexpensive, and perfectly situated for walking tours. You do not have to be a YHA member to stay in any of these. Similar barns, often called bunkhouses, are run by private individuals in these areas – the useful ones are mentioned in the guide. Primitive croft accommodation in the Hebridean Islands is provided by the charitable **Gatliff Hebridean Hostels Trust**, which is allied to the SYHA.

CAMPING AND CARAVANNING

There are hundreds of **campsites** in Britain, charging from £5 per tent per night to around £10 for the plushest sites, with amenities such as laundries, shops and sports facilities. Some YHA hostels have small campsites on their property, charging half the indoor overnight fee. In addition to these official sites, farmers may offer pitches for as little as £2 per night, but don't expect fully tiled bathroms and hair dryers for that kind of money. Even farmers without a reserved camping area may let you pitch in a field if you ask first, and may even charge you nothing for the privilege; setting up a tent without asking is an act of trespass, which will not be well received. **Free camping is illegal** in national parks and nature reserves.

For **North Americans** planning to do a lot of camping, an **international camping carnet** is a sound investment, available from home-motoring organizations, or from *Family Campers and RVers (FCRV)*, 4804 Transit Rd, Building 2, Depew, NY 14043 (☎1-800/245-9755) in the US; 51 W 22nd St, Hamilton, Ontario LC9 4N5 (☎1-800/245-9755) in Canada. The carnet is good for discounts at member sites and serves as useful identifica-

tion. *FCRV* annual membership costs $20, and the carnet an addititional $10.

The problem with many campsites in the most popular parts of Britain – especially the West Country coast, the Welsh coastline and national parks and the Scottish Highlands and islands – is that tents have to share the space with **caravans**. Every summer the country's byways are clogged by migrations of these cumbersome trailers, which are still considerably more numerous than RVs in England. The great majority of caravans, however, are permanently moored at their sites, where they are rented out to families for **self-catering** holidays, and the ranks of nose-to-tail trailers in the vicinity of most of the UK's best beaches might make you think that half the population of Britain shacks up in a caravan for the midsummer break. Visitors from outside Britain

---

SELF-CATERING ACCOMMODATION FIRMS

Brecon Beacons Holiday Cottages, Brynoyre, Talybont-on-Usk, Brecon, Powys LD3 7YS (☎01874/87446). Around 100 cottages, some decidedly quirky, in the Welsh national park.

Coastal Cottages of Pembrokeshire, Abercastle, Dyfed SA62 5HJ (☎01348/837 742). Around 350 cottages, chalets, flats and houses in the Welsh Pembrokeshire coast area.

Country Holidays, Spring Mill, Earby, Lancs BB8 6RN (☎01282/445 095). More than 5000 properties all over England.

Duundas Property Agency, 61–63 Broughton St, Edinburgh EH1 3RJ (☎0131/556 8363). Range of houses throughout Scotland.

English Country Cottages, Grove Farm Barns, Fakenham, Norfolk NR21 9NB (☎01328/864 041). Around 2000 cottages in various parts of rural England.

Finlayson Hughes, 45 Church St, Inverness IV1 1DR (☎01463/224 343). Just under 200 properties across Scotland from castles to bothies.

Forest Holidays, Forestry Commission, 231 Corstorphine Rd, Edinburgh EH12 7AT (☎0131/334 0303). Mostly purpose-built cabins in beautiful woodland areas throughout Britain, often with pony trekking and similar outdoor activities available at or near the site.

Gwyliau Cymreig (*Welsh Holidays*), Snowdonia Tourist Services, Ynys Tywyn, High St, Porthmadog, Gwynedd LL49 9PG (☎01766/513 829). Best and cheapest of the many companies offering

self-catering accommodation in Snowdonia and north Wales.

Landmark Trust, Shottesbrooke, Maidenhead, Berks SL6 3SW (☎01628/825 925). The firm's £8 brochure lists some 150 converted historic properties in England, ranging from restored forts and Martello Towers to a tiny radio shack used in the last war.

National Trust (Enterprises) Ltd, PO Box 536, Melksham, Wilts SN2 8SX (☎01225/791 199). About 200 NT-owned cottages and farmhouses, most set in their own gardens or grounds.

National Trust for Scotland, 5 Charlotte Square, Edinburgh EH2 4DU (☎0131/226 5922). Thirty-seven NTS-owned converted historic cottages and houses around Scotland.

Powell's Cottage Holidays, Dolphin House, High St, Saundersfoot, Dyfed SA69 9EJ (☎01834/812791). Some 250 properties, mainly in south Wales and the Gower.

Quality Cottages, Cerbid, Solva, Haverford, Dyfed SA62 9YE (☎01348/837 871). Coastal cottages throughout Wales.

Rural Retreats, Station Road, Blockley, Moreton-in-the-Marsh, Gloucestershire GL56 9DZ (☎01386/701 177). Upmarket apartments in restored old buildings, many of them listed buildings.

Wales Cottage Holidays, The Bank, Newtown, Powys SY16 2AA (☎01686/625 267). A varied selection of 500 properties all over Wales.

tend to prefer more robust self-catering accommodation, and there are thousands of tourist board-approved properties for rent by the week, ranging from city penthouses to secluded cottages. The least you can expect to pay for four-berth self-catering accommodation in summer would be £150–200 per week, but for something more attractive – such as a small house near the West Country moors – you should budget for twice that amount. The BTA lists include accommodation costing up to £1200 per week.

Detailed annually revised **guidebooks** to Britain's camping and caravan sites include the *AA's Camping and Caravanning in Britain and Ireland*, which lists their inspected and graded sites, and *Cade's Camping, Tourings and Motor Caravan Site Guide*, published by Marwain. The two useful BTA lists are called *Britain: Self-Catering Holiday Homes*, and *City Apartments* – the latter could be useful if you're in a largish party staying in London for a week or two. Alternative sources of information on all types of self-catering accommodation, from canal boats to ex-lighthouses, are *Dalton's Weekly* (available from most newsagents) and the Sunday newspapers, and of course most British travel agents can offer a range of self-catering holiday packages. Some of the more interesting firms offering **accommodation only** are listed in the box opposite.

FOOD AND DRINK

Though the British still tend to regard eating as a functional necessity rather than a focal point of the day, great advances towards a more sophisticated appreciation of the culinary arts have been made in recent years. Every major town has its top-range restaurants, many of them boasting awards for excellence, while it's nearly always possible to eat well and inexpensively thanks chiefly to the influence of Britain's various immigrant communities. However, the pub will long remain the centre of social life in Britain, a drink in a traditional "local" often making the best introduction to the life of a town.

EATING

In many hotels and B&Bs you'll be offered what's termed an **"English breakfast"**, which is basically sausage, bacon and eggs plus tea and toast. This used to be the typical working-class start to the day, but these days the British have adopted the healthier cereal alternative, and most places will give you this option as well. A **"Scottish breakfast"** is likely to include porridge – properly made with genuine oatmeal and traditionally eaten with salt rather than sugar, though the latter is always on offer. You may also be served kippers or Arbroath smokies (delicately smoked haddock with butter), or a large piece of haddock with a poached egg on top. Oatcakes (plain savoury biscuits) and a "buttery" – not unlike a French croissant – will often feature. In larger British towns you won't have to walk far to find a so-called **"greasy spoon"** or **"caff"** (English for café), where the early-day menu will include cholesterol-rich variations on the theme of sausage, beans, fried egg and chips (fries). Establishments where you can just pop in for a continental-style coffee and pastry breakfast are virtually unknown outside the sophisticated zones of London and a few other cities.

For most overseas visitors the quintessential British meal is **fish and chips** (known in Scotland as a "fish supper", even at lunchtime), a dish that can vary from the succulently fresh to the indigestibly oily – in many "chippies" it's little wonder that lashings of salt, vinegar and tomato ketchup or the fruitier brown sauce are common additions. The classier places have tables, but more often they serve takeaway (take-out) food only, sometimes supplying a disposable fork so that you can guzzle your roadside meal with a modicum of decorum. Fish and chip shops can be found on most high streets and main suburban thoroughfares throughout Britain, although in larger towns they're beginning to be outnumbered by **pizza**, **kebab** and **burger** outlets.

Other sources of straightforward food at lunchtime and early evening are "greasy spoons" (which tend to close at around 6–7pm), and **pubs** (which usually stop serving food by 9pm), where you'll often find plain "meat-and-two-veg" dishes: steak and kidney pie, shepherd's pie (minced lamb or beef covered in mashed potato, and baked), chops and steaks, accompanied by boiled potatoes, carrots or some such vegetable. However, a lot of British pubs now take their food very seriously indeed, having separate dining areas and menus that can compete with some of the better mid-range restaurants. In the smallest villages the pub may be the only place you can eat. Another recent development is the growing number of specialist **vegetarian** restaurants, especially in the larger towns, and the increasing awareness of vegetarian preferences in other eating places. In Wales especially you'll come across dozens of small, inexpensive **wholefood cafés**, often doubling up as alternative resource centres. Also on the rise in the major towns are vaguely French **brasseries**, informal bar-restaurants offering simple meals from around £10 per head.

Our restaurant listings include a mix of high-quality and good-value establishments, but if you're intent on a culinary pilgrimage, you would do well to arm yourself with a copy of the *Good Food Guide* (Hodder), which is updated annually and includes nearly 1500 detailed recommendations.

Throughout this book, we've supplied the phone number for all restaurants where you may need to book a table. At places categorized as "**inexpensive**", you can expect to pay under £10 per head, without drinks; "**moderate**" means £10–20, "**expensive**" £20–30, and "**very expensive**" over £30.

Britain has its diverse immigrant communities to thank for the range of foods in the mid-range category. Of the innumerable types of ethnic restaurants offering good-value high-quality meals you'll find **Chinese**, **Indian** and **Bangladeshi** specialities in every town of any size, with the widest choice in London and the industrial cities of northern England. Other Asian restaurants, particularly **Thai** and **Indonesian**, are now becoming more widespread in England, but are generally a shade more expensive, while further up the economic scale there's no shortage of **French** and **Italian** places – by far the most popular European cuisines, though most cities also have their share of **Spanish** tapas bars. **Japanese** food has been one of the success stories of recent years, with diners and sushi bars joining the expense-account restaurants that have been established for some time in the business centres of England.

The ranks of Britain's **gastronomic restaurants** grow with each passing year, with *cordon-bleu* chefs producing high-class French-style dishes, California-influenced menus, internationalist hybrid creations, and traditional British meat and fish dishes that are as delicious as the more arty creations of their cross-Channel counterparts. London of course has the highest concentration of top-flight places, but wherever you are in Britain you're never more than half an hour's drive from a really good meal – some of the very best dining rooms are to be found in the countryside hotels. The problem is that fine food costs more in Britain than it does anywhere else in Europe. If a place has any sort of reputation in foodie circles you're unlikely to be spending less than £30 per head, and for the services of the country's glamour chefs you could be paying up to a preposterous £90.

REGIONAL CUISINE

England is not particularly celebrated for its variety of regional cuisines, though most areas have a speciality or two, generally rather robust in character. Lincolnshire, for example, is known for its **sausages**, Lancashire and Yorkshire for their **black puddings** (a type of sausage), Cornwall for its **pasty** (a stodgy envelope of pastry filled with meat, potatoes and other root vegetables), and Melton Mowbray for its leaden **pork pies**. England's traditional **cakes** – for example, Bath buns, Bakewell puddings or tarts and Eccles cakes – can be found in bakeries on any high street, though they're at their most authentic in their place of origin. A few delicacies are seasonal, such as hot cross buns, available only in the few weeks leading up to Easter. More refined dishes are to be had along the coasts – the best **seafood** is found in Cornwall, while oysters are a speciality in Whitstable – while a few English **cheeses**, notably Stilton, enjoy world recognition. England's regional beers are perhaps more distinctive than its food, however, and you'll find a much stronger emphasis on traditional cooking in Scotland and Wales.

The quality of **Scottish food** has improved by leaps and bounds in recent years. Scottish produce – superb meat, fish and game, a wide range of dairy products and a bewildering variety of traditional baked goodies – is of outstanding quality and has to some extent been rediscovered of late. You'll find that many, but not all, of the best Scottish eating places are included in the *Taste of Scotland* scheme, which aims to promote native cuisine.

The quintessential Scottish dish is **haggis**, a sheep's stomach stuffed with spiced liver, offal, oatmeal and onion and traditionally eaten with bashed neeps (mashed turnips) and chappit tatties (mashed potatoes). Among other native staples is **stovies**, a tasty mash of onion and fried potato heated up with minced beef. Homemade soup is generally welcome in what can be a cold climate: try **Scots broth**, made with various combinations of lentil, split pea, mutton stock or vegetables and barley.

Welsh cooking is similarly in resurgence, as attested by the many restaurants, hotels and pubs displaying the *Taste of Wales* (*Blas ar Cymru*) badge. Traditional dishes, such as the delicious native **lamb**, fresh **salmon** and trout, can be found on an increasing number of menus, frequently combined with the national vegetable, the **leek**. Particularly Welsh specialities include **laver bread** (*bara lawr*), a thoroughly tasty seaweed and oatmeal cake often included in a traditional fried breakfast; **Glamorgan sausages**, a vegetarian combination of local cheese and spices; **cawl**, a chunky mutton broth; and **cockles**, trawled from the estuary north of the Gower.

Dairy products feature highly in such a predominantly rural country, and there's a superb range of Welsh **cheeses**. The best known is Caerphilly, a soft crumbly white cheese that is mixed with beer and toasted on bread to form an authentic Welsh Rabbit (or Rarebit).

DRINKING

The combination of an inclement climate and an English temperamental aversion to casual chat makes the simple **café** a rare phenomenon outside the biggest cities – there are probably more in London's Soho and the surrounding area than in the rest of the country combined. A growing number of pubs now serve **tea and coffee** during the day but in most places you'll attract consternation by asking for a cup; in the more genteel tourist towns (eg Stratford, Harrogate and York), you'll find plenty of **tea shops**, unlicensed establishments where the normal procedure is to order a slice of cake or some other pastry with your tea or coffee – the former is far more popular. Increasingly common in the big cities are **brasseries** or equivalent establishments (see above), where the majority of customers are there for a bite to eat, but where you're generally welcome to spend half an hour nursing a cappuccino or glass of wine.

Nothing is likely to dislodge the **pub** from its status as the great British social institution. Originating as wayfarers' hostelries and coaching inns, pubs have outlived the church and marketplace as the focal points of communities, and at their best they can be as welcoming as the full name – "public house" – suggests. Pubs are as varied as the country's townscapes: in larger market towns you'll find huge oak-beamed inns with open fires and polished brass fittings; in the remoter upland villages there are stone-built pubs no larger than a two-bedroomed cottage; and in the more inward-looking parts of industrial Britain you'll come across no-nonsense pubs where something of the old division of the sexes and classes still holds sway: the "spit and sawdust" public bar is where working men can bond over a pint or two; the plusher saloon bar, with a separate entrance, is the preferred haunt of mutually preoccupied couples, the middle classes and unaccompanied women. Whatever the species of pub, its **opening hours** are daily 11am–11pm (in quieter spots closed between about 3 and 5.30pm), with "last orders" called by the bar staff about twenty minutes before closing time. The legal drinking age is eighteen; unless there's a special family room or a beer garden, children are not usually welcome.

Most pubs are owned by large breweries who favour their own **beers** and **lagers**, as well as some "guest beers", all dispensed by the pint or half-pint. (A pint costs anything from £1.20 to £2, depending on the brew and the locale of the pub; see below for more on types of beer.) **Cider**, the fermented produce of apples, is a sweet, alcoholic beverage produced in the West Country, where it's often preferred to beer. The cider sold in pubs all over England is a fizzy drink that only approximates to the far more potent and less refined **scrumpy**, the type of cider consumed by aficionados of the apple. As with beer, the best scrumpy is available within a short radius of the factory, but the drink has nothing like the variety of beer. **Wines** sold in pubs are generally appalling, a strange situation in view of the excellent range of wine available in off-licences and supermarkets. The wine lists in brasseries and **wine bars** are nearly always better, but the mark-ups are often outrageous, and any members of the party who prefer beer will have to be content with bottled drinks. Nonetheless, many people are prepared to pay the extra in return for a less boozy and male-dominated atmosphere.

BEER

The most widespread type of English beer is **bitter**, an uncarbonated and dark beverage that should be pumped by hand from the cellar and served at room temperature. Though virtually extinct in England, the sweeter, darker "mild" beer and the even stronger **porter** are quite common in Welsh pubs. The indigenous Scottish beer is **ale**, much like the English bitter (in Scotland known as **heavy**). In recent years, boosted by aggressive advertising, **lager** has overtaken beer in popularity, and every pub will have at least two brands on offer, but the major breweries are now capitalizing on a backlash against foreign-sounding, pale, chilly and often tasteless drinks, a reaction in large part due to the work of **CAMRA** (Campaign for Real Ale).

Some of the beer touted as good traditional ale is nothing of the sort (if the stuff comes out of an electric pump, it isn't the real thing), and some of the genuine beers have been adulterated since being taken over by the big companies, but the big breweries do widely distribute some very good beers – for example, *Directors*, produced by the giant Courage group, is a very classy strong bitter. *Guinness*, a very dark, creamy Irish stout, is also on sale virtually everywhere, and is an exception to the high-minded objection to electrically pumped beers (though purists will tell you that the stuff the English drink does not compare

with the home variety). Smaller operations whose fine ales are available over a wide area include Young's, Fuller's, Wadworth's, Adnams, Greene King, Flowers and Tetley's.

Scottish beers are graded by the shilling: a system used since the 1870s and indicating the level of potency – the higher the shilling mark, the stronger or "heavier" the beer. Scotland's biggest name breweries are McEwan's and Younger's, part of the mighty Scottish and Newcastle group, and Tennents, owned by the English firm Bass. The beers produced by these companies tend to be heavier, smoother and stronger than their English equivalents, especially *McEwan's Export*, a mass-produced, highly potent brew, and *Tennents' Fowler's Wee Heavy*, a famously tasty smooth ale. *Younger's Tartan*, though less flavoursome, is Scotland's biggest seller.

However, if you really want to discover how good British beer can be, you should sample the products of the innumerable small **local breweries** producing real ales to traditional recipes. Every region has its distinctive brew, frequently available at free houses – independently run establishments that sell what they please and are generally more characterful than so-called "tied pubs". There are far too many small English breweries to list here, but we've recommended some of the best local brews in the guide. In **Scotland**, Edinburgh's *Caledonian Brewery* makes nine good cask beers, operating from Victorian premises that preserve much of their original equipment. Others to look out for are *Bellhaven*, a brewery near Edinburgh whose 80-shilling *Export* is a typical Scottish ale; *Maclays*, a hoppy, lightish ale brewed in Alloa; and *Traquair*, in the Borders, which does a wonderfully smooth *House Ale*. The dry, fruity *Alice Ale* from Inverness and the *Orkney Brewery's Raven Ale* could be life-savers in the north, where good beer is hard to come by. Among beers worth sampling in **Wales** are the brews produced by the Cardiff-based Brains, whose *Dark*, *Bitter* and *SA Best Bitter* are among the finest pints in the UK. Llanelli-based Felinfoel and Crown Buckley also produce a number of excellent bitters.

If you see a recent CAMRA sticker on the window of a pub, the beer inside is certainly worth a try, but for serious research CAMRA's annual *Good Beer Guide* is essential. Also useful is the *Good Pub Guide* (Vermilion), a thousand-page yearly handbook that rates each pub's ambience and food as well as its beer.

WHISKY

Scotland's national drink is **whisky** – *uisge beatha*, the "water of life" in Gaelic – traditionally drunk in pubs with a half-pint of beer on the side, a combination known as a "nip and a hauf". Whisky has been produced in Scotland since the fifteenth century, and really took off in popularity after the 1780 tax on claret made wine too expensive for most people. The taxman soon caught up with illicit whisky distilling and drove the stills underground, and today many malt distilleries operate on the site of simple cottages that once distilled the stuff illegally. In 1823 Parliament revised its Excise Laws, in the process legalizing whisky production, and today the drink is Scotland's chief export. There are two types of whisky: **single malt**, made from malted barley, and **grain**, which, relatively cheap to produce, is made from maize and a small amount of malted barley in a continuous still. **Blended** whisky, which accounts for more than 90 percent of all sales, is, as the name suggests, a blend of the two types.

Grain whisky forms about 70 percent of the average bottle of blended whisky, but the distinctive flavour of the different blends comes from the malt whisky which is added to the grain in different quantities. The more expensive the blend, the higher the proportion of skilfully chosen and aged malts that has gone into it. Among many brand names, *Johnnie Walker*, *Bells*, *Teachers* and *The Famous Grouse* are some of the most widely available. All have a similar flavour, and are often drunk with mixers such as lemonade or mineral water.

Despite the dominance of the blended whiskies, **single malt whiskies** are infinitely superior, and best drunk neat to appreciate their distinctive flavours. They vary enormously depending on the peat used for drying, the water used, and the type of oak cask in which they are matured, but they fall into four distinct groups – Highland, Lowland, Campbeltown and Islay, with the majority falling into the Highland category and produced largely on Speyside. You can get the best-known blends – among them *Glenlivet*, *Glenmorangie*, *MacAllan*, *Talisker*, *Laphroaig*, *Highland Park* and *Glenfiddich*, the top seller – in most of the pubs.

POST AND PHONES

Virtually all **post offices** (*swyddfa'r post* in Wales) are open Mon–Fri 9am–5.30pm, Sat 9am–12.30 or 1pm; in small communities you'll find sub-post offices operating out of a shop, but these are open the same hours, even if the shop itself is open for longer. Stamps can be bought at post office counters, from vending machines outside, or from an increasing number of newsagents, although in the last case usually only in books of four or ten stamps. A first-class letter to anywhere in the British Isles costs 25p and should arrive the next day; second-class letters cost 19p, taking two to four days to arrive. **Airmail** letters of less than 20g (0.7oz) to EU countries also cost 25p, to non-EU European countries 30p and elsewhere overseas from 41p for 10g. Pre-stamped aerogrammes conforming to overseas airmail weight limits of under 10g cost 39p from post offices.

Public **payphones** are operated by British Telecom (BT) and there should be one within ten minutes' walk of wherever you're standing, unless you're in the middle of a moor. Many BT payphones take all coins from 10p upwards, but an increasing proportion of BT's payphones only accept **phonecards**, available from post offices and newsagents which display BT's green logo. These cards come in denominations of £1, £2, £5 and £10; some BT phones accept credit cards too.

OPERATOR SERVICES

Domestic operator ☎100   International operator ☎155
Domestic directory assistance ☎192   International directory assistance ☎153

INTERNATIONAL CALLS

To **call Britain** from overseas, dial the international access code (☎011 from the US and Canada, ☎0011 from Australia and ☎00 from New Zealand) followed by 44, the area code minus its initial zero, and then the number. To dial **overseas from Britain** it's ☎00 followed by the country code, area code (without the zero if there is one) and subscriber number. Country codes are as follows:

US and Canada ☎ 1   Ireland☎353   Australia☎61   New Zealand☎64

Inland calls are at the cheapest between the hours of 6pm and 8am. **Reduced-rate periods** for most **international calls** are 8pm–8am from Monday to Friday and all day on Saturday and Sunday, though for Australia and New Zealand it's midnight–7am & 2.30–7.30pm daily. Throughout this guide, every telephone number is prefixed by the area code, separated from the subscriber number by an oblique slash. Any number with the prefix ☎0800 or ☎0500 is free to the caller; ☎0345 and ☎0645 numbers are charged at local rate; ☎0981 and ☎0898 numbers, usually information or "entertainment" lines, are charged at the exorbitant premium rate.

OPENING HOURS AND HOLIDAYS

General **shop hours** are Mon–Sat 9am–5.30 or 6pm, although there's an increasing amount of Sunday and late-night shopping in the larger towns, with Thursday or Friday being the favoured evenings for late opening. The big supermarkets also tend to stay open until 8 or 9pm from Monday to Saturday and, in England and Wales, open on Sunday from 10am to 4pm, as do many of the stores in the shopping complexes that are springing up on the outskirts of many major towns. Note that in Scotland you can't buy alcohol in shops on Sundays. Many provincial towns still retain an "early closing day" when shops close at 1pm – Wednesday is the favourite. Not all service stations on motorways are open for 24 hours although you can usually get fuel around the clock in the larger towns and cities.

Unlike in England and Wales, **Scotland's "bank holidays"** mean just that: they are literally days when the banks are closed rather than general public holidays, and they vary from year to year. They include January 2, Good Friday, the first and last Monday in May, the first Monday in August, St Andrew's Day (November 30), Christmas Day (December 25) and Boxing Day (December 26). New Year's Day, January 1, is the only fixed public holiday in Scotland, but all Scottish towns and cities have a one-day holiday in both spring and autumn – dates vary from place to place but normally fall on a Monday. If you want to know the exact dates, you can get a booklet detailing them from *Glasgow Chamber of Commerce*, 30 George Square, Glasgow G2 1EQ.

In England and Wales most fee-charging sites are open on Bank Holidays, when Sunday hours usually apply.

PUBLIC HOLIDAYS IN ENGLAND AND WALES

January 1
Good Friday – late March to early April
Easter Monday – as above
First Monday in May (this public holiday may soon be replaced by a date in October)
Last Monday in May
Last Monday in August
December 25
December 26
Note that if January 1, December 25 or December 26 falls on a Saturday or Sunday, the next weekday becomes a public holiday.

SIGHTS, MUSEUMS AND MONUMENTS

Most attractions in England and Wales are open daily in summer and closed one or two days a week in winter, though the major state museums are open daily all year. In Scotland the tourist season runs from Easter to October and only the biggest museums and most popular indoor attractions are open outside this period, although ruins and gardens are normally accessible year-round. We've given full details of opening hours throughout the guide.

Many of Britain's most treasured sites – from castles, abbeys and great houses to tracts of protected landscape – come under the control of the private **National Trust**, 36 Queen Anne's Gate, London SW1H 9AS (☎0171/222 9251), and **National Trust for Scotland**, 5 Charlotte Square, Edinburgh EH2 4DU (☎0131/226 5922). Both organizations charge an entry fee for the majority of their sites, and these can be quite high, especially for the more grandiose estates. If you think you'll be visiting more than half a dozen of their properties, denoted "NT" or "NTS" in the guide, it's worth taking out **annual membership** (NT £25; NTS £24), which allows free entry to both sets of properties, although you'll only receive mailings from the one that you join.

A great many of Britain's other sites are controlled by the state-run **English Heritage**, 23 Savile Row, London W1X 1AB (☎0171/973 3000); **Historic Scotland**, Longmore House, Salisbury Place, Edinburgh EH9 15H (☎0131/668 8600); and **CADW Welsh Historic Monuments**, Brunel House, 2 Fitzalan Rd, Cardiff CF2 1UY (☎01222/465511), which we've denoted as "EH", "HS" and "CADW" respectively. Annual **membership** of any one of the three (EH £18.50; HS £17; CADW £14) entitles you to half-price entry to properties run by the other two.

A lot of **stately homes** remain in the hands of the landed gentry, who tend to charge in the region of £5 for admission to edited highlights of their domain – even more if, as at Longleat, they've added some theme-park attractions to the historic pile. Many other old buildings, albeit rarely the most momentous structures, are owned by the local authorities, which are generally more lenient with their admission charges, sometimes allowing free access. You may find that a history museum or a similar collection has been installed in the local castle or half-rebuilt ruin, and in these cases

there's usually a modest entry charge. However, municipal art galleries and museums are often free, as are many of the great **state museums** – both the British Museum and the National Gallery are free, for example, though Cardiff's National Museum of Wales is not. On the other hand, these cash-starved institutions are nowadays obliged to request voluntary donations, as are several **cathedrals**. Most cathedrals charge a pound or two for admission to the most beautiful parts of the structure – usually the chapter house or cloister. Churches, increasingly, are kept locked except for services, but when they are open entry is free.

You will certainly have to pay to visit any of Britain's burgeoning **heritage museums**, which in some instances are large multi-building sites staffed by people in period costume, but more often consist of interactive displays – some of which take the form of high-tech animatronic tableaux, while others amount to little more than a few mannequins with video monitors for heads. Tickets for these can cost anywhere between £5 and £10, and expense is not necessarily an indication of quality. However, the most expensive attractions in Britain are those aimed squarely at tourists with cash to spend – Madame Tussaud's and the London Planetarium, the country's number one earner of foreign cash, now charges around £10 admission.

The majority of fee-charging attractions in England have **reductions** for senior citizens, the unemployed, full-time students and children under 16, with under-5s being admitted free almost everywhere. Proof of eligibility will be required in most cases, though even the flintiest desk clerk will probably take on trust the age of a babe-in-arms. The entry charges given in the guide are the full adult charges; as a rule, adult reductions are in the range of 25–35 percent, while reductions for children are around 50 percent.

Finally, foreign visitors planning on seeing more than a dozen stately homes, monuments or gardens might find it worthwhile to buy a **Great British Heritage Pass**, which gives free admission to some 600 sites throughout Britain, many of which are not run by the NT, EH or equivalent organizations. Costing £25 ($39) for seven days, £36 ($58) for fifteen days and £50 ($85) for a month, it can be purchased either in advance or in Britain through most travel agents, *British Airways* offices or the British Travel Centre in London.

THE MEDIA

NEWSPAPERS AND MAGAZINES

English **daily newspapers** are predominantly right-wing, with the Murdoch-owned *Times* and the staunchly Conservative *Daily Telegraph* occupying the "quality" end of the market, trailed by the financially precarious *Independent*, which strives worthily to live up to its self-righteous name, and the *Guardian*, which inhabits a niche marginally to the left of centre. At the opposite end of the scale in terms of intellectual weight and volume of sales is the pernicious *Sun*, the sleaziest occupant of the Murdoch stable; its chief rivals in the sex and scandal stakes are the *Daily Star* and self-consciously ridiculous *Daily Sport*, but the only tabloid that manages anything approximating to a thought-out response to the *Sun*'s reactionary politics is the *Daily Mirror*, and even that paper is now drifting from its former Labour allegiances. The middle-brow daily tabloids – the *Daily Mail* and the *Daily Express* – are uniformly Tory-biased, and show a depressing preoccupation with the royal family and TV celebrities. The scene is a little more varied on a Sunday, when the Guardian-owned *Observer*, England's oldest **Sunday newspaper**, supplements the Sunday editions of the dailies, whose ranks are also swelled by the amazingly popular *News of the World*, a smutty rag known to all as "The News of the Screws".

All the above publications are available in Wales, though they don't cover Welsh news in much depth. The only quality **Welsh daily** is the *Western Mail*, an uneasy mix of local, Welsh, British and token international news, though its attempts to give a Welsh slant to British stories can sometimes be ludicrous. The national Sunday paper, *Wales on Sunday*, is far superior in terms of writing, features and news and sports coverage.

In Scotland, the principal English papers are widely available, often as specific Scottish editions. The Scottish press produces two major daily papers, the liberal-left *Scotsman* and the slightly less-so *Herald*, published in Edinburgh and Glasgow respectively. Scotland's best selling daily paper, though, is the downmarket *Daily Record*, from the same group as the *Daily Mirror*. Many national Sunday newspapers have a Scottish section north of the border, but Scotland's own Sunday "heavy" is the wholly serious and somewhat dull *Scotland on Sunday*. Far more fun is the anachronistic *Sunday Post*, read by over half of the population.

Every town in Britain seems to publish one or more **local papers**, ranging from quality regional news sheets to little more than a collection of adverts. Even these can, however, be a useful source for local events information; we've given details of specific listings magazines in the relevant part of the guide.

When it comes to **specialist periodicals**, British newsagents can offer a range covering just about every subject, with motoring, music, sport, computers, gardening and home improvements all well served. One noticeably poor area is current events – the only high-selling weekly commentary magazine is the *Economist*, which is essential reading in the boardrooms of England. The earnest socialist alternative, the *New Statesman and New Society*, has so few readers that it's stuck with the nickname "The Staggers". The satirical bi-weekly *Private Eye* is a much-loved institution that prides itself on printing the stories the rest of the press won't touch, and on surviving the consequent stream of libel suits. If you feel you can stomach a descent into the scatological pit of the English male psyche, take a look at *Viz*, a bimonthly comic that has managed to lodge its grotesque caricatures in the collective consciousness. Scottish monthly magazines include the widely read *Scots Magazine*, an old-fashioned middle-of-the-road publication that promotes family values. There's a profusion of Welsh monthlies – *Planet*, an English-language overview of the arts, history and politics, is the best of the bunch.

Australians and New Zealanders in London will be gratified by the weekly free magazine, *TNT*, which provides a résumé of news from the home countries as well as adverts for jobs, accommodation and events in the capital. *USA Today* is the most widely available **North American** paper, though only the larger newsagents stock it; *Time* and *Newsweek* are more easily found.

TELEVISION AND RADIO

In Britain there are three terrestrial television stations: the state-owned BBC, with two public service channels, and two independent commercial channels, ITV and Channel Four. Though assailed by critics in the Conservative party, who think that a nationalized TV station should owe a debt of loyalty to the government or that the very notion of a nationalized anything is a Leninist throwback, the **BBC** is just about maintaining its worldwide reputation for in-house quality productions, ranging from expensive costume dramas to intelligent documentaries. BBC2 is the more offbeat and heavyweight BBC channel; BBC1 is avowedly mainstream. Various regional companies together form the **ITV** network, but they are united by a more tabloid approach to programme-making – necessarily so, because if they don't get the advertising they don't survive. **Channel Four**, a partly subsidized institution, is the most progressive of the bunch, with a reputation for broadcasting an eclectic spread of "arty" and minority-pleasing programmes, and for supporting small-budget motion pictures. The principal Welsh channel is **S4C** (*Sianel Pedwar Cymru*), which, like C4, sponsors diverse animation and feature-film projects. Welsh-language programmes are broadcast at lunchtime and for most of the evening, with the rest of the schedule reverting to Channel Four's UK-wide output. Rupert Murdoch's multi-channel BSkyB has a monopoly on the satellite business, presenting a blend of movies, news, sport, reruns and overseas soaps. It has an increasing number of rivals in the form of **cable** TV companies, which are making big inroads in London especially. Within a few years these commercial stations will prob-

ably be making life uncomfortable for the BBC and ITV networks, but for the time being the old terrestrial stations still attract the majority of viewers.

Market forces are eating away rather more quickly at the BBC's **radio** network, which has five stations: Radio One is almost exclusively pop music, with a chart-biased view of the rock world; Two is bland music and chat; Three is predominantly classical music; Four a blend of current affairs, arts and drama; and Five a live sports channel. Radio One has rivals on all fronts, with Virgin running a youth-oriented nationwide commercial network, and a plethora of local commercial stations – like London's Capital Radio and the Kiss FM soul station – attracting large sections of Radio One's target audience. Melody Radio has whittled away at the Radio Two easy-listening market, as has Jazz FM, while Classic FM has lured listeners away from Radio Three by offering a less earnest approach to its subject, though it frequently degenerates into a "Greatest Hits" view of the most renowned composers. The BBC also operates a number of regional stations, but they are usually rather like listening to a broadcast of the local newspapers interspersed with the Top Twenty; the commercial stations, some of them real "fly-by-wire" operations, tend to be far livelier.

One BBC institution that has stayed in front despite the arrival of downmarket pretenders is the *Radio Times*, a weekly publication that gives full details on national TV and radio programmes, not just the ones broadcast by the BBC.

ANNUAL EVENTS

In terms of the number of tourists they attract, the biggest occasions in the English calendar are the rituals that have associations with the ruling classes – from the courtly pageant of the Trooping of the Colour to the annual rowing race between Oxford and Cambridge universities. In Scotland many visitors home straight in on bagpipes, ceilidhs and Highland Games; such anachronisms certainly reflect the endemic British taste for nostalgia, but to gauge the spirit of the nation you should sample a wider range of events. London's large-scale **festivals** range from the riotous street party of the Notting Hill Carnival to the Promenade concerts, Europe's

most egalitarian high-class music season, while the **Edinburgh Festival** and Welsh **National Eisteddfod** are vast cultural jamborees that have attained international status. Every major town in Britain has its own local arts festival, the best of which, along with various other local fairs and commemorative shows, are mentioned in the main part of the guide; the very biggest ones are also listed below.

To see Britain at its most idiosyncratic, take a look at one of the numerous regional celebrations that perpetuate **ancient customs**, the origins and meanings of which have often been lost or conveniently forgotten. The sight of the entire

EVENTS CALENDAR

January 1: Kirkwall Boy's and Men's Ba' Games, Orkney. Mass, drunken football game through the streets of the town, with the castle and the harbour the respective goals. As a grand finale the players jump into the harbour.

Last Tuesday in January: Up-Helly-Aa, Lerwick, Shetland. Norse fire festival culminating in the burning of a specially built Viking longship. Visitors can attend celebrations in the town hall.

End of January: Burns Night. Burns suppers held all over Scotland to commemorate Scotland's greatest poet; haggis, whisky and lots of poetry recital.

February: Scottish Curling Championship held in a different (indoor) venue each year.

Mid-February: Chinese New Year. Festivities in London's Chinatown.

February–March: Five Nations rugby championship.

March: Edinburgh Folk Festival.

March 1: St David's Day. *Hwyrnos* and celebrations all over Wales.

Mid-March: Cheltenham Gold Cup meeting. The country's premier national hunt horseracing event.

Last week of March: University Boat Race. Hugely popular rowing contest on the Thames, between the teams of Oxford and Cambridge.

Shrove Tuesday: Purbeck Marblers and Stonecutters Day, Corfe Castle, Dorset; ritual football game through the streets of the village.

Maundy Thursday: The Queen dispenses the Royal Maundy Money, at a different cathedral every year.

Easter Monday: Hare Pie Scramble and Bottle-Kicking, Hallaton, Leicestershire.

April: Scottish Grand National at Ayr; not quite as testing as the English equivalent steeplechase but an important event on the Scottish racing calendar.

April: Shetland Folk Festival.

First Saturday in April: Grand National meeting, Aintree, Liverpool. Cruelly testing steeplechase that entices most of Britain's population into the betting shops.

April 30–May 3: Minehead Hobby Horse, Minehead, Somerset.

May: Scottish FA Cup Final in Glasgow.

May: Mayfest; Glasgow's recent and very successful answer to the Edinburgh Festival.

May–July: Glyndbourne Opera Festival, East Sussex. The classiest and most snobbish arts festival in the country.

May 1: Padstow Hobby Horse, Padstow, Cornwall.

May 1: Beltane Fire festival on Calton Hill in Edinburgh.

May 8 : Helston Furry Dance, Helston, Cornwall.

Early May: FA Cup Final, Wembley, London. The deciding contest in the premier football tournament.

Late May: Atholl Highlanders Parade at Blair Castle, Perthshire. The annual parade and inspection of Britain's last private army by their colonel-in-chief, the Duke of Atholl.

Late May: Hay-on-Wye Festival of Literature. London's literati flock to the Welsh borders for a week.

Last week in May: Chelsea Flower Show, Royal Hospital, Chelsea, London. Essential event for England's green-fingered legions.

Last week in May: St David's Cathedral Festival. Superb setting for classical concerts and recitals.

Spring Bank Holiday: Monday Cheese Rolling, Brookworth, Gloucestershire. Pursuit of a cheese wheel down a murderous incline – one of the weirdest customs in England.

Late May and early June: Bath International Festival. International arts jamboree.

June–August: Riding of the Marches in the border towns of Hawick, Selkirk, Annan, Dumfries, Duns, Peebles, Jedburgh, Langholm and Lauder. The Rides originated to check the boundaries of common land owned by the town and also to commemorate warfare between the Scots and the English. Nowadays individual Ridings have their own special ceremonies, though they all start with a parade of pipes and brass bands.

June: Shinty Camanachd Cup Final, usually in Inverness. Finals of the intensely competitive games between the northern towns who play Scotland's own stick-and-ball game.

June: Royal Highland Agricultural Show, Ingliston, near Edinburgh. Scotland's biggest and best.

June: Highland Games at Campbeltown, Aberdeen and Grantown-on-Spey.

June: Aldeburgh Festival, jamboree of classical music held on the Suffolk Coast; established by Benjamin Britten.

First week in June: Derby week, Epsom race-course, Surrey. The world's most expensive horse flesh competing in the Derby, the Coronation Cup and the Oaks.

First week in June: Eisteddfod Genedlaethol Urdd. The largest youth festival in Europe, alternating between north and south Wales.

Early June: Cotswold Olympic Games, Chipping Campden, Gloucestershire. Rustic sports festival.

June 12: Trooping the Colour, Horse Guards Parade, London. Equestrian pageantry for the Queen's Official Birthday.

Mid-June: Royal Ascot, Berkshire. High-class horseracing attended by high-class people; the best seats go to royalty and their satellites, while the proles mill around in the outfield.

Mid-June: Cardiff Singer of the World competition. Huge, televised week-long music festival, with a star-studded list of international competitors.

June 24: Midsummer Day Ritual, Stonehenge, Wiltshire.

Last week of June and first week of July: Lawn Tennis Championships, Wimbledon, London. Queues are phenomenal even for the early rounds, and you need to know a freemason or ex-champion to get in to the big games.

July: Scottish Open Golf Championship held at a different venue annually.

July: Glasgow International Folk Festival.

July: Highland Games at Caithness, Elgin, Glengarry, North Uist, Inverness, Inveraray, Mull, Lewis, Durness, Lochaber, Dufftown, Halkirk.

July to early September:The Promenade Concerts, Royal Albert Hall, London. Classical music concerts ending in the fervently patriotic Last Night of the Proms.

First week in July: Henley Royal Regatta, Oxfordshire. Rowing event attended by much the same crew as that which populates the grand-stands at Ascot.

First week in July: Tynwald Ceremony, St Johns, Isle of Man.

Early July: Glastonbury Festival, Somerset. Hugely popular festival, with international bands and loads of hippies. Over £60 entry fee for the three-day event but it can be worth every penny.

Second weekend in July: Gŵyl Werin y Cnapan, Ffostrasol, near Lampeter, Dyfed. The best folk and Celtic music festival in the world.

Second week in July: Llangollen International Music Eisteddfod. Over 12,000 participants from all over the world, including choirs, dancers, folk singers, groups and instrumentalists.

Mid-July: British Open Golf Championship, at a different venue annually. The season's last Grand Slam golf tournament.

Late July: Cambridge Folk Festival. Biggest event of its kind in England.

Late July: Womad, Reading. Three-day world music festival.

Third week in July: Swan Upping, River Thames from Sunbury to Pangbourne; ceremonial registering of the Thames cygnets.

Last week in July: Royal Tournament, Earl's Court Exhibition Centre, London. Precision military displays.

Last week in July to first week in August: Cardiff Street Festival. Includes the Butetown Carnival, a loud, multiracial celebration and party by the bay.

August: Edinburgh International Festival and Fringe. One of the world's great arts jamborees, detailed in full on pp.726-727.

August: Edinburgh Military Tattoo held on the Castle esplanade. Massed pipe bands and drums by floodlight.

August: World Pipe Band Championship at Glasgow.

August: Highland Games at Dunoon (Cowal), Mallaig, Skye, Dornoch, Aboyne, Strathpeffer, Assynt, Bute, Glenfinnan, Argyllshire, Glenurquhart and Invergordon.

First week in August: Royal National Eisteddfod. Wales' biggest single annual event: fun, very impressive and worth seeing if only for the over-blown pageantry. Bardic competitions, readings, theatre, TV, debates and copious help for the Welsh language learner.

August Bank Holiday: Notting Hill Carnival, around Notting Hill, West London. Vivacious celebration by London's Caribbean community – plenty of music, food and floats.

August Bank Holiday: Reading Festival, Berkshire. Three-day indie-rock jamboree.

Last Sunday in August: Plague Memorial, Eyam, Derbyshire.

September: Highland Games at Braemar.

September: Ben Nevis Race for amateurs to the top of the highest mountain in Scotland and back down again.

Early September to early November: Blackpool Illuminations, Lancashire. Five miles of exotic light displays.

EVENTS CALENDAR (cont.)

Late September to early October: Cardiff Festival. Themed annual festival that is one of the UK's largest. Incorportates music, art, drama, opera and literature.

Monday following 1st Sunday after September 4: Abbots Bromley Horn Dance, Abbots Bromley, Staffordshire; vaguely pagan mass dance in mock-medieval costume – one of the most famous ancient customs.

October: The National Mod. Competitive festival of all aspects of Gaelic performing arts, held in varying Scottish venues.

October: Glenfiddich Piping Championships at Blair Atholl for the world's top ten solo pipers.

October: Swansea Festival of Music and the Arts Concerts, jazz, drama, opera, ballet and art events throughout the city.

Late October to early November: Huddersfield Contemporary Music Festival. One of Europe's premier showcases for up-to-the-minute highbrow music.

First Sunday in November: London to Brighton Veteran Car Rally. Ancient machines lumber the 57 miles down the A23 to the seafront.

November 5: Guy Fawkes Night, with nationwide fireworks and bonfires commemorating the foiling of the Gunpowder Plot in 1605. Especially raucous celebrations at Ottery St Mary, Devon and Lewes, East Sussex.

Mid-November: Lord Mayor's Procession and Show, the City of London. Cavalcade to mark the inauguration of the new mayor.

November 30: St Andrew's Day celebrations at St Andrews.

December 31: Tar Barrels Parade, Allendale Town, Northumberland.

December 31: New Year Walk-In, Llanwrtyd Wells, Powys. A boozy stagger around the town.

December 31 and January 1: Hogmanay and Ne'er Day. More important to the Scots than Christmas. Festivities revolve around the "first-footing", when at midnight crowds of revellers troop into neighbours' houses bearing gifts.

---

population of a village kicking a bottle around a hill or throwing cheeses around the fields is not easily forgotten. Some of these strange rituals are mentioned in the guide and included in the list below, but if you'd like a full rundown on such eccentricities as the Britannia Coconut Dancers of Bacup or the ceremony of Dunting the Freeholder in Newbiggin-by-the-Sea, get a copy of *Curious Customs*, an entertaining little book by Martin Green (Impact Books). Bear in mind that at a few of the smaller, more obscure events casual visitors are not always welcome. If in doubt, check with the local tourist office.

Also included in this list are the main **sports** events, which may often be difficult to get tickets for, but are invariably televised. In addition to these, there are of course football matches every Saturday (and some Sundays) from late August till early May, and cricket matches every day throughout the summer – both interesting social phenomena even for those unenthralled by team sports.

SCOTTISH HIGHLAND GAMES

Despite their name, **Highland Games** are held all over Scotland from May until mid-September:

they vary in size and differ in the range of events they offer, and although the most famous are at Oban, Cowal and especially Braemar, often the smaller ones are more fun. They probably originated in the fourteenth century as a means of recruiting the best fighting men for the clan chiefs, and were popularized by Queen Victoria to encourage the traditional dress, music, games and dance of the Highlands; various royals still attend the Games at Braemar. The most distinctive events are known as the "**heavies**" – tossing the caber, putting the stone, and tossing the weight over the bar – all of which require prodigious strength and skill. Tossing the caber is the most spectacular, when the athlete must run carrying an entire tree trunk and attempt to heave it end over end in a perfect, elegant throw. Just as important as the sporting events are the **piping competitions** – for individuals and bands – and **dancing competitions**, where you'll see girls as young as three years old tripping the quick, intricate steps of such traditional dances as the Highland Fling.

The list on the previous pages includes some of the better-known Games; for the smaller, local games, check at individual tourist offices.

OUTDOOR PURSUITS

No matter where you are in Britain, you're never far from a stretch of countryside where you can lose the crowds on a brief walk or cycle ride. For tougher specimens, there are numerous long-distance footpaths, as well as opportunities for the more extreme disciplines of rock climbing and potholing (caving). On the coast and many of the Britain's inland lakes you can follow the more urbane pursuits of sailing and windsurfing, and there are plenty of fine beaches for less structured fresh-air activities or just slobbing around.

WALKING AND CLIMBING

Walking paths trace many of Britain's wilder areas, amid landscapes varied enough to suit anyone. More sedate walkers will be happy enough in England, where many of the footpaths traverse moorlands, but if you're after more demanding exercise, or a feeling of isolation, head for Wales or Scotland. Welsh Snowdonia and the Scottish highlands offer Britain's best climbing and have acted as training grounds for some of the world's greatest mountaineers.

Numerous short walks and several major walks are covered in the guide. However, you should use these notes only as general outlines and always in conjunction with a good **map**. Where possible we have given details of the best maps to use – in most cases one of the *Ordnance Survey* (*OS*) series (see p.20) – along with advice,

leaflets and specialist guidebooks from tourist offices and shops in walking areas. In England and Wales you need to keep to established routes as you'll often be crossing private land, even within the national parks: all *OS* maps mark public rights of way. Scotland, in contrast, has a tradition of free **public access** to most of the countryside, restricted only at certain times of the year.

IN ENGLAND

England's finest **walking** areas are the granite moorlands and spectacular coastlines of **Devon and Cornwall** in the southwest, and the highlands of the north – the low limestone and millstone crags of the **Peak District**, between Sheffield and Manchester; the **Yorkshire Dales**, the stretch of the Pennines to the north of the Peak District; the **North York Moors**, a bleak, treeless upland to the east of the Pennines; and the glaciated Cumbrian Mountains, better known as the **Lake District**. On summer weekends the more accessible reaches of these regions can get very crowded with day-trippers, but at any time of the year you'll find yourself in relative isolation if you undertake one of the **Long Distance Footpaths** (LDPs). Defined as any route over twenty miles long, LDPs exist all over the country and are marked at frequent intervals with an acorn waymarker. Youth hostels are littered along most routes, though you may need a tent for some of the more heroic hikes – like some stretches of the Pennine Way, which, at over 250 miles, are Britain's longest.

The *Long Distance Walkers' Association* (9 Tainters Brook, Uckfield, East Sussex, TN22 1UQ) can provide further information on all the LDPs, while many regional guides are available in outdoor equipment shops. A recommended countrywide guide is *Richard Gilbert's 200 Challenging Walks* (Diadem).

IN SCOTLAND

The whole of Scotland offers good opportunities for gentle hill walking, from the smooth, grassy hills and moors of the **Southern Uplands** to the wild and rugged country of the northwest. Scotland has three **Long Distance Footpaths** (LDPs), each of which takes days to walk, though you can of course just cover sections of them.

SAFETY IN THE SCOTTISH HILLS

Scottish mountains are not high, but, due to rapid weather changes, they are potentially extremely dangerous and should be treated with respect. Every year, in every season, climbers and hill walkers die on Scottish mountains. If the weather looks as if it's closing in, **get down fast**. It is essential that you are properly equipped – even for what appears to be an easy expedition in apparently settled weather – with proper warm and waterproof layered clothing, supportive footwear and adequate maps, a compass (which you should know how to use) and food. Always leave word of your route and what time you expect to return; and remember to contact the person again to let them know that you are back.

The **Southern Upland Way** crosses Scotland from coast to coast in the south, and is the longest at 212 miles; the best known is the **West Highland Way**, a 95-mile hike from Glasgow to Fort William via Loch Lomond and Glen Coe; and the gentler **Speyside Way**, in Aberdeenshire, is a mere thirty miles. The green signposts of the Scottish Rights of Way Society point to these and many other cross-country routes; while in the wilder parts the accepted freedom to roam allows extensive mountain walking, rock climbing, orienteering and allied activities.

Scotland's main **climbing** areas are in the **Highlands**, which boast many challenging peaks as well as great hill walks. There are 279 mountains over 3000ft (914m) in Scotland, known as **Munros** after the man who first classified them: many walkers "collect" them, and it's possible to chalk up several in a day. Serious climbers will probably head for **Glen Coe** or **Torridan** which offer difficult routes in spectacular surroundings. These and some of the other finest Highland areas (Lawers, Kintail, West Affric) are in the ownership of the National Trust for Scotland, while Blaven and Ladhar Bheinn (Knoydart) are John Muir Trust properties; both allow year-round access. Elsewhere there may be restricted access during lambing (dogs are particularly unwelcome during April and May) and deer-stalking seasons (mid-August to the third week in October). The booklet *Heading for the Scottish Hills* (published by the *Scottish Mountaineering Club* or *SMC*) provides such information on all areas. Beginners should contact the **Mountaineering Council of Scotland**, 71 King St (IR), Crieff, Perthshire PH7 3HB (☎01746/654962) for information on courses.

Among the many **guidebooks** available for serious walking and climbing, the *SMC*'s series of *District Guides* offer blow-by-blow accounts of climbs written by professional mountaineers. For other good walking guides see the "Books" section of *Contexts*.

IN WALES

Wales's best walking country is to be found within its three **national parks**. Almost the whole of the northwestern corner of Wales is taken up with the **Snowdonia National Park**, a dozen of the country's highest peaks separated by dramatic glaciated valleys and laced with hundreds of miles of ridge and moorland paths. From Snowdonia, the Cambrian Mountains stretch south to the **Brecon Beacons National Park**, with its striking sandstone scarp at the head of the south Wales coalfield, and lush, cave-riddled limestone valleys to the south. One hundred and seventy miles of Wales' southwestern peninsula make up the third park – the **Pembrokeshire Coast National Park**, best explored by the **Pembrokeshire Coast Path** that traverses the clifftops, frequently dipping down into secluded coves. This is only one of Wales' four frequently walked **Long Distance Paths**. The other three LDPs are the 168-mile long **Offa's Dyke Path** that traces the England–Wales border, the 274-mile **Cambrian Way**, cutting north–south over the Cambrian Mountains, and **Glyndŵr's Way**, which weaves through mid-Wales for 120 miles. For details on specialist walking guides, see *Contexts*, or contact the organizations listed under England, above.

As well as being superb walking country, Snowdonia offers some of Britain's best **rock climbing** and some challenging **scrambles** – ascents that fall somewhere between walks and climbs, requiring some use of your hands. There are a couple of noted climbing spots around the Pembrokeshire coast and in the Brecon Beacons but the vast majority are in **Snowdonia**, with its predominance of low-lying crags and easy access. The best general guide for experienced climbers is *Rock Climbing in Snowdonia* by Paul Williams (Constable). Beginners should contact the *British Mountaineering Council*, Crawford House Precinct Centre, Booth St East, Manchester M13 9RZ (☎0161/273 5835).

CYCLING

Despite the recent boom in the sale of mountain bikes, **cyclists** are treated with notorious disrespect by many motorized road users and by the people who plan the country's traffic systems. Very few of Britain's towns have proper cycle routes, but if you're hell-bent on tackling the congestion, pollution and aggression of city traffic, get a **helmet** and a secure **lock** – cycle theft in Britain is an organized racket, with most machines disappearing overseas. The rural back-roads are infinitely more enjoyable, with a sufficient density of pubs and B&Bs to keep the days manageable – though check what sort of gradients you're likely to enounter, particularly in Wales or Scotland. Your main problem out in the countryside will be finding any spare parts – only inner tubes and tyres are easy to find.

Off-road riding is popular in the highland walking areas, but cyclists in England and Wales should remember to keep to rights of way designated on maps as Bridleways, BOATs ("Byways Open To All Traffic") or RUPFs ("Roads Used As Public Footpaths") and to pass walkers at considerate speeds; access to these paths can sometimes be restricted at peak times in the busiest areas. Footpaths, unless otherwise marked, are for pedestrian use only.

Transporting your bike by **train** is a good way of getting to the interesting parts of Britain without a lot of stressful or boring pedalling; at present, bikes are carried free on suburban trains outside the rush hours of 7.30–9.30am and 4–6pm. On most inter-town routes bikes are carried at £3 per journey. **Bike rental** is available at bike shops in most large towns, but the machines on offer are often pretty derelict – they may be all right for a brief spin, but not for any serious touring. Expect to pay in the region of £8–10 per day, £40–60 per week.

Britain's biggest cycling organization is the **Cycle Touring Club** or CTC (Cotterell House, 69 Meadrow, Godalming, Surrey GU7 3HS; ☎01483/417 217), which supplies members with touring and technical advice as well as insurance. The *Ordnance Survey* is producing a series of excellent regional *Cycle Tour* guides, each covering 24 one-day on- and off-road routes, including details of terrain, gradients, refreshments and places of interest along the way. Recommended nationwide guides are the CTC's 450-page *Route Guide to Cycling in Britain and Ireland* and *Fifty Mountain*

Bike Rides by Jeremy Evans (Crowood). More specifically, there's *England by Bike* by Les Woodland (Cordee) and the regional route guides covering off-road rides in England's Peak District, the Yorkshire Dales and the Lake District produced by *Ernest Press* – although the maps are dire and the books won't last long in muddy or wet conditions.

For those who want a guaranteed hassle-free cycling holiday, there are various companies offering easy-going tours where riders hop from hotel to hotel, with a van carrying all their luggage ahead. One of the most professional outfits is *Country Lanes*, 9 Shaftesbury St, Fordingbridge, Hants SP6 1JF (☎01425/655 022) – accommodation is excellent, food similarly fine, but prices high at £700 for a six-day excursion, including bike rental.

BEACHES

Britain is ringed by fine beaches and bays, many of the best of which are readily accessible by public transport – though of course that means they tend to get very busy in high summer. For a combination of decent climate and good sand, southwest **England** is the best area, especially the coast of north Cornwall and Devon. The other great attraction is the **surfing** – the Atlantic rollers at Bude, Newquay, Perranporth and a few other wide bays are strong enough to attract surfers from Europe, even if the waves aren't exactly Hawaiian. The beaches of England's southern coast become more pebbly as you approach the southeastern corner of the country – resorts round here are more garish than their southwestern counterparts, as exemplified by Brighton. Moving up the east coast, the East Anglian shore is predominantly pebbly and very exposed, making it ideal for those who want to escape the crowds rather than bask in the sun, while right up in the northeast there are some wonderful sandy strands and old-fashioned seaside resorts, though the North Sea breezes often require a degree of stoicism. Over in the northwest, the inland hills of Cumbria are a greater attraction than anything on the coast, though Blackpool has a certain appeal as the apotheosis of the kiss-me-quick holiday town.

Many of **Scotland's** beaches and bays are deserted even in high summer – perhaps hardly surprising given the bracing winds and icy water. Though you're unlikely to come here for a beach holiday, it's worth sampling one or two beaches, even if you never shed as much as a sweater. A

BRITAIN'S DIRTIEST BEACHES

This is a list of British beaches where the shore and bathing waters **failed to meet EU standards** in the last published figures. It was intended that all beaches should reach EU minimum standards by the end of 1995, but, despite great strides having been made, this has not happened yet. An asterisk denotes places that failed for the previous two years as well. The wreck of the Sea Empress in early 1996 may well have long-term consequences for the beaches of south Wales.

ENGLAND

Kent to Dorset

Bournemouth
Brighton
Deal Castle
Folkestone
Hastings
Herne Bay
Hove
Lancing*
Lyme Regis*
Ramsgate*
Ryde (West)
Sandwich Bay*
Southsea
Southwick
Ventnor*
Worthing*

The Southwest

Combe Martin
Ilfracombe
Instow*
Lynmouth
Mounts Bay Wherry (town)*
Paignton
Penzance*
Plymouth Hoe*
Sidmouth
St Ives

East Anglia and the Northeast

Cleethorpes*
Crimdon*
Cromer
Gorleston
Great Yarmouth (South and Pier)*
Leigh-on-Sea
Scarborough (South)
Seaham
Staithes

West Mersea
Whitburn*
Whitly Bay

The Northwest

Allonby (South)*
Blackpool (South Pier)*
Fleetwood*
Heysham*
Lytham St Anne's*
Morecambe (North)*
Roan Head
Seascale*
St Annes (North)*

SCOTLAND

Northeast

Aberdour Harbour
Broughty Ferry
Bruntisland
Cruden Bay
Kinghorn
Kirkcaldy Linktown
Leven East
Lower Largo
St Andrews East
Tayport*
Westhaven

Southern Scotland

Annan*
Ayr*
Drummore
Girvan
Irvine*
Powfoot*
Portobello*
Prestwick*
Saltcoats*
Sandyhills
Stranraer
Turnberry*

WALES

North Coast

Prestatyn (Central)
Penrhyn Bay*
Llandudno West Shore*
Deganwy (North)

West Coast

Llanbedrog
Criccieth (East)
Aberystwyth (Harbour*, South* and Tanybwlch)
Aberaeron (Northern Groyne*, North Harbour and Central Groyne)
New Quay (Traeth Gwyn)
Black Rock Sands
Clarach Bay*
Llangrannog
Aberporth
Gwbert-on Sea at Craig y Gwert
Newport Sands
Pwllgwaelod

South Coast

Broad Haven
Burry Port Beach East
Llanelli Beach*
Goodwich Beach
Saundersfoot
Broughton Bay
Limeslade Bay
Swansea Bay (opposite Black Pill Rock)
Newton Bay
Barry (Watch House Bay)
Whitmore Bay
Jacksons Bay
St Mary's Well Bay
Penarth*

rash of slightly melancholy seaside towns lies within easy reach of Glasgow, while on the east coast, the relatively low cliffs and miles of sandy beaches are ideal for walking. Bizarrely enough, given the low temperature of the water, the beaches in the northeast are beginning to figure on surfers' itineraries, attracting enthusiasts from all over Europe. Perhaps the most beautiful beaches of all are to be found on Scotland's islands: endless, isolated stretches that on a sunny day can seem the epitome of the Scottish Hebridean dream.

In **Wales** the best areas to head for sunbathing and swimming are the Gower Peninsula, the Pembrokeshire coast, the Llŷn and the southwest coast of Anglesey. Wales's southwest-facing beaches offer the best conditions for surfing, key spots being Rhossili, at the western tip of the Gower, and Whitesands Bay near St David's. Winsurfers tend to congregate at Barmouth, Borth, around the Pembrokeshire coast and at The Mumbles. Though the north coast has more resorts than any other section of Wales's coastline, its beaches are certainly not the most attractive and nor is it a good place to swim.

It has to be said that Britain's beaches are not the cleanest in Europe, and many of those that the British authorities declare to be acceptable actually fall below EU standards. Although steps are being taken to improve the situation, far too many stretches of the coastline are contaminated by sea-borne effluent or other rubbish. The box opposite gives the latest state of play. For annually updated, detailed information on the condition of Britain's beaches, the *Good Beach Guide*, compiled by the Marine Conservation Society (David & Charles), is the definitive source.

GOLF

There are over 400 **golf courses** in Scotland, where the game is less elitist, cheaper and more accessible than anywhere else in the world. The game as it's known today took shape in the sixteenth century on the dunes of Scotland's east coast, and today you'll find some of the oldest courses in the world on these early coastal sites, known as "links". If you want a round of golf, it's often possible just to turn up and play, though it's sensible to phone ahead and book, and essential for the championship courses (see below).

Public courses are owned by the local council, while **private** courses belong to a club. You can play on both – occasionally the private courses require that you be a member of another club, and the odd one asks for introductions from a member, but these rules are often waived for overseas visitors and all you need to do is pay a one-off fee. The cost of one round will set you back between around £5 for small, nine-hole courses, up to more than £20 for eighteen holes. Simply pay as you enter and play. In remote areas the courses are sometimes unmanned – just put the admission fee into the honour box. Most courses have **resident professionals** who give lessons, and some rent equipment at reasonable rates. Renting a caddy car will add an extra few pounds depending on the swankiness of the course you are playing.

Scotland's **championship** courses, which often host the British Open tournament, are renowned for their immaculately kept greens and challenging holes, and though they're favoured by serious players, anybody with a valid handicap certificate can enjoy them. **St Andrews** (☎01334/475757) is *the* destination for golfers: it's the home of the Royal and Ancient Golf Club, the worldwide controlling body that regulates the rules of the game. Of its five courses, the best known is the Old Course, a particularly intriguing ground with eleven enormous greens and the world-famous "Road Hole". If you want to play, there's no introduction needed, but you'll need to book months in advance and have a handicap certificate – handicap limits are 24 for men and 36 for women. You could also enter your name for the daily right-to-play lottery – contact the club before 2pm on the day you'd like to play. One of the easiest championship courses to get into is Carnoustie, in Angus (☎01241/853249), though you should still try and book as far ahead as possible. No handicap certificate is required for play here before 1.30pm on Saturday and 11am on Sunday. Other championship courses include Gleneagles in Perthshire (☎0176/ 663543), Royal Dornoch in Sutherland (☎01862/ 810219) and Turnberry in Ayrshire (☎01655/ 331000). A round of golf at any of these will set you back at least £20, double that if you rent a human caddy – and you'll be expected to tip over and above that. Near Edinburgh, Muirfield, considered by professional players to be one of the most testing grounds in the world, is also one of the most reactionary – women can only play if accompanied by a man and aren't allowed into the clubhouse.

SPECTATOR SPORTS

As a quick glance at the national press will tell you, **sport** in Britain is a serious matter, with each defeat of the national side being taken as an index of the country's slide down the scale of world powers. **Football, rugby and cricket** are the major spectator sports, and **horse racing** also has a big following, though a fair proportion of its public has little interest beyond the Grand National, the country's most popular opportunity for a gamble until the National Lottery came along. The calendar is chock-full of one-off quality sports events, ranging from the massed masochism of the London Marathon to the **Wimbledon** championship, one of the world's greatest tennis tournaments.

For the top international events it can be almost impossible to track down a ticket without resorting to the services of a grossly overcharging ticket agency, but for many fixtures you can make credit-card bookings. Should you be thwarted in your attempts to gain admission, you can often fall back on **TV or radio coverage**. BBC Radio 5 has live commentaries on major sporting events, while BBC TV carries live transmission of the big international rugby and cricket matches, though Rupert Murdoch's Sky satellite station makes greater inroads into traditional BBC territory with each passing year. As it is, to watch live Premier League (and some international) football, you'll need to find a set that has the Sky channel – many pubs offer Sky games (sometimes on big screens) to draw in custom.

FOOTBALL

English football teams may have lost ground to the more cultured continentals in recent years, but it is still the most passionately supported sport in the land, and if you have the slightest interest in the game, then catching a **league** or **FA Cup** fixture is a must. The season runs from mid-August to early May, when the FA Cup Final at Wembley (for which tickets are almost impossible to obtain) rounds things off. There are four league divisons for England and Wales: three, two, one and, at the top of the pyramid, the twenty-club **Premier League**. Currently, this is dominated by the big northern English clubs – Liverpool, Manchester United, and Newcastle. In the Midlands, Birmingham's Aston Villa are the strongest club,

while in London the contest is between Arsenal and Tottenham Hotspur (aka Spurs) – the latter are traditionally artistic and the former more artisanal, but lately there hasn't been much to choose between them. **Wales**'s big three teams are Cardiff City, Swansea City and Wrexham, which all play in the second division; the rest of the Welsh clubs play in the feeble Konica League of Wales. **Scotland** has three divisions, each with fewer teams than the equivalent south of the border, and of considerably lower standard. Glasgow Rangers have dominated the top flight in recent years, and are the only Scottish club that currently has the clout or the cash to make big-name signings – they recently brought the trouble-prone Paul Gasgoine, arguably the most talented English player of his generation, back from an ill-starred spell with Italy's Lazio. Rangers' long-standing Glasgow rivals, Celtic, are long on pedigree but short on silverware at the moment.

The team with the biggest following is Manchester United, whose matches are virtually always a sell-out, regardless of how the team is playing. Of the other glamorous English clubs, Liverpool and Newcastle United also command so ardent a following that tickets for their matches are often like gold dust. It's easy enough to get tickets, if booked in advance, for most other Premier League games, unless two local sides are playing each other. In Scotland, only the "Old Firm"clash between Rangers and Celtic is a certain full house.

Most fixtures kick off at 3pm on Saturday (highlights of the day's best games are shown on BBC1's *Match of the Day*, on Saturday night), though there are generally a few mid-week games (usually 7.30pm on Wednesday), and one each on Sunday (kick-off between 2 and 4pm) and Monday (kick-off at 8pm), both broadcast live on Sky TV. Tickets cost from about £15 for Premier games, falling to less than £10 in the lower divisions.

Since the introduction of all-seater Premiership stadiums in 1994, top-flight games have lost their reputation for tribal violence, and there's been a striking increase in the numbers of women and children attending. Nonetheless, it's an intense business, with a lot of foul language, and being stuck in the middle of a few thousand West Ham supporters as their team goes 3–0 down is not one of life's more uplifting experiences.

CRICKET

In the glory days of the Empire the English took cricket to the colonies as a means of instilling the gentlemanly values of fair play while administering a sound thrashing to the natives. These days the former colonies, such as Australia, the West Indies and India, all beat England on a regular basis, so to see the game at its best you should try to get into one of the series of three, five or six **Test matches** played between England and the summer's touring team. These international matches are played in the middle of the cricket season, which runs from April to September. Two of the matches are played in London: the second is always played at Lords, the home of English cricket, and the last is held at The Oval in Kennington, London; the other Test grounds are Trent Bridge (Nottingham), Old Trafford (Manchester), Headingley (Leeds) and Edgbaston (Birmingham). In tandem with the full-blown five-day Tests, there's also a series of one-day internationals, two of which are again usually held in London.

Getting to see England play one of the big teams can be difficult unless you book months in advance. If you can't wangle your way into a Test, you could watch it live on BBC (the Test series is always televised), listen to ball-by-ball commentary on BBC radio, or settle down to an inter-county match, either in the **county championship** (these are four-day games) or in one of the three fast and furious one-day competitions: the **Benson and Hedges Cup** and the **Nat West Trophy** (both knockout competitions), or the **AXA Equity and Law** Sunday league. Of the eighteen county teams in the championship, two are based in London – Middlesex, who play at Lord's, and Surrey, who play at The Oval.

Prices for Test matches cost £15–30 per day; for one-day internationals you can expect to pay £20–40, but tickets for the sparsely attended county games start at as little as £6.

THE RULES OF CRICKET

The laws of cricket are so complex that the official rule book runs to some twenty pages. The basics, however, are by no means as Byzantine as the game's detractors make out.

There are two teams of eleven players. A team wins by scoring more runs than the other team and dismissing all the opposition – in other words, a team could score many runs more than the opposition, but still not win if the last enemy batsman doggedly stays in (hence ensuring a draw). The match is divided into innings, when one team bats and the other fields. The number of innings varies depending on the type of competition; one-day matches have one per team, Test matches and county championship matches have two.

The aim of the fielding side is to limit the runs scored and get the batsmen "out". Two players from the batting side are on the pitch at any one time. The bowling side has a bowler, a wicket keeper and nine fielders. Two umpires, one standing behind the stumps at the bowler's end and one square on to the play, are responsible for adjudicating if a batsman is out. Each innings is divided into **overs**, consisting of six deliveries, after which the wicket keeper changes ends, the bowler is changed and the fielders move positions.

The batsmen score runs either by running up and down from wicket to wicket (one length = one run), or by hitting the ball over the boundary rope, scoring four runs if it crosses the boundary having touched the ground, and six runs if it flies over. The main ways a batsman can be dismissed are: by being "clean bowled", where the bowler dislodges the bails of the wicket (the horizontal pieces of wood resting on top of the stumps); by being "run out", which is when one of the fielding side dislodges the bails with the ball while the batsman is running between the wickets; by being caught, which is when any of the fielding side catches the ball after the batsman has hit it and before it touches the ground; or "LBW" (leg before wicket), where the batsman blocks with his leg a delivery that would otherwise have hit his stumps.

These are the rudimentaries of a game whose beauty lies in the subtlety of its skills and tactics. The captain, for example, chooses which bowler to play and where to position his fielders to counter the strengths of the batsman, the condition of the pitch, and a dozen other variables. Cricket also has a beauty in its esoteric language, used to describe such things as fielding positions ("silly mid-off", "cover point" etc) and the various types of bowling delivery ("googly", "yorker" etc). For beginners, some enlightenment may be gained by watching the TV coverage, or befriending a spectator – cricket fans tend to be congenial types, eager to introduce newcomers to the mysteries of the true faith.

RUGBY

Rugby gets its name from Rugby public school, where the game mutated from football (soccer) in the nineteenth century. A rugby match may at times look like a bunch of weightlifters grappling each other in the mud – as the old joke goes, rugby is a hooligan's game played by gentleman, while football is a gentleman's game played by hooligans – but it is in reality a highly tactical and athletic game. What's more, England's rugby teams have represented the country with rather more success in the last few years than the cricket and football squads, even if they can't quite match the power and attacking panache of the New Zealand and Australian sides.

There are two types of rugby played in Britain. Fifteen-a-side **Rugby Union** is very strong in working-class Wales, especially in the valleys of the former South Wales coal fields, but has upper-class associations in England, where it is the preferred character-building sport of the great fee-paying schools. Another crucial factor in upholding the officer-class image of Rugby Union in England was its maintainence of amateur status, but in 1995 the sport finally went professional. It remains to be seen how this will affect the thirteen-a-side **Rugby League**, which is a professional game played almost exclusively in the north of England (though the final of its knockout trophy is played at Wembley). Union's move towards professionalism was in part brought about by the tendency of League clubs to poach the top Union players – such as Welsh golden boy Jonathan Davies, who defected to Widnes. Davies has now signed for newly salary-paying Cardiff, perhaps presaging a reversal of the traffic. Certainly it seems probable that the hierarchy of Rugby Union will be shaken up by the change in status. Newcastle, seeking to emulate the resurgence of their football team, staged a coup by signing up England Union star Rob Andrew, and might well be soon challenging the current giants of the game – Bath and Leicester – at the top of the championship. As for the League, it's not too much of an exagerration to say that the real competiton in recent years has been for second place – Wigan win whenever they feel like it.

The Union season runs from September until the end of April, finishing off with the **Pilkington Cup**, Union's equivalent of the FA Cup; the League finishes in May, with the **Challenge Cup** final at Wembley. The Pilkington Cup final, international Rugby Union Test matches and some games in the Five Nations Cup (a round-robin tournament between England, Scotland, Wales, Ireland and France) are played at Twickenham stadium in west London. The other international Union grounds are Murrayfield in Edinburgh and Cardiff Arms Park, which is where you'd expect. Unless you are affiliated to one of the 2000 clubs of the Rugby Union, or willing to pay well over the odds at a ticket agency, it is tough to get a ticket for one of these big games – as it is for League internationals, which are played at Wembley or at one of the larger club grounds. For Union and League club games, however, there should be no problem getting tickets at the gate; expect to pay from £5.

TENNIS

Tennis in England is synonymous with **Wimbledon**, the only Grand Slam tournament to be played on grass, and for many players the ultimate goal of their careers. The Wimbledon championship lasts a fortnight, in the last week of June and the first week of July. Most of the tickets, especially those with seats for the main show courts (Centre and No. 1), are allocated in advance to Wimbledon's members, other tennis clubs and corporate "sponsors" – as well as by public ballot (see below) – and by the time these have taken their slice there's not a lot left for the general public.

It is possible, however, to turn up on the day and buy tickets, and if you're rich enough you could buy through ticket agencies (although these sales are technically illegal). On tournament days, queues start to form around dawn and if you arrive by around 7am you have a reasonable chance of securing the limited number of Centre and No. 1 court tickets held back for sale on the day. If you're there by around 9am, you should get admission to the outside courts (where you'll catch some top players in the first week of the tournament). Either way, you then have a long wait until play commences at noon – and if it rains you don't get your money back.

If you want to see big-name players in Britain, an easier opportunity is the **Stella Artois** championship at **Queen's Club** in Hammersmith, London, which finishes a week before Wimbledon. Many of the stars use this tournament to acclimatize themselves to British grass-court conditions. As with Wimbledon, you have to apply for tickets in advance (see below), although there is a limited number of returns on sale at 10am each day.

For the unlucky, there's the consolation of TV coverage, which is pretty well all-consuming for the two weeks that the Wimbledon tournament lasts.

HORSE RACING

For most of the British population there is just one important day in the horse-racing calendar – the first Saturday in April, when the **Grand National**, the "World's Greatest Steeplechase", is run at Liverpool's Aintree course. Millions of people risk a quid or two on the race, and watch the proceedings anxiously on TV, where it's broadcast live and then repeated at least twice before the end of the day. The National is by far the most arduous (some would say cruel) race of the **steeplechasing and hurdling** season, which runs from August to April, with races taking place on Saturdays and midweek at a vast array of courses, ranging from ovals of grass in the depths of the countryside to prestigious venues like Windsor. Ticket prices range from £5 to £30.

The horses and the clientele are often more upmarket when it comes to racing on the **flat**, which is a summer sport, observing an April to September season. Whereas the big events in the steeplechasing season draw a broad-based crowd, the showcase races on the flat are largely about upper-crust networking. That said, thousands of Londoners treat themselves to a day out at Epsom on **Derby Day**, the first Saturday in June. The Derby, a mile-and-a-half race for three-year-old thoroughbreds, is the most prestigious of the five classics of the flat season, and is preceded in the three-day Derby meeting by another classic, **the Oaks**, which is for fillies

only. (The other Classics are the 1000 Guineas, 2000 Guineas – both run at Newmarket – and the St Leger, run at Doncaster.) For sheer snobbery nothing can match the **Royal Ascot** week in mid-June, when the Queen and selected members of the Royal family are in attendance, along with half the nation's blue bloods. As with the Derby, the best seats are the preserve of the gentry, but the rabble are allowed into the public enclosure for a mere £5, and can get considerably closer to the action for around £25, providing they dress smartly. Prices are slightly lower at the country's other flat-racing meetings, where the class divisions of British society are generally less glaring. Many of these meetings take place on courses used for steeplechasing in the winter, though some of the better courses – such as Goodwood – are reserved for the flat.

BETTING

Most of the money spent by Britain's gamblers is blown on the horses, though only a small minority of punters actually goes to the races. At the course itself you can place a bet with one of the independent trackside book-keepers (or "tic-tac men" as they are known, from the bizarre sign language with which they signal the odds), or with the state-run **Tote**, a system by which the total money placed on a race is divided among the winners.

Competing with Tote and the small bookies are the representatives of the big nationwide betting organizations, such as Ladbrokes and William Hill, who make their money by taking bets on anything from the result of the 4.15 at Epsom to the name of the rider who will finish fourth in the Tour de France or the likelihood of snow at Christmas.

Anyone aged eighteen or over can place a bet, on which an eight percent tax is levied – you can have it deducted either from the stake or from your hypothetical winnings.

GAY AND LESBIAN BRITAIN

Homosexual acts between consenting males were legalized in Britain in 1967, but it wasn't until as recently as 1994 that the **age of consent** was finally reduced from 21 to 18 (still two years older than that for heterosexuals). Lesbianism has never specifically been outlawed, apocryphally owing to the fact that Queen Victoria refused to believe that such a thing existed.

As with so many other aspects of British life, attitudes on homosexuality are riven with contradictions. Despite its draconian laws and the sensationalist trash in the tabloid press, England, at least, offers one of the most diverse and accessible lesbian and gay scenes to be found anywhere in Europe. Nearly every town of any size has some kind of organized gay life – pubs, clubs, community groups, campaigning organizations, shops and phone lines – with the major scenes being found in **London, Manchester** and **Brighton**. The Scottish scene is lively in Edinburgh and in Glasgow, but pretty much nonexistent in the more rural areas. In Wales things are a lot more muted, with few venues outside the main centres of Cardiff, Newport and Swansea. We've listed many venues throughout this book, and you'll be able to pick up a free gay listings sheet in almost any one of them.

Of the nationwide **publications**, the weekly *Pink Paper* is informative and contains limited listings; also worth checking are the frothy weekly *Boyz*, and its monthly women's sibling, *Shebang*. The best bet for a comprehensive **national directory** of pubs, clubs, groups, gay accommodation and local lesbian and gay switchboards is the glossy monthly *Gay Times*, available from many newsagents and alternative bookshops. Gay Men's Press produce guidebooks aimed primarily at gay men, although with some lesbian information included too; there's currently *London Scene*, which includes Brighton, and *Northern Scene*, covering an area that stretches from Birmingham up to the Scottish border. Much of the information in such publications applies both to men and women, as the British scene is far more mixed than in most other European nations.

DISABLED TRAVELLERS

Britain has numerous specialist **tour operators** catering for physically disabled travellers, and the number of non-specialist operators who welcome clients with disabilities is increasing. For more **information** on these operators and on facilities for the disabled traveller, you should get in touch with the *Royal Association for Disability and Rehabilitation* (*RADAR*), 250 City Rd, London EC1V 8AF (☎0171/250 3222), which publishes its own guide to holidays and travel abroad (see below), as well as being a good source of all kinds of information and advice. If you're planning a trip to Scotland, contact *Disability Scotland*, Princes House, 5 Shandwick Place, Edinburgh EH2 4RG (☎0131/229 8632), which publishes its own directory and is happy to deal with queries. The *Wales Council for the Disabled*, Llys Ifor, Crescent Road, Caerphilly, Mid-Glamorgan CF8 1XL (☎01222/887325), publishes the *Accessible Wales* booklet (£2). There's also

Mobility International, 228 Borough High St, London SE1 1JX (☎0171/403 5688), which puts out a quarterly newsletter, among other things, that keeps up to date with developments in disabled travel; and the *Holiday Care Service*, 2nd Floor, Imperial Buildings, Victoria Rd, Horley, Surrey RH6 7P2 (☎01293/774 535), which publishes numerous fact sheets on disabled travel abroad and deals with all sorts of queries – it also runs a useful "Holiday Helpers" service.

Mobility International also has a **North American office**, contactable at PO Box 10767, Eugene, OR 97440 (☎503/343-1284). Other useful organizations for North Americans are the *Society for the Advancement of Travel for the Handicapped*, 347 5th Ave, New York, NY 10016 (☎212/447-7284), a non-profit travel-industry referral service that passes queries on to its members; and the *Travel Information Service*, Moss Rehabilitation Hospital, 1200 W Tabor Rd,

Philadelphia, PA 19141 (☎215/456-9600), a telephone information and referral service.

Disabled travellers in **Australia** and **New Zealand** can get information and advice from *ACROD*, PO Box 60, Curtin, ACT 2605 (☎06/682 4333), which has compiled lists of organizations, accommodation, travel agencies and tour operators; *Barrier Free Travel*, 36 Wheatley St, North Bellingen, NSW 2454 (☎066/551 733), a fee-based travel access information service; or the *Disabled Persons Assembly*, PO Box 10, 138 The Terrace, Wellington (☎04/472 2626).

Should you go it alone, you'll find that British attitudes towards travellers with disabilities is often begrudging and guilt-ridden, and are years behind advances towards independence made in North America and Australia. Access to theatres, cinemas and other public places has improved recently, but **public transport** companies rarely make any effort to help disabled people, though some rail services now accommodate wheelchair users in comfort. Wheelchair users and blind or partially sighted people are automatically given 30–50 percent reductions on train fares, and people with other disabilities are eligible for the **Disabled Persons Railcard** (£14 per year), which gives a third off most tickets. There are no bus discounts for the disabled, while of the major **car-rental** firms only *Hertz* offers models with hand controls at the same rate as conventional vehicles, and even these are in the more expensive categories. **Accommodation** is the same story, with modified suites for people with disabilities available only at higher-priced establishments and perhaps at the odd B&B.

Useful **publications** include the *Access* series by the *Pauline Hephaistos Survey Projects*, and RADAR's annually updated *Holidays in the British Isles; A Guide For Disabled People*. Two other publications to look out for are *The World Wheelchair Traveller* by Susan Abbott and Mary Ann Tyrrell (AA Publications), which includes basic hints and advice, and *Nothing Ventured: Disabled People Travel the World* by Alison Walsh (Rough Guides), which has practical advice as well as inspiring accounts of disabled travel worldwide.

DIRECTORY

Cigarettes The last decade has seen a dramatic change in attitudes towards smoking and a significant reduction in the consumption of cigarettes. Smoking is now outlawed from just about all public buildings and on public transport, and many restaurants and hotels have become non-smoking establishments. Smokers are advised, when booking a restaurant table or a room, to check that their vice is tolerated there.

Drugs Likely-looking visitors coming to Britain from Holland or Spain can expect scrutiny from customs officers on the lookout for hashish (marijuana resin). Being caught with possession of a small amount of hashish or grass will lead to a fine, but possession of larger quantities or of "harder" narcotics could lead to imprisonment or deportation.

Electricity In Britain the current is 240V AC. North American applicances will need a transformer and adaptor; Australasian appliances will only need an adaptor.

Laundry Coin-operated laundries (launderettes) are to be found in most British towns and are open about twelve hours a day from Monday to Friday, with shorter hours at weekends. A wash followed by a spin or tumble dry costs about £2, with "service washes" (your laundry done for you in a few hours) about £1 more.

Public toilets These are found at all train and bus stations and are signposted on town high streets. In urban locations a fee of 10p or 20p is usually charged.

Time Greenwich Mean Time (GMT) is used from late October to late March, when the clocks go forward an hour for British Summer Time (BST). GMT is five hours ahead of the US Eastern Standard Time and ten hours behind Australian Eastern Standard Time.

Tipping and service charges In restaurants a service charge is usually included in the bill; if it isn't, leave a tip of 10–15 percent. Some restau-rants are in the habit of leaving the total box blank on credit-card counterfoils, to encourage custom-ers to add another few percent on top of the service charge – if you're paying by credit card, check that the total box is filled in before you sign. Taxi drivers expect a tip in the region of 10 percent. You do not generally tip bar staff – if you want to show your appreciation, offer to buy them a drink.

Videos Visitors from North America planning to use their video cameras in Britain should note that Betamax video cassettes are less easy to obtain in England, where VHS is the commonly used format.

PART TWO

ENGLAND

SCOTLAND

N

CHAPTER 10
**THE
NORTHEAST**

CHAPTER 9
YORKSHIRE

CHAPTER 8
**THE
NORTHWEST**

CHAPTER 7
CENTRAL ENGLAND

WALES

CHAPTER 6
EAST ANGLIA

CHAPTER 4
LONDON TO THE SEVERN

CHAPTER 1
LONDON

CHAPTER 3
**HAMPSHIRE,
DORSET &
WILTSHIRE**

CHAPTER 2
**SURREY, KENT
& SUSSEX**

CHAPTER 5
THE WEST COUNTRY

CHAPTER ONE

LONDON

With a population of nearly seven million, **LONDON** is by far Europe's biggest city, spreading over an area of more than 620 square miles from its core on the River Thames. This is where England's news and money are made, and as far as its inhabitants are concerned, provincial life begins beyond the circuit of the orbital motorway. Londoners' sense of superiority causes resentment in the regions, but it's undeniable that the capital has an unmatched charisma, a unique aura of excitement and success. In most walks of life, it's still the case that if you want to get on, you've got to get on in London.

Despite this dominance, London is the only capital city in Europe that lacks its own governing body, a symptom of over a decade's political indifference to London's special needs. This neglect, compounded by a series of recessions that have bitten ever more deeply into the white-collar economy of the southeast, and by the policies of a government that penalizes the unfortunate, has resulted in a city of ostentatious private affluence and increasing public squalor. Over on the east side of the city, decaying housing estates stand in the shadow of the glossy new tower of Canary Wharf, harbinger of a financial miracle that has never materialized; at night, the West End is packed with theatregoers, while the doorways and shopfronts are becoming the dormitories of the growing band of London's dispossessed.

London should be better than it is, but it is still a thrilling place. The central thoroughfares, buzzing far into the night, are interspersed with quiet squares, explorable alleyways and surprisingly large expanses of greenery – Hyde Park, Green Park and St James's Park are all within a few minutes' walk of the West End shops. The museums and galleries are as varied and as rich as you'll find anywhere, and the majority of the great collections are free, even if such places are now obliged to ask for voluntary donations with increasing aggression. Monuments of the capital's more glorious past are to be seen everywhere, from Roman ruins through great Baroque churches to the architecture of the triumphalist British Empire.

You could also spend days just shopping in London, hobnobbing with the ruling classes in *Harrods*, or sampling the offbeat weekend markets, the seedbed of London's famously innovative street fashions – an inspiration to world-renowned designers, such as Jean-Paul Gaultier. The music and clubbing scenes could keep you going every night of the week, and the mainstream arts are no less exciting, with regular opportunities to catch brilliant theatre companies, dance troupes, exhibitions and opera. Restaurants in London range from Michelin two-star establishments to low-cost high-quality Indian cafés, while scores of London pubs have heaps of atmosphere, especially out of the centre – and an exploration of the further-flung communities is essential to get the feel of this dynamic metropolis.

A brief history of London

The Romans founded Londinium in 43 AD as a stores depot on the marshy banks of the Thames. Despite frequent attacks – not least by Queen Boudicca, who razed it in 61 AD – the port became secure in its position as capital of Roman Britain by the end of the century. London's expansion really began, however, in the eleventh century, when it became the seat of the last successful invader of Britain, the Norman duke **William**

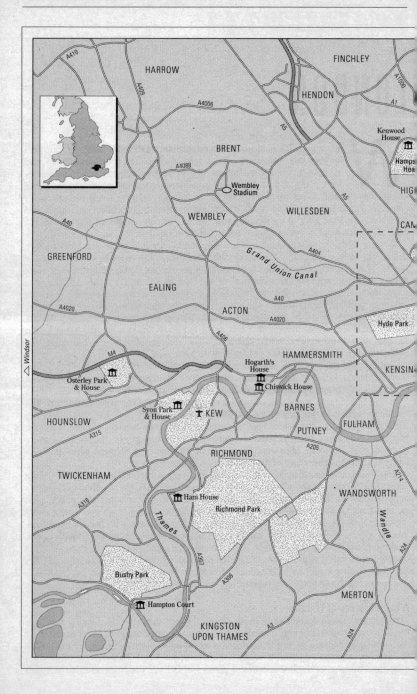

A410

HARROW

FINCHLEY

HENDON

A1000

A1

A4006

A5

Kenwood House

BRENT

Hamps Hea

A4088

HIG

Wembley Stadium

WEMBLEY

WILLESDEN

CAM

A40

Grand Union Canal

A404

GREENFORD

EALING

A40

ACTON

A4020

A4020

Hyde Park

A4020

A406

HAMMERSMITH

KENSIN

M4

Hogarth's House

Osterley Park & House

Chiswick House

Syon Park & House

KEW

BARNES

Hounslow

PUTNEY

FULHAM

A315

RICHMOND

A205

TWICKENHAM

Ham House

WANDSWORTH

A316

Richmond Park

Wandle

A24

Thames

A307

Bushy Park

A308

MERTON

Hampton Court

KINGSTON UPON THAMES

A3

A24

△ Windsor

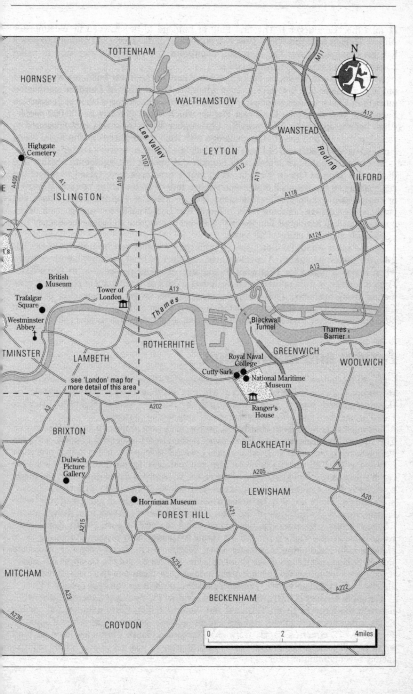

N

TOTTENHAM

HORNSEY

WALTHAMSTOW

WANSTEAD

Highgate
Cemetery

LEYTON

A107

ISLINGTON

A10

A1

A400

A11

A12

A118

ILFORD

A124

A13

British
Museum

Trafalgar
Square

Westminster
Abbey

Tower of
London

A13

Thames

Blackwall
Tunnel

Thames
Barrier

TMINSTER

LAMBETH

ROTHERHITHE

GREENWICH

WOOLWICH

Royal Naval
College

Cutty Sark

National Maritime
Museum

see 'London' map for
more detail of this area

A3

A202

Ranger's
House

BRIXTON

BLACKHEATH

Dulwich
Picture
Gallery

A205

LEWISHAM

A20

Horniman Museum

A21

FOREST HILL

A215

A234

MITCHAM

A3

A222

A236

BECKENHAM

CROYDON

0   2   4miles

Lea Valley

Roding

t's

M11

A12

II (aka the "Conqueror"). The first king of England to be crowned in Westminster Abbey, William built the White Tower – centrepiece of the Tower of London – to establish his dominance over the merchant population, the class that was soon to make London one of Europe's mightiest cities.

Little is left of medieval or Tudor London. Many of the finest buildings were wiped out in the course of a few days in 1666 when the **Great Fire of London** annihilated more than 13,000 houses and nearly ninety churches, completing a cycle of destruction begun the year before by the Great Plague, which killed as many as 100,000 people. Chief beneficiary of the blaze was Sir Christopher Wren, who was commissioned to redesign the city and rose to the challenge with such masterpieces as the Royal Naval Hospital in Greenwich and St Paul's Cathedral, in addition to scores of other churches.

Much of the public architecture of London was built in the eighteenth century and during the reign of Queen Victoria, when grand structures were raised to reflect the city's status as the financial and administrative hub of an invincible empire. However, in comparison to many other European capitals much of London looks bland, due partly to the German bombing raids in World War II, and partly to some postwar development that has lumbered London with the sort of concrete-and-glass mediocrity that gives modern architecture a bad name.

On the other hand, London's special atmosphere comes not from its buildings but from the life on its streets. A cosmopolitan city since at least the seventeenth century, when it was a haven for Huguenot immigrants escaping persecution in Louis XIV's France, today it is truly multicultural, with over a third of its permanent population originating from overseas. This century has seen the arrival of thousands from the Caribbean, the Indian subcontinent, the Mediterranean and the Far East, all of whom play an integral part in defining a metropolis that is unmatched in its sheer diversity.

Arrival and information

Flying into London, you'll arrive at one of the capital's three main international airports, Heathrow, Gatwick or Stansted, each of which is less than an hour from the city centre. (London's fourth airport, City, is used only by business shuttle flights to Brussels, Paris, Amsterdam and a few other European commercial centres.)

Getting into London from **Heathrow**, twelve miles west of the city, couldn't be easier. The **Piccadilly underground line** connects the airport to central London, with one station serving terminals 1, 2 and 3, another serving terminal 4; trains depart every few minutes, cost £3.20 and run between 5am and midnight, taking about forty minutes to reach the centre. If you plan to spend the rest of your arrival day sightseeing, you might consider buying a multi-zone one-day travelcard for £3.90 (see "City Transport", below) at Heathrow. There are also **Airbuses** which run from outside all four Heathrow terminals to several destinations in the city: *Airbus* **A1** (every 20–45 min daily 5.50am– 8.30pm) drops passengers at designated stops in Earl's Court, South Kensington, Knightsbridge and Victoria; *Airbus* **A2** (same frequency daily 5.40am–9.45pm) goes to Notting Hill, Paddington, Lancaster Gate, Marble Arch, Baker Street, Euston and Russell Square. Both routes take about an hour and cost £5, but can be worth the money if you have a lot of luggage to haul. After midnight, the night bus #N97 runs hourly from Heathrow to Trafalgar Square. **Taxis** are plentiful, but will set you back around £35.

Gatwick Airport is thirty miles south of London; the non-stop *Gatwick Express* runs between the airport's South Terminal and Victoria, taking thirty minutes and costing £8.90; it departs every fifteen minutes except between 2am and 5am, when it's hourly. *Flightline 777* **coaches** depart Gatwick's North and South Terminals once an hour between 6.30am and 11.30pm and cost £7.50, arriving at Victoria Coach Station approximately seventy minutes later.

The smaller **Stansted Airport** lies 34 miles northeast of the capital and is served by trains to Liverpool Street (Mon–Sat every 30min 6am–11pm, Sun hourly 7am–11pm), which take 45 minutes and the journey costs £10.

Coming into London from abroad by **coach or train**, you'll almost certainly arrive at Victoria – either at the train station, which serves the English Channel ports, or at the coach station, a couple of hundred yards south down Buckingham Palace Road. *Eurostar* trains using the Channel Tunnel come in at Waterloo's new international terminal. Arriving by train from elsewhere in Britain, you'll come into one of London's numerous mainline British Rail stations, all of which have adjacent underground stations connected to the city centre's tube network. (For details of train connections between other parts of Britain and the mainline stations, see p.138–139.)

Information

The **London Tourist Board** (LTB) has a desk at Heathrow Airport in the underground station concourse for terminals 1, 2 and 3 (daily 8.30am–6.30pm), but the **main central office** is in the forecourt of Victoria station (daily 8am–7pm). Other centrally located offices can be found near Piccadilly Circus in the British Travel Centre, 12 Regent St (Mon–Fri 9am–6.30pm, Sat 9am–5pm & Sun 10am–4pm); in Liverpool Street underground station (Mon–Sat 9am–4.30pm, Sun 8.30am–3.30pm); and at 35–36 Woburn Place in Bloomsbury (daily 7.30am–7.30pm). There are also information counters in the basement of *Selfridges* on Oxford Street, in Greenwich at 46 Greenwich Church St (daily 10am–1pm & 2–5pm; ☎0181/858 6376), and in Richmond, inside the Old Town Hall on Whittaker Avenue (Mon–Fri 10am–6pm, Sat 10am–5pm, plus Sun 10.15am–4.15pm in summer; ☎0181/940 7970). Finally there's an information office, run by the City of London Corporation, opposite the south side of St Paul's Cathedral (April–Sept daily 9.30am–5pm; Oct–March Mon–Fri 9.30am–5pm, Sat 9.30am–12.30pm; ☎0171/323 1456).

The Greenwich, Richmond and St Paul's offices will accept enquiries by phone. The best that the LTB can offer is a spread of pre-recorded phone announcements – these are ninety percent waffle, and the calls are charged at an exorbitant rate. If you're hellbent on increasing the telephone company's profits, phone ☎0171/730 3488 for the day's list of events.

City transport

The fastest way of moving around the city is by **Underground**, or **Tube**, as it's known to all Londoners. Operating from around 5.30am until shortly after midnight, the eleven lines cross much of the metropolis, although south of the river is not well covered and the reliability of certain lines (such as the notorious Northern) is often lousy. Tickets are bought from machines or from a ticket booth in the station entrance hall; the minimum fare for a one-way journey is £1. A **travelcard**, on sale from machines and ticket booths at all tube stations as well as from some newsagents (look for the London Transport sticker), is valid for as many journeys as you want on bus and suburban rail networks, and will quickly save a lot of money. One-day travelcards, valid on weekdays from 9.30am and all day at weekends, cost £3 for the central zones 1 and 2, rising to £3.90 for all six zones (which includes Heathrow). Weekly travelcards are even more economical, beginning at £14.80 for zones 1 and 2, which should cover virtually everything you'll want to see; these cards can only be bought by carriers of a **photocard**, which you can get, free of charge, from tube station ticket booths on presentation of a passport photo.

The network of **buses** is very dense, but you will soon find that the tube is generally quicker, especially in the summer, when central London becomes one large traffic jam.

Bus journeys cost a minimum of 50p, but the average trip in the centre will cost around 80p; normally you pay the driver on entering, although some routes – especially those through the centre – are covered by older buses with an open rear platform and staffed by a conductor. A lot of bus stops are request stops, so if you don't stick your arm out the bus will drive on. Regular buses operate between about 6am and midnight, and a network of **night buses** (prefixed with the letter "N") operates outside this period, routes radiating out from Trafalgar Square at approximately hourly intervals, more frequently on some lines and on Friday and Saturday nights. Fares are twice as expensive on night buses; one-day travel cards aren't valid on them, but weekly ones are.

The principal **London Transport information office**, providing excellent free maps and details of bus and tube services, is at **Piccadilly Circus tube station** (daily 9am–6pm), and there are other desks at Euston, King's Cross, Liverpool Street, Oxford Circus, St James's Park and Victoria stations. There's also a 24-hour phone line for information on all bus and tube services (☎0171/222 1234).

If you're in a group of three or more, London's metered **black cabs** can be an economical way of getting around the centre of town – a ride across the centre, from Euston to Victoria, should cost around £10. A yellow light over the windscreen tells you if the cab is available – just stick your arm out to hail it. (If you want to book one in advance, call ☎0171/272 0272.) London's cabbies are the best trained in Europe – every one of them knows the shortest route between any two points in the capital, and won't rip you off by taking another route. **Minicabs** are less reliable than black cabs, as their drivers are just private individuals rather than trained professionals; however, they are often considerably cheaper, so you might want to take one back from your late-night club. If you want to be certain of a woman driver, call *Ladycabs* (☎0171/254 3501). Few minicabs are metered, so always ask for the price beforehand.

Accommodation

London is a very expensive city and lower-cost **accommodation** in central London tends to be of poor quality. However, the sheer size of the place means that there is little chance of failing to find a room even in midsummer, and the underground network makes accommodation outside the centre a feasible option. There is of course no shortage of top-end accommodation, including such elegant establishments as the *Dorchester*, the *Ritz* and the *Langham*, whose worldwide reputations have ensured a constant stream of guests willing to pay up to £300 per night. All of the **hotels** listed here, however, cost significantly less than that and have been grouped by location rather than in price brackets, with the emphasis on value for money. The capital has plenty of **hostel** space, both in *YHA* properties and student halls, though these can be booked up weeks in advance over the summer.

We've given phone numbers for all our listed accommodation, but if you fail to find something you could always pay someone else to do the phoning round for you. All the LTB offices listed on p.63 operate a **room-reservation service**, for which they charge £5 (£1.50 for hostels), and take fifteen percent of the room fee in advance; credit-card holders can also book through the LTB by phone (☎0171/824 8844). In addition, **Thomas Cook** has accommodation desks at Gatwick airport train station (☎01293/568 459), Victoria station (☎0171/233 6751), King's Cross station (☎0171/837 5681) and Paddington station (☎0171/723 0184). Most of these are open daily from around 7am till 11pm, and will book anything from youth hostels through to four-star hotels for a £5 fee. There are also **British Hotel Reservation Centre** (*BHRC*) desks at both Heathrow underground stations (☎0181/564 8808 & 564 8211), at Stansted Airport (☎01279/662929), at Victoria (☎0171/828 1027) and at 10 Buckingham Palace Rd (☎0171/828 2425). All are open daily from 6am to midnight;

ACCOMMODATION PRICES

Throughout this guide, hotel and B&B accommodation is priced on a scale of ① to ⑨, the number indicating the **lowest price** you could expect to pay per night in that establishment for a **double room** in high season. The prices indicated by the codes are as follows:

① under £20/$30	④ £40–50/$60–75	⑦ £70–80/$105–120
② £20–30/$30–45	⑤ £50–60/$75–90	⑧ £80–100/$120–150
③ £30–40/$45–60	⑥ £60–70/$90–105	⑨ over £100/$150

Hostel accommodation in London is the most expensive in the country, costing as much as £20 per person; the charges we quote are rounded to the nearest 50p.

---

there's no fee for reserving accommodation at Heathrow, Stansted or the Buckingham Palace road office, but the Victoria office charges £3 to reserve a hotel room for you.

A brief word on **London addresses**. Each address ends with a letter giving the geographical location of the street (E for "east", WC for "west central" and so on) and a number that specifies the postal area. This number is not a reliable indication of the remoteness of the locale from the centre, so it's always best to check a map before taking a room at what may sound like a fairly central area.

Hotels and B&Bs

With **hotels** you get less for your money in London than elsewhere in the country – generally breakfasts are more meagre and rooms more spartan than in similarly priced places in the provinces. In high season you should phone as far in advance as you can if you want to stay within a couple of tube stops of the West End, and expect to pay no less than £40 for an unexceptional double room without a private bathroom. If travelling with two or more companions, it's always worth asking the price of the family rooms, which generally sleep four and can save you a few pounds.

The majority of **West End** hotels are out of most people's price range, but there are some notable exceptions within a short walk of **Marble Arch** tube station, close to Oxford Street and the northeastern corner of Hyde Park. Slightly further west, **Paddington** is not an immensely attractive zone, but it lies within walking distance of Hyde Park. For cheap places in this area, check out Norfolk Square and Sussex Gardens, where the small hotels outnumber the residential homes.

For proximity to high-street shops and museums, consider either the Bloomsbury area or South Kensington. The focus of **Bloomsbury** is the British Museum, which stands right by Gower Street, a road packed full of reasonably priced B&B hotels. A ten-minute walk from Gower Street brings you to the West End shopping centres of Tottenham Court Road, Oxford Street and Covent Garden. Across on the other side of the city, plush **South Kensington** is home to three major museums (the Victoria and Albert, the Natural History and the Science museums), with *Harrods* and other upmarket Knightsbridge shops a short walk away.

To the north of here, **High Street Kensington** and adjacent **Notting Hill** offer several good B&Bs in pleasantly grand residential squares. Notting Hill has a vibrant, youthful air about it – expressed every August in the multi-ethnic Notting Hill Carnival, and less extravagantly every weekend with the stalls of Portobello Market. High Street Ken (as it's often called) is a district of traditional chain stores and high-class restaurants, within fairly easy reach of the South Kensington museums.

The area best equipped for travellers on a low budget is the network of streets around **Earl's Court** tube, particularly Penywern Road and Trebovir Road. Here you'll find a huge concentration of bottom-end B&Bs, some offering dormitory accommodation (for about £10 a bed) or at least family rooms, and some with kitchen facilities as well. Earl's Court Road, which cuts through this area, is full of late-night supermarkets, fairly cheap cafés, restaurants and fast-food joints, money exchange booths, discount travel agents and launderettes; there's also a useful travellers' noticeboard, posted next to a newsagents thirty metres left of the Earl's Court tube entrance, which covers part-time job vacancies, short-term accommodation offers and things for sale.

The roads around **Victoria station** also harbour dozens of inexpensive B&Bs – notably along Belgrave Road and Ebury Street – though the area itself lacks the liveliness of Earl's Court and tends to go dead after the offices shut for the night.

Between Marble Arch and Regent's Park

Edward Lear Hotel, 30 Seymour St, W1 (☎0171/402 5401). Comfortable, well-equipped rooms in the former home of the Victorian poet and limerick-writer. Very close to Oxford Street and Hyde Park. Marble Arch tube. ⑤.

Kenwood House Hotel, 114 Gloucester Place, W1 (☎0171/935 3473). Small, but superior B&B midway between Oxford Street and Regent's Park. Baker Street tube. ④.

Hotel La Place, 17 Nottingham Place, W1 (☎0171/486 2323). Upmarket, well-equipped B&B close to the south side of Regent's Park. Baker Street tube. ⑥.

Lincoln House Hotel, 33 Gloucester Place, W1 (☎0171/486 7630). Good-value, recently refurbished B&B, five minutes walk from Oxford Street, Marble Arch or Baker Street tube. ⑤.

London Continental Hotel, 88 Gloucester Place, W1 (☎0171/486 8670). Central, low-cost B&B, with ten percent discount for stays of more than a week. Marble Arch or Baker Street tube. ⑤.

Wigmore Court, 23 Gloucester Place, W1 (☎0171/935 0928). Very popular, friendly hotel just off Oxford Street, offering large, welcoming rooms, and significant discounts outside peak season. Marble Arch or Baker Street tube. ⑤.

Paddington

Ashley Hotel, 15 Norfolk Square, W2 (☎0171/723 3375). A few minutes' walk from Paddington station – all rooms have handbasins or facilities en suite. ⑤.

Dean Court Hotel, 57 Inverness Terrace, W2 (☎0171/229 2961). A favourite with Australian tourists and very close to Hyde Park. Well worth considering for longer stays, as they offer seven nights for the price of six. Queensway or Bayswater tube. ③.

Europa House Hotel, 151 Sussex Gardens, W2 (☎0171/723 7343). Dependable and recently refurbished B&B, with en-suite rooms. Paddington tube. ⑥.

Rhodes House, 195 Sussex Gardens, W2 (☎0171/262 5617). Comfortable, well-furnished B&B; all rooms with shower and TV. Paddington tube. ④.

Saint David's Hotel, 16 Norfolk Square, W2 (☎0171/723 3856). Pleasant, well-appointed B&B in a quiet, attractive square – serves huge breakfasts. Paddington tube. ④.

Sass House, 10–11 Craven Terrace, W2 (☎0171/262 2325). Located near Hyde Park in a pleasant street with a couple of cafés and pubs. Lancaster Gate or Paddington tube. ④.

Tudor Court Hotel, 10 Norfolk Square, W2 (☎0171/723 6553). Nothing spectacular, but perfectly acceptable. Paddington tube. ③.

Westpoint Hotel, 170 Sussex Gardens, W2 (☎0171/402 0281). Rooms are nothing special, but the price is not bad for the area. Paddington or Lancaster Gate tube. ③.

Bloomsbury

Arran House Hotel, 77–79 Gower St, WC1 (☎0171/636 2186). Bright, well-kept B&B, with TV lounge, library, laundry and a garden. Goodge Street tube. ④.

Cosmo-Bedford House Hotel, 27 Bloomsbury Square, WC1 (☎0171/636 4661). Centrally located budget-conscious hotel, 150yds from the British Museum. Russell Square or Holborn tube. ④.

Garth Hotel, 69 Gower St, WC1 (☎0171/636 5761). Good-value, friendly establishment, which serves Japanese breakfast as an option. Tottenham Court Road or Goodge Street tube. ④.

Jesmond Hotel, 63 Gower St, WC1 (☎0171/636 3199). Comfortable and spotless B&B, near the British Museum. Goodge Street tube. ③.

Ridgemount Hotel, 65–67 Gower St, WC1 (☎0171/636 1141). Another good budget B&B. Goodge Street tube. ③.

St Margaret's Hotel, 26 Bedford Place, WC1 (☎0171/636 4277). Small, fresh rooms. Russell Square tube. ⑤.

South Kensington and Knightsbridge

Leicester Court Hotel, 41 Queen's Gate Gardens, SW7 (☎0171/584 0512). Large Victorian house in a quiet square converted to accommodate 40 simply furnished rooms. Gloucester Road or South Kensington tube. ⑧.

Hotel 167, 167 Old Brompton Rd, SW5 (☎0171/373 0672). Nicely furnished Victorian house; all doubles have private bathroom. Gloucester Road tube. ⑧.

Sorbonne Hotel, 39 Cromwell Rd, SW7 (☎0171/589 6636). Fairly basic B&B, but good value given its ideal location, just across the road from the Natural History Museum. For some reason, no children under five allowed. South Kensington tube. ⑤.

South Kensington Guest House, 13 Cranley Place, SW7 (☎0171/589 0021). Plainly furnished B&B in a salubrious street. South Kensington tube. ⑤.

High Street Kensington and Notting Hill

Abbey House Hotel, 11 Vicarage Gate, W8 (☎0171/727 2594). Classy and very comfortable, but with shared facilities only; a place where guests tend to return. High Street Kensington tube. ⑤.

Demetriou Guest House, 9 Strathmore Gardens, W8 (☎0171/229 6709). Good, reasonably priced option in pleasant residential area close to Kensington Gardens. Notting Hill Gate tube. ⑤.

Leinster Hotel, 7–12 Leinster Square, W2 (☎0171/727 4412). Large backpackers' establishment, with a variety of accommodation from singles to five-berth rooms. Notting Hill Gate tube. ②.

Manor Court Chambers, 7 Clanricarde Gardens, W2 (☎0171/792 3361). Small, comfortable B&B in the lively Notting Hill area of west London. Notting Hill Gate tube. ④.

Vicarage Private Hotel, 10 Vicarage Gate, W8 (☎0171/229 4030). Much the same as the neighbouring *Abbey House*. Advance booking essential. High Street Kensington tube. ⑤.

Earl's Court

Beaver Hotel, 57–59 Philbeach Gardens, SW5 (☎0171/373 4553). Quiet and cosy B&B. Earl's Court tube. ③.

Half Moon, 10 Earl's Court Square, SW5 (☎0171/373 9956). Ordinary but inexpensive, with ensuite facilities and TV. Earl's Court tube. ②.

Henley House, 30 Barkston Gardens, SW5 (☎0171/370 4111). Elegantly furnished B&B whose spacious rooms all have TV and bathroom; one of the best in this area. Earl's Court tube. ⑦.

Manor Hotel, 23 Nevern Place, SW5 (☎0171/370 6018). Reasonably priced rooms just off Earl's Court Rd. Earl's Court tube. ③.

Merlyn Court Hotel, 2 Barkston Gardens, SW5 (☎0171/370 1640). Plain but serviceable, with mostly en-suite rooms, in a quiet square off Earl's Court Road. Earl's Court tube. ④.

Oxford Hotel, 24 Penywern Rd, SW5 (☎0171/370 1161). One of the better B&Bs along this popular road. Earl's Court tube. ④.

Rasool Court Hotel, 19 Penywern Rd, SW5 (☎0171/373 8900). The cheapest rooms in this B&B-filled street; basic comfort, and all have satellite TV. Earl's Court tube. ③.

White House Hotel, 12 Earl's Court Square, SW5 (☎0171/373 5903). Basic rooms, but very popular with students. Earl's Court tube. ③.

Windsor House Hotel, 12 Penywern Rd, SW5 (☎0171/373 9087). Simple rooms in a large old Victorian terrace; use of garden and kitchen facilities. Earl's Court tube. ④.

York House, 28 Philbeach Gardens, SW5 (☎0171/373 7519). Roomy B&B that offers big discounts for weekly stays. Earl's Court tube. ④.

Victoria

Chester House, 134 Ebury St, SW1 (☎0171/730 3632). The cheapest of a host of B&Bs along this road, very convenient for Victoria Coach Station and within walking distance of Buckingham Palace. Victoria tube. ④.

Collin House, 104 Ebury St, SW1 (☎0171/730 8031). Some of the most spacious rooms offered by the twenty-odd similar B&Bs along this road. Victoria tube. ⑤.

Easton Hotel, 36–40 Belgrave Rd (☎0171/834 5938). One of the biggest B&Bs in the Victoria area, so worth trying on spec in peak season; rooms adequate for the price. Victoria tube. ③.

Limegrove Hotel, 101 Warwick Way, SW1 (☎0171/828 0458). Just about the least expensive decent rooms in this area – shared facilities, but TVs in every room. Victoria tube. ③.

Melbourne House, 79 Belgrave Rd, SW1 (☎0171/828 3516). Faultless family-run B&B with good amenities. Victoria or Pimlico tube. ⑤.

Oxford House, 92–94 Cambridge St, SW1 (☎0171/834 6467). Very friendly B&B with marvellous food, so reservations essential. Victoria tube. ④.

Stanley House, 19–21 Belgrave Rd, SW1 (☎0171/834 5042). Large, friendly and well-appointed B&B offering a 10 percent discount for weekly stays; all rooms have TV. Victoria tube. ③.

Winchester Hotel, 17 Belgrave Rd, SW1 (☎0171/828 2972). This old town house is one of the best B&Bs in the Victoria area. Victoria tube. ⑤.

Windsor Guest House, 36 Alderney St, SW1 (☎0171/828 7922). Close to Victoria coach and train stations and very inexpensive. Victoria tube. ②.

Hampstead

La Gaffe, 107–111 Heath St, NW3 (☎0171/435 4941). Small but well-appointed hotel in the appealing village-like atmosphere of Hampstead, only two minutes' walk from Hampstead Heath and five minutes' walk from the tube. All rooms have shower and TV, two have four-poster beds and jacuzzis, there's a communal roof garden, and a bar and restaurant downstairs. Hampstead tube. ⑥.

Hampstead Village Guest House, 2 Kemplay Rd, NW3 (☎0171/435 8679). Lovely non-smoking B&B, with a comfortable, homely atmosphere, near the heath. ⑤.

Hostels, student halls and camping

Most *YHA* **hostels** in London are less basic and more expensive than those in the provinces, though there's usually no curfew. They're always busy, especially in summer so you'll have to arrive as early as possible or book in advance. In peak seasons, you're usually limited to a maximum stay of four consecutive nights. A central reservations office, which accepts *Mastercard* and *Visa*, can book you into any of the London *YHA* hostels (☎0171/248 6547). In addition to the official hostels, there's a wide range of **private hostels** which charge roughly the same price; unlike *YHA* hostels, there's no quality control, so standards can vary wildly. Some accommodation in **student halls of residence** is available outside term time, but the prices aren't all that attractive and the rooms get filled quickly. London's **campsites** are all out on the perimeters of the city, offering pitches for around £4, plus a fee of around £3 per person per night (reductions for children and out of season).

YHA hostels

City of London, 36 Carter Lane, EC4 (☎0171/236 4965). In the City – a desolate area at night – but with good public transport links; dorm sizes range from 1–15 beds. £12–23. St Paul's tube.

Earl's Court, 38 Bolton Gardens, SW5 (☎0171/373 7083). Comfortable and fairly capacious, with a friendly atmosphere. £15.50–18. Earl's Court tube.

Hampstead Heath, 4 Wellgarth Rd, NW11 (☎0181/458 9054). One of the biggest and best appointed hostels, set in its own grounds near Hampstead Heath. £12–14.50. Golders Green tube.

Highgate Village, 84 Highgate West Hill, N6 (☎0181/340 1831). A basic hostel, with a midnight curfew, in a very pleasant setting that more than compensates for the walk and longer tube ride to the centre. £8–12. Archway or Highgate tube.

Holland House, Holland Walk, W8 (☎0171/937 0748). This hostel is half in a converted Jacobean house, and half in a 1950s purpose-built block; it's nicely situated and convenient for the centre. £16–18. Holland Park or High Street Kensington tube.

Oxford Street, 14 Noel St, W1 (☎0171/734 1618). In the heart of the West End, but with only 90 beds in 2-, 3- or 4-bedded rooms, it fills up very fast. £14–17. Oxford Circus or Tottenham Court Road tube.

Rotherhithe, Island Yard, Salter Rd, SE16 (☎0171/232 2114). Inconveniently sited on the East London tube line, this large hostel, with 320 beds, makes a viable option in peak season; all rooms have private facilities, and many hold only two beds. £11–23. Rotherhithe tube or bus #P11.

Private hostels

Chelsea Hotel, 33–41 Earl's Court Square, SW5 (☎0171/244 6892). A 260-bed hostel offering dorm beds from £10 per person, and twins with private bathrooms for £25, breakfast included. Facilities include a TV lounge, restaurant, bar with pool table and a laundry. Earl's Court tube.

Maree Hotel, 25 Gower St, WC1 (☎0171/636 4868). Past its prime but still a good deal, with access to a garden, TV lounge, library and laundry. Dorm beds cost £10 per person. Goodge Street tube.

Museum Inn Hostel, 27 Montague St, WC1 (☎0171/580 5360). Excellent central position with 4- to 10-bed mixed dorms for under £15 per person and no curfew. Tottenham Court Road tube.

Quest Hotel, 45 Queensborough Terrace, W2 (☎0171/229 7782). Small, well-worn, but lively hostel, popular with young travellers; 4- or 5-bed dorms cost under £15 per person, including breakfast. Queensway tube.

Hotel Saint Simeon, 38 Harrington Gardens (☎0171/373 0505). Budget accommodation close to the big Kensington museums; dorm beds are £11.50 and double rooms £23.50 per person, including breakfast. Gloucester Road tube.

Student halls

Carr Saunders Hall, 18–24 Fitzroy St, W1 (☎0171/323 9712). Singles and twins at £15 per person including breakfast. Open March, April & July–Sept. Warren Street tube.

International Student House, 229 Great Portland St, NW1 (☎0171/631 3223). Hundreds of beds in a vast complex at the southern end of Regent's Park. Singles at £23, doubles £20 per person. Open all year round. Great Portland Street or Regent's Park tube.

John Adams Hall, 15–23 Endsleigh St, WC1 (☎0171/387 4086). Singles £21 (£19 for students and for stays of six or more nights); doubles £37 (£33 for students or long stays). Open Jan, March, April, July–Sept & Dec. Euston Square tube.

King's Campus Vacation Bureau, 552 Kings Rd, SW10 (☎0171/351 6011). King's College has a range of accommodation (July–Sept), mostly in the Kensington, Chelsea and Westminster areas, with some less expensive alternatives in outlying Hampstead and Wandsworth. Singles £14–22, twin rooms £23–34, all prices including breakfast.

Passfield Hall, 1 Endsleigh Place, WC1 (☎0171/387 3584). Singles £25, doubles £39, including breakfast. Open March, April & July–Sept. Euston Square tube.

Ramsay Hall, 20 Maple St, W1 (☎0171/387 4537). Fairly central and comfortable, with over 400 beds, mostly singles. £19 per person or £18 for stays of a week or longer, including breakfast. Open Jan, March, April, June–Sept & Dec. Warren Street or King's Cross tube.

Campsites

Abbey Wood, Federation Rd, Abbey Wood, SE2 (☎0181/310 2233). Enormous year-round site east of Greenwich, 10 miles from central London. Train from Charing Cross to Abbey Wood.

Crystal Palace, Crystal Palace Parade, SE19 (☎0181/778 7155). All-year site, with maximum one-week stay in summer, two weeks in winter. Mainline train from London Bridge to Crystal Palace or bus #2 or #3.

Hackney Camping, Millfields Rd, Hackney, E5 (☎0181/985 7565). Big and inexpensive but some-what inconvenient, way over in the northeast of the city. Bus #38 from Victoria to Clapton Pond or bus #22a from Liverpool St to Mandeville St. Open mid-June to Aug.

Tent City Summer Tourist Hostel, Old Oak Common Lane, East Acton, W3 (☎0181/743 5708). Dorm accommodation in 14 large tents (single sex and mixed) for £5.50 per night, or you can pitch your own tent for the same price. Offers free accommodation and food plus £30 per week for foreign voluntary workers at the site. Open June–Sept. East Acton tube.

THE CITY

Most of London's big attractions are concentrated **north of the river**, in districts fanning out from **Trafalgar Square**, the site of the National Gallery. From here the wide tree-lined Mall stretches half a mile southwest to **Buckingham Palace**, recently opened to the public. Shooting off south from Trafalgar Square, stately **Whitehall**, a swathe of government offices, brings you to **Westminster** and the Thames, with the **Tate Gallery** a short stroll west along the riverbank.

North and west of Trafalgar Square lies the consumerist core of the **West End**, a lively zone of pubs, restaurants, shops, theatres and cinemas concentrated between **Piccadilly Circus**, **Leicester Square** and **Oxford Street**. The other dynamo of the West End is **Covent Garden**, a couple of minutes' walk northeast of Leicester Square, and within striking distance of **Bloomsbury** to the north, a peaceful, university-dominated retreat presided over by the vast treasure house of the **British Museum**.

The money markets are located over in the eastern part of the inner core, in the district known, confusingly for first-time visitors, as the **City of London**, or simply The City. Modern office buildings dominate the landscape here, but the City has two of London's prime tourist sights, in the shape of **St Paul's Cathedral** and the **Tower of London**. Beyond here, the **East End** has a couple of good little museums among the run-down housing estates, but disappointingly few features attest to its fascinating social history, and over the last decade the whole area has been overshadowed by the **Docklands** developments, the apotheosis of Conservative values. Docklands is the playground of London's newly monied classes, whereas the *ancien régime* prefers to reside on the other side of the West End, in salubrious enclaves such as Mayfair, Knightsbridge and **South Kensington**. All three of these areas boast some fine architectural set-pieces, but the last of them is the one that has the greatest tourist interest, on account of the vast green space of **Hyde Park** and a trio of splendid museums – the Science Museum, the Natural History Museum, and the Victoria and Albert Museum, the world's most extensive showcase of the applied arts.

Lambeth and **Southwark**, the historic but drab quarters across the river from Westminster and The City, have a bunch of impressive performance venues and museums, while north of the centre, beyond the bafflingly powerful pull of **Madame Tussaud's**, you're into a mix of characterful local neighbourhoods and excellent parks – **Regent's Park** is the most elegant, **Hampstead Heath** the largest.

On the outskirts of the city, the grandiose monuments of **Greenwich**, **Windsor** and **Hampton Court** are rich with historic associations, the open spaces of **Richmond** and **Kew** offer an antidote to big-city neurosis, and there are numerous other diversions amid the sprawl, ranging from the bijou **Dulwich Picture Gallery** to the awesome **Thames Barrier**.

Trafalgar Square and The Mall

Trafalgar Square, the confluence of the most congested streets in central London, is always swarming with visitors feeding its flocks of scruffy urban pigeons, or lolling around Edwin Landseer's four gargantuan bronze lions and the nearby fountains. Flanked on the east and west by Canada House and South Africa House, vast reminders of imperial splendour, the square is dominated by **Nelson's Column**, a 185-foot granite pillar topped by a statue of the admiral, commemorating his death at Trafalgar in 1805. On New Year's Eve the square is a heaving mass of drunken revellers; every other night of the year, however, it has a certain grandeur, with floodlights focused on its fountains and column.

At the south end of the square, a small triangular traffic island bearing an equestrian statue of Charles I marks the original site of **Charing Cross**, from where all distances from the capital are measured. The original cross was the last of twelve erected by Edward I to mark the overnight stops on the funeral procession of his wife Eleanor, from Nottinghamshire to Westminster Abbey in 1290. The cross was pulled down in 1647, and a replica built two centuries later in the forecourt of Charing Cross train station, just up the Strand to the east.

The northeastern corner of Trafalgar Square is occupied by the church of **St Martin-in-the-Fields**. An extremely influential design, especially on the church architecture of colonial America, James Gibbs's stately structure combines Corinthian columns and grey stone pediment with a distinctly unclassical spire. Its interior, enlivened by fancy Italian scrolls and cherubs on the plaster ceiling, is best seen while listening to one of the free **lunchtime concerts**. An outdoor market in the grounds sells throwaway clothes and cheap jewellery, and a set of steps leads down to the **crypt**, which has been given over to a popular licensed café. Tucked away in the corner, the brass-rubbing centre (Mon–Sat 10am–6pm, Sun noon–6pm) sells ready-made rubbings, or you can do your own for slightly less.

The National Gallery

Taking up the entire north side of Trafalgar Square, the mighty **National Gallery** (Mon–Sat 10am–6pm, Sun 2–6pm; free; Leicester Square/Charing Cross tube) houses one of the world's great art collections. Established in 1824 when the state bought 38 paintings – including works by Raphael, Rembrandt and Van Dyck – from the Russian-born banker John Julius Angerstein, it now houses pictures from all the major western European schools. The gallery is logically laid out, starting with medieval and early Renaissance works in the new Sainsbury wing, and proceeding broadly chronologically through the West, North and East wings, with the works from each period of each main school arranged together. Don't overlook the lower floor collection, either – where paintings from the main floor are hung, while certain rooms are being refurbished. Another option is to join one of the gallery's free **guided tours** (Mon–Fri 11.30am & 2.30pm, Sat 2 & 3.30pm), which set off from the Sainsbury Wing foyer.

Obviously it is impossible to try to see everything in one go, so it's a good idea to stop off first at the excellent **micro-gallery** in the Sainsbury wing, where touch-screen computer terminals allow you to plan – and print out – a personalized tour. You can also dig out details on individual paintings, artists, movements, techniques and themes from a complete catalogue of the two thousand pictures.

The Sainsbury Wing

Although Prince Charles was outraged upon seeing the original winning design for the **Sainsbury Wing**, blustering that it would be a "monstrous carbuncle on the face of a much-loved and elegant friend", the structure that was eventually built is only timidly postmodern, blending well with the older building. Its main drawback is the compactness of the rooms, which makes it difficult to get a clear view of many of the pictures at peak times – Sunday afternoon, in particular, can be hellish, with snarl-ups created by people trooping in to pay reverence to the **Leonardo Cartoon**, enshrined behind bullet-proof glass in its own dim chapel (room 51). The drawing, *The Virgin and Child with Saint Anne and Saint John the Baptist*, is a study for a painting commissioned by the King of France; like so many of Leonardo's projects it was never completed. Outside the cartoon's room hangs one he did finish – *The Virgin of the Rocks*, a melancholy scene in a brooding landscape.

Room 53 features the extraordinarily vivid **Wilton Diptych**, a portable altarpiece painted by an unknown fourteenth-century artist for the boy King Richard II, who is

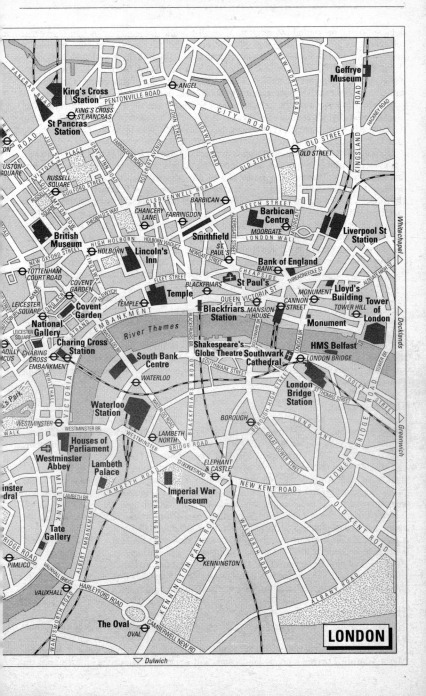

LONDON

depicted being presented by saints to Mary, Jesus and assorted angels. During recent restoration, a minuscule map was discovered in the orb atop the banner, showing a green island, a white castle and a sailing boat, symbolizing Richard's island kingdom.

Paolo Uccello's *Battle of San Romano*, which dominates room 55, is a transitional work, mixing elements of medieval decoration with early Renaissance experiments with linear perspective – note the foreshortened body in the foreground, and the broken lances ranged on the ground. Room 56 introduces the Dutch contingent, notably **Jan van Eyck**'s *Arnolfini Marriage*, one of the few surviving full-length double portraits from the fifteenth century; signed "Van Eyck Was Here" in Latin above the mirror, it served both as a commemorative portrait and a marriage contract.

In room 57, one of **Mantegna**'s early works, *The Agony in the Garden*, demonstrates a convincing use of perspective, with one of the earliest successful renditions of middle distance; nearby, the dazzling dawn sky in the painting on the same theme by his brother-in-law **Giovanni Bellini**, shows the artist's celebrated mastery of natural light. **Botticelli**'s mythological subjects dominate room 58, especially his grandiose *Venus and Mars*, with a naked and replete Mars in a deep post-coital sleep, watched over by a beautifully calm Venus, fully clothed and less overcome. Inspired by a Dante sonnet, the painting was a wedding present – some think it was intended as a headboard for the marital bed, others say it was to decorate the lid of a casket.

Room 61 holds some fine examples of Mantegna's "cameo" paintings, which imitate the effect of classical stone reliefs, reflecting the craze amongst fashionable Venetian society for collecting antique engraved marbles and gems. The largest of them, *The Introduction of the Cult of Cybele*, the artist's last work, was commissioned by Francesco Cornaro, a Venetian nobleman who claimed descent from one of the greatest Roman families. The Venetian theme is continued with Bellini's *Doge Leonardo Loredan*, one of the artist's greatest portraits.

Piero della Francesca's monumental religious paintings are at the opposite end of the wing in room 66. *The Baptism of Christ*, dating from the 1450s, is one of his earliest surviving pictures and displays his immaculate compositional technique, derived from Piero's innovative work as a mathematician.

The West Wing

Displayed in the **West Wing** are the National's High Renaissance works. Room 9, linked to the Sainsbury Wing, has a fine array of Venetian works, including **Titian**'s colourful, early masterpiece *Bacchus and Ariadne* and his very late, much gloomier, *Death of Acteon*, and **Veronese**'s lustrous *The Family of Darius Before Alexander*, a remarkable demonstration of his eye for colour. Next door, in room 8, **Bronzino**'s disturbing and erotic *Venus, Cupid, Folly and Time* and **Raphael's** trenchant *Pope Julius II* keep company with the gallery's works by **Michelangelo**, the most startlingly innovative of which is his unfinished *Entombment*. Michelangelo also provided drawings for the *Raising of Lazarus* by **Sebastiano del Piombo**, the largest painting in the room, which was planned as the altarpiece for Narbonne Cathedral.

Among the the northern Europeans in room 5, **Holbein** stands out, with his portrait *A Lady with a Squirrel and a Starling*, painted in 1527 during the artist's first visit to England. The blue background and the half-length format are familiar Holbein traits, but the presence of the two animals is more mysterious – they may be oblique references to the name of the unidentified sitter, who was probably a regular at the court of Henry VIII.

The North Wing

The North Wing is particularly strong in seventeenth- and eighteenth-century Dutch painting. The Dutch works in room 16 include **Vermeer**'s serene *A Young Woman Standing at a Virginal*, whose subject is now thought to be Vermeer's eldest daughter Maria. **Claude Lorrain**'s poetic landscapes and seascapes, favourites of aristocrats on the Grand Tour, dominate room 19. His moody *Landscape with Psyche Outside the Palace of Cupid* came to be known as the *Enchanted Castle* in the late eighteenth century, when it caught the imagination of the Romantics, supposedly inspiring Keats' *Ode to a Nightingale*. Nearby is the *Landscape with Hagar and the Angel*, the one painting that Sir George Beaumont held onto when donating his collection to the National in 1828. There are more Claude landscapes in room 15, displayed with two Lorrain-influenced **Turner** paintings, according to the English artist's wishes.

Poussin's mythological studies cover much of the wall space in room 20. One of the best pieces is also one of the very few that doesn't derive from a literary source – the dark *Landscape with Man Killed by Snake*, a wonderfully composed study, portraying fear and alarm in a sombre classical landscape. Room 22, in the northwest corner of the North Wing, is completely given over to **Rubens**, including his lurid *Samson and Delilah* and the famous portrait of his sister-in-law, known strangely as *Le chapeau de paille* (The Straw Hat) – the hat is actually black felt, decorated with white feathers.

Two of **Rembrandt**'s self-portraits, painted thirty years apart, regard each other across room 27, the melancholic *Self Portrait Aged 63*, from the last year of his life, making a strong contrast with the sprightly early work.

Velázquez dominates the Spanish paintings in room 29, with his astounding portraits and the remarkable *Rokeby Venus*, an ambiguously narcissistic image that was slashed in 1914 by suffragette Mary Richardson, who loved the painting but was revolted by the way it was leered at. In the adjacent room 32, **Caravaggio**'s melodramatic art is represented by *Christ at Emmaus* and the erotic *Boy Bitten by Lizard*.

Next door, in room 30, **Van Dyck**'s *Portrait of Charles I* is a fine example of the work that made the painter the favourite of the Stuart court, romanticizing the monarch as a dashing horseman. The inscription on the tree declares in Latin that this is Charles, King of England, in case anyone should be confused.

The East Wing

The East Wing, housing paintings from 1700 to 1920, begins in room 33 with some wistful gallantries from **Watteau** and **Fragonard** and a splendid assembly of portraits, including the dapper self-portrait by **Louise Vigée le Brun**, one of only three women artists in the whole collection. Next door, room 34 contains a roll-call of the best of English art: **Turner**'s *Fighting Temeraire*, showing the veteran of Trafalgar being towed to the shipyard at sunset; **Gainsborough**'s feathery and translucent *Morning Walk*; and **Constable**'s *Hay Wain*, a painting so familiar that it's difficult to see it properly any more. In room 37, **Hogarth**'s lively satire on loveless marriage, *Marriage à la Mode*, provides an astringent contrast to **Stubbs**' sleek horses and aristocrats. Room 38 contains **Canaletto**'s glittery vistas of Venice and in room 40, there's the airy draughtsmanship of **Tiepolo**, father and son.

Delacroix, who was profoundly impressed by Constable's dappled application of paint, is shown in room 41 alongside **Ingres**' elegant portrait of the banker's wife *Madame Moitessier*, completed when the artist was 76, having taken twelve years to finish. Also in this room are the only two paintings in the country by **Jacques-Louis David**, as well as the perenially popular, but phoney, *Execution of Lady Jane Grey* by **Paul Delaroche**.

Room 43 has a fine array of Impressionists including **Manet**, whose unfinished *Execution of Maximilian* – one of three versions – was cut into pieces during the artist's lifetime, then bought and reassembled by Degas after Manet's death. Among the other seminal works are **Renoir**'s *Umbrellas* and **Monet**'s *Bathers at La Grenouillère* – and of course, the *Waterlilies* are close at hand. Three magnificent rooms close the proceedings, starring **Van Gogh**'s dazzling *Sunflowers*, **Seurat**'s *Bathers at Asnières*, one of Europe's most comprehensive showings of **Cézanne**, and a few choice works by **Picasso**, dovetailing the National's collection into that of the Tate (see p.82).

The National Portrait Gallery

Around the back of the National Gallery lurks the **National Portrait Gallery** (Mon–Sat 10am–6pm, Sun noon–6pm; free; Leicester Square or Charing Cross tube), which was founded in 1856 to house uplifting depictions of the good and the great. Though it does include some fine paintings among its collection of more than 10,000 portraits, many of the studies are of less interest than their subjects, and the overall impression is of an overstuffed shrine to famous Brits rather than a museum offering any insight into the history of portraiture. However, it is fascinating to trace who has been deemed worthy of our admiration at any moment – warmongers and imperialists earlier this century, writers and poets in the 1930s and, latterly, retired footballers and pop stars.

Best place to start is the **top floor** (level 5), where the sixteenth-century rooms are filled with Tudor royalty, dour prelates, hanged traitors and the only known painting of **Shakespeare** from life, a subdued image in which the Bard sports a gold-hoop earring. Among the seventeenth-century personalities, **Oliver Cromwell** looks dishevelled but resolute in a miniature painted four years before he became Lord Protector. An overdressed, haggard **Charles II** presides over a room crammed full of his mistresses, including Frances Teresa Stuart, upon whom, according to the caption, the King was "mighty hot", and louche Nell Gwynn, the orange-seller turned actress.

The next seven rooms span the eighteenth century, featuring members of the **Kitkat Club**, a group of intellectuals and politicians – including Robert Walpole – who met in a tavern run by one Christopher Cat. Among the various artists and musicians are several fine self-portraits: an energetic, determined **Hogarth**, a perplexed **Sir Joshua Reynolds**, a relaxed **Gainsborough** and **George Stubbs** painted onto a Wedgewood plate. Another room contains both a bold likeness of **Lord Nelson**, and one of the many idealized portraits the smitten George Romney painted of **Lady Emma Hamilton**. The Romantics are represented by **Byron** in dashing Albanian garb and a moody image of **Wordsworth** by the history painter Benjamin Haydon. This portrait, painted in response to Wordsworth's sonnet on another of Haydon's pictures, itself became the subject of Elizabeth Barrett Browning's sonnet *Wordsworth on Helvellyn*.

On the mezzanine floor (level 4) the chronology hiccups, reverting to **Henry VIII** and his predecessors. The space is dominated by the fine larger-than-life Holbein cartoon of the King, a section of a design for a fresco in Whitehall Palace, showing him as a macho buck against a modish Renaissance background. Downstairs (on level 3) are the Victorians and Edwardians, mostly stuffy royalty and stern statesmen – one deteriorated and oddly affecting group, however, shows the **Brontë sisters** as seen by their disturbed brother Branwell; you can still see where he has painted himself out, leaving a ghostly blur between Charlotte and Emily. Also notable on this floor are two great Victorian photographs: one, by Julia Margaret Cameron showing the historian **Thomas Carlyle**, the other, **Isambard Kingdom Brunel** perkily posed in front of colossal iron chains. The twentieth-century displays are changed frequently, although the interwar period (level 2) is more consistent than the most popular section of all, the postwar period (level 1). There are some pretty uninspired paintings here, epitomized by Rodrigo Moynihan's reverential portrait of Margaret Thatcher and Bryan Organ's obsequious renderings of the royals. From time to time a part of the building is given over to a special exhibition, and these are well worth seeing – the photography shows, in particular, are often excellent.

The Mall

The southwestern exit of Trafalgar Square is marked by the imposing **Admiralty Arch**, from where you get a fantastic view down the tree-lined sweep of **The Mall**. This dead-straight avenue – London's nearest equivalent to a Parisian boulevard – was laid out early this century as a memorial to Queen Victoria, along with the triumphal arch itself and, half a mile away, the Victoria Memorial in front of Buckingham Palace. There had, however, been a thoroughfare here since 1660, and Regency architect John Nash was responsible for many of its finest buildings. **Carlton House Terrace**, for example, a graceful stretch of town houses just beyond Admiralty Arch, is typical of his best work, and houses the trendy **Institute of Contemporary Arts**, or ICA (Mon–Sat noon–1am, Sun noon–10.30pm; day pass £1.50), the city's main forum for avant-garde exhibitions, films and performances. Many people pay the day membership for access to the bar alone, one of London's hippest meeting places.

St James's Park and Palace

Flanking nearly the whole length of The Mall, **St James's Park** was originally created for Henry VIII as recreational land between his palaces at Whitehall and St James's. Developed as a public park by Charles II, it was landscaped by Nash into its present elegant appearance for George IV in 1828, in a style that established the trend for Victorian city parks. Today the pretty tree-lined lake is an inner-city reserve for wild-fowl (although the pelicans have been banished to a London Zoo as punishment for preying on London's beloved pigeons) and a favourite picnic spot for the civil servants of Whitehall. The view to Westminster from the bridge is one of the best – and even the insufferably dull facade of Buckingham Palace looks good from here.

North of the park, The Mall passes **St James's Palace**, a lepers' hospital until bon viveur Henry VIII acquired it in 1532 and began the construction of yet another residence. Very little of the sixteenth-century building remains; the brick structure you see today is the result of Nash's restoration and remodelling. An ambassador to the UK is still known as Ambassador to the Court of St James, even though the court has moved down the road. A few lesser royals remain in residence as well as Prince Charles, who moved in after his split with Di, and it's from here that the Queen's Guard sets off to Buckingham Palace for the Changing of the Guard. **Clarence House**, connected to the palace's southwest wing, is the home of the Queen Mother.

Buckingham Palace

The graceless colossus of **Buckingham Palace** (Aug & Sept daily 9.30am–5.30pm; £8; Green Park tube) has served as the monarch's permanent London residence since the accession of Victoria. It began its days in 1702 as the Duke of Buckingham's city resi-dence, built on the site of a notorious brothel, and was sold by the Duke's son to George III in 1762. The building was overhauled in 1812 by Nash and again in 1913, producing a palace that's as bland as it's possible to be. For ten months of the year there's little to do here save watch the **Changing of the Guard**, a thirty-minute cere-mony that many people unaccountably find fascinating (May–Aug daily 11.30am; Sept–April alternate days; no ceremony if it rains).

Since August 1993, however, the hallowed portals have been grudgingly opened for two months of the year, to finance the rebuilding of Windsor Castle after the fire of 1992. Tickets are sold from the tent-like box office in Green Park, at the western end of The Mall; queues vary enormously, but can be more than two hours long, after which there's a further long wait until your allocated visiting time. Once inside, despite the voyeuristic pleasure of a glimpse behind those forbidding walls, it's a bit of an anticli-max: of the palace's 660 rooms you're permitted to see just eighteen, and there's little sign of life, as the Queen decamps to Scotland every summer (see p.889).

Beyond the enormous courtyard, from where you can see the Nash portico that looked over St James's Park until it was closed off by Victoria, you hit the **Grand Hall**, the Duke of Buckingham's original hall. Now a frenzy of red and gold decorated to the taste of Edward VII, it's dominated by Nash's winding, curlicued **Grand Staircase**. Past a range of dull royal portraits, all beautifully lit by Nash's glass dome, the Guard

Room is decorated with Gobelin tapestries and nineteenth-century sculpture, leading into the Green Drawing Room, a blaze of unusually bright green walls, red carpet and enormous chandeliers. Disappointingly, there's no regal throne in the **Throne Room**, just two pink his'n'hers chairs initialled ER and P.

Nash's vaulted **Picture Gallery**, however, stretching right down the centre of the palace, is breathtaking. On show here is a selection of the Queen's art collection (three times larger than the National Gallery's) – among it Rembrandt's *The Shipbuilder and His Wife*, Van Dyck's huge equestrian portrait of Charles I and a portrayal of the King as Saint George by Rubens. It's hard to imagine Prince Charles discoing among all the Old Masters, but it was here that he celebrated his fortieth birthday, having first decked the room out like an harem. Of the remaining rooms a few stand out: the stultifyingly scarlet and gilt **State Dining Room**, for example, and Nash's **Blue Drawing Room**, with thirty fake onyx columns, flock wallpaper and an extraordinary Sèvres porcelain table made for Napoleon. The frothy **White Drawing Room**, full of priceless French antiques, is the incongruous setting of an annual royal prank: when hosting the reception for the diplomatic corps, for some mystifying reason the Queen and family emerge from a secret door behind the fireplace to greet the ambassadors.

You can see a further selection of the monarch's art collection at the **Queen's Picture Gallery** (Tues–Sat 10am–5pm, Sun 2–5pm; £2.50; Victoria tube), a couple of mealy proportioned rooms with no natural light, round the side of the palace on Buckingham Palace Road. Although this is a rotating selection, you'll usually find works by Reynolds, Gainsborough, Vermeer, Rubens, Rembrandt and Canaletto. There's yet more pageantry, in the form of ornate Royal carriages, at the **Royal Mews** (summer Tues–Thurs noon–4pm; winter Wed only; £2), further south on Buckingham Palace Road.

Whitehall to the Tate Gallery

Since the seventeenth century **Whitehall**, the broad avenue connecting Trafalgar Square with Parliament Square, has been the site of nearly all of Britain's key government buildings and civil service offices. The original Whitehall was a palace built for Henry VIII (it was here that he celebrated his marriage to Anne Boleyn in 1533 and died fourteen years later), but little of it survived a fire of 1698 after which, partly due to the dank conditions in this part of town, the royal residence shifted to St James's.

All that remains of the great palace is the elegant Palladian-style **Banqueting House** (Mon–Sat 10am–5pm; £3; Westminster or Charing Cross tube), completed by Inigo Jones in 1622 for James I, and the venue for the great Stuart masques and balls. The weather vane on the north side of the roof was a much later addition, erected in 1686 by James II to warn of the foul "Protestant wind" that might propel William of Orange over the seas from Holland; it did little to protect the King from the Glorious Revolution, however, and, after taking the throne in 1689, William and Mary came to live here for a while. Inside, the one room open to the public is well worth seeing for its ceiling paintings by **Rubens**, glorifying the Stuart dynasty. They were commissioned in 1634 by Charles I – who sixteen years later stepped onto the executioner's scaffold from one of the building's front windows, an event commemorated here on the last Sunday in January with a parade by the Royalist wing of the Civil War Society.

Across the road, po-faced mounted sentries of the Queen's Life Guard and two horseless colleagues, all in ceremonial uniform, are posted from 10am to 4pm at the **Horse Guards** building, on the site of Henry VIII's jousting yard. The mounted guards are changed hourly; those standing have to remain motionless and impassive for two hours before being replaced. Try to time your visit to coincide with the Changing of the Guard (Mon–Sat 11am, Sun 10am), when a squad of twelve mounted troops in full livery arrive from Hyde Park Barracks via Hyde Park Corner, Constitution Hill and the Parade Ground to the rear.

Farther down this west side of Whitehall, opposite Lutyens's stark **Cenotaph**, commemorating "The Glorious Dead" of both world wars, is London's most famous street, **Downing Street**. Number 10 has been the residence of the prime minister since the house was presented to Sir Robert Walpole by George II in 1732; with no. 11 – home of the Chancellor of the Exchequer – and no. 12, it's the only bit remaining of the original seventeenth-century terrace, the rest of the street dating from 1868. The public has been kept at bay since 1990 when Margaret Thatcher ordered a pair of iron gates to be installed at the junction with Whitehall; a highly symbolic act, but less than effective – a year later the IRA lobbed a mortar into Downing Street, coming within a whisker of killing the Cabinet.

In 1938, anticipating Nazi air raids, Winston Churchill decided to vacate Downing Street in favour of a bunker in King Charles Street, which separates the Home Office from the Foreign Office. By 1945 the bunker had become a cramped maze covering more than three acres, including a hospital, canteen and shooting range, as well as sleeping quarters for officers – Churchill, it is said, preferred to rest his head at the Savoy. The restored **Cabinet War Rooms** (daily 10am–6pm; £3.80; Westminster tube) now provide a glimpse of the dark, claustrophobic suites from which Churchill directed wartime operations, including the Map Room, still lined with fading charts studded with coloured pins, and the prime minister's emergency bedroom, complete with a desk from which he made many of his live radio broadcasts.

The Houses of Parliament

The Palace of Westminster, or the **Houses of Parliament**, as it's usually known, stands on the site of a palace built by Edward the Confessor – the seat of all the English monarchs for five centuries until Henry VIII moved the court to Whitehall. Following Henry's death the House of Commons, previously ensconced in the chapter-house of Westminster Abbey, moved into the palace's St Stephen's chapel, thus beginning the building's associations with Parliament. The old palace burned down in 1834, and save for a few pieces buried deep within the interior, everything else is the work of **Charles Barry**, who won the subsequent competition to create something that expressed national greatness through the use of Gothic and Elizabethan styles. The resulting orgy of honey-coloured pinnacles, turrets and tracery, somewhat restrained by the building's blocky symmetry, is the greatest achievement of the Gothic Revival.

Although its not the highest of the three towers, the landmark of the Houses of Parliament is the ornate clock tower known as **Big Ben**, although that's in fact the name of its thirteen-ton main bell. The massive clock looks particularly impressive at night, with the clock face lit up; if parliament is in session another light burns above the face. Inside, the Victorian love of pseudo-Gothic detail is evident in the warren of over one thousand committee rooms and offices, the fittings of which were largely the responsibility of Barry's assistant, **Augustus Pugin**, who was to become the leading ideologue of the Gothic Revival but died in 1852 in Bedlam mental hospital.

Unfortunately, it takes some effort to observe all this at first hand: both the House of Commons (in the north end of the building) and the House of Lords (in the south) have public galleries, but you'll have to queue to get in unless you've obtained a ticket from your local MP or embassy in London several weeks in advance. Debates in the **Commons** – the livelier house – begin at 2.30pm and finish no earlier than 10.30pm each weekday except Friday, when they start at 9.30am and finish at 3pm. Tickets are a must for Question Time, which lasts until about 3.30pm from Monday to Thursday (prime minister's Question Time is on Tuesday and Thursday from 3.15pm until 3.30pm), but access is easier later in the afternoon, or early evening. Those at the front of the queue should be able get into the Commons from about 4.30pm, although occasioanally you might have to wait up to an hour more.

Once inside the Palace, visitors are subjected to various security checks. At the first checkpoint you can peer into, but not enter, one of the few remaining parts of the original palace, the eleventh-century **Westminster Hall**. This cavernous space, unadorned except for its magnificent fourteenth-century oak hammerbeam roof, was once the nation's highest court, and it was here that Guy Fawkes was sent to the Tower for his part in the Gunpowder Plot of 1605. The conspiracy is remembered each year before the State Opening of Parliament, when the yeomen of the guard check the cellars below the House of Lords for latter-day assassins. Other renowned victims who passed through Westminster Hall include Charles I, who was avenged in 1661 when Charles II had Cromwell's head impaled on the roof – where it remained for over twenty years.

From the entrance to Westminster Hall you pass into **St Stephens Hall**, designed by Barry as a replica of the chapel where the Commons met until 1834, with sweeping vaulted ceilings, mosaics, statuary and huge wooden doors. After a further wait the doorkeeper shepherds you through the bustling **Central Lobby**, a good place for MP-spotting. Next stop is a small room where all visitors sign a form vowing not to cause a disturbance, from where long institutional staircases and corridors lead to the **Strangers' Gallery**, rising steeply above the chamber. Everyone is given a guide to the House, which includes explanatory diagrams and notes on procedure, and a Points of Order sheet to help keep up with the matters discussed.

The **House of Lords** (same opening hours as the Commons), or Upper House, a far dozier establishment peopled by unelected Lords and Ladies, is worth a visit simply to see its grandiose chamber of regal gold and scarlet dominated by a canopied gold throne – the queue to get in is always far shorter than for the Commons. Recesses of both Houses occur at Christmas, Easter, and from August to the middle of October.

Westminster Abbey

Westminster Abbey (Mon–Fri 9am–4.45pm, Wed also 6–7.45pm, Sat 9am–2.45pm & 3.45–5.45pm; Westminster tube) deserves a better setting than the western edge of traffic-clotted Parliament Square, for this single building embodies much of the history of England. Founded in the eighth century, rebuilt in the eleventh by Edward the Confessor, then again – in honour of Edward – by Henry III in the mid-thirteenth century, it has been the venue for all but two coronations from the time of William the Conqueror onwards, and the site of all royal burials during the half-millennium between the reigns of Henry III and George II. Scores of the nation's most famous citizens are honoured here, too, and the interior is cluttered with hundreds of monuments, reliefs and statuary – though many of their subjects are buried elsewhere.

Just inside the main entrance is a doleful fourteenth-century portrait of Richard II, the oldest known image of an English monarch painted from life. In the **nave**, two plain floor tablets commemorate Winston Churchill and the Unknown Soldier, while nearby you'll find the florid tombs of Charles James Fox and William Pitt the Younger, and a small plaque on the north wall celebrating "rare Ben Johnson" (sic), marking the spot where the dramatist was buried standing up, to save space.

The best of the monuments, however, lie beyond the choir screen (which incorporates a memorial to Isaac Newton), and to see these you have to pay £3, except on Wednesday evening. You enter via the north choir aisle, also known as **Musicians' Aisle**, which includes memorials to Henry Purcell and Elgar, as well as scientists Darwin and Lister; the north transept, traditionally reserved for statesmen, includes monuments of nineteenth-century prime ministers Peel, Palmerston and Gladstone.

The **central sanctuary**, before the High Altar, is the site of the coronations. On its north side are three wonderful thirteenth-century tombs, one of them that of **Edmund**

Crouchback, founder of the House of Lancaster. Many other royal tombs are clustered in the **Royal Chapels** at the rear of the abbey, the largest of which is **Henry VII's Chapel**, which houses the black marble sarcophagus of Henry and his spouse, resting below an elaborate fan-vaulted Tudor ceiling. Just beyond here, at the very east end, under the Battle of Britain stained-glass window, a plaque marks the spot where Oliver Cromwell rested until the Restoration, whereupon his body was disinterred, hanged at Tyburn and beheaded. The aisle north of this chapel is the resting place of Henry VII's granddaughters, **Queen Elizabeth I** and **Queen Mary**; in the south aisle you'll find the exquisite tomb of Henry's mother, **Margaret Beaufort**.

Entrance to the chapel of **Edward the Confessor**, the most venerable area in the abbey, is over a little bridge from Henry VII's chapel, past a simple wooden effigy of **Henry V**. Canonized in the twelfth century and still adored by Catholic pilgrims for his powers of healing, Edward died a few days after his abbey was consecrated, and his tomb remains at its heart. Its green wooden canopy, made after the original was destroyed in the Reformation, detracts a little from the beauty of the marble casket itself, on which you can still spot traces of the original mosaic and the niches in which pilgrims used to sit, praying for a cure. It's surrounded by some very early effigies – the brass image of **Eleanor I** is one of the most striking, protected by its Gothic wooden canopy, and the outer recesses of **Edward III**'s tomb are decorated with some gleaming bronze figures, visible from the ambulatory. Facing the Confessor's tomb, in front of a fifteenth-century stone screen portraying scenes from his life, is Edward I's **Coronation Chair**, a decrepit oak throne dating from around 1300, squatting above the great slab of the **Stone of Scone** – the Scottish coronation stone pilfered in 1297 by Edward in a demonstration of his mastery of the north.

Arguably the most famous area of the abbey is **Poets' Corner**, in the south transept. The first occupant was **Geoffrey Chaucer**, who was buried here in 1400 not because he was a poet but because he lived nearby, but the trend wasn't followed in earnest until the eighteenth century, since when the transept has been filled with tributes to writers of all shades of talent. On the south wall, the remains of two medieval wall paintings add some muted colour to the wash of grey, and just in front of them stands the memorial to William Shakespeare – who, like T. S. Eliot, Byron, Tennyson and various other luminaries, is not actually buried here. The adjoining **St Faith's Chapel**, reserved for quiet prayer, is gruesomely intriguing for scraps of skin on the door – they are the remains of a foolish soul who attempted to rob the abbey in the 1500s and was flayed to death for his efforts.

Doors on the south side of the nave lead to the **Great Cloister**, rebuilt after a fire in 1298, and paved with yet more funerary slabs. At the eastern end of the cloisters you enter the octagonal **Chapter House** (daily 10.30am–4pm; £2 joint ticket with Pyx chamber & museum; EH), which retains its thirteenth-century decorative paving stones and wall paintings; it was here that Parliament met until 1547. The nearby **Pyx Chamber** (same hours), entered from the east of the cloister, was the sacristy of Edward the Confessor's church and subsequently the royal treasury; it now displays the abbey's plate, and boasts the oldest altar in the building. The vaulted Norman **Undercroft Museum** (same hours) is spookily filled with generations of royal death masks, including those of Edward III and Henry VII. Wax funeral effigies include representations of Charles II, William III and Mary (the King on a stool to make him as tall as his wife), and Lady Frances Stuart, complete with stuffed parrot.

Westminster Cathedral

Just off Victoria Street, which runs southwest off Parliament Square, you'll find one of London's most surprising churches, the stripey neo-Byzantine concoction of the Roman Catholic **Westminster Cathedral** (Mon–Fri 7am–7pm or 8pm in winter, Sat & Sun

7am–8.30pm; Victoria tube). Begun in 1895, it is one of the last and wildest monuments to the Victorian era: constructed from more than twelve million terracotta-coloured bricks, decorated with hoops of Portland Stone, it culminates in a magnificent, tapered campanile which rises to 274 feet (mid-March to Oct daily 9am–5pm; £2). The **interior** is only half finished, and the domed ceiling of the nave – the widest in the country – remains an indistinct blackened mass, free of all decoration. To get an idea of what the place will look like when it's completed, explore the series of **side chapels** – in particular the All Souls Chapel in the north aisle – whose rich, multi-coloured decor makes use of more than one hundred different marbles from around the world.

The Tate Gallery

From Parliament Square the unprepossessing Millbank runs south along the river to the **Tate Gallery** (Mon–Sat 10am–5.50pm, Sun 2–5.50pm; free; Pimlico tube), founded in 1897 with money from Sir Henry Tate, inventor of the sugar cube. The Tate is a difficult collection on which to get a grip, due to the fact that it has to perform two functions – it's both the national collection of British art and the country's main gallery of intenational modern art. To complicate matters further, the English stuff remains on constant show, whereas the twentieth-century collection is partly rehung each year to ensure a decent airing for the whole range. However, even if the Jackson Pollock you were dying to see turns out to be in storage when you arrive, the Tate is always a stimulating place, not least because it presents some of the most intelligent temporary exhibitions in Europe (for which there's an admission charge), ranging from one-artist shows to surveys of entire movements and eras.

The native section has lashings of quintessentially English landscapes by **John Constable**, including the famous *Flatford Mill*, a hoard of portraits by **Gainsborough** and **Reynolds**, and the finest of **Stubbs'** equine studies. On an earthier note, there are **Hogarth**'s naturalistic domestic scenes, and a couple of his satirical works – *The Roast Beef of Old England* is a particularly vicious dig at the French. The visionary strand in English art begins with **Blake** and reaches some sort of summit with the ever-popular **Pre-Raphaelites**, among them Millais' *Ophelia* – whose model posed in a bath and promptly caught a chill, prompting threats of lawsuits from her father – and Holman Hunt's *Awakening Conscience*, the epitome of Pre-Raph sententiousness. An immense assembly of **Turner** paintings, sketches, notebooks and letters occupies the adjoining Clore Gallery, lauded by some as London's boldest postmodern building; this is the world's best Turner collection, and is nearly always crowded – avoid the Sunday rush.

Despite being underfunded compared to the standards of its European and North American rivals, the Tate has first-rate pieces from most of this century's major art movements – Constructivism, Surrealism, Minimalism, Cubism, Pop Art, Dada and Expressionism, abstract and Germanic. It's difficult to predict what will be on display at any one time, but certain names survive every rearrangement: **Picasso**, for example, with works from all of his key periods, and **Matisse**, represented by a sweep of masterpieces ranging from his Fauve paintings through to the jaunty cut-outs of his final years and the progressively more abstract bronze images of a woman's back – displayed off the central sculpture hall, which always features **Rodin**. It's a pretty safe bet that the major Surrealists – **Ernst**, **Dalí** and **Mirò** – will be on display, as will the series of **Rothko** paintings commissioned by the swanky *Four Seasons* restaurant in New York, which found their way to London after the artist suddenly decided he didn't wish his art to be a mere backdrop to the recreation of the wealthy.

The central West End

The West End does not mean quite the same thing to all people: though technically designating that part of central London that lies north of the river and to the west of the City of London, the label is applied by most Londoners to the area in which the theatres, cinemas, shops and restaurants are concentrated – and every Londoner will have a slightly different idea of where this ends. But however ambiguous its borders might be, the West End does have a core district – the area sandwiched between Oxford Street and the axis of Piccadilly and Leicester Square. Whatever hour you wander through, this feels like the heart of London. **Oxford Street** and **Regent Street**, London's most congested shopping zones, are swarming throughout the day, as is **Leicester Square**, the busiest patch of paving in the entire city. Pedestrianized Leicester Square gets even busier at night, with people on their way to the big-screen cinemas, to the theatres on and around **Shaftesbury Avenue**, to the great-value eateries of **Chinatown**, or into **Soho**, a vibrant mix of sleazy sideshows and hip hangouts.

Leicester Square, Chinatown and Soho

Leicester Square is a place to spend money, not to linger: street entertainers cry out for your small change, the mega-cinemas urge you to drop a few quid on the latest Schwarzenegger or Spielberg, the booth of the Society of West End Theatres pulls the queues for its half-price deals, and touts haggle with hapless tourists over the price of dodgy tickets for the top shows. There are no sights as such, unless you count the recently cleaned-up patch of grass at its centre, with its statues of Shakespeare and Charlie Chaplin, as well as busts of Hogarth, Sir Isaac Newton and Reynolds – just three of the many writers and artists who lived here in the eighteenth century.

Chinatown, concentrated off the north side of the square in the roads around **Gerrard Street**, is a self-contained jumble of food shops, restaurants and booksellers, only slightly marred by ersatz touches such as the telephone kiosks rigged out as pagodas. Always worth a visit, the area is especially lively during the Chinese New Year celebrations (late Jan or early Feb), when residents greet the huge papier-mâché lions that dance through the streets.

Carry on across Shaftesbury Avenue and you're into **Soho**, named for the cry that resounded through the district when it was a hunting ground in the 1630s. Soho has absorbed wave after wave of immigrants since the end of the seventeenth century, when Huguenots settled in Bateman Street after fleeing from Louis XIV's intolerant regime, and today many residents are descendants of the Italians, Poles, Greeks and Chinese who later found cheap rents for their workshops and restaurants here. The porn joints that have made this district notorious are still strongly in evidence, especially to the west of Wardour Street, yet Soho retains a certain shabby glamour. It has also long been popular with the city's creative bohos and literati, with the film industry well ensconced around Wardour Street, and media hacks crammed into the members-only *Grouch Club* in Dean Street.

Even today, it's an undeniably lively place, especially along **Old Compton Street**, the main venue for coffee-bar hopping and the hottest place on London's **gay scene**. **Carnaby Street**, on Soho's western fringe, was the centre of Swinging London in the 1960s, but rapidly declined into a depressing avenue of overpriced tack. A recent face-lift, attempting to transform the area into "West Soho", has improved the street a little, but it nevertheless lacks the character and life of Soho proper.

Piccadilly

Piccadilly Circus, the seething junction of, amongst others, Shaftesbury Avenue, Regent Street and Piccadilly, is by no means a picturesque place, not even at night, when its colossal neon advertisements give it a touch of dazzle. Its most famous monument, the aluminium statue known as **Eros** (more properly the *Angel of Christian Charity*), was erected in 1893 in honour of Victorian philanthropist Lord Shaftesbury, eponym of the main drag of London's "Theatreland". Cleaned up to celebrate its centenary, then repaired after a drunk swung from its arm, *Eros* is one of the city's top tourist attractions, a status that baffles all who live here.

The Trocadero and London Pavilion

Overlooking the shiny archer is the three-storey shopping, eating and entertainment mall of **Trocadero** (daily 10am–10pm; Piccadilly Circus tube), originally built as an old music hall. It's even more congested than the streets outside, and the only attractions worth anything more than a passing nod are the **Emaginator** (£3.50 per film), an interactive cinema showing continuous performances of 70mm shorts, and **Segaworld** a virtual reality ride based on Joypolis in Japan. Continuing in the same spirit, the neighbouring **London Pavilion** features the stagey **Rock Circus** (Mon, Wed, Thurs & Sun 11am–9pm, Tues noon–9pm, Fri & Sat 11am–10pm; £6.50), part of the Madame Tussaud group. Billed as an all-singing extravaganza, it's little more than an array of waxen rock legends accompanied by snippets of their hits on malfunctioning headphones.

The Royal Academy of Arts and the Museum of Mankind

West from Piccadilly Circus, traffic-choked **Piccadilly** cultivates a more rarefied and upmarket image, with grand hotels, old shopping arcades and buildings that look as if they were actually designed by an architect. On the south side of the road, **St James's** church, built by Sir Christopher Wren, stands close to one of the favoured emporia of the twin-set and pearls contingent – **Fortnum and Mason**, where a whimsical clock on the facade shows Mr Fortnum and Mr Mason saluting each other on the hour.

Across the road, the **Royal Academy of Arts** (Piccadilly Circus or Green Park tube), occupies the enormous Burlington House, which is fronted with statues of Michelangelo, Titian and Leonardo, among others. Founded by an eminent group of English painters including Gainsborough and Reynolds, the Academy has a fine roll-call of past students, from Turner and Constable to Peter Blake and Elizabeth Frink. As well as being a top-class but conservative art school, the Academy is a prestigious venue for travelling exhibitions, and has a small **permanent collection**, featuring the heavyweights of its formative decades (free guided tours 1pm Tues–Fri). The one big public event in the Academy's calendar is the **Summer Exhibition**, for which anyone can enter paintings, though your chances of gaining acceptance will be greatly enhanced if you stick to portraiture and nice landscapes.

In keeping with the area's haughty tone, the anachronistic **Burlington Arcade**, just west of the Royal Academy, was built in 1819 for Lord Cavendish, to prevent commoners throwing rubbish into his next-door garden. Today it's one of London's most expensive shopping arcades, lined with mahogany-fronted jewellers, gentlemen's outfitters and the like. Bizarrely, it is illegal to whistle, sing, hurry or carry large packages on this small stretch, and the frock-coated and top-hatted footmen (known as Burlington Berties) take the prevention of such criminality very seriously.

At the north end of the arcade, the excellent **Museum of Mankind** (Mon–Sat 10am–5pm, Sun 2.30–6pm; free; Piccadilly Circus or Green Park tube) holds the ethnographic collection of the British Museum, a superb array of domestic, religious and figurative objects from every corner of the globe – there are supposedly so many good spirits here that people send in jinxed and evil items to be exorcised. The place is one great treasure trove: shrunken human heads from Ecuador grinning with sewn-up lips; an impossibly delicate Botswanan hat made from spiders' webs; a pixie cap from Borneo shimmering with fish scales; chunky Polynesian and Hawaiian temple images; rough-hewn Native American totem poles; long skinny Tibetan trumpets. Across the foyer, past the heavy-browed Easter Island statue, Mexican turquoise mosaics fill one room and two large galleries are given over to exhibits of African fetishes, amulets, textiles, weapons, clothes and deities. The first floor reveals a relatively small collection of Meso-American and Pre-Columbian artefacts, including a solid crystal skull which may be Aztec but may be a fake, and unusual Maya woodcarving. Superb temporary shows – which can last a couple of years – have most recently featured the mixed-up world of contemporary New Guinea.

Oxford Street

From Piccadilly Circus the exquisitely designed **Regent Street**, planned by John Nash as the first phase of an avenue leading all the way to Regent's Park (see p.114), curves north to Oxford Circus, passing such famous shops as *Hamley's*, the world's largest toy shop, and the mock-Tudor *Liberty's*. Built on the Roman route to Oxford, **Oxford Street**, which cuts east–west across Regent Street, has been one of the world's busiest shopping streets since early this century, and even recessions and bomb scares haven't made much of a difference to the consumer fever. The east end of the street, from Centre Point to Oxford Circus, is the more downmarket part, with bleak shops full of cut-price jeans, booths selling cheap gifts and policemen's hats, and auctioneers operating out of short-lease shops vacated by traders forced out by sky-high rents – though there's a fair number of nationwide giants here as well, such as *HMV* and *Marks and Spencer*, the great British success story. The west end of the street has *Selfridge's*, *John Lewis* and other classier stores, with exclusive shopping roads feeding into it – **South Molton Street** and **Bond Street** are the preserve of very expensive designer shops, as is **St Christopher's Place**, a pedestrianized alley linking Oxford Street to Wigmore Street on the north side.

The Wallace Collection

One block north of Wigmore Street and just a couple of minutes from Oxford Street, but eons away from its frenetic pace, Hertford House on Manchester Square holds one of London's most important art galleries, the **Wallace Collection** (Mon–Sat 10am–5pm, Sun 2–5pm; free; Bond Street tube). This wonderful array, best known for its eighteenth-century French paintings and decorative art, was bequeathed to the nation by the widow of Sir Richard Wallace, an art collector and, as the illegitimate son of the fourth Marquess of Hertford, inheritor of the elegant mansion and its treasures.

The ground floor has some interesting medieval and Renaissance pieces, an extensive armoury ranged around the central courtyard, and a group of fine nineteenth-century pictures, including Richard Parkes Bonington's translucent watercolours and paintings by his close friend Delacroix. However, the most famous works are on the first floor, the tone of which is set by **Boucher's** sumptuous mythological scenes over the staircase. Here you'll find furniture from the courts of Louis XV and XVI, decorative gold snuff boxes and fine Sèvres porcelain – including mighty wine and ice-cream coolers made for Empress Catherine the Great of Russia and a whimsical pair of vases adorned with elephant-headed candle holders. Of the paintings, portraits include Sir Joshua Reynolds' doe-eyed moppets, Greuze's winsome adolescents drapes, and two by Louise Vigée le Brun, one of the most successful portraitists of pre-revolutionary France. Among the rococo delights are **Fragonard's** coquettes, the most famous of whom flaunts herself to a smitten beau in *The Swing*; some elegiac scenes by **Watteau**;

and Boucher's gloriously florid portrait of Madame de Pompadour, Louis XIV's mistress and patron of many of the great French artists of the period.

In addition to all this French finery there's a good collection from the Dutch and Venetian schools: **de Hooch**'s *Women Peeling Apples*; the contrasting vistas by **Canaletto** and **Guardi**; **Titian**'s *Perseus and Andromeda*; **Rembrandt**'s affectionate portrait of his teenage son, Titus, who was helping administer his father's estate after bankruptcy charges; and **Hals**' arrogant *Laughing Cavalier*, the subject of which remains unknown. In the same vast hall as the Hals you'll find **Velázquez**'s typically searching *Lady with a Fan*, and **Gainsborough**'s deceptively innocent portrait of the actress Mary Robinson, in which she insouciantly holds a miniature of the Prince of Wales, her lover (later George IV).

Covent Garden and Bloomsbury

To the northeast of Trafalgar Square lies Covent Garden, formerly the capital's main fruit and veg market, now an upbeat shopping area revolving round the sensitively preserved market building on Covent Garden piazza. North of here, stylish Floral Street and Neal Street bring you to the edge of Bloomsbury, an area of leafy squares, elegant town houses and intriguing old bookshops. Home to Britain's largest university, the University of London, and its most prestigious museum, the British Museum, the district has long been a magnet for artists and writers, from Dickens through Marx and Lenin to the Oxbridge-educated gang known as the Bloomsbury Set, who clustered round the likes of Virginia Woolf, Lytton Strachey and John Maynard Keynes.

Covent Garden

Glossy **Covent Garden**, which takes its name from the medieval convent garden of Westminster Abbey, became London's first planned square in the 1630s, when Inigo Jones laid out a graceful Palladian-style residential piazza. However, over the next century the tone of the place fell as market traders set up stalls to sell produce to the aristocratic residents. Turkish baths, brothels and gambling dens abounded, and by the early eighteenth century the area was known as "the great square of Venus". At the same time, some of London's most famous coffee houses were concentrated here, frequented by writers such as Boswell and Sheridan, and the **Royal Opera House**, built in 1732 (and rebuilt after a fire in 1809), lent the area a fashionable cachet.

In the 1830s Covent Garden was cleaned up – the slums were torn down and the splendid iron and glass **market hall** was built, housing a vast fruit and vegetable market until the 1970s, when it moved to Nine Elms in Vauxhall. Subsequent plans to demolish the hall to make way for office blocks were thwarted at the last minute by mass protests, and today the restored hall shelters two elegant storeys of shops, a few overpriced restaurants, a pub and art and craft stalls. The western side of the piazza, a semi-institutionalized venue for buskers and street performers, is dominated by the portico of Jones' **St Paul's** church. Known as the actors' church, it is filled with memorials to thespians from Boris Karloff to Gracie Fields, and directly inside the door, the sculptor Grinling Gibbons is remembered by one of his own wooden carvings for St Paul's cathedral. In 1662 the church was, reputedly, the site of the first ever **Punch and Judy** show; commemorated every second Sunday in May by a festival in the delightfully overgrown churchyard, a tranquil respite from the activity outside.

An original flower-market shed on the piazza's east side is occupied by the **London Transport Museum** (daily 10am–6pm; £3.95; Covent Garden tube). It houses a herd of old buses, trains and trams, tracing the history of public transport in London from 1830, when the River Thames was finally abandoned as a main thoroughfare. There's enough interactive fun – driving simulated trains and so forth – to keep children amused, and London Transport's stylish posters, many commissioned from well-known artists, are worthy of an exhibition in themselves.

The rest of the old flower market now houses the **Theatre Museum** (Tues–Sun 11am–7pm; £3), with three centuries of memorabilia from every conceivable area of the performing arts in the west (the entrance is on Russell Street). The corridors of glass cases cluttered with props, programmes and costumes are not especially exciting, and the portrait collection is disappointingly dull. In addition to the permanent exhibits, two special areas host long-term temporary shows – "Slap", a history of stage make-up, is a lot of fun, with videos of the creation of Lloyd Webber's *Phantom of the Opera* and a make-up artist on hand to give you a hideous bullet wound or scar. As well as offering a **booking service** for West End shows and an unusually good selection of cards and posters, the museum is also a resource centre, with a theatre hosting performances, lectures and debates.

The British Museum

The **British Museum** (Mon–Sat 10am–5pm, Sun 2.30–6pm; free; Russell Square, Tottenham Court Road or Holborn tube), occupying a vast plot of land to the north of Great Russell Street, is one of the finest museums on earth. Its creation followed the death of doctor Sir Hans Sloane in 1753, when, upon his suggestion, his heirs sold his collection of over 80,000 curios – from plants and fossils to coins and medals – to the British government. The British Museum, the world's first public museum, was immediately established by an Act of Parliament, and housed in a building bought with funds from a public lottery. As early as 1820, it became clear that more space was needed, and the present structure was purpose-built to accommodate the rapidly expanding collection. Now housing over four million artefacts – a number increasing daily with a stream of new acquisitions, discoveries and bequests – the fourteen-acre Victorian maze of trophy rooms is far too big to be seen in one go. The best advice is to decide which collections you particularly want to see, and concentrate on them – bearing in mind that many are spread over more than one floor. There are **two entrances**: the main one, on Great Russell Street, brings you to the information desk and bookshop, while the smaller doorway on the north side of the building in Montague Place opens onto the Far Eastern galleries.

The Egyptian collection

Beyond the bookshop on the ground floor, just past the entrance to the Assyrian section (see below), two seated black statues of **Amenophis III** guard the entrance to the Egyptian Hall (room 25), where the cream of the British Museum's Egyptian antiquities is on display: the name "Belzoni", scratched under the left heel of the larger statue, was carved by the Italian circus strong man responsible for dragging some of the heftiest Egyptian treasures to the banks of the Nile, prior to their export to England. Nearby, a crowd usually forms around the **Rosetta Stone**, a black slab found in the Nile delta in 1799, whose trilingual inscription enabled scholars to decode Egyptian hieroglyphs for the first time. Beyond the stone, a sombre trio of life-sized granite statues of **Sesotris III** make a doleful counterpoint to the colossal pink-speckled granite head of **Amenophis III**, whose enormous arm lies on the floor next to him. A central atrium flanked with smaller statues – including a rare wooden figure of **Rameses I** from Thebes – contains cases of jewellery, figurines and religious objects, beyond which yet another giant head and shoulders, made of two pieces of different-coloured stone, still bears the hole drilled by French soldiers in an unsuccessful attempt to remove it from the mortuary temple of **Rameses II**. A long dim side gallery is the tomb-like setting for the brightly painted sandstone head of **Mentuhotep**

II, and, completely different in style, the head of an unidentified ruler, formed from smooth green schist that bears an uncanny resemblance to the texture of human skin. A naturalistic and oddly touching tomb painting at the end of the room shows a nobleman hunting wildfowl with his wife and daughter – the sky full of birds, fat fish floating in the river, and an excited tabby cat clutching three dead birds in its claws.

Climbing the west stairs brings you to the **upper floor** and the huge **Egyptian mummy** collection (rooms 60 & 61). The sheer number of exhibits here is overwhelming and it's frustrating that there's little in the way of explanation. Wooden outer caskets scrawled with hieroglyphs fill rooms flanked by brightly decorated mummy cases; the mummies themselves include wistful Roman examples, painted on the outside with the sad faces of their owners. Beyond is an interesting series of less crowded rooms, in which you can see painted pavements, papyrus, domestic objects, and a small room with wax portraits and textiles from Coptic Egypt.

The Mesopotamian and Assyrian collections

Just before reaching the Egyptian sculpture on the ground floor, the attendant gods, their robes smothered in inscriptions, fix their gazes on you, serving as a prelude to the Assyrian finds ranged in a corridor (rooms 19–21) parallel to the Egyptian hall. Guarded by two colossal five-legged, human-headed winged bulls, the collection sets off with a full-scale reconstruction of the **Balawat gates** from Shalmaneser III's palace, leading into rooms lined with reliefs from the **Palace at Nimrud** (883–859 BC); also on display here is a black obelisk carved with hieroglyphs and images of foreign rulers paying tribute to Shalmaneser III.

Another room (17) is lined with splendidly legible friezes, showing **Ashurbanipal's** lion hunts, a "sport of kings" that effectively wiped the beasts out; the succession of graphic death scenes features one in which the King slaughters the cats with his bare hands. From here it's a convenient trot down into the basement, where smaller Mesopotamian friezes and domestic objects include an iron bathtub-cum-coffin from **Ur**, thought to be the first great city on earth, dating from 2500 BC.

On the **upper floor** a series of rooms reached from the west stairs resumes the early story of Mesopotamia. Two of the most extraordinary treasures, fashioned in deep blue lapis lazuli, fragile shell and gold, hail from Ur: the enigmatic **Ram in the Thicket**, a midnight blue and white shell statuette of a goat on its hind legs, peering through golden branches; and the equally mysterious **Standard of Ur**, a small hollow box showing scenes of battle on one side, with peace and banqueting on the other. A selection of Mesopotamian cuneiform tablets scratched with infinitesimal script includes the **Flood Tablet**, a fragment of the Epic of Gilgamesh, perhaps the world's oldest story.

The Ancient Greek collection

Treasures from Ancient Greece are ranged to the side of the Assyrian collection on the ground floor, beginning with Cycladic figures, Minoan artefacts, Archaic black-figured vases and later red-figured vases from Greece's Classical age. Beyond here is a glut of wonders: the marble frieze from the **Temple of Apollo** at Bassae (mezzanine room 6); the reconstructed **Nereid monument**, mighty tomb of a ruler of Xanthos, fronted with Ionic columns and finely carved sea nymphs; and the museum's most famous relics, the **Elgin Marbles**. A huge purpose-built room (the Duveen Gallery; room 8) is devoted to these exquisite friezes, metopes and pedimental sculptures, carved between 447 and 432 BC under the supervision of the great sculptor Pheidias. They were created for the **Parthenon**, the sanctuary of the goddess Athena; the main frieze, resplendent with horseback figures in swirling drapery, probably depicts scenes from a procession in honour of Athena – though one school of thought says it's a celebration of the victory at Marathon. Removed from Athens in 1801 by Lord Elgin, British ambassador to Constantinople, in order to protect them from damage by the Turkish army, the sculptures were bought by the British government in 1816 for £35,000, and have caused more controversy than any other of the museum's trophies. The Greek government has repeatedly requested that they be returned, and commissioned a museum to house them near the Acropolis, but so far there's no sign of the Brits relenting.

Past the Nereid monument in room 9, you come to an enormous caryatid from the **Erechtheion** on the Acropolis, and fragments (in room 12) from two of the Wonders of the Ancient World: two huge figures, a frieze and a marble horse the size of an elephant from the tomb of **King Mausolos at Halicarnassus** (whence derives the term mausoleum); and a sculpted drum from the colossal **Temple of Artemis at Ephesus**. Upstairs are a few rooms dedicated to less spectacular Greek artefacts, including bronzes, terracottas and pottery. The highlight of these first-floor rooms, though, is the **Portland Vase** (room 70), made from cobalt-blue, blown glass, around the beginning of the first millennium, and decorated with opaque white cameos.

The bulk of the British Museum's **Roman statuary** is in the basement's Townley Collection, best approached by the west stairs, which are lined with mosaic pavements. The wonderful carvings include two curiously gentle marble greyhounds, a claw-footed sphinx, assorted nymphs and satyrs, and dozens of portrait busts of emperors and mythological heroes.

Prehistoric and Roman Britain, the Celts and medieval Europe

At the top of the main stairs, an almost intact Romano-British mosaic, centred on the earliest known mosaic representation of Christ, leads into a gathering of domestic objects from Roman Britain, the most famous of these being the 28 pieces of silver tableware known as the **Mildenhall Treasure** (room 40).

Close to the top of the main stairs, a glass case holds the most sensational of the BM's recent finds: the remains of the two-thousand-year-old **Lindow Man**, preserved in a Cheshire bog after his sacrificial death at the hands of Druids. It's an unsettling introduction to the brilliant displays of **Celtic craftwork**, where two of the most distinctive objects are the French bronze wine flasks inlaid with coral. Showing Persian and Etruscan influences, they are supreme examples of Celtic art, with happy little ducks on the lip and rangy dogs for handles. From England there are fabulous heavy golden necklaces, a horned bronze helmet, and fine decorative mirrors and shields, but nothing can rival the Saxon **Sutton Hoo** ship burial. Discovered in Suffolk in 1939, this enormous haul includes silver bowls, gold jewellery decorated with cloisonné enamel, and an iron helmet bejewelled with gilded bronze and garnets. Further on in room 42, among the splendid Viking brooches and coins, are the thick-set **Lewis chessmen**, wild-eyed Scandinavian figures carved from walrus ivory and originally painted dark red, which were discovered in the Outer Hebrides.

The Oriental and Islamic collections

The BM's **Oriental collection** (rooms 33, 34 & 91–94; best approached from the Montague Place entrance) is unrivalled in the West, covering Buddhism, Taoism and Confucianism, and oddities like a third-century BC shamanistic antlered figure that doesn't quite fit anywhere. Outstanding are the ceramic Tang funerary figures, some highly unusual Neolithic axes and jades, and intricate Shang bronze vessels and musical instruments from the eleventh century BC.

Beyond this, a bewildering array of Oriental antiquities includes a **Tibetan** conch shell trumpet decorated with gilt and precious stones, and a filigree altar screen set with bone, shell and semiprecious gems; **Thai** ceramics from Sawankalok; small bronze deities from **Cambodia**; two **Javanese** heads of Buddha in volcanic stone, from the mighty Chandi Borobudur temple; eighteenth-century ivory figures from **Sri**

Lanka; and bronze figures on elaborate thrones from **east India**. The showpiece of the collection, however, is the room of dazzling reliefs, drum slabs and dome sculptures from a second-century Buddhist stupa in southern India.

The museum's **Islamic** antiquities (room 34), from as far apart as Spain and south Asia, are in the gallery adjacent to the north entrance. The pure blues, greens and tomato-reds of the **Iznik** ceramics are particularly fine, as are the monumental **Mongol** lustre tiles and the thirteenth-century astrolobes and celestial globes. Most unusual, however, is the naturalistic green Kashgar jade terrapin, discovered in Allahabad in 1600. On the uppermost level the new **Japanese** gallery is dedicated to temporary exhibitions of prints, cartoons, lacquerwork, silks and some amazing steel blades.

The British Library and the manuscript collection

The museum building is still the home of the **British Library**, currently in the throes of a much delayed move to a new site near St Pancras station. By law the library must preserve a copy of every book, magazine and newspaper printed in Britain, so it's hardly surprising that conditions here are now too cramped. For the time being the **manuscript saloon** (room 30) occupies exhibition space in the east wing, where a selection of ancient manuscripts and precious books are displayed – the **Magna Carta**, **Gutenberg Bible** and (in room 30a) the richly illustrated **Lindisfarne Gospels** are always on show. Classic literary manuscripts include James Joyce's manically scribbled *Finnegans Wake*, a chaotic contrast to Coleridge's fastidious *Kubla Khan* and beautifully handwritten and illustrated copies of *Alice in Wonderland* and *Jane Eyre*. Musical texts range from the Beatles to Brahms, and historical letters include the last – unfinished – correspondence from Lord Nelson to Emma Hamilton during the Battle of Trafalgar. The famous domed **Round Reading Room**, where Karl Marx penned *Das Kapital*, is open to visitors for tours (Mon–Fri 2.15 & 4.15pm).

Minor Bloomsbury museums

A couple of Bloomsbury's lesser museums, although dwarfed by the British Museum, are worth dipping into. The **Dickens House**, 48 Doughty St (daily 10am–5pm; £3; Russell Square tube) is the area's only house museum – surprising, given the plethora of blue plaques marking the residences of local luminaries. The author's home from 1837 to 1839, when he wrote *Nicholas Nickleby* and *Oliver Twist*, the house is cluttered with letters and manuscripts, along with his earliest known portrait (a miniature painted by his aunt in 1830), his quill pens, a Charles Dickens cake decoration, desks he worked at during various stages of his career, first editions, and annotated books he used during extensive lecture tours in Britain and the States. The Drawing Room, where Dickens entertained his literary friends, is restored to the oppressive appearance so fashionable in his day.

Tucked away in the southeast corner of Gordon Square at no. 53, the **Percival David Foundation of Chinese Art** (Mon–Fri 10.30am–5pm; free; Russell Square tube) is a fine collection of ceramics ranging from fragile tea cups to opulent bowls glazed with extraordinarily rich colour. The most famous pieces are the porcelain "David" vases, made in the fourteenth century and aswirl with dragons and fabulous birds – the earliest known use of vivid blue underglaze. Gordon Square itself, once the centre of the Bloomsbury Group, is less landscaped and quieter than Russell Square, used mainly by swotting students from the various university departments in the surrounding buildings. Plaques mark the residences of Lytton Strachey (no. 51) and the Keynes (no. 46), while another (no. 50) commemorates the Bloomsbury Group as a whole (see p.170).

Aldwych and the Inns of Court

The wide crescent of **Aldwych**, forming a neat letter "D" within the eastern section of the Strand, is flanked by the enormous London offices of the Australian and Indian governments, with Bush House – home of the BBC's World Service – hemmed in between them. There are two historic churches here – Gibbs' elegant **St Mary-le-Strand**, with interior carving by Grinling Gibbons, and the official RAF church **St Clement Danes**, designed by Wren with a 115-foot-high tower by James Gibbs – but the area's chief attraction is **Somerset House**, home to the Courtauld Institute.

To the east, hidden away from the main streets, the secluded **Inns of Court** form the centre of judicial London – indeed, of England and Wales, as every barrister must serve some time here before qualifying. Although there are few formal attractions here, with the exception of the beautiful Temple church and the Sir John Soane's Museum, the Inns do make for an interesting stroll, their archaic, cobbled precincts exuding the rarefied atmosphere of an Oxbridge college.

Somerset House and the Courtauld Institute

Standing on the site of a palace begun in 1547 and occupied for a short time by Elizabeth I during the reign of her sister, **Somerset House** was from 1780 to 1838 home to the Royal Academy of Arts. It housed the National Registry of Births and Deaths until 1973, but has recently reverted to its status as an art gallery, although the **Courtauld Institute** (Mon–Sat 10am–6pm, Sun 2–6pm; £3; Temple tube) still shares the building with distinctly unaesthetic Inland Revenue offices. The Courtauld, the first body in Britain to award degrees for Art History as an academic subject, was founded in 1931 as part of the University of London, and has a superb collection, chiefly known for its Impressionists and Post-Impressionists, despite a roster of earlier artists that boasts such names as Rubens, Van Dyck, Tiepolo and Cranach the Elder.

Most visitors head straight for the pretty pink and turquoise room that holds some of the most famous paintings in the world, amongst them **Degas'** *Two Dancers*, **Renoir's** *La Loge*, a version of **Manet's** bold *Déjeuner sur l'herbe*, and the same artist's atmospheric *Bar at the Folies-Bergère*, a nostalgic celebration of the artist's love affair with Montmartre, painted two years before his death. **Cézanne** gets a room practically to himself, featuring one of his series of *Card Players* and several magnificent landscapes, geometrical but lush. Upstairs, the Great Hall, which used to be the main gallery for the Royal Academy, holds changing exhibits from its collection, but whatever the arrangement, it's a safe bet that you'll see familiar paintings by Gauguin, Toulouse-Lautrec, Seurat, Van Gogh and Modigliani.

Temple

Temple, the most interesting of the Inns of Court and, strictly speaking, part of The City (see p.93), actually comprises two Inns, the Middle and Inner Temple. The latter was where Mahatma Gandhi chose to study law in 1888, because, he said, Indian scholars considered it the most aristocratic of the Inns. Outside the half-timbered entrance on Fleet Street stands **Temple Bar**, the latest in a long line of structures marking the boundary between Westminster and the City of London – others have included a simple chain in the twelfth century and Wren's gate built after the Great Fire, topped with spikes and the heads of executed traitors, which was removed in 1878 to ease traffic congestion.

A stroll down Inner Temple Lane brings you to one of London's oldest buildings, the **Temple Church** (Wed–Sun 10am–4pm; closed Aug), built in 1185 by the Knights Templar, an order founded to protect pilgrims on the road to Jerusalem. An oblong chancel was added to the round church in the thirteenth century, and the whole building was damaged in the Blitz, but the original round church still stands, with its recumbent marble effigies and tortured grotesques grimacing in every arch. At the northwestern corner of the choir, behind the decorative altar tomb to Edmund Plowden, builder of the Middle Temple Hall, a stairwell leads up to a tiny cell, less than five feet long, in which disobedient Knights were confined. Much of the church was restored by Wren in 1682, although only his carved oak reredos remains today, and he was also responsible for the elegant red-brick buildings along the northern side of King's Bench Walk, south of the church in the Inner Temple Court.

Medieval law students ate, attended lectures and slept in the **Middle Temple Hall** (open during term time Mon–Fri 10am–noon & 3–4.30pm), which also hosted many of the great Elizabethan masques and plays – reputedly Shakespeare's *Twelfth Night* was premiered here in 1602. Today this triumph of Tudor architecture is worth a visit – it's still the Inns' main dining room – for its fine hammer-beam roof, wooden panelling, decorative Elizabethan screen, portraits of Tudor monarchs, and the small wooden table said to be have been carved from the hatch of one of Sir Francis Drake's ships.

From the Royal Courts of Justice to Gray's Inn

Back across The Strand, the **Royal Courts of Justice**, a daunting nineteenth-century Gothic Revival complex, is where the most important civil cases are tried. The majestic entrance hall is worth a look for its mosaic floor and a small exhibition of legal garb; you can also watch the court proceedings from any one of over fifty public galleries.

The oldest Inn of Court, **Lincoln's Inn** stands at the back of the courts on land originally owned by the Dominicans, bequeathed after 1287 by the Earl of Lincoln to a society of lawyers. Although you can walk around the grounds quite freely, if you want to see the halls you must call at the porter's lodge, at the entrance by Lincoln's Inn Fields. Immediately inside the gate on the southeastern corner of Lincoln's Inn Fields, the seventeenth-century **chapel** has a foundation stone laid by John Donne, once a member of the Inn (Mon–Fri noon–2.30pm). South of here, fifteenth-century lawyers lived in the **Old Hall**, notable for its enormous bay windows and religious painting by Hogarth; from 1733 to 1873 this was the Court of Chancery, where Dickens set the case Jarndyce vs. Jarndyce in *Bleak House*.

The nearby **Sir John Soane's Museum** (Tues–Sat 10am–5pm; free; Holborn tube), on the northern side of Lincoln's Inn Fields, is one of London's best-kept secrets. Soane, architect of the Bank of England, was an avid collector who designed this house not only as a home but as a place to exhibit his art and antiquities after his death. Arranged much as it was in his lifetime, the ingeniously planned house has an informal, treasure-hunt atmosphere, with surprises in every alcove. Sir Joshua Reynolds' *Love and Beauty*, for example, is mounted on mirrors in the open-plan dining-room-cum-library, while Soane's tiny study and drawing room are crammed with fragments of Roman marble and Renaissance bronzes, which continue into the high, narrow corridor, with its glass-tiled floor and unexpected views into other rooms. The **picture room** has false walls that swing back to reveal yet more paintings – a wonderful display, including **Hogarth**'s satirical *Election* series and his morality tale *The Rake's Progress*, as well as **Piranesi**'s drawings of the temples at Paestum.

The flagstoned **crypt** is reached by narrow stairs that lead into the eccentric "monk's parlour", a Gothic folly dedicated to a make-believe padre, complete with tomb, cloister and eerie medieval casts and gargoyles. The hushed sepulchral chamber continues the morbid theme with its wooden mummy case, a model of an Etruscan tomb (complete with skeleton), and the tombstones of Soane's wife and son. You then emerge into a sunny atrium, where the three-thousand-year-old alabaster **sarcophagus of Seti I** is watched over by rows and rows of antique statuary and busts on the ground floor above – an extraordinary sight. At 2.30pm on Saturday a fascinating **free guided tour** takes you round the museum and next door to no. 12, which Soane built for himself in 1792; it now holds an enormous array of architectural drawings, including works by Wren.

North of Lincoln's Inn, **Gray's Inn**, entered from High Holborn, is named for Sir Le Grey, Chief Justice of Chester, who lived in a mansion here in the thirteenth century. The house was used as lodgings for law students in the 1400s, and many more buildings were added during the sixteenth century, but much of what you see today was rebuilt after the Blitz. However, the fabulous Tudor screen and stained glass in the **Hall** are originals (entry by appointment; ☎0171/405 8164).

The City of London

Stretching from Temple Bar in the west to the Tower of London in the east, **The City of London**, also known as the Square Mile, began its days as the fortified heart of Roman London, and soon flourished into a busy trading port. William the Conqueror granted the City certain privileges in exchange for Londoners' acceptance of his rule, at the same time building the Tower of London to warn them not to step out of line; a century later King John agreed to a charter, which still stands, allowing the City to be administered by its own Lord Mayor, elected annually from among the most prominent businessmen. Today the "Corporation of London" retains its independence – with its own police force, for example, and a number of quirky bye-laws.

In the sixteenth century this commercial area, the world's richest port, was the fastest growing city in Europe, but unsanitary conditions and wooden buildings were soon to provoke two devastating disasters: in 1665 the **Great Plague** wiped out about a quarter of London's population, and only a year later the **Great Fire** destroyed four-fifths of the City's buildings. Almost immediately Sir Christopher Wren began his rebuilding programme, setting off with a commemorative obelisk, known simply as **Monument** (April–Sept Mon–Fri 9am–6pm, Sat & Sun 2–6pm; Oct–March Mon–Sat 9am–4pm; £1; Monument tube). Topped with spiky copper flames, the column stands 202ft high, 202ft west from where the conflagration began on the night of September 2, 1666, in a small bakery on Pudding Lane. You can, if you wish, climb the 311 steps to a gallery at the top.

Rebuilt in brick and stone, the City gradually lost its centrality as London swelled beyond its walled boundary; and today, although bustling during the working week, few people actually live here, lending it an eerie desolation after dark. Severely affected by the Blitz, a lot of the City is soulless, and the installation of roadblocks in 1993, after a couple of vastly destructive IRA bombs, has done little to add to its aesthetic charm. However, a few architectural delights do remain, including some beautiful churches – the jewel of which, of course, is St Paul's Cathedral. At the other end of the scale, the construction boom of the Thatcherite eighties, in which nearly fifty percent of the City's office space was rebuilt, produced some extraordinary modern edifices – many of which still stand empty.

Fleet Street

In 1447, William Caxton produced England's first printed book, *Dictes and Sayings of Philosophers*. Half a century later his pupil Wynkyn de Worde moved the Caxton presses from Westminster to **Fleet Street**, to be close to the clergy of St Paul's, and almost immediately clusters of booksellers and printers sprang up along what came to be known as "the Street of Shame". The *Daily Courant*, Britain's first daily paper, started here in 1702, as did *Punch* magazine, devised in 1841 over a tankard of ale in

THE CITY

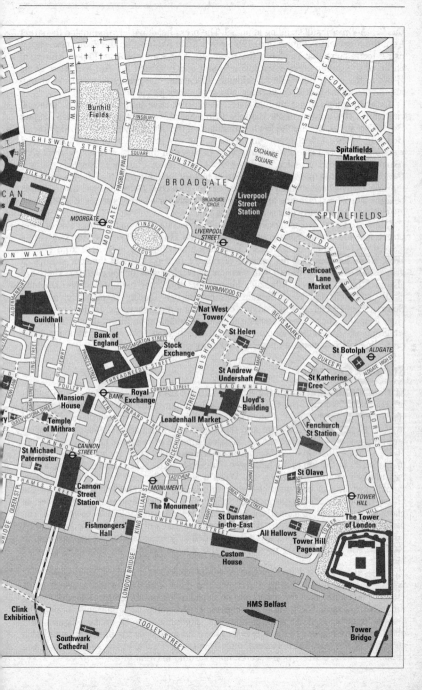

the *Punch Tavern*, still standing at no. 99. The press headquarters dominated the street from the nineteenth century until 1985, when Eddy Shah set up the *Today* newspaper, using technology that rendered the Fleet Street presses obsolete. Rupert Murdoch, baron of the gutter press, soon followed suit and relocated his *Sun* and *News of the World* to the newly developing Docklands, discarding the printers' unions and changing the face of the British newspaper industry for ever.

To learn a little about the old-style Fleet Street, dive into the so-called "printers' cathedral", the church of **St Bride's** (Mon–Sat 8.30am–5.30pm, Sun 9am–7.30pm; Blackfriars tube), behind the Reuters building on the site of Wynkyn de Worde's press. Boasting Wren's tallest tower (incidentally, the inspiration for the traditional tiered wedding cake), St Bride's was extensively damaged in the Blitz, revealing a crypt with remains of Roman mosaics, medieval walls and seven churches. Nestled amongst these relics, a little museum of Fleet Street history includes a print of the front page of the first *Daily Courant* and a 1785 issue of the *Universal Daily Register*, which was to become *The Times*, claiming to be "the faithful recorder of every species of intelligence . . . circulated for a particular set of readers only".

Johnson's Court, one of numerous tiny old alleys clustered on the north side of Fleet Street, leads to Gough Square and **Dr Johnson's House** (May–Sept Mon–Sat 11am–5.30pm; Oct–April closes 5pm; £3; Blackfriars tube). Johnson lived here from 1747 to 1759, while he compiled his seminal dictionary (see p.412), and the four storeys of grey-panelled rooms are lined with portraits and etchings of the irascible wit. There are also pictures of Boswell, Johnson's biographer, and other members of the Doctor's circle, including his black servant Francis Barber. Quirky memorabilia includes Boswell's coffee cup, two first-edition copies of the dictionary, and Dr Johnson's gout chair from the Cock Tavern, another old pub still standing on Fleet Street. The attic, in which he and his six helpers put together the hefty tome, now looks a bit like a classroom, lined with explanatory panels on lexicography.

St Paul's Cathedral

St Paul's Cathedral (Mon–Sat 8.30am–4.15pm; £3, combination ticket with galleries £5; St Paul's tube), the City's finest old building, is the fifth church on this site. Its immediate predecessor, a huge Gothic cathedral, was an unruly place, described in 1598 as a "common passage and thoroughfare . . . a daily receptacle for rogues and beggars however diseased, to the great offence of religious minded people". In 1660, a circus horse named Morocco performed tricks here, including a quick trot up the stairs to the top of the belltower. The Great Fire caused irreparable damage to this unlikely centre of iniquity, and Wren was given the task of building a replacement – just one of over fifty church commissions he received in the wake of the blaze. The architect's design, a compromise solution after several more controversial plans were rejected, is fronted by a double-storey portico flanked by towers, but the most distinctive feature is the **dome**, second in size only to St Peter's in Rome. A London icon since the Blitz, when it stood defiantly unscathed amid the carnage, St Paul's is still a dominating presence on the skyline despite the encroaching tower blocks.

Inside, however, St Paul's creates an impression of plutocratic complacency, typified by the prohibitive entrance charges, the commercialism of the souvenir stalls (soon to be confined to the crypt) and an appalling corporate-sponsored exhibition in the north transept. The body of the church, called "dirty, dark and undevotional" by Queen Victoria, is filled with monuments, predominantly to military figures and obscure statesmen; one of the very few to have survived from the previous cathedral is an effigy of the poet **John Donne**, once Dean of St Paul's, in the south aisle of the choir. The statue actually bears scorch marks from the Great Fire.

A staircase in the south transept leads up to a series of galleries (£2.50) in the dome, which is in fact a triple dome, with an interior cupola separated from the wooden, lead-covered outer skin by a funnel-shaped brick structure. After a relatively painless climb up 250 steps you reach the internal **Whispering Gallery**, so-called because of its acoustic properties – words whispered to the wall on one side are distinctly audible over one hundred feet away on the other. Another 118 steps up, the broad exterior **Stone Gallery** offers a vista of London; the final leg of the climb, 153 fire escape-type steps to the uppermost **Golden Gallery**, is certainly not for the acrophobic.

East of the entrance to the galleries is the staircase to the **Crypt**, the resting place of Wren himself; his son composed the inscription on his tomb, in the east of the Chapel of the Order of the British Empire – *lector, si monumentum requiris, circumspice* (reader, if you seek his monument, look around). The Treasury displays church plate, richly embroidered copes and mitres and bejewelled altar crosses; more interesting, however, are Wren's early plans for the cathedral, and his "Great Model", a wooden replica of the architect's favoured design, which was to have had a dome even larger than the present structure. There are a couple of damaged wooden effigies from the previous cathedral, but the two star tombs are those of **Nelson** and **Wellington**, both occupying centre stage and both with more fanciful monuments upstairs.

The Barbican and Museum of London

A few minutes northwest of St Paul's, the Central Criminal Court, more popularly known as the **Old Bailey**, the name of the street on which it stands, deals with the most serious criminal court cases in a building undistinctive but for its green dome, surmounted by a bronze statue of Justice. This was once the site of the notoriously harsh Newgate prison, whose inmates included Daniel Defoe and the murderer Major Strangeways, who was pressed to death in the courtyard in 1658. From 1783 until 1868 it was the public hangings that drew in the tourists; now you can watch courtroom dramas from the visitors' gallery. Note, however, that no bags or cameras are allowed into the building, and there is no provision for storing them.

Northeast of here, **The Barbican** is the City's only residential complex, a phenomenally ugly and highly expensive ghetto built on the heavily bombed Cripplegate area. Notoriously difficult to find, the **Barbican Arts Centre**, planned as London's answer to the Pompidou Centre, is a maze of walkways and subterranean labyrinths so user-repellent that it has recently been redesigned. It does, nevertheless, house the London Symphony Orchestra, the London chapter of the Royal Shakespeare Company and a good repertory cinema, and holds various free jazz and classical concerts on its many levels. Hidden away in the residential sector, the sixteenth-century **St Giles Church**, next to the artificial lake, is where Oliver Cromwell was married in 1620.

Despite London's long history, very few of its ancient buildings are standing; since World War II, however, Roman, Saxon and Elizabethan remains have been discovered during rebuilding and construction work. Many of these finds are displayed at the **Museum of London** (Tues–Sat 10am–5.30pm, Sun 2–5.50pm; £3, tickets valid for 3 months, free after 4.30pm; Barbican tube), an educational trot through London's past from prehistory to the Blitz, hidden away by the Roman wall excavations at the Barbican's southern corner. Roman relics include marble busts from the **Temple of Mithras**, the remains of which can be found south on Queen Victoria Street. Other highlights include an eighteenth-century gallery, a replica of a Newgate prison cell and a small diorama of the Great Fire, accompanied by a narration of Pepys' account of the blaze. From outside the museum a mile-and-a-half trail, illustrated by explanatory panels, follows the original path of London's **Roman wall** to the Tower of London.

The financial centre

The City has been London's financial centre since the Middle Ages. It was only in 1694, however, that the **Bank of England** was established, to fund the war with France – until then all of London's financial institutions had been dominated by the accounting skills of the Italians. Today all the key money markets, most of which have their origins in the City's sixteenth-century coffee shops, are concentrated around the mighty windowless hulk of the Bank, "The Grand Old Lady of Threadneedle Street". The original building was built in 1734, its colonnaded facade being added fifty years later by Sir John Soane. Today, there's little to see of Soane's work, as much of the sombre edifice was rebuilt in the 1930s. The Bank's **museum** (Mon–Fri 10am–5pm; free; Bank tube), however, contains a reconstruction of Soane's Bank Stock Office, and has a display on currencies and a brain-straining computer on which you can play at wheeling and dealing on the stock market.

Northeast of the Stock Exchange on Old Broad Street, the **NatWest Tower**, a 1970s citadel built on the plan of the National Westminster Bank logo, was the tallest building in Britain until the Canary Wharf tower topped it in 1991. Nearby, on Leadenhall Street, Richard Rogers' glitzy **Lloyd's Building** is one of the City's more controversial new structures, a startling array of glass and blue steel pipes which, despite claims for its ergonomic and environmental efficiency, costs vast sums to maintain. Just south of the Lloyd's building, the picturesque **Leadenhall Market** (Mon–Fri 7am–3pm), a graceful Victorian arcade on the site of the Roman forum, shelters barrows selling exotic seafood, champagne and caviar beneath an elegant glass and iron canopy. The shops and bars remain open until the evening, but it is best to get here at breakfast or lunchtime to catch the market atmosphere.

The Tower of London and around

The **Tower of London** (April, May, Sept & Oct Mon–Sat 9am–6pm, Sun 10am–6pm; June–Aug closes 6.30pm; Nov–March Mon–Sat 9.30am–5pm, Sun 10am–5pm; £8.30; Tower Hill tube), one of London's great landmarks, stands overlooking the river at the eastern boundary of the old city. Usually thought of as a place of imprisonment and death, it has variously been used as an armoury, royal residence and repository of the crown's treasure. It was also the home of the royal menagerie: the keeper of the king's leopard during the reign of Edward II was paid sixpence a day for the sustenance of the beast, one penny for himself.

Originally a fort built by William the Conqueror, by 1100 it had evolved into a huge palace-fortress, dominated by the central White Tower. The inner wall, with its numerous towers, was built in the time of Henry III, and a further line of fortifications was added by Edward I, so much of what's visible today was already in place by the end of the thirteenth century. Although you can explore independently, it's a huge place, with nineteen towers in all, and can be confusing, so it's a good idea to get your bearings on a **free tour**, given every thirty minutes by eminently photographable **Beefeaters**, ex-servicemen in Tudor costume, who can get you into areas otherwise inaccessible.

William's **White Tower**, adorned with corner cupolas in Henry VIII's reign, houses the **Royal Armouries**, a huge array including jousting costumes, gruesome lances and guns, a sixteenth-century "giant's" suit of armour from Germany and a stupendous suit for an elephant. On the second floor, the **Chapel of St John**, London's oldest church, is said to have been where Henry VI was buried after his murder in 1471. Today the once highly decorated blocks of pale Norman limestone are starkly unadorned, the chapel's beauty coming from its smooth curves and perfect rounded apse.

Surrounding the White Tower, **Tower Green** was where the executions took place of those traitors lucky enough to be spared being put to death in front of jeering crowds on Tower Hill. A brass plate marks the spot where Lady Jane Grey, Anne Boleyn, Catherine Howard and four other privileged individuals met their end. They and other noble Tower prisoners, including Thomas More, are buried in the **Chapel of St Peter-ad-Vincula**, a Tudor church close by the scaffold site, only accessible on guided tours. The green is also home to two of the Tower's eight famous **ravens**, their wings clipped so they can't fly away – legend says that the Tower and the kingdom will fall if they do. The birds are descendants of early scavengers attracted by the waste from Palace kitchens, and are the latest in a long line protected by royal decree since the reign of Charles II. They even have their own graveyard, in the moat.

The **Jewel House**, just north of the White Tower, holds the **Crown Jewels**, the majority of which postdate the Commonwealth (1649–60) when many of the royal riches were melted down. These days, the displays are efficient and disappointingly swift – visitors are sped along on moving walkways which allow just 28 seconds' viewing. This mind-blowing display of wealth includes the three largest cut diamonds in the world, the most famous of which, the **Koh-i-Noor**, is set into a crown made for the Queen Mother in 1937 and is displayed seperately near the exit. Equally dazzling is the **Imperial State Crown**, sparkling with a 317-carat diamond, a sapphire from a ring said to have been buried with Edward the Confessor, and assorted emeralds, rubies and pearls. The crowds here are usually phenomenal, so get here as early as possible.

The **Beauchamp Tower**, across the green from the White Tower, is interesting for its graffiti and carvings by prisoners, collected here from other parts of the complex. Prisoners at the **Queen's House**, next door, included Lady Jane Grey and Rudolf Hess, after his unexplained parachute jump into Scotland in 1941. To the south of the White Tower, the **Bloody Tower** contains the room in which the murder by Richard III of the "Princes in the Tower", twelve-year-old Edward V and his younger brother, was thought to have taken place, as well as the quarters where Sir Walter Raleigh spent thirteen years of captivity writing his *History of the World*. Raleigh's study, including an original copy of his book, is re-created on the ground floor, while his sleeping quarters are upstairs. The small exhibition next door on the colonization of Virginia is too dark and cramped to warrant much attention. Below the Bloody Tower, on the waterfront, prisoners were delivered through **Traitor's Gate** after being ferried down the Thames from the courts of justice at Westminster Hall.

The Lanthorn and Wakefield towers, on the wall of the inmost ward, have been reconstructed to represent Edward I's palace, although the king only lived here intermittently. A few panels in the **Lanthorn Tower** describe the king's domestic and public life, accompanied by piped thirteenth-century music, while the **Wakefield Tower**, the second largest in the complex, re-creates two of the King's private chambers, with period-clad actors on hand to answer questions. A copy of the Coronation Chair shows it as it would have originally looked, all gilded and colourful; equally striking are the gaily patterned wall decorations in the Great Hall, where the King spent days playing chess. A tablet on the floor in the state reception room marks the spot where, it is believed, Henry VI was murdered at prayer by Edward IV during the Wars of the Roses. Candlelight and heavy incense enhance the aura of authenticity.

Tower Hill Pageant and Tower Bridge

Tower Hill, where many of the Tower's prisoners were beheaded or hanged, is of little interest now but for the **Tower Hill Pageant** (April–Sept daily 9.30am–5.30pm; Nov–March closes 4.30pm; £5.45; Tower Hill tube), which sounds like some ersatz medieval revelry but is in fact a good little museum. It starts with a subterranean ride like a ghost train, trundling you through various animatronic tableaux, the sound effects and smells (particularly unpleasant at the mass grave of plague victims) making for a surprisingly engaging overview of London's history. You then clamber out and head upstairs to the museum proper, a small but thoughtful arrangement of archeological finds, ranging from Saxon pottery, medieval ear picks and pilgrims' souvenirs to a preserved Roman quay.

The imposing twin towers of **Tower Bridge**, landmarks on the Thames since 1893, support a roadway that can be raised to allow tall ships access to the upper reaches of the Thames – which nowadays happens about ten times a week. Inside the elevated walkways linking the summits of the towers, the brand new **Celebration Story** (April–Oct daily 10am–6.30pm; Nov–March closes 5.15pm; £5; Tower Hill tube) uses state-of-the-art technology to tell the story of the bridge; intended for public use, the walkways were closed from 1909 to 1982 due to their popularity with suicides and prostitutes.

The East End

The East End, spreading east from the City, was a medieval centre for trades banned within London's walls, such as brewing, bell-working and brick-making, and – due to its position near the port – it became a haven for immigrants, from the Huguenots of the seventeenth century to the Bangladeshis of the 1960s and the 1970s. It was always a poor area, and Victorian philanthropists and middle-class social reformers ventured like intrepid explorers into the abyss, returning with outraged reports of overcrowding, drunkenness, prostitution and other moral atrocities. The area swelled in the 1900s as a dormitory town for the fast-growing docks, propagating a mythology that remains entrenched – from Jack the Ripper to the Kray twins, the East End is legendary as the heart of London's underworld. At the same time, the East End's impoverishment made it a breeding ground for radical left-wing politics, but this aspect of East End life has all but vanished, and an alarming number of racist attacks, reminiscent of the fascist attacks against the East End Jews in the 1930s, are perpetrated daily against Asian families.

Visually the East End is uninspiring, dominated by tower blocks and nondescript estates, interspersed with pockets of gentrification where young professionals have snapped up bargain Georgian residences. Apart from a couple of good museums, there are few formal attractions, although tourists do venture out here for the Sunday **markets** in Brick Lane, Spitalfields, Columbia Road and Petticoat Lane (actually on and around Middlesex Street), which sell everything you can imagine. At the opposite end of the scale, many visitors take a river trip or ride the new light railway through **Docklands**, the high-profile development area covering over eight square miles along the river.

Spitalfields and Shoreditch

In 1685, when Louis XIV revoked the Edict of Nantes, French **Huguenots** poured into **Spitalfields**, the area stretching from Liverpool Street Station in the west to Vallance Road and Whitechapel Road in the east, establishing the area as a centre for the silk trade and furniture-making. You can still see the terraces in which they lived, in the narrow roads between Brick Lane and Commercial Street. Many Huguenots worshipped at **Christ Church**, on the corner of Commercial and Fournier streets. Designed by Wren's protegé Nicholas Hawksmoor, it has a grand Italianate portico, octagonal tower, and a graveyard filled with French tombstones. At the other end of Fournier Street – the best preserved of the area's Huguenot streets, lined with restored Georgian houses – the building on the corner has been a Huguenot chapel, Methodist church, a synagogue, and is now a mosque.

Another dominant presence in Spitalfields were the **Jewish** tailors, leather workers and furriers, but since the 1950s the Jewish population has decamped to North London, and the district has become the centre of the **Bengali** community, who continue the rag trade. Its main artery is **Brick Lane**, a street lined with Bengali restaurants, sweet shops and sweat shops and famed for its Sunday flea market.

Further north, at the junction of Shoreditch High Street and Kingsland Road, you come to **St Leonard's Church**, whose bells, according to the nursery rhyme, are the "Bells of Shoreditch". A quarter of a mile or so further north on Kingsland Road, the peaceful **Geffrye Museum** (Tues–Sat 10am–5pm, Sun 2–5pm; free; Old Street or Liverpool Street tube), is housed in eighteenth-century almshouses set back off the road and surrounded by trees. The Geffrye, essentially a furniture museum, was originally established in 1911 for crafts students, when Shoreditch was the centre for English cabinet-making. Today the almshouses are rigged out as living rooms, each in the style of a different era, from the oak-panelled seventeenth century through refined Georgian and cluttered Victorian to Art Deco and 1950s utility.

Whitechapel

In the late nineteenth century, **Whitechapel**, the area south and east of Spitalfields, was a slum known as the "pig market", where sweat-shop workers were hired en masse in the open air. With a grubby fame from the "Jack the Ripper" murders in 1888, Whitechapel has also seen considerable political activity, the most notorious incident being the Battle of Cable Street in 1936, a violent clash between police and 100,000 protesters blocking the path of a fascist march led by Oswald Mosley.

On Whitechapel Road itself, amongst the Halal butchers, textile wholesalers and newsagents, the **Whitechapel Art Gallery** (Tues & Thurs–Sun 11am–5pm, Wed 11am–8pm; usually free; Aldgate East tube), was established in 1901 by the moralistic reformer Samuel Augustus Barnett, who believed poverty was a direct consequence of sin, which in its turn was a result of a lack of high culture. Today the gallery, in a striking crenellated Arts and Crafts building designed by Charles Harrison Townsend, features some of London's best exhibitions of contemporary art.

Further east, the *Blind Beggar Pub*, at the corner with Brady Street, has a place in gangland mythology as a hangout of the Krays – Ronnie Kray killed rival gang leader George Cornell here in 1966. From the pub, a walk north up Cambridge Heath Road brings you something completely different, the **Bethnal Green Museum of Childhood** (Mon–Thurs & Sat 10am–6pm, Sun 2.30–6pm; free; Bethnal Green tube). Designed by Paxton, architect of the Crystal Palace, the museum has a ground floor flanked by intricate dolls' houses, including the only Nuremberg dolls' house outside Germany, made in 1673. Among the jumble of curiosities upstairs are wooden models of nineteenth-century butcher shops, strung with carcasses, and dolls made from found objects, including a little man made from a lobster claw. Beyond the antique automata and moralistic Victorian board games, the museum's doll collection ranges from Native American representations of spirits, through stylish flapper dolls carried by the bright young things of the Jazz Age, to a macabre Shirley Temple.

Docklands

In the sixteenth and seventeenth centuries the **port** was the key to London's wealth, crowded with quays clustered around London Bridge, at that time the only bridge across the Thames. From 1802, new enclosed docks were built to cope with the heavy trade from the imperial dominions, each one walled for security and geared towards different cargoes. However, by the mid-nineteenth century competition from the railways was threatening the docks, and by the 1960s, with the development of modern container ships and the movement of the port to Tilbury, the docks began to close.

For almost two decades the quaysides were a wasteland, until in 1981 the London Docklands Development Corporation (LDDC) was set up to provide state-of-the-art office and residential space in **Docklands**, the 500 acres of land between Tower Bridge and Woolwich. Very soon Rupert Murdoch had shifted his newspapers to Wapping, followed by a few other high-publicity operations, but now, still in recession and with no sign of any decent public transport to link the place to the city centre, Docklands is surreally lifeless, an uneasy mix of drab high-rises, old warehouses converted into expensive apartments, and some startling new architecture – much of it empty. You can view Docklands from a distance on one of the pleasure boats that course up and down the Thames, but those with more than just a passing interest should take the computer-operated **Docklands Light Railway** for the most telling overview of the old and new Docklands. You can tell a lot about this area from the fact that the railway stops running around 9pm from Monday to Friday, and doesn't run at all on Saturdays and Sundays.

The LDDC's first development was **St Katharine's Dock**, a yacht marina immediately east of the Tower of London. Although peopled by smug local office workers, it's an attractive place to sit with a drink, overlooking the boats. East of here, at Limehouse, site of London's first Chinatown, the Thames begins a sudden dramatic horseshoe bend at Limehouse, thus creating the **Isle of Dogs**, originally a marshy peninsula where cattle were fattened for City banquets. In 1802, the peninsula became an island when a canal was cut to form London's first enclosed docks, built to accommodate rum and sugar from the West Indies. Today it is the geographical and ideological heart of the new Docklands, which reaches its apotheosis in **Canary Wharf**, dominated by Cesar Pelli's 800-foot tower, Britain's tallest building. A metaphor for all Docklands stands for, it looks splendid but bankrupted its builders and is vacant beyond the first few storeys.

The **Dockland Visitors Centre**, some way southeast of the tower on Limeharbour (Mon–Fri 8.30am–6pm, Sat & Sun 9.30am–5pm; free; Crossharbour DLR) doubles as a glossy museum of the docks' history and a propaganda machine for the LDDC, with "before and after" photographs and a short film. The centre is also the alighting point for the LDDC **bus tours** (summer daily 9am–4pm; £6), which, depending on the guide (often a genuine East Ender), can offer a salutary overview – an account of "Blood Alley", the sugar warehouse from which the workers would return each day with glassy granules of sugar embedded under their ripped skin, is a corrective to any thoughts about the good old days. Further south, **Island Gardens**, a pleasant park right on the river, and the starting point for the foot tunnel to Greenwich, was reputedly Wren's favourite spot from where to contemplate his masterpieces, the Royal Naval Hospital and the old Royal Observatory across the river (see p.117).

Lambeth and Southwark

The south bank of the River Thames was London's disreputable entertainment district until well into the seventeenth century; today the utterly respectable concert halls and theatres of the South Bank Centre in **Lambeth**, along with the exceptional Museum of the Moving Image, are the only spots to draw tourists across the river in great numbers. However, there are pockets of interest beyond the South Bank. **Southwark**, cradle of Elizabethan theatre, has a range of small museums that are quietly generating a brisk trade despite their inauspicious surroundings, while the Imperial War Museum, further inland, has won awards for its instructive displays.

The South Bank

In 1951 the Festival of Britain, an attempt to revive postwar morale by celebrating the centenary of the Great Exhibition, was held on derelict land south of the Thames. Its only permanent building was the **Royal Festival Hall**, still the most appealing component of what has grown to be the **South Bank Centre**. This predominantly brutalist concrete complex embraces the National Theatre, the National Film Theatre (NFT), a trio of concert halls and the Hayward Gallery, which hosts prestigious, usually contemporary, travelling exhibitions. The Centre's unprepossessing appearance is slightly softened by its location, overlooking river traffic on the Thames, and it can be pleasant to sit by the water with a nighttime drink, or browse through the secondhand bookstalls outside the NFT at the weekend.

The Museum of the Moving Image and the Imperial War Museum

Slotted adroitly under Waterloo Bridge, the **Museum of the Moving Image**, or MOMI (daily 10am–6pm; £5.50; Waterloo tube) covers an impressive amount in a very cramped space, reeling through a spirited history of film and cinema, with actors on hand to enliven the proceedings. It begins with a vast array of optical toys, but the real fun starts in the following rooms, where among the memorabilia, cameras, posters and costumes, you can audition for a screen test in a 1920s-style casting session, make your own cartoons in an animation room, and watch a shoot on a Hollywood film set complete with egotistical director. There's also plenty of opportunity to watch films, often in witty settings: to see the newsreels, for example – including footage of the Hindenberg disaster, Mussolini's pompous posturing, and V-Day celebrations – you climb onto the roof of a news van, thus mimicking the logo of the Pathé newsreels. The television section, pandering shamelessly to twenty- and thirty-something nostalgia, leads to the bit that's most popular with children, where you get to read the television news and be interviewed by a televisual Barry Norman.

From 1815 to 1930 the domed building at the top of Lambeth Road was the infamous Royal Bethlehem asylum, better known as Bedlam, whose inmates were once a form of entertainment for eighteenth-century high society – as shown in Hogarth's paintings in the Soane Museum (see p.92). Now it's the home of the **Imperial War Museum** (daily 10am–6pm; £3.70, free after 4.30pm; Lambeth North tube), an impressively wide-ranging and sober coverage of its subject, with ranks of guns, tanks and fighter planes offset by documents and images attesting to the human damage of war. In addition to the static displays, a good deal of stagecraft is used to convey the misery of combat, with grim walk-through World War I trenches and a re-creation of the Blitz, in which you wander from an air-raid shelter through bomb-ravaged streets accompanied by blaring sirens and human voices. The newest exhibit is Operation Jericho, an extremely realistic flight simulator, which costs extra to play.

Southwark

Southwark, the district ranged around the southern end of London Bridge, was a thriving Roman red-light district, and its brothels continued to do a thriving illegal trade until 1161 when they were licensed by Royal decree. This measure imposed various restrictions on the prostitutes, who could now be fined three shillings for "grimacing to passers-by", and brought in a lot of revenue for the Bishops of Winchester, who owned the area for the four centuries after the Norman Conquest. Under the bishops' rule, bull- and bear-baiting, drinking, cockfighting and gambling were also rife, especially on Bankside, and although after 1556 Southwark came under the jurisdiction of the City, it was not subject to its regulations on entertainment. So Southwark remained the pleasure quarter of Tudor and Stuart London, where brothels and other disreputable institutions banned in the City – notably theatres – continued to flourish until the Puritan purges of the 1640s.

Bankside

Bankside, running along the river east and west of Southwark Bridge, was the most nefarious street of all, known as "Stew's Bank" (from its brothels or "stews") and studded with theatres. Next door to the Bankside Power Station (earmarked to be a new annexe of the Tate Gallery) on the site of Bankside's last bear-baiting amphitheatre, is the almost complete reconstruction of the **Shakespeare Globe Theatre** (daily 10am–5pm; £4; London Bridge tube), which contains a makeshift exhibition of Southwark's theatrical history; it's basically a fund-rasing exercise, though you do get a tour of the work in progress. The original site of the Globe itself, where most of the Bard's later plays were first performed, is marked by a blackened plaque on a brewery wall five minutes' walk away on Park Street, but nothing can be built here as the foundations lie beneath a listed Georgian terrace.

Bankside continues east to the narrow, dark Clink Street, a suitably dismal site for the **Clink Exhibition** (daily 10am–6pm; £2; London Bridge tube), a small museum on the site of a former prison of the same name. The prison was originally a dungeon under the Bishops' Palace – the scrappy remains of which can be seen further along the road – and originated as a pit for disobedient clerics, but when it moved here it became a dumping ground for heretics, debtors, prostitutes and a motley assortment of riverside lowlife, before closing in 1780. Inside, there's some downright prurient material on prostitution, rather less on prison history, plus a few torture devices – particularly gruesome are the spiked iron gags forced between the jaws of uppity women. Serious points could be made about the mores of medieval London, but this is schoolboy stuff.

Southwark Cathedral

Continuing east, Clink Street becomes Cathedral Street, which forms the most pleasant approach to **Southwark Cathedral**, standing close to the southern end of London Bridge. Built in the thirteenth and fourteenth centuries as an Augustinian priory church, it miraculously survived the nineteenth century, which saw its East End chapel demolished to make way for London Bridge, railways built within a few feet of its tower and some heavy-handed Victorian restoration. As if in compensation, the church was granted cathedral status in 1905, and has since had a lot of money spent on it. The cathedral houses hundreds of monuments, including one to the 47 people who died when the *Marchioness* pleasure boat collided with a barge on the Thames in 1989. Others include a thirteenth-century oak effigy of a knight, the brightly painted tomb of poet John Gower, Chaucer's contemporary, and an early twentieth-century memorial to Shakespeare, for whom a birthday service is held here annually. Of the cathedral's original features the splendid choir is the most striking: one of the oldest Gothic stuctures in London, built in 1207, it has a beautiful sixteenth-century stone altar screen.

Old Operating Theatre Museum and Herb Garret

The most educative and strangest of Southwark's museums is the **Old Operating Theatre Museum and Herb Garret** (Tues–Sun 8am–4pm; £2) on St Thomas Street, built in 1821 at the top of a church tower, where the hospital apothecary's herbs were stored. Despite being entirely gore-free, the museum is as stomach-churning as the London Dungeon (see below), for this theatre dates from the pre-anaesthetics era. The surgeons who used this room concentrated on speed and accuracy (most amputations took less than a minute), but there was still a thirty percent mortality rate, many patients simply dying of shock, and many more from bacterial infection, about which very little was known. This is clear from the design of the theatre itself, which has no sink and is made almost entirely of mahogany and pine, which would have harboured bacteria even after vigorous cleaning. Sawdust was sprinkled on the floor to soak up the blood and prevent it dripping onto the heads of the worshippers in the church below.

The London Dungeon, Britain at War and HMS Belfast

A walk past the railway bridges and warehouses of Tooley Street brings you round the back of London Bridge train station to the cold dark vault of the **London Dungeon** (April–Sept daily 10am–6.30pm; Oct–March closes 5.30pm; £6.95; London Bridge tube), a crowd-pleasing show playing on the English fascination with Gothic horror. Among the life-size tableaux are a hanging at Tyburn gallows, a rack with hideous creaking sound effects as the victim's bones are pulled apart, and a man being boiled alive, the general hysteria being boosted by actors dressed as lepers and top-hatted Victorians pouncing out of the darkness. There are long queues for the two "shows" included in the entrance fee. The campy "Theatre of the Guillotine" isn't up to much, but the "Jack the Ripper Experience" is too realistic to be kitsch: an actress dressed as an East End prostitute leads you through a swirling thick yellow fog past dummies and slides of hacked victims, to a morgue where a soundtrack examines the evidence. Womens' groups have picketed the building over this exploitative shocker; you may well emerge in a similar frame of mind.

A little further south on Tooley Street is **Winston Churchill's Britain at War** (April–Sept daily 10am–5.30pm; Oct–March closes 4.30pm; £5; London Bridge tube), which, despite its jingoistic name, is an illuminating exhibition of every aspect of London life during the Blitz. It begins with a rickety elevator ride down to a mock-up of a tube air-raid shelter, a prelude to hundreds of sometimes bizarre wartime artefacts, such as a child's gas mask designed to look like Mickey Mouse. You can sit in an Anderson shelter beneath the chilling whistle of the doodlebugs, tune in to contemporary radio broadcasts and, as a grand finale walk through the chaos of a just-bombed street – pitch dark, noisy, smoky and chokingly hot.

There's more World War II history, from a more aggressive angle, at **HMS Belfast** (summer daily 10am–6pm; winter closes at 5pm; £4; London Bridge tube), a huge battle cruiser permanently moored between Tower Bridge and London Bridge. Following arrows over the ship's seven decks, you wander through cabins, the sick bay and boiler room, scrambling up sheer ladders on the way. There are also various tired-looking displays relating to the D-Day landing and Korea, in both of which the Belfast took part, plus wearisome video coverage of the Falklands War.

The Design Museum

East of the Belfast and Tower Bridge stands **Butler's Wharf**, part of a more sensitive development aimed at restoring the old wharves and warehouses. Backing onto huge old spice warehouses with upper-floor gangways crossing Dickensian narrow streets, Butler's Wharf retains some semblance of historical character, and is also home to the superb riverside **Design Museum** (daily 10.30am–5.30pm; £3.50; London Bridge tube). The stylish white edifice is the perfect showcase for an unpretentious display of contemporary and historical design from cars to fax machines. The two permanent exhibits are constantly evolving: the **Collection Gallery**, on the top floor, examines the factors that have affected design, and the **Review Gallery** acts as a showcase for new ideas, including prototypes and failures. Temporary exhibitions feature the work of important designers, movements or single products – often in settings that put other London museums to shame. The small coffee bar in the foyer serves snacks in a modish environment.

Hyde Park and South Kensington

Hyde Park, the largest of the central London parks, was seized from the Church by Henry VIII to satisfy his desire for yet more hunting grounds, but it was the husband of Queen Victoria who really transformed this area. In 1851 he masterminded the Great Exhibition of the Works and Industry of All Nations, a display of 100,000 creations from around the world including the Koh-i-Noor diamond in a bird cage, an Indian ivory throne, a floating church from Philadelphia, industrial engines, and all manner of china, fabrics and glass. The wonders were housed in the purpose-built **Crystal Palace**, an enormous glass and iron building removed from Hyde Park to southeast London in 1854, where it was destroyed by fire in 1936. The enormous success of the Great Exhibition prompted Albert to propose a "museum village" in neighbouring **South Kensington**, an area that was transformed almost overnight into one of the most fashionable in town. The grand Italianate houses along Queen's Gate, originally called Albert's Road, date from this period, and the district, along with neighbouring Knightsbridge, is still the swankiest shopping area in London. Albert died of cholera in 1861 and never saw his dream fully realized, but South Kensington, with its remarkable cluster of museums and the vast Albert Hall, stands as one of London's most impressive examples of urban planning.

Hyde Park

The best place to enter **Hyde Park** is at Hyde Park Corner, where Constitution Arch celebrates Wellington's victory at Waterloo. A huge equestrian statue of Wellington stands to the north of the arch, facing his former palace, **Apsley House** – known during the Iron Duke's lifetime as Number One, London. The house is now a **Wellington Museum** (Tues–Sun 11am–5pm; £3), which in addition to Wellington's personal effects also features a curious nude statue of the vanquished Napoleon, sculpted by Canova and bought by the Prince Regent in 1816.

Approach the park from Oxford Street and you'll pass **Marble Arch**, which was designed in 1828 by Nash in imitation of the Arch of Constantine in Rome, and shifted here from in front of Buckingham Palace in 1851. This corner of the park, once the site of the Tyburn gallows, is now **Speaker's Corner**, a Sunday forum for soap-box orators since 1872, after riots persuaded the government to license this island of free assembly. It's a place to go to enjoy a little theatre, both from the cranks who expound their views and from the hecklers, a show in themselves.

In the middle of the park the **Serpentine** lake has a popular lido (open in summer), with rowboats for hire and a utilitarian, overpriced café. The nearby **Serpentine Gallery** (daily 10am–6pm; free; Lancaster Gate or South Kensington tube), which hosts lively contemporary art exhibitions and talks, stands in the more tranquil part of the park known as **Kensington Gardens**, close to the **Albert Memorial**. Built in 1876, the memorial is as much a hymn to the glorious achievements of Britain as to the man, though he occupies its central canopy, clutching a catalogue for the Great Exhibition. Unfortunately, the memorial will be obliterated by scaffolding until the year 2000, a fact which would have pleased Albert, who claimed that "I can say, with perfect absence of humbug, that I would rather not be made the prominent feature of such a monument . . . it would upset my equanimity to be permanently ridiculed and laughed at in effigy".

The Prince Consort is also the dedicatee of the **Royal Albert Hall** across the road, completed in 1871, after many fits and starts, by selling seats on a leasehold basis to fund the construction, and today the "ownership" of some seats persists, though this is also the venue for Europe's most democratic music festival, the **Proms**, which from July to September presents top-flight classical concerts for as little as £3.

On the western edge of Kensington Gardens stands **Kensington Palace** (April–Oct Mon–Sat 9am–5.30pm, Sun 11am–5.30pm; £3.90; High Street Kensington tube), which used to be the London residence of Charles and Diana, until Charles moved out to St James's Palace (see p.77). Today the Princess of Wales has apartments on the west side, as do Princess Margaret and Prince and Princess Michael of Kent. On the east side, you are permitted to see a series of relatively unostentatious state apartments filled with portraits, including paintings by Rubens and Van Dyck. Most striking are the King's Gallery, designed by Hawksmoor and with opulent ceilings painted by William Kent, and a display of sumptuous court costumes dating from the mid-eighteenth century. North of the palace, Hawksmoor's exquisite **Orangery**, now a café (daily 10am–6pm), features carving and statues by Grinling Gibbons.

The Victoria and Albert Museum

The **Victoria and Albert Museum** (Mon noon–5.50pm, Tues–Sun 10am–5.50pm; £4.50 donation requested; South Kensington tube) began its days as the Museum of Manufactures, a gathering of objects from the Great Exhibition and a motley collection of plastercasts – it being Albert's intention to rekindle Britain's industrial dominance by inspiring factory workers, students and craftspeople with examples of excellence in applied art and design. This notion disappeared swiftly as exotica poured in from around the world, and today, in addition to being the world's finest collection of decorative arts, the museum encompasses sculpture, musical instruments, paintings and photography all beautifully, if rather haphazardly displayed across a seven-mile, four-storey maze of halls and corridors. In addition, the V&A's temporary shows are among the best in Britain, ranging from surveys of specialized areas of craft and technology to overviews of entire cultures. Floor plans from the information desks at the **main entrance** on Cromwell Road and the **side entrance** on Exhibition Road can help you decide on which areas to concentrate. There are also free guided orientation tours (Mon noon, 12.30pm, 2pm & 3pm, Tues–Sun 11am, noon, 2pm & 3pm).

The ground floor

The ground floor holds the best of the V&A. The **Raphael cartoons** (room 48a), seven full-colour designs for tapestries intended for the Sistine Chapel, are to the left of the main entrance and beyond the museum shop. These drawings, reproduced in countless tapestries and engravings in the seventeenth and eighteenth centuries, were probably more familiar and influential than any of the artist's paintings. Across the hall, the excellent **Dress collection** (room 40) begins from the year 1540 and comes right up to date with Vivienne Westwood's eccentric designs.

There follows a string of superb eastern galleries. The Nehru Gallery (room 41), for example – which shows only a fraction of the biggest assembly of **Indian art** outside the subcontinent – features an exquisitely carved white-jade wine cup belonging to the Emperor Shah Jahan; all manner of jewels, sandstone screens and delicate watercolours; not to mention Tippoo's Tiger, a life-size wooden automaton devouring an officer of the East India Company. Next comes the **Islamic gallery** (room 42), a dramatic gathering of vivid blue tiles and carved wooden pulpits, dominated by the stupendous sixteenth-century Ardabil carpet and the exquisite "Chelsea" carpet, bought in Chelsea but of unknown origin.

The **Medieval treasury** (room 43), full of reliquaries, religious sculpture and other devotional items, including the Norman masterpiece called the Gloucester candlestick, is adjacent to the **Chinese collection** (room 44), which ranges from green-tinged Shang bronzes and Tang horses to ceramics produced in the Cultural Revolution. Next door, the most intriguing objects in the understated **Japanese** room (room 45), amongst all the silk, lacquer and samurai armour, are the tiny jade and marble *netsuke* carvings, portraying such quirky subjects as "spider on aubergine" and "starving dog on a bed of leaves".

Beyond here the two enormous **Cast Courts** were created so that ordinary Londoners, who couldn't afford to travel, would be able to experience the glories of classical and ancient art. Even today the rooms, still painted in heavy Victorian red and green, are an astonishing sight: a life-size replica of Michelangelo's *David* towers opposite Donatello's bronze of the same subject; the colossal cast of Trajan's Column, from the forum in Rome, is sliced in half to fit in the room; while the rest of the space is crammed with full-scale replicas of the doors of Hildesheim cathedral, Spanish altars, the pulpit of Pisa's cathedral and scores of other sculptural masterpieces.

The **British sculpture and architecture** gallery (rooms 50a and 50b) displays an array of funerary monuments and portrait busts. The statue of Handel, created in 1738, was highly radical in its day, showing the composer slouching in inspired disarray, one shoe hanging from his foot. Also here is the original plaster model for the tomb of Victoria and Albert, on which they both appear to be 42 years old (the age Albert died) – Albert is raised slightly higher than the Queen, in accordance with her wishes.

Most of the remainder of the ground floor is given over to the **Italian Renaissance** (rooms 12–20), including a room of Donatello and his followers. Don't miss the museum's original refreshment rooms at the back: the eastern Poynter Room, a wash of decorative blue tiling, is where the hoi polloi ate; the dark green William Morris room, with its Pre-Raphaelite panels, accommodated a better class of diner.

The upper floors

If you go up to the **first floor** from the main entrance, long dark corridors of jewel-coloured stained glass lead you to a series of rooms covering **Britain 1500 to 1750** (rooms 52–58), featuring a restored music room, Spitalfields silks and Huguenot silver, an early seventeenth-century oak-panelled interior thought to have been James I's hunting lodge, and the legendary Great Bed of Ware, a king-sized oak monstrosity mentioned by Shakespeare and Ben Jonson, and thought to have belonged to Edward IV. Beyond here, the **Twentieth-century Galleries** (rooms 70–74) make a diffident attempt to address contemporary questions of design, ranging from Dali's pink Mae West sofa to Alessi kettles, Nike trainers and latex hot pants. On the far side of the massive **silver collection**, you come to a dimly lit room hung with medieval tapestries, and the exemplary **Materials and Techniques Collection**, displaying all manner of lace, Danish cottons, Chinese damask and robes from Palestine and Afghanistan. The heavily-guarded **Jewellery Collection** (rooms 91–93) is equally splendid, sparkling with Egyptian amulets, Celtic chokers, Roman snake bracelets, precious gems and 1960s perspex bangles. Also on this level you'll find medieval ivories and macabre Florentine skeletons amid a show of **European carvings**.

There are more works from eighteenth- and nineteenth-century Britain on the **second floor** (rooms 118–126), with a Chippendale bed, a plaster model of the Albert Memorial and furniture shown at the Great Exhibition. A room devoted to William Morris is adorned with his wallpaper, carpets and tiles, as well as furniture designed by his followers, and the collection comes up to date with a small selection of Henry Moore sculptures. Lastly, also on the second floor, there's the new high-tech **Glass Gallery** (room 131), with touch-screen computers and a spectacular, modern glass staircase and balustrade. The staggering beauty and variety of the glass on display is only slightly tarnished by the lack of any extensive twentieth-century perspective. The **top floor** is given almost exclusively to pottery and earthenware, with Far Eastern ceramics, European porcelain and Islamic tiles, but is often closed in the summer.

The Henry Cole Wing

The **Henry Cole Wing**, named after the museum's first director, can easily be over-looked, as it's only accessible from the Exhibition Road entrance on the ground floor. Highlights here include the **Frank Lloyd Wright** gallery on level 2, centred on an office created by the architect for a Pittsburgh department store owner – a typically organic design in luxuriant wood. Also on this floor is the **European ornamentation** room, demonstrating the influences and fashions in decoration of all kinds: antiquities, Rococo figurines and architectural plans share space with 1920s cotton hangings inspired by Howard Carter's discovery of Tutankhamen's tomb, and kitsch 1950s china.

Portrait miniatures by Holbein, Hilliard and others feature on Level 4, the rest of which is taken up with nineteenth-century oil paintings, densely hung in the manner of their period. The largest collection of Swiss landscape paintings outside Switzerland and sentimental Victorian genre works are unlikely to pull in the crowds, but persevere and you'll discover Carracciolo's *Panorama of Rome*, paintings by the Barbizon School, an Arts and Crafts piano, a Burne-Jones sideboard and several Pre-Raphaelite works. Level 6 is almost wholly devoted to the paintings of **John Constable**, four hundred of whose works were left to the museum by his daughter. The finished works include *Salisbury Cathedral* and *Dedham Mill*, and there are studies for the *Hay Wain* and *Leaping Horse*, plus a whole host of his alfresco cloud studies and sketches.

The Natural History Museum

The **Natural History Museum** (Mon–Sat 10am–5.50pm, Sun 11am–5.50pm; £5.50, free Mon–Fri after 4.30pm, Sat & Sun after 5pm; South Kensington tube), across the way on Cromwell Road, is one of London's finest nineteenth-century buildings, but its contents are a bit of a mish-mash, with some great exhibits peppered amongst others little changed since the museum's opening in 1881. Children seem to enjoy the antiquated glass cases full of dusty birds and animals, but it's the **dinosaurs** that pull in the crowds, a show of massive-jawed skeletons and models much enlivened by a stimulating exhibition on Tyrannosaurus Rex and his pea-brained cronies. Best of all is the grisly life-size animatronic tableau of two reptiles tearing apart a tenontosaurus, with much roaring, slurping and oozing blood. Displays on human biology are mostly old-fashioned and uninspired, but for the non-squeamish the insect room is more engaging, with its giant models of bugs, arachnids and crustaceans, plus real-life displays on the life cycle of the house fly and other unlovely creatures. Opposite the creepy-crawlies is the entrance to the high-tec Ecology gallery, a child-friendly exhibition with a serious message, only slightly marred by the fact it's sponsored by British Petroleum.

The entrance fee includes admission into the former Geological Museum, now known as the **Earth Galleries** (same hours as museum, but closed until at least June 1996), whose main entrance is on Exhibition Road. Its jazziest offering is the "Story of the Earth", an audio-visual introduction to tectonic plates, volcanic eruptions and other acts of God – the earthquake simulator, however, isn't up to much. The gem collection on the ground floor is a dazzling array of flashing diamonds, rubies and emeralds, jades and deep blue lapis lazuli, but the two upper floors, a mercilessly technical explanation of Britain's mineral reserves, hold little interest for non-specialists.

The Science Museum

Established as a technological counterpart to the V&A, the **Science Museum** in Exhibition Road (Mon–Sat 10am–6pm, Sun 11am–6pm; £5, free after 4.30pm; South Kensington tube) unsurprisingly gives a lot of space to British innovation in the era of the Industrial Revolution, highlighting such iconic inventions as George Stephenson's 1813 *Puffing Billy* and his *Rocket* of 1829. The scope of the museum is vast, however, filling seven floors with items drawn from every conceivable area of experimental science, including space travel, telecommunications, time measurement, chemistry, computing, photography and medicine.

On the ground floor, the lovingly presented fire trucks, cars and old trains in the **transport gallery** are deservedly popular, as is the **space gallery**, with a model of the Apollo 10 and videos of life on board a spaceship. The **Launch Pad** on the first floor makes a good attempt to present lively, hands-on demonstrations of basic scientific principles, but much of the rest of the museum is disappointing. Some of it is very heavy-going – you need a PhD to understand some of the chemistry section – while other parts are desperately out of date – "Computing Then and Now" stops abruptly with the behemoths of the mid-1970s.

The best section of the whole museum, the "Science and Art of Medicine" gallery, is all too easily missed, tucked away right on the top floor. Using an anthropological approach, this is a real visual and cerebral feast, galloping through ancient medicine, medieval and Renaissance pharmacy, alchemy, quack doctors, Royal healers, astrology and military surgery. Offbeat artefacts include African fetishes, an Egyptian mummified head, an eighteenth-century Florentine model of a female torso giving birth, George Washington's dentures and an image of Benignus, patron saint of chilblains, crooking his outsize, strangely formed fingers.

Kensington, Knightsbridge and Chelsea

Despite the smattering of aristocratic mansions and the presence of royalty in Kensington Palace, **Kensington** remained little more than a village surrounded by fields until well into the nineteenth century, when the rich finally began to seek new stamping grounds away from the West End. The main draw nowadays are the shops, wooded Holland Park and the former artists' colony clustered around the exotically decorated Leighton House. **Knightsbridge**, to the east, is irredeemably snobbish, revelling in its reputation as the swankiest shopping area in London, largely through *Harrods*, one of London's most popular tourist attractions. To the south of Knightsbridge, **Chelsea**'s repuation as a bohemian quarter is largely undeserved, though its holds a place in popular culture as home to the King's Road, which formed the centre of "Swinging London" in the 1960s, and witnessed the birth of punk in 1976.

Kensington

What makes **Kensington High Street** (or High Street Ken, as the nearby tube is known) stand out from other London shopping streets is its two clothing markets: *Hyper Hyper* – easy to spot thanks to the kitsch caryatids at the entrance – features over seventy stalls run by British designers, while *Kensington Market*, opposite, is a Gothic labyrinth of lock-up shops flogging mainly retro or just cheap clothes, interspersed with hairdressers, a clock repair shop and much more besides. Both places are open Monday to Saturday 10am to 6pm.

A short stroll west along the high street will bring you to the **Commonwealth Institute** (Mon–Sat 10am–5pm, Sun 2–5pm; £1), heralded by a forest of flagpoles and housed in a bold 1960s building with a tent-shaped Zambian copper roof. The giant open-vaulted exhibition hall holds three floors of galleries with rather prosaic school geography lesson displays on each of the nations which, having freed themselves of colonial rule, now make up the Commonwealth. Two paths pass up the side of the Commonwealth Insititute towards the densely wooded **Holland Park**, with its excellent adventure playground. The park is laid out in the former grounds of Holland House – only the east wing of the Jacobean mansion was salvaged after the last war, but it gives a fairly good idea of what the place must have looked like. A youth hostel is linked to the east wing, while a concert tent to the west stages theatrical and musical performances throughout the summer months. Several formal gardens surround the house, drifting down in terraces to the arcades, Garden Ballroom, Orangery and Ice House, which have been converted into a restaurant and art gallery complex.

In the late nineteenth century some of the wealthier artists of the Victorian era founded an artists' colony around the fringes of Holland Park, and several of their highly individual mansions are still standing. First and foremost is **Leighton House**, 12 Holland Park Rd (Mon–Sat 11am–5.30pm; free), the "House Beautiful" created by the architect George Aitchison and Frederic Leighton, who was the only artist ever to be made a peer (albeit on his deathbed). The big attraction is its domed Arab Hall: based on the banqueting hall of a Moorish palace in Palermo, it has a central black marble fountain, and is decorated with Saracen tiles, gilded mosaics and woodwork drawn from all over the Islamic world. The other rooms are less spectacular but, in compensation, are hung with excellent paintings by Leighton and his Pre-Raphaelite friends, Burne-Jones, Alma-Tadema and Millais. Skylights brighten the upper floor, which contains Leighton's vast studio, where his tradition of holding evening concerts continues to this day.

Knightsbridge and Harrods

Most people come to **Knightsbridge** for just one thing: to shop or gawp at **Harrods** (Mon, Tues & Sat 10am–6pm, Wed–Fri 10am–7pm) on Brompton Road. Without doubt the most famous department store in London, it started out as a family-run grocery in 1849, with a staff of two. The current 1905 terracotta building, which turns into a palace of fairy lights at night, is now owned by the Egyptian Al Fayed brothers and employs over 3000 staff, including several ex-army bagpipers who perform daily in the store. The shop occupies four acres spread over seven floors, and is made up of more than 300 departments, a dozen bars and restaurants and even its own pub.

Tourists flock to *Harrods* – it's thought to be the city's third top tourist attraction – with over 30,000 customers passing through each day. Most Londoners limit their visits to the annual sales, with more than 300,000 arriving on the first day of the Christmas Sale. To help keep out the non-purchasing riff-raff, a draconian dress code has been introduced: no shorts, no ripped jeans, no vest T-shirts and no backpacks. In truth, much of what the shop stocks you can buy a great deal more cheaply if you can do without the Harrod's carrier bag, but the store does have a few sections that are real sights. Chief among these are the food halls, with their Arts and Crafts tiling and a surprisingly reasonably priced oyster counter, and the beautiful Art Deco men's hairdressers; both are on the ground floor.

Chelsea

Until the sixteenth century, **Chelsea** was nothing more than a tiny fishing village on the banks of the Thames. Thomas More started its upward trend by moving here in 1520, followed by members of the nobility, including Henry VIII himself. It wasn't really until the latter part of the nineteenth century, however, that Chelsea began to earn its reputation as London's very own Left Bank, a bohemianism formalized by the foundation of the Chelsea Arts Club in 1891 and entrenched in the 1960s, when the likes of David Bailey, Mick Jagger, George Best and the "Chelsea Set" hung out in continental-style boutiques and coffee bars. These days, the area has a more subdued feel, with high rents and house prices keeping things staid, and interior design shops rather than avant-garde fashion the order of the day. The area's other aspect, oddly enough considering its bohemian reputation, is a military one, with central London's main army barracks, the Royal Hospital, home of old veterans known as the Chelsea Pensioners, and the country's army museum.

King's Road
The **King's Road**, Chelsea's main artery, begins at Sloane Square, a leafy nexus on the very eastern edge of Chelsea, which gave its name to the debutantes of the 1980s, the Sloane Rangers, whose most famous alumna was Princess Diana. Sloanes, whose natural habitat is actually further north in Kensington and Knightsbridge, are easily identifiable by their dress code: blue and white pin-striped shirts, cords and brogues for the

men, flick-back hair, pearls and flat shoes for the women, and waxed cotton Barbour jackets for all. The road's household fame, however, came through its role as the unofficial catwalk of the Swinging Sixties. While Carnaby Street (p.83) is still cashing in on its past, and has consequently descended into a tourist quagmire, King's Road has managed to move with the times, through the hippy era, punk and beyond. The "Saturday Parade" of fashion victims is not what it used to be, but posey cafés, boutiques (and antiques) are still what King's Road is all about. And the traditional "Chelsea Cruise", when every flash Harry in town parades his customized motor, still takes place at 8.30pm on the last Saturday of the month, though it's currently located on the Battersea side of the Chelsea Bridge.

Perhaps the road's most famous address of all is **no. 430**, about a mile down the King's Road, where the designer Vivienne Westwood and her then-boyfriend Malcolm McLaren opened a teddy-boy revival store called *Let It Rock*. In 1975 they changed tack and renamed the shop *Sex*, stocking it with proto-punk fetishist gear and displaying simulated burnt limbs in the window. It became a magnet for the likes of John Lydon and John Simon Ritchie, better known as Johnny Rotten and Sid Vicious – the rest, as they say, is history. Now known as *World's End*, the shop, with its landmark backward-clock, continues to sell Westwood's eccentric, fashion-leading clothes.

Military Chelsea

Among the most nattily attired of all the shoppers on the King's Road are the scarlet or navy-blue clad Chelsea Pensioners, the army veterans who live in the nearby **Royal Hospital** (Mon–Sat 10am–noon & 2–4pm, Sun 2–4pm; free), founded by Charles II in 1681 and designed by Wren. The end result – plain, red-brick wings and grassy courtyards, which originally opened straight onto the river – became a blueprint for institutional and collegiate architecture all over the English-speaking world. The two sections of the complex open to visitors are the austere hospital chapel, with its huge barrel vault and the equally grand, wooden-panelled dining hall, with its vast allegorical mural of Charles II and his hospital. In the Soane-designed Secretary's Office, on the east side of the hospital, there's a small museum (opening times as for the hospital), displaying pensioners' costumes, medals and two German bombs.

The concrete bunker next door to the Royal Hospital, on Royal Hospital Road, houses the **National Army Museum** (daily 10am–5.30pm; free). The militarily obsessed are unlikely to be disappointed by the succession of uniforms and medals, but there is very little here for non-enthusiasts, beyond the skeleton of Marengo, Napoleon's charger at Waterloo, and a large model of the battlefield on which 48,000 lost their lives. The temporary exhibitions are often more critical, but otherwise you're better off visiting the infinitely superior Imperial War Museum (p.103).

Chelsea Physic Garden and Carlyle's House

The **Chelsea Physic Garden** is situated at the beginning of Cheyne Walk. Founded in 1673 by the Royal Society of Apothecaries, this is the oldest botanical garden in the country after Oxford's: the first cedars grown in England were planted here in 1683, cotton seed was sent from here to the American colonies in 1732, and the garden contains the country's oldest olive tree. At the entrance (on Swan Walk) you can pick up a map of the garden with a list of the month's most interesting flowers and shrubs, whose labels are slightly more forthcoming than the usual terse Latinate tags. A statue of Hans Sloane, who presented the Society with the freehold, stands at the centre of the garden; behind him there's an excellent tea house, serving delicious home-made cakes and tea, with exhibitions on the floor above.

A short distance from Cheyne Walk, at 24 Cheyne Row, is **Carlyle's House** (Mon–Sat 11am–5pm; NT; £2.80), the Queen Anne house where the historian Thomas Carlyle set up home, having moved down from his native Scotland in 1834. The intellectuals and artists who visited Carlyle – among them Dickens, Tennyson, Chopin, Mazzini, Browning and Darwin – were equally attracted by the wit of his strong-willed wife, with whom Carlyle enjoyed a famously tempestuous relationship. The house itself, made into a museum just fifteen years after Carlyle's death, is a dour abode, kept much as the Carlyles would have had it, and you're positively encouraged to lounge around on the sofas. The top floor contains the garret study where Carlyle tried in vain to escape the din of the street and the neighbours' noisy roosters.

Notting Hill, Marylebone and Regent's Park

To the northwest of Hyde Park lies the hip neighbourhood of **Notting Hill**, a culturally mixed area especially worth visiting for the August bank holiday carnival. Further east the dominating presences on the tourist scene are **Madame Tussaud's** and the **Planetarium**. North of here, and less than five minutes' walk away, is the leafy expanse of Regent's Park, home of **London Zoo**.

Notting Hill

Forty years ago **Notting Hill** was described as "a massive slum, full of multi-occupied houses, crawling with rats and rubbish", and was populated by offshoots of the Soho vice and crime rackets. These insalubrious dwellings became home to a large contingent of Afro-Caribbean immigrants, who had to compete for jobs and living space with the area's similarly down-trodden white residents. Now, the region has been gentrified, with media folk having taken over large houses in the leafy crescents and trendy bars and restaurants springing up all over.

Nowadays, Notting Hill is best known for two things – the **Carnival** (see below) and **Portobello Road market**, a mish-mash of stalls selling anything from valuable antiques to junky bric-a-brac and West Indian vegetables. The initial stretch of

---

NOTTING HILL CARNIVAL

Notting Hill Carnival began unofficially in 1959 as a response to the the previous year's race riots, which took place when bus loads of whites attacked West Indian homes in the area. In 1965, the carnival took to the streets and has grown into the world's biggest street festival outside Rio, with an estimated one million revellers turning up each August bank holiday. During the 1960s, it was little more than a few church hall events and a carnival parade, inspired by that of Trinidad – home of many of the area's immigrants. Today the carnival still belongs to West Indians (from all parts of the city), but there are participants, too, from London's Latin American and Asian communities, and, of course, everyone turns out to watch the bands and parades, and hang out.

The main sights of the carnival are the **costume parades**, known as the *mas*, which take place on the Sunday (for kids' groups) and Monday (adults) from around 10am until late afternoon. The processions consist of floats, drawn by trucks, with costume themes and steel bands – the "pans" which are one of the chief sounds of the carnival (and have their own contest on the Saturday). The parade makes its way around a three-mile route, starting at the top end of Ladbroke Grove, heading south under the Westway, then turning into Westbourne Grove, before looping north again via Chepstow Road, Great Western Road and Kensal Road.

In addition to the parades, there are three or four **stages for live music** – Portobello Green and Powis Square are regular venues – where you can catch reggae, ragga, jungle, a bit of hip-hop and maybe Caribbean soca. And everywhere you go, between Westbourne Grove and the Westway, there are **sound systems** on the street, blasting out reggae and black dance sounds.

London's most popular market contains a mixture of overpriced, touristy stalls and some genuine shops selling classy antiques. In its lower stretches the market gets a lot more funky and the emphasis switches to street clothes and jewellery, odd trinkets, records and books.

Sherlock Holmes, Madame Tussaud's and the Planetarium

A small percentage of tourists emerging from Baker Street tube station are on the trail of English literature's languid super-sleuth, Sherlock Holmes, who lived at 221b Baker Street. That address is today a building society, but further down the road – at no. 239, although the sign on the door says 221b – the **Sherlock Holmes Museum** (daily 9.30am–6pm; £5; Baker Street tube) provides some compensation for the addicted.

Just round the corner on Marylebone Road is **Madame Tussaud's** (Mon–Fri 10am–5.30pm, Sat & Sun 9.30am–5.30pm; £8.35, joint ticket with Planetarium £11.25; Baker Street tube), a place renowned for its wax facsimiles of the rich and famous ever since the good lady arrived in London in 1802 bearing the sculpted heads of guillotined aristocrats. The entrance fee might be extortionate and the dummies inept by *Jurassic Park* standards, but you can still rely on finding London's biggest queues here – an hour's wait is the summertime minimum.

The best photo opportunities come in the first section, a Garden Party of television and sports stars, but the next room, called **200 Years**, is more offbeat. Ranged on a shelf are the heads and limbs of outdated personalities – Muhammed Ali, Nikita Khrushchev – while the very first Tussaud figure, Madame du Barry gently respires (thanks to a motorized heart), close to a fire-damaged model of George IV with a melted eye. The **Grand Hall**, a po-faced gathering of statesmen, clerics, royalty and generals, is lined with oil paintings to add a dash of respectability, but the veracity is a bit suspect – the Princess of Wales is miraculously shorter than her husband, and Margaret Thatcher looks like a kindly aunt. The **Chamber of Horrors**, including the Manson "family" and one of Jack the Ripper's mutilated victims, is unredeemably taste-less, with press clippings gratuitously detailing the exploits of recent serial killers. Tussaud's newest show, the **Spirit of London**, is a bizarre five-minute ride in miniatur-ized black taxi cabs. It begins well, dropping witty visual jokes as it careers through from Elizabethan times through to Swinging London, but becomes just too crazed, ending with a cacophany of punks and Chinese acrobats before shuddering to a halt by a slobbering Benny Hill.

Next door to Madame Tussaud's, the equally crowded **London Planetarium** (same hours; shows every 40min; £4) has an excellent fixed display with a giant revolving Earth circled by satellites, live weather satellite transmissions, images from a space telescope and touch-screen computers. All this is just a taster, however, for the **star show**, in which images collected by satellite and space probes are projected onto a vast dome – the pictures are stunning and the narration ecologically sound.

Regent's Park

Originally one of Henry VIII's many hunting grounds, **Regent's Park** got its name in 1812, when it was landscaped for the Prince Regent by John Nash, as part of a grand scheme to unify central London. The planned grand sweep was only partly realized (Regent Street is its chief vestige), but the park remains, cupped by Nash's graceful residential terraces. In the northern corner of the park, beyond acres of football pitches, lies **London Zoo** (summer daily 10am–5.30pm, winter closes 3pm; £6.95; Camden Town or Regent's Park tube), an institution with a great track record as a research and conservation centre, but which lives constantly under threat of closure due to lack of funds. It's not the most uplifting place for animal lovers: many larger species now live in the more capacious wildlife park at Whipsnade (see p.224), but too many of the Regent's Park inhabitants are housed in concrete and steel hovels – signs outside the cages of big cats ask you not to be distressed if you see them pacing up and down, as if such behaviour were quite normal in the wild. However, some of the enclosures seem as humane as any zoo could make them, and there are some striking architectural features here, like Lubetkin's 1930s spiral-ramped penguin pool and the colossal tent of the Snowden Aviary.

Camden, Hampstead and Highgate

Five minutes' walk northeast from the zoo you're into **Camden Town**, whose vast weekend market – a jumble of clothes, jewellery and ranks of bootleg tapes – is one of the liveliest in the city. One way of soaking up the Camden atmosphere is to take a barge cruise along Regent's canal (from near the zoo): passing elegant waterside houses and run-down semi-industrial landscapes, the cruise terminates at Little Venice, a delightful stretch of houseboats in a swanky west London residential enclave, centred on Warwick Avenue tube. More sedate pleasures are on offer in well-heeled **Hampstead** and **Highgate**, where the major draws are Hampstead Heath, the art collection at Kenwood House, and the wonderfully atmospheric Highgate Cemetery.

Camden Market

Camden Market was confined to Inverness Street until the 1970s when the focus began to shift towards the disused timber wharf and warehouses around Camden Lock, a flight of three locks on the Regent's Canal. The tiny crafts market which began in the cobbled courtyard by the lock has since mushroomed out of all proportion, with everyone trying to grab a piece of the action on both sides of Camden High Street and Chalk Farm Road. More than 100,000 shoppers turn up here each weekend and parts of the market now stay open week-long, though the place is still at its busiest at the weekend. Camden's over-abundance of cheap leather, DM shoes and naff jewellery is compensated for by the sheer variety of what's on offer: from bootleg tapes to furniture and mountain bikes, along with a mass of street fashion that may or may not make the transition to mainstream stores. For all its tourist popularity – it's reputedly the city's fourth largest tourist attraction – this is a market that remains a genuinely hip place.

Hampstead and Highgate

Beyond Camden, up Haverstock Hill, the suburb of **Hampstead** developed as a spa resort in the eighteenth century and retains an upper-crust small-town atmosphere. It's long been a bolt hole of the high-profile intelligentsia, and you can get some idea of its tone from the fact that its MP is the actress Glenda Jackson, who has held the seat for Labour since the 1992 election. An even more lustrous figure is celebrated at **Keats House** (Mon–Fri 2–6pm, Sat 10am–5pm, Sun 2–5pm; free) on Keats Grove, five minutes' walk southeast of Hampstead tube station. The consumptive poet moved into this Regency house in 1818, inspired by the peacefulness of Hampstead and by his passion for girl-next-door Fanny Brawne, whose house is part of the museum. Keats wrote some of his most famous works here, before leaving for Rome, where he died in 1821. Memorabilia include books and letters, an anatomical notebook from his days as a medical student at Guy's and St Thomas' hospitals, and Fanny's engagement ring. A plum tree in the pretty garden is planted on the spot where he is said to have written *Ode to a Nightingale*.

One of the most poignant house museums is the **Freud Museum** (Wed–Sun noon–5pm; £2.50; Finchley Road tube), hidden away in the leafy streets of South Hampstead. Freud fled Vienna after the Nazi invasion of 1938, and arrived a semi-invalid with cancer, which had been diagnosed in 1923 when he was given just five years to live. He lasted sixteen, but died only a year after his arrival in Hampstead. The ground-floor study looks exactly as it did when he lived here, with erotic antiquities, shelves and shelves of books, and his sumptuous couch draped in an opulent Turkish carpet. Upstairs, lively temporary exhibitions illustrate more of the doctor's life, and a small room is dedicated to his daughter, Anna, herself an influential child analyst who lived in the house until her death in 1982.

Hampstead Heath, which lies to the east of Hampstead village, is the closest untamed parkland to central London, offering stupendous views across the metropolis from **Parliament Hill**, the southern part of the Heath. This blustery rise (popular with kite-flyers) is reputedly where Guy Fawkes and his cronies planned to watch the conflagration of the Houses of Parliament in 1605 – hence its name. **Kenwood**, north of Parliament Hill, is a semi-artificial landscape, with splendid gardens of azaleas and rhodedendrons, and a huge grassy amphitheatre in which outdoor classical concerts are held on summer evenings.

Kenwood House (April–Sept daily 10am–6pm; Oct–March closes 4pm; free; Highgate tube), set at the top of a slope sweeping down to the lake, is the Heath's most celebrated sight. Built in the seventeenth century and later remodelled by Robert Adam in Neoclassical style, the house is an attraction in itself, but it's also home to the Iveagh Bequest, a superb collection of seventeenth- and eighteenth-century art from the English, Dutch and French schools. You pass a whimsical Reynolds painting, *Venus Chiding Cupid for Learning to Cast Accounts*, and some good examples of Boucher's flirtatious pastoral scenes, before coming to the Dining Room, where a superb **Rembrandt** self-portrait shares space with Hals' *Man with a Cane* and Vermeer's delicate *Guitar Player*. Paintings by Gainsborough, including the diaphanous *Countess Howe*, caught up in a bold, almost abstract landscape, are on show in the Music Room, alongside works by his more robust contemporary, Joshua Reynolds.

Northeast of the Heath, **Highgate** lacks the literary cachet of its rival, Hampstead, but this equally elegant village compensates by being the home of London's most famous graveyard, **Highgate Cemetery** (Highgate or Archway tube), ranged on both sides of Swains Lane, opened in 1838 as a private venture, and the preferred resting place of many wealthy Victorian families, as well as numerous intellectuals and artists, including Christina Rossetti and George Eliot. The older, more atmospheric and overgrown West Cemetery is no longer in use and only open for guided tours (Mon–Fri noon, 2pm & 3pm, Sat & Sun hourly 10am–4pm; £3), which are well worth joining for the crooked, ivy-covered graves of the famous, the Egyptian Avenue and the ostentatious mausoleums of the Terrace Catacombs. The most publicized denizen of the East Cemetery (April–Sept daily 10am–5pm; Oct–March closes 4pm; £1) is **Karl Marx**, his much visited tomb adorned by a huge bust, placed here in 1956 on a granite plinth inscribed with the words "Workers of the World Unite".

The outskirts

The outskirts of central London are littered with accessible attractions that can fill the best part of a day. To the southeast, the riverside suburb of **Greenwich** is steeped in royal and naval history, boasting some of the finest architecture in all of London, a clutch of good museums and one of the capital's most attractive parks. Also in southeast London, the less spectacular districts of **Dulwich** and **Forest Hill** are enlivened by a first-rate art gallery and an idiosyncratic small museum. Down in the southwest, there are wide open spaces at **Kew**, site of the nation's most spectacular botanical gardens, and at neighbouring **Richmond**, with its vast deer park. In summer, the most pleasant way to reach Kew and Richmond is on a **river cruise** – numerous companies run services between these spots and Greenwich, the Tower of London, Charing Cross and Westminster, with some even venturing upriver to the magnificent Tudor palace of **Hampton Court**. Devotees of the eighteenth century will have a field day in this south-western part of London, as nearby **Chiswick** is home to England's most refined Palladian house, while Robert Adam's finest work can be seen at Syon Park House and Osterley House, both set in regal estates across the river from Kew. Further out, by far the most popular excursion from London is to **Windsor Castle**, often twinned with a trip to **Eton**, thus completing a journey into the heart of the English class system.

Greenwich and Woolwich

"The most delightful spot of ground in Great Britain," according to Daniel Defoe, **GREENWICH** is still one of London's most beguiling spots. At its heart is the outstanding architectural set-pieces of the **Royal Naval Hospital** and the **Queen's House**, courtesy of Wren and Inigo Jones respectively. In addition, there are the tourist draws of the **Cutty Sark**, the **National Maritime Museum** and the **Old Royal Observatory**, plus a Sunday market that pulls in an ever increasing number of Londoners in search of bargains.

Five miles east of central London, Greenwich is quickest reached by rail from Charing Cross or London Bridge (every 30min), although taking a river trip is more scenic, if considerably more expensive. A third possible route takes you on the Docklands Light Railway from Tower Hill to Island Gardens, and where a pedestrian tunnel leads under the Thames to Greenwich – the advantage of this approach being the fabulous view of the Wren buildings from across the river.

The Cutty Sark and St Alfege

Standing in a dry dock next to Greenwich pier, the majestic **Cutty Sark** (April–Oct Mon–Sat 10am–6pm, Sun noon–6pm; Oct–March closes 5pm; £3.25) was built in 1869 to be used on the passage to China, but became obsolete as a tea ship after the opening of the Suez canal, which allowed steamboats a quicker route to the Orient. In the 1880s, however, it was moved to the Australian wool trade, and continued working until 1922. The name comes from Robert Burns' *Tam O'Shanter*, in which Tam is chased by Nannie, an angry witch in a short linen dress, or "cutty sark"; the clipper's figurehead shows her clutching the hair from the tail of Tam's horse. Inside, the ship looks pretty much the same as during its short reign as a tea clipper, the reconstructed living quarters showing the marked difference in conditions for officers and crew. Best of all, though, is the lower hold, with its colourful row of buxom figureheads.

Next to the Cutty Sark, dwarfed by her bulk, is the tiny **Gipsy Moth IV**, the vessel in which Sir Francis Chichester sailed solo round the world in 1965–66 (April–Sept Mon–Sat 10am–6pm, Sun noon–6pm, closed Mon–Fri 1–2pm; Oct closes 5pm; 50p). A short distance further from the river, on Greenwich Church Street, rises one of England's greatest baroque churches, Hawksmoor's **St Alfege**. Dedicated to Alfege, Archbishop of Canterbury, who was murdered here by Vikings in 1012, it was built in 1714 to replace a twelfth-century structure in which Henry VIII was baptized. Much of the interior, including woodcarving by Grinling Gibbons, was flattened in the Blitz, but it has been magnificently repaired.

The Royal Naval College

It's scarcely surprising that the London building that makes the best of its riverbank location should be the **Royal Naval College** which presents an extraordinary facade of pincer-like colonnades to the Thames. It stands on the site of the Palace of Placentia, the Tudor residence where Henry VIII and all three of his children were born, where Henry met Anne Boleyn and where Jane Seymour died in childbirth. Charles II had Placentia demolished and replaced with a palace designed by John Webb, a building later continued by Wren for an entirely different function – the Greenwich Hospital, a home for disabled seamen. Hawksmoor in turn continued the project, and completed the interior, of which only the bombastic **Painted Hall** and the **RNC Chapel** are open to visitors (daily except Thurs 2.30–4.45pm; free).

If you're in need of a bit of refreshment, you could pop into the *Trafalgar Tavern*, on the east side of the college. The pub was frequented by Whig politicians and the Victorian literary set – its legendary whitebait suppers inspired Dickens to use the pub as the setting for the wedding breakfast in *Our Mutual Friend*.

The Queen's House and National Maritime Museum

Greenwich Park was landscaped in 1662 by André le Notre, designer of the gardens at Versailles, to make a suitably elegant setting for the **Queen's House** (daily 10am–5pm; £5.50 combined ticket which also allows admission into the Maritime Museum and the Old Royal Observatory, with a free return visit allowed within twelve months), the earliest example of domestic Palladian architecture in Britain. It was built by Inigo Jones for the wife of James I, but she died before its completion – Henrietta Maria, Charles I's wife, became the first resident. Recent restoration has fitted out the house in Stuart style, shown to particularly dazzling effect in the Queen's Apartment, with its gaudy hand-woven silks and velvets. Next door, the **National Maritime Museum** (same hours as Queen's House) ploughs through seafaring history from 1450 to the present day, with scores of model ships, guns, charts, globes and far too many paintings of ships.

The Old Royal Observatory

The steep slope of Greenwich Park is crowned by the dome of Wren's **Old Royal Observatory** (same hours as Queen's House). The Observatory was set up by Charles II in 1675 to house his astronomer, John Flamsteed, whose task was to study the stars in order to produce accurate navigational maps, as too many explorers were getting lost at sea. Not everything in the observatory is quite as functional as it looks. Beyond the nicely restored **apartments** in which the cantankerous Flamsteed lived, you reach an octagonal domed room containing an eighteenth-century telescope – but this room was never used to map the movement of the stars, acting instead as a reception room in which the king could show off. One of the main problems facing the observatory's workers was that of measuring time differences across the globe, and a very entertaining gallery shows some of the crazy ideas that were offered as solutions.

Flamsteed carried out all real work in what is now called the **Meridian Building**, little more than a shed in the garden, where his first meridian line is marked with pulsing red lights in the floor. Next door, in Halley's Quadrangle Room, you can see the development of sophisticated telescopes and Halley's version of the meridian. A third room reveals yet another meridian, standard from 1700 to 1760, and still used in all Ordnance Survey maps, despite the fact that every other map in the world abides by the present meridian line in the Observatory courtyard, marked by a line of opaque blue glass. The exhibition ends on a soothing note in the Telescope Dome, its enormous Victorian refractor accompanied by videos of space images and New Age music. In addition there are half-hourly presentations (Mon–Sat; £1.50) in the **Planetarium**, housed in the adjoining South Building.

The Ranger's House

The **Ranger's House** (April–Sept daily 10am–6pm; Oct–March Wed–Sun 10am–4pm; £2; EH), a red-brick villa on the southwestern edge of Greenwich Park, houses the

Suffolk collection of art and a wide selection of antique musical instruments. Built in the early eighteenth century, it was lived in after 1749 by the Earl of Chesterfield, who extended the bow window of the large gallery to just within the boundaries of the Royal Park, pushing the rent on the window up to £10 a year, compared to a total rent of six shillings and eight pence on the rest of the house. The high points of the art collection are William Larkin's full-length portraits of a Jacobean wedding party, particularly the twin bridesmaids in slashed silver brocade dresses, and the arrogant Richard Sackville, a dissolute aristocrat resplendent in pompom shoes. The Architectural Study Centre, in the courtyard, is a collection of plaques, mantels, fireplaces and chimneys saved from London's historic buildings – the spiral staircase snaking through the centre of the room was retrieved from the old Covent Garden market hall.

The Thames Barrier

A short boat trip from Greenwich pier (3–5 trips daily; £4 return) passes drab industrial landscapes before gliding towards the gargantuan gleaming fins of the **Thames Barrier**. London has been subject to flooding from surge tides since before 1236, when it was reported that in "the great Palace of Westminster men did row with wherries in the midst of the Hall". With the effects of global warming and rising tides, it became crucial to implement adequate flood protection, and so from 1972 to 1984 the now defunct Greater London Council built the Barrier. It's a mind-blowing feat of engineering, with its ten movable steel gates weighing from 400 to 3700 tonnes each. The **Visitor Centre** (Mon–Fri 10.30am–5pm, Sat & Sun 10.30am–5.30pm; £2.25) on Unity Way is little more than a handful of glossy models, videos and dull statistics; by far the most interesting way to see the Thames Barrier is from the riverbank on the one day a month when it is raised for tests (call ☎0181/854 1373 for dates).

A new attraction, moored a little way east of the Visitors Centre, is the **Russian Submarine**, U-475 Foxtrot (daily 10am–6pm). This sinister Soviet sub carried nuclear weapons and could operate at a depth of 250 yards, making it almost impossible to detect. Very little has been altered inside which means that visitors must be prepared to squeeze through numerous awkward hatches and claustrophobics should stay away.

Dulwich and Forest Hill

Dulwich Village, one of southeast London's prettier patches, is built on land owned in the seventeenth century by the actor Edward Alleyn, who founded **Dulwich College** in 1619 as almshouses and a school for poor boys, on the profits of his whorehouses and bear-baiting pits on Bankside (see p.103). Alleyn is buried in the chapel of the new Dulwich College, a grand Italianate structure with an impressive roll-call of old boys, including Raymond Chandler, P. G. Wodehouse and World War II traitor Lord Haw-Haw, though they tend to keep quiet about the last of the trio.

The original college is a short walk away down College Road, right next to the **Dulwich Picture Gallery** (Tues–Fri 10am–1pm & 2–5pm, Sat 11am–5pm, Sun 2–5pm; £2; West Dulwich BR from Charing Cross), the nation's oldest public art gallery. Designed by Sir John Soane in 1814, it houses the collection assembled in the 1790s by the French dealer Noel Desenfans then bequeathed to Francis Bourgeois, who in turn passed it on to the college. It's a beautifully spacious building, awash in natural light (except for the mausoleum of Desenfans and Bourgeois) and crammed with superb paintings – elegiac landscapes by Cuyp; a fine array of Gainsborough portraits, including his famous Linley Sisters and a likeness of Samuel Linley, said to have been painted in less than an hour; Rembrandt's *Portrait of a Young Man*; one of the world's finest Poussin series; and splendid works by Tiepolo, Hogarth, Van Dyck, Canaletto and Rubens.

If you walk for a mile or so across Dulwich Park and south down Lordship Lane, you'll reach the wacky **Horniman Museum** (Mon–Sat 10.30am–5.30pm, Sun 2–

5.30pm; free; Forest Hill BR), which occupies a striking building designed by Harrison Townsend, architect of the Whitechapel Gallery (see p.101). Horniman, a tea trader with a passion for collecting, financed construction of the purpose-built gallery in 1901, and the museum revels in its Victorian eclecticism. Ethnographic treasures on the ground floor include grotesque masks from Central America, a tiny mummified kitten, an Ethiopian Prince's headdress, and a statue of the goddess Kali dancing on the body of Shiva. Beyond the didactic aquarium, displays on the upper levels are even more diverse: cases of stuffed birds and skeletons share space with half a fruit bat and an orang-utang's foot, while umpteen antique musical instruments join ancient puppets from Poland and Arabian shoes with flaps to scare away scorpions.

Chiswick

The magnificent **Chiswick House** (April–Sept Mon–Sat 10am–6pm; Oct–March Wed–Sun 10am–4pm; Turnham Green tube; EH; £2), was designed in the 1720s by Richard Boyle, Earl of Burlington, the nation's chief proponent of Palladianism, the reaction against the Baroque. Modelled on Palladio's Villa Rotonda near Vicenza, this house was not a residence so much as a "temple to the arts", a showcase for his fine collection and a place to entertain such friends as Swift, Handel, Alexander Pope and William Kent, who painted many of the ceilings and landscaped the gardens. The interior is sober and relatively empty – if you don't have an eye for the finesse of classical architecture, you'll probably get more pleasure from Kent's gardens (daily 8am–dusk; free). Adorned with classical statues from Hadrian's villa at Tivoli, a sunken garden with a pond and a Ionic temple, and a long avenue lined with urns and sphinxes, they also boast a grand stone gateway designed by Inigo Jones and brought here from Beaufort House in Chelsea in 1736.

If you leave Chiswick House gardens by the northernmost exit, beyond the conservatory, it's just a short walk (to the east) along the thunderous A4 road, to **Hogarth's House** (April–Sept Mon & Wed–Sat 11am–6pm, Sun 2–6pm; Oct–March closes 4pm; closed first 2 weeks Sept & last 3 weeks Dec; free), where the artist spent each summer with his wife, sister and mother-in-law from 1749 until his death in 1764. Nowadays, it's hard to beleive that Hogarth came here for peace and quiet, but in the eighteenth century the house was almost entirely surrounded by countryside. In addition to scores of Hogarth's engravings, you can see copies of his satirical series *An Election*, *Marriage à la Mode* and *A Harlot's Progress*, and compare the modern view from the parlour with the more idyllic scene in *Mr Ranby's House*.

Kew and Richmond

More than 50,000 species are grown in the plantations and glasshouses of the **Royal Botanical Gardens** (daily 9.30am–dusk; £4, £1.50 last hour before closing; Kew Gardens tube), created as a pleasure garden in 1731 by Prince Frederick, eldest son of George II, and adapted into a botanical garden in 1759 by Frederick's widow, Princess Augusta. Some of its earliest specimens were brought back from the voyages of Captain Cook, instantly establishing Kew as a leading botanical research centre, and from its original eight acres, Kew has now grown into a giant 300-acre site. Amid the glades, lawns and flowerbeds, the sweltering **Palm House**, an enormous building of glass and iron designed by Decimus Burton in the 1840s, nurtures specimens from most of the world's rainforests and includes an excellent acquarium in the basement; you can cool off in the new **Princess of Wales Conservatory**, which ranges across ten climatic zones. A couple of non-scientific structures also stand within the gardens: the Jacobean red-brick **Kew Palace** (April–Sept daily 11am–5.30pm; £1.20), a three-storey mansion, used mainly as a country retreat by Georges II and III, and decorated to the taste of George III; and the tiny thatched **Queen Charlotte's Cottage** (April–Sept Sat & Sun 11am–5.30pm; 70p, joint ticket with palace £1.50), a summerhouse with flower-painted ceilings.

Richmond, barely a mile upstream from Kew, is accessible by taking a boat or hopping on the tube. Richmond Palace, preferred residence of the Tudors, was mostly destroyed during the Commonwealth, but you can see a few paltry remains on the west side of Richmond Green, a spot flanked by seventeenth- and eighteenth-century houses. It's the river which gives the village most of its character, and Richmond Bridge – an elegant arch built in 1777 – is London's oldest extant bridge. Small jetties nearby have row boats for hire, and cruises to Hampton Court. Richmond's real attraction is the enormous **Richmond Park**, about a mile southeast of the green up Richmond Hill. Once Charles I's hunting ground, this is Europe's largest city park, famous for its red and fallow deer, and for its ancient oaks. Beautiful gardens in the centre feature splendid springtime azaleas and rhododendrons, and a good café with outdoor seating affords spectacular views from the crest of Richmond Hill.

Ham House and Marble Hill

Ham House (April–Sept Mon–Wed 1–5pm, Sat 1–5.30pm, Sun 11.30am–5.30pm; NT; £4), off the beaten track and under-visited, is one of the most appealing of all the historic houses along the river. The best approach is by foot from Richmond riverside, heading southeast along the towpath which eventually leaves the rest of London far behind. Recent restoration has enhanced this period piece, which boasts one of the finest Stuart interiors in the country. The Great Staircase, to the east of the central hall, is stupendously ornate, featuring huge bowls of fruit at the newel posts and trophies of war carved into the balustrade. The rest of the house is equally sumptuous, with lavish plasterwork, silverwork and parquet flooring, Verrio ceiling paintings and rich hangings, tapestries, silk damasks and cut velvets. The Long Gallery, in the west wing, features six "Court Beauties" by Peter Lely and elsewhere there are works by Van Dyck and Reynolds. Another bonus is the formal seventeenth-century gardens, recently restored to something like their former glory.

Not far from Hammerton's Ferry, which takes you across the river from Ham to Twickenham (all year round, weather permitting), is **Marble Hill House** (April–Oct daily 10am–6pm; Nov–Feb Wed–Sun 10am–4pm; EH; free), a stuccoed Palladian villa set in rolling green parkland. Unlike Chiswick, this is no architectural exercise, but a real house, built in 1729 for the Countess of Suffolk, mistress of George II for some twenty years and, conveniently perhaps, also a lady-in-waiting to his wife, Queen Caroline. Her wit and intelligence (though not her beauty) were renowned and she entertained literary figures of the day such as Alexander Pope, John Gay and Horace Walpole. Another royal mistress, Mrs Fitzherbert, the Prince Regent's unofficial wife, later occupied the house in 1795.

Nothing remains of the original furnishings, alas, and though some period furniture has taken its place, the house feels barren. The principal room is the Great Room, a perfect cube whose coved ceiling carries on up into the top-floor apartments. Copies of Van Dyck decorate the walls as they did in Lady Suffolk's day and a further splash of colour is provided by Panini's Roman landscapes above each of the five doors (two of which are purely decorative to complete the symmetery). The other highlight is Lady Suffolk's Bedchamber, featuring an Ionic columned recess – a classic Palladian device.

Syon House and Osterley Park

Across the water from Kew stands **Syon House** (April–Sept Wed–Sun 11am–5pm; Oct Sun only; £3.25; gardens daily 10am–6pm or dusk; £2; Gunnersbury tube then bus

#237/267), granted to the Duke of Northumberland by Elizabeth I and still the family home. Although the house retains its Tudor facade, the opulent interior was redesigned in the mid-eighteenth century by Robert Adam, whose work is seen to best effect in the colourful, columned anteroom. Other rooms feature royal portraits by Lely, Wedgwood pottery and authentic Adam furnishings. While Adam beautified the house, Capability Brown laid out the gardens with an artificial lake and neat lawns – but the Great Conservatory, a prototype for the Crystal Palace, was a Victorian addition. You can also see hundreds of exotic butterflies among the lush greenery of the Butterfly House (summer daily 10am–5pm, winter closes 3.30pm; £2.60).

With architect William Chambers, Adam also redesigned **Osterley Park House** (March Sat & Sun 11am–5pm; April–Oct Wed–Fri 1–5pm, Sat & Sun 11am–5pm; £3.50; NT; park daily 10am–dusk; Osterley tube), an originally Elizabethan mansion three miles west of Syon Park. Of the rooms you're permitted to see, the Drawing Room is the most splendid, with Reynolds portraits on the damask walls and a ceiling centred on a giant marigold, a theme continued in the lush carpet and elsewhere in the house. The Tapestry Room is hung with Gobelin tapestries decorated to Boucher's design, and the State Bedchamber features an outrageous domed bed designed by Adam. Tranquil Osterley Park is one of London's largest estate parks, featuring an eighteenth-century Chinese pagoda, grazing cattle, three lakes and a café in the Tudor stables – it's just a shame about the M4 motorway which cut the estate in half in the 1960s.

Hampton Court

Thirteen miles southwest of London you'll find the finest of Tudor palaces, **Hampton Court Palace** (March–Oct Mon 10.15am–6pm, Tues–Sun 9.30am–6pm; Oct–March Mon closes 4.30pm; £7.50 including maze; BR Hampton Court from Waterloo). Cardinal Wolsey commissioned this immense house in 1516, then handed it to Henry VIII in a vain attempt to win back his favour. Henry enlarged and improved the palace, altering the rooms to suit the tastes of the last five of his six wives, and Hampton Court soon became renowned for its masques, plays and balls, a tradition continued by Elizabeth I. Charles II built the gardens, inspired by what he had seen at Versailles, but it was William III who made the most radical alterations, hiring Sir Christopher Wren to remodel the buildings. Wren intended to tear down the whole palace and start again, but settled upon building the east and south wings, the brick Banqueting House on the river and completing the chapel for Queen Anne. Finally abandoned as a royal residence by George III, Hampton Court was opened to the public by Queen Victoria in 1838.

The royal apartments are divided into six thematic walking tours, for which guided tours and audio tours are available at no extra cost. The highlight of **Henry VIII's State Apartments** is the Great Hall, with its astonishing double hammerbeam roof. Further on is the Haunted Gallery, home to the ghost of Henry's fifth wife, nineteen-year-old Catherine Howard. Another high point is the Chapel Royal, which boasts false timber vaulting wrought in plaster and decorated with gilded, music-making cherubs. The **Queen's Apartments**, approached by the grandiose Queen's Staircase, feature several marvellous marble fireplaces, fiery frescoes, Gobelins tapestries and *Chinoiserie*. The tour of the so-called **Georgian Rooms** takes you through the Cartoon Gallery, hung with Brussels tapestries, some of which are copies of Raphael's cartoons (now in the V&A) for which the room was originally intended. Beyond here, the brightly decorated **Wolsey Closet** is the only room remaining from Wolsey's apartments.

The **King's Apartments**, approached via the magnificent King's Staircase and the armoury of the King's Guard Chamber, are furnished in the same period as the Queen's, with only the throne-like velvet toilet for light relief. The Renaissance Picture Gallery is chock-full of treasures, among them paintings by Tintoretto, Lotto, Bassano, Titian, Parmigianino and Holbein. After the opulence of the rest of the palace, the workaday **Tudor Kitchens** come as something of a relief. To make the most of this route, you really do need the audio tour, which sets the vast complex of reconstructed kitchens alight. Before setting off into the grounds, make sure you visit the Real Tennis court – you might even catch a game of this arcane precursor of modern tennis.

There is plenty more to see in the sixty-acre **grounds** (7am–dusk; free): the Great Vine, grown from a cutting in 1768 and now averaging about seven hundred pounds of black grapes per year; William III's Banqueting House (April–Sept only); and the Lower Orangery, a gallery for **Mantegna**'s heroic canvases, *The Triumphs of Caesar*. The famous **maze** (daily 10am–5pm; £1.80), laid out in 1714, lies north of the palace; beyond here and across Hampton Court Road, Wren's royal road, Chestnut Avenue, cuts through the semi-wild Bushy Park, which sustains a few fallow deer.

Windsor and Eton

Every weekend trains from Waterloo and Paddington are packed with people off on the trail to **WINDSOR**, the royal enclave 21 miles west of London, where they join the human conveyor belt round **Windsor Castle** (March–Oct daily 10am–5pm; Nov–Feb 10am–4pm; £8). Towering above the town on a steep chalk bluff, the castle began its days as a wooden fortress built by William the Conqueror, and numerous later monarchs had a hand in its evolution. Henry II rebuilt it in stone, Henry III and Edward III improved it and George IV restored it. Some of their work was undone by a huge fire in November 1992, which gutted a number of rooms, including St George's Hall, in which monarchs from Edward III onwards held banquets for the Knights of the Garter.

Despite the fire, most of the **State Apartments** (which you enter from the North Terrace) are still open, except at Easter and in June and December, when the Queen is in residence. Highlights include Van Dyck's tryptych of Charles I in the King's Dressing Room; the Queen's Ballroom, dominated by an enormous silver mirror and table, and more Van Dyck paintings; the Queen's Audience Room, decorated with fine Gobelin tapestries; and the vast array of crested helmets and sixteenth-century armour in the Queen's Guard Chamber, which includes an etched gold suit made for Prince Hal. A separate gallery to the left of the main entrance holds exhibitions drawn from the royal art collection (Windsor possesses the world's finest collection of drawings and notebooks by Leonardo da Vinci) and Lutyens' **Queen Mary's Dolls' House** (£1.50), with working lights and plumbing.

A visit to the castle should take in **St George's Chapel** (Mon–Sat 10am–4pm, Sun 2–4pm; closed Jan); a glorious Perpendicular structure, ranking with King's College Chapel in Cambridge (see p.353), it contains the tombs of numerous kings and queens. There are more royal tombs in the Albert Memorial Chapel, built by Henry VII as a burial place for Henry VI and completed by Wolsey, but then coverted into a memorial to Prince Albert, Victoria's husband.

Crossing the footbridge at the end of Thames Avenue in Windsor village brings you to **Eton**, where the *raison d'être* is of course **Eton College** (daily Easter, July & Aug 10.30am–4.30pm; April–June, Sept & Nov 2–4.30pm; £2.20), the ultra-exclusive and inexcusably powerful school founded by Henry VI in 1440 and now charged with educating the heir to the throne, Prince William. Within the rarefied complex you can visit the Gothic chapel, with its medieval wall paintings, and a small self-congratulatory museum telling the history of the school – Percy Bysshe Shelley is a rare rebellious figure in the roll-call of Establishment greats.

EATING, DRINKING AND NIGHTLIFE

No matter what your taste in food, drink or entertainment, you'll find what you're looking for in London, a city that in many ways becomes a more appealing place after dark. The capital's rich ethnic mix and concentration of creative talent gives it a diversity and energy that no other town in England comes close to matching – Birmingham might have a better concert hall, Manchester might have a couple of hot clubs, but nowhere can match the capital's consistent quality and choice. The weekly calendar of gigs, movies, plays and other events is charted most completely in *Time Out*, the main listings magazine, and there are any number of specialist publications for those who want to make sure they are not missing a thing – from solemn books on the foodie shrines of London to esoteric little mags for the rave cognoscenti. However, the listings that follow should be more than enough for any visitor who's planning on spending not more than a couple of months in the city.

Eating

In marked contrast to most of the rest of England, London is a great place to **eat**. You can sample more or less any kind of cuisine here, and – if you have the money – you can experience the very best that the country has to offer. Obviously, there are plenty of places to eat around the main tourist drags of the West End – **Soho** has long been renowned for its eclectic and fashionable restaurants, while **Chinatown**, on the other side of Shaftesbury Avenue, offers value-for-money eating right in the centre of town. But to sample the full range of possibilities you also need to get out of the core of the city – to the **Indian** restaurants of Brick Lane in the East End and Drummond Street near Euston, or to the eateries of Camden and Islington, a short tube ride away to the north. And while there are **haute-cuisine** restaurants in Soho and a few other central spots, many of the better new British and international-style establishments are to be found in the upmarket residential quarters of town.

There are also plenty of spots to pick up a street **snack** or cheap **lunch** – and some of these quick-stop places are good standbys for an evening filler. The inexpensive places that rely on a rapid turnover are listed under "Snacks and quick meals", but there are plenty of more relaxed eateries suitable for a quick bite – check out the pizza and pasta joints (under "Italian"), the Chinese restaurants, many of which do excellent *dim sum*, and the ever expanding ranks of London's bistros (under "French" – the ones with no phone number tend to be open all day).

Eating out in England might not have quite the same social status as it does on the continent, but most of the places we've listed will be busy on most nights of the week, particularly on Friday and Saturday. You're best advised to reserve a table, and with the more expensive places you'll probably be disappointed if you don't plan a week ahead. We've given the phone number for all those restaurants where it's advisable to book.

Snacks and quick meals

Bar Italia, 22 Frith St, W1. A tiny café that's a Soho institution, serving coffee, sandwiches, pizza, etc. Popular with late-night clubbers and those here to watch the Italian league football on the giant screen. Leicester Square tube. Open 24hr.

Bonbonnière, 36 Great Marlborough St, W1. Cheap and plain food served in a dining room at the back of a West End sandwich bar. Oxford Circus tube. Mon–Sat 7.30am–7pm.

Café in the Crypt, St Martin-in-the-Fields church, Duncannon St, WC2. Good-quality buffet food makes this an ideal spot to fill up before hitting the West End for the evening, or after a tour of the National Gallery. Charing Cross tube. Mon–Sat 10am–8pm, Sun noon–6pm.

Centrale, 16 Moor St, W1. Tiny Italian greasy spoon that serves up large plates of pasta and omelettes. You may have to wait for – or share – a table. Unlicensed. Leicester Square tube. Daily noon–9.30pm.

Chelsea Kitchen, 98 King's Rd, SW3. Bargain-basement international dishes served to the impecunious since the 1960s. Sloane Square tube. Mon–Sat 8am–11.45pm, Sun 10am–11.45pm.

China China, 3 Gerrard St, W1. Best Chinatown bet for a quick plate of noodles. Leicester Square tube. Daily noon–midnight.

Food for Thought, 31 Neal St, WC2. Very small Covent Garden vegetarian restaurant – the food is inexpensive and superb but don't expect to linger. Covent Garden tube. Mon–Sat 9.30am–8pm, Sun 10.30am–4pm.

Gaby's, 30 Charing Cross Rd, WC2. Café serving a wide range of home-cooked veggie and Middle Eastern specialities; famously glum staff. Leicester Square tube. Mon–Sat 8am–midnight, Sun noon–10pm.

Maison Bertaux, 28 Greek St, W1. Long-standing Soho patisserie with tables on two floors and lots of cakes. Leicester Square tube. Daily 9am–8pm.

Pho, 2 Lisle St, W1. Vietnamese fast-food café; big bowls of noodle soup. Leicester Square tube. Daily noon–11pm.

Pollo, 20 Old Compton St, W1. The best-value Italian food in town. Always packed, though the queues move quickly. Leicester Square tube. Mon–Sat 11.30am–11pm.

Tokyo Diner, 2 Newport Place, WC2. Brilliant Japanese diner on the edge of Chinatown serving authentic food at a fraction of the cost of its rivals. Try one of the bento meals – an entire meal in a little box. Perfect service; tips not accepted. Leicester Square tube. Daily noon–midnight.

Wagamama, 4 Streatham St, WC1. Hi-tech, licensed Japanese canteen, where the waiters take your orders on hand-held computers. Share long benches and slurp up the huge bowls of noodle soup or stir-fried plates. You'll have to queue, but it moves quickly. Tottenham Court Road tube. Mon–Fri noon–2.30pm & 6–11pm, Sat 1–3.30pm & 6–11pm.

Wren at St James's, 197 Piccadilly, SW1. Veggie and wholefood café by the side of the church. Piccadilly Circus tube. Mon–Sat 8am–7pm, Sun 10am–5pm.

African and Middle Eastern

Calabash, Africa Centre, 38 King St, WC2. Centrally placed basement joint, serving hearty quantities of authentic African food. Moderate. Covent Garden tube. Mon–Fri 12.30–3pm & 6pm–midnight, Sat 6pm–midnight.

La Reash Cous-Cous House, 23–24 Greek St, W1 (☎0171/439 1063). Mainly Moroccan, but with a choice of Middle Eastern *meze* dishes. Huge portions of couscous, both meat and vegetarian. Inexpensive to moderate. Leicester Square tube. Daily noon–midnight.

Osmani, 46 Inverness Street, NW1 (☎0171/267 4682). Titchy North African restaurant with engaging staff and great food. Moderate. Camden Town tube. Mon–Fri 12.30–2.30pm & 7–11pm, Sat & Sun 7–11pm.

American and Mexican/Tex-Mex

Café Pacifico, 5 Langley St, WC2 (☎0171/379 7728). Rated as the best Mexican restaurant in central London, though that isn't much of a title. Fairly quiet during the day, unbelievably noisy in the evening. Good bar. Moderate. Covent Garden or Leicester Square tube. Mon–Sat noon–11.45pm, Sun noon–10.45pm.

Hard Rock Café, 150 Old Park Lane, W1 (☎0171/629 0382). The original "Hard Rock" and the best-known burger joint in town, with permanent queues, loud music and an interior awash with rock memorabilia. Food and drinks are pricey, and quality is questionable, but no one seems to care. Hyde Park Corner tube. Mon–Thurs & Sun 11.30am–12.30am, Fri & Sat 11.30am–1am.

Joe Allen, 13 Exeter St, WC2 (☎0171/836 0651). London branch of the well-known American restaurant group, with the familiar chequered tablecloths and bar-room atmosphere. Burgers are excellent, but you have to ask for them – they are not on the menu. Expensive. Charing Cross or Covent Garden tube. Mon–Sat noon–12.45am, Sun noon–11pm.

Belgian

Belgo Centraal, 50 Earlham St, WC2 (☎0171/813 2233). Hugely popular basement diner-restaurant (with suitably ascetic chairs), where eager waiters in monks' habits dish up Belgian fare and beer. The various price deals are hard to beat – including mussels, frites and a beer for around £5. Covent Garden tube. Inexpensive to moderate. Mon–Fri noon–3pm & 6–11.30pm, Sat noon–11.30pm, Sun noon–10.30pm. The original branch is at 72 Chalk Farm Rd, NW1 (☎0171/267 0718); Chalk Farm tube.

British

Alastair Little, 49 Frith St, W1 (☎0171/734 5183). Austere decor but magnificently inventive cooking, with a menu drawing ideas from Japan and China as well as Europe. Very expensive for dinner, though there's a set lunch for around £25. Leicester Square tube. Mon–Fri noon–3pm & 6–11.30pm, Sat 6–11.30pm.

Bibendum, Michelin House, 81 Fulham Rd (☎0171/581 5817). Magnificent eclectic dishes are served in the upstairs restaurant, one of the country's very best; champagne and exorbitant molluscs are consumed in vast quantities in the downstairs oyster bar. Very expensive. South Kensington tube. Mon–Sat 12.30–2.30pm & 7–11.30pm, Sun 12.30–3pm & 7–10.30pm.

The Criterion, 224 Piccadilly, W1 (☎0171/925 0909). The food is fine, the £10 set menu good value and the decor absolutely dazzling. Moderate to expensive. Piccadilly Circus tube. Mon–Sat noon–11.30pm, Sun noon–5.30pm.

dell'Ugo, 56 Frith St, W1 (☎0171/734 8300). Mediterranean flavours prevail both in the ground-floor café and in the far pricier double-decker restaurant above. A hit with the pace setters of Soho. Inexpensive (in the café) to expensive (upstairs). Leicester Square tube. Mon–Fri noon–3pm & 7pm–midnight, Sat 7pm–midnight.

The Fire Station, 150 Waterloo Rd, SE1 (☎0171/620 2226). The old fire station premises mean plenty of room, but tables are still at a premium, though there's an echoing front bar where you can knock back glasses from the fine wine list while pondering the blackboard menu. Inexpensive. Waterloo tube. Mon–Sat 12.30–2.30pm & 6.30–11.30pm, Sun 12.30–2.30pm; bar open Mon–Sat noon–11pm.

Odette's, 130 Regent's Park Rd, NW1 (☎0171/586 5486). Wide-ranging *cordon bleu* menu, merging Italian, French and even Japanese ideas. Garden at the back and pavement tables in summer. Good wine list. Expensive. Chalk Farm tube. Mon–Fri 12.30–2.30pm & 7–11pm, Sat 7–11pm.

192, 192 Kensington Park Rd, W11 (☎0171/229 0492). Excellent modern-English restaurant, with daily changing menu. Make sure you look your best – staff and clientele are among the most fashionable in London. Moderate to expensive. Ladbroke Grove tube. Daily 12.30–3pm & 6.30–11.30pm.

Chinese/Vietnamese

China City, White Bear Yard, 25 Lisle St, WC2. New restaurant tucked into a little courtyard off Lisle St; fresh and bright, with *dim sum* that's up there with the best and a menu with eminently reasonable prices. Inexpensive. Leicester Square tube. Mon–Sat noon–11.45pm, Sun 11am–11pm.

Chuen Cheng Ku, 17 Wardour St, W1. Massive range of Cantonese dishes; wonderful *dim sum* served up to 6pm. The best dishes are on the Chinese-only menu – ask for the day's special. Moderate. Leicester Square tube. Daily 11am–midnight.

Golden Triangle, 15 Great Newport St, WC2 (☎0171/379 6330). Pleasant, plant-strewn central Vietnamese place with amenable staff and, usually, tables to spare. The menu twists and turns from familiar items – spring rolls, deep-fried squid balls and noodles – through to more interesting Vietnamese specialities. Inexpensive. Leicester Square tube. Daily noon–3pm & 5–11pm.

Mr Kong, 21 Lisle St, WC2 (☎0171/437 7341). Excellent Cantonese food in the heart of Chinatown. Go for the more adventurous "specials" menu. Moderate. Leicester Square tube. Daily noon–1.30am.

Oriental, The Dorchester Hotel, 55 Park Lane, W1 (☎0171/629 8888). Simply the best Chinese restaurant in London, but you'll have to don jacket and tie to taste it. Very expensive. Hyde Park Corner tube. Mon–Fri noon–2.30pm & 7pm–midnight.

Poons, 4 Leicester St and 27 Lisle St (☎0171/437 4549), both WC2 and both Leicester Square tube. The Lisle Street branch, the original *Poons*, is a tatty café quite unlike its smarter Leicester Street offspring, but many think it serves better food. There are other branches in Whiteleys, Queensway (W2) and at 50 Woburn Place (WC1). All inexpensive to moderate. Daily noon–11.30pm.

Poons of Covent Garden, 41 King St, WC2 (☎0171/240 1743). The grander title indicates the culinary distinction of this, the flagship of the Poons empire. Expensive. Covent Garden tube. Daily noon–11.30pm.

Tai Wing Wah, 7–9 Newport Place, WC2 (☎0171/287 2702). A relatively new arrival in Chinatown, already with a good reputation for *dim sum* and politer than average service. Moderate. Leicester Square tube. Mon–Thurs noon–11.30pm, Fri & Sat noon–midnight, Sun 11am–5pm.

East European/Russian

Daquise, 20 Thurloe St, SW7. Something of a cult, with its gloomy Eastern Bloc decor, long-suffering staff and heartily utilitarian Polish food. Good place for a quick bite and a shot of vodka after the South Kensington museums. Inexpensive to moderate. South Kensington tube. Daily 10am–11.30pm.

Gay Hussar, 2 Greek St, W1 (☎0171/437 0973). Nominally Hungarian, but in fact gathering its ideas from all of central Europe, this restaurant has been a Soho institution for years, and claims a longstanding regular clientele. Moderate to expensive. Leicester Square tube. Mon–Sat 12.30–2.30pm & 5.30–10.30pm.

Wódka, 12 St Alban's Grove, W8 (☎0171/937 6513). Perhaps the best choice if you want to experience the best that Polish cuisine has to offer. Watch the bill mount up as you start ladling out the ice-cold flavoured vodkas. Expensive. High Street Kensington tube. Mon–Fri noon–2.30pm & 7–11pm, Sat & Sun 7–11pm.

Fish restaurants

Bentley's, 11–15 Swallow St, W1 (☎0171/734 4756). Creative modern fish cookery in the upstairs restaurant, a simpler (and more entertaining) oyster bar downstairs. Expensive to very expensive. Piccadilly Circus tube. Mon–Fri noon–2.30pm & 6–11pm, Sat 6–11pm.

Café Fish, 39 Panton St, SW1 (☎0171/930 3999). Fishy French-style restaurant (tiger prawns to shark) and wine bar (mussels, fish pie, fish and chips) which opens out onto the pavement in summer. Piccadilly tube. Restaurant; moderate, Mon–Fri noon–3pm & 5.45–11.30pm, Sat 5.45–11.30pm. Wine bar; inexpensive, Mon–Sat 11.30am–11pm.

North Sea Fish Restaurant, 7–8 Leigh St, WC1 (☎0171/387 5892). Top-notch fish and chips in a licensed restaurant heavy on nineteenth-century furnishings. Inexpensive. Russell Square tube. Mon–Sat noon–2.30pm & 5.30–10.30pm.

Sea-Shell, 49–51 Lisson Grove, NW1 (☎0171/723 8703). Already on the tourist circuit, fish and chips don't come much better than this. Inexpensive to moderate. Marylebone tube. Mon–Fri noon–2pm & 5.15–10.30pm, Sat noon–2pm.

French

Bistrot 190, 189 Queen's Gate, SW7. Brasserie classics – stews, sausages, pasta – served with great panache and a hefty price tag. Very popular, but no telephone booking, so expect to queue at the weekend. Expensive. South Kensington tube. Mon–Sat noon–12.30am, Sun noon–11.30pm.

Café Delancey, 3 Delancey St, NW1 (☎0171/387 1985). Spacious Camden brasserie that's always buzzing. Great for breakfast (served all day) and snacks – after dark it transforms into a romantic, candlelit rendezvous. Moderate. Camden Town tube. Daily 8am–midnight.

Café Pelican, 45 St Martin's Lane, W1 (☎0171/379 0309). Popular brasserie with a particularly convincing Parisian-style bar – again, the set meals (from £10) offer the best value. Expensive. Charing Cross tube. Mon–Sat 11am–1am, Sun 11am–10.30pm.

Camden Brasserie, 216 Camden High St, NW1 (☎0171/482 2114). Ever popular north London brasserie, serving reliable char-grilled specials, pasta and French-Med favourites. Moderate. Camden Town tube. Mon–Sat noon–3pm & 6–11.30pm, Sun noon–4.30pm & 5.30–10.30pm.

L'Escargot, 48 Greek St, W1 (☎0171/437 2679). Desperately fashionable with media types; has a New York-style brasserie downstairs and a first-rate French restaurant above. Expensive. Leicester Square tube. Mon–Fri 12.15–2.15pm & 6–11pm, Sat 6–11pm.

Mon Plaisir, 21 Monmouth St, WC2 (☎0171/836 7243). One of London's best imitations of a Parisian bistro, with a good-value set menu and famously chic and *charmant* staff. Expensive. Leicester Square tube. Mon–Fri noon–2pm & 6–11.15pm, Sat 6–11.15pm.

Rotisserie Jules, 6–8 Bute St, SW7. Friendly joint where grilled chicken and chips are the speciality, served speedily. Bring your own booze. Inexpensive. South Kensington tube. Daily 11.30am–11.30pm.

RSJ, 13a Coin St, SE1 (☎0171/928 4554). Regularly high standards of Anglo-French cooking make this a good spot for a meal after an evening at a South Bank theatre or concert hall. Good brasserie in the basement. Moderate (brasserie) to expensive (restaurant). Waterloo tube. Mon–Fri noon–2pm & 6–11pm, Sat 6–11pm.

St Quentin, 243 Brompton Rd, SW3 (☎0171/581 5131). Handy for the South Kensington museums, this bistro-ish French restaurant serves good set-price lunches and dinners. Moderate to expensive. South Kensington tube. Mon–Sat noon–3pm & 7–11.30pm, Sun noon–3.30pm & 6.30–11pm.

Le Tire Bouchon, 6 Upper James St, W1 (☎0171/437 5348). Small, friendly, workaday bistro just off Soho's Golden Square – choose from the ever changing specials or dig into the cheaper set menu. Moderate. Piccadilly Circus tube. Mon–Fri 8am–midnight.

Greek

Jimmy's, 23 Frith St, W1. Basement Greek restaurant that's long been part of the Soho cheap eating scene – mammoth portions of serviceable Greek-Cypriot food with chips. Inexpensive. Leicester Square tube. Mon–Sat 12.30–3pm & 5.30–11pm.

Mega-Kalamaras, 76–78 Inverness Mews, W2 (☎0171/727 9122). The best Greek restaurant in London, serving dishes you won't come across at many others. The menu is in Greek only, though the waiters provide translations; there's a smaller and cheaper branch, *Micro-Kalamaras*, at no. 66 in the same street. Moderate. Bayswater tube. Mon–Sat 7pm–midnight.

Nontas, 14–16 Camden High St, NW1 (☎0171/387 4579). Very good, slightly upmarket Camden Town Greek restaurant with a deservedly popular bar. Inexpensive. Camden Town tube. Mon–Sat noon–2.30pm & 6–11.30pm.

Indian, Bangladeshi and Nepalese

Diwnana Bhel Poori House, 121 Drummond St, NW1 (☎0171/387 5556). Unlicensed, south Indian restaurant, specializing in dosas, bhel poori and vegetarian thalis. Not a place for a night out, but food and prices usually manage to please. Inexpensive. Euston tube. Daily noon–11.30pm.

Gopal's of Soho, 12 Bateman St, W1 (☎0171/434 1621). Unusual nouvelle Indian food of the highest quality. Moderate to expensive. Daily noon–3pm & 6–11.30pm. Piccadilly Circus tube.

Great Nepalese, 48 Eversholt St, NW1 (☎0171/388 6737). One of very few places in London serving genuine spicy Nepalese dishes. Moderate. Euston tube. Daily noon–2.30pm & 6–11.45pm.

Haandi, 161 Drummond St, NW1 (☎0171/383 4557). South Indian vegetarian food is the dominant tendency in this street; the Haandi is a first-rate carnivorous exception. Inexpensive. Warren Street tube. Mon–Sat noon–2.30pm & 6–11.30pm.

Khan's, 13–15 Westbourne Grove, W2 (☎0171/727 5420). Long-established, huge and crowded Indian restaurant, with palms, pillars and pastel blues. Unexceptional food, often lousy service, but great atmosphere. Inexpensive. Bayswater or Queensway tube. Daily noon–3pm & 6–11.45pm.

Mandeer, 21 Hanway Place, W1 (☎0171/323 0660). Well-known central vegetarian restaurant with good-value buffet lunch. Inexpensive to moderate. Mon–Sat noon–3pm & 5.30–10pm. Tottenham Court Road tube.

Namaste, 30 Alie St, E1 (☎0171/488 9242). An award-winning chef has secured the popularity of this East-End Indian, where the menu is a touch more varied than in many of its rivals. Moderate. Aldgate East tube. Mon–Fri noon–3pm & 6–11pm, Sat 7–10pm.

Nazrul, 130 Brick Lane, E1 (☎0171/247 2505). The unlicensed *Nazrul* is among the cheapest of the Brick Lane cafés, drawing a student crowd. Inexpensive. Aldgate East tube. Daily noon–3pm & 5.30pm–midnight, Fri & Sat 5.30pm–1am.

Planet Poppadom, 366 King's Rd, SW3 (☎0171/823 3369). Trendy balti house-brasserie bringing good, quick meals to the King's Road. Choose your own ingredients and hotness. Inexpensive. Sloane Square tube. Mon–Wed 4pm–midnight, Thurs–Sun noon–midnight.

Italian

Amalfi, 29–31 Old Compton St, W1 (☎0171/437 7284). Bright and good-value Soho eatery that's been around for years – whether you want pasta, pizza, meat and fish, or coffee and a cake at a pavement table, there'll be something to tempt you. Inexpensive. Leicester Square tube. Mon–Sat 9am–11pm, Sun 9am–10pm.

Arts Theatre Café, 6 Great Newport St (☎0171/497 8014). Excellent jazz- and blues-washed North Italian café-restaurant in the dimly lit theatre basement, serving a set-price three-course menu that's one of central London's culinary bargains. Inexpensive. Leicester Square tube. Mon–Fri noon–11pm, Sat 6–11pm.

Eagle, 159 Farringdon Rd, EC1 (☎0171/837 1353). Technically a pub, frequented by a loyal crowd of journos and vocal Soho types on an away day tucking into authentic regional Italian food. The day's dishes are chalked up on the board. Inexpensive. Farringdon tube. Mon–Fri 12.30–2.30pm & 6.30–10.30pm.

Peasant, 240 St John St, EC1 (☎0171/336 7726). The second of this area's Cinderella pubs that's forsaken traditional drinking and concentrates on serving up quality Italian food at decent prices. Unlike the nearby Eagle, you can book tables, too. Moderate. Angel or Farringdon tube. Mon–Fri noon–2.30pm & 5.30–11pm, Sat 5.30–11pm.

La Quercia d'Oro, 16a Endell St, WC2 (☎0171/379 5108). Shabby, cheerful, basic trattoria, with big rustic portions and a loud, boisterous crowd. The daily specials on the blackboard are the things to go for – but expect quantity, rather than quality. Moderate. Covent Garden tube. Mon–Fri noon–2.45pm & 6–11.30pm, Sat 6–11.30pm.

PIZZAS

Kettner's, 29 Romilly St, W1. Grand old place with high ceilings and a pianist, though actually part of the *Pizza Express* chain and consequently cheaper than you'd expect from the ambience. Inexpensive to moderate. Leicester Square tube. Mon–Sat 11am–11pm.

Pizza Express, 10 Dean St, W1 (☎0171/437 9595); 30 Coptic St, WC1 (☎0171/636 3232); and numerous other branches all over London. Easily the best of the pizza chains, doing a good line in thin-crust pizzas and great house wine. The Dean Street branch has regular live jazz in the basement; the Coptic Street one is sited in a former dairy. Inexpensive. Daily noon–midnight. Both Tottenham Court Road tube.

Pizzeria Condotti, 4 Mill St, W1 (☎0171/499 1308). Another *Pizza Express* offshoot serving some of the capital's best pizzas in upscale surroundings – reserve at lunchtimes. Moderate. Oxford Circus tube. Mon–Sat 11.30am–midnight.

Japanese and Korean

Benkei, 19 Lower Marsh, SE1 (☎0171/401 2343). Bargain backstreet Japanese diner with a short menu of classics. Great-value set lunches, too. Inexpensive. Waterloo tube. Mon–Fri noon–3pm & 6–10.30pm, Sat 5–10.30pm.

Ikkyu, 67 Tottenham Court Rd, W1 (☎0171/436 6169). Basement Japanese restaurant, good enough for a quick lunch (set meals run £5–10) or a more elaborate dinner. Either way, prices are infinitely more reasonable than elsewhere in the capital, and the food is tasty and authentic. Inexpensive to moderate. Goodge Street tube. Mon–Fri 12.30–2.30pm & 6–10.30pm, Sun 6–10.30pm.

Jin, 16 Bateman St, W1 (☎0171/734 0908). Absolutely authentic Korean food, including great *bulgogi* grilled at a barbecue in the centre of your table. Set meals are pretty good value, but you needn't be frightened by the menu. Moderate. Leicester Square tube. Mon–Sat noon–3pm & 6–11pm.

Spanish and Portuguese

Galicia, 323 Portobello Rd, W10 (☎0181/969 3539). Groovy Notting Hill tapas bar-restaurant, specializing in Galician (northwest Spanish) dishes – octopus is a favourite. Inexpensive to moderate. Ladbroke Grove tube. Tues–Sun noon–2.30pm & 7–11pm; tapas bar Tues–Sun noon–11.30pm.

O Fado, 49 Beauchamp Place, SW3 (☎0171/589 3002). Probably the oldest Portuguese restaurant in London, which speaks volumes for its authenticity. It can get rowdy when the family parties are in, but that's half the enjoyment. Moderate. Knightsbridge or South Kensington tube. Mon–Sat noon–3pm & 6.30pm–12.30am, Sun noon–3pm & 6.30–11.30pm.

Sevilla Mia, 22 Hanway St, W1 (☎0171/637 3756). Hard-to-find basement bar which throbs most nights with Spaniards and their flamenco singing and dancing buddies. The tapas is almost a side issue – and if you come after 8pm or so there'll be nowhere to sit anyway – but it's actually very good. Inexpensive. Tottenham Court Road tube. Mon–Sat 6pm–1am, Sun 7pm–midnight.

Thai, Malaysian and Indonesian

Ben's Thai, Warrington Hotel, 93 Warrington Crescent, W9 (☎0171/266 3134). Worth the trudge from the tube station, as this is top-class Thai food at bargain prices above a highly attractive pub. Inexpensive to moderate. Mon–Sat noon–2.30pm & 6–10pm, Sun noon–2.30pm & 7–9.30pm. Maida Vale tube.

Jakarta, 150 Shaftesbury Ave, WC2 (☎0171/836 2644). All the usual Indonesian and Malaysian dishes at decent prices – the fish and seafood dishes are particularly good. Set lunches around a fiver or so are worth checking out. Moderate. Tottenham Court Road tube. Mon–Sat 6–11.30pm, Sun 5.30–10.30pm.

Melati, 21 Great Windmill St, W1 (☎0171 437 2745). One of the best places in the centre for Malaysian and Indonesian food, with excellent prawn or meat satays and a few more unusual dishes you don't often see. Moderate. Piccadilly Circus tube. Mon–Thurs & Sun noon–11.30pm, Sat & Sun noon–12.30am.

Satay Stick, 6 Dering St, W1 (☎0171/629 1346). There's only one thing to have in a restaurant with a name like this, and it's the best reason to come – the succulent satay is terrific. This place attracts a lunchtime Malaysian crowd, so it's very much the real thing. Moderate. Oxford Circus tube. Mon–Fri noon–3pm & 6–10pm, Sat noon–9pm.

Sri Siam, 14 Old Compton St, W1 (☎0171/434 3544). High-class Thai restaurant, with an unusually extensive list of vegetarian options. Moderate. Leicester Square tube. Mon–Sat noon–3pm & 6–11pm, Sun 6–10.30pm.

Turkish

Efes, 80 Great Titchfield St, W1 (☎0171/636 1953). Vast Turkish kebab restaurant, always packed. Reliably tasty hunks of meat and friendly service. Moderate. Oxford Circus or Great Portland Street tube. Mon–Sat noon–11.30pm.

Sofra, 36 Tavistock St, WC2 (☎0171/240 3773). Good central spot with a bargain set meal and *meze* assortment. Choosing from the menu is more expensive, but the food's good and there's plenty of room to enjoy it – even a conservatory upstairs. Moderate. Covent Garden tube. Daily noon–midnight.

Drinking

Virtually every street in central London has its **pub** and, although you'll find pleasanter places in the outer neighbourhoods, there are one or two watering holes in the tourist zones that retain an element of character. Perhaps the greatest concentrations of unspoilt pubs within a tube hop of the centre are to be found on the east side of town, between Aldwych and the City – some can be uncomfortably packed on weekdays before 8pm, but after that, when the City types have gone home, they are far more appealing.

For drinking beyond the standard 11pm last orders, there are a few late-night bars, chiefly in the West End (Soho especially), though these tend to be cliquey places, which sell the latest overpriced bottled beer. London's **clubs** (see p.134) are generally a lot more fun, though there you can expect to pay even more for your drink than you'll have become used to in London's pubs. Due to a recent relaxation of the English licensing laws, pubs are now allowed to open all day on Sundays. Most pubs in London have taken advantage of the changes and open from 11am–11pm all week. You may find, however, that some of the less busy establishments stick with the old Sunday hours of noon–3pm and 7–10.30pm.

Soho and around

Argyll Arms, 18 Argyll St, W1. One of the more pleasant places in the immediate orbit of Oxford Street, with original etched-glass partitions and wood fittings. Oxford Circus tube.

Coach & Horses, 29 Greek St, W1. Long-standing – and, for once, little-changed – haunt of the ghosts of old Soho, nightclubbers and art students from nearby St Martin's college. Leicester Square tube.

Dog & Duck, 18 Bateman St, W1. Tiny Soho pub that retains much of its old character, beautiful Victorian tiling and mosaics, and a loyal clientele that often includes jazz musicians from nearby Ronnie Scott's club. Leicester Square or Tottenham Court Road tube.

The Edge, 11 Soho Square, W1. A smartly dressed gay and straight crowd hang out at this newly expanded Soho drinking hole. Tottenham Court Road tube. Mon–Sat open til 1am.

ICA Bar, 12 Carlton House Terrace (The Mall), SW1. You have to be a member to drink at the ICA bar – but anyone can join, at £1.50 a day. It's a cool drinking venue, with a noir dress code observed by the arty crowd and cute bar staff. Charing Cross tube. Tues–Sat open till 1am.

Mulligans, 4 Cork St, W1. A fine Irish pub with an odd mix of clientele – Cork Street gallery staff and Irish lads – and the best Guinness in London. Green Park or Piccadilly tube.

Riki-Tik, 23–24 Bateman St, W1. Very trendy bar with futuristic decor and friendly staff. Tottenham Court Road tube. Mon–Sat open till 1am. Charges £3 for entry after 11pm.

Covent Garden and the Strand

Africa Centre, 38 King St, WC2. Noisy, convivial basement bar, attracting Africans and Africaphiles. The beer's awful but that's to miss the point. Covent Garden tube. Mon–Sat 5.30–11pm.

The Coal Hole, 91 Strand, WC2. Former coal heavers' hang-out, next to the Savoy hotel. There's a nice gallery upstairs and a cellar bar down. Charing Cross/Covent Garden tube. Closed Sun.

Gordon's, Villiers St, WC2. Cave-like wine bar right next door to Charing Cross station. The excellent and varied wine list, decent buffet food and genial atmosphere have made it a favourite with the neighbourhood's office workers. Closed at weekends. Charing Cross or Embankment tube.

Lamb & Flag, 33 Rose St, WC2. Busy and highly atmospheric pub, tucked away down an alley between Garrick and Floral streets, where John Dryden was attacked in 1679. Leicester Square tube.

Mars, 59 Endell St, WC2. Gaudi meets Gauguin in this wonderful little designer-squat bar. It's run in very relaxed fashion and features weird bottled beers, flavoured vodkas, a mighty fine menu and a couple of tables outside in summer. Covent Garden tube. June–Aug Mon–Sat 5pm–midnight, Sept–May Mon–Sat noon–midnight.

Punch & Judy, 40 The Market, WC2. Horribly mobbed and expensive, but unbeatable location with a balcony overlooking the Piazza – and a nice cellar bar. Covent Garden tube.

Salisbury, 90 St Martin's Lane, WC2. This is one of the most beautifully preserved Victorian pubs in the capital, with cut, etched and engraved windows, bronze figures and lincrusta ceiling. Overzealous doormen and overcrowding the only drawbacks. Leicester Square tube.

Bloomsbury and Holborn

Cittie of York, 22 High Holborn, WC1. Upstairs is the grand quasi-medieval wine hall, with cubicles once the preserve of lawyers and their clients; below is the cellar, perfect for savouring the distinctive Sam Smith's bitter. Chancery Lane tube. Mon–Fri 11.30am–11pm, Sat 11.30am–3pm & 5.30–11pm.

Museum Tavern, 49 Great Russell St, WC1. Large and characterful old pub, right opposite the main entrance to the British Museum. Tottenham Court Road or Russell Square tube.

Princess Louise, 208 High Holborn, WC1. Old-fashioned place, with high plasterwork ceilings, lots of glass, brass and mahogany, and a good range of real ales. Holborn tube.

The City

Blackfriar, 174 Queen Victoria St, EC4. A gorgeous, utterly original pub, with Art Nouveau marble friezes of boozy monks. Handy for the City sights. Blackfriars tube. Mon & Tues 11.30am–10pm, Wed–Fri 11.30am–11pm.

Fox & Anchor, 115 Charterhouse St, EC1. Smithfield market pub famous for its early opening hours and huge breakfasts served 7–10.30am. Farringdon tube. Mon–Fri 7am–8pm, Sat 8am–11pm, closed Sun.

Hamilton Hall, Liverpool Street Station, EC2. Cavernous, gilded, former ballroom of Great Eastern Hotel, adorned with nudes and chandeliers. Packed out with City commuters tanking up before the train home, but a great place nonetheless.

Lamb, Leadenhall Market, EC3. A great pub right in the middle of Leadenhall Market (close to Lloyd's of London) with pricey but excellent roast beef sandwiches. Liverpool Street tube and train station. Mon–Fri 11am–9pm.

Ye Olde Cheshire Cheese, Wine Office Court, off Fleet St, EC4. A famous seventeenth-century watering hole, with several snug, dark panelled bars and real fires. Popular with tourists, but by no means exclusively so. Temple or Blackfriars tube.

The East End

Dickens Inn, St Katherine's Way, E1. Eighteenth-century timber-framed warehouse transported on wheels from its original site. A remarkable building, but very firmly on the tourist trail. Tower Hill tube.

Prospect of Whitby, 57 Wapping Wall, E1. Flagstone floor, cobbled courtyard and river views. Wapping tube. Mon–Sat 11.30am–3pm & 5.30–11pm, Sun noon–3pm & 7–10.30pm.

Town of Ramsgate, Wapping High St, E1. Dark, narrow medieval pub – located by Wapping Old Stairs which once led down to Execution Dock – with a long and colourful history. Wapping tube.

North London

Flask, 14 Flask Walk, NW3. Convivial Hampstead local, which retains its original Victorian snob screen, serving good food and real ale. Hampstead tube.

Flask, 77 Highgate West Hill, N6. Idyllically situated at the heart of Highgate village green, with a rambling low-ceilinged interior and a summer terrace. Highgate tube.

Fusilier & Firkin, 7–8 Chalk Farm Rd, NW1. Another Firkin pub, right opposite Camden Lock market. Live music Sat afternoons, and heaving with people all weekend. Camden Town tube.

Holly Bush, 22 Holy Mount, NW3. A lovely old gas-lit pub, tucked away in the steep backstreets of Hampstead Village. Hampstead tube. Mon–Fri 11am–3pm & 5.30–11pm, Sat 6–11pm, Sun noon–3pm & 7–10.30pm.

King's Head, 115 Upper St, N1. Busy theatre pub in the heart of Islington with regular live music, a useful late licence, and a bizarre affectation of quoting prices in pre-decimal money. Angel tube.

Waterloo and Southwark

George Inn, 77 Borough High St. London's only surviving coaching inn, dating from the seventeenth century and now owned by the National Trust. Borough or London Bridge tube.

National Film Theatre Bar, South Bank. The only riverfront bar on the South Bank between Westminster and Blackfriars bridges – which is a scandal, considering the views. Lots of outside seating and a congenial crowd. Waterloo tube.

Kensington and Chelsea

Beach Blanket Babylon, 45 Ledbury Rd, W11. Worth a visit if only for the freaked-out decor and the beautiful W11 types who frequent it. Notting Hill tube.

Bunch of Grapes, 207 Brompton Rd, SW3. This High Victorian pub, complete with snob screens, is the perfect place for a post-museum pint. Knightsbridge or South Kensington tube.

Frog and Firkin, 41 Tavistock Crescent. Another of the excellent Firkin chain of pubs; it is handy for Portobello Market and is decorated with an impressive array of hats. Westbourne Park tube.

Grenadier, 18 Wilton Row, SW1. Wellington's local (his horse block survives outside) and his officers' mess; the original pewter bar survives and the Bloody Marys are special. Hyde Park Corner tube. Mon–Sat noon–3pm & 5–11pm, Sun noon–3pm & 7–10.30pm.

Orange Brewery, 37 Pimlico Rd, SW1. Pimlico may be posh, but this is a fairly down-to-earth boozer with its very own micro-brewery. Pimlico tube.

Paviour's Arms, Page St, SW1. Untouched Art Deco pub, close to the Tate Gallery and offering Thai food. Pimlico tube.

Greenwich

Cutty Sark, Lassell St, SE10. The nicest riverside pub in Greenwich – a sixteenth-century building, yet less touristy than the *Trafalgar Tavern* (which is a couple of minutes walk further on, following the river). Maze Hill BR station.

Richard I, Royal Hill, SE10. Popular Greenwich local tucked away off the main drag. Good beer and a garden make it an ideal post-market retreat – and if it's too crowded the *Fox & Hounds* next door is good too. Greenwich BR station.

Trafalgar Tavern, Park Row, SE10. Great riverside position and a mention in Dickens' *Our Mutual Friend* have made this Regency-style inn a firm tourist favourite. Good whitebait and other snacks. Maze Hill BR station.

Chiswick to Richmond

Blue Anchor, 13 Lower Mall, W6. First of Hammersmith's riverside pubs, with a boaty theme and a beautiful pewter bar; most people sit outside and enjoy the river though. Hammersmith tube.

Dove, 19 Upper Mall, W6. Old, riverside pub with literary associations and the smallest back bar in the UK (4ft x 7ft). Ravenscourt Park tube.

White Cross Hotel, Water Lane, Richmond. Closer to the river than its rivals, with a back garden and average pub food. Richmond tube.

Nightlife

On any night of the week London offers a vast range of things to do after dark, ranging from top-flight opera and theatre to clubs with a life span of a couple of nights. The **listings magazine** *Time Out*, which comes out every Wednesday, is essential if you want to get the most out of London, giving full details of prices and access, plus previews and reviews.

Recession may have taken its toll, but London is still a seven-days-a-week party town and maintains its status as the **dance music** capital of Europe and favourite destination of visiting DJs from all over the world. Recent relaxations in attitudes towards late-night licensing have allowed many venues to open until 6am or even later, which has accelerated the move from illegal warehouse parties to purpose-renovated legitimate venues. In the last couple of years the trend has been towards greater musical fragmentation – house is still the dominant club music, but the term covers anything from US garage and deep house, through European trance-techno to the homegrown styles of hard house and the super-fast hardcore/jungle (a reggae offshoot). The jazz and acid jazz scene still thrives, and in addition to dancehall reggae and ragga, the US-led fusion of swingbeat and hip hop is gaining ground with young black kids.

Many of the best events are one-offs or itinerant clubs that rely on word of mouth or mailing lists for publicity – check dance magazines such as *DJ* or *Mixmag*, and pick up the flyers that litter the counters of record shops such as *Black Market* in D'Arblay Street, *Downtown* in Dean Street or *Quaff* at 2 Silver Place (all in Soho). Prices vary enormously, with small midweek nights starting at under £5 and large weekend events charging as much as £25 – around £10 would be the average for a Saturday night, but bear in mind that the mark-up on drinks is phenomenal.

The **live music** scene is amazingly diverse, encompassing all varieties of rock music, from big names on tour at the city's main venues, through to a network of indie and pub bands in more intimate surroundings. There's a fair slice of world music, too, especially African, Latin, Caribbean bands and a smattering of clubs and pubs devoted to Irish music and English roots. Entry prices for gigs run much the same as clubs, though bar prices tend to be lower.

Though a stroll through the West End can create the impression that Lloyd-Webber musicals and revivals of clapped-out plays have a stranglehold on London's **theatres**, the capital is less staid than it might appear. Apart from the classic productions of the major repertory companies, there's a large fringe circuit, staging often provocative pieces in venues that range from proper independent auditoriums to back rooms in pubs. **Cinema** is not as adventurous as it is in some European capitals, with the number of repertory houses diminishing steadily, but there's a decent spread of screenings of general release and re-run films each night of the week. With two opera houses and several well-equipped concert halls, London's programme of **classical**

music is excellent, and the annual Proms season represents Europe's most accessible festival of highbrow music. For most plays and concerts you should be able to get a seat for less than £15 in the West End, or less at venues off the main circuit.

Clubs and discos

Bagley's, King's Cross Goods Yard, off York Way, King's Cross, N1. Vast warehouse-style venue. The perfect place for enormous raves, with a different DJ or ambience in each room. King's Cross tube.

Bar Rumba, 36 Shaftesbury Ave, W1. New West End venue with a programme of all things Latin, jazzy and funky. Live shows too. Piccadilly Circus tube.

Café de Paris, 3 Coventry St, WC2. Following several dark years, the Café has been restored to its old glories and reopened for the city's trendy set. Leicester Square tube.

The Fridge, Town Hall Parade, Brixton, SW2. South London's big night out with a musical policy varying from funk to garage; hosts one of London's biggest gay nights on Tuesdays. Brixton tube.

Gardening Club, 4 Covent Garden Piazza, WC2. Small, trendy and nearly always reliable for a good night's clubbing. Covent Garden tube.

Gossips, 69 Dean St, W1. Dingy basement that seems to have been running forever. Different sounds each night of the week. Tottenham Court Road or Leicester Square tube.

Hippodrome, Charing Cross Road, WC2. London's leading neon palace and a byword for tackiness. Leicester Square tube.

Iceni, 11 White Horse St, W1. Newish club, nicely decked out on two floors and attracting a slightly older crowd. Music from funk and rap to house. Green Park tube.

Maximus, 14 Leicester Square, WC2. Once a super-tacky disco, now playing host to hip club nights. Leicester Square tube.

Ministry Of Sound, 103 Gaunt St, SE1. Large club based on New York's legendary Paradise Garage. The sound system is the best around but the club's past its peak of hipness now. Elephant and Castle tube.

Raw, 112a Great Russell St, WC1. Very clubby and kitsch; bizarre dress is advised. Its Saturday Billion Dollar Babes night is always a sell-out. Tottenham Court Road tube.

Subterania, 12 Acklam Rd, W10. Worth a visit for its diverse (if a tad dressy) club nights on Fridays and Saturdays – if you can get in; also has live music. Ladbroke Grove tube.

UK, Buckhold Rd, SW18. They don't advertise that this is part of Wandsworth's ugly Arndale Centre, but nonetheless it's one of the newest big clubs in town, specializing in cutting-edge British DJs. Wandsworth Town BR from Waterloo.

Velvet Underground, 143 Charing Cross Road, WC2. Very cool, velvet-dripping interior design; happy, housey tunes. Tottenham Court Road tube.

Wag, 35 Wardour St, W1. A hot spot in the mid-eighties, now in need of a major overhaul but still going strong. Piccadilly Circus tube.

Live venues

Academy, 211 Stockwell Rd, SW9. Massive Victorian hall used for concerts and club nights. Brixton tube.

Africa Centre, 38 King St, WC2. African-flavoured music which draws heavily on a London-based African audience. Covent Garden tube.

Astoria, 157 Charing Cross Rd, W1. One of London's best-used venues – a large balconied theatre that has live bands and clubs. Tottenham Court Road tube.

Blue Note, 57 Coronet St, N1. Still one of the trendiest jazz places. Also features African and Latin music. Old Street tube.

Borderline, Orange Yard, Manette St, W1. Intimate venue with diverse musical policy. Good place to catch new bands; also has club nights. Tottenham Court Road tube.

The Forum, 9–17 Highgate Rd, NW5. Perhaps the capital's best medium-sized venue – large enough to attract established bands, but also a prime spot for newer talent. Kentish Town tube.

The Grand, Clapham Junction, St John's Hill, SW11. A grand old theatre, now exclusively a rock venue. Clapham Junction BR from Victoria or Waterloo.

Jazz Café, 5 Parkway, NW1. Slick modern jazz venue with an adventurous booking policy. Camden Town tube.

The Marquee, 105 Charing Cross Rd, W1. Though relocated from the Wardour Street site where the Rolling Stones and innumerable others made their name, this is still one of London's top venues for up-and-coming bands. Tottenham Court Road tube.

Mean Fiddler, 28a Harlesden High St, NW10. Small, rather out-of-the-way venue, with eclectic policy ranging from folk to rock. Willesden Junction tube.

100 Club, 100 Oxford St, W1. After a brief spell as a stage for punk bands, the *100 Club* is back to what it used to be – an unpretentious and inexpensive jazz venue. Tottenham Court Road tube.

Ronnie Scott's, 47 Frith St, W1. The most famous jazz club in London – small, smoky and rather precious. Nonetheless, it's still the place for top-line names. Leicester Square tube.

606 Club, 90 Lots Rd, SW10. London's newest all-jazz venue, located off the untrendy part of the King's Road. Fulham Broadway tube.

Underworld, 174 Camden High St, NW1. Labyrinthine venue, with sporadic club nights; good for new bands. Camden Town tube.

ULU, Manning Hall, Malet St, W1. The best of London's university venues, with an exceptionally cheap bar. Russell Square tube.

Weavers Arms, 98 Newington Green Rd, N1. Intimate pub venue with folk, blues or country bands nightly. Highbury and Islington tube.

Wembley Arena, Empire Way. Main venue for mega-bands. Wembley Park tube.

Gay and lesbian bars and clubs

The **gay scene** in London is livelier than almost anywhere else in Europe, with a vast range of venues from quiet bars to cruisy clubs and frenetic discos – Soho is the rising "gay village", focused on Old Compton Street. Apart from *Time Out*, you should check the up-to-the-minute listings in *Capital Gay* and *The Pink Paper*, weekly free newspapers available in all the places listed below. An excellent source of information on all aspects of gay London is the *London Lesbian and Gay Switchboard* (☎0171/837 7324), which operates around the clock.

Angel, 65 Graham St, N1. Relaxed gay café-bar, attracting a youngish crowd. Angel tube.

The Bell, 257 Pentonville Rd, N1. Popular pub, attracting a mixed crowd. King's Cross tube.

The Black Cap, 171 Camden High St, NW1. North London gay institution – a big venue on the drag scene. Camden Town tube.

Brompton's, 294 Old Brompton Rd, SW5. Long-established gay men's bar, pulling a mixture of tourists, local yuppies and clones. Earl's Court tube.

Compton's of Soho, 53 Old Compton St, W1. Welcoming, long-standing gay pub that has seen a dozen or so new gay cafés, bars and shops grow up around it. Leicester Square tube.

Duke of Clarence, 140 Rothefield St, N1. A down-to-earth women's bar with pool tables and a beer garden. Angel or Highbury and Islington tube.

Fanny's, 305a North End Rd, W14. Predominantly female bar with mixed, bisexual and TV/TS nights, lesbian *Blind Date*, etc. West Kensington tube.

The Fridge, Town Hall Parade, Brixton, SW2. The regular Tuesday-night *Daisy Chain* is one of London's wildest gay and lesbian raves. Brixton tube.

Heaven, under the arches, Villiers St, WC2. A vast complex under Charing Cross station, this is the city's premier gay club – and has occasional mixed nights too. Charing Cross or Embankment tube.

King William IV, 77 Hampstead High St, NW3. Long-established, unpretentious, friendly north London gay pub. Hamsptead tube.

London Apprentice, 333 Old St, EC1. One of the best-known gay pubs in the city. Very busy, fairly cruisy, with a small dance floor downstairs. Old Street tube.

Market Tavern, Market Towers, 1 Nine Elms Lane, SW8. Most people's choice as the best gay pub in south London, with a large dance floor at the front and a quiet bar at the back. Vauxhall tube.

The Village Soho, 81 Wardour St, W1. New chic "gay village" bar. Leicester Square tube.

Theatre and cinema

London's big two **theatre** companies are the **National Theatre**, performing in three theatres on the South Bank (☎0171/928 2252), and the **Royal Shakespeare Company**, whose productions transfer to the two houses in the Barbican after their run in Stratford (☎0171/638 8891). For a show that's had good reviews, tickets under £10 are difficult to come by at either, but it's always worth ringing their box offices for details of standby deals, which can get you the best seat in the house for as little as £5 if you're a student, otherwise £10. Similar deals are offered by many of London's scores of theatres. Venues with a reputation for challenging productions include the *Almeida*, *Royal Court, Young Vic, Tricycle, The Orange Tree, Riverside Studios* and the *ICA*.

A booth in Leicester Square sells half-price tickets for that day's performances at all the West End theatres, but they specialize in the top end of the price range; the Charing Cross Road and Leicester Square areas also have offices that can get tickets for virtually all shows, but the mark-up can be as high as two hundred percent. Don't buy tickets from touts – their mark-ups are outrageous, and there's no guarantee that the tickets aren't fakes.

Leicester Square and its environs – Piccadilly, Haymarket and Lower Regent Street – have the main concentration of big-screen **cinemas** showing new releases; seats tend to cost upwards of £7. The main repertory cinemas in the centre are the **National Film Theatre** on the South Bank and the **ICA**, both of which charge for day membership on top of the ticket price. After a spate of closures, London has very few other repertory cinemas: the *Everyman* in Hampstead has perhaps the most interesting programmes. There are, however, several excellent independent cinemas for new art-house releases – it's always worth checking what's on at the *Renoir* (Russell Square), the *Gate* (Notting Hill), the *Lumière* (St Martin's Lane) and the *Metro* (Rupert Street, near Leicester Square).

Classical music, opera and dance

For **classical concerts** the principal venue is the **South Bank Centre**, where the biggest names appear at the *Festival Hall*, with more specialized programmes being staged in the *Queen Elizabeth Hall* and *Purcell Room* (all three halls ☎0171/928 8800). Programmes in the concert hall of the **Barbican Centre**, Silk Street (☎0171/638 8891), are too often pitched at the corporate audience, though it has the occasional classy recital; for chamber music, the **Wigmore Hall**, 36 Wigmore St (☎0171/935 2141), is many people's favourite. Tickets for all these venues begin at about £5, with cheap standbys sometimes available to students on the evening of the performance.

From July to September each year, the **Proms** at the **Royal Albert Hall** (☎0171/ 589 8212) feature at least one concert daily, with hundreds of standing seats sold for just a couple of pounds on the night. The acoustics aren't the world's best, but the calibre of the performers is unbeatable, and the programme is a fascinating mix of standards and new or obscure works. The hall is so vast that only megastars like Jessye Norman can pack it out, so if you turn up half an hour before the show starts there should be little risk of being turned away.

The **Royal Opera House**, Covent Garden (☎0171/240 1066), has a reputation for dull productions, expensive star names and inexcusable prices (up to £130) – though a few dozen relatively cheap seats (ie under £20) are sold from 10am on the day of the performance, which means you have to start queuing at 8am in most cases. The **English National Opera** at the *Coliseum*, St Martin's Lane (☎0171/836 3161), has more radical producers and is a more democratic institution – tickets begin at £7 and any unsold seats are released on the day of the performance at greatly reduced prices. All works are sung in English at the *Coliseum*. Be warned, however, that both venues look set to be closed for redevelopment for most of 1996.

In addition to the big two opera houses, smaller halls often stage more innovative productions by touring companies such as *Operafactory* and *Opera North* – the *Queen Elizabeth Hall* is a regular venue. Nowadays the *Royal Opera House* has a better reputation for **ballet** than for singing, as its resident **Royal Ballet Company** can call on the talents of Darcy Bussell and Sylvie Guillem, to name just two of its most glamorous stars. Visiting classical companies also appear regularly at *Sadlers Wells* and the *Coliseum*, and less frequently at the *Royal Albert Hall*. London's **contemporary dance** scene is no less exciting – adventurous programmes are staged at the South Bank and at the *ICA*, as well as at numerous more ad hoc venues.

Listings

Airlines *American Airlines*, 421 Oxford St, W1 (☎0345/789 789); *British Airways*, 156 Regent St, W1 (☎0181/897 4000); *Lufthansa*, 23 Piccadilly, W1 (☎0171/408 0322); *TWA*, 200 Piccadilly, W1 (☎0345/737 747); *Virgin Atlantic*, Virgin Megastore, 14 Oxford St, W1 (☎01293/747 747).

Airport enquiries Gatwick (☎01293/535 353); Heathrow (☎0181/759 4321); London City (☎0171/474 5555); Stansted (☎01279/680 500).

American Express 6 Haymarket, SW1 (☎0171/930 4411).

Bicycle rental *On Your Bike*, 22 Duke St Hill, London Bridge, SE1 (☎0171/378 6669); *Evans*, The Cut, Waterloo, SE1 (☎0171/928 4785).

Books *Foyles*, 119 Charing Cross Rd, WC2, is the best-known London general bookshop but is badly stocked and chaotically organized. Neighbouring *Waterstones* is preferable, as is *Books Etc* across the road and *Dillons*, 82 Gower St, WC1 – the university bookshop. For more radical publications, call in at *Compendium*, 234 Camden High St, NW1. Two of London's best art bookshops are *Shipley*, 70 Charing Cross Rd, and nearby *Zwemmer's*. For maps and travel books, go to *Stanford's*, 12 Long Acre, WC2; *The Travellers' Bookshop*, 25 Cecil Court, WC2; or *The Travel Bookshop*, 13 Blenheim Crescent, W11.

Bus station Long-distance coach services depart from Victoria Coach Station, Buckingham Palace Rd (Victoria tube). *National Express* has ticket offices here and at 13 Regent St (timetable info ☎0171/730 0202). European services are operated by *Eurolines*, 52 Grosvenor Gardens, SW1 (☎0171/730 8235).

Car rental Best rates are at *Holiday Autos,* 25 Savile Row, W1 (☎0171/491 1111). The big firms have outlets all over London; ring their central offices to find the nearest one: *Avis* (☎0181/848 8733), *Hertz* (☎0181/679 1799), *Europcar* (☎0345/222 525).

Dentist 24-hr emergency dental service (☎0181/302 8106).

Embassies *Australia*, Australia House, The Strand, WC2 (☎0171/379 4334); *Canada*, 1 Grosvenor Square, W1 (☎0171/258 6600); *Ireland*, 17 Grosvenor Place, SW1 (☎0171/235 2171); *Netherlands*, 38 Hyde Park Gate, SW7 (☎0171/584 5040); *New Zealand*, New Zealand House, 80 Haymarket, SW1 (☎0171/930 8422); *USA*, 5 Upper Grosvenor St, W1 (☎0171/499 9000).

Exchange Shopping areas such as Oxford Street and Covent Garden are littered with private-exchange offices, and there are 24-hr booths at the biggest central tube stations, but their rates are always worse than the banks. Oxford Street, Regent Street and Piccadilly are where you'll find the major branches of all the main banks.

Football London's two top clubs are Tottenham Hotspur, aka Spurs, who play at White Hart Lane (☎0181/365 5050; White Hart Lane BR) and Arsenal, who play at Highbury (☎0171/354 5404; Arsenal tube). You've more chance of getting a ticket for a Premier League game at Chelsea (☎0171/385 5545; Fulham Broadway tube), Queen's Park Rangers (☎0181/749 5744; Shepherd's Bush tube), West Ham (☎0181/472 3322; Upton Park tube) or Wimbledon (☎0181/771 8841; Selhurst Park BR), who play at the stadium of the recently relegated Crystal Palace.

Guided Tours Standard **bus tours** are run by *London Transport Sightseeing Tours* and dozens of rival companies, their open-top double-decker buses setting off every 30min from Victoria station, Trafalgar Square, Piccadilly and other conspicuous spots. Most tours take approximately 90min and cost around £8. Alternatively, you can save yourself the money and the inane commentary by hopping on a real London bus – the #11 will take you past the Houses of Parliament, up Whitehall, along the Strand and on to St Paul's.

Walking tours are infinitely more appealing, covering a relatively small area in much greater detail, mixing solid historical facts with juicy anecdotes; walks on offer range from a literary pub crawl around Bloomsbury to a roam around the remains of the Jewish East End – you'll find them all listed in *Time Out*. Many are organized by *Original London Walks* (☎0171/624 3978), which even offers a Beatles tour, taking you to such famous places as the Abbey Road pedestrian crossing near the EMI studios, which has attracted a steady flow of tourists ever since the Fab Four posed on it for the *Abbey Road* album cover, one sunny morning in August 1969. Most walking tours cost £3–4 and take around two hours.

Hospitals The most central hospitals with 24-hr emergency units are: Guy's, St Thomas St, SE1 (☎0171/955 5000); St Thomas's, Lambeth Palace Rd (☎0171/928 9292); University College, Gower St, W1 (☎0171/387 9300); and the Westminster Hospital, Dean Ryle St, SW1 (☎0181/746 8000).

Left luggage Facilities at London train stations were curtailed in the wake of recent terrorist incidents, and it is impossible to predict when a full service will be resumed. The normal hours are as follows, but you should be prepared to be directed to another station: Charing Cross daily 6.30am–10.30pm; Euston daily 24hr; King's Cross Mon–Sat 7am–8.45pm, Sun 8am–8.45pm; Paddington daily 7am–midnight; Victoria daily 7.15am–10pm; Waterloo Mon–Sat 6.30am–11pm.

London Transport enquiries 24-hr information on ☎0171/222 1234.

Lost property At the train stations: Charing Cross (☎0171/922 6061), Euston (☎0171/922 6477), King's Cross (☎0171/922 9081), Liverpool St (☎0171/922 9158), Paddington (☎0171/922 6773), St Pancras (☎0171/922 6478), Victoria (☎0171/922 6216) and Waterloo (☎0171/922 6135). London transport buses and tube ☎0171/486 2496. Gatwick airport ☎01293/503 162. Heathrow airport ☎0181/745 7727.

Markets *Camden*, Camden High St to Chalk Farm Rd – mainly clothes and jewellery (Thurs–Sun 9am–5pm; Camden Town tube); *Brick Lane* – everything from sofas to antique cameo brooches (Sun dawn to around midday; Aldgate East tube); *Greenwich*, Market Square – small arts and crafts market (Sat & Sun 9am–5pm; Greenwich BR); *Petticoat Lane*, Middlesex St and Goulston St – secondhand clothes (Sun 9am–4pm; Aldgate East or Liverpool Street tube); *Portobello*, Portobello Rd – mostly boho-chic clothes and portable antiques (Fri & Sat 9am–5pm; Notting Hill or Ladbroke Grove tube).

National Express Victoria Coach Station (☎0171/730 8235).

Pharmacies *Bliss*, 5 Marble Arch, W1, is open daily 9am–midnight. The Bliss branch at 50–56 Willesden Lane, NW6, is open daily 9am–2am. Every police station keeps a list of emergency pharmacies in its area.

Police HQ is New Scotland Yard, 1 Drummond Gare, SW1 (☎0171/230 1212); 10 Vine St, W1 (☎0171/437 1212), just off Regent St, is the most convenient West End station.

Post offices The Trafalgar Square post office, 24–28 William IV St, WC2, has the longest opening hours: Mon–Sat 8am–8pm. It's to this post office that Poste Restante mail should be sent.

Train stations and information As a broad guide, Euston handles services to the northwest and Glasgow; King's Cross the northeast and Edinburgh; Liverpool Street eastern England; Paddington western England; Victoria and Waterloo southeast England. For information, call ☎0171/928 5100 for services to eastern and southern England, and eastern and southern London; ☎0171/262 6767 for the south Midlands, west England, west London and south Wales; ☎0171/387 7070 for the north Midlands, north Wales, northwest England and northwest London; and ☎0171/287 2477 for northeast England and eastern Scotland.

Travel agents *Campus Travel*, 52 Grosvenor Gardens, SW1 (☎0171/730 3402); *STA Travel*, 86 Old Brompton Rd, SW7 (☎0171/937 9921); *Council Travel*, 28a Poland St, W1 (☎0171/437 7767); *Trailfinders*, 42–48 Earls Court Rd, W8 (☎0171/937 5400); *Travel Cuts*, 295a Regent St, W1 (☎0171/255 1944)

travel details

It's possible to travel directly from London to scores of English towns; what follows is simply a run-through of the major weekday direct inter-city connections by train and bus. Connections within Greater London are detailed in the appropriate places in this chapter.

Trains from:

London Charing Cross to: Dover (every 30min; 1hr 45min–2hr).

London Euston to: Birmingham (every 30min; 1hr 30min); Carlisle (every 1–2hr; 3hr 45min); Chester (3 daily; 2hr 40min); Crewe (every 30min; 2hr 10min); Liverpool (hourly; 3hr); Manchester (hourly; 2hr 40min).

London King's Cross to: Cambridge (every 30min; 55min); Durham (every 1–2hr; 3hr); Leeds (hourly; 2hr–2hr 20min); Newcastle (every 30min; 2hr 50min); York (every 30min; 1hr 55min).

London Liverpool Street to: Norwich (hourly; 1hr 55min).

London Paddington to: Bath (hourly; 1hr 25min); Bristol (every 30min; 1hr 25min); Exeter (every 1–2hr; 2hr 10min); Oxford (every 30min; 55min); Penzance (8 daily; 5hr); Plymouth (every 1–2hr; 3hr–3hr 40min); Worcester (every 1–2hr; 2hr–2hr 20min).

London St Pancras to: Leicester (every 30min; 1hr 20min); Nottingham (hourly; 1hr 45min); Sheffield (hourly; 2hr 20min).

London Victoria to: Brighton (hourly; 55min); Canterbury (hourly; 1hr 25min); Dover (hourly; 1hr 45min).

London Waterloo to: Portsmouth (twice hourly; 1hr 25min); Southampton (every 20min; 1hr 15min); Winchester (every 20min; 1hr).

Buses from Victoria Coach Station to:

Bath (9 daily; 3hr 5min); **Birmingham** (hourly; 2hr 30min); **Brighton** (every 90min; 1hr 40min); **Bristol** (8–13 daily; 2hr 15min); **Cambridge** (hourly; 2hr); **Canterbury** (every 2hr; 2hr); **Carlisle** (3–4 daily; 5hr 30min); **Chester** (5 daily; 4hr 45min); **Dover** (every 2hr; 2–3hr); **Exeter** (7–8 daily; 3hr 50min); **Gloucester** (9 daily; 3hr 40min); **Liverpool** (5 daily; 4hr 15min); **Manchester** (6 daily; 4hr); **Oxford** (every 15min–1hr; 1hr 30min); **Plymouth** (6 daily; 4hr 30min); **York** (4 daily; 4hr 20min).

CHAPTER TWO

SURREY, KENT & SUSSEX

T he southeast corner of England was traditionally where London went on holiday. In the past, train loads of Eastenders were shuttled to the hop fields and orchards of **Kent** for a working break from the city; boats ferried people down the Thames to the beach at Margate; and everyone from royalty to cuck-olding couples enjoyed the seaside at Brighton, a blot of decadence in the otherwise sedate county of **Sussex**. Adjacent to the capital's southern borders, **Surrey** is the least pastoral and historically significant of the three counties – the home of wealthy metropolitan professionals prepared to commute from what has become known as the "stockbroker belt".

The late twentieth century has brought big changes to the southeast region. In purely administrative terms the three counties have become four, since local govern-ment reorganization split Sussex into East and West. More significantly, many of the coastal towns have faced an uphill struggle to keep their tourist custom in the face of ever more accessible foreign destinations. To make matters worse, the white-collar recession of the early 1990s has hit the southeast hardest of all, disturbing the equilib-rium of this formerly complacent part of England – Brighton, long known as "London beside the sea", now matches the capital with one of the highest proportions of home-less people in the country.

The proximity of Kent and Sussex to the continent has dictated the history of this region, which has served as a gateway for an array of invaders, both rapacious and benign. **Roman** remains dot the three coastal counties – most spectacularly at **Bignor**, near Arundel – and many roads, including the London-to-Dover A2 and Watling Street, follow the stright lines laid by the legionaries. When post-Roman **Christianity** spread through Europe, it arrived in Britain on the **Isle of Thanet** – the northeast tip of Kent, although older orders already existed among the Celts in the north and west of the country. In 597 AD Augustine moved inland and established a monastery at **Canterbury**, still the home of the Church of England and the county's prime historic attraction. (Surprisingly, Sussex was among the last counties to accept the Cross – due more to the region's then impenetrable forest than to its innate ungodliness.)

The last successful invasion of England took place in 1066, when the **Normans** over-ran King Harold's army near **Hastings**, on a site now marked by **Battle Abbey**. The Normans left their mark all over this corner of England and Kent remains unmatched in its profusion of medieval castles, among them **Dover**'s sprawling clifftop fortress guarding against continental invasion and **Rochester**'s huge, box-like citadel, close to the old dockyards of **Chatham**, power base of the formerly invincible British Navy.

Away from the great historic sites, you can spend unhurried days in elegant old towns such as **Rye**, **Royal Tunbridge Wells** and **Lewes**, or enjoy the less elevated charms of the traditional resorts, of which **Brighton** is far and away the best, combin-ing the buzz of a university town with a good-time atmosphere and an excellent range of eating options. Dramatic scenery may be in short supply, but in places the **South Downs Way** offers an expanse of rolling chalk uplands that as much as anywhere in the crowded southeast, gets you away from it all. And of course Surrey, Kent and Sussex harbour some of the country's finest **gardens**, ranging from the lush flower-beds of **Sissinghurst** and the great landscaped estates of **Petworth** and **Sheffield Park**.

Surrey

Effectively a rural suburb of southern London, for those who can afford it, **SURREY** is bisected laterally by the chalk escarpment of the **North Downs** which rise west of Guildford, peak around Box Hill near Dorking and continue east into Kent. The portion of Surrey within the M25 orbital motorway has little natural and virtually no historical appeal, being a collection of satellite towns and light industrial installations serving the capital, although an enjoyable day can be spent at **Sandown Park** or **Epsom** racecourses, or trying the rides at one of Surrey's theme parks, **Thorpe Park** or **Chessington World of Adventures**. Outside the M25's ring Surrey takes on a more pastoral demeanour, with the county town of **Guildford**, the open heathland of Surrey's western borders and **Farnham**, which houses the county's only intact castle.

Guildford

Thirty-five miles southwest of London, **GUILDFORD**, the county capital, is a moderately interesting town, whoses cobbled High Street retains some of its Georgian architectural charm. At the east end of the High Street's pedestrianized section is the **Archbishop Abbot's Hospital** (guided tours by appointment; contact the tourist office for details), a hospice built for the elderly in 1619 and still retaining many original features such as its Flemish stained glass and oak beams. In the early seventeenth century, Guildford became a prominent staging post halfway along the route from London to the Portsmouth docks and the canalization of the River Wey in 1648 reinforced its position on the trade map. The **Guildhall** (guided tours Tues & Thurs 2pm, 3pm and 4pm; free), further along the High Street, is a landmark from this era, though its elaborate Restoration facade and gilded clock belie its Tudor foundations.

Guildford's ruined Norman **Castle** keep (April–Sept daily 10.30am–6pm; 50p) sits on its motte behind the High Street, surrounded by flower-filled gardens. Beneath the castle, the town **museum** (Mon–Sat 11am–5pm; free) houses mementos of local writer Lewis Carroll (aka Rev. Charles Dodgson), author of the children's classic, *Alice's Adventures in Wonderland*. An imaginative sculpture of Alice passing through the looking glass is a recent addition to the Castle Gardens and Dodgson's grave can be visited in the cemetery off The Mount, on the other side of the river.

At the bottom of the High Street runs the **River Wey**, a rather neglected feature of the town, although the once crucial River Wey and Godalming Navigation Canal has been restored into a picturesque waterway. From the *Boat House,* off Millbrook, a couple of hundred yards upstream from where the High Street meets the river, you can **hire boats** and go on a **pleasure cruise** (all year Sun 2.15pm & 3.15pm; 45min; £2.50; late July to early Sept Mon–Sat 2pm & 3.30pm; 90min; £4; ☎01483/504 494).

Finally, it's difficult to miss Guildford's monumentally unremarkable modern Gothic **cathedral**, ostentatiously perched on Stag Hill, a mile northwest of the centre.

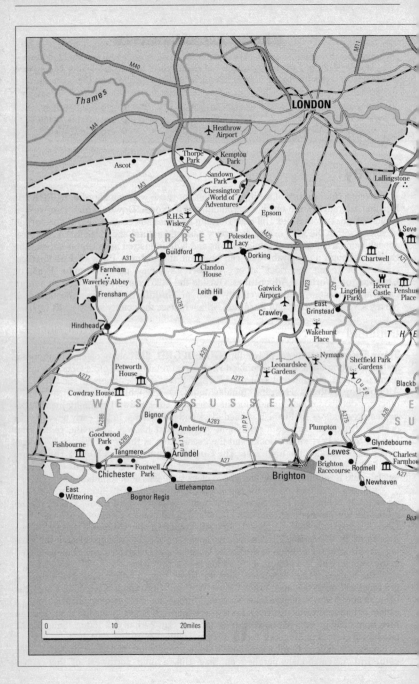

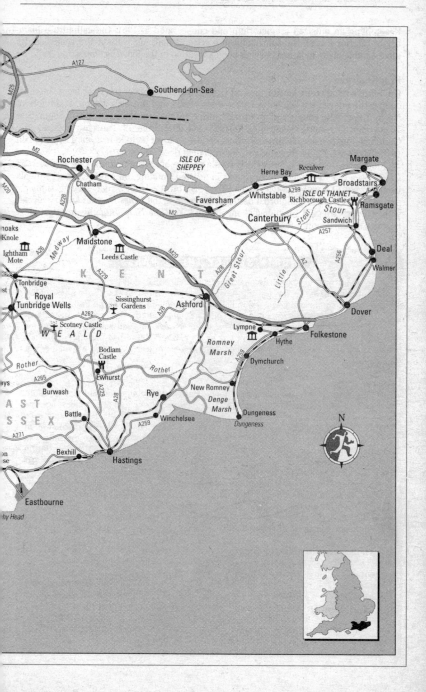

Resembling an outsized crematorium and consecrated in 1961, the cathedral's plain, bright interior has all the spirituality of a concert hall, but without the acoustics. Its most notable claim to fame is having been a location in the film *The Omen*.

Practicalities

Guildford's main **train station** lies off Bridge Street, just over the river from the town centre; the bus station lies between the town centre and the train station, at the foot of North Street. The county's main **tourist office** (May–Sept Mon–Sat 9am–5.30pm, Sun 10am–5pm; Oct–April closed Sun; ☎01483/444 007), is at 14 Tunsgate opposite the Guildhall. Inexpensive **accommodation** options in town include *Hillcote*, 11 Castle Hill (☎01483/63324; ②), or the similar *Greyfriars* next door (☎01483/61795; ②).

The High Street area offers a fairly routine range of **eating** options. *Café de Paris*, 35 Castle St, a busy French-style brasserie in a listed building, offers three-course meals from around £13, with *Cambio*, at 10 Chapel St, off the High Street, serving similarly priced Italian dishes. Guildford's better **pubs** include the *Kings Head* in Quarry Street, with a courtyard and inexpensive meals, and *Ye Olde Ship Inn*, the town's oldest hostelry on Portsmouth Road.

NORTH SURREY THEME PARKS

Within about half an hour's drive southwest of central London lie two popular **theme parks**, both ranking in the top ten most visited attractions in the UK – Chessington comes in at number eight with 1.6 million visitors annually and Thorpe Park at number nine with 1.2 million visitors. Both parks primarily appeal to the 8–14 age group, and can get extremely crowded; an early arrival on summer weekends will avoid long queues for the more popular rides. If it's action you're after, Chessington has the edge, but both sites easily return their seemingly pricey entrance fees with activities that will fill the best part of a day.

Thorpe Park

The purpose-built and water-oriented **Thorpe Park** is well signposted off the A320 south of Staines (April–Oct 10am–5.30pm; £13.25, reductions for children and families; London Waterloo to Staines or Chertsey BR, then bus #58, #561, #586, #950 from Staines or Chertsey, or take the #718 direct from London Victoria Coach Station, which runs in summer only). Set in an old gravel pit next to a concrete works whose machinery is easily mistaken for the latest ride, the park continues to develop new attractions but is still fairly low-key. Swimwear is a good idea for younger children as the better rides can include a soaking, and it allows them to romp around in the play pool. The watery rides provide grins of amusement rather than screams of delight with the *Loggers Leap* involving an exhilarating sixteen-metre drop-off and *Thunder River* being an enjoyable whitish water descent in a huge tyre-like raft. Small children are excluded from these sorts of rides for safety reasons, but are well catered for in the low-adrenalin *Octopus's Garden* and the train or boat ride to the small animal farm.

Chessington World of Adventures

Smaller and more animated, but marginally tackier, **Chessington World of Adventures**, signed off the A243 twelve miles southwest of London (April–Oct daily 10am–5.30pm, July & Aug open till 9.30pm; £14.50, reductions for children; Chessington BR from London Waterloo), used to be a zoo. The best way to get the measure of the place is to take the yellow *Safari Skyway* monorail, which introduces you to the few remaining animals, then hop on the *Chessington Railroad* which does a round tour of the rest of the park. Of the better rides the *Vampire*, *Dragon River* and *Terrortomb* are all fun rather than frightening, although *Rameses Revenge* is slightly scarier.

Farnham and around

Tucked into Surrey's southwestern corner, ten miles west of Guildford along the exposed ridge of the Hog's Back, lies **FARNHAM**. Smaller and more charming than Guildford, Farnham moves at a slower pace and its thousand-year-old origins are more obvious. It is home to Surrey's only intact **Castle**, built around 1160 by Henry de Blois, Bishop of Winchester, as a convenient residence halfway between his diocese and London. Continuously occupied until 1927, the castle now houses a conference venue. Its keep (April–Sept daily 10am–6pm; £2.20; EH), from where there are good views over to the Downs, is the only part open to the public and holds a well shaft excavated from an earlier Saxon structure. Farnham's refined Georgian dwellings are at their best along the broad Castle Street, which links the town centre with the castle. At the bottom, West Street is worth a stroll for its half-timbered buildings with overhanging facades; the buildings now house a mixture of shops, pubs and restaurants.

The **tourist office** is at 28 West St (March–Oct Mon–Sat 10am–5.30pm; Nov–Feb Thurs–Sat 10am–1pm & 2–5.30pm; ☎01252/715 109). Further along the same road *Meads Guest House*, at no. 48 (☎01252/715 298; ③) is a good **accommodation** option, as is the *Stafford House Hotel*, 22 Firgrove Hill (☎01252/724 336; ④), close to the station south of town. The best place for **eating**, the *Vienna Restaurant*, 112 West St (closed Sun), isn't as expensive as it looks, and for reasonable bar meals, try the *Jolly Sailor* pub, 64 West St. The **train station**, with three trains per hour to London Waterloo (45min), is over the river on the south edge of town.

The North Kent Coast

It's a commonly held view that the northern part of Kent is a scenic and cultural wasteland, a prejudice that stems partly from the fact that most visitors only glimpse the area as they race to or from the Channel ports. However, the region has its fair share of attractions, all of which are easily accessible from the capital. The knot of historic sites at **Chatham** and **Rochester** are followed by the seaside towns of **Whitstable**, **Margate** and **Broadstairs**, once popular resorts that make an interesting mix of the stuffy and the purely frivolous.

Rochester

With Chatham and Gillingham, **ROCHESTER** is part of a conurbation known as the Medway Towns, gathered around the River Medway's unsightly tidal reach. Rochester's attractions – the shell of the Norman castle, the superb cathedral and the birthplace of Charles Dickens – are mixed into a centre that, with its proximity to Maidstone and speedy links to the Channel and the capital, is one of Kent's busiest and ugliest industrial areas. Away from High Street, Rochester may not be much to look at, but there's still enough to occupy at least half a day.

The Romans were the first to settle here in numbers, building a fortress on the site of the present **castle** (April–Oct daily 10am–6pm; Nov–March closes 4pm; £2.50; EH), and some kind of fortification has remained here ever since. In 1077, William I gave Gundulf, architect of the White Tower at the Tower of London, the see of Rochester and the job of improving the defences on the Medway's northernmost bridge on Watling Street. The present castle remains one of the best-preserved examples of a Norman fortress in England. The stark one-hundred-foot-high keep glowers over the town, while its interior is all the better for having lost its floors, allowing clear views up and down the dank interior. It has three square towers and a cylindrical one, the southwest tower, which was rebuilt following its collapse during the siege of the castle in 1215, when the bankrupt King John eventually wrested the castle from its archbishop. The outer walls and two of the towers retain their corridors and spiral stairwells allowing access to the uppermost battlements.

The foundations of the adjacent **Cathedral** (daily 8.30–5.30pm; free) were also Gundulf's work, but the building has been much modified over the past nine hundred years. Plenty of Norman touches have endured, notably the richly carved portal and tympanum above the doorway on the west front, which outshines the rest of the building. Some fine paintings also managed to survive the Dissolution, notably those on the pillars and walls of the choir – the thirteenth-century depiction of the Wheel of Fortune shown as a treadmill is a trenchant image of medieval life's relentless slog. The cathedral once enshrined the remains of one St William of Perth, a pious baker from Scotland, who in 1201 embarked on a pilgrimage to the Holy Land, but got only as far as Rochester, where he was murdered and robbed. The monks of Rochester, envying the popular appeal of St Thomas à Becket's shrine at nearby Canterbury, used William's demise as an opportunity to establish a rival shrine – indeed, substantial additions to the cathedral were financed by donations from pilgrims paying their respects to the canonized baker's tomb, which has long since disappeared.

Rochester's most famous son is **Charles Dickens**, who spent his youth around here but would seem to have been less than impressed by the place – it appears in two of his novels as "Mudfog", and "Dullborough". Many town buildings also feature in his novels: the *Royal Victoria and Bull Hotel*, at the top of the High Street, for example, while most of his last book, the unfinished *Mystery of Edwin Drood*, was set here. A gritty picture of Victorian life is conjured up by the tableaux at the **Charles Dickens Centre** in Eastgate House at the east end of the High Street (daily 10am–5.30pm; £2.75). Key scenes from his well-known books are enacted at the push of a button and the whole place is entertaining and informative, whether you're a Dickens enthusiast or not. Further down the High Street stands **Watts' Charity** (March–Oct Tues–Sat 2pm–5pm; free), a sixteenth-century almshouse featuring galleried Elizabethan bedrooms and immortalized in Dickens' short story *The Seven Poor Travellers*.

Not all town museums are worth close scrutiny but Rochester's excellent **Guildhall Museum** (daily 10am–5.30pm; free), at the castle end of the High Street, is an exception. Inside, you'll find a vivid model of King John's siege of the castle and a chilling exhibition on the prison ships or **hulks** once moored near the Medway towns. Following America's gaining of independence in 1776, England was stuck for a place to transport her growing numbers of convicts – an increase caused as much by desperate poverty and draconian sentencing as any wave of criminality. Until the new penal colony of Botany Bay was established a decade or so later, criminals were housed in appalling and overcrowded conditions inside decommissioned naval vessels moored in the Thames. With the clever use of mirrors the exhibit replicates the grim nightmare inside these floating prisons.

Practicalities

The **tourist office** is in Eastgate Cottage, High Street (Mon–Sat 10am–5pm; ☎01634/843 666). Rochester **train station** is at the southeastern end of the High Street, a short walk to the centre of town. As for **accommodation**, you can stay at the aforementioned *Royal Victoria and Bull Hotel*, 16–18 High St (☎01634/846 266; ⑥), for a less expensive option try the **B&Bs** – *Grayling House*, 54 St Margaret's St (☎01634/826 593; ④) or the *Gainsborough* (☎01634/845 596; ②), opposite the train station. A new **youth hostel** is planned for Rochester in 1996 (☎01722/337 515 for details). The town has an unremarkable selection of cafés and **restaurants** – *Casa Lina*, 146 High St, serving pizzas and other Italian staples, is worth a try. Otherwise, try the *Coopers Arms* on St Margaret's Street, just down from the castle and cathedral.

Chatham

Founded by Henry VIII, the port of **CHATHAM** was once the major base of the Royal Navy, many of whose vessels were built, stationed and victualled here, commanding worldwide supremacy from the Tudor era until the end of the Victorian age. Well-sheltered yet close to London and the sea, and lined with tidal mud flats which helped support ships' keels during construction, the port expanded quickly to become England's largest naval base under Charles II. The dockyards were closed in 1984, re-opening soon after as a tourist attraction.

The **Royal Naval Dockyard** (Feb, March & Nov Wed, Sat & Sun 10am–4pm; April–Oct daily 10am–5pm; £5.60) occupies an eighty-acre site about a mile north of the town centre along the Dock Road (bus #182). Behind the stern brick wall you'll find an array of elegantly austere workshops and offices dating from the early eighteenth century, while the main part of the exhibition consists of the Ropery complex including the former rope-making room – at a quarter of a mile long, the longest room in the country. Inside, there are displays on former shipbuilding crafts and the history of the yard, with explanations offered by animated mannequins.

Less interesting by far is the nearby **Fort Amherst** (daily March–Oct 10am–5pm, Nov–Feb 10.30am–4pm; £2.50), built to defend the dockyard in the mid-eighteenth century and extended by brutally treated prisoners-of-war during the Napoleonic era. The fort's honeycomb of tunnels has been restored, but an overlong ninety-minute guided tour fails to bring them to life.

Whitstable

Peculiarities of silt and salinity have made **WHITSTABLE** an oyster-friendly environment since classical times, when the Romans feasted on the region's marine delicacies. Before the modern era, oysters were thought of as poor people's food and during the 1950s the town prospered, with offshore **oyster** beds covering five thousand acres and fishing and seaside tourism bringing additional revenue – but then sea pollution as well as the changing patterns in holidaymaking brought about Whitstable's reversion to humbler status. These days, small-scale boatbuilding and a mildly Bohemian ambience make Whitstable one of the few pleasant spots along the north Kent coast and it's a popular day-trip destination for Londoners.

Back in 1830 Whitstable became the northern terminus for one of Britain's first steam-powered passenger railway services – the so-called "Crab & Winkle Line" which linked the town via a half-mile tunnel (the world's longest at that time) with Canterbury, ten miles to the south. Relics of this line survive at the **Chuffa Trains Railmania Museum**, 82 High St (Mon–Sat 10am–3pm, open till 5pm in school holidays; £1.50), while the town **museum** and **gallery** in Oxford Street (Mon, Tues & Thurs–Sat 10.30am–1pm & 2–4pm; free) explore Whitstable's maritime history, with displays on diving and some good photographs of the town's heyday. Right next door you'll find the **tourist office** (July & Aug daily 10am–5pm; Sept–June Mon–Fri 10am–4pm, Sat 10am–1pm; ☎01227/275 482).

Whitstable's fishing background is reflected in its **eating** places, from any number of fish and chip outlets along the High Street to the very popular *Royal Native Oyster Stores* by the seafront (☎01227/276 856), the town's best restaurant, with its own art-house cinema above. If it's full, *Pearsons Crab & Oyster House* right opposite (☎01227/272 005) is a good second choice. *Tea and Times*, 36 High St, caters for the town's arty fringe and serves a decent English breakfast with freshly brewed coffee and newspapers. For a **drink** check out the *Old Neptune*, standing alone in its white weatherboards on the shore. *Belmont* **B&B** by the rail bridge in Oxford Street (☎01795/272 206; ④), the southern continuation of the High Street, offers **accommodation**, as does *Copeland House*, 4 Island Wall (☎01795/266 207; ⑦), between the High Street and the sea.

The Thanet resorts

The **Isle of Thanet**, a featureless plain fringed by low chalk cliffs and the odd sandy bay, became part of the mainland when the navigable Wantsum Channel began silting up, around the time of the first Roman invasion. This northeastern corner of Kent has witnessed successive waves of incursions. In 43 AD, nearly a century after Julius Caesar's exploratory visit, the Romans got into their stride when they landed near Pegwell Bay and established Richborough port in preparation for the march inland. The Saxons followed them four hundred years later (the island is named after the "tenets", which were fire beacons used to warn local residents of the Saxon's raids) and Augustine arrived here in 597 on a divine mission to end Celtic paganism. The evangelist is supposed to have met King Ethelbert of Kent and preached his first sermon at a spot three miles west of Ramsgate – a cross marks the location at Ebbsfleet, next to Saint Augustine's Golf Club.

Over the next thousand years or so, civilization advanced to the point at which, in 1751, a resident of Margate, one Mr Benjamin Beale, invented the bathing machine, a wheeled cubicle that enabled people to slip into the sea without undue exhibitionism. It heralded the birth of sea bathing as a recreational and recuperative activity, and led to the growth of **seaside resorts**. By the mid-twentieth century the Isle's intermittent expanses of sand had become fully colonized as the "bucket and spade" resorts of the capital's leisure-seeking proletariat. That heyday has passed, but these earliest of resorts still cling to their traditional attractions to varying degrees.

Margate

MARGATE – memorably summarized by Oscar Wilde as "the nom-de-plume of Ramsgate" – is a ragged assortment of cafés, shops and amusement arcades wrapped around a broad bay, a rather less elegant place than the one with which it's been twinned, the Black Sea resort of Yalta. Yet two centuries of tourism are embodied by Margate: at its peak thousands of Londoners were ferried down the Thames every summer's day, to be disgorged at the pier – precursor of all such seaside structures.

Other than the agreeable if small beach, Margate's main attraction along its unashamedly tacky seafront is **Dreamland** on Marine Terrace (most days May–Sept 10.30am–6 or 7pm), an amusement park dating from 1920 and still going strong. Free entry tempts you to buy vouchers for the rides, of which the *Looping Star* roller coaster is the best. If this doesn't appeal you could always visit the **Shell Grotto** (Easter to mid-Oct Mon–Fri 10am–5.30pm, Sat 10am–noon, Sun 10am–4pm; £2), Grotto Hill, off Northdown Road, which claims to be the world's only underground shell temple and has been open to the public since 1835, its passages intricately decorated with shell mosaics – if nothing else, a good place to cool off on a hot day.

The **tourist office** is at 22 High St (Mon–Fri 9am–5pm, Sat & Sun 10am–4pm; ☎01843/220 241) and the **train station** on All Saint's Avenue, just a couple of minutes' walk from *Dreamland*. Margate has plenty of **B&Bs** lining the Regency crescents of the Cliftonville suburb – try the *Durley Dean Hotel*, 9 Ethelbert Crescent (☎01843/292 634; ③), or else there's *Westbrook Bay House*, 12 Royal Esplanade (☎01843/292 700; ④), half a mile west of the train station. Prosaic **seaside food** is on offer at any of the seafront greasy spoons and fish and chip outlets, along with the familiar fast-food chains, but discriminating palates will find little to get excited about.

Broadstairs

Said to have been established on the profits of smuggling, **BROADSTAIRS** is the smallest, quietest and most pleasant of Thanet's three resort towns, overlooking the pretty Viking Bay from its clifftop setting. The town's main claim to fame, though, is as Dickens' holiday retreat: throughout his most productive years he stayed in various hostelries here, and eventually rented an austere dwelling overlooking the bay from Fort Road, since renamed **Bleak House** (mid-March to mid-Oct daily 10am–6pm; £2.50). It was here that he planned the novel of that name as well as finishing *David Copperfield*, and three rooms in the house have been preserved as the author would have known them. There's more of the same at the **Dickens House Museum** in Victoria Parade on the main clifftop seafront (June–Aug daily 2.30–5.30pm; £1).

Broadstairs' **tourist office** is at 67 High St (mid-June to mid-Sept daily 10am–5pm; rest of year Mon–Sat 10am–4pm; ☎01843/862 242) and its **train station** is a ten-minute walk from the seafront. Many **hotels**, restaurants and other establishments cash in on the Dickens angle – he wrote part of *Nicholas Nickleby* at the comfortable but pricey *Royal Albion Hotel* on Albion Street (☎01843/868 071; ⑤). There are several ivy-covered establishments in Belvedere Road, behind the High Street: the *Admiral Dundonald Hotel* at no. 43 (☎01843/862 236; ④) and the *Hanson Hotel* next door (☎01843/868 936; ③) – both are good value. There is also a **youth hostel**, with small bunkrooms and a family atmosphere, just two minutes' walk from the train station, at 3 Osborne Rd (☎01843/604 121). For **food** the *Mad Chef's Bistro*, by the harbour wall down in Harbour Street, serves good local seafood at a reasonable price.

Ramsgate

If Thanet had a capital, it would be **RAMSGATE**, a handsome resort and a working port, with daily ferries crossing the Channel to Dunkerque and Ostend. Rich in robust Victorian red brick, the town is set high on a cliff linked to the seafront and harbour by broad, sweeping ramps, with the villas on the seaward side displaying wrought iron verandahs and bricked-in windows – a legacy of the tax on glazed windows. Overall the port has avoided Margate's vulgarity while retaining some of Broadstairs' class.

The most entertaining sight in Ramsgate is the subterranean **Motor Museum** at West Cliff Hall, just west of the ferry terminal (April–Nov daily 10.30am–5.30pm; Oct–Easter Sun 10am–5pm; £2.50), which spices up its eclectic collection of cars and motorbikes by placing each vehicle in its historical context. A 1905 Rex pushbike is on show alongside a newspaper proclaiming the increase of third-class steamer fares to the USA to £6 and a 1904 De Dion Bouton is displayed along with details of events from the same year – the founding of Rolls Royce and the arrest of a New York woman for a shocking crime, smoking in public. Ramsgate's other sight, the **Clock House Maritime Museum**, in the middle of the harbour (April–Sept Mon–Fri 9.30am–4pm, Sat 2–5pm & Sun 1–6pm; Oct–March Mon–Fri 9.30am–3.30pm; £1), is brightened only by an illuminating section on the Goodwin Sands sandbanks – six miles southeast of Ramsgate – the occasional playing field of the eccentric Goodwin Sands Cricket Club.

The **tourist office** is on Queen Street (Mon–Sat 9.30am–5pm; ☎01843/591086) and the **train station** is about a mile northwest of the centre, at the end of Wilfred Road, off the High Street. *Sally Line* runs **ferries** to Dunkerque five times daily; its Belgian sister company, *Oostende Lines*, runs six ferries a day to Ostend, plus the slightly faster, passenger-only, *Jetfoil* service between three and six times daily (reservations for all the above; ☎01843/595 522). For an overnight **stay** try *Eastwood Guest House*, 28 Augusta Rd (☎01843/591 505; ⑤) or the *Goodwin View Seafront Hotel*, 19 Wellington Crescent (☎01843/591 419; ③). There's a **campsite** at *Nethercourt Hill*, two miles southwest of the town centre (☎01843/595 485). The *Falstaff* pub, on Addington Street by the seafront, does a decent ploughman's lunch, or there's the *Camden Arms*, in nearby La Belle Alliance Square, for good-value fish and chips – for a more formal **restaurant** meal try the *Savoy Hotel*, 43 Grange Rd (☎01843/592 637) which serves excellent seafood dishes.

Canterbury

One of England's most venerable cities, **CANTERBURY** offers a rich slice through two thousand years of history, with Roman and early Christian ruins, a Norman castle, and a famous cathedral that dominates a medieval warren of time-skewed Tudor dwellings. The city began as a Belgic settlement that was overrun by the Romans and renamed **Durovernum**, from where they proceeded to establish a garrison, supply base and system of roads that was to reach as far as the Scottish borders. With the Empire's collapse came the Saxons, who renamed the town **Cantwarabyrig**; it was a Saxon king, Ethelbert, who in 597 welcomed Augustine, despatched by the pope to convert the British Isles to Christianity. By the time of his death, Augustine had founded two Benedictine monasteries, one of which – Christ Church, raised on the site of the Roman basilica – was to become the first cathedral in England.

At the turn of the millennium Canterbury suffered repeated sackings by the Danes until Canute, a recent Christian convert, restored the ruined Christ Church, only for it to be destroyed by fire a year before the Norman invasion. As the new religion became a tool of control, a struggle for power developed between the archbishops, the abbots from the nearby Benedictine abbey and King Henry II, culminating in the assassination

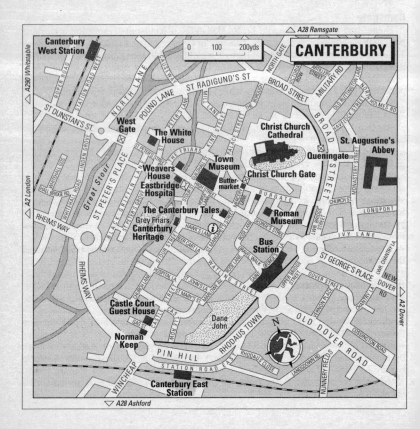

of Archbishop Thomas à Becket in 1170, a martyrdom that effectively established the autonomy of the archbishops and made this one of Christendom's greatest shrines. Geoffrey Chaucer's *Canterbury Tales*, written towards the end of the fourteenth century, portrays the unexpectedly festive nature of pilgrimages to Becket's tomb, which was plundered and destroyed at the orders of Henry VIII.

In 1830 a pioneering passenger railway service linked Canterbury to the sea again, as it had been up till Norman times, and prosperity grew until the city suffered extensive German bombing in the notorious **Baedeker Raids**, when Hitler ordered the destruction of the most treasured historic sites described in the *Baedeker* travel guide series. Today the cathedral and compact town centre, enclosed on three sides by medieval walls, remain the focus for leisure-motivated pilgrims from across the globe.

Arrival, information and accommodation

Canterbury has two **train stations**, Canterbury East for services from London Victoria or Dover Priory, and Canterbury West for slower services from London Charing Cross or Folkestone. The stations are northwest and south of the centre respectively, each a ten-minute walk from the cathedral. *National Express* coaches and local **buses** use the bus station just inside the city walls on St George's Lane. The busy **tourist office** is at 34 St Margaret's St (April–Oct daily 9.30am–5.30pm; Nov–March closes 5pm; ☎01227/766 567), right in the middle of the city centre, off the High Street.

Hotels and B&Bs

Ann's House, 63 London Rd (☎01227/768 767). Restored traditional Victorian villa, with some comfortable rooms. ④.

Cathedral Gate Hotel, 36 Burgate (☎01227/464 381). Built in 1438 and set in the city's medieval heart, this venerable pilgrims' hostelry features crooked floors and exposed timber beams with modern amenities. ⑥.

The Chaucer, Ivy Lane (☎01227/464 427). Fully refurbished with modern comforts but retaining its early-Georgian charm. ⑧.

County Hotel, High St (☎01227/766 266). Four-hundred-year-old hotel in the heart of town, close to everything and with traditionally furnished interior. ⑧.

Maynard Cottage, 106 Wincheap (☎01227/454 991). Inexpensive Jacobean cottage offering B&B just 2min from Canterbury East BR. ④.

St John's Court Guest House, St John's Lane (☎01227/456 425). Good-value guest house, offering B&B in a quiet but central location. ③.

Thanington Hotel, 140 Wincheap (☎01227/453 227). Comfortably converted Georgian building, a 10-min walk from the centre with a pool, games room and friendly, attentive service. ⑥.

The White House, 6 St Peter's Lane (☎01227/761 836). Small and friendly guest house in a fine regency building, midway between the cathedral and Canterbury West BR. ④.

Wincheap Guest House, 94 Wincheap (☎01227/762 309). Good-value B&B, close to Canterbury East station. ③.

Hostels and campsites

KiPPS, 40 Nunnery Fields, (☎01227/786 121). Self-catering hostel-type accommodation in dormitories a few minutes walk from Canterbury East BR; £10 per person.

St Martin's Caravan and Camping Site, Bekesbourne Lane (☎01227/463 216). Large caravan park, one and a half miles east of the city off the A257–Sandwich road.

University of Kent at Canterbury, Giles Lane (☎01227/769 186). Not especially good-value single rooms available during holidays, costing £16–30. Situated on the hill one and a half miles northwest of the city; bland, but with great views.

Youth Hostel, 54 New Dover Rd (☎01227/462 911). Half a mile out of town, and a 15-min walk from Canterbury East station, this friendly hostel is set in a Victorian villa.

The City

Despite the presence of a university and art college, England's second most visited city is fundamentally a fairly conservative and torpid place. It has a population of only 35,000 and is facing something of a crisis on how to deal with its two million annual visitors. The town centre, ringed by ancient walls, is virtually car free, but this doesn't stop the High Street seizing up all too frequently with tourists. Having said that, the very reason for the city's popularity is its rich tapestry of historical sites, combined with a good selection of places to stay, eat and drink, and no visit to southeast England would be complete without, at the very least, a quick stop here.

The Cathedral

Mother Church of the Church of England, seat of the Primate of All England, **Canterbury Cathedral** (daily 8.45am–7pm; £2) is ecclesiastically supreme and fills the northeast quadrant of the city with a befitting sense of authority, even if architecturally it's perhaps not among the country's most impressive cathedrals. A cathedral has stood here since 602, but in 1070 the first Norman archbishop, Lanfranc, levelled that Saxon structure to build a new cathedral. Over successive centuries the masterpiece was heavily modified, and with the puritanical lines of the Perpendicular style gaining ascendancy in late-medieval times, the cathedral now derives its distinctiveness from the thrust of the 235-foot-high **Bell Harry tower**, completed in 1505. The precincts are entered through the superbly ornate early sixteenth-century **Christ Church Gate**, where Burgate and St Margaret's Street meet. This junction, the city's medieval core, is known as the **Buttermarket**, where religious relics were once sold to pilgrims hoping to prevent an eternity in damnation. Passing through the gatehouse you get one of the finest views of the cathedral, foreshortened and crowned with soaring towers and pinnacles.

Once in the magnificent interior, look for the **tomb of Henry IV** and his wife, Joan of Navarre, and for the gilded effigy of Edward III's son, the **Black Prince**, all of them to be found in the Trinity Chapel, behind the main altar. The shrine of **Thomas à Becket**, in the northwest transept, is marked by the Altar of Sword's Point, where a crude sculpture of the assassins' weapons is suspended above the spot where Becket died and was later enshrined – until Henry VIII's act of ecclesiastical vandalism in 1538. Steps from here descend to the low, Romanesque arches of the **Crypt**, one of the few relics of the Norman cathedral and considered the finest such structure in the country, with some amazingly well-preserved carvings on the capitals of the columns. In the cathedral's north flank are the fan-vaulted colonnades of the **Great Cloister**, from where you enter the **Chapter House**, with its intricate web of fourteenth-century tracery supporting the roof and a wall of stained glass, which illustrates scenes from St Thomas's life and death. In 1935, it was a fitting venue for the inaugural performance of T.S. Eliot's *Murder in the Cathedral*.

The rest of the city

Passing through the cathedral grounds and out through the city walls at Queningsgate, or back up Burgate, you'll come to the vestigial remains of **St Augustine's Abbey** (April–Sept daily 10am–6pm; Oct–March Tues–Sun 10am–4pm; £1.80; EH), occupying the site of the church founded by Augustine in 598. Built outside the city because of a Christian tradition which forbade burials within the walls, it became the final resting place of Augustine, Ethelbert and successive archbishops and kings of Kent, although no trace remains either of them or of the original Saxon church. Shortly after the Normans arrived, the church was demolished in the same building frenzy which saw the creation of the cathedral. It was replaced by a much larger abbey, most of which was destroyed in the Dissolution so that today only the ruins and foundations remain.

Nearby, on the corner of North Holmes Road and Pretoria Road is **St Martin's Church**, one of England's oldest churches, built on the site of a Roman villa or temple and used by the earliest Christians. Although medieval additions obscure the original Saxon structure, it was here that King Ethelbert was himself baptized, making this perhaps the earliest Christian site in Canterbury.

Back in the city centre, redevelopment of the Longmarket area a few years ago exposed Roman foundations and mosaics that are now part of the **Roman Museum** (Mon–Sat 10am–5pm, June–Oct also open Sun 1.30–5pm; £1.60). The extant remnants of the larger building are pretty dull and better mosaics can be seen at Lullingstone (see p.165), but the display of recovered artefacts and general design of the museum are tasteful, with Roman domestic scenes re-created, as well as a computer-generated view of Durovernum two thousand years ago.

From here a walk down the High Street to Mercery Lane and a glance up towards Christ Church Gate presents you with one of the most photographed views in the city: a narrow, medieval street of crooked, overhanging houses behind which loom the turreted gatehouse and the cathedral's towers. Turning in the other direction down St Margaret's Street leads to the former church that's now **The Canterbury Tales** (daily April–Sept 9.30am–6.30pm; Oct–March 10am–4.30pm; £4.50), a quasi-educational show based on Geoffrey Chaucer's book, which was the first ever to be printed in English. Genuinely educational and better value is **Canterbury Heritage**, round the corner in Stour Street (Mon–Sat 10.30am–5pm, June–Oct also open Sun 1.30–5pm; £1.60), an interactive exhibition spanning local history from the splendour of Durovernum through to the contemporary literary figures of Joseph Conrad (buried in the cemetery in London Road) and local-born Mary Tourtel, creator of the check-trousered philanthropist Rupert Bear. Back on St Margaret Street, continue to the end to see the simple (but inaccessible) shell of the Norman castle's **keep**.

Where the High Street passes over a branch of the River Stour stands **Eastbridge Hospital** (Mon–Sat 10am–1pm & 2–5pm, Sun 11am–1pm & 2–5pm; free), founded in the twelfth century to provide poor pilgrims with shelter. Downstairs is an exhibition on Chaucer's life, while storytellers in feudal garb recite parts of his book. Over the road is the **Weavers' House**, once inhabited by Huguenot textile workers who had been offered religious asylum in post-Reformation England. At its far end the High Street becomes St Peter's Street, which itself terminates at the two massive crenellated towers of the **West Gate**, between which local buses just manage to squeeze. The only one of the town's seven city gates to have survived intact, its towers house a small **museum** (April–Sept Mon–Fri 11am–1pm & 2–5pm; Oct–March Mon–Fri 2–4pm; 60p), which displays contemporary armaments and weaponry used by the medieval city guard, as well as giving access to the battlements.

Eating, drinking and nightlife

The combination of a large student population and the tourist trade means Canterbury has a good selection of places to **eat and drink**, with many establishments in genuinely old settings. Head for *Tapas en Las Trece*, 13 Palace St, for tasty Spanish snacks (and occasional live music), or the popular, and moderately priced **Café des Amis**, 95 St Dunstans St, for authentic Mexican food. The refined delights of Thai cuisine are available at a reasonable price at *Chaopraya River*, 2 Dover St (☎01227/462 876), while *Kudos*, 52 Dover St (☎01227/761 126), is an inexpensive Chinese restaurant, serving excellent food. For classy Italian dishes at moderate prices, try the *Ristorante Tue e Mio*, a long-established restaurant at 16 The Borough. Finally there's *Fungus Mungus*, an inexpensive veggie café-bar at 34 St Peter's St.

Nightlife in Canterbury keeps a low profile – check what's happening in the free *Fifteen Days* listings magazine available at the tourist office. **Pubs** to go for include the *Bell & Crown*, a cramped medieval hostelry on Palace Street; the *City Arms*, 10 Butchery Lane, the art students' pub; or the *Miller's Arms*, good for a riverside summer-time pint. At *Alberry's* wine bar, opposite the tourist office, you can catch the occasional live music act, while *Cubar*, in Northgate, is a trendy, popular jazz bar. Also in Northgate, the recently revived *Penny Theatre* presents local and global live music. The University puts on a good range of arty **films** (Tues & Thurs 7.30pm during term-time), and also houses the *Gulbenkian Theatre*, a venue which shares the city's more edifying cultural events with the *Marlowe Theatre* in The Friars.

Dover and around

Dover, just 21 miles from the continent (Calais' low cliffs are visible on a clear day), is the southeast's principal cross-Channel port but as a town it is not immensely appealing, even though its key position has left it with a clutch of historic attractions. To its north lie **Sandwich**, once the most important of the Cinque Ports (see box opposite) but now no longer even on the coast, and the pleasant resort towns of **Deal** and **Walmer**, each with its own set of distinctive fortifications as well as a smattering of traditional seaside B&Bs.

Sandwich

SANDWICH, situated on the River Stour four miles north of Deal, is best known nowadays for giving rise to England's favourite culinary contribution when in 1762 the fourth Earl of Sandwich, passionately absorbed in a game of cards, demanded some meat between two bits of bread for a quick snack. Aside from this incident, the town's main interest lies in its maritime connections – it was chief among the Cinque Ports (see box opposite) until the Stour silted up. Unlike other former harbour inlets, however, the Stour hasn't silted up completely and still flows through town, its grassy willow-lined banks adding to the once great medieval port's present charm. By the bridge over the Stour stands the sixteenth-century **Barbican**, a stone gateway where tolls were once collected. Three sixteenth-century pubs, *The Bell Hotel*, *The Crispin* and the *Admiral Owen* cluster within sight of the Barbican and running parallel to the river is **Strand Street**, whose crooked half-timbered facades front antique shops and private homes. The genteel town is separated from the sandy beaches of Sandwich Bay by the **Royal St George** golf course – frequent venue of the British Open tournament – and a mile of nature reserves. The reserve that most ornithologists make for is the **Gazen Salts Nature Reserve**, three miles north of town, across the Stour.

Overlooking the doleful expanse of Pegwell Bay, two miles northwest of Sandwich, is **Richborough Castle** (Easter–Sept daily 10am–6pm; Oct–Easter Tues–Sun 10am–4pm; £1.30; EH), one of the earliest coastal strongholds built by the Romans along what later became known as the Saxon Shore on account of the frequent raids by the Germanic tribe. Like Reculver, ten miles northwest, it guarded the southern entrance to the Wantsum Channel, which then isolated the Isle of Thanet from the mainland. Rumour has it that Emperor Claudius once rode through a triumphal arch erected inside the castle on an elephant on his way to London, but all that remains now within the well-preserved Roman walls are the relics of an early Saxon church. Richborough's historical significance far outshines its present appearance, especially as Pegwell Bay is now blighted by an ugly chemical works.

There's not much **accommodation** of any kind in Sandwich; the *Bell Hotel* by the Barbican (☎01304/613 388; ⑦) is central but pricey; better value is the *Blenheim Cottage* B&B in New Street (☎01304/612 772; ③) or the *Crispin Inn*, an attractive fifteenth-century pub in the village of Worth, a mile or so south of Sandwich (☎01304/

THE CINQUE PORTS

In 1278, Dover, Hythe, Sandwich, New Romney and Hastings – already part of a long-established but unofficial confederation of defensive coastal settlements – were formalized under Edward I's charter as the five **Cinque Ports** (pronounced "sink", despite its French origin). In return for providing England with maritime support when necessary – chiefly in the transportation of troops and supplies to the Continent during times of war – the five ports were given trading privileges and other liberties, which enabled them to prosper while neighbouring ports struggled to survive. Some took advantage of this during peacetime, boosting their wealth by various nefarious activities such as piracy and smuggling of tax-free contraband. Later, Rye and Winchelsea were added to the confederation along with several other "limb" ports on the southeast coast which joined up at various times.

The confederation continued until 1685, when the ports' privileges were revoked. Their maritime services were no longer necessary as Henry VIII had founded a professional navy and, due to a shifting coastline, several of the ports' harbours had silted up anyway. Nowadays, only Dover is still a major working port, though the post of Lord Warden of the Cinque Ports still exists. This honorary title, appointed by the presiding monarch, is currently held by the Queen Mother.

612 081; ④). Your best choices for **meals** in town is the pricey *Fishermans Wharf* on the quayside, which serves excellent seafood; for something less expensive try one of the pubs by the Barbican or *The Haven*, 104 Strand St, for good coffee, light lunches and evening meals.

Deal and Walmer

One of the most unusual of Henry VIII's forts is the diminutive castle at **DEAL**, six miles southeast of Sandwich and site of Julius Ceasar's first successful landfall in Britain in 55 BC. The **castle** (March–Sept daily 10am–6pm; Oct–March Tues–Sun 10am–4pm; £2.50; EH) is situated off the Strand at the south end of town, its rose-petal patterned terraces as much an affectation as a defensive design, based on the premise that rounded walls would be better at deflecting missiles. Inside, the comprehensive display on the other similar forts built during Henry VIII's reign, is well worth a visit. Much more recently, the town was the focal point of Kent's small-scale coal industry, until the pits were shut down during the bitterly fought retrenchments of the 1980s.

Walmer Castle (April–Oct daily 10am–6pm; Nov–March Wed–Sun 10am–4pm; £3.50; EH), a mile south of Deal, is another rotund Tudor fort, albeit with a more conventional interior, commissioned when the castle became the residence of the Lord Warden of the Cinque Ports in 1730. Now it resembles a heavily fortified stately home more than a military stronghold. The best-known Lord Warden was the Duke of Wellington, who died here in 1842, and the house is now devoted primarily to his life and times – prize exhibits include the armchair in which he expired and the original Wellington boots in which he triumphed at Waterloo.

For **accommodation** in this area, *Finglesham Grange* (☎01304/611 314; ④) is a grand-looking B&B in the village of the same name, two miles north of Deal. If you prefer something more cosy, try *Camden Cottage* guest house, 47 Kingsdown Rd, Walmer (☎01304/361 906; ④), just a minute from the beach, or the slightly cheaper *Hardicot Guest House*, also on Kingsdown Road (☎01304/373 867; ④). In Deal there is a trio of places offering accommodation near the roundabout on Beach Street – the best of these is the *Kings Head* pub (☎01304/368 194; ④). For a reasonably priced seafood **meal** try the *Lobster Pot* on Beach Road, Deal, opposite the concrete pier.

Dover

The town authorities have put a lot of effort and money into inducing travellers to stop for a while in **DOVER** before speeding inland to London or Canterbury – a difficult job given that postwar rebuilding has left the town centre downright ugly.

The town's chief attraction is **Dover Castle** (Easter–Sept daily 10am–6pm; Oct–Easter closes 4pm; £5.50; EH), a superbly positioned defensive complex, begun in 1168 and in continuous military use until the 1980s. Exploration of the castle complex begins at the chunky hexagonal remains of the Roman lighthouse. Beside it stands a Saxon-built church, **St Mary in Castro**, dating from the seventh century, with motifs graffitied by irreverent Crusaders still visible near the pulpit. Next is the impressive, well-preserved **keep**, built by Henry II as a palace. Inside it there's a thought-provoking *Making of History* exhibition, and you can climb its spiral stairs to the lofty battlements for views over the sea to France. The castle's other main attraction is its network of underground tunnels dug during the Napoleonic war. Extended during World War II and used as a headquarters to plan the Dunkirk Evacuation, **Hellfire Corner** (entry included in castle entrance fee) – the tunnels' wartime nickname – offers two guided tours, *Underground Hospital* and *Operations*, each around forty

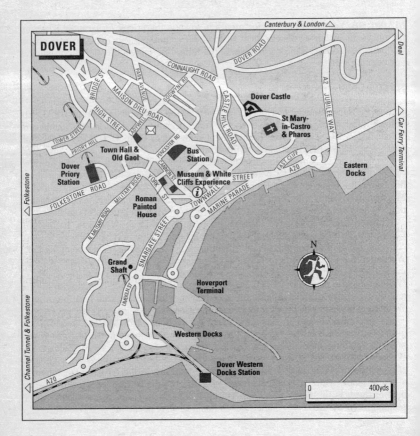

minutes long. The former is spiced up with a little gore, while the latter reveals the quaintly low-tech communications systems and war rooms of the Navy's command post.

The Romans put Dover on the map when, having conquered Europe and decided to move on towards Britannia, they chose Dover harbour as the base for their northern fleet, and erected a lighthouse here to guide the ships into the river mouth. All that remains from this period of the town's history is an ancient guest house, discovered in 1970 during the construction of a car park on New Street. The **Roman Painted House** (April–Oct Mon–Sat 10am–5pm; £1.50), possesses some reasonable Roman wall paintings, the remains of an underground Roman heating system and some mosaics – it's worth a look if you've some time to kill in the town centre.

Views of Dover's famous cliffs are best enjoyed from a boat several miles out to sea, but the **White Cliffs Experience** on Market Square (March–Nov daily 10am–5pm; Dec–Feb closes 3pm; £4.99) – an indoor theme museum with animated mannequins – offers an alternative historical view of the port. Less expensive and less frivolous is the new **museum** below the *White Cliffs* gift shop (daily 10am–5.30pm; £1.15 or included with *White Cliffs* fee), which has three floors packed with informative displays on Dover's past. At the **Old Town Gaol** (Mon–Sat 10am–4.30pm, Sun 2–4.30pm; £3), beneath the Town Hall on Biggin Street, dummies with TVs for heads describe the misery of penal incarceration during Victorian times. The high ground to the west of town, originally the site of a Napoleonic-era fortress, retains one interesting oddity, the **Grand Shaft** (April–Sept Wed–Sun 2–5pm; £1), a triple staircase by which troops could descend at speed to defend the port in case of attack.

Practicalities

Dover has two **train stations**, Dover Priory and Dover Western Docks. **Priory**, a ten-minute walk west of the centre, is linked by regular **shuttle buses** to the Eastern Docks, from where most continental ferries depart, although the fastest trains to Dover are the special boat trains between London Victoria and Western Docks which run about four times daily and take ninety minutes. Next fastest are the hourly services between London Charing Cross and Priory, which take about ten minutes longer, then the ordinary trains linking Victoria with both Priory and Western Docks which take nearly two hours. *National Express* **buses** (every 2hr; journey time 2–3hr) run either to the Eastern Docks or the town-centre **bus station** on Pencester Road, from where frequent shuttle buses service both docks. The **tourist office** is in the town centre on Townwall Street (daily 9am–6pm; ☎01304/205 108).

Nighttime transport to London is poor (the last bus is at 7.45pm, the last train 10.03pm), so late arrivals may have to spend the night in Dover. **Accommodation** is plentiful: *Castle House*, 10 Castle Hill Rd (☎01304/201 656; ④), is a friendly B&B, convenient for the Eastern Dock, as is the *Number One Guesthouse*, 1 Castle Hill Rd (☎01304/202 007; ③). *Linden B&B*, at no. 231, is one of the better B&Bs along the Folkestone Rd (☎01304/205 449; ③). There's a busy **youth hostel**, a mile inland

---

CROSS-CHANNEL FERRIES FROM DOVER AND FOLKESTONE

Dover Eastern Docks to: Calais (*P&O*, 15–24 daily, 75min; *Stena/Sealink*, 4–25 daily, 90min).

Dover Western Docks to: Calais (*Hoverspeed* hovercraft, 9–14 daily, 35min).

Folkestone to: Boulogne (*Hoverspeed SeaCat*, 4–6 daily, 55min).

Reservations: *P&O Ferries* (☎01304/203 388); *Stena/Sealink* (☎01233/647 047); *Hoverspeed* (☎01304/240 241).

from Dover Priory station, in a listed Georgian town house at 306 London Rd (☎01843/604 121), but with an overspill building in Godwyne Road, half a mile north of town.

Given the town's uninspiring appearance, Dover's **pubs** are surprisingly characterful although the town gets a rather rough reputation from its shift workers servicing the docks and ferries. Close to Western Docks, the *Cinque Ports Arms* on Clarence Place has guest beers as well as its standard Fremlin's ales, while the *Park Inn* on Park Street near the Town Hall is a big old place with plenty of real ales to choose from. At the *White Horse* on St James's Street, near the tourist office, local beers are supplemented by some good **meals**, but Dover has few other decent places to eat.

Folkstone to Rye

In Roman times, the **Romney and Denge marshes** – now the southernmost part of Kent – were submerged beneath the English Channel. Then the lowering of the sea levels in the Middle Ages and later reclamation created a forty-square-mile area of marshland which, until the last century, was afflicted by malaria and various other malaises. Contrasting strongly with the wooded pastures of Kent's interior, the sheep-speckled Marshes have an eerie, forlorn appearance, as if still unassimilated with the mainland and haunted by their maritime origins. The ancient town of **Hythe** is on the eastern edge of the reclaimed marshes and is linked with Rye in East Sussex on the marsh's western edge, by the arc of the twenty-three-mile **Royal Military Canal**. **Folkestone**, Kent's other major port, five miles east of Hythe, and site of the British entrance to the **Channel Tunnel**, is a drab and utterly missable introduction to this swathe of coast.

THE CHANNEL TUNNEL

In the autumn of 1994 passenger services through the Channel Tunnel finally began, 160 years after the idea was first suggested by French engineer Aime Thome de Gamond, whose geological survey of the seabed concluded that such a link was feasible. As a result of his work, a tunnel over a mile long was driven out from the English coast in 1882, while French engineers began to dig from Sangatte – the present location of the French terminal. All was all going remarkably well until Queen Victoria became paranoid about the possibility of invasion, and work was halted.

In 1973 a pang of Euro-optimism lead to another attempt until cash problems forced the British to pull out of the "Chunnel", as it was dubbed, and things didn't go any smoother when, at the end of the Eighties, the French and British agreed on proposals for a pair of rail tunnels and a third service tunnel. Britain's biggest-ever civil engineering project was dogged by delays, overspending and disagreements between *Trans Manche Link* (the tunnelers) and *Eurotunnel* (who put up the money), while the British government dithered over the routing of a new high-speed rail link to London, which is not expected to be completed until well into the next century. In the meantime the *Eurostar* travels at close to 200mph from Paris or Brussels to the tunnel, zips through at 100mph to surface at Folkestone and then crawls with the commuter traffic on the overcrowded Network SouthEast lines to its new terminal at Waterloo.

After a series of embarrassing and badly handled teething problems during its first few months of operation, the service has now got into its swing. At present foot passengers still can't catch a train at Folkestone; instead they have to travel up to London, although the new International Terminal being built at Ashford will eventually remedy this.

Folkestone

The tourist appeal of **FOLKESTONE**, seven miles down the coast from Dover, is so insubstantial that local brochures suggest attractions right across the county and even Boulogne as "easily accessible from Folkestone". The only passenger vessels that arrive here these days are the *Hoverspeed SeaCats* from Boulogne, which dock adjacent to **Folkestone Harbour train station** and connect with non-stop trains to London Victoria and **Folkestone Central**, which is served hourly by trains from London Charing Cross. *National Express* **coaches** to London leave from the **bus station** on Bouverie Square, between the Central and Harbour stations.

The **tourist office** is in Harbour Street, near the quayside (daily July–Aug 8am–6.15pm; Sept–June 9am–5.30pm; ☎01303/258 594). If you're stranded in town **overnight**, the plush *Burlington Hotel* on Earls Avenue (☎01303/255 301; ⑥), the *Chilton House Hotel*, 14 Marine Parade (☎01303/249 786; ③) and the *Westward Ho! Hotel*, Clifton Crescent (☎01303/221 515; ③) are the best options among the scores of hotels and B&Bs in town.

Hythe to Dungeness

Separated from Folkestone by the massive earthworks of the Channel Tunnel, **HYTHE** is a sedate seaside resort bisected by the disused waterway of the Royal Military Canal, built as a defensive obstacle during the perceived threat of Napoleonic invasion. Hythe's receding shoreline reduced its usefulness as a port and the nearby coast is now just a sweep of beach punctuated by **Martello Towers**, part of the chain of 74 citadels built along the southeast coastline for the same reasons as the canal.

There's little to do in Hythe other than enjoy its tranquil antiquity, although a ride on the world's largest toy train – or smallest public railway – the **Romney, Hythe & Dymchurch Railway** (*R, H & DR*), a fifteen-inch-gauge line which runs the fourteen miles from Hythe to Dungeness, makes a fun day out. Built in the 1920s as a tourist attraction linking the resorts along the shore, its fleet of steam locomotives are now maintained by volunteers (Easter–Sept daily; March & Oct Sat & Sun only; ☎01797/362 353). At New Romney station, three stops southwest of Hythe, the *R, H & DR* has a permanent **model train** exhibition (same days as the railway 10am–5pm; 60p).

DUNGENESS, six miles south of New Romney, is the southern terminus for the *R, H & DR*, set in the sort of wasteland normally used as an army-firing range, but in this case site of a nuclear power station instead. The barren environment of the Denge Marsh supports a unique floral ecology and all around you'll see tiny communities of wildflowers struggling against the unrelenting breeze. On the road to the power station, the flotsam sculptures in the late film director **Derek Jarman's garden** (still a private home and not a public attraction as such) make an eye-catching sight, though the non-indigenous flora he planted around them has attracted the wrath of the local conservation authorities.

Hythe's **tourist office** (Easter–Sept daily 10am–1pm & 2–5pm; ☎01303/267 799) is situated in the Prospect Road car park, on the road skirting the town centre. For **accommodation** check out the *White House Guest House*, 27 Napier Gardens (☎01303/266 252; ③), just a couple of minutes from the sea, or *Nyanza Lodge*, 87 Seabrook Rd (☎01303/267 315; ④). There are four **campsites** at Dymchurch, six miles along the coast. The *Capri*, 32–34 High St, serves good Italian **food** or try *Ashik*, 1 Red Lion Square, for a better-than-average tandoori.

Rye and Winchelsea

Perched on a hill overlooking the Romney Marshes, the town of **RYE** lies over the county border in East Sussex. Added as a "limb" to the original Cinque Ports, the town then became marooned two miles inland with the retreat of the sea and the silting up of the River Rother. It is now one of the most popular places along the Sussex coast – half-timbered, skew-roofed and quintessentially English, but also very commercialized.

An appraisal of the town is best begun at the **Ypres Tower** in Church Square (April–Oct daily 9am–5.30pm; £1.50); occupying the high point of Rye town, it was formerly used to keep an eye out for cross-Channel invaders and now houses relics from those days. Nearby stands **St Mary's** church, boasting the country's oldest functioning pendulum clock; the ascent of the church tower offers fine views over the clay-tiled roofs and grid of narrow lanes, the most picturesque of which is the cobbled **Mermaid Street**. Henry James, who strangely suggested that "Rye would . . . remind you of Granada", spent the last years of his life at **Lamb House** (April–Oct Wed & Sat 2pm–6pm; £2; NT) at the east end of Mermaid Street. The house's three rooms and garden are of interest chiefly to fans, or to admirers of E.F. Benson, who lived here after James. A plaque in the High Street also testifies that Radclyffe Hall, author of the seminal lesbian novel, *The Well of Loneliness*, was also once a resident of the town.

WINCHELSEA, two miles southwest of Rye and easily reached by train, bus, foot or bike, shares Rye's indignity of having become detached from the sea, but has a very different character. Rye gets all the visitors, whereas Winchelsea feels positively deserted, an impression augmented as you pass through the Strand Gate and see the ghostly ruined church of **St Thomas à Becket**. The original settlement was washed away in the great storm in 1287, after which Edward I planned a new port with a chequerboard pattern of streets. Even at the height of Winchelsea's economic activity, however, not all the plots on the grid were used. The town also suffered from incursions by the French in the fourteenth and fifteenth centuries, at which time the church was pillaged; the remains of the church constitute Sussex's finest example of the Decorated style. Head south for a mile and a half and you get to **Winchelsea beach**, a long expanse of pebbly sand.

Rye **train station** lies on the Hastings–Ashford rail line and is a short walk north of the town; local **buses** use the station forecourt; and the town's **tourist office** is on Strand Quay (April–Oct daily 9am–5.30pm; Nov–March Mon–Fri 11am–1pm Sat & Sun 10am–4pm; ☎01797/226 696). Rye boasts an excellent choice of **accommodation**: *The Old Vicarage Guest House*, 66 Church Square (☎01797/222 119; ⑤), is a lovely Georgian house next to the church; *Jeake's House* on Mermaid Street (☎01797/222 828; ⑤) is one of the best-appointed B&Bs; and *Owlet* B&B, 37 New St, is one of the least expensive options in town (☎01797/222 544; ④). In Winchelsea try *The Country House* (☎01797/ 226 669; ④), a former farmhouse on the Hastings Road, west of town, or the fourteenth-century *Strand House* (☎01797/226 276; ⑤) at the foot of the cliff off the A259. In Rye, the *Mermaid* in Mermaid Street is by far the best **pub**; the pricey *Landgate Bistro* at 5 Landgate (☎01797/222 829) is also recommended; alternatively, you can sample reasonably priced local seafood at the *Old Forge Restaurant* on Wish Street (☎01797/223 227), or the intimate *Gatehouse Restaurant*, 1 Tower St (☎01797/222 327).

Hastings and Battle

During the twelfth and thirteenth centuries, **HASTINGS** flourished as an influential Cinque Port. In 1287 its harbour creek was silted up by the same storm which washed away nearby Winchelsea, forcing the settlement to be temporarily abandoned. These days, Hastings is a curious mixture of traditional seaside resort, arty retreat popular with painters (there's even a street and quarter named Bohemia) and unpretentious fishing port. William, Duke of Normandy, landed at Pevensey Bay, a few miles west of town and made Hastings his base, but his forces met Harold's army – exhausted after quelling a Nordic invasion near York – at **Battle**, six miles northwest of Hastings.

Battle today boasts a magnificent abbey built by William in thanks for his victory, which makes for a good afternoon's excursion from Hastings.

Hastings

Hastings' **Old Town** holds most of the appeal of this fading seaside resort, and even this area lacks a historic or atmospheric focal point. With the exception of the oddly neglected Regency architecture of **Pelham Crescent**, directly beneath the castle ruins, **All Saints Street** is the most evocative thoroughfare, punctuated with the odd, rickety, timber-framed dwelling from the fifteenth century. The thirteenth-century **St Clements** church stands in the High Street, on the other side of The Bourne. By a louvred window at the top of the church's tower rests a cannonball that was lodged there by a Dutch galleon in the 1600s – its poignancy rather lost by a companion fitted in the eighteenth century for the sake of symmetry.

Down by the seafront, the area known as The Stade is characterized by its tall, black weatherboard **net shops**, dating from the mid-nineteenth century. To raise Hastings' tone, the town council attempted to shift the fishermen and their malodorously drying nets from the beach by increasing rents per square foot and these sinister-looking towers were their response. There's a trio of nautical attractions on the adjacent Rock-a-Nore Road: the **Fisherman's Museum** (Mon–Fri 10.30am–5pm, Sat & Sun 2.30–5pm; free), a converted seaman's chapel, offers an account of the port's commercial activities; the neighbouring **Shipwreck Heritage Centre** (Easter–Sept daily 10am–5pm; £1.80), details the dramas of unfortunate mariners; while the **Sea Life Centre** (July & Aug daily 10am–9pm; Sept–June closes 6pm; £4.50), opposite, features walk-through tunnels and magnified tanks housing marine creatures.

Castle Hill, separating the Old Town from the visually less interesting modern quarter, can be ascended by the **West Hill Cliff Railway**, one of two Victorian funicular railways in Hastings (Feb to mid-Dec daily 10am–5.30pm; 65p up, 20p down). On top of the hill is where William the Conqueror erected his first **castle** in 1066, one of several wooden prefabricated structures brought over from Normandy in sections. In the thirteenth century storms caused the cliffs to subside tipping most of the castle into the sea; the surviving ruins, however, offer an excellent prospect of the town. The castle is home to **The 1066 Story** (daily Easter–Sept 10am–5pm; Oct 11am–4pm; £2.50), in which the events of the last successful invasion of the British mainland are described inside a mock-up of a siege tent. More fun is the **Smugglers' Adventure** (daily Easter–Sept 10am–5.30pm; Oct–Easter 11.30am–4.30pm; £3.80; combined ticket with 1066 Story, £5.30), over the hill. Here the labyrinthine St Clement's caves have been converted to house a number of amusing and educational dioramas depicting the town's long history of duty-dodging.

Practicalities

The **train station** is a ten-minute walk from the seafront along Havelock Road; *National Express* services operate from the **bus station** at the junction of Havelock and Queen's roads. The **tourist office** is at 4 Robertson Terrace (Easter–Sept Mon 10.15am–5pm, Tues–Fri 9.30am–5pm, Sat & Sun 10am–5pm; Oct–Easter closed Sun; ☎01424/718 888); a smaller tourist office opens during the summer near the Boating Lake on East Parade. **Accommodation** available in town includes the *Argyle Guest House*, 32 Cambridge Gardens (☎01424/421294; ③) with sea views; timber–framed *Lavender and Lace*, right in the Old Town at 106 All Saints St (☎01424/716 290; ③); and *Lionsdown House*, another Old Town cottage at 116 High St (☎01424/428 168; ④). The nearest **youth hostel** and **campsite** (☎01424/812 373) are in a large manor house at Guestling, three miles along the road to Rye.

For **eating and drinking**, head for the pedestrianized George Street: *Fagins*, at no. 73, is a good bistro; *Café Continental*, at no. 53, serves decent crêpes and light snacks;

and *Platters*, at no. 37, offers inexpensive and wholesome Pakistani and Indian dishes. The best fish and chips in town are at the eat-in *Mermaid*, 2 Rock-a-Nore, right by the beach, while veggies congregate at *La Cucina Verde*, 50 George St. There are more than thirty pubs to choose from in Hastings; the local fishermen's favourite is the *Lord Nelson* on East Bourne St; others to check out are the student hangout by the pier, the *Pig in Paradise*; the ever popular *First in Last Out,* 15 High St in the Old Town; or the creaky-beamed hostelry, *Ye Olde Pump House*, on George Street .

Battle

The town of **BATTLE** – a ten-minute train ride from Hastings – occupies the site of the most famous land battle in British history. Here, on October 14, 1066, the invading Normans overcame the Anglo-Saxon army of King Harold, who was killed not by an arrow through the eye – a myth resulting from the misinterpretation of the Bayeux Tapestry – but from a workaday clubbing about the head. Before the battle took place, William vowed that, should he win the engagement, he would build a religious founda-tion on the very spot of Harold's slaying to atone for the bloodshed and true to his word, **Battle Abbey** (April–Sept daily 10am–6pm; Oct–March closes 4pm; £3; EH) was built four years later and subsequently occupied by a fraternity of Benedictines. The magnificent structure, though partially destroyed in the Dissolution and much rebuilt and revised over the centuries, still dominates the town with the huge Gatehouse, added in 1338, now containing a good audio-visual exhibition on the battle. You can wander through the ruins of the abbey to the spot where Harold was clubbed – the site of the high altar of William's abbey, now marked by a memorial stone.

Though nothing can match the resonance of the abbey, the rest of the town is worth a stroll. At the far end of the High Street, packed with antique shops and other tourist outlets, is the fourteenth-century **Almonry** (Easter–Sept daily 10am–5pm; Oct–Easter Mon–Sat 10am–4pm; Sun noon–4pm; £1) – the present town hall – which contains a miniature model of Battle and the oldest Guy Fawkes in the country. Every year, on the Saturday nearest to November 5, this three-hundred-year-old effigy is paraded along the High Street at the head of a torchlit procession culminating in a huge bonfire in front of the abbey gates; similar celebrations occur in Lewes (see p.168).

The **tourist office** is at 88 High St (April–Sept daily 10am–6pm; Oct–March Mon–Sat 10am–4pm, Sun 1–4pm; ☎01424/773 721). Most of the **accommodation** here is agreeable but expensive – a couple of less pricey **B&Bs** are *Battle Lodge*, Squirrel Corner (☎01424/774 029; ③) and *Great Barn*, 2 Loose Farm Buildings (☎01424/773 829; ③) on the Hastings Road, a couple of miles south of Battle. Town-centre **pubs** serving decent food include the *Old Kings Head* on Mount Street, the *1066* at 12 High St, which serves real ales, and the *Chequers Inn* at Lower Lake, on the High Street.

The Weald

The Weald is usually taken to refer to the region around the spa town of **Royal Tunbridge Wells**, but in fact it stretches across a much larger area between the North and South Downs and includes parts of both Kent and Sussex, though the majority of its attractions are in Kent. During Saxon times, much of The Weald was covered in thick forest – the word itself derives from the Germanic word *wald*, meaning forest and the suffixes -hurst (meaning wood) and -den (meaning clearing) are commonly found in Wealden village names. Now, however, the region is epitomized by gentle hills, sunken country lanes and somnolent villages as well as some of England's most beauti-ful gardens – **Sissinghurst** being the best known.

Burwash, Batemans and Bodiam Castle

Thirteen miles northwest of Hastings on the A265, halfway to Tunbridge Wells, **BURWASH**, with its red-brick and weatherboard cottages and Norman church tower, exemplifies the pastoral idyll of inland Sussex. Half a mile south of the village lies the main attraction, **Batemans** (April–Oct, Mon–Wed, Sat & Sun 11am–5pm; £4; NT), home of the Nobel Prize-winning writer and journalist Rudyard Kipling from 1902 until his death in 1936. Built by a local ironmaster in the seventeeth century and set amid attractive gardens, the house features a working watermill converted by Kipling to generate electricity. Inside, the house is laid out as Kipling left it, with letters, early editions of his work and mementos from his travels on display. Next to the house, a garage houses the last of Kipling's Rolls Royces, one of the many that he owned during his lifetime, although he never actually drove them, preferring the services of a chauffeur.

Bodiam Castle (mid-Feb to Oct daily 10am–6pm or dusk; Nov to New Year's Day Tues–Sun 10am–dusk; £2.50; NT), eleven miles north of Hastings, is a classic, stout, square castle with rounded corner turrets, battlements and a moat. When it was built in 1385 to guard what were the lower reaches of the River Rother, Bodiam was state-of-the-art military architecture, but during the Civil War a company of Roundheads breached the fortress and removed its roof to reduce its effectiveness as a possible stronghold for the King. Over the next 250 years Bodiam fell into neglect until restoration earlier this century by the philanthropic Lord Curzon. Nowadays, the castle particularly appeals to children who enjoy clambering up the narrow spiral staircases which lead to crenellated battlements, and watching the absorbing fifteen-minute video portraying medieval life in a castle. For **accommodation** and **food**, head for the lovely village of **Ewhurst**, two miles southeast, which houses an idyllic country pub, *The White Dog Inn* (☎01580/830 264; ③).

Royal Tunbridge Wells and around

ROYAL TUNBRIDGE WELLS – not to be confused with the more mundane Tonbridge, a few miles to the north – is the home of the mythical whingeing right-wing letter-writer known as "Disgusted of Tunbridge Wells". Most British people, therefore, view it with derision, but don't be misled – this prosperous spa town, surrounded by gorgeous countryside, is an elegant and diverting place. It was founded in 1606, when Lord North discovered a bubbling spring and reached its height of popularity during the Regency period, when such restorative cures were in vogue. The well-mannered architecture of that period, surrounded by parklands in which the rejuvenated gentry exercised, gives the southern and western part of town its special character.

The icon of those genteel times is the **Pantiles**, an elegant lane at the south end of town parallel to London Road, edged with colonnades where the fashionable once gathered to promenade and take the waters. The name reputedly stems from the chunky Kent peg tiles made of baked clay, which still cap the orange roofs of several older buildings in Kent and Sussex. Hub of the Pantiles is the original **Chalybeate Spring** in the Bath House, where a "Dipper" has been employed since the late eighteenth century to serve the ferrous waters. Today's period-dressed incumbent will fetch you a glass from the spring for 25p – or, if you bring your own cup, you can help yourself for free from the adjacent source. Apart from tiles, Tunbridge also produced domestic ceramics, on view with other local relics and historical artefacts in the **Museum and Art Gallery** in Mount Pleasant Road (Mon–Sat 9.30am–5pm; free), the northern continuation of the High Street, itself the northern continuation of the Pantiles.

Tunbridge Wells' **tourist office** is in the Old Fish Market, The Pantiles (Easter–Oct Mon–Fri 9am–6pm, Sat 9.30am–5.30pm, Sun 10am–4pm; Nov–Easter closed Sun; ☎01892/515 675). The **train station**, on the line between London Charing Cross and

Hastings, is also in the town centre, where the High Street becomes Mount Pleasant Road. For **B&B**, *Ephraim Lodge* (☎01892/523 053; ④), on The Common, and the nearby *Jordan House*, 68 London Rd (☎01892/523 983; ③), are good value. The *Swan Hotel* in the Pantiles (☎01892/541 450; ⑥) is pricey but worth a splurge. In keeping with Tunbridge Wells' refined image, there's a good selection of fine **restaurants** – best and most expensive are *Cheevers*, 56 High St (☎01892/545 524), and *Thackeray's House*, 85 London Rd (☎01892/511 921).

Sissinghurst and Leeds Castle

Sissinghurst (April to mid-Oct Tues–Fri 1–6.30pm, Sat & Sun 10am–5.30pm; £5; NT), fifteen miles east of Tunbridge Wells, was described by Vita Sackville-West as "a garden crying out for rescue" when she and her husband took it over in the 1920s. Gradually, they transformed the five-acre plot into one of England's greatest and most popular modern gardens. Spread over the site of an Elizabethan mansion (of which only one wing remains today), the gardens were designed around the linear pattern of the former buildings' walls. Sissinghurst's appeal derives from the way that the flowers are allowed to spill over onto the narrow walkways, defying the classical formality of the great gardens that preceded it. The brick tower Vita restored and used as her study acts as a focal point and offers the best views of the walled gardens. Most impressive are the **White Garden**, composed solely of white flowers and silvery-grey foliage, and the **Cottage Garden**, featuring flora in shades of orange, yellow and red. Sissinghurst gets so busy in summer that timed tickets for half-hourly visits are issued. Food options in the gardens are limited and overpriced – your best bet is to bring a picnic.

Leeds Castle, fifteen miles north of Sissinghurst, on the edge of the North Downs (March–Oct daily 10am–5pm; Nov–Feb closes 3pm; £7.50), is more like a fairytale palace than a defensively efficient fortress. The present stone castle dates from Norman times and is set half on an island in the middle of a lake and half on the mainland surrounded by landscaped parkland. Following centuries of regal and noble ownership (and service as a prison) the castle is now run as a commercial concern, hosting conferences as well as sporting and cultural events. Its interior fails to match the castle's stunning external appearance and, in places, twentieth-century renovations have quashed any of its historical charm; possibly the most unusual feature inside is the dog collar museum. In the grounds, there's a fine aviary with some colourful exotic specimens, as well as manicured gardens and a mildly challenging maze.

Penshurst and Hever Castle

Tudor timber-framed houses and shops line the high street of the attractive village of **PENSHURST**, five miles northwest of Tunbridge Wells. Its village church, St John the Baptist, is capped by an unusual four-spired tower and is entered under a beamed archway which conceals a rustic post office. However, the main reason for coming here is to visit **Penshurst Place** (Easter–Sept daily: house 12.30–5.30pm, grounds 11am–6pm; £4.95), home to the Sidney family since 1552 and birthplace of the Elizabethan soldier and poet, Sir Philip Sidney. The fourteenth-century Barons Hall, built for Sir John de Pulteney, four times Mayor of London, is the chief glory of the interior, with its 60ft-high chestnut roof still in place. The ten acres of grounds include a formal Italian garden with clipped box hedges, and double herbaceous borders mixed with an abundance of yew hedges.

The moated and much-altered **Hever Castle** (mid-March to early Nov noon–6pm; £5), three miles further west, is where Anne Boleyn, second wife of Henry VIII, grew up, and where Anne of Cleves, Henry's fourth wife, lived after their divorce. In 1903, having fallen into disrepair, the castle was bought by William Waldorf-Astor, American

church are the ruins of de Warenne's **St Pancras Priory**, once one of Europe's principal Cluniac institutions, with a church the size of Westminster Abbey. Sadly it was dismantled to build town houses following the Dissolution and is now an evocative ruin surrounded by playing fields.

Returning to the town centre, the **Star Brewery Studio** in Castle Ditch Lane off Fisher Street, displays the creative talents of a collective of artists, bookbinders, carpenters and other artisans; the attached *Star Gallery* (Mon–Sat 10am–5.30pm, Sun 11am–4pm; free) presents a changing series of exhibitions. At the end of Fisher Street, School Hill descends towards Cliffe Bridge, entrance to the commercial centre of the medieval settlement, although Cliffe High Street's appearance is now predominantly nineteenth-century. For the energetic, a path leads up onto the Downs from the end of Cliffe High Street – site of England's worst avalanche disaster in 1836, when a bank of snow slid onto Cliffe village killing eight people. The path passes close to an obelisk, commemorating the seventeen Protestant martyrs.

Practicalities

The **train station**, on Station Road, has hourly services from London Victoria and along the coast to Brighton, Eastbourne, Hastings and the **ferry port** at Newhaven, from where *Stena Sealink* ferries go to Dieppe (4 daily; 4hr; ☎01273/516 699). **Buses** leave from the **bus station** on Eastgate Street, by the river. The **tourist office** (April–Sept Mon–Fri 9am–5pm, Sat 10am–5pm, Sun 11am–3pm; Oct–March Mon–Fri 9am–1pm & 2–5pm; ☎01273/483 448) is at 187 High St. For **accommodation** in town try *Millers*, a timber-framed house at 134 High St (☎01273/475 631; ④) or *Antioch House*, a Jacobean town house with attractive gardens at no. 104 (☎01273/473 057; ④). There's **youth hostel** accommodation eleven miles northeast of Lewes at Blackboys (☎01825/890 607), a rustic wooden cabin with basic facilities, or in the village of Telscombe, six miles south of Lewes (see p.170).

Lewes is home of the excellent Harvey's brewery and most of the **pubs** serve its products. Try the *Black Horse* in Western Road or the *Lewes Arms* just opposite *Star Brewery Studios*. **Food** options include the *Dil Raj,* 12 Fisher St, which serves a range of inexpensive Indian dishes; *La Cucina*, 13 Station St, a moderately priced Italian restaurant; and the *Pai Lin Thai*, 20 Station St, for good, inexpensive Thai food. Pricier options include the brasserie *Twenty Fisher Street*, unsurprisingly at 20 Fisher St, and *Thackery's* at 3 Malling St, over the river on the east side of town, which serves traditional English and French-style food at moderate prices.

Around Lewes: Glyndebourne, Rodmell and Charleston

Glyndebourne, Britain's only unsubsidized opera house, is situated near the village of Glynde, three miles east of Lewes. Founded sixty years ago, the Glyndebourne season is an indispensible part of the high-society calendar, with ticket prices and a distribution system that excludes all but the most devoted opera lovers. On one level, Glyndebourne is a repellent spectacle, its lawns thronged with gentry and corporate bigwigs ingesting champagne and smoked salmon – the productions have massive intervals to allow for an unhurried repast. On the other hand, the musical values are the highest in the country, using young talent rather than expensive star names, and taking the sort of risks Covent Garden wouldn't dream of taking – for example, *Porgy and Bess* is now taken seriously as an opera largely as a result of a great Glyndebourne production. It may be faintly possible for outsiders to acquire tickets in advance by telephone (☎01273/812 321).

Three miles south of Lewes lies the village of **Rodmell**, whose main source of interest is the **Monk's House** (April–Oct Wed & Sat 2–5.30pm; £2; NT), former home of

Virginia Woolf, a leading figure of the Bloomsbury Group (see box below). She and her husband Leonard moved to the weatherboard cottage in 1919 and Leonard stayed there until his death in 1969; both Virginia's and Leonard's remains are interred in the gardens. Nearby lies the River Ouse where Virginia killed herself in 1941 by walking into the water with her pockets full of stones. The house's interior is nothing special and will only really be of interest to Bloomsbury fans, who can look round the study where Virginia wrote several of her novels, and her bedroom, laid out with period editions of her work. Rodmell village also has a very good B&B, *Merlins* (☎01273/486 440; ④), which is right on the South Downs Way and offers a warm welcome. Three miles south of Rodmell, in the village of **Telscombe**, is a quiet **youth hostel** (☎01273/ 301 357), whose simple accommodation is in two-hundred-year-old cottages.

Seven miles east of Lewes, signposted off the A27, is another Bloomsbury Group shrine, **Charleston Farmhouse** (April–July 20 & Sept 6–Oct Wed, Thurs & Sat 2– 5pm; July 21–Sept 5 Wed–Sat 2–5pm; Nov & Dec Sat & Sun 2–4pm; £4.50; bus #125 from Lewes), home to Virginia Woolf's sister Vanessa Bell, Vanessa's husband Clive Bell and her lover Duncan Grant. As conscientious objectors, the trio moved here during World War I so that the men could work on local farms (farm labourers were exempted from military service). The farmhouse became a gathering point for other members of the Group, including the biographer Lytton Strachey, the economist Maynard Kenyes and the novelist E.M. Forster. Duncan Grant continued to live in the house until his death in 1978. All visits to the farmhouse (except Sun) include a fifty-minute guided tour of the interior of the house, where almost every surface is painted

THE BLOOMSBURY GROUP

The **Bloomsbury Group** were essentially a bevy of upper middle-class friends, who took their name from the Bloomsbury area of London, where most of them lived before acquiring country houses in the Sussex countryside. The Group revolved around Virginia, Vanessa, Thoby and Adrian Stephen, who lived at 46 Gordon Square, the London base of the Bloomsbury Group. Thoby's Thursday evening gatherings and Vanessa's Friday Club for painters attracted a whole host of Cambridge-educated snobs who subscribed to Oscar Wilde's theory that "aesthetics are higher than ethics". Their diet of "human intercourse and the enjoyment of beautiful things" was hardly revolutionary, but their behaviour, particularly that of the two sisters (unmarried, unchaperoned, intellectual and artistic), succeeded in shocking London society, especially through their louche sexual practices (most of the group swung both ways).

All this, though interesting, would be forgotten were it not for their individual work. In 1922 Virginia declared, without too much exaggeration, "Everyone in Gordon Square has become famous": Lytton Strachey had been the first to make his name with *Eminent Victorians*, a series of unprecedently frank biographies; Vanessa, now married to the art critic Clive Bell, had become involved in Roger Fry's prolific design firm, Omega Workshop; and the economist John Maynard Keynes had become an adviser to the Treasury (he later went on to become the leading economic theorist of his day). The Group's most celebrated figure, Virginia, married Leonard Woolf and became an established novelist; she and Leonard also founded the Hogarth Press, which published T. S. Eliot's *Waste Land* in 1922.

Eliot was just one of a number of writers, such as Aldous Huxley, Bertrand Russell and E. M. Forster, who were drawn to the interwar Bloomsbury set, but others, notably D. H. Lawrence, were repelled by the clan's narcissism and snobbish narrow-mindedness. Whatever their limitations, the Bloomsbury Group were Britain's most influential intellectual coterie of the interwar years, and their appeal shows little sign of waning – even now scarcely a year goes by without the publication of the biography and or memoirs of some Bloomsbury peripheral.

and the walls are hung with paintings by Picasso, Renoir and Augustus John, alongside the work of the markedly less talented residents. Many of the fabrics, lampshades and other artefacts bear the unmistakeable mark of the Omega Workshop, the Bloomsbury equivalent of William Morris' artistic movement.

Brighton

Recorded as the tiny fishing village of Brithelmeston in the Domesday Book, **BRIGHTON** seems to have slipped unnoticed through history until the mid-eighteenth-century sea-bathing trend established a resort that has never looked back. The fad received royal approval in the 1770s when the decadent Prince Regent, later George IV, began patronizing the town in the company of his mistress, thus setting a precedent for the "dirty weekend", Brighton's major contribution to the English collective consciousness. Trying to shake off this blowsy reputation, Brighton now highlights its Georgian charm, its upmarket shops and classy restaurants and its thriving conference industry. Yet however much Brighton tries to present itself as a comfortable middle-class town, the essence of its appeal is its faintly bohemian vitality, a buzz that comes from a mix of English holidaymakers, thousands of young foreign students from the town's innumerable language schools, a thriving gay community and an energetic local student population from the art college and two universities.

Arrival, information and accommodation

Brighton **train station** is at the head of Queen's Road; *National Express* and *Southdown* **bus services** arrive at Pool Valley **bus station**, tucked just in from the seafront on the south side of the Old Steine. The **tourist office** is at 10 Bartholomew Square, on the southern side of The Lanes (June–Sept Mon–Fri 9am–5.30pm, Sat & Sun 10am–6pm; Oct–May Mon–Sat 9am–5pm, Sun–10am–4pm; ☎01273/323 755), a maze of narrow lanes marking Brighton's Old Town. You'll find most budget **accommodation** clustered around the **Kemp Town** district, to the east of the Palace Pier, with the more elegant and expensive hotels west of the town centre around Regency Square, opposite the West Pier. The only official **campsite** in Brighton is *Sheepcote Vale* (☎01273/626 546), just north of the marina.

Hotels, B&Bs and Guest Houses

Adelaide Hotel, 51 Regency Square (☎01273/205 286). Top-notch guest house in the fancier part of town. ⑦.

Andorra Hotel, 15–16 Oriental Place (☎01273/321 787). At the west end of town, this hotel has comfortable rooms with good facilities and offers reductions for stays of two nights or more. ⑥.

Arlanda Hotel, 20 New Steine (☎01273/699 300). Plusher than average choice in the New Steine square. ⑥.

Cornerways Hotel, 18–20 Caburn Rd (☎01273/731 882). Inexpensive and friendly B&B, a couple of minutes west of the train station. ③.

Four Seasons Guest House, 3 Upper Rock Gardens (☎01273/681 4960. Cosy B&B in the Kemp Town area, with good vegetarian breakfast options. ④.

Georjan, 27 Upper Rock Gardens (☎01273/694 951). Pleasant guest house well situated between the town and seafront. ④.

Lanes Hotel, 70 Marine Parade (☎01273/ 674 231). Attractive hotel with a tiled and balustraded facade right on the seafront with some parking; some of the rooms have four-poster beds. ⑥.

Pier View Hotel, 28 New Steine (☎01273/605 310). Friendly, upmarket guest house in an attractive Regency terrace. ⑥.

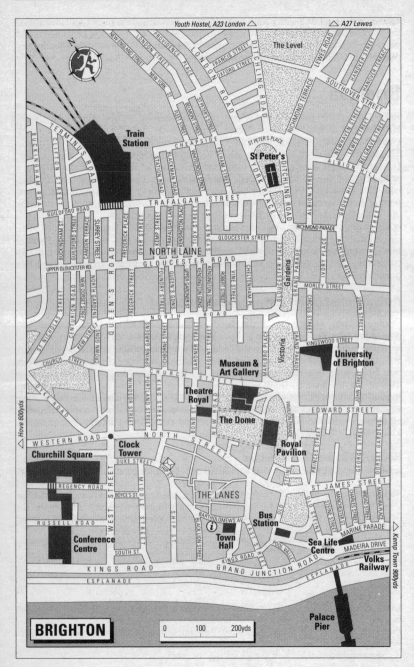

Youth Hostel, A23 London △   △ A27 Lewes

The Level

Train Station

St Peter's

NORTH LAINE

Victoria Gardens

Museum & Art Gallery

University of Brighton

Theatre Royal

The Dome

Clock Tower

Royal Pavilion

Churchill Square

THE LANES

Bus Station

Conference Centre

Town Hall

Sea Life Centre

Volks Railway

Palace Pier

△ Hove 600yds

Kemp Town 900yds △

BRIGHTON

0   100   200yds

Queensbury Hotel, 58 Regency Square (☎01273/325 558). Comfortable guest house in Brighton's definitive Georgian district. ⑤.
Sea Spray, 25 New Steine (☎01273/680 332). Good value B&B with showers in all rooms. ③.
Westbourne Hotel, 46 Upper Rock Gardens (☎01273/686 920). Well appointed B&B close to the seafront and all amenities. ④.

Hostels

Brighton Backpackers, 75 Middle St (☎01273/777 717). Brighton's established independent hostel run by tuned-in owners with a lively, easy-going atmosphere and vivid murals. A new annex just round the corner overlooks the seafront and offers a quieter alternative. £10 for a dorm bed, £25 for a twin room.
Baggies Backpackers, 33 Oriental Place (☎01273/733 740). Spacious house a little west of the centre with large bright dorms, decent showers and plenty of room to spread out. £8 for a bed in a mixed dorm, £9 in a single-sex dorm.
Youth Hostel, Patcham Place, London Rd (☎01273/556 196). Brighton's YHA hostel is housed in a splendid Queen Anne mansion, in parkland four miles north of the sea, close to the junction of the roads to Lewes and London. Take bus #5 or 5a from the town centre.

The Town

Any visit to Brighton inevitably begins with a visit to its two most famous landmarks – the exuberant **Royal Pavilion** and the wonderfully tacky **Palace Pier** – followed by a stroll along the seafront promenade or the pebbly beach. Just as interesting, though, is an exploration of Brighton's car-free **Lanes**, where some of the town's diverse restaurants, bars and tiny bric-a-brac, jewellery and antique shops can be found; or an idle meander through the quaint, but more bohemian, **North Laines** quarter.

The Royal Pavilion

In any survey to find England's most loved building, there's always a bucketful of votes for Brighton's exotic extravaganza, the **Royal Pavilion** (June–Sept daily 10am–6pm; Oct–May closes 5pm; £3.85), which flaunts itself in the middle of the main thoroughfare of Old Steine. The building that originally stood here was a conventional farmhouse. Then in 1787, the fun-loving Prince of Wales commissioned something more regal, and for a couple of decades the prince's south-coast *pied-à-terre* was a Palladian villa, with mildly oriental embellishments. Shortly after becoming Prince Regent, George commissioned John Nash, architect of London's Regent Street, to build an extraordinary confection of slender minarets, twirling domes, pagodas, balconies and miscellaneous motifs imported from India and China and supported on an innovative cast-iron frame, creating an exterior profile that defines a genre of its own – Oriental-Gothic. Queen Victoria was not amused by George's taste in architecture, and shifted the royal seaside residence to the Isle of Wight, taking the pavilion's valuable fittings back to Buckingham and Kensington palaces and selling the building to the town. The pavilion was then pressed into a series of humdrum roles – tea room, hospital, concert hall, radar station, ration office – but has now been brilliantly restored.

Inside the pavilion the exuberant compendium of Regency exotica has been enhanced by the return of many of the objects which Victoria had taken away. One of the highlights – approached via the restrained Long Gallery – is the **Banqueting Room**, which erupts with ornate splendour and is dominated by a one-tonne chandelier hung from the jaws of a massive dragon cowering in a plantain tree. Next door, the huge, high-ceilinged kitchen, fitted with the most modern appliances of its time, has iron columns disguised as palm trees. Nearby, the stunning **Music Room**, the first sight of which reduced George to tears of joy, has a huge dome lined with more than 26,000 individually gilded scales and hung with exquisite umbrella-like glass lamps. After climbing the famous cast-iron staircase with its bamboo-look bannisters, you can go into Victoria's sober and seldom-used bedroom and the North Gallery where the King's portrait hangs, along with a selection of satirical cartoons. More notable, though, is the **South Gallery**, decorated in sky blue with *trompe l'oeil* bamboo trellises and a carpet which appears to be strewn with flowers.

The rest of the town

Across the gardens from the pavilion stands the **Dome**, once the royal stables and now the town's main concert hall, adjoining Brighton's **Museum and Art Gallery** (Tues–Sat 10am–5.45pm, Sun 2–5pm; free), which is entered just around the corner on Church Street. The paintings here are generally nondescript, but there's an interesting collection of classic Art Deco and Art Nouveau furniture as well as Dali's famous sofa, based on Mae West's lips. There's also a large selection of pottery, from basic Neolithic earthenware to delicate porcelain figurines popular in the eighteenth century.

Tucked between the pavilion and the seafront is a warren of narrow, pedestrianized thoroughfares known as **The Lanes** – the core of the old fishing village from which Brighton evolved. Long-established antiques shops, designer outlets and several bars, pubs and restaurants generate a lively and intimate atmosphere in this part of town. **North Laine** is a similar but unpedestrianized precinct, with a more bohemian atmosphere, which spreads north of North Street along Kensington, Sydney, Gardner and Bond streets. Here the shops are more eclectic, selling secondhand records, clothes and New Age objects, and mingle with earthy coffee shops and downbeat cafés.

Most of the seafront is an ugly mix of shops, entertainment complexes and hotels, ranging from the impressively pompous plasterwork of the *Grand* – scene of the IRA's attempted assassination of the Conservative cabinet in 1984 – to the green-glass monstrosity on the seaward side of the Lanes. To fully appreciate the tackier side of Brighton, you must take a stroll along the **Palace Pier** – Brighton's only one, after the West Pier was damaged in a storm in the 1970s, leaving an inaccessible, rusting stump. The Palace Pier has yet to gain a replacement for the splendid theatre that once occupied its seaward end, but every inch of the structure is devoted to fun and money-making, from the cacophonous Palace of Fun and Pleasure Dome with its state-of-the-art video games to the fairground rides and karaoke sessions at the end of the pier.

Right by the pier, on Marine Parade, is the **Sea Life Centre** (daily 10am–6pm; £4.50), one of the best marine life displays of its kind, with a transparent tunnel passing through a huge aquarium – a walk along the bottom of the sea with sharks and rays gliding overhead. Nearby, the antiquated locomotives of **Volk's Electric Railway** (April–Sept; £1 one-way) – the first electric train in the country – run eastward towards the Marina and the nudist beach, usually the preserve of just a few thick-skinned souls.

Eating, drinking and nightlife

Brighton has the greatest concentration of **restaurants** of anywhere in the southeast, outside London. Around the North Laines are a few cheap and cheerful cafés, while for classier establishments head to The Lanes and out towards Hove. Many of the cheaper places fight hard to attract the large student market with discounted deals of around ten per cent, so if you have a student ID, use it. **Nightlife** is hectic and compulsively pursued throughout the year, making Brighton unique in the sedate southeast. Every May the three-week-long **Brighton Festival** takes place in various venues around town. This arty celebration includes fun fairs, exhibitions, street theatre and concerts from classical to jazz; call at the tourist office for more details.

Restaurants

Al Duomo, 7 Pavilion Buildings. Brilliant pizzeria with a genuine wood-burning oven. Has a more intimate sister restaurant *Al Forno*, at 36 East St. Inexpensive.

Black Chapati, 12 Circus Parade (☎01273/699 011). Innovative Asian cooking with Japanese and Thai influences as well as more conventional Indian dishes, which are brilliantly executed. Something of a Brighton landmark despite its out-of-the-way location, more than a mile inland, at the point where the London road enters town. Moderate.

Browns Restaurant, 3–4 Duke St (☎01273/323 501). A mixture of steak, seafood and pasta dishes as well as traditional favourites like Guinness-marinated steak and mushroom pie, served in a sophisticated continental setting with wooden floors, palms and background jazz. Moderate.

Casa Don Carlos, 5 Union St. Small, long-established tapas bar in the Lanes with outdoor seating and daily specials. Also serves more substantial Spanish dishes and drinks. Inexpensive.

English's Oyster Bar, 29–31 East St (☎01273/325 661). Three fisherman's cottages knocked together to house a marble and brass oyster bar and a red velvet dining room. Seafood's the speciality with a mouthwatering menu and better value than you might expect, especially the set menus. Brighton institution famed for its atmosphere as much as its food. Expensive.

Food for Friends, 17 Prince Albert St. Brighton's ever popular wholefood veggie eatery is imaginative enough to please die-hard meat-eaters. It's frequently busy but well worth the squeeze and offers discounts for students. Inexpensive.

Le Gastronome, 3 Hampton Place (☎01273/777 399). Well known for its good-value classic French cuisine, friendly service and outstanding selection of wines. Moderate.

Innocent Bystander, 54 Preston St, off King's Road, near the West Pier. Burgers, vegan breakfasts and the infamous "Gut Buster" breakfast, all accompanied by MTV. Open till 3am. Inexpensive.

Melrose Restaurant, 132 Kings Rd. Traditional and decent seafront establishment which has been serving seafood, roasts and custard-covered puddings for over 40 years. The *Regency Restaurant* next door is a similar and smaller option. Inexpensive.

Piccolo, 58 Ship St. Informal Italian restaurant with pizza and pasta dishes from around £3 and special deals for students. Inexpensive.

Rasa Sayang, 11 Little East St (☎01273/774 545). Dishes from all over southeast Asia – Malaysia in particular – featuring ginger, lemon grass, coconut and spices. Moderate.

The Sanctuary, 51 Brunswick St East, Hove. Cool and arty vegetarian café with soft furnishings and a cosy, relaxed ambience. Deservedly popular despite its not-very-central location. Inexpensive.

Terre-à-Terre, 7 Pool Valley. Good, global, veggie cuisine in a small, modern arty setting. Inexpensive.

Thai Spice Market, 13 Boyces St (☎01273/325 195). Classical Thai interior and cuisine, serving meat, seafood and vegetarian varieties. Moderate.

Yum Yum Noodle Bar, 22–23 Sydney St. Serves anything Southeast Asian – Chinese, Thai, Indonesian and Malaysian noodle dishes at good-value prices. Inexpensive.

Pubs

Cricketers, 15 Black Lion St. Just west of The Lanes, this is Brighton's oldest pub and it looks it too; good pub food.

Dr Brighton's, 16 Kings Rd. Popular gay venue near the Queens Hotel.

Druids Head, 9 Brighton Place. Great, old pub in the heart of the Lanes with the best jukebox in town.

Hand in Hand, 33 Upper St James St. An agreeable pub with its own brewery out the back.

Font & Firkin, Union St. Spacious and imaginatively converted chapel with a bar in place of the altar.

Prince Albert, 48 Trafalgar St. A listed building, popular with students, where live rock and real ale are on the menu.

Queens Head, 10 Steine St. Popular, gay pub in the heart of the town centre.

Smugglers, 10 Ship St. A young crowd packs out this place, with a good jazz club upstairs.

Nightlife

There are a couple of outstanding **clubs**, lots of **live music** and more cinema screens per head than anywhere else in Britain. Midweek entry into the clubs can cost just a couple of pounds and cinema seats are similarly priced before 6pm. For up-to-date details of **what's on**, pick up a free copy of *What's On* from the tourist office, restaurants or pubs. Other listings magazines to watch out for are the monthly *The Punter*

(70p) and *Impact* (50p), which includes *The Queer Guide* supplement detailing gay and lesbian events in the town.

The Basement, Brighton Art College, Grand Parade. Popular nightclub run by local art students and featuring Techno, Ambient and Dub on alternate weeks with a good measure of foot-tapping Psycho, Gothic and Industrial too.

Casablanca, *Churchill Palace Hotel*, 2–5 Middle St. Mostly Brazilian funky jazz and reggae.

Escape, 10 Marine Parade. Brighton's trendiest nightclub packs them in night after night, specializing in funk and rave music.

The Lift, *Pig in Paradise*, Queens Rd. Regular and varied jazz events.

Paradox, 78 West St. The best option after the *Zap Club*. Its *Wild Fruits* gay nights on first Mondays of the month are particularly popular.

The Jazz Place, *Smugglers Inn*, 10 Ship St. Popular jazz venue in the basement with the livelier *Reforming Club* upstairs catering for active ravers and fronting the occasional abstract dance troupe.

Club Revenge, 32 Old Steine. The south's largest gay club with Monday night cabarets plus upfront dance and retro boogie on two floors.

Sussex Club, 5 Regency Square. Small and relaxed lesbian club for over-25s.

Swifts Club, West St. Popular venue for retro sounds from the 60s onwards with the *Cavern* below playing hip-hop, ragga jungle and some truly wicked Street soul.

Zap Club, Kings Rd Arches. Brighton's most durable club, right on the seafront. A popular venue even for Londoners.

Mid-Sussex

The principal attraction of **mid-Sussex** is its wealth of fine gardens, ranging from the majestic **Sheffield Park** to the luscious flowerbeds of **Nymans** and the landscaped lakes of **Leonardslee**. Exploring this region by public transport isn't really feasible unless you take your bike on the train; tourist information is thin on the ground too, so get clued up at Brighton's tourist office before you go.

Sheffield Park and the Bluebell Railway

Ten miles north of Lewes lies the country estate of **Sheffield Park**, its centrepiece a Gothic mansion built for Lord Sheffield by James Wyatt. The house is closed to the public, but you can roam around the hundred-acre **gardens** (April–Nov Tues–Sun 11am–6pm or sunset; £4), which were laid out by Capability Brown, the Christopher Wren of the grassy knoll. A mile south of the gardens lies the southern terminus of the **Bluebell Railway** (May Wed, Sat & Sun; June–Sept daily; Oct–April Sat & Sun; day ticket £7; information ☎01825/722 370), whose vintage steam locomotives chuff nine miles north via Horsted Keynes to Kingscote. Although the service gets extremely crowded on weekends – especially in May, when the bluebells blossom in the woods through which the line passes – it's an entertaining and nostalgic way of travelling through the Sussex countryside and your day ticket lets you go to and fro as often as you like. A vintage bus service connects Kingscote with East Grinstead train station (hourly trains from London Victoria), though plans are afoot to re-lay the remaining two miles of track and link the Bluebell directly with East Grinstead.

Nymans and Leonardslee

Nymans (March–Oct Wed–Sun 11am–7pm or sunset; £3.80; NT), eighteen miles north of Brighton near the village of Handcross, is one of the southeast's greatest gardens. Created by Ludwig Messel, an inspired gardener and plant collector, the gardens contain a valuable collection of exotic trees and shrubs as well as more everyday plants, of which the colourful rhododendrons are particularly prolific. Nymans consists of a series of different enclosures and gardens, the highlight of which is the large, romantic walled garden, almost hidden from sight by an abundance of climbing plants and housing a collection of rare Himalayan magnolia trees. The gardens are centred on the picturesque ruins of a mock-Tudor manor house, now covered in wisteria, roses and honeysuckle, and are laced with gently sloping paths linking the huge beds of rhododendrons, azaleas and roses.

The most picturesque of all the mid-Sussex gardens, though, are those at **Leonardslee** (mid-April to June daily 10am–6pm; July–Oct Mon–Fri 2–6pm, Sat & Sun 11am–6pm; £4), near the village of Crabtree, sixteen miles north of Brighton. Set in a wooded valley, the seventy-acre gardens are crisscrossed by steep paths, which link six lakes, created – like those at Sheffield Park – in the sixteenth century to power water wheels for iron foundries. The range of flora is especially impressive here, featuring many hybrid species of rhododendron that were created specifically for this garden. Wallabies, sika and fallow deer roam freely, adding to the Edenic atmosphere.

Arundel and around

The hilltop town of **ARUNDEL**, eighteen miles west of Brighton, has for seven centuries been the seat of the Dukes of Norfolk, whose fine castle looks over the valley of the River Arun. The medieval town's well-preserved appearance and picturesque setting draws in the crowds on summer weekends, but at any other time a visit reveals one of West Sussex's least spoilt old towns. Arundel also has a unique place in English cricket: traditionally, the first match of every touring side is played against the Duke of Norfolk's XI on the ground beneath the castle.

Arundel Castle, towering over the High Street (April–Oct daily except Sat noon–5pm; £5) is what first catches the eye and, despite its medieval appearance, most of what you see is only a century old. The structure dated from Norman times, but was ruined during the Civil War then lavishly reconstructed during the nineteenth century by the eighth, eleventh and fifteenth dukes. From the top of the keep, you can see the current duke's spacious residence and the pristine castle grounds. Inside the castle, the renovated quarters include the impressive **Barons Hall** and the **library**, which boasts paintings by Gainsborough, Holbein and Van Dyck.

On the edge of the castle grounds, the fourteenth-century **Fitzalan Chapel** houses tombs of past dukes of Norfolk, including twin effigies of the seventh Duke – one as he looked when he died and, underneath, one of his emaciated corpse. The Catholic chapel belongs to the Norfolk estate, but is actually part of the parish **Church of St Nicholas**, whose entrance is in London Road. It is separated from the altar of the main Anglican church by an iron grill and a glass screen. Although traditionally Catholics, the Dukes of Norfolk have shrewdly played down their papal allegiance in sensitive times – such as during the Tudor era when two of the third Duke's nieces, Anne Boleyn and Catherine Howard, became Henry VIII's wives.

Up the High Street away from the river stands the towering bulk of Arundel's Gothic **Cathedral of Our Lady and St Philip Howard** in London Road. The cathedral was constructed in the 1870s by the fifteenth Duke of Norfolk over the town's former Catholic church, with its spire designed by John Hansom, inventor of the Hansom Cab, the earliest taxi. Inside are the enshrined remains of Saint Philip Howard, the fourth Duke's son, exhumed from the Fitzalan Chapel after his canonization in 1970. Following a wayward youth, Howard returned to the Catholic fold at a time when the Armada's defeat saw anti-Catholic feelings soar. Caught fleeing overseas and sentenced to death for praying for Spanish victory, he spent the next decade in the Tower of London, where he died. The cathedral's impressive outline is more appealing than the interior, but it fits in well with the townscape of the medieval seaport, where the antique shop-lined Maltravers and Arun streets are the most attractive thoroughfares.

Practicalities

Arundel **train station** is half a mile south of the town centre on the A27, with **buses** arriving either in the High Street or River Road. The **tourist office** is at 61 High St (Easter–Oct Mon–Thurs 9am–5pm, Fri 9am–6pm, Sat 10am–6pm, Sun 10am–5pm; Nov–Easter Mon–Sat 9.30am–3.30pm; ☎01903/882 268). For **accommodation**, try *Bridge House*, just south of the Queen Street bridge (☎01903/882 779; ③), *Dukes Restaurant*, 65 High St (☎01903/883 847; ④) or, four miles north of Arundel in Amberley, you can stay in luxury at the six-hundred-year-old fortress, *Amberley Castle* (☎01798/931 992; ⑧–⑨). At the other end of the scale, Arundel's **youth hostel** (☎01903/882 204) is in a large Georgian house by the river at Warningcamp, a mile east of town; you can also **camp** at the hostel. First choice for good food is the **restaurant** attached to the *White Hart* pub, 3 Queen St; alternatively try *The Tudor Rose*, 49 High St, or the *Country Kitchen*, 31 Tarrant St, for a good range of vegetarian options. The busiest **pub** in town is the *Eagle* at 41 Tarrant St, which dispenses King & Barnes beer from nearby Horsham, as well as Fuller's London Pride.

Bignor and Petworth

Six miles north of Arundel, the excavated second-century ruins of the **Bignor Roman Villa** (March–May & Oct Tues–Sun 10am–5pm; June–Sept daily 10am–6pm; £3) include some well-preserved mosaics, of which the Ganymede is the most outstanding. The site, first excavated between 1811 and 1819, is superbly situated at the base of the South Downs and features the longest extant section of mosaic in England, as well as the remains of a hypocaust, the underfloor heating system developed by the Romans.

Petworth House (April–Oct Tues–Thurs, Sat & Sun 1–5.30p parking daily 12.30–6pm, free; NT), adjoining the village of Petworth, eleven miles north of Arundel, is one of the southeast's most impressive stately homes. Built in the late seventeenth century, the house contains an outstanding art collection, including paintings by Van Dyck, Titian, Gainsborough, Bosch, Reynolds, Blake and Turner – the last a frequent guest here. Highlights of the interior decor are Louis Laguerre's murals around the **Grand Staircase** and the **Carved Room**, where carvings by Grinling Gibbons and Holbein's full-length portrait of Henry VIII can be seen. The 700-acre grounds were landscaped by Capability Brown and are considered one of his finest achievements.

Chichester

The county town of West Sussex and its only city, **CHICHESTER** is an attractive if stuffy market town, which began life as a Roman settlement – the Roman cruciform street plan is still evident in the four-quadrant symmetry of the town centre, spread around the Market Cross. The city has built itself up as one of southern England's cultural centres, hosting the **Chichester Festival** in early July, its focus a staid programme of middlebrow plays and safe classic productions. The racecourse at Goodwood Park, north of the city, hosts one of England's most fashionable racing events at the same time (see box on p.180). The Gothic cathedral is the chief permanent attraction in the city, but two miles west of the town are the restored Roman ruins of **Fishbourne**, one of the most visited ancient sites in the county.

The City

The main streets lead off to the compass's cardinal points from the **Market Cross**, an ornate, carved-stone rotunda built in 1501 to provide shelter for the market traders, although it appears far too small for its function. West Street, accessible from the award-winning Avenue de Chartres Car Park, is filled by the neat form of the **Cathedral** (Mon–Sat 9.15am–5.15pm, Sun 10am–4pm; guided tours Mon–Sat 11am & 2.15pm; donation requested), whose slender spire – a nineteenth-century addition – is visible out at sea. Building began in the 1070s, but the church was extensively rebuilt following a fire a century later and has been only minimally modified since about 1300, except for the spire and the unique, free-standing fifteenth-century bell tower. The interior is renowned for its contemporary **devotional art**, which includes a stained-glass window by Marc Chagall and an enormous altar-screen tapestry by John Piper.

Other points of interest are the sixteenth-century painting in the north transept of the past Bishops of Chichester, and the fourteenth-century Fitzalan tomb which inspired a poem by Philip Larkin. However, the highlight is a pair of **reliefs** in the south aisle, close to the tapestry – created around 1140, they show the raising of Lazarus and Christ at the gate of Bethany. Originally highly coloured, the reliefs once featured semi-precious stones set in the figures' eyes and are among the finest Romanesque stone carvings in England.

Across South Street in the well-preserved Georgian quadrant of the city known as the Pallants, you'll find **Pallant House**, 9 North Pallant (Tues–Sat 10am–5.15pm; £2.50). Stone dodos stand guard over the gates of this fine mansion, which houses artefacts and furniture from the early eighteenth century. Modern works of art are also included, among them pieces by Henry Moore and Barbara Hepworth and George Sutherland's portrait of Walter Hussey, the former Dean of Chichester, who commissioned much of the cathedral's contemporary art.

Continuing in an anticlockwise direction around the town, and crossing East Street to head north up Little London, brings you to the **Town Museum** (Tues–Sat 10am–5.30pm; free), housed in an old corn store. Inside, the modest but entertaining display on local life includes a portable oven carried by Joe Faro, the city pieman, as well as the portable stocks used for the ritual humiliation of petty criminals. The **Guildhall** (June–Sept Tues–Sat 1–5pm; free), a branch museum within a thirteenth-century Franciscan church in the middle of Priory Park, at the north end of Little London, has some well-preserved medieval frescoes. Formerly a town hall and court of law, the poet, painter and visionary William Blake was tried here for sedition.

Practicalities

Chichester's **train** and bus **stations** are at the foot of South Street, ten minutes' walk from the centre, via the **tourist office** at 29a South St (Mon–Sat 9.30am–5.30pm; ☎01243/775 888). If you want to splash out on **accommodation**, there are two comfortable and characterful inns in the centre of town: the *Ship* on North Street (☎01243/778 000; ⑧), and the much older *Dolphin and Anchor* on West Street (☎01243/785 121; ⑥). Less expensive **B&B** options include the central *Riverside Lodge*, 7 Market Ave (☎01243/783 164; ④), in the Pallants quarter, or 148 Broyle Rd (☎01243/798 662; ③), on the north side of town close to the Festival Theatre. You can **camp** at the *Earnley Beach Centre*, Clappers Lane, Earnley, six miles southwest of town (☎01243/673 533), a large site with its own bar and private beach, and a popular spot for windsurfing.

Both the *Ship* and the *Dolphin and Anchor* are good places for a **drink**, or you could try the *Rainbow*, 56 St Paul's Rd, a little way out of the centre – it has an excellent range of Sussex beers. For something to **eat**, South Street has the *Medieval Crypt Brasserie* at no. 12, and *Micawbers* next door which specializes in seafood. For a mediterranean menu try the stylish *Little London Restaurant* in Little London, off East Street.

HORSE-RACING IN SOUTHEAST ENGLAND

A popular way to spend a day out in southeast England is to go to the races at one of the many tracks in the region. **Glorious Goodwood** and the **Derby week** are the fashionable meetings to attend, as is the **Royal Ascot** in Berkshire, but the less well-known courses, such as Brighton, Fontwell Park and Kempton Park, offer equally entertaining meetings throughout the year. For course locations, see chapter map on p.142–143. Generally it'll cost you around £8–10 to get into a "basic" enclosure, but you can pay much higher prices for admission into the grandstand and more exclusive enclosures, where the social event often takes precedence over the racing.

Ascot (☎01344/22211; 10min walk from Ascot BR). No account of racing in southeast England would be complete without Ascot, the jewel in the crown of English racecourses. Admission is expensive but the facilities and atmosphere make it worth the price. The week-long *Royal Meeting* in mid-June is the one to attend, and to dress up for, with a selection of outrageous hats, outfits and Royals on display, especially on Ladies' Day. The racecourse hosts less glamorous meetings throughout the rest of the year.

Brighton (☎01273/682 912; Brighton BR with connecting buses on race days). Overlooking Brighton Marina at the east end of town, Brighton's racecourse has a U-shaped track and is one of the few courses in England that doesn't form a complete circuit; binoculars are useful and can be hired. The racecourse's situation, on top of the South Downs overlooking the English Channel, makes it particularly appealing for a day out. Regular meetings take place from April to September with the three-day meeting in early August providing the best action.

Epsom Downs (☎01372/726 311; Epsom Downs or Tattenham Corner BR with connecting buses on race days). Home of two of England's most famous races, the *Derby* and the *Oaks*, both of which take place during Derby week, the first week in June. The *Derby* has been run for nearly two hundred years and is the time when Epsom really comes alive – a fun day out for all classes of persons. There are very few meetings at other times: an evening meeting at the end of June and July and a two-day event at the end of August.

Fishbourne Roman Palace

Fishbourne (March–Nov daily 10am–6pm; Dec–Feb Sun only 10am–4pm; £3.50), two miles west of Chichester (Fishbourne BR or bus #700 from Chichester), is the largest and best-preserved Roman palace in the country. Roman relics have long been turning up in Fishbourne and in 1960 a workman unearthed their source – the site of a depot used by the invading Romans in 43 AD which later probably became the vast, hundred-room palace of the Romanized Celtic aristocrat, Cogidubnus. A pavilion has been built over the north wing of the excavated remains, where floor mosaics depict Fishbourne's famous dolphin-riding cupid as well as the more usual geometric patterns. Like the remains at Bignor (see p.178), only the residential wing of the former quadrangle has been excavated – other parts of the dwelling fulfilled mundane service roles and probably lacked the mosaics which give both sites their singular appeal. The underfloor heating system has also been well restored and an audio-visual programme gives a fuller picture of the palace as it was in Roman times. The extensive gardens attempt to re-create the appearance of the palace grounds as they would have been then.

Fontwell Park (☎01444/441 111; Barnham BR with connecting buses on race days). Midway between Arundel and Chichester, Fontwell Park is a lesser-known racecourse which makes it a friendly and welcoming venue for first-time race-goers. One-day meetings take place once or twice a month from August to May.

Goodwood Park (☎01243/774 107; 4 miles from Chichester BR with connecting buses on races days). Goodwood boasts a wonderful location, on a lush green hill overlooking Chichester with the South Downs as a backdrop. Even if you have only the mildest interest in the sport, and no interest in betting, it's worth a visit for the main meeting, *Goodwood Week* – or "Glorious Goodwood" to its fans; held in late July, it's second only to Ascot in its social cachet. There are plenty of other meetings from May to late September.

Kempton Park (☎01932/782 292; 5-min walk from Kempton Park BR). Just fifteen miles from London, this popular course has excellent facilities, including covered enclosures for inclement meetings; the majority of the fixtures are run on the flat. Racing takes place all year with evening meetings in April and from June to August. A highlight is the very popular two-day Christmas Festival which starts on Boxing Day.

Lingfield Park (☎01342/834 800; 10-min walk from Lingfield BR). Has an all-weather synthetic track so that races can be run here when they would have to be abandoned elsewhere, but unfortunately this hasn't really caught on with the public and crowds are poor. If you want a lively atmosphere, stick to the turf (grass) events – especially the Turf National Hunt at the beginning of December and the Turf Flat in early May.

Plumpton (01444/441 111; Plumpton BR). Eight miles out of Brighton, this course has one of the sharpest tracks in the country (leading to it being nicknamed the "Wall of Death"), with extremely tight bends and a downhill back straight. Facilities here are good and races take place all year except in June and July.

Sandown Park (☎01372/463 072; 10-min walk from Esher BR). Only 14 miles from Central London, this hugely popular venue near Esher has been frequently voted "Racecourse of the Year" over the past decade. Atmosphere, an excellent location and superb facilities all add up to a great day's racing with the *Whitbread Gold Cup* towards the end of April, and the *Coral-Eclipse Stakes* in early June, bringing out the crowds and well worth attending.

travel details

Trains

Battle to: Hastings (30 daily; 10min); London Victoria (30 daily; 1hr 20min); Tunbridge Wells (30 daily; 30min).

Brighton to: Chichester (17 daily; 55min); Gatwick Airport (19 daily; 25min); Hastings (20 daily; 1hr 30min); Lewes (20 daily; 20min); London Victoria (28 daily; 55min); London King's Cross (17 daily; 1hr 15min); Rye (18 daily; 1hr 30min).

Broadstairs to: London (27 daily; 1hr 50min); Ramsgate (27 daily; 10min).

Canterbury to: Dover (hourly; 20min); London Charing Cross and Victoria (63 daily; 1hr 50min); Ramsgate (hourly; 15min).

Chatham to: London Victoria (51 daily; 1hr 5min); Dover (hourly; 50 min).

Chichester to: Brighton (17 daily; 55min); London Victoria (2 hourly; 1hr 50min).

Dover to: Canterbury (hourly; 20min); Folkestone (hourly; 20min); London Charing Cross and Victoria (19 daily; 2hr).

Eastbourne to: Gatwick Airport (hourly; 40min); Hastings (30 daily; 40min); Lewes (30 daily; 25min); London Victoria (17 daily; 2hr 55min).

Folkestone to: Dover (hourly; 20min); London (19 daily; 1hr 45min).

Gatwick Airport to: Brighton (19 daily; 25min); London Victoria (every 15min; 30min).

Hastings to: Battle (30 daily; 10min); Brighton (20 daily; 1hr 30min); Eastbourne (30 daily; 40min); Gatwick Airport (hourly; 1hr 25min); London Charing Cross or Victoria (30 daily; 1hr 55min); Rye (20 daily; 20min); Tunbridge Wells (30 daily; 45min).

Lewes to: Brighton (every 30min; 20min); Eastbourne (30 daily; 25min); London Victoria (17 daily; 3hr 20min).

Maidstone to: London (29 daily; 1hr 5min).

Margate to: Canterbury (hourly; 20min); London Victoria (29 daily; 1hr 40min).

Ramsgate to: Broadstairs (29 daily; 10min); Canterbury (hourly; 15min); London Victoria and Charing Cross (29 daily; 1hr 50min).

Rochester to: Dover (hourly; 1hr); London Victoria or Charing Cross (41 daily; 55min).

Rye to: Brighton (18 daily; 1hr 30min); Hastings (20 daily; 20min).

Sandwich to: Dover (hourly; 15min); Ramsgate (hourly; 10min); London Victoria (20 daily; 2hr 30min).

Sevenoaks to: London Victoria (26 daily; 1hr 5min).

Tunbridge Wells to: Battle (30 daily; 30min); Hastings (30 daily; 45min); London (28 daily; 1hr 30min).

Whitstable to: London Victoria (27 daily; 1hr 20min); Ramsgate (27 daily; 35min).

Buses

All buses go to Victoria Coach Station

Brighton to: London (9 daily; 1hr 45min); Portsmouth (1 daily; 1hr 45min).

Canterbury to: London (10 daily; 1hr 50min).

Chichester to: London (2 daily; 3hr).

Dover to: London (13 daily; 2hr 45min).

Eastbourne to: London (5 daily; 2hr 15min).

Folkestone to: London (7 daily; 2hr 30min).

Hastings to: London (5 daily; 3hr 30min).

Ramsgate to: London (6 daily; 2hr 45min).

Rochester to: London (hourly; 1hr).

Tunbridge Wells to: London (4 daily; 1hr 30min).

CHAPTER THREE

HAMPSHIRE, DORSET AND WILTSHIRE

The distant past is perhaps more tangible in **Hampshire**, **Dorset** and **Wiltshire** than in any other part of England. Predominantly rural, these three counties overlap substantially with the ancient kingdom of **Wessex**, whose most famous ruler, Alfred, repulsed the Danes in the ninth century and came close to establishing the first unified state in England. Before Wessex came into being, however, many earlier civilizations had left their stamp on the region. The chalky uplands of Wiltshire boast several of Europe's greatest Neolithic sites, including **Stonehenge** and **Avebury**, while in Dorset you'll find **Maiden Castle**, the most striking Iron Age hill fort in the country, and the **Cerne Abbas Giant**, source of many a legend. The Romans tramped all over these southern counties, leaving the most conspicuous signs of their occupation at the amphitheatre of **Dorchester** – though that town is more closely associated with the novels of Thomas Hardy and his distinctively gloomy vision of Wessex.

None of the landscapes of this region could be described as grand or wild, but the countryside is consistently seductive, its appeal exemplified by the crumbling fossil-bearing cliffs around **Lyme Regis**, the managed woodlands of the **New Forest**, or the gentle, open curves of **Salisbury Plain**. Its towns are also generally modest and slow-paced, with the notable exceptions of the two great maritime bases of **Portsmouth** and, to a lesser extent, **Southampton**, a fair proportion of whose visitors are simply passing through on their way to the more genteel pleasures of the **Isle of Wight**. This is something of an injustice, though neither place can compete with the two most interesting cities in this part of England – **Salisbury** and **Winchester**, each of which possesses a stupendous cathedral amid an array of other historic sights. Of these counties' great houses, **Wilton**, **Stourhead**, **Longleat** and **Kingston Lacy** are the ones that attract the crowds, but every cranny has its medieval church, manor house or unspoilt country inn – there are few parts of the country in which an aimless

---

ACCOMMODATION PRICE CODES

Throughout this guide, hotel and B&B accommodation is priced on a scale of ① to ⑨, the number indicating the **lowest price** you could expect to pay per night in that establishment for a **double room** in high season. The prices indicated by the codes are as follows:

① under £20/$30	④ £40–50/$60–75	⑦ £70–80/$105–120
② £20–30/$30–45	⑤ £50–60/$75–90	⑧ £80–100/$120–150
③ £30–40/$45–60	⑥ £60–70/$90–105	⑨ over £100/$150

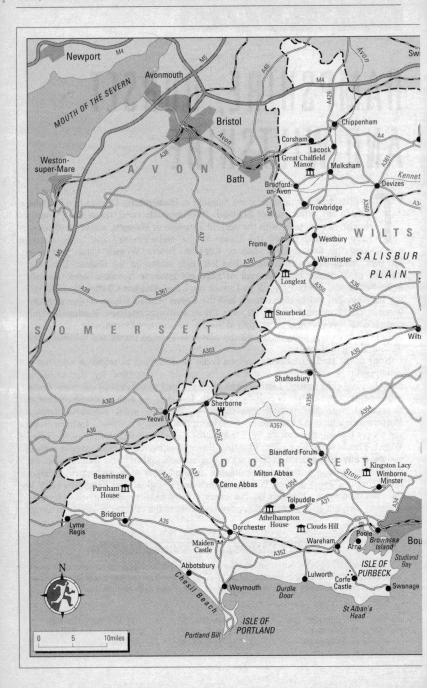

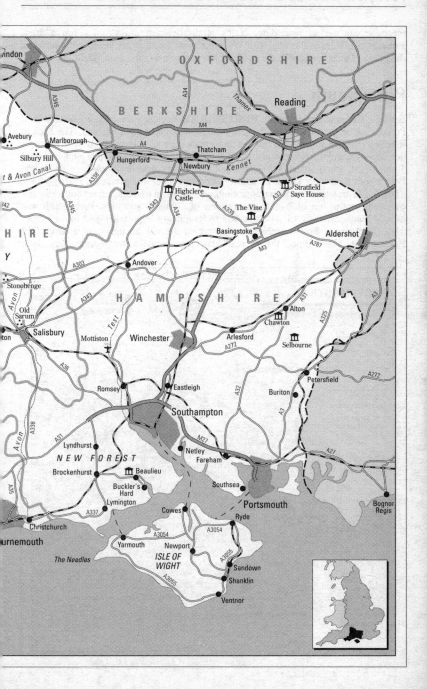

meander can be so rewarding. If it's straightforward seaside fun you're after, **Bournemouth** leads the way, with Weymouth and Lyme Regis heading the ranks of the minor resorts, along with the yachties' havens over on the Isle of Wight.

Portsmouth

Britain's foremost naval station, **PORTSMOUTH** occupies the bulbous peninsula of Portsea Island, on the eastern flank of a huge, easily defended harbour. The ancient Romans raised a fortress on the northernmost edge of this inlet, and a small port developed during the Norman era, but this strategic location wasn't fully exploited until Tudor times, when Henry VII established the world's first dry dock here and made Portsmouth a royal dockyard. It has flourished ever since and nowadays Portsmouth is a large industrialized city, its harbour clogged with naval frigates, ferries bound for the continent or the Isle of Wight, and swarms of dredgers and tugs. Portsmouth was heavily bombed during the last war due to its military importance and tower blocks from the nadir of British architecture now give the city an ugly profile. Only **Old Portsmouth**, based around the original harbour, preserves some Georgian and a little

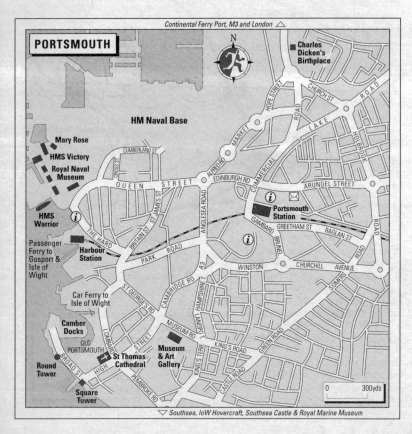

Tudor character. East of here is **Southsea**, a residential suburb of terraces with a half-hearted resort strewn along its shingle beach, where a mass of B&Bs face stoic naval monuments and tawdry seaside amusements.

The Royal Naval Base

For most visitors, a trip to Portsmouth begins and ends at the **Historic Ships**, in the **Royal Naval Base** (daily March–Oct 10am–6pm; Nov–Feb 10.30am–5pm; last entry 90min before closing) at the end of Queen Street. The complex comprises three ships and as many museums, with each ship visitable separately (£4.95 each), though most people do the lot on an all-inclusive ticket (£9.90) which will easily take half a day. Note that visits to the *Victory* are guided, with limited numbers at set times, and you may have to wait up to a couple of hours to take your turn.

Nearest the entrance to the complex is the youngest ship, **HMS Warrior**, dating from 1860. It was Britain's first armoured, or "iron-clad" battleship, complete with sails and steam engines, and was the pride of the fleet in its day. Longer and faster than any previous naval vessel, and the first to be fitted with washing machines, the *Warrior* was described by Napoleon III as a "black snake amongst the rabbits". Despite the weaponry, including rifles, pistols and sabres, the *Warrior* was never challenged nor even fired a cannon in her 22 years at sea. **HMS Victory** was already forty years old when she set sail from Portsmouth for Trafalgar on September 14, 1805, returning victorious three months later, but bearing the corpse of Admiral Nelson. Shot by a sniper from a French ship at the height of the battle, Nelson expired below decks three hours later, having been assured that victory was in sight. The usual fate of casualties at sea was to be sewn into their hammocks with a cannon ball and thrown overboard, but Nelson didn't wish to be buried at sea, so his body was preserved in a huge vat of brandy pending his eventual burial in St Paul's Cathedral. In a shed behind the *Victory* are the remains of the **Mary Rose**, Henry VIII's flagship, which capsized before his eyes off Spithead in 1545 while engaging French intruders, sinking swiftly with almost all her seven-hundred-strong crew. In 1982 a massive conservation project raised the remains of the hull, which silt had preserved beneath the seabed. The ship itself is a bit disappointing; the exhibition close to the *Warrior*, displaying thousands of objects which were found near the wreck, is rather more absorbing.

Opposite the *Victory* various buildings house the exhaustive **Royal Naval Museum**. Tracing the story from Alfred the Great's fleet to the present day, this is the most resistible attraction in the complex. The naval theme is continued at **Submarine World** on Haslar Jetty in Gosport (April–Oct daily 10am–5.30pm; Nov–March closes 4.30pm; £4), reached by taking the passenger ferry from Harbour train station jetty (daily 5.30am–midnight, every 15min; £1.20 return), just south of the entrance to the Royal Naval Base. Allow yourself a couple of hours to explore these slightly creepy vessels – a guided tour inside *HMS Alliance* gives you an insight into life on board and the museum elaborates evocatively on the long history of submersible craft.

Old Portsmouth, Southsea and Porchester Castle

Back at the Harbour train station in Portsmouth, it's a well-signposted twenty-minute walk south to what remains of **Old Portsmouth**. Along the way in the High Street, you pass the simple **Cathedral of St Thomas**, whose twelfth-century features have been obscured by postwar development. The High Street ends at a maze of cobbled Georgian streets huddling behind a fifteenth-century wall protecting the **Camber**, or old port, where Walter Raleigh landed the first potatoes and tobacco from the New World. Nearby, the Round and Square Towers, which punctuate the Tudor fortifications, are popular vantage points for observing nautical activities. The remainder of Portsmouth has little else of interest apart from **Dickens' Birthplace** at 393

Commercial Rd (March–Oct daily 10.30am–5.30pm; £1) half a mile north of the town centre, where Dickens was born in 1812.

Southsea's main attraction is the **D-Day Museum** on Clarence Esplanade (April–Oct daily 10am–5.30pm; Nov–May 10am–5pm; £3.50), relating how Portsmouth had a chance to avenge its wartime bombing by being the main assembly point for the D-Day invasion, code-named "Operation Overlord". Next door to the museum, the squat profile of **Southsea Castle** (daily 10am–5.30pm; £1.50), built from the remains of Beaulieu Abbey (see p.198), may have been the spot where Henry VIII watched the *Mary Rose* sink in 1545. A mile further along the shoreside South Parade, just past South Parade pier, the **Royal Marines Museum** (daily 10am–5pm; £3) describes the origins and greatest campaigns of the Navy's elite fighting force. Outside, a junior assault course gives aspirant young commandos a chance to get in shape.

The city's outstanding monument is six miles away – just past the burgeoning marina development at Port Solent – where, in the third century, the Romans founded **Portchester Castle** (April–Sept daily 10am–6pm; Oct–March Tues–Sun 10am–4pm; £2; EH). Over twenty feet high and incorporating some twenty bastions, this Roman fort is the finest surviving example in northern Europe and is so robust that the Normans felt no need to alter it when they moved in. In later years a castle was built within its precincts by Henry II, which Richard II extended and Henry V used as his garrison when assembling the army that was to fight the Battle of Agincourt. Today its grassy enclosure makes a sheltered spot for a congenial game of cricket.

Practicalities

Portsmouth's main **train station** is in the city centre, but the line continues to **Harbour Station**, the most convenient stop for the main sights and old town. Passenger ferries leave from the jetty at the Harbour station to Ryde, on the Isle of Wight (see p.190) and Gosport, on the other side of Portsmouth Harbour (see p.187). *Wightlink* car ferries depart from the ferry port off Gunwharf Road for Fishbourne on the Isle of Wight (see p.190). There are three **tourist offices** (daily 9.30am–5.30pm) in Portsmouth: one on The Hard, by the entrance to the dockyards (☎01705/826 722); another opposite the main train station, at 103 Commercial Rd (☎01705/838 382); and a third at the Continental Ferry Port (☎01705/838 635).

One of the nicest **places to stay** is *The Sally Port*, 57–58 High St (☎01705/821 860; ⑥), an old pub opposite the cathedral, which serves good bar food. *Albatross Guest House*, 51 Waverley Rd (☎01705/828 325; ③), is one of many good value Southsea B&Bs. The official **youth hostel** (☎01705/375 661; bus #12 from city centre), is in an attractive Tudor manor on Old Wymering Lane, in Cosham, ten minutes west of Corsham train station. Alternatively, there's a forty-bed hostel, *Southsea Lodge*, at 4 Florence Rd in Southsea (☎01705/832 495; bus #4 to South Parade Pier). *Bistro Montparnasse*, 103 Palmerston Rd, stands out from the many restaurants in this part of Southsea for its good-quality French and seafood dishes; a cheaper alternative is the wholefood *Country Kitchen*, 59a Marmion Rd, Southsea. Two pubs on Bath Square in Old Portsmouth, with good food, beer and views over the harbour, are *Spice Island* and the *Still &West*.

Southampton

A glance at the map gives some idea of the strategic maritime importance of **SOUTHAMPTON**, which stands on a triangular peninsula formed at the place where the rivers Itchen and Test flow into Southampton Water, an eight-mile inlet from the Solent. Sure enough, Southampton has figured in numerous stirring events: it witnessed the exodus of Henry V's Agincourt-bound army, the Pilgrim Fathers' final departure in the *Mayflower* in 1620, and the maiden voyages of such ships as the *Queen Mary* and the *Titanic*. Unfortunately, since its pummelling by the Luftwaffe and some disastrous postwar planning, the thousand-year-old city is now a sprawling conurbation low on most tourists' list of priorities.

King Canute is alleged to have commanded the waves to retreat at Southampton – not, as legend has it, from a misguided sense of his kingly powers, but to rebuke his overweening courtiers. Whatever his motive, the task would have been especially difficult here, for Southampton, like other Solent ports, enjoys the phenomenon of "double tides" – a prolonged period of high water as the Channel swirls first up the westerly side of the Solent, then, two hours later, backs up round Spithead. This means that exceptionally large vessels can berth here and, even though ocean-going liners are rare nowadays, there'll certainly be some large-scale vessels either in the Eastern Docks, or in the **Western Docks**, home to England's largest commercial dry dock.

Core of the modern town is the **Civic Centre**, a short walk east of the train station. Its clock tower is the most distinctive feature of the skyline, and it houses an excellent **art gallery** that's particularly strong on twentieth-century British artists such as Sutherland, Piper and Spencer (Tues–Fri 10am–5pm, Thurs till 8pm, Sat 10am–4pm, Sun 2–5pm; free). The **Western Esplanade**, curving southward from the station, runs alongside the best remaining bits of the old city **walls**. Rebuilt after a French attack in 1338, they feature towers with evocatively chilly names like Windwhistle, Catchcold and **God's House Tower** – the last of these, at the southern end of the old town in Winkle Street, houses a good **museum of archaeology** (Tues–Fri 10am–5pm, Sat 10am–4pm, Sun 1–5pm; free). Best preserved of the city's seven gates is **Bargate**, at the opposite end of the old town, at the head of the High Street; an elaborate structure, cluttered with lions, classical figures and machicolations (defensive apertures used to drop missiles), it was formerly the guildhall and courthouse.

Other ancient buildings survive amid the piecemeal redevelopment of the High Street area. The oldest church is **St Michael's**, to the west of the High Street, with a twelfth-century font of black Tournai marble. The nearby **Tudor House museum**, in Bugle Street (same times as God's House Tower museum), is an impressive fifteenth-century, timber-framed building, outshining its exhibits of Victorian and early twentieth-century social history, a banqueting hall and a reconstructed Tudor garden. On the opposite side of the High Street, the ruined **Holy Rood** church stands as a monument to the merchant navy men killed in World War II. Down at the southwest corner of the old town, by the seafront, the **Wool House** is a fine fourteenth-century stone warehouse; formerly used as a jail for Napoleonic prisoners, it now houses a **maritime museum** (Tues–Fri 10am–1pm & 2–5pm, Sat 10am–1pm & 2–4pm, Sun 2–5pm; free) with accounts of the heyday of ocean liners including the tragedy of the *Titanic*.

If you're an aviation enthusiast you should visit the **Hall of Aviation** in Albert Road South, by the car ferry terminal (Tues–Sat 10am–5pm, Sun noon–5pm, plus Mon 10am–5pm in school holidays; £3). Dedicated to local aviation designer R. J. Mitchell, it has sixteen of his aircraft on display, including the Spitfire, the Sandringham Flying Boat and the Supermarine seaplane, which in 1931 won the Schneider Trophy by whizzing round the Isle of White at an average speed of 340mph.

Practicalities

The **train station** is centrally located in Blechynden Terrace, west of the Civic Centre; the **bus** and **coach stations** are immediately south and north of the Civic Centre. The **tourist office** is at 9 Civic Centre Rd (Mon–Sat 9am–5pm, Thurs opens 10am; ☎01703/221 106). Southampton isn't a wildly attractive **place to stay**, but there are plenty of possibilities in the centre: *Elizabeth House* at 43–44 The Avenue (☎01703/224 327; ⑤) or *Linden*, just north of the train station on The Polygon (☎01703/225 653; ③).

For grander lodging, try the four-hundred-year-old *Star* (☎01703/339 939; ⑤) or *Dolphin* (☎01703/339 995; ⑦) hotels, both at the bottom of the High Street and both providing comfortable accommodation. There's not a great choice of original **eating** places in town either: try *Buon Gusto*, at 1 Commercial Rd, an inexpensive Italian restaurant; *The Town House*, 59 Oxford St, for vegetarian specialities; or *Kuti's Brasserie*, 39 Oxford St, a top-class, moderately priced Indian restaurant. As for pubs, the tiny, old *Platform Tavern* in Winkle Street at the south end of the High Street, is your best bet.

The Isle of Wight

Having achieved county status after years of being lumped in with Hampshire, the **ISLE OF WIGHT** still has difficulty in shaking off its image as a mere adjunct of rural southern England – comfortably off, scrupulously tidy and desperately unadventurous. Yet the Isle of Wight – less than 23 miles at its widest point – packs a surprising variety of landscapes and coastal scenery within its bounds. The island is divided fairly neatly by a chalk spine that runs east to west across its centre: north of the ridge is a terrain of low-lying woodland and pasture, deeply cut by meandering rivers; to the south is open chalky downland fringed by high cliffs. Two **Heritage Coast** paths follow the best of the shoreline and, what's more, the island harbours several historic buildings and a splendid array of well-preserved Victoriana clad in fretted bargeboards and pseudo-Gothic gables. All of which is scarcely surprising, since the founding Victorian herself felt most at home here – **Osborne House**, originally designed as a summer retreat for the royal family, became Victoria's permanent home after Albert died.

If you're dependent upon **public transport**, pick up the *Southern Vectis* bus route map and timetable from the tourist office or bus station at your point of arrival. The company's hourly *Island Explorer* buses (routes #7 and #7A) run all round the island in about four hours. A *Rover Ticket* allows you unlimited travel on the bus network, costing £5.95 for a summer Day Rover and £22.50 for a Weekly Rover, with discounts of about thirty percent in winter (information ☎01703/522 456). The **rail line** is a short east-coast stretch linking Ryde, Sandown and Shanklin. **Bikes** are carried free on all ferry services, but beware that in summer the island's narrow lanes can get very busy.

Ryde and around

As a major ferry terminal, **RYDE** is the first landfall many visitors make on the island, but one where few choose to linger, despite some grand nineteenth-century architecture and decent beach amusements. Reaching out over the shallows of Ryde Sands, the functional half-mile-long pier is where the ferries dock and former London Underground rolling stock carries the seasonal throngs inland. Union Street rises steeply from the pier's base to the town centre and at its crest sits All Saints church whose spire acts as a landmark from vantage points all across the east of the island and even from parts of the mainland.

The **tourist office** (Aug daily 9.15am–7.45pm; Sept–July closes 5.45pm ☎01983/562 905), **bus station**, *Hovercraft* terminal and Esplanade train station are all located near the base of the pier. **Boat trips** to the Solent forts leave from Ryde jetty; for details contact *Solent Cruises* (☎01983/564 602). **Accommodation and** fine Italian cooking are available just over the road from the jetty in the *Biskra House Hotel and Restaurant*, 17 St Thomas St (☎01983/567 913; ④). Other **B&Bs** to try include *Trentham Guest House*, 38 The Strand (☎01983/563 418; ②), or *Vine Guest House* at 16 Castle St (☎01983/566 633; ②) – both are south of the Esplanade. *Joe Daflo's Café Bar* at 24 Union St has an appealing continental menu, while the *Redan* at no. 70 is an unusual and inexpensive pub and coffee shop combination.

As elsewhere on the island, just a couple of miles can remove you from an undistinguished urban setting into one of idyllic rusticity. Just ouside the village of **BINSTEAD**, two miles west of Ryde's centre, lies **Quarr Abbey**, founded in 1132, but now little more than an ivy-clad archway, hanging picturesquely over a farm track. In 1907 a new abbey was founded just west of the ruins, a striking rose-brick building with Byzantine overtones. Just south of Ryde, the **Isle of Wight Stream Railway** (Easter–Sept, up to 7 daily departures 10am–5pm; ☎01983/884 343; £5.50) starts its delightful ten-mile round trip to Smallbrook on the main Ryde–Shanklin line to the east. Though it doesn't stop anywhere of interest along the way, the impeccably restored carriages in traditional green livery pass through lovely unspoilt countryside.

The village of **BRADING**, four miles south of Ryde on the busy A3055, boasts a cornucopia of sites spanning two millennia. Just south of the village are the remains of **Brading Roman Villa** (April–Oct Mon–Fri 10am–5.30pm, Sat & Sun 10.30am–5.30pm; £2), one of two Roman "villas" on the island (the other is in Newport; see p.572) which were probably sites of bacchanalian worship. The Brading site is renowned for its superbly preserved mosaics, including intact images of Medusa and depictions of Orpheus and Iao, both known to have associations with the cult of Bacchus.

Nunwell House (July–Sept Mon–Wed & Sun 10am–5pm; £2.80), signposted off the A3055 less than a mile northwest of Brading, was where, in 1647, Charles I spent his last night of freedom before being taken to Carisbrooke Castle and eventual execution in Whitehall. The house has been in the Oglander family for nearly nine hundred years, with the present building being a mix of Jacobean and Georgian styles with Victorian additions. Nunwell sits in five acres of lovely gardens and remains very much a family home of the present owners, whose military legacy is reflected inside in a small exhibition commemorating the Home Guard, the defence force of volunteers recruited during the early years of World War II when the island prepared to resist Nazi occupation.

Sandown and Shanklin

SANDOWN is the island's holidaymaking epicentre and possesses the island's only surviving pleasure **pier**, bedecked with amusement arcades, cafeterias, dodgems and a large theatre with nightly entertainment in season. Those with children might consider a visit to **Jack Corney's Zoological Gardens** (Easter–Oct daily 10am–6pm; Nov–

Easter Sun only 10am–5pm; £3.99) at Yaverland, just east of town, which houses an exhaustive selection of spiders and snakes, including huge pythons and the deadly taipan, as well as some frisky lemurs and monkeys, tigers, panthers and other big cats.

Possibly being separated from the shore by a hundred foot-cliffs has preserved **SHANKLIN** from the tawdry excesses of its northern neighbour. It hasn't stopped the promotion of the Old Village's rose-clad, thatched charm with the same zeal as Sandown's pier. Nevertheless, with the adjacent **Shanklin Chine** (Easter to mid-Oct daily, 10am–5pm; June–Sept closes 10pm; £2), a twisting pathway descending a mossy ravine and decorated at night with fairy lights, it all adds up to a picturesque spot, popular since early Victorian times when local resident John Keats drew his Romantic imagery from the environs.

Sandown's **tourist office** (Easter–July, Sept & Oct daily 9am–6pm; July & Aug closes 8.45pm; Nov–Easter Mon–Sat 9.30am–5pm; ☎01983/403 886) is at the base of the pier. The Shanklin equivalent is at 67 High St (same times; ☎01983/862 942). Both towns have *Island Line* train stations about half a mile inland from their beachfront centres. For **accommodation**, try *St Catherines Hotel*, 1 Winchester Park Rd (☎01983/402 392; ④), a comfortable B&B five minutes from Sandown beach, or the attractive Victorian *Osbourne House Hotel*, 20 Esplanade (☎01983/862 501; ③), near Shanklin beach. More secluded is *Alverstone Manor*, 32 Luccombe Rd (☎01983/862 586; ⑥), a mile from the Old Village in Shanklin. *Sandown Youth Hostel* (☎01983/402 651) is in a converted house in the town centre on Fitzroy Street. **Food** options in Sandown include the *Kings Bar Café*, a continental-style licensed café on the High Street with great views over the sea. In Shanklin, head for the *Fisherman's Cottage Free House*, an atmospheric seafaring pub at the southern end of the Esplanade on Appley Beach, serving wholesome food. Alternatively, you could try the excellent *Sea Food Restaurant* in the *Seacourt Hotel* in Lake, between Sandown and Shanklin.

Ventnor and around

The attractive seaside resort of **VENTNOR** sits at the foot of St Boniface Down (787ft), the island's highest point. The Down periodically disintegrates into landslides creating the jumbled terraces known locally as the **Undercliff**, whose sheltered, south-facing aspect and mild winter temperatures have turned Ventnor into a fashionable health spa. Thanks to these unique factors, the town possesses rather more character than the island's other resorts, its Gothic Revival buildings clinging dizzily to zigzagging bends. The floral terraces of the **Cascade** curve down to the slender Esplanade and narrow beach, where former boatbuilders' cottages now provide more recreational services. From the Esplanade, it's a pleasant mile's stroll to Ventnor's famous **Botanical Gardens**, where 22 landscaped acres of subtropical vegetation flourish.

Ventnor's **tourist office** is at 34 High St (Easter–Oct daily 9.30am–5.30pm; ☎01983/853 625). For **accommodation**, try the *Spyglass Inn* (☎01983/855 338; ④) on Ventnor's Esplanade, which boasts a great location, or the *Bonchurch Inn* (☎01983/852 611; ③), off the Shute in the suburb of Bonchurch. Also in Bonchurch is the *Peacock Vane Hotel* (☎01983/520 019; ⑤), a stylish Victorian house in its own grounds. The best of the many **restaurants** in Ventnor town centre is the *Thistle Café*, 30 Pier St, offering inexpensive seafood and vegetarian meals as well as a decent all-day breakfast.

Appuldurcombe House and St Catherine's Point

Follow the B3327 for a couple of miles inland, over St Boniface Down to Wroxall, where a track leads left for half a mile to the ruins of **Appuldurcombe House** (daily April–Sept 10am–6pm; £1.40; EH), built in the late eighteenth century in the Palladian style, its gardens landscaped by Capability Brown. The house was the home of Lord Yarborough before impecunity and neglect led to its semi-abandonment earlier this century. What makes Appuldurcombe unusual is that it has been preserved in this state of decay, a partially roofed but intact shell where the evidence of a former owner's extravagant raising of all floor levels and doorways is clear.

A footpath runs southwestwards along the coast to the most southerly tip of the island, **St Catherine's Point**, with St Catherine's Oratory, a prominent landmark known locally as the "Pepper Pot", on the downs behind. In fact it's a medieval light-house, reputedly built in 1325 as an act of expiation by Walter de Goditon who attempted to pilfer a cargo of wine owned by a monastic community whose ship was wrecked off Atherfield Point in 1313. A short distance west lies **Blackgang Chine** (Easter to late May & late Sept to Oct daily 10am–5pm;, late May to late Sept closes 10pm; £4.50), which opened as a landscaped garden in 1843, and gradually evolved into a theme park, possibly the world's first, now offering a half-dozen exhibits from Smugglerland to Dinosaurland, a giant maze and a rendition of a Victorian Quay.

Yarmouth and around

Situated at the mouth of the River Yar, the pleasant town of **YARMOUTH** was the island's first purpose-built port. Although razed by the French in 1377, the port began to prosper again after **Yarmouth Castle** (April–Oct daily 10am–6pm; £2; EH), tucked between the quay and the pier, was built by Henry VIII. Although there is little more to see in town, Yarmouth, linked to Lymington in the New Forest by car ferry, makes an appealing arrival or departure point. The **tourist office** is on Yarmouth Quay (Easter to mid-Nov daily 9.30am–5.15pm; mid-Nov to Dec Mon–Fri 10am–4pm; ☎01983/760 015). There's a good range of **accommodation** in town – *Jireh House* in St James's Square (☎01983/760 513; ③) is a seventeenth-century guest house with tearooms, which serves evening meals in summer; or try the cosy *Bugle Hotel* (☎01983/760 272; ⑤) opposite, also one of the town's many good **pubs**. There's good **food** too at the Bugle's *Poachers Restaurant, Barnacles* on Bridge Street or *Gossips* at the base of the pier.

Yarmouth is also a good base for exploring the isle's western tip, whose focal points are **Alum Bay**'s multichrome cliffs, best viewed from the chair lift (£1.75 return), and the chalk stacks of **The Needles**, best seen from a boat trip leaving from Alum Bay (*Needles Pleasure Cruises*; 20min; £2; ☎01983/754 477), or from the tunnel by the Old Battery, a fort dating from 1862. Taking the southern road from Freshwater Bay you'll pass the *Farringford Hotel*, on Bedbury Lane (☎01983/752 500; ⑧), Tennyson's former home. There's also a **youth hostel** between the Needles and Yarmouth, at Totland Bay (☎01983/752 165).

Cowes and around

COWES, at the island's northern tip, is inextricably associated with sailing craft and boatbuilding: Henry VIII built a castle here to defend the Solent's expanding naval dockyards and in the 1950s the world's first hovercraft made its test runs here. In 1820 the Prince Regent's patronage of the yacht club gave the port its cachet with the *Royal Yacht Squadron*, now one of the world's most exclusive sailing clubs, permitted to fly the St George's Ensign, guaranteeing free entry to all foreign ports. Only its three hundred members and their guests are permitted within the hallowed precincts of the club house in the remains of Henry VIII's castle, and the club's landing stage is sacro-sanct. The first week of August sees the international yachting festival known as **Cowes Week**, which visiting royalty turns into a high society gala, although most summer weekends see some form of yachting or powerboat racing off Cowes.

The town is bisected by the River Medina with West Cowes being the older and more interesting half, its High Street meandering up from the waterfront Parade. Along the High Street you'll find shops reflecting the town's gentrified heritage, with boatyards, chandlers and *Bekens'* famous yachting gallery – a photo by Bekens of your yacht is considered as prestigious as a family portrait by Snowdon. Cowes **tourist office** is at the Arcade, Fountain Quay (April–June daily 9am–4pm; July–Oct closes 5pm; Nov–March Tues & Wed 9am–4.30pm, Fri 9am–4pm, Sat & Sun 10am–3pm; ☎01983/291 914). **Boat trips** upriver and around the harbour leave from The Parade; for details contact *Solent Cruises* (☎01983/564 602).

Central **accommodation** options include the *Union Inn* (☎01983/293 163; ③) in Watch House Lane; the *Wishing Well Guest House* (☎01983/297 322; ④), 10b High St; or the *Doghouse* (☎01983/293 677; ⑤), on Crossway Road, East Cowes. The town boasts a decent selection of places to **eat**: *Baan Thai,* 10 Bath Rd, and the *Ocean Tandoori,* 38 Birmingham Rd (the east end of the High Street) both offer good-quality oriental food at moderate prices. There are numerous wholesome snack and sandwich shops along the High Street as well as traditional pub meals served at the *Fountain*, *Anchor* and *Harbour Lights*, all on the High Street.

Osbourne House and Whippingham

A floating bridge (pedestrians free, cars 60p) connects West Cowes to the more industrial East Cowes, where the only place of interest is Queen Victoria's family home, **Osbourne House** (April–Oct daily 10am–6pm; £5.50; EH) signposted one mile southeast of town. The house was built in 1845–51 by Prince Albert and Thomas Cubitt, as an Italianate villa with balconies and large terraces overlooking the landscaped gardens towards the Solent. The state rooms, used to entertain visiting dignitaries, possess an expected formality while the private apartments feel more homely like an affluent family's holiday residence, which is what Osbourne was – far removed from the pomp and ceremony of state affairs in London.

Following Albert's death, the desolate Victoria spent much of her time at Osbourne where she eventually died in 1901. Since that time and according to her wishes the house has remained virtually unaltered, allowing an unexpectedly intimate glimpse into Victoria's family life. A mile south of Osbourne is another of Albert's architectural extravaganzas, the Gothic Revival **Whippingham Church** (Easter–Oct Mon–Fri 10am–5.30pm). The German Battenburg family, who later adopted the anglicized name, Mountbatten, have a chapel here and the parents of the present Queen's late uncle, Earl Mountbatten, the island's last governor, are buried in the churchyard.

Newport and Carisbrooke Castle

NEWPORT, the capital of the Isle of Wight, sits at the centre of the island at a point where the Medina's commercial navigability ends. Apart from a few pleasant old quays dating from its days as an inland port, the town serves as the island's municipal and commercial centre, where *Marks & Spencers*, *Sainsburys* and other familiar chain stores draw in the shoppers. The town's main attraction is the hilltop fortress of **Carisbrooke Castle** (April–Oct daily 10am–6pm; Nov–March closes 4pm; £3.50; EH), on the southwest outskirts. The austere Norman keep's most famous visitor was Charles I, detained here (and caught one night ignominiously jammed between his room's bars while attempting escape) prior to his execution in London. The **museum** in the centre of the castle features many relics from his incarceration as well those of the last royal resident, Princess Beatrice, Queen Victoria's youngest daughter. The castle's other notable curiosity is the sixteenth-century well house where donkeys still trudge inside a huge, hamster-like, treadmill to raise a barrel 160ft up the well shaft.

Winchester

Nowadays a tranquil, handsome market town, set amid docile hay meadows and water-cress beds, **WINCHESTER** was once the fifth largest town in Roman Britain. It was **Alfred the Great**, however, who really put Winchester on the map, when he made it the capital of his Wessex kingdom in the ninth century. For the next couple of cent-uries it ranked alongside London, its status affirmed by William the Conqueror's coro-nation in both cities, and his commissioning of the local monks to prepare the **Domesday Book**. It wasn't until after the Battle of Naseby in 1645, when Cromwell took the city, that Winchester began its decline into provinciality. Hampshire's county town now has a scholarly and slightly anachronistic air, embodied by the ancient almshouses that still provide shelter for senior citizens of "noble poverty" – the pensioners can be seen wandering the town in medieval black or mulberry-coloured gowns with silver badges. A trip to this secluded old city is a must – not only for the magnificent **cathedral**, chief relic of Winchester's medieval glory, but for the all-round well-preserved ambience of England's Middle Age capital.

The City

The first minster to be built in Winchester was raised by Cenwalh, the Saxon king of Wessex in the mid-seventh century, and traces of this building have been unearthed adjacent to the present **Cathedral**, which was begun in 1079. Its construction lasted for three hundred years, producing a church whose elements range from early Norman to Perpendicular styles. The exterior is not its best feature – squat and massive, the cathe-dral crouches stumpily over the tidy lawns of the Cathedral Close. The interior is rich and complex, however, and its 556-foot nave makes this Europe's longest medieval church. Outstanding features include its carved Norman font of black Tournai marble, the fourteenth-century misericords (the choir stalls are the oldest complete set in the country) and some amazing monuments – Bishop **William of Wykeham's Chantry**, halfway down the nave on the right, is one of the best. Jane Austen, who died in Winchester, is commemorated by a stone close to the font, though she's recorded simply as the daughter of a local clergyman. Above the high altar lie the mortuary chests of pre-Conquest kings, including Canute, while William Rufus, killed hunting in the New Forest in 1100 (see p.197), lies in the presbytery. The Norman crypt contains the tomb of Saint Swithun, originally buried outside in the churchyard. When his remains were interred inside the Cathedral where the "rain of heaven" could no longer fall on him, he took revenge and the heavens opened for forty days, hence the legend that if it rains on St Swithun's Day (July 15) it will continue for another forty.

The Norman **crypt** is open only in the summer, since it's flooded for much of the winter – the cathedral's original foundations were dug in marshy ground, and at the beginning of this century a steadfast diver, William Walker, spent five years replacing the rotten timber foundations with concrete. If you catch it open, though, have a look inside at the fourteenth-century statues of William of Wykeham and Saint Swithun as well as Anthony Gormley's standing figure, one of the country's most adventurous recent ecclesiastical commissions.

Walk west along the High Street, north of the cathedral, and you'll pass close to the **City Museum** on The Square (Mon–Fri 10am–5pm, Sat 10am–1pm & 2–5pm, Sun 2–5pm; Oct–March closed Mon; free), a basic local history display, and eventually arrive at **Great Hall** in Castle Street (April–Oct daily 10am–5pm; Nov–March closes 4pm), the vestigial remains of a thirteenth-century castle destroyed by Cromwell. Sir Walter Raleigh heard his death sentence here in 1603, though he wasn't finally dispatched until 1618, and Judge Jeffreys held one of his Bloody Assizes in the castle after Monmouth's rebellion in 1685. The main interest now, however, is a brightly painted

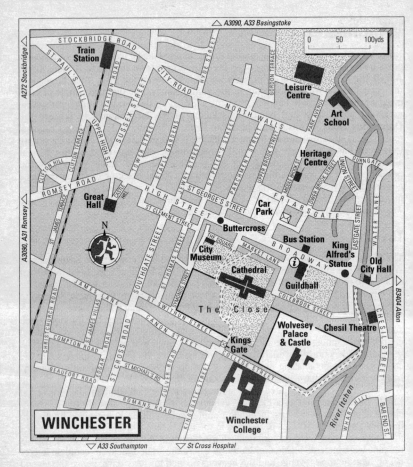

eighteen-foot disc slung on one wall like some curious antique dartboard. This is alleged to be King Arthur's Round Table, but the woodwork is probably fourteenth-century, later repainted as a PR exercise for the Tudor dynasty – the portrait of Arthur at the top of the table bears an uncanny resemblance to Henry VII.

If instead you walk east, past the Guildhall and the august bronze statue of King Alfred on the Broadway, you reach the River Itchen and the **Old City Mill** (April–Sept daily 11am–4.45pm; March & Oct Sat & Sun, noon–4pm; 90p; NT), now part-occupied by a youth hostel. Turning right before the bridge you pass what remains of the Saxon walls, which bracket the ruins of the twelfth-century **Wolvesey Castle** (Easter–Sept daily 10am–6pm; £1.50) and the Bishop's Palace, built by Christopher Wren. Immediately to the west up College Street stand the buildings of **Winchester College**, the oldest public school in England – established in 1382 by William of Wykeham for "poor scholars", it now educates few but the wealthy and privileged. The cloisters and chantry are open during term time, the chapel is open all year. The thirteenth-century **Kings Gate**, at the top of College Street, is one of the city's original medieval gateways, housing St Swithun's church.

Practicalities

Winchester **train station** is about a mile northwest of the cathedral on Stockbridge Road; if you arrive by **bus**, you'll find yourself on the Broadway, opposite the **tourist office** in the imposing Guildhall (late May to Sept Mon–Sat 10am–6pm, Sun 11am–2pm; Oct–May Mon–Sat 10am–5pm; ☎01983/01962/840 500). The classiest **accommodation** is at the *Wykeham Arms*, 75 Kingsgate St (☎01962/853 834; ⑦), where the art of inn-keeping has not yet vanished. Nearly as central but not as expensive is the *Portland House Hotel*, 63 Tower St (☎01962/865 195; ⑤), a Georgian house in a quiet mews between the cathedral and the train station. *Delbrook*, on Hubert Road (☎01962/865 093; ④) is a pleasant Edwardian-era, family-run B&B by the water meadows near St Cross, one mile south of the city centre. Winchester has an exceptionally lovely **youth hostel**, in a converted eighteenth-century mill on Water Lane (☎01962/853 723).

The city's best **pub** is the *Wykeham Arms*, 75 Kingsgate St, unprepossessing from outside but inside a maze of characterful, intimate spaces with imaginative, moderately priced food. The *Eclipse Inn*, on The Square, is an archetypally picturesque old inn specializing in inexpensive steak and kidney pies. A good-value lunch spot is the *Cathedral Refreshment Rooms*, on The Close, run by the Friends of Winchester Cathedral. *Nine The Square*, 9 Great Minster St, offers inexpensive light meals at the downstairs wine bar, while *Noatt's*, Jewry Street, is a cheap café/restaurant, serving home-cooked dishes with Thai, Carribean and Mediterranean influences.

The Watercress Line and Chawton

Alresford, six miles east of Winchester, is the beginning of the **Mid-Hants Watercress Line** (July & Aug daily; Feb–June, Sept, Oct & Dec intermittent sevices; £7.50 day pass; ☎01962/734 866), a jolly, steam-powered train, so named because it passes through the former watercress beds which once flourished here. The train chuffs ten miles east to Alton, with gourmet dinners served on board on Saturday evenings and traditional Sunday lunches too.

A mile southwest of Alton lies **CHAWTON**, where Jane Austen lived from 1809 to 1817 during the last and most prolific years of her life and where she wrote or revised almost all her six books, including *Sense and Sensibility* and *Pride and Prejudice*. **Jane Austen's house** (Jan & Feb Sat & Sun 11am–4.30pm; March, Nov & Dec Wed–Sun 11am–4.30pm; April–Oct daily 11am–4.30pm; £2), in the centre of the village, is a plain red-brick building, containing first editions of some of her greatest works.

The New Forest

The name of the **NEW FOREST** is misleading, for much of this region's woodland was cleared long before the Normans arrived, and its poor sandy soils support only a meagre covering of heather and gorse in many areas. The forest was requisitioned by William the Conqueror in 1079 as a game reserve, and the rights of its inhabitants soon became subservient to those of his precious deer. Fences to impede their progress were forbidden, and terrible punishments were meted out to those who disturbed the animals – hands were lopped off, eyes put out. Later monarchs gradually restored the forest-dwellers' rights, and today the New Forest enjoys a unique patchwork of ancient laws and privileges, enveloped in an arcane vocabulary dating from feudal times. The forest boundary is the "perambulation", and owner-occupiers of Forest land have common rights of obscure practices such as "turbary" (peat-cutting), "estover" (firewood-collecting), and "mast" (letting pigs forage for acorns and beech mast), as well as the right of pasture, permitting domestic animals to graze freely.

The **trees** of the New Forest are now much more varied than they were in pre-Norman times, with birch, holly, yew, Scots pine and other conifers interspersed with the ancient oaks and beeches. The main wooded areas are around **Lyndhurst**, the "capital" of the New Forest, and one of the most venerable trees is the much visited **Knightwood Oak**, just off the A35 three miles southwest of Lyndhurst, which measures about 22 feet in circumference at shoulder height. The most obvious species of New Forest **fauna** are the New Forest **ponies** (reputedly descendants from the Armada's small Spanish horses which survived the battle), now thoroughly domesticated – you'll see them grazing nonchalantly by the roadsides and ambling through some villages. The local deer are less likely to be seen now that some of the faster roads are fenced, although several species still roam the woods, including the tiny **Sika deer**, descendants of a pair which escaped from Beaulieu in 1904.

Covering about 144 square miles – a third now in private ownership, the rest administered by the Forestry Commission – the New Forest is one of southern England's main rural playgrounds, and about eight million visitors annually flock here to enjoy a breath of fresh air, often after spending hours in traffic jams. To get the best from the region, you need to walk or ride through it, avoiding the places cars can reach. There are 150 miles of car-free gravel roads in the forest, making cycling an appealing prospect. The *Ordnance Survey Leisure Map* of the New Forest is worth getting if you want to explore in any detail, and in Lyndhurst you can pick up numerous specialist walking books and natural history guides. The forest also has nine Forestry Commission **campsites** – to make a booking and obtain the necessary permit, call or write to the Queen's House, High St, Lyndhurst, Hants SO43 7NH (☎01703/283 771); and there's a **youth hostel** in Cottesmore House, Cotts Lane, Burley (☎01425/403 233).

Lyndhurst and Brockenhurst

LYNDHURST, its town centre skewered by an agonizing one-way system, isn't a particularly interesting place, though the brick **parish church** is worth a glance for its William Morris glass, Lord Leighton fresco, and the grave of one Mrs Reginald Hargreaves, better known as Alice Liddell, Lewis Carroll's model for Alice. It's mainly valuable for the resources of the **New Forest Museum & Visitor Centre** off the High Street (daily 10am–5pm; ☎01703/282 269) where you can buy bus passes and maps for cycling and riding; *AA Bike Hire* in Gosport Lane **rents bikes** (☎01703/283 349). For **accommodation** try *Forest Cottage* (☎01703/283 461; ③), a B&B at the west end of the High Street, or *Ormonde House* (☎01703/282 806; ⑤) on Southampton Road. *Le Café Parise* sells snacks and the *Crown Hotel* does larger meals – both are on the High Street.

BROCKENHURST, three miles to the south of Lyndhurst, is a useful centre for visitors without their own transport. There's a train station right in town and by the level crossing *New Forest Cycle Hire* (☎01590/624 204) offers **bikes for rent** for £6–10 a day. The town also has some decent places to **stay**: try the *Cottage Hotel* on Sway Road (☎01590/62 2296; ⑥) or *Cater's Cottage*, Latchmoor (☎01590/623225; ③), an above-average B&B on the southern outskirts of Brockenhurst; while a short distance further south in Setley, there's a B&B at *Setley Lodge* (☎01590/622 146; ③). The *Snakecatcher* on Lyndhurst Road is a pleasant **pub** with terrific bar food.

Beaulieu and Buckler's Hard

The village of **BEAULIEU** (originating from the French, but pronounced "Bewley"), in the southeast corner of the New Forest, was once the site of one of England's most influential monasteries, a Cistercian house founded in 1204 by King John – in remorse, it is said, for ordering a group of supplicating Cistercian monks to be trampled to death. Built using stone ferried from Caen and Quarr on the Isle of Wight , the **abbey** managed a self-sufficient estate of ten thousand acres and became a famous sanctuary,

---

RUFUS STONE

The Forest's most visited site, the **Rufus Stone**, stands a few hundred yards from the M27 motorway, three miles northwest of Lyndhurst. Erected in 1745, the monument marks the putative spot where the Conqueror's ghastly son and heir, **William II** – aka William Rufus after his ruddy complexion – was killed in 1100. The official version is that a crossbow bolt fired by a member of the royal hunting party glanced off a stag and struck the king in the heart. Sir William Tyrrell took the rap for the "accident" and fled incriminatingly to France, though he later swore on his deathbed that he had not fired the fatal arrow. As William II was a tyrant with many enemies, his death probably was a political assassination – a strong suspect was William's brother Henry, also in the shooting party, who promptly raced to Winchester to claim the crown, leaving Rufus to be carted ignominiously to the Cathedral by a passing charcoal burner. The stone is remarkably unimpressive for such a landmark: the Victorians encased it in a protective layer of metal to deter vandals, and now it can't be seen at all clearly.

---

offering shelter to Queen Margaret of Anjou among many others. The abbey was dismantled soon after the Dissolution, and its refectory now forms the parish church, which, like everything else in Beaulieu has been subsumed by the Montagu family who have owned a large chunk of the New Forest since one of Charles II's illegitimate progeny was created Duke of the estate.

The estate has been transformed with a prodigious commercial vigour into **Beaulieu** (Easter–Oct daily 10am–6pm; Nov–Easter closes 5pm; £7.50), a tourist complex comprising **Palace House**, the attractive if unexceptional family home, the abbey and the main attraction, Lord Montagu's **National Motor Museum**. An undersized monorail and a more fitting old London bus ease the ten-minute walk between the entry point and Palace House. The house, formerly the abbey's gatehouse, contains masses of Montagu-related memorabilia while the undercroft of the adjacent abbey houses an exhibition depicting medieval monastic life. Inside the celebrated Motor Museum, a collection of 250 cars and motorcycles includes a Formula One McLaren, spindly antiques and recent classics, as well as a couple of svelte land-speed racers such as the record-breaking *Bluebird*. The entertaining *Wheels*, a dizzying ride-through display, takes you on a trip through the history of motoring.

If Beaulieu amply deserves its name, **BUCKLER'S HARD**, a couple of miles downstream on the River Beaulieu, has an even more wonderful setting. It doesn't look much like a shipyard now, but from Elizabethan times onwards dozens of men o' war were assembled here from giant New Forest oaks. Several of Nelson's ships, including *HMS Agamemnon*, were launched here, to be towed carefully by rowing boats past the sandbanks and across the Solent to Portsmouth. The largest house in this carefully restored hamlet of shipwrights' cottages – now an overrun part of the Montagu estate – belonged to Henry Adams, the Master Builder responsible for most of the Trafalgar fleet. The **Maritime Museum** stands at the top of the village, tracing the history of the great naval ships (Easter–May daily 10am–6pm; June–Sept closes 9pm; Oct–Easter closes 4.30pm; £2.75).

Lymington

The most pleasant point of access for the Isle of Wight (see p.190) is **LYMINGTON**, a sheltered haven linked by ferry to Yarmouth and now one of the busiest leisure harbours on the south coast. Rising from the quay area, the old town is full of cobbled streets and Georgian houses and has one unusual building – the partly thirteenth-century church of **St Thomas the Apostle**, with a cupola-topped tower built in 1670.

Places to **stay** in town include *Albany House*, Highfield (☎01590/671 900; ④), a Regency house near the public gardens, and *Wheatsheaf House*, a quaint listed building on Gosport Lane, (☎01590/679 208; ③). *Monet's Brasserie* (☎01590 672 007; ⑤), opposite Safeways on Stanford Road, specializes in local seafood and has a couple of rooms for B&B. The town's best **pubs** are the *Chequers* on Ridgeway Lane, on the Pennington (west) side of town; the *Bosun's Chair* on Station Road; and the harbourfront *Ship Inn*, on the quayside, with seats outside overlooking the water.

Signposted two miles east of Lymington, the **Sammy Miller Museum** on Gore Road, New Milton (daily 10am–4.30pm; £3), gives classic motorcycles the "Beaulieu" treatment. Many of the once eminent British marques from Ariel to Vincent are displayed, as well as exotica from MV, NSU and several acclaimed trials bikes ridden by Sammy Miller himself, one of Britain's most successful trials riders.

Bournemouth and around

Renowned for its clean sandy beaches, the resort of **Bournemouth** is the nucleus of Europe's largest non-industrial conurbation stretching between Lymington and Poole harbour. The resort has a single-minded holidaymaking atmosphere, though neighbouring **Poole** and **Christchurch** are more interesting historically. North of this coastal sprawl, the pleasant old market town of **Wimborne** has one of the area's most striking churches, while the stately home of **Kingston Lacy** contains an outstanding collection of old masters and other paintings.

Bournemouth

BOURNEMOUTH dates only from 1811, when a local squire, Louis Tregonwell, built a summer house on the wild, unpopulated heathland that once occupied this stretch of coast, and planted the first of the pine trees that now characterize the area. Sadly, the blandly modern town that you see today has little to remind you of Bournemouth's Victorian heyday. Bournemouth does, howvever, abound in public gardens – over two thousand acres of them, most notably **Compton Acres** (March–Oct daily 10.30am–6.30pm or dusk; £3.90), at the west end of town, off the Poole road. Here you'll find seven gardens each with a different international theme, the best of which are the elegantly understated Japanese Garden, and the more familiar, formal Italian Garden.

The excellent **Russell-Cotes Museum** on East Cliff Promenade (Tues–Sun 10am–5pm; £1.50, Sat & Sun free), is central Bournemouth's sole non-horticultural attraction. It houses a collection of oriental souvenirs gathered from around the world by the Russell-Cotes family, hoteliers who grew wealthy during Bournemouth's late-Victorian tourist boom. The benefactors' lavishly decorated former home, featuring unusual stained glass and ornate painted ceilings, is jam-packed with their eclectic collections of which the Japanese artefacts are especially interesting. About a mile and a half east of the museum in the suburb of Boscombe, the **Shelley Rooms** in Shelley Park off Beechwood Avenue (Tues–Sun 2–5pm; free) house memorabilia relating to the Romantic poet Percy Bysshe Shelley, the husband of Mary Shelley, who wrote the gothic horror tale *Frankenstein* in 1818 when aged only 21. She is buried with the poet's heart in the graveyard of St Peter's Church, just east of The Square.

Practicalities

The **train station** is just under a mile east of the centre; frequent **buses** run into town from the bus station opposite. The **tourist office** is on Westover Road, in the centre of town (Sept to mid-July Mon–Sat 9.30am–5.30pm, Sun 10am–5pm; mid-July to Aug Mon–Sat 9.30am–7pm, Sun 10am–5pm; ☎01202/291 715). Bournemouth has **accommodation** to suit all budgets: try *Sea Dene Hotel*, 10 Burnaby Rd (☎01202/761 372; ③), near the beach at Alum Chine, or *Chine Grange*, 25 Durley Chine Rd (☎01202/553 021; ④); *Tudor Grange*, 31 Gervis Rd, East Cliff (☎01202/291 472; ④–⑤) has an attractive interior and gardens; the Edwardian *Langtry Manor*, 26 Derby Rd, East Cliff (☎01202/290 550; ⑧–⑨) is the former hideaway of Edward VII and his mistress, Lillie Langtry.

The *Butlers Crab & Ale House*, 165 Old Christchurch Rd, is one of the most popular **pubs**, specializing in local seafood; at no. 136 on the same street, the *L'Odeon Jazz Club* is a laid-back jazz club with a moderately priced **restaurant**. Alternatives to the usual seaside resort entertainment include the *Pavilion Theatre,* with its own ballroom, and the *Winter Gardens*, home of Bournemouth's symphony orchestra. Things get lively during the middle two weeks of May, when the *Bournmouth International Festival* of art, dance and music takes place.

Christchurch

CHRISTCHURCH, five miles east of Bournemouth, is best known for its colossal parish church, **Christchurch Priory** (Mon–Sat 9.30am–5pm, Sun 2.15–6pm; admission by donation), bigger than most cathedrals. Built on the site of a Saxon minster dating from 650 AD but exhibiting chiefly Norman and Perdendicular features, the church is the longest in England at 311ft; its fan vaulted North Porch is also the country's biggest. Fine views can be gained from the top of the 120-ft tower (Mon–Sat 9.30am–5pm, Sun 2.15–6pm; 50p). The area round the old town quay has a carefully preserved charm. The **Red House Museum and Gardens** (Tues–Sat 10am–5pm, Sun 2–5pm; £1.80, Nov–Feb free) on Quay Road contains an affectionate collection of local memorabilia, and **boat trips** (several daily Easter to mid-Oct; ☎01202/429 119) can be taken from the grassy banks of the riverside quay east to Mudeford or upriver to the *Tuckton Tea Rooms* to the east of Bournemouth.

Accommodation options around town are fairly pricey; try the central *Kings Arms Toby Hotel*, 18 Castle St (☎01202/484 117; ⑤), or the *Avonmouth Hotel*, 95 Mudeford (☎01202/483 434; ⑧). For **something to eat**, try *La Mamma Pizza* at 51 Bridge St which serves Italian classics at moderate prices, or the slightly pricier French restaurant, *Le Petit St Tropez*, at 3 Bridge St. Recommended **pubs** include the *King's Arms Hotel* right by the priory with a nice garden area, or check out Christchurch's oldest pub, *Ye Olde George Inn*, 2a Castle St, which also has a good restaurant.

Poole

POOLE, west of Bournemouth, is an ancient seaport on a huge, almost landlocked harbour. The town developed in the thirteenth century and was successively colonized by pirates, fishermen and timber traders, more recently replaced by companies speculating for oil in the shallow waters – the harbour's environmental significance ensures that the extraction process is carefully disguised. The old quarter by the quayside is worth exploring: the old Custom House, Scaplen's Court and Guildhall are the most striking of over a hundred historic buildings within a fifteen-acre site.

Other quayside attractions are the Poole Pottery showroom and crafts centre, and the regular boats over to **Brownsea Island**, in the middle of the harbour (April–Oct daily 10am–8pm or dusk). Now a National Trust property, this five-hundred-acre island of heath and woodland is famed for its red squirrels and other wildlife – and for its role in the Boy Scout movement, formed in the wake of a boys' camping expedition led here by Lord Baden-Powell in 1907. The **Waterfront Museum** in Poole relates the story of the Scouts and other aspects of local history (Mon–Sat 10am–5pm, Sun 2–5pm; £1.95). Over the road, **Scaplen's Court** (same hours; £1.25) is a late-medieval building where local history is further expanded, but in a more characterful setting.

For **accommodation**, try the handsome *Antelope Hotel* at the quay end of the High Street (☎01202/672 029; ⑤). Smaller hotels include the *Sea Witch* at 47 Haven Rd, Canford Cliffs (☎01202/707 697; ⑤) and *Norfolk Lodge,* 1 Flaghead Rd, Canford Cliffs (☎01202/708 614; ⑤), both of which are convenient for the Sandbanks beaches. Less central but great value is the *Harbour Lights Hotel*, 121 North Rd, Parkstone (☎01202/748 417; ③). There's a collection of good **restaurants** at the southern end of the High Street; look out for *Mez Creis* seafood restaurant at no. 16 (both open 7pm till late), or *Toppers*, further down. On the Waterfront, *Corkers* has a café-bar downstairs and a restaurant above, serving traditional English dishes and seafood.

Wimborne Minster and Kingston Lacy

An ancient town on the banks of the Stour, just a few minutes' drive north from the suburbs of Bournemouth, **WIMBORNE MINSTER**, as the name suggests, is mainly of interest for its great church, the **Minster of St Cuthberga**. Built on the site of an eighth-century monastery, its massive twin towers of mottled grey and tawny stone dwarf the rest of the town – the church was even more imposing before its spire fell down during a service in 1600. What remains today is basically Norman with later features added – such as the Perpendicular west tower, which bears a figure dressed as a grenadier of the Napoleonic era, who strikes every quarter-hour with a hammer. Inside, the church is crowded with memorials and eye-catching details – look out for the orrery clock inside the west tower, with the sun marking the hours and the moon marking the days of the month, and for the organ with trumpets pointing out towards the congregation instead of pipes. The **Chained Library** above the choir vestry (Mon–Fri 10.30am–12.30pm & 2–4pm; 40p), dating from 1686, is Wimborne's most prized possession and one of the oldest public libraries in the country.

Wimborne's older buildings stand around the main square near the minster, and are mostly from the late eighteenth or early nineteenth century. The **Priest's House** on the High Street started life as lodgings for the clergy, then became a stationer's shop. Now it is an award-winning **museum** (April–Oct Mon–Sat 10.30am–4.30pm, Sun 2–4pm; £1.50), each room furnished in the style of a different period. A working Victorian kitchen, a Georgian parlour and an ironmonger's shop are among its exhibits, and a walled garden at the rear provides an excellent place for summer teas.

Kingston Lacy (April–Oct daily except Thurs & Fri noon–5.30pm; £5.50; NT), one of the country's finest seventeenth-century country houses, lies two miles northwest of Wimborne Minster, in 250 acres of parkland grazed by a herd of Red Devon cattle. Designed for the Bankes family, who were exiled from Corfe Castle after the Roundheads reduced it to rubble, the Queen Anne brick building was clad in grey stone during the nineteenth century by Charles Barry, co-architect of the Houses of Parliament. William Bankes, then owner of the house, was a great traveller and collector, and the **Spanish Room** is a superb scrap book of his Grand Tour souvenirs. Kingston Lacy's **picture collection** is also outstanding, featuring Titian, Rubens, Velazquez, and many other old masters. Be warned, though, that this place gets so swamped with visitors that the National Trust has to issue timed tickets at busy weekends.

The Isle of Purbeck

Though not actually an island, the **ISLE OF PURBECK** – a promontory of low hills and heathland jutting below Poole Harbour – does have an insular and distinctive feel. Reached from the east by the ferry from Sandbanks, at the narrow mouth of Poole harbour, or by a long and congested landward journey via the bottleneck of **Wareham**,

Purbeck can be an effortful destination, but its villages are immensely pretty, none more so than **Corfe Castle**, with its majestic ruins. **Swanage**, a low-key seaside resort, is flanked by more exciting coastlines, all accessible on the Dorset Coast Path. Like Portland, further west, the area is pockmarked with stone quarries – Purbeck marble is the finest grade of the local oolitic limestone.

Wareham

The grid pattern of its streets indicates the Saxon origins of **WAREHAM**, and the town is surrounded by even older earth ramparts known as The Walls. A riverside setting adds to its charms, though the major road junction at its heart causes gridlock in summer, and the scenic stretch along The Quay also gets fairly overrun. Nearby lies an oasis of quaint houses around **Lady St Mary's** church, which contains the marble coffin of Edward the Martyr, murdered at Corfe Castle in 978 by his stepmother, to make way for her unready son Ethelred.

St **Martin's Church**, at the north end of town, dates from Saxon times, but its most striking feature is a romantic effigy of **T.E. Lawrence** in Arab dress, which was originally destined for Salisbury Cathedral, but rejected by the Dean there who disapproved of Lawrence's sexual proclivities. Lawrence was killed in 1935 in a motorbike accident on the road from Bovington, after returning to Dorset from his Middle Eastern adventures. His simply furnished cottage is at **Clouds Hill**, seven miles northwest of Wareham (Easter–Oct Wed–Fri & Sun 2–5pm; £2.20; NT). In Wareham the small **museum** next to the town hall in East Street (Easter–Oct 11am–1pm & 2–5pm) displays some of Lawrence's memorabilia as does the absorbing but overpriced **Tank Museum** in Bovington Camp, five miles west of Wareham (daily 10am–5pm; £5).

The town hall on East Street contains the **tourist office** (Easter–June, Sept & Oct Mon–Sat 9am–5pm; July & Aug daily 9am–5pm; Nov–March Mon–Sat 9.30am–1pm). Wareham's best **accommodation** options are *The Anglebury Restaurant*, 15 North St, with inexpensive rooms (☎01929/552 988; ②) or *The Old Granary Restaurant* (☎01929/ 552 010; ⑤) on The Quay, with views over the river.

Corfe Castle

The romantic ruins crowning the hill behind the village of **CORFE CASTLE** (Feb– Nov 10am–5.30pm or dusk if earlier; Dec & Jan Sat & Sun noon–3.30pm; £3; NT) are perhaps the most evocative in England. The family seat of Sir John Bankes, Attorney General to Charles I, this Royalist stronghold withstood a Cromwellian siege for six weeks, gallantly defended by Lady Bankes. One of her own men eventually betrayed the castle to the Roundheads, after which it was reduced to its present gap-toothed state by gunpowder. Apparently the victorious Roundheads were so impressed by Lady Bankes' courage that they allowed her to take the keys to the castle with her – they can still be seen in the library at the Bankes' subsequent home, Kingston Lacy (see above).

The village is well stocked with tea rooms and gift shops and has a couple of good pubs too: *The Fox* on West Street and, below the castle ramparts, *The Greyhound* which serves excellent seafood and has a few rooms (☎01929/480 205; ⑤). For **B&B**, try *Brook Cottage*, 5 East St (☎01929/480 347; ③), or the Tudor-beamed *Cartshed Cottage* at Whiteway Farm, one mile east in Church Knowle (☎01929/480 801; ④).

Swanage

Purbeck's largest seaside resort is **SWANAGE**, which boasts a pleasant sandy beach and an ornate town hall, the facade of which once adorned the Mercer's Hall in the City of London and was brought back here as ballast after delivering a cargo of stone. The town's station is the southern terminus of the **Swanage Steam Railway** (☎01929/424 276; returns from £4), which runs as far as Corfe Castle. Swanage is also a good base for exploring **Shell Bay**, to the north, a magnificent long beach of icing-sugar sand, backed by a remarkable heathland ecosystem that's home to all six British species of reptile – adders are quite common, so be careful.

At the top end of the beach a **ferry** (every 20min, 7am–11pm) crosses the mouth of Poole harbour connecting the Isle of Purbeck with Sandbanks in Poole. The **tourist office** is by the beach on Shore Road (Easter–Oct daily 10am–5pm; Nov–Easter Mon–Thurs 10am–5pm, Fri 10am–4pm; ☎0929/422 885), and there's a **youth hostel**, with good views across the bay, on Cluny Crescent (☎01929/422 113). There are scores of **B&Bs** in Swanage; you'll find a handy trio on Kings Road near the train station, or try the *Purbeck Hotel,* 19 High St (☎01929/425 160; ③), which also has a decent pub. Swanage has a wide variety of **places to eat,** the best of which is the excellent *Galley,* 9 High St (☎01929/427 299), specializing in well-prepared local fish dishes.

Lulworth Cove and Durdle Door

Highlights of the coast beyond Swanage are the grey-white chalk and limestone cliffs between Durlstone Head and St Alban's Head. Further west still, the geology of the coast changes to blackish beds of shale, which turn into a semi-fluid morass in wet weather, leaving limestone layers above unsupported. At **Lulworth Cove**, a perfect shell-shaped bite in the coastline formed when the sea broke through a weakness in the cliffs and then gnawed away at them from behind, forming a circular cave which eventually collapsed to leave a bay enclosed by sandstone cliffs. Lulworth's scenic charms are well known, and as you descend the hill through the quaint thatch-and-stone village of West Lulworth in summer the sun glints off the metal of a thousand car roofs in the car park behind the cove. The fee to park here (£3) includes entry to the **Lulworth Heritage Centre** where the mysteries of the local geology are explained.

Immediately west of the cove you come to **Stair Hole**, a roofless sea cave riddled with arches that will eventually collapse to form another Lulworth, and a couple of miles west is **Durdle Door**, a famous limestone arch that appeals to serious geologist and casual sightseer alike. Most people take the uphill route to the arch which starts from the car park but, if you want to avoid the steep climb, you can drive a mile from the village towards East Chaldon and park at the *Durdle Door Caravan Park* (☎01929/ 200 400) for a small fee.

West Lulworth is the obvious **place to stay or eat** on this section of coast: best of the bunch are the *Castle Inn* (☎01929/400 311; ④), *Cromwell House Hotel* (☎0929/400 253; ⑤) and *Newlands Farm* (☎01929/400 376; ④), an early nineteenth-century farmhouse. The **youth hostel** at the end of School Lane West (☎01929/400 564) is a plain chalet with small rooms, just a stone's throw away from the Dorset Coast Path. In **East Lulworth**, the *Weld Arms* also has rooms (☎01929/400 211; ③) and the easily missed *Sailor's Return* in East Chaldon, four miles northwest of Lulworth Cove, is locally unsurpassed for its mouthwatering pub food.

Dorchester and around

The county town of Dorset, **DORCHESTER** still functions as the main agricultural centre for the region, and if you catch it on a Wednesday when the market is in full swing you'll find it livelier than usual. For the local tourist authorities, however, this is essentially **Thomas Hardy**'s town – he was born at Higher Bockhampton, three miles east of here, is buried in Stinsford, a couple of miles northeast, and spent much of his life in Dorchester itself, where his statue now stands on High West Street. The town appears in his novels as "Casterbridge", and the countryside all around Dorchester provided the landscapes of his books, particularly the wild heathland to the east ("Egdon Heath"), and the eerie yew forest of Cranborne Chase. The real Dorchester has a pleasant central core of mostly seventeenth-century and Georgian buildings, while to the southwest of town looms the massive hill fort of **Maiden Castle**, the most impressive of Dorset's many pre-Roman antiquities.

Dorchester was Durnovaria to the Romans, who founded the town in about 70 AD. The original Roman walls were replaced in the eighteenth century by tree-lined avenues called "Walks" (Bowling Alley Walk, West Walk and Colliton Walk), but some traces of the Roman period have survived. At the back of County Hall excavations have uncovered a fine Roman villa with a well-preserved mosaic floor, and on the southeast edge of town you'll find **Maumbury Rings**, where the Romans held vast gladiatorial combats in an amphitheatre adapted from a Stone Age site. The gruesome traditions continued into the Middle Ages, when gladiators were replaced by bear-baiting and public executions or "hanging fairs".

Continuing the sanguinary theme, after the ill-fated rebellion of the Duke of Monmouth (another of Charles II's illegitimate offspring) against James II, **Judge Jeffreys** was appointed to punish the rebels. His "Bloody Assizes" of 1685, held in the Oak Room of the **Antelope Hotel** on Cornhill, sentenced 292 men to death. In the event, 74 were hanged, drawn and quartered, and then their heads were stuck on pikes throughout Dorset and Somerset; the luckier suspects were merely flogged and transported to the West Indies. Judge Jeffreys lodged just round the corner from the *Antelope* in High West Street, where a half-timbered restaurant now capitalizes on the lurid association.

In 1834 the **Shire Hall**, further down High West Street, witnessed another cause célèbre, when six men from the nearby village of **Tolpuddle** were sentenced to transportation for banding together to form the Friendly Society of Agricultural Labourers, in order to present a request for a small wage increase on the grounds that their families were starving. After a public outcry the men were pardoned, and the Tolpuddle Martyrs passed into history as founders of the trade union movement. The room in which they were tried is preserved as a memorial to the martyrs, and you can find out more about them in Tolpuddle itself, eight miles east on the A35, where there's a fine little museum (Tues–Sat 10am–5.30pm, Sun 11am–5.30pm; free).

The best place to find out about Dorchester's history is in the engrossing **Dorset County Museum** on High West Street (Mon–Sat 10am–5pm; £2), where archeological and geological displays trace Celtic and Roman history, including a section on Maiden Castle. Pride of place goes to the re-creation of Thomas Hardy's study, where his pens are inscribed with the names of the books he wrote with them. Other museums in town include the small **Dinosaur Museum** (daily 9.30–5.30pm; £2.75) in Icen Way, appealing chiefly to children. Best of all is **Tutankhamun: The Exhibition** in the High Street (daily 9.30am–5.30pm; £3.50), a fascinating and thorough exploration of the young pharaoh's life and afterlife through to the eventual discovery of his tomb in 1922. Everything from the mummified remains, complete burial chamber and the celebrated golden mask has been carefully and atmospherically re-created with painstaking detail.

Practicalities

Dorchester has two **train stations**, both of them to the south of the centre: trains from Weymouth and London Waterloo (up to 8 daily) arrive at Dorchester South, while Bristol trains use the Dorchester West station. Most **buses** stop around the car park on Acland Road, to the east of South Street. The **tourist office** is in Antelope Walk (April–May & Oct Mon–Sat 9am–5pm; June–Sept Mon–Fri 9am–6pm, Sat 9am–5pm, Sun 10am–2pm; Nov–March Mon–Fri 10am–3pm, Sat 10am–2pm; ☎01305/267 992).

Dorchester has a good selection of **accommodation**, with the best value being the *Casterbridge Hotel*, 49 High East St (☎01305/264 04; ⑤), a superior Georgian guest house, and *Maumbury Cottage*, 9 Maumbury Rd (☎01305/266 726; ③), a small, friendly and central B&B. The *King's Arms*, High East Street, (☎01305/265 353; ⑦), a historic local landmark, has pricey rooms but serves good food, including vegetarian dishes. The nearest **youth hostel** is at Litton Cheney (☎01308/482 340), halfway between Dorchester and Bridport, and the closest **campsite** is the *Giant's Head Caravan and Camping Park*, Old Sherborne Road (☎01305/341 242), half a mile north of town. When it comes to **food**, your best bet is a pub meal; try the *Royal Oak* or the *Old Ship Inn*, both on High West Street and both highly recommended.

Maiden Castle

One of southern England's finest prehistoric sites, **Maiden Castle** stands on a hill two miles or so south of Dorchester. Covering about 115 acres, it was first developed around 2000 BC by a Stone Age farming community and then used during the Bronze Age as a funeral mound. Iron Age dwellers expanded it into a populous settlement and fortified it with a daunting series of ramparts and ditches, just in time for the arrival of Vespasian's Second Legion. The ancient Britons' sling stones were no match for the more sophisticated weapons of the Roman invaders, and Maiden Castle was stormed in a bloody massacre in 43 AD. What you see today is a massive series of grassy concentric ridges about sixty feet high, creasing the surface of the hill. The main finds from the site are displayed in the Dorset County Museum (see above).

Weymouth to Bridport

Whether George III's passion for sea bathing was a symptom of his eventual madness is uncertain, but it was at the bay of **Weymouth** that in 1789 he became the first reigning monarch to follow the craze. Sycophantic gentry rushed into the waves behind him, and soon the town, formerly a workaday harbour, took on the elegant Georgian stamp which it bears today. A likeness of the monarch on horseback is even carved into the chalk downs northwest of the town, like some guardian spirit. Weymouth nowadays plays second fiddle to the vast resort of Bournemouth to the east, but it's still a lively family holiday destination, with several costly new attractions to augment its more sedate charms.

Just south of the town stretch the giant arms of Portland Harbour, and a long causeway links Weymouth to the strange five-mile-long excrescence of the **Isle of Portland**. West of the causeway, the eighteen-mile bank of pebbles known as **Chesil Beach** runs northwest in the direction of **Bridport**.

Weymouth

Weymouth had long been a port before the Georgians popularized it as a resort – it's possible that a ship unloading a cargo here in 1348 brought the Black Death to English shores, and on a happier note it was from Weymouth that John Endicott sailed in 1628 to found Salem in Massachusetts. A few buildings survive from these pre-Georgian times: the restored **Tudor House** in Trinity Street (June–Sept Tue–Fri 11am–4pm; £1.50) and the ruins of **Sandsfoot Castle**, built by Henry VIII, overlooking Portland Harbour. But Weymouth's most imposing architectural heritage stands along the Esplanade, a dignified range of bow-fronted and porticoed buildings gazing out across the graceful bay, an ensemble rather disrupted by the garish **Clock Tower** commemorating Victoria's jubilee. The more intimate quayside of the Old Harbour, linked to the Esplanade by the main pedestrianized throroughfare St Mary's Street, is lined with waterfront pubs from where you can view the passing yachts, trawlers and ferries.

Weymouth's slightly faded gentility is now counterbalanced by a number of "all weather" attractions, like the **Sea Life Park** in Lodmoor Country Park east of the Esplanade (daily 10am–6pm or later in summer; £4.50), where you can get close to sharks and rays and wander among multichrome birds in the 33°C tropical house.

Other attractions include the **Deep Sea Adventure** at the Old Harbour (Easter–June, Sept & Oct 10am–5.30pm; July & Aug 10am–10pm; £3.50), which describes the origins of modern diving and the sobering story of the Titanic disaster. Over the river on Hope Square, **The Timewalk** (daily 9.30am–5.30pm; £4), housed in Brewer's Quay, contains an entertaining walk-through exhibition of Weymouth's maritime and brewing past. A 15-min walk southwards, the Palmerstone-era **Nothe Fort** (May–Sept daily 10.30am–5.30pm; £2) has a number of displays on military themes plus a museum on the centuries-old practice of coastal defence, made obsolete in 1956 by advancing technology.

Practicalities

Weymouth **train** station is a couple of blocks west of the Bay, where you'll find the **tourist office**, at the northern end of the Esplanade (summer daily 9.30am–6pm; winter Mon–Sat 10am–4pm; ☎01305/765 221). For **accommodation** in the centre, try the *Chatsworth*, 14 Esplanade (☎01305/785 012; ⑤); *Bay Lodge*, 27 Greenhill (☎01305/782 419; ④), a better than average B&B with sea views; or *Cavendish House*, 5 Esplanade (☎01305/782 039; ④). *Perry's*, 4 Trinity Rd (☎01305/785 799), is an attractive **restaurant** overlooking the quayside, serving good-value seafood (open evenings only). Veggies should head for the *Wholefood Café*, 21 East St, while those on the hunt for fish and chips should make their way to the family-run *Seagull Café*, Trinity Road. The *Nothe Tavern*, on Barrack Road, is one of Weymouth's better **pubs**, doing a good range of food and Eldridge Pope beer, with harbour views from the garden.

Portland

Stark, wind-battered and treeless, the **ISLE OF PORTLAND** is famed above all for its hard white limestone, which has been quarried here for centuries – Wren used it for St Paul's Cathedral, and it clads the UN headquarters in New York. It was also used for the six-thousand-foot breakwater that protects Portland Harbour – the largest artificial harbour in Britain, which was built by convicts in the mid-nineteenth century. Poorer grades of Portland stone are pulverized for cement – the industrial stone-crushing plant is a prominent and unlovely feature of the island.

The causeway road by which Portland is approached stands on the easternmost section of the Chesil shingle. To the east you get a good view of the harbour, a naval base since 1872, but now jeopardized by the post-Cold War rundown of Britain's defences. The first place you come to, **Fortuneswell**, overlooks the huge harbour and is itself surveyed by a 450-year-old Tudor fortress, **Portland Castle** (April–Sept daily 10am–6pm; Oct 10am–4pm; £2; EH), commissioned by Henry VIII. Easton, the main village on the island, is home to Pennsylvania Castle (now a hotel), built in 1800 for John Penn, governor of the island and a grandson of the founder of Pennsylvania. Two miles east, near Church Ope Cove, there's a small **museum** (Easter–Sept daily 10.30am–1pm & 1.30–5pm; Oct–Easter closed Wed & Thurs; £1.10) housed in a seventeenth-century cottage, with exhibitions on local shipwrecks, smuggling and quarrying.

The museum also houses the **tourist office** (daily 9.30am–5pm; ☎01305/785 747) and nearby you can see the ruins of St Andrews Church and eleventh-century Rufus Castle. The craggy limestone of the island rises to 496 feet at **Portland Bill**, where a lighthouse has guarded the promontory since the eighteenth century (the present one dates from 1906, open in summer); the *Old Higher Lighthouse* now provides **B&B** accommodation (☎01305/822 300; ③).

Chesil Beach and Bridport

Chesil Beach is the strangest feature of the Dorset coast, a two-hundred-yard wide, fifty-foot high bank of pebbles that extends for eighteen miles, its component stones gradually decreasing in size from fist-like pebbles at Portland to "pea gravel" at Burton Bradstock in the west. This sorting is an effect of the powerful coastal currents, which make this one of the most dangerous beaches in Europe. Though not a swimming beach, Chesil is popular with sea anglers, and its wild, uncommercialized atmosphere makes an appealing antidote to the south coast resorts. Chesil Beach encloses a brackish lagoon called The Fleet for much of its length – setting for J. Meade Faulkner's classic smuggling tale, *Moonfleet*.

At the point where the shingle beach attaches itself to the shore is the pretty village of **ABBOTSBURY**, all tawny ironstone and thatch. The village **Swannery** (March–Oct daily 10am–6pm; £3.50), a wetland reserve for mute swans, dates back to medieval times, when presumably it formed part of the abbot's larder. Other attractions include the **Sub-Tropical Gardens** (March–Oct daily 10am–5pm; Nov–Feb closes 3pm; £3.50), where delicate species thrive in the micro-climate created by Chesil's stones, which act as a giant radiator to keep out all but the worst frosts. Up on the downs two miles inland is a monument to **Thomas Hardy**, this time not the writer, but the flag captain in whose arms Admiral Nelson expired. If you want to **stay** in Abbotsbury try *Swan Lodge* B&B, 1 Rodden Row (☎01305/871 249; ④) or the handsome *Ilchester Arms* in the village centre, which also serves fine **food** (☎01305/871 243; ⑤).

BRIDPORT, just beyond the far end of Chesil Beach, is a nice old town of brick rather than stone, with unusually wide streets, a hangover from its rope-making days when cords made of locally grown hemp and flax were stretched between the houses. If you want to know about the rope and net industry head for the tatty little fishing resort of **West Bay**, Bridport's access to the sea, where the **Harbour Museum** (April–Sept daily 10am–6pm; 50p), will fill you in about "Bridport daggers" (hangmen's nooses) and more besides. West Bay has one bright spot, the *Riverside Restaurant and Café*, a renowned but informal fish place with good views out to sea. Back in Bridport there's **B&B** at *Britmead House*, 154 West Bay Rd (☎01308/422 941; ⑤) and *Cranston Cottage*, 27 Church St (☎01308/456 240; ③). The Bridport **tourist office** is at 32 South St (April–Oct Mon–Sat 9am–5pm; Nov–March closes 3pm; ☎01308/42401).

Lyme Regis

LYME REGIS, Dorset's most westerly town, shelters snugly between steep hills, just before the grey, fossil-filled cliffs lurch into Devon. Its intimate size and undeniable photogeneity make Lyme so popular that in high summer car-borne crowds jostle with pedestrians for the limited space along its narrow streets. For all that, the town lives up to the classy impression created by its regal name, which it owes to a royal charter granted by Edward I in 1284. It has some upmarket literary associations to further bolster its self-esteem – Jane Austen resorted to a seafront cottage here and penned *Persuasion*, while novelist John Fowles is the town's most famous current resident. *The French Lieutenant's Woman*, filmed on location here, did more than any tourist board production ever could to place the resort firmly on the map.

Colourwashed cottages and elegant Regency and Victorian villas line its seafront and flanking streets, but Lyme's best-known feature is a briskly practical reminder of its commercial origins. As you walk along the seafront and out towards **The Cobb**, the curving harbour wall first constructed in the thirteenth century, look for the outlines of ammonites in the walls and paving stones. The cliffs around Lyme are a complex layer-cake of limestone, greensand and unstable clay, a perfect medium for preserving fossils, which are exposed by landslips of the waterlogged clays. In 1811 after a fierce storm caused parts of the cliffs to collapse, twelve-year-old Mary Anning, a keen fossil-hunter, discovered an almost-complete dinosaur skeleton, a thirty-foot ichthyosaurus now displayed in London's Natural History Museum (see p.109).

Hammering fossils out of the cliffs is frowned on by today's conservationists, and is in any case rather hazardous. Hands-off inspection of the area's complex geology can be enjoyed on both sides of town: to the west lies the **Undercliff**, a fascinating jumble of overgrown landslips, now a nature reserve. East of Lyme, the Dorset Coastal Path is closed as far as jaded **Charmouth** (Jane Austen's favourite resort), but at low tide you can walk for two miles along the beach then, just past Charmouth, rejoin the coastal path to the headland of **Golden Cap**, an outcrop of sandstone crowned with gorse.

Lyme's excellent **Philpot Museum** on Bridge Street (April–Oct Mon–Sat 10am–5pm, Sun 10am–noon & 2.30–5pm; £1) provides a crash course in local history and geology, while **Dinosaurland** on Coombe Street (April–Oct daily 10am–7pm; Nov–May Sat & Sun 10am–5pm; £3.20) fills out the story on ammonites and other local fossils. Also worth seeing is the small **marine aquarium** on The Cobb (Easter–Oct 10am–5pm; £1.20), where local fishermen bring unusual catches, and the fifteenth-century **parish church** of St Michael the Archangel, up Church Street, which contains a seventeenth-century pulpit and a massive chained Bible.

Practicalities

Lyme's nearest **train station** is in Axminster, five miles north; the hourly #31 **bus** (Mon–Sat) runs from here to Lyme Regis. The helpful **tourist office** is on Church Street by the museum (April–Oct Mon–Fri 10am–6am, Sat & Sun 10am–5pm; ☎01297/442 138). Lyme's sole seafront **hotel** is the pricey *Bay Hotel* on Marine Parade (☎01297/442 059; ⑦). However, the *Old Monmouth Hotel* is centrally located at 12 Church St (☎01297/442 456; ③) as is the nearby *Coombe Street Gallery* (☎01297/442 924; ②), 33 Coombe St. Reasonably priced **meals** can be had at the *Kersbrook Hotel* on Pound Road, which is also a pleasant place to **stay** (☎01297/442 596; ⑦), or *Bensons* on Broad Street, serving mostly French-style dishes in elegant surroundings. The best **pubs** are the *Royal Standard* on Ozone Parade, or the *Pilot Boat* on Bridge Street, which also does smashing seafood meals.

Inland Dorset and Southern Wiltshire

The main pleasures of inland Dorset come from unscheduled meandering through its ancient landscapes and tiny rural settlements, many of which boast preposterously winsome names such as Ryme Intrinseca, Piddletrenthide, Up Sydling and Plush. The county's most visited village is **Cerne Abbas**, due to its rumbustious chalk-carved giant. The major tourist honey pots, though, are the towns of **Blandford Forum**, **Shaftesbury** and **Sherborne**, the landscaped garden at **Stourhead** across the county boundary in Wiltshire, and the brasher stately home at **Longleat**, an unlikely hybrid of safari park and historic monument.

Blandford Forum

BLANDFORD FORUM, the gateway into mid-Dorset from Bournemouth, owes its latinate name not to the Romans but to medieval pedantry – the original Saxon name *Cheping*, meaning "market", was translated as *forum* by Latin-speaking tax officials in the thirteenth century. The Romans weren't far away, however – their main route from Old Sarum to Dorchester ran through the Iron Age fortification of Badbury Rings, just east of the town, where it made an uncharacteristic bend. In 1731 Blandford was all but destroyed by fire, the fourth such conflagration since the end of the sixteenth century. The phoenix that rose from these ashes was designed by the unfortunately named Bastard brothers, John and William, whose "Blandford School" produced buildings characterized by mellow dapplings of brick and stone.

Sleepy Blandford still boasts one of the most harmonious and complete Georgian townscapes in England, with its centrepieces being the **Town Hall** and the **Church of St Peter and St Paul**, built in 1739. Outside, the church's distinguishing feature is the cupola perched on its handsome square tower; inside it has fine box pews and huge Ionic columns. It doesn't quite look as John Bastard intended, though: the church was altered at the end of the nineteenth century, when the chancel was sawn off the nave, stuck on wheels, rolled out the way so that a new section could be built in the gap, and then stuck back on to the extension. The town **museum** in Bere's Yard, opposite the church (April–Sept Mon–Sat 10am–4pm; 50p) offers a pithy account of local history.

Blandford's **tourist office** is in the car park on West Street (April–Oct daily 10am–5.30pm; ☎01258/454 770). There are many **B&B**s along Whitecliff Mill Street, the best of which is *Methuen*, at no. 25 (☎01258/452 834; ④), a detached Georgian house five minutes from the town centre. The local Hall & Woodhouse brewery supplies many local **hostelries** – *The Greyhound*, in quiet Greyhound Place, is a good-looking pub with outdoor seating and great food.

Cerne Abbas

The most visited site in Dorset lies a further ten miles west, just off the A352, on the regular bus route between Dorchester and Sherborne (#216). **CERNE ABBAS** has bags of charm in its own right, with gorgeous Tudor cottages and abbey ruins, not to mention a clutch of decent pubs. Its main attraction, however, is the enormously priapic **giant** carved in the chalk hillside, standing 180 feet high and flourishing a club over his disproportionately small head. The age of the monument is disputed, some authorities believing it to be pre-Roman, others thinking he might be a Romano-British figure of Hercules, but in view of his prominent feature it's probable that the giant originated as some primeval fertility or protective symbol. Today it is in the care of the National Trust, who do their best to stop people wandering over it and eroding the two-foot trenches that form the outlines – a school of thought maintains that lying on the outsize member will induce conception.

Shaftesbury

Ten miles north of Blandford, **SHAFTESBURY** perches on a spur of lumpy green-gold hills, with severe gradients on three sides of the town. On a clear day views from the town are terrific – one of the best vantage points is **Gold Hill**, quaint and cobbled and very steep. The local history museum (Easter–Sept daily 11am–5pm; 50p) at the top is worth a glance – its contents include a collection of locally made buttons. Pilgrims once flocked to Shaftesbury to pay homage to the bones of Edward the Martyr, brought to the **Abbey** in 978, though now only the footings of the abbey church survive, just off the main street (Easter–Sept daily, Oct Sat & Sun 10.30am–5.30pm; £1). **St Peter's** church on the market place is one of the few reminders of Shaftesbury's medieval grandeur, when it boasted a castle, twelve churches and four market crosses.

The **tourist office** is on Bell Street (Easter–Oct daily 10am–5pm; ☎01747/853 514). The *Mitre Inn* on the High Street serves good pies and has **rooms** (☎01747/852 488; ④) as has *The Knoll* in Bleke Street (☎01747/855 243; ④). A mile south of town near Cann, on the scenic A350 to Blandford, *Saxon Rise Farm* (☎01747/854 515; ③) offers **B&B** with great views.

Stourhead

Landscape gardening was a favoured mode of display among the grandest eighteenth-century landowners, and **Stourhead**, ten miles northwest of Shaftesbury, is one of the most accomplished survivors of the genre. The Stourton estate was bought in 1717 by Henry Hoare, who commissioned Colen Campbell to build a new villa in the Palladian style. Hoare's heir, another Henry, returned from his Grand Tour in 1741 with his head full of the paintings of Claude and Poussin, and determined to translate their images of well-ordered, wistful classicism into real life. He dammed the Stour to create a lake, then planted the terrain with blocks of trees, domed temples, stone bridges, grottoes and statues, all mirrored vividly in the water. In 1772 the folly of King Alfred's Tower was added and today affords fine views across the estate and into neighbouring counties. The house itself is fairly run-of-the-mill, though it has some good Chippendale furniture (garden daily 9am–7pm or sunset; £4.20; house April–Oct Sat–Wed noon–5.30pm; £4.30; tower £1.50; combined ticket £7.50; NT). A mile to the southeast in the showpiece village of **Stourton**, also now owned by the National Trust, the *Spread Eagle Inn* is a good place to have lunch.

Longleat

If Stourhead is an unexpected outcrop of Italy in Wiltshire, the African savannah intrudes even more bizarrely at **Longleat** (house Easter–Sept 10am–6pm; Oct–Easter closes 4pm; £4; safari park March–Oct 10am–6pm; £6.50; combined ticket £10), south of the road from Warminster to Frome. In 1946 the Sixth Marquess of Bath became the first stately home-owner to open his house to the paying public on a regular basis to help make ends meet, and in 1966 he turned Longleat's Capability Brown landscapes into a drive-through **safari park** – the first in the country. Once committed to such commercial enterprise, the bosses of Longleat knew no limits: other attractions now include the world's largest hedge maze, a Doctor Who exhibition, a hi-tech simulation of the world's most dangerous modes of travel, and the Seventh Marquess' steamy murals encapsulating his interpretation of life and the universe (children may not be admitted). Beyond the brazen razzmatazz, though, there's an exquisitely furnished Elizabethan house, with the largest private library in Britain and a fine collection of pictures, including Titian's *Holy Family*.

Longleat is about four miles from the train stations of Frome and Warminster, between which bus #53 shuttles roughly every hour – though be prepared to walk the two and a half miles from the entrance of the house to its grounds. Car-less visitors must survey the lions, tigers, giraffes, elephants, zebras and hippos from a safari bus for an extra £1.

Sherborne

Tucked away in the northwest corner of Dorset, the attractive town of **SHERBORNE** was once the capital of Wessex, holding cathedral status until Old Sarum usurped the bishopric in 1075. This former glory is embodied by the magnificent **Abbey Church** (Mon–Sat 8am–4pm, Sun 8am–6pm), which was founded in 705, later becoming a Benedictine abbey. Most of its extant parts date from the fifteenth-century rebuilding, and it is one of the best examples of Perpendicular architecture in Britain, particularly noted for its outstanding **fan vaulting**. The church also has a famously weighty peal of bells, led by "Great Tom", a tenor bell presented to the abbey by Cardinal Wolsey. Among the abbey church's many tombs are those of Alfred the Great's two brothers, Ethelred and Ethelbert, located in the northeast corner. The **almshouse** on the opposite side of the Abbey Close was built in 1437 and is a rare example of a medieval hospital; another wing provides accommodation for Sherborne's well-known public school.

Sherborne also has two "castles", both associated with Sir Walter Raleigh. Queen Elizabeth I first leased, then gave Raleigh the twelfth-century **Old Castle** (daily 10am–6pm; £1.30; EH), but it seems that he despaired of feudal accommodation and built himself a more comfortably domesticated house, **Sherborne Castle** (Easter–Sept Thurs, Sat & Sun 1.30–5.30pm; £3.60), in adjacent parkland. When Sir Walter fell from the Queen's favour by seducing her maid of honour, the Digby family acquired the house and have lived there ever since; portraits, furniture and books are displayed in a whimsically Gothic interior, remodelled in the nineteenth century. The Old Castle fared less happily, and was pulverized by Cromwellian cannonfire for the obstinately Royalist leanings of its occupants. The **museum** on Half Moon Street (Tues–Sat 10.30am–4.30pm, Sun 2.30–4.30pm; 50p) includes a model of the Old Castle and photographs of parts of the fifteenth-century Sherbourne Missal, a richly illuminated tome weighing nearly fifty pounds, now housed in the British Library.

The **tourist office** is at 3 Tilton Court, Digby Road (Easter–Oct Mon–Sat 9.30am–5.30pm; Nov–Easter Mon–Sat 10am–3pm; ☎01935/815 341). For an **overnight stay** try *The Half Moon Hotel* on Half Moon Street (☎01935/812 017; ③), the *Britannia Inn* on Westbury Road, just down from the abbey (☎01935/813 300; ③) or the *Cross Keys Hotel*, 88 Cheap St (☎01935/812 492; ④), which has a few tables out front for drinks and meals. *Oliver's* on Cheap Street and the *Church House Gallery* close to the abbey on Half Moon Street, are both good for teas and light lunches.

Salisbury

SALISBURY, huddled below Wiltshire's chalky plain in the converging valleys of the Avon and Nadder, looks from a distance very much as it did when Constable painted his celebrated view of it from across the water meadows, even though traffic may clog its centre and military jets scream overhead from local air bases. Prosperous and well kept, Wiltshire's only city is designed on a pleasantly human scale, still dominated by the cathedral's immense spire – though sadly, the condition of the cathedral itself remains problematic, and scaffolding will blur its elegant silhouette for the foreseeable future. The town itself sprang into existence in the early thirteenth century, when the bishopric was moved from **Old Sarum**, an ancient Iron Age hill fort which now stands on the northern fringe of the town, just a bit closer than **Wilton House** to the west, one of Wiltshire's great houses.

The City

Begun in 1220, **Salisbury Cathedral** (May–Aug daily 8am–8.15pm; Sept–April closes 6.30pm; admission by donation of £2.50) was mostly completed within forty years and is thus uniquely consistent in its style, with one extremely prominent exception – the **spire**, which was added a century later and at 404 feet is the highest in England. Its survival is something of a miracle, for the foundations penetrate only about six feet into marshy ground, and when Christopher Wren surveyed it he found the spire to be leaning almost two and a half feet out of true. The tie-rods inserted by Wren arrested the problem, but didn't cure it, and engineers are now at work on it again.

The interior is over-austere after James Wyatt's brisk eighteenth-century tidying, but there's an amazing sense of space and light in its high nave, despite the sombre pillars of grey Purbeck marble, which are visibly bowing beneath the weight they bear. Monuments and carved tombs line the walls, where they were neatly placed by Wyatt, and in the north aisle there's a fascinating clock dating from 1386, one of the oldest functioning clock mechanisms in Europe. Other features not to miss are the vaulted colonnades of the **cloisters** and the octagonal **chapter house** (Mon–Sat 10am–5pm, Sun 1–5pm; 30p), its walls decorated with a frieze of scenes from the Old Testament. The **library**, which is only open for research purposes, contains a rare original copy of the Magna Carta.

Surrounding the cathedral is **The Close**, the largest and most impressive in the country, a peaceful precinct of lawns and mellow old buildings. Most of the houses have seemly Georgian facades, though some, like the Bishop's Palace and the deanery, date from the thirteenth century. **Mompesson House**, built by a wealthy merchant in 1701, is a fine example of a Queen Anne house and contains some beautifully furnished eighteenth-century rooms and a superbly carved staircase – the entry price includes a

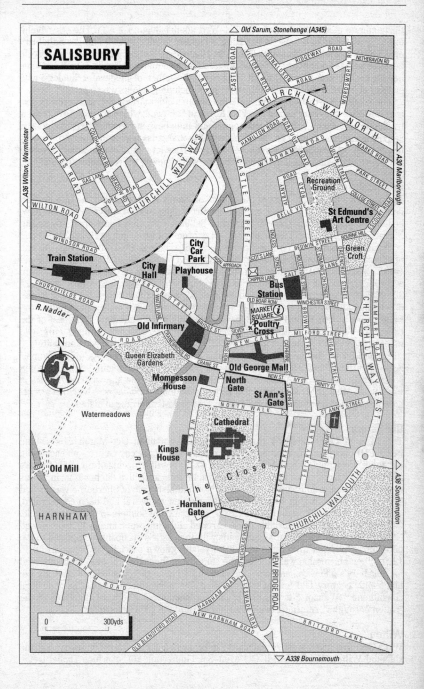

thirty-minute guided tour (April–Oct Sat–Wed noon–5.30pm; £3; NT). The other building to head for in The Close is the **King's House**, in which you'll find the **Salisbury and South Wiltshire Museum** (Mon–Sat 10am–5pm, Sun 2–5pm; £2.50) – an absorbing account of local history. It includes a good section on Stonehenge as well as focusing on the life and times of Keith Pitt-Rivers, the father of modern archeology who excavated many of Wiltshire's prehistoric sites, including Avebury (see p.217).

The Close's **North Gate** opens onto the centre's older streets, where narrow pedestrianized alleyways bear names like Fish Row and Salt Lane, which are indicative of their trading origin. Many half-timbered houses and inns have survived all over the centre, and the last of four market crosses, **Poultry Cross**, stands on stilts in Silver Street, near the Market Square. Salisbury's market, held on Tuesdays and Saturdays, still serves a large agricultural area, as it did in earlier times when the city grew wealthy on wool.

Practicalities

Trains arrive half a mile west of the centre, on South Western Road; the **bus station** lies north of the Market Place, on Endless Street. The **tourist office** is on Fish Row, just off the Market Place (June & Sept Mon–Sat 9am–6pm, Sun 11am–4pm; July & Aug Mon–Sat 9am–7pm, Sun 11am–5pm; Oct–May Mon–Sat 9am–5pm; ☎01722/334 956).

For **accommodation**, try the *Victoria Lodge*, 61 Castle St (☎01722/330 749; ③), one of several inexpensive B&Bs along this road; the *Clovelley Guest House*, on Mill Road (☎01722/322 055; ④) near the train station; or the oak-beamed *Old Bakery*, 35 Bedwin St (☎01722/320 100; ④), closer to the city centre. *The Old Bell*, 2 St Ann St (☎01722/327 958; ⑤) is an attractive inn near the cathedral, or else there's *Glen Lyn Guest House*, 6 Bellamy Lane, Milford Hill (☎01722 327 880; ④), ten minutes' walk east of the centre. **Salisbury's youth hostel** is in a 220-year-old building ten minutes' walk east of the cathedral, on Milford Hill (☎01722/327 572). *Coombe Nurseries Caravan Park*, two miles to the west in Netherhampton (☎01722/328 451) is a well equipped **campsite**.

For **food and drink**, sample the popular *Michael Snell Tea Rooms*, on St Thomas' Square, or the *Bishops Mill Tavern*, a popular pub with outdoor seating, right in the city centre on Bridge Street. Another pub worth mentioning is the atmospheric *Haunch of Venison* on Minster Street, which also serves good food. *Sunflowers*, 4 Ivy St, is a vegetarian restaurant specializing in good-value Thai and Mediterranean dishes.

Old Sarum

The ruins of **OLD SARUM** (April–Sept daily 10am–6pm; Oct–March closes 4pm; £1.40; EH) occupy a bleak hilltop site two miles north of the city centre – an easy walk, but there are plenty of buses: #3, #5, #9 or #X19. Possibly occupied up to 5000 years ago then developed as an Iron Age fort whose double protective ditches remain, it was settled by Romans and Saxons before the Norman bishopric of Sherborne was moved here in the 1070s. Within a couple of decades a new cathedral had been consecrated, and a large religious community was living alongside the soldiers in the central castle. Old Sarum was an uncomfortable place, parched and windswept, and in 1220 the dissatisfied clergy – additionally at loggerheads with the castle's occupants – appealed to the pope for permission to decamp to Salisbury (still known officially as New Sarum) in 1220. When permission was granted, the stone from the cathedral was commandeered for Salisbury's gateways, and once the church had gone the population waned. By the nineteenth century Old Sarum was deserted, but it continued to exist as a political constituency (William Pitt was one of its representatives), the most notorious of the "rotten boroughs", returning two MPs right up until the 1833 Reform Act.

Wilton

WILTON, five miles west of Salisbury, is renowned for its carpet industry and the splendid **Wilton House** (April–Oct Mon–Sat 11am–6pm; £6), of which Daniel Defoe wrote, "One cannot be said to have seen anything that a man of curiosity would think worth seeing in this county, and not have been at Wilton House." The Tudor house, built for the First Earl of Pembroke on the site of a dissolved Benedictine abbey, was ruined by fire in 1647 and rebuilt by Inigo Jones, whose classic hallmarks can be seen in the sumptuous Single Cube and Double Cube rooms, so called because of their precise dimensions. Sir Philip Sidney, illustrious Elizabethan courtier and poet, wrote part of his magnum opus *Arcadia* here – the dado round the Single Cube Room illustrates scenes from the book. The easel **paintings** are what makes Wilton really special, however – the collection includes Van Dyck, Rembrandt, two of the Brueghel family, Poussin, Andrea del Sarto and Tintoretto. In the grounds, the famous **Palladian Bridge** has been joined by ancillary attractions including an adventure playground, garden centre and an audio-visual show on the colourful Earls of Pembroke, all designed to subsidize a massive programme of structural renovation.

Salisbury Plain and northwards

The Ministry of Defence is the landlord of much of **SALISBURY PLAIN**, the 100,000 acres of chalky upland to the north of Salisbury. Flags warn casual trespassers away from MoD firing ranges and tank-training grounds, while rather stricter security cordons off such secretive establishments as the research centre at Porton Down, Britain's centre for chemical and biological warfare. As elsewhere, the army's residency has ironically saved much of the Plain from modern agricultural chemicals, thereby inadvertently nurturing species all but extinct in more trampled landscapes.

Though now largely deserted except by forces' families living in ugly, temporary-looking barracks quarters, Salisbury Plain once positively throbbed with communities. Stone Age, Bronze Age and Iron Age settlements left hundreds of burial mounds scattered over the chalklands, as well as major complexes at Danebury, Badbury, Figsbury, Old Sarum (see above) and, of course, the great circle of **Stonehenge**. North of Salisbury Plain, beyond the A342 Andover–Devizes road, lies the softer Vale of Pewsey, traversed by the Kennet canal. **Marlborough**, to the north of the Vale, is the centre for another cluster of ancient sites, including the huge stone circle of **Avebury**, the mysterious grassy mound of **Silbury Hill** and the chamber graves of **West Kennet**.

(Malmesbury, though in Wiltshire, is covered in the following chapter, on p.244, as it feels more closely allied to the Cotswolds area than to the rest of its county, from which it's cut off by the M4 and rail line.)

Stonehenge

No ancient structure in England arouses more controversy than **STONEHENGE** (April to mid-July daily 10am–6pm; mid-July to Sept closes 8pm; Sept–March closes 4pm; £3; NT & EH), that mysterious ring of monoliths nine miles north of Salisbury. While archeologists argue over whether it was a place of ritual sacrifice and sun-worship, an astronomical calculator or a royal palace, the guardians of the site struggle to accommodate its year-round crowds, resentful at no longer being able to walk among the stones. Annual battles between the police and gatherings of Druids and New Age travellers trying to celebrate the summer solstice are a thing of the past since the passage of the draconian Criminal Justice Act – but the site is nonetheless securely patrolled on midsummer's dawn. Conservation of Stonehenge, one of UNESCO's 380 designated World Heritage Sites, is obviously an urgent priority, and the current custodians are trying to address the dissatisfaction that many feel on visiting this landmark. A new visitor centre is planned a mile and a half from the stones at Larkhill, and a rerouting of the nearby roads is projected. In the meantime, visitors are issued with handsets programmed to dispense a range of information on the site – some of the soundtrack is interesting, but much is misleading and patronizing.

What exists today is only a small part of the original prehistoric complex, as many of the outlying stones were plundered by medieval and later farmers for building materials. The construction of Stonehenge is thought to have taken place in several stages. In about 3000 BC the outer circular bank and ditch were constructed, and the massive Heel Stone placed outside the entrance to the central enclosure; just inside the ditch was dug a ring of 56 pits, which at a later date was filled with a mixture of earth and human ash. Around 2100 BC the first stone circle was raised within the earthworks, comprising approximately eighty great blocks of dolerite (bluestone), whose ultimate source was Preseli in Wales. Some archeologists have suggested that these monoliths were found lying on Salisbury Plain, having been borne down from the Welsh mountains by a glacier in the last Ice Age, but the lack of any other glacial debris on the plain would seem to disprove this theory. It really does seem to be the case that the stones were cut from quarries in Preseli and dragged or floated here on rafts, a prodigious task in view of the fact that some are twenty-five feet high and weigh as much as forty tons. Scientists recently claimed to have dated a bluestone's removal from its source, which may finally solve some part of the enigma.

The crucial phase in the creation of the site came in 1500 BC, when the incomplete bluestone circle was transformed by the construction of a circle of twenty-five **trilithons** (two uprights crossed by a lintel) and an inner horseshoe formation of five trilithons. Hewn from Marlborough Downs sandstone, these colossal stones (called sarsens) were carefully dressed and worked – for example, to compensate for perspectival distortion the uprights have a slight swelling in the middle, the same trick as the builders of the Parthenon were to employ several hundred years later. More bluestones were used to form a small circle and horseshoe within the trilithons, but the purpose of all this work remains baffling. The symmetry and location of the site (a slight rise in a flat valley with even views of the horizon in all directions), as well as its alignment towards the points of sunrise and sunset on the summer and winter solstices, tend to support the supposition that it was some sort of observatory or time-measuring device.

Marlborough

An obvious base from which to explore Salisbury Plain is **MARLBOROUGH**, a peaceful spot now that the M4 deflects traffic from the old stagecoach route passing through the town. It's a handsome town too: the wide High Street, a dignified assembly of Georgian buildings, has a fine Perpendicular church standing at each end, and half-timbered cottages rambling up the alleyways behind. The famous public school is not especially old – it was established in 1843 – but incorporates an ancient coaching inn among its red-brick buildings.

Marlborough **tourist office** is in the car park on George Lane (Easter–Oct Mon–Sat 10am–5pm; Nov–Easter Mon–Sat 10am–4.30pm; ☎01672/513 989) and there are several inns and guest houses offering **accommodation** along the High Street. Top of the range are *Ivy House* (☎01672/515 333; ⑦) and the *Castle and Ball* (☎01672/515 201; ⑨); less expensive B&B options include the *Merlin* pub (☎01672/512 151; ④) and *Mrs Waite*, 5 Reeds Ground, London Road (☎01672/513 926; ③). **Eating** is no problem in central Marlborough: the bistro food at *Ivy House* is reasonable, while *Polly's Tea Rooms* serves good snacks.

Silbury Hill, West Kennet and Avebury

The neat green mound of **Silbury Hill**, five miles west of Marlborough, is probably overlooked by a majority of drivers whizzing by on the A4. At 130 feet it's no great height, but when you realize it's the largest prehistoric artificial mound in Europe, and was made by a people using nothing more than primitive spades, it commands more respect. It was probably constructed around 2600 BC, but like so many of the sites of Salisbury Plain, no one knows quite what it was for, though the likelihood is that it was a burial mound. You can't actually walk on the hill – so having admired it briefly from the car park, cross the road to the footpath that leads half a mile to the **West Kennet Long Barrow**. Dating from about 3250 BC, this was definitely a chamber tomb – nearly fifty burials have been discovered at West Kennet.

Immediately to the west, the village of **AVEBURY** stands in the midst of a **stone circle** (April–Oct daily 11am–5.30pm; Nov to mid-Dec Sat & Sun 11.30am–4pm; free) that rivals Stonehenge – the individual stones are generally smaller, but the circle itself is much wider and more complex. A massive earthwork 20 feet high and 1400 feet across encloses the main circle, which is approached by four causeways across the inner ditch, two of them leading into wide avenues stretching over a mile beyond the circle. The best guess is that it was built soon after 2500 BC, and presumably had a similar ritual or religious function to Stonehenge's. The structure of Avebury's diffuse circle is quite difficult to grasp unless you see a plan of it beforehand, so you should first of all drop into the **Alexander Keiller Museum**, at the entrance to the site, which displays excavated material and explanatory information (April–Oct daily 10am–6pm; Nov–March Mon–Sat 10am–4pm; £1.50; NT & EH). Thus clued up, you can wander round the peaceful circle, accompanied by sheep and cattle grazing unconcernedly among the stones. The placid **village** of Avebury, half inside the circle, is on good bus routes from Marlborough and Devizes, with the *Red Lion* pub (☎01672/539 266; ③) providing a few rooms and serving reasonable meals.

Devizes

DEVIZES, seven miles down the A361 from Avebury at the mouth of the Vale of Pewsey, is a pleasant place, with some attractive eighteenth-century houses, a stately semicircular market place and a couple of fine churches, St Mary's and St John's. It's chiefly worth a stop, however, for the excellent **museum** at 41 Long St (Mon–Sat 10am–5pm; £1.75, free Mon), housing an exceptional collection of prehistoric finds from barrows and henges throughout the county. Star exhibit is the so-called *Marlborough Bucket*, decorated with bronze reliefs from the first century BC.

Devizes has a very helpful **tourist office** at 39 St John's St (Easter–Oct Mon–Sat 10am–5.30pm, Sun 10am–noon & 1.30–5.30pm; Nov–Easter Mon–Sat 10am–4.30pm; ☎01380/729 408). The best place **to stay** is the listed, timber-framed *Long St Guest House* on Long Street (☎01380/724 245; ⑤); less expensive are the *Craven B&B* on Station Road (☎01380/723 514; ③) and the *White Bear Inn* on Market Street (☎01380/722 583; ③). If you just want to **eat**, try the *Wiltshire Kitchen* on St John's Street, just off the market square, which serves good lunches and snacks, as does the *Grindle Grill Café* near the cinema on Market Place. Also on Market Place, you'll find the *Seafood Restaurant* which provides more substantial meals.

Lacock and Corsham Court

LACOCK, ten miles northwest of Devizes, is the perfect English feudal village, albeit one gentrified by the National Trust to within a hairs' breadth of natural life, and besieged by tourists all summer. Appropriately for so photogenic a spot, it has a fascinating museum dedicated to the founding father of photography, Henry Fox Talbot, a member of the dynasty which has lived in the local **Abbey** since it passed to Sir William Sharington on the Dissolution of the monasteries in 1539. His descendant, Henry Fox Talbot, was the first to produce a photographic negative, and the **Fox**

Talbot Museum (April–Oct daily 11am–5.30pm; £2.40; NT), in a sixteenth-century barn by the abbey gates, captures something of the excitement he must have experienced as the dim outline of an oriel window in the abbey steadily imprinted itself on a piece of silver nitrate paper. The postage-stamp-sized result is on display in the museum. The abbey itself (April–Oct daily except Tues 1–5.30pm; £4.20; NT), preserves a few monastic fragments amid the eighteenth-century Gothic, while the church of **St Cyriac** contains the opulent tomb of the nefarious Sir William Sharington, buried beneath a splendid barrel-vaulted roof.

Another sight within a short drive of Lacock is **Corsham Court** (Easter–Sept Tues–Sun 2–6pm; Oct, Nov & Jan–Easter Tues–Thurs, Sat & Sun 2–4.30pm; £3.50), three miles west. It dates from Elizabethan times, though what you see now bears the Georgian stamp of Nash and Capability Brown, and the house contains a fine collection of art, including pieces by Caravaggio, Rubens, Reynolds and Michelangelo. The village of **Corsham** is another dignified little cloth-making town of Bath stone, riddled with underground limestone quarries and a long railway tunnel engineered by Brunel. The delightfully Chaucerian-sounding hostelry, *At the Sign of the Angel*, back in Lacock, is a good if expensive hotel and restaurant (☎01249/730 230; ⑧).

Bradford on Avon and around

With its buildings of mellow auburn stone, reminiscent of the townscapes over the county border in Bath and the Cotswolds, **BRADFORD ON AVON** is the most appealing town in the northwest corner of Wiltshire. Sheltering against a steep wooded slope, it takes its name from its "broad ford" across the Avon, replaced in the thirteenth century by a **bridge** that was in turn largely rebuilt in the seventeenth. The domed structure at one end is a quaint old jail converted from a chapel. The local industry, based on textiles like that of its Yorkshire namesake, was revolutionized with the arrival of Flemish weavers in 1659, and many of the town's handsome buildings reflect the prosperity of this period. Yet Bradford's most significant building is the tiny **St Laurence** church on Church Street, an outstanding example of Saxon architecture dating from about 700. Wrecked by Viking invaders, and later used as a school and a simple dwelling, it was rehabilitated by a local vicar in 1856. Its distinctive features are the carved angels over the chancel arch.

Bradford's **train station** is on St Margaret's Street close to the town centre. A well-equipped **tourist office** is based in the public library on Bridge Street (April–Oct daily 10am–5pm; Nov–March closes 4pm; ☎01225/865 797). Bradford has a good range of **accommodation**, none more characterful than *Bradford Old Windmill*, a non-smoking B&B at 4 Mason's Lane (☎01225/866 842; ⑥) that offers an imaginative vegetarian menu. *Priory Steps* (☎01225/862 230; ⑤), closer to the centre on Newtown, has excellent views over a roofscape of weavers' cottages. The *Riverside Inn,* 49 St Margaret's St (☎01225/863 526; ④), lives up to its name, but has basic rooms without private facilities. For light lunches or cakes, try the *Bridge Tea Rooms* on Bridge Street; for alcohol or more substantial food, head for the *Bunch of Grapes* **pub** on Silver Street.

travel details

Trains

Bournemouth to: Brockenhurst (every 20min; 25min); Dorchester (hourly; 40min); London (hourly; 1hr 25min); Poole (every 20min; 10–15min); Southampton (every 20min; 35min); Weymouth (hourly; 50min); Winchester (hourly; 1hr).

Dorchester to: Bournemouth (hourly; 40min); Brockenhurst (hourly; 55min); London (hourly; 2hr 20min); Weymouth (hourly; 10min).

Portsmouth to: London (every 20–30min; 1hr 30min); Southampton (every 20–30min; 40min); Winchester (hourly; 50min).

Ryde (Isle of Wight) to: Shanklin (every 30min; 20min).

Salisbury to: London (hourly; 1hr 30min); Portsmouth (hourly; 1hr 40min); Southampton (every 40min; 30min).

Southampton to: Bournemouth (every 15–20min; 30min); Brockenhurst (every 10–15min; 15min); London (every 30min; 1hr 15min); Portsmouth (every 20–30min; 40min); Salisbury (every 40min; 30min); Weymouth (hourly; 1hr 25min); Winchester (every 30min; 10min).

Winchester to: Bournemouth (hourly; 1hr); London (every 30min; 75min); Portsmouth (hourly; 50min); Southampton (every 30min; 10min).

Buses

Bournemouth to: London (10 daily; 2hr 25min); Lyndhurst (6 daily; 1hr 45min); Poole (every 10min; 10min).

Dorchester to: London (2 daily; 3hr 45min); Poole (4 daily; 1hr 15min); Salisbury (5 daily; 1hr 45min); Weymouth (every 30min; 25min).

Lyndhurst to: Bournemouth (6 daily; 1hr 45min); Poole (6 daily; 1hr 55min); Southampton (hourly; 25min).

Lymington to: Beaulieu (5 daily; 35min)

Poole to: Bournemouth (every 10min; 10min); Corfe (every 30min; 50min).

Portsmouth to: London (8 daily; 2hr); Southampton (hourly; 30min); Winchester (11 daily; 1hr 55min).

Salisbury to: London (4 daily; 3hr); Poole (hourly; 2hr); Stonehenge (hourly; 40min).

Southampton to: London (8 daily; 2hr 30min); Winchester (8 daily; 25min).

Weymouth to: Dorchester (every 30min; 25min).

Winchester to: London (6 daily; 2hr); Portsmouth (11 daily; 1hr 55min); Southampton (8 daily; 25min).

CHAPTER FOUR

FROM LONDON TO THE SEVERN

The slab of land **between London and the Severn River** is a disparate region of Roman towns and New Towns, tree-clad hills and rolling downs, encompassing no fewer than seven counties. The chief physical link within this swathe of England is the **River Thames**, whose 215-mile course from its source in the western Cotswolds makes it the second longest river in the country. Transport routes create a further continuity, the oldest of them being the **Ridgeway**, a prehistoric track running the length of the Chiltern hills and continuing southwest into Wiltshire. Of more practical use to the majority of visitors, the M40/A40 road slices right through the heart of central southern England, linking London to Gloucester via Oxford and the Cotswolds, while the M4 motorway and the rail line between London and Bristol marks the region's approximate southern edge. It is scarcely surprising that this is not an area in which you can easily find many remote and unpopulated spots.

Of the places covered in this chapter, **St Albans** is rather stranded on the fringes of London, an island of Roman and medieval history in a knot of motorways and new towns like Welwyn Garden City, Stevenage and Hemel Hempstead. But the amorphous developments surrounding the cathedral town also conceal a few surprises, not least **Hatfield House**, one of the country's finest ancestral homes. Neighbouring Bedfordshire, mostly flat agricultural land with a hint of industrial Midlands, is not a county you'd cross England to visit. The best of adjacent **Buckinghamshire** lies in the **Chiltern Hills**, which rise in the south of Bedfordshire and peter out in Oxfordshire. These picturesque chalk uplands, with their heavy covering of beech trees, are best explored from **Henley-on-Thames**. **Berkshire**, which extends from the M25 all the way west to beyond Newbury, is blighted in its eastern part by fairly hideous towns such as Reading and Slough, though the former is a major rail junction that you may well need to make use of. By contrast, the Berkshire Downs, divided from the Chilterns by the Thames but linked to them by the Ridgeway, include the **Vale of the White Horse**, one of the highlights of this whole region.

Bordering Berkshire to the north, **Oxfordshire** is firmly centred on its county town. With its ancient university, superb museums and lively student population, **Oxford** can keep you busy for days, and it's an excellent base for the **Cotswolds**, which lie mostly in **Gloucestershire**. Throughout the Cotswolds, beautifully preserved mansions and churches attest to the fortunes made through the medieval wool trade, and the remarkable continuity of Cotswold architecture has created villages as attractive as any in England, though the tourist deluge makes some spots nightmarish in summer. Tourism is less of a nuisance in the southern areas of the Cotswolds, around the busy working towns of **Cirencester** and **Stroud**, and of course there's plenty of good walking country in which to escape the crowds.

In the west, the land drops sharply from the Cotswold escarpment down to **Cheltenham**, a once elegant Regency spa most famous these days for its horse racing. It's a rather staid place, however, with much less to offer than **Gloucester**, with its superb cathedral and rejuvenated docklands. From here, the Vale of Gloucester follows the route of the **Severn** northeast towards Worcestershire, the stone cottages of the Cotswolds giving way to the thatched, half-timbered and red-brick houses which are characteristic of **Tewkesbury**, a solidly provincial town with a superb abbey.

St Albans and around

ST ALBANS is a well-blended medley of medieval and modern features grafted onto the site of Verulamium, the town founded by the Romans soon after the invasion of 43 AD. It was here, in 209 AD, that a Roman soldier became the country's first Christian martyr when he was beheaded for giving shelter to a priest. Pilgrims later flocked to the town that had come to bear his name, where the place of execution was marked by a hilltop cathedral, once one of the largest churches in the Christian world. A day's visit should suffice to explore St Albans' small centre, but an overnight stay is recommended, not least to try out some of the excellent pubs.

The City

An abbey was constructed in St Albans in 1077, on the site of a Saxon one founded by King Offa of Mercia, and despite subsequent alterations – like the ugly west front – the legacy of the Normans remains the most impressive aspect of the city's **Cathedral**. The sheer scale of their design is breathtaking: the nave, almost 300 feet long, is the longest medieval nave in Britain, even if it isn't the most harmonious – the massive Norman pillars on the north side stand out from those in the later Early English style, some of which retain thirteenth- and fourteenth-century paintings, the detail clear though the ochre colours are much faded. Contrastingly crisp black and white geometric designs decorate the Norman arches in the nave and in the transepts at the base of the tower, where the impact of the original design reaches its peak, as the tower is a virtually unadulterated Norman relic. Behind the high altar an elaborate stone reredos (a clumsy construction compared with the Gothic rood screen) hides Saint Alban's fourteenth-century shrine. The tomb was almost completely destroyed during the Dissolution, but the Victorians patched it up and further restoration has been done recently. Some of the carving on the Purbeck marble remains remarkably clear: a scene on the west end depicts the saint's martyrdom.

Leaving the cathedral past the shop and cafeteria, you reach the **abbey gate**, the only other part of the original complex to have survived the Dissolution. Down Abbey Lane, past the *Fighting Cocks* (one of the oldest pubs in the country) and across the trickle of the River Ver, you reach **Verulamium Park**, the heart of the Roman city. Verulamium nowadays fulfils a role primarily as a city park, though it has fragments of the old Roman wall and, in a small brick hut, the remains of a town house with its under-floor heating system and mosaic floor. The city's finest Roman heritage occupies the excellent **Verulamium Museum** on the northern edge of the park (Mon–Sat

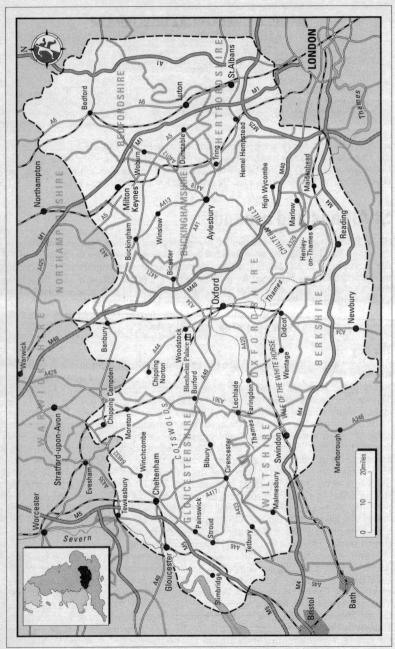

10am–5.30pm, Sun 2–5.30pm; £2.50), where cabinets are crammed with local finds, including exquisite jewellery, amphoras and coins in almost mint condition. The **Verulamium Theatre** (daily summer 10am–5pm, winter 9am–4pm; £1), across the busy road from the museum, was built around 140 AD but reduced to the status of municipal rubbish dump by the fifth century. It's nothing but a small hollow in comparison with the Colosseum, but the site is impressive if only for the fact that nothing else quite like it exists in Britain.

You can walk back to the centre along St Michael's Street, over one of the prettier stretches of the Ver, past a sixteenth-century mill (now a museum and café), and up the gently curving Fishpool Street, a quiet road lined with medieval inns and handsome Georgian houses. Off the northern end of St Peter's Street, on Hatfield Road, the **City Museum** (Mon–Sat 10am–5pm, Sun 2–5pm; free) provides a thorough history of St Albans from Boudicca to the building of the M25. You can also learn about Matthew Paris, the most famous occupant of St Albans abbey – his chronicles, covering events before and during his own lifetime in the thirteenth century, are some of the wittiest and most detailed written in medieval Europe. The museum uses reproductions of some of his manuscripts to tell the city's early history, including an illustration of the martyrdom of Alban which leaves absolutely nothing to the imagination.

Practicalities

Trains from King's Cross arrive at St Albans' City Station, ten minutes' walk east of the main drag, St Peter's Street. Trains from Euston serve the small Abbey Station at the bottom of Holywell Hill, a more strenuous ten-minute walk south of the centre. Most **buses** terminate at City Station, but virtually all services stop along St Peter's Street too. The **tourist office** is in the Town Hall, at the bottom of St Peter's Street (Mon–Sat 9.30am–5.30pm; ☎01727/864 511). There are several **B&Bs** near the City Station, such as the *Ellenbeigh Guest House* at 33 Alma Rd (☎01727/833 393; ③) or, a couple of doors along, *Care Inns*, at no. 29 (☎ 01727/867 310; ③). You can't move for **pubs** in St Albans – the Campaign for Real Ale has its headquarters here, and seems to have a good influence. *The Goat*, on Sopwell Lane, serves excellent food and beer, and has jazz on Sunday lunchtimes. *The Garibaldi*, on next-door Albert Street, combines good beers and an imaginative menu with outside tables. The low prices at *Cosa Nostra*, an Italian **restaurant** at 67 Lattimore Rd, pull a steady stream of customers, or you could try the *New Gulshan*, the best Indian restaurant in town, at 141 Victoria St.

Hatfield

Hatfield House (late March to mid-Oct Tues–Sat noon–4pm, Sun 1.30–5pm; £5), six miles east of St Albans, is one of the most impressive houses in England. Henry VIII and his heirs used the original building as a country retreat, though for Elizabeth, kept here by her half-sister Mary, it was more a prison than a home. James I, on inheriting the throne, decided he disliked Hatfield and did a house swap with his Chief Minister, Sir Robert Cecil, whose descendants still live here. From the awesome brick exterior to the dark wood panelling inside, Hatfield House has a grand and heavy atmosphere, but some magnificent Tudor and Jacobean portraits bring the **interior** alive, supplying a roll-call of the important people of the day. Elizabeth I provides a central theme, her memorabilia including a pair of the queen's silk stockings and an extraordinary pedigree tracing her descent from Adam and Eve via Noah and King Lear. The banqueting hall survives from the Tudor building but is rarely open, being used mainly for "Elizabethan banquets". The extensive grounds include part of the **formal gardens** laid out by John Tradescant, the greatest gardener ever engaged by the Stuarts.

Hatfield House can be reached easily on public transport, its entrance being opposite the train station of **HATFIELD** town, on the King's Cross–Cambridge line; frequent local buses also serve London and neighbouring towns. At first sight Hatfield smacks of suburbia, but the old centre – a short walk south of the station – is well worth exploring. Climb the steep Fore Street to the **church**, which has a window by the Pre-Raphaelite artist Edward Burne-Jones, and the tomb of Sir Robert Cecil, a macabre affair with Cecil's effigy resting over a skeleton. The *Eight Bells* pub at the bottom of Fore Street serves a good pint and a reasonable lunch.

The Chilterns

The chalk downs of the **Chiltern Hills** extend roughly from Luton to Reading, two unattractive towns that give little indication of their closeness to marvellous walking country, where pretty villages and homely pubs escape the touristic overkill that afflicts the Cotswolds. The most attractive area lies immediately south of High Wycombe – another depressing place, where you may need to change buses – and the M40, which hacks a route straight through the beech-clad hills. **Marlow** and **Henley** are the best bases for exploring the hills and the Thames Valley, which runs along the southern edge of the Chilterns. Some of the best walks incorporate stretches of the ancient Ridgeway path.

Woburn

Not strictly speaking in the Chilterns, but a worthwhile detour nevertheless, **Woburn Abbey** (April–Oct Mon–Sat 11am–4pm & Sun 11am–5pm; Dec–March Sat & Sun 11am–4pm; £6.50) is set in parkland, some twelve miles northwest of Luton, off the M1. The eighteenth-century house, called an "abbey" since it was built on the site of a Cistercian foundation, contains some superb pictures to sustain interest throughout the grand and rather cluttered state rooms. Some of the finest **Tudor portraits** in the country hang in the Long Gallery, with works by Canaletto, Rembrandt and Gainsborough as other highlights. You can explore the grounds immediately around the house on foot, but only motorists can enter the part given over to **Woburn Safari Park** (March–Oct daily 10am–sunset; £7.90; Nov–Feb Sat & Sun 11am–3pm; £5), the largest drive-through wildlife reserve in Britain. The animals include endangered species such as the African white rhino and bongo antelope, and appear to be in excellent health. The Bengal tigers can be unnervingly playful, but a posse of guards tours around in orange Land Rovers on the lookout for drivers in distress – the main danger is an overheated engine, a common problem in high season when the traffic achieves rush-hour congestion. For this reason, turn up as early as possible.

The **train stations** at Flitwick, Leighton Buzzard and Bletchley are all about six miles away, but you can reach the town direct by **bus** from Milton Keynes (which is on the main line from London to Birmingham); neither buses nor trains run on Sundays.

Whipsnade Zoo and Tring

Whipsnade Zoo (summer Mon–Sat 10am–6pm, Sun 10am–7pm; closes sunset in winter; £7.30), the free-range menagerie of the Zoological Society of London, perches high up on the downs between Dunstable and Tring, seven miles southwest of Luton. Whipsnade runs a number of major breeding programmes; there is a flourishing cheetah population, and the rare Burmese elephant has also been bred successfully. Most animals, from sleek tigers to harmless wallabies, are kept in large enclosures, separated from the public by a fence or a ditch. The Discovery Centre, which adopts a more overtly educational approach, lets you watch nervy golden tamarinds and other jungle species at close quarters. You can drive around the zoo (an extra £6 per car is payable March–Nov), but it's possible to see everything perfectly well on foot, or you

---

THE RIDGEWAY

The **Ridgeway** has existed for around five thousand years and was probably once part of a route extending from the Wash in Norfolk to the Dorset coast. Today it is defined by the Countryside Commission as running from **Ivinghoe Beacon** near Tring to **Overton Hill**, 85 miles southwest in Wiltshire, crossing five counties. Skirting any densely populated areas, it follows the top of the ridge for most of its course, except where the Thames slices through the ridge at the **Goring Gap**, which marks the transition from the wooded valleys of the Chilterns to the more open Berkshire Downs. It's not a consistently magnificent footpath, but it does offer a number of archeological diversions, the finest of them being in the **Vale of the White Horse** and around **Avebury** (see p.217). There are several youth hostels within reach of the Ridgeway and a *Ridgeway Information and Accommodation Guide* is available from the Ridgeway Officer, Dept. of Leisure and Art, Countryside Service, Holton, Oxford OX33 1QQ (☎01865/810 224).

---

could hop on the free motorized train that stops at the main enclosures. There's also a steam train (for which you must pay), which takes you closer to the animals.

Six miles southwest of Whipsnade, the small and unremarkable town of **TRING** is the surprising location for an annexe of London's Natural History Museum. **Tring Zoological Museum** (Mon–Sat 10am–5pm, Sun 2–5pm; £2.20) houses the largest such collection ever put together by one person, in this case Lord Walter Rothschild (1868–1937), an enthusiastic and eccentric zoologist. Even if you balk at the idea of admiring stuffed animals, it's hard not to be stirred by the beauty of the birds of paradise or the freakishness of the quagga, a relative of the zebra extinct since the 1880s. One of the world's biggest collections of fleas includes two dressed in clothes by a Mexican woman in 1905.

You can get to Tring by **train** on the Euston–Northampton rail line, though the station is a twenty-minute walk east of town. To get to Whipsnade from Tring, take the #61 Luton–Aylesbury bus, and pick up the #43 at Dunstable; otherwise, alight at the Whipsnade turn-off, from where it's a mile up the hill to the zoo.

Henley-on-Thames and around

Three counties – Oxfordshire, Berkshire and Buckinghamshire – meet at **HENLEY-ON-THAMES**, a long-established stopping place for travellers between Oxford and London. Its brick and half-timbered buildings are certainly elegant, particularly along the main street, but Henley is an affluent commuter town that lacks warmth at the best of times and becomes positively arrogant during the **Royal Regatta**, the world's most important amateur rowing tournament. Established in 1839, it's the boating equivalent of the Ascot races, a quintessentially English parade ground for the rich, aristocratic and aspiring, whose champagne-swilling antics are watched by even larger numbers of hoi polloi. The competitions, featuring past and potential Olympic rowers, run from the last Wednesday in June for five days. Information is available from the Regatta Headquarters on the Berkshire side of the Thames (☎01491/572 153).

A branch line runs north to Henley from the Paddington–Reading **rail** line, but you usually have to change trains at Twyford, five miles south; there are no services on Sundays between September and May. *Thames Transit* **buses** #390 between Oxford and London stop in New Street. The **tourist office** (April–Sept daily 10am–7pm; Oct–March closes 4pm; ☎01491/578 034) is in the basement of the town hall, at the top of Hart Street. The best **B&Bs** are dispersed along the quiet streets, south of Hart Street, near the train station and include the *Avalon* at 36 Queen St (☎01491/577 829; ③). In summer you can **camp** at the *Swiss Farm Caravan Park*, a mile north on the Marlow

Road (☎01491/573419). For food, your best bet are the **pubs**: the *Angel* by the bridge, the *Three Tuns* and the *Argyll* further up. Brakspears, the local brewery, presides over most of Henley's pubs like a feudal dynasty and fortunately produces good ale.

Five miles north of Henley lies **Stonor Park**, a Tudor mansion nestled in a fold of the Chilterns on the edge of the village of Stonor. Many of the Stonor family, refusing to renounce Catholicism, were imprisoned and deprived of their land, though they were later reinstated, and their descendants still live here. From the outside, the rich ochre brickwork and fine proportions of the **house** (May to late Sept Wed & Sun 2–5.30pm; July to late Aug also Thurs 2–5.30pm; Aug also Sat 2–5.30pm; £4) make an enduring impact, but the interior lacks cohesion and contains little old family furniture. Nevertheless there are some interesting memorabilia relating to the Jesuit scholar and missionary Edmund Campion, who took refuge here but was eventually executed in 1581 and later canonized. The chapel frieze, carved from tea chests by a Polish artist during World War II, was given by Graham Greene, a family friend who was staying here when he wrote *Our Man in Havana*. The pleasant grounds are open more regularly than the house (March–Oct daily 11am–6pm; Nov & Dec closes 4pm; £3).

Marlow, Cookham and Cliveden

MARLOW, ten miles downstream, is a clone of its neighbour, with pleasant Georgian architecture, swarms of tourists in summer and its own regatta. But it is smaller and more relaxed than Henley, and you can while away an hour watching boats go through the lock or tracing Marlow's literary connections. In 1817 Percy Bysshe Shelley and his wife Mary moved to an unmarked house on West Street (between Hayes Place and the school) and stayed for a year – just long enough for him to compose the *Revolt of Islam* and for her to write *Frankenstein*. T.S. Eliot lived down the road at no. 31 for a time in 1918, and Jerome K. Jerome wrote parts of *Three Men in a Boat* in the *Two Brewers* on St Peter's Street, Marlow's best **pub**. Even so, the fact that the easiest way to reach Cookham is by train from Marlow station is the main reason to come here.

On sunny weekends people flock to **COOKHAM**, three miles southeast of Marlow, for its riverside setting, for its pubs, and because this quaint village was once the home of **Stanley Spencer** (1891–1959), one of Britain's greatest – and most eccentric – artists. The Bible dominated Spencer's education, and in many of his later works he transposes the Biblical tales to his own surroundings, transforming Cookham into an earthly paradise in which even the most ordinary objects and people are holy. Spencer's Christianity was extremely unorthodox, however, following a private religious system he called the "Church of Me", and making no distinction between sacred and profane love. In his paintings, the result is a world in which mundane scenes become overwhelmingly sensual, but Spencer's fixation with sexuality had less happy consequences: he divorced his first wife, Hilda, in order to marry his bisexual mistress, Patricia Preece, who exploited him financially and constantly humiliated him. Throughout this miserable second marriage Spencer continued writing to Hilda, a passionate correspondence that continued even after her death in 1950.

Spencer's greatest achievement is generally considered to be his murals in the Sandham Memorial Chapel at Burghclere in Hampshire, but several of his visionary Cookham-based pictures, including the wonderful but unfinished *Christ Preaching at Cookham Regatta*, are on display in the old **Wesleyan Chapel** on the High Street (Easter–Oct daily 10.30am–5.30pm; Oct–Easter Sat & Sun 11am–5pm; 50p). Spencer and Patricia lie together in the churchyard, just to the left of the path leading up to the south porch. Cookham Rise **train station**, two stops from Marlow, is a ten-minute walk west across the common from the main village. The *Bel and the Dragon* pub, with ancient beams and comfy leather chairs, pulls a good pint and serves homemade food.

High up on a ridge to the east of Cookham, **Cliveden** was designed last century by Sir Charles Barry, architect of the Houses of Parliament – a connection reinforced by the fact that Nancy Astor, the first woman to be elected to the House of Commons, once lived here. Impressive if only for its size, Cliveden's redeeming feature is its position, which provides the country's finest views of the Thames. The National Trust has been reduced to leasing Cliveden as a £300-a-night hotel, but you can visit the west wing of the house (April–Oct Thurs & Sun 3–6pm; £1) and glimpse guests sipping tea in the oak-panelled hall or waiters laying tables in the gilt-laden dining rooms – an echo of the period when Nancy Astor hosted England's most glittering political and literary gatherings here. The grounds (March–Oct daily 11am–6pm; Nov & Dec closes 4pm; £4) in the vicinity of the house are teeming with people at weekends, but you can find peace and quiet 200 feet below in the woods along the river.

Oxford

The university might dominate central **OXFORD** both physically and mentally, yet the wider city has developed out of the prosperity generated not by the colleges but by the nearby Cowley factory, which launched Britain's first mass-produced car in the 1920s. Thousands of workers have been laid off over the last decade, but the motor industry remains vital to the city's economy. Oxford first blossomed under the Normans, when the cathedral was built and Oxford was chosen as the royal residence. It seems that the presence of **Henry I**, the so-called "Scholar King", helped attract students in the early twelfth century, their numbers increasing with the expulsion of English students from the Sorbonne in 1167. The first colleges, founded mostly by rich bishops, were essentially ecclesiastical institutions – reflected in both their design (most had cloisters and a chapel) and discipline (until 1877 lecturers were not allowed to marry, and women have been granted degrees only since 1920).

Tension between the university and the city – or "Town" and "Gown" – has existed as long as the university itself, a fact epitomized during the **Civil War**, when the colleges sided with Charles I (who turned Oxford into the Royalist capital of England) while the city backed the Parliamentarians. The privileges enjoyed by the colleges – until 1950 the university had two MPs of its own, for example – have stoked resentment that still flares into the occasional confrontation, but a non-communicative coexistence is more typical. Given that thousands of tourists and foreign-language students also invade the city throughout the year, it is no surprise that Oxford's 120,000 permanent inhabitants tend to keep themselves to themselves. For all its idiosyncrasies, Oxford should not be missed, and can keep you occupied for several days. The university buildings include some of England's greatest architecture, and the city can also boast some excellent museums and numerous bars and restaurants.

Arrival, information and accommodation

Oxford **train station** is fifteen minutes' walk west of the centre, linked by a shuttle bus. Long-distance **buses** terminate at the Gloucester Green bus station at the bottom of George Street, less than five minutes from the centre; some buses from the surrounding area, including the Cotswolds, terminate on St Giles instead. Intense competition between private companies means that **city buses** run reasonably frequently, most leaving from Cornmarket. The Oxford Bus Company produces a useful map of routes within the city, which you can pick up at the Gloucester Green station or at the **tourist office** in the Old School, also in Gloucester Green (Mon–Sat 9.30am–5pm, also Sun 10am–3.30pm in summer; ☎01865/726 871), where you can buy

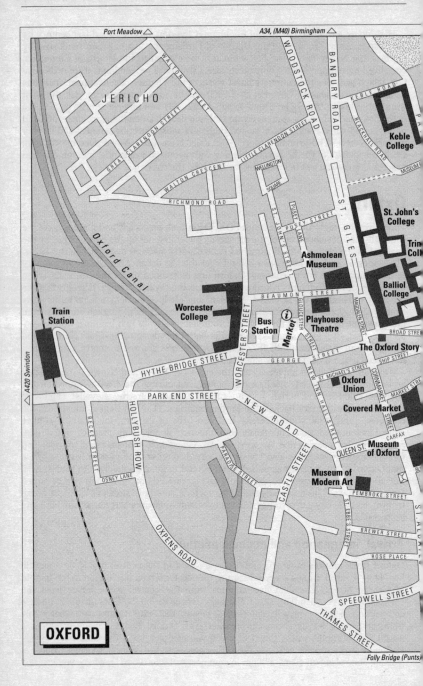

Port Meadow △

A34, (M40) Birmingham △

JERICHO

WALTON STREET

GREAT CLARENDON STREET

LITTLE CLARENDON STREET

WOODSTOCK ROAD

BANBURY ROAD

KEBLE ROAD

BLACKHALL ROAD

Keble College

WALTON CRESCENT

RICHMOND ROAD

WELLINGTON SQUARE

ST. JOHN'S STREET

PUSEY STREET

PUSEY LANE

ST. GILES

St. John's College

Trin Coll

Oxford Canal

Ashmolean Museum

Balliol College

Worcester College

BEAUMONT STREET

GLOUCESTER STREET

MAGDALEN STREET

Train Station

WORCESTER STREET

Bus Station

Market

ⓘ

Playhouse Theatre

BROAD STREET

The Oxford Story

A420 Swindon △

HYTHE BRIDGE STREET

GEORGE STREET

NEW INN HALL STREET

ST. MICHAEL'S STREET

SHIP STREET

CORNMARKET

PARK END STREET

BECKET STREET

HOLLYBUSH ROW

PARADISE STREET

NEW ROAD

Oxford Union

Covered Market

MARKET STREET

OSNEY LANE

CASTLE STREET

QUEEN ST.

CARFAX

Museum of Oxford

Museum of Modern Art

PEMBROKE STREET

ST. EBBE'S STREET

ST. ALDATE

OXPENS ROAD

BREWER STREET

ROSE PLACE

OXFORD

SPEEDWELL STREET

THAMES STREET

Folly Bridge (Punts)

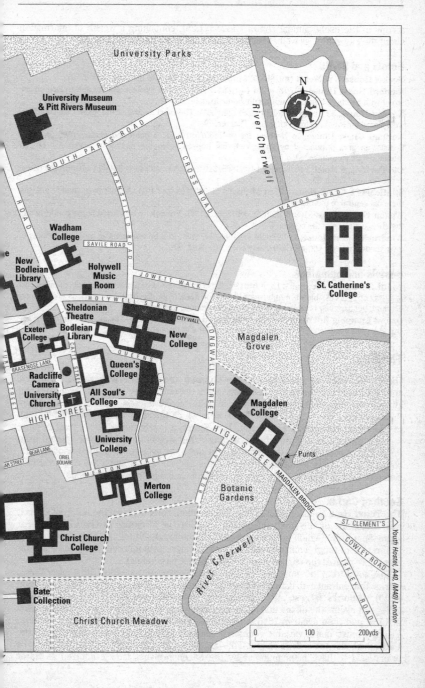

a copy of the useful annual *Oxford Guide* (£1.25), containing a wealth of information about the city sights, as well as services, pubs and restaurants in the area.

Hotels and B&Bs

Becket House, 5 Becket St (☎01865/724 675). Quiet, and close to the train station. ③.

Nanford Guest House, 137 Iffley Rd (☎01865/244 743). The liveliest and cheapest place on the street with plenty of room, though hardly home-from-home. ③.

Newton House, 82 Abingdon Rd (☎01865/240 561). The most central of the south Oxford B&Bs, well placed for evening strolls along the Thames. ③.

Norham Guest House, 16 Norham Rd (☎01865/515 352). A quiet and genteel place in north Oxford, an area dominated by large Victorian houses belonging mostly to academics. Fifteen minutes' walk from town. ④.

Old Parsonage Hotel, 1 Banbury Rd (☎01865/310 210). A small classy hotel in a handsome house at the top of St Giles. ⑨.

St Michael's Guest House, 26 St Michael's St (☎01865/242 101). Almost permanently full, but the most central of the B&Bs. ④.

Walton Guest House, 169 Walton St (☎01865/52137). Friendly, with simple home comforts and the cheapest place in the centre. ③.

Windrush Guest House, 11 Iffley Rd (☎01865/247 933). Run by a welcoming couple and closer to town than other east Oxford B&Bs; only open July–Sept. ④.

Hostels and camping

Youth Hostel, 32 Jack Straw's Lane (☎01865/62997). Off the Marston Road a couple of miles east of the centre, accessible on minibuses #13, #14 or #14A from the High Street. Beds are in great demand, but camping is available in the attractive wooded grounds.

Oxford Camping International, 426 Abingdon Rd (☎01865/246 551). The closest campsite to the city, just over a mile south of Carfax. Take bus #35 or #36 from St Aldates.

The City

Oxford straddles the confluence of the **Thames** and the **Cherwell** rivers. In theory, and on most maps, the former is known within the city as the "Isis", but few locals actually use the term. Central Oxford's main point of reference is **Carfax**, overlooked by the Saxon remnant of St Martin's tower, from which the city's main axes radiate. Many of the oldest colleges face onto the High Street, a lovely though busy road rippling through the centre, or onto streets running either side of it: most can be spotted from the tangle of bikes around the entrance. Owing to the ever-growing number of visitors, colleges have restricted opening hours to the afternoon only and a few charge admission too, though in some cases only at weekends and during holiday periods.

South of Carfax

The **Town Hall**, an ostentatious Victorian creation, spreads down the hill from Carfax, with a staircase on the south side giving access to the **Museum of Oxford** (Tues–Sat 10am–5pm; free), which makes good use of photographs to tell the history of the city. In the face of tough competition this museum often gets ignored, but you'll learn far more here than at the *Oxford Story* in Broad Street (see below).

Just down from the museum, the huge **Tom Tower**, designed by Christopher Wren, marks the entrance to **Christ Church** (Mon–Sat 10.30am–4.30pm, Sun 2–4.30pm; £2.50), Oxford's largest, most prestigious and some would say most pretentious college. It claims the distinction of having been founded twice, first by Cardinal Wolsey in 1525, and then again in 1546 following the cardinal's fall from grace and decease. Visitors must enter via the Memorial Garden, which takes you directly to the **Cathedral**, also the college chapel. This largely Norman building once formed part of a priory said to have been founded by the Saxon princess later canonized as **Saint**

ON THE RIVER

Punting is a favourite summer pastime both among students and visitors, but handling a punt – a traditional flat-bottomed boat ideal for the shallow waters of the Thames and Cherwell – requires some practice. The Cherwell, though much narrower than the Thames and therefore trickier to navigate, provides more opportunities for pulling to the side for a picnic – an essential part of the punting experience. For **boat rental**, Magdalen Bridge, at the east end of the High, is the most central place, but in summer it's so busy that you're better off going north to the Cherwell Boat House by Wolfson College off Banbury Road. From the Thames boat station at Folly Bridge, south of St Aldates, you'll have to punt a fair way along a broad stretch of river before being able to turn off onto the Cherwell. Expect to pay about £7 per hour for a boat, with a £25 deposit.

The other boats most commonly seen on the Thames belong to the university **rowing clubs**, which started up in the early nineteenth century, when top hats were *de rigueur*: the first Oxford-Cambridge boat race (now staged in London) took place in 1829. Rowers practise mainly along the stretch between Folly Bridge and Iffley, also used for college races. The so-called **Torpids** are held at the end of February and the **Eights** at the end of May – the latter are the most important and therefore attract the largest crowds.

Frideswide, whose shrine was the impetus to Oxford's growth. The cathedral has been hacked about but it still possesses a lovely freshness and sense of space. The Norman legacy remains in the glorious choir, where massive Norman columns rise to delicate fifteenth-century stone vaulting. The **shrine of St Frideswide**, by the Lady Chapel, had to be rebuilt following its destruction during the Dissolution, but it retains the first-known example of natural foliage in English sculpture, a splendid confection of leaves dating from around 1290. A window in the adjacent Latin Chapel depicts the life of the saint, one of the earliest works by Pre-Raphaelite luminary Edward Burne-Jones, who also created some windows in the south aisle.

From the cathedral you enter the striking but unfinished **Tom Quad**, its raised terrace originally designed for a cloister. Through the smaller Peckwater quad you reach Canterbury quad, where the **Christ Church Picture Gallery** (Easter–Sept Mon–Sat 10.30am–1pm & 2–5.30pm, Sun 2–5.30pm; winter closes 4.30pm; £1) provides a pokey home for works by many of Italy's finest artists from the fifteenth to eighteenth centuries, including some by Leonardo da Vinci and Michelangelo.

Christ Church Meadow stretches south from the college, where you can follow a shady path first south along the Thames and then north by the Cherwell. Back on St Aldates and just south of Christ Church, the **Bate Collection** (Mon–Fri 2–5pm; free) contains England's most comprehensive collection of European woodwind instruments. In addition to rows of flutes and clarinets, there are all sorts of other instruments on show, from medieval crumhorns, looking like rejected walking sticks, to the country's finest gamelan, which is played regularly.

Back towards Carfax and off to the left along Pembroke Street, the **Museum of Modern Art** or Moma (Tues, Wed, Fri & Sat 10am–6pm, Thurs 10am–9pm & Sun 2–6pm; £2.50) is always worth checking out. The gallery usually has two exhibitions on the go, featuring international contemporary art in a wide variety of media; the basement cafeteria serves good coffee and vegetarian food as well.

East of Carfax – the High Street and around

As you walk east along the **High Street** from Carfax, the first building to demand attention is **St Mary's** or the University Church. Its handsome Baroque porch, flanked by chunky corkscrewed pillars, and the elaborately pinnacled tower take precedence over an unexceptional interior. Across the High from St Mary's, an alley called Magpie Lane leads to Merton Street, cobbled and uncharacteristically tranquil, and to **Merton**

College (Mon–Fri 2–5pm, Sat & Sun 10am–5pm; winter Sat & Sun closes 4pm; free), historically the city's most important college. Balliol and University colleges may have been founded earlier, but it was Merton – opened in 1264 – which set the model for Oxbridge colleges, being the first to gather its students and tutors together in one place. Furthermore, unlike the other two, Merton retains some of its original medieval buildings, which are therefore the oldest part of the university.

The best of the thirteenth-century architecture can be seen in the **Mob Quad**, a delightful courtyard complete with mullioned windows and Gothic doorways, and in the **Chapel**, where the painted windows in the choir, dating from around 1300, were donated by Henry de Mamesfeld, an egocentric who appears as a kneeling figure 24 times. A curious monument in the antechapel shows Thomas Bodley (founder of Oxford's most important library) surrounded by masculine-looking women in classical garb. Merton's other gem is its fourteenth-century **Library**, one of the finest medieval libraries in Britain. Much of the woodwork, including the panelling, screens and book-cases, dates from the Tudor period, but some fittings are original.

Back on the High, **University College** (known as "Univ"), founded in 1249, has a rightful claim to be the city's first college, but nothing of that period survives – what you see dates mostly from the seventeenth century. A year Univ may prefer to forget is 1811, when it expelled **Percy Bysshe Shelley** for distributing a paper called *The Necessity of Atheism*. Guilt later induced Univ to accept a memorial to the poet after he drowned in Italy in 1822: the white marble monument, showing the limp body of the poet borne by winged lions and mourned by the muse of poetry, occupies a shrine-like room by Staircase 3. The college's most famous recent alumnus was Bill Clinton, the non-inhaling Rhodes Scholar.

Queen's College, across the road from Univ, cuts an altogether more impressive figure. The only Oxford college to have been built in one period (1672–1760), Queen's benefitted from the skills of some of the country's finest architects: Nicholas Hawksmoor did much of the work and his teacher, Christopher Wren, designed the chapel, a grand room with a ceiling of cherubs and foliage and a massive oak screen. Unfortunately, the chapel can be visited only on a tour arranged at the tourist office.

Oscar Wilde's college, **Magdalen** (term-time Mon–Fri 2–6pm, Sat, Sun & Easter hols noon–6pm; June–Sept daily 11am–6pm; April–Sept £1.50), pronounced "Maudlin", dominates the eastern end of the High, its majestic medieval tower worthy of a cathe-dral. A handsome reredos saves the **Chapel** from complete gloom, but you must admire it from a distance since a stone screen confines you to the ante-chapel, a spirit-less room that contains a great rarity – a contemporaneous copy of Leonardo da Vinci's *Last Supper*, which was used as a guide for the restoration of the original in Milan; the Royal Academy has lent it to the college until 1998. The adjacent **cloisters**, with bizarre and grotesque stone figures perched atop delicate buttresses, are the best in Oxford, and Magdalen boasts better **grounds** than most too: a bridge across the Cherwell joins **Addison's Walk**, which you can follow round a water meadow where rare wild fritillaries flower in spring. Deer graze in a fenced-off park on the river's west bank, some of them destined for the college dining tables. Magdalen also has a fine choir, whose annual duties include singing madrigals from the top of the church tower at 6am on May 1. Pubs open especially for this May Day event and the din made by drunken students often drowns out the singing.

The small **Botanic Gardens** (daily 9am–5pm) opposite Magdalen predate all others in the country, being first planted in 1621, on the site of a medieval Jewish cemetery. Bounded by a curve of the Cherwell, they provide a peaceful escape from the High.

Retracing your steps back to Queen's, you can cut north up Queen's Lane, past some of the best gargoyles in Oxford, to **New College** (term-time Mon–Fri 2–4pm; free; Sat, Sun & hols 11am–5pm; £1). Founded in 1379, the college has splendid Perpendicular architecture in the Front Quad, though the addition of an extra storey in 1675 spoiled the overall effect. The **Chapel** has been mucked about too, yet it remains the finest in Oxford after the cathedral, not so much for its design as its contents. The antechapel contains some original fourteenth-century glass, but the Nativity in its west window was designed by Sir Joshua Reynolds in 1777, a not entirely successful departure for England's famous portrait painter. Beneath it, shoved up against the wall, stands the wonderful *Lazarus* by Jacob Epstein – Khrushchev, after a visit to the college, claimed that the memory of this haunting sculpture kept him awake at night. On the south wall a war memorial by Eric Gill lists 228 students killed in World War I. A magnificent nineteenth-century stone reredos takes up the entire east wall, consisting of about fifty canopied figures, mostly saints and apostles, with Christ as the centrepiece. An archway on the east side of Front Quad leads through to the grounds – a pleasant lawn skirted by the best-preserved part of the thirteenth-century **city walls**. You can leave the college either through the north entrance into Holywell Street or back the way you came and into New College Lane: heading west along either street brings you to the top of Broad Street.

The Broad Street area

Oxford's most monumental architecture prevails over the eastern end of Broad Street. The semicircular **Sheldonian Theatre**, placed with its facade directed away from the street, was Christopher Wren's first major work: a reworking of the Theatre of Marcellus in Rome, it was conceived in 1663 at the tender age of 31, when Wren's main job was as Professor of Astronomy. Designed as a stage for university ceremonies, it now functions mainly as a concert hall. The interior, painted in gold and a dull brown, lacks any sense of drama, and even the views from the cupola (50p) are disappointing.

Wren's colleague Hawksmoor designed the **Clarendon Building**, set at right angles to the Sheldonian and now part of the university library. Across the courtyard, a doorway leads to the **Old Schools Quad**, a beautifully proportioned, symmetrical space created in the seventeenth century by an unknown architect. On the east side, the so-called Tower of the Five Orders of Architecture gives a lesson in design, with tiers of columns built according to the five classical styles: from top to bottom, Tuscan, Doric, Ionic, Corinthian and Composite.

One of the country's great centres of learning occupies the building opposite. Set up by Thomas Bodley in the seventeenth century, the **Bodleian Library** is now the second largest library in the UK. An estimated eighty miles of shelves are distributed among various buildings, including the ugly modern annexe on the other side of Broad Street. While only members can enter the main part, you can go on a guided tour of Duke Humfrey's library (Mon–Fri 2pm & 3pm, Sat 10.30am & 11.30am; £2), founded in 1439 and restored by Bodley – sign up for a tour in the Exhibition Room, on the south side of the quad. The painted beams are glorious, and you'll be shown a selection of precious manuscripts and books, but an aura of ancient scholarship is far more tangible in the less visited Merton library (see above). Entered through the shop on the west side of the quad, the **Divinity School** (Mon–Fri 9am–5pm, Sat 9am–12.30pm; free), has a fifteenth-century vaulted ceiling, a riot of pendants and decorative bosses best seen on a bright sunny day, when light streams onto the still fresh stone.

The **Radcliffe Camera** (closed to the public) seems rather isolated behind the Old Schools Quad, but this only adds to the majesty of this mighty Italianate rotunda, built from 1737 to 1749 by James Gibbs, architect of London's St Martin in the Fields. For a less intimidating perspective, climb the 125-step tower of the University Church (May–Sept Mon–Sat 9.15am–7pm; Oct–April closes 4.30pm; also all year Sun 12.30pm–5pm; £1.40), which backs onto Radcliffe Square. The views can't be bettered, particularly over **All Souls College** (March–Oct Mon–Fri 2–4.30pm; Nov–Feb Mon–Fri 2–4pm; free), with its twin mock-Gothic towers (the work of Hawksmoor) and a coloured sundial designed by Wren.

Back on Broad Street, a series of classical heads, their eyes blackened by pollution, stare menacingly across the street at *Blackwells*, Oxford's largest and most famous bookshop, continuing along the front of the **Museum of the History of Science** (Tues–Sat noon–4pm; free), where microscopes and early calculators are immaculately displayed alongside Islamic and European astrolabes that seem more like works of art than tools of science. **Exeter College** (daily 2–5pm; closed Christmas week; free), next to the museum but entered from Turl Street, has Oxford's most elaborate **Chapel**: modelled by Sir Gilbert Scott on Sainte Chapelle in Paris, it's a cramped conglomeration of fussy neo-Gothic features. A tapestry of the *Adoration of the Magi*, by William Morris and Edward Burne-Jones who met at Exeter, is ill served by its setting. The chapel in **Trinity College** (March–Oct 2–5pm; £1) couldn't be more different. Grinling Gibbons did some of his finest carving here, a distinctly secular performance with cherubs' heads peering out from delicate foliage. **Balliol** (daily 2–5pm; free), next door, is as left-wing as Trinity is Conservative, and is an unexceptional assembly of buildings, haphazardly gathered around two quads.

The **Oxford Story** (daily summer 9.30am–5pm, winter 10am–4pm; £4.50), towards the Cornmarket end of Broad Street, involves sitting at a desk and being pulled sluggishly past scenes illustrating the history of the university, while listening to a commentary through headphones. You can spend a more pleasurable half-hour around the corner at the **Oxford Union** in St Michael's Street, home of the university debating society, where many budding politicians – Edward Heath and Tony Benn among them – have tried out their oratory skills. The original debating hall, shaped rather like an upturned boat and now the union library (term-time Mon–Sat 9.30am–7pm; hols Mon–Sat 10am–5pm; only open to students), is decorated with Pre-Raphaelite murals illustrating the Arthurian legend, created (but never completed) in the 1850s by William Morris, Rossetti, Burne-Jones and a few like-minded friends. The position of the windows between the badly faded panels makes a full appreciation of the murals difficult, but they remain a fascinating oddity.

The Ashmolean, University and Pitt Rivers museums

The university's best museums grew up around the collections of **John Tradescant**, gardener to James I. During extensive travels around the world he built up a huge collection of artefacts and natural specimens which became known as Tradescant's Ark. The collection eventually passed to the university, was split up – mainly between the Ashmolean and the Pitt Rivers museums – and has been added to ever since.

The **Ashmolean** (Tues–Sat 10am–4pm, Sun 2–4pm; free), the oldest public museum in the country, was established as a home for the Tradescant Ark in 1683, occupying what is now the History of Science Museum in Broad Street. Now in a mammoth Neo-classical building on Beaumont Street, the Ashmolean houses the university's vast collection of art and archaeology. If you don't have time to make more than one visit, you'll have to just pick out the highlights. Downstairs, the **Egyptian** displays should not be missed: in addition to the well-preserved mummies and coffins, there are unusual frescoes, rare textiles from the Roman and Byzantine periods and several fine examples of relief carving, such as on the shrine of Taharqa. The Eastern Art section includes superb Islamic ceramics and early Chinese pottery. On the first floor, the Beazley Room contains an excellent display of Greek vases from the Geometric Period. A small part of the Ashmolean's original collection can be seen in the Tradescant Room, an offbeat group of exhibits including Guy Fawkes's lantern and Oliver Cromwell's death mask. The oldest known North American Indian garment and other ethnographical objects give a taste of what you'll find in the Pitt Rivers.

The Department of Western Art straddles the first and second floors. The Fortnum Gallery has the best of the **Italian art**, notably Piero di Cosimo's *Forest Fire* and Paolo Uccello's *Hunt in the Forest*, followed by a strong showing of **French paintings**, with

Pissarro, Renoir, Cézanne and Bonnard all well represented, plus a small number by Picasso. Look out for what's on in the Eldon Gallery, which stages exhibitions from the Ashmolean's vast hoard of **prints**, and for the Michelangelo and Raphael drawings by the staircase; these include some of Raphael's finest sketches. Up on the second floor, the Combe Gallery is devoted to mostly nineteenth-century **British paintings**; Samuel Palmer's visionary paintings run rings around the rest, though there's lashings of Pre-Raphaelite stuff from Rossetti, Holman Hunt and cohorts.

By the *Lamb and Flag* pub on St Giles, around the corner from the Ashmolean, an alley cuts through to Parks Road and the **University Museum** (Mon–Sat noon–5pm; free), opposite the mottled brick facade of Keble College. The building, constructed under the guidance of John Ruskin, looks more like a cross between a railway station and a church than a museum – particularly inside, a neo-Gothic fusion of cast-iron and glass, featuring soaring columns and capitals decorated with animal and plant motifs.

The museum's natural history displays, despite the presence of a few dodo fragments, are outdone by the **Pitt Rivers Museum** (Mon–Sat 1–4.30pm; free), reached through a door at the far end. Founded in 1884 from the bequest of Grenadier Guard turned archeologist Augustus Lane Fox Pitt-Rivers, this is one of the world's finest ethnographic museums and an extraordinary relic of the Victorian age, arranged like an exotic junk shop with each bulging cabinet labelled meticulously by hand. The exhibits, brought to England by several explorers, Captain Cook among them, range from totem poles and mummified crocodiles to African fetishes and gruesome shrunken heads from Ecuador. For a breather afterwards, go and sit in the University Parks on the banks of the Cherwell.

Eating, drinking and nightlife

With so many students to cater for, Oxford has developed a huge choice of places to eat and drink. Oxford is not a town for wild nights: lovers of **classical music** are well catered for, but the city has a fairly paltry offering of other forms of entertainment. Listings are given in the *Oxford Times*, out on Friday, in *Daily Information* (weekly out of term-time), a broadsheet pasted up in pubs and cafés; and in *This Month in Oxford*, a monthly booklet which you can pick up free at the tourist office. *First Word*, a free monthly paper, has information about gigs in and around Oxford; you can usually get a copy at the *Philanderer and Firkin* or *Freud's Art Café* (see below). Tickets to most musical events are on sale at *Blackwells Music Shop*, 38 Holywell St (☎01865/792 792).

Snacks and cafés

Convocation Coffee House, Radcliffe Square, attached to the University Church. Ideal for coffee and cake or quiche-and-salad lunches. Open daily 9.30am–6pm.

Nosebag, 6 St Michael's St. A civilized but unassuming cafeteria, with Laura Ashley decor. The hot and cold food attracts queues at lunchtime; not so in the evening, when it's a good place for a quick but wholesome meal. Open daily.

St Giles Café, 52 St Giles. Oxford's favourite greasy spoon. The huge fry-ups and the best coffee in town pull an interesting mix of people. The most regular customer, the poet Elizabeth Jennings, is an almost permanent fixture.

Restaurants

Aziz, 230 Cowley Rd (☎01865/798 033). Lively, spacious and bright Indian restaurant. Delicious food, with a wide range of vegetarian dishes. Open daily. Inexpensive.

Bangkok House, 42 Hythe Bridge St (☎01865/200 705). Best oriental restaurant in town, with superb Thai food and excellent service. The mixed starter and the coconut-milk curries are particularly good. Open daily except Sun & Mon lunch. Moderate.

Bath Place Restaurant, 4–5 Bath Place, Holywell St (☎01865/792 812). If you want to splash out, this is the place to do it. Post-nouvelle food, from pasta with wild mushrooms to brill in red wine and cinnamon sauce. Intimate ambience, slowish service. Expensive.

Blue Coyote, 36 St Clements. Unpretentious, good atmosphere. New Mexican dishes and steak feature heavily; superlative nachos. Blues played on Sun. Open daily. Inexpensive.

Browns, 5–9 Woodstock Rd. Buzzing and stylish restaurant with abundant foliage. Main courses from hamburgers to fresh salmon; large helpings, quality not immaculate. No booking allowed but queueing is part of the experience. Open daily – also for breakfast. Moderate.

Gee's Brasserie, 61 Banbury Rd (☎01865/58346). Chic conservatory setting, but not as expensive as it looks. The unusual menu includes char-grilled vegetables with polenta, a variety of steaks and a wide choice of breads. Open daily for lunch and dinner plus brunch at weekends. Moderate.

Hi-Lo Jamaican Eating House, 68 Cowley Rd. Legendary West Indian restaurant where the owner charges what he thinks you can afford. Exciting though limited meat-oriented menu (goat often features), with heavy reggae beat to accompany your meal. Open daily. Inexpensive to expensive, depending on your luck.

La Cantina, 15 Magdalen St. Tasty Mexican food, loudish music and noisy with conversation from the predominantly young clientele. Jugs of sangria and tequila slammers recommended. Open daily. Inexpensive.

Pizza Express, Golden Cross, Cornmarket. Lovely Tudor building and the best-value pizzas in central Oxford. Expect a 30-min wait at weekends. Open daily. Inexpensive.

Taj Mahal, 16 Turl St (☎01865/245 564). Without doubt, the best Indian restaurant in the centre. Polite, friendly service and good tandoori dishes. Vegetarian versions of most curries. Open daily. Inexpensive.

Pubs and bars

Bar Celona, Little Clarendon St. A small Hispanic-style bar; good place to share a bottle of wine and a plate of nachos.

Bullingdon Arms, 162 Cowley Rd. Irish pub known affectionately as the "Bully" and the most popular watering hole in east Oxford. Live music Wed nights, plus impromptu sessions.

Eagle and Child, 49 St Giles. Known variously as the "Bird and Baby", "Bird and Brat" or "Bird and Bastard". Once the haunt of J.R.R. Tolkien, C.S. Lewis and other Anglican literary types, it attracts a fairly genteel mix of professionals and academics.

Freud's Art Café, Walton Street. The drinks are overpriced, the service poor, the live music of variable quality and £3 admission is charged on Saturdays. Good points: interesting building (a Greek Revival church) and open late (Mon & Tues until midnight, Wed–Sun until 2am).

Jolly Farmers, Paradise Street. Oxford's most popular gay pub; mainly male and a crush at weekends.

King's Arms, 40 Holywell St. Prone to student overkill at term-time weekends, but otherwise very pleasant, with snug rooms at the back. Good choice of beers.

The Turf, Bath Place, off Holywell Street. Small seventeenth-century pub with a fine range of beers, and mulled wine in winter. Abundant seating outside.

Nightlife

In addition to the city's main concert halls, certain college chapels – primarily Christ Church, Merton and New College – are good venues for classical recitals. Student productions dominate the city repertoire, but the quality of acting varies, particularly when they tackle Shakespeare, the favourite for the open-air college productions put on for tourists during the summer. Venues for **folk**, **jazz** and other popular music are thin on the ground, but at least they make for a better evening than the city's nightclubs.

Apollo, George Street (☎01865/244 544). Known locally as the "Appalling", but the UK's top opera and ballet companies occasionally break up the monotonous programme of ageing pop acts and pantomimes.

Holywell Music Room, 32 Holywell St. This small, plain, Georgian building opened in 1748 as the first public music hall in England. Haydn once conducted here. It has a varied programme, from straight classical to experimental music, with occasional jazz.

Northgate Hall, 16 St Michael's St. A lesbian and gay centre with discos on certain nights (eg women only Friday, mixed on Saturday). Vastly improved since it got a late licence, but still unpredictable.

Old Fire Station, 40 George St (☎01865/794 494). Has found a niche for itself as a testing ground for West End musicals; tickets for these workshop productions are cheap by London standards. Also live jazz and blues Fri and Sat nights.

Oxford Venue, 196 Cowley Rd (☎01865/790 501). The best bet for a good night of live music. Folk and world music most Tues nights, plus other bands Thurs and Sat, but the venue is liable to sporadic closure. A disco sometimes follows the concerts, usually until 2am.

Park End Club, 37 Park End St. A slick outfit, currently the most popular mainstream club in Oxford, with a couple of prosecutions for overcrowding. Open until 2am.

Pegasus Theatre, Magdalen Road (☎01865/722 851). Low-budget, avant-garde productions dominate the programme of this east Oxford theatre.

Philanderer and Firkin, 56 Walton St. Good indie bands play here, both local and moderately well-known ones on nationwide tours. The small room above the pub cannot cope with the crowds attracted by the latter. Go prepared to sweat.

Playhouse, Beaumont Street (☎01865/798 600). The city's best theatre. Professional touring companies perform a mixture of plays, opera and concerts, with the odd production by Oxford University Dramatic Society (OUDS), the top student group.

Sheldonian Theatre, Broad Street. Hard seats and less-than-perfect acoustics, but still Oxford's top concert hall. Tickets and programme available from *Blackwells Music Shop* (see p.235).

Around Oxford

If you have a car, it is possible to go on day trips into the Chilterns and Cotswolds from Oxford. Those reliant on the buses will be more restricted, though **Blenheim Palace** is a straightforward ride from the city. Renting a bicycle is strongly recommended if you want to explore the **Vale of White Horse**, to the southwest of the city.

Blenheim Palace

Military achievement nowadays is rewarded with a medal or promotion, but in 1704, as a thank you for his victory over the French in the Battle of Blenheim, John Churchill, First Duke of Marlborough, got money to build himself the only non-royal residence in the country grand enough to bear the name "palace". The result, at Woodstock, seven miles northwest of Oxford, was the gargantuan **Blenheim Palace** (mid-March to Oct daily 10.30am–5.30pm; £7), designed by Sir John Vanbrugh, architect of Castle Howard in Yorkshire. The current Marquess of Blandford, whose antics – ranging from possession of drugs to burglary and assault – fill the tabloids from time to time, is sadly not untypical of the clan. Other than the First Duke of Marlborough, the only other distinguished family member was **Sir Winston Churchill**, born here in 1874. Several rooms are dedicated to the wartime prime minister, who is buried with his parents and wife in the graveyard of **Bladon** church, visible to the southeast.

The Italianate palace, the country's greatest example of Baroque civic architecture, is too awesome to be beautiful and is more a monument than a house – as was always Vanbrugh's intention. **Inside**, the highlights include the dining salon with its murals by Louis Laguerre, furniture from Versailles, stone and marble carvings by Grinling Gibbons, and several fine gold-leaf ceilings by Nicholas Hawksmoor. Unfortunately, you don't get much of a chance to relish it all, since the guides whisk visitors through Blenheim in around 45 minutes. Formal **gardens** stretch southwards from the palace, but the palace **grounds** (daily 9am–4.45pm; £4 with car, £1 for pedestrians), landscaped by Capability Brown, remain the chief attraction. Fine vistas fan out in every direction, including from Vanbrugh's own bridge up to the Column of Victory, erected by Sarah Jennings and topped by a statue of her husband posing heroically in a toga. There are two **entrances** to Blenheim Palace, one just south of Woodstock on the Oxford road and another through the Triumphal Arch at the west end of Park Street.

The Vale of the White Horse

Extending southwest from Oxford, the **Vale of the White Horse** takes its name from the prehistoric figure carved into the chalk of the Berkshire Downs above Uffington, eighteen miles from the city. Burial mounds and Iron Age forts pepper the downs, linked by the Ridgeway path which runs along the top. Most paths follow the old drove roads, along which sheep were once taken to and from the market, but nowadays horses are almost as common as sheep. The well-drained downland turf provides an ideal training ground for racehorses, and special areas known as "gallops" are used by numerous local stables, particularly around Lambourn on the southern slopes.

White Horse Hill, six miles along the Ridgeway west of Wantage, follows close behind Stonehenge and Avebury in the hierarchy of Britain's ancient sites, though it attracts nothing like the same number of visitors. Carved into the north-facing slope of the downs, the 374-foot-long **horse** looks like something created with a few swift strokes of an immense brush. Some people have suggested it was a glorified signpost, created to show travellers where to join the Ridgeway. In Victorian and Edwardian times the best-loved legend, popularized in a ballad by G. K. Chesterton, claimed that it was cut by King Alfred as an emblem of his victory over the Danes at the Battle of Ashdown, fought nearby in 871 AD. The first record of the horse's existence dates from the time of Henry II, but recent research has suggested that its origin goes back some two thousand years earlier, as far back as the second millennium BC, making it by far the oldest chalk figure in Britain.

Legend has it that the small flat-topped and possibly artificial hillock below the horse, known as **Dragon Hill**, was where Saint George killed and buried the dragon, a theory supposedly proved by the bare patch at the top and the channel down the side, where blood trickled from the creature's wounds. **Uffington Castle**, the prehistoric fort above the horse, now shown to date back to the same era as the White Horse, provides a grazing ground for sheep and the best vantage point in the area for visitors. The Ridgeway runs along its south side and continues west two miles to **Waylands Smithy**, a five-thousand-year-old burial mound encircled by trees. It is one of the best neolithic remains along the Ridgeway, though heavy restoration has rather detracted from the mystery of the place. Among a number of conflicting myths, the most durable suggests that Waylands Smithy was named after an invisible smith who made invincible armour and reshod travellers' horses.

White Horse Hill can be reached up two narrow roads leading off the B4507, a Roman route otherwise known as the Portway, which follows a lovely undulating route along the foot of the downs; the only public transport to White Horse Hill is bus #97 between Wantage and Faringdon (Wed, Fri & Sat). **UFFINGTON**, six miles west of Wantage, is the closest village to the horse, thirty minutes' walk due south. A metropolis compared with the other villages along the Portway, Uffington has a couple of **B&Bs**, the better being *The Craven* on Fernham Road (☎01367/820 449; ④). There is limited **camping** space at Britchcombe Farm, in a fabulous spot by the Portway just east of the Uffington turn-off.

The Cotswolds

The limestone hills of the **Cotswolds** are preposterously photogenic, strewn with countless picture-book villages built by merchants enriched by the wool trade. Wool was important here as far back as the Roman era, but the greatest fortunes were made between the fourteenth and sixteenth centuries, during which period many of the region's fine manors and churches were built. Largely bypassed by the Industrial Revolution, which heralded the area's commercial decline, much of the Cotswolds is a relic, its architecture preserved in often immaculate condition. Numerous churches are decorated with beautiful Norman carving, for which the local limestone was ideal: soft and easy to carve when first quarried, but hardening after long exposure to the sunlight. The use of this local stone is a strong unifying characteristic, though its colour modulates as subtly as the shape of the hills, ranging from a deep golden tone in **Chipping Campden** to a silvery grey in **Painswick**.

The consequence of all this is that the Cotswolds have become one of the country's main tourist attractions, with many towns afflicted by plagues of tea and souvenir shops – this is Morris Dancing country. To see the Cotswolds at their best, visit in winter or avoid the most popular towns and escape into the hills themselves. This might be a tamed landscape, but there is good scope for walks, either in the gentler valleys that are most typical of the Cotswolds or along the dramatic escarpment which marks the boundary with the Severn valley. A long-distance path called the **Cotswold Way** runs along the top of the ridge, stretching about one hundred miles from Chipping Campden to Bath. A number of prehistoric sites provides added interest along the route, with some – such as **Belas Knap** near Winchcombe – being well worth a diversion.

There are few large settlements in this region, the biggest true Cotswold town being **Cirencester**, a buzzing community dating back to the Romans. Nearby **Cheltenham** actually sits on the wrong side of the western escarpment and has little in common with Cotswold wool towns, but it likes to present itself as a gateway to the hills.

The eastern approaches

Most of the towns and villages covered in this section, apart from **Burford**, aren't strictly part of the Cotswolds, but rather are satellites to the region, often built of the same local limestone. As the eastern gateway to the Cotswolds, Burford is busy, but this area enjoys greater tranquillity than you'll find in the heart of the hills.

Lechlade and around

LECHLADE marks the westernmost navigable point of the Thames and thus in summer is teeming with pleasure boats, but for most people it's handy as a springboard for exploring the southern fringe of the Cotswolds. For **overnight stops** try the *Red Lion* (☎01367/252 373; ③), or the *Flour Bag* B&B (☎01367/252 322; ③), which doubles as a bakery. You can pitch a tent at the St John's Priory **campsite** (☎01367/252 360), a mile southeast along the A417. The boating fraternity congregates at the *Trout*, a real anglers' pub next door to the campsite, with stuffed fish on the wall (and live jazz); a footpath leads there across the meadow from by the church.

There's lots to see around Lechlade, like the tiny church at **INGLESHAM**, by a farm about a mile south. Its oldest parts are Saxon and the whole building breathes history, its wooden screens twisted with age, its stone floor worn and uneven. You can walk to the church along the east bank of the Thames, though you must rejoin the A361 for a short distance at the end. Isolated among fields just three miles east of Lechlade, **KELMSCOTT** has become a place of pilgrimage for devotees of **William Morris**, who used the Tudor manor as a summer home. The simple beauty of the house (April–Sept Wed 11am–1pm & 2–5pm; £5) is enhanced by the decor created by Morris or his Pre-Raphaelite friends, including Burne-Jones and Rossetti. Morris and his wife Jane are buried in the shadow of the minuscule village church. Kelmscott is a pleasant stroll along the north bank of the Thames from Lechlade.

Burford and the Windrush Valley

The **River Windrush**, flanked by gentle hills, meanders between willows alongside the busy A40, a contrastingly peaceful valley – at least until you reach **BURFORD**, twenty miles from Oxford. The time to appreciate the town's magnificent sloping High Street is not in summer, when cars battle for space while tourists fight it out on the pavements and in the antique shops. But the huge **parish church**, originally Norman but remodelled in the fifteenth century, is a delight at any time. An unusual monument to Henry VIII's barber, Edmund Harman, shows four Amazonian Indians, said to be the first representation of native Americans in Britain.

Spare a morning to follow the footpath along the Windrush through **Widbrook**, a hamlet with an idyllic medieval chapel built in the middle of a field on the site of a Roman villa, and on to **Swinbrook**, just under three miles east of Burford. The church in this immaculate village contains a monument showing six members of the Fettiplace family reclining comically on their elbows: the Tudor effigies rigid and stony-faced, their Stuart counterparts stylish and rather camp. The best place for **lunch** or a drink is the *Swan Inn* in Swinbrook.

Many of Burford's old inns have metamorphosed into expensive **hotels**, but the *Highway Hotel* at 117 High St (☎01993/822 136; ④) is good value and there are several **B&Bs**, including the *Dower House* on Westhall Hill (☎01993/822 596; ③), a short walk north across the river.

The northern Cotswolds

Following the Windrush upstream from Burford takes you north to **Bourton-on-the-Water**, a landlocked Weston-super-Mare and a nightmare of coaches and screaming children. **Stow-on-the-Wold**, ten miles north of Burford, is by contrast horribly genteel, though as the highest town in the Cotswolds it has some merits as a vantage point – and it does have a **youth hostel** (☎01451/830 497). The main sources of interest in this area lie farther north.

Moreton-in-Marsh and around

MORETON-IN-MARSH, fifteen miles north of Burford, has more of a buzz than most Cotswold towns, particularly on Tuesdays, when the High Street disappears beneath a huge market. But the thing not to miss in Moreton is the **Batsford Arboretum** (March–Oct daily 10am–5pm; £2), a fifteen-minute walk from the High Street. The largest private collection of rare trees in the country, it was planted in the 1880s by Lord Redesdale following his return from a posting in Tokyo. The hilly gardens have a distinctly Japanese flavour, and you can sit here amid magnolias and Chinese pocket-handkerchief trees enjoying wonderful views over the Evenlode valley. Moreton has better bus services than most other towns in the region, and is also on the London–Oxford–Worcester **rail** line. There's little in the way of **hotels**, however, *Moreton House* (☎01608/650 747; ③) being the best value of those on the High Street.

Two miles southwest of Moreton along the A44, just before you reach Bourton-on-the-Hill, you come to the bottom of the drive leading to the blue onion domes and miniature minarets of **Sezincote** (May–Sept Thurs & Fri 2.30–5.30pm; garden Jan–Nov same hours; £4 house, £2.50 garden), tucked gracefully if incongruously among the Cotswolds. Built in the early nineteenth century, the house was a collaboration between architect Samuel Pepys Cockerell, and artist Thomas Daniell, both of whom had spent time in India and been inspired by Moghul architecture. The end result so impressed the Prince Regent in 1806 that he ordered Brighton Pavilion to be built along these exotic lines. Inside, a curious classical-cum-Chinese style takes precedence; outside, temples, statues and unusual trees and shrubs are scattered about the small but exquisite garden.

Chipping Campden

CHIPPING CAMPDEN, six miles northwest of Moreton, gives a better idea than anywhere else in the Cotswolds as to what a prosperous wool town might have looked like in the Middle Ages. The houses have undulating, weather-beaten roofs and many retain their original mullioned windows, while the fine Perpendicular **church** dates from the fifteenth century, the zenith of the town's wool-trading days. Inside, an ostentatious monument commemorates the family of Sir Baptist Hicks, a local benefactor who built the nearby almshouses and the market hall in the High Street. The town's other main sight is the **Woolstaplers Museum** (April–Oct daily 10am–5pm; Nov & Dec Sat & Sun only 10am–5pm; £2), more an orderly junk shop than a museum, bulging with everything from old matchboxes to dusty typewriters.

A fine panoramic view rewards those who make the short but severe hike up the Cotswold Way northwest to **Dover's Hill** (follow Hoo Lane north off the High St). Since 1610 this natural amphitheatre has been the stage for an Olympics of rural sports, though the event was suspended last century when games such as shin-kicking became little more than licensed thuggery. A more civilized version, the **Cotswolds Games**, has been staged each June since 1951 – no shin-kicking, but still the odd bit of hammer-throwing.

Such a museum piece as Chipping Campden must inevitably cope with herds of visitors in summer. Try to stay overnight and explore in the evening or at dawn, when the streets are empty and the golden hues of the stone at their richest. You can't move for **guest houses** along the High Street. *Haydon House* on the corner of Church Street (☎01386/840 275; ④) has fewer lacy trimmings than most, as does the *Volunteer Inn* (☎01386/840 688; ③) on Park Road. Most other **pubs** have rooms but are in a different price bracket, such as the *Noel Arms* (☎01386/840 317; ⑧). The standard of pubs is good, but the *Eight Bells Inn*, around the corner from the church, is particularly cosy.

Winchcombe, Sudeley and around

WINCHCOMBE, twelve miles southwest of Chipping Campden, has an attractive blend of stone and half-timbered buildings and a couple of museums, but the real attractions are Sudeley Castle, Belas Knap and Hailes Abbey, all located just outside the town (see below). **Buses** from Cheltenham to Winchcombe run hourly; services from Chipping Campden run only three times a week (Tues, Thurs & Sat). There are plenty of **B&Bs** in Winchcombe, the best being the *Great House* on Castle Street (☎01242/602 490; ③); the *Gower House* at 16 North St (☎01242/602 616; ③) offers a good though noisier alternative. The *Old Corner Cupboard*, a thirteenth-century **pub** on Gloucester Street, has good beers, no music and a friendly atmosphere.

A short walk west of Winchcombe, **Sudeley Castle** (April–Oct 11am–5pm daily; £4.95) was once a favourite country retreat of Tudor and Stuart monarchs, though it never belonged to the royal family. It has a particularly strong connection with Catherine Parr, the sixth wife of Henry VIII, who came to live here after her marriage to Thomas Seymour, Lord of Sudeley, following the king's death. During the Civil War the house became a base for the Royalists (Charles I sought refuge here several times), then was later all but destroyed by the Parliamentarians. What remained stood empty until 1830, when the ruins were bought by the Dent family, whose work re-created an extremely handsome exterior but not the atmosphere of a fifteenth-century home. The motley collection inside includes paintings by Turner and Constable, a bed Charles I once slept in and the tooth of Catherine Parr, whose tomb is in the chapel. The real joy of Sudeley lies outside: in the **Queen's Garden**, with its huge yew hedges cut like masonry; in the creeper-covered ruins of the banqueting hall; and, above all, in the setting, with the green slopes of the escarpment behind.

Up on the ridge overlooking Winchcombe, the Neolithic long barrow of **Belas Knap** occupies one of the most breathtaking spots in the Cotswolds. Dating from around 3000 BC, this is the best-preserved burial chamber in England, stretching out like a strange sleeping beast cloaked in green velvet. The two-mile climb up the Cotswold Way from Winchcombe contributes to the fun, giving good views back over Sudeley Castle. The path strikes off to the right near the entrance to Sudeley; when you reach the road at the top, turn right and then left up into the woods, from where it's a ten-minute hike to Belas Knap.

Hailes Abbey (Easter–Sept daily 10am–6pm; Oct closes 5pm; Nov–March closes 4pm; £2), a two-mile stroll northeast of Winchcombe, was once one of England's great Cistercian monasteries. Pilgrims came here from all over the country to pray before the abbey's phial of Christ's blood, a relic shown to be a fake at the time of the Dissolution, when the thirteenth-century monastery was demolished. Not much of the original complex remains beyond the foundations, but some cloister arches survive, worn by wind and rain. The ruin is undramatic, but Hailes is still worth visiting for the attached museum, the tranquillity of the spot and for the nearby **church**, which is older than the abbey and contains beautiful wall paintings dating from around 1300. The cartoon-like hunting scene was probably a warning to Sabbath-breakers.

Cheltenham

Until the eighteenth century **CHELTENHAM** was like any other Cotswold town, but then the discovery of a spring in 1716 transformed it into Britain's most popular **spa**. During Cheltenham's heyday, a century or so later, the royal, the rich and the famous descended in hordes to take the waters, which were said to cure anything from constipation to worms. Nowadays, it's not a place you're likely to want to linger in, though it is a natural stopping-off place; the haughty elegance of the Regency architecture, characterized by fancy ironwork and Greek columns, also makes for a pleasant change after the homely Cotswolds. The town is also a thriving arts centre, famous for its festivals of music (July) and literature (October) – and then, of course, there's the racecourse, Britain's main steeplechasing venue, whose three-day National Hunt Festival in March attracts 40,000 people each day.

The focus of Cheltenham, the broad **Promenade**, sweeps majestically south from the High Street, lined with the town's grandest houses, smartest shops and most genteel public gardens. A short walk north of the High Street, through the ugliest part of the centre, brings you to **Pittville**. Planned as a spa town to rival Cheltenham, it was never completed and is now mostly parkland, where you can stroll along a few solitary Regency avenues and visit the grandest spa building, the domed **Pump Room**, whose chief function is as a concert hall – though you can sample England's only naturally alkaline water for free here. Once you've had your fill of old spa architecture, the **Art Gallery and Museum** on Clarence Street (Mon–Sat 10am–5.20pm; free) marks the high point of Cheltenham. It is good on social history, and provides a good background to the nineteenth-century crafts movement and its centres of activity in the Cotswolds.

All **buses** arrive at the station in Royal Well Place, just west off the Promenade. The **train station** is on Queen's Road, southwest of the centre; buses F and G run into town every ten minutes, or else it's a twenty-minute walk. The **tourist office** is at 77 Promenade (Mon–Fri 9.30am–6pm, Sat 9.30am–5pm, Sun 10am–4pm; ☎01242/226 554). The best **B&Bs** are the *Brennan* at 21 St Luke's Rd (☎01242/525 904; ③) or the livelier *Cross Ways* at 57 Bath Rd (☎01242/527 683; ③). The *Lawn Hotel* at 5 Pittville Lawn (☎01242/526 638; ③), near the park, is quieter and excellent value; nearby is the more upmarket *Regency House* at 50 Clarence Square (☎01242/582 718; ⑤). The nearest **campsite** is Longwillows in Woodmancote (☎01242/674 113), below Cleeve Hill, the highest point along the Cotswold escarpment (1083ft), accessible on bus D from Pittville Street. Cheltenham makes a good base for exploring the Cotswolds by **bike**: rental is available from *Loose Tubes*, 22 Moorend Park Rd (☎01242/575 967).

Restaurants in central Cheltenham cater mainly for the upper end of the market, in which price range is *Below Stairs* at 103 Promenade (closed Sun; moderate; ☎01242/ 234 599), serving scrumptious fish and seafood. Lower down the price scale are *Prima Pasta*, 33 Promenade, a good place to relax over a coffee, and *Pizza Piazza* at the bottom of Montpellier Street. Cheltenham's **pubs** are dreary; the *Restoration Inn*, on the High Street, is one of the few survivals from the town's pre-spa days.

Cirencester

Fifteen miles south of Cheltenham, on the very fringes of the Cotswolds, **CIRENCESTER** (Corinium) ranked second only to Londinium in size and importance under the Romans. A provincial capital and a centre of trade, it flourished for three centuries and had one of the largest forums north of the Alps. Few Roman remains are visible in Cirencester itself thanks to the destruction meted out by the Saxons in the sixth century. The new occupiers built an abbey (the longest in England at the time), but the town's prosperity was restored only with the wool boom of the Middle Ages, when the wealth of local merchants financed the construction of one of the finest Perpendicular churches in England. Cirencester has survived as one of the most affluent towns in the area, hence the much vaunted title "Capital of the Cotswolds", and has an endearingly old-fashioned atmosphere, generated partly by shops that haven't changed for decades.

Cirencester's heart is the delightful swirling **Market Place**, on Mondays and Fridays packed by traders' stalls. An irregular line of eighteenth-century facades along the north side contrast with the heavier Victorian structures opposite, but the parish church of **St John the Baptist**, built in stages during the fifteenth century, predominates. The extraordinary flying buttresses which support the tower had to be added when it transpired that the church had been constructed upon a filled-in ditch. The church's three-tiered south porch – large enough to function as the town hall at one stage – leads to the nave, where slender piers and soaring arches create a superb sense of space, enhanced by clerestory windows that bathe the nave in a warm light. The church contains much of interest, including a wineglass **pulpit**, carved in stone in around 1450 and one of the few pre-Reformation pulpits to have survived in Britain. North of the chancel, superb fan vaulting hangs overhead in the **chapel of St Catherine**, who appears in a still vivid fragment of a fifteenth-century wall painting. Outside, one of the best views of the church is from the **Abbey Grounds**; site of the Saxon abbey, it's now a small park skirted by the modest river Churn and a fragment of the Roman city wall.

Few medieval buildings other than the church have survived in Cirencester. The houses along the town's most handsome streets – Park, Thomas and Coxwell – date mostly from the seventeenth and eighteenth centuries. One of those on Park Street houses the **Corinium Museum** (April–Oct Mon–Sat 10am–5pm & Sun 2–5pm; Nov–March Tues–Sat 10am–5pm & Sun 2–5pm; £1.50), which devotes itself mainly to the Roman era. Given that the museum has one of the largest Roman collections in Britain, the number of exhibits on display is disappointing, but a lot of space is taken up by **mosaic pavements**, which are among the finest in the country.

Practicalities

The **tourist office** (April–Oct Mon–Sat 9.30am–5.30pm; Nov–March Mon–Sat 9.30am–4.30pm), in the Corn Hall on the Market Place, is excellent and has an **accommodation** list outside. A string of **B&Bs** lines Victoria Road, a short walk east: *Apsley Villa* at no. 16 (☎01285/653 489; ③) and *Warwick Cottage* at no. 75 (☎01285/656 279; ③) are cheaper than most. If you've more money to spare, stay at the *Corinium Court Hotel* (☎01285/659 711; ⑤) or the *White Lion Inn* (☎01285/654 053; ④), both on Gloucester Street, one of Cirencester's quietest and most attractive streets. There is a **youth hostel** in **Duntisbourne Abbots** (☎01285/821 682), five miles west but not accessible by bus (see below). The most accessible **campsite** is at *Perrotts Brook* (☎01285/831 301), two miles north on the A435; any Cheltenham-bound bus will drop you there.

The *Number One* **restaurant**, next to the Brewery Arts Centre, off Cricklade Street, is inexpensive and veggie, while the centre's theatre has a buzzing café on the first floor (Mon–Sat). Cirencester has a good choice of **pubs**, their clientele swollen by tweedy students from the Royal Agricultural College. One pub they don't frequent is the atmospheric *Courtyard Bar*, a room half obscured beneath a veil of smoke and packed with OAPs; it is tucked down a passageway behind the *Kings Head* on the Market Place. You can rent **bikes** at *Pedal Power*, 5 Ashcroft St (☎01285/640 505).

Malmesbury

The striking half-ruin of a Norman abbey prevails over the small hill town of **MALMESBURY**, one of the oldest boroughs in England. Lying eleven miles south of Cirencester, it's not part of the Cotswolds geologically, though the town's early wealth was based on wool. Malmesbury certainly lacks the tweeness of the Cotswold towns to the north, with new housing estates encircling the centre, and modern developments marring views over the Avon. But none of this can detract from the splendour of the abbey, a majestic structure with some of the country's finest Romanesque sculpture.

The High Street, which begins at the bottom of the hill by the old silk mills and heads north across the river and up past a jagged row of ancient cottages, ends up at the octagonal **Market Cross**. Built in around 1490 to provide shelter from the rain, nowadays it is a favourite haunt of the local youth, whatever the weather. Nearby, the eighteenth-century **Tolsey Gate** leads through to the **Abbey** (daily 10am–4pm). Founded in the seventh century and once a powerful Benedictine foundation, the abbey burnt down in about 1050; the twelfth-century building which replaced it was damaged during the Dissolution, other parts collapsing at a later date. The **nave** is the only substantial Norman part to have survived, which it has done beautifully. A multitude of figures, in three tiers depicting scenes from the Creation, the Old Testament and the life of Christ, surround the doorway of the south porch, the pride of the abbey, while inside the porch the Apostles and Christ are carved in deep relief. To the left of the high altar, the pulpit virtually hides the **tomb of King Athelstan** (died 940), grandson of Alfred the Great and the first Saxon to be recognized as King of England; the tomb is empty, the location of the king's remains being unknown.

Malmesbury has other illustrious connections. It was, for example, the birthplace of **Thomas Hobbes** (1588–1679), the moral and political philosopher who suggested in his book *Leviathan* that the only way to avoid social chaos was for people to surrender their rights to an all-powerful authority, an ideology that has led to his being claimed as a precursor by the Left and Right alike. Another local celebrity is **Elmer the Monk**, who in 1005 attempted to fly from the abbey tower with the aid of wings: he limped for the rest of his life, but won immortal fame as the "flying monk".

There are several **B&Bs** in town: the **tourist office** (☎01666/823 784) in the Town Hall has an accommodation list outside. The *Whole Hog* wine bar, overlooking the Market Place, serves good, inexpensive **food**, including Wiltshire ham and Malmesbury sausages. *Fables* at the top of Silver Street, off Cross Hayes, is better for teas and coffees and also does food. The *Guild Hall Bar* on Oxford Street, opposite the tourist office, is a free house with good ale and pool.

Stroud and around

Five heavily-populated valleys converge at **STROUD**, twelve miles west of Cirencester, creating an exhausting jumble of hills and a sense of high activity untypical of the Cotswolds. The bustle is not a new phenomenon. During the heyday of the wool trade the Frome river powered 150 mills, turning Stroud into the centre of the local cloth industry. Some of the old mills have since been converted into flats, others contain factories – a few even continue to make cloth, including the so-called Stroudwater Scarlet used for military uniforms.

The town's interest centres around its industrial past: for general background you could spend half an hour at the **Lansdown Hall Museum** (Mon–Fri 10am–5pm, Sat 10am–4pm), which is due to move to new premises at the Mansion House, in Stratford Park Leisure Centre – check current situation with the tourist office. Industrial archeology is strewn the length of the Frome valley – the so-called Golden Valley. Council offices occupy one of the valley's finest mills, **Ebley Mill**, a twenty-minute walk west of the centre along the old Stroudwater Canal – for the best view you should then walk south across the field to the village of **Selsley**.

The unused **Severn and Thames Canal** east of Stroud cuts a more picturesque route, particularly beyond Chalford, three miles east, where houses perch precariously on the hillside. Walk thirty minutes along the towpath from here and you'll end up at the mouth of the **Sapperton tunnel**, more than two miles long and a great feat of eighteenth-century engineering. It is unsafe to go inside, so seek sustenance at the nearby *Daneway Inn* instead, or walk up to the hilltop village of **Sapperton**, a world away from the hurly-burly of the Frome valley.

Trains on the London–Gloucester rail line stop at Stroud; bus services arrive at Russell Street or the station on Merrywalks. The **tourist office** (daily 10am–5pm) is in the Subscription Rooms on Kendrick Street. Most guest houses are at the top of uninviting hills, but the **B&B** at 1 Whitehall (☎01453/750 766; ②) overlooks a quiet – and level – street just east of the centre. The *London Hotel* at 30 London Rd (☎01453/579 992; ④) offers the best value among the smarter places. You'll find the nearest **youth hostel** and **campsite** at Slimbridge (see below). For **food** in the daytime go straight to *Mills Café* in Withey's Yard off the High Street, which sells various wholesome concoctions. Vegetarian and organic meals are also served on Union Street at *The Pelican*, which calls itself an "ethnic pub" and has tatty leather sofas and live jazz and folk.

Uley and Slimbridge

The B4066 cuts a glorious route along the valley ridge southwest of Stroud, passing through **ULEY**, six miles from town. Boasting one of the best settings in the region, the **church** lords it over the small green and the *Old Crown* pub, where the local brews include one called Pigor Mortis. **Uley Bury**, among the largest hill forts in Britain, extends along the ridge above the village. The path from the church takes you up the shortest and steepest route, though motorists can opt to drive up to the car park right by the fort. Fences prevent you from clambering on top of the bury, but you can walk around the edge – a distance of about two miles – and take in some staggering views.

Eight miles southwest of Stroud, out of the Cotswolds, **SLIMBRIDGE** sits in a narrow corridor between the M5 and the Severn – a surprising location for Britain's largest wildfowl sanctuary, the **Slimbridge Wildfowl and Wetlands Centre** (summer daily 9am–5pm, winter closes 4pm; £4.70), covering 880 acres between Sharpness Canal and the river. Geese, swans, ducks and a huge gathering of flamingos make up the bulk of the birdlife. While some birds are resident all year round, many are migratory: the greatest numbers congregate in the winter months, when Bewick swans, for example, migrate from Russia. There is a comfortable, purpose-built **youth hostel** (☎01453/890 275) and a **campsite**, the *Tudor Caravan Park* (☎01453/890 483), midway between the village and the wildfowl centre, about half a mile from each. The only **buses** to go anywhere near Slimbridge are those between Gloucester and Bristol or Dursley, which stop by the turn-off on the A38, just over a mile east of the village.

Painswick

The A46 and the B4070 are equally attractive routes linking Stroud and Cheltenham, but the former has the edge because after four miles you reach the old wool town of

PAINSWICK, where ancient buildings jostle for space on narrow streets running downhill off the busy main street. The fame of Painswick's **church** stems not so much from the building itself as from the surrounding **graveyard**, where 99 yew trees, cut into bizarre bulbous shapes resembling lollipops, surround a collection of eighteenth-century table tombs unrivalled in the Cotswolds.

However, it's the **Rococo Garden** (mid-Jan to Nov Wed–Sun 11am–5pm; £2.60), about half a mile north up the Gloucester road and attached to Painswick House (not open to the public), that ranks as the town's main attraction. Created in the early eighteenth century and later abandoned, the garden is being restored to its original form with the aid of a painting dated 1748. Although unfinished, it is already beautiful and the country's only example of Rococo garden design – a short-lived fashion typified by a mix of formal geometrical shapes and more naturalistic, curving lines. With a vegetable patch as an unusual centrepiece, the Painswick garden spreads across a sheltered gully – for the best vistas, walk round anticlockwise. In February and March people flock to see the snowdrops which smother the slopes beneath the pond.

The number of **guest houses** and **hotels** attests to the amount of people who find Painswick a more congenial place than Stroud. For quiet and reasonable rooms try the *Thorne Guest House* on Friday Street (☎01452/812 476; ④), or *Cardynham House* on St Mary's Street (☎01452/813 536; ③) near the *Royal Oak* **pub** (the best in town). Alternatively, you might consider heading out of town to the village of Edge, half a mile west, where *Upper Dorey's Mill* (☎01452/812 459; ③) offers plenty of rural atmosphere in a disused cloth mill (non-smokers only).

Gloucester

For centuries life was good for **GLOUCESTER**. Under the Romans, it became a *colonia* or home for retired soldiers – the highest status a provincial Roman town could dream of. Commercial prestige came with trade up the Severn, while the city's political importance hit its peak under the Normans, when William the Conqueror met here frequently with his council of nobles. The Middle Ages saw Gloucester's rise as a religious centre, but also saw its political and economic decline: navigating the Severn as far up as Gloucester was so difficult that most trade gradually shifted south to Bristol. In a brave attempt to reverse the city's demise, a canal was opened in 1827 to link Gloucester to Sharpness, on a broader stretch of the Severn further south. Trade picked up for a time, but it was only a temporary stay of execution.

Ironically, the canal is busy once again, though this time with pleasure boats. The Victorian dockyards too have undergone a facelift and are touted as the city's great new tourist attraction – and indeed they house some of the region's best museums. Gloucester's most magnificent possession, however, is the **cathedral**, its tower visible for miles around. Few other buildings in the city have survived the ravages of history and the twentieth century, with the centre a mish-mash of medieval ruins swallowed up by ugly new buildings.

The City

Gloucester lies on the east bank of the Severn, its centre spread around a curve in the river. **The Cross**, once the entrance to the Roman forum, marks the heart of the city and the meeting point of Northgate, Southgate, Eastgate and Westgate streets, all Roman roads. **St Michael's Tower**, the remains of an old church and now the tourist office, overlooks it. The main shopping area lies east of the Northgate–Southgate axis, with the cathedral and the docks, the focus of interest, to the west of it. The bus and train stations are opposite one another across Bruton Way, five minutes' walk east of the Cross.

The Cathedral

The superb condition of Gloucester **Cathedral** (daily 8am–6pm) is striking in a city that has lost so much of its past. As a place of worship it shot to importance after the murder at Berkeley Castle of Edward II in 1327: Bristol and Malmesbury wouldn't take his body, but Gloucester did, and the martyr's shrine became a major place of pilgrimage. The money generated helped finance the conversion of the church into the country's first and greatest example of the Perpendicular style; the magnificent 225-foot tower crowns the achievement.

Beneath the reconstructions, some Norman aspects remain, best seen in the **nave**, flanked by sturdy pillars and arches adorned with immaculate zigzag mouldings. Only when you reach the choir and transepts can you see how skilfully the new church was built inside the old, the Norman masonry hidden beneath the finer lines of the Perpendicular panelling and tracery. The **choir** has extraordinary fourteenth-century misericords, and also provides the best vantage point for admiring the east window, completed in around 1350 and – at almost eighty feet tall – the largest medieval window in Britain. Beneath it, to the left is the **tomb of Edward II**, immortalized in alabaster and marble and in good fettle apart from some graffiti. In the nearby **Lady Chapel**, delicate carved tracery holds a staggering patchwork of windows, virtually creating walls of stained glass. There are well-preserved monuments here too, but the tomb of Robert II, back in the **presbytery**, is far more unusual. Robert, eldest son of William the Conqueror, died in 1134, but the painted wooden effigy dates from around 1290. Dressed as a crusader, he lies unnaturally with his arms and legs crossed, his right hand gripping his sword ready to do battle with the infidel.

The innovative nature of the cathedral's design can perhaps be best appreciated in the **cloisters**, completed in 1367 and featuring the first fan vaulting in the country. The fine quality of the work is outdone perhaps only by Henry VII's Chapel in Westminster Abbey, which it inspired. Back inside, an exhibition in the upstairs galleries (reached from the north transept) traces the history of the cathedral, putting it into context with that of the city as a whole.

Southgate and Westgate streets

The most interesting parish church in Gloucester is **St Mary de Crypt** on Southgate Street, mostly late medieval but with some of its original Norman features. A soft, soothing light filters through the stained-glass windows, and a sixteenth-century wall painting of the Adoration of the Magi in the chancel shows unusual detail for work of that period. Greyfriars runs alongside St Mary's, past the ruins of a Franciscan church and the Eastgate Market to the **City Museum** on Brunswick Road (Mon–Sat 10am–5pm; July–Sept also Sun 10am–4pm; free), with a good archeological collection including a fragment of the Roman city wall, preserved *in situ* below ground level.

Westgate Street, quieter and many times more pleasant than its three Roman counterparts, retains several medieval buildings. One of them, a creaking timber-framed house at the bottom of the street, contains the **Folk Museum** (Mon–Sat 10am–4pm, also summer Sun 10am–5pm; free), which illustrates the social history of the Gloucester area using an impressive collection of objects, from huge wrought-iron cheese presses to salt-filled rolling pins used to scare off witches. College Court alley leads from Westgate Street to the haven of the cathedral, passing the Beatrix Potter shop and museum (☎01452/526 467) – only for the seriously obsessed.

The Docks

The **Docks** complex was developed during the fifty years following the opening of the Sharpness canal in 1827. The import of corn represented the bulk of the port's business at that time, and huge **warehouses** were built for storing the grain. Fourteen of them have survived, mostly now converted into offices, shops and museums, a redevelopment at its most crudely commercial in the **Merchants' Quay** shopping centre, an oversized greenhouse full of forlorn shoppers.

The museums, however, are excellent. The **Robert Opie Museum of Packaging and Advertising** (March–Oct daily 10am–5pm; Nov–Feb Tues–Sun 10am–5pm; £2.95) gathers together a collection of packets and tins spanning almost a century, from late Victorian times to the 1980s. The first part takes you through the last hundred years decade by decade – something of a nostalgia trip, going back to the good old days of British manufacturing industry. Look out for the "Nasti" toilet roll, with a picture of Hitler and the catchphrase "a unique sanitary bum paper".

The much bigger **National Waterways Museum** (same times; £4.25), in the southernmost Llanthony Warehouse, completely immerses you in the canal mania which swept Britain in the eighteenth and nineteenth centuries, touching on everything from the engineering of the locks to the lives of the horses that trod the towpaths. You walk around to a lively background of recordings, including imaginary dialogues spoken in good West Country accents and readings of contemporary accounts; there's also a series of excellent hands-on displays, particularly on the top floor where you can steer your own narrow boat (harder than it looks) or build a canal on a computer.

The **Regiments of Gloucestershire Museum** (Tues–Sun 10am–5pm; £2.75), in the old customs house, does an award-winning job of making a potentially dull or alienating subject fascinating. It doesn't rely on the displays of uniforms and miscellaneous memorabilia used in most military museums, but concentrates on all aspects of life as a soldier, both in war- and peacetime.

Practicalities

The **tourist office** is in St Michael's Tower on the Cross (Mon–Sat 10am–5pm; ☎01452/421 188). Judging from the amount of **accommodation** in the city centre, Gloucester doesn't expect many visitors to stay overnight. Of the few **hotels** near the Cross, the *Lamprey* at 56 Westgate St (☎01452/522 355; ③) and the *New Inn* at the bottom of Northgate Street (☎01452/522 177; ③) offer the best value. The *Beaufort* **B&B** at 31 Spa Rd (☎01452/306 034; ③) is quieter and just a stone's throw from the docks.

You'll find some of the best **food** in the city at the *Undercroft Restaurant* in the cathedral, and at the café-bar in the Guildhall on Eastgate Street; the latter is open until 11pm and is always lively. Another good place for vegetarians is the *Down to Earth* café in the Eastgate Market. *Ye Olde Fish Shoppe* on Hare Lane, a Gloucester institution, occupies a sixteenth-century building and is the fanciest takeaway for miles. For pizzas go to *Pizza Piazza* at Merchant's Quay. Of the town's **pubs**, the rambling fifteenth-century *New Inn* on Northgate Street has a good atmosphere and a splendid galleried courtyard, but for really tasty food go to the *Tailor's House* on Westgate Street – don't miss the hot beef sandwiches at lunchtime, so go early.

Tewkesbury and around

The small market town of **TEWKESBURY**, ten miles north of Gloucester, stands hemmed in by the Avon and Severn rivers, which converge nearby, and the threat of floods has curbed expansion more efficiently than any conservation-conscious planning office could. In addition to the pressure of space, the comparatively unchanging face of Tewkesbury is also due to the fact that it almost completely missed out on the Industrial Revolution. Elegant Georgian houses and medieval timber-framed buildings still line several of the town's main streets – especially Church Street – and the Norman **abbey** has survived as one of the greatest in England. Some old buildings inevitably fell to postwar bulldozers, however, particularly along the High Street, and recent years haven't been kind to the town's economy.

The site of **Tewkesbury Abbey** was first selected for a Benedictine monastery in the eighth century, but virtually nothing of the Saxon complex survived a sacking by the Danes, and a new abbey was founded by a Norman nobleman in 1092. The work took about sixty years to complete, with some additions made in the fourteenth century. Two hundred years later the Dissolution brought about the destruction of most of the monastic buildings, but the abbey itself survived thanks to a buy-out in which the local people paid Henry VIII £453 for the property. The sheer scale of the abbey's exterior makes a lasting impact: its colossal **tower** is the largest Norman tower in the world, while the west front's soaring recessed arch – 65 feet high – is the only exterior arch in the country to boast such impressive proportions. In the nave, fourteen stout Norman pillars steal the show; the roof of the fourteenth-century **choir** is equally staggering. The brightly painted bosses include a ring of Yorkist suns, said to have been put there by Edward IV after the defeat of the Lancastrians at Tewkesbury in 1471, the last important battle of the Wars of the Roses. The abbey's medieval **tombs** celebrate Tewkesbury's greatest patrons, the Fitzhamons, De Clares, Beauchamps and the Despensers, who turned the building into a mausoleum for themselves. Don't miss the macabre so-called **Wakeman Cenotaph**, in the ambulatory, carved in the fifteenth century, with a decaying corpse being consumed by snakes and other creatures.

Practicalities

The **tourist office** at 64 Barton St (Mon–Sat 10am–4.30pm; also summer Sun 10am–4pm; ☎01684/295 027) has free town and walking maps, plus a small museum upstairs. There are several **guest houses** and **B&Bs** on Barton Road, the busy Evesham road, including the *Bali-Hai* at no. 5 (☎01684/292 049; ②). More genteel are the *Crescent Guest House* at 30 Church St (☎01684/293 395; ③) or the quiet *Carrant Brook House* on Rope Walk (☎01684/290 355; ④). There's a caravan site in the park by the abbey (☎01684/296 876), but **campers** should head for the campsite in Twyning (☎01684/292 145), three miles north and accessible on Worcester bus #373.

The town has a curious line in **tea shops**, several of which make you feel as if you're in someone's sitting room; try the one in the *Bible Bookshop* on Nelson Street. Its **pub** equivalent is the ancient *Berkeley Arms* on Church Street, which is popular with pensioners and serves astoundingly cheap but distinctly basic food. If quality of food takes priority over local colour, you'll do better at *Ye Olde Black Bear* at the top of the High Street, which also pulls some of the best pints in town. *Le Bistro André* at 78 Church St (closed Sun; expensive; ☎01684/290 357) is a lively French restaurant serving anything from snails to venison.

Deerhurst

Before the construction of Tewkesbury's abbey, **DEERHURST**, just south of the town, was the most prestigious religious centre in the area. As the chief monastery in the Saxon kingdom of Hwicce, it was considered a suitable venue for the meeting in 1016 between the English king Edmund Ironside and Cnut (Canute) the Dane, at which the partition of England was agreed. Deerhurst's importance declined after 1100, but two outstanding buildings date back to the village's heyday.

The monastery church of **St Mary's**, some of which dates back to the eighth century, is a chronological jumble, but the interior remains remarkably simple considering. It also contains several very rare features, like the series of curious windows and holes which puncture the nave walls: these small triangular piercings, cut by the Saxons, are said to represent the eyes of God. In the north aisle, a ninth-century font of golden Cotswold stone has intricate spiral decoration unique for that period. Outside, a sign directs you to a stylized carved angel high up on the wall of the ruined apse; though also Saxon, the relief looks more Celtic in inspiration.

The nearby **Odda's Chapel**, which also clings to another building (in this case a half-timbered cottage), lay neglected until last century, its Saxon masonry smothered underneath plaster. It is only slightly younger than St Mary's, having been built in 1056 by Odda in honour of his brother Aelfric, both relatives of the king. The small chapel, just forty feet long, has survived in good condition apart from a few damp patches. The original dedicatory inscription is in the hands of the Ashmolean Museum in Oxford, but a copy has been put in its original place.

Deerhurst is four miles south of Tewkesbury by road, but only two miles on foot across the fields or along the Severn. Alternatively, you can catch the #50 **bus** from Tewkesbury to Gloucester, which runs three times a day and stops at Deerhurst.

Bredon Hill

The most important Iron Age fort in the area once crowned **Bredon Hill**, six miles northeast of Tewkesbury and visible for miles around in the flat Severn Vale. Excavation of the site revealed more than fifty bodies all hacked to pieces, seemingly the victims of a final assault by unknown attackers in the first century AD. Inside the rampart, a huge expanse covering eleven acres, an eighteenth-century tower called Parson's Folly is an incongruous centrepiece, but the views are supreme, with deer often grazing on the slopes. Bredon Hill can be approached from various places around the southern foot of the hill. From **Overbury**, one of the prettier villages, the climb takes less than an hour. If you're relying on public transport, buses bound for Evesham from Tewkesbury pass through the village of **Bredon** (none on Sun), from where you should allow about three hours to walk to the hill and back.

travel details

Trains

Cheltenham to: Gloucester (1–2 hourly; 10min); London (1–2 hourly; 2hr).

Gloucester to: Cheltenham (1–2 hourly; 15min); London (1–2 hourly; 2hr); Stroud (Mon–Sat 1–2 hourly, 5 on Sun; 15min).

Henley to: London (hourly; 30–60min).

Milton Keynes to: London (every 30min; 40min).

Oxford to: London (1–2 hourly; 1hr 30min); Moreton-in-Marsh (hourly; 40min); Worcester (hourly; 1hr 10min).

St Albans to: London (14 daily; 20–35min).

Buses

Cheltenham to: Burford (6 daily, 2 on Sun; 45min); Cirencester (Mon–Sat 5 daily; 40min); Gloucester (every 15–30min; 30–45min); London (11 daily; 2hr 40min); Moreton-in-Marsh (8 daily; 1hr); Oxford (4–6 daily; 1hr 30min); Stroud (7 Mon–Sat; 45min); Tewkesbury (Mon–Sat hourly, 2 on Sun; 30min); Winchcombe (hourly; 25min).

Cirencester to: Cheltenham (6 daily; 40min); Gloucester (8 daily; 50min); Lechlade (5–7 daily; 20min); London (8 daily; 2hr 30min); Malmesbury (4–6 daily Mon–Sat; 45min); Stroud (4 daily Mon–Sat; 45min); Tetbury (5 daily Mon–Sat; 45min).

Gloucester to: Cheltenham (every 15–30min; 30–45min); Cirencester (8 daily; 50min); Ledbury (3 daily Mon–Sat; 1hr); Oxford (2 daily; 1hr 30min); London (9 daily; 3hr 40min); Stroud (hourly Mon–Sat; 30min); Tewkesbury (10 daily; 35–55min); Worcester (5 daily; 1hr 30min).

Henley to: Marlow (every 30 min; 20min); Oxford (9 daily; 75min); London (8 daily; 1hr 40min).

Oxford to: Burford (5 daily; 40min); Cheltenham (4–6 daily; 1hr 10min); Gloucester (3 daily; 2hr); Henley (8 daily; 75min); London (every 15min–1hr; 1hr 45min); Tewkesbury (2–4 daily; 2hr 30min); Worcester (1 daily; 2hr) .

Stroud to: Cheltenham (7 daily Mon–Sat; 45min); Cirencester (4 daily Mon–Sat; 45min); Gloucester (hourly Mon–Sat; 30min); Painswick (8 daily Mon–Sat; 10min); Tetbury (4 daily Mon–Sat; 35min).

Tewkesbury to: Cheltenham (hourly Mon–Sat, 2 on Sun; 30min); Gloucester (10 daily; 35–55min); Oxford (2–4 daily; 2hr 30min–3hr); Worcester (Mon–Sat 10 daily; 35–70min).

CHAPTER FIVE

THE WEST COUNTRY

England's **West Country** – comprising the counties of Avon, Somerset, Devon and Cornwall – is a region encompassing everything from genteel, cosy villages to vast Atlantic-facing strands of golden sand and wild expanses of granite moorland. It would be impossible to do justice to this great peninsula by basing yourself in any one place – the country beckons ever westwards into rural backwaters where increasingly exotic place names and idiosyncratic pronunciations recall that this was once England's last bastion of Celtic culture.

The biggest city in the West Country is also its easternmost – **Bristol**, a cosmopolitan and sophisticated place which, although overrun by traffic and defaced by office blocks, preserves traces of every phase in its long maritime history. Bristol is within reach of some superb countryside, and only a few miles from Georgian **Bath**, whose symmetrical honey-toned terraces perfectly exploit its scenic location. The exquisite cathedral city of **Wells** lies close at hand, over the Somerset border and just up the road from **Glastonbury**, one of many sites steeped in Arthurian legend in this part of the country. On the border with Devon, **Exmoor** offers a foretaste of the wilderness to be found on **Dartmoor**, which takes up much of the southern half of Devon. The greatest of the region's massifs, Dartmoor lies between **Exeter** and **Plymouth**, the West Country's only major cities except for Bristol. Exeter is by far the more interesting, dominated by the twin towers of its medieval cathedral; Plymouth, though holding some reminders of its role as an Elizabethan naval port, is for the most part spoiled by postwar development.

Warmed by the Gulf Stream, and enjoying more hours of sunshine than virtually anywhere else in England, this part of the country can sometimes come fairly close to the atmosphere of the Mediterranean, and indeed Devon's principal resort, **Torquay**, styles itself the capital of the "English Riviera". Cornwall too has its concentrations of tourist development – chiefly at **St Ives**, **Newquay** and **Falmouth** – but this county is essentially less domesticated than its agricultural neighbour. In part this is due to the overbearing presence of the turbulent Atlantic, which is never more than half an hour's drive away, and gives Cornwall's old fishing ports an almost embattled character, especially on the north coast. The fortified headland of **Tintagel** and the clenched little harbour of **Boscastle** are typical of Cornwall's craggy appeal, but the full elemental power of the ocean can best be appreciated on Cornwall's twin pincers of **Lizard Point** and **Land's End**, where the splintered cliffs resound to the constant thunder of the waves. And there's another factor contributing to Cornwall's starker feel: unlike Devon, this county was once considerably industrialized, and is dotted with remnants of its now defunct mining industries, their ruins presenting a salutary counterpoint to the tourist-centred seaside towns.

The best way of exploring the coast of Devon and Cornwall is along the **South West Way**, Britain's longest waymarked footpath, which allows the dauntless hiker to cover almost six hundred miles from the Somerset border to the edge of Bournemouth in Dorset. Getting around by **public transport** in the West Country can be a convoluted and lengthy process, especially if you're relying on the often skimpy bus network. By train, you can reach Bristol, Exeter, Plymouth and Penzance, with a handful of branchlines wandering off to the major coastal resorts – though there's nothing like the extensive network enjoyed by the Victorians.

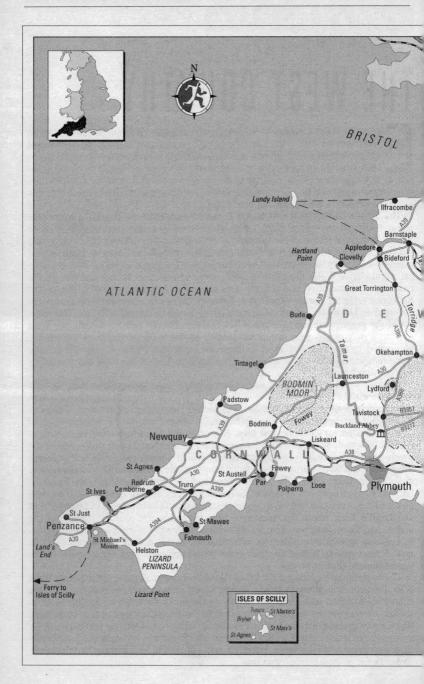

N

BRISTOL

Lundy Island

Ilfracombe

Barnstaple

Hartland
Point
Appledore
Clovelly
Bideford

ATLANTIC OCEAN

Great Torrington

D   E

Torridge

Bude

Okehampton

Tintagel

BODMIN
MOOR

Launceston

Lydford

Padstow

Fowey

Tavistock

Bodmin

Buckland Abbey

Newquay

Liskeard

C O R N W A L L

A38

St Agnes

St Austell

Fowey

Redruth
Camborne

Truro

Par

Polperro

Looe

Plymouth

St Ives

St Just

St Mawes

Penzance

Land's
End

St Michael's
Mount

Falmouth

Helston

LIZARD
PENINSULA

Ferry to
Isles of Scilly

Lizard Point

ISLES OF SCILLY

Tresco   St Martin's
Bryher
St Mary's
St Agnes

Built in the mid-fourteenth century, they have been continuously occupied by members of the cathedral clergy ever since.

On the other side of the cathedral – and accessible through the cathedral shop – are the cloisters, from which you can enter the tranquil grounds of the **Bishop's Palace** (Easter–Oct Tues–Thurs 10am–6pm, Sun 2–6pm; except Aug daily 10am–6pm; £2.50). The residence of the Bishop of Bath and Wells, the palace was walled and moated as a result of a rift with the borough in the fourteenth century, and the imposing gatehouse still displays the grooves of the portcullis and a chute for pouring oil and molten lead on would-be assailants. Its tranquil gardens contain the springs from which the city takes its name – and which still feed the moat as well as the streams flowing along the gutters of Wells' High Street – and the ruined, thirteenth-century **Great Hall**.

Practicalities

Wells **bus station** is off Market Street, while the **tourist office** is on Market Place (daily April–Oct 9.30am–5.30pm; Nov–March 10am–4pm; ☎01749/672 552). Among the best **B&Bs** are the seventeenth-century *Tor Guest House* overlooking the cathedral (☎01749/672 322; ④), and the no-smoking *Bekynton House*, 7 St Thomas St (☎01749/ 672 552; ③). On the High Street there's the *Red Lion*, a nice old coaching inn off Market Place (☎01749/672 616; ⑤), and *The Star Hotel* at no. 18 (☎01749/670 500; ⑥). *Chapel's* on Union Street (off the High Street) is a modern café-bar offering dishes like pork in cider and fisherman's pie as well as snacks. The Italian-run *Ancient Gate House* on Sadler Street (closed Sun; ☎01749/679 085) is also worth trying; on the same street at no. 5, *Ritcher's* combines a downstairs bistro with an evening-only restaurant in a plant-filled loft serving top-notch dishes (closed Wed & Sun; ☎01749/679 085). Excellent wholefood is served at *The Good Earth* on Priory Road (closed Sun), or you can find decent **pub** fare at the *City Arms* on Cuthbert Street, formerly the city jail.

The Mendips

The **Mendip Hills**, rising to the north of Wells, are chiefly famous for Wookey Hole – the most impressive of many caves in this narrow limestone chain – and for the **Cheddar Gorge**, where a walk through the narrow cleft might make a starting point for more adventurous trips across the Mendips. From Monday to Saturday there's an hourly bus to Wookey Hole from Wells (#172), from where there's also an hourly bus to the gorge (#126 or #826).

Wookey Hole

Hollowed out by the River Axe a couple of miles outside Wells, **Wookey Hole** is an impressive cave complex of deep pools and intricate rock formations, but it's folklore rather than geology that takes precedence on the guided tours (daily March–Oct 9.30am–5.30pm; Nov–Feb 10.30am–4.30pm; closed Dec 17–25; £5.40). Highlight of the tour is the alleged petrified remains of the Witch of Wookey, a "blear-eyed hag" who was said to turn her evil eye on crops, young lovers and local farmers until the Abbot of Glastonbury intervened – he dispatched a monk who drove the witch into the inner cave, sprinkled her with holy water and turned her into stone. Some substance was lent to the legend when an ancient skeleton – in fact Romano-British – was unearthed here in 1912, together with a dagger, sacrificial knife and a big rounded ball of pure stalagmite, the so-called witch's ball. Beside her were found two skeletons, the remains of goats tied to a stake. At the end of the hour-long tour, you can visit a functioning Victorian paper mill by the river, and rooms containing speleological exhibits. On a less earnest note is the range of amusements laid on by Madame Tussauds, owners of the complex – notably a collection of gaudy, Edwardian fairground pieces.

Cheddar Gorge

Six miles west of Wookey on the A371, **CHEDDAR** has given its name to Britain's best-known cheese – most of it now mass-produced far from here – and is also renowned as a centre for strawberry growing. However, the biggest selling point of this rather plain village is the **Cheddar Gorge**, lying beyond the neighbourhood of Tweentown about a mile to the north. Cutting a jagged gash across the Mendip Hills, the limestone gorge is an impressive geological phenomenon, though its natural beauty is undermined by the minor road running through it and by the Lower Gorge's mile of shops, coach park and **tourist office** (summer daily 10am–5.30pm; winter Mon–Fri noon–5pm, Sat & Sun 10am–5pm; ☎01934/744 071). Few trippers venture further than the first few curves of the gorge, beyond the shops, which admittedly holds its most dramatic scenery, though each turn of the two-mile length presents new, sometimes startling vistas. At its narrowest the path squeezes between cliffs towering almost 500ft above, and if you don't want to follow the road as far as **Priddy**, the highest village in the Mendips, you can reach more dramatic destinations by branching off onto marked paths to such secluded spots as **Black Rock**, just two miles from Cheddar, or **Black Down** (1067ft), the Mendips' highest peak. Clifftop paths winding along the rim of the gorge provide an alternative to walking next to the road.

Beneath the gorge, the **Cheddar Caves** (Easter–Sept daily 10am–5.30pm; Oct–Easter closes 4.30pm; £5) were scooped out by underground rivers in the wake of the Ice Age, and later occupied by primitive communities. The bigger of the two main groups, **Gough's Caves**, is made up of chambers with names like Solomon's Temple, Aladdin's Cave and the Swiss Village, all arrayed with tortuous rock formations that resemble organ pipes, waterfalls and giant birds. **Cox's Caves** (same ticket), entered lower down the main drag, have floodlighting that picks out subtle pinks, greys, greens and whites in the rock, and a set of lime blocks known as the Bells, which produce a range of tones when struck. The Fantasy Grotto, attached to Cox's Caves, is the kids' favourite, with high-tech light and laser effects playing on its gushing waterfall.

Outside again, close to Cox's Cave, the 274 steps of **Jacob's Ladder** (same ticket as caves) lead to a clifftop viewpoint towards Glastonbury Tor, Exmoor and the sea. It's a muscle-wrenching climb – anyone not in a state of honed fitness can reach the same spot via a narrow lane winding up behind the cliffs. You can also survey the panorama from **Pavey's Lookout Tower** nearby.

Among Cheddar's handful of **B&Bs**, try *Chedwell Cottage* on Redcliffe Street (☎01934/743 268; ③; closed Dec), or the *Clementine*, Old Station Road (☎01934/743 651; ③). Otherwise there is a **youth hostel** opposite the fire station, off the Hays (☎01934/742 494), and three **campsites**, two near the centre of Cheddar – *Froglands* (☎01934/742 058) and across the road *Church Farm* (☎01934/743048) – and the far more luxurious *Broadway House* (☎01934/742 610), on the outskirts of the village off the A371 to Axbridge.

Glastonbury

Six miles south of Wells, **GLASTONBURY** lies at the centre of the so-called **Isle of Avalon**, a region rich with mystical associations. At the heart of it all is the early Christian legend that the young Christ once visited this site, a story that is not as far-fetched as it sounds. The Romans had a heavy presence in the area, mining lead in the Mendips, and one of these mines was owned by **Joseph of Arimathea**, a well-to-do merchant said to have been related to Mary. It's not completely impossible that the merchant took his kinsman on one of his many visits to his property, in a period of Christ's life of which nothing is recorded. It was this possibility to which William Blake referred in his *Glastonbury Hymn*, better known as *Jerusalem*: – "And did those feet in ancient time/ Walk upon England's mountains green?" Another legend relates how

Joseph was imprisoned for twelve years after the crucifixion, miraculously kept alive by the **Holy Grail**, the chalice of the Last Supper, in which the blood was gathered from the wound in Christ's side. The Grail, along with the spear which had caused the wound, were later taken by Joseph to Glastonbury, where he founded the abbey and commenced the conversion of Britain.

According to the official version, however, **Glastonbury Abbey** (June–Aug 9am–6pm; Sept–May 8.30am–dusk; £1.50) was a Celtic monastery founded in the fourth or fifth century – making this the oldest Christian foundation in England – and enlarged by Saint Dunstan, under whom it became the richest Benedictine abbey in the country. The original building was destroyed by fire in 1184 and the ruins are the rather scanty remains of what took its place, reduced to their present state at the Dissolution. Hidden behind walls at the centre of town, surrounded by grassy parkland and shaded by trees, the ruins only hint at the extent of the building, which was financed largely by a constant procession of medieval pilgrims. Most prominent and photogenic remains are the transept piers and the shell of the Lady Chapel, with its carved figures of the Annunciation, the Magi and Herod.

The abbey's **choir** introduces another strand to the Glastonbury story, for it holds what is alleged to be the tomb of **Arthur and Guinevere**. As told by William of Malmesbury and Thomas Malory, the story relates how, after being mortally wounded in battle, King Arthur sailed to Avalon where he was buried alongside his queen. The discovery of two bodies in an ancient cemetery outside the abbey in 1191 – from which they were transferred here in 1278 – was taken to confirm the popular identification of Glastonbury with Avalon. In the grounds, the fourteenth-century abbot's kitchen is the only monastic building to survive intact, with four huge corner fireplaces whose flues meet a great central lantern. Look out for the thorn that grows nearby, supposedly from the original **Glastonbury Thorn** that was said to have sprouted from the staff of Joseph of Arimathea when he landed here to convert the country. The plant grew for centuries on a nearby hill known as Weary-All, and despite being hacked down by puritans, lived long enough to provide numerous cuttings whose descendants still bloom twice a year (May & Dec). Only at Glastonbury do they flourish, it is claimed – anywhere else they die after a couple of years.

On the edge of the abbey grounds, the medieval abbey barn forms the centrepiece of the engaging **Somerset Rural Life Museum** (April–Oct Mon–Fri 10am–5pm, Sat & Sun 2–6pm; Nov–March Mon–Fri 10am–5pm, Sat 11am–4pm; £1), illustrating a range of local rural occupations, from cheese- and cider-making to peat-digging, thatching and farming.

From the ruins it's a mile-long hike to **Glastonbury Tor**, at 521ft a landmark for miles around. The conical hill is topped by the dilapidated **St Michael's Tower**, sole remnant of a fourteenth-century church; it commands stupendous views encompassing Wells, the Quantocks, the Mendips, the once marshy peat moors rolling out to the sea, and sometimes the Welsh mountains. Pilgrims once embarked on the stiff climb here with hard peas in their shoes as penance – nowadays people come to feel the vibrations of crossing ley lines. If you don't fancy the steep ascent, there's an easier path further up Wellhouse Lane, the road that leads to the Tor Park from the centre of town. At the bottom of Wellhouse Lane, in the middle of some public gardens, the **Chalice Well** (daily March–Oct 10am–6pm; Nov–Feb 1–4pm; £1) is meant to be the hiding place of the Holy Grail. The reddish waters were considered to have curative properties, making the town a spa for a brief period in the eighteenth century.

Back in town, you might take a glance at the fifteenth-century church of **St John the Baptist**, halfway along the High Street. The tower is reckoned to be one of Somerset's finest, and the **interior** has a fine oak roof and stained glass illustrating the legend of St Joseph of Arimathea, both from the period of the church's construction. The Glastonbury thorn in the churchyard is the biggest in town. Further down the street, the fourteenth-century **Tribunal** was where the abbots presided over legal cases; it later became a hotel for pilgrims, and now holds a small museum of finds from the Iron Age lake villages that once fringed the marshland below the Tor (Easter–Sept Mon–Thurs & Sun 10am–5pm, Fri & Sat 10am–5.30pm; Oct–Easter Mon–Thurs & Sun 10am–4pm, Fri & Sat 10am–4.30pm; £1.50).

Practicalities

Glastonbury's **tourist office** is in the Tribunal on the High Street (Easter–Sept Mon–Thurs & Sun 10am–5pm, Fri & Sat 10am–5.30pm; Oct–Easter Mon–Thurs & Sun 10am–4pm, Fri & Sat 10am–4.30pm; ☎01458/832 954). **Bicycles** can be rented at *Pedalers*, 8 Magdalene St. The nearest **youth hostel** (☎01458/442 961) lies a couple of miles outside the village of Street, an easy bus ride away, and there's a decent **campsite** at *Ashwell Farm House*, Ashwell Lane, below the Tor (☎01458/832 313).

Among the town's less expensive **accommodation** choices, the seventeenth-century *Waterfall Cottage*, 20 Old Wells Rd, boasts a garden and views (☎01458/831 707; ②). *The Bolthole*, 32 Chilkwell St, is a comfortable **B&B** (Easter–Oct; ☎01458/832 800; ③), though not as grand as *Chalice Hill House* (☎01458/832 459; ⑤), on nearby Dod Lane, headquarters of the Ramala Centre, a meditation hostel which also offers accommodation without strings, including use of tennis court and heated pool. Another retreat, the *Shambhala Healing Centre*, offers much the same package on Coursing Batch, abutting the Tor (☎01458/833 081; ③). If you prefer a more medieval mood, opt for the oak-panelled *George and Pilgrims*, on the High Street (☎01458/831 146; ⑥).

There are some decent **cafés** wedged between the esoteric shops of Glastonbury's High Street, including the *Excalibur* and *Deacon's Coffee House*, which also does inexpensive home-cooked meals. The *Blue Note Café* is another good place to hang out over coffees and cakes, often with live music.

Taunton and the Quantocks

Travelling west from the Glastonbury region into Devon, your route could take you through **Taunton**, which makes a handy starting point for excursions into the gently undulating **Quantock Hills**, a mellow landscape of snug villages set in scenic wooded valleys or "combes". Public transport is fairly minimal round here, but there are horse-riding facilities at many local farms, and you can see quite a lot on the **West Somerset Railway** between Bishops Lydeard and the coastal resort of Minehead, with stops at some of the thatched, typically English villages along the west flank of the Quantocks.

Taunton

TAUNTON, Somerset's county town, lies in the fertile Vale of Taunton Deane, wedged between the Quantock, Brendon and Blackdown hills. The region is famed for its production of cider and scrumpy (its less refined cousin), while Taunton itself is host to one of the country's biggest cattle markets. Taunton's **Castle**, started in the twelfth century, staged the trial of royal claimant Perkin Warbeck, who in 1490 declared himself to be the Duke of York, the younger of the "Princes in the Tower", sons of Edward IV, who had been murdered seven years earlier. Most of the castle was pulled down in 1662, but a part of it now houses the **County Museum** (Mon–Sat 10am–5pm; £1.50), which includes a portrait of Judge Jeffreys among other memorabilia of local interest. Overlooking the county cricket ground are the pinnacled and battlemented towers of the town's two most important churches: **St James** and **St Mary Magdalene**, both fifteenth-century though remodelled by the Victorians. St Mary's is worth a look inside for its roof bosses carved with medieval masks.

Otherwise Taunton should only detain you as a base to visit the Quantock villages or Exmoor. **Information** is handled by the library on Corporation Street (Mon, Tues & Thurs 9.30am–5.30pm, Wed & Fri 9.30am–7pm, Sat 9.30am–4pm; ☎01823/274 785). If you want to stay here, head for Wellington Road in the centre, where there are three **B&Bs**: *Brookfield* at no. 16 (☎01823/272 786; ②), *Lilacs* at no. 18 (☎01823/326 420; ③) and *Acorn Lodge* at no. 22 (☎01823/337 613; ②). The most atmospheric place in town is next to the museum: *The Castle*, Castle Green (☎01823/272 671; ⑨), a battlemented, wisteria-clad, 300-year-old hotel exuding old-fashioned good taste and expense accounts. For a snack or **meal**, walk for about ten minutes down East Street from Fore Street to *Porter's*, a congenial and inexpensive wine bar at 49 East Reach.

The Quantock Hills

Geologically closer to Devon than Somerset, the **Quantock Hills** are a cultivated outpost of Exmoor, similarly crossed by clear streams and grazed by red deer. Just twelve miles in length, the range is enclosed by a triangle of roads leading up from Bridgwater and Taunton, within which snake a tangle of narrow lanes connecting secluded hamlets, reached by local buses from the area's two main towns.

Bishops Lydeard and Combe Florey

North of Taunton, the first villages you pass through on the A358 give you an immediate introduction to the flavour of the Quantocks. **BISHOPS LYDEARD**, four miles up, has a splendid church tower in the Perpendicular style, and the church's interior is also worth a look for its carved bench ends, one of them illustrating the allegory of a pelican feeding its young with blood from its own breast – a symbol of the redemptive power of Christ's blood. The village is the terminus of the **West Somerset Railway**, the longest private line in Britain, linked by buses from Taunton train station. From March to October steam and diesel trains depart up to five times daily, stopping at restored stations on the way to Minehead, some twenty miles away (see p.275).

Nether Stowey and around

Eight miles northwest of Taunton on the A39, the pretty village of **NETHER STOWEY** is best known for its association with **Samuel Taylor Coleridge**, who walked here from Bristol at the end of 1796, to join his wife and child at their new home. This "miserable cottage", as Sara Coleridge called it, was visited six months later by William Wordsworth and his sister Dorothy, who soon afterwards moved into Alfoxton House, near Holford, a couple of miles down the road. Coleridge composed some of his best poetry at this time, including *The Rime of the Ancient Mariner* and *Kubla Khan*, and the two poets in collaboration produced the *Lyrical Ballads*, the poetic manifesto of early English Romanticism. Many of the greatest figures of the age came to visit the pair, among them Charles Lamb, Thomas de Quincey and William Hazlitt, stirring the suspicions of the local authorities in a period when England was at war with France. Spies were sent to track them and Wordsworth was finally given notice to leave in June 1798.

In **Coleridge's cottage** (April–Sept Tues–Thurs & Sun 2–5pm; £1.50; NT), not such an "old hovel" now, you can see his parlour and reading room. The nearby village library has a **Quantock Information Centre** furnishing material on routes and local **accommodation**. A good choice in the village is *Castle Cottage* at 12 Castle St (☎01278/733 453; ③), a seventeenth-century house which also serves light meals and teas to non-guests. **Holford** has the *Quantock House*, a beautiful Elizabethan thatched cottage (☎01278/741 439; ③), and a **youth hostel** (☎01278/741 224), in whose grounds you can camp, a signposted two-mile walk from Holford's centre. If you want to do some horseback trekking, contact *Mill Farm* (☎01278/732 286) at **Fiddington**, near Nether Stowey – also a useful **campsite**.

Exmoor

A high bare plateau sliced by wooded combes and splashing rivers, **EXMOOR** can be one of the most forbidding landscapes in England, especially when its sea mists fall. When it's clear, though, the moorland of this national park reveals rich swathes of colour and an amazing diversity of wildlife, from buzzards to the short and stocky **Exmoor ponies**, a species closely related to prehistoric horses. In the treeless heartland of the moor around Simonsbath, it's not difficult to spot these unique animals, though fewer than five hundred now remain, and of these there are only about 120 that are pure-bred and free-living. Much more elusive are the **red deer**, England's largest native wild animal, of which Exmoor supports England's only wild population; around seven hundred are thought to inhabit the moor today.

Endless permutations of **walking routes** are possible along a network of some six hundred miles of footpaths and bridleways. **Horseback** is another way of getting the most out of Exmoor's desolate beauty, and stables are dotted throughout the area – the most convenient are mentioned below. There are four obvious bases for inland walks: **Dulverton** in the southeast, site of the main information facilities; **Simonsbath** in the centre; **Exford**, near Exmoor's highest point of Dunkery Beacon; and the attractive village of **Winsford**, close to the A396 on the east of the moor. Exmoor's coastline offers an alluring alternative to the open moorland, all of it accessible via the **South West Way**, which embarks on its long coastal journey at **Minehead**, though there is more charm to be found further west at the sister villages of **Lynmouth** and **Lynton**, just over the Devon border.

Dulverton

The village of **DULVERTON**, on the southern edge of the national park near Brompton Regis, is the Park Authority's headquarters and so makes a good introduction to Exmoor. **Information** on the moor is available at the Visitor Centre at the Guildhall, near the river off Bridge Street (April–Oct daily 9.30am–5.30pm; Nov–March Mon–Sat 10am–3pm; ☎01398/323 841). **Accommodation** in Dulverton includes *Town Mills* (☎01398/323 124; ③), an old millhouse in the centre of the village. If you hanker after beams and four-posters, try the *Lion Hotel* in Bank Square (☎01398/323 444; ⑤). *Crispin's*, in a nook off 26 High Street, does moderately priced carnivorous and vegetarian **food**. Moorland **riding** in the area and tuition is offered at *West Anstey Farm*, two miles west of Dulverton, which also offers accommodation (☎01398/341 354; ②).

Winsford, Exford and Dunkery Beacon

Five miles north of Dulverton, **WINSFORD** lays good claim to being the moor's prettiest village. A scattering of thatched cottages ranged round a sleepy green, it is watered by a confluence of streams and rivers – one of them the Exe – giving it no fewer than seven bridges. *Larcombe Foot* (April–Dec; ☎01643/851 306; ③), a mile to the north, offers excellent **B&B** overlooking the Exe, and there's a **campsite** nearby at *Halse Farm* (March–Oct; ☎01643/851 259). **Horse-riding** can be arranged at *Tufters* (☎01643/851 318), less than half a mile from the campsite. *The Royal Oak*, a thoroughly thatched and rambling old inn on the village green, can offer you drinks, snacks and full **restaurant meals**, though the rooms are pricey (☎01643/851 455; ⑦).

The hamlet of **EXFORD**, an ancient bridging point on the River Exe, is popular with walkers for the four-mile hike from here to **Dunkery Beacon**, Exmoor's highest point at 1700ft. The village also holds Exmoor's main **youth hostel**, a large Victorian house in the centre (☎01643/831 288). *Westermill Farm* (☎01643/831 238) provides a secluded **campsite** on the banks of the Exe. Three miles east at Luckwell Bridge, and convenient for Dunkery Beacon, *Cutthorne* (Feb–Nov; ☎01643/831 255; ④) is a secluded eighteenth-century farmhouse offering **B&B**.

THE SOUTH WEST WAY

The South West Way, the longest footpath in Britain, starts at Minehead and tracks the coastline along Devon's northern seaboard, round Cornwall, back into Devon, and on to Dorset, where it finishes close to the entrance to Poole Harbour. The path was conceived in the 1940s, but it is only in the last ten years that – barring some insignificant gaps – the full **600-mile route** has been open, much of it on land owned by the National Trust, and all of it well signposted with the acorn symbol of the Countryside Commission.

The relevant Ordnance Survey maps can be found at most village shops on the route, while many newsagents, bookshops and tourist offices will stock books or pamphlets containing route plans and details of local flora and fauna. The Countryside Commission in conjunction with Ordnance Survey produces a series of books (published by Aurum Press) describing different parts of the path, while the **South West Way Association**, Windlestraw, Penquit, Ermington, Devon PL21 0LU (☎01752/896 237) publishes an annual guide to the whole path, including accommodation lists, ferry timetables and so forth.

Simonsbath and around

At the centre of the National Park stands **Exmoor Forest**, the barest part of the moor, scarcely populated except by roaming sheep and a few red deer – the word "forest" denotes simply that it was a hunting reserve. In the middle of it stands the village of **SIMONSBATH** (pronounced "Simmonsbath"), home to the Knight family, who bought the Forest in 1818 and, by introducing tenant farmers, building roads and importing sheep, brought systematic agriculture to an area that had never before produced any income. The Knights also built a wall round their land – parts of which can still be seen – as well as the intriguing Pinkworthy (pronounced "Pinkery") Pond, four miles to the northwest, whose exact function has never been explained. The *Exmoor Forest Hotel* (☎01643/831 341; ④) offers comfortable **accommodation**, and also space for free **camping**. There's a decent restaurant here too, *Boevey's*, in a converted barn attached to the *Simonsbath House Hotel* (both Feb–Nov; ☎01643/831 259; ⑧). Two miles outside the village on the Brayford road, the *Poltimore Arms* at **Yarde Down** is a classic country **pub**, serving excellent food including vegetarian dishes.

Minehead and Dunster

Once a chief port on the Somerset coast, **MINEHEAD** quickly became a favourite Victorian watering hole with the arrival of the railway and has ever since retained a cheerful holiday-town atmosphere. Steep lanes containing some of the oldest houses link the two quarters of **Higher Town** on North Hill, and the livelier **Quay Town**, the harbour area. It is in Quay Town that the **Hobby Horse** performs its dance in the town's three-day May Day celebrations, snaring maidens under its prancing skirt and tail in a fertility ritual resembling the more famous festivities at Padstow (see p.317).

The **tourist office** is midway between Higher Town and Quay Town at 17 Friday St, off the Parade (April–Oct Mon–Sat 9.30am–5pm, July & Aug also Sun 10am–1pm; Nov–March Mon–Sat 10am–4pm; ☎01643/702 624). If you want to **stay** in Minehead, *Avill House* on Townsend Road (☎01643/704 370; ②) is bright and good value for money, a short walk from the seafront past the tourist office. Up a bracket, the *Mayfair Hotel*, 25 The Avenue (April–Nov; ☎01643/702 719; ④) is central, plush, and has lots of rooms. There's a **youth hostel** a couple of miles southeast, outside the village of Alcombe (☎01643/702 595), in a secluded combe on the edge of Exmoor.

The old village of **DUNSTER** is about a mile from the first stop on the **West Somerset Railway**, three miles inland of Minehead. The main street is dominated by the towers and turrets of **Dunster Castle** (house April–Sept daily except Thurs & Fri

11am–5pm; Oct closes 4pm; grounds daily April–Sept 11am–5pm, Feb, March & Oct to mid-Dec closes 4pm; house & grounds £4.80, grounds only £2.70; NT), most of whose fortifications were demolished after the Civil War. After that the castle became something of an architectural showpiece, and Victorian restoration has made it into something more like a Rhineland schloss than a Norman stronghold. On a tour of the castle you can see a bedroom once occupied by Charles I, a fine seventeenth-century carved staircase and a richly decorated banqueting hall. The grounds include terraced gardens and riverside walks – and drama productions are periodically staged here in summer. The nearby hilltop tower is a Georgian-Gothic folly, **Conygar Tower**, dating from 1776.

Despite the influx of seasonal visitors, Dunster village preserves relics of its woolmaking heyday: the octagonal **Yarn Market**, in the High Street below the castle, dates from 1609, while the three-hundred-year-old **water mill** at the end of Mill Lane is still used commercially (July & Aug daily 11am–5pm; April–June, Sept & Oct closed Sat; £1.50; NT) – a decent place to eat lunch in its riverside garden. You could **stay** in the elegant old *Dollons House* (a non-smoking house), 10 Church St (☎01643/821 880; ④).

Porlock

The real enticement of **PORLOCK**, six miles west of Minehead, is its extraordinary position in a deep hollow, cupped on three sides by the hogbacked hills of Exmoor. Unfortunately the thatch-and-cob houses and dripping charm of the village's long main street have led to invasions of tourists, some of whom are also drawn by the place's literary links. According to Coleridge's own less than reliable testimony, it was a "man from Porlock" who broke the opium trance in which he was composing *Kubla Khan*, while the High Street's beamed *Ship Inn* prides itself on featuring prominently in the Exmoor romance *Lorna Doone* (see below), and in real life having sheltered the poet Robert Southey, who staggered in rain-soaked after an Exmoor ramble.

The best **accommodation** in town is on the High Street, where the *The Ship* (☎01643/862 507; ③) has plenty of atmosphere and the Victorian *Lorna Doone Hotel* offers rooms, all with private bath and TV (☎01643/862 404; ④). Further down, the *Cottage* is smaller and quainter (☎01643/862 687; ③). Both this and the *Lorna Doone* serve snacks, meals and teas.

WALKS FROM LYNTON AND LYNMOUTH

The major year-round attraction in these parts is walking, not only along the coast path but inland. The one-and-a-half-mile tramp to **Watersmeet**, for example, follows up the East Lyn river to where it is joined by Hoar Oak Water, a tranquil spot transformed into a roaring torrent after a bout of rain. From the fishing lodge here – now owned by the National Trust and open as a café and shop in summer – you can branch off on a range of less trodden paths, for instance three quarters of a mile south to **Hillsford Bridge**, the confluence of Hoar Oak and Farley Water.

North of Watersmeet, a path climbs up **Countisbury Hill** and the higher **Butter Hill** (nearly 1000ft), giving riveting views of Lynton, Lynmouth and the north Devon coast, and there is also a track leading to the lighthouse at **Foreland Point**, close to the coastal path. East from Lynmouth you can reach the point via a fine sheltered shingle beach at the foot of Countisbury Hill – one of a number of tiny coves, accessible on either side of the estuary.

From Lynton, an undemanding expedition takes you west along the North Walk, a mile-long path leading to the **Valley of the Rocks**, a steeply curved heathland dominated by rugged rock formations. At the far end of the valley, herds of wild goats range free, as they have done here for centuries.

If you walk two miles west over the reclaimed marshland, you'll come to the minute harbour of **PORLOCK WEIR**, which gives little inkling of its former role as a hard-working port trafficking with Wales. It's a peaceful spot, giving onto a bay that enjoys the mildest climate on Exmoor. An easy stroll from here would be a couple of miles west along the South West Way to **St Culbone**, a tiny church – claimed to be the country's smallest – sheltered within woods once inhabited by a leper colony.

Lynton and Lynmouth

West from Porlock, the road climbs 1350 feet in less than three miles, though there is a gentler and more scenic toll road alternative to the direct uphill trawl. Nine miles along the coast, on the Devon side of the county line, the Victorian resort of **LYNTON** perches above a lofty gorge with splendid views over the sea. Almost completely cut off from the rest of the country for most of its history, the village struck lucky during the Napoleonic Wars, when frustrated Grand Tourists – unable to visit their usual continental haunts – discovered in Lynton a domestic piece of Swiss landscape. Coleridge and Hazlitt trudged over to Lynton from the Quantocks, but the greatest spur to the village's popularity came with the publication in 1869 of R.D. Blackmore's Exmoor melodrama *Lorna Doone*, a book based on the outlaw clans who inhabited these parts in the seventeenth century. Since then the area has become indelibly associated with the swashbuckling romance. The imposing **Town Hall** on Lee Road epitomizes the Victorian-Edwardian accent of Lynton. It was the gift of publisher George Newnes, who also donated the nearby hydraulic cliff railway connecting Lynton with Lynmouth (Easter–Oct Mon–Sat 8am–1pm & 2–7pm; 50p).

Lynton's **tourist office** is in the town hall (Mon–Sat 10am–5pm; ☎01598/752 225). There's a good choice of inexpensive **B&Bs**, among them *Cranleigh House*, 36 Lee Rd (☎01598/752 249; ②), and the more central *St Vincent* on Castle Hill (☎01598/752 244; ③), a whitewashed, Georgian house with spacious bedrooms and a garden. The *Lynhurst Hotel*, Lyn Way (☎01598/752 241; ③), further out from the centre, enjoys striking views over the valley. There is a **youth hostel** (☎01598/753 237) about a mile inland from Lynton's centre, signposted off Lynbridge Road. **Snacks** and coffees are served at *The Old Bank Café* (closed Sun night & Feb) opposite St Mary's church.

Five hundred feet below Lynton, **LYNMOUTH** lies at the junction and estuary of the East and West Lyn rivers, in a spot described by Gainsborough as "the most delightful place for a landscape painter this country can boast". The picturesque scene was shattered in August 1952 when Lynmouth was almost washed away by floodwaters coming off Exmoor, a disaster of which there are many reminders around the village. Having recovered its calm, Lynmouth is ruffled now by the summer crowds, though nothing could compromise the village's unique location. Shelley spent his honeymoon here with his sixteen-year-old bride Harriet Westbrook, making time in his nine-week sojourn to write his polemical *Queen Mab* – two different houses claim to have been the Shelleys' love nest. R.D. Blackmore stayed in **Mars Hill**, the oldest part of the town, its creeper-covered cottages framing the cliffs behind the Esplanade.

Lynmouth has a **National Park Visitor Centre** at the harbour (April–Sept daily 9.30am–6.30pm; Oct closes 5.30pm; ☎01598/752 509). The most evocative place to stay is the **B&B** at 1 The Esplanade, right on the harbour (☎01598/752 321; ③). Next door is the *Rising Sun Hotel* (☎01598/753 223; ⑧), a fourteenth-century thatched inn. Other good choices are the posh *Bath Hotel*, Harbourside (☎01598/752 238; ⑤) and the *Orchard House Hotel*, 12 Watersmeet Rd (March–Oct; ☎01598/753 247; ③). *Prior's Cottage*, overlooking the river on Harbourside, does inexpensive **lunches**, though you'll find better fare at the *Rising Sun* and at the *Bath Hotel*, which charges a modest £16 for a five-course supper.

DEVON

With its rolling meadows, narrow lanes and remote thatched cottages, **Devon** has long been the urbanite's ideal vision of a pre-industrial, "authentic" England, and a quick tour of the county might suggest that this is largely a region of cosy, gentrified villages inhabited largely by retired folk and urban refugees. Certainly Devon suffers from an excess of cloying nostalgia, but its popularity has a positive side to it as well – chiefly that zealous care is taken to preserve the undeveloped stretches of countryside and coast in the condition that has made them so popular. Pockets of genuine tranquillity are still to be found all over the county, from Dartmoor villages with an appeal that goes deeper than mere picturesqueness, to quiet coves on the spectacular coastline.

Devon has played a leading part in England's **maritime history**, and reminders of the great names of Tudor and Stuart seafaring can be found in the two main towns of **Exeter** and **Plymouth**. These days the nautical tradition is perpetuated by yachtspeople taking advantage of Devon's numerous creeks and bays, especially on its southern coast. Land-bound tourists flock to the sandy beaches and seaside resorts, of which **Torquay** on the south coast and **Ilfracombe** on the north are the busiest, though the most attractive are those which have retained something of their nineteenth-century elegance, such as Sidmouth, Dartmouth and Salcombe. Other seaside villages retain a low level of fishing activity but otherwise live on a stilted Old World image, of which **Clovelly** is the supreme example. **Inland**, Devon is characterized by swards of lush pasture and a scattering of sheltered villages, the county's low population density dropping to almost zero on **Dartmoor**, the wildest and bleakest of the West's moors.

Exeter

EXETER's sights are richer than those of any other town in Devon or Cornwall, the legacy of an eventful history since its Celtic foundation and the establishment here of the most westerly Roman outpost. After the Roman withdrawal, Exeter was refounded by Alfred the Great and by the time of the Norman Conquest had become one of the largest towns in England, profiting from its position on the banks of the River Exe. The expansion of the wool trade in the Tudor period sustained the city until the eighteenth century, and Exeter has maintained its status as commercial centre and county town, despite having much of its ancient centre gutted by World War II bombing.

Arrival, information and accommodation

Exeter has two **train stations**, Exeter Central and St David's, respectively serving the London–Salisbury and the Bristol–Taunton lines. **Buses** stop at the station off Paris Street, right across from the **tourist office** (Mon–Fri 9am–5pm, Sat 9am–1pm & 2–5pm; ☎01392/265 700).

For real luxury **accommodation**, look no further than the *Rougemont Hotel*, Queen Street (☎01392/54982; ⑧), or the *The Royal Clarence Hotel*, Cathedral Yard (☎01392/58464; ⑨), built in 1769, and reputedly the first inn in England to be described as a "hotel." Period trappings for half the price can be had at *The White Hart*, 65 South St (☎01392/79897; ④), an old coaching inn in the centre, while Pre-Raphaelite etchings decorate the individually furnished *Raffles*, 11 Blackall Rd (☎01392/70200; ③). For conveniently located **B&Bs**, try the Georgian *Park View Hotel*, 8 Howell Rd (☎01392/71772; ③) for St David's; *Maurice*, 5 Bystock Terrace (☎01392/213 079; ②) for Central Station; and *The Edwardian*, 30 Heavitree Rd (☎01392/76102; ③) for the bus station.

The official **youth hostel**, 47 Countess Wear Rd (☎01392/873 329) lies two miles outside the city; take minibus #K or #T from High Street or South Street to Topsham Road, a 15-min ride, then walk for another 10min. Alternatively, the *University Halls of Residence*, Stoker Road (☎01392/211 500), offer accommodation at various sites around the city for £9.95 per person in single or double rooms (March, April & July–Sept).

The City

The most distinctive feature of Exeter's skyline, **St Peter's Cathedral** is a stately monument made conspicuous by the two great Norman towers flanking the nave. Close up, it is the facade's ornate Gothic screen that commands attention: its three tiers of sculpted figures – including Alfred, Athelstan, Canute, William the Conqueror and Richard II – were begun around 1360, part of a rebuilding programme which left only the Norman towers from the original construction. The cathedral boasts the longest unbroken **Gothic ceiling** in the world, its **bosses** vividly sculpted – one shows the murder of Thomas à Becket. The **Lady Chapel** and **Chapter House** – respectively at the far end of the building and off the right transept – are thirteenth-century, but the main part of the nave, including the lavish rib vaulting, are from the full flowering of the English Decorated style, a century later. There are many fine examples of sculpture from this period, including, in the minstrels' gallery on the left side, angels playing musical instruments and, below them, figures of Edward III and Queen Philippa. Dominating the cathedral's central space are the huge organ pipes installed in the seventeenth century, harmonizing perfectly with the linear patterns of the roof and arches. In the **choir** don't miss the sixty-foot **bishop's throne** or the **misericords** – decorated with mythological figures around 1260, among the oldest in the country.

Outside, a graceful statue of Richard Hooker, one of Exeter's early bishops, surveys the **Cathedral Close**, a motley mixture of architectural styles from Tudor to Regency, though most display Exeter's trademark red brickwork. One of the finest buildings is the Elizabethan **Mol's Coffee House**, impressively timbered and gabled. Some older buildings can also be found amid the banal concrete of the modern town centre, including Exeter's finest civic building, the fourteenth-century **Guildhall**. Standing not far from the cathedral on the pedestrianized High Street, it's fronted by an elegant Renaissance portico, and the main chamber merits a glance for its arched roof timbers, which rest on carved bears holding staves, symbols of the Yorkist cause during the Wars of the Roses. Just down from here, opposite **St Petrock's** – one of medieval Exeter's six surviving medieval churches in the central area – you'll find the impossibly narrow Parliament Street, just 25 inches wide at this end.

On the west side of Fore Street, the continuation of the High Street, a turning leads to **St Nicholas Priory** (Easter–Oct Mon–Sat 1–5pm; £1.25), part of a small Benedictine foundation that became a merchant's home after the Dissolution; the interior has been restored to what it might have looked like in the Tudor era. On the other side of Fore Street, trailing down towards the river, cobbled **Stepcote Hill** was once the main road into Exeter from the west, though it is difficult to imagine this steep and narrow lane as a main thoroughfare. Another of central Exeter's ancient churches, **St Mary Steps**, stands surrounded by mainly Tudor houses at the bottom, with a fine seventeenth-century clock on its tower and a late Gothic nave inside.

Exeter's centre is bound to the southwest by the River Exe, where the port area is now mostly devoted to leisure activities, particularly around the old **Quayside**. Pubs, shops and cafés share the space with handsomely restored nineteenth-century warehouses and the smart **Custom House**, built in 1681, its opulence reflecting the former importance of the cloth trade. Next door, the Quay House from the same period has an information desk and, upstairs, a video on Exeter's history (Easter–Oct). You can cross

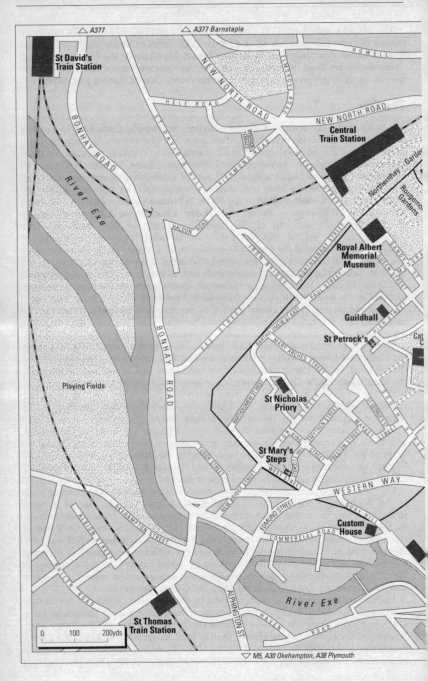

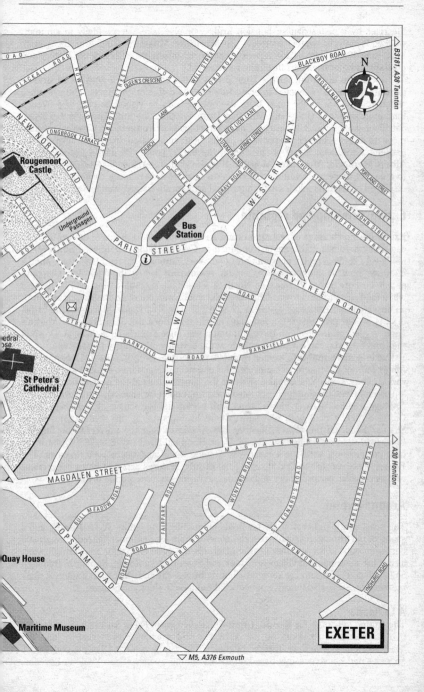

EXETER

the river by a pedestrian suspension bridge, or else take a ferry (daily in summer, weekends only in winter) to reach the **Maritime Museum** (July–Aug 10am–6pm; Sept–June 10am–5pm; £4.25), a partly waterborne ensemble reflecting the history and diversity of water transport throughout the world.

Back at the north end of the High Street is the entrance to a network of **underground passages** excavated to bring water to the cathedral precincts. The passages, which resemble a public toilet from the outside, can be visited as part of a twenty-minute guided tour (July–Sept Mon–Sat 10am–5.30pm; Oct–June Tues–Fri 2–5.30pm, Sat 10am–5.30pm; £2.25). Nearby, Castle Street leads to **Rougemont Castle**, now little more than a perimeter of red-stone walls best appreciated from the surrounding gardens. On Queen Street at the end of the parks, you could drop in at the **Royal Albert Memorial Museum** (Mon–Sat 10am–5.30pm; free), the closest thing in Devon to a county museum. Exuding the Victorian spirit of wide-ranging curiosity, this well-displayed collection includes a distinguished array of silverware, watches and clocks.

Eating, drinking and nightlife

Exeter has no shortage of restaurants and pubs within a short radius of the centre. You can enjoy a substantial breakfast or lunch at *Coolings Wine Bar* (closed Sun eve) in medieval Gandy Street. For a touch of Old World atmosphere try *Mad Meg's*, once a nunnery, now an inexpensive basement **restaurant** below the Pickwick shopping arcade on Fore Street. *Herbie's*, 15 North St (closed all-day Sun & Mon eve) is the only wholefood restaurant in town. Alluring garlic smells waft out of *La Rosina* (closed Sun), an unpretentious trattoria-pizzeria at 27 South St. The *Well House*, in front of the cathedral, is an old **pub** offering good-value lunches, as does the *Ship Inn* in St Martin's Lane – and it prides itself on the claim that it was once Francis Drake's local. Down at the Quayside, you can eat sitting outside at the seventeenth-century *Prospect Inn*.

Exeter's main **nightlife** venue is the **Arts Centre** (☎01392/421 111) behind the Albert Memorial Museum, staging regular non-mainstream films, exhibitions, gigs and various workshops. You can also soak up the latest sounds at the nearby *Cavern Club*, in Queen Street, off Gandy Street (also open from noon for snacks), the *St Anne's Well Brewery*, a pub on Lower North Street with occasional live music, at *Timepiece*, Little Castle Street, a club with alternative/indie leanings, or at the students' union on Stocker Road. Of the town's theatres, the *Northcott*, near the university on Stocker Road (☎01392/54853), and the *Barnfield*, on Barnfield Road (☎01392/70891), have the best productions, with the former also staging ballet and opera performances. The **Exeter Festival**, in the first three weeks of July, features jazz and blues concerts as well as classical performances and cabaret, at various venues around town.

Around Exeter

The coast south and east of Exeter holds an architectural oddity, **A La Ronde**, and a string of old-fashioned seaside resorts, none of them over-commercialized, though still best seen outside the summer peak. **Sidmouth** is a good choice for an overnight stop, as are the neighbouring villages of **Beer** and **Seaton**. A La Ronde, Exmouth, Budleigh Salterton and Sidmouth are served by hourly **buses** #57 and #X57 from Exeter. A mini-bus service, #899, also hourly, connects Sidmouth with Beer and Seaton.

A La Ronde

The Gothic folly of **A La Ronde**, (April–Oct daily except Fri & Sat 11am–5.30pm; £3), two miles outside Exmouth off the A376, was the creation of two cousins, Jane and Mary Parminter, who were inspired by their 1790s European Grand Tour to construct a sixteen-sided house possibly based on the Byzantine basilica of San Vitale in Ravenna.

The end product is filled with mementos of the Parminters' tour as well as a number of their more offbeat creations, such as a frieze made of feathers culled from game birds and chickens. In the upper rooms is a gallery and staircase completely covered in shells, too fragile to be visited, though part of it can be glimpsed from the completely enclosed octagonal room on the first floor – a closed-circuit TV system enables visitors to home in on details. The women intended that the house should be inherited only by female descendants, though the conditions of Mary Parminter's will (she died in 1849) were broken at the end of the nineteenth century when the building was inherited by the Reverend Oswald Reichel. Reichel added the dormer windows on the second floor, which give out superb views over the Exe Estuary to Haldon Hill, and Dawlish Warren.

Exmouth and Budleigh Salterton

EXMOUTH started as a Roman port and went on to become the first of the county's resorts to be popularized by holidaymakers in the late eighteenth century. Overlooking lawns, rock pools and a respectable two miles of beach, Exmouth's Georgian terraces once accommodated such folk as the wives of Nelson and Byron – installed at nos. 6 and 19 The Beacon respectively. The town's unhurried air contrasts sharply with the cranes and warehouses of the docks beyond the Esplanade. The best place to **stay** in terms of location is *The Manor Hotel*, The Beacon (☎ 01395/274 477; ⑤).

Four miles to the east, bounded on each side by red sandstone cliffs, **BUDLEIGH SALTERTON** continues the genteel theme – its thatched and whitewashed cottages attracted such figures as Noël Coward and P.G. Wodehouse, and John Millais painted his famous *Boyhood of Raleigh* on the shingle beach here. (Sir Walter Raleigh was born in East Budleigh, a couple of miles inland.) Three miles east, Ladram Bay is a popular pebbly beach sheltered by woods and beautiful eroded cliffs. If you want to stay in the area, contact the **tourist office** on Fore Street (June & Sept Mon–Sat 10am–5pm; July & Aug daily 10am–5pm; reduced opening hours in winter; ☎01395/445 275).

Sidmouth

Set amidst a shelf of crumbling red sandstone, cream-and-white **SIDMOUTH** is the chief resort on this stretch of coast and boasts nearly five hundred buildings listed as having special historic or architectural interest, among them the stately Georgian homes of **York Terrace** behind the Esplanade. Moreover, the **beaches** are better tended than many along this coast, not only the mile-long main town beach but also Jacob's Ladder, a cliff-backed shingle and sand strip beyond Connaught Gardens to the west of town. To the east, the South Devon Coast Path (part of the South West Way) climbs steep Salcombe Hill to follow cliffs that give sanctuary to a range of birdlife including yellowhammers and green woodpeckers, as well as the rarer grasshopper warbler. Further on, the path descends to meet one of the most isolated and attractive beaches in the area, **Weston Mouth**.

The **tourist office** is on Ham Lane, off the eastern end of the Esplanade (Easter–Oct daily 10am–5pm; Nov–Easter Mon–Sat 10am–1pm; ☎01395/516 441). Of the **B&Bs**, *Ferndale*, 92 Winslade Rd (March–Oct; ☎01395/515 495; ②), a Victorian house a mile from the sea, is one of the cheapest; closer to the seafront, there's *The Old Farmhouse*, on Hillside Road (Feb–Nov; ☎01395/512 284; ④). There's more choice in the string of guest houses along Salcombe Road, including 1 Salcombe Villas (☎01395/577 222; ③). For **snacks** in town, *Osborne's* on Fore Street offers light meals, while two hundred yards from the seafront, on Old Fore Street, the *Old Ship* and *Anchor* **pubs** provide excellent bar meals and suppers as well as a good range of ales.

Beer and Seaton

Eight miles east along the coast, the fishing village of **BEER** lies huddled within a small sheltered cove between gleaming white headlands. A stream rushes along a deep channel dug into Beer's main street, and if you can ignore the crowds in high summer much of the village looks unchanged since the times when it was a smugglers' eyrie, its inlets used by such characters as Jack Rattenbury, who published his *Memoirs of a Smuggler* in 1837. The village is best known for its quarries, which were worked from Roman times until the last century: **Beer Stone** was used in many of Devon's churches and houses. *Bay View* (☎01297/20489; ②), overlooking the sea on Fore Street, is easily the best of the **B&Bs**, and Beer's **youth hostel** is on a hillside half a mile northwest, at Bovey Combe, Townsend (☎01297/20296).

SEATON, a smooth stroll less than a mile eastwards, has a steep, pebbly beach like Beer's, but this is a much more developed resort, mutating from a placid, slow-moving haven at its western end to a much gaudier affair to the east. One of the main attractions is the open-top **tramway** which follows the path of the old railway line to the inland village of Colyton. Seaton's **tourist office** is on the Esplanade (April–Oct 9am–5pm, closed Thurs & Sun afternoons; Nov–March daily 9am–1pm; ☎01297/21660). On Trevelyan Road, at the eastern end of the Esplanade, you'll find *Beach End* (☎01297/23388; ③), a bright and roomy Edwardian **B&B** or, just across from the tourist office, *Beaumont* on Castle Hill (☎01297/20832; ③), on the west side – both have sea views.

The "English Riviera" region

The wedge of land between Dartmoor and the sea contains some of Devon's most fertile pastures, backing onto some of the country's most popular coastal resorts. Chief of these is **Torbay**, an amalgam of **Torquay**, **Paignton** and **Brixham**, together forming the nucleus of an area optimistically known as "**The English Riviera**". To the south the port of **Dartmouth** offers another calmer alternative, linked by riverboat to historic and almost unspoilt **Totnes**.

Torquay

The coast is heavily urbanized around **Torbay**, a tourist conglomeration entirely dedicated to the exploitation of the bay's sheltered climate and exuberant vegetation. **TORQUAY**, the largest component of this super-resort, comes closest to living up to the self-penned "English Riviera" sobriquet, sporting a mini-corniche and promenades landscaped with flowerbeds. The much vaunted palm trees (actually New Zealand cabbage trees) and the coloured lights that festoon the harbour by night contribute to the town's unique flavour, a slightly frayed combination of the exotic and the classically English. Torquay's transformation from a fishing village began with its establishment as a fashionable haven for invalids, among them the consumptive Elizabeth Barrett Browning, who spent three years here. In recent years the most famous figures previously associated with Torquay – crime writer Agatha Christie and traveller Freya Stark – have given way to the fictional TV hotelier Basil Fawlty, whose jingoism and injured pride perfectly encapsulate the town's adaptation to the demands of mass tourism.

The town is focused on the small **harbour** and marina, where the mingling crowds can seem almost Mediterranean, especially at night. To one side stands the copper-domed **Pavilion**, an Edwardian building that originally housed a ballroom and assembly hall, now refurbished with shops. Behind the Pavilion, limestone cliffs sprouting white high-rise hotels and apartment blocks separate the harbour area from Torquay's main beach, **Abbey Sands**. If this gets too crowded, follow the pretty half-mile coastal walk north through Daddyhole Plain, a large chasm in the cliff caused by a landslide locally attributed to the devil ("Daddy"). The path descends to meet the seawall at **Meadfoot Beach**, where boats and pedalos can be hired. If you're searching for something a little more low-key, continue round the point to where a string of beaches extends as far as the cliff-backed coves of **Watcombe** and **Maidencombe**.

The **train station** is off Rathmore Road, next to the Torre Abbey gardens; most **buses** leave from outside the Pavilion. Torquay's **tourist office** is in the Pavilion (July–Sept daily 9am–5pm; Oct–June closed Sun; ☎01803/297 428). There's plenty of **accommodation** in Torquay: try *Claver Guest House*, 119 Abbey Rd (☎01803/297 118; ②), or the *Chesterfield Hotel*, 62 Belgrave Rd (☎01803/292 318; ③), close to the train station and the marina. Behind the station, on Old Mill Road, the Victorian *Torbay Rise* (☎01803/605 541; ③) stands on a hill overlooking the harbour. There is a surprisingly high standard of cuisine in Torquay's **restaurants**, one of the best being the *Mulberry Room*, 1 Scarborough Rd (☎01803/213 639), where the menu is colour-coded according to its cholesterol content. The earthier *Jingles*, 34 Torwood St, offers low-priced Tex-Mex meals, and you can find an amazingly eclectic range of dishes at the otherwise traditional *Hole in the Wall* **pub** at 6 Park Lane.

Paignton

Not so much a rival to Torquay as its complement, **PAIGNTON** lacks the gloss of its neighbour, but also its pretensions. Activity is concentrated at the southern end of the wide town beach, around the small harbour that nestles in the lee of the appropriately named Redcliffe headland. Otherwise diversion-seekers could wander over to **Paignton Zoo** (summer daily 10am–6pm; winter closes 5pm; £5.50), a mile out on Totnes Road, or board the **Torbay Steam Railway** (June–Sept daily; April, May, Oct & Dec less frequent), which connects with Paignton's other main beach – **Goodrington Sands** – before trundling alongside the Dart estuary to Kingswear, seven miles away. You could make a day of it by taking the ferry from Kingswear to Dartmouth, then a river-boat up the Dart to Totnes, and finally a bus back to Paignton.

Paignton's bus and train stations are next to each other off Sands Road. Five minutes away, the seafront has a **tourist office** (summer daily 9am–5.15pm, June & Sept closes 6pm, July & Aug closes 7pm; winter closed Sun; ☎01803/558 383). If you need a place to **stay**, you could do worse than *St Weonard's Hotel*, 12 Kernou Rd (☎01803/558 842; ③), a hundred yards from the seafront. The harbour area has a few **pubs** and **restaurants**, including the inexpensive *Harbour Light* and the nearby *Pier Inn*.

Brixham

From Paignton, it's a fifteen-minute bus ride down to **BRIXHAM**, the prettiest of the Torbay towns. Fishing was for centuries Brixham's lifeblood and it still supplies fish to restaurants as far away as Bristol. Among the trawlers on Brixham's quayside is moored a full-size reconstruction of the **Golden Hind**, the surprisingly small vessel in which Francis Drake circumnavigated the world. The harbour is overlooked by an unflattering statue of William III, a reminder of his landing in Brixham to claim the crown of England in 1688. From here, steep lanes and stairways thread up to the older centre around Fore Street, where the bus from Torquay pulls in. From the harbour, you can reach the promontory of **Berry Head** along a path winding up from the *Berry Head House Hotel*. Fortifications built during the Napoleonic War are still standing on this southern limit of Torbay, which is now a conservation area, attracting colonies of nesting seabirds and affording fabulous views.

The town's **tourist office** (Mon, Fri & Sun 10am–5pm, Tues–Thurs & Sat 9am–5.15pm; ☎01803/852 861) is on the quayside, next to William's statue. **Accommodation** includes two B&Bs on King Street, overlooking the harbour: *Sampford House* at no. 59 (☎01803/857 761; ③) and the *Harbour View Hotel*, at no. 65

(☎01803/853 052; ③), the latter a former harbour master's house. Behind the quay-side, at 11 Prospect Rd, the *Brioc Hotel* (☎01803/853 540; ②) also offers good value. The nearest **youth hostel** (☎01803/842 444) is four miles away, one and a half miles from Churston Bridge (bus #106 or #100), or one stop on the *Paignton & Dartmouth Steam Railway* (April–Oct & part of Dec). Brixham offers fish and more fish, from the takeaway shops on the harbourside to the moderately priced *Poopdeck* **restaurant** at 14 The Quay, above the *Harbourside Bookshop*. For a relaxed pint, try the *Blue Anchor* on Fore Street, with coal fires and low beams.

Totnes

Most of the Plymouth buses from Paignton and Torquay make a stop at **TOTNES**, on the west bank of the River Dart. The town has an ancient pedigree, its period of great-est prosperity occurring in the sixteenth century when this inland port exported cloth to France and brought back wine. Some handsome structures from that era remain, and there is still a working port down on the river, but these days Totnes has mellowed into a residential market town, enjoying an esoteric fame as a centre of the book trade and even attracting a New Age arts-and-crafts crowd.

The town centres on the long main street that starts off as Fore Street, site of the town's **Museum** (April–Oct Mon–Fri 10.30am–5pm, July & Aug also Sat 11am–3pm; £1), which occupies a four-storey Elizabethan house at no. 70. Showing how wealthy clothiers lived at the peak of the town's success, it is packed with domestic objects and furniture, and also has a room devoted to local mathematician Charles Babbage (1791–1871), whose "analytical engine" was the forerunner of the computer. Fore Street becomes the **High Street** at the East Gate, a much retouched medieval arch. Beneath it, Rampart Walk trails off along the old city walls, curling round the fifteenth-century church of **St Mary's**. Inside, an exquisitely carved rood screen stretches across the full width of the red sandstone building. Behind the church, the

---

FRANCIS DRAKE

Born around 1540 near Tavistock, **Francis Drake** worked in the domestic coastal trade from the age of thirteen, but was soon taking part in the first English slaving expeditions between Africa and the West Indies, led by his Plymouth kinsman John Hawkins. Later Drake was active in the secret war against Spain, raiding and looting merchant ships in actions unofficially sanctioned by Elizabeth I. In 1572 he became the first Englishman to sight the Pacific, and soon afterwards, on board the Golden Hind, became the first one to **circumnavigate the world**, for which he received a knighthood on his return in 1580. The following year Drake was made mayor of Plymouth, settling in Buckland Abbey (see p.290), but was back in action before long – in 1587 he "singed the king of Spain's beard" by entering Cadiz harbour and destroying 33 vessels that were to have formed part of Philip II's **armada**. When the replacement invasion fleet appeared in the English Channel in 1588, Drake – along with Raleigh, Hawkins and Frobisher – played a leading role in wrecking it. The following year he set off on an unsuccessful expedition to help the Portuguese against Spain, but otherwise most of the next decade was spent in rela-tive inactivity in Plymouth, Exeter and London. Finally, in 1596 Drake left with Hawkins on a raid on Panama, a venture that cost the lives of both captains.

Drake has come to personify the Elizabethan age's swashbuckling expansionism and patriotism, but England's naval triumphs were as much the consequence of John Hawkins' humbler work in building and maintaining a new generation of warships as they were of the skill and bravery of their captains. Drake was simply the most flamboy-ant of a generation of reckless and brilliant mariners who broke the Spanish hegemony on the high seas, laying the foundations for England's later imperialist policies.

eleventh-century **Guildhall** (Easter–Oct Mon–Fri 10am–1pm & 2–5pm; 60p) was originally the refectory and kitchen of a Benedictine priory. Granted to the city corporation in 1553, the building still houses the town's council chamber, which you can see together with the former jail cells and courtroom.

Totnes Castle (April–Sept daily 10am–6pm; Oct daily 10am–4pm; Nov–March Wed–Sun 10am–4pm; £1.50; EH) on Castle Street – leading off the High Street – is a classic Norman structure of the motte and bailey design, its simple crenellated keep atop a grassy mound offering wide views of the town and Dart valley. Totnes assumes a much livelier air at the bottom of Fore Street, at river level. This is the highest navigable point on the **River Dart** for sea-going vessels, and there is constant activity around the ships coming in from and leaving for European destinations. More locally, there are also cruises to Dartmouth between Easter and October and near the railway bridge you can board a steam train of the **South Devon Railway** on its run along the course of the Dart to Buckfastleigh, adjacent to Buckfast Abbey (see p.293).

Totnes' **tourist office** is on The Plains, at the bottom of Fore Street (summer daily 9.30am–5pm; winter closed Sun; ☎01803/863 168). There are a couple of basic **B&Bs** at 2 Antrim Terrace (☎01803/862 638; ③) and 1 Castle View Terrace (☎01803/862 555; ②), both below the castle, and both for non-smokers, or you could pamper yourself at *The Old Forge* in Seymour Place (☎01803/862174; ④). The **youth hostel** (☎01803/862 303), in a sixteenth-century cottage, lies next to the River Bidwell two miles from Totnes and half a mile from Shinner's Bridge (bus #X80). *Willow*, 87 High St, is an inexpensive vegetarian **restaurant**, while the *Elbow Room*, a two-hundred-year-old converted cottage and cider press on North Street, serves inexpensive meals and also does B&B (☎01803/863 480; ④). There are also several decent **pubs**: the *Bull Inn*, at the top of the High Street, or the riverside *Steampacket*, on St Peter's Quay.

Dartmouth

South of Torbay, and eight miles downstream from Totnes, **DARTMOUTH** has thrived since the Normans recognized the potential of this deepwater port for trading with their home country, and today its activities embrace fishing, freight and a booming leisure industry – as well as the education of senior service's officer class at the Royal Naval College, built on a hill overlooking the port at the start of this century.

Behind the enclosed boat basin at the heart of town stands Dartmouth's most photographed building, the four-storey **Butterwalk**, built in the seventeenth century for a local merchant. Richly decorated with woodcarvings, it overhangs the street on eleven granite columns, forming an arcade now holding shops and Dartmouth's small **Museum** (Mon–Sat April–Oct 11am–5pm; Nov–March 1.15–4pm; £1), mainly devoted to maritime curios, including old maps, prints and models of ships. Nearby **St Saviour's**, rebuilt in the 1630s from a fourteenth-century church, has long been a landmark for boats sailing upriver. The building stands at the head of Higher Street, the old town's central thoroughfare and the site of another tottering medieval structure, *The Cherub* inn. More impressive is **Agincourt House** on the parallel Lower Street, built by a merchant after the battle for which it is named.

Lower Street leads down to **Bayard's Cove**, a short cobbled quay lined with well-restored eighteenth-century houses, where the Pilgrim Fathers touched en route to the New World. A twenty-minute walk from here along the river takes you to **Dartmouth Castle** (April–Sept daily 10am–6pm; Oct daily 10am–4pm; Nov–March Wed–Sun 10am–4pm; £2; EH), one of two fortifications on opposite sides of the estuary. The site includes coastal defence works from the last century and from World War II, though the main interest is in the fifteenth-century castle, the first in England to be constructed specifically to withstand artillery. The castle was never actually tested in action, and consequently is excellently preserved. If you don't relish the return walk, you can take advantage of a ferry back to town (April–Sept every 15min).

Continuing south along the coastal path brings you through the pretty hilltop village of **Stoke Fleming** to **Blackpool Sands** (45min from the castle), the best beach in the area. The unspoilt cove, flanked by steep, wooded cliffs, was the site of a battle in 1404 in which Devon archers repulsed a Breton invasion force sent to punish the privateers of Dartmouth for their raiding across the Channel. Summer cruises depart from Dartmouth's quay up the River Dart to Totnes; this is the best way to see the river's deep creeks and the various houses overlooking the river, among them the **Royal Naval College** and **Greenway House**, birthplace of Walter Raleigh's three seafaring half-brothers, the Gilberts, and later rebuilt for Agatha Christie.

Dartmouth's **tourist office** is on Mayor's Avenue (April–Sept Mon–Sat 9am–5pm, Sun 10am–4pm; Oct–March Mon–Sat 10am–4.30pm; ☎01803/834 224). The hilltop **accommodation** choices at least have views: try 6 Combe Close (☎01803/834 180; ②), off Clarence Hill, or *Oaklands* at 6 Vicarage Hill (☎01803/833 274; ③). There is more character at *The Captain's House*, 18 Clarence St (☎01803/832 133; ③), but Dartmouth's best is *The Royal Castle Hotel* (☎01803/833 033; ⑧), right on the central quay, converted from two seventeenth-century merchants' houses. Dartmouth has a good range of **restaurants** like *Bayard's* at 25 Lower St (☎01803/833 523), serving moderately priced fish and vegetarian dishes, or *Cutter's Bunch*, a more upmarket French bistro a few doors down at no. 33 (☎01803/832 882). *Billy Budd's*, 7 Foss St (Tues–Sat; ☎01803/834 842), is another candlelit bistro that excels in seafood dishes and homemade ice cream.

Plymouth

PLYMOUTH's predominantly bland and modern face belies its great historic role as a naval base, when it enjoyed the patronage of such national heroes as John Hawkins and Francis Drake. It was from here that the latter sailed to defeat the Spanish Armada in 1588, and 32 years later the port was the last embarkation point for the Pilgrim Fathers, whose New Plymouth colony became the nucleus for the English settlement of North America. The sustained prominence of the city's Devonport dockyards as a shipbuilding and military base made it a target in World War II, when the Luftwaffe reduced much of the old centre to rubble. Subsequent reconstruction has done nothing to enhance the place. That said, it would be difficult to spoil the glorious vista over **Plymouth Sound**, the basin of calm water at the mouth of the combined Plym, Tavy and Tamar estuaries, which has remained largely unchanged since Drake played his famous game of bowls on the Hoe before joining battle with the Armada.

The Town

A good place to start a tour of the town is **Plymouth Hoe**, an immense esplanade studded with reminders of the great events in the city's history. Resplendent in fair weather, with glorious views over to sea, the Hoe can also attract some pretty ferocious winds, making it well-nigh impossible to explore in wintry conditions. Approaching from the Civic Centre – the hub of the town centre – the most distinctive landmark is a tall white naval war memorial, standing alongside smaller monuments to the defeat of the Spanish Armada and to the airmen who defended the city during the wartime blitz, and a rather portly statue of Sir Francis Drake, gazing grandly out to the sea. Appropriately, there's a bowling green back from the brow.

In front of the memorials the red-and-white-striped **Smeaton's Tower** (Easter–Oct 10.30am–5pm; 80p) was erected in 1759 by John Smeaton on the treacherous

Eddystone Rocks, fourteen miles out to sea. When replaced by a larger lighthouse in 1882, it was reassembled here, where it gives the loftiest view over Plymouth Sound. Below Smeaton's Tower is the **Plymouth Dome** leisure complex (daily winter 9am–sunset; summer 9am–7.30pm; £3.50, combined Dome and Tower ticket £4.05), which includes tricksy audio-visual exhibitions of Plymouth's history and the lives of local heroes such as Drake, the Mayflower Pilgrims and Captain Cook. On the seafront, Plymouth's workaday **Aquarium** (daily April–Oct 10am–6pm; Nov–March 10am–5pm; £2) stands in front of the uncompromising **Royal Citadel**, constructed in 1666 to intimidate the populace of the only town in the southwest to be held by the Parliamentarians in the Civil War. Though still used by the military, there are guided tours through some of its older parts, including the seventeenth-century Governor's House and the Royal Chapel of St Katherine (tours May–Sept 11.30am & 2pm; £2.50); tickets are available from the Plymouth Dome or the tourist office.

Round the corner is **Sutton Harbour**, the old town's quay, still used by the trawler fleet and scene of a boisterous early-morning fish market. The **Mayflower Steps** here commemorate the sailing of the Pilgrim Fathers and a nearby plaque lists the names and professions of the 102 Puritans on board. All three of Captain Cook's voyages to the South Seas, Australia and the Antarctic also started from here, as did the nineteenth-century transport ships to Australia, carrying thousands of convicts and colonists. The **Barbican** district, which edges the harbour, is the heart of old Plymouth. Most of the buildings are now shops and restaurants, but off the quayside, New Street holds most of the oldest buildings, among them the **Elizabethan House** (April–Oct Wed–Sun 10am–5pm), a captain's dwelling with a lovely old pole staircase.

On the edge of the district, the mainly seventeenth-century **Merchant's House Museum** at 33 St Andrew St (Easter–Sept Mon–Fri 10am–1pm & 2–5.30pm, Sat 10am–1pm & 2–5pm; £1.05) goes into various aspects of Plymouth's history. Opposite stands the city's chief place of worship, **St Andrew's**, a reconstruction of a fifteenth-century building that was almost completely gutted by a bomb in 1941. The entrails of the navigator Martin Frobisher are buried here, as are those of Admiral Blake, the Parliamentarian who died as his ship entered Plymouth after destroying a Spanish treasure fleet off Tenerife.

Practicalities

Plymouth's **train station** is off Saltash Road, from where bus #30 or #43 leaves every ten or fifteen minutes for the central Royal Parade. The **bus station** is just over St Andrew's Cross from the Royal Parade, at Bretonside. The **tourist office** (summer Mon–Sat 9am–5pm, Sun 10am–4pm; winter Mon–Fri 9am–5pm, Sat 10am–4pm; ☎01752/264 849) is off Sutton Harbour at 9 The Barbican.

Most of the city's **accommodation** is immediately south of here, on or around the long Citadel Road: try *The Lawns* at no. 171 (☎01752/229 474; ②), or *Avalon* at no. 167 (☎01752/668 127; ②). On the other side of the Hoe, the *Osmond Guest House*, 42 Pier St (☎01752/229 705; ②), is close to the seafront, and offers a pick-up service from the train station. The *Bowling Green Hotel* overlooks Francis Drake's fabled haunt on Plymouth Hoe, at 9–10 Osborne Place, Lockyer St (☎01752/667 485; ③). If everywhere central is booked up, try *Phantele* (☎01752/561 506; ②), a budget choice at 176 Devonport Rd, on the west side of town. Plymouth's **youth hostel** (☎01752/562 189) is also on this road, at Belmont House – a short walk from Devonport train station, or bus ride from the centre (*Citybus* #33A or #34A, or *Western National* #15A , #14A or #81).

Most of Plymouth's good **restaurants** are located in and around the Barbican area. One of the most interesting is the moderately priced *Sima Sina* at 54 Notte St, specializing in Greek and Middle Eastern cuisine; three doors down is the popular *Eastern Eye* Indian restaurant. Nearby Southside Street harbours the *Barbican Pasta Bar* and the *Piermaster's*, which serves fresh fish landed at the nearby harbour (closed Sun). *Plymouth Arts Centre*, 38 Looe St, also has a self-service vegetarian restaurant until 8pm, though the major reason for coming here is to see its film and live performances. The *Dolphin* pub on Southside Street, a landmark in the Barbican, is crowded with fishermen in the morning and boisterous boozers at night. On the other side of town, the *Brown Bear* on Chapel Street is a traditional beamed pub in the Devonport dock district, patronized by beer and food aficionados.

Around Plymouth

Best of the local day excursions are to **Mount Edgcumbe**, where woods and meadows provide a welcome antidote to the urban bustle, and are within easy reach of some fabulous sand. East of Plymouth, the aristocratic opulence of **Saltram House** includes some fine art and furniture, while to the north of town you can visit Drake's old residence at **Buckland Abbey**.

Mount Edgcumbe

Lying on the Cornish side of Plymouth Sound and visible from the Hoe, **Mount Edgcumbe** features a Tudor house, landscaped gardens and acres of rolling parkland and coastal paths. The **house** (April–Oct Wed–Sun 11am–5pm; £3.60) is a reconstruction of the bomb-damaged Tudor original, though inside the predominant note is eighteenth-century, the rooms elegantly restored with authentic Regency furniture. The highlight, though, is the **grounds**, including impeccable gardens divided into French, Italian and English sections – the first two a blaze of flowerbeds adorned with classical statuary, the last an acre of sweeping lawn shaded by exotic trees. You can reach the house by the passenger **ferry** to Cremyll, leaving at least hourly from Admiral's Hard (bus #34 from the Guildhall); in summer there's also a direct motor launch between the Mayflower Steps and the village of **Cawsand**, an old smugglers' haunt two hours' walk from the house. Cawsand itself is just a mile from the southern tip of the huge **Whitsand Bay**, the best bathing beach for miles around.

Saltram House

The remodelled Tudor mansion **Saltram House** (April–Sept Mon–Thurs & Sun 12.30pm–5.30pm; £5; NT), two miles east of Plymouth off the A38, is Devon's largest country house, featuring work by the great architect Robert Adam and fourteen portraits by **Joshua Reynolds**, who was born in the nearby village of Plympton. Showpiece is the Saloon, a fussy but exquisitely furnished room dripping with gilt and plaster, and set off by a huge Axminster carpet especially woven for it in 1770. Saltram's landscaped park provides a breather from this riot of interior design, though it is marred by the proximity of the road. You can get here on the hourly #22 bus from Royal Parade to Cott Hill, from where it's a ten-minute signposted walk.

Buckland Abbey

Six miles north of Plymouth, close to the River Tavy and on the edge of Dartmoor, stands **Buckland Abbey** (April–Oct daily except Thurs 10.30am–5.30pm; Nov–March Sat & Sun 2–5pm; house & grounds £4, grounds only £2; NT), once the most westerly of England's Cistercian abbeys. After its dissolution Buckland was converted to a private home by the privateer Richard Grenville (cousin of Walter Raleigh), from whom the estate was acquired by Sir Francis Drake in 1582, the year he became mayor of Plymouth. It remained his home until his death, though the house reveals few traces of Drake's residence. There are, however, numerous maps, portraits and mementos of his buccaneering exploits on show, most famous of which is Drake's Drum, which was said to beat a supernatural warning of impending danger to the country. The house stands in majestic grounds which contain a fine fourteenth-century **Great Barn**, buttressed and gabled and larger than the abbey itself. To get to the abbey, take the #83, #X83 or #84 bus to Tavistock, changing at Yelverton to the #55 minibus.

Dartmoor

Occupying the main part of the county between Exeter and Plymouth, **DARTMOOR** is southern England's greatest expanse of wilderness, some 365 square miles of raw granite, barren bogland, sparse grass and heather-grown moor. It was not always so desolate, as testified by the remnants of scattered Stone Age settlements and the ruined relics of the area's nineteenth-century tin-mining industry. Today desultory flocks of sheep and groups of ponies are virtually the only living creatures to be seen wandering over the central fastnesses of the National Park, with solitary birds – buzzards, kestrels, pipits, stonechats and wagtails – wheeling and hovering high above.

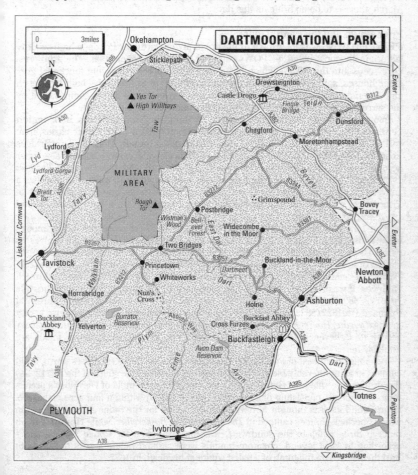

The core of Dartmoor, characterized by tumbling streams and high tors chiselled by the elements, is **Dartmoor Forest**, which has belonged to the Duchy of Cornwall since 1307, though there is almost unlimited public access. Camping is permitted out of sight of houses and roads, but fires are strictly forbidden. Though networks of sign-posts or painted stones do exist to guide **walkers**, map-reading abilities are a prerequisite for any but the shortest walks, and a good deal of experience is essential for longer distances. Information on walks and on pony-trekking centres can be found at the National Park Visitor Centres in Dartmoor's major towns and villages, and from information points in smaller villages.

Much to the irritation of locals and visitors alike, the **Ministry of Defence** has appropriated a significant portion of northern Dartmoor, an area that contains Dartmoor's highest tors and some of its most famous beauty spots. The MoD firing ranges are marked by red and white posts; when firing is in progress, red flags or red lights signify that entry is prohibited. As a general rule, you can assume that if no warning flags are flying by 9am between April and September, or by 10am from October to March, there is to be no firing on that day.

Princetown and the central moor

PRINCETOWN owes its growth to the proximity of Dartmoor Prison, a high-security jail originally constructed for POWs captured in the Napoleonic War. The grim presence seeps into the village, which has a somewhat oppressed air and functional grey stone houses, some of them – like the parish church of St Michael – built by French and American prisoners. What Princetown lacks in beauty is amply compensated by the surrounding country, the best of which lies immediately to the north.

Information on all of Dartmoor is given by the main **National Park information centre**, on the village's central green (daily summer 10am–5pm, winter closes 4pm; ☎01822/890 414). The best place to stay is *Lamorna*, a friendly **B&B** on Two Bridges Road (☎01822/890 360; ②). Two pubs in Princetown's central square also offer accommodation, the *Devil's Elbow* (☎0822/890 232; ②) and the *Plume of Feathers* (☎0822/890 240; ③), which claims to be the oldest building in town, and also has a convenient **campsite** and staple bar food. At Rundlestone, one mile northwest of Princetown, a row of miners' houses has been converted into a basic **youth hostel** (☎01822/890 433).

Four miles northeast of Princetown, the largest and best preserved of Dartmoor's **clapper bridges** crosses the East Dart river at **POSTBRIDGE**, to which it gives its name. Used by tin-miners and farmers since medieval times, these simple structures consist of huge slabs of granite supported by piers of the same material. Walkers from Postbridge can explore up and down the river, or press further south through **Bellever Forest**, on the edge of which lies one of Dartmoor's two **youth hostels** (☎01822/88227). There's also a YHA camping barn close to Bellever Forest at Runnage (☎01822/88222); farmhouse breakfasts are available. You'll find more luxury in the *Lydgate House Hotel*, half a mile southwest of Postbridge and offering easy access to Bellever Forest (March–Dec; ☎0822/88209; ④); inexpensive meals are available here.

Two miles northeast of Postbridge, the solitary *Warren House Inn* offers warm, firelit comfort in an unutterably bleak tract of moorland. About a mile south of the B3212, lies the Bronze Age village of **Grimspound**, the completest example of Dartmoor's prehistoric settlements, consisting of 24 circular huts scattered within a four-acre enclosure. Grimspound itself is thought to have been the model for the Stone Age settlement in which Sherlock Holmes camped in *The Hound of the Baskervilles*, while **Hound Tor**, an outcrop three miles to the southwest, was the inspiration for Conan Doyle's tale – according to local legend, phantom hounds were sighted racing across the moor to hurl themselves on the tomb of a hated squire at his death in 1677.

Buckland, Widecombe and the southeastern moor

Four miles east of the crossroads at Two Bridges, **Dartmeet** marks the place where the East and West Dart rivers merge after tortuous journeys from their remote sources. Crowds home in on this beauty spot, but the valley is memorably lush and you don't need to walk far to leave the car park and ice-cream vans behind. From here the Dart pursues a more leisurely course, joined by the River Webburn near the pretty moorland village of **BUCKLAND-IN-THE-MOOR**, one of a cluster of moorstone-and-thatched hamlets on this southeastern side of the moor.

Four miles north, another popular Dartmoor village, **WIDECOMBE-IN-THE-MOOR**, is set in a hollow amid high granite-strewn ridges. Its church of **St Pancras** provides a famous local landmark, its pinnacled tower dwarfing the fourteenth-century main building, whose interior boasts a beautiful painted rood screen. Look out here too for the carved one-eared rabbits – an alchemist's symbol – above the communion rail. The nearby **Church House** was built in the fifteenth century for weary churchgoers from outlying districts, and was later converted into almshouses. Widecombe's other claim to fame is the traditional song, *Widdicombe Fair*: the **fair** is still held annually on the second Tuesday of September, but is now primarily a tourist attraction. You can **stay** in Widecombe in the plain *Sheena Tower* (Feb–Nov; ☎01364/621 308; ③); half a mile out, Higher Venton Farm (☎01364/621 235; ③) is a peaceful thatched longhouse close to a couple of good pubs. You can **camp** at Cockingford Farm, one and a half miles south of Widecombe (March–Nov; ☎01364/621 258).

A couple of miles east, the Dart weaves through a wooded green valley to enter the grounds of **Buckfast Abbey** (daily May–Oct 9am–5pm; Nov–April 10am–4pm; free), a modern monastic complex occupying the site of an abbey founded in the eleventh century by Canute. The present buildings were built by exiled French Benedictine monks who consecrated their new abbey in 1932, though work on the other monastic buildings has continued until recently. The church itself is in a traditional Anglo-Norman style, following the design of the Cistercian building razed in 1535, and shows examples of the monks' dexterity in making stained-glass windows – which, along with honey, handicrafts and tonic wine, help to keep the community funded.

The northeastern moor

The essentially unspoilt market town **MORETONHAMPSTEAD**, lying on the north-eastern edge of the moor, makes an attractive entry point from Exeter – and, inciden-tally, shares with Woolfardisworthy (near Bideford) the honour of having the longest single-word place name in England. Local **information** is handled by *Brambles* tea room, in the main square. There is classy **accommodation** in the central *White Hart* (☎01647/440 406; ⑥), a Georgian posting house that also provides meals, and at *Cookshayes*, on the edge of the village at 33 Court St (March–Oct; ☎01647/440 374; ③), offering good home cooking. The Steps Bridge **youth hostel** (☎01647/252 435) sits on the outskirts of **Dunsford**, three miles northeast of Moretonhampstead and right on the boundary of the National Park. Its woodland setting overlooking the Teign Gorge makes it a popular overnight stop for hikers, and it's close to the main **park information centre** in these parts (April–Oct daily 10am–5pm; ☎01647/252 018).

Moretonhampstead has a historic rivalry with neighbouring **CHAGFORD**, a Stannary town (a chartered centre of the tin trade) that also enjoyed prosperity as a centre of the wool trade. It stands on a hillside overlooking the River Teign, with a fine fifteenth-century church on its edge and enough attractions within and around to keep its pubs and hotels in business. The ancient *Three Crowns*, next to the former guildhall on the main square, is one of a number of decent **pubs** in the village, and offers **accommodation** in raftered rooms (☎01647/433 444; ④). An alternative is the *Georgian Lawn House* (☎01647/433 329; ③), close to the centre on Mill Street.

There are numerous walks to be made in the immediate vicinity, for instance downstream along the Teign to the twentieth-century extravaganza of **Castle Drogo** (April–Oct daily except Fri 11am–5.30pm; £4.60; grounds only April–Oct 10.30am–5.30pm; £2; NT), which occupies a stupendous site overlooking the Teign gorge. Having retired at the age of 33, grocery magnate Julius Drewe unearthed a link that suggested his descent from a Norman baron, and set about creating a castle befitting his pedigree. Begun in 1910, to a design by **Sir Edwin Lutyens**, it was not completed until 1930, but the result was an unsurpassed synthesis of medieval and modern elements. Paths lead from Drogo east to the beauty spot of **Fingal's Bridge**, where shaded green pools hold trout and salmon. The *Angler's Rest* pub has an adjoining restaurant.

Okehampton

The main centre on the northern fringes of Dartmoor, **OKEHAMPTON** grew prosperous as a market town for the medieval wool trade, and some fine old buildings survive between the two branches of the River Okement that meet here, among them the prominent fifteenth-century tower of the **Chapel of St James**. Across the road from the seventeenth-century town hall, a granite archway leads into the **Museum of Dartmoor Life** (Easter–May & Oct Mon–Fri 10am–5pm; June–Sept daily 10am–5pm; £1.60), an excellent overview of habitation on the moor since earliest times. Loftily perched above the West Okement, **Okehampton Castle** (April–Sept daily 10am–6pm; Oct daily 10am–4pm; Nov–March Wed–Sun 10am–4pm; £2; EH) is the shattered hulk of a stronghold laid waste by Henry VIII; its ruins include a gatehouse, Norman keep and the remains of the Great Hall, buttery and kitchens.

The **tourist office** (April–Oct Mon–Sat 10am–5pm, plus Sun in peak season; ☎01837/53020) is on Fore Street next to the museum and the *White Hart* (☎01837/52730; ②). There's plenty of other decent **accommodation** in the centre of town, with two B&Bs on Station Road: *Meadow Ley* at no. 65 (☎01837/53200; ②) and, two doors down, *Hill House* (☎01837/54706; ②). Half a mile north of the centre, there's another B&B at Upcott House, Upcott Hill (☎01837/53743; ③). There's a small **campsite** three quarters of a mile east of Okehampton on the B3260, *Yertiz* (☎01837/52281). In the centre of town, *The Coffee Pot* in Fairplace Terrace is a cheap retreat for coffees and meals, tucked away behind the museum.

Lydford

Five miles southwest of Okehampton, the village of **LYDFORD** boasts the sturdy but small-scale Lydford Castle, a Saxon outpost, then a Norman keep and later used as a prison. The lovely old *Castle Inn* sits right next to the castle, and provides a fire-lit sixteenth-century bar, a pricey but first-rate **restaurant**, and excellent **accommodation** (☎01822/820 242; ④). The chief attraction here, though, is **Lydford Gorge** (April–Oct 10am–5.30pm; Nov–March 10.30am–3pm as far as the White Lady Waterfall only;

£2.80; NT), whose main entrance is a five-minute walk downhill. Two routes – one above, one along the banks – follow the ravine burrowed through by the River Lyd as far as the hundred-foot White Lady Waterfall, coming back on the opposite bank. Overgrown with thick woods, the one-and-a-half-mile gorge is alive with butterflies, spotted woodpeckers, dippers, herons and clouds of insects. The full course would take you roughly two hours at a leisurely pace, though there is a separate entrance at the south end of the gorge if you only want to visit the waterfall. In winter months, when the river can flood, the waterfall is the only part of the gorge open.

Tavistock

The main town of the western moor, **TAVISTOCK** owes its distinctive Victorian appearance to the building boom that followed the discovery of copper deposits here in 1844. Originally, however, this market and Stannary town on the River Tavy grew around what was once the West Country's most important Benedictine abbey, established in the eleventh century, scanty remnants of which survive in the churchyard of **St Eustace**, a mainly fifteenth-century building with some fine monuments inside and a William Morris window in the south aisle. If you can, try to catch the town's bustling Friday market, a fixture since 1105.

Half a mile south of Tavistock, on the Plymouth Road, stands a statue of Francis Drake, who was born and raised on Crowndale Farm, a mile south of town; the statue on Plymouth Hoe is a replica of this one. On the same road, at no. 48, is a reliable **B&B**, *Mallards Guesthouse* (☎01822/615 171; ③); another good choice is the Georgian *Eko Brae* at 4 Bedford Villas, in the Springhill quarter of town (☎01822/614 028; ③). There is a National Park **tourist office** in the town hall on Bedford Square (April–Oct Mon–Sat 10am–5pm, plus Sun in peak season; ☎01822/612 938) and **bikes** can be rented from *Tavistock Cyles*, Paddons Row, Brook Street (☎01822/617 630).

North of Tavistock, a four-mile lane wanders up to **Brent Tor**, 1130ft high and dominating Dartmoor's western fringes. Access to its conical summit is easiest along a path gently ascending through gorse on its southwestern side, leading to the small church of St Michael at the top. Bleak, treeless moorland extends in every direction, wrapped in silence that's occasionally pierced by the shrill cries of stonechats and wheatears. A couple of miles eastwards, **Gibbet Hill** looms over Black Down and the ruined stack of the abandoned Wheal Betsy silver and lead mine.

North Devon

From Exeter the A377 runs alongside the scenic Tarka Line rail line to **North Devon**'s major town, **Barnstaple**. Within easy reach of here, the resorts of **Ilfracombe** and **Woolacombe** draw the crowds, though the fine sandy beaches surrounding the latter give ample opportunity to find your own space. The river port of **Bideford** gives its name to a long bay that holds another beach resort, **Westward Ho!**, as well as the precipitous village of **Clovelly**, perhaps Devon's most famous beauty spot. Inspiring coastal walks follow the bay, particularly to the stormy **Hartland Point** and beyond. Away from the coast, there is plenty of scope for walking and cycling along the Tarka Trail long-distance path, passing through some of the region's loveliest countryside, while for a complete break, the tiny island of **Lundy** provides further opportunities for stretching the legs and clearing the lungs.

Barnstaple

BARNSTAPLE, at the head of the Taw estuary, makes an excellent springboard, being well connected to the resorts of Bideford Bay, Ilfracombe and Woolacombe, as well as to the western fringes of Exmoor. The town's centuries-old role as a market-place is perpetuated in the daily bustle around the huge timber-framed **Pannier Market** off the High Street, alongside which runs **Butchers Row**, its 33 stalls now converted to a variety of uses. In the High Street itself, fourteenth-century **St Anne's Chapel** was converted into a grammar school in 1549, and later numbered amongst its pupils John Gay, author of the *Beggar's Opera*. Retaining its old fittings, it now contains a small **museum** on the history of education (May–Oct Tues–Sat 10am–1pm & 2–4.30pm; free). The riverside is the pleasantest place to stroll, with the colonnaded eighteenth-century **Queen Anne's Walk** – built as a merchants' exchange – providing some architectural interest.

A well-equipped **tourist office** adjoins the library in Tuly Street, near Castle Green (Mon–Fri 9am–7pm, Sat 9.30am–5pm; ☎01271/388 584). There are plenty of **places to stay** in town, two of them at the bottom of the High Street: the *Georgian Nelson House* 99 Newport Rd (☎01271/45929; ②) and, around the corner on Victoria Road, the equally spacious *Ivy House* (☎01271/71198; ②). A little further out on Landkey Road is the first-rate *Mount Sandford* (☎01271/42354; ③), which has a beautiful garden, and serves dinner. On a plusher note, the *Royal and Fortescue Hotel* off The Square on Boutport Street (☎01271/42289; ⑤) offers a pampered environment. Among the best moderately priced **restaurants** in town are the Italian *Vienetta* on Boutport Street and *Room at the Top* on Bear Street, which also has a good vegetarian selection. For gourmet dining, head south of the centre, to *Lynwood House* on Bishops Tawton Road (☎01271/43695; ⑥), which serves a moderate set-lunch and expensive but choice seafood dishes in the evening.

Ilfracombe and around

The most popular resort on Devon's northern coast, **ILFRACOMBE** is essentially little changed since its evolution into a Victorian and Edwardian tourist centre, large-scale development having been restricted by the surrounding cliffs. Nonetheless, the relent-

---

THE TARKA LINE AND THE TARKA TRAIL

Henry Williamson's *Tarka the Otter* (1927), rated by some as one of the finest pieces of nature writing in the English language, has been appropriated as a promotional device by the Devon tourist industry. As parts of the book are set in the Taw valley, it was inevitable that the Exeter to Barnstaple rail route – which follows the Taw for half of its length – should be dubbed the **Tarka Line**. Leaving hourly from Exeter St David's station, this branch line cuts through the sparsely populated heart of Devon, the biggest town en route being **Crediton**, ancient birthplace of Saint Boniface (patron saint of Germany and the Netherlands) and site of the bishopric before its transfer to Exeter in the eleventh century.

Barnstaple forms the centre of the figure of eight traced by the **Tarka Trail**, which tracks the otter's wanderings for a distance of over 180 miles. To the north, the trail penetrates Exmoor then follows the coast back, passing through Williamson's home village of **Georgeham** on its return to Barnstaple. South, the path takes in Bideford, following a disused railway line to Meeth, and continuing as far as Okehampton before swooping up via Eggesford, the point at which the Tarka Line joins the Taw valley.

Twenty-three miles of the trail follow a former railway line that's ideally suited to **bicycles**, and there are rental shops at Barnstaple (near the train station), Instow and Bideford. A good ride from Barnstaple is to **Torrington** (15 miles south), where you can eat at the *Puffing Billy* pub, formerly the train station. Tourist offices give out leaflets on individual sections of the trail, but the best overall book is *The Tarka Trail Guide* (Devon Books, £3.95), available from tourist offices or bookshops.

less pressure to have fun and the ubiquitous smell of chips can become oppressive, though in summer you can always pop down to the small harbour and escape on a coastal tour, a cruise to Lundy Island (see p.300) or a fishing trip.

An attractive stretch of coast runs east out of Ilfracombe, beyond the grassy cliffs of Hillsborough, where a succession of undeveloped coves and inlets are surrounded by jagged slanting rocks and heather-covered hills. Three miles to the east, above the almost enclosed Watermouth Bay, lies **Watermouth Castle** (April–Oct Mon–Fri 11am–4pm), an imposing nineteenth-century mansion, best admired from the outside unless you have kids, who will appreciate the water shows, dungeons and carousel.

The best **beaches** in the area are around **Morte Point**, five miles west of Ilfracombe. Below the promontory stretches a rocky shore whose menacing sunken reef inspired the Normans to give it the name Morte Stone. A break in the rocks makes space for the pocket-sized **Barricane Beach**, famous for the tropical shells washed here from the Caribbean by the Atlantic currents. Luckily there's room for everyone on the two miles of **Woolacombe Sand**, a broad, west-facing expanse much favoured by surfers and families alike. The quieter southern end is bracketed by **Baggy Point**, where from September to November the air is a swirl of gannets, gulls, shags, cormorants and shearwaters. Round the point, **Croyde Bay** is another surfers' delight, more compact than Woolacombe, with stalls on the sand renting surfboards and wet suits.

From Barnstaple, *Red Bus* #62 and #308 – actually yellow – and *Filer's* #301 and #304 run several times an hour to Ilfracombe, with the #308 also calling at Croyde. The Ilfracombe **tourist office** is on the Promenade (Mon–Fri 10am–5pm, Sat 1–5pm, Sun 10am–2pm; ☎01271/863 001). One of Ilfracombe's less expensive **hotels** is *Kinvara*, very central at 6 Avenue Rd (☎01271/863 013; ②), but if you want views, try the *Cavendish* at 9 Larkstone Terrace (March–Oct; ☎01271/863 994; ④). Alternatively, the *Harbourside Hotel*, a little out of the centre at Larkstone Terrace (☎01271/862 231; ③), is good value, with sea views. Ilfracombe's **youth hostel**, Ashmour House, is a Georgian building above the harbour on Hillsborough Terrace (☎01271/865 337). Near the bus station on Broad Street, the *Landpiper Inn* has a good selection of **food**.

Bideford Bay

Bideford Bay (sometimes called Barnstaple Bay) encapsulates the variety of Devon, encompassing the downmarket beach resort of **Westward Ho!**, the savage wind-lashed rocks of **Hartland Point** and the photogenic village of **Clovelly**. **Instow** and **Appledore**, sheltered towns in the mouth of the Torridge estuary, have a lower-key attraction, while **Bideford** itself is mainly a transit centre, with some decent accommodation and bus connections to all the towns on the bay, and regular boats for Lundy.

Bideford

Like Barnstaple, nine miles to the east, the estuary town of **BIDEFORD** formed an important link in the north Devon trade network, mainly due to its **bridge**, which still straddles the River Torridge. First built in 1300, the bridge was reconstructed in stone in the following century, and subsequently reinforced and widened, hence the irregularity of its 24 arches, no two of which have the same span. Bideford's greatest prosperity arose in the seventeenth and eighteenth centuries, when it enjoyed a flourishing trade with the New World, and today the tree-lined quay along the west riverbank is still the focal point for the knot of narrow shop-lined streets.

From the Norman era until the eighteenth century, the port was the property of the Grenville family, whose most celebrated scion was **Richard Grenville** (1541–91), commander of the ships that carried the first settlers to Virginia, and later a major player in the defeat of the Spanish Armada. Grenville also featured in *Westward Ho!*, the historical romance by **Charles Kingsley**, who wrote part of the book in

Bideford and is thus commemorated by a statue at the quay's northern end. Behind, **Victoria Park** extends up the riverbank, containing guns captured from the Spanish in 1588.

Opposite the park is the **tourist office** (Easter–June, Sept & Oct Mon–Thurs 10am–5pm, Fri & Sat 10am–6pm, Sun 10am–1pm; July & Aug Mon & Sat 10am–6pm, Tues–Thurs 10am–5pm, Fri 10am–7pm, Sun 10am–4pm; Nov–Easter Mon–Fri 9am–4pm; ☎01237/477 676). A useful **B&B** nearby is *The Cornerhouse* at 14 The Strand, two minutes from Victoria Park (☎01237/473 722; ②). Further out, on Northam Road, is the attractive *Mount Hotel* (☎0237/473 748; ④), set in its own walled gardens, while the *Royal Hotel* provides a touch of class (☎01237/472 005; ④), just over the old bridge on Barnstaple Street. Cooper Street, running up from the quay, has a good-value **restaurant**, *The Cavalier*, at the top of the street, on Mill Street, the *Heavitree Arms* has bar snacks. For exploring the Tarka Trail by **bike**, there's *Bideford Bicycle Hire*, Torrington Street (☎01237/424 123), two hundred yards south of the bridge on the far riverbank.

Appledore and Instow

The old shipbuilding port of **APPLEDORE**, near the confluence of the Taw and Torridge rivers, still has several operating boatyards and a small sailing fleet moored in the river, but the peaceful pastel-coloured Georgian houses give little hint of the extent of the industry in earlier times. There are a few **B&Bs** overlooking the estuary on Marine Parade, including *Riverside Guest House* at no. 4 (☎01237/478 649; ②); otherwise try *Ship House* on Newquay Street (☎01237/476 140; ③).

In summer foot passengers can take the ferry (April–Oct every 20min) across to **INSTOW**, whose sandy beach stretches in a long line, broadening to a muddy flat at low tide. There's another good accommodation option here, the no-smoking *Pilton Cottage*, Victoria Terrace, Marine Parade (☎01271/860 202; ③), across the road from the beach. Three quarters of a mile inland, Worlington House **youth hostel** (☎01271/860 394) occupies a large Victorian country house overlooking the estuary.

Westward Ho!

WESTWARD HO!, three miles northwest of Bideford, is the only English town to be named after a book. After the publication of Kingsley's historical romance in 1855, speculators recognized the tourist potential of what was then an empty expanse of sand and mud pounded by Atlantic rollers, and the town's first villa was built within a decade. Rudyard Kipling spent four years of his youth here, as described by him in *Stalky and Co*, and his presence is recalled in Kipling Terrace – the site of his school – and **Kipling Tors**, the heights at the west end of the three-mile sand and pebble beach.

Kingsley didn't think much of the new resort when he paid a visit, and he certainly wouldn't care for it now, with its spawn of amusement arcades, caravan sites and holiday chalets, and its sub-standard sea water. You might content yourself with the walk along the beach towards the west, or the excellent views from the Tors.

Clovelly

The impossibly picturesque village of **CLOVELLY**, which must have featured on more calendars, biscuit boxes and tourist posters than anywhere else in the West Country, was put on the map in the second half of the nineteenth century by two books: Charles Dickens' *A Message From the Sea* and, inevitably, *Westward Ho!* – Charles Kingsley's father was rector here for six years. To an extent, the tone of the village has been preserved since then by limiting hotel accommodation and precluding holiday homes, but on crowded summer days it's impossible to see past the artifice. The first hurdle to surmount is the horrific **visitor centre**, where you are charged £1.80 for access to the centre's shops, snack bars, audio-visual show and car park. Walkers, cyclists and users of public transport have right of way to the village, though it involves a tiresome detour round the oversized complex. Below the centre, the cobbled, traffic-free main street plunges past neat, flower-smothered cottages where sledges are tethered for transporting goods – the only way to carry supplies since the use of donkeys ceased.

At the bottom lies Clovelly's stony beach and tiny harbour, snuggled at the bottom of a cleft in the cliff wall. A lifeboat operates from here, and a handful of fishing boats are the only remnants of a fleet which provided the village's main business before the herring stocks became depleted. The jetty was built in the fourteenth century to shelter the coast's only safe harbour between Appledore and Boscastle in Cornwall. If you can't face the return climb, take the Land Rover which leaves about every fifteen minutes from behind the *Red Lion* (Easter–Oct 9.30am–5.30pm) back to the top of the village. It is here, immediately below the visitors centre, that Hobby Drive begins, a three-mile walk you can make along the cliffs through woods of sycamore, oak, beech, rowan and the occasional holly, with grand views over the village.

You can reach Clovelly by *DevonBus* #319 from Bideford. There are just two **hotels** in the village: the *New Inn* (☎01237/431 303; ③), halfway down the High Street, and, enjoying the best position of all, the *Red Lion* (☎01237/431 237; ⑥) at the harbour. Below the *New Inn* is a small **B&B**, *Donkey Hill Cottage* (☎01237/431 601; ③) where you are advised to reserve rooms a long way in advance. There's a greater selection of guest houses a twenty-minute walk up from the visitor centre in Higher Clovelly: go for *The Old Smithy* on the main road (☎01237/431 202; ③) or *Fuchsia Cottage* on Burscott Lane (☎01237/431 398; ②), with views from its first-floor rooms. If you want to **eat** here, your best option is the *Red Lion* which offers a three-course dinner for £15.75.

Hartland Point and around

You could drive along minor roads to **Hartland Point**, ten miles west of Clovelly, but the best approach is on foot along the coastal path. Shortly before arriving, the path touches at the only sandy beach between Westward Ho! and the Cornish border, **Shipload Bay**. The headland presents one of Devon's most dramatic sights, its jagged black rocks battered by the sea and overlooked by a solitary lighthouse 350 feet up. South of Hartland Point, the saw-toothed rocks and near-vertical escarpments defiantly confront the waves, with spectacular waterfalls tumbling over the cliffs. This sheer stretch of coast has seen dozens of shipwrecks over the centuries, though many must have been prevented by the sight of the tower of fourteenth-century **St Nectan's** – a couple of miles south of the point in the village of Stoke – which acted as a landmark to sailors before the construction of the lighthouse. At 128 feet, it is the tallest church tower in North Devon, and overlooks a weathered old graveyard containing memorials to various members of the Lane family – of the Bodley Head and Penguin publishing empire – who were associated with the area; inside, the church boasts a finely carved rood screen and a Norman font, all overlooked by a repainted wagon-type roof. Tea and homemade scones are served at *Stoke Barton Farm*, just opposite, which also provides **B&B** (☎01237/441 238; ③) and basic camping facilities.

Half a mile east of the church, gardens and lush woodland surround **Hartland Abbey** (May & June Wed only 2–5.30pm; July–Sept also Sun 2–5.30pm; £3.50), an eighteenth-century country house incorporating the ruins of an abbey dissolved in 1539. There are just three pubs and a café in **HARTLAND** itself, further inland, while **HARTLAND QUAY** is a scatter of houses round the remains of a once busy port, financed in part by the beneficence of the mariners Raleigh, Drake and Hawkins, but mostly destroyed by storms in the last century. However, the *Hartland Quay* **hotel** provides an excellent opportunity to stay in the area (☎01237/441 218; ③), and there is a **youth hostel** in a converted Victorian schoolhouse at Elmscott, two miles south and about half a mile inland (☎01237/441 367). The only public transport is the *Filers Travel* bus from Barnstaple – alight at Hartland.

Lundy Island

There are fewer than twenty full-time residents on **Lundy**, a tiny windswept island twelve miles north of Hartland Point. Now a refuge for thousands of marine birds, Lundy has no cars, just one pub and one shop – indeed little has changed since the Marisco family established itself here in the twelfth century, using the shingle beaches and coves to terrorize shipping along the Bristol Channel. The family's fortunes only fell in 1242 when one of their number, William de Marisco, was found to be plotting against the king, whereupon he was hanged, drawn and quartered in London.

After the Mariscos, Lundy's most famous inhabitants were Thomas Benson, MP for Barnstaple in the eighteenth century – who was discovered using slave labour to work the granite quarries, and later found guilty of a massive insurance fraud – and **William Hudson Heaven**, who bought the island in 1834 and established what became known as the "Kingdom of Heaven." His home, **Millcombe House**, an incongruous piece of Georgian architecture in the desolate surroundings, is one of many relics of former habitation scattered around the island, like the castle standing on Lundy's southern end, erected by Henry III following the downfall of the Mariscos.

Tracks and footpaths interweave all over the island, and walking is really the only thing to do here. Inland, the grass, heather and bog is crossed by dry-stone walls and grazed by ponies, goats, deer and the rare Soay sheep. The shores – mainly cliffy on the west, softer and undulating on the east – shelter a rich variety of **birdlife**, including kittiwakes, fulmars, shags and Manx shearwaters, which often nest in rabbit burrows. The most famous birds, though, are the **puffins** after which Lundy is named – from the Norse *Lunde* (puffin) and *ey* (island). They can only be sighted in April and May, when they come ashore to mate. Offshore, grey seals can be seen all year round.

The *Oldenburg* crosses to Lundy **from Bideford** throughout the year apart from a few weeks in January and February, with additional sailings **from Ilfracombe** (1–4 weekly) and **from Clovelly** from April to September. From Bideford sailings increase in frequency from twice a week in winter to four times in midsummer, taking two and a quarter hours (reservations ☎01237/470 422). **Accommodation** on the island can be reserved months in advance, but B&B reservations can only be made within two weeks of the proposed visit through the Landmark Trust (☎01237/431 831).

CORNWALL

When D.H. Lawrence wrote that being in **Cornwall** was "like being at a window and looking out of England," he wasn't just thinking of its geographical extremity. Virtually unaffected by the Roman conquest, Cornwall was for centuries the last English haven for a **Celtic culture** elsewhere eradicated by the Saxons – a land where princes communed with Breton troubadours, where chroniclers and scribes composed the epic tales of Arthurian heroism, and where itinerant men from Welsh and Irish monasteries disseminated an elemental and visionary Christianity. Primitive granite crosses and a crop of Celtic saints remain as traces of this formative period, and though the Cornish language had ebbed away by the eighteenth century, it is recalled in Celtic place names that have grown more exotic as they have become corrupted over time.

Another strand of Cornwall's folkloric character comes from the **smugglers** who thrived here right up until the last century, exploiting the sheltered creeks and hidden anchorages of the southern coasts. For many fishing villages, such as Polperro and Mousehole, contraband provided an important secondary income, as did the looting of the ships that regularly came to grief on the reefs and rocks. Further distinguishing it from its neighbour, Cornwall has also had a strong **industrial economy**, based mainly on the mining of **copper** and **tin** in the north, centred on the towns of Redruth and St Agnes, and in the south on the deposits of **china clay**, which are still being mined in the area around St Austell.

Nowadays, of course, Cornwall's most flourishing industry is tourism. The repercussions of the holiday business on Cornwall have been uneven, for instance shamefully defacing **Land's End** but leaving Cornwall's other great promontory, **Lizard Point**, untainted. Examples of what happens when all the stops are pulled out can be seen in the thronged resort of **Falmouth** and its north-coast equivalent, **Newquay**, the West's chief surfing centre, though the quainter villages, such as **Mevagissey**, **Polperro** and **Padstow**, have also succumbed to the sellout. Others, such as **Boscastle** or **Charlestown**, are hardly touched, however, and you couldn't wish for anything more remote than **Bodmin Moor**, a tract of wilderness in the heart of Cornwall – and even **Tintagel**, site of what is fondly known as King Arthur's castle, has preserved its sense of desolation. Other places have reached a happy compromise with the seasonal influx, like **St Ives**, **Fowey** and **Bude**, or else are saved from over-exploitation by sheer distance, as is the case with the **Isles of Scilly**.

From Looe to Veryan Bay

The southern strip of the Cornish coast from Looe to Veryan Bay holds a string of medieval harbour towns tarnished by various degrees of commercialization, but there are also a few spots where you can experience the best of Cornwall, including some wonderful coastline. The main rail stop is **St Austell**, the capital of Cornwall's china clay industry, though there is a branch line connecting nearby **Par** with the north coast at Newquay. To the east of St Austell Bay, the touristy **Polperro** and **Looe** are easily accessible by bus from Plymouth, and there's a rail link to Looe from Liskeard. The estuary town of **Fowey**, in a niche of Cornwall closely associated with the author Daphne du Maurier, is most easily reached by bus from St Austell and Par, as is **Mevagissey**, to the west.

Looe and Polperro

LOOE was drawing crowds as early as 1800, when the first "bathing machines" were wheeled out, but the arrival of the railway in 1879 was what really packed its beaches. Though Looe now touts itself as something of a shark-fishing centre, most people come here for the sand, the handiest stretch being the beach in front of East Looe – the busier half of the river-divided town. If you walk a mile eastwards you'll find a cleaner spot to swim at **Millendreath**.

East Looe's **tourist office** is at the Guildhall on the main Fore Street (Easter–Oct daily 10am–5pm; Nov–Easter Mon–Sat 10am–noon; ☎01503/262 072). There's plenty of **accommodation** here: try *Osbourne House*, a converted cottage in Lower Chapel Street, close to the harbour (March–Oct & Dec; ☎01503/262 970; ③), or *Sea Breeze*, a B&B further up the same street (☎01503/263 131; ③) – both have moderately priced restaurants. Other eateries include the harbourside *Loft*, specializing in lobster and other seafood, and the inexpensive *Golden Guinea* on Fore Street, a seventeenth-century building that does a brisk trade in staple seaside meals as well as cream teas.

From the bus stop and car park at the top of the village, it's only a five-minute walk to neighbouring **POLPERRO**, following the River Pol down to the minuscule harbour. The tight-packed houses rising on each side of the stream present an undeniably pretty sight, little changed since the village's heyday of smuggling and pilchard fishing, but the "discovery" of Polperro has almost ruined it, its straggling main street – The

Coombes – now an unbroken row of tourist shops and fast-food outlets. Best places to **stay** are *New House* on Talland Hill (☎01503/272 206; ③), right on the harbour, or *Lanhael House*, a period building with gardens and pool safely removed from the mêlée above the car park (☎01503/272 428; ③). The *Plantation Café*, on The Coombes, is good for cream teas and snacks; also on the main road, *The Kitchen* is famous for its sausages but also offers fish dishes.

Fowey

The ten miles west from Polperro to **Polruan** are among the best stretches of the coastal path in south Cornwall, giving access to some beautiful secluded sand beaches. There are frequent ferries across the River Fowey from Polruan, giving a fine view of the quintessential Cornish port of **FOWEY** (pronounced "Foy"), a cascade of neat, pale terraces at the mouth of one of the peninsula's greatest rivers. The major port on the county's south coast in the fourteenth century, Fowey finally became so ambitious that it provoked Edward IV to strip the town of its military capability, though it continued to thrive commercially, coming into its own as the leading port for china clay shipments in the last century. In addition to the bulkier freighters sailing from wharves north of the town, the harbour today is crowded with trawlers and yachts, giving the town a brisk, purposeful character lacking in many of Cornwall's south coast ports.

Fowey's steep layout centres on the church of **St Fimbarrus**, a distinctive fifteenth-century construction replacing a church that was sacked by the French. Behind St Fimbarrus stands **Place House**, an extravagance belonging to the local Treffry family, with a Victorian Gothic tower grafted on to the fifteenth- and sixteenth-century fortified building. Below the church, the **Ship Inn**, sporting some fine Elizabethan panelling and plaster ceilings, was originally home to the Rashleighs – a recurring name in the annals of this region – and held the local Roundhead HQ during the Civil War. From here, Fore Street, Lostwithiel Street and the Esplanade fan out, the **Esplanade** leading to a footpath that gives access to some splendid walks around the coast. Past the remains of a blockhouse that once supported a defensive chain hung across the river's mouth, lies the small beach of **Readymoney Cove**, so called either because it was where smugglers buried their ill-gotten gains, or because it was where the flotsam of shipwrecks came ashore. Close by stand the ruins of **St Catherine's Castle**, built by Thomas Treffry on the orders of Henry VIII, and offering fine views across the estuary.

Fowey is the terminus of the thirty-mile **Saints' Way** from Padstow, but there are plenty of short-range targets for the less ambitious. North of Fowey, the **Hall Walk** is a scenic four-mile circular hike that involves crossing the river on the car ferry (at the car park north of town) to **Bodinnick**, walking downstream on the other side, crossing the footbridge over the narrow creek of Pont Pill then taking the passenger ferry back from Polruan. The walk passes a memorial to "Q", alias of Sir Arthur Quiller-Couch, who lived on Fowey's Esplanade between 1892 and 1944, and whose writings helped popularize the place he called "Troy Town".

Practicalities

Separated from eastern routes by its river, Fowey is most accessible by frequent #24 and #24A buses from St Austell. There is a small **tourist office** in the town's post office (July & Aug Mon–Sat 9am–5.30pm, Sun 10am–1pm; Sept–June Mon–Fri 9am–1pm & 2–5.30pm, Sat 9am–1pm; April–June & Sept also Sat 2–5pm; ☎01726/833 616). All of the central pubs offer **B&B**: try the *Ship* (☎0726/833 751; ③) or *Safe Harbour* (☎01726/833 379; ③), both on Lostwithiel Street. The *Wheelhouse* B&B (☎01726/832 452; ③) and the plusher *Marina Hotel*, on the Esplanade (☎01726/833 315; ⑤), both have gardens and river views. There is a **youth hostel** in the nearby riverside hamlet of Golant at *Penquite House* (☎01726/833 507). The nearest **campsite** is at *Yeate Farm* (April–Oct; ☎01726/870 256), on the eastern bank of the river, three quarters of a mile up from the Bodinnick ferry crossing. Fowey has some good **restaurants**, among them *The Restaurant* at 3 The Esplanade, specializing in lobster, and *Food For Thought* on the quay, that serves mainly French dishes – both are moderately priced. The area is also well provided with worthy **pubs**, such as Golant's *Fisherman's Arms*, the *Old Ferry Inn* at Bodinnick, and Polruan's excellent *Lugger Inn*.

St Austell and its bay

It was the discovery of china clay, or kaolin, in the downs to the north of **ST AUSTELL** that spurred the town's growth in the eighteenth century. An essential ingredient in the production of porcelain, kaolin had till then only been produced in northern China, where the high ridge, or *kao-lin*, was the sole known source of the raw material. Still a vital part of Cornwall's economy, the clay is now mostly exported for use in the manufacture of paper, as well as paint and medicines. The conical spoil heaps left by the mines are a feature of the local landscape, especially on Hensbarrow Downs to the north, the great green and white mounds making an eerie sight.

St Austell's nearest link to the sea is at **CHARLESTOWN**, an easy downhill walk from the centre. This unassuming and unspoilt port is named after the entrepreneur Charles Rashleigh, who in 1791 began work on the harbour in what was then a small fishing community two miles south of St Austell, widening its streets to accommodate the clay wagons passing through daily . The wharves are still used, loading clay onto vessels that appear oversized beside the tiny jetties. Behind the harbour, the **Shipwreck Museum** (daily April–Sept 10am–5pm; Oct–March 10am–4pm; £2.95) is entered through tunnels once used to convey the clay to the docks, and shows a good collection of photos and relics as well as tableaux of historical scenes.

On each side of the dock the coarse sand and stone **beaches** have small rock pools, above which cliff walks lead around St Austell Bay. Eastwards, you soon arrive at overdeveloped **Carlyon Bay**, whose main resort is **Par**. The beaches here get clogged with clay – the best swimming is to be found futher on at the sheltered crescent of **Polkerris**. The easternmost limit of St Austell Bay is marked by **Gribbin Head**, near which stands Menabilly House, where Daphne Du Maurier lived for 24 years – it was the model for the "Manderley" of *Rebecca*. The house is not open to the public, but you can walk down to Polridmouth Cove, where Rebecca met her watery end.

Trains on the main London–Penzance line serve St Austell, with most services also stopping at Par. *Roselyn Coaches* runs an hourly **bus** service linking St Austell, Charlestown, Par and Polkerris. Charlestown has two really attractive places **to stay**: *T'Gallants* (☎01726/70203; ③), a smart Georgian B&B at the back of the harbour, and the *Pier House Hotel* (☎01726/67955; ⑤), with a premium harbourside location and a good **restaurant**. Behind *T'Gallants*, the *Rashleigh Arms* offers real ale and a range of food, though the finest **pub** is the *Rashleigh Inn* at Polkerris. The best **campsite** in St Austell Bay is *Par Sands* (April–Oct; ☎01726/812 868), next to Par beach.

Mevagissey to Veryan Bay

MEVAGISSEY was once known for the construction of fast vessels, used for carrying contraband as well as pilchards. Today the tiny port might display a few stacks of lobster pots, but the real business is tourism, and in summer the maze of backstreets is saturated with day-trippers, converging on the inner harbour and overflowing onto the large sand beach at **Pentewan** a mile to the north, despite the poor water quality.

Past the headland to the south of Mevagissey, the small sandy cove of **Portmellon** retains little of its boatbuilding activities but is freer of tourists. Further still, **GORRAN**

HAVEN, a former crab-fishing town, has a neat rock-and-sand beach and a footpath that winds round to the even more attractive **Vault Beach**, half a mile south. South of here juts the most striking headland on Cornwall's southern coast, **Dodman Point**, cause of many a wreck and topped by a stark granite cross built by a local parson as a seamark in 1896. The promontory holds the substantial remains of an Iron Age fort, with an earthwork bulwark cutting right across the point.

Curving away to the west, the elegant parabola of **Veryan Bay** is barely touched by commercialism. Just west of Dodman Point lies one of Cornwall's most beautiful coves, **Hemmick Beach**, an excellent swimming spot with rocky outcrops affording a measure of privacy. Visually even more impressive is **Porthluney Cove**, a crescent of sand whose centrepiece is the battlemented **Caerhays Castle** (May–Oct Mon–Sat 11am–4pm; £2.80), built in 1808 by John Nash. A little further on, the minuscule and white-washed **Portloe** is fronted by jagged black rocks that throw up fountains of sea spray, giving it a good, end-of-the-road kind of atmosphere. Sequestered inland, **VERYAN** is best known for its curious circular nineteenth-century white houses. A lane from Veryan leads down to one of the cleanest swimming spots on Cornwall's southern coast, **Pendower Beach**. Two thirds of a mile long and backed by dunes, Pendower joins with the neighbouring **Carne Beach** at low tide to create a long sandy continuum. If you want to stay in Veryan, try the *New Inn*, a friendly **B&B** which serves wholesome **meals** (☎01872/501 362; ③).

Practicalities

From St Austell's train station, buses #26 and #26a leave hourly for Mevagissey, some continuing to Gorran Haven. Veryan and Portloe are reachable on #306 from Truro. The old *Ship Inn* (☎01726/843 324; ③) in Mevagissey offers reasonable **accommodation**; otherwise try *Mevagissey House* (March–Oct; ☎01726/842 427; ③), on Vicarage Hill. You might be better off staying in Portmellon, where the weathered old *Rising Sun Inn* (☎01726/843 235; ③) confronts the sea. In Gorran Haven, the well-situated *Llawnroc Inn* (☎0726/843 461; ③) is the only budget option. The nearest **youth hostel** (☎01726/843 234) is in a former farmhouse at **Boswinger**, a remote spot half a mile from Hemmick Beach, and a mile from the bus stop at Gorran Church Town (bus #26). Boswinger also has a **campsite**, *Sea View* (Easter–Sept; ☎01726/843 425), overlooking Veryan Bay. There's no shortage of **restaurants** in Mevagissey, most specializing in fish – for location you might try the large harbourfront *Shark's Fin Hotel*. The *Cellar Bar* on Church Street and the *Fountain Inn* on Fore Street are pubs that serve food.

St Mawes to Falmouth

Lush tranquillity collides with frantic tourist activity around **Carrick Roads**, the complex estuary basin to the south of **Truro**, the region's main centre for transport and accommodation. On the eastern shore, the luxuriant **Roseland** peninsula is a backwater of woods and sheltered creeks between the River Fal and the sea. **St Mawes** is the main draw here, chiefly on account of its castle, a twin of Pendennis across the neck of the estuary in **Falmouth**, a major resort at the end of a branch line from Truro, itself a stop on the main line to Penzance.

St Mawes and the Roseland peninsula

Stuck on the end of a prong of land at the bottom of Carrick Roads, secluded, unhurried **ST MAWES** has an attractive walled seafront below a hillside of villas and abundant gardens. Out of sight at the end of the seafront stands small and pristine **St Mawes Castle** (April–Sept daily 10am–6pm; Oct daily 10am–4pm; Nov–March Wed–

Sun 10am–4pm; £1.50; EH). Built during the reign of Henry VIII, to a clover-leaf design, with a central round keep surrounded by robust gun emplacements, the castle owes its excellent condition to its early surrender when under siege by Parliamentary forces in 1646. The dungeons and gun installations contain various artillery exhibits as well as some background on local social history.

Out of St Mawes, you could spend a pleasant afternoon poking around the Roseland peninsula between the Percuil River and the eastern shore of Carrick Roads. It's only two and a half miles to the scattered hamlet of **ST JUST-IN-ROSELAND**, where the strikingly picturesque church of St Just stands right next to the creek, surrounded by palms and subtropical shrubbery, its gravestones tumbling down to the water's edge. A couple of miles further north, the chain-driven King Harry **ferry** (summer daily 8am– 9pm; winter Mon–Sat 8am–7pm; £1.80 per car) crosses the River Fal about every twenty minutes, docking close to **Trelissick Gardens** (March–Oct Mon–Sat 10.30am– 5.30pm, Sun 12.30–5.30pm; March & Oct closes 5pm; £3.40; NT), which are celebrated for their hydrangeas and other Mediterranean species.

In summer, there's a **ferry** from St Mawes to the southern arm of the Roseland Peninsula, which holds the twelfth- to thirteenth-century church of **St Anthony's** and the **lighthouse** on St Anthony's Head, marking the entry into Carrick Roads. There's also a ferry crossing from St Mawes to Falmouth. St Mawes makes an attractive – though pricey – place **to stay**. Right on the seafront, *St Mawes Hotel* (March–Nov; ☎01326/270 266; ⑨) enjoys a glorious view over the estuary; the price includes dinner. You'll find a more relaxed reception down the road at *The Rising Sun* (☎01326/270 233; ⑦), also with a good restaurant. Less expensive rooms can be found at inland B&Bs and farmhouses, for example *Commerrans Farm* (☎01872/580 270; ③), two and a half miles outside St Just. There's a decent **campsite** at Trethem Mill, three miles inland of St Mawes (April–Oct; ☎01872/580 504). In St Mawes itself, the *Victory Inn* is a good old oak-beamed **pub** just off the seafront.

Truro

TRURO, seat of Cornwall's law courts and other county bureaucracies, has a distinctly small-scale provincial feel, even if its Georgian houses do reflect the prosperity that came with the tin-mining boom of the 1800s. Blurring the town's overall identity, its modern shopping centre stands alongside the powerful but chronologically confused **Cathedral**. Completed in 1910, this was the first Anglican cathedral to be built in England since St Paul's, but it incorporates part of the fabric of the old parish church that previously occupied the site. The airy interior's best feature is the neo-Gothic baptistry, with its emphatically pointed arches and elaborate roof vaulting. To the right of the choir, St Mary's aisle is a relic of the original Perpendicular building, other fragments of which adorn the walls, including – in the north transept – a colourful Jacobean memorial to local Parliamentarian John Robartes and his wife. The only other item to keep you in Truro is the **Royal Cornwall Museum** (Mon–Sat 10am–5pm; £1.50) housed in an elegant Georgian building on River Street. The exhibits include minerals, toys and paintings by Cornish artists.

Truro's **tourist office** is on Boscawen Street (Mon–Fri 9am–1pm & 2–5pm; ☎01872/ 74555). Buses stop nearby at Lemon Quay, or near the train station on Richmond Hill. Best **accommodation** near the train station is *The Gables*, 49 Treyew Rd (☎01872/ 42318; ②); *The Bay Tree*, which lies halfway between the station and the centre at 28 Ferris Town (☎01872/40274; ③); and *Patmos* at 8 Burley Close (☎01872/78018; ②), where Lemon Street meets Falmouth Road. The nearest **campsite** is Carnon Downs, a couple of miles outside Truro on the Falmouth road (April–Oct; ☎01872/862 283). *Butchers* **restaurant** on Quay Street offers Italian dishes, while *The Feast* is an excellent wholefood restaurant at 15 Kenwyn St. If you feel like a culinary adventure, eat Vietnamese at *Linda's* (closed Sat lunch & Sun; ☎01872/222 109) on Little Castle Street.

On the corner of Francis and Castle streets, the *Wig and Pen* is a decent **pub** with bar food and a separate restaurant, while the *Globe Inn* next door also serves hot snacks.

Falmouth

The construction of Pendennis Castle on the southern point of Carrick Roads in the sixteenth century prepared the ground for the growth of **FALMOUTH**, then no more than a fishing village. The building of its deepwater harbour was proposed a century later by Sir John Killigrew, and Falmouth's prosperity was assured when in 1689 it became chief base of the fast Falmouth Packets, which sped mail to the Americas. This century, though, Falmouth has shed most of its Cornishness, and, barring its castle, has little to offer anyone who wants to get away from the hard sell.

The long **High Street** is crammed with humdrum bars and cafés, though at its southern end, Arwenack Street, it does have the Tudor remains of the Killigrews' **Arwenack House**. The peculiar granite pyramid standing opposite the house, built in 1737, is probably intended to commemorate the local family, though its exact significance has never been clear. Apart from this, the centre of town only offers a clamber up the precipitous 111 steps of **Jacob's Ladder** from The Moor, the old town's main square, to give a bird's-eye view of the harbour. From the Prince of Wales Pier, below The Moor, frequent ferries leave for St Mawes, accompanied in summer by boats touring the local estuaries.

Standing sentinel at the tip of the promontory that separates Carrick Roads from Falmouth Bay, **Pendennis Castle** (daily April–Sept 10am–6pm; Oct–March 10am–4pm; £2.20; EH) shows little evidence of its five-month siege by the Parliamentarians during the Civil War, which ended only when half its defenders had died and the rest been starved into submission. Facing right out to sea on its own pointed peninsula, the stout ramparts offer the best all-round views of Carrick Roads and Falmouth Bay. Beyond Pendennis Point stretches a long sandy bay with various **beaches** backed by expensive hotels. If you wanted to swim, the best spot is from **Swanpool Beach**, accessible by cliff path from the more popular **Gyllyngvase Beach** – or walk a couple of miles further on to **Maenporth**, from where there are some fine clifftop walks.

Falmouth's **tourist office** is off The Moor, on Killigrew Street (Mon–Thurs 8.45am–5.15pm, Fri 9am–4.45pm, Sat 9am–5pm; July & Aug also Sun 10am–4pm; ☎01326/312 300). Most of the town's **accommodation** is in the south part of town, for example the good-value *Ivanhoe* at 7 Melvill Rd (☎01326/319 083; ③). For the beach area, expect to pay more: *Chellowdene* (May–Sept; ☎01326/314 950; ③) on the parallel Gyllyngvase Hill has more reasonable rates than most. There's a perfectly sited **youth hostel** inside Pendennis Castle (☎01326/311 435). Among the overdeveloped caravan parks on the coast south of Falmouth, a decent-sized **campsite**, *Tremorvah Tent Park* (☎01326/312 103), stands one mile outside town on the Swanpool road. The best fish in town is to be found at *The Seafood Bar*, Lower Quay Hill (evenings only; closed Sun; ☎01326/315 129). The *Quayside Inn*, further up on Arwenack Street, is the pick of the **pubs**. Falmouth makes a convenient base for exploring the Carrick Roads and Helford estuaries: you can **rent bikes** from *Blazing Saddles*, 29 Killigrew St (☎01326/211 980).

The Lizard peninsula

If the generally flat and treeless **Lizard peninsula** can be said to have a centre, it is **Helston**. From Falmouth, bus #2 takes fifty minutes to reach Helston, then makes a stop at Porthleven on its way to Penzance. Bus #320 from Truro (Mon–Sat) passes through Helston on the way to **Mullion** and the village of **The Lizard**, while from Helston the #326 leaves at least five times daily from Monday to Saturday, passing through Gweek, St Keverne and **Coverack**.

The east coast to Lizard Point

To the north of the peninsula, the snug hamlets sprinkled in the valley of the **River Helford** are a complete contrast to the rugged character of most of the Lizard. At the river's mouth stands **MAWNAN**, whose granite church of St Mawnan-in-Meneage is dedicated to the sixth-century Welsh missionary Saint Maunanus – Meneage, rhyming with vague, means "land of monks". Upstream on the south side, **Frenchman's Creek** is one of a splay of creeks and arcane inlets running off the river, and was the inspiration of Daphne du Maurier's novel of the same name – her evocation of it holds true: "still and soundless, surrounded by the trees, hidden from the eyes of men".

You can get over to the south bank by the seasonal ferry from Helford Passage to **Helford**, an agreeable old smugglers' haunt. South of here, on the B3293, the road meets the coast at the fishing port of **COVERACK**, whose name – "Hideaway" – gives some indication of its one-time role as a centre of contraband. Three miles offshore lurk the dreaded **Manacles** rocks, the cause of numerous shipwrecks over the centuries, many of which were gleefully claimed by the local wreckers. Coverack has a few decent **places to stay**, including the pleasant *Bakery Cottage* (☎01326/280 474; ②), with home cooking; at the seafront, ask in the *Harbour Lights* restaurant about vacancies in a neighbouring cottage (☎01326/280 507; ③). There's a **youth hostel** just west of Coverack's centre in a country house overlooking the bay (☎01326/280 687); the hostel also runs windsurfing courses.

On the south tip of the promontory, beyond the safe and clean swimming spot of **Kennack Sands**, a white lighthouse marks **Lizard Point**. Below, a lifeboat is stationed in a tiny cove, just up from the ceaselessly churning sea. A mile inland sits the nondescript village called simply The Lizard, where you can sleep and eat at *The Caerthillian* (☎01326/290 019; ②), which has an inexpensive **restaurant** with dishes ranging from coq au vin and poached salmon to homemade pizzas. A mile westward lies the peninsula's best-known beach, **Kynance Cove**. With its sheer hundred-foot cliffs, its stacks and arches of serpentine rock and its offshore islands, the beach has an irresistible wild grandeur, and the water quality is excellent – but take care not to be stranded on the islands by the tide, which submerges the entire beach at its flood.

The west coast

Four miles north of Kynance Cove, **MULLION**, the Lizard's biggest village, has a fifteenth- to sixteenth-century church dedicated to the Breton **Saint Mellane** (or Malo), with a dog door for canine churchgoers. In the centre of the village, *Alma House* (☎01326/240 509; ③) provides good **accommodation** with a superb **restaurant** attached. A mile away on the coast, **Mullion Cove** has more rock sculptures and a small beach outside its sheltered harbour, though the neighbouring beaches of **Polurrian** and **Poldhu** are more popular with surfers. At the cliff edge, the Marconi Monument marks the spot from which the first transatlantic radio transmission was made in 1901. The freshwater **Loe Pool**, three miles north, is separated by a shingle bar from the sea, and is one of the two places claiming to be where the sword Excalibur was restored to its watery source (the other is on Bodmin Moor).

Nearby **Porthleven** is a sizeable port that once served to export tin ore from the Stannary town of **HELSTON**, three miles inland. This transport junction is best known for its **Furry Dance** (or Floral Dance), which dates from the seventeenth century. Held on May 8 (unless this falls on a Sunday or Monday, when the procession takes place on the nearest Saturday), it's a stately procession of top-hatted men and summer-frocked women performing a strange, rather solemn dance through the town's streets and gardens. Other than this, the town's most famous attraction is the garish **Flambards Theme Park** (April to mid-July & mid-Aug to Oct 10am–5.30pm; mid-July to mid-Aug 10am–7.30pm; £6.95), a riot of pseudo-Victoriana. Helston **tourist office** (Easter–Oct Mon–Fri 10am–1pm & 2–5.30pm, Sat 10am–1pm & 2–5pm; slightly shorter hours in winter; ☎01326/565 431) is at 79 Meneage St. Just along the street at no. 95 is

Hutchinson's award-winning fish and chip shop. For a drink or a **pub** meal, check out the *Blue Anchor* at 50 Coinagehall St, once a fifteenth-century monastery rest house, now a cramped pub with flagstone floors and mellow beer brewed on the premises.

The Penwith peninsula

Though more densely populated than the Lizard, the **Penwith peninsula** is a more rugged landscape, with a raw appeal that is still encapsulated by **Land's End**, despite the commercial paraphernalia superimposed on that headland. The seascapes, the quality of the light and the slow tempo of the local fishing communities made this area a hotbed of artistic activity in the late nineteenth century, when the painters of **Newlyn**, near **Penzance**, established a distinctive school of painting. More innovative figures – among them Ben Nicholson, Barbara Hepworth and contructivist Naum Gabo – were soon afterwards to make **St Ives** one of England's liveliest cultural communities, and their enduring influence has recently been marked with the opening of a St Ives branch of the Tate Gallery, showcasing the modern artists associated with the locality.

From Penzance, **buses** #1 and #4 go straight to Land's End in about an hour, whereas the #6B (Mon–Fri 4 daily) takes in Newlyn, Mousehole aand Lamorna Cove. North of Land's End, the comparatively neglected headland of Cape Cornwall is served by the #10 bus from Penzance to St Just, while Zennor, St Just, Sennen Cove and Land's End are served by open-top bus from St Ives (June–Sept 3 daily).

Penzance and around

Occupying a sheltered position at the northwest corner of Mount's Bay, **PENZANCE** has always been a major port, but most traces of the medieval town were obliterated at the end of the sixteenth century by a Spanish raiding party. Today the dominant style of Penzance is Georgian, particularly at the top of **Market Jew Street** (from *Marghas Jew*, meaning "Thursday Market"), which climbs from the harbour and the train and bus stations. At the top of the street stands the green-domed Victorian **Market House** before which stands a statue of **Humphry Davy** (1778–1829), the local woodcarver's son who pioneered the science of electrochemistry, and invented the life-saving miners' safety lamp, which his statue holds.

Turn left here into **Chapel Street**, which has some of the town's finest buildings, including the flamboyant **Egyptian House**, built in 1835 to contain a geological museum but subsequently abandoned until its restoration twenty years ago. Across the street, the **Union Hotel** dates from the seventeenth century, and originally housed the town's assembly rooms: the news of Admiral Nelson's victory at Trafalgar and the death of Nelson himself were first announced from the minstrels' gallery here in 1805. At no. 19, the **Maritime Museum** (Easter–Oct Mon–Sat 10am–5pm; £1.50) holds a good collection of seafaring articles, including an array of items salvaged from local wrecks and a full-size section of an eighteenth-century man o' war.

If your interest is roused by the art scene that flourished hereabouts at the turn of the century, head for Morrab Road, between the promenade and Alverton Street (a continuation of Market Jew Street), where the town's **Museum** (Mon–Fri 10.30am–4.30pm, Sat 10.30am–12.30pm; £1) holds the biggest collection of the works of the Newlyn School – the colony of artists who gathered here around the Irish painter Stanhope Forbes (1857–1948) – impressionistic maritime scenes, frequently sentimentalized but often bathed in an evocatively luminous light. Newlyn itself, one of Cornwall's biggest fishing ports, lies immediately south of Penzance.

Penzance's **tourist office** (Mon–Fri 9am–5pm, Sat 10am–1pm; summer Sat until 5pm; ☎01736/62207) is right next to the train and bus stations near the harbour.

Among the numerous **guest houses** on Morrab Road, try *Kimberley House* at no. 10 (☎01736/62727; ②); on Chapel Street, there's the seventeenth-century *Trevelyan Hotel* (☎01736/62494; ③). *Queen's Hotel*, The Promenade (☎01736/62371; ⑤), has lashings of old-fashioned comfort, or you can splash out on the *Union Hotel* in Chapel Street (01736/62319; ⑤). The **youth hostel**, housed at Castle Horneck, Alverton (☎01736/62666), is two miles from Penzance station (bus #B, #5 or #10B as far as the *Pirate Inn*). *Richmond's* **restaurant** on Chapel Street (closed Sun) is good for inexpensive seafood suppers while delicious meat and fish recipes are offered at *Harris's*, 46 New St (closed Sun & Mon lunch). Penzance has a couple of characterful **pubs**: the *Admiral Benbow* on Chapel Street, crammed with gaudy ships' figureheads and other nautical items, and the *Turk's Head*, on the same street, which dates back to the thirteenth century. For **bike rental** head for *Geoff's Bikes* on Victoria Place (☎01736/63665).

St Michael's Mount

Buses from Penzance bus station leave every thirty minutes for Marazion, five miles east, from where the medieval chimneys and towers of **St Michael's Mount** (April–Oct Mon–Fri 10.30am–4.45pm; Nov–March Mon, Wed & Fri 10.30am–3.45pm; £3.50; NT) can be seen a couple of hundred yards offshore. A vision of the archangel Michael led to the building of a church on this granite pile around the fifth century, and within three centuries a Celtic monastery had been founded here. The present building derives from a chapel raised in the eleventh century by Edward the Confessor, who handed over the abbey to the Benedictine monks of Brittany's Mont St Michel, whose island abbey was the model for this one. After the Civil War, when it was used to store arms for the Royalist forces, it became the residence of the St Aubyn family, who still inhabit the castle. The fortress-isle has a tamer, more pedestrian feel than its prototype off the Breton coast, but its eye-catching site demands a first-hand inspection from anyone travelling along this part of the Cornish littoral. A good number of its buildings date from the twelfth century, but the later additions are more interesting, such as the battlemented **chapel** and the seventeenth-century decorations of the Chevy Chase Room, the former refectory. At low tide the promontory can be approached via a cobbled causeway; at high tide there are boats from Marazion, and in summer there's also a direct ferry from Penzance.

Mousehole to Land's End

Accounts vary as to the derivation of the name of **MOUSEHOLE** (pronounced "Mouzle"), though it may be from a smugglers' cave just south of town. In any case, the name evokes perfectly this minuscule harbour, cradled in the arms of a granite breakwater three miles south of Penzance. The village attracts more visitors than it can handle, so hang around until the crowds have departed for a walk through its tight tangle of lanes and a drink in the *Ship Inn*. Half a mile inland, the churchyard at **Paul** holds a monument to Dolly Pentreath, a resident of Mousehole who died in 1777 and was reputed to have been the last person to speak only the Cornish language.

Three miles south round the coast, **Lamorna Cove** is squeezed between granite headlands, linked by a flower-bordered lane to the tiny village of **LAMORNA**, where an old flour mill jostles for attention with a comfortable old pub, the *Lamorna Inn*, also known as *The Wink* – as the sign shows, it was the wink that signified that contraband spirits were available. The *Lamorna Cove Hotel* (☎01736/731 411; ⑤), about half a mile above the cove, has a pool, gardens and wonderful views.

PORTHCURNO's name means "Port Cornwall", but its beach of tiny white shells suggests privacy and isolation rather than the movement of ships. Steep steps lead up from here to the cliff-hewn **Minack Theatre**, created in the 1930s and since enlarged to hold 750 seats, though the basic Greek-inspired design has remained intact. The spectacular backdrop of Porthcurno Bay makes this one of the country's most inspiring theatres. The summer season lasts seventeen weeks from May to September, presenting a gamut of plays, opera and musicals, with tickets costing just £5 (box office Mon–Fri 9–11.45am; ☎01736/810 181). Bring a cushion, a rug and an umbrella.

Nothing can quite destroy the potency of **Land's End**, the extreme western tip of England, but the presence of the colossal theme park built here in 1987 comes close to violating irreparably the spirit of the place. Nothing could trivialize this majestic headland more than **The Land's End Experience** (daily summer 10am–6pm; winter 10am–5pm; £5.50), which substitutes a tawdry panoply of lasers and unconvincing sound effects for the real open-air experience. The location is still a public right of way, so you're not obliged to buy a ticket to reach the point, where turf-covered cliffs sixty feet high provide a platform to view the Irish Lady, the Armed Knight, Dr Syntax Head and the rest of the Land's End outcrops. Beyond them you can spot the Longships lighthouse, a mile and a half out to sea, and sometimes the Wolf Rock lighthouse, nine miles southwest, or even the Isles of Scilly, 25 miles away.

Whitesand Bay to Zennor

To the north of Land's End the rockscape changes from granite to slate, the rounded cliffs falling away at **Whitesand Bay** to reveal a glistening mile-long shelf of beach that offers the best swimming on the Penwith peninsula. The rollers make for good surfing and boards can be rented at **Sennen Cove**, the more popular southern end of the beach. There are a few places to **stay** around the southern end of the strand, including *Myrtle Cottage* (☎01736/871 698; ②), which also has a cosy café open to non-residents, and the nearby *Polwyn Cottage*, tucked away on Old Coastguard Row (☎01736/871 349; ③). If all else fails, try the *Sennen Cove Hotel*, visible from the strand, which has great views, but is otherwise fairly second-rate (☎01736/871 275; ③).

Cape Cornwall, three miles northward, shelters another superb beach, overlooked by the chimney of the Cape Cornwall Mine, which closed in 1870. Half a mile inland the grimly grey village of **ST JUST-IN-PENWITH** was a centre of the tin and copper industry, and the rows of trim cottages radiating out from Bank Square are redolent of the close-knit community that once existed here. The tone is somewhat lightened by the grassy open-air theatre where the old Cornish miracle plays were staged; it was later used by Methodist preachers as well as Cornish wrestlers. The village has a **youth hostel** on its outskirts (☎01736/788 437); a traditional Cornish pub, *The Star Inn* off Bank Square, which serves brilliant breakfasts and also has **rooms** (☎01736/788 767; ②); and the *St Just Tea Rooms*, which provides decent lunches and snacks.

East of St Just, the landscape is all rolling moorland and an abundance of granite, the chief building material of **ZENNOR**. D.H. Lawrence and Frieda came to live here in 1916: "It is a most beautiful place," Lawrence wrote, "lovelier even than the Mediterranean." The Lawrences were soon joined by John Middleton Murry and Katherine Mansfield, with the hope of forming a writers' community, but the new arrivals soon left for a more sheltered haven near Falmouth. Lawrence stayed on to write *Women in Love*, before being given notice to quit by the local constabulary, who suspected Lawrence and his German wife of unpatriotic sympathies. His Cornish experiences were later described in *Kangaroo*. At the bottom of the village, the *Wayside Inn* is an outdoor **Museum** dedicated to Cornish life from prehistoric times (April–Sept 10am–6pm; £1.85). Nearby, the *Tinners Arms*, where Lawrence stayed before moving into Higher Tregerthen, is a homely place to drink and **eat**.

St Ives

East of Zennor, the road runs for four hilly miles on to the steeply built town of **ST IVES**, a place that has smoothly undergone the transition to holiday haunt from its previous role as a centre of the fishing industry. So productive were the offshore waters that a record sixteen and a half million fish were caught in one net on a single day in 1868, and the diarist Francis Kilvert was told by the local vicar that the smell was sometimes so great as to stop the church clock. By the time the reserves dried up around the early years of this century, St Ives was beginning to attract a vibrant **artists' colony**, precursors of the wave later headed by Ben Nicholson, Barbara Hepworth (second of Nicholson's three wives), Naum Gabo and the potter Bernard Leach, who in the 1960s were followed by a third wave including Terry Frost, Peter Lanyon, Patrick Heron, Bryan Winter and Roger Hilton.

Sunday painters dominate the dozens of galleries sandwiched between the town's restaurants and bars – the place to view the better work created in St Ives is the new **St Ives Tate Gallery** overlooking Porthmeor Beach, on the north side of town (April–Oct Mon, Wed, Fri & Sat 11am–7pm, Tues & Thurs 11am–9pm, Sun 11am–5pm; Nov–March Tues–Sun 11am–5pm; £3). The beachfront, viewed through a grand concave window, is a constant presence inside the airy and gleaming white building, creating a dialogue with the gallery's paintings, sculptures and ceramics, most of which date from the period 1925 to 1975. Apart from these, the Tate has some specially commissioned contemporary works on view. The museum's rooftop **café** is one of the best places in town for tea and cake.

The Tate ticket also admits you to the **Barbara Hepworth Museum** (April–Oct Mon–Sat 11am–7pm, Sun 11am–5pm; Nov–March Tues–Sun 11am–5pm; £1.50), a short distance away on Back Street, near the High Street on Barnoon Hill. One of the foremost non-figurative sculptors of her time, Hepworth lived in the building from 1949 until her death in a studio fire in 1975. Apart from the sculptures, which are arranged in positions chosen by Hepworth in the house and garden, the museum has masses of background on her art, from photos and letters to catalogues and reviews. A few Hepworths are scattered around the town, including a tender *Madonna* in the harbourside church of **St Ia** – a fifteenth-century building dedicated to the female missionary who was said to have floated over from Ireland on an ivy leaf.

After visiting the Tate, devotees of Bernard Leach's Japanese-inspired ceramics can visit his studio, the **Leach Pottery**, run by his wife Janet in the village of Higher Stennack, three quarters of a mile outside St Ives on the Zennor road (bus #16, #17 or #17a). Janet Leach also runs the *New Craftsman* shop in Fore Street with some examples of her husband's work alongside her own.

The wide expanse of **Porthmeor Beach** dominates the northern side of St Ives, the stone houses tumbling almost onto the yellow sands. Unusually for a town beach, the water quality is excellent, and the rollers make it popular with surfers. East out of town, a string of magnificent golden beaches line **St Ives Bay** – the strand is especially fine on the far side of the port of Hayle, at the mouth of the eponymous river.

Practicalities

The **train station** is off Porthminster Beach, just north of the **bus station** on Station Hill. The **tourist office** is in the Guildhall, on Street An Pol, two minutes' walk away (July & Aug Mon–Sat 9am–6pm, Sun 9am–1pm; Sept–April Mon–Thurs 9am–5.30pm, Fri 9am–5pm, plus May Sat 10am–1pm, June Sat 9am–5.30pm; ☎01736/796 297). You can rent **surfing equipment** from *WindanSea* and *Headworx*, both on Fore Street.

A convenient **place to stay**, for the bus and train stations, is *Chy-Roma*, 2 Seaview Terrace (☎01736/797 539; ③). *The Grey Mullet*, 2 Bunkers Hill (☎01736/796 635; ③), oak-beamed and bedecked with flowers, is just twenty yards from the harbour, while *Gowerton*, 6 Sea View Place (☎01736/796 805; ③), is on the harbour, overlooking the pier. *Kandahar*, 11 The Warren (☎01736/796 183; ③) is one of several **B&Bs** edging the seafront below the bus station, but the best place by far is the *Garrack Hotel*, Burthallan Lane (☎01736/796 199; ⑦), within walking distance of Porthmeor Beach. Family-run, the hotel has an indoor pool and sauna, and an excellent though pricey restaurant. St

---

GETTING TO THE ISLANDS

The islands are accessible by sea or air. **Boats from Penzance to St Mary's** are operated by the *Isles of Scilly Steamship Company* on the South Pier (☎01736/62009). Sailings take place daily at different times according to day and season and take nearly three hours; single tickets are £35, with discounts for students, families and children. There are ferries between each of the inhabited islands, though these are sporadic in winter.

The main departure points for **flights** are **Exeter** (Mon–Sat 1–3 daily; 50min; returns from £75; enquiries ☎01392/67433), **Newquay** (July–Sept Tues, Thurs & Fri 8.50am & 3.25pm; 35min; returns from £60; enquiries ☎01637/860 551) and **Land's End**, near St Just (Mon–Sat hourly until 5.15pm; 15min; returns from £50; enquiries ☎01736/787 017). In addition to these, **helicopter** flights from the heliport a mile east of Penzance are run by *British International Helicopters* (summer Mon–Sat hourly 8am–6pm, less frequently in winter; returns from £55; enquiries ☎01736/63871). All the prices quoted are for cheap day returns, but most of the flights offer discounts for children, and it's always worth asking about special offers, such as "short break" deals. Most landings are at St Mary's, though there are some flights which go direct to Tresco.

Ives has no **campsite** on the seafront, though *Ayr* (April–Oct; ☎01736/795 855) has a good sea prospect, half a mile west of the town centre, above Porthmeor Beach.

Wilbur's Café, on St Andrew's Street, has a lively atmosphere and is the best place for inexpensive **food**, closely followed by *Peppers*, 22 Fore St, a pizza and pasta parlour, also serving fish and steaks. *The Grapevine*, a bistro and coffee house on the High Street, is good for fresh local fish, as is the *Pig 'n' Fish*, Norway Lane (closed Sun, Mon & Nov to mid-March).

The Isles of Scilly

The **Isles of Scilly** are a compact archipelago of about a hundred islands 28 miles southwest of Land's End, none of them bigger than three miles across, and only five of them inhabited – **St Mary's**, **Tresco**, **Bryher**, **St Martin's** and **St Agnes**. In the annals of folklore, the Scillies are the peaks of the submerged land of Lyonesse, a fertile plain that extended west from Penwith before the ocean broke in, drowning the land and leaving only one survivor to tell the tale. In fact they form part of the same granite mass as Land's End, Bodmin Moor and Dartmoor, and despite rarely rising above one hundred feet, they possess a remarkable variety of landscape. All are swept by an energizing briny air filled with the cries of sea birds, and though the water is cold the beaches are clean and alluring enough to tempt you into the shallow bays. Other points of interest include Cornwall's greatest concentration of prehistoric remains, some fabulous rock formations, and masses of **flowers**. Along with tourism, the main source of income here is flower-growing, for which the equable climate and the long hours of sunshine – their name means "Sun Isles" – makes the islands ideal.

Free of traffic, theme parks and amusement arcades, the Scillies are a welcome respite from the tourist trail, the main drawbacks being the shortage of accommodation – making advance booking essential at any time – and the high cost of reaching the islands. If you're coming between May and September, try to time your visit to be here on a Friday evening to witness the weekly **gig races**, the most popular sport on the Scillies, performed by six-oared vessels some thirty feet in length. Some of the boats used are over a hundred years old, built originally to carry pilots to passing ships.

St Mary's

The island of **ST MARY'S** holds the overwhelming majority of the archipelago's population and most of its tourist accommodation. From the airport there are buses to shuttle passengers the mile to **HUGH TOWN**, straddling a neck of land at the southwestern end of the island. Ferries from Penzance dock on the north side of town, under a knob of land still known as The Garrison, where the **Star Castle**, built in Elizabeth I's reign after the scare of the Spanish Armada, has been converted into a hotel. The best remnants of early human settlement on the Scillies are to be found at **Halangy Down**, three quarters of a mile north of Hugh Town. Dating from around 200 BC, it's an extensive complex of stone huts, chief of them a structure built around a courtyard with interconnecting buildings.

The sheltered bay of Porthcressa, a short way south, has the town's best bathing **beach** and offers bike rental at *Buccabu Bike Hire*, a good way to get around the island if you don't want to take advantage of the circular **bus** service (4–7 daily), though neither is ideal for exploring the remoter coastal sections. From Porthcressa another path wanders south to skirt the **Peninnis Headland**, passing some impressive sea-sculpted granite rocks. The path follows the coast to **Old Town Bay**, around which the modern houses of **OLD TOWN** give little hint of its former role as the island's chief port. The town has cafés and a sheltered south-facing beach.

Three quarters of a mile up, **Porth Hellick** is the next major inlet on the island's southern coast, marked by a rugged quartz monument to the fantastically named Sir Cloudesley Shovell, who in 1707 was washed up here from a shipwreck which claimed four ships and nearly 1700 lives. On one side of the bay is another rock shape, the **Loaded Camel**, near which a gate leads to a 4000-year-old **barrow**, probably used by the Bronze Age people from the Iberian peninsula, who were the Scillies' first colonists. **Pelistry Bay**, on the northeastern side of St Mary's, less than two miles from Hugh Town, is one of the most secluded spots on the island, its crystal-clear waters sheltered by the outlying **Toll's Island**, joined to St Mary's at low tide by a slender strand.

Hugh Town's **tourist office**, on Porthcressa Beach (Mon–Sat 8.30am–5pm; ☎01720/422 536), has information on accommodation for all the Scillies. The town is relatively well supplied with **B&Bs**: Porthcressa Road has the small *Pieces of Eight* (☎01720/422 163; ③), and *The Boathouse*, on the Thoroughfare (☎01720/422 688; ③). Close by, the *Harbourside Hotel* is one of St Mary's best options, in a superb position on the main quay (☎01720/422 352; ⑦); higher up, in The Garrison, there's *Veronica Lodge* (closed Dec; ☎01720/422 585; ③). The island's only **campsite** is at *Garrison Farm* near the playing field at the top of the promontory (March–Oct; ☎01720/422 670). The *Pilot's Gig* is a basement **restaurant** below the Garrison Gate at the end of Hugh Street, specializing in fish. Further down, the *Nut Rock Café* has very basic meals and does takeaway packed lunches. In The Garrison, the *Star Castle Hotel* has a good-value fixed-price menu, and you can also snack cheaply in the hotel's *Dungeon Bar*.

Tresco

After St Mary's, **TRESCO** is the most visited island of the Scillies, yet the boat loads of visitors somehow manage to lose themselves on the two-miles-by-one island, the second largest in the group. Once the private estate of a priory, Tresco still retains a cloistered, slightly privileged air, and it has none of St Mary's short-term budget accommodation. Boats generally pull in at **New Grimsby**, halfway up the west coast, though may also land at Old Grimsby, on the east coast, or the southernmost point of Carn Near. Whichever the case, it is only a few minutes' walk to the entrance to **Abbey Gardens** (daily 10am–4pm; £4), featuring a few ruins from the priory amid subtropical gardens laid out in 1834. Many of the plants were grown from seeds taken from London's Kew Gardens, others were brought here from Africa, South America and the Antipodes. The entry ticket also admits you to **Valhalla**, a collection of figureheads and other curiosities taken from shipwrecked vessels.

You don't need to walk far to find alluring sandy beaches: one of the best – **Appletree Bay** – is only a few steps from the southern ferry landing at Carn Near. **Old**

Grimsby, on the island's eastern side, has another couple of lovely sand beaches, looking out to a submarine-shaped rock offshore. The main quay at **New Grimsby** is the departure point for boat excursions and the town boasts another gorgeous sandy bay. Half a mile north of here, **Charles' Castle**, built in the 1550s, overlooks the lagoon-like channel separating Tresco from Bryher. The castle was badly designed, its guns unable to depress far enough to be effective, and it was superseded in 1651 by **Cromwell's Castle**, a gun tower built below it next to a lovely sandy cove. Northwest from here, a path winds across the moor to the northern coast's **Piper's Hole**, a deep underground cave accessible from the cliff edge.

Apart from the exclusive *Island Hotel* at the centre of the island (☎01720/422 883; ⑨), the only **accommodation** on the island is the *New Inn* at New Grimsby (☎01720/422 844; ⑧). The latter has a **restaurant** with a three-course set menu, and you can eat pub snacks in its garden. For gourmet cuisine splash out at the *Island Hotel*, specializing in fresh fish.

Bryher

Covered with a thick carpet of bracken, heather and moss, **BRYHER** is the wildest of the inhabited islands, but the seventy-odd inhabitants have introduced some pockets of order in the form of flower plantations, mostly confined to the small settlement around the quay and climbing up the slopes of **Watch Hill**. It is the exposed western seaboard that takes the full brunt of the Atlantic, nowhere more spectacularly than at the aptly named **Hell Bay**, cupped by a limb of land on the northwestern shore. In contrast to this sound and fury, peace reigns in the southern cove of **Rushy Bay**, one of the best beaches in the Scillies. From the quay, there is a daily boat service to the other islands, and frequent tours to seal and bird colonies as well as fishing expeditions. You could make a quick hop to the small isle of **Samson**, deserted since 1855 when the last impoverished inhabitants were ordered off by the island's proprietor.

Kenython is the cheapest of Bryer's **B&Bs** (April–Oct; ☎01720/422 885; ②), though there is a **campsite** at Jenford Farm on Watch Hill (☎01720/422 886). There is a **bar** and **restaurant** at the island's one hotel, the *Hell Bay* (March–Oct; ☎01720/422 947; ⑧), which is near the pool below Gweal Hill. You can also eat inexpensively at the *Vine Farm Café*, on Watch Hill, and *Fraggle Rock Café*, near the post office.

St Martin's

The main landing stage at **ST MARTIN'S** is on the southern promontory, at the head of the majestic sweep of **Par Beach** – a fitting entry to the island that boasts the best of the Scillies' beaches. From the quay, a road leads up to **HIGHER TOWN**, the main concentration of houses and location of the only shop. The waters hereabouts are among the clearest in Britain, and are much favoured by scuba enthusiasts; contact the *St Martin's Diving Centre* (☎01720/422 848) for tuition. Beyond the church, follow the road westwards to **LOWER TOWN**, a cluster of cottages on the western extremity. The town overlooks the uninhabited isles of **Teän** and **St Helen's**, the latter holding the remains of a tenth-century oratory, monks' dwellings and a chapel, as well as a pest house, erected in 1756 to house plague carriers entering British waters.

Along the southern shore, the gentler side of the island, you'll find the long strand of **Lawrence's Bay** and large areas of flowerbeds. On the northern side, the coast is rougher, with the exception of **Great Bay**, a beautiful secluded half-mile of sand, ideal for swimming. From its western end, you can climb across boulders at low tide to the hilly and wild **White Island**, on the northeastern side of which is a vast cave, **Underland Girt**, accessible at low tide. At **St Martin's Head** on the northeastern tip of the main island lies the red and white Daymark erected in 1683 (not 1637 as inscribed) as a warning against shipping. Below St Martin's Head, on the southeastern shore, lies another fine beach, **Perpitch**, looking out to the scattered Eastern Isles, slivers of rock to which boats take trippers to view puffins and grey seals.

St Martin's has two **B&Bs**, *Glenmoor Cottage* (☎01720/422 816; ③) and *Polreath* (☎01720/422 046; ④), both in Higher Town. In Middletown, there is a **campsite** (☎01720/422 888), just off the road near Lawrence's Bay. The only **pub** on the island is the *Sevenstones Inn* in Lower Town, where snacks are available.

St Agnes

Visitors to the southernmost island of **ST AGNES** disembark at **Porth Conger**, from where a road leads to the western side of the island, on the way passing the **Old Lighthouse**, one of the oldest in the country – dating from 1680 – and the most significant landmark on St Agnes. From here the right-hand fork leads to **Periglis Cove**, a mooring for boats on the western side of the island, while the left-hand fork goes to **St Warna's Cove**, where the patron saint of shipwrecks is reputed to have landed from Ireland, the exact spot being marked by a holy well. **Beady Pool**, an inlet on the eastern side of the headland, gained its name from the trove of beads washed ashore from the wreck of a seventeenth-century Dutch trader; some of the reddish-brown stones still occasionally turn up. The eastern side of St Agnes faces the smaller isle of **Gugh**, linked by a sand bar at low tide, when a lovely sheltered beach is formed.

Least expensive of the **B&Bs** on St Agnes is *Downs Cottage* (March–Nov; ☎01720/422 704; ③), situated near the Old Lighthouse and the post office, followed by nearby *Smugglers Cottage* (☎01720/422 375; ③), and *Covean Cottage*, above Porth Conger (Jan–Oct; ☎01720/422 620; ④). There's a good **campsite** at *Troy Town Farm* above Periglis Cove (☎01720/422 360), enjoying superb views over to the Western Rocks. Just above the jetty at Porth Conger, the *Turk's Head* serves pasties to go with its beer.

Redruth to Bude

Though generally harsher than the county's southern seaboard, the north Cornish coast is punctuated by some of the finest beaches in England, the most popular of which are to be found around **Newquay**, the surfers' capital. Other major holiday centres are to be found down the coast at the ex-mining town of **St Agnes** and north round the Camel estuary, where the port of **Padstow** makes a good base for some remarkable beaches. North of the Camel, the coast is an almost unbroken line of cliffs as far as the Devon border, the gaunt, exposed terrain making a melodramatic setting for **Tintagel**, though the strand at **Bude** attracts legions of surfers and holidaymakers. Parts of the more westerly stretches are littered with the derelict stacks and castle-like ruins of the engine-houses that once powered the region's **copper** and **tin mines**, industries that at one time led the world.

Redruth and around

In the 1850s **REDRUTH** and neighbouring **CAMBORNE**, with which it is now amalgamated, accounted for two thirds of the world's copper production, the 350 pits employing some 50,000 workers, many of whom were forced to emigrate when cheaper deposits of tin and copper were discovered overseas at the turn of the century. The simple granite mine buildings bear a family resemblance to the numerous Methodist chapels in the area – testimony to the success enjoyed by the nonconformist sects in Cornwall. Between 1762 and 1786 the grassy hollow of Gwennap Pit, outside **St Day**, a mile southeast of Redruth, was the site of huge gatherings of miners and their families to hear John Wesley preach. The first visits to Cornwall by the founder of Methodism were met with derision and violence, but he later won over the tough mining communities who could find little comfort in the gentrified established church. At one time Wesley estimated that the congregation at Gwennap Pit exceeded 30,000 noting in his diary, "I shall scarce see a larger congregation till we meet in the air." The present tiered amphitheatre was created in 1805, and is today the venue of Methodist meetings for the annual Whit Monday service.

The town's former harbour lies two and a half miles away at **PORTREATH**, a surfing beach that enjoys the cleanest water on this stretch. The village is within walking distance of the awe-inspiring **Hell's Mouth**, a cauldron of waves and black rocks at the base of two-hundred-foot cliffs five miles down the coast at the top of St Ives Bay; it's also just three miles south of **Porthtowan**, another popular surfing beach.

You can find several **B&B**s in Redruth, among them the attractive *Lansdowne House*, five minutes from the bus and train stations at 42 Clinton Rd (☎01209/216 002; ③). Portreath has the basic *Cliff House*, just off the harbourside (March–Oct; ☎01209/ 842 008; ③), and *Sycamore Lodge* on Primrose Terrace (☎01209/842 784; ③).

St Agnes and around

Though its last tin mines closed as recently as 1986 and the village is surrounded by ruined chimney stacks, **ST AGNES** today gives little hint of the conditions in which its population once lived, the straggling streets of uniform grey cottages now housing retired people, whose immaculate flower-filled gardens are admired by the troops of holidaymakers striding up and down the steep terrace called Stippy-Stappy.

Well connected by bus, St Agnes makes a useful stopover for exploring the coast in the area. At the end of a steep valley below St Agnes, **Trevaunance Cove** is the site of several failed attempts to create a harbour for the town. Its fine sandy beach is a favourite with surfers and other bathing enthusiasts, despite the poor water quality. West of St Agnes lies one of Cornwall's most famous vantage points, **St Agnes Beacon**, 630ft high, from which views extend inland to Bodmin Moor and even across the peninsula to St Michael's Mount. A short distance away, the headland of **St Agnes Head** has the area's largest colony of breeding kittiwakes, and the nearby cliffs also shelter fulmars and guillemots, while grey seals are a common sight offshore.

A good place to **stay** in St Agnes is *Trearren*, a spacious house on a private road in the centre – turn left five hundred yards past *Barclay's* on the one-way system (☎01872/552 017; ②). The most intriguing **pub** is the *Railway Inn* on Vicarage Road, which has a good selection of ales and snacks. One of the area's choicest **hotel-restaurants** occupies a spectacular position at Trevaunance Point overlooking Trevaunance Cove: the ivy-clad *Trevaunance Point Hotel* (☎01872/553 235; ⑧), ex-home of actor Claude Rains, serves wonderful moderately priced fish dishes as well as a six-course vegetarian binge. In Trevaunance Cove itself, there's *Sea Spray* on Quay Road (☎01872/552 991; ④) – it has superb views of the cove, though the nearby *Driftwood Spars Hotel* has more character (☎01872/552 428; ⑤). On the clifftop outside Perranporth, the **youth hostel** (☎01872/573 812), in a former coastguard's station, enjoys great views towards Ligger Point at the north end of the beach.

Newquay

It is difficult to imagine a lineage for **NEWQUAY** that extends more than a few years back, but the "new quay" was built in the fifteenth century in what was already a long established fishing port. Up to then it had been more colourfully known as Towan Blistra, and was concentrated in the sheltered west end of the bay. The town was given a boost in the nineteenth century when its harbour was expanded for coal import and a railway was constructed across the peninsula for china clay shipments. With the trains came a swelling stream of seasonal visitors, drawn to the town's superb position on a knuckle of cliffs overlooking fine golden sands and Atlantic rollers, natural advantages which have made Newquay the premier resort of north Cornwall.

The centre of town is a brisk parade of shops and restaurants, partly pedestrianized, from which lanes lead to ornamental gardens and sloping lawns on the clifftops. Below, adjacent to the small harbour in the crook of the massive Towan Head, **Towan Beach** is the most central of the seven miles of firm sandy beaches that follow in an almost unbroken succession. You can reach all of them on foot, though for some of the further ones, such as the extensive **Watergate Bay**, you can take local buses #53 and #56 or *City Hoppas* A, B, C and D. The beaches get unbearably crowded in season, and all are popular with surfers, particularly Watergate and – west of Towan Head – **Fistral Bay**, the largest of the town beaches. On the other side of East Pentire Head from Fistral, **Crantock Beach** – reachable over the Gannel River by ferry or upstream footbridge – is usually less crowded, and has a lovely backdrop of dunes and undulating grassland.

Newquay's **train station** is off Cliff Road, a couple of hundred yards from the **bus station** on East Street. The **tourist office** lies opposite the bus station at Marcus Hill (May–Sept Mon–Sat 9am–6pm, Sun 10am–5pm; Oct–April Mon–Sat 9am–5pm; ☎01637/871 345). For **accommodation** near the bus station, try *Claremont House*, 35 Trebarwith Crescent (☎01637/875 383; ③), conveniently placed for the beaches. *Sunset House*, 17 Atlantic Rd (☎01637/875 470; ③), is a reliable choice, while fans of Fistral Beach will appreciate the proximity of *Links Hotel* on Headland Road (☎01637/873 211; ③). The area's **campsites** are all mega-complexes, but *Sunnyside* a couple of miles inland by train on Quintrell Downs (☎01637/873 338), at least has separate tent space. *Porth Beach* (☎01637/876 531) is right next to one of Newquay's best beaches.

There's no lack of places to **eat**, but most are mediocre. *JJ's Pizzeria*, on the corner of Beachfield Avenue offers a decent lunch, and *Maharajah* is a good Indian restaurant at 39 Cliff Rd. Otherwise your best bet is *The Cavalier* **pub** right next to the train station, where you can eat cheap tapas as well as bar food. For **surfing equipment**, go to *Fistral Surf Shop* at 1 Beacon Rd on the harbour side of the headland; lessons are run by the *Offshore Surfing School* on Tolcarne Beach. And if you want to explore the surf-head/rave culture, check out *The Lizzy*, a music venue in the *Pentire Hotel*, half a mile out of the centre between Fistral and Crantock beaches.

Padstow and around

The small fishing port of **PADSTOW** is nearly as popular as Newquay, but has a very different feel. Enclosed within the estuary of the Camel – the only river of any size that empties on Cornwall's north coast – the town long retained its position as the principal fishing port on this coast, and still has something of the atmosphere of a medieval

THE SAINTS' WAY

Padstow's St Petroc church is the traditional starting point for one of Cornwall's oldest walking routes, the **Saints' Way**. Extending for some thirty miles between Cornwall's north and south coasts, and connecting the principal ports of Padstow and Fowey, the path originates from the Bronze Age when traders preferred the cross-country hike to making the perilous sea journey round Land's End. The route was later travelled by Irish and Welsh missionaries crossing the peninsula between the fifth and eighth centuries, in order to visit some of the principal shrines of Cornwall's Celtic culture.

Skirting Bodmin Moor, the reconstructed Saints' Way is rarely dramatic, though it passes a variety of scenery and several points of interest along the way, from Neolithic burial chambers to medieval churches and the more austere lines of Wesleyan chapels. The route is well marked and can be walked in stages, the country paths that constitute it stretching for two to six miles each; although it crosses several trunk roads, these do not impinge too much. Pick up guides and leaflets giving detailed directions in the local tourist offices.

town. Its chief annual festival is also a hangover from times past, the **Obby Oss**, a May Day romp where one of the locals garbs himself as a horse and prances through the town preceded by a masked and club-wielding "teaser" – a spirited if rather institutionalized re-enactment of old fertility rites.

On the hill overlooking Padstow, the church of **St Petroc** is dedicated to Cornwall's most important saint, a Welsh or Irish monk who landed here in the sixth century, later died here, and gave his name to the town – "Petrock's Stow". The building has a fine fifteenth-century font, an Elizabethan pulpit and some amusing carved bench ends. The walls are lined with monuments to the local Prideaux family, who still occupy nearby **Prideaux Place**, an Elizabethan manor house with richly furnished rooms and formal gardens (April–Sept Mon–Thurs & Sun 1.30–5pm; house & grounds £3.50, grounds only £2). The harbour is jammed with launches and boats offering cruises in Padstow Bay, while a regular **ferry** (summer daily; winter closed Sun) carries people across the river to **ROCK** – close to the sand-engulfed church of **St Enodoc** (John Betjeman's burial place) and to the good beaches around Polzeath (see p.318).

The coast on the **south side** of the estuary also offers some good **beach** country, which you can reach on buses #55, #56 and #56a. Out of Padstow, the rivermouth is clogged by **Doom Bar** which, apart from thwarting the growth of Padstow as a port, has scuppered some three hundred vessels. Round **Stepper Point** you can reach the sandy and secluded Harlyn Bay and, turning the corner southwards, **Constantine Bay**, the area's best surfing beach. The dunes backing the beach and the rock pools skirting it make this one of the most appealing bays on this coast, though the tides can be treacherous and bathing hazardous near the rocks. Three or four miles further south lies one of Cornwall's most dramatic beaches, **Bedruthan Steps**. Traditionally held to be the stepping stones of a giant called Bedruthan (a legendary figure conjured into existence in the nineteenth century), these slate outcrops can be readily viewed from the clifftop path, at a point which drivers can reach on the B3276.

Practicalities

Padstow's **tourist office** is on the harbour (May, June & Sept Mon–Fri 10am–5pm, Sat 10am–1pm, Sun 11am–4.30pm; July & Aug daily 10am–7pm; Oct–April Mon–Fri 10am–12.30pm; ☎01841/533 449). Central **accommodation** includes the *London Inn* on Landawell Street (☎01841/532 554; ③), converted from a row of fishermen's cottages in 1802, and the *Old Ship Hotel*, Mill Square (☎01841/532 357; ④). The nearest **youth hostel** has stunning views and is excellently sited almost on the beach at Treyarnon Bay (☎01841/520 322; bus #55, #56 or #56a). Behind the hostel there is a **campsite** at Trethias Farm (April–Sept; ☎01841/520 323). Padstow's quayside is lined with snack bars and pasty shops as well as pubs where you can sit outside, such as the *Shipwright's* on the harbour's north side. There is also a smartish **restaurant** here, the *Old Custom House*, serving game as well as vegetarian dishes, but the best is the very expensive *Seafood Restaurant*, at Riverside (Mon–Sat; ☎01841/532 485) – one of England's top fish restaurants. In the cramped backstreets off the main strip, you'll find *Rojano's* offering pizza and pasta on Mill Square. The nautical-flavoured *London Inn* (see above) does good food, as does the *Old Ship*, where you can eat outside.

Polzeath to Port Isaac

Facing west into Padstow Bay, the beaches of and around **POLZEATH** are the finest in the vicinity, pelted by rollers which make this one of the best surfing sites in the West Country – though Daymer Bay still falls short of EU standards of water cleanliness (see p.48). *Pheasants Rise*, Trebetherick (☎01208/863 190; ③), is a useful **B&B** a few minutes' walk from both Polzeath and Daymer bays, and the Tristram **campsite** (☎01208/862 215) sits on a cliff overlooking the beach. Polzeath has a small **tourist**

office behind the beach (April–Oct daily 10am–5pm; ☎01208/862 488). On the beach, the *Cornish Chough* does full meals as well as cream teas; the *Oyster-Catcher* pub is a lively evening hangout just up the hill. *Surf's Up* on the beach offers **surfing** tuition; the gear can be rented from shops.

The next settlement of any size is **PORT ISAAC**, northeast of Polzeath, wedged in a gap in the precipitous cliff wall and seemingly immune to the fashionable currents sweeping the rest of the coast. Only seasonal trippers ruffle the surface of life in this cramped harbour town, whose narrow lanes focus on a couple of pubs at the seafront, where a pebble beach and rock pools are exposed by the low tide. The village offers good **accommodation**, best of all the sixteenth-century *Slipway Hotel* (☎01208/880 264; ⑤), opposite the harbour, with a bar and excellent restaurant. Cheaper choices are outside the centre and away from the sea, among them *Fairholme* (March–Oct; ☎01208/880 397; ③) at 20 Trewetha Lane, and *The Homestead* (☎01208/880 064; ②) on Tintagel Terrace. The *Golden Lion* is Port Isaac's most cheerful **pub** and has an adjoining bistro. Crab is what Port Isaac is famous for; you can buy it to take away at a shop on the harbourfront, or try it at the *Slipway Hotel* or the moderately priced *Old School*, at the top of the village (☎01208/880 721; ③).

Tintagel and Boscastle

East of Port Isaac, the coast is wild and unspoiled, making for some steep and strenuous walking, and providing an appropriate backdrop for the black, forsaken ruins of **Tintagel Castle** (April–Sept daily 10am–6pm; Oct–March daily 10am–4pm; £2.20; EH). It was the twelfth-century chronicler Geoffrey of Monmouth who first popularized the notion that this was the **birthplace of King Arthur**, son of Uther Pendragon and Ygrayne, but by that time local folklore was already saturated with tales of King Mark of Cornwall, Tristan and Iseult, Arthur and the knights of Camelot. Twin influences were at work in Geoffrey's story, which merges the historic figure of Arthur – now thought to have been a Celtic warlord who resisted the Saxon advance in the fifth century – with a separate body of legend centring on the missionary activity of the Celtic monastery that occupied this site in the sixth century. Tintagel is certainly a plausibly resonant candidate for the abode of the Once and Future King, but the **castle** ruins in fact belong to a Norman stronghold that was once occupied by the earls of Cornwall, who after sporadic spurts of rebuilding allowed it to decay, most of it having washed into the sea by the sixteenth century. The remains of the **Celtic monastery** are still visible on the headland and are an important source of knowledge of how the country's earliest monastic houses were organized.

The best approach to the site is from **Glebe Cliff** to the west, where the parish church of **St Materiana** sits in isolation. From the village of **Tintagel** the shortest access is from the signposted path, a well-trodden route. The only item of note in this dreary collection of cafés and B&Bs is the **Old Post Office** (daily April–Sept 11am–5.30pm; Oct 11am–5pm; £2; NT), a rickety-roofed slate-built fourteenth-century construction. The village has plenty of **accommodation**. *The Hunter's Rest* on Atlantic Road (☎01840/770 559; ②) is one of a terrace of B&Bs looking out over the cliff. The *Old Malt House* (March–Oct; ☎01840/770 461; ③) and the *Tintagel Arms Hotel* (☎01840/770 780; ④), both on Fore Street, are conveniently located for the castle. Three quarters of a mile outside the village at Dunderhole Point, past St Materiana, the offices of a former slate quarry now house a **youth hostel** (☎01840/770 334). At the end of Atlantic Road, the *Headland* site offers scenic **camping** (☎01840/770 239).

Three miles east of Tintagel, the port of **BOSCASTLE** lies compressed within a narrow ravine drilled by the rivers Jordan and Valency, its tidy riverfront bordered by thatched and lime-washed houses giving on to the twisty harbour. Above and behind, a collection of seventeenth- and eighteenth-century cottages can be seen on a circular walk, starting either from Fore Street or the main car park. The walk traces the valley of the Valency for about a mile to reach Boscastle's graceful **parish church**, tucked away in a peaceful glen. Another mile and a half up the valley lies another church, **St Juliot's**, restored by Thomas Hardy when he was plying his trade as a young architect. It was while he was working here that he met Emma Gifford, whom he married in 1874, a year after the publication of *A Pair of Blue Eyes*, the book that kicked off Hardy's literary career. It opens with an architect arriving in a Cornish village to restore its church, and is full of descriptions of the country around Boscastle.

Boscastle's best **accommodation** is *St Christopher's Hotel* (March–Oct; ☎01840/250 412; ③), a restored Georgian manor house at the top of the High Street. The *Old Coach House* on Tintagel Road (☎01840/250 398; ③) is another well-equipped old building. The harbour has a lovely old **youth hostel** (☎01840/250 287); nearby, you can eat at the *Harbour Café*, which serves hot meals all day. The village has three good **pubs**, though the *Napoleon* has the advantage of a good vegetarian menu among its bar meals and a spacious garden with distant views of the sea. The *Cobweb* is busier but rates highly on atmosphere and has live music on Saturdays.

Bude and around

There is little distinctively Cornish in Cornwall's northernmost town of **BUDE**, four miles west of the Devon border. Built around an estuary surrounded by a fine expanse of sands, the town has sprouted a crop of holiday homes and hotels, though these have not unduly spoiled the place nor the magnificent cliffy coast surrounding it.

Of the excellent beaches hereabouts, the central **Summerleaze** is clean and wide, growing to such immense proportions when the tide is out that a sea-water swimming pool has been provided near the cliffs. The mile-long **Widemouth Bay**, two and a half miles **south** of Bude, is the main focus of the holiday hordes – it has the cleanest water monitored between Bude and Polzeath, though bathing can be dangerous near the rocks at low tide. Surfers also congregate five miles down the coast at **Crackington Haven**, wonderfully situated between 430-foot cliffs at the mouth of a lush valley, though the water quality is poor. The cliffs on this stretch are characterized by remarkable zigzagging strata of shale, limestone and sandstone, a mixture which erodes into vividly contorted detached formations.

To the **north** of Bude, acres-wide **Crooklets** is the scene of **surfing** and life-saving demonstrations and competitions. A couple of miles further, **Sandy Mouth** holds a pristine expanse of sand with rock pools beneath the encircling cliffs. The water quality is up to EU standards despite the seaborne litter, and myriad wildflowers dot the country around. It is a short walk from here to another surfers' delight, **Duckpool**, a tiny sandy cove flanked by jagged reefs at low tide. The beach is dominated by the three-hundred-foot **Steeple Point**, at the mouth of a stream that flows through the **Coombe Valley**. Once the estate of the master Elizabethan mariner Sir Richard Grenville, the valley is now managed by the National Trust, who have laid out a one-and-a-half-mile nature trail alongside the wooded stream, half a mile inland.

Between Duckpool and the Devon border stretch five miles of strenuous but exhilarating coast. The only village along here is **Morwenstow**, just south of **Henna Cliff**, at 450 feet the highest sheer drop of any seacliff in England after Beachy Head, affording magnificent views along the coast and beyond Lundy to the Welsh coast.

Practicalities

Bude's **tourist office** is in the centre of town at The Crescent (April–Sept daily 9am–5.30pm; ☎01288/354 240). For **accommodation**, *Clovelly House*, 4 Burn View (Jan–Oct; ☎01288/352 761; ②), and *Links View*, 13 Morwenna Terrace (closed Dec; ☎01288/352 561; ②), are both near the golf course. *Dorset House* is a grander hotel on Killerton Road (☎01288/352 665; ③), while the best of the lot is the *Falcon Hotel*, an old coaching inn on Breakwater Road (☎01288/352 005; ⑤). Among the hotels around Crooklets Beach, try the *Inn on the Green*, (☎01288/356 013; ④). Bude's nearest **campsite** is *Wooda Park* (April–Oct; ☎01288/352 069), away from the sea at Poughill (pronounced "Poffil"), two miles north of Bude. The *Falcon Hotel* offers good food at its bar and has a more formal and expensive **restaurant**, which specializes in seafood. For snacks and salads, try the central *Carriers Inn* on the Strand, which has seating outside. There's a choice of **surfing equipment rental** outlets, including *XTC* on Morwenna Terrace and *Zuma Jay* on Belle Vue Lane.

Bodmin and Bodmin Moor

Bodmin Moor, the smallest, mildest and most accessible of the West Country's great moors, has some beautiful tors, torrents and rock formations, but much of its fascination lies in the strong human imprint, particularly the wealth of relics left behind by its **Bronze Age** population, including such important sites as Trethevy Quoit and the stone circles of The Hurlers. Separated from these by some three millennia, the churches in the villages of St Neot's, Blisland and Altarnun are among the region's finest examples of fifteenth-century art and architecture.

Bodmin

The town of **BODMIN** lies on the western edge of Bodmin Moor, equidistant from the north and south Cornish coasts and the Fowey and Camel rivers, a position that encouraged its growth as a trading town. It was also an important ecclesiastical centre after the establishment of a priory by Saint Petroc, who moved here from Padstow in the sixth century. The priory disappeared but Bodmin retained its prestige through its church of St Petroc, built in the fifteenth century and still the largest in Cornwall. Though officially the county town, Bodmin sacrificed much of its administrative role by refusing access to the Great Western Railway in the 1870s, as a result of which much local business transferred down the road to Truro. Bodmin does have a train stop now, though **Bodmin Parkway** station lies three miles outside town, with a regular bus connection to the centre.

Bodmin's most prominent landmark is the **Gilbert Memorial**, a 144-foot obelisk honouring a descendant of Walter Raleigh and occupying a commanding location on Bodmin Beacon, a high area of moorland near the centre of town. Below, at the end of Fore Steet, stands **St Petroc's** church; inside it has an extravagantly carved twelfth-century font and an ivory casket that once held the bones of Petroc, while the south-west corner of the churchyard holds a sacred well. Close by, the notorious **Bodmin Jail** (Easter to mid-Oct daily except Sat 10am–6pm; £2.80) glowers malevolently on Berrycombe Road, redolent of the public executions that were guaranteed crowd-pullers until 1862, when the hangings retreated behind closed doors. You can visit part of the original eighteenth-century structure, including the condemned cell and some grisly exhibits chronicling the lives of the inmates.

From Parkway it's less than two miles' walk to one of Cornwall's most celebrated country houses, **Lanhydrock** (April–Sept Tues–Sun 11am–5.30pm; Oct Tues–Sun 11am–5pm; house & grounds £5.40, grounds only £2.50; NT), originally seventeenth-century but totally rebuilt after a fire in 1881. The granite exterior remains true to its original form, but the 42 rooms show a very different style, including a long picture gallery with a plaster ceiling depicting scenes from the Old Testament and – most illuminating of all – servants' quarters that reveal the daily workings of a Victorian manor house. The grounds have magnificent beds of magnolias, azaleas and rhododendrons, and a huge area of wooded parkland bordering onto the River Fowey.

Practicalities

Bodmin's **tourist office** (May–Aug Mon–Sat 10am–5pm; Sept Mon–Fri 10am–5pm; Oct–April Mon–Fri 10am–1pm; ☎01208/76616) is at the bottom of St Nicholas Street. Basic **B&B** is available at 21 Boxwell Park, a ten-minute walk from St Petroc's church off Launceston Road (April–Oct; ☎01208/73641; ③). Larger and better equipped is *Lignano*, on the outskirts of town at 68 Castle Hill (☎01208/74184; ②). Outside town, adjoining the Lanhydrock estate, the handsome Georgian farmhouse of *Treffry Farm* (March–Oct; ☎01208/74405; ③) has rooms and a separate cottage that sleeps six. There's a good **campsite** on Old Callywith Road, a ten-minute walk from the centre (March–Sept; ☎01208/73834).

Off Fore Street, the *Hole in the Wall* **pub** on Crockwell Street has an agreeable back-room bar in what used to be the debtors' prison, with exposed fourteenth-century walls enclosing a collection of antiquities and bric-a-brac. You can drink in the courtyard in summer, bar lunches are available, and there's an upstairs **restaurant** specializing in fish. Finally, you can rent **bikes** at *Cycle Revolution* on Honey Street, off Turf Street near St Petroc's (☎01208/72557).

Bodmin Moor

Just ten miles in diameter, **BODMIN MOOR** is a wilderness on a small scale, its highest tor rising to just 1375ft from a platform of 1000ft. Yet the moor conveys a sense of loneliness quite out of proportion to its size, with scattered ancient remains providing in places the only distraction from an otherwise empty horizon. Aside from its tors, the main attractions of the landscape are the small Dozmary Pool, a site steeped in myth, and a quartet of rivers – the Fowey, Lynher, Camel and De Lank – that rise from remote moorland springs and effectively bound the moor to the north, east and south.

Blisland and the western moor

BLISLAND stands in the Camel valley on the western slopes of Bodmin Moor, three miles northeast of Bodmin. Georgian and Victorian houses cluster around a village green and a church whose well-restored interior has an Italianate altar and a startlingly painted screen. On **Pendrift Common** above the village, the gigantic **Jubilee Rock** is inscribed with various patriotic insignia commemorating the jubilee of George III's coronation in 1809. From this seven-hundred-foot vantage point you look eastward over the De Lank gorge and the boulder-crowned knoll of **Hawk's Tor**, three miles away. On the shoulder of the tor stand the Neolithic **Stripple Stones**, a circular platform once holding 28 standing stones, of which just four are still upright. Blisland lies just a couple of miles east of the **Merry Meeting** crossroads, a point near the end of the Camel Trail. Best of the local accommodation is *Moss Farm*, midway between Blisland and Hawk's Tor near the hamlet of Bradford (☎01208/850 628; ③); the farm also has pitches for **camping** and offers **pony-trekking**.

Bolventor and Dozmary Pool

The village of **Bolventor**, lying at the centre of the moor midway between Bodmin and Launceston, is an uninspiring place close to one of the moor's chief focuses for walkers and sightseers alike – **Jamaica Inn** (☎01566/86250; ⑤). A staging post even before the precursor of the A30 road was laid here in 1769, the inn was described by Daphne du Maurier as being "alone in glory, four square to the winds", and the combination of its convenient position and its association with her has led to its growth into a hotel and restaurant complex. One corner exhibits the room where the author stayed in 1930, soaking up inspiration for her smuggler's yarn. At the other end of the building is a **Museum of Curiosities** (Easter–Oct 10am–4pm, open till 8pm during school holidays; winter 11am–4pm; £1.95) a fairground miscellany of Victorian toys, mummified and stuffed animals, a collection of pipes and a guinea pigs' cricket match.

The inn's car park is a useful place to leave your vehicle and venture forth on foot. Just a mile away, along what must be the most travelled path on the moor, **Dozmary Pool** is another link in the West Country's Arthurian mythologies – after Arthur's death Sir Bedevere hurled Excalibur, the king's sword, into the pool, where it was claimed by an arm raised from the depths. Loe Pool, near Porthleven on the Lizard, also claims the same honour (see p.307). Despite its proximity to the A30, the diamond-shaped lake usually preserves an ethereal air, though it's been known to run dry in summer, dealing a bit of a blow to the legend that the pool is bottomless.

The lake is also the source of another, more obviously Cornish legend, that of John Tregeagle, a steward at Lanhydrock, whose unjust dealings with the local tenant farmers in the seventeenth century brought upon his spirit the curse of endlessly baling out the pool with a perforated limpet shell. As if this were not enough, his ghost is further tormented by a swarm of devils pursuing him as he flies across the moor in search of sanctuary; their infernal howling is sometimes audible on windy nights.

Liskeard and St Neot

Liskeard, a bus and rail junction just off the southern limits of the moor, makes a decent overnight stop, with accommodation at *Elnor*, 1 Russell St (☎01579/342 472; ③) and *The Nebula*, 27 Higher Lux St (☎01579/343 989; ④). From here, buses go on to **ST NEOT**, one of Bodmin Moor's prettiest villages, approached through a lush wooded valley. Its fifteenth-century **church** contains some of the most impressive stained-glass windows of any parish church in the country, the oldest glass being the fifteenth-century **Creation Window**, at the east end of the south aisle. Next along, **Noah's Window** continues the sequence, but the narration soon dissolves into windows portraying patrons and local bigwigs, while others present cameos of the ordinary men and women of the village.

This southern edge of the moor is far greener and more thickly wooded than the northern reaches, due to the confluence of a web of rivers into the Fowey. One of the moor's best-known beauty spots is a couple of miles east, below Draynes Bridge, where the Fowey tumbles through the **Golitha Falls**, less a waterfall than a series of rapids. Dippers and wagtails flit through the trees, and there's a pleasant woodland walk you can take to the dam at the Siblyback Lake reservoir just over a mile away: follow the river up to Draynes Bridge, then walk north up a minor road until a path branches off on the right after a half-mile, leading down to the water's edge.

Camelford and the northern tors

The northern half of Bodmin Moor is dominated by its two highest tors, both of them easily accessible from **CAMELFORD**, a town once associated with King Arthur's Camelot, while Slaughterbridge, which crosses the River Camel north of town, is one of the contenders for his last battleground. The town's modest **North Cornwall Museum** (April–Sept Mon–Sat 10am–5pm; £1.25) in the centre contains domestic items and exhibits showing the development of the local slate industry, and also has a **tourist office** (same times; ☎01840/212 954). Although it lacks excitement, Camelford makes a useful touring base. Among its **accommodation** is the central *Camelford House*, 3 Victoria Rd (☎01840/212 470; ③), and *The Countryman Hotel* at no. 7 on the same street (☎01840/212 250; ③). The *Mason's Arms* on Market Place also has rooms and a beer garden (☎01840/213 309; ②) and *The Orangery*, opposite Camelford House, makes a convenient coffee stop. There are two **campsites** in the area, at *King's Acre* (April–Oct; ☎01840/213 561) and *Lakefield Caravan Park*, Lower Pendavey Farm (April–Oct; ☎01840/213 279).

Rough Tor, the second highest peak on Bodmin Moor at 1311ft, is four miles' walk southeast from Camelford. The hill presents a different aspect from every angle: from the south an ungainly mass, from the west a nobly proportioned mountain. A short distance to the east stand the Little Rough Tor, where there are the remains of an Iron Age camp, and Showery Tor, capped by a prominent formation of piled rocks. Easily visible to the southeast, **Brown Willy** is, at 1375ft, the highest Bodmin peak in Cornwall, as its original name signified – Bronewhella, or "highest hill". Like Rough Tor, Brown Willy shows various faces, its sugar-loaf appearance from the north sharpening into a long multi-peaked crest as you approach. The tor is accessible by continuing from the summit of Rough Tor across the valley of the De Lank, or, from the south, by footpath from Bolventor. The easiest ascent is by the worn path which climbs steeply up from the northern end of the hill.

Altarnun and the eastern moor

ALTARNUN is a pleasant, granite-grey village snugly sheltered beneath the eastern heights of the moor. Its prominent **church**, dedicated to St Nonna, mother of David, patron saint of Wales, contains a fine Norman font and 79 bench ends carved at the beginning of the sixteenth century, depicting saints, musicians and clowns. The village also has a Methodist chapel, over the door of which there is an effigy of John Wesley – a regular visitor to the neighbourhood – by Nevill Northey Burnard (1818–78), a local sculptor who, despite the praise of his contemporaries, ended his days in a Redruth poorhouse. Outside the village, *Trecollas Farm* (March–Oct; ☎01566/86386; ②) offers good accommodation and a four-course breakfast.

South of Altarun, **Withey Brook** tumbles 400ft in less than a mile of gushing cascades before meeting up with the River Lynher, which bounds Bodmin Moor to the east. Beyond the brook, on **Twelve Men's Moor**, lie some of Bodmin Moor's grandest landscapes. The quite modest elevations of Hawk's Tor (1079ft) and the lower Trewartha Tor appear enormous from the north, though they are overtopped by **Kilmar**, highest of the hills on the moor's eastern flank at 1280ft. Withey Brook starts life about six miles from Altarun on **Stowe's Hill**, site of the moor's most famous stone pile, **The Cheeswring**, a precarious pillar of balancing granite slabs, marvellously eroded by the wind. Gouged out of the hillside nearby, the disused Cheesewring Quarry is a centre of rock climbing. A mile or so south down Stowe's Hill stands an artificial rock phenomenon, **The Hurlers**, a wide complex of three circles dating from about 1500 BC. The purpose of these stark upright stones is not known, though they owe their name to the legend that they were men turned to stone for playing the Celtic game of hurling on the Sabbath.

The Hurlers are easily accessible just outside **MINIONS**, Cornwall's highest village, three miles south of which stands another Stone Age survival, **Trethevy Quoit**, a chamber tomb nearly nine feet high, surmounted by a massive capstone. Originally enclosed in earth, the stones have been stripped by centuries of weathering to create Cornwall's most impressive megalithic monument. Bus #278 from Liskeard (Mon–Sat 6 daily) calls at St Cleer and Darite, both of which are close to Trethevy Quoit; alternatively, it's a three-mile walk from Liskeard.

travel details

Trains

Bath to: Bristol (every 20min; 15min); London (hourly; 1hr 25min).

Bodmin to: Exeter (hourly; 1hr 40min); London (9 daily; 4hr); Penzance (hourly; 1hr 20min); Plymouth (hourly; 50min).

Bristol to: Bath (every 20min; 15min); Exeter (hourly; 1hr 20min); London (every 30min; 1hr 30min); Penzance (5 daily; 4hr); Plymouth (8–9 daily; 2hr); Truro (5 daily; 3hr).

Exeter to: Bodmin (hourly; 2hr); Bristol (hourly; 1hr 10min); Exmouth (11–24 daily; 25min); Honiton (10 daily; 30min); Liskeard (hourly; 1hr

40min); London (15 daily; 2hr 40min); Par (hourly; 1hr 50min); Penzance (hourly; 3hr 15min); Plymouth (hourly; 1hr 10min); Torquay (4–24 daily; 45min); Truro (hourly; 2hr 30min).

Falmouth to: Truro (Mon–Sat 13 daily; 22min).

Liskeard to: Exeter (hourly; 1hr 30min); London (9 daily; 3hr 30min); Looe (7–12 daily, no Sun service Oct–June; 35min); Penzance (hourly; 1hr 40min); Plymouth (hourly; 30min); Truro (hourly; 50min).

Newquay to: Par (Mon–Sat 5 daily, also Sun 5 daily in summer; 50min).

Penzance to: Bodmin (hourly; 1hr 20min); Bristol (6 daily; 4hr); Exeter (hourly; 3hr); Liskeard (hourly; 1hr 20min); London (8 daily; 5hr); Par (hourly; 1hr 5min); Plymouth (hourly; 2hr); St Ives (Mon–Sat 9 daily; 22min); Truro (hourly; 30min).

Plymouth to: Bodmin (hourly; 40min); Bristol (hourly; 2hr 30min); Exeter (hourly; 1hr); Liskeard (hourly; 25–40min); London (hourly; 3hr 45min); Par (hourly; 50min); Penzance (hourly; 2hr); St Erth (hourly; 1hr 45min); Truro (hourly; 1hr 15min).

St Ives to: Penzance (Mon–Sat 9 daily; 22min); St Erth (Mon–Sat every 30min; 12min).

Torquay to: Exeter (4–22 daily; 45min).

Truro to: Bristol (hourly; 3hr 40min); Exeter (hourly; 2hr 20min); Falmouth (9–13 daily; 20min); Liskeard (hourly; 48min); London (hourly; 4hr 45min); Penzance (hourly; 45min); Plymouth (hourly; 1hr 15min).

Buses

Bath to: Bristol (every 15–30min; 40min); Exeter (3 daily; 2hr 50min–3hr 25min); Frome (Mon–Sat hourly; 55min); London (9 daily; 3hr 5min); Salisbury (1–7 daily; 1hr 25min–2hr 5min); Wells (hourly; 1hr 20min).

Bodmin to: Bristol (3 daily; 3hr 30min); Newquay (3 daily; 45min); Plymouth (3 daily; 1hr); St Austell (Mon–Sat 13 daily; 55min).

Bristol to: Bath (every 15–30min; 50min); Bodmin (3 daily; 3hr 30min); Exeter (3–9 daily; 1hr 40min); Falmouth (1 daily; 5hr); Frome (Mon–Sat hourly; 1hr 40min); Glastonbury (3–12 daily; 1hr 30min); London (8–17 daily; 2hr 15min); Newquay (3 daily; 4hr 20min); Plymouth (6 daily; 2hr 40min); St Austell (3 daily; 3hr 55min); Torquay (5 daily; 2hr 45min–3hr 35min); Truro (5 daily; 4hr 30min); Wells (4–12 daily; 1hr).

Exeter to: Bath (3 daily; 2hr 50min–3 hr 10min); Bristol (5–9 daily; 1hr 40min–2hr); Falmouth (1 daily; 3hr 50min); London (8 daily; 3hr 50min); Plymouth (6 daily; 1hr); St Austell (4 daily; 2hr–3hr 30min); Torquay (7–8 daily; 1hr 5min); Truro (4 daily; 2hr 30min–4hr).

Falmouth to: Bristol (1 daily; 5hr 15min); Exeter (1 daily; 4hr 10min); Plymouth (2 daily; 2hr 30min); St Austell (2 daily; 1hr 5min); Truro (2 daily; 30min).

Glastonbury to: Bristol (4–12 daily; 1hr 22min); Frome (1 daily; 45min); Taunton (Mon–Sat 5 daily; 1hr 35min); Wells (Mon–Sat hourly, Sun every 2hr; 16min).

Newquay to: Bodmin (3 daily; 50min); Bristol (3–4 daily; 4hr 50min); Plymouth (4 daily; 1hr 25min–2hr); St Austell (Mon–Sat 5–7 daily; 1hr 10min).

Penzance to: Plymouth (8 daily; 3–4hr); St Austell (8 daily; 1hr 35min–2hr 15min); St Ives (5 daily; 25min); Truro (8 daily; 1hr 5min–1hr 40min).

Plymouth to: Bodmin (3 daily; 1hr); Bristol (6 daily; 2hr 45min); Exeter (6 daily; 1hr); Falmouth (2 daily; 2hr 10min); London (6 daily; 4hr 30min); Newquay (3 daily; 1hr 45min); Penzance (8 daily; 3hr 20min); St Austell (8 daily; 1hr 20min); St Ives (5 daily; 2hr 55min); Torquay (12 daily; 1hr 40min); Truro (8 daily; 1hr 55min).

St Austell to: Bodmin (Mon–Sat 10 daily; 55min); Bristol (3 daily; 4hr 15min–5hr 40min); Exeter (4 daily; 2hr 25min–3hr 50min); Falmouth (2 daily; 55min); Newquay (Mon–Sat 5–7 daily; 1hr 10min); Penzance (7 daily; 2hr 45min); Plymouth (8 daily; 1hr 20min); St Ives (5 daily; 1hr 35min); Truro (8–11 daily; 35–50min).

Taunton to: Glastonbury (Mon–Sat 5 daily; 1hr 35min); Wells (Mon–Sat 5 daily; 1hr 50min).

Torquay to: Bristol (8 daily; 2hr 45min–3hr 35min); Exeter (6–7 daily; 1hr); London (6–7 daily; 5hr).

Truro to: Bristol (5 daily; 4hr 50min); Exeter (4 daily; 2hr 55min–4hr 20min); Falmouth (2 daily; 20min); Penzance (8 daily; 1hr 5min–1hr 40min); Plymouth (8 daily; 1hr 55min); St Austell (8–11 daily; 35–50min); St Ives (5 daily; 1hr).

Wells to: Bath (3–11 daily; 1hr 20min); Bridgwater (Mon–Sat 5–9 daily; 1hr 20min); Bristol (4–12 daily; 1hr); Frome (Mon–Sat hourly; 1hr); Glastonbury (Mon–Sat hourly, Sun every 2hr; 15min); Taunton (Mon–Sat 6 daily; 1hr 50min).

CHAPTER SIX

EAST ANGLIA

Strictly speaking, **East Anglia** is made up of just three counties – Suffolk, Norfolk and the old county of Cambridgeshire – which were settled by Angles from Holstein in the fifth century, though in more recent times, it's come to be loosely applied to include Essex and what used to be Huntingdonshire. As a

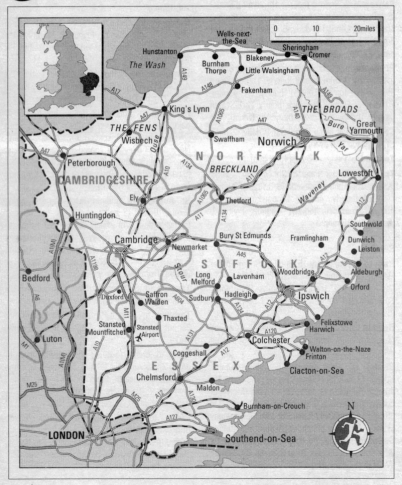

region it's renowned for being featureless and boring, and of course such clichés always contain more than a grain of truth – if you're looking for mountains, you've come to the wrong place. But there are also numerous spots that refuse to conform to the dull stereotype: parts of Suffolk are positively hilly, and its coastline can induce vertigo; you won't find a finer selection of medieval churches than in Norfolk and Suffolk; and even in the indisputably flat fenlands there are gems such as Ely to savour.

Of all the East Anglian counties, **Suffolk** is the most varied. Its undulating southern reaches, along the River Stour, are home to picturesque, well-preserved little towns which enjoyed immense prosperity during the heyday of the region's woollen trade, from the thirteenth to the sixteenth centuries. **Bury St Edmunds** can boast not just the ruins of its once prestigious abbey, but also has some fine Georgian architecture on its grid-plan streets and a new museum that draws in the crowds. Even the much maligned county town of **Ipswich** has more to offer than it's generally given credit for – few other towns can claim an Elizabethan mansion and a masterpiece of modern architecture within walking distance of one another. Despite unrelenting coastal erosion and the decline in traditional industries such as fishing, the coastline also has much to offer: **Aldeburgh** hosts one of the best music festivals in the country, while **Southwold** is an archetypal Edwardian seaside resort.

Norfolk, as everyone knows thanks to Noel Coward, is very flat. Fewer people realize that, though it is now one of the emptiest and most peaceful counties in England, it was once the most populous. Its capital, **Norwich**, is still East Anglia's largest city, renowned for its Norman cathedral and castle, and for its high-tech Sainsbury Centre, a provocative collection of twentieth-century art. The one part of Norfolk which has been well and truly discovered is the **Broads**, a unique landscape of reed-ridden waterways that have been over-exploited by farmers and boat hire companies for the last twenty years. Too far from London to attract day-trippers, the Norfolk coast – with the exception of touristy **Great Yarmouth** and, to a lesser extent, the Victorian resort of **Cromer** – remains one of the most unspoilt in England, with the Cley marshes and Blakeney Point among the country's top nature reserves. Meanwhile, sheltering inland, are two outstanding stately homes – **Blickling Hall** and **Holkham** – with more within easy striking distance of **King's Lynn**, itself an ancient maritime trading port.

Cambridge is, rightly so, the one place in East Anglia everyone visits – home to a world-renowned university and one of the most beautiful towns in England. The rest of Cambridgeshire is dominated by the landscape of the **Fens**, for centuries an inhospitable marshland, which eventually was drained to provide rich alluvial farming land. Its one great highlight is the cathedral town of **Ely**, stranded on one of the few areas of raised ground in the fens, an easy and popular day trip from Cambridge. The old county of Huntingdonshire, now the western part of Cambridgeshire, has very little to attract the visitor, except perhaps **Peterborough**, where you can admire another of East Anglia's great cathedrals.

Essex, not properly part of East Anglia, has a bad reputation with the rest of the English, its inhabitants the butt of numerous jokes. Essex man and woman are brash,

ACCOMMODATION PRICE CODES

Throughout this guide, hotel and B&B accommodation is priced on a scale of ① to ⑨, the number indicating the **lowest price** you could expect to pay per night in that establishment for a **double room** in high season. The prices indicated by the codes are as follows:

① under £20/\$30	④ £40–50/\$60–75	⑦ £70–80/\$105–120
② £20–30/\$30–45	⑤ £50–60/\$75–90	⑧ £80–100/\$120–150
③ £30–40/\$45–60	⑥ £60–70/\$90–105	⑨ over £100/\$150

uncultured Tory-voting *nouveaux riches*, so the myth goes, and though there are people who conform to this stereotype, they are probably no more common in Essex than anywhere else in the southeast of England. Inevitably, however, its proximity to London has turned many places into soulless commuter towns. Chelmsford's position at the geographical centre of Essex has made it the county's capital, but it's **Colchester** which has the most to offer in the way of sights.

Colchester

If you visit anywhere in Essex, it should be **COLCHESTER**, fifty miles or so northeast of London, which prides itself on being England's oldest town. There is documentary evidence of a settlement here at least as early as the fifth century BC, and by the first century AD the town was the capital of King Cunobelin – better known as Shakespeare's Cymbeline. When the Romans invaded Britain in 43 AD they chose Colchester (Camulodunum) as their new capital, though it was soon eclipsed by London and became a retirement colony for legionaries. The first Roman temple in the country was erected here, and in 60 AD the colony was the focus of Boudicca's abortive revolt (see box opposite) – a millennium later the conquering Normans built one of their mightiest strongholds here. But the conflict that most marked the town came in 1648 during the Civil War, when Colchester was subjected to a gruelling eleven-week siege by the Parliamentarian army led by Lord Fairfax. Today, a university town and a major army base in the heart of prosperous Essex, Colchester still bears the traces of the events that shaped its past.

The Town

Most visitors start off at the town's rugged, honey-coloured **Castle**, the perfect introduction to Colchester's long history. Begun less than ten years after the Battle of Hastings, it boasts a phenomenally large keep – the largest in Europe at the time – built on the site of the defunct Roman temple, the foundations of which are still visible at the foot of the castle. The **Museum** within the castle (March–Nov Mon–Sat 10am–5pm, Sun 2–5pm; Dec–Feb closed Sun; £2.50) contains the best of the region's Anglo-Roman archaeological finds, although that amounts to little more than a handful of mosaics, tombstones and statues. The Boudicca revolt and the 1648 siege are also covered in depth, and you can sign up for a guided tour of the underground tunnels.

The castle stands at the eastern end of the wide **High Street**, which lies pretty much along the same route as it did in Roman times. The most arresting building is undoubtedly the flamboyant **Town Hall**, built at the turn of the century, and topped by a statue of Saint Helena, mother of Constantine the Great and daughter of "Old King Cole" of the nursery rhyme – who, some say, gave the town its name. Immediately north of the High Street is the so-called **Dutch Quarter**, where Flemish refugees settled in the sixteenth century to assist the town's ailing cloth trade. The area still makes a nice place to wander, particularly along West and East Stockwell streets. South of the High Street, much of the medieval street plan has been subsumed into a vast open-air shopping precinct. The two reasons for venturing here are both in Trinity Street: the thoroughly Saxon **Holy Trinity Church**, now a museum of social history (April–Oct Tues–Sat 10am–noon & 1–5pm; free) and, down a passageway opposite, **Tymperleys Clock Museum** (April–Oct Tues–Sat 10am–1pm & 2–5pm; free). The latter is housed in a wonderful fifteenth-century timber-framed house, with its own garden, worth a visit in itself as much as for the beautiful Colchester-made clocks within.

At the western end of the High Street is the town landmark, **"Jumbo"**, a disused nineteenth-century water tower, which is considerably more imposing than the nearby

BOUDICCA

Boudicca – popularly known as Boadicea – was the widow of Prasutagus, chief of the Iceni tribe of Norfolk, who had allied themselves to the Romans during the conquest of Britain in 43 AD. Five years later, when the Romans attempted to disarm them, Prasutagus and the Iceni revolted but were easily put down. On Prasutagus' death, the Romans ignored his will and confiscated his property – when Boudicca protested, the Romans flogged her and raped her daughters. Boudicca quickly rallied the Iceni and their allies, then in 60 AD set off on a rampage through southern Britain.

As the ultimate symbol of Roman oppression, the Temple of the Deified Claudius in Colchester was the initial focus of hatred, and once Colchester had been demolished Boudicca laid waste London and St Albans too, massacring over 70,000 citizens and inflicting crushing defeats on the Roman units stationed there. She was far from squeamish, ripping traitors' arms out of their sockets, and torturing every Roman and collaborator in sight. She was eventually defeated by the Roman governor Suetonius Paullinus in a pitched battle which cost the Romans just four hundred lives, and the Britons countless thousands. Boudicca committed suicide, while the Romans took their revenge on the surviving rebel tribes.

Balkerne Gate. This is the largest surviving Roman gateway in the country, though at only a touch over six feet in height, it's far short of spectacular. The town's **Roman Walls**, to which the gate is joined, are somewhat more impressive, though the overall effect of this particular section is spoiled by the adjacent ring road. With a little time to spare, it's worth strolling down East Hill, a continuation of the High Street east of the castle. Splendid Georgian houses line the top end of the hill, one of which is now the **Hollytrees Museum** (Tues–Sat 10am–noon & 1–5pm; free), containing a collection of costumes, toys and decorative arts from the eighteenth to the twentieth century.

Practicalities

Services from London and Harwich arrive at the mainline **Colchester North Station**, fifteen minutes' walk north of town. The **bus station** is off Queen Street, a little to the south of the castle. The **tourist office** is on the corner of Queen Street and the High Street (April–Oct Mon, Tues, Thurs & Fri 9am–5pm, Wed, Sat & Sun 10am–5pm; Nov–March closed Sun; ☎01206/282 920). There's a cheap **B&B** at 13 Worcester Rd (☎01206/866 825; ②), off Guildford Road, north of East Hill, and a couple of reasonable ones in Roman Road, the *Old Manse* at no. 15 (☎01206/451 54; ③) being the nicer. Colchester abounds in fantastically old **hotels**, including the fifteenth-century *Red Lion*, 43 High St (☎01206/577 986; ⑤), and the *Rose and Crown*, East Gates (☎01206/866 677; ⑤), which claims to be the oldest in England. Otherwise, there's a **youth hostel** in a beautiful Georgian house at the bottom of East Hill (March–Dec; ☎01206/867 982), while the **campsite** is on Cymbeline Way (☎01206/45551; a 30-min walk or take bus #15 or #17 from North Station), just by the A12 Colchester turn-off and more invitingly, by the Lexden nature reserve.

The most consistent **restaurant** in Colchester is the *Warehouse Brasserie* in Chapel Street, just off St John's Street; alternatively, try the leafy, upmarket Italian joint, *La Piazza*, on West Stockwell Street (☎01206/760 680). Colchester's oysters have been highly prized since Roman times, and you still enjoy the local variety at *Franco's*, an Italian seafood place on East Hill. As for **pubs**, there's the aforementioned *Rose and Crown* and *Red Lion,* as well as the *Foresters Arms* on Castle Road to recommend, plus the *Playhouse*, a converted theatre on St John's Street. As for **nightlife**, the *Colchester Arts Centre*, next to the Balkerne Gate (☎01206/577 301), puts on a good programme of folk, jazz and theatre in a converted Victorian church.

The Stour Valley and the wool towns

The **Stour Valley** forms the border between Essex and Suffolk for much of its length, and signals the beginning of East Anglia proper. Compared to much of the region it is positively hilly, and as such is one of the prettiest parts of Suffolk. It comes as little surprise that two of the greatest English artists – Constable and Gainsborough – who were both born here, spent much of their time painting the local landscape. To the north and east of **Sudbury**, the largest town on the Stour, the rolling hills and green pastures are scattered with exquisitely preserved medieval villages, whose former prosperity is embodied by their ostentatious churches and wealth of half-timbered cottages. This rich architectural heritage was paid for by the merchants who settled in the **Suffolk wool towns**, which formed the nucleus of East Anglia's weaving trade during the thirteenth and fourteenth centuries. This trade went into decline in Tudor times, though most of these towns continued spinning cloth for the next three hundred years. The Industrial Revolution left all but Sudbury behind, but allowed the preservation of these villages, which now make most of their money from tourism.

Flatford Mill and Dedham

"I associate my careless boyhood to all that lies on the banks of the Stour" wrote John Constable, who was born in 1776 to a miller in East Bergholt, nine miles northeast of Colchester. The house in which he was born has long since disappeared, so it has been left to **Flatford Mill** – where Constable painted his most famous canvas, *The Haywain* (now in the National Gallery in London) – to take up the painter's cause. The National Trust now owns the sixteenth-century thatched **Bridge Cottage** (April, May & Oct Wed–Sun 11am–5.30pm; June–Sept daily 10am–5.30pm; Nov Wed–Sun 11am–3pm; free), which overlooks the scene and is stuffed full of Constabilia – and has installed a tea room with tables by the river. The granary next door contains mezzotints of Constable's works; the mill itself (not the one he painted, but a Victorian replacement) is now a NT field study centre; beyond stands **Willy Lott's Cottage** (closed to the public), which does actually feature in the painting.

The nearest village to the mill is **DEDHAM**, which has a smattering of mildly diverting attractions of its own. You can grab a bite to **eat** at the *Marlborough Head* pub, opposite Constable's old school, or eat in gourmet-style at the expensive *Le Talbooth* (☎01206/323 150), a riverside house which also offers stylish **accommodation** in nearby *Maison Talbooth*, Stratford Road (☎01206/322 367; ⑨); a cheaper alternative is *May's Barn Farm*, off Long Road West (☎01206/323 191; ③).

Sudbury

Fifteen miles northwest of Colchester, **SUDBURY** has doubled in size in the last thirty years, to become easily the most important town in this part of the Stour valley. Sudbury's most famous export is **Thomas Gainsborough**, the leading English portraitist of the eighteenth century, whose statue stands on Market Hill, the town's predominantly Victorian market place. **Gainsborough's House** (mid-April to Oct Tues–Sat 10am–5pm, Sun 2–5pm; Nov to mid-April Tues–Sat 10am–4pm, Sun 2–5pm; £2.50), where the painter was born in 1727, is at 46 Gainsborough St, west off the main square. None of the portraits of high-society ladies with which he made his name are to be found in the museum's collection, which is dominated by lesser-known landscapes and portraits, but the house itself – with a Georgian facade but a Tudor interior – is a good enough reason to pay a visit.

Sudbury is fifteen miles northwest of Colchester along the A134, and half an hour by **train** (change at Marks Tey); its **tourist office** is in the town hall on Market Hill

(April–Oct Mon–Sat 10am–4.45pm; ☎01787/881 320). There's little reason to hang around Sudbury, though you could use it as a base for exploring the wool towns. If so, try *St Faith's Villa* on Queen's Road (☎01787/374 627; ②), or *Litchgate*, 45 Clarence Rd (☎01787/373 429; ②), a homely, central **B&B**. For a pricier option, there's the *Mill Hotel* on Walnut Tree Lane (☎01787/375 544; ⑤), in a converted mill, with the Stour still running under it.

Long Melford

True to its name, **LONG MELFORD**, four miles north of Sudbury on the A134, has possibly the longest main street in the country – two miles in total – dotted with timber-framed houses, many of which are now antique shops. At its northern end, the street opens up into a wide sloping green beyond which stands a collection of sixteenth-century almshouses presided over by the village's mighty **Holy Trinity** church. Built in the fifteenth century, around the same time as Lavenham's (see below), it is one of the most majestic of the so-called wool churches, with a fine array of stained glass, including one window decorated with three rabbits representing the Holy Trinity.

To the east of the green, behind a high brick wall, is **Melford Hall** (April–Oct Sat & Sun 2–5.30pm; May–Sept also Wed & Thurs; £2.70; NT), a turreted red-brick Tudor mansion, once a country retreat for the abbots of Bury St Edmunds. The interior is mostly eighteenth-century and Regency, and there's a display of watercolours by Beatrix Potter, a distant relative of the owners. Just past the green, a mile-long lime-tree drive heads off northwest to **Kentwell Hall** (April to mid-June Sun only 11am–5pm; mid-June to mid-July Sat & Sun 11am–5pm; mid-July to Sept daily 11am–5pm; Oct Sun only noon–5pm; £4.30), a moated Tudor mansion that's still in private hands. Aside from the house itself, there's a brick rose maze, a fifteenth-century moathouse, a working "Tudor" farm, and touristy "historical recreations", which take place from mid-June to mid-July, most summer weekends and bank holidays.

Lavenham

Four miles east of Long Melford, off the A134, lies **LAVENHAM**, formerly centre of the region's wool trade and today one of the most visited villages in Suffolk, thanks to its unrivalled array of perfectly preserved half-timbered houses. Lavenham's most celebrated building is its cream-coloured timber-framed **Corpus Christi Guildhall** (April–Oct daily 11am–5pm; £2.50; NT), a relatively new structure for this venerable town, having been built in the sixteenth century. The hefty entry fee allows you to view an exhibition on the woollen industry and a much altered interior.

Better value is the **Little Hall** (Easter–Oct Wed, Thurs, Sat & Sun 2.30–5.30pm; £1), a fifteenth-century house to the east of the Guildhall, which contains a small collection of furniture and *objets d'art*. The other building which opens its doors to the public is the **Priory** on Walter Street (mid-March to Oct daily 10.30am–5.30pm; £2.50), founded by Benedictine monks, now thoroughly renovated and displaying modern stained-glass windows and other works by the Hungarian artist Ervin Bossanyi, with a delightful herb garden out back. If you arrive by car, as most people do, you might as well park opposite the Perpendicular church of **St Peter and St Paul**, at the top of Church Street, which the local merchants endowed with a 141-foot flint tower.

Double **rooms** at *The Swan* (☎01787/247 477; ⑨), a splendid fifteenth-century inn, cost around £110; for less than half the price, there's the equally ancient *Angel Hotel* (☎01787/247 388; ⑤) or *Angel Corner* (☎01787/247 168; ③), both on the main square overlooking the Guildhall. If you need any help, the **tourist office** is located on Lady Street (Easter to mid-May Mon–Fri 10am–1pm & 2–4.45pm, Sat & Sun 10am–4.45pm; mid-May to Sept daily 10am–4.45pm; ☎01787/248 207).

Bury St Edmunds

BURY ST EDMUNDS started out as a Benedictine abbey, founded in 945 AD to house the remains of Edmund, King of East Anglia, who was tortured and beheaded here by the marauding Danes in 869 AD. Before its dissolution in 1539, the abbey became one of the richest in the country, rebuilt on a grand scale by the Normans in the eleventh and twelfth centuries. Nowadays Bury makes its money from sugar and beer, and is better known for its graceful Georgian streets and its flower gardens than for its ancient monuments. Nevertheless, it's the prettiest place of any size in Suffolk, and with the recent opening of the fascinating Manor House museum, demands a day of anyone's time.

The town is still laid out along its original Norman grid plan, and slopes gently down to the confusingly named **Angel Hill**, a broad, L-shaped space, displaying a fine array of Georgian buildings. A twelfth-century wall runs along the east side of Angel Hill, with the bulky but ornate fourteenth-century Abbey Gate forming the entrance to the abbey gardens and ruins. The **abbey ruins** themselves are like nothing so much as petrified porridge, with little to remind you of the grandiose Norman church where 25 barons met in 1214, and vowed to force the Magna Carta on King John. Nowadays, thanks to the efforts of the local council, it is the award-winning **garden** and the suntrap rose garden, hemmed in by giant yew hedges, which are the best features of the abbey grounds. The only significant remnant of the abbey is a section of the **west front**, whose rubbled remains have been integrated into a set of Georgian houses and later attached to a polygonal tower, soon to house an exhibition on the abbey.

Backing onto the abbey ruins is Bury's **Cathedral** (daily June–Aug 8.30am–8pm; Sept–May 8.30am–5.30pm), with chancel and transepts added as recently as the 1960s. That its thousand-odd kneelers are often cited as one of its major highlights gives an idea of the paucity of the interior, notwithstanding the newly painted hammerbeam roof. In fact, it was a toss-up between this place and **St Mary's church**, further down Crown Street, as to which would be given cathedral status in 1914, though the presence of the tomb of Mary Tudor in the latter may have something to do with the eventual decision.

Round the corner from St Mary's, in Honey Hill, is the newly opened **Manor House** (Mon–Sat 10am–5pm, Sun 2–5pm; £2.50), housed in a Georgian mansion built by the wife of the first Earl of Bristol as a *pied-à-terre* party house. A superb collection of clocks and watches is the core of the museum; the accompanying paintings are less compelling, but the whole place is well served by a computerized public information system. The museum also mounts extremely popular temporary exhibitions on art and textiles, often based on TV and film costume dramas.

At the far end of Crown Street stands Bury's most important industrial concern after the local sugar factory, the pungent **Greene King brewery** (tours booked through the tourist office Mon–Thurs; £2.50), whose powerful Abbot Ale is an intense bitter-sweet beer to be quaffed with caution. The brewery and the National Trust are joint owners of the elegant Regency **Theatre Royal** opposite (Mon–Sat 10am–8pm; free), built in 1819 by William Wilkins.

The main shopping area is in the upper part of town around Cornhill and Buttermarket, a wedge-shaped market place culminating in the flint-walled **Moyse's Hall** (Mon–Sat 10am–5pm, Sun 2–5pm; free), one of the few surviving Norman houses in England, dating from around 1180. Over the years it has served as a police station, synagogue, prison, workhouse and, since 1899, the local museum, whose most intriguing exhibit is a miniature church made out of snail shells.

Practicalities

The **train station** is ten minutes' walk north up Northgate Street from Angel Hill, where the **tourist office** is situated at no. 6 (Easter–May Mon–Fri 9.30am–5.30pm, Sat

10am–3pm; June–Sept also Sun 10am–3pm; ☎01284/764 667). If the *Angel Hotel* (☎01284/753 926; ⑧) is beyond your budget, there's always the *Olde White Hart* (☎01284/755 547; ④), an even older inn on Southgate Street. The tourist office will reserve a **B&B** for you, or you could try calling at 54 Guildhall St (☎01284/762 745; ③) or 16 Cannon St (☎01284/761 776; ②).

Bury has a good range of **restaurants**: *Mortimer's*, 30 Churchgate St, like its sister outfit in Ipswich, serves wonderfully fresh fish and seafood at moderate prices, while the *Cupola House* in the Traverse does slightly cheaper food. Another good place worth investigating for lunch is *The Sanctuary*, off Hatter Street, which serves French-influenced dishes. One **pub** you must visit is the *Nutshell*, on The Traverse, which, at sixteen feet by seven and a half, is Britain's smallest. And for beer connoisseurs, Greene King's brewery tap is the ancient-looking *Dog & Partridge*, 29 Crown St.

Ickworth

Three miles southwest of Bury along the A143, **Ickworth House** (April–Oct Tues, Wed & Fri–Sun 1–5pm; £4.30; NT) is quite unlike any other English stately home: an extraordinary elliptical rotunda with twin curving wings, reminiscent of an Austrian Baroque chateau. It was built by the enormously rich fourth Earl of Bristol to house his vast private art collection, which includes works by Titian, Velasquez, Hogarth, Gainsborough and Reynolds. A semi-formal Italian **garden** (daily April–Oct 10am–5pm, Nov–March 10am–4pm; £1.50) adjoins the house, and there's a deer enclosure in the woodland to the west of the house. If you don't have your own transport, the Haverhill bus (Mon–Sat only), will drop you off at the end of the mile-long drive.

Ipswich

Situated at the head of the Orwell estuary, **IPSWICH** was a rich trading port in the Middle Ages, but its appearance today is mainly the result of a revival of fortunes in the Victorian era. Despite the insensitive urban planning which has been inflicted on the town over the last century, the two magnificent surviving reminders of old Ipswich – Christchurch Mansion and the Ancient House – are reason enough to spend an afternoon here. And the recently renovated quayside is also worth investigating, if only to dine out in one of its restaurants and pubs.

The ancient Saxon market place, **Cornhill**, is still the town's focal point and boasts a bevy of imposing Victorian edifices. To get to Ipswich's most famous building, walk halfway along Tavern Street, and duck down the mock-Tudor arcade known as The Walk to Buttermarket, on which stands the **Ancient House** (also known as Sparrowe's House). The exterior of this Tudor building was decorated around 1670 with one of the finest examples of sculpted plasterwork in the country (a technique known as "pargeting"), a riot of white stucco depicting four of the continents. Since the house is now a bookshop, you're free to take a peek inside to view yet more of the decor, including the hammerbeam roof on the first floor.

From the Ancient House, head up Dial Lane and back onto Tavern Street, where two wonderful mock-Tudor shops, built in the 1930s, face the *Great White Horse Hotel*, which appears in Dickens' *Pickwick Papers*. Heading north up Northgate Street will bring you eventually to **Christchurch Mansion** (Tues–Sat 10am–5pm, Sun 2.30–4.30pm; free), a handsome Tudor building, sporting seventeenth-century Dutch gables and set in 65 acres of **parkland**, an area larger than the town centre itself. The mansion's labyrinthine interior is well worth exploring, with period furnishings and a moderately good collection of paintings by Constable and Gainsborough, as well as more contemporary exhibitions.

From the centre, head south down St Peter's Street, lined with some fine half-timbered houses, and you will eventually reach Ipswich's tranquil **Wet Dock**, the largest in Europe when it opened in 1845 and looking much as it was then. The smell of malt and barley still wafts across the dockside, and several of the granaries continue to function, while other warehouses have been turned into pubs, restaurants and offices. Halfway along the quayside stands the proud Neoclassical **Customs House**, built for the opening of the dock.

Practicalities

Ipswich **train station** is on the south bank of the Orwell, ten minutes' walk from Cornhill along Princes Street. The **bus station** is more central, occupying the Old Cattle Market, one block south of the Ancient House. The **tourist office** (Mon–Sat 9am–5pm; ☎01473/258 070) occupies St Stephen's Church in St Stephen's Lane, between the bus station and the Ancient House. If you wish to follow in the footsteps of George II, Lord Nelson and Dickens, **stay** at the *Great White Horse*, Tavern Street (☎01473/256 558; ④). Alternatively, try *Mount Pleasant*, 103 Anglesea Rd (☎01473/251 601; ④) or *Finches Hotel*, 29 Burners St (☎01473/221 124; ②), both within easy walking distance of Christchurch Park and the town centre. One of the best areas for **restaurants** is down by the Wet Dock: the *Wherry Quay* does à la carte French dinners, while *Mortimer's on the Quay* specializes in fish and seafood. If you're looking for something cheaper, try the *Malt Kiln* **pub**, or the vegetarian *Café Marno*, 14 Nicholas St. For evening **entertainment**, the *Ipswich Film Theatre*, in the Corn Exchange, behind the town hall, shows mainstream and art movies, while the newly established *Wolsey Studio*, St George's Street, puts on an adventurous programme of contemporary drama.

The Suffolk Coast

The **Suffolk Coast** feels detached from the rest of the county: the road and rail lines from Ipswich to Lowestoft funnel traffic five miles inland for most of the way, and patches of woodland make the separation still more complete. Coastal erosion continues to plague the region, and has contributed to the virtual extinction of the local fishing industry and, in the case of **Dunwich**, has destroyed virtually the entire town. What is left, however, is undoubtedly one of the most unspoilt shorelines in the country, if you leave aside the Sizewell nuclear power station. The sleepy isolation of **Orford** is rarely broken even in the height of summer, and even more well-established resorts like **Southwold** have managed to escape the lurid fate of other English seaside towns. The Suffolk coast is also host to East Anglia's most compelling cultural gathering, the three-week-long **Aldeburgh Festival**, which takes place every June.

Orford

A tiny village on the other side of the storm-racked Forest of Rendlesham from Woodbridge, **ORFORD** is dominated by its twelfth-century Norman **Castle** (April–Dec daily 10am–6pm; Jan–March Wed–Sun 10am–4pm; EH; £2), built on high ground to the southwest of the village by Henry II, and under siege within months of its completion from Henry's rebellious sons. All that remains now is the lofty keep, though you can get an idea of the scale of the original fortifications from the displays inside. From the top of the keep you get a great view across Orford Ness, a six-mile-long spit of shingle deposits that has all but blocked off Orford from the sea since Tudor times.

Whilst in Orford, be sure to visit *Richardson's Smokehouse* in Bakers Lane, one of the few **smokehouses** still to employ the traditional oak-wood methods of smoking meat and fish. The *Butley Orford Oysterage*, at the top of Bakers Lane, is equally tempting, with a very reasonably priced menu, including **fresh oysters** and smoked fish. **Rooms**

BENJAMIN BRITTEN AND THE ALDENBURGH FESTIVAL

Benjamin Britten was born in Lowestoft in 1913, and was closely associated with this part of Suffolk for most of his life. However, it was during his self-imposed exile in the USA during World War II – he was a conscientious objector – that Britten first read the work of the nineteenth-century Suffolk poet, George Crabbe. Crabbe's *The Borough*, a grisly portrait of the life of the fishermen of Aldeburgh, was the basis of the libretto of Britten's best-known opera, *Peter Grimes*, which was premiered in London in 1945 to great acclaim.

In 1947 Britten founded the English Opera Group and the following year launched the **Aldeburgh Festival** as a showpiece for his own works and those of his contemporaries. He lived in the town for the next ten years, achieved much of his best work as a conductor and pianist there, and for the rest of his life composed many works specifically for the festival, most notably his masterpiece for children, *Noye's Fludde*, and the last of his fifteen operas, *Death in Venice*.

By the mid-1960s, the festival had outgrown the parish churches in which it began, and moved into a collection of disused malthouses, three miles west on the River Alde at **Snape Maltings**, which were converted into one of the finest concert venues in the country. In addition to the concert hall, there's now a recording studio, a music school, various shops and a tea room, as well as a pub, the *Plough and Sail*.

For more information on the Aldeburgh Festival, contact the **festival box office** on the High Street (Mon–Sat 9.30am–5pm; ☎01728/453 543), which can also answer general enquiries on the town out of season when the tourist office is closed. Tickets for the concerts, talks, exhibitions and other special events go on sale to the public around the middle of April, and often sell out fast for the big-name recitals; prices range from £5 to £25. There are concerts at other times of the year at the Maltings, such as the Proms season in August, and the week-long Britten Festival at the end of October.

are available at the *Crown & Castle* (☎01394/450 205; ⑥), near the castle, and the *King's Head* (☎01394/450 271; ④), on the other side of Market Hill. The nearest **campsite** is set in Rendlesham Forest near Butley off the B1084 (April–Oct; ☎01394/450 707). Down by the quayside, you can book a **boat trip** for Havergate Island, an RSPB reserve famous for its avocets.

Aldeburgh and Thorpeness

ALDEBURGH is best known for its annual arts festival, the brainchild of composer **Benjamin Britten**, who is buried in the village churchyard alongside the great tenor Peter Pears, his lover and musical collaborator. Outside of June, when the festival takes place, Aldeburgh is the quietest of places, with just a small fishing fleet selling its daily catch from wooden shacks along the shore. The wide main street and the backstreets which surround it are all that's left of a once extensive medieval town, scoured away by centuries of erosion – consequently the seafront is something of a hotchpotch, as it was not designed to face the sea. Aldeburgh's oldest building, the **Moot Hall** (Easter–May Sat & Sun 2.30–5pm; June & Sept daily 2.30–5pm; July & Aug daily 10.30am–12.30pm & 2.30–5.30pm; 45p), a short distance north along the seafront, is now a museum. Built out of a mixture of red brick, flint and timber, it stood in the town centre when it was first constructed around 1500, but is now only a few yards from the beach.

Aldeburgh's **tourist office** (April–Oct Mon–Fri 9am–5.15pm, Sat & Sun 10am–5.15pm; ☎01728/453 637) is located in the cinema on the High Street. Getting hold of **accommodation** should be no problem, except of course in June; *Austins Hotel* (☎01728/453 932; ⑤), with its superb restaurant, and the *Brudenell Hotel* on The Parade (☎01728/452 071; ⑥), are the town's two top hotels. The festival box office can

DUNWICH

Seat of the King of East Anglia, a bishopric and once the largest port on the Suffolk coast, the ancient city of **Dunwich**, eight miles north of Aldeburgh, reached its peak of prosperity in the twelfth century. Over the last millennium, however, something like a mile of land has been lost to the sea, a process which continues at the rate of about a yard a year. The whole of the medieval city now lies under the ocean, including all twelve churches, the last of which toppled over the cliffs in 1919 – you can still see it peeping out of the water occasionally at low tide. All that remains is one gravestone, a few metres from the precipice, and the ruins of Greyfriars monastery, which lay to the west of the city. In the one small street of terraced houses that now makes up Dunwich, there's a **Museum** (April–Sept daily 11.30am–4.30pm; Oct daily noon–4pm; free) which contains a model of the lost city, and recounts its steady demise. If the museum's closed, you can always inspect the prints and maps of old Dunwich a few doors down in the village's last surviving pub, the *Ship Inn*. A walk along the beach will reveal the crumbling cliffs, and the fishing boats that still sell their daily catch off the shingle.

also recommend B&Bs in the area, and there's a **youth hostel** in Blaxhall, housed in a former village school a couple of miles west of Snape Maltings (☎01728/688 206). The nearest **campsite** is the *Church Farm Caravan Site*, just north of Aldeburgh on the Thorpeness Road (April–Oct; ☎01728/453 433).

Southwold

Perched on more robust cliffs on the other side of the River Blyth, **SOUTHWOLD**'s days as a busy fishing port are also long gone, though a small fleet still brings in herring, sprats and cod in season. For the last hundred years, however, Southwold has made more money as a genteel seaside resort, with tea rooms and bookshops in its unspoilt, mostly Georgian High Street, a fine array of Victorian boarding houses lining the seafront and a long line of beach huts along the shore. The town's sights – such as they are – are clustered near St James's Green: the gleaming white lighthouse, the much admired Saxon church and the town brewery.

The local **tourist office** is in the town hall, on the market place (Easter–Sept Mon–Fri 11am–1pm & 1.45–5pm, Sat 10am–1pm & 1.45–5.30pm, Sun 11am–1.15pm & 1.45–4pm; ☎01502/724 729). Two comfortable Georgian **hotels** are located near the old market square: the *Swan* (☎01502/724 729; ⑧) and the *Crown* (☎01502/722 275; ⑥), and there's a good choice of **B&Bs** such as *Acton Lodge* (☎01502/723 217; ④), on the front itself, North Parade. The moderately expensive **restaurant** in the *Crown* is the one to go for if you've got the money to spare; nearer the seafront are two pleasant little **pubs**, the *Lord Nelson* and the *Sole Bay Inn*, both of which serve the town's most famous export, Adnam's bitter.

Norwich

One of the five largest cities in Norman England, **NORWICH** once served a vast hinterland of cloth producers in the eastern counties, whose work was exported from here to the continent. Its isolated position beyond the Fens meant that it enjoyed closer links with the Low Countries than with the rest of the country – it was, after all, quicker to cross the North Sea than go cross-country to London. The local textile industry was further enhanced by an influx of Flemish and Huguenot weavers, who made up more than a third of the population in Tudor times. With the onset of the Industrial Revolution, Norwich lost ground to the northern manufacturing towns, though this

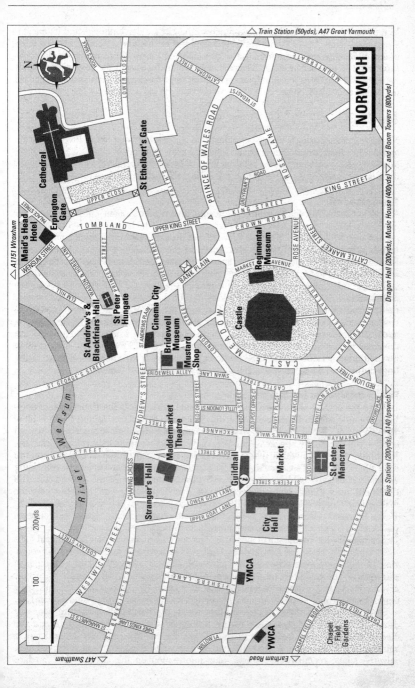

NORWICH

△ Train Station (50yds), A47 Great Yarmouth

▷ Dragon Hall (200yds), Music House (400yds) and Boom Towers (800yds)

▷ Bus Station (200yds), A140 Ipswich

△ Earlham Road

◁ A47 Swaffham

◁ A1151 Wroxham

Cathedral
Maid's Head Hotel
Erpington Gate
St Ethelbert's Gate
St Andrew's & Blackfriars' Hall
St Peter Hungate
Cinema City
Bridewell Museum
Mustard Shop
Castle
Regimental Museum
Maddermarket Theatre
Stranger's Hall
Guildhall
Market
City Hall
St Peter Mancroft
YMCA
YWCA
Chapel Field Gardens

TOMBLAND
UPPER KING STREET
UPPER CLOSE
LOWER CLOSE
PALACE STREET
WENSUM STREET
ELM HILL
WAGON & HORSE LANE
PRINCES STREET
QUEEN STREET
ST ANDREW'S PLAIN
ST ANDREW STREET
PRINCE OF WALES ROAD
CATHEDRAL STREET
MOUNTERGATE
ROSE LANE
KING STREET
KING STREET
CROWN ROAD
GREYFRIARS ROAD
ST VEDAST
ST FAITH'S LANE
ROSE AVENUE
CATTLE MARKET STREET
MARKET AVENUE
BELL AVENUE
FARMER'S AVENUE
CASTLE MEADOW
LONDON STREET
SWAN LANE
BRIDEWELL ALLEY
BEDFORD STREET
CASTLE STREET
WHITE LION STREET
RED LION STREET
OLD POST OFFICE CT
LITTLE LONDON ST
DAVEY PLACE
ROYAL ARCADE
GENTLEMAN'S WALK
HAYMARKET
ORFORD PLACE
EXCHANGE STREET
DOVE STREET
LONDON STREET
PUDDING LANE
ST PETER'S STREET
THEATRE STREET
LOWER GOAT LANE
UPPER GOAT LANE
ST GILES STREET
FISHERS LANE
POTTERGATE
CHARING CROSS
ST BENEDICT'S STREET
WESTWICK STREET
ST GEORGE'S STREET
DUKE STREET
COSTANY STREET
THREE KINGS LANE
ST MARGARET'S ST
ST MARGARET'S LANE
VICTORIA
CHAPEL FIELD NORTH
CHAPEL FIELD EAST
POTTERGATE
ROUGE HILL
BANK PLAIN
River Wensum

0 100 200yds

lack of success has helped preserve much of the city's older buildings and its ancient street plan. Since the 1980s, however, Norwich has been enjoying something of a mini-boom, which has made it one of the richest cities in the southern half of England. As East Anglia's unofficial capital, Norwich also lies at the hub of the region's transport network and serves as a useful base for visiting the Broads, and even as a springboard for the north Norfolk coast.

The City

Norwich is a surprisingly hilly city, tucked into a sweeping bend of the River Wensum, and the irregular street plan, a Saxon legacy, makes orientation confusing. There are, however, plenty of landmarks to help you find your way: the cathedral with its giant spire, the Norman castle on its commanding mound and the distinctive clock tower of City Hall.

The Cathedral

Norwich **Cathedral** (daily summer 7.30am–7pm; winter 7.30am–6pm; free) is easy enough to locate, thanks to its prickly octagonal spire which rises to a height of 315ft, second only to Salisbury. It is best viewed from the east, where the thick curves of the flying buttresses, the rounded excrescences of the ambulatory chapels – unusual in English cathedrals – and the straight lines of the main body can all be seen. The **interior** is pleasantly light thanks to the pale pink stone and clear glass of much of the nave, where the thick pillars are a powerful legacy of the Norman builders who began the cathedral in 1096. As you walk round, look out for the cathedral's superb examples of medieval art: the misericords in the presbytery; the *Despenser Reredos*, a fourteenth-century painted panel in St Luke's Chapel; and the medieval frescoes in the treasury, above the north side of the ambulatory. Accessible from the south aisle of the nave are the cathedral's unique two-storey **cloisters**, built between 1297 and 1310. They contain a remarkable set of sculpted **bosses** depicting scenes from the Bible, similar to the ones in the main nave, but close enough to be viewed without binoculars.

From Tombland to the Market

Leaving the cathedral close via the two medieval gates – Ethelbert and Erpingham – brings you out onto **Tombland**, the old Saxon market place. At the north end of Tombland, fork left at the *Maid's Head Hotel*, and **Elm Hill** – more a gentle slope than a hill – will eventually appear on the left. As you pass along its cobbles, admiring the half-timbered houses which make it Norwich's most photographed spot, be sure to take a look at Wright's Court, down a passageway at no. 43, one of the few remaining enclosed courtyards which were once a feature of the street. At the far end Elm Hill opens out into a triangular space centred on a plane tree, planted on the spot where the eponymous elm tree from Henry VIII's time once stood. Beyond lies the church of **St Peter Hungate** (Mon–Sat 10am–5pm; 50p), now a brass-rubbing centre and museum of church art, with a few musical instruments thrown in.

One block west, on the north side of St Andrew's Plain, two adjoining medieval halls – **St Andrew's Hall** and **Blackfriars Hall** – have served as public venues for centuries, though they were originally the nave and chancel, respectively, of a Dominican monastery. The buildings off the former cloisters (known as "The Garth") are now given over to the adjacent School of Fine Arts. You can gain access to both halls throughout the day, since the crypt now serves as a coffee bar (daily 10am–4.30pm).

South of the Plain, down Bridewell Alley, stands the **Bridewell Museum** (Mon–Sat 10am–5pm; £1.40 includes entry to the Strangers' Hall, St Peter Hungate and the Regimental Museum), built as a private house, for centuries the city jail and now a museum of local industry. Its collection is a wonderful potpourri of old machines, adverts, signs, reconstructed shops, plus information on the all-important mustard industry. For more on the latter, you can pop round the corner to the Colman's-run **Mustard Shop**, 3 Bridewell Alley (Mon–Sat 9.30am–5pm), with a history of the company and a bewildering variety of its produce on sale.

Continuing west along Bedford Street and Pottergate, turn right by St John Maddermarket, now a Greek Orthodox church, passing under the church tower to emerge at **Maddermarket Theatre**, built in 1921 in the style of an Elizabethan playhouse. Nearby, through an archway just off Charing Cross, is **Strangers' Hall** (Mon–Sat 10am–5pm; £1), one of Norwich's more interesting museums, illustrating domestic life through the ages. The house itself is an architectural treat, built for a merchant in the fourteenth century but lived in by a succession of immigrant weavers who gave the place its current name. Inside, the highlights are the fifteenth-century Great Hall, the Walnut Room and the pale green Georgian dining room, but the museum also boasts one of the finest costume collections in the country – underwear is the speciality.

From Strangers' Hall, head up St Gregory's Alley and Lower Goat Lane and you will eventually arrive at the city's nine-hundred-year-old **market place** (closed Sun), covered with a blanket of stripey awnings and presided over by three very different but equally imposing buildings. The oldest of the trio is the **Guildhall**, built in the fifteenth century in flint and stone, which now houses the tourist office and an exhibition of the civic regalia and silver plate (Mon–Fri 2–3.30pm; free), the finest in the country after London. The rather severe **City Hall**, built in a Swedish style in the 1930s, commands the heights of the market place, but it's **St Peter Mancroft** (Mon–Fri 9.30am–4.30pm, Sat 10am–12.30pm; free), Norwich's finest parish church, with its frilly fifteenth-century tower, which steals the show. Below the church is another unmistakeable landmark, the bubble-gum-pink pub, *Sir Garnett Wolseley*, sole survivor of the 44 ale houses that used to crowd the market place.

The wide pavement of the **Gentlemen's Walk**, the town's main promenade, runs along the bottom of the market place. Halfway along the Walk, the lime-green **Royal Arcade** has been beautifully restored to reveal the swirl and blob of the Art-Nouveau tiling, ironwork and stained glass. The arcade's eastern facade, further from the Walk, is actually the better of the two, and will take you conveniently to the foot of the castle.

The Castle and King Street

High on a mound in the centre of town stands the twelfth-century **Castle Keep** (Mon–Sat 10am–5pm, Sun 2–5pm; £2.20), replete with blind arcading, an unusually decorative touch on a military structure. You can join a guided tour of the battlements and dungeons (the castle served as the county gaol for over six hundred years), or simply wander at will around the museum and art gallery inside. The latter contains a selection of work by the early nineteenth-century Norwich School of landscape painters, whose leading lights were John Sell Cotman and John Crome.

On leaving the castle, follow the signs to the **Royal Norfolk Regimental Museum**, (same times as castle; £1) situated below the castle on Market Avenue, but connected to the castle via a winding stairwell, the gloomy Prisoners' Tunnel and a claustrophobic reconstruction of a World War I trench. The museum itself recounts the conflicts of the twentieth century in a fairly even-handed way, while upstairs are displays on the early history of the Royal Norfolk regiment, founded in 1685.

If you've any energy left, you might like to visit the newly restored **Dragon Hall**, 115–123 King St (April–Oct Mon–Sat 10am–4pm; Nov–March Mon–Fri 10am–4pm; £1), which was built as a cloth showroom for merchant and town mayor Robert Toppes. Inside, the timber-framed Great Hall holds the brightly coloured, medieval wooden dragon which gives the place its name. A right turn just past the hall up St Julian's Alley leads to **St Julian's church** (daily 7am–6pm) and adjoining monastic cell. This was the retreat of Saint Julian, a Norwich woman who took to living here after experiencing visions of Christ in 1373; her mystical *Revelations of Divine Love* was the first widely distributed book written by a woman in the English language, and has been in print ever since.

UEA and the Sainsbury Centre

The **University of East Anglia** (UEA), on the western outskirts of the city, is a modern architectural monument of sorts, with its "ziggurat" halls of residence, designed in the 1960s by Denys Lasdun, and the high-tech **Sainsbury Centre for Visual Arts** (Tues–Sun noon–5pm; £1), an amazing piece of architectural art built by Norman Foster in 1977. The hangar-like interior houses one of the most unusual collections of sculpture and painting in the country, donated by the family who own the Sainsbury supermarket chain, in which the likes of Giacometti, Bacon and Henry Moore rub shoulders with Mayan and Egyptian antiquities. Be sure to check out the bizarre Reserve Collection Display, presenting more of the same in the subterranean compact storage unit. To get to the UEA site, take bus #12, #14, #15, #23, #26, #27, #33 or #35 from Castle Meadow.

Practicalities

Norwich **train station** is on the east bank of the River Wensum, ten minutes' walk east of the castle keep which overlooks the city centre; **buses** terminate at Surrey Street, five minutes' walk south of the castle. The **tourist office** (June–Sept Mon–Sat 9.30am–6pm; Oct–May Sun only 9.30am–5.30pm; ☎01603/666 071) is in the Guildhall on the market place. The city has **accommodation** to suit all budgets, from the *Maid's Head Hotel*, on Tombland (☎01603/761 111; ⑦), where Elizabeth I once stayed, to *Meadow House*, 64 Bishopsgate (☎01603/627 307; ③), east of the cathedral. For the very cheapest **B&Bs**, you'll have to forsake the city centre and head west down Earlham Road – try *Rosedale*, at no. 145 (☎01603/453 743; ②) or *Aberdale Lodge*, at no. 211 (☎01603/502 100; ②). The large **youth hostel**, at 112 Turner Rd (April–Aug; ☎01603/627 647) has comfortable facilities. The **campsite** closest to the centre is *Lakenham* (April–Sept; ☎01603/620 060), a mile or so south on Martineau Lane, off King Street.

If you're only visiting the cathedral, and need a bite to **eat**, *Pizza One* is conveniently located on Tombland, or try the delicious homemade meals, cakes and scones at the half-timbered *Briton Arms* at the top of Elm Hill. Veggies should home in on the *Tree House*, above the *Rainbow* wholefood shop on Dove Street. Norwich excels in no-nonsense **pubs** like the *Plough* on St Benedicts Street, and the *Red Lion*, on St George Street, the art students' local which serves incredibly cheap food. By way of contrast, you could try the *Gardeners/Murderers*, a loud maze of a pub on Timberhill, perenially popular with the city's youth. *Marco's* is another popular pub on St Andrew's Street, with **live music** most evenings, but the *Waterfront*, 139–41 King's St, is Norwich's principal **club** and alternative music venue.

On the St Andrew's Plain, the sixteenth-century Suckling House has been converted into an art-house **cinema**, *Cinema City,* with a pleasant bistro attached. The *Norwich Arts Centre*, Reeves Yard, St Benedicts Street, hosts a **jazz festival** in the last two weeks of November, and offers the most eclectic year-round programme of cultural events, with everything from acid jazz to small-scale theatre. Norwich also boasts a permanent **puppet theatre** in the former Church of St James, on Whitefriars – performances are at 10.30am and 2.30pm every Saturday.

The Norfolk Broads

Three rivers – the Yare, Waveney and Bure – meander across the marshland to the east of Norwich, converging on Breydon Water before flowing into the sea at Great Yarmouth. In places these rivers break out into wide expanses of water known as "broads", which for years were thought to be natural lakes. In fact they're the result of extensive peat cutting – peat being a valuable source of energy in a region where wood was scarce – which created pits later flooded when sea levels rose in the thirteenth and fourteenth centuries. One of the most important wetlands in Europe, providing a haven for such species as swallowtail butterflies, kingfishers, great crested grebes and Cetti's warblers, the **Norfolk Broads** are also the county's major tourist attraction.

The Broads' delicate ecological balance suffered badly during the 1970s and 1980s: the careless use of fertilizers poisoned the water with phosphates and nitrates, encouraging the spread of algae; the decline in reed cutting – previously in great demand for thatching – made the broads unnavigable in parts; while the enormous increase in pleasure-boat traffic began to erode the banks. National park status was accorded to the area in 1988, and efforts are now underway to clear the waters and protect the Broads' ecosystem from commercial agriculture and mass tourism.

The best way to see the Broads is of course by boat, and you could happily spend a week or two exploring the 125 miles of lock-free navigable waterways, visiting the various churches and windmills en route. The next best mode of transport is cycling, and least satisfactory of all is driving. Public transport is patchy, though there are trains from Norwich to **Wroxham**, **Reedham** and **Acle**, as well as more infrequent bus services. In addition, there's the **Bure Valley Railway** (April–Sept & Dec; ☎01263/733 858), a narrow-gauge line that connects Wroxham with Aylsham, near Blickling Hall.

Practicalities

There are various information centres dotted around the Broads. The easiest to get to by road is the **Broadland Conservation Centre** (Easter–Oct Mon–Thurs & Sun 10.30am–5.30pm, Fri & Sat 2–5.30pm; £1), a thatched building on the edge of Ranworth Broad eight miles northeast of Norwich, which has a viewing platform, with binoculars on hand, from which you can spot the herons, crested grebes and terns which thrive in the marshes. More information on boat hire and accommodation can be gleaned from Hoveton **tourist office** (April–Oct daily 9am–1pm & 2–5pm; ☎01603/782 281).

Should you need **accommodation**; there's the *Red Roof Farmhouse* on Ludham Road (☎01692/670 604; ③) in Potter Heigham, the nominal capital of the Broads, or *The Mount*, 93 Norwich Rd (☎01603/783 909; ③), in Wroxham on the River Bure, but Norwich, Great Yarmouth and even Lowestoft are equally feasible launching pads. The main agents for **boat rental** are *Blakes* of Wroxham (☎01603/782 911) and *Hoseasons* of Lowestoft (☎01502/501 010); prices start at £500 a week for four people in peak season. Several boatyards in Wroxham and Potter Heigham offer cruises and rent boats for the day – phone or ask at the tourist board in Hoveton for details . There are numerous places offering **bike rental**, such as *Just Pedalling* in Coltishall (☎01603/737 201) and *Etna* in Reedham (☎01493/700346).

Great Yarmouth

First and foremost, **GREAT YARMOUTH** is a seaside resort, its promenade a parade of amusement arcades and rainy-day attractions, dead as a dodo in winter, heaving in summer. As such Yarmouth has more in common with the downmarket Essex resorts than with the rest of the county coastline. But Yarmouth is also a port with a long history, and despite the extensive wartime bomb damage, it retains a handful of sights that give some idea of the place Daniel Defoe thought "far superior to Norwich".

Arriving by train or car from Norwich, initial impressions are favourable thanks to the appealing jumbo-pencil pinaccles of the fourteenth-century church of **St Nicholas**, which boasts the widest nave in the country, and consequently a rather impressive west front. The church stands at the northern end of the broad market place, centre of which was medieval Yarmouth, but now mostly undistinguished. The one exception is the **Hospital for Decayed Fishermen**, founded in 1702, which opens out into a lovely little courtyard flanked by Dutch gables, its central cupola topped by a chilly-looking statue of the fishermen's friend, Saint Peter.

Despite considerable wartime damage, great swathes of the **medieval walls** remain, including many of the original towers – one of the best-preserved parts is along Ferrier Road, just north of St Nicholas. Other interesting features of the old town are the narrow parallel alleys, known locally as "rows", which used to link the river with the shoreline. Sixty-nine have survived, and at the **Old Merchant House** in Row 117 (April–Sept daily 10am–1pm & 2–6pm; £1.20), three blocks west of the town hall along South Quay, you can join up with one of English Heritage's guided tours of several of them. For more on Yarmouth's past, head for the nearby **Tolhouse Museum**, off Yarmouth Way (summer Mon–Fri & Sun 10am–1pm & 2–5pm), once the town's courthouse and jail, or the **Elizabethan House Museum** (Easter hols Mon–Fri 1–5pm, Sun 2–5pm; June–Sept daily except Sat 10am–5pm) back on South Quay, which concentrates on domestic life. A combined ticket costing £1 covers entry to the Tolhouse Museum, the Elizabethan House Museum and the Maritime Museum (see below).

The vast majority of tourists simply head for the Victorian-built seafront, **Marine Parade**. The biggest attractions nowadays are the *Marina* (daily 10am–10pm), a big sports complex with an aquaslide and wave machine, and the *Kingdom of the Sea* (daily 10am–dusk; £4), where you come face to face with sharks and other sea creatures. Also on Marine Parade is the town's **Maritime Museum** (summer daily except Sat 10am–5pm), which traces the history of the herring industry and the inland waterways; you can also visit the **Lydia Eva** steam drifter on the Town Quay (July–Oct daily 10am–4.30pm; free), sole survivor of the three thousand drifters which used to fish for herring in the area.

Practicalities

Great Yarmouth's **train station** is a good fifteen-minute walk from the seafront, across the river, past the big church, and then four or five blocks east; **buses** terminate one block from the sea on Wellesley Road. There are two **tourist offices** in Yarmouth: one in the town hall (Mon–Fri 9am–5pm; ☎01493/846 345), and one on Marine Parade (April, May & mid-Sept to mid-Oct daily 10am–1pm & 2–5pm; June to mid-Sept Mon–Sat 9.30am–5.30pm, Sun 10am–5pm; ☎01493/842 195). The *Royal*, 4 Marine Parade (☎01493/842 026; ④) is Yarmouth's finest **hotel**, or else there are countless cheap **B&Bs**: *Marine Beach*, 49 Marine Parade (☎01493/331 313; ②), for sea views, or *The Willow*, 26 Trafalgar Rd (☎01493/332 355; ②). Yarmouth's **youth hostel** is off North Drive at 2 Sandown Rd (☎01493/843 991). The **restaurant** situation is pretty dire. Far and away the best place is the fairly expensive *Seafood Restaurant*, 85 North Quay (☎01493/856 009), just up from St Nicholas, which does a superb fish soup and Mediterranean-influenced seafood dishes. The *Anna Sewell House* restaurant, next door to the church, on the edge of the market place, serves cheap English food plus a few vegetarian dishes, and as the name suggests was the childhood home of Anna Sewell, author of *Black Beauty*. The **pub** scene is not much better, with the notable exception of the venerable *Duke's Head* on Hall Quay, near the town hall.

The north Norfolk coast

The out-and-out bad taste of Great Yarmouth's seafront is an inauspicious start to the Norfolk coast, but it is an atypical one. For the next thirty miles, there are no estuaries, no harbours and very little habitation – until you reach **Cromer**, an attractive Victorian seaside town whose bleak and blustery cliffs have been attracting tourists for over a century. West of **Sheringham**, the shoreline becomes a ragged patchwork of salt marshes, dunes and shingle spits which forms an almost unbroken series of nature reserves, sheltering a fascinating range of flora and fauna. The other major attraction along this northern stretch of the coast is the large number of stately homes a short distance inland – some, like **Blickling** and **Holkham Hall**, among the finest in the country.

Cromer

Dramatically poised on a high bluff, **CROMER** is by far the most memorable of the Norfolk coastal resorts. The church tower, at 160ft the tallest in Norfolk, attests to the port's medieval wealth, but it was the advent of the railway in the 1880s which heralded the most frenetic building activity. Sadly the *Hotel de Paris* is the sole survivor of the bevy of grand Edwardian hotels which once backed onto the old town. A small fleet of crab boats resting on the beach with their attendant tractors is all that remains of the town's traditional industry. Cromer's pier was badly damaged in a storm in November 1993, but has since been repaired and now houses the **Cromer Lifeboat Museum** (May–Oct daily 10am–4pm; free), detailing the adventures of the local lifeboat crew, who are kept extremely busy along a coast with little natural shelter.

Cromer's **train station** is a short walk along the A148 to Fakenham; **buses** terminate at Prince of Wales Road, next to the **tourist office** (daily April to mid-July, Sept & Oct 10am–4/5pm; mid-July to Aug 9.30am–6/7pm; Nov–March 10am–4pm; ☎01263/512 497). The place to **stay**, naturally enough, is the flamboyant Gothic *Hotel de Paris* (☎01263/513 141; ⑤). Cheaper places are readily available just off Runton Road, like *The Knoll*, 23 Alfred Rd (☎01263/512 753; ③). *Monroe's*, in Garden Street, is the best chippy in town; *The Dolphin*, further down the same street, does a wide range of **pub food** including such classic vegetarian dishes as nut roast; for the local speciality, fresh crab, try the *Cromer Grill*, again in Garden Street.

Felbrigg and Blickling

Just a couple of miles southwest of Cromer, **Felbrigg Hall** (April–Oct daily except Tues & Fri 1–5pm; £4.60; NT) doesn't create a strong initial effect – the entrance front is Jacobean, but the rest is a fairly unexceptional extension built in the 1780s. The interior, however, retains some magnificent seventeenth-century plasterwork ceilings along with sundry *objets d'art* from a Windham Grand Tour. Alternatively, you can skip the hall, pay a visit to the tea rooms in the converted stables and then explore the chestnut woods of the **park** and gardens (same days as hall 11am–5pm; £1.80). St Margaret's church at the southeastern tip of the park contains a fine collection of brasses, while the extensive walled garden, featuring a lovely octagonal dove house, hosts an open-air music festival in mid-June.

Few stately homes are as immediately appealing as **Blickling Hall** (April–Oct Tues, Wed & Fri–Sun 1–5pm; £4.90; NT), set in a sheltered, wooded valley ten miles south of Cromer and a mile or so west of the A140 to Norwich – the main approach, flanked by fifteen-foot-high yew hedges, is unforgettable. The house was built around 1620 for Sir Henry Hobart, the Lord Chief Justice, in a style which harks back to Tudor times. First impressions are deceptive, however, for the early seventeenth-century interior has mostly vanished, replaced by fairly standard Georgian furnishings, the one exception being the superb 1620s plasterwork ceiling in the Long Gallery. The hall's other valuable possession is the gargantuan tapestry depicting Peter the Great, given to one of the family by Catherine the Great, which hangs in its own specially designed room. If you're in need of more sustenance than the hall's tea room can provide, head for the *Buckinghamshire Arms* just by the gravel entrance. Better still, you could picnic in the hall's fantastic **gardens** (same hours as Blickling hall except daily in July & Aug; £2.50) which include a mile-long lake, an orangery and a pyramidal mausoleum.

Cley

A few miles to the west of Sheringham, the sea disappears from view behind a shingle barrier that was built in an attempt to prevent a repetition of the flood of 1953, which claimed over a thousand lives. Just south of the barrier lie the **Cley Marshes**, established as the first nature reserve in the country in 1926, and attracting a bewildering variety of waders – and, of course, "twitchers". There are several places to park along the southern border of the marshes on the A149, but without a permit (available from the warden in the last building on the way out of Cley east on the A149; ☎01263/740 380; £3 a day), you can only use the public hide on the A149, or walk along the East Bank. The shingle barrier culminates in the final wispy sand and shingle spit of **Blakeney Point**, famed for its colonies of terns and seals, and accessible on foot, though it's a long trudge across the shingle (alternatively, you can join one of the boat trips from Blakeney or Morston – see below).

The most obvious base for the area is the once-busy wool port of **CLEY-NEXT-THE-SEA**, a tiny village of flint cottages strung out along the A149 and down a series of narrow back alleys. The original village was destroyed in a fire in 1612, which explains why Cley's rather grand fourteenth-century **church** seems somewhat abandoned at the very southern edge of the current village. The Black Death brought construction to a sudden halt, hence the contrast between the stunted chancel and tower and the splendid nave, which boasts five fine medieval brasses and some wonderful fifteenth-century bench ends depicting animals and grotesques.

There are several **B&B**s to choose from, including the village pub, the *George & Dragon* (☎01263/740 652; ④), *Whalebone House* (☎01263/740 336; ③), a tea room on the main street, and *Cley Mill* (☎01263/740 209; ④), which is attached to an eighteenth-century **windmill** (Easter–Sept daily 2–5pm; £1.50). The nearest **bike rental** outfit is *Glaven Valley Cycle Hire* (☎01263/741 172), a couple of miles south of Cley in Glandford. Cley's other great draw is the excellent *Cley Smoke House,* selling local smoked fish and other delicacies, and *Picnic Fare*, unquestionably the finest deli in East Anglia, housed in an old forge on the main street.

Blakeney

To get a really good view of the seals on Blakeney Point, you need to take one of the boat trips which depart from the quay (or "staithe", as they're known in these parts) at **BLAKENEY**, a mile or so to the west of Cley. The harbour is served by one of the channels which pierce their way through the sand and shingle; since the channel is flooded for only a few hours at high tide, you'll need to check the blackboard on the quayside for the departure times of the boats. Depending on the timing of the tides, you may have to leave from the quay at neighbouring Morston, which lies a mile further west. Other points of interest in Blakeney – which boasts a lovely, narrow, meandering high street flanked by modest pebble-covered cottages – include the remains of the thirteenth-century guildhall, signposted from the quay, and the parish church which, in addition to its main west tower, has an unusual beacon tower at the eastern end, which originally doubled as a lighthouse.

Blakeney's quayside **accommodation** is dominated by none-too-cheap hotels, the least expensive being the sixteenth-century *Manor Hotel* (☎01263/740 376; ⑤). B&Bs don't come much cheaper than *Bramble Lodge*, opposite the garage on the A149 (☎01263/740 191; ③), or the best of the village's pubs, the *King's Head* (☎01263/740 341; ④), also on the quayside. Also worth considering is *Morston Hall* (☎01263/741 041; ⑨) in neighbouring Morston, a luxurious hotel, where dinner, bed and breakfast costs £70 per person per night – the restaurant is one of the finest in East Anglia (around £25 per head) and is open to non-residents. Last of all, if you're looking for **bike** or **canoe rental**, contact *Blakeney Point Sailing School* (☎01263/740 704), which also runs sailing courses for beginners and upwards.

Wells-next-the-Sea

Despite its name, **WELLS-NEXT-THE-SEA** is situated a good mile or so from open water. In Tudor times, when it enjoyed much easier access to the sea, it was one of the great ports of eastern England. It's still one of the most attractive towns on the north Norfolk coast, and the only one to remain a commercially viable port. There's nothing specific to see amongst its narrow lanes but, nicely sheltered from the offshore winds, it makes a very good base for exploring the surrounding coastline.

The town divides into three distinct areas, starting with the broad rectangular green to the north, lined with oak and beech trees and some very fine Georgian houses, and known as **The Buttlands** since the days when it was used for archery practice. South of here are the narrow lanes of the town centre – **Staithe Street**, the miniature main street, has some interesting shops for browsing. At the bottom end of Staithe Street stands the **quay**, a rash of amusement arcades and the road to the local beach, which is shadowed by a high bank erected to consolidate the narrow channel to the sea, and a tiny seasonal narrow-gauge railway which runs roughly every forty minutes and will save you the long trek to the beach.

The **tourist office** is on Staithe Street (March to mid-July & Oct Mon–Sat 10am– 5pm, Sun 10am–4pm; mid-July to Sept Mon–Sat 9.30am–7pm, Sun 9.30am–6pm; ☎01328/710 885). If you're looking for **accommodation**, the *Crown*, on The Buttlands (☎01328/710 209; ⑤) and the *Scarborough House*, Clubbs Lane (☎01328/710 309; ④) are two of the nicest hotels in Wells; *Mill House*, Northfield Lane (☎01328/710 739; ③) is slightly less expensive. There's also a **campsite** by the beach, *Pinewoods Caravan and Camping* (March–Oct; ☎01328/710 439). Wells has some excellent **restaurants** starting with *The Moorings*, by the quay on Freeman Street (☎01328/710 949), which offers unusual and beautifully prepared dishes at around £15 for a three-course set menu. *Nelson's*, on Staithe Street, is a tea and coffee shop which does hot food for under £5; or for **pub** food and a pint of ale, head for the *Crown* on The Buttlands.

Holkham Hall

One of the most popular outings from Wells is to **Holkham Hall** (June–Sept Mon– Thurs & Sun 1.30–5pm; Easter, May & Spring Bank Hols Sun & Mon 11.30am–5pm; £3), a couple of miles to the west, designed by eighteenth-century architect William

---

NELSON

Norfolk's local hero is **Horatio Nelson**, born September 29, 1758, in the village of Burnham Thorpe, four miles southwest of Wells. Nelson joined the navy at the tender age of twelve, and was sent to the West Indies, where he met and married Frances Nisbet, retiring to Burnham Thorpe in 1787. Back in action again by 1793, his recklessness cost him first the sight of his right eye, and shortly afterwards his right arm. His personal life was equally eventful: he was a notorious womanizer, whose infatuation with Emma Hamilton, wife of the ambassador to Naples, caused the eventual break-up of his marriage. His finest hour was during the Battle of Trafalgar in 1805, when he led the British navy to victory against the combined French and Spanish fleet, getting himself mortally wounded in the process.

Nelson's father was the local rector, and it was the admiral's express wish that he be buried in the **parish church**. He in fact lies in St Paul's Cathedral, but the church has become something of an unofficial shrine to the local boy, its cross and lectern made out of timbers taken from the *Victory*, its south aisle housing a permanent exhibition on his life. The other place to head for is the **village pub** (no prizes for guessing the name) where Nelson held a farewell party for the locals in 1793, and where you can down a tot of "Nelson's Blood" rum, served by the landlord, Les Winter, who has written no fewer than three books on the man.

Kent for the Earl of Leicester and still owned by the family. The severe, sandy-coloured Palladian exterior belies the warmth and richness of the interior, which retains much of its original decoration. The marble splendour of the entrance hall gives way to the rich colours of the state rooms, which are hung with a **painting collection** that has been depleted over the years but still boasts canvases by Van Dyck, Gainsborough, Rubens, Titian and Poussin. The **park** (always open) is laid out on sandy, saline land that was reclaimed in 1722, and stretched right to the sea until the coastline receded. The focal point of the design, by Kent or Capability Brown, is the eighty-foot obelisk, from which you can view both the hall to the north and the triumphal arch to the south.

In common with the rest of the north Norfolk coast, there's plenty of **birdlife** to observe in and around the park – the large lake is inhabited by greylag and Canada geese and has a cormorant roost on the island. There's also a deer park close by. If you leave the estate by the north gate, and head for the sea, you'll reach **Holkham Bay**, one of the finest sandy beaches on this stretch of coast. On either side lies a nature reserve of sand dunes backed by a pine plantation – waders inhabit the mud and sand flats, while further inland you can see warblers, flycatchers and redstarts.

King's Lynn

An ancient port built on an improbably marshy location, **KING'S LYNN** straddles the mouth of the Great Ouse, a mile or so before it flows into the Wash. Strategically placed to supply seven English counties, the merchants of Lynn grew rich importing fish from Scandinavia, timber from the Baltic and wine from France, while exporting wool, salt and corn to the Hanseatic ports. Timber and grain still pass through Lynn, along with Skoda cars from the Czech republic and many other products. The town itself suffered badly during the 1950s and 1960s when much of the old centre was demolished to make way for commercial development. As a result, Lynn lacks the concentrated historic charm of towns such as Bury St Edmunds, though it does have a number of well-preserved buildings, the oldest guildhall in the country, and a handful of excellent stately homes within easy reach.

Lynn's historic core lies in the two blocks between the High Street and the quayside. A good place to begin is the **Saturday Market Place**, the older and lesser of the town's two market places. Lynn's prettiest building, the **Trinity Guildhall**, graces the north side of the market place, its chequered flint facade extending across buildings from four different periods, from the original guildhall of 1421 to the neo-Gothic extension of 1895. To the right is the **Old Gaol House** (April–Oct daily 10am–5pm; Nov–March closed Wed & Thurs; £2), housing the tourist office, a small museum on crime and punishment and, in the guildhall undercroft, an exhibition of the town's rich collection of civic regalia. The treasures include King John's Cup and Sword, the latter a gift to the town prior to the king's ill-fated dash across the Wash, during which he lost the crown jewels.

On the whole, the old harbour has lost its charm – even the gentle Georgian curve of Queen Street, featuring Clifton House with its barley-sugar columns, is now marred by traffic diverted from the pedestrianized High Street. At the end of Queen Street is Purfleet, one of a number of creeks which used to divide the town into three islands, overlooked by **Customs House**, an attractive Palladian building with a rooftop balustrade and cupola. On King Street, with its much wider berth, stands Lynn's most precious building, the **St George's Guildhall** (April–Sept Mon–Fri 10am–5pm, Sat 10am–1pm & 2–5pm; Oct–March Mon–Fri 11am–4pm, Sat 11am–1pm & 2–4pm; £1), built in 1420, the oldest surviving guildhall in England, once an Elizabethan theatre, and now the Fermoy arts centre. Beyond the guildhall is the later and much larger **Tuesday Market Place**, with the pastel-pink *Duke's Head Hotel* from 1689 and the Neoclassical Corn Exchange standing out against an unspectacular assemblage.

Before calling it a day, it's worth strolling up St Nicholas Street and North Street, past the slowly subsiding chapel of St Nicholas, which sports an ornate two-tiered south porch. At the far end of the street is Lynn's most chastening museum, **True's Yard** (daily 9.30am–4.30pm; £1.80), all that remains of Lynn's North End fishing community, which was levelled in the slum clearances of the 1930s. Guided tours, often by old Northenders, take you behind the present-day tea rooms to two tiny cottages, consisting of just one small room on each floor, in which families of ten or more used to live, most without running water.

Practicalities

From the **train station**, it's a short walk down Waterloo Street to the **bus station**, which itself lies on the eastern edge of the town centre. The **tourist office** is in the Old Gaol House (Mon–Thurs 9.15am–5pm Fri & Sat 9.15am–5.30pm; May–Sept also Sun 10am–3pm; ☎01533/763 044). **Accommodation** presents few problems except during the arts festival at the end of July. Lynn's finest is the *Duke's Head* on the Tuesday Market Place (☎01533/774 996; ⑦), though the *Tudor Rose*, a fifteenth-century inn on St Nicholas Street (☎01533/762 824; ⑤) is also highly recommended. For more reasonably priced **B&Bs**, try *The Beeches*, 2 Guanack Terrace, off London Road (☎01533/776 664; ③), or the nearby *Fairlight Lodge*, 79 Goodwins Rd (☎01533/762 234; ②). The town's central **youth hostel** is in Thorseby College, College Lane (☎01533/772 461). For somewhere really special to **eat**, try *Rococo*, an expensive, modish little outfit on the Saturday Market Place (☎01533/771 483). Cheaper possibilities are the *Riverside Restaurant*, round the back of the Fermoy arts centre, or the *Tudor Rose*.

Around King's Lynn

One thing in King's Lynn's favour is the number of stately homes within a twenty-mile radius of the town. The architectural gem is **Houghton Hall**, one of the finest Palladian mansions in the country, though the mellow red brick of **Oxburgh Hall** is more immediately appealing and **Sandringham**, the Queen's country residence, is the most popular. The area also holds some fine Norman ruins at **Castle Rising** and **Castle Acre**. Of the five, Sandringham and Castle Rising are the only ones directly accessible by public transport from Lynn.

Castle Rising

Situated at the centre of extensive earthworks, the twelfth-century keep of **Castle Rising** (April–Sept daily 10am–6pm; Oct–March Wed–Sun 10am–4pm; £1.30; EH), though ruined, is in remarkably good condition, with much of its original decoration intact – blind arcading and ox-eye windows on the outside and vaulted ceilings and ornamented fireplaces inside. The nearby village is laid out on a grid plan and contains a quadrangle of beautiful seventeenth-century almshouses, whose elderly inhabitants still go to church in the red cloaks and pointed black hats, the colours of the original benefactor, the Earl of Northampton. Buses #410 and #411 from King's Lynn stop off at the *Black Horse* pub in the village, five miles northeast of King's Lynn.

Sandringham House

Local buses continue from Castle Rising past the seven-thousand-acre estate of the neo-Jacobean **Sandringham House** (Easter–Sept daily 11am–4.45pm; closed for 2 weeks late July or early Aug; £4), bought in 1861 by Queen Victoria for her son, the future Edward VII. The house museum contains an exhibition of royal memorabilia from dolls to cars. More arresting are the beautifully maintained grounds (Easter–Sept 10.30am–5pm; £3), a gallimaufry of rhododendrons and azaleas in spring and early summer. The estate's sandy soil is also ideal for game birds, which was the attraction of the place for the terminally bored Edward, whose tradition of New Year shooting parties is still followed by the royals, despite considerable protests.

Houghton Hall

Five miles due east of Sandringham is the early Palladian masterpiece of **Houghton Hall** (Easter–Sept Thurs & Sun 2–5pm; £4), unbelievably rejected by the future Edward VII in favour of Sandringham. It was built in the 1730s for the country's first prime minister, Sir Robert Walpole, to designs by Colen Campbell. As at Holkham, the fairly plain exterior – enlivened a little by James Gibbs' Baroque topping – gives no hint of the lavishness of the state rooms, of which the most fabulously grandiose is the Stone Hall. Sadly, the family's great art collection now hangs in the St Petersburg Hermitage, having been sold to Catherine the Great to pay off the debts of an errant earl. Instead, you can view the Sèvres porcelain, Mortlake tapestries and the twenty thousand model soldiers, or, more interestingly, visit the stables – used for breeding heavy horses and Shetland ponies – and seek out the white fallow deer in the park.

Castle Acre

CASTLE ACRE stands on one of the few hilltops in Norfolk, twelve miles east of King's Lynn, approached via a narrow flint gateway, all that remains of the **castle** built as a manor house by William de Warenne shortly after the Conquest. The village itself nestles within the grounds of the outer bailey, which has worn back down to the original Roman earthworks, while to the west, on the banks of the River Nar, there are more extensive ruins of a Cluniac **priory** also founded by Warenne (April–Sept daily 10am–6pm; Oct–March Wed–Sun 10am–4pm; £2.20; EH). The most significant feature left standing is the highly decorated late-Norman west front, while the elegant adjacent priory lodge now contains a small museum.

Oxburgh Hall

Some eighteen miles southeast of King's Lynn, on the edge of Breckland, stands **Oxburgh Hall** (April–Oct Sat–Wed 1–5pm; £4; NT), built in 1482 by the Bedingfeld

---

THE FENS

One of the strangest of all English landscapes, the **Fens** cover a vast area from just north of Cambridge right up to Boston in Lincolnshire. For centuries, they were an inhospitable wilderness of quaking bogs and marshland, punctuated by clay islands on which small communities eked out a livelihood cutting peat for fuel, using reeds for thatching, and living on a diet of fish and wildfowl. Piecemeal land reclamation took place throughout the Middle Ages, but it wasn't until the seventeenth century that the systematic draining of the fens was undertaken – amid fierce local opposition – by the Dutch engineer **Cornelius Vermuyden**. The transformation of the fens had unforseen consequences: as it dried out, the peaty soil shrank to below the level of the rivers, causing further flooding, a situation only exacerbated by the numerous windmills, erected to help drain the fens, but which actually resulted in further shrinkage. It wasn't until the advent of steam-driven pumps in the 1820s that the fens were finally turned into the valuable agricultural land which you now see.

At **Wicken Fen** (daily dawn–dusk; £2.50; NT), seven miles southeast of Ely, you can visit one of the few remaining areas of undrained fenland. Its survival is thanks to a group of Victorian entomologists who donated the land to the National Trust in 1899, making it the oldest nature reserve in the UK. The six hundred acres are undrained but not uncultivated – sedge-and reed-cutting are still carried out to preserve the landscape as it is – and the reserve also features the last surviving wind pump in the fens.

family, whose staunch Catholicism never faltered throughout the turbulent times of the Reformation. The approach to the hall is via an eighty-foot ceremonial gateway, matched by the main gate tower of the house itself. The exterior is wonderful – an archetypal medieval manor house, surrounded by a moat strewn with water-lilies, its dappled brickwork exuding warmth. However, aside from the tapestries executed by the imprisoned Mary Queen of Scots, the rooms themselves, redecorated in Victorian times, are disappointing. The most exquisite Bedingfeld legacy – the family's sixteenth-century terracotta tomb – is just outside the grounds of the hall in the partly ruined parish church.

Ely

ELY began its life as a seventh-century Benedictine abbey built on the Isle of Ely, a rare patch of upland in the soggy fens. Until the draining of the fens in the seventeenth century, this was to all intents and purposes a true island – the name Ely means "eel island" – surrounded by treacherous marshland, accessible only with the aid of "fen-slodgers" who knew the terrain. Under Hereward the Wake, the island became a centre of Anglo-Saxon rebellion, holding out against the Norman invaders until 1071. To mark their victory, the Normans constructed a new "cathedral of the fens", a towering structure visible for miles across the flat landscape. With a population of less than ten thousand, Ely has changed very little since medieval times, and the cathedral remains its main attraction.

The best way of approaching the **Cathedral** (daily summer 7am–7pm, winter 7.30am–6pm; £2.60) is to head up Station Road from the train station, and take the second right into Broad Street. Halfway along the street, turn left into the rural haven of the cathedral close, from where you get by far the best **view** – the crenellated towers to the west end perfectly balanced by the prickly finials to the east, with the famous timber lantern rising above them. At the top of the hill, pass through the medieval Ely Porta, once the main entrance to the monastery, and turn right to reach the lopsided **west front** – its northwest transept fell down in a storm in 1701.

The first things to strike you as you enter the **nave** are the sheer length of the building, and the lively nineteenth-century painted ceiling, largely the work of amateurs. The procession of plain late-Norman arches, built around the same time as Peterborough, leads to the architectural feature which makes Ely so special, the **octagon** – the only one of its kind in England – built in 1322 to replace the collapsed central tower. Its construction, employing the largest oaks available in England to support some four hundred tons, is one of the wonders of the medieval world, and the effect, as you look up into this Gothic dome, is breathtaking.

When the central tower collapsed, it fell eastwards, hence the fussier decorative style of the rebuilt choir. The presbytery, beyond, was built in the thirteenth century to house the relics of **Saint Ethelreda**, founder of the abbey in 673, who, despite being twice married, is honoured liturgically as a virgin. At the far eastern end are two fantastically ornate chantry chapels from the sixteenth century, which together once housed over two hundred statues lost during the Reformation. The other marvel at Ely is the **Lady Chapel**, in actual fact a separate building accessible via the north transept. It, too, lost its wealth of sculpture and all its stained glass during the Reformation, but its wide fan vaulting remains an exquisite example of English Gothic. A startling variety of stained glass, dating from 1240 to the present day, is on view in the **Stained Glass Museum** (March–Oct Mon–Sat 10.30–4pm, Sun noon–3pm; Nov–Feb Sat & Sun only; £1.50) in the north triforium.

In addition to the cathedral, Ely also boasts the finest collection of medieval domestic architecture in the country, much of it now used by the King's School, a mixed boarding school which trains the cathedral's choristers – there's a small map and guide to the **monastic buildings** available from the cathedral. Perhaps the most evocative is the one on Firmary Lane, which was originally the main hall of the monks' infirmary. Another medieval ensemble lies to the west of here, backing onto The Gallery, a street named after the overhead passage that once connected the cathedral with the Bishop's Palace on the green.

Practicalities

Ely lies on a major rail intersection, with direct trains from as far afield as Liverpool, Norwich and London. The **tourist office** is in Oliver Cromwell's House (May–Sept daily 10am–6pm; Oct–March Mon–Sat 10am–5pm; ☎01353/662 062), and contains a small museum on the man. *The Black Hostelry* (☎01353/662 612; ④) is a superb **B&B** within the complex of medieval buildings on Firmary Lane; other attractive possibilities are *The Post House* (☎01353/667 184; ③), a seventeenth-century house on Egremont Street, or try the B&B also on Egremont Street, at no. 31 (☎01353/663 118; ③). There are plenty of **tea rooms** and a few restaurants in Ely; one of the former which serves decent hot meals is *Dominique's*, 8 St Mary's St (Wed–Sun). Ely's friendliest **pub** is the *Prince Albert*, on Silver Street, which has a garden round the back.

Cambridge

An agricultural market town at heart, **CAMBRIDGE** is, on the whole, a much quieter and more secluded place than Oxford, but what really sets it apart from its scholarly rival are "The Backs" – the green swathe of land straddling the languid River Cam – which overlook the backs of the old colleges, and provide the town's most enduring image. Tradition has it that Cambridge was founded in the late 1220s by scholastic refugees from Oxford who fled the town after one of their number was lynched by hostile townsfolk – the first proper college wasn't founded until 1271, however. Rivalry has existed between the two institutions ever since – epitomized by the annual Boat Race on the River Thames – while internal tensions between "town and gown" have inevitably plagued a place where, from the late fourteenth century onwards, the university has tended to dominate local life. The first (but by no means the last) rebellion against the scholars occurred during the Peasants' Revolt of 1381, and had to be put down with armed troops by the Bishop of Norwich; five townsfolk were hanged as a result.

In the sixteenth century, Cambridge became a centre of church reformism, educating some of the most famous Protestant preachers in the country including Cranmer, Latimer and Ridley, all of whom were martyred in Oxford by Mary Tudor. Later, during the Civil War, Cambridge once again found itself at the centre of events: Cromwell himself was both a graduate of Sidney Sussex and the local MP, while the university was largely Royalist. The nineteenth century witnessed the biggest changes in the balance between town and gown: the number of students increased dramatically, while the university itself lost its ancient privileges over the town, which was expanding rapidly thanks to the arrival of the railway. This century, change has been much slower coming to Cambridge, particularly when it comes to equality of the sexes: only three colleges accepted women until the mid-1970s, with some colleges holding out until the late 1980s.

Arrival, information and accommodation

Stansted, London's third airport, with its striking new terminal building designed by Norman Foster, is just thirty miles south of Cambridge (bus every hour; direct train only once daily). Closer at hand, the **train station** is a mile or so southeast of the city

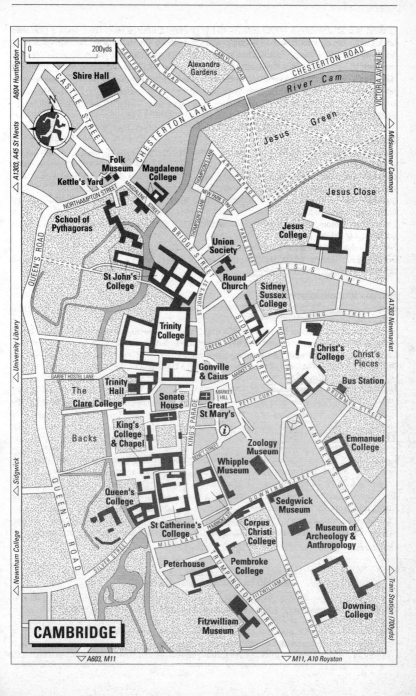

0   200yds

Shire Hall

Alexandra Gardens

CHESTERTON ROAD

River Cam

Jesus Green

CHESTERTON LANE

Jesus Close

Folk Museum

Magdalene College

Kettle's Yard

School of Pythagoras

Union Society

Jesus College

St John's College

Round Church

Sidney Sussex College

Trinity College

Christ's College

Christ's Pieces

Bus Station

Gonville & Caius

Trinity Hall

The Clare College

Senate House

Market Hill

Great St Mary's

Emmanuel College

King's College & Chapel

Zoology Museum

Whipple Museum

Backs

Queen's College

Sedgwick Museum

St Catherine's College

Corpus Christi College

Museum of Archeology & Anthropology

Peterhouse

Pembroke College

Downing College

Fitzwilliam Museum

CAMBRIDGE

A604 Huntingdon

A1303, A45 St Neots

Queen's Road

University Library

Sidgwick

Newnham College

A603, M11

M11, A10 Royston

VICTORIA AVENUE

Midsummer Common

A1303 Newmarket

Train Station (700yds)

centre; the shuttle bus #1 runs into town every eight minutes until 6pm, with a skeleton service continuing until 9pm. The **bus station** is centrally located on Drummer Street, right by Christ's Pieces. Cambridge is a cycling city, with almost every student owning one; for **bike rental** near the train station, go to *Geoff's*, 65 Devonshire Rd (April–Sept daily 9am–5.30pm; Oct–March closed Sun). Cambridge **tourist office** is conveniently situated in the ornate, domed former public library on Wheeler Street, behind the town hall (Easter–Sept Mon–Fri 9am–6/7pm, Sat 9am–5pm, Sun 10.30am–3.30pm; Oct–Easter Mon–Fri 9am–5.30pm, Sat 9am–5pm; ☎01223/322 640) .

Hotels and B&Bs

Arundel House Hotel, 53 Chesterton Rd (☎01223/367 701). Big Victorian hotel on the far side of Jesus Green. ④.

Dresden Villa, 34 Cherry Hinton Rd (☎01223/247 539). Guest house close to the train station. ④.

Hamilton Hotel, 156–58 Chesterton Rd (☎01223/365 664). Small, reliable hotel. ③.

Lensfield Hotel, 53 Lensfield Rd (☎01223/355 017). Good location just round the corner from the Fitzwilliam Museum. ⑤.

Lyngamore House, 35–37 Chesterton Rd (☎01223/312 369). Least expensive of the lot on a street packed full of B&Bs. ②.

Netley Lodge, 112 Chesterton Rd (☎01223/363 845). B&B not far from the river. ③.

Six Steps, 93 Tenison Rd (☎01223/353 968). One of several B&Bs in this road, close to the train station. ③.

Hostels and campsites

Carpenter's Arms,182 Victoria Rd (☎01223/351 814). Dorm accommodation above a pub for £11 a night.

Youth Hostel, 96 Tenison Rd (☎01223/354 601). Situated close to the train station, with a small courtyard garden and games room. Open all year, but very busy from March onwards.

Cambridge Camping and Caravanning Club Site, Cabbage Moor, Great Shelford (April–Oct; ☎01223/841 185). Three miles south of the city centre – take the A10, then turn left onto the A1301. BR station; Great Shelford.

Highfield Farm Campsite, Long Rd, Comberton (☎01223/262 308). Three miles west of the city centre; take the A603, cross over the M11 and then turn right into the B1046; bus #118 goes there from the centre.

The City

Cambridge's main shopping street is Bridge Street, which becomes Sidney Street, St Andrew's Street and finally Regent Street; the other main thoroughfare is the procession of St John's Street, Trinity Street, King's Parade and Trumpington Street. The university developed in the land west of this latter route along the banks of the Cam, and now forms a continuous half-mile parade of colleges from Magdalene to Peterhouse, with sundry others scattered about the periphery. The account below starts with King's College, whose chapel is the university's most famous landmark, and covers the rest of the town in a clockwise direction.

COLLEGE OPENING TIMES

Admission charges to the colleges have only very recently been introduced, and only tend to apply to the most popular ones in the centre of town. However, it's a creeping trend, so don't be surprised if other, lesser-known colleges start following suit. The opening times listed in the text were correct at the time of going to press, but are liable to change as the colleges assess the efficacy of these new arrangements. It's also worth noting that all colleges close their doors to the public in May, during the exam season.

King's College

Henry VI cleared away half of medieval Cambridge to make room for **King's College** (term-time Mon–Sat 9.30am–3.30pm, Sun 1.15–2.15pm; out of term Mon–Sat 9.30am–3.30pm, Sun 10am–4.30pm; £2), founded in 1441. The overall layout of his Great Court survives, but much of the existing college is a neo-Gothic design by William Wilkins, built in the early nineteenth century. The one element of Henry's plan that is left standing is Cambridge's most celebrated building – **King's College Chapel**, on the north side of Great Court; tourists must enter via Trinity Lane. Committed to canvas by Turner and Canaletto, eulogized in three sonnets by Wordsworth, it's now perhaps best known for its **boys' choir**, who process across the college grounds in their antiquated garb to sing evensong (Tues–Sun 5.30pm). The chapel's simple design is offset by the richly decorated interior, which boasts extravagant fan vaulting, supported by a wall of sixteenth-century stained glass, which somehow survived the Reformation. The intricately carved organ screen, financed by Henry VIII, is one of the earliest examples of Italianate Renaissance wood carving in England; behind the altar hangs Rubens' *Adoration of the Magi*, donated anonymously to the college in 1962.

Like Oxford's New College, King's enjoyed an exclusive supply from one of the country's public schools – in this case, Eton. The first non-Etonians were only accepted in 1873, and until 1851 the college claimed the right to award its students degrees without taking any examinations. Times have changed since those days, and if anything, King's is now one of the more progressive colleges, having been among the first to admit women in 1972. Among its most famous alumni are E.M. Forster, who described his experiences in *Maurice*; film director Derek Jarman; and John Maynard Keynes, whose economic theories did much to improve the college's finances when he became the college bursar.

From King's Parade to Clare College

King's Parade, originally the medieval High Street, is inevitably dominated by the college and chapel, but the higgledy-piggledy shops opposite are an attractive foil to William Wilkins' screen, which replaced the west side of the street. At the far end of King's Parade is **Great St Mary's**, the university's pet church, whose tower (Mon–Sat 10am–4.45pm, Sun 12.30–4.30pm; £1.20) gives out a good overall view of the colleges and a bird's-eye view of the colourful market place, east of the church. Opposite the church stands **Senate House**, an exercise in Palladian classicism by James Gibbs, and the scene of graduation ceremonies on the last Saturday in June, when champagne corks fly around the rabbit-fur collars and black gowns.

A short way along Trinity Street is the main entrance to **Gonville and Caius College**, known simply as Caius (pronounced "keys"), after the co-founder John Keys, who latinized his name, as was the custom with men of learning. The design of the college owes much to Keys, who placed a gate on each side of two courts, each representing a different stage on the path to academic enlightenment: the Gate of Humility, through which the student entered the college, now stands in the Fellows' Garden; the Gate of Virtue, sporting the female figures of Fame and Wealth, marks the entrance to Caius Court; while the Gate of Honour, capped with sundials and decorated with classical motifs, leads to Senate House.

Senate House Passage leads past the Gate of Honour to two well-concealed colleges. The first, **Trinity Hall**, has little to detain you, though its Elizabethan library retains several of its original chains designed to prevent students from purloining the texts. **Clare College** (daily 10am–4.30pm; £1.50), to the south, is one of seven colleges founded, rather surprisingly, by women. Its plain period-piece courtyards, completed in the early eighteenth century, lead to one of the most picturesque of all the bridges over the Cam, **Clare Bridge**, studded with ornamental stone balls. Beyond lie the Fellows' Gardens, among the loveliest of the college gardens open to the public.

Trinity and St John's

Trinity College (daily 10am–6pm; £1.50) is the largest of the Cambridge colleges, has the largest courtyard and is the third largest landowner in the country. It comes as little surprise then that its list of famous alumni is longer than any other college: literary greats from Dryden to Byron, Tennyson and Nabokov; the Cambridge spies Blunt, Burgess and Philby; two prime ministers, Balfour and Baldwin; Isaac Newton, Lord Rutherford, Vaughan Williams, Pandit Nehru, Edward VII, George VI, Bertrand Russell, Ludwig Wittgenstein, and that other great philosopher, Prince Charles.

A statue of Henry VIII, who founded the college in 1546, sits in majesty over Trinity's Great Gate, his sceptre replaced with a chair leg by a student wit. The vast asymmetrical expanse of **Great Court** displays a fine array of Tudor buildings, the oldest of which is the fifteenth-century clock tower; the annual race against its midnight chimes is now common currency thanks to the film *Chariots of Fire*. The centrepiece of the court is the delicate fountain, in which, legend has it, Lord Byron used to bathe naked with his pet bear – the college forbade students from keeping dogs. To get through to Nevile Court, you must pass through the "screens passage", a common feature of Oxbridge colleges, separating the hall from the kitchens.

The delightfully symmetrical Nevile Court, with its elegant cloisters, is where Newton first calculated the speed of sound. At the far end, the courtyard is enclosed by the university's most famous building after King's College Chapel, the **Wren Library** (term-time Mon–Fri 9am–5pm, Sat 9am–1pm; out of term closed Sat). Viewed from the outside, it's impossible to appreciate the scale of the interior thanks to Wren's clever device of concealing the internal floor level. In contrast to many modern libraries, natural light pours into the white stuccoed interior, which contrasts wonderfully with the dark limewood bookcases, which house numerous valuable manuscripts including Milton's *Lycidas*, Wittgenstein's journals, and A.A. Milne's *Winnie the Pooh*.

Another Tudor gatehouse marks the entrance of **St John's College** (March–Oct daily 10am–4.30pm; £1.50), founded 35 years earlier than Trinity by the Bishop of Rochester on behalf of Lady Margaret Beaufort, mother of Henry VII – her coat of arms, held aloft by two spotty, mythical beasts with revolving horns, decorates the entrance. Wordsworth, who lived above the kitchens on F Staircase, described the three successive courts which lead to the river as "gloomy", and they continue to exhibit some of the university's most lugubrious brickwork. The arcade on the far side of Third Court leads through to the celebrated **Bridge of Sighs**, a covered bridge built in 1831 but in most other respects very unlike its Venetian namesake. The bridge is closed to the public, and in any case is best viewed either from a punt or from the much older, more stylish Wren-designed St John's Bridge, to the south.

From Magdalene to Jesus

Just round the corner from St John's Northampton Street entrance, off Castle Hill, is **Kettle's Yard** (Tues–Sun 2–4pm; free), a deceptively spacious open-plan conversion of some old slum dwellings, originally owned by the art critic and curator, Jim Ede (1895–1990). The house is packed full of works of art, including many by the St Ives' primitivist Alfred Wallis, but it is much more than a simple gallery – it's the sense of art within a living space, amid house plants, lounge chairs and an extensive library of art books, which make the place so special. In 1970 a formal exhibition gallery (Tues–Sat 12.30–5.30pm, Sun 2–5.30pm; free) was added as a forum for contemporary artists.

Heading south down Castle Hill you cross over into Magdalene Street, straddled by **Magdalene College** (pronounced "maudlin"; daily 8am–6.30pm; free), the last of the colleges to admit women – it succumbed in 1988. In the second of the college's sixteenth-century courtyards stands the **Pepys Building** (Mon–Sat Sept–Easter 11.30am–12.30pm; Easter–Aug 11.30am–12.30pm & 2.30–3.30pm), named after the Magdalene boy whose entire library has been on display here in its original red oak bookshelves, since 1742 when it was bequeathed to the college along with his famous diary (though this remained undiscovered until the nineteenth century).

Cross the river via Magdalene Bridge, site of the old Roman ford, onto Bridge Street, at the end of which stands the **Round Church**, built in the twelfth century on the model of the Holy Sepulchre in Jerusalem. The spire is a nineteenth-century addition, but the Norman pillars remain inside; the church now houses the town's brass-rubbing centre. Set back from the road, behind the church, is the **Union Society**, a bastion of male-dominated debating culture which only began to admit women in the 1960s. The society likes to think of itself as a miniature House of Commons – its debating chamber is designed as such – and its formalized debates continue to attract many of the leading politicians and speakers of the day, though it is now attended almost exclusively by the university's more ambitious and reactionary elements.

The wide open spaces and intimate cloisters of **Jesus College**, a short way down Jesus Lane from the Round Church, are reminiscent of a monastic institution – and with good reason, for the college was founded in 1496 by the Bishop of Ely on the grounds of a suppressed Benedictine nunnery. The main red-brick gateway is approached via a distinctive walled walkway strewn with bicycles and known as "The Chimney". Much of the ground plan of the nunnery has been preserved, especially around Cloister Court, the prettiest of the college's courtyards. The college chapel, occupying the former priory chancel and looking more like a medieval parish church, was imaginatively restored in the nineteenth century, using ceiling designs by William Morris and pre-Raphaelite stained glass. The poet Samuel Taylor Coleridge was the college's most famously bad student, absconding in his first year to join the Light Dragoons, and returning only to be kicked out for a combination of bad debts and unconventional opinions.

St Andrew's Street

To get to St Andrew's Street from the Round Church, you must pass down Sidney Street, named after **Sidney Sussex College**, one of the most unprepossessing of the old Cambridge colleges, thanks to the mock-Gothic cement rendering that was plastered over the college walls in the 1830s. The college's only claim to fame is that Oliver Cromwell studied here, and in 1960 it was the lucky recipient of Oliver

---

ON THE RIVER

One activity you should have a go at while in Cambridge is **punting**, even though first-timers tend to find themselves zigzagging across the water, and punt jams are very common on the stretch of the Cam along the Backs in summer. Prices range between £5 to £7 an hour, with up to six people in each punt. *Scudamores*, at Mill Lane and Magdalene Bridge, is the biggest outfit; *Trinity Punts* from Trinity College Backs is cheaper but tends to have longer queues; several outlets on Granta Place hire out punts for the less frequented upper river. If you find it all too daunting you can always hire a **chauffeur punt** from the *Spade & Becket* pub on Jesus Green.

As well as punting, Cambridge is famous for its **rowing clubs**, which are clustered along the north bank of the river on Midsummer Common, the only stretch of water that is punt-free. The most important inter-college races are the **May Bumps**, which, confusingly, take place in the first week of June; fight your way to the bar of the *Fort St George* on Midsummer Common and watch the spectacle.

Cromwell's head, now buried in a secret location in the college chapel. At the point where Sidney Street becomes St Andrew's Street, you pass the turreted gateway of **Christ's College** (daily 9.30am–noon; free), featuring the coat of arms of the founder, Lady Margaret Beaufort, who also founded St John's. Passing through First Court you come to the Fellows' Building, attributed to Inigo Jones, whose central arch gives access to the **Fellows' Garden** (Mon–Fri 9.30am–noon). The poet John Milton is said either to have planted or composed beneath the garden's elderly mulberry tree, though it's likely he did neither; Christ's other famous undergraduate was Charles Darwin, who showed little academic promise and spent most of his time hunting and shooting.

Further up St Andrew's Street is **Emmanuel College**, founded in 1583 to train a new generation of Protestant clergy following the Reformation. Its rather uninspiring Neoclassical facade hides a much more imaginative display within, including Wren's fanciful chapel and cloister, which deliberately echo those at Peterhouse (see below). Still further up the street is the uncompromisingly Neoclassical ensemble of **Downing College**, established in 1800 and unique amongst Cambridge colleges in being laid out like a campus around a central lawn, rather than enclosed in separate courtyards.

From St Catherine's to Peterhouse

The final foursome of colleges in the town centre begins with **St Catherine's College**, founded in 1473 by the provost of King's on land just to the south of that college. "Catz", as it is popularly known, has little to entice, especially when compared with **Corpus Christi College**, opposite, founded by two of the town's guilds in 1352. Ignore the first court and head north into Old Court, which dates from the foundation of the college, and is where Christopher Marlowe wrote *Tamburlaine* before graduating in 1587. The college library, on the south side, contains a priceless collection of Anglo-Saxon manuscripts, while the north side is linked by a gallery to **St Bene't's Church**, which served as the college chapel, but is of much earlier Saxon origin.

Queens' College (March–Oct daily 10am–12.15pm & 2–4.15pm; £1), halfway down Silver Street, is the most oversubscribed college, and it's not difficult to see why. Cloister Court is a fairy-tale Elizabethan courtyard with galleried arcades, and the exquisite President's Lodge is the last remaining half-timbered building in the university. Be sure to pay a visit to the college hall, off the screen's passage, which features interior decor by William Morris, and portraits of Erasmus and one of the co-founders, Elizabeth Woodville, wife of Edward IV. Equally eye-catching is the wooden **Mathematical Bridge** over the Cam, a copy of the mid-eighteenth-century original which, it was claimed, would stay in place even if the nuts and bolts were removed.

Back on Trumpington Street, **Pembroke College** contains Wren's first ever commission, the college chapel, paid for by his Royalist uncle, erstwhile bishop of Ely and a college fellow, in thanks for his deliverance from the Tower of London after seventeen years' imprisonment. Outside the library there's a statue of William Pitt the Younger, who entered the college at fifteen and was prime minister at twenty-five, just one of a long list of college alumni which includes poets Edmund Spenser and Thomas Gray, TV wit Clive James and the current poet laureate, Ted Hughes.

Across the road from Pembroke is the oldest and smallest of the colleges, **Peterhouse**, founded in 1284. Few of the original buildings have survived, except the thirteenth-century hall on the south side (open daily 9.30am–noon), which was considerably remodelled inside by William Morris. Peterhouse used the church next door – Little St Mary's – as the college chapel, until the present one, with its light-hearted Baroque gables, was erected in the main court in 1632.

The Fitzwilliam Museum

Of all the museums in East Anglia, the **Fitzwilliam Museum**, on Trumpington Street (Tues–Fri Lower Galleries 10am–2pm, Upper Galleries 2–5pm, Sat both 10am–5pm, Sun both 2.15–5pm; free), stands head and shoulders above the rest. The building itself is a splendidly fanciful interpretation of Neoclassicism, built in the mid-nineteenth century to house the vast collection bequeathed by Viscount Fitzwilliam in 1816. The museum's **Lower Galleries** contain a wealth of antiquities including Egyptian sarcophagi and mummies, fifth-century BC black- and red-figure Greek vases, plus a bewildering display of European porcelain, including Meissen figures. The array of Spanish and Italian earthenware is equally overwhelming, but be sure to persevere to the far end of the galleries where the fantastic Chinese vase collection resides, and where a stylish new gallery of Korean ceramics has just been built.

The **Upper Galleries** concentrate on painting and sculpture. Van Dyck, Gainsborough and Reynolds all feature in the central hall, while next door the nineteenth-century section includes several works by William Blake; pre-Raphaelite classics by Millais, Rossetti, Ford Madox Brown and Burne-Jones; a handful of Sickert's Camden Town nudes; as well as paintings by Stanley Spencer, Modigliani, Picasso and a fair smattering of French Impressionists. The Italian section boasts works by Fra' Filippo Lippi and Simone Martini, Titian and Veronese, while Frans Hals and Ruisdael feature in the Flemish section. The twentieth-century gallery is packed with an eclectic selection including the likes of Robert Rauschenberg, Lucian Freud, David Hockney, Henry Moore, Ivon Hitchens, Ben Nicholson and Barbara Hepworth.

Eating, drinking and nightlife

Students are not the world's greatest customers for restauranteurs, so although the **takeaway** and **café** scene is good in the centre, and Cambridge abounds in excellent **pubs**, fine **restaurants** are few and far between. During term-time, there's a bit more **nightlife**, with numerous student drama productions, classical concerts and gigs culminating in the traditional orgy of excess following the exam season, though the more firmly town-based venues, like the Corn Exchange, put on events throughout the year. For all the week's events, check the listings section of the student weekly, *Varsity*.

Cafés and snacks

CB1, 32 Mill Rd. The worldwide web has reached Cambridge, in this café for keen surfers. Daily 9am–midnight.

Café Rouge, 25–26 Bridge St. London-based brasserie chain that serves French classics and coffee. Mon–Sat 8am–11pm, Sun 10am–10.30pm.

Clowns, 54 King St. Real Italian-style cappuccino and cakes, and plenty of newspapers at this popular student café. Daily 9am–midnight.

Fitzbillies, 52 Trumpington St. French patisserie baking the best pastries in town, with a café upstairs. Mon–Thurs 9am–5.30pm, Fri & Sat 9am–9pm, Sun 11.30am–4.30pm.

Restaurants

Brown's, 23 Trumpington St. Lively cheap restaurant in the former outpatients department. No bookings. Mon–Sat 11am–11.30pm, Sun noon–11.30pm. Inexpensive to moderate.

Effes, 78 King St. Hugely popular Turkish restaurant, with great char-grilled meats prepared under your nose. Daily until midnight. Moderate.

King's Pantry, 9a King's Parade. The only vegetarian restaurant in Cambridge. Mon–Sat 8am–5pm & 6.30–9.30pm, Sun 8am–5.30pm. Inexpensive.

Midsummer House, Midsummer Common (☎01223/692 99). Riverside restaurant specializing in top-notch French cuisine. Tues–Fri noon–2pm & 7–9.30pm, Sat 7–9.30pm, Sun noon–2pm. Expensive.

Panos, 154 Hills Rd (☎01223/212 958). Best Greek restaurant in town – try the scotch steak or any of the other charcoal grills. Mon–Fri noon–2pm & 7–10pm, Sat 7–10pm. Moderate.

Pizza Express, 28 St Andrew's St. Superior pizza chain with intimate branch at above address and grander, marbled hall at 7a Jesus Lane (in the former Pitt Club). Both branches open daily until midnight. Inexpensive.

Twenty-Two, 22 Chesterton Rd (☎01223/351 880). Exclusive, evenings-only English restaurant by the banks of the Cam, with good-value fixed-price menus. Closed Sun & Mon. Moderate to expensive.

Pubs

Boathouse, 14 Chesterton Rd. The most pleasant of the riverside pubs, slightly out of town on the north side of the Cam.

Eagle, Bene't St. A thoroughly ancient inn with a cobbled courtyard where Crick and Watson sought inspiration in the 1950s, at the time of their discovery of DNA.

Elm Tree, Elm St. A cosy little local behind the police station, on the east side of Parker's Piece park.

Free Press, Prospect Row. The food and beers are excellent; the clientele mostly from the university's rowing fraternity.

Live & Let Live, 40 Mawson Rd. Great open-plan free house hidden in the backstreets close to the train station.

Maypole, Park St. Small, central pub whose popular landlord, Mario, is a world-class cocktail shaker.

Zebra, 80 Maid's Causeway. Very popular for its pub food and convenient for the Grafton shopping centre.

Music, nightlife and other entertainment

When it comes to **classical music**, the King's College choir is of course the main attraction, though the choral scholars who perform at the chapels of St John's and Trinity are also exceptionally good. *Cambridge Footlights* are among the better student **theatre** productions to be staged at the *ADC Theatre*, on Park Street. Until the city's main rep theatre, the *Arts Theatre*, reopens after its lengthy refurbishment, the beautifully restored *Corn Exchange*, behind the town hall, will continue be the main venue for opera, ballet and musicals as well as **rock gigs**. Another place to hear live bands is *The Junction* on Clifton Road, which also features comedy acts and dance groups. Cambridge has its own *Arts Cinema*, off Market Street, showing a wide selection of **films** including old and new classic art films; in addition, during term-time, each of the colleges has its own cinema club, with very cheap admission – listings from *Varsity*.

June and July are the busiest times in Cambridge's calendar of events. The fortnight of post-exam celebrations, which takes place in the first two weeks of June and is confusingly known as **May Week**, herald the ball and garden party season, and include boat races, known as the "May Bumps", on the Cam by Midsummer Common. The vaguely hippie **Strawberry Fair**, descendant of the town's famous medieval Stourbridge Fair which was discontinued in 1934, takes place in mid-June on Midsummer Common, with bands, theatre, stalls and much more besides – all for free. By contrast, you'll have to pay up to £50 for a tent pitch and entry into the three-day **Cambridge Folk Festival**, held annually at the end of July, and attracting a wide variety of loosely folk-based acts. Also in the last fortnight of July, Cambridge puts on a large-scale **international arts festival**, which has even attracted a separate fringe festival in recent years.

Around Cambridge

The landscape immediately around Cambridge is unrelentingly flat and dull – you have to travel a good ten miles south before there's a break to the monotony. Of the two most popular day trips, **Duxford**, the outpost of the Imperial War Msueum, is of specialist interest; **Audley End**, on the other hand, has slightly more universal appeal.

Duxford

Eight miles south of Cambridge, and visible from the M11, are the giant hangars of the **Imperial War Museum** (daily April to mid-Oct 10am–6pm; mid-Oct to March 10am–4pm; £6), based at Duxford airfield. The flat landscape of East Anglia has a special place in aviation history for having the largest number of wartime airfields in the country. Duxford itself was a Battle of Britain station, equipped with Spitfires, and there's a reconstructed Operations Room in one of the control towers. Most of the exhibits are postwar military and civil aircraft, from the Sunderland flying boat to the Vulcan B2 bombers which were used for the first and last time in the Falklands, but the newest thrill is the recently opened land warfare building at the far end of the airfield.

Audley End

Easier to get to by public transport, the palatial Jacobean mansion of **Audley End** (April–Sept Wed–Sun noon–6pm; £5.40; EH) is just fifteen miles south of – and less than half an hour by train from – Cambridge. Built by the Earl of Suffolk at no small expense, it was sufficiently grand to tempt Charles II to purchase it, and from 1669 and 1701 it was used on and off by successive sovereigns. More than thirty rooms are now open to the public, including the Great Hall, with its richly carved wooden screen of 1605, and several other chambers designed by Robert Adam. The magnificent grounds were laid out by Capability Brown and now contain, among other things, a miniature railway.

Peterborough

Even if you're only passing through **PETERBOROUGH**, in the far northwestern corner of Cambridgeshire, you should make a point of visiting the city's superb **Cathedral** (May–Aug Mon–Sat 7.45am–7.30pm, Sun 8am–5.30pm; Sept–April Mon–Sat 7.30am–6.15pm, Sun 7.45am–5pm). The Danes destroyed the first monastic church built on this spot in 870, while its replacement burnt down in 1116 – the foundations are still visible beneath the cathedral. Work began the following year on the present structure and was completed within the century. The one significant later addition is the thirteenth-century **west front**, one of the most magnificent in England, made up of three grandiloquent, deeply recessed arches, marred slightly by an incongruous central porch added in 1370.

The **interior** is a wonderful example of pure Norman architecture– round-arched rib vaults and shallow blind arcades line the nave – with a flat wooden vault whose painted ceiling from 1220 is one of the most important pieces of medieval art in Europe. You must pay 20p to illuminate it, and you need a pair of binoculars fully to appreciate its wealth of decoration. **Catherine of Aragon**, Henry VIII's first wife, whom he divorced in 1533, thus precipitating the English Reformation, is buried in the north aisle of the presbytery under a slab of black Irish marble. Mary Queen of Scots was buried in a corresponding spot in the south aisle, but was later transferred to Westminster Abbey.

The cathedral lies through the medieval Western Foregate, to the east of the pedestrianized town centre, whose most elegant building is the free-standing **Guildhall**, a seventeenth-century structure with slender arcading. To get to the cathedral from the **train** or **bus station**, walk south to the beginning of Cowgate, and then continue due east. The **tourist office** is on Bridge Street, not far from the cathedral (summer Mon–Fri 9am–5pm, Sat 10am–4pm; ☎01733/317 336). For **picnic provisions**, be sure to stock up at *Elton Dairy*, ten minutes' drive west of Peterborough, which specializes in Scottish seafood, including Loch Fyne oysters and smoked salmon.

travel details

Trains

Cambridge to: Bury St Edmunds (8 daily; 40min); Ely (hourly; 15min); Ipswich (6 daily; 1hr 20min); King's Lynn (hourly; 45min); London King's Cross (every 30min; 55min); Norwich (16 daily; 1hr); Peterborough (hourly; 50min).

Colchester to: Ipswich (every 30min; 25min); London Liverpool Street (every 30min; 50min); Norwich (hourly; 1hr 5min).

Ely to: King's Lynn (hourly; 30min); Peterborough (hourly; 30min).

Ipswich to: Bury St Edmunds (10 daily; 30min); Ely (7 daily; 1hr); London Liverpool Street (every 30min; 1hr 10min); Norwich (hourly; 45min); Peterborough (7 daily; 1hr 50min).

Norwich to: Ely (hourly; 50min); Cromer (every 1–2hr; 50min); Great Yarmouth (hourly; 30min); London Liverpool Street (hourly; 2hr); Peterborough (hourly; 1hr 30min).

Peterborough to: London King's Cross (every 30min; 1hr).

Buses

Bury St Edmunds to: Colchester (8 daily; 2hr); Lavenham (10 daily; 25min); Long Melford (10 daily; 45min); Sudbury (10 daily; 1hr).

Cambridge to: Bury St Edmunds (5 daily; 50min); Huntingdon (6 daily; 1hr); London (hourly; 2hr); Peterborough (6 daily; 1hr 50min); Stansted Airport (7 daily; 40min).

Colchester to: Dedham (4 daily; 30min); Lavenham (8 daily; 1hr 30min); Long Melford (every 1–2hr; 1hr); Sudbury (every 1–2hr; 50min).

Ipswich to: Aldeburgh (2–6 daily; 1hr 45min); Orford (1–2 daily; 1hr 15min).

King's Lynn to: Castle Rising (hourly; 15min); Peterborough (6 daily; 1hr 15min); Sandringham (8 daily; 25min).

Sheringham to: Blakeney (3–5 daily except Mon & Sat; 20min); Wells-next-the-Sea (1–5 daily except Mon & Sat; 50min).

Sudbury to: Bury St Edmunds (hourly; 50min); Long Melford (hourly; 5min); Lavenham (Mon–Sat hourly; 25min).

CHAPTER SEVEN

CENTRAL ENGLAND

Central England is the most diffuse region of the country, bracketed to the west by the Welsh border and to the north by the lower reaches of the Pennines, but otherwise difficult to define geographically. At least there can be no doubt about the location of its economic and demographic focus – **Birmingham**, Britain's second city and once the world's greatest industrial metropolis. Long saddled with a reputation as a culture-hating, car-loving backwater, Birmingham has redefined its image in recent years with some bold artistic and redevelopment projects, most notably the construction of the complex that houses the country's best concert hall. Although it may still be few people's idea of a good-looking town, it's the liveliest spot in the entire region, with nightlife encompassing everything from Royal Ballet productions to all-night raves, and a great spread of restaurants and pubs.

The conurbation clinging to the western side of Birmingham, known as the **Black Country**, more amply fulfils the negative stereotypes, although even here you'll find a few pleasant surprises, in the shape of some excellent museums and galleries. The region to the south of this West Midlands industrial zone, crossed by the wide and fertile vales of the rivers **Severn** and **Avon**, holds central England's biggest tourist draws – **Stratford-upon-Avon**, a place now almost throttled to death by Shakespeare-related paraphernalia, and the castle of nearby **Warwick**. The crowds and commercialism of these two towns are uncharacteristic of the rest of the southern Midlands, a predominantly pastoral region typified by lush orchards and quaint villages and by the low-key old cathedral cities of **Hereford** and **Worcester**, two of England's more attractive county towns.

To the north of Birmingham and the Black Country, **Staffordshire** and **Shropshire** bear substantial patches of industry and plentiful reminders of the Industrial Revolution – principally at **Ironbridge**. Both counties have their share of more seductively historic towns – such as **Lichfield** and **Ludlow** – but perhaps their greatest appeal lies in the varied landscapes to be found between the fringes of the Peak District and the Welsh border. Parts of Staffordshire and virtually all of **Shropshire** are remarkably beautiful, their hills rising ever higher towards the mountains of Wales, peaking at the raw uplands of the **Long Mynd** and **Wenlock Edge**.

Most tourists bypass the counties of the East Midlands – **Nottinghamshire**, **Leicestershire**, **Northamptonshire** and **Lincolnshire** – on their way to more obvious destinations. It's true they miss little of overriding interest, though **Nottingham** and **Leicester** are quite boisterous cities and the rural beauty of much of

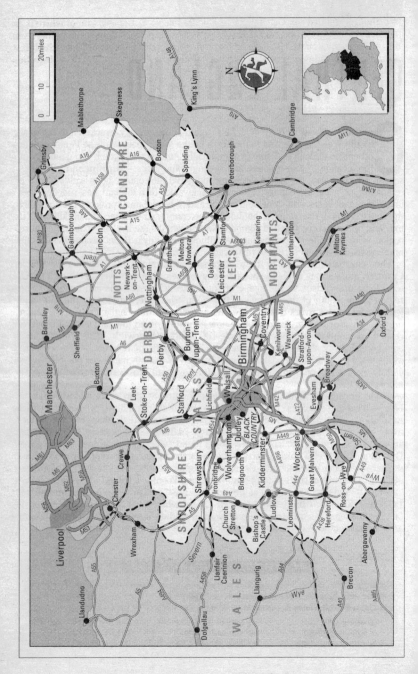

Northamptonshire can match that of the better-known Cotswolds. **Lincolnshire** is an agricultural backwater in comparison to its neighbours, but its sights – as distinct from the mostly dreary landscape – are far more diverting, most remarkably the cathedral at **Lincoln**, the alluring stone-built town of **Stamford**, and the superb parish **churches** that are spread out across the county.

Stratford-upon-Avon

STRATFORD-UPON-AVON is an unremarkable market town with a pedigree that's unexceptional but for one little detail: in 1564, the wife of a local merchant, John Shakespeare, gave birth to **William Shakespeare**, probably the greatest writer ever to use the English language. Consequently, this ordinary little place is nowadays all but smothered by package-tourist hype and tea-shoppe quaintness, representing the worst of "England-land" heritage marketing.

Arrival, information and accommodation

The **train station** is on the northeastern edge of town, ten minutes' walk from the centre. Local **bus services** arrive at the central Bridge Street; *National Express* **coaches** arrive at the lower end of the street, opposite *McDonald's*. Stratford's **tourist office** (April–Oct Mon–Sat 9am–6pm, Sun 11am–5pm; Nov–March Mon–Sat 9am–5pm; ☎01789/293 127) is on Bridgefoot, at the river end of Bridge Street; pick up a free copy of the *Observer This Week* for local events and information. Many of the town signposts point towards a tourist information centre in Rother Street – this is, in fact, the *Guide Friday* tourism centre, which basically exists to sell tickets for its bus tours of the town and environs. The official tourist office will sell you an all-in ticket for all five **Shakespeare Birthplace Trust** properties (£8), or a **Town Heritage Trail** (£5.50) for the three Trust properties in Stratford.

As one of the most congested tourist traps in Britain, Stratford's **accommodation** is distinctly pricey and gets reserved well in advance. In peak months, and during the Shakespeare birthday celebrations around April 23, it is essential to book ahead. One of the cheapest options is *Bronhill House*, 260 Alcester Rd (☎01789/299 169; ②), near the station. Two on Evesham Road are *Clomendy Guest House*, at no. 157 (☎01789/266 957; ③), and *Naini-Tal*, at no. 63A (☎01789/204 956; ③). *Eastnor House Hotel*, 33 Shipston Rd (☎01789/268 115; ④), is just over the main river bridge from the centre, while the *Falcon Hotel*, Chapel Street (☎01789/279 953; ⑧), is a half-timbered old inn right at the heart of the town. The **youth hostel** is on the edge of the pretty riverside village of Alveston, two miles east on the B4086 (Mon–Sat *Stratford Blue* bus #18; ☎01789/297 093). The *Stratford Racecourse* **campsite** is one mile southwest of the town centre on Luddington Road (Easter–Sept; ☎01789/267 949); hourly bus #218 (Mon–Sat) passes the site.

The Town

Bridge Street is the main thoroughfare of Stratford, leading down to the main road bridge over the Avon, with the other major town centre streets running off it in a roughly medieval grid pattern. At its west end, Bridge Street divides into **Henley Street**, home of the Birthplace Museum, and **Wood Street**, which leads up to the wide **market place**. Running along the townside bank of the Avon are **Waterside** and its continuation, **Southern Lane**, the main route to the theatres, Holy Trinity church and the area known as **Old Town**.

The Birthplace Museum

Top of everyone's Bardic itinerary is the **Birthplace Museum**, a restored half-timbered building amongst a sea of overpriced shops and twee tea rooms on Henley Street (March–Oct Mon–Sat 9am–5.30pm, Sun 9.30am–5.30pm; Nov–Feb Mon–Sat 9.30am–4pm, Sun 10am–4pm; £2.75). The museum is actually two buildings knocked into one. The west half, now fitted out in the style of a sixteenth-century domestic interior, was the business premises of the poet's father, who would appear to have worked as a glover, though some argue that he was a wool merchant or a butcher. Neither is it certain that Shakespeare was born in this building nor that he was born on April 23, 1564 – it's just known that he was baptized on April 26, and it's an irresistible temptation to place the birth of the national poet three days earlier, on St George's Day. However, both suppositions are now treated as fact at this shrine, where the east half of the building – bought by John Shakespeare in 1556 – displays a range of exhibits relating to a life which remains almost as enigmatic as those of Shakespeare's forgotten contemporaries.

Chapel Street

Follow the High Street south from the junction of Bridge and Henley streets, and you'll eventually come to another Birthplace Trust property, **Nash's House** and **New Place** on Chapel Street (March–Oct Mon–Sat 9.30am–5pm, Sun 10am–5pm; Nov–Feb Mon–Sat 10am–4pm, Sun 10.30am–4pm; £1.90). The house was the property of Thomas Nash, first husband of Shakespeare's granddaughter, Elizabeth Hall, and is mostly taken up by a very dry history of Stratford. The gardens contain the foundations of New Place, Shakespeare's last residence, demolished in 1759 by its owner, Reverend

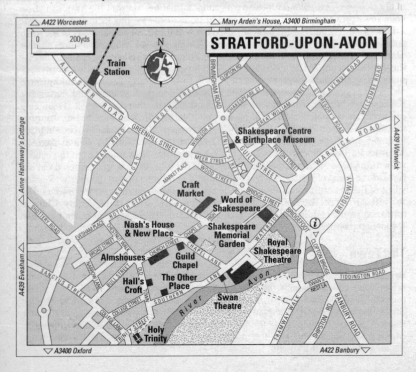

Francis Gastrell, who was fed up with the volume of pilgrims coming to see the property, having already tried to stem the tide by cutting down a mulberry tree that Shakespeare himself was reputed to have planted. An alleged descendant of the notorious mulberry occupies the central lawn of the superb gardens, which also has some beautiful flowerbeds and lavish topiary. The adjoining **Shakespeare Memorial Garden**, entered from Chapel Lane (March–Oct Mon–Sat 9am–dusk, Sun 10am–dusk; Nov–Feb Mon–Fri 9am–4pm, Sun noon–4pm), affords excellent views over the New Place gardens.

The theatres

There was no theatre in Stratford in Shakespeare's day – it was not until 1769 that Stratford organized any event in honour of him, and that was a festival put together by London-based actor-manager **David Garrick**, which featured no dramatic performances at all. From then on, the idea of building a permanent home in which to perform Shakespeare's works gained momentum, and the feasibility of building a theatre in backwater Stratford grew immensely with the advent of better roads and the railways. The first Memorial Theatre opened in 1879, on land donated by local beer magnate **Charles Flower**, who also funded the project.

After a fire in 1926 the competition held for a replacement was won by the only woman applicant, **Elisabeth Scott**. Her theatre, overlooking a beautiful scene of lush meadows and willow trees on the northern banks of the Avon, is today the **Main House**, presenting a constant diet of Shakespeare's works. At the back, the burnt-out original theatre was converted in 1980 into a replica "in-the-round" Elizabethan stage – named **The Swan**, it's used for works by Shakespeare's contemporaries, classics from all eras, and one annual piece by the man himself. A third auditorium, the **The Other Place**, in nearby Southern Lane, showcases modern and experimental pieces.

During the day you can inspect the RSC's trove of theatrical memorabilia at the **RSC Collection** (summer Mon–Sat 9.30am–6pm, Sun noon–4.30pm; winter Mon–Sat same hours, Sun 11am–3.30pm; £2), entered through the Swan Theatre, or go on a **backstage tour** (Mon–Wed & Fri 1.30pm & 5.30pm, except matinee days or during previews, and 4 tours on Sun; £4, with admission to the RSC Collection; information ☎01789/412 602). If you have the energy, you could go on a tour immediately after the evening performance, starting at the stage door of the Main House (Mon–Sat; £3).

Each of these options is a far more satisfying way of learning about Shakespeare's craft than is the nearby **World of Shakespeare** at 13 Waterside (daily summer 9.30am–9.30pm; winter 9.30am–5.30pm; £3.50), an audio-visual Elizabethan pageant that patronizes, confuses and bores you in 25 minutes flat.

The Old Town

South of the theatres, the street passes some quiet public gardens on the river's edge before entering the serene **Old Town**, a district focused on **Holy Trinity Church** (summer Mon–Sat 8.30am–6pm; winter Mon–Sat 8.30am–4pm, Sun 2–5pm). Aside from its interest as Shakespeare's burial place, Holy Trinity is a fine Gothic structure, most of it built between the thirteenth and fifteenth centuries, topped by an eighteenth-century replacement of its original wooden spire. Quite unusually, the chancel is built on a slight skew from the line of the nave – supposedly to represent Christ's inclined head on the cross. A small fee is payable to see Shakespeare's tomb, on the north side of the chancel, and the copies of the registers of his birth and death.

The Old Town is also home of one of the town's most impressive medieval houses, the Birthplace Trust's **Hall's Croft**, close to the foot of Church Street (March–Oct Mon–Sat 9.30am–5pm, Sun 10am–5pm; Nov–Feb Mon–Sat 10am–4pm, Sun 10.30am–4pm; £1.90). The former home of Shakespeare's elder daughter, Susanna, and her doctor husband, John Hall, the Croft has been preserved as a fascinating museum of

---

TICKETS FOR THE RSC

As the Royal Shakespeare Company works on a repertory system, you could stay in Stratford for a few days and see four or five different plays. Tickets for the **Main House** start at around £5 for a restricted view, rising to £40, although you should be able to get pretty good seats for less than £20. However, very popular shows get booked up months in advance, in which case you'll have to do a little early-morning queueing. **Swan** tickets are generally between £9 and £30, with tickets for **The Other Place** hovering between £13 and £17.

The Main House **box office** (☎01789/295 623) serves as the central booking agent for all three houses, although you collect your tickets from the theatre in question. The box office opens at 9.30am, with one hundred Main House tickets kept back for that evening's performance – for a real blockbuster, arriving to queue at 5am would not be too early. Alternatively, a limited number of cheaper **standing tickets** can be booked for the Main House or The Swan, although these can sell out just as quickly as the seats. **Returns** are fairly scarce, although if you've no other option turn up about an hour before the performance and try pestering the box office right through until the curtain goes up. The RSC runs a **ticket availability information line** (☎01789/269 191).

Elizabethan medicine. Having perused Hall's casebooks – noting that Joan Chidkin of Southam "gave two vomits and two stools" after being "troubled with trembling of the arms and thighs" – you can suffer vicariously at the displays of eye-watering forceps and other implements. The best view of the building itself is at the back, in the neatly manicured walled garden.

Anne Hathaway's Cottage and Mary Arden's House

Of the remaining two Birthplace Trust properties, **Anne Hathaway's Cottage** (March–Oct Mon–Sat 9am–5.30pm, Sun 9.30am–5.30pm; Nov–Feb Mon–Sat 9.30am–4pm, Sun 10am–4pm; £2.30) is the one that can be reached on foot, as it's just over a mile west of the centre in **Shottery**, a walk signposted from Evesham Place, south of the market place. Alternatively, the *Guide Friday* tour bus visits the site, or you can catch the *Avon Shuttle* bus. The cottage of the woman who in 1582 became Shakespeare's wife is an extensive thatched house of very low rooms, containing some fine period furniture but – like most of the Birthplace Trust properties – little in the way of labelling, presumably to encourage visitors to buy the official guide books. To add to the commercial pressure, the route through the house forces you through various tacky souvenir shops before releasing you into the adjoining picnic orchard and the **Shakespeare Tree Garden**, a patch planted with species mentioned in the plays.

The last of the Birthplace Trust sites is **Mary Arden's House** (March–Oct Mon–Sat 9.30am–5pm, Sun 10am–5pm; Nov–Feb Mon–Sat 10am–4pm, Sun 10.30am–4pm; £3.20), three miles to the north in Wilmcote, and reached by train (Mon–Sat), bus #228, or *Guide Friday* tour bus. Mary Arden was Shakespeare's mother, the only unmarried daughter when her father, Robert, died in 1556. Unusually for the time, she inherited the house and land, thus becoming one of the neighbourhood's most eligible women – John Shakespeare, eager for self-improvement, married her within a year. The house is a well-furnished example of an Elizabethan country farm, and though labelling is, once again, rather scant, there's a host of informative guides to fill in the details of family life and traditions. Grouped around the house and courtyards is the **Shakespeare Countryside Museum**, helping to place the plays in their rural context: quarrying, farming, falconry, smithying and wheelwrighting are all explained or demonstrated.

Eating and drinking

Stratford is used to feeding and watering millions of visitors, so finding refreshment is never difficult – it can, however, be prohibitively expensive. The greatest concentration of restaurants is on Sheep Street, where your best bet is *The Opposition* at no. 13 (☎01789/269 980), which serves imaginative international dishes in a busy atmosphere. *Fatty Arbuckle's*, 9 Chapel St (☎01789/267 069), is a cosy and moderately priced bistro that also gets phenomenally packed. An alternative is *Café Sol*, Swan's Nest Lane (☎01789/297 733), a modern Spanish and Mexican restaurant overlooking the river. The busiest fish-and-chip shop is run-of-the-mill *Barnaby's*, because it's close to the theatre, but the *Kingfisher Fish Bar*, 13 Ely St (☎01789/292 513), just a five-minute walk away, is more traditional and less expensive.

The *Dirty Duck*, on Waterside, is the infamous actors' **pub**, stuffed to the gunwales every night with a vocal entourage of RSC employees and hangers on – essential viewing. The other place frequented by the acting fraternity is the late-licence bar of the *Arden Thistle Hotel*, also on Waterside, opposite the RSC. The *Froth and Elbow* is a deservedly popular real-ale bar in the beautifully ornate *Shakespeare Hotel* on Chapel Street. Out of the immediate tourist area, *Recession*, on the corner of Guild Street and Birmingham Road, has good beer and a young, mainly local crowd. The *Queen's Head*, 54 Ely St, attracts a friendly mixed, straight and gay crowd.

Around Stratford: Charlecote and Alcester

Stratford Blue buses run out into many of the surrounding villages; their travel shop in the tourist office has full details. One particularly attractive route is that of the #18 to Warwick and Leamington, which passes through **CHARLECOTE**, four miles east of Stratford off the B4086. Here you'll find **Charlecote Park** (April–Oct daily except Mon & Thurs 11am–5.30pm; £4; NT), a huge country estate centred on an ornate Elizabethan mansion. The house, furbished in a rather heavy Victorian reworking of Elizabethan style, is awash with souvenirs of the British Empire, paintings of the estate and portraits of the Lucy family, who have lived here since 1247. The real pleasures of Charlecote are the vast park, the gardens, watered by the rivers Avon and Dene, and the croquet lawn – you can rent equipment from the gatehouse. Grazing throughout the estate are herds of fallow deer, whose ancestors are said apocryphally to have been poached by the young William Shakespeare.

Two great country houses near the picturesque market town of **ALCESTER** (pronounced "Ulster"), eight miles west of Stratford, are reasonably accessible by bus. **Coughton Court**, a couple of miles north of Alcester (April & Oct Sat & Sun noon–5pm; May–Sept daily except Thurs & Fri noon–5pm; £4.50, grounds only £2.50; EH) is a beautiful Elizabethan house, set in formal grounds that encompass two adjacent parish churches. Displays inside the house include the dress worn by Mary Queen of Scots at her execution. Buses #208 and #228 from Stratford via Alcester stop outside.

One mile southwest of Alcester lies the Palladian pile of **Ragley Hall** (April–Sept daily except Mon & Fri 11am–5pm, grounds 10am–6pm; £4.50, grounds only £3.50). Home of the Marquess of Hertford, the house displays a suitably grand array of trappings that include intricate Baroque plasterwork and an exquisite eighteenth-century furniture collection. The current marquess' more contemporary tastes can be seen in the extravagant mural of the *Temptation of Christ* by Graham Rust, which took the artist some fifteen years to complete. Many people come to Ragley and ignore the hall, as the extensive parkland and well-designed adventure playground provide enough diversion in themselves. The only bus that goes there directly is the Sunday *Cotswold Connection* bus #166; at other times you'll have to walk from Alcester.

Warwick and around

Although not a scintillating place, **WARWICK** has one of the county's more intriguing townscapes since the centre was ravaged by fire in 1694, a disaster that has left Warwick with a Georgian core edged by untouched medieval buildings. The homely dimensions of the town are disrupted only by the hideous 1960s county hall, and of course by the famous castle.

The Town

Warwick Castle (daily April–Oct 10am–6pm; Nov–March 10am–5pm; £8.25) is locally proclaimed the "greatest medieval castle in Britain", and if bulk equals greatness, then the claim is valid, although much of the existing structure owes its stature to extensive nineteenth-century restoration. The first fortress at Warwick was raised in 914 by Ethelfleda, daughter of Alfred the Great; most of the older parts of the present castle date from the fourteenth century, however, a period when the local Beauchamp family played a prominent part in the Hundred Years War. Prisoners were brought to Warwick from the battlefields of France and incarcerated in the **dungeons** of Caesar's Tower, which include a fearsome *oubliette*, a tiny cell where prisoners were left to perish forgotten by their captors.

Madame Tussaud's, the present owners, have certainly made their mark with a display based on the theme of a **royal weekend party**. This extravaganza of waxwork nobility, including the young Churchill at a piano, fills the private apartments which were rebuilt in 1870 after fire damage. The larger state rooms, as yet free of waxy gentry, ooze opulence with paintings and furniture fit for a royal palace. The **Cedar Drawing Room**, lavishly panelled in 1790, contains the *pièce de resistance* – a sixteenth-century Italian table depicting a woman in the four stages of pregnancy. A newer display, **Kingmaker**, adds smells and atmospheric sounds to a lifelike waxwork scene of the preparations for Richard Earl of Warwick's final battle in 1471. For more serious historians, the **gatehouse** houses an exhibition of the life of Richard III, which examines his part in the death of the young princes (see p.989).

In the 74 acres of gardens surrounding the castle, where on summer weekends armoured knights joust in contests, you'll find a Victorian rose garden and Capability Brown's **Peacock Garden** whose strutting tenants are known to seek tit-bits in local pubs. The Victorian boathouse on river island offers perfect views towards the high walls of the castle. Another good viewpoint is the private **Mill Garden** (donations requested) at the lower end of quaint, cobbled Mill Street, which slopes down from the back of the castle. The glorious garden leads down to the river's edge and the mossy stumps of the old bridge that led out of Warwick when Mill Street was the main through-route.

Near the castle entrance in Castle Street is the half-timbered **Oken's House**, now home of the **Doll Museum** (Easter–Sept Mon–Sat 10am–5pm, Sun 2–5pm; £1), a rather fey and specialist collection. Continue over Jury Street and up Church Street to reach the magnificent church of **St Mary**, which was largely wrecked in the great fire of 1694, and rebuilt as a weird Gothic-Renaissance amalgam. One part remained untouched, however – the **Beauchamp chapel**, a glorious specimen of Perpendicular style. It's packed with tombs from the fifteenth and sixteenth centuries, of which the finest is the painted monument to Robert Dudley, Earl of Leicester, one of Elizabeth I's most influential advisers.

The nearby market place is home to the eighteenth-century Shirehall, now a branch of the **Warwickshire Museum** (Mon–Sat 10am–5.30pm, also Sun 2.30–5pm from May–Sept; free). Apart from the standard geological and wildlife exhibits, it has some good displays on the county's history, including a huge 1647 tapestry map of the county and a well-made video about the 1694 fire. Down towards the station is the other main branch of the museum, the Jacobean **St John's House** in St John's (Tues–Sat 10am–12.30pm & 1.30–5.30pm; also May–Sept Sun 2.30–5pm; free), with displays of period costume and some rather tatty social history exhibitions.

Practicalities

Warwick's **tourist office** is in the Courthouse on Jury Street, midway between St Mary's and the castle (daily 9.30am–4.30pm; ☎01926/492 212). Local **B&Bs** include the excellent *Seven Stars* pub in Friars Street (☎01926/492 658; ②), *Austin House* at 96 Emscote Rd (☎01926/493 583; ③), and the *Avon Guest House* at 7 Emscote Rd (☎01926/491 367, ③). There's a well-appointed town-centre **campsite**, the *Racecourse*, off Hampton Road (March–Oct; ☎01926/495 448). Most of the good **pubs** and **restaurants** are around Smith Street – although there seems to be little choice except Indian or Italian food. Of the latter, the best and most reasonable is *Piccolino's Pizzeria* at 31 Smith St (☎01926/491 020). Alternatively, on the corner of Smith and St Nicholas Church streets is the *Angry Cheese* bistro, good for an all-day range of inexpensive bar meals and snacks. In St Nicholas Church Street, the *New Bowling Green* **pub** is a popular, old-fashioned sort of place with a beautiful garden. Two pubs on Saltisford (the Birmingham road) also stand out – the *King's Head*, possibly the least touristy of the town centre pubs, and the *Antelope*, the sole gay pub in the area.

Kenilworth

To the north of Warwick is the rather nondescript **KENILWORTH**, little more than a slightly upmarket dormitory to Coventry. It does, however, have one remarkable sight – the **Castle** from which Scott took his inspiration (April–Sept daily 10am–6pm; Oct–March Tues–Sun 10am–4pm; £2; EH). Begun in the twelfth century – the keep dates from then – the castle eventually passed into the hands of John of Gaunt, who transformed it into a magnificent fortified home. His son, Henry IV, used it as a royal residence, and it remained one until 1563, when Elizabeth I gave the castle and the title of Earl of Leicester to her minion Robert Dudley. Kenilworth then became one of England's most fashionable playgrounds, hosting spectacular pageants and entertainments, but following Dudley's death the castle slid into gradual decay, hastened by the attention of Cromwell's troops in the Civil War. Today, the red sandstone ruins still maintain a tremendous presence, with large remnants from each era still easily discernible.

Coventry

Back at the start of the fifteenth century, **COVENTRY** was far larger and more important than Warwick, its wealth founded on the cloth, thread and dyeing industries, precursors of the engineering plants that were to become the staple of the city's economy. Nowadays it has a downbeat and depressed air. Its motor production lines have waned to near-extinction, and the city is lumbered with some of England's ugliest urban planning, a direct result of the Luftwaffe raid of November 14, 1940, which devasted not just Coventry's armaments factories but much of the old town.

Today, Coventry has just one thing going for it: its modern **Cathedral**, built by Sir Basil Spence, and one of England's most inspirational examples of postwar architecture. Raised in 1962 alongside the shell of the old **Cathedral of St Michael**. Spence's pink-sandstone replacement – dedicated with a performance of Benjamin Britten's specially written *War Requiem* – gave the city a cathedral of overwhelming grace and lightness, thanks in part to the luminescent stained glass that soars to the ceiling. On the cathedral's outside wall, by the main steps, Jacob Epstein's *St Michael and the Devil*

LADY GODIVA

Coventry's most famous citizen was **Lady Godiva**, wife of Leofric, eleventh-century Earl of Mercia, whose taxation policies supposedly prompted his spouse to protest by riding through the town's streets naked. The equally apocryphal story of Peeping Tom – the one town inhabitant who dared look at her as she passed by – is played out every hour in the gloriously tacky **clock** in Broadgate.

fight for the soul of the world, while within the cathedral, all lines focus on another striking piece of modern religious art, the 75-foot **tapestry** of *Christ in Majesty* by Graham Sutherland. A canopied walkway links the new cathedral with the ruins of the old, used every three years as an atmospheric venue for the **Coventry Mystery Plays** – the next cycle is due to be held in 1996.

Few people chose to **stay** in Coventry, but if you're stuck try the *Arlon Guest House*, 25 St Patrick's Rd, in the city centre (☎01203/225 942; ③), or *Brookfields*, just west of the centre on 134 Butt Lane (☎01203/404 866; ③). From July to September, single rooms are available at the univeristy *Priory Halls of Residence* for £16.50 a night (☎01203/838 445); the **tourist office** on Bayley Lane can also help with bookings (☎01203/832 303). Spon Street has a variety of **food** options; try *Tete à Tete* at no. 188 for a snack, or *Ostler's* at no. 166 for something more substantial. Alternatively, *The Juicy Pear* at 100 Hay St in the Cathedral quarter is a lively café-bar and restaurant in a sixteenth-century building, with live music at weekends.

Worcestershire

In geographical terms, **Worcestershire** can be compared to a huge saucer, with the low-lying plains of the Vale of Evesham and Severn Valley rising to a lip of hills: the Malverns in the west, the Cotswolds in the south, the Abberley and Clee hills to the northwest and the Clents and Lickeys in the northeast. Watering the central plains are the rivers Severn and Avon, meandering through the principal city of **Worcester** and many of the county's most attractive market towns. The northern fringes of the county are populated by industrial and overspill towns that have more in common with the Birmingham conurbation than the rural lifestyle portrayed in *The Archers*, the BBC's never-ending radio soap, loosely based on life in mid-Worcestershire.

Worcester

Right at the heart of the county, both geographically and politically, **WORCESTER** is a robust, slightly schizophrenic city, where timbered Tudor and refined Georgian buildings are overshadowed by charmless modern developments. The chief offender is the new CrownGate Shopping Centre, which obliterates a large swathe of the city centre, but perhaps the biggest single influence on the city is the River Severn, which flows along Worcester's west flank. Because the Severn is prone to flood, building is prohibited in the meadows flanking the river, leaving clear space by the cathedral, which rises high above the muddy brown river on the eastern bank.

The City
Worcester's skyline is dominated by the squat sandstone bulk of its **Cathedral**, a rich stew of architectural styles, and best approached from the path that runs along the river's edge and through a gate bearing marks of the city's flood levels. The oldest section of the cathedral is its many-columned **crypt**: built underneath the Saxon monas-

tery founded here by Saint Oswald in 983, it is the largest Norman crypt in the country. The large circular **Chapter House**, off the cloisters, is the other main Norman portion, and has the distinction of being the first such building constructed without the use of a central supporting pillar. Inside the main part of the cathedral, the western end of the twelfth-century **nave** displays the transition between the rounded Norman and pointed Gothic arches. The pillars of the nave are decorated with bunches of fruit, carved by stonemasons from Lincoln, most of whom succumbed to the Black Death, leaving inferior successors to finish the job.

Built in the mid-twelfth century, the Early English **east end** is one of the most elaborate sections, with the choir's forest of slender pillars soaring over the intricately worked choir stalls. In front of the **high altar** is the tomb of England's most reviled monarch, King John, who died in 1216 and who ended up in Worcester after explicitly instructing that he was to be buried between the tombs of Saint Wulstan and Saint Oswald – not that there was any other city eager to take his corpse. On the south side of the chancel is the cathedral's richest monument: **Prince Arthur's Chantry**, a delicate lacy pattern of carved stonework built as a memorial in 1504 by King Henry VII for his young son, Arthur, who died on his honeymoon with Catherine of Aragon – later to become the first wife of his younger brother, Henry VIII.

Tucked behind the cathedral in Severn Street, alongside an eighteenth-century canal, is the **Dyson Perrins Museum** (Mon–Fri 9.30am–5pm, Sat 10am–5pm; £3.25, including admission to the factory), dedicated to Worcester's famous porcelain industry, which dates back to the mid-eighteenth century. Up behind the Royal Worcester works on the busy Sidbury dual carriageway is the oldest building in the city, the **Commandery Civil War Centre** (Mon–Sat 10am–5pm, Sun 1.30–5.30pm; £3.15). This was Charles II's headquarters leading up to the Battle of Worcester in 1651 but is now empty, save for a few exhibits on the events of the Civil War, focusing on the trial of Charles I and the background to Cromwell's victory.

Friar Street, which forks off Sidbury just up from the Commandery, by the *Olde Talbot Hotel*, is blighted by some garish 1960s developments, but these give way to Worcester's most complete thoroughfare of Elizabethan and Tudor buildings, including the **Tudor House Museum** (daily except Thurs & Sun 10.30am–5pm; £1.50). The display starts with an examination of Worcester during World War II, interesting chiefly because it's a typical picture of ordinary life throughout the war years. The remainder of the rather chaotic museum is given over to anodyne reconstructions of Edwardian and Victorian shops, offices and domestic settings. Almost opposite is **The Greyfriars** (April–Oct Wed & Thurs 2–5.30pm; £2.10; NT), a largely fifteenth-century town house, whose principal attraction is the rambling walled garden at the back.

Many people flock to the area on the trail of **Sir Edward Elgar**, whose statue faces the cathedral at the bottom of the High Street. His **birthplace** – a tiny, rustic cottage in **Lower Broadheath**, a couple of miles west of Worcester (buses #312, #419 and #420), is now open as a museum (daily except Wed May–Sept 10.30am–6pm; Oct to mid-Jan & mid-Feb to April 1.30–4.30pm; £3). The crowded rooms contain Elgar's musical manuscripts, personal correspondence in his spidery handwriting, press cuttings, photographs and miscellaneous mementos centred on the desk at which he worked.

Practicalities

Of the two Worcester **train stations**, Foregate Street is the more central, although some InterCity services stop only at Shrub Hill, a fifteen-minute walk to the east of the city centre. The **bus** and **coach station** is situated on the city side of the main river bridge, behind the CrownGate Shopping Centre. The **tourist office** (Mon–Sat April–Sept 10.30am–5.30pm; Sept–March 10.30am–4pm; ☎01905/726 311) is located in the handsome Georgian Guildhall, towards the cathedral end of the High Street. **Bike rental** is available from *Peddlars* on Barbourne Road (☎01905/24238).

For accommodation, the best **hotel** options are the huge *Fownes' Hotel*, occupying an old glove factory at the cathedral end of City Walls Road (☎01905/613 151; Mon–Fri ⑦, Sat & Sun ③), and the nearby *Loch Ryan* at 119 Sidbury (☎01905/351 143; ④). **B&Bs** include the *Abbeydore*, 34 Barbourne Rd (☎01905/26731; ②), *Osborne House*, 17 Chestnut Walk (☎01905/22296; ③), or *Wyatt Guest House* at 40 Barbourne Rd (☎01905/26311; ②). There is a **campsite** three miles north of Worcester at the *Millhouse* at Hawford (☎01905/451 283; hourly buses to Kidderminster).

Best of the **café-bars** along Friar Street is *Heroes* at no. 26–32. The best Indian **restaurant** is the *Bombay Palace* at 38 The Tything (☎01905/613 969; moderate), while *Thyme Table* on Angel Street serves an excellent range of vegetarian dishes (☎01905/610 505; moderate). The friendly *Worcester Arts Workshop* in Sansome Street contains gallery space, a theatre and a café, making it a useful place to find out about local events. Of the fine crop of **pubs** run by the local Jolly Roger brewery, the *Brewery Tap* at no. 50 is the best, with excellent food and occasional live music. Another Jolly Roger house is the *Cardinal's Hat*, at 31 Friar St, its small, crowded rooms stuffed full of quirky memorabilia; it also does good-value lunches.

Malvern

One of the most exclusive and refined areas of the Midlands, **Malvern** is the generic name for a string of towns stretched along the lower slopes of the **Malvern Hills**, which rise sharply out of the flat plains like a line of gnarled old shoulders. The main centre of the region is **GREAT MALVERN**, which is served by rail from Worcester, Birmingham and London. This pretty town was firmly established in the Victorian era, when crino-lined gentry came to take the spa waters, making the steep hike up to St Anne's Well on the hill behind town, which still has a more or less constant flow of fresh water. The peculiarities of Malvern's curing waters are explained in the town **Museum**, housed in the delicately proportioned Abbey Gateway on Abbey Road (Easter–Oct daily except Wed in school terms, 10.30am–5pm; 50p). Nineteenth-century cartoons show unwitting patients packed into cold wet sheets, or hopping gaily away from their crutches and wheelchairs, while Dr Wall's theories of hydropathy throw some light on the popularity and subsequent decline of this questionable cure.

The main sight in town is the nearby **Priory**, its patchwork exterior contrasting with the ordered, serene interior, which is especially notable for its stained glass and hundreds of detailed wall tiles, all added to the building in the mid-fifteenth century. The window of the north transept, in particular, is one of the best pieces of medieval stained glass in Britain. Among the priory's graves is that of Darwin's granddaughter, who died here as a child despite being bathed with Malvern water.

The **tourist office**, in the Winter Gardens complex on Grange Road (summer daily 10am–5pm; winter closed Sun; ☎01684/892 289), issues free local maps and information packs, as well as selling three excellent large-scale maps of the Malvern hills, with geological and nature notes. This is a great area to explore on a bike – you can rent from *Spokes and Saddles*, 202–10 Worcester Rd, Malvern Link, less than a mile from the centre of town or one stop up the rail line (☎01684/576 141). The Winter Gardens is also the principal home of the long-established **Malvern Festival**, supported for decades by George Bernard Shaw, held in May and now including a lively fringe.

Accommodation is plentiful – right in the heart of the main town is the rambling old *Great Malvern Hotel*, Graham Road (☎01684/563 411; ⑥). **B&Bs** include *Kylemore*, 30 Avenue Rd (☎01684/563 753; ②), *Ashford Cottage*, 32 North Malvern Rd (☎01684/565 350; ②) and *Elm Bank*, 52 Worcester Rd (☎01684/56605; ③). The homely **youth hostel**, serving excellent meals, is a couple of miles south of Great Malvern, off the main A449 at 18 Peachfield Rd, Malvern Wells (☎01684/569 131). The nearest **camp-**

site is at *Odd Fellows Pub*, four miles southwest in Colwall (☎01684/540 084) – the infrequent bus #675 to Ledbury passes by.

Herefordshire and the Forest of Dean

Shackled to Worcestershire by government bureaucrats since 1974, **Herefordshire** is a more lethargic, isolated county than its relucant twin, with an agricultural economy unaffected by the industrial advances of its neighbour. When the counties separate in 1997, it may have a little more difficulty securing an economic balance, but will retain its orchards and hop fields among the rolling pasture land that makes the area one of the Midlands' most appealing rural pockets. Most of the settlements of any size lie on the fertile plains of the rivers **Wye** and **Lugg**, which crisscross their way between England and Wales, flanked in the east by the undulating green slopes of the Malverns and in the west by the starker, purple humps of the Black Mountains.

The county town, **Hereford**, is fairly small in comparison with other major centres in England, but its distance from any other large areas of population give it the status and feeling of a larger, self-contained city. Secondary market towns such as **Leominster**, **Ross-on-Wye** and **Ledbury** are old-fashioned, sleepy places struggling hard to find a modern identity that doesn't depend upon a neatly packaged tourist image. To the south, the westernmost triangle of Gloucestershire, divorced from the rest of the county by the Severn, contains the **Forest of Dean**, great swathes of which remain untainted.

Hereford

A cathedral city since its inception around 700 AD, **HEREFORD** occupies a splendid position amidst some of the least spoilt rural landscapes in England, remaining firmly rooted in its agricultural base – the local **cider** industry is one of the city's biggest trades, something that local companies and the tourist board have not been slow to capitalize on. The Wye meanders around the southern side of the city centre, with the medieval Wye Bridge and its twentieth-century neighbour, Greyfriars Bridge, connecting the two banks. The cathedral and its close sit on the northern bank, at the heart of the city centre, with the main shopping streets spreading out around it.

The **Cathedral** is a curious building, an amalgam of many different periods that do not always unite to eye-pleasing effect. The rather dumpy red-sandstone **tower** was constructed in the early fourteenth century, eclipsing the western tower built by the Normans, which collapsed under its own weight in 1786. As a result of the accident, a great section of the **nave** was destroyed, leaving restorers and architects with a problem that has never been satisfactorily resolved. Even to this day, the nave lacks the grandeur of many other English cathedrals, despite the surviving Norman arches at its eastern end. The **northern transept**, however, is a flawless exercise in thirteenth-century taste; designed by Bishop Aquablanca, probably to house his own tomb, it has soaring windows that are among the finest extant examples of Early English architecture. On the opposite side of the church, in the Norman **south transept**, unusual features include a German *Adoration of the Magi* that dates from the sixteenth century and an early fireplace, one of the few still surviving within an English church.

In the late 1980s, dire financial difficulties prompted the cathedral authorities to plan the sale of their most treasured possession, the **Mappa Mundi**. This parchment map was drawn in 1289, and at 65 by 53 inches it is the largest known example of such a work from that period. Its detail is astonishing, showing the complete world from its centre at Jerusalem to the very edges of the void, where Britain and Ireland sit right on the extremity of civilization. Eventually, a scheme was hatched to keep the map in

Hereford by raising funds from shareholders and visitors. To that end, the Mappa Mundi is presented as part of an exhibition in the cathedral's **crypt** (Easter–Oct Mon–Sat 10am–4.15pm; Nov–Easter Mon–Sat 10.30am–3.15pm; £3) that includes a video on the map and its significance. Also housed in the cathedral is the world's largest **Chained Library** (80p), a collection of some 1600 books and manuscripts from the eighth to the fifteenth century.

There's not much else to see in Hereford, though the main thoroughfare, **High Town**, holds the lively Butter Market and some fine Georgian buildings. Cider-heads should stumble over the ring road to the west of the city centre for the **Cider Museum and King Offa Distillery** in Pomona Place, off Whitecross Road (April–Oct daily 10am–5.30pm; Nov–March Mon–Sat 1–5pm; £1.95), and the nearby **Bulmers' Cider Factory** in Plough Lane, which organizes very popular tours (Mon–Fri 10.30am, 2.15pm & 7.30pm; £2.95; tours must be pre-booked – call ☎01432/352 000).

Practicalities

The **tourist office** is almost directly opposite the cathedral at 1 King St (May–Sept daily 9am–5pm; Oct–April closed Sun; ☎01432/268 430). **Bike rental** is available from *Coombes Cycles* at 94 Widemarsh St (☎01432/354 373). Hotel **accommodation** includes the *Somerville* on Bodenham Road (☎01432/273 991; ④) and the *Hereford Moat House* on Belmont Road (☎01432/354 301; ⑥). Pick of the B&Bs are *Richmond House*, 57 Edgar St (☎01432/271 769; ③) and *Bowes Guest House*, 23 St Martin's St, south of the Wye Bridge (☎01432/267 202; ②).

A great place for inexpensive and wholesome **food** is *The Marches*, on Union Street. Other dependable choices include the similarly inexpensive *Firenze* pasta and pizza place at 21 Commercial Rd, the moderate *Paradise* Thai restaurant at 50 Widemarsh St (☎01432/279 971) and, for cheap and filling daytime food, *Café 89* on East Street. In a city that makes such a big deal of its **cider** industry, you should at least show the courtesy of sampling some of the finished product in one of the city's **pubs** – the *Commercial Hotel* near the train station on Commercial Road, the old-world *Black Lion* on Bridge Street, the *Orange Tree* on King Street or the riverbank *Lancaster*, over the Wye Bridge on St Martin's Street, which attracts a trendy crowd.

Leominster and Croft Castle

LEOMINSTER (pronounced "Lemster"), thirteen miles north of the county town on the Hereford–Shrewsbury rail line, is Herefordshire's second town. The extremely pretty centre is a largely half-timbered patchwork of medieval streets with overhanging gables, grouped around the swarthy red **Priory Church**. It preserves several original Norman features, from the rounded windows in the clerestory and the sturdy pillars of the north nave to the carved "Green man" fertility spirit by the west door; the central nave is enhanced by the delicate traceries of a Perpendicular west window. Also in the priory is a rare example of a **ducking stool**, used to dunk dishonest tradesmen, scolds and the odd wayward wife up until 1809. The **tourist office** is just off the central Corn Square at 6 School Lane (April–Sept Mon–Fri 9.30am–5.30pm, Sat 9am–5pm; Oct–March Mon–Sat 10am–4pm; ☎01568/616 460); they will sort out local accommodation.

The major sight within a short radius of Leominster is **Croft Castle** (April & Oct Sat & Sun 2–5pm; May–Sept Wed–Sun 2–6pm; £3.10; NT), five miles northwest. The castle itself maintains the sturdy pink-stone towers and walls built in the fourteenth and fifteenth centuries, but was much augmented during the next three centuries by an assortment of extravagant owners. Mock-Gothic castellated bays lie each side of the gabled front and, inside the castle, there's an exuberant Georgian-Gothic staircase. One Thomas Johnes, who in 1750 bought the castle from the Croft family (whose descendants bought it back in 1923), was responsible for the kitsch Blue and Gold Room, with its vast gaudy chimney place. Croft Castle's parkland covers over a thousand acres, in which you can find a series of beautifully kept tree avenues, the best of which is the silver birch line leading from Cock Gate. Still in the grounds, one mile north of the castle, is the hill fort of **Croft Ambrey**, reached after a fairly steep walk from the castle. It was inhabited for nearly four hundred years until about the time of the birth of Christ, but there is little to see today except for some stunning panoramic views.

Ledbury and Eastnor

Fourteen miles east of Hereford, along the main railway line to Worcester, lies **LEDBURY**, a town famous for its much filmed Church Lane, a jumble of Tudor and Stuart architecture winding to the door of the massive parish church. The **Old Grammar School**, near the top of Church Lane, has been converted into a rather bland heritage centre, which lacks the local flavour captured in the **Butcher Row Folk Museum** opposite (Easter–Sept daily 11am–5pm; free). At the other end of the lane, tucked behind the tourist office in the council buildings, is the **Painted Room** (Mon–Wed & Fri 10am–2pm, Thurs 10am–1pm; donations requested), featuring a set of bold symmetrical floral designs painted on wattle and daub walls, possibly by the sons of the constable who is thought to have lived here in the sixteenth century. Ledbury's other main curiosity is the **Market Hall**, a Tudor beamed building raised on wooden columns, on the main road at the end of Church Lane. Built in the early seventeenth century, it's used today as a covered market at weekends. The **tourist office** is at 1 Church Lane (May–Sept daily 10am–1pm & 2–5pm; Oct–April closed Sun; ☎01531/636 147).

Two miles east of Ledbury stands **Eastnor Castle** (Easter to end Sept Sun noon–6pm; July & Aug also Mon–Fri noon–6pm; £3; EH), a massive mock-medieval pile built in 1812 on the whim of the first Earl Somers, who wanted a home in the style of the Marcher fortresses of Edward I. Many of the age's finest architects, designers and landscapists were involved in this ambitious project, leaving a rich legacy of phantasmogoric decor, particularly in the drawing room, designed and furnished by the young Augustus Pugin, and the extraordinarily high baronial hall, the centrepiece of the castle. Lavish tapestries and portraits, designed in the style of earlier centuries to bolster the earl's fantasies, hang on the walls of the main hall and entrance lobby.

Ross-on-Wye and the Forest of Dean

ROSS-ON-WYE, perched high above a loop of the river fifteen miles to the south of Hereford, is the obvious base for exploring the Forest of Dean and the Welsh borderland. It's a relaxed town, its streets having a pleasing sense of proportion, thanks mainly to the efforts of pioneering seventeenth-century town planner, John Kyrle, also responsible for laying out **The Prospect**, the walled clifftop garden behind the tapering spire of the parish church. The town's other attractions are its **shops** – especially its antique and bookshops – rather than its museums, which are rather twee.

The **tourist office** is on the main Broad Street (summer Mon–Sat 9am–5pm, Sun 10am–1pm; winter Mon–Sat 10am–4pm; ☎01989/562 768). **Accommodation** includes the relaxed *Arches Country House* on Walford Road (☎01989/563 348; ③), *Edde Cross House*, Edde Cross Street (☎01989/565 088; ④; no smoking) and *Vaga House* on Wye Street (☎01989/563 024; ③). **Restaurants** vary from the basic *Oat Cuisine*, a daytime wholefood café on Broad Street, to *Meader's*, at the bottom of Copse Cross Street, with Hungarian specialities (☎01989/562 803; moderate to expensive). Of the **pubs**, the *King Charles II* on Broad Street comes complete with its original oak-beamed courtyard. **Bikes** can be rented from *Revolutions*, also on Broad Street (☎01989/562 639).

The **youth hostel** at **Welsh Bicknor** (☎01594/860 300) is sited in a Victorian rectory, amid dramatic scenery six miles down the Wye, just over a mile from **GOODRICH**, home of an imposing sandstone castle (daily April–Sept 10am–6pm; Oct–March 10am–4pm; £2; EH). The castle commands clear views beyond the encircling river to the hills and forests of Gloucestershire; its position guaranteed its importance from the twelfth century until its final battering in the Civil War. Though damaged, it presents an interesting survey of changing architectural styles, from the Norman keep to the Medieval banqueting hall. Stagecoach R#61 (Mon–Fri 6 daily, Sat 4; 15min) from Ross to Monmouth stops at Goodrich.

The road leading south from Goodrich winds to **Symond's Yat**. Don't be tempted to visit Jubilee Park, an over-congested tourist trap, but if you've any interest in birds, head for Symond's Yat Rock, a promontory jutting out above the forest at the end of a pleasant three-mile walk from Welsh Bicknor youth hostel. A pair of peregrines nest here each year, their hide guarded by the *RSPB* who have telescopes and binoculars on hand for visitors.

The Forest

Although forestation is now rather patchy, the central knot of the **FOREST OF DEAN** – the part between Coleford and Cinderford – is still large enough to be able to escape the crowds. There are, it is said, around two thousand miles of paths in the forest, threaded between some twenty million trees, predominantly silver birch, huge oaks and old ash trees. Greenery and wild flowers have swamped many of the industrial workings and buildings that are dotted through the forest – the remains of the coal mines and foundries that flourished here from the era of the Romans until this century. Most of the forest's population centres are connected by a fairly regular **bus** service – check with the Gloucestershire public transport line (☎01452/527 516).

The picturesque village of **ST BRIAVELS**, fifteen miles south of Ross near the Wye, is home to one to England's most impressive **youth hostels**, occupying the foreboding Norman castle once used by King John as a hunting lodge (☎01594/530 272). From St Briavels, the B4228 leads into the forest proper, becoming increasingly touristy as it does so. Four miles along the road from St Briavels, at the *Lambsquay Hotel*, a road branches off to the **Clearwell Caves** (March–Oct 10am–5pm; £2.90), nine caverns with some good lighting effects and displays on the history of the forest and its people.

A mile further on is **COLEFORD**, bereft of trees but the most attractive of the larger forest towns and home of the main **tourist office**, just off the market place on Gloucester Road (Mon–Sat 10am–5pm; summer also Sun 10am–2pm; ☎01594/836 307). This is the principal **accommodation** base for the forest, with the excellent *Forest House Hotel* on Cinder Hill (☎01594/832 424; ③) and *Mrs Hailes* at Rookery Farm, Newland, just over a mile outside town (☎01594/832 432; ③).

The B4226 runs from Coleford right through the heart of the forest, to **CINDERFORD**, a soulless grey town six miles to the east. No buses run along the road, but it's only a few miles from Coleford to the Beechenhurst Enclosure, a picnic site, park information centre and starting point for nature walks and the **Forest of Dean Sculpture Trail**, an easy walk littered with contemporary artwork and sculptures including a giant chair on the crest of a hill. The forest is also a great place to cycle – miles of tracks are clearly marked. *Pedalabikeaway*, 500 yards west of Beechenhurst (July & Aug 10am–5pm; April–June & Sept closed Mon; Oct–March Sat & Sun (only) 10am–5pm ☎01989/770 357) rents trail bikes, Victorian trikes, wheelchair tandems and mountain bikes at very reasonable rates. If you want to ride into the forest from Coleford, try *Riders of Lydney* at the Crown Inn, just outside town in Colway (☎01594/836620), who offer a drop-off and collection service.

Birmingham

If any city can be described as the first purely industrial city, it is **BIRMINGHAM**. Whereas many northern and Midland cities grew on a handful of staple industries, "Brum" turned its hand to every kind of manufacturing, gaining the epithet "the city of 1001 trades". It was here that the pioneers of the Industrial Revolution – James Watt, Matthew Boulton, William Murdock, Josiah Wedgwood, Joseph Priestley and Erasmus Darwin (grandfather of Charles) – formed the Lunar Society, a melting pot of scientific and industrial ideas that spawned the world's first purpose-built factory, the distillation of oxygen, the invention of gas lighting and the mass production of the steam engine. A Midlands market town swiftly mushroomed into the nation's economic dynamo – in the fifty years up to 1830 the population more than trebled to 130,000.

Now the second largest city in Britain, with a population of one million, Birmingham has long outgrown the squalor and misery of its boom years, and its industrial legacy is chiefly to be seen in a crop of excellent heritage museums, an extensive network of canals and a multi-racial population that makes this one of Britain's most eclectic conurbations. The shift to a post-manufacturing economy is symbolized by the brand new city-centre conference centre and by the enormous National Exhibition Centre on the outskirts, while Birmingham's cultural initiatives – enticing a division of the Royal Ballet to take up residence here, and building a fabulous new concert hall for the City of Birmingham Symphony Orchestra – have no equal outside the capital.

Arrival, information and accommodation

Birmingham's **airport** is eight miles east of the city centre at Elmdon; the main terminal is connected to Birmingham International train station, from where there are regular services into the centre. **New Street train station**, to which all InterCity and the vast majority of local services go, is right in the heart of the city; trains on the Stratford-upon-Avon and Warwick lines usually use **Snow Hill** and **Moor Street** stations, both about ten minutes' signposted walk from New Street. *National Express* **coach** travellers are dumped in the grim surroundings of **Digbeth coach station**, from where it is a ten-minute uphill walk to the centre. *London Express* coaches arrive at Colmore Row, close to the cathedral.

Free accommodation booking, maps and transport information are provided by all the city's **tourist offices**. Equidistant from New Street station are those at 2 City Arcade, off New Street (Mon–Sat 9.30am–5.30pm; ☎0121/643 2514) and the Central Library, Chamberlain Square (Mon–Fri 9am–8pm, Sat 9am–5pm; ☎0121/236 5622). There are also offices open Monday to Friday 9am to 5pm and during major conferences in the International Convention Centre (ICC) in Centenary Square and two in the National Exhibition Centre, next to the airport.

With cheaper accommodation being generally out of the city centre, you are likely to be using local **buses** at some point: *West Midlands Travel* (*WMT*) is the largest operator (the blue and silver buses), although vehicles of every hue can be seen jostling for custom on the city's streets. The off-peak day pass for *WMT* buses is good value for money (£2.20) and can be bought on the first bus used.

B&Bs and cheaper **hotels** are concentrated two miles west along the A456 **Hagley Road** (buses #9, #19, #120, #123, #124, #126, #136–8, #192, #193, #292) and in **Acocks Green**, four miles southeast of the centre (trains from Moor Street or Snow Hill, or buses #1, #11, #37 or #38). Central hotels are generally geared up to the expense-account trade, but the ICC tourist office offers cut-price *Warm Hearted Weekends* (☎0121/780 4321) in most of the city-centre hotels, with prices starting at around £18 per person per night. These are available for Friday, Saturday and Sunday nights all

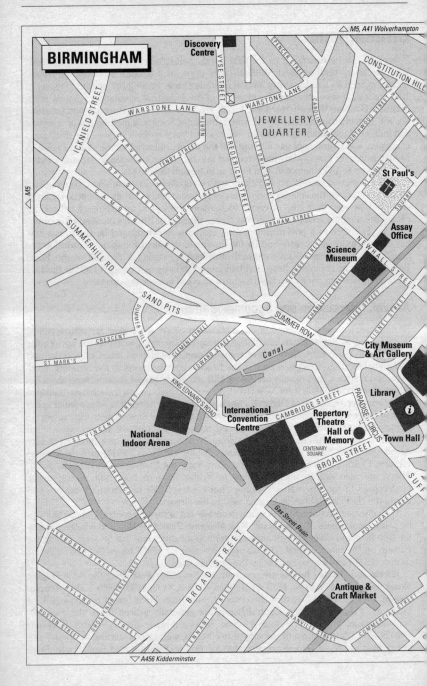

BIRMINGHAM

△ M5, A41 Wolverhampton

Discovery Centre

CONSTITUTION HILL

SPENCER STREET

ICKNIELD STREET

WARSTONE LANE

VYSE STREET

WARSTONE LANE

JEWELLERY QUARTER

LIVERY STREET

NORTHWOOD STREET

CAROLINE STREET

△ M5

CARVER STREET

POPE STREET

TENBY STREET

TENBY STREET NORTH

FREDERICK STREET

VITTORIA STREET

St Paul's

ST PAUL'S SQUARE

CAMDEN STREET

ALBION STREET

GRAHAM STREET

Assay Office

NEWHALL STREET

SUMMERHILL RD

SAND PITS

GEORGE STREET

CHARLOTTE STREET

Science Museum

SUMMER HILL ST

CRESCENT

ST MARK'S

SUMMER ROW

FLEET STREET

LIONEL STREET

City Museum & Art Gallery

CLEMENT STREET

EDWARD STREET

Canal

CAMBRIDGE STREET

Library

PARADISE CIRCUS

ℹ

KING EDWARD'S ROAD

International Convention Centre

Repertory Theatre

Hall of Memory

Town Hall

ST VINCENT STREET

National Indoor Arena

CENTENARY SQUARE

BROAD STREET

SUFF

SHEEPCOTE STREET

BRIDGE STREET

HOLLIDAY STREET

SHERBORNE STREET

Gas Street Basin

GAS STREET

RYLAND STREET

BROAD STREET

BERKLEY STREET

COMMERCIAL STREET

RUSTON STREET

GROSVENOR STREET WEST

TENNANT STREET

Antique & Craft Market

GRANVILLE STREET

▽ A456 Kidderminster

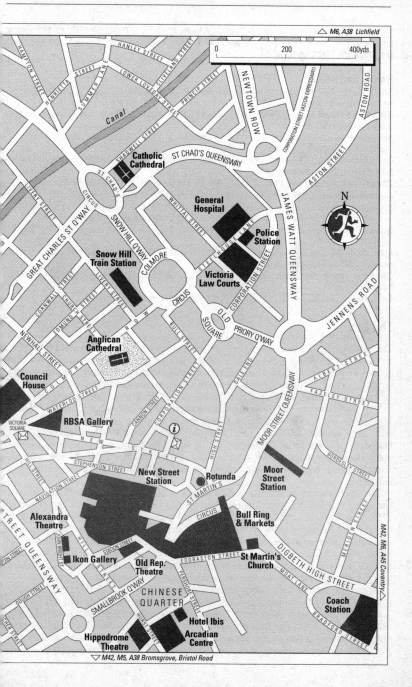

year round and every night in July and August. In the centre of town there are also a couple of places offering B&B for gay and lesbian visitors – see the "Lesbian and Gay Birmingham" section on p.384.

Hotels and B&Bs

Atholl Lodge Guest House, 16 Elmdon Rd, Acocks Green (☎0121/707 4417). Comfortable guest house in a popular area. ②.

Ashbourne Guest House, 3 Elmdon Rd, Acocks Green (☎0121/707 2324). Small, well-furnished and fairly cosy B&B. ③.

Ashdale House, 39 Broad Rd, Acocks Green (☎0121/706 3598). Well-situated B&B, serving good vegetarian and organic food. ③.

Campanile Hotel, 55 Irving St (☎0121/622 4925). Slightly downbeat but handily placed just off Bristol Street, in the city centre. ⑥.

Cook House, 425 Hagley Rd (☎0121/429 1916). One of the best-value hotels in the area. ③.

Greenway House, 978 Warwick Rd, Acocks Green (☎0121/706 1361). Homely B&B. ③.

Hotel Ibis, Ladywell Walk, Arcadian Centre (☎0121/622 6010). Chintzy and rather anonymous, but well situated in the heart of the Chinese Quarter, near the major theatres and nightclubs. ④.

Kennedy Guest House, 38 York Rd (☎0121/454 1284). A low-key and functional B&B, near Hagley Road. ②.

Lyby Guest House, 14–16 Barnsley Rd (☎0121/429 4487). Off Hagley Road, well placed for the trendy suburb of Bearwood. ②.

Old Farm Hotel, 108 Linden Rd, Bourneville (☎0121/458 3146). Friendly hotel, just 250 yds from *Cadbury World*. ⑤.

Town House, 435 Hagley Rd (☎0121/429 2482). Good B&B for single rooms. ③.

The City

The focus of the city centre is where the main shopping thoroughfares of New Street and Corporation Street meet at right angles, just outside the shopping complex that houses New Street station. These streets contain an array of samey chainstores and tarted-up precincts; more interesting are the multifarious **markets** in and around the infamous **Bull Ring**, yawning under the Rotunda at the intersection of New and High streets. Bulls used to be tethered and baited here, in the belief that if the animal died angry, the meat was better. The Bull Ring indoor shopping centre is scarcely a more edifying spectacle, fulfilling every miserable cliché about 1960s town planning – thankfully, it is due to be demolished by the end of the century. On the far side of the complex, on the edge of the market stalls, stands **St Martin's**, the city's parish church, dating back to the fourteenth century, but completely rebuilt in the late nineteenth.

The finest church in the city is **St Philip's**, a bijou example of English Baroque, occupying a grassy knoll on Colmore Row, west of Corporation Street. Consecrated in 1715 as an overspill for the packed St Martin's, it became the city's cathedral in 1905 at the expense of the parish church, largely due to its superior position in a less congested, more upmarket corner of the city centre. The church was extended in the 1880s, when four new stained-glass windows were commissioned from local boy Edward Burne-Jones, a leading light of the Pre-Raphaelite movement. The windows are typical of his style: intensely coloured, fastidiously detailed, and rather sentimental.

One of the world's most comprehensive collections of Pre-Raphaelite art, including an entire room of Burne-Jones' work, is housed in the **City Museum and Art Gallery** in Chamberlain Square (Mon–Sat 9.30am–5pm, Sun 2–5pm; free), two hundred yards along Colmore Row. The overwrought ranks of pieces by Rossetti, Holman Hunt, Millais and Madox-Brown are more than most eyes can take, though some of the portraits avoid the fussiness of the big allegorical and religious paintings. England's largest provincial museum contains a lot more than just masses of Pre-Raphs. A good collection of eighteenth- to twentieth-century British art includes a thorough survey of watercolour landscapes from 1750 to 1850 and numerous works by David Cox, Constable's Birmingham contemporary. The international collection has its main strengths in seventeenth-century Italian works, and a small showing of Impressionists.

Birmingham's industrial prowess is amply demonstrated throughout the museum. The ground-floor Industrial Gallery, housed in the original Victorian building complete with ornate skylights and huge gaslights, contains beautiful stained glass and local ceramics – and leads to the genteel Edwardian tea room, one of the most pleasant places in Birmingham for a midday break. Elsewhere in the building you'll find galleries devoted to silver, base metalwork and jewellery. Upstairs is a large and rather old-fashioned natural history collection, linked to a couple of rooms looking at ancient worlds. Tucked down by the back entrance off Great Charles Street are two interesting local history galleries, which focus mainly on the industrial beginnings and development of the city. The adjoining Gas Hall is one of the country's most impressive venues for touring art exhibitions.

Chamberlain Square is also bounded by the huge municipal monolith of the domed **Council House**, and the classical **Town Hall** (1832–46), based on the Roman temple in Nîmes. The rather stark **Central Library**, which would seem to be based on a multi-storey car park, brings the tone down a little and its entrance attracts a variety of soap-box speakers, airing their views on religion and politics. The central focus is a fountain commemorating Joseph Chamberlain (1836–1914), whose political career took him from the Birmingham mayor's office to national prominence as leader of the Liberal Unionists and figurehead of the resistance to Irish home rule. On the steps lies a statue of the city's first MP, Thomas Attwood, his coat-tails tumbling down the concrete.

On its south side Chamberlain Square opens onto the beautifully refurbished Victoria Square, where the old-fashioned gallery of the **Royal Birmingham Society of Artists** (Mon–Sat 10.30am–5pm; free), on the corner of New Street, hosts some interesting temporary exhibitions. On the other side, walk through the hideously kitsch Paradise Forum – entered through the library complex – to get to Centenary Square, laid out as a complement to the showpiece **International Convention Centre** (ICC) and the *Birmingham Repertory Theatre*. Centre-stage on the wide paving is a butter-coloured sculpture called *Forward*, a simplistically rousing image of the city's history by Birmingham-born Raymond Mason.

On the canals at the back of the ICC, turn left for the bright, boat-filled **Gas Street Basin**, or turn right for a canalside wander up to the huge dome of the National Indoor Arena, where the canal forks. Go right for an interesting walk down a lock flight for half a mile to the **Museum of Science and Industry** on Newhall Street (Mon–Sat 9.30am–5pm, Sun 2–5pm; free) – take the steps immediately before the tunnel under Telecom Tower. The museum's coverage of Birmingham's industrial past ranges from dusty exhibits unaltered since the 1950s to the latest in interactive technology. The transport section is especially good, including a selection of Midlands-made cars, the chain-driven Mercedes used by German Chancellor Hindenburg, and the *City of Birmingham*, a locomotive so vast that its section of the museum had to be built around it. In amongst the factory machines lurks the world's oldest working steam engine, a Watt and Boulton original, built in Birmingham in the 1780s. Upstairs is an enjoyable hands-on gallery, the Light on Science, containing dozens of experiment stations at which you can play with prisms, light and mirrors, make sound sculptures and so on.

Further up the canal, you reach the Pugin-designed **St Chad's Catholic Cathedral** (1839–41), the first Catholic cathedral to be built in England since the Reformation. Perhaps more rewarding is Birmingham's two-hundred-year-old **Jewellery Quarter**, immediately northwest of the science museum, and well signposted all over the city centre. Bucklemakers and toymakers first colonized the area in the 1750s, opening the way for hundreds of silversmiths, jewellers and goldsmiths. Although their industry has waned, there are still around five hundred jewellery-related companies in the quarter, many of which can be visited. Amongst the traders and bargain-hunters thronging the streets, don't miss the beautifully proportioned Georgian **St Paul's Square** and church, and the engrossing **Jewellery Quarter Discovery Centre**, 77–79 Vyse St (Mon–Fri 10am–4pm, Sat 11am–5pm; £2). Built around a factory that was abandoned in 1980 but had remained virtually unchanged since the 1950s, the museum brilliantly evokes the atmosphere of the old works, where dozens of workers would be wedged into tiny, hot and noisy spaces to churn out earrings, brooches and rings. The factory comprises the second part of the museum visit – the first section is a visitor centre detailing the growth and decline of the trade in Birmingham.

Bournville

Most remarkable of Birmingham's suburbs is the planned Quaker village of **BOURNVILLE**, four miles southwest of the city centre (train from New Street or buses #83, #84, #85 & #85a from Digby). In 1879 George and Richard **Cadbury**, whose father had started the firm in the hope of producing a cheap chocolate-based non-alcoholic drink to replace beer, moved the family's business out of the squalid city centre to this custom-made "factory in a garden". Once decent working conditions had been achieved for their employees, the Cadburys set about improving the living conditions of the wider working-class people of Birmingham, constructing a workers' village of some eight thousand houses. Much influenced by the utopian ideas of William Morris and the Arts and Crafts movement, the Bournville scheme included gardens for every house, extensive parkland, a mock half-timbered parade of shops next to a village green, and a pair of uprooted Tudor houses, **Selly Manor** and **Minworth Greaves** on Maple Road, now open as a museum of Tudor and Jacobean furniture (Tues–Fri 10am–5pm; £1). The **Cadbury World** museum, tacked onto the huge factory off Linden Road (tour bookings ☎0121/451 4108; £4.90), takes visitors through the histories of the cocoa bean and the Cadbury dynasty – with excellent displays on advertising – but for chocoholics the point of the tour is the opportunity to gorge on free samples from the production line and stock up on the cut-price finished product.

Edgbaston

EDGBASTON was first developed in the 1790s by the Calthorpe family as a genteel residential estate from which industry and commerce were explicitly banned, and an air of privilege still pervades this suburb to the immediate southwest of the city centre. The **Birmingham Botanical Gardens**, in the north of Edgbaston on Westbourne Road (Mon–Sat 9am–8pm or dusk, Sun 10am–8pm or dusk; £3.20), were opened in 1832 for the private pleasure of Edgbaston's denizens, but have now grown into fifteen acres of plants, lakes and glasshouses for the delectation of the masses. Buses #3, #10, #21–3, #29 and #103 from the city centre pass close.

The finest of Birmingham's 149 public parks is **Cannon Hill Park**, off the Pershore and Edgbaston roads two miles south of central Birmingham – buses #45 and #47 from the city centre stop nearby. Apart from usual urban park attractions, Cannon Hill is also home to the excellent **Midland Arts Centre** (see p.385), which has a good bar and café. On the Pershore Road side of the park, the **Birmingham Nature Centre** (March–Oct daily 10am–5pm; Nov–March Sat & Sun 10am–dusk; free) holds a dowdy collection of cuddly animals and fearful spiders and snakes, founded as a way of showing poor city kids a slice of the country.

Birmingham University, on the southern fringe of Edgbaston (trains from New Street or buses #61–64, #83–85 and #142–144), is visible for miles around thanks to the 325-foot clock tower that dominates the campus. Its hidden secret is the **Barber Institute of Fine Arts**, on Edgbaston Park Road (Mon–Sat 10am–5pm, Sun 2–5pm; free), whose superb gallery contains a world-class collection of European masters from the thirteenth century onwards. Notable pieces include a fine collection of Rembrandt studies, a Rubens landscape and Degas' *Jockeys Before the Race*, a characteristically audacious piece of off-centre composition. The Barber also houses a good collection of Impressionists, including Monet, Pissaro and Boudin, as well as works by Magritte, Bellini, Gwen John, Whistler, Van Gogh, Gaugin and Turner.

The Tolkien Trail

An extraordinary number of visitors to Birmingham are here to follow the trail of **J.R.R. Tolkien**, author of *The Hobbit* and *Lord of the Rings*, who lived in many different parts of Birmingham between the ages of three and nineteen – a **Tolkien Trail** leaflet is available from the tourist offices. A prime Tolkien site lies four miles southeast of the city centre at **Sarehole Mill** on Cole Bank Road, Hall Green (March–Oct daily 2–5pm; free), reached by bus #4. The writer spent four years of his early childhood in a house opposite this eighteenth-century brick corn mill, and many of his literary ideas were inspired by the building and its gloomy lake – his drawing of Hobbiton and Sandyman's Mill in *The Hobbit* allegedly bears a striking resemblance to the then rural hamlet of Sarehole. Other places that influenced Tolein can still be visited – notably the spectacularly ornate Catholic **Oratory church**, just beyond Five Ways on the Hagley Road (open mornings) and the nearby **Perrot's Folly**, Monument Road (Mon–Fri 10am–5pm; £1.50), a curious 98-foot castellated tower built by the local landowner in 1758.

Eating, drinking and nightlife

Birmingham's central **restaurants** have a reputation as soulless places which empty as the evening wears on. It's true that many places are geared towards the grey-suit market, but there are a couple of central areas to find decent, reasonably priced restaurants around the Chinese Quarter at the top of Hurst Street – also the focus of the gay scene. Birmingham's gastronomic speciality is the **Balti**, a delicious kashmiri stew cooked and served in a wok-like dish called a *karahi*, with nan bread instead of cutlery. Overpriced Balti houses have opened up in the centre, but by far the best Balti houses are in the inner-city southern suburbs of **Balsall Heath** and **Sparkhill**. The best of these are listed here – all are unlicensed, so take your own booze. The city-centre **pubs** vary as much as you'd expect, but more traditional pubs abound throughout the centre and out into the livelier suburbs of Moseley and Balsall Heath.

Nightlife ranges from clubs that are publicized on a word-of-mouth basis, through to pubs and larger music venues. Birmingham's showpiece **Symphony Hall** and the resident Birmingham Royal Ballet are the spearheads of the city's resurgent high-cultural scene, and the social calendar gets an added boost from the range of new **festivals**, all of which offer many events for free. These include **Towards the Millennium**, a multi-media arts festival between February and April, the **Women's Festival** in March, the **Readers' and Writers' Festival** in May, the **Jazz Festival** in July, the **Comedy Festival** in September and the **Film and TV Festival** in October.

For current information on all events, performances and exhibitions, pick up a free copy of *What's On Birmingham and Midlands* (not to be confused with the inferior *What's On West Midlands*) from tourist offices, galleries or public venues.

Restaurants

Bambos, 61 Station St (☎0121/643 5621). An upstairs city-centre Greek restaurant – excellent food, complemented by all-singing, plate-smashing frolics. Moderate.

Chung Ying, 16–18 Wrottesley St (☎0121/622 1793). The best Cantonese dishes in the Chinese Quarter, and always busy. Moderate.

Diwan, 3b Alcester Rd, Moseley. Although the decor is like a cross-channel ferry, the Baltis here are superb. Bus #50 stops outside. Inexpensive.

Punjab Paradise, 377 Ladypool Rd, Balsall Heath (☎0121/449 4110). One of the city's classic Balti houses, specializing in milder dishes. Bus #50 to the Moseley Dance Centre, then a 10-min walk. Inexpensive.

Royal Naweed, 44 Woodbridge Rd, central Moseley. Dependable Indian, invariably busy and well situated for good local pubs. Bus #50. Inexpensive.

Shah Faisal, 348–50 Stratford Rd, Sparkhill. Large and very tasty Baltis in very traditional, pink surroundings. Buses #2, #4–6, #12, #31, #37 or #41. Inexpensive.

Teppanyaki, Arcadian Centre, Hurst St (☎0121/622 5183). The city's first Japanese restaurant, swiftly gaining an excellent reputation. Expensive.

Warehouse Café, 54 Allison St, Digbeth (☎0121/633 0261). Imaginative and 100 percent vegan café, above *Friends of the Earth*. Moderate.

Pubs

James Brindley, next to the *Hyatt Hotel* off Bridge Street. Popular with businesspeople in the week, but Sat and Sun jazz brunches give the place a different air. Great canalside location.

Old Contemptibles, 176 Edmund St. Real old spit-and-sawdust saloon, incongruously packed with grey suits at lunch and in the early evening. Excellent lunchtime food.

The Old Fox, Arcadian Centre, Hurst St. Over-modernized but popular pub, with an excellent selection of beer and amiable atmosphere.

Prince of Wales, Cambridge St. An old-fashioned haunt with long-standing custom from the Repertory Theatre, now pulling them in from the neighbouring ICC.

Prince of Wales, 118 Alcester Rd, Moseley. Best of the suburban pubs in the balti belt – very popular with students and young trendies. Bus #50.

The Victoria, John Bright St. An elaborately tiled and smokey Irish pub, next to the Ikon Gallery; best-value lunchtime food in the city centre.

Clubs

Baker's, 163 Broad St. A small, artily designed disco-club with a wide range of speciality evenings.

Bobby Brown's, 48 Gas St. A stylish club overlooking the canal basin; mixed music diet primarily aimed at the over-25s.

The Cave, *Cave Arts Centre*, 516 Moseley Rd, Balsall Heath. Lots of Afro-Caribbean jiving and occasional reggae.

The Institute, opposite Digbeth coach station. The nightclub with the widest appeal, hosting regular live music in the huge old Digbeth Civic Hall.

Moseley Dance Centre, 572 Moseley Rd, Balsall Heath. Trendiest Sat night out in town – assorted 1970s/1980s/rave discos. Bus #50.

Ronnie Scott's, 258 Broad St. Second of the maestro's jazz clubs, good also for big names in blues and world music.

Lesbian and gay Birmingham

Fountain Inn, 102 Wrentham St (☎0121/622 1452). A mainly male real-ale pub with B&B accommodation (③) and occasional cabaret.

The Fox, 17 Lower Essex St. A mainly female pub with excellent atmosphere and courtyard garden.

The Jug, 27 Water St. An idiosyncratic, high-camp club on the edge of the Jewellery Quarter; the only main venue out of the Hurst Street area's "gay village".

The Nightingale, 37 Thorp St. The city's foremost gay club, loud and fun. Due to move soon round the corner to Lower Essex Street.

Partners, Albany House, 27–35 Hurst St. A mixed, loud, lively and young cellar bar.

The Village, 152 Hurst St (☎0121/622 4742). A mainly male and enjoyably stylish café-bar, with daytime and early evening food, a garden and B&B accommodation (③).

Tin Tins, 308 Bull Ring Centre, opposite New Street station on Smallbrook Queensway. A mixed, ravey club.

Classical music, theatre and dance

Alexandra Theatre, Suffolk Street Queensway (☎0121/643 1231). Home of Gilbert and Sullivan revivalists the D'Oyly Carte, and venue for populist musicals, farces and plays interspersed with one-night alternative fare.

Cave Arts Centre, 516 Moseley Rd, Balsall Heath (☎0121/440 0288). A largely black arts centre, including theatre and comedy.

Hippodrome Theatre, Hurst Street (☎0121/236 4455). Home of the Birmingham Royal Ballet and regular hosts of the Welsh National Opera. Also touring plays and big pre- and post-West End productions.

Midlands Art Centre, Cannon Hill Park, Edgbaston (☎0121/440 0888). Venue for touring theatre companies and some local groups.

Old Rep Theatre, Station St (☎0121/616 1519). Britain's oldest repertory theatre, now home to the imaginative Birmingham Stage Company.

Repertory Theatre, Centenary Square (☎0121/236 4455). Mixed diet of classics and new work, including some local and experimental writing in the Studio.

Symphony Hall, International Convention Centre, Centenary Square (☎0121/212 3333). Acoustically one of the most advanced concert halls in Europe, home of the acclaimed City of Birmingham Symphony Orchestra (CBSO) under the baton of Simon Rattle, as well as a venue for touring music and opera.

Town Hall, Victoria Square (☎0121/235 3942). The CBSO's old home is still used for classical and rock concerts, as well as a venue for stand-up comedy.

Listings

Airport enquiries ☎0121/767 5511.

Banks *Lloyds*, 125 Colmore Row; *Midland*, 130 New St; *NatWest*, 103 Colmore Row.

Bookshops *Bookscene*, 35 Pallasades Shopping Centre; *Dillons* 128 New St; *Waterstone's*, 24 High St.

Bus enquiries Local services ☎0121/200 2700; *London Express* ☎0121/200 3334; *National Express* ☎0121/622 4373.

Car rental *A1 Discount Car Hire*, 30 Digbeth St (☎0121/622 7100); *Bristol Street Motors*, 156–82 Bristol St (☎0121/666 6000); *Budget*, 95 Station St (☎0121/643 0493).

Cricket Warwickshire County Cricket Ground, Edgbaston Rd, Edgbaston (☎0121/446 4422).

Exchange *American Express*, 17 Martineau Square, off Corporation Street (☎0121/233 2141); *Thomas Cook*, 50 Corporation St (☎0121/236 9711) and 99 New St (☎0121/643 3120).

Football Aston Villa, based at Villa Park (☎0121/327 5353) are the city's big club. One-time rivals, Birmingham City, based at St Andrews (☎0121/772 0101), are threatening a revival.

Hospital General Hospital, Steelhouse Lane (☎0121/236 8611).

Laundry Nearest to the city centre is *Washmore* at 49 Bristol Rd. Convenient for the hotels and B&Bs listed above is *Washland*, 58 Yardley Rd, Acocks Green.

Left luggage New Street station (Mon–Sat 6.45am-8.45pm, Sun 11.15am–6.45pm).

Lesbian and Gay Switchboard Daily 7–10pm ☎0121/622 6589; *Unison* lesbian & gay group ☎0121/643 6084.

Police Main city-centre stations in Steelhouse Lane (☎0121/626 6010) and on the corner of Digbeth and Allison streets (☎0121/626 6020).

Post Office Main post office at 1 Pinfold St, on the corner with Victoria Square.

Train enquiries Long-distance services ☎0121/643 2711; local services ☎0121/200 2700.

Women's advice and information centre Devonshire House, Digbeth (☎0121/773 6952; open for visitors Tues & Thurs 10am–4pm).

The Black Country

The area known as the **Black Country** might now appear to be an undifferentiated mass sprawling from the western side of Birmingham, but in fact it's composed of several tightly knit industrial communities, which have gradually expanded until each is touching its neighbours. Some of these towns grew on the basis of one or two staple products – leather in Walsall, locks in Willenhall, glass in Stourbridge – whilst the rest exploited the abundant local resources (chiefly coal and limestone) to develop a range of industries, with heavy engineering predominant. Although many of the older trades have long gone, this is still an area where manufacturing is regarded as the only real work, so it's unsurprising that the Black Country's industrial heritage is the main reason for visiting the area.

Dudley

The ancient borough of **DUDLEY**, eight miles west of Birmingham (bus #87 or #126), is dominated by its ruined Norman **Castle**, sadly an integral part of a dreadful **zoo** that straggles over the hill (Easter to mid-Sept daily 10am–4.30pm; rest of year closes 3.30pm; £4.95). The most visitable attraction in Dudley – indeed, the whole of the Black Country – is the **Black Country Museum** on the Tipton Road, over the far side of Castle Hill from the town centre (March–Oct daily 10am–5pm; Nov–Feb Wed–Sun 10am–4pm; £5). Buildings from the surrounding district – shops, a chapel, a pub, workshops, forges and homes – have been re-erected here and populated with local people in period costume, mimicking forms of labour that once employed thousands in these parts. For added authenticity (and more money) you can take a trip down to an underground coal seam, or you can escape the past on a canal trip into a tunnel under Castle Hill, through some spectacularly floodlit limestone caverns.

Walsall

WALSALL, ten miles northwest of Birmingham (train or buses #51, #951 or #952), is a pleasantly stoic town, now attempting to diversify into tourism after years as a centre of the leather industry. Its prime attraction is the **Museum and Art Gallery** on Lichfield Street (Mon–Fri 10am–6pm, Sat 10am–4.45pm; free), which contains a superb collection donated by the widow of Sir Jacob Epstein. As well as Epstein's own work, it features art by Van Gogh, Picasso, Rodin, Renoir and Matisse.

Wolverhampton and around

WOLVERHAMPTON, fifteen miles northwest of Birmingham, is an unattractive mix of Victorian civic architecture and hideous 1960s shopping malls, but the **Museum and Art Gallery** on Lichfield Street (Mon–Sat 10am–6pm; free) is a great deal more interesting than many comparable municipal collections, especially in its range of Pop Art and contemporary pieces. The other reason for venturing into Wolverhampton is to visit the two fine country houses that sit on the edge of the town.

Four miles west is the mock-half-timbered **Wightwick Manor** at Wightwick Bank, off the A454 (March–Dec Thurs & Sat 2.30–5.30pm; house and garden £4.50; NT). Built in 1887, it was designed by Edward Ould, a devotee of William Morris, and the fabulously ornate furnishings, fittings and paintings all reflect the Pre-Raphaelite influence. The fine garden (March–Dec Wed & Thurs 11am–6pm; £2) is maintained in its original form, complete with plump orchards and ostentatious topiary. Buses #516 and #890 from Wolverhampton stop at the bottom of the road.

Four miles to the north of town, off the A460, is **Moseley Old Hall** (April–Oct Wed, Sat & Sun 2–2.30pm also Tues July & Aug 2–5.30pm; £3.30; NT), now sheltering in the lee of the M54 and Fordhouses prison. King Charles II took refuge here on escaping from the Battle of Worcester in 1651 – you can see the bed he slept in and the hole in which he sheltered for the best part of two days as Parliamentarian troops scoured the area. The timber-framed Elizabethan house and, in particular, the formal seventeenth-century gardens are very well maintained. Buses #870–2 and #613 from Wolverhampton pass nearby, leaving a ten-minute walk to the hall.

Shropshire

One of England's largest, least spoiled and least populated counties, **Shropshire** stretches from its long and winding border with Wales to the very edge of the urban West Midlands. The remotest and most beautiful parts of the county are the southern and western fringes, where the hills become increasingly barren and dramatic as they approach the Welsh mountains. Scything across the southern part of the county are the twin ridges of **Wenlock Edge** and the blustery **Long Mynd**, excellent focal areas for walking, hang-gliding and youth hostelling. The River Severn flows into the county from Wales through the county town of **Shrewsbury**, on to **Ironbridge**, where it was harnessed for some of Britain's earliest industrial sites, and then through the hilltop town of **Bridgnorth**.

Ironbridge and around

The nearest Shropshire town to the West Midlands conurbation, both geographically and culturally, is **IRONBRIDGE**, the collective title for a cluster of small villages huddled in the wooded Severn valley, to the south of the new town of Telford. Ironbridge was the crucible of the Industrial Revolution, an achievement encapsulated by its famous span across the Severn gorge – engineered by Abraham Darby in 1779, it was the world's first iron bridge. This Abraham Darby was the third innovative industrialist of that name – the first one started iron-smelting in the Severn gorge back in 1709, then the second invented the forging process that made it possible to produce massive single items in iron. Under the guidance of such creative figures as the third Abraham Darby and Thomas Telford, this area's factories churned out engines, rails, wheels and other heavy-duty iron pieces in quantities unmatched in England.

Manufacturing has now vanished, but the surviving monuments make the **Ironbridge Gorge Museum** the best industrial heritage museum in the country. The museum is in fact seven museums and an assortment of other attractions spread over six square miles. The best way to tour the museum sites is with a **passport** ticket (£8), allowing unlimited access to all of the sites in any calendar year. All sites open at 10am every day, going through until 5pm, except between June and August, when they close at 6pm – though some of the smaller exhibits close sometimes in winter. A free **bus** operates throughout the summer between the sites. The place to begin is at the southern end of the **bridge** itself, where the old **tollhouse** contains an exhibition on the bridge's construction and significance. On the opposite (northern) bank of the river, a few hundred yards upstream towards the power station cooling towers, is the **Museum of the River** (£2 if visited singly). Though in places little more than a PR exercise for the local privatized water company, it still has plenty to enjoy – especially the forty-foot model of the gorge in the 1790s. From here, Dale Road leads north, past the youth hostel, to the **Coalbrookdale Museum of Iron** (£3), which ranges from displays on the first use of iron four thousand years ago to some superb examples of Victorian and Edwardian ironwork. Linked to the museum is the **Elton Gallery**, showing a rotating collection of industrial art, and the rebuilt Darby **iron furnace**. One hundred yards up from the furnace, **Rosehill House** (£2), contains the possessions of a Quaker ironmaster from the early nineteenth century.

The other museums lie to the east of the bridge in the village of **COALPORT**. Most impressive of them is the **Blists Hill Open Air Museum** (£6), a mile up the hill from the riverbank. Staffed by period-dressed employees, the rambling site encloses various reconstructed Victorian buildings – among them a school, a stinking candle-makers, a doctor's surgery complete with horrific instruments, a gas-lit pub, a working wrought-iron works and a slaughterhouse. Further east along the river's edge are the **Tar Tunnel** (80p), where bitumen oozes from the walls, and the **Coalport China Museum** (£3), whose disused conical bottle kilns are the setting for a mix of social history and elegant examples of the porcelain and china for which Coalport was famous. On the opposite bank of the river, accessible either by footbridge from near the Tar Tunnel or the roadbridge a mile upstream, is the **Jackfield Tile Museum** (£3). Housed in an old tile factory, it's an interesting examination of the beginnings of the coal industry in the area (which survived right up until 1979), leading into a superbly ornate Victorian tile showroom. The **Maws Craft Centre**, just past the museum, springs to life towards the end of June when the *Jackfield and Ironbridge Bluegrass and Roots Festival* attracts local and national bands for three days of mellow music. Other events which take place in the gorge annually are the *Lion's Raft Race* (June) and the frenzied *Coracle Regatta* (Aug) – check with the tourist board for exact dates.

Practicalities

Ironbridge is accessible by regular bus from Telford, or *Williamson's* coach #X96, which runs daily between Shrewsbury, Ironbridge, Telford and Birmingham. The main **tourist office** (April–Oct 9am–6pm; Nov–March 9am–5pm; ☎01952/432 166) is next to the bridge on the northern bank. Pick of the **hotels** are the *Tontine*, on The Square by the bridge (☎01952/432 127; ⑥), and *Ye Olde Robin Hood*, on Waterloo Street, Ironbridge (☎01952/433 100; ⑥), both old Victorian coaching inns. **B&Bs** include *Woodlands Farm* on Beech Road, Ironbridge (☎01952/432 741; ②), or right next to the bridge, the *Post Office House* at 6 The Square (☎01952/433 201; ③). The **youth hostel** is in the old Workers' Institute opposite the Coalbrookdale Museum of Iron (☎01952/ 433 281); there's a **campsite** at the *Severn Gorge*, a mile from Blists Hill on the Bridgnorth Road, Tweedale (☎01952/684 789). For something other than pub **food**, try the moderately priced *Oliver's Vegetarian Bistro* on the High Street. Best bet for good beer in cosy surroundings is the *Coalbrookdale Inn*, past the Museum of Iron, while a potent local brew is served up in the modest *All Nations Pub*, opposite Blists Hill.

Much Wenlock

MUCH WENLOCK, five miles southwest of Ironbridge, is unfailingly quaint, a patch-work of Tudor, Jacobean and Georgian buildings, their style captured perfectly by the Guildhall, sitting pretty on the sturdy oak columns of the Butter market. Set amid fine topiary in a dipped basin of green fields on the edge of the tiny town is the skeletal ruin of the eleventh-century **priory** (April–Oct daily 10am–6pm; Nov–March Wed–Sun 10am-4pm; £2; EH), which boasts some solid Norman carving in its chapter House and lavatorium. If the place appeals, try the *Old Barn* at the end of High Street (☎01952/728 191; ③), a homely B&B, or splash out at the *Talbot Inn* in the town centre (☎01952/727 077; ⑧), an eccentrically run guest house and **pub** serving excellent **food**.

Bridgnorth

Nine miles further down the A458 lies **BRIDGNORTH**, a quirky split-level market town with some excellent architecture and with enough evening life to make it worth stopping in. The Low Town is the northern terminus of the **Severn Valley Railway** (operates April–Oct & Christmas; ☎01299/403 816), one of the longest and most picturesque steam railways in Britain, running sixteen miles to Kidderminster; buses from Shrewsbury, Kidderminster, Ludlow or Wolverhampton call at the High Town.

Low Town bestrides the banks of the muddy Severn around the base of the sandstone rock on which is perched the older and more interesting **High Town**, whose skyline is dominated by the precarious castle keep and the domed tower of St Mary's church. Connecting the two halves on the river side of the town are a series of steps that wind their way up the sandstone cliff under tightly packed houses, which arch over the narrow passageways. For those without the energy, there is the century-old **cliff railway** (Mon–Sat 8am–8pm, Sun noon–8pm; 30p), clanking up Britain's steepest rail gradient to connect Underhill Street with Bank Street.

High Town is centred on the High Street, a wide, handsome thoroughfare packed with long-established family firms and antique shops, and crowned by its seventeenth-century **Town Hall**, which straddles wooden arches in the middle of the street. The street runs north to south, with the northern end funnelling under one of the old fortified town gates, **Northgate**. South past the town hall, the nostalgiac **Costume and Childhood Museum** (Mon–Sat 10.30am–5pm, Sun 2–5pm; £1.25), housed in the nineteenth-century market hall, incorporates art and geological galleries.

High Street becomes West Castle Street and leads down to the town gardens, in which the ruins of the twelfth-century **castle** are splayed. Its virtual annihilation by Cromwell's troops in 1646 left just the bulk of the keep, leaning at an angle of seventeen degrees from the vertical. The gardens lead down to **Castle Walk**, a pleasant walled pathway that winds along the cliff edge a hundred feet above the river. Thomas Telford's **St Mary's** church, resplendent above Castle Walk, is large and airy and topped out with a square, pillared tower that stands out for miles around.

Bridgnorth's well-stocked **tourist office** is in the library on Listley Street, off the High Street (Mon–Wed, Fri & Sat 9.30am–5pm; April–Oct also Thurs 10am–5pm & Sun 11am–5pm; ☎01746/763 358). There's plenty of **accommodation** in High Town, including the *Croft Hotel*, St Mary's Street (☎01746/762 416; ④), in the centre of High Town, or *St Leonard's Gate* B&B, 6 Church St (☎01746/766 647; ③). There's a **campsite** at *Stanmore Hall* (☎01746/761 761), two miles east of town on the Stourbridge road. Cheap and filling **food** is served at the *Tudor Room*, right underneath Northgate at the top of the High Street, and at *Pizza Lodge*, opposite the main post office at 10 Bank St, open every day for steaks, burgers and pizzas. For a quiet pint, head for the enjoyably downbeat *Railwayman's Arms*, at the Severn Valley Railway station, where a fine selection of real ales is served amid lashings of train memorabilia.

Shrewsbury and around

SHREWSBURY, Shropshire's county town, sits in a loop of the River Severn, a three-hundred-yard spit of land being all that keeps the town centre from being an island. It would be difficult to design a better defensive site, and fortifications were first built on this narrow neck in the fifth century, after the departure of the Roman legions from the nearby garrison at Wroxeter. The Normans, realizing the strategic potential of the site, built the first stone castle, which was expanded by Edward I in the late thirteenth century. As the town grew prosperous on the back of the Welsh wool trade its status grew relentlessly, reaching its ascendancy when Shrewsbury briefly became capital-in-exile for King Charles I during the early years of the Civil War. The eighteenth century saw the town evolve as a stagecoach post on the busy London to Holyhead route, and although this traffic withered on the arrival of the railways, the town had by then become the host of a lively social season, patronized by the sort of people who could afford to send their progeny to the famous Shrewsbury School. The top-notch gatherings might have gone, but Shrewsbury still exudes an air of complacent prosperity, and preserves some of the best Tudor and Jacobean streetscapes in England.

The Town

The sandstone **Castle**, sitting high above the castellated train station, rests on the site of fortifications that go back a millennium and a half. Today's buildings date mainly from the thirteenth century, although the great architect and engineer Thomas Telford was brought in during the 1790s to shore up the ruins and turn the castle into an extravagant private home for local magnate Sir William Pulteney. Now home to the dull **Shropshire Regimental Museum** (Mon–Sat 10am–5pm; summer also Sun noon–5pm; £1), the castle also hosts the annual *World Music Day* and open-air Shakespeare plays (both July) which make the most of the castle's dramatic setting.

Castle Gates winds up the hill from the station into the heart of the river loop on which the town was founded. From the town's raised core, **The Square**, Shrewsbury's famed Tudor and Jacobean buildings cascade down steep gradients and along tiny, cobbled alleyways. **Wyle Cop** tumbles east towards the **English Bridge** and the floodlights of the riverside soccer stadium; behind The Square and Wyle Cop, the maze of alleys around Butcher Row and Fish Street hide numerous offbeat shops, some good pubs and cafés, and an excellent **craft centre** housed in a deconsecrated church. South of The Square is College Hill, home of the **Clive House Museum** (Mon 2–5pm, Tues–Sat 10am–1pm & 2–5pm; £1), the Georgian-facaded town house of Lord Clive of India. Inside is an old-fashioned and rather cursory examination of the man, together with an exquisite collection of eighteenth- and nineteenth-century Coalport porcelain.

On Barker Street, running west towards the Welsh Bridge, is Shrewsbury's best museum and the main showpiece for both the town and its county, **Rowley's House** (Mon–Sat 10am–5pm; summer also Sun noon–5pm; £2). An ostentatious 1590s house with a seventeenth-century brick residence tacked on, it houses jumbled displays relating to local life, with the most interesting exhibits coming from the nearby Roman city of **Wroxeter**, including a unique silver mirror from the third century AD. On the western side of town, the pristine **Quarry Park**, home of the celebrated annual August **flower festival**, runs gently down to the river's edge, overlooked by the wedding-cake tower of the town's most celebrated church, **St Chad's**. England's largest round church, St Chad's was consecrated in 1792 as a replacement for the parish church that had collapsed as the clock struck four one morning in 1788.

Beyond the arc of the river is Shrewsbury's most important ecclesiastical building, the **Abbey**, now locked in the middle of a traffic intersection up Abbey Foregate. Founded in the 1080s by Roger de Montgomery, who was also responsible for the first stone castle here, the abbey was a Benedictine monastery that became a major political and religious force in Shropshire until the Dissolution. Unusually, the church and monastery buildings were not destroyed by the king's henchmen – indeed, the abbey church continued life as a parish church for the eastern side of Shrewsbury. Inside, the best feature is the huge west window of heraldic glass, dating from the fourteenth century. Underneath it is the original Norman door, and four of the nave pillars and their connecting arches also date from the original church.

The monastery stood largely intact until the 1830s when a new road swept away most of the buildings, leaving only a pile of crumbling remains. These have since been converted into a new heritage centre, **The Quest** (daily 10am–5pm; £3.95), which re-creates the living conditions of medieval monks, basing the whole thing around Ellis Peters' *Brother Cadfael* stories – Shropshire-based tales of medieval monastic sleuthing. For Cadfael fans there's a mystery to be solved through clues hidden in barrels of corn, clothes chests and haunted bedrooms, as well as a replica of the author's study. For the more historically inquisitive the scriptorium, complete with quills, natural pigments and calligraphic stamps, and the garden planted with herbs used by medieval medics, will prove more inspiring.

Practicalities

The **tourist office** is right in the heart of the town in The Square (Easter–October Mon–Sat 9.30am–6pm, Sun 10am–4pm; Nov–Easter Mon–Sat 9.30am–5.30pm; ☎01743/ 350 761). **Accommodation** includes *The Castle Vaults*, a warm and enjoyable pub at 16 Castle Gates (☎01743/358 807; ③), and the *Sandford House*, St Julian's Friars (☎01743/ 343 829; ③). Town-centre **B&Bs** include *Pryce's Villa Guest House*, 15 Monkmoor Rd, off Abbey Foregate (☎01743/356 217; ②); *Abbey Court House*, 134 Abbey Foregate (☎01743/364 416; ③); and the *College Hill*, 11 College Hill (☎01743/365 744; ③). The **youth hostel**, housed in a former Victorian ironmasters' house, is beyond the abbey at The Woodlands, Abbey Foregate (☎01743/360 179).

For daytime **food**, try the *Bear Steps* coffee house, in St Alkmund's Square, where you can sit outside under the half-timbered rafters, or the *Goodlife Wholefood Restaurant* in Barrack's Passage, off Wyle Cop. For evening food, there's the *Koh-i-noor Tandoori Restaurant*, St Julian's Friars (☎01743/362 832), which serves inexpensive curries and baltis, or *The Karakoram*, down by the Welsh Bridge on Frankwell Quay (☎01743/244 444), for similarly priced continental dishes. The *Castle Vaults* (see above), serves good Mexican food and excellent beer. The *Severn Stars* on Coleham Head is a relaxed folk-music **pub** just over the English Bridge from the town centre. More lively entertainment can be found on Howard Street, behind the train station, at *The Buttermarket*, which has a jazz and roots club every Thursday (☎01743/365 913).

Around Shrewbury: Hawkstone Park

A common activity for eighteenth- and nineteenth-century gentry was to convert their estates into pleasure parks for strolling, hunting and contemplating nature – **Hawkstone Park** (daily 10am–dusk; £3.50), which lies about ten miles north of Shrewsbury between Hodnet and Weston, is an outstanding example of this. The park, which consists of a maze of tree-lined avenues, high ridges and sandstone cliffs, was designed by the Hill family, who owned the estate from 1748 until 1895. On one ridge is a tall monument, a tower with 150 spiral steps leading to its windswept balcony. More unusual features along the one- or two- hour circular walk around the park include Swiss Bridge – two tree trunks spanning a deep gully – a hermit's cave, and a curious set of dim and eerie grottos on Grotto Hill, from the top of which the views stretch for miles across the plains to the Welsh hills. Parts of the path are a little tricky underfoot, especially towards Foxes Knob, a sandstone outcrop reached via dark passageways snaking through the rock. Bus #572 runs from Shrewsbury to Hodnet (30min) on Tuesdays and Sundays, from where it's a two-mile walk to the park.

The Long Mynd and Wenlock Edge

The **Long Mynd** and **Wenlock Edge**, two long ridged hills on opposite sides of the main A49 and rail line to the south of Shrewsbury, offer some of England's most beautiful countryside, with astounding views from the tops and a wealth of remote villages in which walkers can stop for a refreshing pint. The main centre for both hills is **CHURCH STRETTON**, accessible from Shrewsbury and Ludlow by train or bus #435. A pleasant if slightly touristy village, it has the **Shropshire Hills Information Centre** in Church Street (Easter & May–Oct Mon–Sat 10am–6pm, Sun noon–5pm; ☎01694/ 723 133), where you can pick up free literature on outdoor pursuits in the area. **Accommodation** is available at the *Belvedere Guest House*, Burway Road (☎01694/722 232; ④), *Littlebrook*, 38 Ludlow Rd (☎01694/722 307; ③), or *Highcliffe*, ten minutes' walk from the town on Madeira Walk (☎01694/722 908; ②). **Bike rental** is available from *Longmynd Cycles*, Sandford Court, Sandford Avenue (☎01694/722 367).

The **youth hostel** at **Bridges** (☎01588/650 656), five miles' hike west from Church Stretton near Ratlinghope, is a splendid base for walks, sitting between the Long Mynd and the **Stiperstones**, a remote range of boggy heather dotted with ancient cairns and earthworks. Eight miles east of Church Stretton, on the lower western slopes of Wenlock Edge near Longville-in-the-Dale, there's a **youth hostel** in the sumptuous surroundings of Wilderhope Manor (☎01694/771 363).

Craven Arms, the next stop down the rail line, is half a mile north of the tiny village of **STOKESAY**, which contains one of the most appealing manor houses in Britain. **Stokesay Castle** (April–Oct daily 10am–6pm; Nov–March Wed–Sun 10am–4pm; £2.30; EH) is the name for a collection of leaning, half-timbered buildings that span a period of over three hundred years, gathered around a neat grassy courtyard. The main block is the thirteenth-century fortified manor, with a vast banqueting hall that retains its central fireplace, rush-matted floor and unusually large old windows. Across the central courtyard is the black and yellow gatehouse, built more than three hundred years after the manor house yet forming a harmonious group with the main building and the tiny parish church, just over the lane. Although the church was largely rebuilt in the mid-seventeenth century, some of the original Norman features can still be seen.

BISHOP'S CASTLE, midway between Offa's Dyke and the southern edge of the Long Mynd, is a real treat – uncluttered, very pretty and full of fine secondhand book-shops and junk shops. **Buses** drop you at the bottom of the High Street, which winds past half-timbered frontages to the miniature Georgian **Town Hall** – this was England's smallest borough until 1967 – and the lurching **House on Crutches**. Stroll up past the town hall and veer to the right to reach the most renowned building in Bishop's Castle, the seventeenth-century **Three Tuns brewery** and its time-warped pub on Salop Street, which serves up traditional home brew. What must be England's most eccentric **tourist office** is housed in a secondhand shop called *Old Time*, at 29 High St (daily 10am–10pm; ☎01588/638 467; ②) – they can sort out **accommodation**, and offer rooms of their own. The *Castle Hotel* in Castle Square, at the top of High Street (☎01588/638 403; ④) is a wonderful **pub** and **restaurant**, with the added attraction of its own bowling green.

Five miles south of Bishop's Castle (Mon–Sat, bus #741–745), the modest village of **CLUN**, an excellent base for forest walks and jaunts on Offa's Dyke, embraces a **castle** (dawn–dusk; free) built soon after the Norman conquest to defend the Welsh borders. After several attacks it was finally abandoned in the sixteenth century and its most striking feature today is a vast grey-stone tower, raised on a mound cradled by the river below. *Clun Farm* on High Street (☎01588/640 432; ②) is one of the better **B&Bs**. The small **youth hostel** (☎01588/640 582) is in a converted watermill, just under a mile from the castle.

Ludlow

Tucked away in the southwestern corner of Shropshire, nearly thirty miles south of Shrewsbury, **LUDLOW** is one of the most picturesque towns in the Midlands. A strate-gically pivotal centre in the bitter wars between the expansionist English and tenacious Welsh, it boasts a vast eleventh-century **Castle** (daily Feb–May, Oct & Nov 10.30am–4pm; May–Oct 10.30am–5pm; £2), which served as the government seat for Wales and the Marches throughout the seventeenth century – in the 1950s, Ludlow was even considered as a candidate for the official capital of Wales. With much of its masonry intact and a spectacular setting above the River Teme, the castle makes a fine open-air theatre during the **Ludlow Festival** every June and July.

The castle entrance opens out on to the main market place, home of the new town **Museum** (Mon–Sat 10am–5pm; summer also Sun 10.30am–5pm; £1) and the intri-guing **Castle Lodge** (daily 10am–5pm; £1), predominantly Elizabethan in style, but influenced by occupants from the fourteenth century. In the ground-floor oak-panelled rooms, stained windows depict the coats of arms of Germans summoned by Henry VIII to help sack England's monasteries. In low beamed chambers upstairs, there's a display of Ludlow's chequered history, which omits the popular rumour that Mary Queen of Scots hid from Elizabeth's henchmen in the lodge's basement.

To the south of the castle lies a medieval grid of streets, most of them rebuilt during the eighteenth century and little touched since. **Broad Street** is the most attractive, containing many of Ludlow's five hundred listed buildings in its lines of half-timbered Tudor and red-brick Georgian houses. The town centre is bounded on the western side by the River Teme and on the eastern side by the old main road through the town, part of which is the old **Bull Ring**, home of the *Feathers Hotel*, one of England's finest Jacobean buildings. Reaching high over the surrounding Georgian rooftops is the 135-foot tower of the parish church of **St Laurence**, which easily lives up to the expectations created from afar: the fifteenth-century interior is magnificently proportioned, with vast windows allowing light to flood the mellow walls and floors. Saint Laurence is depicted in nearly thirty different tableaux of amazing detail on the east window of the chancel, while the church's **misericords** are among the finest in central England.

The **tourist office** (Mon–Sat 10am–5pm; summer also Sun 10.30am–5pm; ☎01584/ 875 053) is underneath the museum on the market place. First choice for accommodation is the very beautiful *Feathers Hotel* in the Bull Ring (☎01584/875 261; ⑨), an intricately decorated Jacobean pile; there are also cheery pub B&Bs at the *Wheatsheaf Inn*, next to the Town Gate on Lower Broad Street (☎01584/872 980; ③), and the *Blue Boar Inn* on Mill Street (☎01584/872 630; ③). The **youth hostel** (☎01584/872 472) is at the bottom of Lower Broad Street and there's a **campsite** a mile to the west of town at North Farm, Whitcliffe (☎01584/872 026). **Bike rental** is available from *Pearce Engineering* in Fishmore (☎01584/876 016). **Food** comes cheapest from *Aragon's*, in the northeastern corner of the market place on Church Street – a marked contrast to the generally overpriced tea rooms that litter the town, one exception being *DeGrey's Café* in Broad Street. Two **pubs** for good beer and better than average bar food are the *Horse and Jockey* on Old Street and the *Globe*, off the market place on Market Street.

Staffordshire

The miscellaneous and low-key landscapes of **Staffordshire** don't enthrall too many people, but the county packs in coach loads of visitors owing to the presence of **Alton Towers** – Britain's answer to Disney glitter, and the nation's most popular tourist attraction. The white-knuckle rides take vastly more money than do the hoteliers in the cathedral city of **Lichfield**, at the southern end of Staffordshire, and the main historic attraction hereabouts. It's not quite the only town worth visiting: there's the moorland town of **Leek**, and the old brewing capital of **Burton** – the latter ranking second behind Alton Towers in the popularity stakes. Neither Stoke-on-Trent, Staffordshire's largest city famous for its potteries, nor Stafford, the county town, need delay you at all, and there's nothing compulsive about Derby, a city closer in character to Staffordshire

ALTON TOWERS

Britain's largest amusement park and most popular tourist attraction, **Alton Towers** (mid-March to early Nov 9am–7pm or dusk; £16.50; ☎01538/702 200), fifteen miles east of Stoke, preserves its number one ranking by introducing new and more terrifying rides each season; if the white-knuckle stuff is too strong for you, there are endless food outlets to escape into, along with landscaped and themed gardens, and an array of less stressful fairground attractions.

SAMUEL JOHNSON

Eighteenth-century England's most celebrated wit and critic, **Samuel Johnson** was born above his father's bookshop in Lichfield's market square in 1709. From Lichfield he went to Pembroke College, Oxford, which he left in 1731 without having completed his degree. Disgruntled with academia, Johnson returned to Staffordshire as a teacher, before settling in Birmingham for three years, a period that saw his first pieces published in the *Birmingham Journal*.

In 1735 Johnson married Elizabeth Porter, a Birmingham friend's widow twenty years his senior, returning to his home district to open a private school in the village of Edial, three miles southwest of Lichfield. The school was no great success, so after two years the Johnsons abandoned the project and went to London with the young David Garrick, their star pupil. Journalism and essays were the mainstay of the Johnsons' penurious existence until publisher Robert Dodsley asked Samuel to consider compiling a **Dictionary of the English Language**, a project that nobody had undertaken before, and which was to occupy him for eight years prior to its publication in 1755. Massively learned and full of mordant wit ("lexicographer: a writer of dictionaries; a harmless drudge"), the *Dictionary* is one of Johnson's greatest legacies, although he was financially and emotionally stretched to breaking point by the workload it imposed upon him. Money problems continued to dog the writer – in 1759 he wrote the novel *Rasselas* in one week, in order to raise money for his mother's funeral – but a degree of financial stability came at last in the early 1760s, when the new king, George III, granted him a bursary of £300 per year.

In 1763 Johnson met James Boswell, a pushy young Scot who clung tenaciously to the cantankerous older man until he learned to like him. Their journey to Scotland resulted in one of the finest travel books ever written, **A Journey to the Western Isles of Scotland** (1775), in which Johnson's fascinated incredulity at the native way of life makes for utterly absorbing reading. Other publications from his final decade included a preface to Shakespeare's plays, a series of political tracts and the magnificent **Lives of the English Poets**. However, the work by which he is now best known is not one that he himself wrote – it is Boswell's **The Life of Samuel Johnson**, commenced on its subject's death in 1784, published in 1791, and still the English language's most full-blooded biography.

than to most of its own county. The best of Derbyshire is to be found in the Peak District – the southernmost part of the Pennines (see The Northwest).

Lichfield

The small city of **LICHFIELD**, a slow-moving but amiable place in the south of the county, demands a visit for one reason – its magnificent **Cathedral**. Standing on the site of a shrine built for the relics of Saint Chad around 700 AD, the cathedral was begun in 1085, substantially rebuilt in the thirteenth and fourteenth centuries, and is unique in possessing three spires – an appropriate distinction for a bishopric that once extended over virtually all of the Midlands. The **west front** is adorned by over one hundred statues of Biblical figures, English kings and the ancestors of Christ, some of them dating back to the thirteenth century but most of them nineteenth-century replacements of originals destroyed by Cromwell's troops. Even the central spire was demolished during the skirmishes – Lichfield justly claims to be the cathedral that was most damaged during the Civil War. Extensive and painstaking rebuilding and restoration work, which was begun immediately on the restoration of the monarchy in 1660, has gone on ever since, although the bulk of it was only completed by the end of the nineteenth century.

The **interior** is no less impressive, even if the dimensions are quite compact. The finest part of the main body of the church is the east end, where the choir, which is set at an angle of ten degrees to the line of the nave, contains the oldest surviving bit of the cathedral's structure – the first three bays are in the Early English style. On the south side of the choir nave stands a two-storey thirteenth-century extension whose upper level, with its fine minstrels' gallery, is where the head of Saint Chad used to be displayed to the faithful. Most impressive of all is the **Lady Chapel** at the furthest point of the east end, containing magnificent sixteenth-century windows from the Cistercian abbey at Herkenrode in Belgium, brought to England in 1802. However, the cathedral's greatest treasures are displayed in the beautiful **Chapter House**, where you'll find the eighth-century **Lichfield Gospels**, illuminated manuscripts of the complete gospels of Matthew and Mark and a fragment of the gospel of Luke. St Michael's Chapel, in the south transept, contains a bust of the city's most famous son, Samuel Johnson.

If you walk a couple of hundred yards south from the cathedral to Breadmarket Street, on the corner of the market place, you'll come to the **Samuel Johnson Birthplace Museum** (daily 10am–5pm; £1). Crammed with books, manuscripts and pictures, the museum pays handsome tribute to the great man. Opposite Johnson's house, in the middle of the market square, is the twelfth-century church of **St Mary**, home to the **Lichfield Heritage and Treasury Exhibition** (daily 10am–5pm; £1), an overdesigned presentation of the city's history, with illuminating sections on the Civil War and Regency periods. On either side of the market square stand ponderous statues of Samuel Johnson and his biographer, James Boswell; near Boswell's is a memorial to Edward Wightman, who in 1612 was burnt at the stake for heresy on this spot – the last person to be so punished for that crime.

Practicalities

Trains from Birmingham arrive at the central Lichfield City station, but many others use Lichfield Trent Valley station, on the northern fringe of the city, from where there's a frequent shuttle service to City station. The **tourist office** is in Donegal House, a warm red-brick house tucked in the southwestern corner of the market square on Bore Street (April–Oct Mon–Sat 9am–6pm, Sun 2–5pm; Nov–March Mon–Sat 9am–5pm; ☎01543/252 109). **Accommodation** is available in the *Duke of York* pub, east of the market square on Church Street (☎01543/255 171; ③), or the following **B&Bs**: *Altair House*, 21 Shakespeare Ave (☎01543/252 900; ③); the centrally located *Mrs Duval's* at 21–23 Dam St (☎01543/264 303; ③); or *Mrs Rule's*, Stowe Hill, at the top of Auchinleck Drive (☎01543/254 806; ③). For **food**, try the Chinese *Lee Gradens*, Tamworth Street; the *Prince of India*, 9 Bore St; or, on the other side of the market square, the oak-beamed *Propino Bibo*, 3–5 Lombard St. The *Horse and Jockey* on Sandford Street is a good, no-frills **pub**, but for bar food go to the *Greyhound* on Upper St John Street.

Burton-on-Trent

Twelve miles northeast of Lichfield along the ruler-straight Roman-built Ryknild Street (now the A38) lies **BURTON-ON-TRENT**, the major brewing town in Britain, with little to attract tourists save its store of good beer. Devotees of the hop can follow their noses to the **Bass Museum Brewery**, Horninglow Street (Mon–Fri 10am–4pm, Sat & Sun 10.30am–4pm; £3.45), where displays about the brewing process, the history of the industry in Burton, and even the Bass company's dray horses, culminate in a sample from the bar. You can extend your visit to include a tour of the **brewery** (£1.20), if there's enough demand. Serious ale-heads should sign up for one of the **brewery tours** at Ind Coope in Station Street (☎01283/531 111 ext. 2500), where £7.50 gets you a meal and two half-pints or £13 allows you a meal plus unlimited beer. Group bookings are preferred – if you're alone, they'll add you in with a visiting party.

Burton's **tourist office** is housed in the Octagon Centre on New Street (Mon–Fri 10am–5.30pm, 10am–4pm; ☎01283/516 609). There's **accommodation** at the *Abbey*

Lodge Hotel, 1 Meadow Rd, Burton Bridge (☎01283/530 657; ③), or the *Westlake Guest House* at 204 Ashby Rd (☎01283/546 717; ②). For **food**, traditional curry can be consumed at *George's Tandoori Restaurant*, 48–49 Station St (☎01283/33424), and the *Curry Centre*, 133 High St (☎01283/67362), both moderately priced. There's also an inexpensive daytime bistro at the trendy *Brewhouse Arts Centre* on Union Street. Unsurprisingly, Burton is stuffed with good **pubs** like the tap pub of the *Burton Bridge Brewery*, on Bridge Street, or the *Blue Posts*, a good Bass pub on the High Street. Further down the High Street, there's the Bass local, the *Dog Inn*, which is near two fine Marston's pubs, the *Anchor* (New Street) and the *Leopard* (Lichfield Street).

Nottinghamshire

With a population of over 270,000, **Nottingham** is one of England's big cities, a manufacturing centre for bikes, cigarettes, pharmaceuticals and lace – though it's more famous for its association with **Robin Hood**, the legendary thirteenth-century outlaw. Unfortunately the lair of Hood's bitter enemy, the Sheriff of Nottingham, is long gone, and today the city is at its most diverting in the Lace Market, whose cramped streets are crowded with the mansion-like warehouses of the Victorian lacemakers. The county town is flanked to the north by the gritty towns and villages of what was, until recently, the Nottinghamshire coalfield, and to the south by the commuter villages of the Nottinghamshire Wolds, neither of them areas that are going to hold your attention. Moving east, the thin remains of **Sherwood Forest** form The Dukeries, named after the five dukes who owned most of this area and preserved at least part of the ancient broad-leaved forest. Three of the four remaining estates – Thoresby, Worksop and Welbeck – are still in private hands, but **Clumber Park** is now owned by the National Trust and offers charming woodland walks. Beyond lies the market town of **Southwell**, whose main attraction is its fine Norman Minster.

Nottingham

Controlling a strategic crossing over the Trent, the Saxon town of **NOTTINGHAM** was built on one of a pair of sandstone hills whose 130-foot cliffs look out over the valley. What was once "one of the most beautiful towns in England", according to Daniel Defoe, was transformed, in the second half of the eighteenth century, by the expansion of the lace and hosiery industries. Within the space of fifty years, Nottingham's population increased from 10,000 to 50,000, the resulting slum becoming a hotbed of radicalism. In the 1810s, a recession provoked the hard-pressed workers into action. They struck against the employers and, calling themselves **Luddites**, after an apprentice turned protestor by the name of Ned Ludlam, raided the factories to smash the knitting machines – just the first of several troubled periods. The worst of Nottingham's slums were eventually cleared in the late nineteenth century, when the city centre assumed its present structure, with the main commercial area ringed by alternating industrial and residential districts. Crass postwar development has embedded the remnants of the city's past in a townscape that will be dishearteningly familiar if you've seen a few other English commercial centres.

The Town
The **Old Market Square** is still the heart of the city, an airy open area watched over by the neo-Baroque **Council House**. From here, it's a five-minute walk west up Friar Lane to **Nottingham Castle** (daily 10am–5pm; Mon–Fri free, Sat & Sun £1), whose heavily restored gateway stands above a folkloric bronze of Robin Hood, with plaques depicting his Merry Men on the wall behind. Beyond the gateway, lawns slope up to

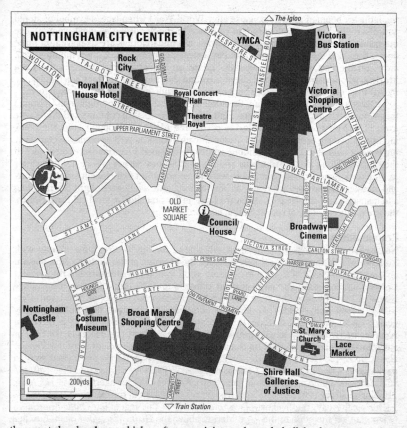

the squat ducal **palace**, which – after remaining a charred shell for forty years – was opened as the country's first provincial museum in 1878. The mansion occupies the site of the castle's upper bailey and, just outside the main entrance, two sets of steps lead down into the maze of ancient caves that honeycomb the cliff beneath. One set leads into **Mortimer's Hole** (tours Mon–Sat 3–6 daily; 50p), a 300-foot shaft along which, so the story goes, the young Edward III and his chums crept in October 1330 to capture the Queen Mother, Isabella, and her lover, Roger Mortimer – his would-be usurpers and the murderers of his father, Edward II. The interior of the ducal mansion boasts the **Story of Nottingham Galleries**, a lively and entertaining account of the city's development – in particular, look out for a small but exquisite collection of late medieval **alabaster carvings**, an art form for which Nottingham once had an international reputation. It's worth walking up to the top floor too, for a turn round the main **picture gallery**, a curious assortment of nineteenth-century romantic paintings in which the works of Richard Parkes Bonington are the most distinguished.

A couple of minutes' walk east of the castle is the **Costume Museum**, 51 Castle Gate (daily 10am–5pm; free), the best of the city's other museums. In the 1760s, Nottingham saw the earliest experiments to produce machine-made lace, but it was not until the 1840s that the city produced the world's first fully machined lace garments. After that the industry boomed until its collapse after World War I when lace, a symbol of an old and discredited order, suddenly had no place in the wardrobe of most women. The museum's lace-trimmed dresses, accessories and underclothes are displayed on three floors, the changing fashions illustrated by a sequence of dioramas. A few minutes' walk away, on the east side of the Market Square up along Victoria Street, is the **Lace Market**, whose narrow lanes and alleys surround the church of **St Mary's**, a handsome, mostly fifteenth-century structure built on top of the hill that was once the Saxon town.

St Mary's abuts High Pavement, the administrative centre of Nottingham in Georgian times, and here you'll find the **Shire Hall**, whose Neoclassical columns and dome date from 1770. Now housing the **Galleries of Justice** (daily 10am–5pm; £3.95), the building boasts two superbly preserved Victorian courtrooms as well as some spectacularly unpleasant old cells. The surrounding sandstone-trimmed Victorian warehouses are at their most striking along **Broadway** and adjacent **Stoney Street**, where – at the corner of Woolpack Lane – a particularly fine warehouse boasts an extravagent stone doorway and slender high-arched windows, as well as long attic windows to light the mending and inspection rooms. Nearby, on Byard Lane, is the first shop of local lad **Paul Smith**, the great success story of recent British fashion.

Practicalities

Nottingham **train station** is on the south side of the city centre, a five-minute walk from the Market Square. Most long-distance buses arrive at the **Victoria bus station** on the oppposite side of town, a five-minute stroll from the centre through the *Victoria Centre* shopping mall. The city's **tourist office** is on the ground floor of the Council House at 1 Smithy Row (summer Mon–Fri 8.30am–5pm, Sat 9am–5pm, Sun 10am–4pm; winter closed Sun; ☎0115/947 0661). Nottingham has around fifty **hotels**, mostly geared up for the business trade. In the centre, the plushest place to stay is the *Royal Moat House Hotel*, in the Royal Centre on Wollaton Street (☎0115/941 4444; ⑤–⑨). For a comfortable mid-range hotel on the northern edge of the city centre, try the *Regency House Hotel*, 198 Derby Rd (☎0115/947 4520; ⑤). The city's **B&Bs** are tucked away in the suburbs – one exception is *Greenwood Lodge*, 5 Third Ave, Sherwood Rise (☎0115/962 1206; ③), a mile or so north of the centre. An even cheaper alternative is *The Igloo*, 110 Mansfield Rd (☎0115/947 5250), a backpackers' haven in the centre.

During the day, the liveliest place to **eat** at is at the vegetarian *Out-to-Munch*, 15 Goosegate, on the edge of the Lace Market above the *Hiziki Wholefood Shop*. Another slightly more expensive vegetarian option is the *Salamander* restaurant, 23 Heathcote St. Two excellent Indian restaurants are *Anilas Indian Restaurant*, 23 Goldsmith St, and *Saagar Tandoori*, 473 Mansfield Rd, a mile or so north of the city centre. As for **pubs** head for the *Lincolnshire Poacher*, 161 Mansfield Rd, which has the city's widest selection of bottled and real ales. *The Peacock*, 11 Mansfield Rd, is equipped with push-button bells to ring for waiter service, while the *Newmarket Inn*, on Parliament Street, is more low-key. *Ye Olde Trip to Jerusalem Inn* is an incredible pub carved into the rock below the castle, and puportedly a meeting point for soldiers gathering for the Third Crusade.

Nottingham's **nightclub** scene is boisterous and fast-moving. *Deluxe*, a huge place spread over three floors on James's Street, is currently the city's trendiest club, though *The House*, a newish club on the corner of Huntingdon and King Edward streets, looks set to rival it. *Rock City*, on Talbot Street, is a giant-sized, very busy nightclub, with different music and a different crowd each night. For **live music**, both popular and classical, most big names play at the *Royal Centre Concert Hall* on Wollaton Street. On a more sedate note, the *Broadway Cinema*, 14 Broad St, is the best **cinema** in town, featuring the pick of mainstream and avant-garde films. *Gatsbys*, on Huntingdon Street, is the most popular of the city's **gay** bars, with a busy active scene, while *Triangles*, at the top of North Sherwood Street, is Nottingham's main **lesbian** pub, slightly cliquey but worth a visit for some serious drinking.

West of Nottingham: Wollaton Hall and Eastwood

From the city centre, bus #25 runs three miles west to **Wollaton Hall**, a flamboyant Elizabethan mansion built for Sir Francis Willoughby in the 1580s by the architect of Longleat, Robert Smythson (see p.211). Perched on top of a grassy knoll, the hall presents a grand facade of chimneys, turrets and tiers to the surrounding parkland, but the interior, refashioned in the nineteenth century, now houses a tedious natural history museum (Mon–Sat 10am–4pm, Sun 1–4pm; Mon–Fri free, Sat & Sun £1).

D.H. Lawrence was born in the coalmining village of **EASTWOOD**, about six miles west of Nottingham. The mine closed years ago, and Eastwood's something of a post-industrial eyesore, but Lawrence's childhood home, a tiny two-up, two-down terraced house, has survived, refurbished as the **D. H. Lawrence Birthplace Museum**, 8a Victoria St (daily April–Oct 10am–5pm; Nov–March 10am–4pm; £1.50), though none of the original furnishings and fittings have lasted. **Buses** #R12 and #R13 depart for the thirty-minute trip to Eastwood every half-hour.

North of Nottingham: Newstead Abbey and Hardwick Hall

In 1539, Henry VIII granted **Newstead Abbey** (house April–Sept daily noon–6pm; grounds daily April–Sept 9am–8pm, Oct–March 9am–5pm; £3.50, grounds only £1.60), eleven miles north of Nottingham, to Sir John Byron, who demolished most of the church and converted the prior's lodgings into a family home. In 1798, **Lord Byron** inherited Newstead, then little more than a ruin. He restored part of the building, but most of the present structure dates from later renovations, which created the incoherent mansion of today. Inside, the poet's old apartments house a modest display of manuscripts and memorabilia, but most people come here to visit the surrounding **gardens**, a delightful combination of lake, Gothic waterfalls, yew tunnels and Japanese-style rockeries, complete with odd-looking pagodas. **Bus** #63 leaves hourly for the 25-minute trip to the gates of Newstead Abbey, a mile or so from the house.

Four miles northwest of Newstead Abbey, just over the Derbyshire border, lies **Hardwick Hall** (house April–Oct Wed, Thurs, Sat & Sun 12.30–5pm or sunset; gardens same months daily noon–5.30pm; house & gardens £5.50, gardens £2; NT), a startling sixteenth-century house whose walls comprise more glass than stone. Inside, there's a magnificent show of furniture and tapestries, many of which were listed in an inventory taken in 1601; outside, Longhorn cattle roam the grounds, mingling with a flock of Whiteface Woodland sheep.

Sherwood Forest and Clumber Park

Most of **Sherwood Forest**, once a vast royal forest of oak, birch and bracken covering all of west Nottinghamshire, was cleared in the eighteenth century, and nowadays it's difficult to imagine the protection it provided for generations of outlaws, the most famous of whom was **Robin Hood**. There's no "true story" of Robin's life – the earliest reference to him, in Langland's *Piers Plowman* of 1377, treats him as a fiction – but to the balladeers of fifteenth-century England, who invented most of the folklore, this was hardly the point. For them, Robin was a symbol of yeoman decency, a semi-mythological opponent of corrupt clergymen and evil officers of the law. In the early tales, although Robin shows sympathy for the peasant, he has rather more respect for the decent noble-man, and he's never credited with robbing the rich to give to the poor. This and other parts of the legend, such as Maid Marion and Friar Tuck, were added later.

Robin Hood may lack historical authenticity, but it hasn't discouraged the county council from spending thousands of pounds sustaining the **Major Oak**, the dilapidated tree where Maid Marion and Robin are supposed to have married. The Major Oak is a few minutes' walk from the entrance to **Sherwood Forest Country Park** (daily dawn–dusk; free), half a mile north of the village of Edwinstowe, itself twenty-odd miles north of Nottingham. Beside the park entrance, the **visitor centre** (daily 10.30am–4.30pm; free) retells the outlaw's story in the "Robyn Hode and Mery Scherwode" exhibition; the surrounding 450 acres of oak and silver birch is crisscrossed with footpaths.

North of Ollerton, Edwinstowe's immediate neighbour, the A614 trims the edge of Thoresby Park to reach, after six miles, the eastern entrance to **Clumber Park** (daily dawn–dusk), four thousand acres of park and woodland lying to the south of Worksop. The estate was once the country seat of the Dukes of Newcastle and it was here in the 1770s that they constructed a grand mansion overlooking Clumber Lake. The house was dismantled in 1938, when the duke sold the estate, and today all that remains of the lakeside buildings are the Gothic Revival **Chapel** (daily 10am–4pm), built for the seventh duke in the 1880s, and the adjacent stable block, which now houses a National Trust office (April–Oct daily 1–5pm), shop and café, two miles or so from the A614.

East Midlands **bus** #33 leaves Nottingham hourly for the fifty-minute trip to Edwinstowe, before travelling on up the west side of Clumber Park en route to Worksop – get off at Carburton for the two-mile walk to the NT office in Clumber Park. There's also a **campsite** (April–Sept; ☎01909/482 303) in the walled garden a few minutes' walk north of the chapel. Amongst the villages within easy striking distance of the park, unassuming **Edwinstowe** has a couple of hotels and a handful of **B&Bs**, the cheapest of which is *The Cottages*, 1 Church St (☎01636/824 383; ②).

Southwell

SOUTHWELL, some fourteen miles northeast of Nottingham, is a sedate backwater distinguished by **Southwell Minster**, whose twin west towers are visible for miles around, and the fine mansions facing it along Church Street. Built at the beginning of the twelfth century – although some elements were added later – the Norman design predominates, from the imposing west towers through to the forceful, dog-tooth-decorated doorways. Inside, the nave's heavy stonework ends abruptly with the clumsy mass of the fourteenth-century screen, beyond which lies the Early English **Choir** and the amazing **Chapter House**. The latter is embellished with naturalistic foliage dating from the late thirteenth century – the earliest carving of its type in England.

The **bus** service from Nottingham to Southwell is excellent, so there's no real reason to stay, though there are several decent **hotels** and **B&Bs**, including the *Bramley Apple*, near the minster at 51 Church St (☎01636/813 675; ③), with modest rooms and serving good, inexpensive meals. Another option is *The Old Forge*, 2 Burbage Lane (☎0636/813 257; ④), a comfortable four-bedroomed B&B, a few minutes' walk north of the minster.

Leicestershire

The compact county of **Leicestershire** is one of the more anonymous of the English shires, though **Leicester** itself is saved from mediocrity by its role as a focal point for Britain's Asian community. To the west of Leicester, a series of industrial settlements are enlivened by the substantial remains of the castle at **Ashby-de-la-Zouch**. In the northeast lie **Melton Mowbray**, the pork-pie capital of the world, and **Belvoir Castle**, exhibiting the art collection of the Duke and Duchess of Rutland.

Leicester

On first impression **LEICESTER** is a drearily modern place, but further inspection reveals traces of the town's rich medieval and Roman past. The Romans developed

Ratae Coritanorum (Leicester's predecessor) as a fortified town on the Fosse Way, the military road running from Lincoln to Cirencester. Subsequently, its medieval castle became the base of the Earls of Leicester, the most distinguished of whom was Simon de Montfort, who forced Henry III to convene the first English Parliament in 1265. Since the late seventeenth century, Leicester has been a centre of the hosiery trade and it was this industry that attracted hundreds of Asian immigrants to settle here in the 1950s and 1960s. Today, about a third of Leicester's population is Asian and the city elected the country's first Asian MP, Keith Vaz, in 1987. There's also a large Afro-Caribbean community, which stages the country's second biggest street festival, after the Notting Hill Carnival (see p.113), on the first weekend in August.

The Town

Leicester's landmark Victorian **clock tower** stands on the west side of the city centre at East Gates, midway between the bus and train stations. From here, the old High Street runs west to Silver Street, which becomes Guildhall Lane and leads to **St Martin's Cathedral**, a much modified eleventh-century structure that incorporates a fine medieval wooden roof in the north porch. Next door is the **Guildhall** (Mon–Sat 10am–5.30pm, Sun 2–5.30pm; free), a half-timbered building which has served, variously, as the town hall and police station, but is now a small museum, displaying fearsome-looking manacles and the like.

From the Guildhall, it's a short walk west to the ring road and, just beyond, the Saxon church of **St Nicholas**, reached by keeping to the right of the *Holiday Inn*. The adjacent **Jewry Wall**, a chunk of Roman masonry 18ft high and 73ft long, was a part of the Emperor Hadrian's public baths, although his grand scheme was spoilt by the engineers, who miscalculated the line of the aqueduct that was to pipe in the water, and so bathers had to rely on a hand-filled cistern replenished from the river. The **Jewry Wall and Archaeology Museum** (Mon–Sat 10am–5.30pm, Sun 2–5.30pm; free), abutting the baths, charts Leicester's history from prehistoric to medieval times. Highlights include a fine assortment of Roman relics – from Fosse Way milestones to the splendid Peacock mosaic pavement – and some beautiful medieval glass.

Dodging the traffic, cross St Augustine Road to the south to arrive at the **Castle Gardens**, which, running alongside a canalized portion of the Soar, incorporate the **castle motte**, the mound where Leicester's Norman fortifications once stood. Walking through the gardens, you re-emerge on the Newarke, the location of the **Newarke Houses Museum** (Mon–Sat 10am–5.30pm, Sun 2–5.30pm; free), two Jacobean houses that make a delightful setting for an extensive exploration of the town's social history. Behind the museum, in Castle View, is the attractive church of **St Mary de Castro** (open Wed & Fri lunchtime, Thurs pm & Sat 2–5pm), whose mixture of architectural styles incorporates several Norman features, notably a five-seater sedilia in the chancel. In the vicinity of the church lie the scant remains of the medieval castle, including the ruined Turret Gateway, tucked behind the brick facade of the courthouse.

Nearby, stranded between the carriageways of the ring road, is the distinctive **Magazine Gateway**, once the medieval entrance to the Newarke. Of more interest is the modern **Jain Centre**, on Oxford Street, reached by the pedestrian underpass near the *Magazine*. The rites and beliefs of the Jains, a long-established Indian religious sect, focus on an extreme reverence for all living things – traditional customs include the wearing of gauze masks to prevent the inhalation of passing insects. The centre's splendid marble-fronted building contains one of the few Jain temples in western Europe and visitors may enter the lobby or, better, view the interior (Mon–Fri 2–5pm; call first if visiting outside these hours on ☎0116/254 3091).

From the Jain Centre, it's about ten minutes' walk southeast to New Walk, a tree-lined promenade that's the home of the **Leicestershire Museum and Art Gallery** (Mon–Sat 10am–5.30pm, Sun 2–5.30pm; free). Upstairs you'll find the country's largest collection of German Expressionists, as well as works by Walter Sickert, Jacob Epstein, Laura Knight and Stanley Spencer. On the ground floor, the Egyptian Gallery features a collection of mummies brought from Egypt as souvenirs in the 1880s.

About half a mile north of the city centre, **Abbey Park** is a pleasant place to take a stroll, though nothing remains of the Augustinian abbey where Cardinal Wolsey died in 1530, on his way to London to face charges of high treason. Not far away, to the northeast of the park, the area of **Belgrave** has become the focus of Leicester's Gujarati community, and the Belgrave Road is lined with Asian goldsmiths and jewellers, saree shops and Asian restaurants. During Diwali, the Hindu Festival of Light held in October or November, there are illuminations the length of the road, drawing thousands of Asian visitors from all over the country.

Practicalities

Leicester **train station** is situated on London Road just to the southeast of the city centre, and ten minutes' walk from **St Margaret's bus station**, which is on the north side of the centre, just off Gravel Street. There's a **tourist office** at the bus station (Mon–Sat 9am–5pm; summer Sun also10am–4pm; ☎0116/251 1301) and another at 7/9 Every St on Town Hall Square (Mon–Fri 9am–5.30pm, Sat 9am–5pm; Easter–Sept also Sun 10am–4pm; ☎0116/265 0555). For **hotel** accommodation, *Spindle Lodge* has a pleasantly quiet setting, south of the train station at 2 West Walk, off New Walk (☎0116/255 1380; ⑤) or, close by, there's the family-owned *Belmont Hotel*, on De Montfort Street (☎0116/254 4773; ⑦, or ⑤ at weekends). One of the cheapest places to stay is *Richard's Backpackers Hostel*, 157 Wanlip Lane, Birstall (☎0116/267 3107; ①), on the northern edge of town; take bus #61 or *Midland Fox* #125 from the Haymarket.

The most famous and longest established of the **Indian restaurants** on the Belgrave Road is *Bobbys*, at no. 154–56, which is strictly vegetarian and uses no garlic or onions; other alternatives include the *Sayonara Thali*, at no. 49, and *Friends Tandoori*, at no. 43. In the centre, *The Case*, on Hotel Street, is a chic place to eat and during the day the *Bread and Roses*, below *Blackthorn Books* on the High Street, serves good vegetarian food. As for **pubs**, the *Rainbow and Dove*, on Charles Street, attracts real ale enthusiasts; the *Charlotte*, on Oxford Street, features bands on most nights; and the *Magazine*, Newarke Street, is a student haunt. On the **gay and lesbian** scene, the best pubs are the *Dover Castle*, Dover Street, and the *Pineapple*, on Burleys Way. The *Phoenix Arts Centre*, Newarke Street (☎0116/255 4854), is the best venue in town for the performing arts and doubles up as an independent cinema, while Leicester's *Coliseum Centre*, Belgrave Road (☎0116/266 9477), showcases acts from India.

Melton Mowbray and Belvoir

MELTON MOWBRAY is famous for pork pies, an unaccountably popular English snack made of compressed balls of meat and gristle encased in wobbly jelly and thick pastry. The pie is the traditional repast of the fox-hunting fraternity, for whom the town of Melton, lying close to the region's most important hunts – Belvoir, Cottesmore and Quorn – has long been a favourite spot. The antics of the aristocratic huntsmen are legend – in 1837 the Marquis of Waterford literally painted the town's buildings red, hence the saying – but with the snowballing opposition to blood sports, the days of the tally-ho brigade may be numbered. If you want to sample the genuine traditional hunters' pie, it is available in Melton only at *Dickinson & Morris*, on Nottingham Street.

Heading northeast from Melton Mowbray along the A607, it's about ten miles to the lip of the escarpment overlooking the rich farmland of the Vale of Belvoir (pronounced "beaver"). Down below in the valley, on the largest hill around, stands **Belvoir Castle** (April–Sept Tues–Thurs & Sat 11am–5pm, Sun 11am–6pm; Oct Sun only 11am–5pm; £4.25), an incoherent castellated pile, rebuilt several times over the centuries, most recently in 1816. The castle may not be much to look at, but the Duke and Duchess of Rutland's hoard of art is another story. Highlights include the enormous Gobelin tapestries and paintings by Jan Steen and David Teniers the Younger, and Hans Holbein's portrait of Henry VIII. German-born Holbein was introduced to the king on his second visit to England, in 1532, and Henry was so pleased by his first portraits, which picked a delicate line between flattery and honesty, that he kept him employed until the artist's death in 1543. Belvoir also attracts hundreds of day-trippers for its weekend "medieval" jousts or some other special event.

Oakham and around

Well-heeled **OAKHAM**, some twenty-five miles east of Leicester, has a long history as a market town, its prosperity bolstered by Oakham School, a late sixteenth-century foundation that's become one of the country's more exclusive public schools. The town's stone terraces and Georgian villas are too often interrupted by the mundanely modern to assume any grace, though the L-shaped Market Place, where the sturdy awnings of the octagonal Butter Cross shelter the old town stocks, is a delight. On the north side of the Market Place stands the **Banqueting Hall** (April–Oct Tues–Sat 10am–1pm & 2–5.30pm, Sun 2–5.30pm; Nov–March Tues–Sat 10am–1pm & 2–4pm, Sun 2–4pm; free), all that remains of the town's castle except for the odd fragment of wall. Built for Walkelin de Ferrers in 1191, the hall is a good example of Norman domestic architecture; inside, the whitewashed walls are covered with horseshoes, the result of the ancient custom by which every lord or lady, king or queen, is obliged to present an ornamental horseshoe when they first set foot in Oakham.

Close by, Oakham School is housed in a series of impressive ironstone buildings along the west edge of the Market Place. On the right-hand side of the school, a narrow lane allows sight of more of the buildings on its way to **All Saints'** church, whose heavy tower and spire rises high above the town. Dating from the thirteenth century, the church is distinguished by the medieval carvings along the piers beside the chancel, with Christian scenes and symbols set opposite dragons, grotesques, devils and demons. Finally, there's the sizeable **Rutland County Museum** (Mon–Sat 10am–5pm, Sun 2–4pm), a brief signposted walk from the Market Place along the High Street, where an assortment of agricultural tools and Rutland County mementos is enlivened by a lithograph of a disconcertingly huge prize-winning heifer.

HALLATON HARE PIE SCRAMBLE AND BOTTLE KICKING

Hallaton, eleven miles southwest of Oakham, is Leicestershire's most attractive village, its postcard prettiness composed of neat ironstone cottages around a well-kept village green, embellished by a medieval church, a conical Butter Cross and a duck pond. Every Easter Monday, this tranquil scene is disturbed by the **Hare Pie Scramble and Bottle-Kicking** contest, when the inhabitants of Hallaton fight for pieces of pie with the people of nearby Medbourne. The participants gather at the *Fox Inn* by the village pond, then proceed to kick small barrels of ale round a hill and across a stream, as has been the custom for several hundred years – though no one has the faintest idea why. The village **Museum** (May–Oct Sat & Sun 2.30–5pm; free) does its best to shed some light on the business.

With regular services from Leicester and Peterborough, Oakham **train station** lies on the west side of town, five minutes' walk from the centre. **Buses** connect the town with Leicester, Nottingham and Melton Mowbray, arriving at St John Street, close to the Market Place. Should you decide to stay, the **tourist office**, at the library on Catmose Street (Mon–Wed 9.30am–7pm, Thurs 9.30am–1pm, Fri 9.30am–5pm, Sat 9.30am–1pm; ☎01572/724 329), will book accommodation at no charge. Alternatively, there are a couple of handy **B&Bs** near the High Street on Northgate, at no. 20 (☎01572/756 153; ②), and at no. 27 (☎01572/755 057; ②), whilst the *Whipper-In Hotel*, on the Market Place (☎01572/756 971; ⑥), features lushly decorated bedrooms and a liberal sprinkling of antiques. For **food**, the *Whipper-In* also serves excellent bar snacks, as does the *Rutland Angler*, nearby on Mill Street.

Northamptonshire

NORTHAMPTONSHIRE's three largest towns – **Northampton**, Kettering and Corby – are of limited appeal, but outside of these, the county is a swathe of rural beauty, modest hills and patchy woodland, cradling immaculately preserved villages, country estates and magnificent churches. Among these is the country's finest Saxon church at **Brixworth**; the idyllic village of **Sulgrave**, ancestral home of George Washington; **Boughton House**, whose art collection rivals any in the country; and **Geddington**, home of Edward I's beautiful memorial to his queen.

Northampton and around

If it wasn't for the great fire that swept through **NORTHAMPTON** in 1675, the county town might have more going for it – as it is, despite its setting by the River Nene, the place is bland and predominantly modern. Its churches and sparse Georgian remains, however, harbour a few architectural surprises and it's the obvious place to gather information before checking out the rest of the county.

The most prominent feature of central Northampton is the heavy clock tower and a lavish glass dome of **All Saints Church** (daily 9am–3pm), south of Market Square on George Row. The church's pillared portico is reminiscent of St Paul's Cathedral and topped by a statue of Charles II in a toga, raised to commemorate his donation of a thousand tons of timber after the 1675 fire. East of All Saints, along St Giles Street lies the **Guildhall** (tours Tues 2.15pm; £1.50; Thurs 2.15pm; £2.50), built in three stages (1864, 1892 and 1992) yet perfectly symmetrical. Ornate carvings surround the arches of the earlier structure; among them you can spot scenes central to the county's history – look out for Mary Queen of Scots with her head on the block, the Battle of Naseby and the Great Fire.

The **Central Museum and Art Gallery** (Mon–Wed, Fri & Sat 10am–5pm, Thurs 10am–8pm, Sun 2–5pm; free), a hundred yards south on Guildhall Road, marks the town's industrial heritage with an exceptional display of shoes, belonging to everyone from Queen Victoria to Elton John. The most original, though, is a *kadaitcha*, made by Australian aborigines from emu feathers and women's hair, and used to fool trackers. North of Market Square, up Sheep Street is Northampton's oldest building, the **Church of the Holy Sepulchre** (May–Sept Tues noon–4pm, Wed noon–2pm & Fri 2–4pm; free), built in 1100 and one of only four round churches in the country.

Just outside town, Riverside Park is the site chosen for a new **National Fairground Museum**, due to open in 1996. Beneath a large marquee, the museum will pack in the largest surviving dodgems and a traditional galloping horse roundabout among a whole collection of fairground memorabilia dating from the eighteenth century; ask at the tourist office for details of opening hours.

Practicalities

A tiny section of the castle, where Thomas à Beckett was tried in 1164, remains beside Northampton's **train station**, ten minutes' walk west of the centre. Buses and coaches pull into the **bus station** on Lady's Lane, five minutes' walk from the **tourist office** (Mon–Fri 9.30am–5pm, Sat 9.30am–4pm; summer also Sun 10.30am–2.30pm; ☎01604/ 22677) opposite the Guildhall at 10 St Giles St. The plushest **hotel** in the centre is *The Angel* on Bridge Street (☎01604/21661; ⑦), a popular eighteenth-century coaching inn. Further out of town, at 407 Wellingborough Rd, *Abington Park Guest House* (☎01604/ 35072; ③) is a cosy **B&B**; nearby *Abington Lodge*, 13 Ardington Rd (☎01604/33128; ③), offers similar facilities.

For **food**, there's the excellent *Laughing Lentil* at 48 Bridge St, a homely, vegetarian restaurant; in the evening try *Coconut Grove*, 15 Wellington Place (☎01604 38187) for moderately priced, spicy Caribbean food. On Gold Street, *The Mine* serves Mexican specialities in an intimate setting. As for **nightlife**, the town's *Royal Theatre*, on Guildhall Road, retains its glamorous nineteenth-century interior, while the newer *Derngate*, on the same street, has the best acoustics. *Roadmender* pub on Lady's Lane hosts live jazz and rock, while the popular *Zone & Ritzy* on Weedon Road is your best bet for a night out clubbing.

Brixworth, Earls Barton and Stoke Bruerne

At **BRIXWORTH**, six miles north of Northampton (bus #62 or #X61), is the Anglo-Saxon church **All Saints Church** (daily 10am–5pm), whose most unusual feature is a cylindrical stair-turret added to the western clock tower in the ninth century. Inside, the uncluttered nave's whitewashed walls set off the stonework, also prominent in the triple archway set high up on the west wall. At the east end the rounded apse, modelled on the Roman basilica style, has been modified, but still incorporates three eighth-century pillars.

Another ecclesiastical gem lies six miles east of Northampton at **EARLS BARTON** (buses #45, 46 or 47 from Northampton), a growing village encircling **All Saints Church** (daily 9am–5pm). The church's eighty-foot tower is typically Saxon, a solid stone block whose beamed effect suggests an earlier timber construction. The rest of the church is newer, though Norman arcading in the choir has not been eclipsed by medieval additions which include a fine painted screen.

Seven miles south of Northampton, the Grand Union canal enters England's longest navigable tunnel at **STOKE BRUERNE**. Before the advent of steam tugs in the 1870s, boats were pushed through the two-mile-long Blisworth tunnel by "legging" before being relieved by a tow-horse. This exhaustive task is fully explained in the excellent **Canal Museum** (April–Oct daily 10am–6pm; Nov–March Tues–Sun 10am–4pm; £2.50), housed in a converted corn mill half a mile from the tunnel at the top of a flight of five locks. Outside the museum, there's the obligatory pub, *The Boat Inn*, stocked with narrow boat trinkets, the moderate to expensive *Bruernes Lock Restaurant* and the delightful *Old Chapel Tea Rooms*, which has a superb display of local art work. On the canalfront *Wharf Cottage* offers very cosy **rooms** (☎01604/862 174; ③).

Sulgrave

Fifteen miles southwest of Northampton in the picturesque village of **SULGRAVE**, is the home of George Washington's ancestors, **Sulgrave Manor** (April–Oct Mon, Tues, Thurs & Fri 2–5.30pm, Sat & Sun 10.30am–1pm & 2–5.30pm, Aug opens 10.30am; March, Nov & Dec closes 4.30pm; £3). Built in 1539, the house was in the family until 1656, when Colonel John, great grandfather of the American president, set sail for the New World. Despite the fact that George Washington never set foot in the place, Sulgrave has taken on the air of a shrine to American democracy, with a small

museum dedicated to the man. The house is actually relatively free of Washington memorabilia, leaving the architecture to speak for itself, though on most summer weekends the house is taken over by local historians dressed in period costume. **Accommodation** is available in the village at the excellent *Star Inn* (☎01295/760 389; ④), which also does good bar meals.

Rothwell, Rushton and Harrington

Just off the A6, fifteen miles north of Northampton, **ROTHWELL** (pronounced "Rowell") is an unremarkable market town but for its centre, a square market place with **Jesus Hospital**, barely changed since it was built in 1535, and the spireless **Holy Trinity Church** (10am–noon) flanking its southern side. Inside, there's a fine set of thirteenth-century sedilia beside choir stalls carved with mythical animals and wide-eyed faces; and don't miss the thousand or so bones stored in the macabre charnel. The focus of the market square – the scene of Rothwell Fair in the week following Trinity Sunday – is **Market House**, built in 1577 by Thomas Tresham, a convert to Catholicism who stood by his faith despite Elizabeth I's Protestant controls. He was imprisoned and heavily fined, but was so passionate about his belief that he expressed it in architecture, building curious monuments based on auspicious religious themes.

Tresham's most bizarre conception is the **Triangular Lodge** (April–Sept daily 10am–6pm; £1.50; EH) in **RUSHTON**, two miles east of Rothwell. A play on the Trinity, the lodge has three sides, dedicated to the Father, the Son and the Holy Ghost and each is 33ft long, with three windows and three gables. Even the central chimney topping the three storeys is triangular. Built of limestone and ironstone to give a striped effect, this was the recusant's only completed building, and certainly his most ingenious. Only two of the date stones around the lodge are "true" – his release from prison in 1593, and the construction of the lodge in 1595. The rest form an arithmetical puzzle: subtracting 1593 from the other figures gives the date of the crucifixion, the Virgin Mary's death and so forth. The entrance on "God's" side leads inside, where the whitewashed walls are interrupted only by triangular windows and fireplaces.

Five miles west of Rushton, just outside the tiny village of **HARRINGTON**, the intriguing **Carpet Baggers Aviation Museum** (March–Oct Sat & Sun 10am–5pm; £2) occupies the site of a World War II intelligence base. This is a specialist interest museum, run by ex-carpet baggers who were instrumental in sending secret agents to the continent. Part of the museum contains crushed remains of planes, mangled engine parts, bombs and bullets collected from the area by a dedicated member of the Carpet Baggers Association. A second building, where Colonel Colby devised the CIA, is stocked with 1940s photographs and newspapers, leaflets dropped into Europe by the Americans, and a selection of weapons. The café, in the original intelligence room, has a video showing the making of PLUTO, an eighty-mile-long pipeline built in Corby to carry fuel under the Channel to the continent in time for D-day in 1944.

Boughton and around

None of Northamptonshire's stately homes is as grand or opulent as **Boughton House** (house Aug daily 2–5pm; £4.50 grounds May–Sept daily except Fri 1–5pm; £1.50; free for disabled visitors), the centre of an 11,000-acre estate, which lies northeast of Northampton between Kettering and Corby, incorporates five villages and has been owned by the Dukes of Buccleuch and their ancestors, the Montagus, for five hundred years. The present duke is Europe's largest private landowner with assets worth an estimated £200 million. The house, open for just one month a year, contains rooms hung with superlative works by Gainsborough, Van Dyck and El Greco. Forty Van Dycks in the **Drawing Room** include a self portrait and studies of Charles I and

Rubens, hanging above the oldest-known English rugs in existence, borrowed on occasions by the royal family to place beneath the throne in Westminster Abbey. The highlight of William III's **state apartments** (£1) is the collection of Raphael cartoons, and the ceilings showing the *Rape of Proserpina* and the twelve constellations. There's also an unrivalled **armoury**, the **Audit Room Gallery**, filled with a vast collection of Louis XVI Sèvres crockery, as well as 350 acres of parkland to visit.

Geddington

When Queen Eleanor, cherished wife of Edward I, died in 1290 at Harby, near Lincoln, her embalmed body was carried in state to Westminster Abbey, and a memorial built at each resting point of the cortège. The most complete of the three surviving monuments graces the centre of **GEDDINGTON**, the largest village of the Boughton estate. Mounted on a stepped platform, the **Eleanor Cross** stands like a spire, culminating in a cluster of sumptuously carved points above three figures of Eleanor, overlooking the town she had stayed in when accompanying Edward on royal hunts. Part of Geddington Chase (the royal forest) still lies beyond the village, but the only remains of thirteenth-century architecture, other than the cross, are sections of the church and the sturdy triple-arched bridge that crosses the shallow River Ise. **Bus** #8 makes six daily journeys from Kettering to Geddington (except Sun), stopping close to *The Star Inn* and *Eleanor House Tea Shop & Restaurant*, both good places for a snack.

Lincolnshire

The obvious place to start a visit to **LINCOLNSHIRE** is **Lincoln** itself, where the cathedral, the third largest church in England, remains the region's outstanding attraction. The coast, so different from the rest of the county, is encapsulated by **Skegness**, a typically brash English seaside resort. Delightful **Stamford**, in the southwest corner of the county, is an alternative base to Lincoln, an attractive town boasting one of the great monuments of Elizabethan England, **Burghley House**. It also stands not too far away from the **The Fens**, whose most appealing villages lie along the A17, a road that runs close to the old fenland port of **Boston**, now Lincolnshire's second town. The other chief town of southern Lincolnshire is **Grantham**, birthplace of Margaret Thatcher and the site of a splendid medieval church.

Lincoln

Reaching high into the sky from the top of a steep hill, the triple towers of the mighty cathedral of **LINCOLN** are visible for miles across the flatlands. In 47 AD the Romans occupied the Celtic settlement of Lindon and built a fortified town which subsequently became, as Lindum Colonia, one of the four regional capitals of Roman Britain. Today, only fragments of the Roman city survive, mostly pieces of the third-century town wall, but these are outdone by reminders of Lincoln's medieval heyday, when the town became a centre of the wool trade with Flanders – that is, until 1369 when the wool market was transferred to neighbouring Boston.

It was almost five hundred years before the town revived, the recovery based upon its manufacture of agricultural machinery and drainage equipment for the fenlands. As the nineteenth-century town spread south down the hill and out along the old Roman road, the Fosse Way, so Lincoln became a place of precise class distinctions: the "Up hill" area, sloping north from the cathedral, became synonymous with middle-class respectability, "Down hill" with the proletariat. It's a distinction that remains – locals selling anything from secondhand cars to settees still put "Up hill" in brackets to signify a better quality of merchandise.

The City

Approached through the arch of medieval Exchequergate, the west front of **Lincoln Cathedral** (summer Mon–Sat 7.15am–8pm, Sun 7.15am–6pm; winter Mon–Sat 7.15am–6pm, Sun 7.15am–5pm) is a glorious sight, a cliff face of blind arcading mobbed by decorative carving. Most striking of all is the extraordinary band of twelfth-century carved panels which depict Biblical themes with a passionate initimacy, their inspiration being a similar frieze at Modena cathedral in Italy. The west front's apparent homogeneity is deceptive, and further inspection reveals two phases of construction – the small stones and thick mortar of much of the facade belong to the original church, completed in 1092, whereas the longer stones and finer courses date from the early thirteenth century. These were enforced modifications, for in 1185 an earthquake shattered much of the Norman church, which was then rebuilt under the auspices of **Bishop Hugh of Avalon**, the man responsible for most of the present cathedral, with the notable exception of the fourteenth-century towers.

The cavernous **interior** is a fine example of Early English architecture, with the nave's pillars conforming to the same general design yet differing slightly, their varied columns and bands of dark Purbeck marble contrasting with the oolitic limestone that is the building's main material. Looking back up the nave from beneath the central tower, you can also observe a major medieval botch: Bishop Hugh's roof is out of alignment with the earlier west front, and the point where they meet has all the wrong angles. It's possible to pick out other irregularities too – the pillars have bases of different heights, and there are ten windows in the north wall and nine in the south – but these are deliberate features, reflecting a medieval aversion to the vanity of symmetry. Pre-Christian images are still visible around the cathedral; above the doorway to the left of the decorative stone rood screen at the head of the nave, the Cheeky Green Man (an early fertility symbol) peers out from behind some foliage, watched by the beady eye of a stealthy dragon.

Beyond the central tower lies **St Hugh's Choir**, its fourteenth-century misericords carrying an eccentric range of carvings, with scenes from the life of Alexander the Great and King Arthur mixed up with Biblical characters and folkloric parables. Further on is the Gothic **Angel Choir**, which was completed in 1280 – its roof is embellished by dozens of finely carved statuettes, including the tiny Lincoln Imp (see below). Finally, a corridor off the choir's north aisle leads to the wooden-roofed **cloisters** and the ten-sided **Chapter House**.

From the cathedral, it's a short walk across to **Lincoln Castle** (summer Mon–Sat 9.30am–5.30pm, Sun 11am–5.30pm; winter closes 4pm; £2). The castle walls incorporate bits and pieces from the twelfth to the nineteenth century, with the earliest remains, the **Lucy Tower**, built on the mound of the first Norman keep. Behind the walls, in the spacious castle grounds, is the dour red-brick old jail, now housing one of the four surviving copies of the **Magna Carta** and an exhibition on "Law and Liberty", based around the remarkable **prison chapel**. Here, prisoners were locked in high-sided cubicles where they could see the preacher and his pulpit but not their fellow internees, an arrangement founded in the pseudo-scientific theory that defined crime as a contagious disease. Unfortunately for the theorists, their system of "Separation and Silence" drove many prisoners crazy, and it had to be abandoned, though nobody bothered to dismantle the chapel.

Leaving the castle via the west gate, you reach **The Lawn**, formerly a lunatic asylum and now a leisure complex incorporating a modest exhibition on mental health and a large tropical glasshouse, the **Sir Joseph Banks Conservatory**, named after the local botanist who travelled with Cook on his first voyage to Australia. From The Lawn, it's a five-minute walk north along Union and then Burton Road to the Victorian barracks, where the musty **Museum of Linconshire Life** (Mon–Sat 10am–5.30pm; also May–Sept Sun 10am–5.30pm & Oct–April Sun 2–5.30pm; £1) has an idiosyncratic assortment of bygones, including several mind-boggling early farm machines.

"Up hill" Lincoln has many other historic remains, notably several slabs of Roman wall, with the most prominent being the second-century **Newport Arch**, which straddles Bailgate, once the main north gate into the city. There's also a bevy of medieval stone houses, at their best on and around Steep Hill as it cuts down to the city centre. In particular, look out for the tidily restored twelfth-century **Jew's House**, a reminder of the Jewish community that flourished in medieval Lincoln, that now houses the *Jew's House Restaurant* (see below). The **Usher Gallery**, Lindum Road (Mon–Sat 10am–5.30pm, Sun 2.30–5pm; 80p), is on the hillside too, its well-presented displays featuring some fine watercolours of the cathedral and its environs, and an eclectic collection of watches and clocks dating from the seventeenth century.

Practicalities

Both Lincoln **train station**, on St Mary's Street, and the **bus station**, close by off Norman Street, are located "Down hill" in the city centre. From either, it's a steep, twenty-minute walk to the cathedral (bus #7 and #8). The main **tourist office** (summer Mon–Thurs 9am–5.30pm, Fri 9am–5pm, Sat & Sun 10am–5pm; winter same hours except Sat & Sun 11am–3pm; ☎01522/529 828) is at 9 Castle Hill, between the cathedral and the castle. For a **hotel** near the cathedral, try the delightful eighteenth-century *D'Isney Place Hotel* (☎01522/538 881; ⑥) on Eastgate. There are also several **B&Bs** nearby: try *the Old Rectory*, 19 Newport (☎01522/514 774; ③), *Newport Guest House*, 26 Newport (☎01522/528 590; ③), or *Mrs Taylor*, 1 Limelands, off Mill Road (☎01522/512 061; ③). Lincoln **youth hostel**, 77 South Park (☎01522/522 076), a Victorian villa opposite South Common park, is half a mile south of the train station. The nearest **campsite** is at *Hartsholme Country Park* (March–Oct; ☎01522/686 264), about three miles southwest of the centre and served by bus #10.

Geared up for the tourist industry, the **pubs and restaurants** around the cathedral tend to be overpriced, though you can still get a good inexpensive traditional English dish at *Browns Pie Shop*, 33 Steep Hill. Alternatively, the *Victoria*, on Union Street opposite The Lawn, serves great-value meals and snacks along with a vast array of guest beers. For a more formal dinner (evenings only), try the French restaurant, *Cosy Bistro 7* on Gordon Road, just off Bailgate (☎01522/375 777; moderate) or the plush *Jew's House Restaurant* on Steep Hill, which serves excellent but expensive meals. The big and brash *Stadz Café*, by the foot of Steep Hill, is a popular spot with local ravers.

Skegness

SKEGNESS has been a busy resort ever since the railways reached the Lincolnshire coast in 1875. Its heyday was before the 1960s, when the Brits took themselves off to sunnier climes, but it still attracts thousands of city dwellers each year, who come for the wide, sandy beaches and for a host of attractions ranging from nightclubs to bowling greens. Every inch the traditional English seaside town, Skegness shadows many of its rivals by keeping its beaches clean and its parks spick and span, whilst *Funcoast World*, a massive leisure complex in neighbouring Ingoldmells, has Europe's largest indoor "fun pool". But it's still easy to escape the hurly-burly – just head four miles south along the coastal road to **Gibraltar Point Nature Reserve**, where a series of footpaths criss-cross a narrow strip of salt marsh, sand dune and beach. You can reach the reserve by walking along the beach from Skegness.

The **tourist office** (April–Sept daily 9am–6pm; Oct–March Mon–Fri 9am–5pm, Sat 10am–4pm, Sun noon–4pm; ☎01754/764821), is behind the beach in the Embassy Centre on Grand Parade. Skegness **bus** and **train** stations are ten minutes' walk inland from the clock tower beside the tourist office, straight up Lumley Road. A series of convenient **B&Bs** and **guest houses** are strung out along South Parade and

Drummond Road, a few minutes' walk from the Embassy Centre: try the *Belle View Hotel*, 12 South Parade (☎01754/765 274; ②), *Singlecote*, 34 Drummond Rd (☎01754/764 698; ②) or *Scarborough House*, 54 South Parade (☎01754/764 453; ③).

The Lincolnshire Fens

The Lincolnshire section of **The Fens**, the great chunk of eastern England extending from Cambridge to Boston, encompasses some of the most productive farmland in Europe. Since the time of the Roman occupation this flat, treeless terrain has slowly been reclaimed from the marshes and swamps that once drained into the Wash, but it nonetheless remained an uncomfortable place for centuries. As a medieval chronicler described it, "There is in the middle part of Britain a hideous fen which [is] oft times clouded with moist and dark vapours having within it divers islands and woods as also crooked and winding rivers". These conditions spawned the distinctive culture of the so-called **fen slodgers**, who embanked small portions of marsh to create pastureland and fields, supplementing their diets by catching fish and fowl, and gathering reed and sedge for thatching and fuel. Their economy was threatened by the large-scale land-reclamation schemes of the late fifteenth and sixteenth centuries, and time and again the fenlanders sabotaged progress by breaking down the banks and dams. But the odds were stacked against the saboteurs, and the great landowners eventually drained huge tracts of the fenland: by the end of the eighteenth century the fen slodgers' way of life had all but disappeared. Nonetheless, the Lincolnshire fens remain a distinctive area of introverted little villages, with just one major settlement, the old port of **Boston**.

Boston

BOSTON, bisected by the muddy River Witham as it nears the Wash, was England's second largest seaport in the thirteenth and fourteenth centuries, its flourishing economy dependent on the wool trade with Flanders. The town's medieval merchants, revelling in their success, built the magnificent church of St Botolph, whose 272-foot tower still presides over the town and the fenland. The church was completed in the early sixteenth century, but by then Boston was in decline as trade drifted west towards the Atlantic and the Witham silted up. The town's fortunes only revived in the late eighteenth century when, after the nearby fens had been drained, it became a minor agricultural centre with a modest port that has, in recent times, been modernized for trade with the EU.

Mostly edged by Victorian red-brick buildings, the narrow streets of Boston's cramped centre radiate out from the massive bulk of **St Botolph** (Mon–Sat 8.30am–4.30pm, Sun 8.30am–4pm; winter closes Sun noon). Most of the church's exterior masonry, embellished by the high-pointed windows of the Decorated style, dates from the fourteenth century, but the huge and distinctive **tower** (£2), whose lack of a spire earnt the church the nickname Stump, is of later construction, topped by an octagonal lantern built in the early sixteenth century. Visible from twenty miles away, it once sheltered a beacon that guided travellers from the fens and the North Sea. The highlight of St Botolph's light and airy interior, apart from the trip up the tower, are the chancel's fourteenth-century **misericords**, bearing a lively mixture of vernacular scenes, such as organ-playing bears and a pair of medieval jesters squeezing cats in imitation of bagpipes. There's also the **Cotton Chapel**, dedicated to John Cotton, vicar here in 1612 and later a leading light among the Puritans of Boston, Massachusetts. In the early seventeenth century, Lincolnshire's Boston became a centre of Nonconformism, providing a stream of emigrants for the colonies of New England.

It was here, too, that some of the **Pilgrim Fathers** were caught by the authorities in 1607, after their failed attempt to escape religious persecution by slipping across to Holland. They were imprisoned for thirty days in the **Guildhall** (Mon–Sat 10am–5pm;

April–Sept also Sun 1.30–5pm; £1, free on Mon), on South Street near St Botolph, which now accommodates a small museum containing several old cells, one of which has been returned to its seventeenth-century appearance.

It's ten minutes' walk east from Boston **train station** to the town centre – on the way you'll pass West Street's *Regal* cinema, which overlooks the **bus station**. Close to St Botolph is the **tourist office**, in the *Blackfriars Arts Centre* on Spain Lane (Mon–Sat 9am–5pm; ☎01205/356 656). Boston has several reasonably convenient **B&Bs**, among them *Mrs Waters* at 16 Sleaford Rd (☎01205/352 253; ③), just west of the train station, and *Mrs Cannell*, at Fleetwood, Raybrook Close (☎01205/362 941; ②), north of the centre off Tattershall Road. For **food**, *TEMS*, in Shodfriars Hall on South Street by the Guildhall, serves inexpensive bar snacks and more filling meals in an adjoining restaurant; the *White Hart Hotel*, on Bridge Foot, does decent inexpensive food, too.

Stamford

STAMFORD is delightful, a handsome little limestone town of yellow-grey seventeenth- and eighteenth-century buildings edging narrow streets that slope up from the River Welland. It was here that the Romans forded the River Welland, establishing a fortified outpost that the Danes subsequently selected for one of their regional capitals. Later the town became a centre of the medieval wool and cloth trade, its wealthy merchants funding a series of almshouses known as "callises", after Calais, the English-occupied port through which most of them traded. Indeed, Stamford Cloth became famous throughout Europe for its quality and durability, a reputation confirmed when Cardinal Wolsey used it for the tents of the "Field of the Cloth of Gold", the conference of Henry VIII and Francis I of France outside Calais in 1520. Stamford was also the home of William Cecil, Elizabeth's chief minister, who built his splendid mansion, Burghley House, close by. After the collapse of the wool trade, the town prospered as an inland port and, in the eighteenth century, as a staging point on the Great North Road from London. More recently, Stamford escaped the three main threats to old English towns – the Industrial Revolution, wartime bombing and postwar development – and was designated the country's first Conservation Area in 1967. Thanks to this, its unspoilt streets lent themselves perfectly to the filming of the recent TV adaptation of George Elliot's *Middlemarch*.

The Town

Above all, it's the harmony of Stamford's architecture that pleases, rather than any specific sight. There are, nevertheless, a handful of buildings of some special interest in the centre, beginning with the church of **St Mary's**, set beside a mixed Georgian and medieval close on St Mary's Street. The church, with its splendid spire, has a small, airy interior that incorporates the Corpus Christi chapel, whose intricately embossed, painted and panelled roof dates from the 1480s.

From St Mary's, several lanes thread through to the carefully maintained High Street, where Ironmonger Street leads north to Broad Street, the site of **Browne's Hospital** (May–Oct Sat & Sun 2.30–5pm), the most extensive of the town's almshouses. This paupers' hospital was inelegantly remodelled by the Victorians, but the chapel preserves much of its fifteenth-century stained glass, as does the nearby church of **St John**, just to the west on Red Lion Square. Back on Broad Street, the **Stamford Museum** (April–Sept Mon–Sat 10am–5pm, Sun 2–5pm; Oct–March Mon–Sat 10am–12.30pm & 1.30–5pm; 50p) features a tasteless exhibit comparing the American midget Tom Thumb with the Leicester fat man, Daniel Lambert.

Down the hill from St Mary's, on the other side of the Welland, is the **George Hotel**, on High Street St Martin's, a splendid old coaching inn whose Georgian facade supports one end of the gallows that span the street – not a warning to criminals, but an advertising hoarding. Close by, the late fifteenth-century church of **St Martin's** shelters the magnificent tombs of the lords Burghley, with a recumbent William Cecil carved beneath twin canopies. Just behind, the early eighteenth-century effigies of John Cecil and his wife show the couple as Roman aristocrats, propped up on their elbows to gaze across at their distinguished ancestor.

From St Martin's church, it's a fifteen-minute stroll south along High Street St Martin's to **Burghley House** (tours April–Sept daily 11am–5pm; £5.10), an extravagant Elizabethan mansion standing in parkland landscaped by Capability Brown. The house itself was completed in 1587 after 32 years' work, its mellow-yellow ragstone exterior, with its dainty cupolas, pyramidal clock tower and skeletal balustrading planned by **William Cecil**, the long-serving advisor to Elizabeth I. A shrewd and cautious man, Cecil steered his queen through all sorts of difficulties, from the wars against Spain to the execution of Mary Queen of Scots, vindicating Elizabeth's assessment of his character when she appointed him in 1550: "You will not be corrupted with any manner of gifts, and will be faithful to the state".

With the notable exception of the Tudor kitchen little remains of Burghley's Elizabethan interior. Instead, the house bears the heavy hand of John, the fifth Lord Burghley, who toured France and Italy in the late seventeenth century, commissioning furniture, statuary and tapesteries, as well as buying up old Florentine and Venetian paintings, such as Paolo Veronese's *Zebedee's Wife Petitioning our Lord*. To provide a suitable setting for his Old Masters, John brought in Antonio Verrio and his assistant Louis Laguerre, who between them covered many of Burghley's walls and ceilings with frolicking gods and goddesses. These gaudy and gargantuan murals are at their best in the Heaven Room, an artfully painted classical temple that adjoins the Hell Staircase, where the entrance to the inferno is through the gaping mouth of a cat. Have a close look also at the fine portraits in the Pagoda Room, in particular the querulous Elizabeth I and a sublimely self-confident Henry VIII by Joos van Cleve.

Finally, if you're in Stamford in June, July or August, head out to **Tolethorpe Hall**, a beautiful Elizabethan mansion that's home to *Stamford Shakespeare Company*. The troupe gives outdoor performances, but the audience is safely covered by a vast open-fronted marquee; call ☎01780/54381 for details of performances.

Practicalities

Stamford **train station** is five minutes' walk from the town centre. The **bus station** lies on the north side of the river off All Saints' Street, a brief walk from the **tourist office**, at the east end of Broad Street (April–Sept Mon–Sat 10am–5pm, Sun 2–5pm; Oct–March Tues–Sat 10am–12.30pm & 1.30–5pm; ☎01780/55611). Stamford has several expensive **hotels**, two of the best being the *Garden House*, which occupies an attractive eighteenth-century building on High Street St Martin's (☎01780/63359; ⑦), and the plush *George Hotel* (☎01780/55171; ⑨), the old coaching inn just down the street. There are also a handful of comfortable and convenient **B&Bs**: try *Mrs Harvey*, 20 St Mary's St (☎01780/63265; ②), or *Mrs Ward*, 5 Barn Hill, off Red Lion Square (☎01780/51559; ③). For **food**, the *Bay Tree* coffee house, on St Paul's Street off the High Street, sells cheap and tasty snacks during the day, while *Candlesticks*, 1 Church Lane, offers good-quality meals from a wide-ranging, inexpensive menu, as does the restaurant of the *Garden House*. Alternatively, the *Lord Burghley* inn, on Broad Street, serves excellent and substantial bar meals, with the *Hole in the Wall* on Cheyne Lane offering similar food and live blues bands on Friday nights.

Grantham and around

GRANTHAM, midway between Stamford and Lincoln, was once a major staging point on the Great North Road from London, but today its lengthy high street is no more than a provincial thoroughfare flanked by an unappetizing combination of modern offices and Victorian red brick.

Grantham's pride and joy is the church of **St Wulfram's** (Mon & Thurs–Sat 9am–12.30pm & 2–5.30pm, Tues 9am–12.30pm), set within its own close on Swinegate, behind and to the left of the Guildhall, standing halfway along the main drag. St Wulfram's most obvious feature is its 282-foot-high central spire, a fourteenth-century construction whose angular lines are emphasized by pointed blind arcading, slim window openings and the narrowest of columns. Inside, highlights are the sinuous Decorated window tracery in and around the south chancel aisle and the late sixteenth-century **chained library** (Mon, Thurs & Fri 10am–noon & 2–4pm) above the south porch. The high altar is of interest too, not for itself, but because its position prompted a bitter wrangle in 1627. Believing the altar should be more conspicuous, the High-Church party turned it round to look down the nave, but the Puritans objected and came to move it back again. The resulting brawl, something of a *cause célèbre*, hardened attitudes in the run-up to the Civil War.

Beside the church is King's public school, whose original sixteenth-century classroom, with its mullioned windows and high-pitched stone roof, fronts Church Street. This was where **Isaac Newton** received his initial education in the 1650s. There's a statue of the great physicist and mathematician outside the Guildhall and a room of mementos, including a plaster-cast death mask, in the adjacent **Museum** (April–Sept Mon–Sat 10am–5pm, Sun 2–5pm; Oct–March Tues–Sat 10am–12.30pm & 1.30–5pm; 50p), which also has a display on **Margaret Thatcher**, who was born in Grantham in 1925. In a moment of gay abandon, Mrs Thatcher gave several of her dresses to the museum, although her absurd handbags and threatening hairstyle were always more memorable. Her childhood home is up along the main street at 2 North Parade: originally a grocer's store, it's since been turned into a chiropodist's surgery.

Grantham **train station** is ten minutes' walk from the Guildhall: follow Station Road to the four-way junction and turn right along Wharf Road, where you'll also find the **bus station**. Next door to the Guildhall is the **tourist office** (summer Mon–Sat 9.30am–5pm, Sun 10am–3pm; winter closed Sun; ☎01476/66444). The handiest **B&B** is the *Archway House*, by St Wulfram's at 15 Swinegate (☎01476/61807; ④), whilst the *Beehive Inn*, close by on Castlegate, serves tasty **bar snacks**.

Belton House

The honey-coloured limestone facade of **Belton House** (April–Oct Wed–Sun 1–5.30pm; gardens & park 11am–5pm; combined ticket £4.30; NT), three miles northeast of Grantham, is Restoration design at its finest, its delicate symmetry enhanced by formal gardens and by a later landscaped park. Belton was built in the 1680s for a local family of lawyer-landowners, the Brownlows, whose subsequent climb up the aristocratic ladder prompted them to remodel the interior of their home in the sumptuous Neoclassical style of the late eighteenth century. Entry is through the Marble Hall, where a sequence of family portraits, including three by Reynolds, are framed by the intricate limewood carvings that remain Belton's most distinctive feature. Several of them, both here and in the **saloon**, are thought to be the work of **Grinling Gibbons**, the great Rotterdam-born woodcarver and sculptor. Belton is also noted for its pastel-shaded, Adam-style plasterwork ceilings and, on display in the Chapel Drawing Room, a pair of splendid tapestries, which, despite their Indian and Japanese themes, were made in John Vanderbank's workshop in Soho, London. It's easy to reach Belton by **bus** from Grantham: service #601 runs roughly every hour from Monday to Saturday.

travel details

Trains

Birmingham New Street to: Birmingham International (every 15–30min; 15min); Coventry (every 15–30min; 25min); Great Malvern (every 30min; 1hr); Hereford (10 daily; 1hr 50min); Kidderminster (every 30min; 30min); Leicester (hourly; 50min); Lichfield (every 15min; 45min); London (every 30min; 1hr 40min); Nottingham (hourly; 1hr 45min); Shrewsbury (hourly; 1hr 20min); Stoke-on-Trent (hourly; 55min); Stourbridge (every 15min; 20min); Walsall (Mon–Sat every 30 min; 25min); Wolverhampton (every 30min; 20min); Worcester (every 30min; 55min).

Birmingham Snow Hill to: Stratford-upon-Avon (Mon–Sat hourly; 50min); Warwick (Mon–Sat hourly; 40min).

Grantham to: London (hourly; 1hr 40min); Nottingham (8 daily; 45min); Skegness (hourly; 1hr 30min).

Hereford to: Birmingham (10 daily; 1hr 50min); Great Malvern (13 daily; 30min); Leominster (hourly; 15min); London (4 daily; 2hr 55min); Ludlow (hourly; 25min); Shrewsbury (hourly; 55min); Worcester (13 daily; 40min).

Leicester to: London (hourly; 1hr 20min); Melton Mowbray (hourly; 15min); Nottingham (every 30min; 20min); Oakham (hourly; 30min); Stamford (hourly; 50min).

Lincoln to: Gainsborough (hourly; 25min); Leicester (hourly; 1hr 30min); London (hourly; 2hr 40min); Nottingham (hourly; 1hr).

Northampton to: Birmingham (hourly; 1hr 10min); Coventry (hourly; 40min); London Euston (17 daily; 1hr 10min–1hr 40min).

Nottingham to: Leicester (hourly; 25min); Lincoln (hourly; 50min); London (hourly; 1hr 40min); Manchester (hourly; 2hr 20min); Newark (hourly; 35min); Sheffield (hourly; 1hr 15min).

Shrewsbury to: Birmingham (hourly; 1hr 20min); Crewe (hourly; 45min); Hereford (hourly; 55min); Ludlow (hourly; 30min); Leominster (hourly; 45min).

Stamford to: Leicester (hourly; 30min); London (hourly; 2hr); Oakham (hourly; 10min).

Stratford-upon-Avon to: Birmingham (Mon–Sat hourly; 50min); Warwick (Mon–Sat 8 daily; 25min).

Worcester to: Birmingham (every 30min; 55min); Hereford (13 daily; 40min); Kidderminster (every 30min; 20min); London (12 daily; 1hr 50min).

Buses

Birmingham to: Burton-on-Trent (Mon–Sat hourly; 1hr 30min); Dudley (every 30min; 50min); Hereford (Mon–Sat 6 daily; 3hr); Ironbridge (5 daily; 1hr); Kidderminster (hourly; 1hr); Leicester (5 daily; 1hr); Leominster (Mon–Sat 6 daily; 2hr 30min); Lichfield (Mon–Sat; hourly 1hr); London (hourly; 2hr 30min); Ludlow (Mon–Sat hourly; 2hr); Nottingham (5 daily; 1hr 20min); Shrewsbury (5 daily; 1hr 45min); Stratford-upon-Avon (hourly; 1hr); Wolverhampton (every 30min; 1hr); Worcester (every 30 min; 1hr 30min).

Boston to: Skegness (2 daily; 1hr 10min); Spalding (5 daily; 1hr 10min).

Bridgnorth to: Ironbridge (Mon–Sat 6 daily; 35min); Ludlow (Mon–Fri 2 daily; 1hr 15min); Much Wenlock (Mon–Sat 8 daily; 20min); Shrewsbury (Mon–Sat 6 daily; 1hr); Wolverhampton (hourly; 50min).

Burton-on-Trent to: Birmingham (Mon–Sat hourly; 1hr 30min); Lichfield (Mon–Sat hourly; 30min).

Coventry to: Kenilworth (Mon–Sat hourly; 25min); Stratford-upon-Avon (Mon–Sat hourly; 1hr 15min); Warwick (Mon–Sat hourly; 20min).

Grantham to: Nottingham (5 daily; 1hr 10min); Stamford (Mon–Sat 2 daily; 1hr 15min).

Hereford to: Birmingham (Mon–Sat 5 daily; 3hr); Great Malvern (1 daily; 45min); Leominster (Mon–Sat 2 hourly; 45min); London (3 daily; 4hr 15min); Worcester (Mon–Sat 8 daily; 1hr–1hr 25min).

Leicester to: Ashby-de-la-Zouch (hourly; 1hr); Foxton (2 daily; 30min); London (hourly; 2hr 30min); Melton Mowbray (hourly; 50min); Northampton (6 daily; 1hr 20min).

Lincoln to: Boston (3 weekly; 1hr 30min); Grantham (hourly; 1hr); London (1 daily; 4hr 50min); Louth (4 daily; 1hr 10min); Skegness (Mon–Sat 5 daily, 1 on Sun; 1hr 45min); Sleaford (5 daily; 1hr 15min); Stamford (1 daily; 1hr 25min); Woodhall Spa (2 weekly; 50min).

Ludlow to: Birmingham (Mon–Sat hourly; 2hr); Bishop's Castle (Mon–Sat 3 daily; 55min); Bridgnorth (Mon–Fri 1 daily; 1hr 15min); Church Stretton (Mon–Sat 6 daily; 30min); Hereford

(Mon–Sat 7 daily; 55min); Leominster (Mon–Sat 7 daily; 25min); Shrewsbury (Mon–Sat 5 daily; 1hr 20min).

Northampton to: Birmingham (5 daily; 2hr); Brixworth (7 daily; 15min); Coventry (5 daily; 1hr 10min); Daventry (every 30min; 30min); Heathrow Airport (4 daily; 3hr); Kettering (18 daily; 40min–1hr 10min); Leicester (10 daily; 1hr 30min); Lincoln (1 daily; 3hr); London (3–4 daily; 2hr); Nottingham (1 daily; 2hr 25min); Oundle (4 daily; 1hr 30min).

Nottingham to: Leicester (hourly; 45min); London (every 2hr; 2hr 40min); Northampton (1 daily; 2hr 25min); Skegness (1 weekly; 2hr).

Shrewsbury to: Birmingham (4 daily; 1hr 45min); Bishop's Castle (Mon–Sat 3 daily; 1hr 45min); Bridgnorth (Mon–Sat 6 daily; 1hr 10min); Church Stretton (Mon–Sat 5 daily; 45min); Ironbridge (6 daily; 45min); Ludlow (Mon–Sat 5 daily; 1hr

20min); London (4 daily; 3hr); Much Wenlock (Mon–Sat 6 daily; 45min).

Stamford to: London (1 daily; 3hr 40min); Nottingham (1 daily; 1hr 15min).

Stoke-on-Trent (Hanley) to: Alton Towers (1 daily; 1hr); Birmingham (9 daily; 1hr); Buxton (3 daily; 1hr); London (6 daily; 3hr); Shrewsbury (6 daily; 1hr 50min).

Stratford-upon-Avon to: Alcester (Mon–Sat 6 daily; 35min); Birmingham (hourly; 1hr); Blenheim Palace (3 daily; 1hr 10min); Coventry (Mon–Sat hourly, 5 on Sun; 1hr 15min); Kenilworth (hourly; 55min); Warwick (hourly; 25min); Worcester (2 on Sun; 1hr 45min).

Worcester to: Birmingham (every 30min; 1hr 30min); Great Malvern (every 30min; 30min); Hereford (Mon–Sat 8 daily; 1hr 30min); London (1 daily; 3hr 25min); Stratford-upon-Avon (2 on Sun; 1hr 45min).

CHAPTER EIGHT

NORTHWEST ENGLAND

Within the **northwest** of England lie some of the ugliest and some of the most beautiful parts of the country. The least attractive zones of this region are to be found in the inchoate sprawl connecting the country's third and sixth largest conurbations, Manchester and Liverpool, but even here the picture isn't unrelievedly bleak, as the cities themselves have an uningratiating appeal. Set on the Mersey estuary, **Liverpool** is the more immediately appealing, its Georgian townhouses and twin cathedrals overlooking the docks that once made the city's fortune. Though the wharves are now redundant, many of the riverside buildings have been redeveloped and are now home to two of the north of England's best museums. In **Manchester** only a handful of Victorian Gothic buildings lend any grace to the cityscape, but the Castlefield area boasts a top-class industrial museum on the site of the world's oldest passenger railway station. Where Manchester really scores over its rival, however, is in the buzz of its club scene, intermittently at the leading edge of the country's youth culture.

You don't have to get far out of the built-up corridor before the scenery improves dramatically. To the southeast of Manchester, the soft contours of the **Peak District** offer great country for moderately strenuous walks, as well as the diversions of the former spa town of **Buxton**, the limestone caverns of **Castleton**, and a couple of fine country houses. The hills, which form the southern tip of the Pennine range, melt away to the west into undulating, pastoral **Cheshire**, where the county town of **Chester** sits encircled by England's finest set of ancient city walls. Among the coastal resorts to the north of the cities, **Blackpool** stays top of the league by supplying undemanding entertainment with more panache than its neighbours – but for anything more culturally invigorating you'll have to continue north to the historically important town of **Lancaster**, with its Tudor castle.

The highlight of the entire northwest is of course the **Lake District**, a tightly packed landscape of lustrous water and superb peaks – the highest in England. Offering walks ranging from stern ridge-top hikes to quieter lakeside ambles from the bustling villages of **Windermere**, **Ambleside** and **Grasmere**, the Lake District also attracts hundreds of literary pilgrims, the residences of Wordsworth, Ruskin and Beatrix Potter getting as crowded in high summer as the Midlands' shrines to William Shakespeare. The Cumbrian coast – lair of the Sellafield nuclear plant – is best passed through quickly, though two ecclesiastical sites, **Cartmel Priory** and the ruins of

---

ACCOMMODATION PRICE CODES

Throughout this guide, hotel and B&B accommodation is priced on a scale of ① to ⑨, the number indicating the **lowest price** you could expect to pay per night in that establishment for a **double room** in high season. The prices indicated by the codes are as follows:

① under £20/$31	④ £40–50/$62–78	⑦ £70–80/$108–124
② £20–30/$31–46	⑤ £50–60/$78–93	⑧ £80–100/$124–155
③ £30–40/$46–62	⑥ £60–70/$93–108	⑨ over £100/$155

Furness Abbey, justify a detour, as does **Eskdale**, a superb approach to the central lakes. To the east, the peaceful riverside towns of the **Eden valley** separate the lakes from the near wilderness of the northern Pennines. All roads north converge on Cumbria's county town, **Carlisle**, a place that sadly bears few traces of a pedigree that stretches back beyond the construction of Hadrian's Wall. Finally, the semi-autonomous **Isle of Man**, only 25 miles off the coast and served by ferries from Liverpool and Heysham, provides a terrain almost as rewarding as that of the Lake District but without the seasonal overcrowding.

Manchester

Inevitably, first impressions of **MANCHESTER** take in the monuments to a history of prosperity and decline that is still unfolding. Stoic tower blocks and empty shells of mills and factories reach for the skyline beside rows of shabby back-to-back houses. All this reinforces traditional images of the struggling post-industrial city, but Manchester is being treated to a facelift, prompted by high crime rates in ugly council estates, and by the city's likely selection as the venue for the Commonwealth Games in the year 2002. Old buildings are being cleaned, new ones built, the canals are being tidied up and inner-city estates revamped in a concerted effort to pull Manchester out of the doldrums of the Sixties and Seventies. These changes can only improve the already buzzing cultural scene: a mixture of classical concerts, theatre, Chinese and Asian festivals and the north's hottest clubs catering to the "Madchester" youth, England's largest student population and a blossoming gay community whose passion for all night dancing is taking the city's club culture to new heights.

Manchester's lack of homogeneity is surprising, considering its rapid growth from what was little more than a village in 1750 to the world's major cotton-milling centre in only a hundred years. The spectacular rise of **Cottonopolis**, as it became known, came from the production of competitively priced imitations of expensive Indian calicoes, using machines evolved from Arkwright's first steam-powered cotton mill, which opened in 1783. The rapid industrialization of the area brought prosperity for a few but a life of misery for the majority, and the discontent of the poor came to a head in 1819 when eleven people were killed at **Peterloo**, in what began as a peaceful workers' demonstration against the oppressive Corn Laws. Exploitation had worsened by the time Friedrich Engels arrived in 1842 to work in his father's cotton plant – the suffering he witnessed was a seminal influence on the co-author of the *Communist Manifesto*.

Waterways and railway viaducts form the matrix into which the city's principal buildings have been bedded – as early as 1772 a canal was cut to connect the city to the coal mines at Worsley, and the railway to Liverpool, opened in 1830, was the world's first passenger line. The **Manchester Ship Canal**, constructed to entice ocean-going vessels into Manchester and away from burgeoning Liverpool, was completed in 1894, and played a crucial part in reviving Manchester's competitiveness. A century later, with the docks, mills and canals no longer in use, it's the splendid behemoths of Victorian Gothic standing proud amid unsightly sixties architecture that echo the city's past. Looking towards a brighter future, Manchester's planners are taking more sensitive steps to improve the lot of communities in inner-city suburbs such as Hulme and Moss Side, both scarred by gang violence and drug dealing, giving tenants a say in the design of new estates and encouraging local businesses. These projects, like the schemes to ease the problems of homelessness that have mushroomed since the late eighties, are the first steps towards changes that will take years to come into effect.

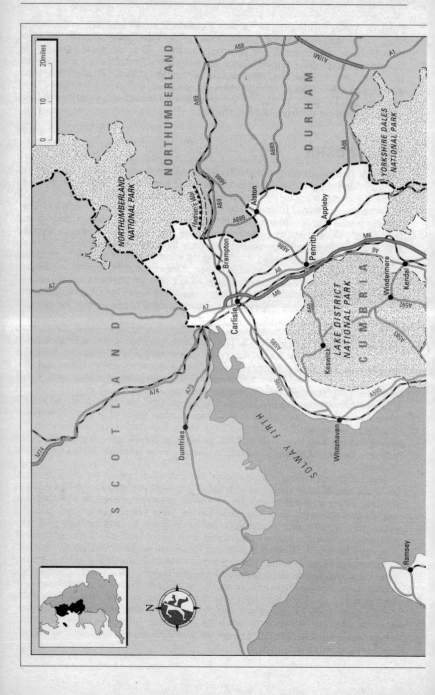

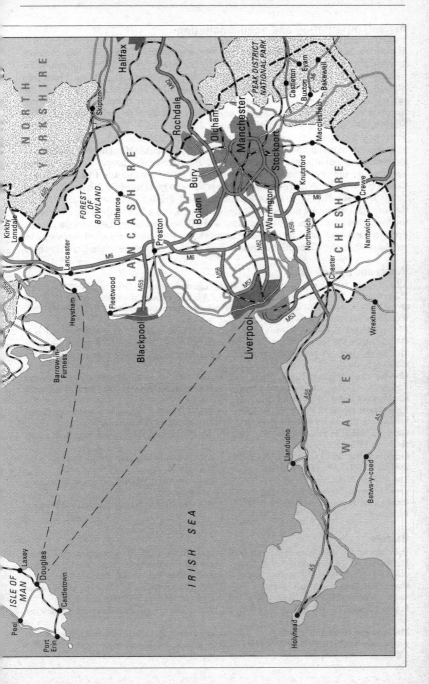

Arrival, information and accommodation

Manchester's three main **train stations** form the points of a triangle that encloses much of the city centre, two of them linked by the smart new *Metrolink*, vanguard of a welcome return to trams on Britain's streets. Intercity trains all pull into **Piccadilly Station**, on the east side, from where you can walk a few hundred yards west into the city's core or hop on the *Metrolink* downstairs (buy your ticket on the platform). Regional routes to points south, east and west call both here and at **Oxford Road Station**, five minutes' walk south of the St Peter's Square *Metrolink* stop. **Victoria Station**, in the north, services the northern hinterland and Bradford.

A second terminal and new rail link to Piccadilly make **Manchester Airport** an increasingly popular point of entry to Britain. The fractionally cheaper *747 Express* bus also runs to the city, dropping you on Portland Street outside the **Chorlton Street Coach Station**, from where *National Express* services go to most British destinations.

The **tourist office** (Mon & Sat 10am–5pm, Tues–Fri 9am–5pm; ☎0161/234 3157) in the town hall extension on central St Peter's Square, has a free **map** of the city centre, the free *What's On* monthly listings paper and will book accommodation for no charge. Free rail and bus route maps and information on the latest travelcard deals can be picked up from the **Piccadilly Gardens Bus Station**, hub of the urban bus network.

Hotels and B&Bs

Albert Vault, 169 Chapel St (☎0161/834 4024); **Egerton Arms**, 2 Gore St (☎0161/834 3182); **Salford Arms**, 146 Chapel St (☎0161/839 9548). A bunch of pubs all offering similar B&B type accommodation half a mile along Bridge Street from the city centre; take bus #7, #11, #30, #31, #61, #64, #66 or #68 from Piccadilly. ③.

Bloom's Hotel, 11 Blooms St (☎0161/236 7198). A new hotel, housed in a renovated warehouse in the heart of the gay village (but not exclusively gay), with tasteful decoration and saunas. ④.

The Crown Inn, 321 Deansgate (☎0161/834 1930). Very central B&B accommodation above a traditional pub. ③.

Crowne Plaza Midland Hotel, Peter St (☎0161/236 3333). Once the terminus hotel for Central Station (now G-Mex) and the place where Rolls met Royce for the first time, the building is the apotheosis of Victorian brickwork. ⑨.

Elton Bank Hotel, 62 Platt Lane, Rusholme (☎0161/4224 6449). Two miles from the city centre, overlooking Platt Fields park and convenient for the curry houses of Rusholme. ②.

Gardens Hotel, 55 Piccadilly (☎0161/236 5155). An accommodating three-star place with a bathroom and TV in each room. ⑤.

Grafton Hotel, 56–58 Grafton St (☎0161/273 3092). Six knocked-through terrace houses, by the medical school south of the university; popular with groups. ③.

The Palace Hotel, Oxford Street (☎0161/236 9999). An Alfred Waterhouse glazed-tile extravaganza, opposite the Cornerhouse arts centre. ⑨, ⑦ at weekends.

Rembrandt Hotel, 33 Sackville St (☎061/236 1311). Comfortable, friendly, central and predominantly gay. ②.

Hostels

Bookings for the four university hostels must be made through the accommodation office (Mon–Fri; ☎0161/247 2958). *Cavendish Hall*, *Loxford Tower* and *Woolton Hall* only take weekly bookings at £53 for a single room self-catering; only at *Montgomery House* can you stay less than a week.

Cavendish Hall, Cavendish St (☎0161/247 1338). Accommodation in 200 single-bed students' rooms, 5min south of Oxford Road station; available July to mid-Sept. Breakfast included.

Loxford Tower, Lower Chatham St (☎0161/247 1334). Close to Cavendish Hall, with the same set-up.

Montgomery House, Desmesne Rd, Whalley Range (☎0161/226 3434). Three miles from the city centre; take bus #101, #102, #105 or #108. Available June to mid-Sept. A single room costs £8.50 a night.

Woolton Hall, Whitworth Lane (☎061/224 7244). Single student rooms by the Owen's Park campus, a couple of miles south along Oxford Road. B&B or bed only. Available June to late Sept. Virtually any bus from Oxford Road station goes there.

Youth Hostel, Potato Wharf, Castlefield (☎0161/839 9960). Pristine new hostel, overlooking the canal, opposite the Museum of Science and Industry. The en-suite rooms sleep one to four people (you can pay more to have the room to yourself) and the bunks convert into double beds; facilities for disabled people are available. £8.20–£11.60 per bed. G-Mex Metrolink.

The City

If Manchester can be said to have a centre, it's **St Peter's Square** and the cluster of buildings focused on it: the town hall, the largest municipal library in the world and the lavish *Midland Hotel*. Behind the *Midland*, the huge vault of the former Central Station now functions as the **G-Mex** exhibition centre, part of a general spruce-up spreading west to the Castlefield district, home to the city's two most popular tourist attractions. Most of the rest of the city's attractions and the majority of eating and drinking spots are scattered over a broad expanse to the north along **Deansgate** and east towards **Piccadilly Gardens**. A few more string out along the main southern artery **Oxford Road**, strictly Oxford Street until a quarter of a mile out but always referred to by the former name.

St Peter's Square and around

Manchester could claim little architectural merit without its Victorian neo-Gothic buildings. One of its boldest, Alfred Waterhouse's **Town Hall**, divides St Peter's Square from the more harmonious Albert Square to the north, where guided tours of the building set off about twice a month (see tourist office for details). On most days you can wander inside and climb one of the grand staircases to the **Great Hall**, with its double hammerbeam roof and paintings by Ford Madox Brown depicting decisive moments from Manchester's past: its Roman foundation, John Kay inventing the flying shuttle that transformed cotton weaving, and so forth.

To see Brown's achievement in the context of his peers, stroll across St Peter's Square to Charles Barry's porticoed **City Art Gallery** (Mon–Sat 10am–5.45pm, Sun 2–5.45pm; free guided tours Sat & Sun 2.30pm; free), where the array of high Victorian art includes the country's finest public collection of Pre-Raphaelite works. Ground-floor galleries are used for touring exhibitions, leaving the upper floor free for the permanent collection. Canaletto's *The Church of San Giorgio Maggiore, Venice*, in the second room is almost overshadowed by the sheer enormity of James Barry's *The Birth of Pandora* beyond and the oddity of George Stubbs' *Cheetah and Stag with Two Indians*, a scene set against a Derbyshire landscape. Two rooms on, visitors tend to gather around Ford Madox Brown's masterpiece *Work*, which contrasts the honest toil of navvies with the idleness of the rich. Nearby hangs Brown's Byron-inspired *Prisoner of Chillon*, painted in 1843 before he was swept up by the Pre-Raphaelite wave – there's also a fair showing by Holman Hunt and his Pre-Raph confrères. In the last room, Pierre Adolphe Valette's *Albert Square, Manchester*, a dreary, grey scene, blurred by rain, is as true of today's view of Albert Square as when it was painted in 1910. Most twentieth-century work is displayed in changing exhibitions held in the **Athenaeum Gallery** (same times; free), around the corner on Princess Street.

Castlefield

Fifteen minutes' walk southwest of the town hall lies the rapidly developing area of **Castlefield**, until a few years ago a wasteland of railway viaducts and supermarket-trolley-filled canals. The castle-in-the-field itself is a **Roman fort** whose reconstructed but scant remains can be seen a hundred yards from the considerably more diverting

Museum of Science and Industry (daily 10am–5pm; £4) – one of the most impressive museums of its type in the country, mixing technological displays with trenchant analysis of the social impact of industrialization. The entry ticket is valid all day, thus allowing a decent lunch break – and you need it, especially if you want to catch any of the huge array of Lancashire-made steam engines progressively fired throughout the day in the **Power Hall**. Pride of place, though, goes to a working replica of Robert Stephenson's *Planet* – for which his father George's *Rocket* was the prototype. Built in 1830, the *Planet* reliably attained a scorching 30mph but had no brakes; the museum's version does, and uses them at weekends (Easter–Nov Sat & Sun noon–4pm; Dec–Easter Sun only), dropping passengers a quarter-mile away at the **world's oldest passenger railway station**. It was here that the *Rocket* arrived on a rainy September 15, 1830, after fatally injuring Liverpool MP William Huskisson at the start of the inaugural passenger journey from Liverpool. A reconstructed Victorian sewer below the station illustrates the problems of 1870s sanitation, while the improvements brought about by domestic electricification are brought home in a suite of period rooms. At weekends in the **Textile Gallery**, the museum's comprehensive selection of carding machines, bobbin threaders and cotton looms crash into action. The **Air and Space Gallery**, across the road, is an anomaly in that it barely touches on Manchester at all.

As a tourist attraction, though, the museum can't compete with the **Granada Studios Tour** (April–Sept daily 9.45am–7pm; Oct–March Mon–Fri 9.45am–5.30pm, Sat & Sun 9.45am–6.30pm; last entry 3hr before closing; £11.99), entered around the corner on Water Street. Each year 700,000 people file through the studio doors, into an American-style street scene, complete with cops and friendly baseball players, and then undergo ten different "experiences", ranging from a motion simulator to a smoothly orchestrated backstage tour. But it's the allure of Britain's longest-running soap opera that keeps the turnstiles moving, even though most of the footage for *Coronation Street* is now shot elsewhere. Nonetheless, most of the punters are happy enough to marvel at the stars on celluloid prior to wandering around the set used for outdoor sequences and into the *Rovers Return* for a pint.

North of the town hall

About ten minutes' walk north of Castlefield, and slightly nearer to the town hall, you'll find the city's finest example of Victorian Gothic, the beautifully detailed **John Rylands Library** on Deansgate (Mon–Fri 10am–5.30pm, Sat 10am–1pm; free). Now part of Manchester University, it was founded in 1890 by Enriquetta Ryland to house the theological works collected by her late husband, and now displays Bibles in more than three hundred languages among its million-strong general collection.

From the library, continue up Deansgate and left onto Bridge Street to reach the Pumphouse, home to **The People's History Museum** (Tues–Sun & Bank Hols 11am–4.30pm; £1, free on Fri), an exhibition recording the lives and protests of England's working class over the last two hundred years. Banners, press reports and charters show the struggles of suffragettes, reformers and radicals, fighting for equal representation, votes and fair pay; trade unionism is also well documented. Copies of anti-government cartoons printed in the *Manchester Guardian* in the 1800s show distaste with parliamentary decisions and this theme is brought up to date with an overview of Thatcher's policies; on a lighter note there are also displays devoted to the country's favourite football teams. Planned extensions will make this one of the country's fullest representations of the voice of the working class.

Northeast of here stands St Ann's Square and the **Royal Exchange**, formerly the Cotton Exchange, which employed seven thousand people until trading finished on December 31, 1968 – the trading board still shows the last day's prices for American and Egyptian cotton. The hall's immense glass domed roof now tops the **Royal Exchange Theatre**, the country's largest theatre-in-the-round, which sits in the middle of the exchange like a lunar landing pod. The pedestrianized area around St Ann's Square and the adjacent King Street provides Manchester's best shopping, boasting most of the popular designer and high-street outlets as well as a smattering of bars and coffee houses.

The small, Perpendicular **Cathedral**, between Cross Street and Deansgate, is not one of the country's great religious structures, but does claim the widest nave in England and a fine array of misericords depicting everything from dragon-slaying to backgammon playing. The cathedral's choristers are trained in **Chetham's Hospital School**, which lurks almost unnoticed in front of Victoria Station. This fifteenth-century manor house became a school and a free public library in 1653, then was transformed into a music school in 1969. There are **free recitals** (Mon–Fri 1pm) during term-time and a half-hour tour following the concert on Wednesdays. In front of the Cathedral, set off Corporation Street, the **Old Corn Exchange** is now home to an "alternative" shopping arcade, that wins hands down over the Arndale Centre for imaginative gifts, bizarre records and antiques, and a plethora of fortune tellers.

Oxford Road

Another Gothic Revival building, half a mile south along Oxford Road, houses the **Manchester Museum** (Mon–Sat 10am–5.30pm; free), whose extensive Egyptian collection doesn't quite counterbalance the humdrum geological and ethnographic sections. Keep plodding south for another half-mile to reach the city's modern art collection, in the red-brick **Whitworth Gallery** (Mon–Sat 10am–5pm, Thurs to 9pm; free). As you walk in you confront Jacob Epstein's African-influenced nude, *Genesis*, which caused mass protest at its unveiling and later became part of a Modern Art freak show in Blackpool. Works by British staples Moore, Frink and Hepworth set off contributions from lesser-known sculptors, while in another gallery the museum's strong assembly of watercolours by Turner, Constable and Blake fight for prominence. Appropriately enough, given Manchester's cotton connections, the gallery displays the country's widest range of textiles outside London's Victoria and Albert Museum.

Salford Museum and Art Gallery

No artist is more closely linked with an English city than Lowry is with Manchester, now home to the most extensive Lowry exhibition in the country. **Salford Museum and Art Gallery**, in Peel Park next to the University (Mon–Fri 10am–4.45pm, Sun 2–5pm; free), illustrates his early views on the desolation and sadness of Manchester's mill workers and his changing outlook in later life when he repeated earlier paintings changing the greys and sullen browns for lively reds and pinks. Lowry also expanded his repertoire as he grew older, capturing mountain scenes and seascapes in broad sweeps of his brush, and painting full-bodied realistic portraits which are far less known than his matchstick crowds. In addition to the Lowry exhibition the museum has an impressive Victorian art collection, a gallery for temporary exhibitions and, on the ground floor, an atmospheric reproduction of a nineteenth-century street. Frequent buses from the city centre stop outside the museum, while trains from Oxford Road station and Metrolink trams from St Peter's Square take just seven minutes to reach Salford Crescent, a couple of minutes' walk from the museum.

Eating, drinking and nightlife

The bulk of Manchester's eating, drinking and entertainment places are scattered around the city centre and along the area bordering Oxford Road all the way to Rusholme – a narrow band from which few Mancunians stray. The greatest central concentration of **restaurants** is around Portland Street, where the country's largest **Chinatown** has a host of cheap places to eat, while out at Rusholme you'll find the best

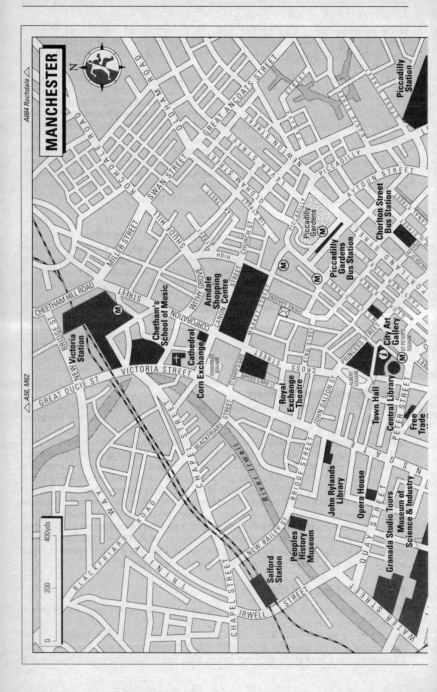

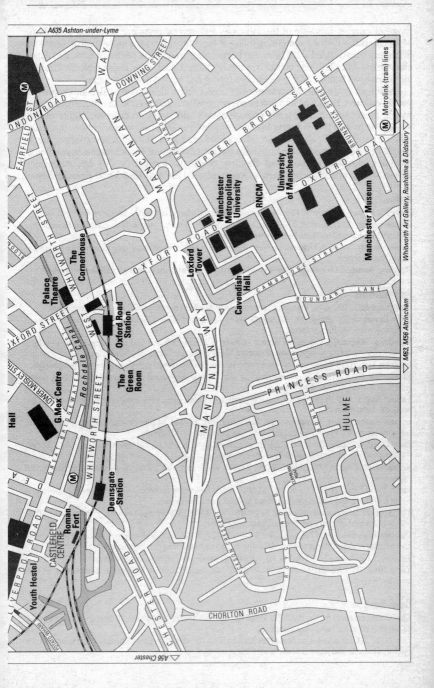

△ A635 Ashton-under-Lyme

DOWNING STREET

FAIRFIELD ST

LONDON ROAD

Ⓜ Metrolink (tram) lines

GROSVENOR STREET

UPPER BROOK STREET

BRUNSWICK STREET

OXFORD ROAD

University of Manchester

Manchester Museum

Whitworth Art Gallery, Rusholme & Didsbury ▷

The Cornerhouse

Palace Theatre

OXFORD STREET

WHITWORTH STREET

Manchester Metropolitan University

RNCM

Loxford Tower

Cavendish Hall

CAMBRIDGE STREET

BOUNDARY LANE

OXFORD STREET

WHITWORTH STREET WEST

Oxford Road Station

The Green Room

MANCUNIAN WAY

PRINCESS ROAD

M63, M56 Altrincham ▷

Hall

G.Mex Centre

Rochdale Canal

Bridgewater Canal

HULME

LOWER MOSLEY STREET

DEANSGATE

Ⓜ

Deansgate Station

WHITWORTH STREET

LIVERPOOL ROAD

Youth Hostel

CASTLEFIELD CENTRE

Roman Fort

CHESTER ROAD

CHORLTON ROAD

◁ A56 Chester

range of **curries** this side of the Pennines and several restaurants serving until 3am. Most city **pubs** dish up something filling at lunchtime, but for a more modish snack or drink, European-styled **café-bars** are burgeoning around the centre of town and especially in the so-called "gay village" on the Rochdale Canal, their decor typically consisting of exposed beams, primary-coloured piping and a good deal of chrome.

For fifteen years now, Manchester has been vying with London as Britain's capital of **youth culture**. Banks of fly posters advertise what's going on in the numerous clubs which, as elsewhere, frequently change names and styles on different nights of the week. The best of the enduring live-music clubs are listed below; entry prices normally range from £2 to £5, and they are all licensed until 2am, though some continue for a couple of alcohol-free hours. For the broadest coverage of Manchester's happenings, including **classical music and theatre**, check the fortnightly *City Life* magazine, whose listings are only marginally supplemented by the dire *Manchester Evening News*.

Cafés

Affleck's Palace, Oldham St. Five floors of boutiques and several cafés – the best is on the top floor.

Cornerhouse, 70 Oxford St. The place to sip a cappuccino after viewing the galleries, though the ground-floor bar suffers from being rather pretentious.

Green Room, 54–56 Whitworth St West. Industrially styled vegetarian café attached to the city's main fringe theatre.

Howling Smith, 3 Oldham St. Low-key underground café with the best fruit milkshakes around.

Restaurants

Café Yaqoub, 2 Union St. Bargain-basement curry house in the middle of the city. Inexpensive.

Café Istanbul, 79 Bridge St. An open-fronted restaurant with delicious Turkish dishes and an extensive wine list. Inexpensive.

Dimitri's Taverna, 1 Campfield Arcade, corner of Liverpool Road and Deansgate. A good-value, low-key place offering a wide range of eastern Mediterranean dishes. Moderate.

Eastern Touch, 76 Wilmslow Rd. One of the best of the low-priced curry restaurants. Inexpensive.

El Macho, 103 Portland St. Wide range of only slightly Anglicized Mexican meals washed down with jugs of margaritas. Moderate.

Fallen Angel, 263 Upper Brook St. Excellent vegetarian café, with imaginative meals and huge portions. Inexpensive.

Indian Cottage, 501 Claremont Rd, Rusholme (☎0161/224 0446). One of the swankier Asian restaurants, with a good tandoori menu and an indoor pond. Moderate.

Jade Garden, 54 Faulkner St. Cantonese with gaudy decor but good lunch specials and a better than usual range of vegetarian dishes. Inexpensive.

Koreana, 40 King St (☎0161/236 9338). Korean restaurant with excellent set menus. Moderate to expensive.

Little Yang Sing, 17 George St (☎0161/228 7722). Basement forerunner of its bigger brother (see below). Dingier and with a smaller menu but still good. Moderate.

The Market Restaurant, 104 High St (☎0161/834 3743). Adventurous eclectic cuisine makes this one of Manchester's very best restaurants. Expensive.

Punjab Sweethouse, 177 Wilmslow Rd (☎0161/225 2960). Superb all-vegetarian Indian restuarant, specializing in *dosas*, *thalis* and special sweets; also does takeaway. Inexpensive.

Tandoori Kitchen, 131 Wilmslow Rd. Excellent Persian specialities. Inexpensive.

Yang Sing, 34 Princess St (☎0161/236 2200). Amongst the best Cantonese restaurants in the country. Expensive.

Café-bars

The Conservatory, 5 Old Bank St. Head for the downstairs bar where all beers and spirits cost £1.10; also good for lunchtime snacking.

Dry 201, 28 Oldham St. The first of the café-bars on the scene, *Dry* was started by the now defunct Factory Records and houses Manchester's first Internet café.

The Grinch, 5–7 Chapel Walks, off Cross Street. A good selection of beer and cocktails are on offer in this pricier-than-average spot, with a decent Mediterranean-style menu.

Isobar, 35–43 Oldham St. Very popular, chic bar serving excellent food throughout the day and late into the night.

J.W. Johnson's, 78 Deansgate. The place to be seen with the city's rich kids, wannabes and the *Manchester United* youth team. Has outdoor seating and an imaginative menu.

Manto, 46 Canal St. The smartest and most interesting café-bar, with a gay/straight balance, displaying bizarre art on the walls and supplying newspapers with Sunday brunch.

Metz, 3 Brazil St. New, classy bar and restaurant, opposite *Manto* and with a similar gay/straight mix; great for a pre-club drink or two.

Night & Day, Oldham Street. Unpretentious, cosy café-bar with a late licence Sat & Sun, excellent food and live music – jazz, blues, Latin and funk – from local musicians.

TeN, 10 Tariff St. More informal and cosy than the other café-bars, with sounds ranging from techno to Latin, and a £1 cover charge which includes a plate of vegetable chilli.

Pubs

The Beer House, 6 Angel St, off Rochdale Road. The best place for ale-tasting, with a constant stock of more than thirty brands of beer.

Circus Tavern, 86 Portland St. Manchester's smallest pub; good beer too.

Corbieres Wine Cavern, behind *Waterstones* on St Ann's Square. Largely a student bar with a jukebox reflecting Manchester's stamp on the contemporary music scene.

Dukes '92, Castle St. Huge old warehouse on the Duke of Bridgewater's canal in Castlefield, classily revamped with art on the walls. Serves a wide range of pâtés and cheeses.

Flea and Firkin, corner of Oxford and Grosvenor streets. Predominantly student-filled beer-hall style pub, with brewery on site.

The Granby, 84 Princess St. Open until 2am though you'll have to arrive before 11pm if you want to avoid the cover charge.

Joshua Brooks, 106 Princess St. Popular with local students for a pre-club drink, this pub has a large flag-stoned basement with loud music, and a good selection of guest and bottled beers.

The Lass o' Gowrie, 1 Charles St. Glazed tiles on the outside and a micro-brewery inside make this one of the better studenty pubs.

Marble Arch, 73 Rochdale Rd. Real ale house with scores of bottled beers and a great atmosphere.

The Mark Addy, corner of Stanley and Bridge streets. A pub serving a choice of 50 cheeses and 8 pâtés (including vegetarian). Eat inside, or outside by the River Irwell.

O' Shea's, 80 Princess St. Incredibly popular Irish pub, with live music nights, Guinness and good food.

Clubs and music venues

Academy, Oxford Road, on the university campus (☎0161/275 2930). Box-like venue for new and established bands.

Band on the Wall, 25 Swan St (☎0161/832 6625). Cosy club with a great reputation for its live bands – world and folk music Wed, reggae Fri. If there's no queue, you have to knock on the door to get in.

The Brickhouse, 66 Whitworth St West (☎0161/236 4418). Indie, techno, Seventies, depending on the night.

Equinox, Bloom St. One of Manchester's best venues for heavy house and classic disco. Open until early morning, but be prepeared to queue.

PJ.Bells, 85 Oldham St (☎0161/834 4266). Live music most nights. Heavily jazz, blues and funk oriented. Excellent Sun night jazz jam session.

Haçienda, 11–13 Whitworth St West (☎0161/236 5051). The best-known club in Manchester featuring mainly DJ-led dance music. Once at the cutting edge and still not far off it.

Oscar's, Cooper St. Mainstream dance and funk hits for disco divas. Don't go in trainers – you won't get in! Free admission.

Paradise Factory, 112–16 Princess St (☎0161/273 5422). Hottest club on the scene, occupying the old Factory Records building. There's a gay night on Fri, with a women's den upstairs.

The Ritz, Whitworth St West (☎0161/236 4355). A one-time ballroom where they still spread talc on the floor Wed and Thurs. On Fri and Sat it's a suits and stilettos disco, with Mon as "alternative night".

Classical music, theatre and cinema

Manchester is blessed with the North's most highly regarded orchestra – **The Hallé**, currently based at the Free Trade Hall, 46 Peter St (☎0161/834 1712), but due to be rehoused at the mammouth Bridgewater Hall, opposite G-Mex, where concerts are scheduled to start in autumn 1996. The **Royal Northern College of Music** (RNCM) on the corner of Oxford Road and Hulme Street also stages top-quality classical and modern jazz concerts (☎0161/273 4504). Of the excellent theatre companies, the most innovative stagings are at the *Contact Theatre*, 15 Oxford Rd (☎0161/274 4400), a mile south of the centre, which puts on predominantly modern works. *The Green Room*, 54–56 Whitworth St West (☎0161/236 1677), has a rapidly changing fringe programme which includes dance, mime and cabaret. Established drama is most likely to get an imaginative airing at the *Royal Exchange* (☎0161/833 9833), which sells seats on the day for around £5. There are seven mainstream **cinema** screens at the *Odeon*, 1 Oxford St; for art-house films, check out the *Cornerhouse*, 70 Oxford St.

Listings

Bookshops *Waterstone's*, 92 Deansgate, is the northwest's largest bookshop. *Frontline Books*, 1 Newton St, is Manchester's foremost outlet for radical literature.

Exchange *American Express*, 39 Deansgate (☎0161/835 3121); *Thomas Cook*, 23 Cross St (☎0161/839 0832) and 2 Oxford St (☎0161/236 8575). The only late-night exchanges, other than the big hotels, are at the airport (6am–midnight) and at the youth hostel (daily 7am–11pm).

Football Tickets for Manchester United matches at Old Trafford (trains from Oxford Road; ☎0161/872 1661) are like gold dust. Manchester City, the poorer cousins, play at Maine Road in Rusholme (buses #98 and #111; ☎0161/226 1191). United offers tours of Old Trafford and its museum (Tues–Sun 9.30am–4pm; £5, or £3 for museum only; ☎0161/877 4002); City's humbler tour is free (Aug–May Mon–Fri 10am & 2pm; ☎0161/226 1191).

Hospital Manchester Royal Infirmary, 13 Oxford Rd (☎0161/276 1234).

Laundry *Mr Bubbles*, 244 Wilmslow Rd (daily 8am–10pm). Take any bus along Oxford Road.

Pharmacy *Cameolord Ltd*, 7 Oxford St (daily 8am–midnight).

Police Bootle St (☎0161/872 5050).

Post Office The main office is at 26 Spring Gardens.

Women *The Pankhurst Centre*, 60–62 Nelson St, inside the hospital grounds (☎0161/273 5673). Located in the house where Emmeline Pankhurst and her daughters once lived, it brings together half a dozen women's organizations and hosts the cosy *Annie Kenney's Vegetarian Café*.

■ MANCHESTER'S GAY SCENE

Manchester has one of Britain's most vibrant **gay** scenes, centred along the Rochdale Canal between Princess and Sackville Streets. Early evenings kick off by the lock at the trendy *Manto* café-bar, at *Metz* opposite, or over the road at the more macho *New Union*. A camp neon Liberty beckons you to grind the night away at *New York, New York* and *Equinox*, both on Bloom Street, or beyond to the funky house sounds of *La Câge*, *Equinox*'s upstairs bar. *Central Park*, on Sackville Street, is open 2am–3pm most Sundays (get a membership card on Sat; £7), while *Manto* serves breakfast accompanied by rave music (Sun 2am–6am). The *Haçienda* (see above) celebrates the last Wednesday of each month with a "no-hets" *Flesh Night*. For further info, try the *Gay drop-in Centre* on Sidney Street (☎0161/274 3814) with its coffee bar, meeting rooms and Helpline. Manchester also has a **Gay Switchboard**, operating daily 4–10pm (☎0161/274 3999).

The Peak District

In 1951 the modest hills and dales of the **PEAK DISTRICT**, at the southern tip of the Pennine range, became Britain's first national park. Wedged between Manchester, Sheffield and Derby, it is effectively the backyard for the fifteen million people who live within an hour's drive of its boundaries, though somehow it accommodates the huge influx with the minimum of fuss.

Landscapes in the Peak District come in two forms. The brooding high moorland tops of **Dark Peak**, fifteen miles east of central Manchester, take their name from the underlying gritstone, known as millstone grit for its former use – a function commemorated in the millstones demarcating the park boundary. Windswept, mist-shrouded and inhospitable, the flat tops of these peaks are nevertheless a firm favourite with walkers on the **Pennine Way**, which meanders from the tiny village of **Edale** north to the Scottish border. Altogether more forgiving, the southern limestone hills of the **White Peak** have been eroded into deep forested dales populated by small stone villages and often traced by walking trails along former rail routes. The limestone is riddled with complex cave systems around **Castleton** and under the region's largest centre, **Buxton**, an elegant former spa town just outside the park's boundaries, at the end of an industrialized corridor reaching out from Manchester. Two of the country's most distinctive manorial piles, **Chatsworth House** and **Haddon Hall**, stand near **Bakewell**, a town famed locally not just for its cakes but also for its **well-dressing**, a possibly pagan ritual of thanksgiving for water that is observed in about twenty Peak villages throughout the summer.

Your own transport is a boon in the Peaks, where **trains** penetrate only as far as Buxton from the north and cut through Edale on the Manchester to Sheffield route, augmented by a barely adequate network of local **buses**. There's plenty of **accommodation** here, mostly in B&Bs, with a dozen youth hostels and numerous campsites scattered among them.

Buxton

BUXTON was founded in 79 AD by the Romans, who discovered a spring from which 1500 gallons of pure water gushed out every hour at a constant 28°C, and so famous did the spring become that Mary Queen of Scots was allowed by her captors to come here for treatment of her rheumatism. Its heyday came in the last two decades of the eighteenth century, with the fifth Duke of Devonshire's grand design to create a northern answer to Bath or Cheltenham, a plan thwarted by the climate but not before some distinguished eighteenth-century buildings had formed the gracious Lower Buxton.

The town has now effectively deserted its heritage. **St Ann's Hotel**, its grandest architectural feature – modelled on the Royal Crescent in Bath – has been boarded up for several years, though a million-pound government grant looks set to preserve at least the structure. The thermal baths were closed in 1972, leaving only the Perrier-owned bottling plant by the train station, and **St Ann's Well** on the Crescent, where local people still come to fill their bottles, as reminders of the town's *raison d'être*. The nearby Pump Room is reduced to housing the **Micrarium** (April–Oct daily 10am–5pm; £2.50), where a few dozen interactive displays explicate the world of the microbe.

To the left of the Crescent stands the thousand-seat **Opera House** (tours Sat 11am; £1), the main venue for the **Buxton Opera Festival** held during the last two weeks of July. At the opposite end of the Crescent, the glass and cast-iron canopy hides the entrance to the Cavendish Arcade shopping centre, which makes a hash of preserving the eighteenth-century bath houses.

Behind the well and Micrarium, an attractive park known as **The Slopes** leads up to the Market Place and the **Buxton Museum and Art Gallery** on Terrace Road (Tues–

Fri 9.30am–5.30pm, Sat 9.30am–5pm; £1), which houses a collection of ancient fossils, rocks and pots found in the Peak District, among them jaw bones from Neolithic lions and bears. The displays on the first floor document local history from the Bronze Age to more recent times. The top of the Slopes offers the best prospect over St Ann's Hotel to the **Palace Hotel** and the **Devonshire Hospital**; the latter, built in 1790 as a riding school, is covered by what for a long time was the world's widest domed roof.

As rewarding as any of Buxton's architectural attractions is **Poole's Cavern** (Easter–Oct 10am–5pm; April, May & Oct closed Wed; £3.40), a mile up the hill to the south. The guided-tour patter is irksome, but the orange and blue-grey stalactite formations are amazingly complex and the chambers impressively large. A twenty-minute walk up through the Grinlow Woods from the mouth of the cave leads to **Solomon's Temple**, a Victorian folly with great views across Buxton and beyond.

Practicalities

Frequent train services from Manchester terminate two minutes' walk from the centre at the **train station**, which is also a stop for the two-hourly #R1 Nottingham–Manchester bus. Although the town isn't actually in the National Park, its **tourist office** in the old Natural Baths on the Crescent (daily March–Sept 9.30am–5pm; daily Nov–Feb 10am–4pm; ☎01298/25106) covers the whole of the Peak District.

Accommodation is plentiful, especially along Compton Road, which runs parallel to London Road. *Brightside* at no. 3 (☎01298/24425; ②) and *Griff Guesthouse* at no. 2 (☎01298/23628; ③) are both good, though *Hartington Hotel*, 18 Broad Walk (☎01298/22638; ③), is only a couple of pounds more and overlooks Pavilion Gardens. It is a twenty-minute walk to the **youth hostel**, set in wooded grounds, at the end of London Road (☎01298/22287), and a further five from there up Dukes Drive to the nearest campsite, *Lime Tree Park* (March–Oct; ☎01298/22988).

The densest collection of **restaurants** and a couple of lively pubs pack around Market Place, with the fine pizzas from *Firenze Pizzeria Ristorante*, 3 Eagle Parade, and the inexpensive curries at *Malik Tandoori*, 1 Market Place, standing out. During the day *Dandelion Days* on Bridge Street, by the railway viaduct, has an exceptional range of vegetarian meals.

Castleton and around

The limestone hills of the White Peaks are riddled with water-worn cave systems, best explored in the four show caves within walking distance of **CASTLETON**, ten miles northeast of Buxton. The closest, the **Peak Cavern** (Easter–Oct daily 10am–5pm; £3) is tucked in a gully at the back of the town, its gaping mouth once providing shelter for a rope factory and a small village, of which a vague floor plan remains. It is only fifteen minutes' walk along the road, or less over the fields, to **Speedwell Cavern** (daily 9.30am–5.30pm or dusk; £4.50), entered by boat through a half-mile-long tunnel that was blasted out in search of lead. The boat ride is fun but all you get to see is one cavern containing The Bottomless Pit, a pool where 40,000 tons of mining rubble were dumped without raising the water level.

The other two caves are the world's only source of the sparkling fluorspar known as **Blue John**. Highly prized for ornaments and jewellery for the past 250 years, this semi-precious stone comes in a multitude of hues from blue though deep red to yellow depending on its hydrocarbon impurities. Before being cut and polished it must be soaked in pine resin, a process originally carried out in France, where the term *bleu-jaune* provided the source of its English name. The **Treak Cliff Cavern** (daily March–Oct 9.30am–5.30pm; Nov–Feb daily 9.30am–4.30pm; £3.95), just along the hillside from Speedwell, contains the best examples of the stone in situ and a good deal more in the shop. The cavern also has finer stalactites than the **Blue John Cavern**, fifteen minutes' walk further on (daily

9.30am–6pm or dusk; £4), which compensates by diving deeper into the rock. Narrow steps and sloping paths follow an ancient watercourse through whirlpool-hollowed chambers down to the Dining Room Cavern, where a former owner once held a banquet.

On the surface, the dominant feature of Castleton is **Peveril Castle** (daily April–Sept 10am–6pm; Oct–March 10am–4pm; £1.30), from which the village gets its name. Begun by William I's illegitimate son William Peveril to protect the king's rights to the forest that then covered vast areas of the Peak District, the keep and much of the curtain wall still stand, commanding great views of the Hope Valley, and of the tourists recovering from their caving expeditions in the cafés and pubs below.

Manchester trains stop at Hope **train station** two miles away, linked to Castleton by the hourly #272 bus from Sheffield. All buses stop a hundred yards short of the **Peak National Park Information Centre**, Castle Street (Easter–Oct daily 10am–1pm & 2–5.30pm; Nov–Easter Sat & Sun 10am–1pm & 2–5pm; ☎01433/620 679). The following **places to stay** are both central, *Bargate Cottage*, Market Place (☎01433/620 201; ④) and *Cryer House*, Castle Street (☎01433/620 244; ③), as is the lively **youth hostel**, on Market Place (☎01433/620 235), which dates from the fifteenth century. For a filling meal, try *Ye Olde Cheshire Cheese* on How Lane, which also does B&B (☎01433/620 330; ④), or the Peak Hotel, also on How Lane, which serves equally good bar meals. There is a **campsite**, *Losehill Hall*, half a mile out on the Sheffield road (March–Nov; ☎01433/620 636).

Edale

There's almost nothing to **EDALE** except for a couple of pubs, a train station and a sign pointing to the beginning of the 250-mile **Pennine Way**, which runs from *The Old Nag's Head* across England's backbone to Kirk Yetholm on the Scottish border. An excellent **circular walk** (9 miles; 1300ft; 5hr) uses the first part of the Pennine Way, leading up onto the bleak gritstone table top of **Kinder Scout** (2088ft), below which the village cowers. En route you pass, **Kinder Downfall**, Derbyshire's highest cascade, and scene of the Kinder Scout Trespass of 1932, when dozens of protesters walked onto unused but private land, five subsequently getting prison sentences. It turned out to be the turning point in the fight for public access to open moorland, leading three years later to the formation of the Ramblers' Association.

The *Ramblers' Hotel* (☎01433/670 268; ③), close to the train station, is the most convenient **place to stay** and serves good bar meals, though *The Old Nags Head*, four hundred yards north, has a better ambience. The nearest **youth hostel**, the *Edale YHA Activity Centre* (☎01433/670 302) is a mile and a half east of Edale station, and is accessible along the road to Nether Booth or through the *Fieldhead* campsite (☎01433/70216) behind the **National Park Information Centre** (daily 9am–5.30pm), two hundred yards north of the train station.

Bakewell and around

BAKEWELL, flanking the banks of the River Wye midway between Buxton and Matlock, is known primarily known for **Bakewell Pudding**, a wonderful flakey, almond-flavoured confection invented here around 1860 when a cook botched a recipe for strawberry tart. Almost a century before this fortuitous mishap, the Duke of Rutland set out to develop a spa here to surpass the work his rival, the Duke of Devonshire, was doing at Buxton. The frigidity of the water made failure inevitable, leaving only Bath Gardens beside Rutland Square as a reminder of the venture.

If you're staying here as a base for a visit to Chatsworth or Haddon Hall (see below), you could pop into the **Church** to look at its handsome sixteenth-century tombs: one of local bigwig Sir George Vernon, the other of his daughter Dorothy Manners and her husband John Manners. After that, you might carry on up the hill behind the church to the **Bakewell Old House Museum**, Cunningham Place (April–Oct daily 2–5pm; £1.80), a Tudor house once owned by Richard Arkwright, now housing rustic tools and costumes from Bakewell's past. The energetic can head off along the **Monsal Trail**, which cuts eight miles north through some of Derbyshire's finest limestone valleys to Wyedale, three miles east of Buxton.

Buses stop at Rutland Square, very close to the **tourist office** in Old Market Hall (daily Easter–Oct 9.30am–5.30pm; Nov–Easter 9.30am–5pm; closed Thurs afternoon; ☎01629/813 227). For **accommodation**, try the tranquil, sylvan *Woodlands*, Burton Close (☎01629/812 543; ④), off the Matlock road ten minutes' walk south, or the homely *Bridge B&B*, overlooking the Wye on Bridge Street (☎01629/812 867; ③). *Erica Cottage*, Butts Road (☎01629/813 241; ②), is five minutes' walk from Rutland Square up King Street and about as central as the **youth hostel**, Fly Hill (☎01629/812 313). *Aitch's Wine Bar & Bistro*, 4 Buxton Rd (☎01629/813 895; moderate) is the best **restaurant**, though the bar meals at the *Castle Inn* on Bridge Street are perfectly adequate. For something a bit more lively, try *Scotties Bar and Restaurant*, beneath the bridge, where you can hear live jazz and blues on Thursday, Friday and Saturday nights. Two excellent bakeries, *The Old Original Pudding Shop* on Rutland Square and *Bloomer's* on Matlock Street, both claim to bake Bakewell Pudding to the original recipe.

Chatsworth House and Haddon Hall

The main reason to stop in Bakewell is to visit two fine but very different country houses. The simple, understated **Haddon Hall** (July & Aug Tues–Sat 11am–6pm; April–June & Sept daily 11am–6pm; £4.50), two miles south of Bakewell and on the #R1 bus route, is one of the finest medieval manor houses in England. The Vernons owned it for four hundred years until 1558 when the sole heir, **Dorothy Vernon**, married John Manners, scion of another powerful family who later became Dukes of Rutland. Their union is commemorated on their joint tomb in Bakewell church, but the romantic story of their elopement is probably apocryphal. At the start of the eighteenth century, when the Devonshires outdid the Rutlands by building Chatsworth next door, the hall fell into two centuries of neglect, thereby sparing it from Georgian and Victorian meddling. Restoration early this century revealed the **chapel**'s wall paintings of exotic plants and animals, plastered over at the Reformation. Across the courtyard, the fourteenth-century kitchens – originally detached from the house for fear of fire – are now connected by a passage to the banqueting hall, complete with a beautifully restored roof. A couple of less interesting domestic rooms lead to the house's highlight, the **Long Gallery**, built by John Manners for indoor promenades during bad weather.

Chatsworth House (late March to Oct daily 11am–4.30pm; house & grounds £5.75, grounds only £3), four miles west of Bakewell off the A619, was built in the seventeenth century by the first Duke of Devonshire, and has been in the family ever since.

The monumental Palladian frontage beautifully sets off the hundred acres of formal gardens, but they are tiny in comparison to the vast **park**, redesigned in the 1750s by Capability Brown. In the 1820s, the sixth Duke instigated more substantial changes when he added the north wing and set Joseph Paxton (creator of London's Crystal Palace) to work on the gardens, creating the **Emperor Fountain**. At 296ft, it was the world's highest gravity-fed jet but now attains a meagre third of that. Inside the house, a maze of balconies and grand staircases lead eventually to the **State Apartments**, their ceilings daubed with overblown cherubic figures. None of the rooms is finer than the **Dining Room** in the north wing, its table set as it was for the visit of George V and Queen Mary in 1933, and its wall hung with seven Van Dykes. Vases of the semi-precious Blue John stone (see p.431) flank the door through to the **Sculpture Gallery**, where exhausted visitors can admire a Rembrandt and a Franz Hals before falling out into the gardens. The hourly #170 **bus** (#58 on Sun) from Bakewell to Baslow can drop you within a mile of the house, but the mile-and-a-half walk south from Baslow through the deer park avoids the busy approach road.

Eyam

Within a year of September 7, 1665, the attractive hillside settlement of **EYAM** (pronounced "Eem"), eight miles north of Bakewell, had lost three quarters of its population of 350 to the bubonic plague, a calamity that earned it the enduring epithet, "The Plague Village". The first victim was one George Viccars, a tailor who is said to have released some infected fleas from a package of cloth brought from London to one of the so-called **plague cottages** next to the church. The ensuing epidemic was prevented from spreading by a self-imposed quarantine led by the rector, William Mompesson, who arranged for food to be left at places on the parish boundary – such as **Mompesson's Well**, half a mile up the hill to the north. (Payment was made with coins left in pools of disinfecting vinegar – the stone bowls in which they were immersed can still be seen.)

Mompesson's grave lies in the shadow of a richly carved eighth-century **Celtic cross** in the churchyard, while panels inside the church tell more of the village's history, highlighting a number of minor sites dotted around the town. The most harrowing of these are the **Riley Graves**, half a mile east of the village, where a Mrs Hancock buried her husband, three sons and three daughters within eight days in August 1666. Six years after the plague ended **Eyam Hall** (Wed, Thurs, Sun & Bank hols 11am–5.30pm; £3.25) was built for Thomas Wright a hundred yards west of the church, possibly in an attempt to install his son as the squire of the depleted village. Wright's heirs have lived in it ever since, building up a fine collection of furnishings that can be seen on fascinatingly anecdotal hour-long guided tours.

Buses #65 and #67 between Sheffield and Buxton run along Church Street where you'll find one of the village's few **B&Bs**, the comfortable *Delf View House* (☎01433/631533; ④). It is a stiff twenty-minute walk uphill to Eyam **youth hostel**, a large Victorian house on Hawkhill Road (☎01433/630 335). The best place to **eat** is the moderately priced *Miner's Arms* on Water Lane off the main square.

Cheshire

For the most part, Cheshire is a county of rolling green countryside and country manor houses, interspersed with dairy farms from whose churns emerge tons of delicious, crumbly, white Cheshire cheese. The county town, **Chester**, with its complete circuit of town walls and partly Tudor centre, is as alluring as any of the country's northern towns, capturing the essence of what has always been one of England's wealthiest rural counties. By contrast Crewe, the only other Cheshire town of any appreciable size, is a place where you may find yourself having to change trains, but are unlikely to want to stay. Far more enjoyable are the villages of the **Cheshire Plain**, set in a landscape that conjures archetypal images of pastoral England.

Chester

In 1779 Boswell wrote to Samuel Johnson: "Chester pleases me more than any town I ever saw." **CHESTER** has changed since then, but not so much. A glorious two-mile ring of medieval and Roman walls encircles a neat kernel of Tudor and Victorian buildings, including the unique raised arcades called the "Rows". Under the Romans Deva Castra, as it was known, became their largest known fortress in Britain. Later, trade routes to Ireland made Chester the most prosperous port in the northwest, a status it recovered after the English Civil War, which brought a two-year-long siege to the town at the hands of the Parliamentarians. By the middle of the eighteenth century, however, silting of the port had forced the Irish trade to be rerouted first through Parkgate on the Dee estuary, and then to Liverpool. Things improved a little with the industrial revolution, as the canal and railway networks made Chester an important regional trading centre, a function it still retains.

Arrival, information and accommodation

Most bus services from Liverpool arrive at **Chester bus station**, close to the northern city walls and to Northgate Street, where you'll find the main **tourist office** in the town hall (May–Oct Mon–Sat 9am–7.30pm, Sun 10am–4pm; Nov–April Mon–Sat 9am–5.30pm, Sun 10am–4pm; ☎01244/318 356). Most other buses use the **bus exchange** just behind the town hall. From the **train station** it's a ten-minute walk to the Eastgate Clock, where St John Street leads to the **Chester Visitor Centre**, Vicars Lane (daily Easter–Oct 9am–7pm; Nov–Easter 9am–7pm; ☎01244/351 609), which has much the same information, but also books tickets for Irish ferries.

In high summer, it's a good idea to book **accommodation** in advance. One of the cheapest places around is *R & A Davies*, centrally located at 22 Cuppin St (☎01244/340 452; ②). Brook Street, near the train station, boasts a bevy of B&Bs, one of the best being the *Ormonde Guesthouse*, 126 Brook St (☎01244/328 816; ②). Sixteenth-century *Castle House*, 23 Castle St (☎01244/350 354; ④), is excellent, as is the seventeenth-century *Chester Town House*, 23 King St (☎01244/350 021; ④). For all the amenities, head for the *Pied Bull* (☎01244/325 829; ⑦), an old coaching inn on Northgate Street. The **youth hostel**, 40 Hough Green (☎01244/680056), is twenty minutes' walk from The Cross – cross Grosvenor Bridge and turn right at the roundabout. It is 500 yards along on the right. The easiest **campsite** to get to is *Chester Southerly Caravan Park* (March–Nov; ☎01829/270 791; bus #1 from the bus station), three miles away off the A55, served by all Wrexham-bound buses.

The Town

The main thoroughfares of Chester's Roman grid plan meet at **The Cross**, where the town crier welcomes visitors to the city (April–Sept Tues–Sat noon & 2pm). Both sides of all four streets are lined by **The Rows**, unique galleried arcades running on top of the ground-floor shops. The engaging black and white tableau is a blend of genuine Tudor houses and Victorian half-timbered imitations, with the finest Tudor buildings on Watergate Street – though Eastgate Street is perhaps the most picturesque, leading to the filigree Jubilee Clock. The origin of The Rows is still controversial – they were first recorded soon after the fire that wrecked Chester in 1278, and may originally have been built on top of the heaped rubble left after the blaze.

For a good introduction to the town, head south from the Cross to the **Chester Heritage Centre**, Bridge Street Row (Mon–Sat 11am–5pm, Sun noon–5pm; £1), which gives an overview of Chester's history from Roman times to the Industrial Revolution. Don't overlook the medieval carved oak roof of what used to be St Michael's church. Whether you want a baked potato or not, *Spudulike*, uphill at 43 Bridge St, warrants a moment's diversion for the well-preserved Roman hypocaust (early central heating), part of a bathhouse that extended under the *Lawley's China Shop* around the corner at 18 St Michael's Row, where a piece of mosaic is visible in the basement.

You can get the best insight into Chester's Roman heritage at **Dewa Roman Experience** (daily 9am–5pm; £3.50), tucked away on Pierpoint Lane which joins Bridge Street at the Yorkshire Bank. You're free to touch the archeological finds on show after following an armoured soldier through Roman street scenes and an excavation of Roman, Saxon and medieval buildings.

North of The Cross, another Roman fragment is visible through a window set into the side wall of the neo-Gothic town hall, which stands across Northgate Street from the heavily restored **Cathedral**, entered through the Georgian Abbey Square. Taking the role of cathedral in 1541 after the Dissolution of the Monasteries, this Benedictine church is dedicated to Saint Werburgh, a seventh-century Saxon princess who became Chester's patron saint. Parts of the eleventh-century structure can still be seen in the north transept but the highlights in an otherwise simple interior are the fourteenth-century choir stalls, with their intricately carved misericords. Doors in the north wall of the nave lead into the shady sixteenth-century cloisters, encircling a small garden.

East of the cathedral, steps provide access to the top of the two-mile girdle of the medieval and Roman **city walls** – the most complete set in Britain, though in places the wall is barely above street level. You can walk past all its turrets and gateways in an hour or two, calling first at the fifteenth-century **King Charles Tower** (April–Oct Sat 10am–5pm; Sun 2–5pm; 50p), in the northeast corner. So named because Charles I is said to have stood here in 1645 watching his troops being beaten on Rowton Moor, it now houses a small but interesting exhibition on the siege of Chester, immediately after the Royalist defeat. The **Water Tower** (same times as King Charles Tower; 50p), at the northwest corner, houses a display charting, among other aspects of the city's trading past, the changes brought about by the gradual silting of the River Dee. South from the tower you'll see **Roodee**, England's oldest racecourse, laid out on a silted bow where the Roman docks once stood. Races are still held here in May, June and July; the tourist office has further details.

Until nineteenth-century excavation work, much of the wall near the Water Tower was propped up by scores of sculpted panels and engraved headstones, now on display at the **Grosvenor Museum** on Grosvenor Street (Mon–Sat 10.30am–5pm, Sun 2–5pm; free), located near the southern end of Roodee. The back of the museum opens into a preserved Georgian house complete with rickety floors and sloping stairs. Across the road on Castle Street, the dull **Cheshire Military Museum** (Mon–Fri 9am–5pm, Sat & Sun 9am–noon & 1pm–5pm; 50p) inhabits part of the same complex as the **Norman Castle** (Easter–Sept daily 10am–6pm; Oct–Easter 10am–4pm; free), founded by William the Conqueror but most of it little older than the Greek Revival Assize Courts on the same site. The castle's history is explained in a couple of cells in the guard room, but the gracefully simple St Mary de Castro chapel is the main attraction.

South of the castle the wall is buried under the street, but it rises again alongside the **Roman Gardens** (unrestricted access), at the southeast corner, where Roman foundations dug up during redevelopment have been liberally distributed. Across the road, half of the **Roman Amphitheatre** has been excavated (Easter–Sept 10am–6pm; Oct–Easter 10am–1pm & 2–4pm; free); it is estimated to have held seven thousand spectators, making it the largest in Britain, but the stonework is barely head-high now.

The partly ruined **Church of St John the Baptist**, a little to the east, was founded by the Saxon princess Aethelflaeda and briefly served as the cathedral of Mercia.

Though smaller than St Werburgh's it is considerably more impressive, the solid Norman pillars of the nave rising to a Transitional triforium and Early English clerestory. Outside are the ruins of the northwest tower, which collapsed in 1881, possibly weakened by its use as a Parliamentarian gun emplacement during the Civil War.

From the southern edge of the city walls, steps lead to The Groves, on the banks of the Dee, where *Bithells Boats* runs half-hour cruises on the river (every 15min: April–Nov 10am–6.30pm; Dec–March Sat & Sun 11–4pm; £2.50) and two-hour trips in the summer (daily 11am; Wed & Sat also 8.15pm).

Eating and drinking

You can't walk more than a few paces in Chester without coming across somewhere good to **eat or drink**, as often as not in a medieval crypt or Tudor building. For inexpensive bistro-style dishes during the day, try the *Cathedral Refectory* in the thirteenth-century monks' dining room. Another inexpensive choice is *Telford's Warehouse*, a Mexican-Italian restaurant in a pub built partly over the turning basin of the Shropshire Union Canal, on Raymond Street. Slightly more expensive, the highly praised *Garden House*, 1 Rufus Court (☎01244/313 251), specializes in vegetarian fare, but also serves fish, meat and game. Alternatively, there's *Francs*, 14 Cuppin St (☎01244/317 952), an excellent and very French bistro, or *Mama Mia*, 87 Werburgh St (☎01244/314 663), an imaginative pizzeria with speciality fish and vegetarian dishes.

For a wide choice of ales, the best **pub** to head for is *The Ale Taster*, an intimate pub by the river on The Groves, while *The Crypt*, 28 Eastgate St, serves good bar food in a thirteenth-century rib-vaulted basement. *Ye Olde Boot Inn*, Eastgate Row, is a characterful pub with a backroom where fourteen Roundheads were killed and the highbacked seat was once used by soliciting prostitutes. Wine, real ales and good bar meals can be had at *Watergates*, a cosy wine bar in a crypt formerly used as a wine merchants, on Watergate Square. For live music or comedy, check out *Alexander's Jazz Theatre and Café Bar*, 2 Rufus Court, a chic, continental style café-bar with tapas from the counter.

Around Chester

There are two main attractions in the environs of Chester: the **zoo** and the **boat museum** at Ellesmere Port. On a Sunday you can get a *Cheshire Bus* Adventurer ticket (£3 on the bus), which gives unlimited bus travel throughout the county and a discount on entry charges to the zoo and museum.

CHESTER ZOO

Chester's most popular attraction, **Chester Zoo** (April–Sept 10am–5.30pm; Oct–March 10am–6pm; £7), is one of the best in Europe and, after London, is the second largest in Britain, spreading over 110 landscaped acres. The zoo is well known for its conservation projects and has had recent success with a pair of Asiatic lions who, within four months of their introduction from north India in 1994, became the parents of three healthy cubs. Animals are grouped by region in large paddocks viewed from a maze of pathways or from the creeping monorail (80p). The zoo entrance is signposted off the A41 to the north of town and reached by bus #40 every ten minutes from the bus exchange or the #11c and #12c *Merseybus* to Liverpool.

ELLESMERE PORT BOAT MUSEUM

It's claimed that the **Ellesmere Port Boat Museum** (April–Oct 10am–5pm; Nov–March 11am–4pm; closed Fri and some Thurs; £4.50) seven miles north of Chester, has Britain's largest collection of floating canal vessels, a contention that seems completely plausible when you see the flotilla. Scores of barges are scattered throughout the canal basin and staircase of locks where the Shropshire Union Canal meets the refinery-lined River Mersey at the head of the Manchester Ship Canal. Indoor exhibits trace the history of canals and their construction, and you can take a short ride on a narrow boat (£1.50). The museum is five minutes' walk from Ellesmere Port train station (change at Hooton from Chester) or take buses #2 or #3 from Chester bus station.

The Cheshire Plain

Chester is no measure of the rest of the county, a region of lush pastureland and unflustered little towns strung together by hedgerowed lanes. Perhaps because of the familiarity of the landscape, the Danes took a liking to the **Cheshire Plain**, leaving the names of the River Dane and **Knutsford** (Canute's ford) as evidence of their occupation. Since that time farming has continued to be the mainstay of the county's economy, but salt mining around Northwich and silk manufacture in Macclesfield have contributed in their day. Once the main centre of southern Cheshire, **Nantwich** has benefited from the rise of nearby Crewe and is today a sleepy town packed with four-hundred-year-old houses and shops.

Knutsford

While conquering the greater part of England between 1015 and 1018 the Danish king Knut (Canute) is said to have crossed Lily Stream at the spot where the winding streets and eighteenth-century houses of **KNUTSFORD** now stand. From medieval times it was important locally for its market and coaching inns, but today is a quiet wealthy community that makes much of its having been the model for Cranford in the book of the same name by **Elizabeth Gaskell**; she spent a few childhood years here and is buried outside the Unitarian church by the train station. Admirers of Mrs Gaskell can identify the houses mentioned in the novel, but for most visitors the buildings raised by Manchester glovemaker and philanthropist **Richard Watt** will have a more immediate appeal – though their loosely Mediterranean style may not be to everyone's taste. The most visible buildings are the terracotta-roofed Ruskin Rooms on Drury Lane, built as a reading and recreation place for the townspeople, and The King's Coffee House, King Street, which now houses the highly regarded and expensive *La Belle Epoque* restaurant (☎01565/633 060), with its Art-Nouveau interior.

Trains on the Manchester–Chester line stop each hour except for Sundays, when a bus from Manchester's *Metrolink* terminus at Altrincham is the easiest way to get here. The **tourist office** is right opposite the station on Toft Road (Mon–Thurs 8.45am–5pm, Fri 8.45am–4.30pm; ☎01565/632 611) and can fill you in on Gaskellian associations. Pilgrims might want to **stay** at *The Royal George Hotel*, King Street (☎01565/634151; ⑦), which features in several of Gaskell's novels, but those seeking cheaper accommodation will be hard pressed. *Mrs Morton*, 8 Lee Close (☎01565/633 596; ③) and *Krakatoa*, Manor Park South (☎01565/651 157; ③) have only one room each.

Nantwich

In 1583 **NANTWICH** was almost entirely destroyed by fire. Such was the town's importance for its salt production that Elizabeth I donated £1000 and ordered a nationwide appeal to help with rebuilding. A largely pedestrianized centre makes a good place to amble around and see Cheshire's second-best set of timber-framed buildings, with an essential stop being the predominantly fourteenth-century **Church of St Mary**, where the ribbed vaulting in the chancel has bosses depicting the Virgin's life. The church and neighbouring **Sweetbriar Hall** are two of the three buildings to survive the fire – the other was the timber-framed Elizabethan **Churche's Mansion** in Hospital Street.

The *Crown Hotel* on the High Street is perhaps the most striking of the black-and-white buildings, the gallery on the top floor now converted into separate rooms. It's also one of the most atmospheric and lively spots in town for a drink. Elements of the town's former cottage industries of cheese-, salt- and shoemaking are showcased in the small **Nantwich Museum** on Pillory Street (April–Sept daily except Wed & Sun 10.30am–4.30pm; Oct–March also closed Mon; free).

The **train station** sees hourly traffic on the Manchester–Crewe–Cardiff line and is only five minutes' walk from the **tourist office**, Church House, Church Walk (Mon–Fri 8.45am–5.15pm plus Sat morning in summer; ☎01270/610 983). Pick of the **accommodation** is the *Crown Hotel* on the High Street (☎01270/625 283; ⑥), followed by *The Red Cow*, 51 Beam St (☎01270/628 581; ③) across from the **bus station**. *Churche's Mansion*, Hospital Street (☎01270/625 933) is the best **restaurant**; good inexpensive fare is on offer at *The Lamb* on Hospital Street.

Liverpool

If one city in England could be said to stand as a symbol of a nation in decline, it would be **LIVERPOOL**. Once the country's main transatlantic port and the empire's second city, it's associated now with resilience to adversity. For years Liverpool has lived with poverty and mass unemployment, but nothing has broken its extraordinary spirit of community, a spirit that emerged strongly in the aftermath of the Hillsborough football stadium disaster of 1989, when the deaths of 95 Liverpool supporters seemed to unite the whole city. Acerbic wit and loyalty to one of the city's two top-flight football teams are the linchpins of scouse culture – though Liverpool makes great play of its musical heritage, which is reasonable enough from the city that produced the Beatles.

This is a city built on trade. Although it gained its charter from King John in 1207, Liverpool remained a humble fishing village for half a millennium until the silting-up of Chester and the booming slave trade prompted the building of the first dock in 1715. From then until the abolition of slavery in Britain in 1807, Liverpool was the apex of the **slaving triangle** in which firearms, alcohol and textiles were traded for African slaves, who were then shipped to the Caribbean and America. The holds were filled with tobacco, raw cotton and sugar for the return journey. After abolition the port continued to grow into a seven-mile chain of docks, not only for freight but also to cope with wholesale European **emigration**, which saw nine million people from half of Europe leave for the Americas and Australasia between 1830 and 1930. Some never made it further than Liverpool and contributed to a five-fold increase in population in fifty years. An even larger boost came with immigration from the Caribbean, China and especially Ireland, in the wake of the potato famine in 1845. The resulting mix became one of Britain's earliest multi-ethnic communities, described by Carl Jung as "the pool of life".

The docks were busy until the middle of this century when a number of factors led to the port's present moribund state: cheap air fares saw off the lucrative liner business; trade with the dwindling Empire declined while European traffic boosted south-eastern ports at Tilbury, Harwich and Southampton; and containerization meant reduced demand for handling and warehousing. Successive Labour-led city councils have tried to alleviate the depressed economy, with the most extreme measures being during Derek Hatton's control from 1983 to 1986. Defying Margaret Thatcher's impositions on local government spending, the council maintained jobs and services at the cost of a massive negative budget, a course of action which eventually led the central Labour party to disqualify the Hatton clique. While Hatton survived prosecution for fraud, a more moderate Labour group was installed on Merseyside, but no solution has yet been found to the city's economic haemorrhage.

Liverpool's legacy of magnificent municipal buildings – best seen en masse from across the water or on the Mersey ferry – are the chief attractions of the cityscape, along with its two **cathedrals**. The city's mercantile past and aspects of its recent history are well covered in a number of museums and galleries, especially in the rejuvenated warehouses of **Albert Dock**, site of the **Tate Gallery**. These sights can easily sustain a day or two – and make time to drop into one of Liverpool's many late-closing bars, the surest way to get the feel of the place.

Arrival, information and accommodation

Mainline trains pull in to **Lime Street** station, which faces the **bus station** along the curve of Roe Street. *National Express* buses stop on Islington Street, just north of Lime Street. The suburban *Merseyrail* system calls at four underground stations in the city including Lime Street and **Central**, under the main post office where Ranelagh Street meets Bold Street. Pick up timetables, maps and the comprehensive *Merseyside Pocket Guide* (25p) at the **Merseyside Welcome Centre**, in Clayton Square Shopping Centre (Mon–Sat 9.30am–5.30pm; ☎0151/709 3631), or the **tourist office**, Atlantic Pavilion, Albert Dock (daily 10am–5.30pm; ☎0151/708 8854).

Hotels and B&Bs

Belvedere, 83 Mount Pleasant (☎0151/709 2356). Convenient and cheap hotel. ③.

Britannia Adelphi Hotel, Ranelagh Place (☎0151/709 7200). Liverpool's premier hotel, once catering to passenger liner custom. Now slightly faded, it is still worth dropping in for afternoon tea in the chandeliered lounge, and the weekend discounts are massive. ⑥.

Feathers Hotel, 119–25 Mount Pleasant (☎0151/709 9655). A converted and modernized terrace of Georgian houses. Frequent winner of the Merseyside Tourist Board Hotel of the Year Award. ③.

Lord Nelson, Lord Nelson St (☎0151/709 4362). Conveniently located just behind Lime Street Station. ④.

Redcroft, 12 Parkfield Rd (☎0151/727 3723). Three miles out from the centre (bus #20, #21, #32 or #82), but close to Sefton Park and the pubs and restaurants of Lark Lane. ②.

Shaftsbury Hotel, Mount Pleasant (☎0151/709 4421). Being the backdrop for the lovers' tryst in *Letter to Brezhnev* doesn't guarantee high standards, but at least it's central. ④.

Hostels

Embassie Youth Hostel, 1 Falkner Square (☎0151/707 1089). A private hostel with dorm beds and a continental breakfast for £8.50. Twenty minutes' walk from Lime Street station; bus #80.

John Moores University, Cathedral Park, St James Rd (☎0151/709 3197). In the shadow of the cathedral. Self-catering accommodation (July–Sept) at £14 per bed; book through the tourist office.

University of Liverpool Halls of Residence, Greenbank Lane (☎0151/794 6405). Inconveniently situated four miles out of the centre (bus #80) and only open during university vacations. B&B costs £12.50 in a single room; book through the tourist office.

YMCA, 56 Mount Pleasant (☎0151/709 9516). Separate floors for men and women. Double (£21.50) and single (£12) rooms are basic, but there is no curfew and the restaurant has bargain meals.

YWCA, 1 Rodney St (☎0151/709 7791). Recently upgraded single rooms for women only, at £10 a night. Centrally heated and with communal kitchens.

The City

The main sights are fairly widely scattered throughout the centre of Liverpool but you can easily walk between most of them, through cityscapes ranging from soulless shopping arcades to the regal Georgian Terraces around Rodney Street. Even the walk from the Anglican cathedral through the shops to Albert Dock will only take half an hour.

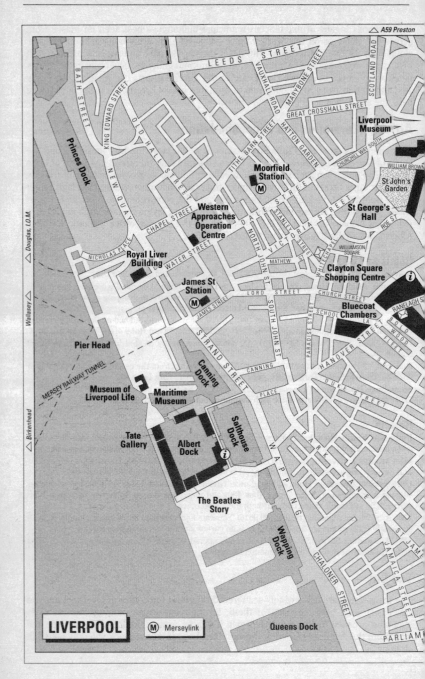

△ A59 Preston

LEEDS STREET

VAUXHALL ROAD

MARYBONE STREET

SCOTLAND ROAD

GREAT CROSSHALL STREET

BATH STREET

KING EDWARD STREET

OLD HALL STREET

NEW QUAY

TITHE BARN STREET

HATTON GARDEN

CHURCHILL WAY SOUTH

WILLIAM BROWN

Liverpool Museum

Princes Dock

Moorfield Station (M)

St John's Garden

CHAPEL STREET

DALE STREET

STANLEY STREET

VICTORIA STREET

ROE ST

Western Approaches Operation Centre

NICHOLAS PLACE

WATER STREET

NORTH JOHN ST

MATHEW

St George's Hall

WILLIAMSON SQUARE

WHITECHAPEL

Royal Liver Building

James St Station (M)

JAMES STREET

LORD   STREET

SOUTH JOHN ST

PARADISE STREET

SCHOOL LA

CHURCH STREET

Clayton Square Shopping Centre (i)

RANELAGH S

BOLD

WOOD

FLEET

SEE

Bluecoat Chambers

Pier Head

STRAND STREET

CANNING

HANOVER STREET

DUKE STREET

MERSEY RAILWAY TUNNEL

Canning Dock

PLACE

△ Wallasey

△ Birkenhead

△ Douglas, I.O.M.

Museum of Liverpool Life

Maritime Museum

Tate Gallery

Albert Dock (i)

Salthouse Dock

PARK LANE

WAPPING

JAMACA STREET

The Beatles Story

Wapping Dock

CHALONER STREET

JAME

PARLIAM

LIVERPOOL

(M) Merseylink

Queens Dock

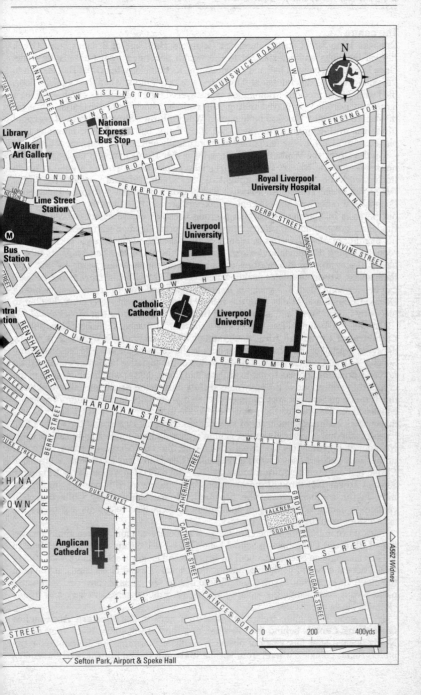

N

Library
Walker
Art Gallery

National
Express
Bus Stop

NEW ISLINGTON

ISLINGTON

ST ANNE STREET

BRUNSWICK ROAD

LOW HILL

KENSINGTON

PRESCOT STREET

HALL LANE

LONDON

ROAD

PEMBROKE PLACE

Royal Liverpool
University Hospital

Lime Street
Station

LORD
NELSON ST

M

Bus
Station

DERBY STREET

IRVINE STREET

MINSHULL ST

Liverpool
University

BROWNLOW HILL

SMITHDOWN LANE

ntral
tion

BENSHAW STREET

MOUNT PLEASANT

Catholic
Cathedral

Liverpool
University

ABERCROMBY SQUARE

GROVE STREET

HARDMAN STREET

HOPE STREET

RONEY STREET

BERRY STREET

DUKE STREET

MYRTLE STREET

CATHERINE STREET

HINA
OWN

ST GEORGE STREET

UPPER DUKE STREET

HOPE STREET

CATHERINE STREET

FALKNER
SQUARE

GROVE STREET

A562 Widnes

Anglican
Cathedral

STREET

PARLIAMENT STREET

MULGRAVE STREET

UPPER

PRINCES ROAD

STREET

0   200   400yds

▽ Sefton Park, Airport & Speke Hall

The centre

Opposite Lime Street station stands **St George's Hall**, one of Britain's finest Greek Revival buildings and a testament to the wealth generated from transatlantic trade. Once Liverpool's concert hall and crown courts, its tunnel-vaulted Great Hall is open to the public for the odd craft fair and for three weeks in August when the exquisite floor, tiled with 30,000 precious Minton tiles, is uncovered. The hall's Willis organ – the third largest in Europe – is played during July recitals; check with the tourist office for details. To the right, classical buildings on William Brown Street house the **Liverpool Museum and Planetarium** (Mon–Sat 10am–5pm, Sun noon–5pm; museum free, planetarium £1.20), where temporary exhibits usually outclass the permanent displays.

Up the street, the **Walker Art Gallery** (Mon–Sat 10am–5pm, Sun noon–5pm; free) houses one of the country's finest provincial art collections. There's a good range of Italian work on show, the highlight being Simone Martini's expressive *Christ Discovered in the Temple*. An assertive Rembrandt self-portrait is displayed alongside Poussin and other seventeenth-century masters across the hall in the Audley Gallery, but here, as in Manchester, British painting occupies centre stage. George Stubbs, England's greatest animal painter, shows off his preoccupation with horse anatomy in his painting of *Molly Longlegs* in room 2, while Turner's maturing style is captured in room 6 through the romantic *Linlithgo Palace* and the much later *Landscape*, its subject barely discernible in the washes of colour. Contemporaneous work by the Pre-Raphaelites, whose nostalgiac fastidiousness is typified by Millais' *Lorenzo and Isabella*, can be viewed in room 3. A group of Impressionists, and Post-Impressionists including Degas, Cézanne and Monet drag the collection into the twentieth century, leading to pieces by Lucian Freud and an archetypal Hockney, *Peter Getting Out of Nick's Pool*.

On the hill behind Lime Street rises the funnel-shaped Catholic **Metropolitan Cathedral of Christ the King**, denigratingly known as "Paddy's Wigwam". A rapidly decaying symbol of modernism, it was built in the 1960s in the wake of the revitalizing Second Vatican Council, and was raised on top of the tentative beginnings of Sir Edwin Lutyens' grandiose project to outdo St Peter's in Rome, bits of which can be seen in the crypt. At the other end of the aptly named Hope Street, the **Anglican Cathedral** looks much more ancient but was completed eleven years later in 1978, after 74 years in construction. The last of the great Neo-Gothic structures, Sir Giles Gilbert Scott's masterwork claims a smattering of superlatives: Britain's largest and the world's fifth largest cathedral, the world's tallest Gothic arches and the highest and heaviest bells. Not enough important people have died to fill out the stark pillarless interior, but a visit to the finely detailed Lady Chapel and a look at Elizabeth Frink's last work, a bronze of Christ, pad out the free **guided tours** (☎0151/709 6271). On a clear day, a trip up the 330-foot **Tower** (£1) through the cavernous belfry is rewarded by views to the Welsh hills. In the southern arcade the **Elizabeth Hoare Embroidery Collection** (£3) contains a manageable display of sumptuous ecclesiastical vestments and traces the art's history from the thirteenth century.

Back down in the core of the city, just west of Central Station, the beautifully proportioned **Bluecoat Chambers** in School Lane (Tues–Sat 10.30am–5pm; free) was built in 1717 as an Anglican boarding school for orphans and is now a contemporary art gallery with a decent café and bookshop, hosting occasional jazz and blues bands. If you're in the mood for expenditure, you could nip into nearby **Quiggins**, a converted warehouse packed with ever-changing shoplets hawking records, posters, jewellery and trendy clothing, plus a cheap café.

It's a good ten-minute trek northwest from here to the **Western Approaches Operations Centre**, behind the town hall at 1 Rumford St (daily 10am–4pm; £3.99). Newly opened after fifty years of obscurity, it fills about a third of the hundred-room underground complex where, from spring 1941 until the end of the war, the Anglo-

THE BEATLES IN LIVERPOOL

Liverpool has sustained its musical impetus ever since the Sixties and is still turning out some excellent bands, but none is ever likely to eclipse the Beatles. **Mathew Street**, five minutes' walk west of Central station, is where *The Cavern* used to be; once the womb of Merseybeat, it's become a little enclave of Beatles nostalgia, most of it bogus. The club no longer exists, having been covered over by the Cavern Walks Shopping Arcade, with an awful bronze statue of the boys in the atrium. A couple of pubs, *The Abbey Road* and *Lennon's Bar*, raise no more than a token toast to the soul of Beatlemania, embodied better at *The Beatles Shop*, 31 Mathew St, with the "largest range of Beatles gear in the world". A walk around the corner onto Stanley Street reveals Eleanor Rigby sitting on her park bench.

Misplaced in the Albert Dock, **The Beatles Story** (Easter–Oct daily 10am–6pm and later in July & Aug; Nov–Easter Mon–Fri 11am–5pm, Sat & Sun 10am–6pm; £4.95) is a spiritless but informative show, tracing The Beatles' rise from the early days at The Cavern (re-created here) to their disparate solo careers, ending with John Lennon's death. John is further commemorated with a new exhibition of photos in the shop adjoining the museum. Dedicated pilgrims will get more from the two-hour **Beatles Magical History Tour** (£6.50), on board a customized double-decker bus staffed by guides with – in some cases – first-hand acquaintance with the Beatles. It leaves Albert Dock daily at 2.20pm, visiting Strawberry Fields (a Salvation Army home), Penny Lane (an ordinary suburban street), and the terraced houses where the lads grew up. The local bus #19 also passes Penny Lane and Strawberry Fields, but then you miss the anecdotes.

Beatlemania is wholeheartedly celebrated on August Bank Holiday Monday (the last Monday of the month) at the culmination of the annual **Mathew Street Festival**, filling the town centre with wannabe Beatles, jiving to the sounds of tunes that have been hummed and strummed in Liverpool since the first concert rocked the Cavern in the 1960s.

American air-sea campaign was orchestrated. Much of the original furniture and many of the huge wall maps have been restored or replicated to re-create the map room, nerve centre of the so-called "Citadel", where the staff spent virtually all their time during the most intense periods of activity.

Pier Head and Albert Dock

Though the tumult of shipping which once fought the current here has gone, the **Pier Head** landing stage remains the embarkation point for the **Mersey Ferries** to Woodside (for Birkenhead) and Seacombe. Ride one if only for the magnificent views of the Liverpool skyline and the prominent Liver Insurance Building – it's topped by the "Liver Birds", a couple of cormorants which have become the symbol of the city. Straightforward ferry shuttles operate only in the rush hours; at other times the boats run circular **sightseeing cruises** (hourly Mon–Fri 10am–3pm, Sat & Sun 10am–7pm; £2.75) complete with sappy commentary and repeated renditions of Gerry Marsden's *Ferry 'cross the Mersey*.

Albert Dock, five minutes' walk south, started to decline at the beginning of this century, as the new deep-draught ships were unable to berth here, and last saw service in 1972. A decade later the site was given a complete scrub-down and refit, with much of the space in the former warehouses being turned over to speciality shops and monuments to the more meaningful economic activities that used to take place here. The **Maritime Museum** (daily 10.30am–5.30pm; £2.50 for the day) fills one wing and in summer takes over part of Canning dock for floating displays. Spread over four floors, it has sections on Britain's Customs and Excise, the history of Liverpool's evolution as a port and shipbuilding centre, and models of seacraft from Samoan rafts to opulent passenger liners. An illuminating display details Liverpool's pivotal role as a springboard for emmigrants – the Irish potato famine and a multiplicity of European wars, combined with the lure of gold and free land, brought people scurrying here to buy their passage to North America or Australia. To cater for them, short-stay lodging houses sprang up all over the centre, as illustrated in an 1854 street scene complete with enthusiastic role-players (Wed–Sun).

The latest addition to the museum, entitled *Transatlantic Slavery – Against Human Dignity*, is both enlightening, shocking and refreshingly honest, and banishes years of Eurocentric excuses, to expose the true horror of the exploitation of African slaves who were kidnapped, abused and sold as property. The slave trade continued for four hundred years up to 1900; even after official abolition in 1807 the number of slaves shipped to sugar plantations in the Americas ran into the millions. The conditions endured by slaves on the transatlantic voyage are illustrated by a reconstruction of a slave ship, echoing with haunting voices reading from diaries of slaves and slavers, telling of rape, torture and death. The exhibition winds up with a video of Africans resident in Britain airing their views on the impact of slavery and the legacy of racism, after which head for the museum's excellent top-floor café, approached through a hall hung with nineteenth century racist propoganda, countered by protest cartoons from the abolitionist camp.

The same entry ticket gets you into the Piermaster's House, the Cooperage and the **Museum of Liverpool Life** (same hours), across the dock outside. Particularly revealing about the hardships that have moulded the resilient scouse character, it has excellent sections on the role of trade unions, the women's suffrage movement and the social unrest that led to the Toxteth riots. It is not all doom and gloom though – Merseyside football gets good coverage, as does the homegrown soap *Brookside*.

The neighbouring **Tate Gallery Liverpool** (Tues–Sun 10am–6pm; free) is the country's foremost twentieth-century art showcase outside the capital, drawing from the same pool of paintings and sculpture as its London cousin, and often displaying them more successfully in its spacious and well-lit rooms. One floor is devoted to large long-term installations like the "New Realities" exhibition on postwar European art, while other rooms are occupied by briefer retrospectives and an ever-changing display of individual works.

The outskirts

Located by Liverpool's airport, six miles southeast of the centre, **Speke Hall** (April–Oct Tues–Sun 1–5.30pm; Nov to mid-Dec Sat & Sun 1–4.30pm; house and gardens £3.40; gardens April to mid-Dec Tues–Sun noon–4pm; £1) is one of the country's finest examples of Elizabethan timbered architecture. Sitting in an oasis of rhododendrons, the house encloses a beautifully proportioned courtyard overlooked by myriad diamond panes. Highlights of the interior are the Jacobean plasterwork in the Great Parlour and the Great Hall's carved oak panel. The #80 bus to the airport runs within half a mile of the entrance.

For a glimpse of one of the more benign aspects of Merseyside's industrial past, take the *Merseyrail* under the river to **Port Sunlight**, a garden village created in 1888 by industrialist William Hesketh Lever for the workers at his soap factory. The project, similar in scope to those of Titus Salt at Saltaire near Bradford and John Cadbury at Bourneville in Birmingham (see p.382), is explained at the **Port Sunlight Heritage Centre**, 95 Greendale Rd (April–Oct daily 10am–4pm; Nov–March Mon–Fri noon–4pm; 20p), set amid the open-planned housing estates. Off Greendale Road, a little further from Port Sunlight station, the **Lady Lever Art Gallery** (Mon–Sat 10am–5pm; Sun noon–5pm; free) houses a small collection of English eighteenth-century furniture and Pre-Raphaelite paintings, by artists such as Rosetti.

Eating, drinking and nightlife

Although short on top-notch **restaurants**, Liverpool has several perfectly serviceable places with an emphasis on value for money. Most are around Hardman and Bold streets, on Albert Dock, and along Nelson Street, heart of Liverpool's Chinatown, which now stretches around the corner onto Berry Street. If you don't mind a fifteen-minute bus ride (#20, #21, #32 or #82), you could make for Lark Lane in Aigburth, close to Sefton Park, which is packed with a dozen great eating and drinking spots.

Liverpool's **pubs** stay open later than most, with about a dozen now serving until 1am or 2am, and their numbers ever increasing. Though good places just for a drink, many also act as venues for up-and-coming bands, who tend to disappear from the local circuit as soon as they achieve fame. Big-name bands frequently play the *Royal Court Theatre* on Roe Street opposite Lime Street station, though the range is much narrower than in Manchester. *In Touch*, a free monthly guide available at tourist offices, lists all concerts, exhibitions, gigs and events in and around the city. The rise of late-opening bars has stolen a good deal of trade from the **clubs**, which are mainly notable for their lack of pretence, fashion playing second string to dancing and drinking. Liverpool's **gay scene** doesn't amount to much, being limited to an area between Victoria and Dale streets, around Stanley Street.

The *Royal Liverpool Philharmonic Orchestra*, up with Manchester's *Hallé* as the northwest's best, dominates the city's **classical music scene** and often plays at the excellent *Everyman Theatre* on Hope Street. The Anglican Cathedral is also a favourite spot for classical concerts, with its good acoustics and inexpensive tickets. The *Unity Theatre*, Hope Place (☎0151/709 4988), puts on the most adventurous range of contemporary **theatre**, while the *Everyman*, 1 Hope St (☎0151/709 4776) presents everything from Shakespeare to Jarman. The *Playhouse Theatre* (☎0151/709 8363) on Williamson Square offers more mainstream shows. The three-screen **arthouse cinema**, *051 Media Centre*, is at the bottom of Mount Pleasant.

Cafés and snacks

Acorn Gallery and Bistro, 16 Newington. Great wholefood quiches, bakes and salads in a small first-floor art gallery off Renshaw Street.

Anglican Cathedral Refectory. Appetizing snacks and lunches.

Av-u-et Café, St John's Market. Comfortable place for tea, coffee and light lunches.

Café Tabac, 126 Bold St. Licensed café with bohemian leanings. Open until 11pm (5pm on Sun).

Everyman Bistro, 9–11 Hope St. Lunchtime and early-evening bistro in the basement of the theatre with great quiche, pizza and salad type meals for around a fiver.

Largo Bistro, 20 Colquitt St. Similar fare to the *Acorn*, in spare surroundings taking up half of a keyboard shop off Bold Street. Occasional live music Thurs–Sat.

Restaurants

L'Alouette, 2 Lark Lane (☎0151/727 2142). Contemporary French cuisine in intimate surroundings. Moderate.

Armadillo Restaurant, 20 Mathew St (☎0151/236 4123). An airy venue serving light and tasty dishes with a vegetarian bias. The menu is more extensive in the evening, but you can eat for half the price if you arrive before 6.30pm. Moderate to expensive.

Bistro Bali, Edward Pavilion, Albert Dock (☎0151/708 0514). A select range of Indonesian dishes, with vegetarians well catered for. Moderate.

Casa Italia, 40 Stanley St (☎0151/227 5774). Lively trattoria with better than average pasta and pizza dishes. Inexpensive.

Elham, 95 Renshaw St (☎0151/709 1589). Highly rated Lebanese food. Moderate.

The Gardens, 4 Brownlow Hill (☎0151/709 5225). Thai, Malay and Chinese cuisine. Open to 4am at the weekend. Moderate.

Keith's Wine Bar, 107 Lark Lane. The trendiest place in this part of town to eat a full meal for under £5. Many people come here just to sample the dozens of wines on offer. Inexpensive.

Orient, 54 Berry St. Good-value Peking and Shanghai cuisine. Moderate.

Que Pasa Cantina, 94–96 Lark Lane (☎0151/727 0006). The city's best Mexican. Moderate.

Ristorante del Secolo, 40 Stanley St (☎0151/236 4004). Upstairs and upmarket from the *Casa Italia*, this is Liverpool's top Italian place, with a seafood-oriented menu. Wear your best clothes. Moderate.

Valparaiso, 4 Hardman St (☎0151/708 6036). Chilean and other Latin-American dishes. Early evening specials before 7.30pm. Moderate.

Pubs, bars and clubs

Baa Bar, 43–45 Fleet St. Liverpool's only continental-style bar; DJs late in the week bring a lively and varied mix of styles.

Beat Bar Club, 1 Mount Pleasant. Part of the *051 Media Centre*, with a variety of club nights.

Black Horse and Rainbow, 21–23 Berry St. Late-closing pub which brews its own beer and has bands upstairs.

The Blue Angel, 108 Seal St. A long-standing studenty club known locally as "The Razz".

The Casablanca, 29 Hope St. Unmarked but for a single white bulb, "The Casa" is a seedy dive with a disco that holds a special place in the heart of Liverpool clubbers.

Cream, Wolstenholme Square, off Hanover Street. One of Liverpool's most popular clubs, often featuring big names as "secret" gigs. Hosts an all-nighter (10.30pm–6.30am) on the last Friday of every month, when queues stretch to the end of the street.

The Flying Picket, 24 Hardman St. A friendly pub tucked in behind the Trade Union centre. Upstairs is one of the best places for local bands.

Guignan's, Slater Street. The best of several Irish-themed pubs to have sprung up in recent years. Open until 2am often with live bands and no cover charge.

Hardy's, Hardman St. Open most nights for non-stop dancing, with regular 80s, house and indie nights.

The Lisbon, 35 Victoria St. Traditional pub with mixed gay and straight clientele.

Mardi Gras, 59 Bold St. Long-standing student favourite, with indie bias.

The Philharmonic, 36 Hope St. A good and often packed watering hole where the main attractions are the gilded wrought-iron gates and the marble decor in the gents.

Listings

Bookshops Most of the bookshops are along Bold Street: *Dillons* at no. 14, *Waterstones* at no. 52 and the more radical *News from Nowhere* at no. 112.

Exchange *American Express*, 54 Lord Street (☎0151/708 9202); *Thomas Cook*, 75 Church St (☎0151/709 2152).

Ferries The *Isle of Man Steam Packet Company* (☎01624/661 661) runs Liverpool's last long-distance ferry service from Princes Dock, just by Pier Head, to Douglas every Saturday evening and more frequently in summer. Buy tickets from the tourist office.

Festivals Annual festivities include **Summer Pops** (July) when the *Royal Philarmonic* sets itself up beneath a huge marquee on King's Dock to perform a series of classical concerts; **Brouhaha Street Theatre Festival** (Aug) involves performances by a host of European theatre groups; the **Mathew Street Festival** is a free shindig, with local and national street performers playing the best of the Beatles.

Football Everton play at Goodison Park (bus #19; ticket office ☎0151/523 6666). Liverpool play at Anfield (bus #17; ticket office ☎0151/260 8680); a 45-min guided tour around Anfield is possible (Mon–Fri 2pm & 3pm; £1.50; booking essential on ☎0151/263 2361).

Horse racing The first Saturday in April is **Grand National Day** at Aintree – the "World's Greatest Steeplechase". The race is the culmination of a meeting that starts on the previous Thursday, with prices ranging from £5 to £30. If you go, catch the *Merseyrail* to Aintree and buy a ticket on the gate or book on ☎0151/523 2600.

Hospital *Royal Liverpool University Hospital*, Prescot St (☎0151/706 2000).

Laundry *Liver Launderette*, 2b Princess Rd (Mon–Fri 9am–6pm, Sun 9am–4pm).

Pharmacy *Moss Chemists*, 68–70 London Rd. Open daily until 11pm.
Police Canning Place, entrance on Hope St (☎051/709 6010).
Travel information For details of bus and train links throughout Merseyside, call ☎0151/236 7676.

Lancashire

LANCASHIRE's industrial prominence in the last century was primarily due to the cotton-mill towns around Manchester and to the thriving port of Liverpool. Today, neither of those cities are part of the county, having been excised when England's first substantial county boundary changes since the Domesday Book were enacted in 1974. The urban counties of Merseyside and Greater Manchester chopped off the southern section of Lancashire while Cumbria grabbed a substantial northern chunk leaving Lancashire little more than half its former size.

The towns of present-day south Lancashire – Burnley, Accrington, Blackburn and Preston – are bound by a shared past to the Liverpool and Manchester conurbations, but these run-down places offer little of interest. Bus and train travellers may have to change at Preston, however, especially if you are heading for the luridly entertaining resort of **Blackpool**, twenty miles to the west. The historic county town of **Lancaster** is losing much of its former administrative role to the more centrally placed Preston, but has far more allure, with its Norman castle, Georgian streets and smattering of decent museums. Many visitors press on north from Lancaster, missing the barren fells of the **Forest of Bowland** which occupies most of the east of the county. Public transport is difficult and much of the land is private, but for all that it can be an attractive alternative to the overcrowded Lake District to the north.

Blackpool

Shamelessly brash **BLACKPOOL** is the archetypal British seaside resort, its **Golden Mile** of piers, fortune tellers and bingo halls making no concessions to anything but low-brow fun-seeking. Swimming is essentially off limits until the planned sewage system is complete (planned for 1997), but sixteen million people still come here each year, and love every minute. The coming of the railway in 1840 made Blackpool. The **Wintergardens**, with its barrel-vaulted ballroom, the baroque **Grand Theatre** on Church Street, and other refined diversions were built to cater to the tastes of the first influx, but it was the Central Pier's "open-air dancing for the working classes" that heralded the crucial change of accent. Suddenly Blackpool was favoured destination for the "Wakes Weeks", when whole Lancashire mill towns descended for their annual seven days' holiday.

In summer, virtually every visitor calls in at the **Pleasure Beach** (March–Easter Sat & Sun 10am–8pm; Easter to end June Mon–Fri 2pm–6 or 8pm, Sat & Sun 10am–10pm; end June to Nov 5 daily 10am–11pm), forking out up to £3 for "White Knuckle" rides including *The Big One*, the world's fastest roller-coaster (85mph) which involves a terrifiying near-vertical drop from 235ft. Across the road, the **Sandcastle** (Easter–Oct daily 10am–6pm; £4.20) is the only place you are likely to want to swim. With every aquatic diversion kept at a constant 29°C it can be a welcome respite from the biting sea air. Next door, the **Crystal Maze** (daily 10am–5pm; £3.99) gives you the chance to compete in an adventurous team game, while **Coronation Street World** (April–Nov daily 10am–10pm; Dec–March Sat & Sun 10am–10pm; £5.99), in the same complex as the *Sandcastle*, provides diversion for fans of Manchester's famous soap.

When other resorts close up for the winter, Blackpool's main season is just beginning, as over half a million light bulbs are used to create **The Illuminations**, which decorate the promenade from September 1 to November 5. This is really the best time to visit, when the ancient, wooden trams are dusted off and put into service from **Blackpool Tower** – the skyline's only touch of grace – to the South Pier. The **Tower World** theme park (Easter to early Nov daily 10am–11pm; Nov–Easter Sat 10am–11pm, Sun 10am–6pm; £6) offers a ride up the 500-foot imitation of the Parisian landmark, plus a visit to the Edwardian ballroom and Moorish-inspired circus between the tower's legs. Both still function, though in the spirit of the times the circus is now animal-free; for performing elephants and monkeys, visit the Russian Circus at the Pleasure Beach (summer only).

The small aquarium in Tower World doesn't match up to its neighbour in the **Sealife Centre** (daily 10am–6pm, open to 10pm summer Fri & Sat; £4.50), where eight-foot sharks loom at you as you march through a glass tunnel. After that it is downhill all the way. **Louis Tussauds Waxworks**, opposite Central Pier (daily 10am–10pm; £3) is just what you would expect, plus an adults-only anatomy section for an extra pound. The **piers**, once Blackpool's pride, are packed with amusement arcades and venues for unfunny comedians and has-been entertainers.

Practicalities

Getting to Blackpool either by train or *National Express* bus is likely to involve a change at Preston, twenty miles to the east. Trains from there arrive at Blackpool North, a few steps along High Street from the combined *National Express* and local bus depot, and five minutes' walk along Talbot Road from the main **tourist office**, 1 Clifton St (Easter to early Nov Mon–Sat 9am–5pm, Sun 10am–3.45pm; rest of year Mon–Thurs & Sat 8.45am–4.45pm, Fri 8.45am–4.15pm; ☎01253/21623).

Blackpool claims to have more **hotel beds** than Portugal – a plausible boast – and prices are generally low, but rise on weekends during the Illuminations. *Ardern*, 99 Coronation St (☎01253/20717; ②) is central, fairly basic but good. *Crooked House* at 9 Nelson Rd, off Lytham Road between Central and South piers (☎01253/346 179; ③), has satellite TV in all rooms. For a vegetarian and vegan guest house, there's the non-smoking *Wildlife Hotel*, 39 Woodfield Rd (☎0253/46143; ②), off the promenade between Central and South piers. At the quieter, northern end of town, the family-run *Southern House Private Hotel*, 1A King Edward Ave (☎01253/352 712; ③), also does low-cost evening meals. The best of the guest houses catering for Blackpool's blossoming **gay** scene is *Raffles Hotel*, set back from the central pier at 73 Hornby Rd (☎01253/26401; ②), which welcomes gay, lesbian and straight guests and serves great value evening meals. The best nearby **campsite** is *Underhill Farm*, Preston New Road (☎0253/63107), three miles east on bus routes #154 and #155.

Toeing the British seaside line, **eating** revolves around fish 'n' chips and greasy Formica tables. One highlight though is *Robert's Oyster Bar*, 92 Promenade, near the base of the tower, where you wash down your oysters with a Guinness from *The Mitre* pub around the corner. If you really want a blow-out try the inspired French dishes at the expensive *September Brasserie*, 15–17 Queen St (☎01253/23282), the only place in Blackpool to win plaudits from foodies. Of the **pubs**, *Raikes Hall Hotel*, half a mile inland on Liverpool Road, has good beer and occasionally decent jazz bands, and a place in local history – the Great Blondin once performed his tightrope act here. Later, you'll find the liveliest venues are *Funny Girls*, a transvestite-run bar on Queen Square close to North Pier and *Main Entrance*, at the Palace Nightclub on the seafront at the south of the tower. *Flamingos*, opposite the train station at the top of Talbot Road is the largest and liveliest gay club outside London, with four storeys of dance floors. For live rock music, *The 'Tache* on Cookson Street is best.

The Forest of Bowland

In stark contrast to the conurbations of Manchester and Merseyside, much of northern Lancashire is occupied by thinly populated grouse moorland known as the **Forest of**

Bowland – the name "forest" is used in its traditional sense of "a royal hunting ground", and much of the land still belongs to the Crown. What few trees do grow here are clustered in the valleys, which are accessible only by unclassified roads that follow former cattle-droving tracks. The best of these is the **Trough of Bowland**, which cuts northwest towards Lancaster from Dunsop Bridge, Newton and Slaidburn, the three tiny settlements in the heart of the region. **SLAIDBURN** is the most attractive of the trio. The *Hark and Bounty Inn* (☎01200/446 246; ④) dates back to the thirteenth century and dishes up some excellent bar meals, or across the road there is the simple King's House **youth hostel** (☎01200/446 656).

Public transport is limited to five daily buses to Dunsop Bridge, Newton and Slaidburn (two going on to Settle in Yorkshire), from the market town of **CLITHEROE**, deep in the wooded Ribble valley on the forest's southern fringes. The town's served by buses from Preston and trains from Manchester Victoria. The **tourist office**, next to the **Norman Keep** at 12 Market Place (April–Sept Mon–Sat 9am–5pm, Sun 10.30am–3.30pm; Oct–March Mon–Sat 9am–5pm; ☎01200/25566) is the main source of information for the Forest of Bowland and is just five minutes walk from the town's empty Norman keep, which towers above the Ribble valley floor. An obvious local target is Pendle Hill, a couple of miles to the east, where the ten **Pendle Witches** allegedly held the diabolic rites that led to their hanging in 1612. The evidence against them came mainly from one small child, but nonetheless a considerable mythology has grown up around the witches, whose memory is perpetuated by a hilltop gathering each Halloween. If you need to spend the night in Clitheroe, try *Brooklyn*, 32 Pimlico Rd (☎01200/28268; ④), or *Mrs Haselwood*, 8 Lingfield Ave (☎01200/22360; ②).

Lancaster and around

LANCASTER hugs the south bank of the River Lune around the wharves which made it an important port on the slave triangle, and it's the legacy of predominantly Georgian buildings from the period of the slave trade that gives the town its character, though it goes back at least as far as the Roman occupation. For centuries it has been Lancashire's county town, but since the boundary changes in 1974 is losing its importance, with Preston taking over much of the county's administration.

Lancaster Castle (Easter–Oct daily 10.30am–5pm except during court sessions; £2.50) has been the city's focal point from Roman times to the present day. Its major role now is as crown court and prison, but about a quarter of the building can be visited on a tour beginning around the back in the Shire Hall. The eight-foot-thick walls of the thirteenth-century Hadrian's Tower encircle a room hung with instruments of torture used on the prisoners who were slammed up in the lightless cells next door, which you are invited to experience briefly. The castle's neighbour, the formerly Benedictine **Priory Church of St Mary** (Easter–Oct daily 9.30am–6pm), has a Saxon doorway at the west end and some finely carved fourteenth-century choir stalls.

A two-minute walk down the steps between the castle and church brings you to the seventeenth-century **Judges' Lodging** (July–Sept Mon–Fri 10am–1pm & 2–5pm, Sat & Sun 2–5pm; Easter–June & Oct Mon–Sat 2–5pm; £1.20), now home to two museums. The ground and first floors house furniture by Gillows of Lancaster, one-time boat-builders who, in the eighteenth century, took to cabinet-making with the tropical timber which came back as ballast in their boats. Their high-quality work earned them contracts to fit the great Cunard transatlantic liners, the Queen Mary and Queen Elizabeth. The finely worked pieces on display mainly come from the earlier period, with an especially beautiful Regency writing desk and a magnificent billiards table – Gillows are credited with first putting the slate under the baize. The top floor is given over to a predictable **Museum of Childhood**.

Continuing down the hill and left onto Dameside you arrive on the riverbank, where the top floor of one of the warehouses is taken up by part of the salt-smelling **Maritime Museum**, St George's Quay (Easter–Oct daily 11am–5pm; Nov–Easter daily 2–5pm; £1.50), entered through the Old Customhouse. The museum's ample coverage of life on the sea and inland waterways of Lancashire is complemented by the revamped **City Museum** on Market Street, five minutes' walk east of the Judges' Lodging (Mon–Sat 10am–5pm; free), which explores the town's wider history through displays on Neolithic, Roman, medieval and Georgian Lancaster.

For a panorama of Morecambe Bay and the Cumbrian fells, take bus #8 or #27 and haul yourself up the 220-foot **Ashton Memorial** (Easter–Sept daily 10am–5pm; Oct–Easter Mon–Fri 11am–4pm, Sat & Sun 10am–4pm; 50p), a lavish self-celebration raised in 1807 in Williamson Park, Lancaster's highest point, by local statesman and lino magnate Lord Ashton. The grounds, which include a **butterfly and palm house** (same hours; £3.50 includes memorial entry), were given to the town by Ashton's father, who employed cotton workers to landscape it when the American Civil War caused a cotton famine.

Practicalities

Lancaster is a frequent stop on the west-coast rail line from London to Scotland and the north–south coach routes. You may have to change here for the daily **ferries to the Isle of Man** from **Heysham**. From the combined local bus and *National Express* station on Cable Street it's a five-minute walk to the **tourist office**, 29 Castle Hill (July & Aug daily 9.30am–6pm; Easter–June & Sept Mon–Sat 10am–5pm; Oct–Easter Mon–Sat 10am–4pm; ☎01524/32878), which is well signposted from the **train station**, a hundred yards away in Meeting House Lane.

Castle Park, which runs beside the castle, turns into West Road where you'll find a couple of good **B&Bs**: *Mrs Buckingham* at no. 35 (☎01524/381 489; ③) and *Mrs Gardner* at no. 50 (☎01524/67602; ③). To be right in the centre, try the *Duke of Lancaster Hotel*, a family-run pub on Church Street (☎01524/32136; ④), or for a little more peace, the excellent *Edenbreck House*, Sunnyside Lane (☎01524/32464; ③), which is at the end of Ashfield Avenue, ten minutes' walk up Meeting House Lane.

For **meals**, cheapest decent options are *Pizza Margherita*, 2 Moor Lane, and *Shabab*, a curry house beside the tourist office on Castle Hill. There's nothing very stylish in Lancaster, but you could try the wholesome meals at *O'Malleys Café* on Bashful Alley, close to the castle, or the popular and the slightly more expensive cajun and ribs joint *Crow's*, 10 King St (☎01524/382 888). Of an evening, most of the young crowd pile into the cellar **bar** at *The Merchants 1688*, 29 Castle Hill, leaving *The Ring O' Bells*, 52 King St, to cater to those seeking a more traditional ambience.

The Lake District

The Lake District is England's most hyped scenic area, and for good reasons. Within an area a mere thirty miles across, sixteen major lakes are squeezed between the steeply pitched faces of England's highest mountains, an almost alpine landscape that's augmented by waterfalls and picturesque stone-built villages packed into the valleys. The heart of the region is **Scafell**, a volcanic dome that had already been weathered into its present shape before the last Ice Age, when glaciers flowed off its flanks to gouge their characteristic U-shaped valleys. As the ice withdrew, terminal moraines of sediment dammed the meltwater, so that the main lakes now radiate like immense spokes from the hub of Scafell.

Human interaction has also played a significant part in the shaping of the Lake District. Before Neolithic peoples began to colonize the region around five thousand

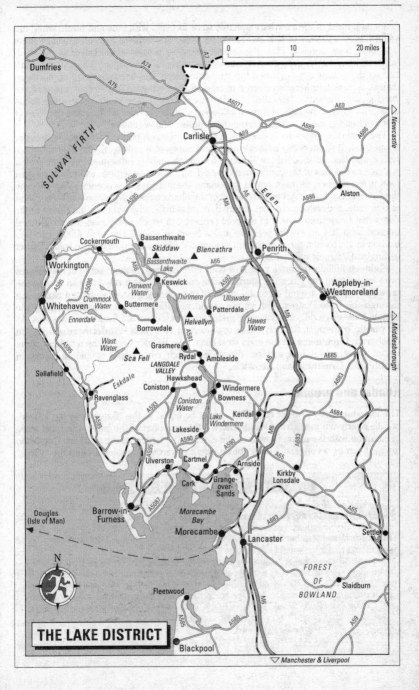

THE LAKE DISTRICT

years ago, most of the now bare uplands were forested with pine and birch, while the valleys were a thicket of oak and alder. As these first settlers learned to shape flints into axes, they began to clear the upland forests, a process accelerated by the road-building Romans. An even greater impact was made by the Norse Vikings in the ninth and tenth centuries, who farmed the land extensively and left their mark on northern dialect: a mountain here is referred to as a "fell", a waterfall is a "force", streams are "becks", and the suffix "-thwaite" indicates a clearing. In later centuries grazing flocks of sheep cropped the hills of their wild flowers, while charcoal-making and the mining of copper and graphite further altered the contours and vegetation.

Two factors spurred the first waves of tourism: the reappraisal of landscape brought about by such painters as Constable and the writings of Wordsworth and his contemporaries, and the outbreak of the French Revolution and its subsequent turmoil, which put paid to the idea of the continental Grand Tour. At the same time, as the war pushed food prices higher, farmers began to reclaim the hillsides, a tendency sanctioned by the General Enclosure Act of 1801. Most of the characteristic dry stone walls were built at this time, a development that alarmed Wordsworth, who wrote in his *Guide to the Lakes* that he desired "a sort of national property, in which every man has a right and interest who has an eye to perceive and a heart to enjoy". His wish finally came to fruition in 1951 when the government designated 880 square miles of the Lake District as England's largest national park.

Eighteen million visitors a year now pour into the park, making some of the villages even busier than the cities the tourists have come from. As a rule you can escape the crowds by getting around on foot – some of the country's most celebrated **walks** run through the Lake District, with an almost unchartable network of paths tracking the broken knife-edge ridges or weaving easier courses around the flanks onto the tops. As for **public transport**, the only Lakes town served by train is **Windermere**, which you reach from Oxenholme on the main west-coast line. Windermere is the terminus of the Lakes' most useful bus service, the #555, which runs every couple of hours to **Ambleside**, **Grasmere** and **Keswick**.

Kendal and around

The limestone-grey town of **KENDAL** might be billed as the "Gateway to the Lakes", but it's nearly ten miles from Windermere – the true start of the lakes – and has more in common with the market towns to the east. As the largest of the southern Cumbrian towns it can be a congested place, but it offers rewarding rambles around the "yards"

WALKING IN THE LAKE DISTRICT

The walks detailed in this section range from those which will barely raise the pulse to hands-on scrambles too steep to take your dog up. All can be attempted in strong-soled shoes in dry weather, but a little rain or snow makes the likes of Sharp Edge (Blencathra) and Striding Edge (Helvellyn) a dangerous proposition. Before starting out, you should check the weather forecast on ☎017687/75757.

Almost all these walks require a good contour map and even non-walkers spending more than a day or so in the Lakes would benefit from one. The best general map of the area is the Ordnance Survey inch-to-the-mile (1:63,360) *Touring Map and Guide* 3, with hill shading and illustrated text on the back. Better for serious walking are the 1:50,000 *OS Landranger* 89, 90, 96 and 97, or even the 1:25,000 *OS Outdoor Leisure* series, which cover the whole Lake District except the northern flanks of Skiddaw, and are detailed enough to show fences. Many shops and tourist offices also sell the *Lakeland Leisure Walks* series (£1), each volume containing five easy to moderate walks centred on one of the major towns.

and "ginnels" which make an engaging maze on both sides of Highgate and Stricklandgate, the main street. Strolling around or following one of the walks organized through the tourist office will take you past restored almshouses, mullioned shopfronts and trade signs like the pipe-smoking Turk outside the snuff factory on Lowther Street. The "Kendal green" cotton cloth, actually yellow wool, was worn by English archers and earned Kendal a mention in Shakespeare's *Henry IV*, but today the town's most visible product is **Kendal Mintcake**, a solid block of sugar and peppermint oil, an energy-giving confection that has been hoisted to the top of the world's highest mountains. You'd think these must be the only places where people would be desperate enough to eat the stuff, but you see it for sale everywhere.

Of the town's three museums (all April–Oct Mon–Sat 10.30am–5pm, Sun 2–5pm; Nov–Easter Mon–Fri 11am–4pm, Sat & Sun 1–4pm; £2.50 each, combined ticket £5), the least interesting is the **Kendal Museum**, opposite the train station, which traces Cumbria's natural history, redeemed only by a tuneful slate xylophone and reverential displays on the life of **Alfred Wainwright** (1907–91). In 1952 this one-time borough treasurer, dissatisfied with the accuracy of existing maps across the fells, embarked on what became a series of 47 walking guides, all but two of them painstakingly handwritten with mapped routes and delicately drawn views. Ironically the popularity of his purple-prosed pocket guides has led to the ravaging of the land he so adored, especially on his most trekked route, the "Coast to Coast" from St Bees in Cumbria to Yorkshire's Robin Hood's Bay, much of which is not on designated rights-of-way and often crosses sensitive wildlife areas and archeological sites.

The other two museums are in the Georgian Abbot Hall and its stable block, by the river to the south. The main hall, painstakingly restored to 1760s' townhouse style, houses the **Art Gallery**, where cherubic portraits by Kendal-born society painter George Romney line the walls, along with works by Ruskin, Turner and lesser local artists. Few can compete with the furniture designed and built by Gillows of Lancaster (see p.449), whose chairs, writing desks and games tables have all survived in excellent condition. The small modern art collection upstairs is rounded out with Barbara Hepworth's *Oval Form*, gracing the grass between the hall and the stables which house the **Museum of Lakeland Life and Industry**, where reconstructed rooms make a fairly vivid presentation of rural trades and crafts. The mock-up study of Arthur Ransome, author of the children's classic *Swallows and Amazons*, is enlivened by memorabilia from his stint as *Manchester Guardian* reporter during the Russian Revolution; John Cunliffe, inventor of Postman Pat, gets similar treatment next door.

Next door, the wide aisles of the Early English parish church (Easter–Oct daily 9.20am–4.30pm; Nov–Easter daily 9.20am–noon and 2–4pm; free) house a number of family chapels, including that of the Parr family, who once owned the ruined **Kendal Castle**, on a hillock to the east. It's claimed as the birthplace of Katherine Parr, Henry VIII's sixth wife, but the story is probably apocryphal – she was born in 1512, at which time the building was in an advanced state of decay.

Practicalities

Kendal's **train station** is the first stop on the Windermere branch line, just five minutes from the **Oxenholme** main line station. By catching bus #41 or #41A to the town hall from Oxenholme (every 20min) you can avoid the wait for the next train. The **tourist office** (Easter–Oct daily 9am–6pm; Nov–Easter Mon–Sat 9am–5pm; ☎01539/ 725 758) is in the town hall on Highgate and sells coach tickets. *National Express* coaches stop on Blackhall Road opposite the bus station on their way south, but opposite the post office on Stricklandgate going north.

As usual, B&Bs form the mainstay of the budget **accommodation**, much of it along the road to Windermere. A couple of places close to the train station are *Ivy Cottage*, 27

Castle St (☎01539/723 949; ②), and the slightly grander *Bridge House*, 65 Castle St (☎01539/722 041; ③). Closer to the centre are *Hillside Guest House*, 4 Beast Banks (☎01539/722 836; ③), just off All Hallows Lane opposite the town hall, and *Da Franco's Hotel and Restaurant*, 101 Highgate (☎01539/722 430; ④). Less convenient but worth the effort for the views and swimming pool is the non-smoking *Holmfield*, 41 Kendal Green (☎01539/720 790; ③), reached off Green Road, ten minutes' walk along Windermere Road. Cheapest of all is the **youth hostel**, 118 Highgate (☎01539/724 066), which has plenty of smaller, family rooms and is attached to *The Brewery* arts centre, housing a theatre, galleries, a café-restaurant and, bar and hosting good live bands throughout the year. The most convenient **campsite** is *Ashes Lane*, off the Windermere Road (mid-March to mid-Jan; ☎01539/821 119), reached by bus #555.

As for **places to eat**, you can get inexpensive lunches in *Waterside Café* and *Wholefood Shop* on Gulfs Road, by the river at the bottom of Lowther Street. The wood-beamed *Farrers Tea & Coffee Merchants*, 13 Stricklandgate, serves good drinks and cakes, only to be outdone by *1657 – The Chocolate House*, on Branthwaite Brow. The *Sizzling Wok*, 3 Stramongate, does inexpensive Cantonese fare; or try the pizzas and moderately priced Italian dishes at *Da Franco's* (see above). In a similar price range is *The Moon*, 29 Highgate, with a mainly vegetarian menu. For evening entertainment *The Brewery,* with a bar, cinema and live music, is a good bet; otherwise try the *Ring o' Bells* by the church or *The Wool Pack*, opposite *Farrers* on Stricklandgate.

Sizergh Castle and Levens Hall

Two of Cumbria's grandest stately homes lie within easy reach of Kendal. The closest, just two miles to the south, is **Sizergh Castle** (April–Oct daily except Fri 1.30–5.30pm; £3.30; NT), tucked away off the A591 amid acres of parkland. Sizergh is more of a grand manor house than a castle, but owes its epithet to the fourteenth-century peel tower (which you'll often see spelt "pele tower" in the north of England) at its core, one of the best examples of the towers built throughout the region as safe havens, during the protracted border raids of the Middle Ages. Like much of the rest of the house the Great Hall underwent significant changes in Elizabethan times, when extensions were added to the house and most of its rooms were panelled in oak with their ceilings layered in elaborate plasterwork. Each room is hung with portraits of the family and their royal aquaintances and stocked with exquisite furniture, including an extraordinary bedstead made from a pew that once stood in Kendal parish church. Little has changed in the Banqueting Hall since the fourteenth century save for the loss of an upper storey and the addition of a partition at the east end, added to provide more private sleeping quarters for the heads of the family.

Two miles south of Sizergh, **Levens Hall** (April–Sept 11am–5pm; £4.20, gardens only £2.50), also built around an early peel tower, is more uniform in style than Sizergh, since the bulk of it was built or refurbished in classic Elizabethan style between 1570 and 1640 by James Bellingham. Not long afterwards, the Bellinghams lost the whole estate in a hedonistic spate of gambling and it was later bought by the privy purse to James II and ancestor of the present owners, the Bagots. The main entrance opens into the spacious Great Hall, its panelled walls lined with countless coats of arms; to the left of the hall are the large and small drawing rooms. The other end of the Great Hall leads to the most splendid apartment, the dining room, panelled not with oak but with goat's leather, printed with a deep green floral design – one goat was needed for every forty or so squares. Upstairs, the bedrooms offer glimpses of the beautifully trimmed topiary garden below, where yews in the shape of pyramids, peacocks and top hats stand between blooming bedding plants.

Windermere, Bowness and around

WINDERMERE town was all but non-existent until 1847 when a railway terminal was built, making England's longest lake (after which the town is named) an easily accessible resort. Most of the guest houses and amenities built for the Victorians still stand, stretching a mile downhill to its older twin town, **BOWNESS**. Windermere is the transport hub for the southern Lakes, and the arrival point for trains and coaches from further south, but Bowness has more to entertain and is more attractive, spilling down to the piers of the lake. Together the two towns make Cumbria's most popular resort; packed with trinket shops and souvenir-hunting tourists they're victims of their own popularity and are overrun for much of the year.

They're particularly full on summer weekends, which is when you'll probably want to head out onto the lake in a rowboat, available for rent at the pier, or on a **ferry**. The short ferry across the water to Sawrey (every 20min; 20p, or £1 for a car) from just south of Bowness opens up the western side of the lake, while the *Windermere Lake Cruises* operate stylish steamers to Lakeside (summer only; hourly; £3.30 single, £5 return) or to Ambleside (summer only; every 30min; £3.20 single, £5 return) with a round-the-lake ticket for £8. You can get a closer look at the ferries at the **Windermere Steamboat Museum** (mid-March to Oct daily 10am–5pm; £2.80), situated on the shore 500 yards north of Bowness. Star exhibit among the wonderfully sleek and burnished craft is the 1850 *Dolly*, allegedly the world's oldest mechanically driven boat, and extremely well preserved after spending 65 years at the bottom of Ullswater.

In Bowness, **The World of Beatrix Potter** (daily Easter–Sept 10am–6.30pm; Oct–Easter 10am–4pm; £2.75), an overdone display of drawings of farmyard animals, will soon rid you of any enthusiasm you might have had for the children's story-writer. It's better to visit Potter's crowded home, **Hill Top** (April–Oct daily except Thurs & Fri 11am–5pm; £3.30; NT) in Near Sawrey, two miles from the cross-lake ferry on the other side of the lake. Equally popular is the short walk up to **Orrest Head** (784ft), giving a 360° panorama from the Yorkshire Fells to the Langdales and Troutbeck Valley; the path branches off the main road a hundred yards south of the train station.

Practicalities

National Express coaches stop outside the **train station** only a few yards from the **Windermere tourist office**, Victoria Street (daily Easter–Oct 9am–6pm; Nov–Easter 9am–5pm; ☎015394/46499). Among the information available is *Walks in the Countryside* (20p), a particularly useful leaflet if you are planning to stay at the **youth hostel** (☎015394/43543). It is almost a mile uphill from Troutbeck Bridge, itself a mile north of Windermere along the A591, or the leaflet outlines a preferable (if longer) cross-country route via Orrest Head; there's also a mini-bus shuttle service to the hostel from Windermere station.

The nearest **B&Bs** are on the High Street, off Victoria Street, with the bulk of the rest lining Oak and Broad streets. Three particularly helpful and comfortable ones are: *Heather Cottage*, 11 Broad St (☎015394/44616; ②); *Yorkshire House*, 1 Upper Oak St (☎015394/44689; ②); and the non-smoking *Village House*, 5 Victoria St (☎015394/46041; ②). College Road, at the bottom of Victoria Street, has a couple more comfortable places: *Ashleigh Guesthouse* at no. 11 (☎015394/42292; ③) and *The Archway* at no. 13 (☎015394/45613; ④), both serving dinner on request. In Bowness, *Montclare House* (☎015394/42723; ①) on Cragbrow (the main street), offers B&B and very cheap lunches. The only close **campsite** is *Braithwaite Fold* (April–Oct; ☎015394/42177) near the ferry to Sawrey, half a mile south of the **Bowness tourist office**, Glebe Road (April–Oct daily 9.30am–5.30pm or 7.30pm; Nov & Dec Sat & Sun 10am–4pm).

The Village Restaurant, 1 Cross St (☎015394/43429), is one of the better **places to eat** in Windermere, serving a moderately priced menu of pâtés, pizza and fresh fish dishes; the *Oriental Kitchen*, Crescent Road, serves a broad range of Cantonese fare. In Bowness, the excellent Anglo-Italian cuisine of the *Porthole Eating House*, 3 Ash St, (☎015394/42793), is the upmarket choice. *Tom Broster's Restaurant*, Queen's Square (☎015394/43535) does less expensive fish dishes and operates as a cheaper daytime café, while *Rastelli's* on Lake Road serves brilliant pizzas and *Vinegar Jones*, on the same road, cooks the best fish and chips around. For a drink, try *The Hole in't Wall* **pub**, in Falbarrow Road off Queen's Square, behind the Bowness church; it's the town's oldest hostelry, has open fires and oozes atmosphere.

Bike rental is available from *Lakeland Leisure*, on Lake Road, Bowness (☎015394/44786), and **boat** and **board rental** from *Gilly's Landing* in Bowness. An extravagant but memorable way of getting the best views of the Lake District is by **hot-air balloon**. The *Windermere Balloon Company* offers morning or evening trips, leaving from the south end of Lake Windermere, at around £140 per person for a one-to-two-hour flight; call ☎01229/581 779 for details.

South to Lakeside

To avoid the crowds in town, take a ferry the five or so miles from Bowness to **Lakeside**, on the quieter southern reaches of Lake Windermere. Lakeside is also the terminus of the **Lakeside and Haverthwaite Railway** (April–Nov 6 or 7 daily; £3.10 return), whose steam-powered engines chuff along four miles of track through the forests of Backbarrow Gorge.

Less than a mile northwest of Lakeside, below Finsthwaite Heights, stands one of England's only working mills, **Stott Park Bobbin Mill** (daily April–Sept 10am–6pm, Oct 10am–4pm; £2.30; EH). Founded in 1835 to supply the textile industry, the mill diversified to manufacture products such as spade handles, yo-yos and toggles, though commercial production finally ceased in 1971. Former workers guide visitors through the processes of cutting, boring, roughing and drying on machinery that hasn't changed since it was introduced in the mid-nineteenth century.

Ambleside, the Langdale Valley and Grasmere

AMBLESIDE is very much at the heart of the southern lakes region, making it a first class base for walkers, but also granting it high-season crowds second only to Windermere. The cosy town centre consists of a cluster of grey-green stone houses, shops and B&Bs hugging a circular one-way system, which loops round just south of the narrow gully of stony Stock Ghyll. The rest of town lies a mile south at **Waterhead** (referred to as Ambleside on ferry timetables), a harbour on the shores of Windermere that's filled with ducks, swans and rowboats. There are quieter shores a few minutes' walk further south for picnics or, if the weather's good, a bracing dip in the lake.

It's Ambleside's overall prettiness that attracts rather than any particular sight, but you could look in on the grass-covered floor plan of the second century Roman **Galava Fort** at Waterhead (dawn–dusk; free), or the mural of the rush-bearing ceremony in **St Mary's Church**, whose spire is visible from all over town. A couple of hundred yards north, **Bridge House** (Easter–Oct 10am–5pm), now a shop and National Trust centre, straddles Stock Ghyll – legend has it that a Scotsman built the two-storey two-roomed house to evade land taxes. Behind this is **Adrian Sankey's Glass Works** (Mon–Sat 9am–5.30pm, Sun 9.30am–5.30pm; 30p), where you can watch glass being blown, then splash out on one of the unique finished products.

National Express **coaches** stop on Lake Road, 600 yards south of the local bus stop in King Street. The main **tourist office**, Old Courthouse, Church Street (Easter–Oct daily 9am–5pm; Nov–Easter Fri & Sat 9am–5pm; ☎015394/32582) is around the corner from King Street. Lake Road, running between Waterhead and Ambleside, is lined with dozens of **B&Bs**, but the following are worth trying first: *Eversly*, Low Gale (☎015394/

WALKS FROM AMBLESIDE

An excellent full day's walking and sightseeing from Ambleside takes in Rydal Mount, Dove Cottage, Grasmere (see opposite for all three) and Loughrigg Fell (1099ft), a nine-mile hike. For **Rydal Mount**, either follow the A591 all the way, or turn left down Stoney Lane on the outskirts of Ambleside then cross the footbridge and turn right to follow the minor road until it meets the main road again. By Rydal Mount, a bridleway leads to Dove Cottage and Grasmere. The return route loops around the other side of Grasmere and Rydal Water lakes, initially on the minor road for a mile then branching left onto the path along **Loughrigg Terrace**, with its superb lake views. The terrace circles **Loughrigg Fell** and returns to Rydal, but by taking a path to the top of the Fell you can return to Ambleside from the west.

The walk over **Wansfell** to **Troutbeck** and back (6 miles) has more extensive views and is a little tougher. Stock Ghyll Lane runs up the left bank of the tumbling stream to one of the more attractive waterfalls in the region, **Stock Ghyll Force**. The path then rises steeply to **Wansfell Pike** (1581ft) and down into Troutbeck village, with *The Mortal Man* pub a short detour to the left, though you may have to follow the road further to the delightful seventeenth-century *Queen's Head Hotel*, open all day. Retracing your steps, continue south on the minor road to **Townend** (April–Oct Tues–Fri & Sun 1–5pm; £2.50; NT), a seventeenth-century yeoman farmer's house. The road on the right leads onto the flanks of Wansfell and around past the viewpoint at **Jenkin Crag** back to Ambleside.

33311; ②), off Lake Road up the 55 steps opposite Kelsick Road; *Shirland*, Compston Road (☎015394/32999; ②); *The Waterwheel Guesthouse*, Bridge Street (☎015394/33286; ③), right by the bridge across Stock Ghyll; or *Holme Lea Guesthouse*, Church Street (☎015394/32114; ②). There's a large and often crowded **youth hostel** in Waterhead on the A591 (☎015394/32304); for **bike rental**, try *Biketreks* on Market Place.

Best place for a daytime coffee or an expensive evening **meal** is *The Glass House* (☎015394/32581), a renovated fulling mill with water wheel on Rydal Road next to *Adrian Sankey's*. The small and homely, moderately priced *Stampers Restaurant*, tucked beneath Birkett's Bakery on Church Street, has a good range of filling meals, while *Zeffirelli's*, on Compston Road specializes in inexpensive vegetarian pizzas and pasta and offers a three-course dinner and cinema ticket special. *Pippins*, on Lake Road, is great for all-day breakfasts and healthy snacks. The *Golden Rule* **pub**, on Smithy Brow by Stock Ghyll, is a favourite of locals and climbers, and *The Sportsman* on North Road has a basement disco (£2), which is licensed until midnight.

The Langdale Pikes

Three miles west of Ambleside, **Skelwith Bridge** is the start of **Great Langdale Valley**, a classic U-shaped glacial valley overlooked by the prominent rocky summits of the **Langdale Pikes**, the most popular of central Lakeland fells. If you don't mind company, stop outside the *New Dungeon Ghyll Hotel*, four miles past Skelwith Bridge and take the little lane indicated by the "Stickle Ghyll" sign. The path (4 miles; 2400ft ascent; 4hr) follows the beck straight up to Stickle Tarn, around to the right then left up to Pavey Ark. Two more adventurous routes to the top of **Pavey Ark** (2297ft) can be easily seen on the crags above Stickle Tarn: **Jack's Rake** trail ascends the face right to left, and is probably the hardest commonly used route in the Lake District, requiring a head for heights and steady footing. From near its base, an easier route rises to the right. It is fairly easy from then on to **Harrison Stickle** (2414ft), down to the stream forming the headwaters of Dungeon Ghyll and slowly up to **Pike of Stickle** (2326ft). Backtracking a short distance, a path leads to the right almost parallel with Dungeon Ghyll, back to the start.

The traditional stopping place for anyone visiting the valley is the *Old Dungeon Ghyll Hotel* (☎015394/37272; ⑤), seven miles northeast of Ambleside at the end of the

B5343; it offers great four-course dinners in its lively bar. Midway between here and Ambleside, *Elterwater* **youth hostel** (☎015394/37245) is the most convenient budget accommodation, just over the river from **Elterwater** village, a mile and a half west of Skelwith Bridge, though *High Close* **youth hostel** (☎015394/37313) has a more spectacular setting, high on the road over Red Bank from Skelwith Bridge to Grasmere.

Rydal and Grasmere

A mile and a half north along the A591 from Ambleside, the hamlet of **RYDAL** consists of an inn, a few houses and **Rydal Mount** (March–Oct daily 9.30am–5pm; Nov–Feb daily except Tues 10am–4pm; £2.50), home of William Wordsworth from 1813 to his death in 1850. Parts of the house have been recently redecorated, but furniture and portraits give a good sense of its former occupants, as does Wordsworth's airy attic study. For many, the highlight is the garden, which has been preserved as Wordsworth designed it. You can stay in Rydal at the licensed *Nab Cottage* (☎015395/ 35311; ④), a quiet and cosy retreat, once the home of Thomas de Quincey.

Three miles further on, the tiny village of Grasmere further exploits the Wordsworth seam, but is pretty enough to justify a visit even if the poet doesn't stir you. The village of **GRASMERE** consists of an intimate cluster of grey-stone houses on the old packhorse road which runs beside the babbling River Rothay. A great smell leads you to *The Gingerbread Shop*, converted from the schoolhouse where Wordsworth once taught. It is by the back entrance to **St Oswald's Churchyard**, where the poet, his sister and many other members of his family are buried beneath the yews. Inside the church you can admire the unique twin naves, split by a solid arched partition.

On the outskirts of the village is **TOWN END**, where William and Dorothy Wordsworth lived from 1799 to 1808 at **Dove Cottage** (March–Oct Mon–Sat 10am–4.30pm, Sun 11am–4.30pm or later; £4), the house in which William wrote some of his best poetry. Guides bursting with anecdotes lead you around rooms which reflect Wordsworth's guiding principle of "plain living but high thinking" and are little changed now but for the addition of electricity and internal plumbing. This maxim, however, was only temporary as Wordworth was raised in comfortable surroundings and returned to a relatively high standard of living when he moved to Rydal. If you visit the cottage, you've already paid for the **Museum** full of paintings, manuscripts and bric-a-brac once belonging to the Wordsworth, Coleridge and Thomas de Quincey.

Grasmere's **accommodation** tends to be a little more expensive than Ambleside's. Top of the pile is the superb *White Moss House* (☎015394/35295; ⑨), a house once owned by Wordsworth, a mile south on the A591, at the northern end of Rydal Water. In the village itself, *Titteringdales Guesthouse*, on Pye Lane (☎015394/35439; ③), and *Undercrag* (☎015394/35349; ③), a hundred-yard walk up Easedale Road, are both comfortable. Grasmere has no campsite but two **youth hostels**: *Butterlip How*, 150 yards north on Easedale Road (☎015394/35316), and *Thorney How*, a characterful former farmhouse, just under a mile further along the road (☎015394/35581). If these are full, the **tourist office** (April–Oct daily 9.30am–5pm; ☎015394/35245), tucked in behind the Grasmere Garden Centre at the south end of the village, can help out.

The best **restaurant** for miles around is the expensive *White Moss House* (see above). Bar meals are available in the village pubs, while *Piggy in the Middle*, Broadgate, can't be beaten for cappuccinos, pizzas and sandwiches, and *The Rowan Tree Licensed Restaurant*, Langdale Road, serves very tasty vegetarian dishes on a terrace overlooking the river.

Coniston Water

In certain circles **Coniston Water** is renowned not for its tranquil beauty but as the one-time venue for just about the noisiest sporting activity known to humanity. In the mid-1960s, the long uninterruptedly glass-like surface of Coniston attracted the atten-

WRITERS IN THE LAKE DISTRICT

William Wordsworth was not the first to praise the Lake District – Thomas Gray wrote appreciatively of his visit in 1769 – but he dominates its literary landscape, not solely through his poetry but also through his still useful *Guide to the Lakes*. Born in Cockermouth in 1770, he was sent to school in Hawkshead before a stint at Cambridge, a year in France and two in Somerset. In 1799 he returned to the Lake District, settling in the Grasmere district, where he spent the last two thirds of his life with his sister **Dorothy**, who not only transcribed his poems but was an accomplished diarist as well.

Wordsworth and fellow poets **Samuel Taylor Coleridge** and **Robert Southey** formed a clique that became known as the **"Lake Poets"**, a label based more on their fluctuating friendships and their shared passion for the region than on any common subject matter in their writings. A fourth member of the Cumbrian literary elite was the critic and essayist **Thomas De Quincey**, chiefly known today for his *Confessions of an English Opium-Eater*. One of the first to fully appreciate the revolutionary nature of Wordsworth and Coleridge's collaborative *Lyrical Ballads*, De Quincey became a long-term guest of the Wordsworths in 1807, taking over Dove Cottage from them in 1809. He stayed there until 1820, but it was only in the 1830s that he started writing his *Lake Reminiscences*, offending Wordsworth and Coleridge in the process.

Meanwhile, after short spells at Allan Bank and The Vicarage, both in Grasmere, the Wordsworths made **Rydal Mount** their home, supported largely by William's position as Distributor of Stamps for Westmorland and his later stipend as Poet Laureate. After his death in 1850, William's body was interred in St Oswald's churchyard in Grasmere, to be joined five years later by Dorothy and by his wife Mary four years after that.

Inspired by Wordsworth's writings and by the terrain itself, the social philosopher and art critic **John Ruskin** also made the Lake District his home, settling at Brantwood outside Coniston in 1872. His letters and watercolours reflect a deep love of the area, also demonstrated by his unsuccessful fight to prevent the damming of Thirlmere. Much of Ruskin's feeling for the countryside permeated through to two other literary immigrants, **Arthur Ransome**, writer of the children's classic *Swallows and Amazons*, and **Beatrix Potter**, whose favourite Lakeland spots feature in her children's stories.

tion of national hero **Donald Campbell**, who in 1955 had set a world water-speed record of 202mph on Ullswater, bumping it up to 276mph nine years later in Australia. On January 4, 1967 he set out to better his own mark on Coniston Water, but just as his jet-powered *Bluebird* hit an estimated 320mph, a patch of turbulence sent it into a somersault. Campbell's shoes, helmet, oxygen mask and teddy bear mascot were recovered from the water, but his body and boat were destroyed completely – the tragic moment was recorded by photographs, now on display at the Windermere Steamboat Museum (see p.455).

Coniston village and Brantwood

A memorial plaque to Campbell decorates the green in the slate-grey village of **CONISTON**, hunkered below the craggy and copper-mine-riddled bulk of Coniston Old Man. Boat speeds are now limited to 10mph, a graceful pace for the sumptuously uphol-stered **Steam Yacht Gondola** (April–Oct 4 or 5 daily; £4.30 return; NT), built in 1859, which leaves Coniston Pier for hour-long circuits, calling at Park-a-moor landing stage then Brantwood. The *M.V. Ruskin* (April to mid-Nov daily 4–8pm; £3 including 50p off house entry) also makes the trip to the magnificently sited **Brantwood**, two and a half miles by road from Coniston (mid-March to mid-Nov daily 11am–5.30pm; mid-Nov to mid-March Wed–Sun 11am–4pm; £3.25), where art critic and moralist **John Ruskin** lived from 1872 until his death in 1900. Champion of J.M.W. Turner and the Pre-Raphaelites, and proponent of the supremacy of Gothic architecture, Ruskin insisted upon the indivisibility of ethics and aesthetics, and was appalled by the conditions in which the captains of industry made their labourers work and live, while expecting him to applaud their patronage of the arts. A video expands on his philosophy and whets the appetite for rooms full of his watercolours, doing justice to a man who greatly influenced such disparate figures as Proust, Tolstoy, Frank Lloyd Wright and Gandhi.

The **tourist office**, 16 Yewdale Rd (April–Oct daily 10am–5pm; ☎015394/41533) will help you find **accommodation**, which is plentiful. In the centre the best choices are *Lakeland House* on Tiberthwaite Avenue (☎015394/41303; ③), opposite the Campbell memorial, and, just a few doors along, the *Crown Hotel* (☎015394/41243; ③). A slate-flagged farmhouse has been turned into *Thwaite Cottage* (☎015394/41367; ③), half a mile out on the Hawkshead road, though vegetarians might prefer *Beech Tree Guesthouse*, Yewdale Road (☎015394/41717; ③), where four-course dinners are on offer. The *Sun Hotel* (☎015394/41248; ⑥), uphill from the bridge in the centre of Coniston, has the best rooms in town and an excellent moderately priced **restaurant**.

Of the two **youth hostels**, *Coniston Holly Row* (☎015394/41323) is closer, just a few minutes' walk north of Coniston on the Ambleside road, but *Coniston Coppermines* (☎015394/41261) is more peaceful, in dramatic mountain setting a mile or so up a small road between *The Black Bull*, which does hearty bar meals, and the *Co-Op*. The nearest **campsite** is the year-round *Coniston Hall Campsite and Sailing Club*, Haws Bank (☎015394/41223; reservations essential), a mile south of town by the lake.

Hawkshead

Greystone **HAWKSHEAD** was an important wool market at the time Wordsworth was studying at **Hawkshead Grammar School** (Easter–Oct Mon–Sat 10am–12.30pm & 1.30–5pm, 4.30pm in Oct, Sun 1–5pm; £1.75), where pride of place is given to the desk on which William carved his signature. While there he attended the fifteenth-century **Church** above the school, which harks back to Norman and Romanesque designs in its rounded pillars and patterned arches. Its chief interest is in the 26 pithy psalms and Biblical extracts illuminated with cherubs and flowers, painted on the walls during the seventeenth and eighteenth centuries.

From its knoll the churchyard gives a good view over the village's twin central squares and the **Beatrix Potter Gallery** on Main Street (April–Oct daily except Fri 10.30am–4.30pm; £2.50; NT), occupying rooms once used by her solicitor husband. With their timed-entry ticket, best bought early in summer, fans get bustled into rooms full of Potter's original illustrations, though the less devoted might find displays on her life as keen naturalist, conservationist and early supporter of the National Trust more diverting. The National Trust shop opposite can lend you the key to the **Hawkshead Courthouse** (April–Oct daily 10am–5pm; free), situated half a mile to the north where the Coniston road branches, the last remaining manorial building from the time when the area was controlled by Furness Abbey (see p.467).

If the weather looks promising, time is better spent amongst the remarkable sculptures in **Grizedale Forest**, which drapes over the Furness Fells separating Coniston Water from Windermere. There's no public transport to the forest, but you can **rent bikes** from the campsite in Hawkshead or from the **Grizedale Forest Centre** (Feb–Dec daily 10am–5pm; ☎01229/860 369), four miles further on, or just head out on foot along ten miles of the Silurian Way, which links the majority of the fifty-odd stone and wood sculptures scattered amongst the trees. Since 1977 artists have been invited to come here, often for six months at a time, to create a sculptural response to their surroundings using natural materials. Some of the resulting works are startling, as you round a bend to find a hundred-foot-long wave of bent logs or a drystone wall slaloming the conifers. Pick up a map from the centre and take a picnic.

Some contend that Wordsworth briefly boarded at what is now *Anne Tyson's Cottage* (☎015394/36405; ③), on Wordsworth Street behind the fifteenth-century *Minstrels Gallery* on the main square, just one of many good tea rooms. All four of the village's pubs also have accommodation, with the *The King's Arms Hotel*, The Square (☎015394/36372; ④), being one of the best and serving **bar meals** a cut above the others. *Greenbank Country House Hotel*, fifty yards north of the square on Main Street (☎015394/36497; ③), is also very good. The **youth hostel**, *Esthwaite Lodge* (☎015394/36293), is a mile to the south in a Regency mansion with good family rooms, and the *Croft Caravan and Camping Site* (mid-March to Oct; ☎015394/36374) could hardly be more central – it's on Lonsdale Road, right in the village. **Camping** is also available in the heart of Grizedale Forest; ask at the centre for details.

Keswick and Derwent Water

Standing on the shores of Derwent Water at the junction of the main north–south and east–west routes through the Lake District, **KESWICK** makes a good base for exploring the delightful Borrowdale – the start of many walking routes to the central peaks around Scafell Pike – or Skiddaw and Blencathra, which loom over the town. Popular throughout the year, the town is a fine place to amble around in the sun, and has one of northern England's wackier museums too.

Granted its market charter by Edward I in 1276, Keswick was important for wool and leather until around 1500, when these trades were supplanted by the discovery of local graphite. **The Cumberland Pencil Museum**, Main Street (daily 9.30am–4pm; £2.50) tells the story, beginning with its early application as moulds for cannon balls. With the Italian idea of putting Borrowdale graphite into wooden holders, Keswick became an

---

WALKS FROM KESWICK

The most obvious hike from Keswick is the **Derwent Water Circuit** (9–10 miles; 3hr), outlined in a leaflet from the tourist office. You could tackle parts of the circuit by hopping on the **Keswick Launch**, which from Easter to November runs right around the lake calling at seven points. Going anticlockwise from Keswick, the main points of interest are: the woodlands and moulded landscapes of **Lingholm Gardens** (April–Oct daily 10am–5pm; £2.50); the 120-foot **Lodore Falls**; the drystone **Ashness Bridge**, one of Cumbria's most photographed vistas; and **Friar's Crag**, from where pilgrims left for St Herbert's Island in the middle of the lake, to seek the hermit's blessing.

Rising sharply through coniferous forests above Keswick, **Latrigg Fell** (4–6 miles; nine-hundred-foot ascent; 2–3hr) gives splendid views across Derwent Water to Borrowdale and the high fells. Follow Station Road past the youth hostel and then right up Spooney Green Lane across the A66, then skirt the west flank before zig-zagging to the summit from the north. Return either directly down the southern gully or follow the longer eastern ridge to Brundholme, returning through Brundholme wood or along the railway path.

More demanding, but the easiest of the true mountain walks, is **Skiddaw** (5 miles; 3000ft ascent; 5hr), a smooth mound of splintery slate. Follow the walk above, skirting the west flank of Latrigg, but continue straight ahead when the path branches right to the Latrigg summit. It is pretty much a steady walk (with a possible diversion up Little Man along the way) before reaching a false summit and finally the 3054-foot High Man. A far more exciting ascent (4 miles; 4–5hr) starts from the east shore of Bassenthwaite Lake not far from the *Ravenstone Hotel* (☎017687/76240; ⑤). The climb begins in the shade of Dodd Wood and joins Longside Edge, winding around to the summit from the west and finishing up with a steep scramble over scree. The best way down is to follow the "Allerdale Ramble" around the crags of Broad End back to Millbeck, a mile and a half north of Keswick, or to the southern end of Dodd Wood, from where an easy path cuts back to the *Ravenstone Hotel*. You can stay out in the middle of the hills at the *Skiddaw House* **youth hostel** (phone *Carrock Fell* hostel: ☎016974/78325), one of the most remote buildings in England, 1500 feet above sea level and with no motor vehicle access.

important pencil-making town, and remained one until the late eighteenth century, when the French discovered how to make pencil graphite cheaply by binding the common amorphous graphite with clay. Keswick's monopoly was quickly broken, and only the factory which owns the museum still survives. Inside, a mock-up of the long-defunct Borrowdale mine leads through a potted history of modern graphite use.

The town also makes its contribution to the local adulation of Squirrel Nutkin's creator, with the multi-media **Beatrix Potter's Lake District**, Packhorse Court (July & Aug daily 10am–5.30pm; April–June & Sept–Oct daily 10am–5pm; Nov–March Sat & Sun 12–4pm; £2.50; NT), explaining the writer's conservation work in the region. Even more of an acquired taste is "**Cars of the Stars" Motor Museum**, Standish Street (Easter to early Jan daily 10am–5pm; £2.99), showcasing The Saint's Volvo, James Bond's Lotus, Lady Penelope's Rolls Royce and so on. In Station Road you'll find **Fitz Park Museum and Art Gallery** (Easter–Oct daily 10am–4pm; £1), a quirky collection of ancient dental tools, fossils and some prized manuscripts and letters written by the Lakeland Poets.

Keswick's most celebrated landmark, the nearby **Castlerigg Stone Circle**, is made especially resonant by its magnificent mountain backdrop. From the end of Station Road, take the rail line path for half a mile, then turn onto the minor road to the right where the path runs under the road – the site's a mile further. Thirty-eight hunks of Borrowdale volcanic stone, the largest almost eight feet tall, form a circle a hundred feet in diameter, another ten blocks delineating a rectangular enclosure within. The array probably had an astronomical or timekeeping function when it was erected four to five thousand years ago.

Practicalities

Most buses and *National Express* coaches to Whitehaven from Manchester or London go from beside the supermarket on Main Street. *Mountain Goat* buses to Buttermere (May–Sept 2 or 3 daily) and York (4 weekly, via Harrowgate) stop on Central Car Park Road outside *S&S Travel*, which sells coach tickets and holds **left luggage** for £1 per day. The **tourist office** is in Moot Hall on Market Square (April–June, Sept & Oct daily 9.30am–5.30pm; July & Aug closes 7pm; Nov–March closes 4pm; ☎017687/72645), and the **National Park Information Centre**, 31 Lake Rd (daily April–Oct 9.30am–5.30pm; Nov–March 10am–4pm) also runs a *bureau de change*.

WALKS FROM BORROWDALE – SCAFELL, SCAFELL PIKE AND GREAT GABLE

The rugged area of fells at the head of Borrowdale contains one of the finest looking mountains in England – **Great Gable** (2949ft) – and the highest point in England, **Scafell Pike** (3205ft), its summit close to the second highest point in the Lakes, **Scafell** (3162ft). A loop taking in Scafell Pike and Scafell (8 miles; 3000ft ascent; 6hr) leaves Seathwaite via Stockley Bridge, branching to the right up Styhead Ghyll to Sty Head, then follows the Corridor Route approaching the Scafell Pike summit from the northwest. From there you have to negotiate Lord's Rake, a narrow ridge leading to **Scafell** half a mile to the southwest. The return from Scafell Pike starts northeast past Broad Crag path, continuing down to Esk Hause, where you turn left before branching right along Grains Ghyll to Seathwaite.

The easier of two approaches to **Great Gable** starts near the *Honister Hause* youth hostel and follows a path (6 miles; 2200ft ascent; 4hr) past Green Gable (2628ft), Grey Knotts and Brandreth, returning along an almost parallel path to the west. The second route (8 miles; 3000ft ascent; 6hr) starts at Seatoller and follows the road to Seathwaite cutting right up Sour Milk Ghyll, approaching again via Green Gable and using either of the paths mentioned above to descend to Honister Hause, from where a path to the left of the road takes you back to Seatoller.

Several decent **B&Bs** cluster along Bank Street, near the tourist office, and Southey Street, near the start of the Penrith road. Just about the cheapest central rooms are at *The Bridgedale Guesthouse*, 101 Main St (☎017687/73914; ②). Other good places include *Greenside Vegetarian Guesthouse*, 48 St John St (☎017687/74491; ③), and the *George Hotel*, 3 St John St (☎017687/72076; ④), the oldest hotel in Keswick. *The Great Little Tea Shop*, 26 Lake Rd (☎017687/73545; ③), does B&B and inexpensive vegetarian meals, ten percent of the profits going to conservation groups. A converted woollen mill by the river houses Keswick's **youth hostel**, Station Road (☎017687/72484). The nearest **campsite** (Feb–Nov; ☎017687/72392) is less than ten minutes' walk from the centre, down by the lake; turn left off Main Street beside the supermarket.

The tastiest of many **places to eat** is the licensed, self-service *Mayson's*, 33 Lake Rd, serving mouthwatering bakes, pies and stir-fries. After a cold day on the fells, *Abraham's Tea Rooms* in *George Fisher's* comes to your aid with warming mugs of glüwein and good café fare. The *Four in Hand* on Lake Road is the best **pub** (with excellent bar food); the *Queen's Head* off High street is the rowdiest.

Borrowdale and Buttermere

It is difficult to overstate the beauty of **Borrowdale**, with its bucolic river flats, at the head of Derwent Water, overshadowed by the peaks of Scafell and Scafell Pike, the highest in England. Walks on these start from **Seatoller**, eight miles south of Keswick, which can be reached on bus #79 from Keswick (5–9 daily). No bus continues from Seatoller over the Honister Pass into the equally striking **Buttermere** – that is accessible directly from Keswick on the *Mountain Goat* service (May–Sept 2–3 daily), which follows an unclassified road through Derwent Fells. Neither valley has a village of any size, but several hotels and B&Bs are strung out along the main road, to complement the four well-spaced youth hostels and campsites (all open Easter–Oct).

The *Derwent Water* **youth hostel** (☎017687/77246), based in an old mansion with fifteen acres of grounds sloping down to the lake, is a couple of miles south of Keswick along the B5289. Just before the hostel, a narrow road branches left for a steep climb to the photogenic Ashness Bridge and *Ashness Farm* **campsite** (☎017687/77361), both half a mile along. Back on the B5289, head three miles south past the *Borrowdale Hotel* (☎017687/77224; ⑧), which has an excellent if expensive restaurant, to the **Bowder Stone**. Controversy surrounds the origin of this house-sized lump of rock, pitched precariously on edge. Some say it came from the fells above, others contend it was brought by the last Ice Age from Scotland. In Borrowdale's only hamlet, **Rosthwaite**, the *Royal Oak Hotel* (☎017687/77214; ④) has more comfortable accommodation than the valley's second **youth hostel** (☎017687/77257), sitting back off the road at the end of the village opposite *Chapel House Farm* **campsite** (☎017687/77602). Another mile on, **Seatoller** is no more than a National Trust information centre, a car park and a few slate-roofed houses clustered around the moderately priced *Yew Tree Restaurant* (☎017687/77634) and the *Seatoller House* **B&B** (March–Nov; ☎017687/77218; ④). There's an informal **campsite** in a field by the beck along the road to **Seathwaite**, a popular base for walks up the likes of Great Gable and Scafell Pike (see box opposite).

Continuing west from Seatoller, a steep mile and a quarter grind gets you to the car park at the top of Honister Pass, by the *Honister Hause* **youth hostel** (☎017687/77267), starting point for walks to Great Gable. The road follows Gatesgarthdale Beck for three miles and makes a dramatic descent into the **Buttermere** valley by *Gatesgarth Farm* **campsite** (☎017687/70256), then runs another mile beside the lake to a fourth **youth hostel** (☎017687/70245) just before Buttermere village. The village has two hotels: *The Bridge Hotel* (☎017687/70252; ⑨, including B&B, afternoon tea and dinner) and *The Fish Hotel* (☎017687/70253; ⑤, including dinner). Of the **B&Bs**

nestling in secluded spots in the valley, the best is *Pickett Howe* (☎01900/85444; ⑤), a delightful seventeenth-century farmhouse in Brackenthwaite at the western end of Crummock Water.

Cockermouth

The farming community of **COCKERMOUTH**, midway between the industrial coast and Keswick at the confluence of the Cocker and Derwent rivers, is yet another station on the Wordsworth trail: the **Wordsworth House** on Main Street (April–June Mon–Fri 11am–5pm; July–Oct Mon–Sat 11am–5pm; £2.40; NT) is where William and Dorothy were born and spent their first few years. The blockish eighteenth-century building was nearly replaced by a bus station in the 1930s, but was saved and given to the National Trust who have furnished it with imports from their vaults. Some of the original features remain and the kitchen has been put to good use as a café, but on a warm day the walled garden beside the river is more pleasurable than the house.

Once you've paid homage to the Wordsworths, Cockermouth has a triad of minor attractions in store. Next door to the Wordsworth House, you can get your hands dirty at **The Printing House** (Easter–Oct Tues–Sat 10am–4pm; £1.50), where visitors are invited to tackle some of the seventy-odd printing machines ranging from wood-block to Linotype. Otherwise it's a toss-up between **The Cumberland Toy and Model Museum**, Banks Court (Feb–Nov daily 10am–5pm; £1.50), and the hour-long **Jenning's Brewery Tour**, Brewery Lane (April–Oct Mon–Fri 11am & 2pm; July–Sept also Sat 11am; £2.70), which culminates with a tasting.

All **buses** stop on Main Street, from where you follow the signs to the **tourist office** in Riverside car park, off Market Place (April–June & Oct Mon–Sat 10.30am–4.30pm; July–Sept Mon–Sat 10am–6pm, Sun 2–5pm; Nov–March Mon–Sat 10.30am–4pm; ☎01900/822 634). Two of the best **B&Bs** are just a couple of minutes from the centre: *Castlegate Guest House*, on Castlegate (☎01900/822 441; ③), and *Manor House*, 23 St Helen's St (☎01900/822 416; ③). Ten minutes' walk south along Station Road, then Fern Bank brings you to the **youth hostel** (☎01900/822 561) in a seventeenth-century watermill. **Eating** well in Cockermouth isn't a problem, with *The Riverside Restaurant*, 2 Main St (☎01900/823 871) offering a moderately priced gamey menu, and the *The Quince and Medlar*, 12 Castlegate (☎01900/823 579) serving excellent vegetarian dishes. The *Trout* in Crown Street has good bar meals and fine beer.

WALKS FROM GLENRIDDING

Helvellyn (3114ft) is the most popular of the four 3000-foot mountains in Cumbria, and one of the most frequently chosen routes over it is the circuit from Glenridding over Striding Edge and Swirral Edge, two rocky ridges that surround Red Tarn and converge at the flat summit (7 miles; 2600ft ascent; 5–6hr). You are unlikely to be alone or get lost on the yard-wide approaches but the four memorials on Striding Edge are suitable warning of the dangers. Purists walk the tops, the more cautious use the safer path just off the crest.

Paths from two alternative starting points meet at the beginning of **Striding Edge**: a steep one from Glenridding car park, and an easier one from the broad-bottomed Grisedale valley, half a mile south of Glenridding. After you've negotiated Striding Edge, a right turn at the summit leads northeast to the less demanding **Swirral Edge**, via the col from where a route leads down to Red Tarn, then follows the beck to the disused slate-quarry workings and the Helvellyn hostel, two miles from Glenridding. Another route, of equal duration, climbs back up to Catstycam and drops down the northern ridge path into Keppel Cove, where you cross the dam and continue to the hostel.

Ullswater

Wordsworth declared **Ullswater** "the happiest combination of beauty and grandeur, which any of the Lakes affords", a judgement that still holds good. Much of Ullswater's appeal derives from its serpentine shape, a result of the complex geology of this area: the glacier that formed the trench in which the lake now lies had to cut across a couple of geological boundaries, from granite in the south, through a band of Skiddaw slate, to softer sandstone and limestone in the north.

The chief lakeside settlements, **PATTERDALE** and **GLENRIDDING**, are less than a mile apart at the southern tip of Ullswater – at over seven miles long, Cumbria's second longest lake – each with a smattering of cafés and B&Bs but not otherwise notable except as a base for one of the most popular scrambling routes in the country (see the box opposite). If you're not in the mood for a strenuous clamber, you could take a trip on the **Ullswater Steamer** (Easter–Oct 2 or 3 daily; £3 one-way) from Glenridding to Pooley Bridge, at the northern end of the lake.

The steamer also chugs from Glenridding to **Howtown** (Mar–Oct 4–9 daily; £2.40 one-way), a small settlement halfway along the lake. A popular walk from Howtown back to Patterdale (4.5 miles; 2hr 30min) follows the shore of Ullswater around Hallin Fell (or over, climbing 263ft) to Sandwick, then crosses fields before rejoining the shore at Long Crag for the final two miles to the south end of the lake. A more strenuous and rewarding route (8 miles; 2631ft ascent; 4–5hr) from Howtown follows Fusedale Beck and climbs up to the High Street, a broad-backed ridge that was once a Roman road. After meeting the highest point, **High Raise** (2632ft), the path arches round a horseshoe of steep craggy drops, crosses a boggy patch of land to **Angle Tarn**, and winds down to Goldmill Beck in the valley floor next to Patterdale.

An alternative excursion is to **Gowbarrow Park**, three miles to the north of Glenridding, where the A5091 meets the A592; the hillside still blazes green and gold in spring, as it was doing when the Wordsworths visited; it's thought that Dorothy's recollections of the visit in her diary inspired William to write his famous *Daffodils* poem. The car park at Gowbarrow is also the start of an easy, brief walk up to **Aira Force**, a bush-cloaked seventy-foot waterfall that's spectacular in spate and can be viewed from bridges spanning the top and bottom of the drop.

Apart from the *Ullswater Steamer* the only **public transport** is the summer-only bus service between Penrith and Patterdale (Mon–Fri 3–5 daily, 1 continuing to Bowness over the Kirkstone Pass). **Accommodation** is abundant, the best place being the lakeside *Glenridding Hotel* (☎017684/82228; ⑦), right in the centre of Glenridding. Other good spots are the *Fairlight Guest House* (☎017684/82397; ②) by Glenridding's central car park, and the *Moss Grey Guest House and Café* (☎017684/82500; ③) near the shops in Glenridding, where *Gillside Caravan & Camping* (March–Oct; ☎017684/82346) lurks behind the summer-only **tourist office** (☎017684/82414). There's a **youth hostel** in Patterdale (☎017684/82394), while the *Helvellyn* youth hostel (☎017684/82269) is in a dramatic setting up Glenridding valley, by the disused quarries (see box). In the same buildings is the very basic "stone tent" called *Swirral Bothy*, which must be reserved in advance through Keswick tourist office (☎017687/72803).

The Cumbrian coast

Furness, the southern quarter of Cumbria, was part of Lancashire until 1974 and in many ways shares that county's industrial heritage, so don't expect the **Cumbrian coast** to match the spectacular scenery inland. Apart from fast access by road and rail to the southwestern section of the lakes, the greatest appeal of this region is in the monastic abbey at **Cartmel**, the ruins of **Furness Abbey** and the **Eskdale** valley, a good base for walks, served by a narrow-gauge rail line.

Cartmel

A train to Cark-in-Cartmel followed by a two-mile bus journey will get you to **CARTMEL**. The village is dominated by the proud **Church of St Mary** (daily summer 9am–5.30pm; winter 9am–3.30pm), the only substantial remnant of the Augustinian priory that stood here from the twelfth century until the Dissolution. A diagonally crowned tower is the most distinctive feature outside, while the light and spacious Norman-transitional interior climaxes at a splendid chancel, illuminated by the 45-foot-high **East Window**. You can spend a good half-hour scanning the immaculate misericords and numerous tombs, chief among them the **Harrington Tomb** in the Town Choir, to the south of the chancel – the weathered figure is that of John Harrington, who rebuilt this section in 1340. The choir went on to act as the parish church when the rest of the building was abandoned following the reformation, the nave only regaining its cover in the 1620s thanks to the munificence of local landowner, George Preston. Before you leave, peruse the grave stones on the church floor, reminders of men and women swept away by the tide while crossing the sands. Another priory relic is the **Priory Gatehouse** (April–Oct Tues–Sun 11am–5pm; free), now housing an art gallery upstairs. You'll pass the gatehouse en route to the racecourse whose delightful setting by the River Eea deserves a look even if the races (held on the last weekend in May and August) aren't in action.

The Cavendish (☎015395/36240; ④), on Cavendish Street, sits on the site of a monastic guest house and is the oldest and most characterful of the town's **pubs**, offering good food, award-winning *Lakeland Gold* beer, comfortable accommodation and a jazz festival on the second last weekend in August. Around the corner on Market Square, *Market Cross Cottage* (☎015395/36143; ③) is a cosy **B&B** that also serves meals.

Ulverston

The south coast railway line winds westwards from Cartmel to **ULVERSTON**, a close-knit market town, which formerly prospered on the cotton, tanning and iron-ore industries. The mainstay of the economy today is a rather unsightly chemical works, but the plant doesn't mar Ulverston's prettiness, which is enhanced by its dappled grey limestone cottages and a jumble of cobbled alleys zig-zagging off the central market place.

The first thing you'll notice on the approach to Ulverston is what looks like a lighthouse high on the hill to the north of town. This is the **Hoad Monument**, built in 1850 to honour locally born Sir John Barrow, a former secretary of the admiralty. However, Ulverston's most famous son is Stan Laurel, the wimpering, head-scratching half of Laurel and Hardy, who are celebrated in a mind-boggling collection of memorabilia at the **Laurel and Hardy Museum** on Upper Brook Street (daily 10am–4.30pm; £2). The eccentric showcase of hats, photos, letters, press cuttings and props leads into a 1920s style cinema with almost constant screenings of the duo's films.

Down from the museum, in Lower Brook Street, Ulverston's **Heritage Centre** (daily except Wed & Sun 9.30am–4.30pm; 50p) is a little bland, but gives a good overview of the town's history and its various industrial achievements. The other main attraction is the glass factory, *Cumbria Crystal*, on Lightburn Road, close to the railway bridge (Mon–Thurs 9am–4pm, Fri 9am–3pm; £1) where you can watch the crystal-making process from blowing to painstaking carving.

Ulverston train **station**, serving the Cumbrian coast railway, is only a few minutes' walk from the town centre, where **buses** arrive on Victoria road from Cartmel (#535), Grange-over-Sands and Barrow (#570), and Windermere (#518). The **tourist office** is close by, in Coronation Hall on County Square (Mon–Sat 9am–5pm; ☎01229/587 120). Though Ulverston's nightlife is modest, it has some good accommodation. Pick of the

B&Bs are *The Whitehouse*, a three-hundred-year-old beamed cottage on Market Street (☎01229/583 340; ③), and *Dyker Bank Guest House* at 2 Springfield Rd, just up from the station (☎01229/582 423; ③). The nearest **campsite** is two miles down the coast at *Bardsea Leisure Park* (☎01229/584 712). There are plenty of cafés in Ulverston; for a larger **meal**, try *The Ship's Wheel*, renowned for its frothy coffees and traditional cooking, or *The Rose & Crown*, with live music on Wednesday nights, both on King Street.

Barrow-in-Furness

With rows of terraced houses and the shipyard cranes piercing the skyline, **BARROW-IN-FURNESS** has a distinctly industrial feel, that's been the town's hallmark since it grew up around a booming iron industry in the nineteenth century. Steel works and shipbuilding followed, making Barrow one of England's busiest ports, but the steel works closed in 1983 and orders for military seacraft fell in the late 1980s, though these have picked up since. Given Barrow's reliance on this business, it's hardly surprising that the only exhibition centre here is **The Dock Museum** (April–Oct Tues–Sun 10.30am–5pm; Nov–March Wed–Fri 10.30am–4pm, Sat & Sun 12–4pm; free), a newly established showcase for *VSEL*, the company in charge of the industry. The museum's situation in the dried out graving dock where ships were once repaired is of more interest than its contents, which record the town's shipbuilding history with dioramas, pictures and video clips.

The region's wealth used to be concentrated at **Furness Abbey** (April–Sept daily 10am–6pm; Oct daily 10am–4pm; Nov–March Wed–Sun 10am–4pm; £2.20; EH), a set of roofless red-,sandstone arcades and pillars hidden in a wooded vale a mile and a half out of town on the Ulverston road (bus #6 stops within half a mile). Now one of Cumbria's finest ruins, it was once the most powerful abbey in the northwest, possessing much of southern Cumbria as well as land in Ireland and the Isle of Man. By the fourteenth century it had become such a prize that the Scots raided it twice, though it survived until Henry VIII chose it to be the first of the large abbeys to be dissolved. The massive slabs of stone-ribbed vaulting and richly embellished arcades are the equal of any of Yorkshire's far busier abbey ruins, and there's a small museum housing some of the best carvings and a superb collection of photos.

Barrow's **tourist office** is located at Forum 28, Duke Street (Mon–Sat 9.30am–5pm; ☎01229/870 156); a few low-cost **B&B**s can be found along Abbey Road and Church Street, about fifty yards south of the office. *Mr Beecroft*, 119 Abbey Rd (☎01229/829 574; ②) is about the cheapest, with *Infield Guesthouse*, 276 Abbey Rd (☎01229/831 381; ②) being perhaps a little more comfortable. The nearest **campsite** is *South End Caravan Site* (March–Oct; ☎01229/472 823), towards the south tip of Walney island.

Eskdale

On its way between Barrow and Whitehaven, the Cumbrian coast railway stops at **RAVENGLASS**, a sleepy estuary village with a single main street. This is the starting point for the toy-like **Ravenglass and Eskdale Railway**, known affectionately as *La'al Ratty* and opened in 1875 to carry ore from the Eskdale mines to the coastal railway. The tiny train, running on a 15-inch gauge track, takes forty minutes to wind its way through seven miles of forests and fields between the fell sides of the Eskdale valley to **Dalegarth** station (£5.70 return), a popular starting point for walks back to the coast or up to Lakeland's peaks (see box). The narrow road along the dale from Ravenglass is the only east–west link from the central lakes to the coast, winding over the hair-raising one-in-three **Hardknott Pass**, the steepest grade in England, and the slightly more manageable **Wrynose Pass**.

Three miles beyond Dalegarth station and 800ft up, the remains of granaries, bath houses and the commandant's quarters for **Hardknott Roman Fort** command a strategic and panoramic position. Over Hardknott pass, the road drops to Cockley Beck, at

---

WALKS FROM ESKDALE

An easy riverside walk (2 miles; negligible ascent; 1hr) starts 200 yards east of Dalegarth station down a track to St Catherine's church opposite the road to Boot, the nearest village. In low water you can cross the river below the church by stepping stones; you turn right then left up a path beside a stream to **Stanley Ghyll Waterfall**. Returning along the path beside the stream, a branch on the left leads back to Dalegarth station via a bridge over a swimming hole. If you don't cross the stepping stones, you can take a path following the right bank to Doctor Bridge where you can cross and double back for Stanley Ghyll or continue to the road and the *Woolpack Inn*.

The inn is a common starting point for the **Woolpack Round** (16 miles; 5500ft; 8–10hr), topping the two highest mountains in England and several others which aren't much lower. It is not easy going and a certain amount of scrambling is required, but the views and the varied terrain make this one of the finest Lakeland walks. The conical **Harter Fell** (2130ft) to the east is the first objective, reached by a road from almost opposite the *Woolpack Inn* to Penny Hill Farm, from where a path heads steeply up to the south, gradually turning east to the summit. The route down across peaty turf (unmarked on OS maps) follows a spur to the top of Hardknott Pass then up to **Hard Knott** (1802ft), from where you follow a broad ridge to **Crinkle Crags** (2676ft) and the beginning of a long skyline traverse sweeping around to the north and west. Clearly defined paths then guide you over **Bow Fell** (2959ft) and **Esk Pike** (2904ft) to the col at **Esk Hause** (2490ft), the heart of the Lake District, from where valleys fan out in all directions. The rise up to **Great End** (2986ft) and along to the huge cairn on **Scafell Pike** (3205ft) is but a prelude to the walk's crux, the scramble down into the gully of Micheldore and climb up the craggy Broad Stand to the summit of **Scafell** (3163ft). From here it is all downhill past Slight Side (2500ft) to the south, then over grass and heather back to *The Woolpack*.

---

the head of quiet Dunnerdale, where an unclassified road branches south to Duddon Bridge. The Wrynose Pass road continues east to the col, where the **Three Shire Stone** marks the old boundary of Cumberland, Westmorland and Lancashire. Beyond, it's seven miles' descent past the foot of the Langdale valley to Ambleside.

From Dalegarth Station it is 500 yards to *Hollins Farm* **campsite** (☎019467/23253), another three quarters of a mile to the *Woolpack Inn* (☎019467/23230; ④) and a further 400 yards to *Eskdale* **youth hostel** (☎019467/23219).

East Cumbria: The Eden Valley and Penrith

Along with the Lune Valley around Kirkby Lonsdale, the **Eden Valley** splits the Pennines from the Lake District fells. Although it is one of the most attractive sections of motorway in the country, the M6 – following the main London–Penrith–Glasgow rail line – misses the best of the valley. Far better are the smaller roads through the attractive market towns of **Kirkby Lonsdale**, Sedburgh and Kirkby Stephen to the former county town of **Appleby-in-Westmorland**. The hub of east Cumbrian transport is **Penrith**, though it isn't on the **Settle to Carlisle Line**, a magnificent rail route through open scenery via Appleby-in-Westmorland and Kirkby Stephen.

Kirkby Lonsdale

Close to the point where Cumbria, Lancashire and Yorkshire meet, the flint and limestone houses of quaint **KIRKBY LONSDALE** sit on a rise above the River Lune, which provides the focus for the town's two main sights. Ten minutes' walk south from Market Square, the three-arched **Devil's Bridge** was a stone-built crossing by 1380 and until the construction of its more recent counterpart was the main route into Yorkshire. A path from Devil's Bridge follows the Lune to the base of a steep flight of steps that re-enters the town behind St Mary's Church at **Ruskin's View**. Turner painted the view over the valley from here but it was John Ruskin who, with typical overstatement, declared: "I do not know in all my own country, still less in France or Italy, a place more naturally divine, or a more priceless possession". In fact, the views improve if you continue up the elevated path beyond the viewpoint.

Kirkby Lonsdale has frequent **bus** connections from Lancaster (1 daily continuing to Settle), and a very helpful **tourist office** at 24 Main St (Easter–Oct daily 9am–1pm & 2–5pm; Nov–Easter Mon & Thurs–Sat 9am–1pm & 2–5pm; ☎015242/71437). Pick of the accommodation is at *The Sun Hotel* on Market Street (☎015242/71965; ④), which also has some of the best bar **meals**; best B&Bs are *The Courtyard*, Fairbank (☎015242/71613; ②), and *Hillside* at 31 New Rd (☎05242/71426; ②). The nearest **youth hostel** (☎015242/41444) is six miles away in Ingleton, Yorkshire, close to White Scar Caves, but there's no longer a bus link there.

Appleby-in-Westmorland

One-time county town of Westmorland, **APPLEBY-IN-WESTMORLAND**, ten miles northwest of Kirkby Stephen, is protected on three sides by a loop in the River Eden. The fourth was defended by the now privately owned **Appleby Castle** (April–Oct daily 10am–5pm; £3.50), where rare species of farm animals are bred on the grounds. You can climb to the top of the Norman keep, which was restored by **Lady Anne Clifford**, who after her father's death in 1605 spent 45 years trying to claim her rightful inheritance. A triptych known as *The Great Picture*, which she commissioned to commemorate her eventual success, is displayed in the Great Hall (closed Mon & Sat) along with other fine paintings and porcelain. She also founded the **almshouses** on Boroughgate, the town's backbone, which runs from High Cross, former site of the cheese market outside the castle, to Low Cross, site of the general Saturday market.

The town is usually peaceful, but changes its character completely in June when the **Appleby Horse Fair** takes over nearby Gallows' Hill, as it has done since 1750. Britain's most important gypsy gathering, it draws hundreds of chrome-plated caravans and more traditional horse-drawn "bow-tops", as well as the vehicles of scores of tinkers, New-Age travellers and sightseers. A week of road racing, hair-raising stunts and fortune telling culminates on the second Wednesday of June, the day for the horse trading. The whole week gets the support of the local council but only some of the residents, many complaining about the disruption and the boisterous revelry which forces some publicans to shut up shop for the week.

The Settle to Carlisle **rail line** is the best way to get to Appleby, although the X74 Carlisle to Darlington **bus**, via Penrith, comes through twice daily (not Sun). The **tourist office**, in the Moot Hall on Boroughgate (April–Sept Mon–Sat 10am–5pm, Sun noon–4pm; Oct–March Mon–Thurs 10am–noon, Fri & Sat 10am–noon & 2–4pm; ☎017683/51177), ten minutes' walk from the station. The top **hotel** in town is the *Tufton Arms Hotel*, Market Square (☎017683/51593; ⑥); at the other end of the scale, there's **B&B** at 17 Barrowmoor Rd (☎017683/61610; ②), a mile west of the castle. The closest **campsite** is at *Dufton Hall* (☎017683/51573; ③), three miles away in Dufton, which also has the closest **youth hostel** (☎017683/51236). There is no shortage of **places to eat**: try the *Tufton Arms Hotel*, which dishes up extra-large bar meals, while the *Royal Oak* is renowned for its Cumberland sausages.

Penrith

The deep red buildings of **PENRITH**, thirteen miles northwest of Appleby, were built from the same rust-red sandstone used to construct the castle in the fourteenth century, as a bastion against raids from the north; it's now a crumbling ruin, opposite the train station. More impressive are the remains of **Brougham Castle** (April–Sept daily 10am–4pm Oct 10am–6pm; £1.30; EH), a mile and a half south of Penrith by the River Eamont. Passed down through the influential Clifford family to Lady Anne (see above), the castle overlaps the site of a Roman fort and contains a collection of tombstones commemorating Britons who adopted Roman customs and the Latin language. You have to travel further for the most dramatic local sight, the prehistoric stone circle known as **Long Meg and her Daughters**. Standing outside a ring of stones nearly 400ft in diameter, Long Meg is the tallest stone at 18ft and has a profile like the face of an austere old lady. The stone family, said by some to be a coven of witches turned to stone by a magician, is in Little Salkeld, six miles north of Penrith and just over a mile's walk from Langwathby on the Settle to Carlisle railway.

Trains from Manchester, London, Glasgow and Edinburgh pull into Penrith, five minutes' walk south of the **bus station** on Albert Street. Around the corner on Middlegate the **tourist office** (April–Oct daily 10am–6pm; Nov–March Mon–Sat 10am–5pm; ☎01733/67466) shares a seventeenth-century school house with a small local museum. The bulk of the useful **B&Bs** line Victoria Road, though *George's Place*, off Middlegate at 7 Queen St (☎01768/66635; ②), is even more central. The closest **campsite** is *Lowther Caravan Park* (☎01768/63631), a mile south along the A66 at Eamont Bridge. During the day, some of the best-value **food** is at *The Arcade Café*, Devonshire Arcade; later, try the inexpensive pizza and pasta at *Nunzio's*, Corn Market, or *Chataways Bistro* (☎01768/890 233), whose imaginative food is enhanced by its setting on the edge of St Andrews churchyard.

Carlisle

CARLISLE, the county town of Cumbria and its largest city, was originally a Celtic settlement, then became a Roman town during the construction of Hadrian's Wall. Long after the Romans had gone, the Saxon settlement was repeatedly fought over by the Danes and the Scots, the latter losing it finally to the Normans of William Rufus. The struggle with the Scots continued for centuries: William Wallace was repelled in 1297, Robert the Bruce eighteen years later, and Bonnie Prince Charlie's troops took Carlisle and held it for a few months before surrendering to the Duke of Cumberland.

Chief relic of all this mayhem is **Carlisle Castle** (daily summer 9.30am–6pm; winter 9.30am–4pm; £2; EH), built by William Rufus on the site of a Celtic hill fort at the apex of the town walls, now reached by an underpass at the end of Castle Street. During nine hundred years of continuous military use, it has undergone considerable changes, most evident in its outer bailey, which is filled with fairly modern buildings named after battles from the Napoleonic Wars and World War I. Apart from the Gatehouse, with its reconstructed warden's quarters, only the **inner bailey** is of great interest. It was here, in 1568, that Elizabeth I kept Mary Queen of Scots as her "guest". A table which may once have been used by her is kept in the **Military Museum** in the former armoury, but much more interesting are the displays in **The Keep** and the elegant heraldic carvings done by prisoners in a top-floor alcove. The castle was recaptured from Bonnie Prince Charlie's troops in 1745, but the story of "the licking stone" in the dungeon providing sustenance for the Scottish prisoners is probably apocryphal. More credible is the claim they were the first to sing, "You'll take the high road and I'll take the low road", referring to their poor prospects of returning to Scotland alive.

A good deal more history is on offer at **Tullie House Museum and Art Gallery** across Castle Way from the castle entrance (Mon–Sat 10am–5pm, Sun noon–5pm; £3.30), which takes an imaginative if lightweight approach to Carlisle's turbulent past. Special emphasis is put on life on the edge of the Roman Empire and on a dramatic attempt to convey the intensity of the feuds between the "Reivers", border families who lived beyond the jurisdiction of the Scottish and English authorities from the fourteenth to the seventeenth century.

Christianity was established in Carlisle by Saint Kentigern, who became the first bishop and patron saint of Glasgow. However, the present **Cathedral** (daily summer 7.45am–8.30pm; winter 7.45am–6pm), a hundred yards south along Castle Street, wasn't founded until the twelfth century and has been considerably altered since. Parliamentary troops during the Civil War destroyed all but two powerful arches of the original eight bays of the Norman nave, their simplicity now a foil for the ornate choir stalls and the glorious **East Window**, which features some of the finest pieces of fourteenth-century stained glass in the country, although two thirds of it is a faithful nineteenth-century restoration. In the northwest corner of the nave, steps lead down to the **Treasury**, containing glittering chalices and communion sets, Henry VIII's charter of the foundation of the Dean and Chapter in 1541, and a cutaway section of the foundations which have so poorly supported the arches above.

Practicalities

Emerging from the train station, you can't miss **The Citadel**, built in the nineteenth century on the site of a medieval fortress but serving only as council offices. Its twin drum towers make a grand entrance to English Street which leads to the main square where the **tourist office** (June–Aug Mon–Sat 9.30am–6pm, Sun 11am–4pm; Sept–May Mon–Sat 9.30am–5pm; ☎01228/512 444) is housed in the Elizabethan former town hall. The office organizes guided tours and coach trips to Hadrian's Wall; you can also leave bags here for 30p per day. The **bus station** is off Lowther Street, close to the centre.

Budget **accommodation** is concentrated between Victoria Place and Warwick Road: try *Howard House*, 27 Howard Place (☎01228/29159; ②), or *Redruth Guesthouse*, 46 Victoria Place (☎01228/21631; ②). The *County Hotel*, on the southern continuation of English Street at 9 Botchergate (☎01228/31316; ⑤), is one of the more appealing central hotels. The **youth hostel** (☎01228/23934) in Etterby, a mile and a quarter northwest of the centre, may soon cease to exist, so enquire first; if it's still going, take the #62 bus to St Ann's Hill from the train station. The nearest **campsite** is *Orton Grange* (☎01228/710 252) on the A596 four miles southwest of the city – take bus #300.

If you like your **food** spicy, *Zapotec: the Kitchens of Mexico and Spain*, 18 Fisher St (☎01228/512 209; moderate) is a good bet, or make for Cecil Street, just outside the city walls to the east, where *Cecil's Treat* at no. 36 (☎01228/514 868; moderate) offers a menu ranging from Beef Wellington to peanut roast.

The Isle of Man

The **ISLE OF MAN**, almost equidistant from Ireland, England, Wales and Scotland, is stuck with the reputation of being a tax haven for greedy Brits and a refuge for the sort of people who think that even Victorian values were a bit on the lax side. It is, however, one of the most beautiful spots in Britain, a mountainous, cliff-fringed island just thirty-one miles by thirteen, into which are shoehorned austere moorlands and wooded glens, fine castles, beguiling narrow-gauge railways and scores of standing stones and Celtic crosses. The earliest substantial human traces are Mesolithic flint workings from about 6000BC, predating the Neolithic farming settlements by about three millennia. Saint Patrick is said to have come here in the fifth century bringing Christianity, which struggled for a while when the Vikings established garrisons here in the eleventh century, though they converted while they reigned as **Kings of Mann** (deriving, like the modern "Man", from the pre-Roman but unexplained *Mona*). The Scots under Alexander wrested power from the Norsemen in 1275, the beginning of an ultimately unsuccessful 130-year struggle with the English over control.

The distinct indentity of the island remained intact, however, and many true Manx inhabitants, who comprise a mere forty percent of the island's population, insist that the Isle of Man is not part of England, nor indeed of the UK. Indeed, the island has its own government, **Tynwald**, arguably the world's oldest democratic parliament, which has run continuously since 979 AD. Tynwald consists of two chambers, the 24-member House of Keys and the smaller, more elite Legislative Assembly, both presided over by a lieutenant-governor who is appointed by the British monarch, the Lord of Man, and the island remains a crown dependency. To further complicate matters, the island maintains a unique associate status in the EU, neither contributing nor receiving funds but enjoying the same trading rights. The island has its own sterling currency, worth the same as the mainland curency; its own laws, though they generally follow Westminster's; an independent postal service; and a Gaelic-based language which nearly died out but is now once again being taught in schools. It also, of course, produces its own tailless version of the domestic cat.

For most of its history, crofting and fishing interspersed with a good bit of smuggling have formed the basis of the economy. Tourism began to flourish during the late Victorian and Edwardian eras, but in recent years the real money-spinner has been the **offshore finance industry**, exploiting the island's low income tax and absence of death duties. Whole streets in **Douglas**, the capital, are taken up by consultancies and the island is dotted with the houses and swanky cars of British tax exiles. This hasn't helped the island's image problem, which largely stems from its archaic human rights legislation. Homosexuality was illegal here until 1992, while the death penalty and corporal punishment were only abolished in 1993, in response to pressure from Westminster and the European Community. With such a record, it might seem perverse that in 1881 Tynwald became the first government to see fit to grant women a vote, although this was limited to property owners and empowered very few.

Though the landscapes are wonderful, the island's main tourist draw is the **TT (Tourist Trophy) motorcycle races** in the first two weeks in June, a frenzy of speed and burning rubber that's shattered the island's peace annually since 1907. Thousands of bikers swamp the place to watch a non-stop parade of maniacs hurtling round the lanes at speeds well in excess of 100mph. Don't come at this time unless you have booked well in advance.

Douglas

DOUGLAS, heart of the offshore financial industry, also has the vast majority of the island's hotels and good restaurants, and it makes as good a base as any, since all roads lead here. A product of Victorian mass tourism, Douglas displays many similarities to Blackpool, just across the water: five-storey terraces back the mile-and-a-half-long curve of the promenade and its tram tracks, and the town even makes a paltry attempt to emulate the illuminations. The seafront vista has changed little since Victorian times, and is still trodden by heavy-footed cart horses pulling trams. The **Gaiety Theatre** (guided tours Sat 10.30am), on Harris Promenade, is fronted by a stained-glass canopy and boasts a lush, lapis-blue interior designed by Frank Matcham.

The **Manx Museum**, Kingswood Grove (Mon–Sat 10am–5pm; free), five minutes' walk inland up Church Road and Crellins Hill, is the prime Manx heritage showcase and should definitely be visited before heading off around the island. A Neolithic farming community begins a sequence of imaginative reconstructions that culminates in a Victorian street scene complete with ancient tram cars. More recent activities get run-of-the-mill treatment with collections of TT motorbikes and boards explaining the capital's financial wheeling and dealing.

With the exception of the museum and theatre, the sights of Douglas are also the means of getting out of it. Little is left of the network of railways which once covered the island, but two century-old **rail** services still provide the best public transport to all the major towns and sights except for Peel. The carriages of the **Steam Railway** rock their fifteen-mile course from Douglas to Castletown and Port Erin at a spirited pace (Easter–Oct 10am–5pm 4–6 daily; £6.20 return to Port Erin). The rolling terrain due north of Douglas is covered by an **Electric Railway**, its single wooden carriage resembling a tramway more than a train, and running seventeen miles from Derby Castle Station (horse-drawn tram or #2 bus) to Ramsey (Easter–Oct 5–15 daily; £5 return). Ten minutes' walk from the first station is the beginning of another railway, the short **Groundle Glen Railway** (Easter & summer Sun 11am–4.30pm; £1.50 return), which goes three quarters of a mile out onto the headland and back. If you plan to spend a whole day on the trains, it may be worth getting a *day rover* ticket (£8.80, child £4.40), which covers the electric and steam routes as well as the trip to Snaefell summit.

Practicalities

Ferries all dock by the Sea Terminal at the southern end of the waterfront. Fifty yards beyond the forecourt taxi rank, the Lord Street **bus station** is the hub of the island's dozen or so bus routes. North Quay runs 300 yards west from here alongside the fishing port to Douglas Station, terminus of the steam railway to Port Erin, while the waterfront runs a mile and a half north to Derby Castle Station for the **electric railway** to Laxey and Ramsey. *Eurocycles* on Victoria Road, off Broadway (☎01624/624 909) rents reliable **bikes**. The **tourist office** is in the Sea Terminal building (Easter & mid-May to Sept daily 9am–7.30pm; April & Oct daily 9am–5pm; Nov–Easter Mon–Thurs 9am–5.30pm, Fri 9am–5pm, Sat 9.30am–12.30pm; ☎01624/686 766).

As for **B&Bs**, if proximity to the ferry terminal is your chief concern then go for *The Walpole Hotel*, Walpole Avenue (☎01624/674 965; ③). *Seanook*, 10 Empire Terrace (☎01624/676 830; ②), and *Seafield*, 14 Empire Terrace (☎01624/674 372; ②) are about the cheapest; or if you want a bit more comfort, try the distinctively styled *Edelweiss Hotel*, Queen's Promenade (☎01624/675115; ④), set slightly back from the front. The nearest **campsite** backs onto *Nobles Park Grandstand* on Glencrutchery Road, a mile north of the tourist office (mid-June to mid-Sept; ☎01624/621 132). *Glenlough Farm* (☎01624/851326) over three miles west at Union Mills, is the closest all-year site.

Several good **restaurants** nestle amongst the general dross. The *Bay Room Restaurant*, amongst the sculptures in the Manx Museum, and *Greens Vegetarian Restaurant*, in the ticket office at the steam railway station, both dish up great inexpensive food – though they close early. The formal *Waterfront Restaurant*, North Quay (☎01624/673 222), offers the island's finest and most expensive dining experience though the inexpensive *Blazers* next door is run by the same people. Otherwise, try the cosy *Scotts Bistro*, a few steps to the north at 5–7 John St in Douglas' oldest building; its imaginative menu includes queenies, a unique Manx scallop. The lively *Bushy's Brew* **pub** on Victoria Street has a juke box built into the back of an old Ford Anglia and serves own-brewed "Old Bushy Tail", which will soon revive flagging spirits.

The rest of the island

Modern Douglas is atypical of an island which prides itself on its Celtic and Norse heritage, and it's the vestiges of the distant past – the castles at the former capital **Castletown** and the west coast port of **Peel** – that make the most obvious destinations. To the north, **Laxey** is an attractive proposition for its huge **waterwheel** and the meandering train ride to the barren summit of **Snaefell**, the island's highest peak. From its summit you get an idea of the range of the Manx scenery, the finest parts of which are to be found in the seventeen officially designated National Glens, most of them linked by ninety-mile **Raad Ny Foillan** (Road of the Gull) coastal footpath, which passes several of the island's numerous smaller sites: hill forts, Viking burial ships and Celtic crosses, all pinpointed in the Manx Museum.

The **narrow-gauge trains** are the most enjoyable way to get to Laxey, Ramsey, Castletown and Port Erin but **buses** are often quicker. The most useful routes are: #1 to Port Erin and Port St Mary via the airport and Castletown, #5 and #6 to Ramsey via St Johns and Peel, and #15 to Ramsey via Laxey and the picturesque Dhoon Glen.

Laxey, Snaefell and Ramsey

The brooding presence of **Snaefell** hangs heavy over the straggling town of **LAXEY**, seven miles north of Douglas. Filling a narrow valley, Laxey spills down from the train station to a small harbour and pebbly beach, squeezed between two bulky headlands. Inland and uphill from the train station is Laxey's pride, the **"Lady Isabella" Waterwheel** (Easter–Sept daily 10am–5pm; £2). At 72ft across, it's the largest working wheel in the world – a slightly bogus claim since it doesn't actually drive anything – which used to pump water from the local lead mines until 1929. The mechanism and its relation to the mine is all well explained – and if that doesn't interest you, the climb up the spiral stairs is reason enough to drop by.

The half-hour Electric Railway ride from Douglas drops you at the station used by the **Snaefell Mountain Railway** (Easter–Oct daily 10.30am–3.30pm; £4.75 return) which runs to the island's highest point. Every few minutes, a tramcar begins its thirty-minute wind through increasingly denuded moorland to the inelegant café and bar at the top of **Snaefell** (2036ft), from where you can see England, Wales, Scotland and Ireland on a clear day. The tram stops as it crosses the road below the summit, allowing people to visit **Murray's Motorcycle Museum** (summer daily 10am–5pm; £2).

There are several **guest houses** to chose from, though it's advisable to book in advance. You'll find welcoming rooms at *Narrowgate House* (☎01624/861966; ③) on Old Laxey Hill or, closer to the harbour at Ny Creggan, *Fairy Cottage* offers an imaginative vegetarian breakfast menu (☎01624/861412; ③). The nearest **campsite** is on Quarry Road (April to mid-Sept; ☎01624/861241), signposted off Minorca Hill which branches right off the Ramsey Road after half a mile. The *Mines Tavern,* by the station, serves lunches, and in the evening you can try the *Riverside Studio* close to the waterwheel (☎01624/862 121), which also has live jazz and blues at weekends, or the slightly less expensive *Mona Lisa*, an Italian bistro on Glen Road.

RAMSEY marks the northern terminus of the Electric Railway, 45 minutes beyond Laxey. The Victorian tourist boom left behind the island's only iron pier and a series of grand terraces along the front, which raise the tone of an otherwise uncomfortable composite of new and old buildings. Ramsey makes a good base for a day's **cycling**; bikes can be rented from *Ramsay Cycles* on Bowring Road ☎01624/814 076).

Accommodation is fairly limited but a couple of good bets are *Eskdale*, Queen's Drive West (☎01624/813 283; ③) just back from the pier, and *Whitestones*, The Vollan, Mooragh Promenade (☎01624/813 824; ③) at the north end of the prom, past the grassy field which passes for the town's sole **campsite**.

St Johns and Peel

The only main road across the island follows a deep twelve-mile-long furrow between the northern and southern ranges from Douglas to Peel. A hill at **ST JOHNS**, nine miles along it, is the original site of **Tynwald**, the ancient Manx government, which derives its name from the Norse *Thing Völlr*, meaning "Assembly Field". Nowadays the word refers to the Douglas-based House of Keys and Legislative Council, but acts passed in the capital only become law once they have been proclaimed here on July 5 (ancient Midsummer's Day) in an annual open-air parliament that also hears the grievances of the islanders. Tynwald's four-tiered grass mound stands at the other end of a processional path from the village church.

PEEL, its harbour naturally protected by St Patrick's Isle, boasted a monastery as far back as the seventh or eighth century, parts of which remain inside the ramparts of the red sandstone **Peel Castle** (Easter–Sept daily 10am–5pm; £2). The Vikings built the first fortifications and the site became the residence of the Kings of Mann until 1220, when they moved to Castle Rushen in Castletown. The English continued strengthening the fortress, eventually completing a fifteen-foot curtain wall around the islet. Only this is in good repair, leaving the huge ward dotted with miscellaneous remains, including the Gothic vaults of St Germain's Cathedral.

A couple of **places to stay** huddle together at the end of Marine Parade: *Fernleigh* (☎01624/842 435; ③) and *Waldick Hotel* (☎01624/842 410; ④); or there's the *Peel Camping Park*, Derby Road (☎01624/842 341), signposted about half a mile out on the Douglas road. If you are looking for something more than the waterfront cafés, head for *Kingallons Bistro* (☎01624/844 366; moderate) on the east quay near the harbour; for something a bit less expensive, try the **pub** next door, *Creek Inn*, which serves a delicious array of fish pâtés.

Castletown and Port Erin

The sleepy harbour and low-roofed cottages of **CASTLETOWN**, the island's capital from the twelfth century until 1869, are all dominated by **Castle Rushen** (Easter–Sept daily 10am–5pm; £3), one of the most complete and compact medieval castles in Britain. Formerly home to the island's legislature and still the site of the investiture of new lieutenant-governors, the present structure was started around the thirteenth century, its limestone walls well under way by the time the last Viking monarch, Magnus, died here in 1256. The heavy defences, comprising three concentric rings of stone-clad ramparts, fosses and a complex series of doors and portcullises, must have made entry a forbidding objective. Once inside, it's worth pressing on through the five floors of rooms, furnished in medieval and seventeenth-century styles, if only for the rooftop viewpoint.

Castletown's **tourist office** (Easter–Sept daily 10am–5pm) is in the Old Grammar School, built around 1200, and located towards the beach, across the central car park. The **Steam Railway** station is five minutes' walk from the centre of Castletown, which is also on the #8 **bus** route between Peel and Port Erin, and the #1 route between Douglas and Port Erin. There's only one **B&B**, *Rowans* on Douglas Street (☎01624/823 210; ③), close to the beach across the footbridge from Castle Rushen. Castletown has a good range of **restaurants**: the *Chablis Cellar*, 21 Bank St, does inexpensive lunches and evening meals at the weekend, while *The Viking Inn* by the harbour serves good food at reasonable prices.

Plans for the southern branch of the steam railway beyond Castletown included the speculative construction of a new resort, **PORT ERIN**, six miles to the west. The elegant station is still here, 75 minutes' ride south of Douglas, with one of its engine sheds converted into a small **railway museum** (daily 10am–noon & 1–4pm; free). A century on, an arm of guest houses stretches out towards the slate headland to the north of the deeply indented Port Erin Bay, while the other side of the town is taken up by the breakwater and small harbour. Behind the harbour, the **Marine Interpretation Centre** (April–Oct Mon–Fri 9am–5pm; free) explains the complexities of the shoreline ecology – best experienced on the **Calf Island Cruises** (April–Oct 4–6 daily; £6) to the Calf of Man bird sanctuary, half a mile off the southwest coast. Keen birdwatchers can stay in the **hostel** on the island, which must be booked in advance with *Manx National Heritage* at the Manx Museum, Douglas (☎01624/67522; ①).

Epworth on Church Road (☎01624/832 431; ②) is one of the best simple **B&Bs**, or for a sea view, try the rooms at the *Balmoral Hotel* on the Promenade (☎01624/833 126; ③). The beachfront cafés do inexpensive meals, but there is no middle ground before you get up to the expensive *Falcon's Nest* on Station Road (☎01624/834 077), which is also the most lively place for an evening drink, and often has live music on Saturdays.

travel details

Trains

Appleby-in-Westmorland to: Carlisle (6 daily; 40min).

Blackpool to: Manchester (hourly; 1hr 10min); Preston (hourly; 30min).

Buxton to: Manchester (hourly; 50min).

Carlisle to: Appleby (6 daily; 40min); Barrow-in-Furness (5 daily; 2hr 20min); Lancaster (hourly; 1hr); London (8 daily; 4hr 20min); Manchester (2 daily; 2hr 30min); Preston (21 daily; 1hr 20min–1hr 40min).

Chester to: Knutsford (hourly; 50min); Liverpool (every 30min; 45min); London (3 daily; 3hr 30min); Manchester (every 30min; 1hr–1hr 20min); Northwich (hourly; 30min).

Crewe to: Chester (hourly; 20min); Carlisle (11 daily; 2hr 10min); Liverpool (18 daily; 45min); London (every 30min; 2hr); Manchester (every 30min; 50min); Nantwich (8 daily; 10min); Oxenholme (11 daily; 2hr 10min).

Lancaster to: Barrow-in-Furness (17 daily; 1hr); Carlisle (hourly; 1hr); Heysham (1 daily; 30min); Morecambe (every 40min; 10min).

Liverpool to: Chester (every 30min; 45min); London (hourly; 2hr 35min); Manchester (hourly; 50min); Preston (14 daily; 1hr 5min).

Manchester to: Barrow-in-Furness (3–7 daily; 2hr 10min–2hr 30min); Blackpool (hourly; 1hr 10min); Buxton (hourly; 50min); Cardiff (10 daily; 3hr 10min); Carlisle (2 daily; 2hr 30min); Chester

(every 30min; 1hr–1hr 20min); Liverpool (every 30min; 50min); London (hourly; 2hr 35min); Northwich (hourly; 30min); Oxenholme (4–6 daily 40min–1hr 10min); Penrith (2–4 daily; 2hr) Preston (15 daily; 55min).

Oxenholme (Kendal) to: Birmingham (6–8 daily 2hr 30min–3hr); Carlisle (14–18 daily; 40–50min) Edinburgh (5–9 daily; 2hr 20min–3hr 30min) Glasgow (7–10 daily; 2hr 30min–3hr); London Euston (5–7 daily; 3hr 30min–5hr); Manchester (3–9 daily; 1hr 40min); Penrith (14–18 daily 30min); Preston (1–2 hourly; 30–40 min).

Preston to: Barrow-in-Furness (4–8 daily; 1hr 15min); Blackpool (hourly; 30min); Carlisle (15–21 daily; 1hr 20min–1hr 40min); Liverpool (14 daily 1hr 5min); London (17 daily; 3hr); Manchester (15 daily; 55min); Oxenholme (15–23 daily; 35min); Penrith (12–15 daily; 1hr–1hr 10min).

Buses

Blackpool to: London (4 daily; 6hr); Manchester (every 2hr; 1hr 50min); Preston (every 2hr; 35min); Windermere (2 daily; 1hr 40min).

Carlisle to: Appleby (1 daily; 1hr 15min); Keswick (1–4 daily; 1hr 30min–2hr); Lancaster (4–5 daily; 1hr 10min–4hr 30min); London (3–4 daily; 5hr 30min); Manchester (2–3 daily; 2hr 30min); Windermere (3 daily; 2hr 20min).

Chester to: Liverpool (Fri–Mon 1 daily; 1hr); London (5 daily; 4hr 45min); Manchester (4 daily 1hr 15min).

Kendal to: Ambleside (hourly; 40min); Cartmel (7 daily; 1hr); Grasmere (every 1–2hr; 1hr); Keswick (every 1–2hr; 1hr 25min); Lancaster (hourly; 1hr); Manchester (1–3 daily; 2hr 45min); Windermere/Bowness (hourly; 30min).

Keswick to: Ambleside (every 1–2hr; 55min); Buttermere (2–3 daily; 30min); Carlisle (1–4 daily; 1hr 30min–2hr); Cockermouth (7 daily; 35min); Grasmere (every 1–2hr; 40min); Kendal (every 1–2hr; 1hr 25min); Lancaster (5–10 daily; 2hr 50min); Manchester (1–3 daily; 3hr 50min); Windermere (every 1–2hr; 1hr).

Lancaster to: Barrow-in-Furness (1 daily; 2hr); Carlisle (4–5 daily; 1hr 10min–4hr 30min); Kendal (hourly; 1hr); Keswick (5–10 daily; 2hr 50min); Kirkby Lonsdale (6 daily; 1hr); London (2–3 daily; 5hr 40min); Manchester (2 daily; 2hr); Windermere (hourly; 1hr 45min).

Liverpool to: Blackpool (Fri–Mon 1 daily; 2hr); Bristol (1 daily; 4hr); Chester (Fri–Mon 1 daily; 1hr); London (5 daily; 4hr 15min); Manchester (hourly; 1hr); Preston (2 daily; 1hr).

Manchester to: Blackpool (every 2hr; 1hr 50min); Carlisle (2–3 daily; 2hr 30min); Chester (4 daily; 1hr 15min); Kendal (1–3 daily; 2hr 45min); Keswick (1–3 daily; 3hr 50min); Lancaster (2 daily; 2hr); Leeds (hourly; 1hr 35min); Liverpool (hourly; 1hr); London (6 daily; 4hr); Preston (9 daily; 1hr 10min); Windermere (1–3 daily; 3hr).

Windermere to: Ambleside (every 20min–1hr; 15min); Barrow-in-Furness (1–3 daily; 1hr 35min); Carlisle (3 daily; 2hr 20min); Grasmere (every 1–2hr; 30min); Kendal (hourly; 30min); Keswick (every 1–2hr; 1hr); Lancaster (hourly; 1hr 45min); Manchester (1–3 daily; 3hr).

Ferries

Douglas to: Belfast (2 weekly in summer; 5hr); Dublin (2 weekly in summer; 4hr 45min); Fleetwood (1 weekly in summer; 3hr 20min); Heysham (6–8 weekly; 3hr 45min); Liverpool (1–4 weekly; 4hr 30min).

Fleetwood to: Douglas (1 weekly in summer; 3hr 20min).

Heysham to: Douglas (6–9 weekly; 3hr 45min).

Liverpool to: Douglas (1–4 weekly; 4hr 30min).

CHAPTER NINE

YORKSHIRE

ew visitors pass through **YORKSHIRE**, England's largest county, without spending time in history-soaked **York**, for centuries England's second city. Famed primarily for its Minster, the city is an ensemble of tiny medieval alleys, castle ruins, tucked-away churches, riverside gardens and top-notch museums. In the prosperous north and east of the county York's mixture of medieval, Georgian and Victorian architecture is mirrored in miniature by towns such as **Beverley**, centred on another soaring minster, **Richmond**, banked under a crag-bound castle, and **Ripon**, gathered around its honey-stoned cathedral. **Knaresborough** shares similar attributes, but is overshadowed by the faded gentility of neighbouring **Harrogate**, a spa town of little general interest, geared these days towards the conference trade rather than health-seeking hopefuls. Yorkshire's other spa, **Scarborough**, is now a port and seaside town that is unlikely to make a big impression, and much the same goes for **Hull**, chief port of the southern Yorkshire region now designated as Humberside. If you're in a hurry to see the best of the coast, pass them by in favour of briny towns such as **Whitby** or the plentiful undeveloped stretches of shore.

Few places could be in such marked contrast to York as the cities of the other Yorkshire, the former capitals of England's textile and heavy-engineering industries. In the south, **Sheffield** and its blighted surroundings are the twice-struck victims of industrial collapse, hit first by a contraction in the steel industry, and more recently by the forced closure of mines that once tapped the most productive coalfields in Britain. Further north in the conurbation around **Leeds** and **Bradford**, nineteenth-century world leaders in textiles, manufacturing went into a fatal tailspin a decade or more earlier. Having hit rock bottom first, they have had more time for fresh initiatives, so that whereas Sheffield is still on its uppers, Leeds, and to a lesser extent Bradford, present less downbeat visions of urban decline. Leeds makes little play for tourists but boasts a couple of fine galleries, whilst Bradford chases visitors with grim determination, waylaying people on their way to **Haworth** – birthplace of the Brontë sisters – with its **Hockney gallery** and **National Museum of Photography, Film and Television**.

If you see anything of Yorkshire's dour heartland it may well be no more than a glimpse as you make for the **Dales**, a lovely patchwork of limestone hills and serene valleys northwest of Leeds, ranging from the gentle, grassy spans of **Wharfedale** and **Wensleydale** to the majestic heights of Ingleborough, Whernside and Pen-y-ghent, and the wilder valleys of **Swaledale**, **Dentdale**, **Ribblesdale** and **Malhamdale**. Numerous stone-built villages provide often idyllic centres from which to walk, the whole area being covered by tracks, long-distance paths and old drove roads, most waymarked by the **Yorkshire Dales National Park**, which has information centres and smaller information points in many centres. Less visited and less obviously pretty, but still well worth several days, is the country's other national park, the **North York Moors**, divided into bleak upland moors and a tremendous rugged coastline.

The county is also scattered with a host of **historic sites and buildings**. These include not only the more predictable roster of stately homes, among which **Castle Howard** stands out, but also imperious relics of the Industrial Revolution, from the civic splendour of Leeds Town Hall to the Italianate pastiche of **Saltaire**, a millworkers' village on the outskirts of Bradford. In an earlier age, before the Reformation, Yorkshire had more monastic houses than any other English county, centres not only of religious retreat but also of a commercial acumen that was to lay the foundations of the region's great woollen industry. Many beautifully situated ruins survive today at **Fountains**, **Rievaulx**, **Bolton Abbey**, **Whitby** and elsewhere, graceful counterpoints to the more stolid remains of the **castles** at York, Richmond, Scarborough and Pickering – the foremost of more than twenty castles raised in Yorkshire by the Normans. York boasts some **Roman** remains, while near Pickering you'll find Wade's Causeway, Britain's finest surviving stretch of Roman road; still more ancient are the prehistoric barrows and dykes that ripple over the Dales and North York Moors.

Sheffield

Like many of its neighbours, **SHEFFIELD**, Yorkshire's second city, has had its days of glory, but unlike Leeds it has yet to provide the sort of urban renewal that's going to tempt any but the most die-hard of tourists. Its former prosperity was based on steel, in particular on cutlery, having been almost synonymous with the latter from as early as the fourteenth century. Technological advances in steel production turned it into one of the country's foremost centres of heavy and specialist engineering, soon creating a city of Victorian elegance and racking poverty, a mixture that characterized most northern industrial towns. Luftwaffe bombing in World War II destroyed many of the city's civic buildings, most of which were replaced with the worst sort of postwar brutalism, and a downturn in the steel industry has all but put paid to the city's pre-eminence.

For most casual visitors, central Sheffield's main draw is likely to be the award-winning **Ruskin Gallery** (Mon–Sat 10am–5pm; free) in Norfolk Street, midway between the Crucible Theatre and the Town Hall; the latter, one of the few Victorian edifices to escape bombing, is topped by the figure of Vulcan, the Roman god of fire and metalworking. The gallery houses the collection of the Guild of St George, founded by John Ruskin in 1875 to "improve" the working people of Sheffield, and their education must have been wonderfully eclectic if the collection is anything to go by – a bulging library is complemented by an intriguing pot-pourri of watercolours, minerals, paintings and medieval illuminated manuscripts. A new Ruskin Craft Gallery (same hours) organizes special exhibitions and workshops of contemporary crafts.

One block east of the Ruskin Gallery is the **Graves Art Gallery** (Mon–Sat 10am–5pm; free), located on the top floor of the City Library on Surrey Street. Despite a few European paintings it leans most heavily towards nineteenth- and twentieth-century British artists like Turner, Nash, Gwen John and the Pre-Raphaelites. Parts of the city's nineteenth-century collection are also held at the **Mappin Art Gallery** (Tues–Sat 10am–5pm, Sun 11am–5pm; free) in Weston Park near the university, a mile west of the city centre (bus #52 from the High Street).

Sheffield's best museums are those devoted to its industrial past, though none are in the city centre. The **City Museum** (Tues–Sat 10am–5pm, Sun 11am–5pm; free), adjacent to the Mappin, contains the definitive collection of cutlery and Sheffield ware, but

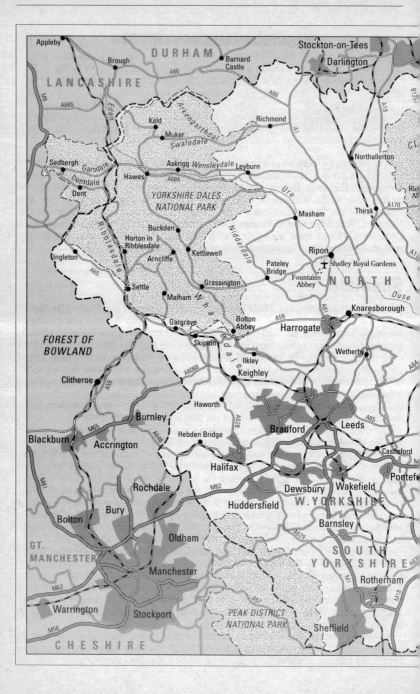

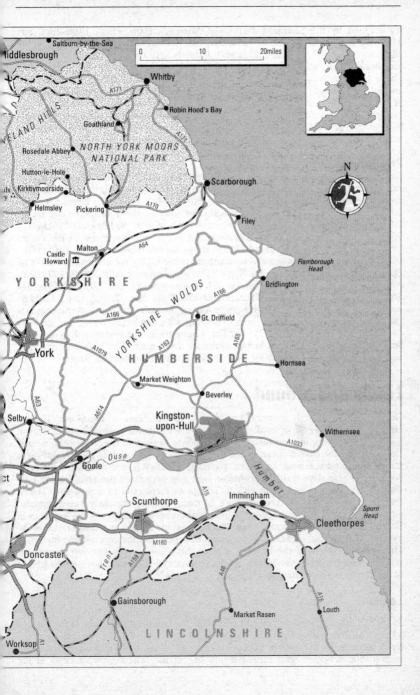

it's eclipsed by the **Sheffield Industrial Museum** (Mon–Thurs 10am–4pm, Sun 11am–4.45pm; £2.50), located off Alma Street on Kelham Island, one mile north of the city centre (bus #47/48 from Flat Street). Exhibits here reveal the depth of the city's industrial output, ranging from a colossal 12,000-horsepower steam engine to a silver-plated penny-farthing made for the Tsar of Russia. Further afield, the **Abbeydale Industrial Hamlet** (Tues–Sat 10am–5pm, Sun 11am–5pm; £2.50), five miles southwest of central Sheffield on Abbeydale Road South (bus #97 from High Street) contains an eighteenth-century scythe works that's powered by four water wheels, together with a two-hundred-year-old steel furnace, two furnished houses from the same era, and a water-driven forge and grinding wheel for sharpening cutlery.

Practicalities

Sheffield's **train station** is east of the city centre off Sheaf Square; the bus station is two hundred yards further north on Pond Street. Walk west along Howard Street to reach the main **tourist office**, on Union Street (Mon–Fri 9.30–5.15pm, Sat 9.30–4.15pm; ☎0114/273 4671); there's also a smaller office on the train station concourse. For **accommodation** try the small but central *Rutland Arms*, 86 Brown St (☎0114/272 9003; ③); the *Priory Lodge*, 40 Worstenholme Rd, a mile southwest of the centre (☎0114/258 4670; ③); or *Parklands*, 113 Rustings Rd, two miles southwest (☎0114/267 0692; ③). First choice among the **restaurants** is the highly recommended *Parkes La Bonne Bouche*, 130 Penistone Rd North (Thurs–Sat evening only; ☎0114/233 8388). Also excellent are the *Mediterranean*, 271 Sharrowvale Rd; *Mr BB's Brasserie*, 344 Sharrowvale Rd, for vegetarian food; and *Antonio's Flying Pizza*, 255 Glossop Rd, a long-established and rumbustious Italian place. Among the **pubs** the top weekend choice is the *Washington* on Fitzwilliam Street, heaving with black-clad types; the studenty *Broomhill*, 484 Glossop Rd; or *The Fat Cat*, a more traditional real-ale pub in old steel-land on Alma Street. The best-known **clubs** are *The Drop* at City Hall, Barker's Pool, and the *Leadmill*, 6/7 Leadmill Rd, now rivalled by *Capital* on Matilda Street.

Leeds and around

During the nineteenth century **Leeds** and its satellites – **Bradford**, Halifax, Huddersfield and a host of smaller centres – were the world's mightiest producers of textiles, an industry first nurtured by the monastic houses of the Moors and nearby Dales. In time the advent of canals and technical innovations such as the harnessing of steam power turned what had been a cottage industry into a dynamic large-scale economy. These days ruthless economic logic has devastated the area, leaving only disused textile mills and great civic buildings as memorials to a past age. Today, though, a new vigour is creeping back to many areas, particularly Leeds, and for anyone interested in social history or industrial archeology there can be few areas in Britain with so many dedicated museums and historic sites. For a taste of the broad swathes of moorland on Leeds' doorstep, most people join the coach-borne hordes to **Haworth**, birthplace of the Brontës, a place that's now wretchedly over-visited, but remains surrounded by the bleakly attractive countryside that infuses the best known of the Brontë books, *Wuthering Heights*.

Leeds

In 1847 Charles Dickens described **LEEDS** as "the beastliest place, one of the nastiest I know," an observation that many visitors might have applied to the city until compara-tively recently. Now, however, improved communications, a major clean-up and urban rejuvenation schemes have turned it into one of the fastest growing cities in the country, a financial and administrative centre that's also home to Opera North, the noted West Yorkshire Playhouse and a triennial international piano competition that ranks among the world's top musical events. Furthermore, the city art gallery has the best collection of British twentieth-century art outside London, together with a neighbouring gallery devoted to locally born sculptor Henry Moore.

There's much to be said for wandering around Leeds city centre for an hour or so, first to explore the brimming, shop-filled **Arcades** – Thornton, Queens, Burton, Grand and Market Street – and then to take in some of its proud Victorian architecture, notably the **Corn Exchange**, on Call and Vicar lanes, and **Leeds Town Hall**, north of the train station on Victoria Square, the finest such building in the country. Equally impressive is the Leeds Markets area, on the east side of the city centre, particularly the newly restored **Kirkgate Market**, the largest market in the north of England. Housed in a superb Edwardian building, it's a descendant of the medieval woollen markets that were instrumental in making Leeds the early focus of the region's textile industry.

After that, your first port of call should be the **Leeds City Art Gallery** on The Headrow (Mon, Tues, Thurs & Fri 10am–5.30pm, Wed 10am–9pm, Sat 10am–4pm; free). The gallery is noted for its Henry Moore Collection – with pieces by Jacob Epstein, Barbara Hepworth and others, as well as Moore – and for its outstanding twentieth-century art, amongst which local painters figure large, notably L.S. Lowry and landscapist Atkinson Grimshaw, together with the founder of the Camden Town Group, Walter Sickert. A major new gallery, **The Henry Moore Sculpture Centre** (same hours), complementing the museum's collection, is housed in an adjacent Victorian merchant's warehouse, with its own entrance at 11–15 Cookridge St.

Leeds City Museum (Tues–Fri 10am–5.30pm, Sat 10am–4pm; free) on the first floor of the Central Library on The Headrow is a compact but rather pedestrian run-through of local history. Far more interesting is the vast **Armley Mills Museum** (Tues–Sat 10am–5.30pm, Sun 2–5pm; £1.20) off Canal Road, which runs between Armley and Kirkstall Road about a mile from the city centre (*Yorkshire Rider* bus from the Corn Exchange). There's been a mill on the site since at least the seventeenth century, and the present building was one of the world's largest woollen mills until its closure in 1969. Displays recount the whole story of Leeds' industrial history, with plenty of working machinery, together with a definitive account of how cloth was made, from the fleece off the sheep's back to great rolls of finished cloth.

Practicalities

Leeds City **train station** is off City Square on the southern flank of the city centre, which also houses the **tourist office** in The Arcade (Mon–Fri 9.30am–5pm, Sat 9.30am–12.30pm & 1.30–4pm; ☎0113/242 5242). The **coach station** is on Wellington Street, which leads west off City Square, while the local **bus station** is a sprawling terminal on St Peter's Street, close to the Leeds market area. Good-value **hotels** in the centre include the *Griffin*, 31 Boar Lane (☎0113/242 2555; ⑤) and the *Wellesley*, Wellington Street (☎0113/243 0431; ⑤). You'll find less expensive accommodation near the university campus, a mile northwest of the centre, with three good places on Woodsley Road: *Manxdene Hotel* at no. 154 (☎0113/243 2586; ③), *Avalon Guest House* at no. 132 (☎0113/243 2545; ③) and *Moorlea Hotel* at no. 146 (☎0113/243 2653; ③).

The Cornucopia in the Corn Exchange, Call Lane, is the city's most atmospheric **café**; *Brasserie Forty Four*, 44 The Calls, is the best of Leeds' brasserie-**restaurants**; the best Italian is *Bibi's*, Minerva House, 16 Greek St (☎0113/242 0905). Three quality Asian and Indian restaurants to try are *Nafees*, 69a Raglan Rd, the *Darbar*, 16–17 Kirkgate and *Ayesha*, Victoria Road, all inexpensive and very popular. **Pubs** to head for include the traditional *Victoria*, Great George Street, and the long-famous *Whitelocks*, Turk's Head Yard, off Briggate. *The Pack Horse*, on Woodhouse Lane, is *the* student pub. The best **clubs** are *The Warehouse*, 19 Somers St, *The Phoenix*, 58 Francis St and

The Music Factory, 174 Briggate. Leeds also has a big reputation for **high culture**: *Opera North* is based at *The Grand Theatre*, 46 New Briggate and there's top-class theatre at the *West Yorkshire Playhouse*, Quarry Hill Mount.

Harewood

Harewood House (April–Oct daily 11am–5.15pm; Feb, March & Nov Sun only; garden opens 1hr earlier; £5.95 for bird gardens, house and grounds), eight miles north of Leeds, was designed and decorated by one the greatest architectural teams ever assembled under one roof. Conceived in 1759 by York architect John Carr, the building was finished by Robert Adam, the furniture was made by Thomas Chippendale and the landscaped gardens were laid out by Capability Brown. Georgian purists might lament some of the Victorian additions, but the ensemble is still outstanding, and is further enhanced by paintings by artists of such mettle as Turner, El Greco and Giovanni Bellini. One of the more unusual features outside is the **Bird Garden**, four acres of aviaries caging over 150 species. There are frequent buses to Harewood from Leeds.

Bradford

In its Victorian heyday **BRADFORD** – England's fourth largest metropolitan area – was the world's biggest producer of worsted cloth, its skyline etched black with mill chimneys, and its hills clogged with some of the foulest back-to-back houses of any northern city. The town has left this nether world behind and is valiantly laying on tourist attractions to rinse away its associations with urban decrepitude – but although there are the unexpected pleasures of the National Museum of Photography, Film and Television and the village of Saltaire, with its David Hockney gallery, you couldn't make out a case for seeing much else in the city.

The only thing of general interest in the city centre is the **National Museum of Photography, Film and Television** (Tues–Sun 10.30am–6pm; free), five minutes' walk north of the bus and train stations, and opposite the beautifully eye-catching Alhambra Theatre. Founded in 1983, it has become the most visited national museum outside London, attracting 750,000 visitors a year. The ground floor kicks off with the **Kodak Museum**, a museum-within-a-museum which houses the contents of Kodak's private collection. Like the floors which follow, it's crammed with memorabilia and hundreds of cameras, all haphazardly displayed. Sadly, there's little continuity, but for anyone with any technical or professional interest, the place will be a revelation, and if the hands-on gizmos don't appeal there are all sorts of nostalgic nuggets to grab the attention. The museum also contains Europe's largest cinema screen (52ft by 64ft), which puts on four daily screenings (£3.90), drawn from the handful of IMAX films available – a Rolling Stones concert, the Grand Canyon, shark-infested waters and a few other pulse-quickening scenarios.

Any approach to Bradford is dominated by the staggering profile of Manningham Mill and its Italianate chimney, just one of several sites and small museums which recall the city's industrial past. All of these, however, pale in comparison to **Saltaire**, a model industrial village and textile mill north of Bradford city centre, built in the style of the Italian Renaissance between 1852 and 1872, and modelled on buildings of the Italian Renaissance, by the industrialist **Sir Titus Salt**, who built his fortune on the innovative use of alpaca and mohair. Salt's Mill was the biggest factory in the world when it opened, and was surrounded by schools, hospitals, a train station, parks, baths, wash-houses, 45 almshouses and around 850 houses. The style and size of each dwelling was designed to reflect the place of the head of the family in the factory hierarchy, one example – for all Salt's philanthropic vigour – of his rigid adherence to the prevailing class orthodoxy. Similarly, of the village's 22 streets, all – bar Victoria and Albert streets – were named after members of his family. Even more tellingly, the church, strategically placed directly outside the factory gates, was the first public building finished, and, of course, the village contained not a single pub.

The mill is planned to become a glitzy shopping centre but at present its centrepiece is the **1853 Gallery** (daily 10am–6pm; free), an entire floor of the old spinning shed given over to the world's largest collection of the works of Bradford-born **David Hockney**. All phases of the artist's career are covered, from his student days through the Californian swimming pool period up to his present experiments with fax, Xerox machines and Polaroids. Many works are for sale, hinting at the hard-nosed business ethic behind the mill's present set-up. You can catch trains to Saltaire station from Bradford, or take buses #663–669 – ask to be dropped at Victoria Street.

Practicalities

Trains and **buses** both arrive at **Bradford Interchange** on Croft Street, a little to the south of the city-centre grid. There's also a much smaller station at Forster Square, across the city, for trains to Keighley. The **tourist office** (Mon–Sat 9.30am–5.30pm, Sun 1–5.30pm; ☎01274/753 678) shares the lobby of the National Museum. In the unlikely event you'll want to **stay** overnight, the best-value guest houses within half a mile of the centre are the *Ivy*, 3 Melbourne Place (☎01274/727 060; ②) and the *New Beehive Inn*, Westgate (☎01274/721 784; ③). More central and luxurious is the *Pennington Midland Hotel*, by the station on Foster Square ☎01274/735 735; ⑤).

Bradford's large Asian and Indian population have made the city famous for its **curry houses**. The *Kashmir*, 27 Morley St, Bradford's first ever curry house and still one of the best, is a simple café-style place two minutes west of the Alhambra and the National Museum. Also close are the *Taj Mahal* almost next door at 25 Morley St, the *International*, 40–42 Mannville Terrace, and the *Bombay Tandoori*, 3b Wilton St. All of these are open until 2am, every day. Slightly further afield, Bradford's – and therefore Britain's – finest curries are to be found at *Mumtaz Paan House*, 386–92 Great Horton Rd (daily 11.30am–midnight), parallel to Morley Street.

Haworth

Of English literary shrines probably only Stratford sees more visitors than the quarter of a million who swarm annually into **HAWORTH** to tramp the cobbles once trodden by the **Brontë** sisters. Quite why the sheltered life of the Brontës should exert such a powerful fascination is a puzzle, though the contrast of their pinched provincial existences with the brooding moors and the tumultous passions of *Wuthering Heights* probably forms part of the answer. Whatever the reasons, the village's steep, cobbled main street is lost during the summer under huge crowds, herded by multilingual signs around the various stations on the Brontë trail.

Of these the **Parsonage** (daily April–Sept 10am–5pm; Oct–March 11am–4.30pm; closed Jan 15–Feb 9; £3.60), at the top of the main street, is the obvious focus, a modest Georgian house bought by Patrick Brontë in 1820 to bring up his family, five years prior to the death of his wife and two eldest offspring. The surviving four children – Anne, Emily, Charlotte and their dissipated brother, Branwell – spent most of their lives in the place, which is now furnished as it was in their day, and filled with the sisters' pictures, books, manuscripts and personal treasures. You can see the sofa on which Emily died in 1848, aged just 28, for example, and the footstool on which she sat outside on fine days writing *Wuthering Heights*. Charlotte's tiny shoes and wedding clothes are also here: her marriage took place in the nearby **church**, which also holds the Brontë graves (except for Anne's, which is in Scarborough). Branwell, however, by all accounts, spent less time in the Parsonage than his sisters, preferring hours of alcoholic excess in the *Black Bull*, a pub within staggering distance of the Parsonage near the top of Main Street.

If you've come this far you should try some of the well-signed **walks** onto the surrounding moors, many described by the sisters themselves, particularly those to the spots which are popularly – but in most cases wrongly – said to have been the inspiration for locations in the novels. The most popular run to **Brontë Falls**, **Bridge and Chair**, reached via West Lane and a track from the village, and to **Top Withens**, a mile beyond, a ruin fancifully thought to be the model for Wuthering Heights (2hr round trip). A plaque here bluntly points out that "the buildings, even when complete, bore no resemblance to the house she [Emily] described." The moorland setting, however, beautifully evokes the flavour of the book, and to enjoy it further you could walk on another two and a half miles to **Ponden Hall**, perhaps the Thrushcross Grange of *Wuthering Heights* (this section of path, incidentally, forms part of the Pennine Way).

Practicalities

There are frequent buses to Haworth from Bradford, just eight miles away, though the nicest way of getting here is to take a train from Leeds (or Bradford's Forster Square station) to **Keighley**, then change to the private steam trains of the *Keighley and Worth Valley Railway* (mid-June to Aug Mon–Fri 4 daily, Sat & Sun 8 daily; Sept to mid-June Sat & Sun and school hols 1 daily; £4.80 return) for the five-mile run to Haworth, whose station is half a mile from the village centre. Haworth **tourist office** is at the top of the hill at 2–4 West Lane (daily 9.30am–5.30pm; ☎01535/642 329).

The **youth hostel**, *Longlands Hall* (☎01535/642 234), a former mill owner's mansion, overlooks the village a mile from the centre at Longlands Drive, Lees Lane, off the Keighley Road. If you want luxury **accommodation**, head for *The Old White Lion Hotel*, 6 West Lane (☎01535/642 313; ⑤); *Weaver's*, at no. 15 (☎01535/643 822; ⑥), which also has one of the best **restaurants** in the county; or join Bramwell's ghost in the *Black Bull Hotel*, Main Street (☎01535/642 249; ④). Less expensive places on the same street include *The Apothecary* at no. 86 (☎01535/643 642; ③), *Brow View* at no. 6 (☎01535/644 270; ③) and *Heather Cottage Tea Room* at nos. 25–27 (☎01535/644 511; ③).

The Yorkshire Dales

Yorkshire's **DALES** – from the Viking word *dalr* (valley) – form a lovely and varied upland area of limestone hills and pastoral valleys at the heart of the Pennines, wedged between the Lake District to the west and the North York Moors to the east. One of the country's ten national parks, the region is crammed with opportunities for outdoor activities: the whole park is criss-crossed by several long-distance footpaths; there's a specially designated circular cycle way; and a host of centres geared up for caving and other more specialist pursuits.

Most approaches are from the industrial towns to the south, via the **Settle and Carlisle Railway** or from towns such as **Skipton**, **Settle** and **Ingleton**, which lie dotted along the main A65 road. This makes southern dales like **Wharfedale** the most visited, and neighbouring **Airedale** is also immensely popular, thanks to the fascinating and accessible scenery squeezed into its narrow confines around **Malham**. **Ribblesdale**, approached from Settle, is more sombre and less visited, as is **Kingsdale**, crowned by Whernside, one of the Dales' famous **Three Peaks** – a summit which also overlooks **Dentdale** to the north, which with **Garsdale** is one of the least known but most beautiful of the valleys. Moving north, there are two parallel dales, **Wensleydale** and **Swaledale**, the latter pushing Dentdale as the most rewarding overall target, and flowing east via **Richmond**, an appealing historic town.

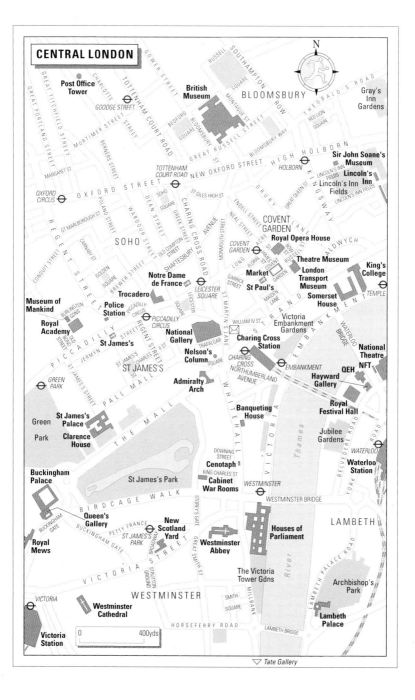

CENTRAL LONDON

N

GREAT TITCHFIELD STREET
GREAT PORTLAND STREET
GOWER STREET

Post Office Tower

CHARLOTTE STREET
TOTTENHAM COURT ROAD

GOODGE STREET

RUSSELL SQUARE
SOUTHAMPTON ROW

British Museum

MONTAGUE ST
BEDFORD SQUARE
BLOOMSBURY SQUARE

BLOOMSBURY

THEOBALD'S ROAD
RED LION SQUARE

Gray's Inn Gardens

MORTIMER STREET
BERNERS STREET

MARGARET ST

BEDFORD SQ
GREAT RUSSELL STREET
BLOOMSBURY WAY

TOTTENHAM COURT ROAD
NEW OXFORD STREET
ST GILES HIGH ST

HIGH HOLBORN
HOLBORN
KINGSWAY
LINCOLN'S INN FIELDS

Sir John Soane's Museum
Lincoln's Inn
Lincoln's Inn Fields

OXFORD CIRCUS
OXFORD STREET
POLAND STREET

REGENT STREET
GT. MARLBOROUGH ST
WARDOUR STREET
DEAN STREET
SOHO SQUARE
GREEK STREET
CHARING CROSS ROAD
ENDELL STREET
DRURY LANE
GREAT QUEEN ST

SOHO

CONDUIT STREET
CARNABY ST
GOLDEN SQUARE
BREWER STREET
OLD COMPTON STREET
SHAFTESBURY AVENUE
MONMOUTH STREET
NEAL STREET
LONG ACRE
FLORAL ST

COVENT GARDEN
Royal Opera House

COVENT GARDEN
Market
St Paul's

Theatre Museum
London Transport Museum

ALDWYCH

King's College

Somerset House

TEMPLE

Notre Dame de France

GARRICK STREET
MAIDEN LANE

LEICESTER SQUARE

BOND STREET
Museum of Mankind

BURLINGTON GDNS

Trocadero
Police Station

Royal Academy

PICCADILLY
REGENT STREET
PICCADILLY CIRCUS

St James's

JERMYN STREET

National Gallery

Nelson's Column

WILLIAM IV ST

Charing Cross Station

Victoria Embankment Gardens

EMBANKMENT

WATERLOO BRIDGE

National Theatre

QEH
NFT

ST JAMES'S ST
ST CHARLES ST
ST JAMES'S SQ

ST JAMES'S

TRAFALGAR SQUARE

CHARING CROSS
NORTHUMBERLAND AVENUE

EMBANKMENT

Hayward Gallery

GREEN PARK

PALL MALL

Admiralty Arch

ST JAMES'S STREET

Royal Festival Hall

Banqueting House

WHITEHALL

VICTORIA

Thames

Green Park

St James's Palace

Clarence House

THE MALL

DOWNING STREET

Cenotaph
KING CHARLES ST
Cabinet War Rooms

Jubilee Gardens

WATERLOO

Waterloo Station

BELVEDERE ROAD

Buckingham Palace

St James's Park

BIRDCAGE WALK

BUCKINGHAM GATE

Queen's Gallery

PETTY FRANCE

New Scotland Yard

ST JAMES'S PARK

BROADWAY

WESTMINSTER

WESTMINSTER BRIDGE

Houses of Parliament

LAMBETH

Royal Mews

VICTORIA

STRUTTON GROUND

Westminster Abbey

STOREY'S GATE
GREAT SMITH ST

River

LAMBETH PALACE ROAD

VICTORIA

Westminster Cathedral

WESTMINSTER

SMITH SQUARE
MILLBANK

The Victoria Tower Gdns

Archbishop's Park

Victoria Station

0   400yds

HORSEFERRY ROAD

LAMBETH BRIDGE

Lambeth Palace

▽ Tate Gallery

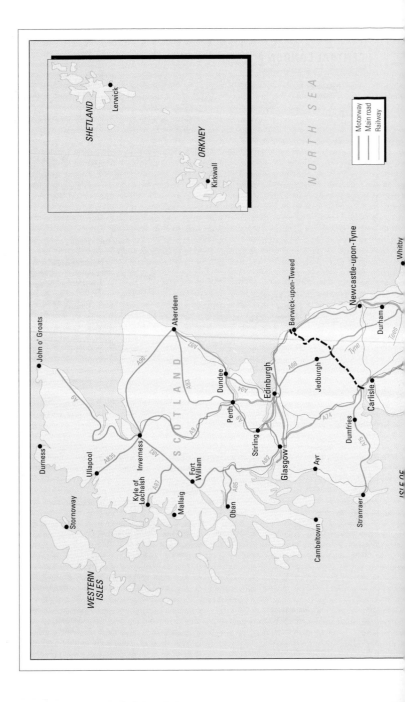

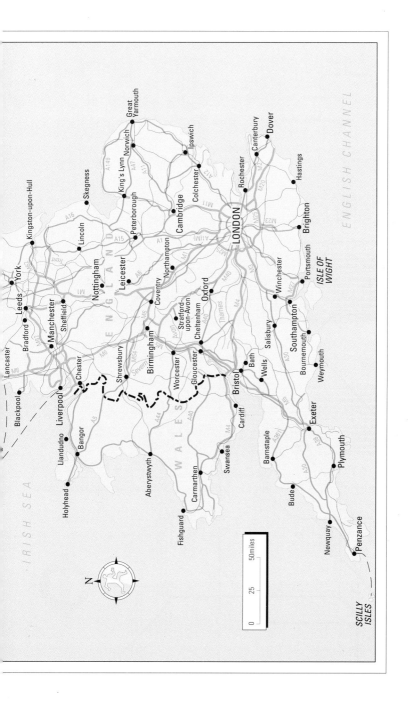

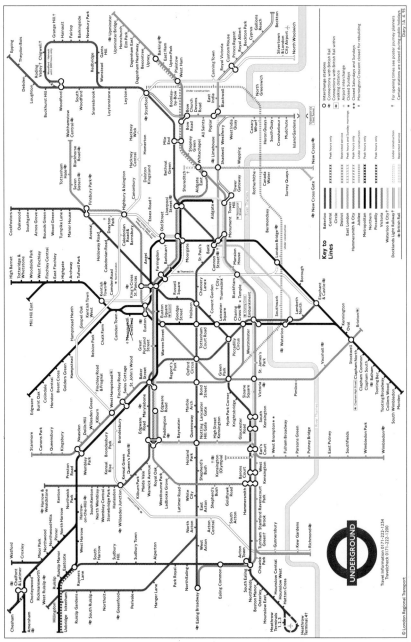

UNDERGROUND

Travel Information 0171-222-1234
Travelcheck 0171-222-1200

© London Regional Transport

Diary 1A 4. 95

Key to Lines

Bakerloo
Central
Circle
District
East London
Hammersmith & City
Jubilee
Metropolitan
Northern
Piccadilly
Victoria
Waterloo & City †
Docklands Light Railway†
British Rail

Peak hours only
Restricted service
Peak hours and Sunday mornings
Under construction
Peak hours only
Peak hours only

Under construction
Restricted service

Interchange stations
Connections with British Rail
Connections with British Rail within walking distance
Airport interchange
Airport interchange
Closed Saturdays and Sundays
Closed Sundays
Morningston Crescent closed during construction for rebuilding

† For opening times see poster journey planners
Certain stations are closed during public holidays

Skipton

SKIPTON rightly belongs to Airedale, but as a vital transportation hub, any trip to the southern dales is going to pass through here, particularly if you want to see Wharfedale, five miles to the east. Apart from practical advantages, however, the town's worth an hour or so in its own right, particularly on one of its four weekly **market** days (Mon, Wed, Fri & Sat), when the streets and pubs are filled with what seems like half the Dales' population.

Sceptone, or "Sheeptown" was a settlement long before the arrival of the Normans, whose **Castle** (Mon–Sat 10am–dusk, Sun 2pm–dusk; Oct–Feb closes at 4pm; £3.20) provided the basis for the present fortress, among England's best preserved, thanks mainly to the efforts of Anne Clifford, who rebuilt much of her family seat between 1650 and 1675 following the depredations of the Civil War. Little survives in the way of furniture or fittings, but the slit windows, six towers and beautiful **Conduit Court** all very much look the part.

Lady Anne also displayed her restorative skills on the **Church of the Holy Trinity** on Masket Street, which has a fine bossed fifteenth-century roof, beautiful chancel screen (1533) and a twelfth-century font crowned with an odd Jacobean cover. Also worth seeing elsewhere is the town hall's pithy **Craven Museum** (April–Sept Mon–Fri 11am–5pm, Sat 10am–noon & 1–5pm, Sun 2–5pm; Oct–March Mon–Fri 2–5pm, Sat 10am–noon & 1.30–4.30pm; free), a brief introduction to the geology, flora, fauna, folk history and archeology of Craven, the name of the region cradled between Wharfedale and the Lancashire border. After that, drop into the **High Corn Mill** on nearby Ellerbeck, a working watermill that's stood since the Domesday Book.

The **tourist office** is near the town hall, off the High Street (Mon–Sat 10am–5pm, Sun 2–5pm; ☎01756/792 809). There's plenty of **accommodation** – try *Bourne House Guest House*, 22 Upper Sackville St (☎01756/792 633; ②), *Peace Villas*, 69 Gargrave Rd (☎01756/790 672; ②) or the *Unicorn Hotel*, Devonshire Place, off Keighley Road (☎01756/794 146; ②). You can **rent bikes** from *Eric Burgess Cycles* on Water Street (☎01756/794 386). The best **pub** in town is the *Royal Shepherd* on Canal Street.

Wharfedale

The River Wharfe flows into the Ouse, south of York, but **WHARFEDALE** proper starts just east of Skipton with **Bolton Abbey** and then continues north in a broad, pastoral swathe scattered with villages as picture-perfect as any in northern England. **Grassington** is the main centre, with lesser hamlets – mainly in Upper Wharfedale – making less frenetic bases. Upland roads lead from the head of the valley up minor dales to cross the watershed into Wensleydale, though the most attractive itinerary would take you up lonely **Littondale** to Arncliffe, a village almost too good to be true, and then over the tops to either Malham or Ribblesdale.

Bolton Abbey and the Strid

BOLTON ABBEY, five miles east of Skipton, is the name of a whole village rather than an abbey, a confusion compounded by the fact that the place's main monastic ruin is known as **Bolton Priory**. This formed part of an Augustinian community founded by Cecily de Romille in 1120 at nearby Embsay, but moved here in the 1150s by her daughter, Alice, to commemorate the drowning of her son in the Strid (see below). Turner painted the site, and Ruskin described it as the most beautiful in England, though the priory is now mostly ruined, a consequence of the Dissolution – only the nave, incorporated into the village church in 1170, survived in almost its original state.

To get here from Skipton, take the irregular *Keighley & District* bus #76 (1 on Wed, Fri & Sat), and for **information** visit the village post office (☎01756/710 533).

The priory is also the starting point for several highly popular riverside walks, including a section of the **Dales Way** footpath that follows the river's west bank to take in Bolton Woods and the **Strid** (from "stride"), an extraordinary piece of white water two miles north of the abbey, where softer rock has allowed the river to funnel into a cleft just a few feet wide. Numerous people have drowned trying to make the leap (the river here is 30ft deep), the quite obvious dangers underlined by the lifebelts hung nearby. As one local guide puts it, "there is no record of anyone failing to jump the Strid more than once." Access to the river's east bank is from the priory; for the west bank walk to the Cavendish Memorial, three hundred yards north of the village on the B6160, where a small toll is payable to reach the water.

Accommodation locally is limited. At Bolton Abbey the main **hotel** is the sumptuous *Devonshire Arms*, owned by the Duke of Devonshire (☎01756/710 441; ⑦) – if you can't afford a room here, at least drop into its bar for an excellent lunchtime snack. Easier on the pocket is **B&B** at *Hesketh House Farm*, in the village (☎01756/710 332; ②). There's a **camping barn** at Barden run by *High Gamsworth Cottage* (☎01756/720 630; ①) – sleeping bags are required, and B&B is also available. *Holme House Farm*, a quarter of a mile south of Barden, also has B&B (☎01756/720 661; ③).

Grassington

GRASSINGTON, nine miles from Bolton Abbey, is Wharfedale's popular main village, dreary on its outskirts but Georgian at the centre. *Keighley & District* **buses** #71 and #72 run between Skipton and the village roughly hourly except on Sunday, with about five daily pushing into the upper valley as far as Buckden (see below). The **National Park Information Centre** (April–Oct daily 10am–4pm; Nov–March most Sat & Sun 10am–4pm; ☎01756/752 748) on Hebden Road, across from the bus station, books **accommodation** for a small fee and provides wide-ranging information, particularly on the region's long lead-mining tradition. B&Bs include *Kirkfield*, Hebden Road (☎01756/752 385; ③), with airy rooms and views; 16 Wood Lane (☎01756/752 841; ③); and *Craiglands*, Brooklyn (☎01756/752 093; ③). Costlier places with good reputations are the *Grassington House Hotel*, The Square (☎01756/752 406; ④), and the *Black Horse Hotel*, just off The Square (☎01756/752 770; ③). There's also a **youth hostel** (☎01756/752 400) housed in the sevententh-century rectory of the unspoilt village of **Linton**, a mile to the southwest. The nearest **campsite** is *Mason's* at Ainhams, Appletreewick (☎01756/720 236). To **rent bikes**, an ideal way to explore the upper valley, contact the *Hardware Shop*, 5 Chapel St.

Upper Wharfedale and Littondale

Wharfedale's scenery above Grassington grows still more impressive, starting a mile north with a tract of ancient woodland, **Grass Wood**, and followed two miles later by **Kilnsey Crag**, a dramatic, glacially carved overhang. Information on the crag and its surroundings can be gleaned from the national park information point at Kilnsey Park on the southern edge of **KILNSEY** village (☎01756/753 114). You can **stay** in Kilnsey below the cliff at the *Tennant Arms* (☎01756/752 301; ②) or at the **bunkhouse barn**, *Skirfare Bridge Dales Barn* (☎01756/752 465; ①), half a mile further north, at the junction of the Littondale road (see below).

A mile beyond the outcrop a road branches off left into **Littondale**, an empty, pristine dale with stunning scenery and views, especially at Hesleden Bergh, where a road climbs over the moors to Stainforth in Ribblesdale, and above **ARNCLIFFE**, as idyllic a village as you'll find. On foot the ideal way to see the dale is to follow the valley-floor footpath from Arncliffe to Litton (2.5 miles), then continue the three miles up to **HALTON GILL**, where there's a bunkhouse barn at *Ellershaw Farm*

(☎01756/770 226; ①). For more comfort – and good beer into the bargain – stay in Arncliffe at the ivy-covered *Falcon* (☎01756/77205; ③), or at the similarly ancient and unspoilt *Queen's Arms* hostelry in Litton (☎01756/770 208; ③). B&B is also available in Litton at *Grange Cottage* (☎01756/752 527; ②), and there's a **campsite** a mile and a half southeast of Arncliffe at Hawkswick Cote Farm (☎01756/770 226). For more details of local walks, contact the **National Park Information Point** at Litton post office (☎01756/770 200).

The landscapes in the last six miles of Wharfedale and its continuation, **Langstrothdale**, hardly suffer by comparison with Littondale, a large proportion of their moors and valleys forming part of the National Trust's vast Upper Wharfedale Estate. **KETTLEWELL** (Norse for "bubbling spring"), three miles north of Kilnsey, is the main centre for the upper dale, a far more attractive proposition for a weekend's walking or relaxing than Grassington, with a campsite just to the north and the *Whernside House* **youth hostel** (☎0765/760 232). Other accommodation in the village is excellent, notably the superb *Langcliffe House Guest House* (☎01756/760 243; ③), *Fold Farm B&B* (☎01756/760 886; ③) and *Dale House Hotel* (☎01756/760 836; ③).

Take time to explore the valley and villages to the north, either via the vale's single lonely road or the Dales Way path, both of which push to the dale's upper limit. **STARBOTTOM**'s *Fox & Hounds* pub has ancient flagged floors and a huge fire, with three rooms for rent (☎01756/760 269; ③), while top-notch pub accommodation is available in **BUCKDEN** at the *Buck Inn* (☎01756/760 228; ③). A mile upstream you might walk along the river to **HUBBERHOLME** and the *George* (☎01756/760 223; ②), the favourite pub of archetypal Yorkshireman, J.B. Priestley, who's buried in the churchyard nearby. There's also a **bunkhouse barn** here at *Grange Farm* (☎01756/760 259; ①). Higher up the valley, superbly placed for walkers – particularly on the Dales and Pennine Ways – is a further bunkhouse at *Cam Farm* (☎0860/648 045; ①), three miles west of Oughtershaw in the remote upper reaches of Langstrothdale.

Malhamdale

A few miles west of Wharfedale lies **MALHAMDALE**, the uppermost reaches of Airedale and one of the national park's most heavily visited regions, thanks to its three outstanding natural features, Malham Cove, Malham Tarn and Gordale Scar. All three attractions are within easy hiking distance of Malham village, so any walking you do locally is likely to be in company, with the Pennine Way further adding to the column of walkers processing through the area.

Malham

Unless you come off-season some idea of what to expect in **MALHAM** comes at the vast peripheral car park, likely to be packed solid with hikers and day-trippers. Approach by public transport is on the twice-daily *Pennine* #210 bus from Skipton or the daily *Ingfield Northern* bus from Settle (schooldays only). Once you've arrived, the best way to deal with the crowds is to visit the **National Park Information Centre** on the southern edge of the village (Easter–Oct daily 9.30am–5pm; Oct–Easter Sat & Sun 10am–4pm; ☎01729/830 363) and then make straight for Malham Cove or Gordale Scar, each little more than a mile distant.

Something of the village's off-peak charm can be enjoyed in the evening when the trippers have gone home, though you'll need to book ahead to stay at the swish, centrally placed **youth hostel** (☎01729/830 321). There's a **bunkhouse barn** immediately north of the national park centre at Hill Top (☎01729/830 320; ①) and several **B&Bs**, cheapest of which is *Friars Garth*, on the eastern edge of the village (☎01729/830 328; ①), followed by the central *Sparth House Hotel* (☎01729/830 332; ②) and, opposite, the excellent *Miresfield Farm* (☎01729/830 414; ①–②). You can **camp** at

Townhead Farm (☎01729/830 287), near the cove, and under Gordale Scar at *Gordale Scar House Campsite* (☎01729/830 333).

Malham Cove, Malham Tarn and Gordale Scar

Malham Cove appears in spectacular fashion a mile north of Malham, a white-walled limestone amphitheatre rising 300ft above its surroundings. Like Gordale Scar's ramparts to the east it was formed by a shear along the Mid-Craven Fault, a geological tear that runs 22 miles from Wharfedale to Kirkby Lonsdale in Cumbria. Still visible on the clifftop are the black stains left by an earlier waterfall, once higher than Niagara, which accorded to patchy local records dried up during the eighteenth century.

A great motorway of a track leads to the cove, passing some of England's most visible prehistoric field banks, or lynchets, en route. Fewer people make the haul to the top, where the rewards are fine views and the famous **limestone pavement**, an expanse of clints (slabs) and grikes (clefts) created by water seeping through weaker lines in the limestone rock. Unusual plants and ferns such as dog's mercury and hart's-tongue shelter in the crevices, making this a favoured spot for botanists.

To the northwest rises the great bulk of Fountains Fell, its name a link with Fountains Abbey many miles to the east, erstwhile owner of huge estates in Craven. A simple walk over the moors, either via the Pennine Way or the more interesting dry valley to the west, brings **Malham Tarn** suddenly into sight, a lake created by an impervious layer of glacial debris. This, too, is an area of outstanding natural interest, its numerous waterfowl protected by a nature reserve on the west bank – visible from a nature trail which forms part of the Pennine Way on the east bank.

Unless your interests are ornithological, however, it's best to avoid the long haul round the lake and make do with the view alone before turning south for **Gordale Scar**, also easily seen from Malham village. Here the cliffs are if anything more spectacular than at Malham Cove, complemented by a deep ravine to the rear caused by the collapse of a cavern roof. A little to the south of the scar, off the road, lies **Janet's Foss**, a gem of a waterfall set amidst green-damp rocks and overarching trees.

It's usually possible to take in Malham's trio of sights in a clockwise circular **walk** from Malham (8 miles; 3hr 30min), the only problem being at Gordale Scar, where after heavy rain the water in the beck may make it difficult to scramble down the stream-cut gorge for the last leg back to Malham. If you don't want to see the Tarn and open moorland the walk is easily cut short by taking a waymarked track from the northern edge of the pavement above Malham Cove down to Gordale Bridge and thus onto Gordale Scar (5 miles; 2hr 30min).

Ribblesdale

RIBBLESDALE, further west, is a less coherent dale, its scenery more dour and brooding than the bucolic valleys to the east. It's entered from **Settle**, southern terminus for the **Settle to Carlisle Railway**, among the most scenic rail routes in the country. After **Stainforth**, close to one of the more noted of the Dales' many waterfalls (or "forces"), the valley's only village of any size is **Horton in Ribblesdale**, a focus not only for the Ribble Way and Pennine Way, but also where most people start the famous **Three Peaks Walk**, an arduous hike around the Dales' highest peaks.

Like Skipton a base for Wharfedale, **SETTLE** is one of the Dales' gateway villages – terminus of the **Settle and Carlisle Railway**, well placed for upper **Ribblesdale** to the north and a pleasant enough base if you haven't the time to find a more intimate overnight stop within the national park. The **tourist office** is in the town hall (Mon–Sat daily 10am–5pm; ☎01729/825 192), on the village's seventeenth-century market square, while the best places to **stay** are *Penmar Court Guest House*, Duke Street (☎01729/823 258; ②); *Oast Guest House*, 5 Penyghent View, Church Street (☎01729/

822 989; ③); *Halsteads*, 3 Halsteads Terrace (☎01729/822 823; ③); and the *Royal Oak Hotel*, Market Place (☎01729/823 102; ⑤). A good simple place to **eat** is the *Car and Kitchen*, on the Market Place.

STAINFORTH, two miles north of Settle, makes a good base for walks in the lower valley, with several B&Bs and a **youth hostel** set in extensive grounds about a quarter of a mile south of the centre (☎01729/823 577). A good local trek is down to the National Trust-owned Stainforth Bridge, a seventeenth-century packhorse bridge just a stone's throw from Stainforth Force waterfall and the **campsite** at Little Stainforth (☎01729/822 200). The best of the area's short walks climbs up to another waterfall, **Catrigg Force**, a mile east of the village, easily reached by an unmetalled lane.

Mine workings old and new detract slightly from **HORTON IN RIBBLESDALE**, a noted walking centre and base for some of the Dales' key cave and limestone pavement scenery. The *Pen-y-ghent Café* (also known as the *Three Peaks Café*) here is a **National Park Information Point** (☎01729/860 333) and an unofficial headquarters for the famous **Three Peaks Walk**, a 24-mile, 12-hour circuit of Pen-y-ghent (2273ft), Whernside (2414ft) and Ingleborough (2376ft). The village is most convenient for the ascent of Pen-y-ghent, arguably the most dramatic of the three summits, three miles to the east on the Pennine Way; the other peaks are more easily climbed from Ingleton, Chapel-le-Dale or Dentdale. Finally, be sure to walk, cycle, drive or take a train to the head of the valley, where the **Ribblehead Viaduct** cuts a superb profile, backed by some of the most uncompromising moors in the entire national park.

Accommodation in Horton is much in demand: B&Bs include *Wagi's* at Townend Cottage (☎01729/860 320; ③), *Burnside* (☎01729/860 223; ③) and *South House Farm*, Selside (☎01729/860 271; ③). The largest place in town is the *Crown Hotel* (☎01729/860 209; ③). There's a central tents-only **campsite** at *Holme Farm* (☎01729/860 281). Should you find yourself up in the wild country at Ribblehead, or stranded having missed the last train, salvation's at hand in the shape of the *Station Inn* (☎015242/41274; ③) and *Gearstone Farm* (☎015242/41405; ③), within a mile of the station. The *Station Inn* also has a bunkhouse barn.

The Western Dales

The **WESTERN DALES** is a term of convenience for a couple of tiny dales running north from **Ingleton**, a village perfectly poised for walks up Ingleborough and Whernside, and for **Dentdale**, one of the loveliest valleys in the national park. (Much of this region has been hived off into Cumbria, to the disgust of its erstwhile Yorkshire population.) Unless you have a car, any extensive exploration is difficult, though Ingleton is linked by bus to Skipton and Settle, and the Settle and Carlisle Railway offers access to upper Dentdale, with fine walks possible virtually off the station platforms. Ingleton has most accommodation, but **Dent** is by far the best village, with a cobbled centre barely altered in centuries.

Ingleton and around
INGLETON caters for a fair share of tourists, as well as cavers and climbers, but while the village is pleasant enough there's little specific to see. It sits at the confluence of two streams, the Twiss and the Doe, their beautifully wooded valleys perhaps the area's best features. The circular **Falls' Walk** up the Swilla Glen (4.5 miles; 2hr 30min; £1.59 admission) is the town's main attraction, passing the Pecca Falls and Thornton Force in the course of its progress up the tree-hung vale. Paths then lead east via Twistleton Hall to the head of the Doe at Beezley Farm (refreshments) where a signed path takes you down the valley back to Ingleton by way of Beezley and Snow Falls. Serious hikers congregate in Ingleton to tackle **Ingleborough**, one of the Three Peaks, reached by a slightly laborious route to the east (3 miles; 2hr 30min).

An *Ingleton Waterfalls Trail* leaflet is available from the **tourist office** (May–Oct daily 10am–4.30pm; ☎015242/41049) in the community centre car park in the centre of the village. They also have lists of the village's **accommodation**, among which there's a **youth hostel** (☎015242/41444), located centrally in a lane between the market square and the swimming pool. Among a dozen other overnight options the best guest house is *Ingleborough View*, Main Street (☎015242/41523; ②), followed by the *Langber County Guest House*, Tatterthorne Lane (☎015242/41587; ②). There are two good hotels: the *Springfield*, Main Street (☎015242/41280; ③) and the *Moorgarth Hall Country House*, New Road (☎015242/41946; ④). Another possible base is the **Hill Inn** (☎015242/41256; ②), in the nearby village Chapel-le-Dale, on the road to Ribble Head (see above); built in 1615 – Turner and John Buchan are listed among its drinkers – it's a lively, unpredictable place, with occasional live music and lots of climbers and cavers. Rooms are available and there's a **campsite** nearby.

Four miles southeast of Ingleton lies **CLAPHAM**, yet another seductive little village, all of it protected as a conservation area. Check into the **National Park Information Centre** (April–Oct daily 10am–5pm; Nov–March occasional Sat & Sun; ☎015242/51419) alongside the car park, for a leaflet on the nature trail (1.5 miles; 50min; 20p toll) through Clapdale Woods to **Ingleborough Cave** (March–Nov daily; Feb daily except Mon & Fri; Dec–Jan Thurs, Sat & Sun 10am–5pm; £3.50), the Pennines' oldest show cave. The trail footpath – the only access – was laid out with numerous exotic trees and flora, most brought to Britain by Reginald Farrer, a scion of the family who own Ingleborough Hall and the surrounding estate. Follow the footpath beyond the caves and after a little over a mile you reach **Gaping Gill**, probably the most famous of the Dales' many potholes; carry on another two miles northwest from Gaping Gill and you arrive at the summit of Ingleborough – better than the haul up from Ingleton. Clapham has a good **hotel**, the *New Inn* (☎015242/51203; ④) and a more reasonable guest house, *Arbutus House*, Riverside (☎015242/51240; ④), as well as *The Flying Horseshoe* pub (☎015242/51229; ③), a mile from the village by the railway station.

Dentdale

Any rail or road route to **Dentdale** has plenty of scenic rewards, but the most breath-taking is from Ingleton up Kingsdale and down Deepdale, with the vast whalebacks of Gragareth and Whernside rising to each side of the windblown little road. There's next to nothing to do locally except walk or revel in the scenery, but there are few better spots to do either, with **DENT** village (4 miles west of Dent Head train station) an unbeatable base, its grass-grown, cobbled streets clustered around the *The Sun Inn* (☎015396/25208; ③) to create as seductive a Dales village as you'll find. In addition to *The Sun* there are a handful of other overnight possibilities, namely *Smithey Fold* (☎015396/25368; ②) and *Low Laning House* (☎015396/25537; ②), both private houses, and the *Stone Close Guest House* (☎015396/25231; ④), which has a superb café-restaurant too. There's also a **campsite** on the western edge of the village, *High Laning Farm* (☎015396/25239). Dent **youth hostel** is about six miles east up the valley at *Dee Side House* (☎015396/25251). Note that close to the Dent Head station is the hamlet of **COWGILL**, with a neat guest house, *Birk Rigg* (☎015396/25367; ②), and the larger *Sportsman's Inn* (☎015396/25282; ③).

Wensleydale

Best known of the Dales to outsiders, if only for its cheese, **WENSLEYDALE** is the largest, least varied and most serene of the national park's dales. Named after a now inconsequential village rather than its river (the Ure), it contains one of the area's biggest towns in **Hawes**, plus several well-known waterfalls – notably Aysgarth Falls –

and, as it opens into the Vale of York, a handful of lesser attractions, ranging from **Middleham Castle** to Theakston's brewery in **Masham**.

The dale is traversed by the national park's only east–west main road (A684), and linked by high moor roads to virtually all the park's other dales of note. Although the scenery is less spectacular than in other valleys, hiking possibilities are as plentiful as elsewhere, with the **Pennine Way** crossing the valley at Hawes. Public transport is restricted, limited to summer-only *Yorkshire Dales National Park* **buses** from Garsdale Head station, a twice-daily postbus from Hawes to Bedale (via Leyburn), and the infrequent *United* #159 from Ripon to Hawes and #26 to Hawes from Richmond.

Hawes

HAWES – from the Anglo-Saxon *haus*, a mountain pass – is head of Wensleydale in all respects: its chief town, its main hiking centre and home of its tourism, cheese and rope-making industries, all three coming together in the **Dales Countryside Museum**, housed in Station Yard's former train station and warehouses (Easter–Oct daily 9am–5pm; £1.50). The comprehensive and well-presented collection, garnered by Dales' chroniclers Marie and Joan Ingilby, embraces lead mining, farming, peat-cutting, knitting (hand-knitted hosiery was a speciality) and all manner of rustic minutiae. In a long shed alongside, the Hawes Ropeworks presents popular demonstrations of traditional rope-making (daily 9am–5.30pm; free). The **National Park Information Centre** shares the same buildings (daily 10am–5pm; ☎01969/667 450).

A mile out of town to the north, people cough up the 60p toll at the *Green Dragon Pub* to walk to **Hadrow Force** – about all the fall is worth for much of the year, for though this is the highest above-ground waterfall in the country (Gaping Gill and other potholes have longer underground drops) there's often barely a trickle dribbling over the edge. Summer brass-band recitals in the natural amphitheatre make for a more surreal attraction. One of the best but toughest local **walks** follows the Pennine Way immediately west of the *Green Dragon* to Great Shunner Fell (5 miles one way; 2hr 30min). Far more people, however, drive the parallel road over to Thwaite for the views and the **Buttertubs**, a series of deeply eroded natural wells five miles north of Hawes.

There's a smart, purpose-built **youth hostel** (☎01969/667 368) at Lancaster Terrace, at the junction of the main A684 and B6255. **Guest houses** to aim for include *East House*, Gayle Lane (☎01969/667 405; ②), *White Hart Inn*, Main Street (☎01969/667 259; ③) and the excellent *Old Station House*, Hardraw Road (☎01969/667 785; ③). The best **hotel** in town is the *Cocketts Hotel*, Market Place (☎01969/667 312; ④); the best **pub** is the *Board Inn* on the Market Place, particularly on Tuesday, when it's crammed with farmers and market traders. If you're **camping**, head for the *Bainbridge Ings Site* (☎01969/667 354), just south of the main road, half a mile east of the village.

Aysgarth and around

AYSGARTH, nine miles east of Hawes, is the vortex that sucks in the dale's biggest crowds, courtesy of the twin **Aysgarth Falls** – the Upper nearer the village to the east, and the more spectacular Lower Falls half a mile beyond. Broad rather than high, falling in a series of limestone steps, both are impressive only in spate, whilst in summer the riverbanks alongside are choked with picnicking families. A nature trail is marked through the surrounding woodlands and there's a big car park and **information centre** (April–Oct daily 9.30am–4.30pm, plus occasional Sat & Sun in winter; ☎01969/663 424) on the north bank. This makes the river's south bank slightly quieter, a bank you could follow by footpath for a couple of miles before cutting south across the main road at Eshington Bridge for West Burton village and paths back to Aysgarth.

In Aysgarth the church of **St Andrew's** is worth a look for its carved pews and one of Yorkshire's finest rood screens (1500), possibly removed from nearby Jervaux Abbey. Immediately below the church is an old water-driven mill, now the **Yorkshire**

Carriage Museum (daily 9.30am–8pm; £1.50), housing fifty-plus coaches, hearses, fire engines and estate vehicles. The mill produced one of history's more famous sartorial job lots: the red flannel shirts worn by the Italian soldiers of Garibaldi's 1860 army of unification. Aysgarth has a trio of **B&Bs** and one **hotel**: *Marlbeck* (☎01969/663 610; ③), *Wensleydale Farmhouse* (☎01969/663 534; ③), *Low Gill Farm* (☎01969/663 554; ③) and *Stow House Hotel* (☎01969/663 635; ⑤). There's a **youth hostel** (☎01969/663 260) on the south side of the village, just a minutes' walk from the Falls, and a **campsite**, *Westholme Caravan Park* (☎01969/663 268), half a mile east on the A684.

Wensley and Middleham Castle

A few miles east of Aysgarth, Wensleydale broadens into a low-hilled pastoral valley, the border of the national park marking the end of classic Dales scenery and the start of the Vale of York's more mundane flats. **Leyburn** occupies almost the last piece of straggling high ground on the valley's north edge, but if you're coming from Aysgarth you'd do better to leave the A684 at **WENSLEY**, another beguiling place wound around a green village square. The church of the **Holy Trinity** ranks as one of the Dales' finest, founded in the thirteenth century but with fabric from the five centuries that followed, the most impressive an extravagant box pew and a sixteenth-century rood screen removed from Easby Abbey (see below).

The vast ruins of **Middleham Castle** (April–Sept daily 10am–6pm; Oct–March Tues–Sun 10am–4pm; £1.10; EH), two miles southeast of Leyburn, were originally built by the Normans to guard the route from Skipton to Richmond; the castle gained added historical resonance when it passed by marriage to the future Richard III in 1471. The keep is one of England's largest, despite being slighted after Richard's defeat at Bosworth Field. Beyond Middleham, Wensleydale all but peters out, though beer fans might want to check out **MASHAM**, seven miles southeast of Middleham, home of Theakston's brewery and **Old Peculier** (sic) ale, an essential point of pilgrimage. You can take tours (with tastings) around the brewery, or sample the stuff in the *White Bear*.

Swaledale and Richmond

The national park's northernmost dale, **SWALEDALE** is rivalled only by Dentdale for the lonely grandeur of its landscapes. Narrow and steep-sided in its upper reaches, it emerges rocky and rugged in its central tract, running past the idyllic villages of Muker, Thwaite and **Keld** before more typically pastoral scenery cuts in at Reeth. The *United* **bus** #30 runs up the valley as far as Keld from Richmond.

Keld

Aim to start any tour of Swaledale as high as possible, preferably by coming over the Buttertubs Pass from Hawes and heading up-valley on the Kirkby Stephen road to take in the desolate scenery of short side-valleys such as Stone Dale, Whitsun Dale and Birkdale. **KELD** makes an ideal hiking centre – the Pennine Way and Coast to Coast paths cross here – and is surrounded by relics of the lead-mining industry that once brought a prosperity of sorts to much of the valley. Here you'll also see the incredible profusion of ancient field barns, or **laithes**, for which the dale is renowned, the legacy of a system of husbandry that dates back to Norse times.

Any number of **walks** are possible locally, the shortest being to **Kisdon Force**'s triple-stacked waterfall and its wooded gorge, half a mile east of the village, though the best is the hike along the River Swale to Muker (see below), below the circular bulk of Kisdon hill (2.5 miles; 1hr 30min). The valley road cuts round Kisdon to the south, following part of the so-called **Corpse Way**, a lane used by those paying their last respects when the nearest church was ten miles away at Grinton – footpaths follow its still obvious route down the valley. Keld's busy **youth hostel** is *Keld Lodge*, an old shooting lodge (☎01748/886 259), though B&B at *East Stonesdale Farm* (☎01748/886 374; ③), stunningly situated close to Kisdon Force, is a more tempting proposition.

Thwaite to Reeth

One of Swaledale's attractions is the possibility of walking on footpaths that link villages all the way down the valley to Reeth. **THWAITE**, another attractive Norse-founded settlement, is the first hamlet south of Keld, with **accommodation** at *Kearton Guest House* (☎01748/886 277; ③). North of **GUNNERSIDE**, midway between Thwaite and Reeth, the little Gunnerside Gill valley contains the best of the area's old lead mines, all easily seen on a six-mile circular walk from the village, covered by a special trail leaflet available from the village post office's summer-only **National Park Information Point** (☎01748/886 220). There's a **bunkhouse barn** at the *Punch Bowl Inn* (☎01748/886 233; ①) at **LOW ROW**, a couple of miles further east, with inexpensive B&B and evening meals also available.

A couple of miles east lies **REETH**, the dale's main village, its cove-table cottages gathering around a triangular green. There a steady procession to the **Tan Hill Inn** at the very top of the dale, the highest pub in England, built to serve the coal mines that fed the lead mines and smelting mills of the lower dale. If the area's lead-mining heritage appeals, drop into Reeth's **Folk Museum** (Easter–Sept daily 10.30am–6pm; 85p), also home to the local **tourist office** (same times; ☎01748/884 373). There are plenty of **B&Bs** in Reeth itself, including *Galway House*, The Green (☎0748/84507; ③) and *Hackney House*, Bridge Terrace (☎0748/84302; ②). The nearest **youth hostel**, *Grinton Lodge* (☎01748/884 206) is housed in a former shooting lodge in the hills, ten minutes' walk above **Grinton**, just half a mile south of Reeth.

Richmond

Although marginalized on the national park's northeasternmost borders, **Richmond** is the Dales' singlemost tempting historical town, thanks mainly to the magnificent **Castle**, whose ranging walls and colossal keep cling to a precipice above the Swale (April–Oct daily 10am–6pm; Nov–March Tues–Sun 10am–4pm; £1.80; EH). Begun around 1070 by Alan Rufus, first Norman Earl of Richmond, it retains many features from its earliest incarnation, principally the gatehouse, curtain wall and Scolland's Hall, the oldest Norman great hall in the country. Legend, however, links it to earlier times, notably to King Arthur, who's reputed to lie in a local cave awaiting England's hour of need. The castle was roofed with Swaledale lead, and its building and upkeep paid for over the centuries with a levy of two pence per muleload of lead coming down the dale.

Most of medieval Richmond – all cobbled streets and narrow wynds – sprouted around the castle, but much of the town now radiates from the **Market Place**. Victorian and Georgian buildings hem the square, though the most unusual structure is the defunct Holy Trinity church, built in 1135 and now a museum for North Yorkshire's Green Howards regiment. Just out of the square stands the **Theatre Royal**, built in 1788, making it one of the England's oldest theatres. It's unassuming from the outside, but the tiny interior has been called one of England's finest pieces of Georgian architecture (tours March–Oct Mon–Sat 11am–4.45pm; free). If you have time, wander out to the beautifully situated **Easby Abbey** (same times as castle; free), a mile southeast of the town centre and reached by a wooded riverside path. Founded in 1152, the abbey is now ruined, but the remains are extensive, and in places – notably the thirteenth-century refectory – still remarkably intact.

The **tourist office**, at Friary Gardens on Queens Road (daily summer 9.30am–5.30pm; winter 9.30am–4.30pm; ☎01748/850 252), is helpful in finding **accommodation**, among the best of which is the *Black Lion* on Finkle Street (☎0748/823 121; ③), also the most alluring of the town's many **pubs**. B&Bs to try include 27 Hurgill Rd (☎0748/824 092; ③) and the excellent *West End Guest House*, 45 Reeth Rd (☎0748/824 783; ③). If you want to push the boat out, bed down in the luxury of the *King's Head*

Hotel, Market Place (☎0748/850 220; ⑨). There are no **restaurants** in town other than a cheap Chinese and Indian, and the best bet for food is to head for one of the town's pubs – the *King's Head*, in particular, serves reasonable bar meals.

Harrogate to Ripon

Somewhat off the beaten track unless you're driving between York and the Dales, **Ripon** – despite its ancient cathedral – would hardly merit a visit on its own were it not for **Fountains Abbey**, Britain's largest monastic ruin and its most beautiful. Easily seen from Ripon, it has the added bonus of being the focal point of **Studley Royal**, an eighteenth-century landscaped garden complete with lake, temples, water-garden and deer park. With time and transport you could take in a handful of other historic buildings nearby, though the better excursions are perhaps made from the refined spa town of **Harrogate**: either to **Knaresborough** for its castle, or to **Nidderdale**, an often overlooked adjunct to the Dales proper – for which Harrogate's bus and train connections make the town a perfect gateway.

Harrogate

HARROGATE is Yorkshire's tea-shop capital and the very picture of genteel respectability, albeit one that's frayed around the edges. It owes its airy, planned appearance and early prosperity to the discovery of Tewit Well in 1571, the first of over eighty ferrous and sulphurous springs that were to turn the town into one of the country's leading spas. These days local pockets are lined more by a year-round panoply of conferences, shows and festivals, but many monuments to past splendours are left standing. Most notable of these are the Royal Hall, the Opera House, the **Royal Baths and Assembly Rooms** off Crescent Road (where you can take a Turkish Bath in Victorian surroundings) and the 120-acre **Valley Gardens**. Site of half the original springs, the gardens are now a continuation of the **Stray**, a jealously guarded green belt that curves around the south of the town centre and is connected to it by West Park. Three minutes' walk from the Assembly Rooms stands the **Royal Pump Room**, built over the sulphur well that feeds the Royal Baths. If you don't want to take the cure here, you could just drop in to the **museum**, which recreates something of the town's health-fixated past (Mon–Sat 10am–5pm, Sun 2–5pm; £1.50).

Harrogate's **tourist office** is in the Royal Baths and Assembly Rooms (summer Mon–Sat 9am–6pm, Sun 1–4pm; winter Mon–Fri 9am–5.15pm, Sat 9am–1pm; ☎01423/525 666). For **accommodation**, try the central *Ruskin Hotel*, 1 Swan Rd (☎01423/502 045; ⑤) or *Fountains*, 27 King's Rd ☎01423/530 483; ④). Of Harrogate's many **festivals,** the most noteworthy are the flower shows (second weeks of April & Sept), the Hallé Orchestra festival (third week in June), the Great Yorkshire Show (second week in July) and the antiques show (second half of Sept). Queen of the tea shops is *Betty's*, located at 1 Parliament St. If you're after something stronger try *Hales Bar*, 1 Crescent Rd – all gaslights and mirrors. Best of Harrogate's **restaurants** is *Millers*, 1 Montpellier Mews (☎01423/530 708); if you can't afford its prices, you might want to try the fish at *Drum and Monkey*, 5 Montpellier Gardens.

Knaresborough

A three-mile hop from Harrogate by bus or train, **KNARESBOROUGH** rises spectacularly above the River Nidd's limestone gorge, its old town houses, pubs, shops and gardens clustered together on the wooded northern bank. The rocky crag above the town is crowned by the stump of a **Castle** dating back to Norman times (May–Sept daily 10.30am–5pm; £1.50); built on the site of Roman and Anglo-Saxon fortifications, it's now little more than a fourteenth-century keep thanks to Cromwell's wrecking tactics during the Civil War. It was here that Henry II's knights fled after the murder of Thomas à Becket in Canterbury Cathedral; here, too, that Richard II was held before being removed to Pontefract, where he was murdered in 1400. In Castle Yard, close to the castle entrance, stands the **Old Court House Museum**, with an original Tudor court and displays on local history (same times & ticket as castle).

The town's two novelty acts are to be found out in the southeastern suburbs. **Mother Shipton's Cave** (daily Easter–Oct 9.30am–5.45pm; Nov–Easter 10am–4.45pm; £3.95) was home to a sixteenth-century soothsayer who predicted the defeat of the Armada, the Great Fire of London, world wars, cars, planes, iron ships – falling short, however, in the most important oracular chestnut of them all, the End of the World, which she predicted would take place in 1881. Close by is an equally tourist-thronged spot, the **Dropping Well**, where dripping, lime-soaked waters coat everyday objects – gloves, hats, coats, toys – in a brownish veneer that sets rock-hard in a few weeks.

The **tourist office** is at 35 Market Place (May–Sept Mon–Sat 10am–5.30pm, Sun 2–5pm; ☎01423/866 886). If you fancy staying overnight the best of the basic **B&Bs** are the *Crown*, High Street (☎01423/862 122; ③) and *Ebor Mount*, 18 York Place (☎01423/864 033; ③). For something more plush opt for the *Villa Hotel*, 47 Kirkgate (☎01423/865 370; ④) or the town's best, *The Dower House*, Bond End (☎01423/863 302; ⑥). Far and away the best **pub** in town is *Mother Shipton Inn* at Low Bridge, a fine, traditional stone building with a maze of rooms, snugs and alcoves, and a great garden looking over the river to the town's famous rail viaduct.

Nidderdale

The rumours claim **NIDDERDALE** was excluded from the Yorkshire Dales National Park so that reservoirs and other landscape-scarring features could go ahead unencumbered by planning restrictions. Despite these developments, the dale's beautiful upper reaches stand comparison with its more famous neighbours, yet remain relatively unknown and under-visited. Onward itineraries are pretty limited, however: unless you take the wild road north to Masham and Wensleydale (see p.492), you'll have to backtrack at least to **Pateley Bridge**, the dale's main village, to find a way out of the valley.

Ripley

The lower vale is a patchwork of farming land, its first obvious distraction coming at **RIPLEY**, a village whose bizarre appearance is due to a whim of the Ingilby family, who between 1827 and 1854 rebuilt it in the manner of an Alsace-Lorraine village, for no other reason than they liked the style. Summer crowds pile in for the cobbled square, original stocks and the twee cottages, not to mention the Ingilby house, parkland and **Castle** (gardens March Thurs–Sun 11am–4pm; April–Oct daily 11am–5pm; Nov & Dec daily 11am–3.30pm; castle April, May & Oct Sat, Sun & bank hols 11.30am–4.30pm; June & Sept Thurs–Sun 11.30am–4.30pm; July & Aug 11.30am–4.30pm; gardens only £2.25, castle and gardens £3.75) – the last with a museum of armour, weapons, furniture and the like. Close to the bridge over the village beck, look in on **All Saints'** church, whose stonework bears the indentations of musket balls, said to be caused by the execution of Royalist soldiers after the Battle of Marston Moor. The graveyard also contains the "Kneeling" or "Weeping" cross, a stone with eight niches to receive the knees of penitents – the only one of its kind in the country.

Pateley Bridge and around

Workaday **PATELEY BRIDGE** serves as the dale's focus, housing the **tourist office** at 14 High St (April–Sept daily 10am–5pm; ☎01423/711 147) and acting as a base for campers, cavers and visitors of every shade. Its **Nidderdale Museum** (Easter–Sept daily 2–5pm; winter Sun only; 80p), in the old council offices on the edge of the village, provides a run-through of dale life in days gone by. After that, you could stroll the **Panorama Walk** (2 miles; 1hr), signed from the top of the High Street.

Five miles west of the village on the Grassington road lie the **Stump Cross Caverns**, one of England's premier show caves, though only one massive stalagmite-filled cavern of the three-mile complex is open to the public (Easter–Oct daily 10am–5.30pm; winter Sat & Sun 10.30am–4pm; £3.20). About the same distance east of the village, off the B6265, are the extraordinary **Brimham Rocks**, six hundred acres of strangely eroded millstone grit outcrops scattered over one-thousand-foot high moors, all under the protection of the National Trust, who have a useful **information centre** at Brimham House (April–Oct daily 9am–6pm; free). **Views** from here are superlative, stretching over the Vale of York, with York Minster visible on clear days.

North of Pateley Bridge, above the Gouthwaite Reservoir, Nidderdale closes in and the scenery is superb. Part of the reservoir is a restricted-access **nature reserve**, but plenty of geese, waders and waterfowl can be seen year-round from the surrounding roads and tracks. In the upper valley there's also the **How Stean Gorge**, a terrific ice-gouged ravine of surging waters and overhanging rocks.

Ripon

The unassuming market town of **RIPON** only really diverts by virtue of its **Cathedral**, a building which seems at first glance small and not terribly impressive, only a closer look revealing its treasures. The first church on the site was founded in 672 by Saint Wilfrid, its original crypt still extant below the central tower. The rest of the building was destroyed by the Danes in the ninth century, then a second church fell foul of the Normans, part of whose replacement remains, though the bulk of the present building dates from the reign of Archbishop Roger of York (1154–81). The subtle, twin-towered **west front** probably dates from around 1250, though it shows a great variety of styles, also repeated in the central tower. Inside, be sure to take a close look at the **choir**'s misericords, full of painted figures of miserable clergymen, executed by the same team that carved the similarly impressive stalls at Beverley (see p.512). In Saint Wilfrid's treasure-laden **crypt**, notice the narrow hole on the north side, the so-called St Wilfrid's Needle; the ability to crawl through it is taken as a sign of chastity.

The town's other focus is its **Market Place**, linked by Kirkgate to the cathedral. A ninety-foot obelisk built in 1780 dominates the square, a blustering conceit in stone, raised by William Aislabie to celebrate his sixty years as the local MP. At its apex stands a horned weather vane, an allusion to the "Blowing of the Wakeman's Horn", a ceremony – now something of a tourist attraction – which may date from 886, when Alfred the Great reputedly granted Ripon a charter (which would make it England's oldest chartered town) and an ox's horn was presented for the setting of the town's watch. The last official Wakeman died in 1637, but the horn is still blown nightly at 9pm in the square's four corners and outside the house of the incumbent mayor. The half-timbered **Wakeman's House** stands on the square, now a small gift shop selling local crafts (Mon–Sat 9am–5.30pm), and the town's **tourist office** (April–Oct Mon–Sat 10am–5.30pm, Sun 2–7pm; ☎01765/604 625).

Places to **stay** include: *Marrick House*, 21 Iddesleigh Terrace (☎01765/01765/602 707; ③), near the Minster; *The Coopers*, 36 College Rd (☎01765/603 708; ③), a quiet spot overlooking the countryside; *Bishopton Grove House*, Bishopton (☎01765/600 888; ③), a Georgian house in a peaceful corner of the town; *Crescent Lodge*, 42 North St (☎01765/602 331; ④), a Georgian lodge just five minutes from the Market Place; and the *Unicorn Hotel*, the Market Place (☎01765/602 202; ⑤), Ripon's finest. Top place to **eat** in Ripon is the *Old Deanery*, on Minster Road.

Fountains Abbey and Studley Royal

It's tantalizing to imagine how the English landscape might have appeared had Henry VIII not dissolved the monasteries, with all the artistic ruin and impoverishment precipitated by that act. **Fountains Abbey**, four miles southwest of Ripon, gives a good idea of what might have been, and is the one ruin amongst Yorkshire's many monastic fragments you should make a point of seeing. Linked to it are the gardens of **Studley Royal**, landscaped in the eighteenth century to form a setting for the abbey, but only reunited as a single 680-acre National Trust estate in 1983.

The site is signed off the B6265 Ripon to Pateley Bridge Road, ten miles north of Harrogate. The closest **rail** link is Harrogate, with a bus connection to Ripon; a **bus** (#143) also runs to Ripon from York train station. **Bus** #145 runs close to the abbey from Ripon (Thurs & Sat only).

The abbey and gardens are **open** daily except Friday in November, December and January, for the following hours: April to September 10am to 7pm, October to March 10am to 5pm, or dusk if earlier. Except when the abbey is shut, Fountains Hall is open daily from April to September from 11am to 6pm, closing two hours earlier in other months; admission is £4, though you don't have to pay to get into Studley's deer park (all year in daylight hours) or St Mary's Church (Easter & May–Sept daily 1–5pm).

The Abbey

Beautifully set in a narrow, wooded valley, through which the River Skell flows, **Fountains Abbey** was founded in 1133 by thirteen dissident Benedictine monks from the wealthy abbey of St Mary's in York (perhaps encouraged by the success of Rievaulx, founded a year earlier) and formally adopted by the Cistercians two years later (see box). Within a hundred years St Mary's *ad fontes* had become the wealthiest Cistercian foundation in England, a century which saw the three main phases of the

---

THE CISTERCIANS

England's monastic tradition received a boost in the middle of the twelfth century when Norman landlords, seeking to secure spiritual salvation and raise a bit of cash, handed over portions of their estates to various religious orders, often to dissident offshoots of the Benedictines such as the **Cistercians**. Committed to toil, self-sufficiency and prayer, the movement was founded at Cîteaux in Burgundy, in reaction to the arrogant affluence of the Cluniacs, who themselves had earlier reacted against the same perceived fault in the Benedictines. Fountains found itself in the vanguard of the movement, founded just five years after Waverley, the first Cistercian foundation in England.

Besides the core of priest-monks common to all Benedictine communities – whose obligatory presence at choir seven times daily left little time for work outside the cloister – the Cistercians uniquely had a second tier of lay-brethren known as **conversi**, or "bearded ones". At Fountains, around forty monks were complemented by two hundred such *conversi*. The new recruits – often skilled farmers and masons – ventured far from the mother house, returning only for major festivals and feast days. They were organized into **granges** (farms) to run flocks of sheep, drain land (hence Yorkshire's many "Friar's Ditches"), clear pasture, mine stone, lead or iron – even, in a couple of cases, to run a stud farm and sea-fishing business. Fountains' holdings in the Craven area of the Dales alone totalled over a million acres.

The Cistercians' success prompted the Augustinians (Kirkham and Guisborough) and Benedictines (York and Whitby) to follow suit, though within a hundred years much of their early vigour had been lost, partly as a result of an economic downturn which followed the Black Death. Granges were broken into smaller units and leased to a new class of tenant farmer, as the Cistercians joined the older orders in living off rents rather than actively developing their own estates.

Abbey's structural development: the church's nave and transepts (1135–47), the domestic buildings (1147–79), and the church's east end (1220–47). Only the church's domineering tower belongs to a latter period (1498–1526). At the Dissolution the Abbey was sold to Sir Richard Gresham, and ultimately became a source of building stone for the nearby **Fountains Hall** (see below). Further desecration was avoided when in 1768 it became part of Studley Royal under William Aislabie, who extended the landscaping exploits of his father to bring the ruined abbey within the estate's orbit.

Most immediately eye-catching is the abbey **church**, in particular the Chapel of the Nine Altars at its eastern end, whose delicacy is in marked contrast to the classic Cistercian austerity of the rest of the nave. A great sixty-foot-high window rises over the chapel, complemented by a similar window at the nave's western doorway, over 370ft away. Equally grandiose in scale is the **undercroft** of the Lay Brothers' Refectory off the cloister, a stunningly vaulted space over 300ft long that was used to store the monastery's annual harvest of fleeces. Its sheer size gives some idea of the abbey's entrepreneurial scope, some thirteen tons of wool a year being turned over, most of it sold to Venetian and Florentine merchants. The monks soon became speculators, buying wool from local farmers to sell in addition to their own production.

The size of the Refectory, the **Lay Brothers' Dormitory** above it, and the **Lay Brothers' Infirmary** over the river, all give an idea of the number of lay brothers at the abbey: all are substantially larger than the corresponding monks' buildings, of which the most prepossessing are the **Chapter House** and **Refectory** – notice the huge fireplace of the tiny **Warming Room** alongside the refectory, the only heated space in the entire complex. Outside the abbey perimeter, between the gatehouse and bridge, are the Abbey Mill and **Fountains Hall**, the latter a fine example of early seventeenth-century domestic architecture.

Studley Royal

A bucolic riverside walk, marked from the abbey car park (2 miles; 1hr) takes you through the abbey and past Fountains Hall to a series of ponds and ornamental gardens, harbingers of **Studley Royal** (which can also be entered via the village of Studley Roger). This lush medley of lawns, lake, woodland and **Deer Park** was laid out in 1720 by John Aislabie, MP for Ripon and Chancellor of the Exchequer until his involvement with the South Sea Company – one of the great financial scandals of the century – forced his resignation. Apart from the various contrived **views** of the abbey, the garden's best moments are its cascades and **water gardens**, fed by canals from the Skell, and its artfully arranged buildings such as the Temple of Piety and Banqueting House, the latter probably designed by Colen Campbell, a pioneer of English Palladianism. Just within the park stands the church of **St Mary's** (1871), sumptuous to the point of gaudiness, but neatly approached by an avenue of limes that frame the distant towers of Ripon cathedral.

York

YORK is the north's most compelling city, a place whose history, said George VI, "is the history of England". This is perhaps overstating things a little, but it reflects the significance of a metropolis that until the Industrial Revolution was second only to London in population and importance, not only at the heart of the country's religious life, but also a key player in some of the major events that have shaped the nation. These days a more provincial air hangs over the city, and – in summer at least – the feeling that York has been turned into a heritage site for the benefit of tourists. That said, no trip to this part of the country is complete without a visit to York. York's university and colleges also provide the spur for a reasonably healthy nightlife.

A brief history of York

The **Romans** chose York's swampy position, at the confluence of two minor rivers, as the site of a military camp during their campaigns against the Brigantians in 71 AD, and in time this fortress became a city – **Eboracum**, capital of the Empire's northern European territories and one of its most important administrative centres. The base for Hadrian's northern campaigns, it was also ruled for three years by Septimius Severus, one of two emperors to die in the city. The other, Constantine Chlorus, was the father of Constantine the Great, first Christian emperor and founder of Constantinople, who was with him at his death and was proclaimed Roman Emperor here – the only occasion an emperor was enthroned in Britain.

The city emerged as a **Saxon** vassal, Eoforwic, and later became the fulcrum of Christianity in northern England. It was here, on Easter Day in 627, that Bishop Paulinus, on a mission to establish the Roman Church, baptized King Edwin of Northumbria in a small timber chapel built for the purpose. Six years later the church became the first minster and Paulinus the first Archbishop of York. In 867 the city fell to the **Danes**, who renamed it **Jorvik**, and later made it the capital of eastern England (Danelaw), following a treaty in 886 between Alfred the Great and Guthrum the Dane. Later Viking raids culminated in the **Battle of Stamford Bridge** (1066) six miles east of the city, where English King Harold defeated the Norse King Harald – a Pyrrhic victory in the event, for his weakened army was defeated by the Normans just a few days later at the Battle of Hastings, with well-known consequences for all concerned.

Stone walls were thrown up during the thirteenth century, when the city became a favoured Plantaganet retreat and commercial capital of the north, its importance reflected in the new title of Duke of York, bestowed ever since on the monarch's second son. The 48 **York Mystery Plays**, one of only four surviving such cycles, date from this era, created by the powerful guilds which rose with the city's woollen industry. During the **Civil War** Charles I established his court in the strongly pro-Royalist city, inviting a Parliamentarian siege which was eventually lifted by Prince Rupert of the Rhine, a nephew of the king. Rupert's troops, however, were routed by Cromwell and Sir Thomas Fairfax at the **Battle of Marston Moor** in 1644, another seminal battle in England's history, which took place just six miles west of York. It's said that only the fact that Fairfax was a local man saved York from destruction.

The city's eighteenth-century history was marked by its emergence as a social centre for Yorkshire's landed elite. Whilst the Industrial Revolution largely passed it by, the arrival of the railways brought renewed prosperity, thanks largely to the enterprise of pioneering "Railway King" **George Hudson**, lord mayor during the 1830s and 1840s. Chocolate, in the shape of Terry and Rowntree-Nestlé, is now the financial mainstay, together with the proceeds from several million annual tourists.

Arrival, information and accommodation

Direct mainline **trains** from all over the country arrive at **York Station**, just outside the city walls on the south side of the River Ouse, a short walk from the historic core. **Buses** drop off and pick up on Rougier Street, 200 yards north of the train station, alongside a tourist-cum-*National Express* office. Local buses board principally at the train station, Rougier Street and on Piccadilly. The main **tourist office** is 200 yards west of the Minster in the De Grey Rooms, Exhibition Square (July & Aug Mon–Sat 9am–7pm, Sun 10am–6pm; April–June, Sept & Oct Mon–Sat 9am–6pm, Sun 10am–6pm; Nov–March Mon–Sat 9am–5pm, Sun 10am–2pm; ☎01532/621 756); there are smaller offices on the train station (April–Oct Mon–Sat 9.30am–8pm, Sun 11am–6pm; Nov–March Mon–Sat 9.30am–5.30pm, Sun 11am–5pm; ☎01904/621 756) and on Rougier Street (Mon–Sat 9am–6pm, Sun 10am–5pm; ☎01532/620 557).

YORK

△ A1036 Malton

△ A19 Thirsk

Black Swan Inn

St Anthony's Hall

JEWBURY

ST MAURICE'S ROAD

MONKGATE

ST JOHN STREET

LORD MAYOR'S WALK

Merchant Taylor's Hall

Bedern Hall

BEDERN

ALDWARK

ST ANDREWGATE

SAINT SAVIOURGATE

SPEN LANE

HUNDGATE

DUNDAS STREET

MONKGATE

Monk's Bar

St William's College

COLLEGE STREET

DEANGATE

GOODRAMGATE

GOODRAMGATE

600

KING'S SQUARE

COLLIERGATE

SHAMBLES

Open Air Market

Treasurer's House

Holy Trinity

LOW PETERGATE

GRAPE LANE

CHURCH STREET

PARLIAMENT STREET

Minster Library

Dean's Park

York Minster

MINSTER YARD

MINSTER YARD

St Michael-le-Belfrey

HIGH PETERGATE

LITTLE STONEGATE

STONEGATE

SWINEGATE

DAVYGATE

NEW STREET

CONEY STREET

Mansion House

CLAREMONT TERRACE

PORTLAND STREET

GILLYGATE

BOOTHAM ROW

Bootham Bar

EXHIBITION SQUARE

ST LEONARD'S PLACE

DUNCOMBE PLACE

BLAKE STREET

ST HELEN'S SQUARE

Library

Assembly Rooms

Guildhall

LENDAL

MUSEUM STREET

City Art Gallery

King's Manor

MARYGATE

St Mary's Abbey

The Yorkshire Museum

Museum Gardens

Lendal Bar

LENDAL BRIDGE

WELLINGTON ROW

BOOTHAM

SAINT MARY'S

GROSVENOR TERRACE

BOOTHAM TERRACE

MARYGATE

FREDERIC STREET

LONGFIELD TERRACE

SYCAMORE TERRACE

BOOTHAM TERRACE

QUEEN ANNE'S ROAD

LEEMAN ROAD

UNION TER

N

△ Youth Hostel

▽ (100yds)

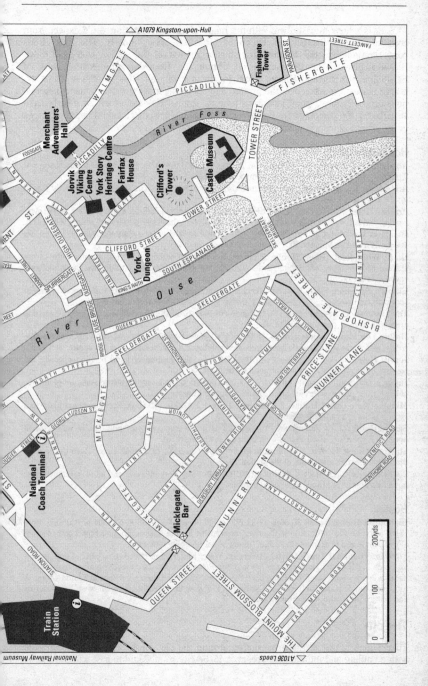

△ A1079 Kingston-upon-Hull

Fishergate Tower

FAWCETT STREET

PARAGON ST

PICCADILLY

FISHERGATE

WALMGATE

River Foss

TOWER STREET

FOSSGATE

Merchant Adventurers' Hall

PICCADILLY

Castle Museum

Jorvik Viking Centre

York Story Heritage Centre

Fairfax House

Clifford's Tower

CASTLEGATE

TOWER STREET

ST.

COPPERGATE

HIGH OUSEGATE

SPURRIERGATE

CLIFFORD STREET

KING STREET

OUSEGATE

York Dungeon

SOUTH ESPLANADE

KING'S RAITH

SKELDERGATE BRIDGE

TERRY AVENUE

River Ouse

Ouse

BRIDGE ST OUSE BRIDGE

QUEEN'S RAITH

SKELDERGATE

SKELDERGATE

ST DENYS ROAD

RICHMOND ST

CROMWELL ROAD

KYME STREET

NEWTON TERRACE

BAILE HILL TERRACE

CLEMENTHORPE

BISHOPGATE STREET

PRICE'S LANE

NUNNERY LANE

NORTH STREET

MICKLEGATE

FETTER LANE

BISHOPHILL JUNIOR

BISHOPHILL SENIOR

VICTOR STREET

FAIRFAX STREET

HAMPDEN STREET

LOWER PRIORY STREET

ST BENEDICT ROAD

ST BENEDICT ROAD

NORTHOLME ROAD

SWANN STREET

GEORGE HUDSON ST

TANNER ROW

National Coach Terminal ⓘ

TOFT GREEN

TRINITY LANE

PRIORY STREET

KINGSBURY TERRACE

Micklegate Bar

MICKLEGATE

NUNNERY LANE

DALE STREET

SCARCROFT LANE

STATION ROAD

QUEEN STREET

SOUTH PARADE

THE MOUNT

BLOSSOM STREET

MOSS STREET

EAST MOUNT ROAD

PARK STREET

Train Station ⓘ

0   100   200yds

△ A1036 Leeds

National Railway Museum

York is a busy tourist town, with the range of **accommodation** you'd expect, from countless cheap B&Bs to a clutch of top-notch luxury hotels. The main B&B concentrations are the **Mount** area (turn right out of the station and head down Blossom Street), the side streets off Clifton and **Bootham** (immediately west of Exhibition Square) and **Haxby Road** (north of town; take bus #1, #2a or #3). City-centre places are thinner on the ground and obviously in far greater demand; reservations are definitely a good idea from June to August. If you're stuck for a bed, make straight for the station or De Grey tourist offices; there's also a useful board of places in the station office window if you arrive after hours.

Hotels and B&Bs

Abbeyfields Guest House, 19 Bootham Terrace (☎01904/636 471). B&B in a Victorian house just 5 minutes' walk from the centre; all rooms with bathrooms and TV. ③.

Ambleside Guest House, 62 Bootham Crescent (☎01904/637 165). Quiet B&B perfectly placed for the city centre. ③.

Arndale Hotel, 290 Tadcaster Rd (☎01904/702 424). Highly commended hotel with walled garden overlooking the racecourse a mile south of the centre. Many rooms have four-posters and whirlpool baths. ③.

Bootham Bar Hotel, 4 High Petergate (☎01904/658 516). A refined eighteenth-century hotel just 100 yards from the Minster. ⑤.

Dairy Wholefood Guest House, 3 Scarcroft Rd (☎01904/639 367). Half a mile south of the station; rooms heavy on Habitat and Laura Ashley. Offers choice of traditional or wholefood/vegetarian breakfasts. ③.

Elliott's, Sycamore Place, Bootham Terrace (☎01904/623 333). Friendly, peaceful and convenient spot with comfy rooms, big breakfasts, good bar snacks and a fine restaurant. ④.

The Hazelwood, 24–25 Portland St, Gillygate (☎01904/626 548). Good rooms in a quiet residential area, with a small, pleasant garden. ④.

Holme Lea Manor Guest House, 18 St Peter's Grove, Bootham (☎01904/623 529). Comfortable rooms with period touches in a quiet, tree-lined cul-de-sac a few minutes from the centre. ③.

Jorvik Hotel, 72 Marygate, Bootham (☎01904/653 511). Extremely good position opposite the western entrance to St Mary's Abbey and gardens. ④.

Judge's Lodging, 9 Lendal (☎01904/638 733). Located in the lovely eighteenth-century residence of the former Assize Court judges; a minute from the Minster. ⑧.

Minster View Guest House, 2 Grosvenor Terrace (☎01904/655 034). Recommended place in a quiet position immediately west of the Minster. ③.

Saxon Hotel, 71–73 Fulford Rd (☎01904/622 106). Pleasant, very friendly family-run Victorian hotel off Fishergate, just a 10-min walk from the town centre. ④.

Staymor Guest House, 2 Southlands Rd (☎01904/626 935). In a small street close to the river three quarters of a mile south of the station. ②.

23 St Mary's, 23 St Mary's, Bootham (☎01904/622 738). Very pleasant and amiable family-house hotel just west of St Mary's Abbey and gardens. ⑤.

Hostels

Bishophill House Youth Hostel, 11–13 Bishophill Senior Rd (☎01904/625 904 or 630 613). Non-IYHF place on the south side of the river, convenient for the station, Rougier Street and old city. Dorm, single and twin rooms available; late-night bar and bike rental too.

York International Youth Hostel, Haverford, Water End, Clifton (☎01904/653 147). Large, superior-grade IYHF hostel , formerly the home of the Rowntrees, York's chocolate-making dynasty. It's about a 20-min walk along Bootham from the tourist office and then a left turn at Clifton Green. A nicer and quicker approach from the station is to follow the riverside footpath west. Small dorms and licence for alcohol with evening meal.

The city

Take a look at one of the maps dotted around the city centre and you're confronted with a baffling and intimidating prospect. If the city council and tourist office are to be believed, there are around sixty churches, museums and historic buildings crammed within York's walls. In fact the tally of things you really want to see is surprisingly limited, with most sights within easy walking distance of one another. Even so, it's hard to get round everything in less than two days, and equally difficult to stick to any rigid itinerary. The **Minster** is the obvious place to start, followed by the cluster of buildings that circle it; then you might cut south to the **Shambles**, central to the city's old centre and pedestrianized grid, or walk around **the walls** from the Minster to **Exhibition Square** and **Museum Street** for the city's art gallery, museum and St Mary's Abbey, evocative ruins surrounded by the city's loveliest gardens. Thereafter you could walk through the main shopping streets to take in the **Merchant Adventurers' Hall**, most striking of the city's smaller medieval buildings, then deal with **Clifford's Tower** and the nearby Jorvik Viking Centre and **Castle Museum**. Lastly, be sure to leave time to take in the slightly outlying **National Railway Museum**, a superb museum whose appeal goes way beyond railway memorabilia.

York Minster

York Minster (daily 7am–dusk; £1.50 donation requested) ranks as one of the country's most important sights, a fact not lost on the thousands who throng its colossal and, it must be said, strangely unatmospheric interior. Seat of the Archbishop of York, it is Britain's largest Gothic building and home to countless treasures, not least of which is the world's largest medieval stained-glass window and an estimated half of all the medieval stained glass in England. In addition to the main body of the church, any complete tour of the building, which took 250 years to complete, should also include the foundations, crypt, chapter house and the great central tower.

In its earliest incarnation the Minster was probably the wooden chapel used to baptize King Edwin of Northumbria in 627. After its stone successors were destroyed by the Danes, the first significant foundations were laid around 1080 by the first Norman archbishop, Thomas of Bayeaux. The oldest surviving fabric, in the south transept, dates from 1220 and the reign of Archbishop Walter de Grey, who also began work on a new north transept in 1260. A new **Chapter House** (Mon–Sat 10am–6.30pm, Sun 1–6.30pm; 60p), in the Decorated style, appeared in 1300, and a new nave in the same style was completed in 1338. The Perpendicular choir was realized in 1450 and the western towers in 1472. In 1480, the thirteenth-century central tower, which had collapsed in 1407, was rebuilt, bringing the Minster to more or less its present state.

In the 1960s, in the course of investigating subsidence that had begun to affect the building, it was found that the 20,000-ton, 234-foot central tower was resting on only a shallow bed of loose stones, a discovery which prompted a £2 million project that was to involve packing the foundations with thousands of tons of concrete and over six miles of reinforced steel rods. That wasn't the end of the church's troubles, though. In 1984 lightning struck the Minster, unleashing a disastrous fire which raged through the south transept, destroying the timber-framed central vault and all but two of its extraordinary roof bosses.

Nothing else in the Minster can match the magnificence of the **stained glass** in the nave and transepts. The West Window (1338) contains distinctive heart-shaped upper tracery (the "Heart of Yorkshire"), whilst in the nave's north aisle, the second bay window (1155) contains slivers of the oldest stained glass in the country. In the fifth bay notice the window showing Saint Peter attended by pilgrims (1312), with the funeral of a monkey among the fascinating details in its lower scenes. Moving down to the crossing, the north transept's Five Sisters Window is named after the five fifty-foot lancets, each glazed with thirteenth-century *grisaille*, a distinctive frosted, silvery-grey glass. Opposite, the south transept contains a sixteenth-century, 17,000-piece Rose Window, commemorating the 1486 marriage of Henry VII and Elizabeth of York, an alliance which marked the end of the War of the Roses.

The greatest of the church's 128 windows, however, is the majestic East Window (1405), at 78ft by 31ft the world's largest area of medieval stained glass in a single window. Its themes are the beginning and the end of the world, the upper panels showing scenes from the Old Testament, the lower sections mainly episodes from Revelations. Notice also the glass of the transeptal bays, midway down the south wall of the choir, with their scenes from the lives of saints Cuthbert and William of York. The tombs of William, a twelfth-century archbishop of York, and of Cuthbert, ordained bishop in 685, stood near the high altar until the Reformation, and were credited with numerous miracles.

Before leaving the main body of the interior, give some time to the north transept's four-hundred-year-old wooden clock with its oak knights, and the stone **choir screen**, knotted with incredibly intricate carvings and decorated with life-size figures of English monarchs from William I to Henry VI – all except the latter carved in the last quarter of the fifteenth century. Most of the choir dates from restorations following a fire in 1829. The painted **stone shields** round much of the nave and choir are those of Edward II and the barons who in 1309–10 held a "parliament" in York. Amongst the many **tombs**, those with most interest are the monument to Walter de Grey, a beautiful grey-green canopy protecting a recumbent stone figure in the south transept, and the tomb of the ten-year-old William, second son of Edward III, in the choir aisle.

Be sure also to go down to the **crypt** (60p), which transmits the most powerful sense of antiquity, as it contains portions of Archbishop Roger's choir and sections of the 1080 church, including pillars with fine Romanesque capitals. The font stands over the supposed site of Paulinus' timber chapel, while a small illuminated doorway opens onto the base of a pillar belonging to the guardhouse of the original Roman camp. The **foundations**, or undercroft, are more intriguing still (Mon–Sat 10am–6.30pm; Sun 1–6.30pm; £1.80). Most of the area's seven separate chambers are now a museum, fitted into a space excavated during the 1960s restoration, whose concrete consequences contrast with capitals, sculpture and fabric from the present Minster, its Norman predecessor, and the ancient Roman fort. Fragments of the last include the tribune where Constantine the Great was probably proclaimed emperor. Amongst the church relics in the adjoining treasury are silver plate found in Walter de Grey's tomb and the eleventh-century *Horn of Ulf*, presented to the Minster by a relative of King Canute.

Access to the foundations is from the south transept, also the entrance to the **Central Tower**, which you can climb for rooftop views over the city (daily 10am–6pm; £2). Finally, pop into the **Chapter House**, an architectural novelty whose buttressed octagonal walls remove the need for a central pillar, otherwise a common feature of this type of building (same hours as foundations; 60p).

Around the Minster

Past the Minster's west front a gateway leads into **Dean's Park**, a quiet green oasis bordered by a seven-arched fragment of arcade from the Norman archbishop's palace and by **York Minster Library** (Mon–Fri 9am–5pm; free), housed in the thirteenth-century chapel of the same palace. Among its more interesting exhibits is the baptismal entry for Guy Fawkes, removed from **St Michael-le-Belfry**, immediately south of the Minster. The church was built in 1536 and is bursting with seventeenth-century brasses and medieval stained glass.

Walk through Dean's Park with the Minster on your right, then through the gate at the top to reach the **Treasurer's House** in Chapter House Street, a glorious seventeenth-century town house that stands on the site of houses used by the Minster's treasurers until the Dissolution. Now owned by the National Trust, it offers exhibitions and videos which trace the site's changing fortunes, together with the paintings and furniture of industrialist Frank Green, who lived here from 1895 to 1930 (April–Oct daily 10.30am–5.30pm; £3).

Just around the corner in College Street stands **St William's College**, an eye-catching half-timbered building studded with oriel windows, initially dedicated to the great-grandson of William the Conqueror (first Archbishop of York) and built in its present guise in 1467 for the Minster's chantry priests. During Charles I's three-year residence it served time as the Royal Mint and the king's printing press; these days it is a conference hall and home of the more prosaic York Brass Rubbing Headquarters (Mon–Sat 10am–5pm, Sun 12.30–5pm).

The walls

Down from the college, College Street opens out into Goodramgate, with **Monk's Bar** at its northern end – tallest of the city's four main gates and a point of access to the city's superb **walls**. Although much restored, they date mainly from 1327–77 and the reign of Edward III, though fragments of Norman work survive, particularly in the gates (or "bars"), whilst the northern sections still follow the line of the Roman ramparts. The only break in the walls is east of Monk's Bar, where the city was first protected by the marshes of the River Foss and later by the deliberately flooded area known as King's Pool. As elsewhere in England the suffix "-gate" is a legacy of the Danes, derived from a Scandinavian word for street.

If you want just a taste of the walls' best section – with great views of the Minster and swathes of idyllic-looking gardens – take the ten-minute stroll west from Monk's Bar to Exhibition Square (see below) and **Bootham Bar**, the only gate on the site of a Roman gateway. A stroll round the walls' entire two-and-a-half-mile length will take you past the southwestern **Micklegate Bar**, built to a Norman design reputedly using ancient stone coffins as building stone. It was then used to exhibit the heads of executed criminals. **Walmgate Bar** in the east is the best-preserved and has traditionally been the city's strongest bar; it was unsuccessfuly undermined by the Roundheads during the Civil War, its present slight sag said to be a consequence of that episode.

Goodramgate and the Shambles

East of Goodramgate, in a confusing labyrinth of quiet residential streets, are clustered **Bedern Hall**, a medieval lodging for the Minster's priests; the plain-faced **St Anthony's Hall**, once home to the eponymous guild, and the **Merchant Taylors' Hall** and **Black Swan Inn**, both pictures of medieval half-timbered perfection. The Merchant Taylors' guild established a weaving workhouse to prevent "laytering and ydleness of vacabunds and poor follc"; a small upstairs museum explicates their good work (daily 8.30am–5pm; £1.80). At the south end of Goodramgate, **Our Lady's Row**, the oldest houses in the city (1316), stands hard against **Holy Trinity**, a much altered thirteenth-century church known for its east window, jumbled box pews and saddleback tower, an unusual feature in English churches.

The **Shambles**, off King's Square at the southern end of Goodramgate, could be taken as the epitome of medieval York, though the crowds and self-concious quaintness take the edge of what otherwise would be a perfect medieval thoroughfare. Flag-stoned, almost impossibly narrow and lined with perilously leaning houses, it was the home of York's butchers, its erstwhile stench and squalor now difficult to imagine, though old meat hooks still adorn the odd house. At no. 35, there's a **shrine** (closed to the public) to Margaret Clitherow, the Catholic wife of a butcher, martyred in 1586 for allegedly sheltering priests: she was pressed to death with rocks piled on top of a board on the city's Ouse Bridge. Newgate **market** lies off the Shambles, together with the core of the city's shopping streets.

Exhibition Square and Museum Street

Exhibition Square holds the city's main tourist office and provides the focus of a fine collection of sights. Dominating its southern flanks is the **City Art Gallery**, an extensive collection of British, early Italian and northern European paintings (Mon–Sat 10am–4.30pm, Sun 2.30–4.30pm; free). Most are decidedly second-division, but the gallery is worth a few minutes for its special exhibitions and twentieth-century British painters like Gwen John, Spencer and Sickert, all well represented on the end wall of the upstairs gallery. Look out in particular for the extraordinary G-strings and scarlet posing pouches in Stanley Spencer's Crucifixion scene.

Left of the gallery as you face it stands **King's Manor**, founded in 1270 and enlarged in 1490 to provide lodgings for the abbot of nearby St Mary's Abbey. After the Dissolution it was ceded to the Lord President of the Council of the North, effectively making it northern England's royal headquarters: Henry VIII, James I and Charles I all stayed here at one time or another. It's now a university hall of residence.

South of Exhibition Square on Museum Street stands the entrance to the **Yorkshire Museum** (April–Oct daily 10am–5pm; Nov–March Mon–Sat 10am–5pm, Sun 1–5pm; £3). The museum scores most highly on its archeological sections, which run from fragments of a Roman gateway and a reconstructed Roman kitchen through to impressive displays of Viking and Anglo-Saxon artefacts. Quite whether the medley is worth the admission, however, is open to question. Part of the museum basement incorporates the fireplace and chapter house of **St Mary's Abbey**, whose further ruins lie around the beautifully laid-out **Museum Gardens**, the abbey's former grounds (abbey and gardens free). Founded around 1080 by Stephen of Lastingham (see p.518) and enlarged by William Rufus, the abbey became an important Benedictine foundation, additionally significant as it was from here that disenchanted monks fled to found Fountains Abbey (see p.499). The fact that the abbey controlled the city's brothels at the time can hardly have helped the Benedictine cause.

Directly opposite the museum and garden entrance, Lendal leads off Museum Street to a trio of notable civic buildings, first of which is the **Assembly Rooms** on Blake Street, built between 1732 and 1736 by the third Earl of Burlington, one of England's earliest champions of Palladianism. An epicentre of chic during York's eighteenth-century social heyday, the building attempted to emulate London's grander salons; its 52-columned Central Hall is a tribute to the Egyptian Hall of the capital's Mansion House. Be sure to search the rotundas's mural of Roman York, in which Burlington had himself painted as Constantine the Great. York's own **Mansion House** (by appointment only), built in 1725 and private home of the city's mayor, is in St Helen's Square, formerly the city's main Roman gate. The 600-year-old **Guildhall** behind was almost totally destroyed by bombing in 1942, but has been restored to an almost mirror image of its original, timber-roofed state (May–Oct Mon–Thurs 9am–5pm, Fri 9am–4pm, Sat 10am–5pm, Sun 2–5pm; Nov–April closed Sat & Sun; free).

Walk down Davygate from St Helen's Square to the musty church of **St Mary's Pavement**, worth a glance for its wooden ceiling and old glass. Beyond the church on the left is the entrance to the **Merchant Adventurers' Hall**, where the overpowering whiff of wood polish prepares you for one of the finest medieval timber-framed halls in Europe (mid-March to mid-Nov daily 8.30am–5pm; mid-Nov to mid-March Mon–Sat 8.30am–3pm; £1.80). The beautiful building was raised by the city's most powerful guild, dealers in wool from the Wolds, woollens from the Dales and lead from the Pennines, commodities that were traded for exotica from far and wide. An icon brought back from Russia gives some some idea of the organization's commercial scope.

York Castle and around

York's final group of monuments cluster around **York Castle**, something of a misnomer, because little survives of the fortress, one of two established by William the Conqueror. The perilously leaning **Clifford's Tower**, though, is as evocative a piece of military engineering as you could wish for: a stark and isolated stone keep built on one of William's mottes between 1245 and 1262 (daily April–Sept 10am–6pm; Oct–March

10am–4pm or dusk; £1.50; EH). The old Norman keep was destroyed in 1109 during one of the city's more shameful historical episodes, when 150 Jews were put inside the tower for their own protection during an outburst of anti-Semitic rioting. The move did little to appease the mob, however, and faced with starvation or slaughter the Jews committed mass suicide by setting the tower on fire.

Immediately east of the tower lies the excellent **Castle Museum** (April–Oct Mon–Sat 9.30am–5.30pm, Sun 10.30am–5.30pm; Nov–March Mon–Sat 9.30am–4pm, Sun 10.30am–4pm; £4.20), a remarkable collection founded by a Dr Kirk of Pickering, who realized, even eighty years ago, that many of the everyday items used in rural areas were in danger of disappearing. He took the unusual step of accepting bric-a-bric from his patients in lieu of fees. A whole range of early craft, folk and agricultural ephemera is now complemented by costumes, militaria, workshops and two entire reconstructed streets. In particular look for the lovely corridor of old hearths and fireplaces, Kirk's fetishistic collections of truncheon and biscuit moulds, and some magnificently archaic televisions and washing machines. Be certain to take a look upstairs at the military displays and the rambling dungeons and period rooms, all of which are well worth seeing. Pride of place in this upper section is a dazzling **Viking helmet**, discovered during the Coppergate excavations and the only one of its kind ever found.

If Kirk's legacy is an old-style museum at its best, the castle's other nearby distractions, by contrast, are firmly in the Disney mould. Best known is Coppergate's horrendously over-visited **Jorvik Viking Centre** (daily April–Oct 9am–7pm; Nov–March 9am–5.30pm; £4.25), a multi-million pound affair that takes you on a twenty-minute ride back through time to experience the sights, smells and sounds of a riverside Viking village – with the voice of Magnus Magnusson for company. Get here bang on opening time to have any chance of beating the queues, and leave time to potter around the site museum, devoted to artefacts found during excavations of Coppergate's real Viking village, now lost beneath a monumentally awful shopping centre.

In a similar mode, but less persuasive are the nearby Friargate Wax Museum, the predictably salacious Dungeon Museum in Clifford Street, and the more informative **York Story Heritage Centre** on Castlegate (Mon–Sat 10am–5pm, Sun 1–5pm; same ticket as Castle Museum). If the Centre's "100 Years of History" doesn't appeal, drop into the adjacent **Fairfax House**, recently restored to take an eighteenth-century collection of fine arts left by Noel Terry, scion of one of the city's chocolate dynasties.

National Railway Museum

The **National Railway Museum** on Leeman Road (Mon–Sat 10am–6pm, Sun 11am–6pm; £4.20), ten minutes' walk from the station, is a must if you have even the slightest interest in railways, history, engineering or Victoriana. It's a huge museum in the modern mould, and has already won a Museum of the Year award. The main hall contains some fifty locomotives dating from 1829 onwards, all stunningly restored, among them the *Mallard*, at 126mph the world's fastest steam engine. This machine and many others are still in working order, and pull steam specials all over the country on Wednesdays and Saturdays during the summer. There's also plenty of rolling stock, some from as early as 1797, the plush splendour of the royal carriages and the bleak segregation of classes in the Victorian coaches being particularly eye-opening.

Eating, drinking and nightlife

In keeping with much else in the city, most of the pubs are relentlessly and self-consciously old-fashioned, though the majority serve perfectly good lunchtime snacks and evening meals. The tea shops are also much of a muchness, with the exception of *Betty's*, the ultimate tea-and-scones experience. If you want something at the higher end of the culinary spectrum, the city also has a scattering of well-regarded restaurants, though most spots are mid-range places aimed at the average tourist and the less than well-heeled student. Students also provide the impetus for healthy helpings of live music and nightlife, much of it detailed in free weekly handouts *York Journal What's On* and *YourKmusic*.

Snacks and cafés

Betty's, St Helen's Square. If there are tea shops in heaven they'll be like *Betty's*, a York institution founded in 1919 and now with over 400 items on its menu, nearly all of them home-made; a dozen or so fish and meat hot dishes – not to mention extraordinary puddings – make *Betty's* as enticing in the evenings as it is during the day. There's also a shop where you can buy fine-grade teas and coffees, and some of the tea-shop staples – like pikelets and Yorkshire fat rascals. Daily 9am–9pm.

Miller's Yard Vegetarian Restaurant, Gillygate. Good-value vegetarian food from a sparsely decorated workers' co-op that uses organic ingredients wherever possible; a takeaway service is also available.

Oscar's, 8 Little Stonegate. Unassuming from the outside, this bustling bistro has an excellent varied menu and a courtyard for alfresco eating; a pub atmosphere at lunchtime, more laid-back in the evening. Daily 11am–10pm.

Taylor's, 46 Stonegate. Pricier than some places, but owned by *Betty's* and in the same league; over 100 years old, it's the picture of a classic tea shop.

Restaurants

Kites, 13 Grape Lane (☎01904/641 750). The food has been described as "hippy gourmet", the atmosphere is correspondingly laid-back. Moderate to expensive.

Lawries, 2 Jubbergate. The city's finest deli downstairs and a reasonably priced café-restaurant upstairs in a lovely half-timbered building. Moderate.

Melton's, 7 Scarcroft Rd (☎01904/634 341). Simple, classy cooking; very good fish and poultry dishes, and imaginative vegetarian food too – Thurs is non-meat day. Expensive.

19 Grape Lane, 19 Grape Lane (☎01904/636 366). Cramped but renowned restaurant serving top-quality modern British food. Expensive.

The Rubicon, 5–7 Little Stonegate. Good non-smoking, unlicensed vegetarian restaurant. Inexpensive to moderate.

Pubs

Black Swan, Peasholme Green. York's oldest pub and a Grade II listed building with some superb sixteenth-century features. Reasonable lunchtime food.

Fox Inn, Holgate Rd. Informal, comfortable pub, founded in 1776 and sympathetically restored.

Golden Ball, Cromwell Rd, Bishophill. Perhaps the city centre's nicest and most archetypal "local"; nice beer garden tucked away at the back.

Hole in the Wall, High Petergate. Very close to the Minster, yet rarely crowded; very friendly, and mighty portions of good bar food.

King's Arms, King's Staithe. Close to the Ouse Bridge, this pub has a fine riverside setting – and accordingly gets very busy in summer.

Lowther, King's South. A widely revered and reviled pub; *the* meeting place for students, alternative types and assorted lowlife.

Spread Eagle, Walmgate. One of the city's most popular old-fashioned pubs; lunchtime and early evening food and occasional live music.

Nightlife

Most bigger bands bypass the city, but the **pub-music** scene flourishes and there are a few biggish local venues – the best are the *Bonding Warehouse*, Skeldergate, *Fibbers*, Stonebow and the *Spotted Cow*, the last also a venue for some of York's better club nights. Jazz and folk crop up in pubs like the *Black Swan* on Peasholme Green and the *Punch Bowl* on Stonegate. The **York Arts Centre** (☎01904/627 129) south of the river on Micklegate also hosts more esoteric gigs, as well as less mainstream theatre. Musicals, pantos and more upmarket theatre find their home in the *Theatre Royal*, St Leonard's Place (☎01904/623 568).

Humberside

An artificial creation cobbled together in 1974 from parts of Lincolnshire and Yorkshire's old East Riding, **HUMBERSIDE** nevertheless has a distinct character, distinguished by a strong seafaring tradition – exemplified by **Hull** and Grimsby – and by the flatlands that stretch northwards from Hull to meet the Yorkshire Wolds, a crescent-shaped ridge of hills that falls to the sea at Flamborough Head. Lonely beaches, wild foreshores and forgotten seafront villages provide further coastal attractions, especially if you're here to indulge in birdwatching, but the region's resorts – Filey, Bridlington and Cleethorpes – are now rather melancholy places. **Beverley**, the area's only town worth visiting for its own sake, can be reached by infrequent **bus** from York or by bus from Hull, which is linked to Doncaster on the main London–York **train** line.

Hull

HULL's most famous adopted son, the poet Philip Larkin, wrote: "I wish I could think of just one nice thing to tell you about Hull, oh yes . . . *it's very nice and flat for cycling,*" capturing something of the character of a town fixed in the national psyche as a place of terminal dullness. The town – rarely known by its full grandiose title of Kingston-upon-Hull – undoubtedly suited the poet's curmudgeonly temperament, but he might have mentioned Hull's self-reliant and no-nonsense atmosphere, or that the docks and old centre, now being restored after years of neglect, are surprisingly appealing, boasting one of England's largest parish churches and a couple of decent museums.

Hull's maritime pre-eminence dates back to 1299, when it was laid out as a seaport by Edward I. It quickly became England's leading harbour, and was still a vital garrison when it refused to admit Charles I in 1642, the first overt act of rebellion of what was to become the English Civil War. Close links with the sea continue – Ross and Bird's Eye fish-processing plants are still major employers – and the town's maritime legacy is detailed in the **Town Docks Museum** (Mon–Sat 10am–5pm, Sun 1.30–4.30pm; free), located at the town's epicentre on the east side of Queen Victoria Square, immediately north of Prince's dock (300yds east of the train station). Marine art lurks across the road in the **Ferens Art Gallery** (Mon–Sat 10am–5pm, Sun 1.30–4.30pm; free), distinguished by twentieth-century British pieces and the odd Old Master from Constable, Frans Hals and Canaletto.

Leave Queen Victoria Square on its east side by Whitefriar Gate side, turn right on Trinity Lane after two hundred yards, and you're in front of **Holy Trinity**, among the largest parish churches in the country. Its transepts and chancel, notable for their early use of brick, date from around 1300, the nave from a century later, the central tower a century after that. Outside stands the oldest secular building to have survived the World War II bombing that destroyed some ninety percent of Hull – the **Old Grammar School** (same hours as Ferens Gallery; free), built in 1538, and now a small museum of local life, archives and period photographs.

Hull **tourist office** is in the Central Library on Albion Street (Mon 10am–8pm, Tues–Thurs 9am–8pm, Fri 9am–5.30pm, Sat 9am–4.30pm; ☎01482/223 344). The most central **B&B** options are the *Clyde House Hotel*, 13 John St, Kingston Square (☎01482/ 214 981; ③) and the family-run *Pines Hotel*, 138 Spring Bank (☎01482/215 477; ③); more upmarket is the *Royal Hotel*, 170 Ferensway (☎01482/325 087; ⑦). For **restaurants**, Hull's best includes the expensive *Cerutti's*, on Nelson Street (☎01482/328 501) overlooking the Humber, and the top-quality, moderately priced, Italian restaurant *Operetta*, 56–58 Bond St (☎01482/218 687). Veggies should head for the *Tropicana*, on Beverley Road, which serves delicious Malaysian dishes. Of Hull's many **pubs**, the historical *Old White Harte*, 25 Silver St is a student favourite; less busy but just as atmospheric is the *Old Blue Bell*, Market Place. Hull's **clubs** are cheap, unpretentious and fun: the *Adelphi*, 89 De Grey St is a student stalwart, *Spiders* on Cleveland Street caters for the Goth population, and the more mellow *Welly Club* is on Wellington Lane.

Beverley

If Hull's somewhere you can either take or leave, **BEVERLEY** by contrast ranks as one of northeast England's premier towns, its Minster the superior of many an English cathedral, its tangle of old streets, cobbled lanes and elegant Georgian and Victorian terraces the very picture of a traditional market town. Over 350 buildings are listed as possessing historical or architectural merit, and though you could see its first-rank offerings in a morning this is one of a handful of places in this part of the world that you might want to stay in for its own sake. Beverley is most easily reached by bus from Hull, though there are also two or three buses daily from York as well.

Approaches to the town are dominated by **Beverley Minster's** twin towers, visible for miles across the wolds and airy flatlands (Mon–Sat 9am–dusk, Sun 2.30am–5pm). Initiated as a modest chapel, the minster became a monastery under John of Beverley, Bishop of York, buried here in 721 and canonized in 1037. Fires and the collapse of the central tower in 1213 paved the way for two centuries of rebuilding, funded by bequests from pilgrims paying homage to the saint, and the result was one of the finest Gothic creations in the country. The **west front**, which crowned the work in 1420, is widely considered without equal, its survival due in large part to Baroque architect Nicholas Hawksmoor, who restored much of the church in the eighteenth century.

Similar outstanding work awaits in the **interior**, most notably the **Percy Tomb** on the north side of the altar, thought to be the tomb of Lady Idoine Percy (d. 1365), its sumptuously carved canopy one of the masterpieces of medieval European ecclesiastical art. Alongside it on the right stands the **Fridstol**, a "sanctuary chair" dating from Athelstan's reign (924–39) which provided safe haven for men on the run. The north transept – aisled, like the transepts at York Minster – harbours another remarkable tomb, behind the second column on the right as you stand with your back to the main altar, bearing the effigy of an unknown fourteenth-century priest. Other incidental carving throughout the church is magnificent, much of it on a musical theme, particularly the 68 misericords of the oak **choir** (1520–24), one of the largest and most accomplished in England. John of Beverley is buried in the crossing at the top of the nave, and you should take time to study the doughty Norman **font** on the right of the nave.

Beverley's other great church, **St Mary's**, nestles alongside the **North Bar**, sole survivor of the town's five medieval gates. A chapel once attached to the Minster, it's a tantalizing amalgam of styles, from the south porch's Norman arch to the thirteenth-century chancel and fifteenth-century Perpendicular elements of the tower and nave. Inside, the chancel's painted panelled ceiling (1445) contains portraits of English kings from Sigebert (623–37) to Henry VI, executed at about the same time as the eye-catching rood screen and misericords. Amidst the carvings, the favourite novelty is the so-called **Pilgrim's Rabbit**, said to have been the inspiration for the White Rabbit in Lewis Carroll's *Alice in Wonderland*.

Practicalities

The **tourist office** is in the Guildhall on Register Square (April–Oct Mon–Fri 9.30am–5.30pm, Sat 9.30am–5pm, Sun 10am–2pm; Nov–March Mon–Fri 9.30am–5.30pm, Sat 10am–4pm; ☎01482/867 430). The least expensive **B&Bs** are at 4 Ellerker Rd (☎01482/868 617; ②) and at 45 Grove Park (☎01482/867 871; ②). Two **guest houses** stand out: the central *Eastgate*, 7 Eastgate (☎01482/868 464; ②), and *Oak House*, 43 North Bar Without (☎01482/881 481; ③). Of the **pubs**, the *Windmill Inn*, 53 Lairgate (☎01482/862 817; ③) has a dozen rooms for rent. The **youth hostel** (☎01482/881 751) occupies a restored Dominican friary that was mentioned in the *Canterbury Tales*; it's located in Friar's Lane, off Eastgate, just a hundred yards southeast of the Minster.

The North York Moors

Virtually the whole of the **North York Moors**, from the Hambleton and Cleveland hills in the west to the cliff-edged coastline, is protected by one of the country's ten national parks. The moors are lonely, heather-covered, flat-topped hills cut by deep, steep-sided valleys, and views here stretch for miles, interrupted only by giant cultivated forests, pale shadows of the woodland that covered the region before it was cleared by Neolithic and later tribes. Barrows and ancient forts provide memorials of these early settlers, mingling on the high moorland with the Roman remains of **Wades Causeway**, the battered stone crosses of the first Christian inhabitants, and the ruins of great monastic houses such as **Rievaulx**.

The **western moors** are preceded by several appealing villages and historic monuments, notably **Castle Howard**, best seen from **Helmsley**, one of the two pivotal centres in the park's southern reaches. The **central moors** offer the best walking and the most noted landscapes, principally Bransdale, Farndale and Rosedale, with Helmsley or **Pickering** equally good bases. **Hutton-le-Hole** is perhaps the perfect picture-postcard village in the region, closely followed by **Thornton-le-Dale**. Popular long-distance paths cross the park, notably the **Cleveland Way**, which follows the coast and northern moors, and the **Lyke Wake** and **Coast to Coast** walks.

The northern moors, traversed by just a handful of mostly minor roads, are best approached by steam, using the **North York Moors Railway** between Pickering and the Grosmont BR station, one of the most scenic lines in Britain. Be sure to pick up the free *Moors Connecter*, a summary of all rail and **bus routes** on and around the moors, available from tourist offices and park information centres. On Sundays from May 30 to September 26 there are also special **Moorbus** services, running between points not usually served by public transport.

The western moors

The **western moors** are marked on their western edge by the scarp of the Hambleton Hills – crowned by the Cleveland Way – and the ruler-straight line of the A19 road between Middlesbrough and **Thirsk**, a useful railhead for the region. To the east they are closed by Rye Dale, one of the region's more bucolic valleys, and the B1267 from **Helmsley**, by far the area's nicest village and its best base for explorations. Most outings are likely to centre less on the scenery – except for the walks and staggering views from **Sutton Bank** on the A170 – than on a cluster of historic buildings, of which the most prepossessing is **Rievaulx Abbey**, easily seen from Helmsley, as is **Castle Howard**, one of England's greatest Baroque creations. It's closely followed by **Mount Grace Priory**, to the north of Thirsk, and then by Osgodby Hall, Shandy Hall, **Byland Abbey**, Newburgh Priory and **Nunnington Hall**, grouped conveniently close together on a minor road loop from Thirsk to Helmsley – an alternative to the A170.

Coxwold and Byland Abbey

The first diversion if you're following the main A170 route from Thirsk to Scarborough is **COXWOLD**, as attractive a little village as they come. The majority of its many visitors are here on a literary pilgrimage, come to pay homage to the novelist **Laurence Sterne**, who is buried by the south wall in the churchyard of **St Michael's**, where he was vicar from 1760 until his death in 1768. The church, with its odd octagonal tower, is worth closer scrutiny, particularly the three-decker pulpit and medieval stained glass,

---

WALKS FROM SUTTON BANK

The main A170 road enters the National Park as it climbs five hundred feet in half a mile to **Sutton Bank** (960ft), a phenomenal viewpoint whose panorama extends across the Vale of York to the Pennines on the far horizon. At the top stands a lavish North York Moors **National Park Information Centre** (April–Oct daily 10am–5pm; Nov–March Sat & Sun 11am–4pm; ☎0845/597 426), full of background on the short but superlative waymarked walks you can make from here.

Sutton Bank lies at the end of the **Cleveland Way** (see p.522), which provides the main path **north**. You can follow this along the top of a wooded escarpment before doubling back via Dailstone Farm (4 miles; 1hr 30min), but a more varied loop (2.5 miles; 2hr), part of the **Sutton Bank Nature Trail**, drops steeply through woodland from the Cleveland Way after half a mile to **Gormire**, the National Park's only natural lake, a mysterious sheet of water with no visible inlets or outlets – local legend claims it hides an entire village.

To the **south** of the A170 the marked **White Horse Nature Trail** (2.5 miles; 1hr 30min) skirts the crags of Roulston Scar, passing the Yorkshire Gliding Club en route to the **Kilburn White Horse**, northern England's only turf-cut figure – but unlike its ancient southern counterparts, a rather sham affair cut in 1857 and only white because it's covered in imported chalk chippings. You could make a real walk of it by dropping a couple of miles down to **Kilburn** village, synonymous with woodcarving since the days of "Mouse Man" Robert Thompson (d. 1955), whose woodcarvings – marked by his distinctive mouse motif – are found in York Minster and Westminster Abbey.

---

but most people head for **Shandy Hall** (house June–Sept Wed 2–4.30pm, Sun 2.30–4.30pm; gardens June–Sept daily except Sat 11am–4.30pm; house and gardens £2.50, gardens only £1.50), Sterne's home, now a museum crammed with literary memorabilia. It was here that he wrote *A Sentimental Journey through France and Italy* and the wonderfully eccentric *The Life and Opinions of Tristram Shandy, Gentleman*, which prompted Samuel Johnson loftily and misguidedly to declare "nothing odd will last".

Of the village's many lovely buildings, the *Fauconburg Arms*, a superb old **pub** in Main Street, has the most to recommend it – it has a restaurant and **rooms** too (☎013476/214; ④). The pub is named after the Viscount who married Mary, daughter of Oliver Cromwell, whom he brought to live in **Newburgh Priory**, half a mile south of the village (April to mid-June Wed & Sun 2–6pm; £3.50). Raised on the site of an Augustinian monastery founded in 1150, the house is famous for reputedly containing a **tomb** with the headless body of **Oliver Cromwell**. The story claims that Mary brought her father's body here after it was exhumed from Westminster Abbey in readiness to be "executed" at Tyburn in revenge for Cromwell's part in the Civil War. Resourceful Mary is supposed to have exchanged Oliver's corpse with that of some ordinary Joe, but it's not quite clear how this tale can be made to tally with the fact that Oliver's body had been mummified before its burial, and thus would have been expected to resemble the recently deceased leader.

Laurence Sterne talked of "A delicious Walk of Romance" from Coxwold to **Byland Abbey**, founded by Cistercians in 1177 just two miles northeast of the village (April–Sept daily 10am–6pm; Oct daily 10am–4pm; Nov–March Wed–Sun 10am–4pm; £1.30; EH). His description captures the appeal of the ruins, which though larger in ground area than the Cistercian houses at Fountains and Rievaulx, are far less well preserved, leaving the haunting location and stark west front as the abbey's most memorable aspects. Other colossal but skeletal remains include the lay brothers "lane", a rare example of the corridor which kept abbey servants at a remove from the cloister and the ordained monks. Equally unusual are some fine thirteenth-century green-and-yellow tiled floors, seen to best effect in the south transept chapels.

Nunnington Hall

Moving eight miles due east from Byland through Ampleforth – famous for its Catholic public school – and Oswaldkirk brings you to **Nunnington Hall** (April–Oct Tues–Thurs & Sat 2–6pm, Sun noon–6pm, July & Aug also Fri 2–6pm; £3.50, garden only £1; NT), a part-Tudor manor house stranded in the flats of lower Rye Dale about six miles south of Helmsley. The pannelled bedrooms and vast main hall are impressive, but the principal diversion is the famous **Carlisle Collection**, 22 miniature rooms each furnished and decorated in different styles. The house, woods and gardens are all supposed to be haunted, though the most notable presence are peacocks strutting the garden lawns. The only public transport is the *Scarborough & District* **bus** #128 between Helmsley and Scarborough, which stops at **Wombleton**, three miles away.

Castle Howard

Immersed in the deep countryside of the Howardian Hills ten miles south of Helmsley, **Castle Howard** (March–Nov daily 10am–5pm; £6, grounds only £4) is the seat of one of England's leading aristocratic families and among the country's grandest stately homes. After breasting a straggling line of circular walls marking the estate's thousand-acre extent, roads from any of the above towns enter clipped parkland and tidy country-side dotted with towers, obelisks and blunt sandstone follies that peek above the trees. Designed by Vanbrugh in 1699 and almost forty years in the making, the colossal main house is full of furniture by Sheraton and Chippendale, paintings by the likes of Gainsborough, Veronese, Rubens and Van Dyck, and room after room of decorative excess – all trinkety *objets d'art*, gaudy friezes and monumental pilasters. Outside, the stables have been converted into the **Costume and Regalia Gallery**, Britain's largest private collection of period clothes. Gracious formal gardens stretch in all directions, sloping gently in one direction to a large artifical lake, and in the other to the distant, Hawksmoor-designed Howard family mausoleum. Public transport to the house is poor; in summer there are just two *Yorkshire Coastliner* **buses** a day (1 on Sun) from York, and three (1 on Sun) from Malton and Pickering.

Helmsley

One of the moors' most appealing villages, **HELMSLEY** makes a perfect base for the western moors, and if you have transport, for the central moors as well. Local life revolves around a large cobbled market square (market day is Fri), dominated by a vaunting monument to the second Earl of Feversham, whose family were responsible for rebuilding most of the village in the last century. Close to the square, overlooking the village's western fringe, is **Helmsley Castle**, its unique twelfth-century D-shaped keep ringed by massive earthworks (April–Oct daily 10am–4pm; Nov–March Wed–Sun 10am–4pm; £2; EH). After a three-month siege during the Civil War it was "slighted" by Sir Thomas Fairfax, the Parliamentary commander, and much of its stone was plundered by townspeople for local houses.

To the southwest of the village, overlooking a wooded meander of the Rye, stands the Fevershams' country seat, **Duncombe Park**, probably designed by Vanbrugh at about the same time as Castle Howard (April & Oct Wed & Sun; May & June Wed–Sun; July–Sept daily; house and gardens 11am–4.30pm on these days; parkland and shop 10.30am–5pm on these days; house, gardens and parkland £4.50; gardens and parkland £2.75; parkland only £1). The grounds are more appealing than the house, boasting swathes of landscaped gardens, including Britain's tallest ash and lime trees.

You can reach Helmsley by *Stephenson's* **bus** #94 from Malton, #57 from York and #141 from Thirsk; from Scarborough take the *Scarborough & District* #128. There's a **tourist office** in the town hall on the Market Place (April–Oct daily 9.30am–6pm; Nov–March Sat & Sun 10am–4pm; ☎01439/770173), with information on the two

long-distance footpaths from the village: the Cleveland Way and the **Ebor Way**, a gentle seventy-mile route to Ilkley that links with the Dales Way.

There's plenty of other **accommodation**, including the classy *Feversham Arms*, 1 High St (☎01439/770 766; ⑤), and *Feathers Hotel*, 1 Market Place (☎01439/770 275; ⑥). If you're not treating yourself, go for B&B at 20 Ashdale Rd (☎01439/7703 24; ③) or 41 Ashdale Rd (☎01439/770 488; ③). The purpose-built **youth hostel** (☎01439/770 433) is a quarter of a mile east of the Market Place at the junction of Carlton Road and Carlton Lane. Best place for a snack, light lunch or seriously priced dinner is *Monet's*, 19 Bridge St – it has a lovely terrace for alfresco eating, and has rooms for rent (☎01439/770 618; ⑤). The *Black Swan* on the main square is also well known for teas and good, if pricey, evening meals.

Rievaulx Abbey and Terrace

From Helmsley you can hike the opening two miles of the Cleveland Way then half a mile through Rievaulx village to **Rievaulx Abbey**, once one of England's greatest Cistercian abbeys, and with 200,000 visitors a year, the most heavily visited historic building on the moors (daily April–Sept 10am–6pm; Oct–March 10am–4pm; £1.80; EH). Founded in 1132, the abbey became the mother-church of the Cistercians in England (see p.499), quickly developing from a series of rough shelters on the deeply wooded banks of the Rye to become a flourishing community with interests in fishing, mining, agriculture and the woollen industry. Nemesis came with the Dissolution, when many of the walls were razed and the roof lead stripped – the beautiful ruins, however, still suggest the abbey's former splendour. They are at their best in the triple-arched nave, oriented from north to south instead of the conventional west-east axis because of the valley's sloping site. The *Tees & Middlesbrough* #294 **bus** runs from Helmsley to Rievaulx (Fri only).

Although they form some sort of ensemble with the abbey, there's no access between the ruins and **Rievaulx Terrace and Temples** (April–Oct daily 10.30am–6pm or dusk; £2.50; NT), a site entered from the B1257. This half-mile stretch of grass-covered terraces and woodland was laid out as part of Duncombe Park in the 1750s, and as with Studley Royal at Fountains, the Terrace was engineered partly to enhance the views of the abbey. The resulting panorama over the ruins and the valley below are superb, and this makes a great spot for a picnic or simply for strolls along

---

THE LYKE WAKE WALK

One of England's more macho long-distance paths, the **Lyke Wake Walk** was founded in 1955 as a light-hearted idea: anyone who completed the forty-mile hike in less than 24 hours became a member of the Lyke Wake Club and qualified for a badge in the shape of a coffin. As word spread it became something of a cult, the net result being deeply eroded paths and mountains of litter – to the extent that the National Park authority discourages large groups. The path isn't marked on most maps for the same reason. Although still the most popular walk on the moors, it has recently become less choked with groups, and is complemented by another trans-moors route, Wainwright's similarly controversial Coast to Coast walk.

The Lyke Wake starts at **Osmotherely** (like the North York Moors section of Wainwright's walk) and shadows the Cleveland Way for a while along the northern edge of the Cleveland Hills before dropping to the sea at Ravenscar by way of Fylingdales. It links numerous prehistoric sites, following the age-old tracks of monks, miners and smugglers. The path's **name**, incidentally, comes from a dialect poem, the *Lyke Wake Dirge*, the story of a journey across one of the "burial routes" that linked the Moors' ancient burial mounds. It recalls the ancient practice of waking (keeping vigil) over a dead body (the lyke).

the lawns and woodland trail. Tuscan and Ionic Temples lie at opposing ends of the Terrace, the latter with a fine painted ceiling, excellent furniture and a permanent exhibition on eighteenth-century English landscape design.

Mount Grace Priory

Ten miles north of Thirsk, the fourteenth-century **Mount Grace Priory** (daily mid-April to Sept 10am–6pm; Oct 10am–4pm; £2.20; NT & EH), the most important of England's nine Carthusian ruins and the only one in Yorkshire, provides a striking contrast to its more grandiose and worldly Cistercian counterparts. The Carthusians took a vow of silence and lived, ate and prayed alone in their two-storey cells, each separated from its neighbour by a privy, small garden and high walls. The incumbents were given their meals through a hatch, specially angled to prevent the monks from seeing their waiters. The foundations of the cells are still clearly visible, together with one which has been reconstructed to suggest its original layout and the monks' way of life. Other substantial remains include the ruins of the gatehouse and the walls and tower of the priory church, which divides the site's two main courtyards.

Once you've seen the priory don't overlook the nearby **Lady Chapel**, nor some great short walks, notably along the Cleveland Way north of the ruins to the 982-foot summit of Scarth Wood Moor and then down to Cod Beck Reservoir (3 miles; 1hr). If you're heading for the priory by car it's best to use the minor road which crosses Osmotherley Moor and the Cleveland Hills to the east and then follows Rye Dale to Helmsley, a neat way of seeing a good slice of the western moors. By public transport catch a **train** to **Northallerton**, six miles to the southwest, and then the *United-Tees & District* **bus** from Northallerton to Middlesbrough (Mon–Sat 9 daily), alighting at Priory Road End, half a mile from the priory.

The central moors

The **central moors**, bounded by Rye Dale in the west and by Newton Dale in the east, form the heart of the North York Moors. They contain their highest, wildest moors, such as Baydale, Westerdale and Wheeldale, and their most attractive valleys: Bransdale, loneliest and least-known; **Farndale**, renowned for its spring swathes of daffodils; **Rosedale**, fringed by the dark depths of Cropton Forest; and **Newton Dale**, traversed by the privately run **North York Moors Railway**. The line may well be the only part of the region you'll see unless you hike or have access to a car or bike, for public transport is all but unheard of, linking only the main centres – Helmsley, Kirkbymoorside and **Pickering**, the last the railway's southern terminus and the best overnight base unless you plump for B&B options in the Dales or fight for accommodation in the Moors premier showpiece village, **Hutton-le-Hole**. Also within easy reach of Pickering is **Thornton-le-Dale**, another high-ranking contender for prettiest village in Yorkshire, and **Dalby Forest**, whose unending ranks of conifers are redeemed by a superb forest drive and a large number of specially marked trails.

Hutton-le-Hole and Lastingham

One of Yorkshire's quaintest villages, **HUTTON-LE-HOLE** has become so great a tourist attraction that you'll have to come off-season to get much pleasure from its tidy gardens, its stream crossed village green and the sight of sheep wandering freely through the lanes. Apart from the sheer photogeneity of the place, the big draw is the **Ryedale Folk Museum** (Easter–Oct daily 10am–5.30pm; £2.50), an ever-expanding set of displays over a two-acre site. Local life is documented from the era of prehistoric flint tools, through Romano-British artefacts and pottery, to a series of reconstructed buildings, notably a sixteenth-century house, a glass furnace, a crofter's cottage and a nineteenth-century blacksmith's shop. The museum also houses an **information** centre (Easter–Oct daily 10am–5.30pm; ☎01751/417 367). Try to **stay** at the village's *Burnley House Hotel* (☎01751/417 548; ③), a fine Georgian house; there's alternative accommodation at the less smart *Barn Hotel* (☎0751/417 311; ③), the *Hammer and Hand* B&B (☎01751/417 300; ③) or at *Westfield Lodge* (☎01751/417 261; ③).

About a mile and a half east of Hutton-le-Hole in **LASTINGHAM**, itself no slouch in the scenic stakes, stands **St Mary's**, a superb little church, built over Lastingham Abbey, a Benedictine house founded in 654 by monks Cedd and Chad from Lindisfarne, both of whom were later canonized. The monastery was destroyed by the Danes and then partly rebuilt by monks from Whitby, who left in 1087 to found St Mary's in York without finishing their work here. The present church, however, preserves the early **Norman crypt**, one of Yorkshire's great ecclesiastical treasures. Burial place of Saint Cedd, the crypt was once one of Northumbria's most sacred points of pilgrimage. Today its heavy vaults and massive columns still shelter the head of an eighth-century Anglo-Saxon cross, a wealth of interesting stonework and other pre-Norman relics. The village is tiny, with just one cosy pub, a post-office-cum-shop, and a couple of lovely eighteenth-century **B&Bs**, *Holywell House* (☎01751/417 624; ③) and *Prospect House* (☎01751/417 559; ③).

Farndale

FARNDALE, the North York Moors' best-known dale, is entered by minor roads from Hutton-le-Hole or from **Gillamoor** a little to the west, the latter known for its so-called Surprise View over the valley's southern flanks. Further up the vale the country lanes are packed in spring with tourists come to see the area's wild **daffodils**, protected by a 2000-acre nature reserve. Controversy recently flared up when the main paths through the woods and meadows were surfaced to deal with the sheer number of visitors.

The flowers grow in several parts of the dale, but the best area is north of **Low Mill**, where the roads from Gillamoor and Hutton-le-Hole meet, about four miles north of the latter. Take the **path** beside the car park (signposted "High Mill") over the bridge and turn left to follow the track alongside the River Dove for about fifty minutes – as well as the thousands of daffodils, notice the alder trees, whose Gaelic name, *ferna*, may well have given Farndale its name. At High Mill cut up to **Church Houses**, turn right on the tarmac for about three quarters of a mile and at Mackeridge House take the track back to Low Mill via Bragg Farm (keep left of the farm, ignoring a footpath signed right), Bitchagreen and High Wold House (3.25 miles; 2–2hr 30min).

It goes without saying that there are any number of walks up on **Rudland Rigg** and **Farndale Moor** – a particularly good route follows the old mine railway across Farndale Moor into Rosedale (see below). The best road route cuts east from Church Houses up on to Farndale Moor to meet a high moor road from Hutton-le-Hole that curves around the head of Rosedale before dropping down to Rosedale Abbey.

Rosedale

ROSEDALE, just a couple of miles east of Farndale, is slightly wilder and steeper, seen by fewer visitors, and has a good network of wild upland roads ranging over its moors, which are densely studded with ancient stone cross and prehistoric tumuli. The largest of its three communities, **Rosedale Abbey**, preserves only few fragments of the Cistercian priory (1158) which gave it its name, most of them incorporated into the parish church. Now somnolent in the extreme, in the last century the village had a population of over five thousand, most employed in the **ironstone workings** whose remnants lie scattered all over the lonely high moors roundabout. The first mine opened in 1851, some three million tons of ore being excavated between 1856 and 1885. Horse-drawn wagons dragged the stone by pack road to Pickering until the opening of a remarkable moorland railway which connected with the main Esk Dale line at Battersby to carry ore north to the ironworks of Teeside.

THE NORTH YORK MOORS RAILWAY

One of the northeast's big tourist draws, the volunteer-run **North York Moors Railway** (Moorsrail for short) connects Pickering with the Middlesbrough–Whitby BR line at Grosmont, eighteen miles to the north. The line was completed by **George Stephenson** in 1835, just nine years after the opening of the Stockton and Darlington Railway, making it one of the earliest lines in the country. Even by the standards of later projects it was a remarkable feat of engineering, navigating 1-in-15 gradients and using thousands of tons of brushwood and heather-stuffed sheepskins to provide bedding for the track through the dale's extensive bogs. For twelve years carriages were pulled by horse, steam locomotives only arriving in 1847. The line closed in 1965 and was formally reopened in 1973.

Most people make a full return journey for the superb scenery of the roadless **Newton Dale**, but if you want to combine some walking with the ride trains, stop en route at one of three minor stations. The first is **Levisham**, perfect for walks to Levisham village, where the *Horseshoe Inn* is a favourite target (1.5 miles), to Lockton (1 mile beyond), and to the **Hole of Horcum**, a bizarre natural hollow gouged by the glacial meltwaters that carved out Newtondale – the seven-mile circuit is one of the Moors' best short walks. The second stop, **Newtondale Halt**, is ideal for walks to the Hole of Horcum, just south, back to Pickering, or through the extensive local woods on trails specially marked by the Forestry Commission. The final stop, **Goathland**, has more facilities than its predecessors and is close to the *Mallyan Spout* pub, described in the *Times* as serving "the best pub grub in England". *Wheeldale Lodge* **youth hostel** (☎01947/86350) is located in lonely moorland three miles southwest of the village, and there's also a **campsite** at *Brow House Farm*, a mile and a half southwest of the station.

Scheduled Moorsrail services operate between late March and early November, with trains running hourly to thrice-daily depending on the time of year (for information ring ☎01751/472 508; recorded timetable ☎01751/473 535). Moorsrail's only drawbacks are the **fares**, which exceed even those of BR – a day return along the whole line costs £8.50. Part of its attraction, of course, are the steam trains, though be warned that diesels are pulled into service when the fire risk in the forests is high.

Pickering

The biggest centre for miles around, and self-proclaimed "Gateway to the Moors", **PICKERING** is a handy place to stay if you're touring. Its undoubted big pull, and biggest plus if you're using public transport, is the **North York Moors Railway** (see box). Whilst waiting for a train you could happily potter around the informal **Beck Isle Museum of Rural Life** on Bridge Street (late March to Oct daily 10am–5pm; £1.75) or the church of **St Peter and St Paul**, famed for a Norman font and extensive fifteenth-century frescoes, discovered in 1851 but painted over again by the local vicar who feared they'd provoke idolatory. Although crude and rather heavy-handedly restored, the scenes are still compelling, including Herod's feast, Saint George and the Dragon and the martyrdom of Thomas à Becket. Finally, stroll up to the fine motte and bailey **Castle** on the hill north of the market place (April–Sept daily 10am–6pm; Oct daily 10am–4pm; Nov–March Wed–Sat 10am–4pm; £2; EH). Started in 1180, it was reputedly used by every English monarch up to 1400 as a base for hunting in nearby Blandsby Park. Eight monarchs certainly put up here, and possibly a ninth, Richard II, was kept here as a prisoner shortly before his murder in Pontefract.

Plenty of **buses** run to Pickering from Malton, Leeds and York (the *Yorkshire Coastliner* #840 or #842), and hourly from Scarborough (*Scarborough & District* #128). See the box above for details of NYMR trains. The swish **tourist office**, on Eastgate Square (April–Oct daily 9.30am–6pm; Nov–March Mon–Sat 10am–4.30pm; ☎01751/473 791) will book **accommodation**, the best of which is the *White Swan* on the Market Place (☎01751/472 288; ⑥). Amongst the numerous **B&Bs**, first choices are: 103

Westgate (☎01751/472 500; ②), *Kirkham Garth*, Whitby Road (☎01751/474 931; ②) and *Old Manse*, Middleton Road (☎01751/476 484; ③). The nearest **youth hostel** is at *The Old School*, Lockton (☎01751/460 376), five miles northeast off the A169 – about two miles cross-country walk from the NYMR station at Levisham.

Stape, Cawthorn Camps and Wheeldale Roman Road

Comprising just a few farms and isolated houses seven miles north of Pickering, **STAPE** is an archetypal high moors community, perfectly placed to act as a halfway house for walks between Moorsrail stations or a base for walks in **Cropton Forest**. It's also a walk away from the best-preserved stretch of Roman road in Europe, **Wheeldale Roman Road**, a mile of the road that ran from York to bases on the coast: the fact that it's plumb in the middle of open moorland only adds to its appeal. It's signed off the unmetalled road from Stape to Goathland, perhaps the wildest and most adventurous north–south route over the Moors. As an adjunct to the road, visit the fascinating **Cawthorn Camps**, two miles south of Stape, the only Roman camps of their kind in the world. The site's jumbled collection of earthworks, spreading over 103 acres, puzzled archeologists for years, as all the previously discovered Roman marching camps in Europe were built on precise geometrical plans. It's now known that this was a military training area, troops from York's Ninth Legion garrison being sent here on exercises, many of which obviously involved building camps. Pickering's tourist office will provide details of isolated B&Bs in the neighbourhood, and *Wheeldale Lodge* **youth hostel** lies five miles to the north (see box on p.519).

Thornton-le-Dale and Dalby Forest

THORNTON-LE-DALE , just two miles east of Pickering, hangs onto its considerable charm despite the main A170 Scarborough road scything through its centre. Most of the houses, pubs and shops are fairly alluring, none more so than the thatched cottage near the parish church, which features in so many ads, magazine covers, chocolate boxes and calendars that it's been described as the most photographed house in Britain. There are too many cafés, gift shops and other people around for most tastes, but the old market cross, stocks and various stream-side strolls are well worth half an hour if you can get here off season.

A minor road from Thornton-le-Dale leads to **Low Dalby**, three and a half miles to the north, where a **Forestry Commission information centre** (May–Oct daily 10am–5.30pm; ☎01751/60295) marks the main western entrance to the monumental expanse of **Dalby Forest**. The centre has information not only on the forest, one of the first to be planted after the foundation of the Forestry Commission in 1919, but also on wildlife, picnic spots and the range of marked trails scattered around the woods, varying in length from one to sixteen miles. There's also a toll road here (£2) which indicates the start of a nine-mile **forest drive** that emerges close to Harkness, four miles from Scarborough.

The Yorkshire coast

A bracing change after the flattened seascapes of East Anglia and Holderness, the **Yorkshire coast** is the southernmost stretch of a cliff-edged shore that stretches almost unbroken to the Scottish border. **Scarborough**, a schizophrenic mixture of spa and sleaze, is the biggest town here, and the ideal launching pad for exploring pockets of coast to the south and the more spectacular littoral to the north. **Robin Hood's Bay** is the most popular of the many Yorkshire villages with fishing and smuggling traditions, and **Whitby** too has a touch too many visitors, attracted by its ruins and cobbled streets, though overall it's probably the best stopover if you want a quick taste of the area. Heading to virtually any of the smaller coastal hamlets will bring you to similar-looking but far quieter spots, and for those who want to sample the most dizzying cliff-tops, the **Cleveland Way** provides a marked path along virtually the entire coast.

Scarborough

The oldest resort in the country, **SCARBOROUGH** was "the Queen of the Watering Places" to the Victorians, then was transformed into a holiday haven for workers from the industrial heartlands. Though no longer as popular as it was before the age of air travel, it still has the traditional ingredients of a beach resort, from kitsch amusement arcades and Kiss-Me-Quick hats to the more refined pleasures of a spa, a tight-knit old town and a genteel round of quiet parks and gardens – of which the Valley and South Cliff gardens are the best.

Only the town's **Castle** (daily April–Oct 10am–6pm; Nov–March 10am–4pm; £1.50; EH), mounted on a jutting headland between two golden-sanded bays east of the town centre, rates highly in the historical building stakes. Bronze and Iron Age relics have been found on the wooded castle crag, together with fragments of a fourth-century Roman signalling station, Saxon and Norman chapels, and a Viking camp, reputedly built by a Viking with the nickname of *Scardi* (or "harelip"), from which the town's name derives. The present castle consists mainly of a three-storey keep (1158–64), a thirteenth-century barbican and raking buttressed walls which trace the cliff edge. Although besieged many times, the fortifications were never taken by assault, its only fall coming after a siege during the Civil War when the Parliamentarians starved the garrison into surrender, after which it was slighted. It took a further pounding from an infamous German naval bombardment of the town in 1914. As you leave the castle drop into the church of **St Mary's** (1180), immediately below on Castle Road, whose grave-yard contains the tomb of Anne Brontë, who died here in 1849.

After the castle, the chief distraction is the unexpected concentration of Pre-Raphaelite art in the church of **St-Martin-on-the-Hill** on Albion Road. The Victorian-Gothic pile has a roof by William Morris, an *Annunciation* triptych by Burne-Jones, a pulpit with four printed panels by Rossetti, stained glass by Morris, Burne-Jones and Ford Madox Brown, and an east wall whose tracery provides the frames for *Angels* by Morris and *The Adoration of the Magi* by Burne-Jones.

Scarborough's **tourist office** is at St Nicholas Cliff (daily summer 9.30am–6pm; winter 10am–4pm; ☎01723/373 333), a quarter of a mile east of the **train station**. Scarborough's better-regarded **accommodation** options include the *Rex*, 9 Crown Crescent (☎01723/373 297; ②), *Howdale Hotel*, 121 Queen's Parade (☎01723/372 696; ③) and *Riviera*, St Nicholas Cliff (☎01723/372 277; ⑤). The **youth hostel** occupies a converted water mill on Burniston Road, Scalby Mills (☎01723/361 176), two miles north of the town on the A165 and ten minutes' walk from the sea. For **drinking**, try the easy-going *Leeds Arms* on St Mary's Street in the old town, the old-fashioned *Hole in the Wall* on Vernon Street or the *Highlander* in the *Stresa Hotel* on the Esplanade, South Cliff, with great views, and numerous beers, four of which come from the brew-ery behind the hotel. A long-established and popular **restaurant** is the *Lanterna*, 33 Queen St, where the emphasis is on Mediterranean dishes, Italian in particular.

Hayburn Wyke and Ravenscar

At **Hayburn Wyke**, a tiny and tranquil bay mostly owned by the National Trust, Hayburn Beck runs though scrub and woodland before tumbling onto the rocky beach in a small waterfall. The waters have carved away layers of the surrounding boulder clay, making this a good spot to forage for fossils, but it's an equally attractive spot if you simply want to enjoy the scenery. The Cleveland Way cuts through from

THE CLEVELAND WAY

The **Cleveland Way**, one of England's ten premier long-distance National Trails, starts at **Filey Brigg**, south of Scarborough and follows a route that embraces both the cliff scenery of the north Yorkshire coast and the northern rim of the North York Moors and Cleveland Hills to the west. The horseshoe-shaped route terminates 93 miles later at Helmsley, though an unofficial "Missing Link" joins Helmsley to Filey, thus completing a circular walk.

If you don't want to tackle the whole thing then it's easy to walk short stages, particularly on the coastal portion, where taxis and buses are more common. The outstanding high cliff sections are (from north to south): Hayburn Wyke to Robin Hood's Bay (7 miles), Robin Hood's Bay to Whitby (6 miles), Sandsend to Runswick Bay to Staithes (7 miles), and Staithes to Skinningrove, the section with the highest cliffs (5 miles).

There are **youth hostels** at Scarborough (see p.521), Robin Hood's Bay (see p.523), Whitby (see p.525) and Osmotherley (☎01609/883 575), YHA camping barns at Kildale (no phone) and Farndale (☎01904/621 756), and plenty of B&B and small hotel accommodation on the coast. The OS Touring Map *North York Moors* marks the entire path; for more detail you need OS Landranger **maps** nos. 93, 94, 100 and 101. Several guides are available, the best being *National Trail Guide: Cleveland Way* by Ian Sampson (Aurum Press) and *Walking the Cleveland Way and The Missing Link* by Malcolm Boyes (Cicerone Press).

Scarborough, six miles to the south, but road access takes you only as far as the *Hayburn Wyke Hotel*, an arrangement which keeps the bay area and the adjoining 34-acre nature reserve remarkably unspoilt.

A back-lane drive, or one of the Cleveland Way's more exhilarating passages – a four-mile hike over the 500-foot ramparts of **Beast Cliff** – bring you to the village of **RAVENSCAR**, 600ft above the sea in the lee of tumuli-spotted **Stoupe Brow** (871ft), the last upland gasp of Fylingdales Moor to the west. (The village marks the end of the Lyke Wake Walk – see p.516.) Views to the north around the sweep of Robin Hood's Bay are superb, particularly from the mock-battlemented *Raven Hall Hotel*, constructed on the site of an old Roman signal station, and which was used as a hideaway for George III when his bouts of madness kept him from the public gaze. There's a small charge for non-patrons to wander the hotel's panoramic cliff-edge terraces.

Close by are a National Trust shop and **Coastal Centre (**April, May & Sept Sat & Sun 10.30am–5.30pm; June–Aug daily same hours; ☎01723/870138), which has displays on the village's dead-end streets and isolated houses, part of an 1895 scheme to create "another Scarborough," an enterprise foiled by the cliffs' unstable geology. Also featured are the **fossils** that can be found on the coast immediately below; it's well worth scrambling down the path to the left of the hotel, but take great care on the fore-shore, where the tide is fast-rising – explore on the ebb tide only and don't be tempted into swimming. The most detailed exhibits, however, relate to the area's **alum mines**. Quarries dot the Old Peak cliffs and the ridges of Stoupe Brow, where alum was mined between 1640 and 1862, the mineral being used in the leather and textile industry to fix dyes, and in the manufacture of candles and parchment. The industry declined in the nineteenth century, and the last mine closed in 1871, and a marked trail from the centre takes you past recently re-excavated workings

B&B is available in Ravenscar at *Bide-A-While*, 3 Lorings Rd (☎01723/870 643; ②), and at *Smugglers Rock*, a Georgian country house with good views (☎01723/870044; ③); Bent Rigg Farm, just to the east of the village, has **B&B** and space for **camping** (☎01723/870 475; ②). The *Raven Hall* hotel (see above), has a great location but stratospheric prices (☎01723/870 353; ⑨).

Robin Hood's Bay

Although known as Robbyn Huddes Bay as early as Tudor times, there's nothing except half-remembered myth to link **ROBIN HOOD'S BAY** with Sherwood's legendary bowman – locals anyway prefer the old name, Bay Town. Perhaps the best-known and most heavily visited spot on the coast, the village fully lives up to its reputation, with narrow streets and pink-tiled cottages toppling down the cliff-edge site, evoking the romance of a time when this was both a hard-bitten fishing community and smugglers' den *par excellence*.

From the car park in the upper part of the village, it's a 1-in-3 walk down the hill to Bay Town proper, little more than a couple of narrow streets that lead down to a curving, rocky shoreline. The gift shops and cafés are complemented by all too predictable "themed" attractions, notably the **Smuggling Experience** (Easter to mid-Oct daily 10am–6pm; £1.50), which is unashamedly aimed at children. You'll probably have more fun tackling a straightforward local **walk**, either to Boggle Hole (1 mile south), returning inland via South House Farm and the path along the old Whitby railway, or to the National Trust-owned headlands and Cleveland Way to the north.

Whitby, seven miles north, has the nearest train station and tourist office (see below). **Accommodation** is plentiful, but often in short supply during high season: try *Moor View House*, Main Street (☎01947/880 576; ③), *Rosegarth*, Thorpe Lane (☎01947/880 578; ②) or the *Victoria Hotel*, Station Road (☎01947/880 205; ②). You can also stay at the seventeenth-century *Dolphin* in King Street (☎01947/880 337; ③), the oldest pub in town, with a reputation for excellent **food**, or at the *Laurel*, Main Street (☎01947/880 400; ③), one of Yorkshire's smallest pubs, which has a bar carved from solid rock. Boggle Hole's **youth hostel** is one of Yorkshire's most popular, a former mill in a wooded ravine about a mile south of Robin Hood's Bay at Mill Beck, Fylingthorpe (☎01947/880 987). Note that a torch is essential after dark.

Whitby

Historical associations, atmospheric ruins and intrinsic charm make **WHITBY** a first-choice overnight stop whether you're exploring the coast, heading inland for the moors, or pushing on to Durham and Northumberland. Divided by the River Esk, the town splits into two distinct halves, the old town to the east and the newer town across the way on the West Cliff, home to the modern quay, hotels, shops and the various arcades, bingo halls, souvenir stalls and suchlike. Virtually everything you want to see is in the old town, principally the **Abbey** and **St Mary's Church**, the inspiration for Bram Stoker's *Dracula*; the **Lifeboat Museum**; and the **Captain Cook Memorial Museum**; leaving the West Cliff with only a modest museum and the Sutcliffe Gallery, the latter a collection of photographs of old Whitby.

The Town

Climb the famous 199 steps of the **Church Stairs** from the north end of Church Street, the old town's main drag, and you come first to the bizarre church of **St Mary's**, an architectural dog's dinner dating back to 1110, boasting a Norman chancel arch, a profusion of eighteenth-century panelling and box pews unequalled in England, and a unique triple-decker pulpit – note the built-in ear trumpets, added for the benefit of a nineteenth-century rector's deaf wife. The Cholmley family pew, in particular, almost obscuring the chancel, is superb, a capricious confection of twisting wooden columns. Notice also the galleries arranged like a ship's decks, and the roof, constructed by seventeenth-century naval carpenters as if part of a ship's cabin.

In climbing the Church Stairs you'll have followed in the fictional footsteps of Bram Stoker's **Dracula**, who in the eponymous novel takes the form of a large dog that bounds up the steps after the wreck of the ship bearing his coffin. In the graveyard he claims Lucy as his victim, taking refuge in the grave of a suicide victim, which he then uses as a base for his nocturnal forays. The Dracula connection has proved a huge attraction to Goths who come to Whitby from far and wide. The town even hosts a Dracula convention/ball at least twice a year, when the streets are over-run with Goths in Regency dress, wedding gowns, top hats and capes. For more on the count, pick up details of the *Dracula Trail* – which ends at the church – from the tourist office.

The ruins of **Whitby Abbey** (April–Sept daily 10am–6pm; Oct–March 10am–4pm; £1.50; EH), beyond St Mary's, might be paltry in extent but they are wonderfully evocative, the nave, soaring north transept and lancets of the east end giving a hint of the building's former delicacy and splendour. Its monastery was founded in 657 by Saint Hilda of Hartlepool, daughter of King Oswy of Northumberland, and by 664 had become important enough to host the Synod of Whitby, an event of seminal importance in the development of English Christianity. It settled once and for all the question of determining the date of Easter, and adopted the rites and authority of the Roman rather than the Celtic Church. One of the burning issues decided was whether priests should shave their tonsures in the shape of a ring or a crescent. **Caedmon**, one of the brothers at the abbey during its earliest years who was reputedly charged with looking after Hilda's pigs, has a twenty-foot cross in his memory which stands in front of St Mary's, at the top of the Stairs. His nine-line *Song of Creation* is the earliest surviving poem in English, making the abbey not only the cradle of English Christianity, but also the birthplace of English literature. The original abbey was destroyed by the Danes in 867 and refounded by the Benedictines in 1078, though most of the present ruins – built slightly south of the site of the Saxon original – date from between 1220 and 1539.

Whitby likes to make a fuss of **Captain Cook**, who served an apprenticeship here under John Walker, a Quaker ship-owner, and used Whitby-built ships on three of his pioneering voyages. The most famous, the *Endeavour*, was of a local type known as a "cat". Used mainly in the coal trade, they were slow and broad-bottomed, designed for inshore and difficult river work, specifications that were to prove perfect for Cook's surveys of the South Sea islands and the Australian coast. The **Captain Cook Memorial Museum** (April–Oct daily 9.45am–5pm; March Sat & Sun 11am–3pm; £1.50), housed in Walker's old house in Grape Lane, contains an impressive amount of Cook memorabilia. Matters maritime are further explored in the **Whitby Lifeboat Museum** (irregular hours; free), the best museum of its kind in the country, located near the harbourside on Pier Road. Whitby lifeboat crews over the years have won more RNLI gold medals for gallantry than any other crew in Britain; you'd envy none of them the job, particularly after seeing one exhibit, the last RNLI hand-rowed boat, a flimsy-looking craft used until well into this century. The **Pannet Park Museum and Art Gallery** (May–Sept Mon–Sat 9.30am–5.30pm, Sun 2–5pm; Oct–April Mon & Tues 10.30am–1pm, Wed–Sat 10.30am–4pm, Sun 2–4pm; £1) in the Pannet gardens across the river in West Cliff also has a room devoted to Cook, together with rooms devoted to Whitby's seafaring tradition, its whaling industry in particular.

Practicalities

Whitby's **train** and **bus stations** are adjacent to one another on Station Square, a couple of blocks south of the bridge to the old town; the **tourist office** is right outside the train station (daily May–Sept 9.30am–6pm; Oct–March 10am–4.30pm; ☎01947/ 602674). Easily the most atmospheric place to **stay** in town is the eighteenth-century *White Horse and Griffin* (☎01947/604 857; ④) on Church Street in the old town; on the same street is the *Shepherd's Purse*, at no. 95 (☎01947/820 228; ③). For low-cost sea views try *Ashford*, 8 Royal Crescent (☎01947/602 138; ②) or *Boulmer*, 23 Crescent Ave (☎01947/604 284; ③). For a touch more style, try the *Old West Cliff Hotel*, 42 Crescent Ave (☎01947/603 292; ④) or *Seacliff Hotel*, North Promenade (☎01947/603 139; ④).

The **youth hostel**, East Cliff (☎01947/896 350), is a converted stable a stone's throw from St Mary's, and there's also a private hostel, *Harbour Grange*, Spital Bridge, on the eastern side of the river (☎01947/600 817).

Most **restaurants** also serve primarily fish and chips; the best of these is *Trenchers*, close to the tourist office on New Quay Road. Otherwise, the most enjoyable meals are to be had at the *White Horse and Griffin* (see above); once a week a good, local blues band plays. Also highly recommended is the *Shepherd's Purse Wholefood Restaurant* (see above) at the rear of its health-food shop in old Whitby's cobbled main street. The *Duke of York* **pub** on Church Street, at the bottom of the 199 steps, has harbour views, while the mock-rustic *Tap & Spile* on new Quay Road is the real ale haunt. There are regular year-round **gigs** at several pubs, climaxing with the annual **Whitby Folk Week**, held in the last week in August. A special festival campsite is usually set up, but if you want regular accommodation for this week, book well in advance.

travel details

Trains

Harrogate to: Knaresborough (every 30min; 15min); Leeds (every 30min; 45min); York (hourly; 30min).

Hull to: Leeds (hourly; 1hr); London (15 daily; 3hr); York (10 daily; 1hr).

Knaresborough to: Harrogate (every 30min; 15min); Leeds (every 30min; 45min); York (hourly; 30min).

Leeds to: Bradford (every 15min; 20min); Harrogate (every 30min; 35min); Hull (hourly; 1hr); Knaresborough (every 30min; 45min); London (every 30min; 2hr); Settle (3–8 daily; 1hr); Sheffield (every 30min; 45min–1hr 15min); Skipton (hourly; 40min); York (every 30min; 40min).

Pickering to: Grosmont (May–Oct 4–8 daily; 1hr).

Scarborough to: York (8–15 daily; 45min).

Sheffield to: Leeds (every 30min; 45min–1hr 15min); London (every 45min; 2hr); York (hourly; 1hr 20min).

Whitby to: Middlesbrough (Mon–Sat 4 daily; 1hr 30min).

York to: Bradford (every 45min; 1hr); Harrogate (hourly; 35min); Hull (hourly; 1hr); Leeds (every 30min; 40min); London (every 30min; 2hr); Scarborough (8–15 daily; 45min); Sheffield (hourly; 1hr 20min).

Buses

Helmsley to: Malton (Mon–Sat 3 daily; 1hr); Pickering (Mon–Sat 7 daily, 3 on Sun; 40min); Rievaulx Abbey & Sutton Bank (June–Sept 5 on Sun, Tues & Wed only; 30min); Scarborough (3–7 daily; 1 hr); York (Mon–Sat 3daily; 1hr 30min).

Pickering to: Castle Howard (May–Sept 1–3 daily; 30min); Helmsley (3–7 daily; 40min); Hutton-le-Hole (June–Sept 5 on Sun, Tues & Wed only; 35min); Low Dalby (June–Sept 6 on Sun, Tues & Wed only; 30min); Rosedale Abbey (1 on Mon; June–Sept 5 on Sun, Tues & Wed; 30min); Scarborough (Mon–Sat hourly, 6 on Sun; 1hr); Whitby (5 daily; 1hr); York (Mon–Sat hourly, 3 on Sun; 1hr 20min).

Scarborough to: Helmsley (3–6 daily; 1hr 35min); Hull (1 daily; 2hr); Leeds (hourly; 3hr); Malton (hourly; 1hr); Middlesbrough (4–8 daily; 2hr); Pickering (hourly; 1hr); Robin Hood's Bay (hourly; 45min); Whitby (hourly; 1hr); York (hourly; 1hr 45min);

Settle to: Horton-in-Ribblesdale (4–9 daily; 20min); Lancaster (Mon–Sat 3 daily; 1hr 35min).

Skipton to: Grassington (Mon–Sat 2 daily; 45min); Buckden (1 daily; 1hr); Ingleton (Mon–Sat 3 daily; 35min); Keighley (Mon–Sat hourly; 30min); Malham (Mon–Sat 5 daily; 40min–1hr 5min).

Whitby to: Castle Howard (May–Oct 1 daily; 1hr 15min); Grosmont (July–Sept 7 daily; 25min); Goathland (Mon–Fri 2 daily; 30min); Hull (1 daily; 2hr 45min); Malton (5 daily; 1hr 25min); Middlesbrough (10 daily; 1hr); Pickering (5 daily; 1hr); Robin Hood's Bay (hourly; 25min).

York to: Beverley (4 daily; 1hr 15min); Bradford (5 daily; 1hr 45min); Castle Howard (1–2 daily; 1hr); Hull (5 daily; 1hr 30min); Leeds (10 daily; 45min); London (4 daily; 4hr 20min); Pickering (Mon–Sat hourly, 4 on Sun; 1hr 20min); Sheffield (4 daily, 2hr 15min); Whitby (3–5 daily; 2hr 20min).

CHAPTER TEN

NORTHEAST ENGLAND

F or England's northeastern region – in particular the counties of **Northumberland** and **Durham** – the centuries between the Roman invasion and the 1603 union of England and Scotland were a period of almost incessant turbulence. To mark the empire's limit and to contain the troublesome tribes of the far north, **Hadrian's Wall** was built along the seventy-odd miles between the North Sea and the east coast, an extraordinary military structure that is now one of the country's most evocative ruins. When the Romans departed the northeast was plunged into chaos and divided into unstable Saxon principalities until order was restored by the kings of Northumbria, who dominated the region from 600 until the 870s. It was they who nourished the region's early Christian tradition, which achieved its finest flowering with the creation of the **Lindisfarne Gospels** on what is now known as Holy Island. The monks abandoned their island at the end of the ninth century, in advance of the Vikings' destruction of the Northumbrian kingdom, and only after the Norman Conquest did the northeast again become part of a greater England.

The Norman kings and their immediate successors repeatedly attempted to subdue Scotland, passing effective regional control to powerful local lords. Their authority is recalled by a sequence of formidable coastal fortresses, most impressively those at **Bamburgh**, **Alnwick** and **Warkworth**, and also by **Durham Cathedral**, the magnificent twelfth-century church of the Prince Bishops of Durham, who ruled the whole of County Durham. Long after the northeast had ceased to be a critical military zone, its character and appearance was transformed by the **Industrial Revolution**. Coal had been mined here for hundreds of years, but exploitation only began in earnest towards the end of the eighteenth century, when two main coalfields were established – one dominating County Durham from the Pennines to the sea, the other stretching north along the Northumberland coast from the Tyne. The world's first **railway**, the **Darlington and Stockton** line, was opened in 1825 to move coal to the nearest port for export, while local coal and ore also fuelled the foundries of Middlesbrough and Consett, which in turn supplied the shipbuilding and heavy-engineering companies of Tyneside. The region boomed, creating a score of sizeable towns, amongst which Newcastle was pre-eminent – as it remains today, despite an economic decline that began in the 1920s.

Most visitors dodge the depressed industrial areas, bypassing the unsightly towns along the **Tees Valley** – Darlington, Stockton, Middlesborough and Hartlepool – on the

---

ACCOMMODATION PRICE CODES

Throughout this guide, hotel and B&B accommodation is priced on a scale of ① to ⑨, the number indicating the **lowest price** you could expect to pay per night in that establishment for a **double room** in high season. The prices indicated by the codes are as follows:

① under £20/$30	④ £40–50/$60–75	⑦ £70–80/$105–120
② £20–30/$31–45	⑤ £50–60/$75–90	⑧ £80–100/$120–150
③ £30–40/$45–60	⑥ £60–70/$90–105	⑨ over £100/$150

way to **Durham**, from where it's a short hop to **Newcastle**, an earthy city distinguished by some fine Victorian buildings. North, past the old colliery villages, the brighter parts of the Northumberland coast boast some fine castles, **Holy Island**, the extravagant ramparts of **Berwick-upon-Tweed**, a string of superb if chilly beaches, and the desolate archipelago of the **Farne Islands**. Inland there are the scenic Durham **dales** and the harsh landscapes of **Northumberland National Park**, a huge chunk of moorland and tree plantations that edges the most dramatic portion of Hadrian's Wall. The wall is easily visited from **Hexham**, where you can also pick up the region's main hiking trail, the **Pennine Way**.

Durham

The view from **DURHAM** train station is one of the finest in northern England – a panoramic prospect of Durham cathedral, its towers dominating the skyline from the top of a steep sandstone bluff within a narrow bend of the River Wear. This dramatic site has been the resting place of Saint Cuthbert since 995, when his body was moved here from nearby Chester-le-Street, over one hundred years after his fellow monks had fled from Lindisfarne in fear of the Vikings, carrying his coffin before them. Cuthbert's hallowed remains made Durham a place of pilgrimage for both the Saxons and the Normans, who began work on the present cathedral at the end of the eleventh century. In the meantime, William the Conqueror, aware of the defensive possibilities of the site, had built a castle that was to be the precursor of ever more elaborate fortifications.

Subsequently, the bishops of Durham were granted extensive powers to control the troublesome northern marches of the kingdom, ruling as semi-independent princes, with their own army, mint and courts of law. The bishops were at the peak of their power in the fourteenth century, but thereafter their office went into decline, especially in the wake of the Reformation, yet they clung to the vestiges of their powers until 1836, when they ceded them to the Crown. They abandoned Durham Castle for their palace in Bishop Auckland and transferred their old home to the fledgling **Durham University** – and so matters rest today, cathedral and university monopolizing a city centre which remains an island of privilege in what is otherwise a moderately sized, working-class town at the heart of the old Durham coalfield.

The City

Surrounded on three sides by the River Wear, Durham's centre is readily approached by two small bridges which lead from the western, modern part of town across the river to the spur containing castle and cathedral. The commercial heart of this "old town" area is the triangular **Market Place**, inappropriately dominated by an equestrian statue of the Third Marquis of Londonderry, a much hated nineteenth-century colliery owner – in the words of John Doyle, a pitman from Horden, "His Lordship reached three score and ten/A very fine performance when/One thinks how many did him scorn/And wished him dead 'ere he was born." Flanking the square are the **Guildhall** and **St Nicholas' Church**, both now modernized beyond distinction. The **Market Hall**, which still holds a lively market (Thurs & Fri 9am–4pm, Sat 9am–4.30pm), is buried in the vaults of the buildings that line the west side of the square.

The Cathedral

From Market Place, it's a five-minute walk up the steep and cobbled Saddler Street to the majestic **Durham Cathedral** (daily May–Sept 7.15am–8pm; Oct–April 7.15am–6pm; admission by donation), facing the castle across the manicured Palace Green. Standing on the site of an early wooden Saxon cathedral, built to house the remains of

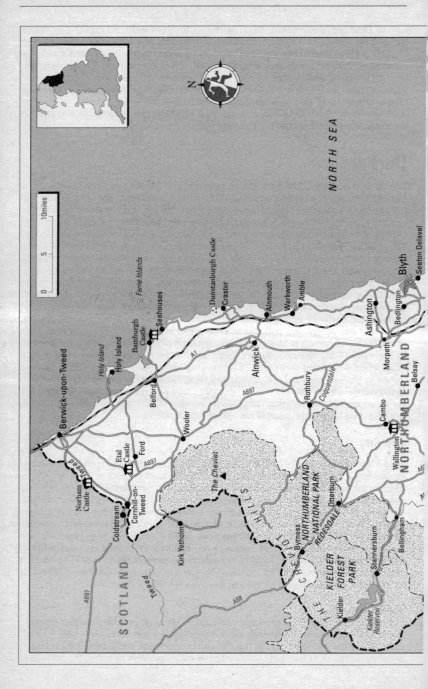

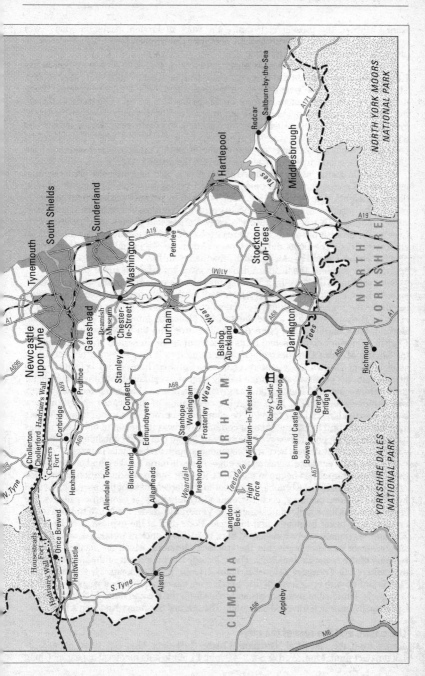

Saint Cuthbert, the present cathedral – the work of French master masons – was completed in 1133, and has survived the centuries pretty much intact, a supreme example of the Norman-Romanesque style.

Entry is through the **northwest porch**, where a replica of the lion-head **Sanctuary Knocker** is a reminder of the medieval distinction between secular and religious law. The church used to be ringed by wooden crosses and, once a fugitive reached them, he or she could claim sanctuary from the lay authorities for up to 35 days. In theory, this right to sanctuary was universal, but in practice it was mostly used by the rich to give them time to arrange their affairs before they went into exile. Rarely did anyone try to stop these wealthy runaways from reaching safety and, after the prescribed period, the monks gave their "guests" a robe of Saint Cuthbert, which extended the church's protection while they made their way to the nearest port.

The awe-inspiring **nave**, completed in 1128, is a bold and inventive structure that uses pointed arches for the first time in England, raising the vaulted ceiling to new and dizzying heights. The weight of the stone is borne by massive pillars, their heaviness relieved by striking Moorish-influenced geometric patterns – chevrons, diapers and vertical fluting. Most of the cathedral's early fixtures and fittings were destroyed by Cromwell's Scottish prisoners, who were deposited inside the church after the battle of Dunbar in 1650. The Scots did not, however, damage the gaudily painted, sixteenth-century **Prior Castell's clock**, which now hangs in the south transept, because it sported their emblem, the thistle. A door here gives access to the tower (£1).

Separated from the nave by a Victorian marble screen is the **choir**, where the dark-stained Restoration stalls are overshadowed by the vainglorious **bishop's throne**, reputedly the highest in medieval Christendom, built on the orders of the fourteenth-century Bishop Hatfield, whose militaristic alabaster tombstone lies just below. Beyond, the **Chapel of the Nine Altars** dates from the thirteenth century, its Early English stonework distinguished by its delicacy of detail. Here, and around the adjoining **Shrine of Saint Cuthbert**, much of the stonework is Frosterley marble, each dark shaft bearing its own fancy pattern of fossils. Cuthbert himself lies beneath a plain marble slab, his presence and shrine having gained a reputation over the centuries for their curative powers. The legend was given credence in 1104, when the saint's body was exhumed for reburial here, upon the completion of the eastern end of the new Norman cathedral, and was found to be completely uncorrupted, more than 400 years after his death on Lindisfarne. Almost certainly, this was the result of his fellow monks having (unintentionally) preserved the body by laying it in sand containing salt crystals – though to medieval eyes, here was testament enough to the saint's potency.

Back near the entrance, stuck on the edge of the ravine at the west end of the church, the **Galilee Chapel** was begun in the 1170s, its light and exotic decoration in imitation of the Great Mosque of Cordoba, a contrast to the forcefulness of the nave. Subdivided by twelve slender columns, each surrounded by a medley of geometric patterns, the chapel contains the simple tombstone of the **Venerable Bede**, the Northumbrian monk credited with being England's first historian. Bede died at the monastery of Jarrow in 735, and his remains were transferred here in 1020. An ancient wooden doorway opposite the main entrance leads into the spacious **cloisters**, which are flanked by what remains of the monastic buildings. These include the undercroft of the monks' dormitory, where the **Treasury** (Mon–Sat 10am–4.30pm, Sun 2–4.30pm; £1, senior citizens 80p) is stuffed with ecclesiastical bric-a-brac, from altar plate, bishops' rings and seals to vestments, illuminated manuscripts and relics from the life and times of Saint Cuthbert – principally his much travelled oak coffin. The original Sanctuary Knocker is here, too.

The castle and the rest of the city

Across from the cathedral, **Durham Castle** (July–Sept Mon–Sat 10am–noon & 2–4.30pm; Oct–June Mon, Wed & Sat 2–4.30pm; £1.50) lost its medieval appearance long ago, during refurbishments arranged by a succession of Prince Bishops, but the university went further by renovating the old keep as a hall of residence. It's only possible to visit the castle on a 45-minute guided tour, highlights of which include rapid visits to the fifteenth-century kitchen, a climb up the enormous hanging staircase, and the jog down to the so-called "Norman chapel" – in fact the medieval treasure room. In the Great Hall, the miniature suits of armour above the Musicians' Gallery were, according to Royalist propaganda, issued to young boys by Cromwell, who sent them into battle ahead of his regular troops as a human shield.

Below the castle and the cathedral are the wooded banks of the **River Wear**, where a pleasant footpath runs right round the peninsula. It takes about thirty minutes to complete the circle, passing a succession of bridges with fine vantage points over town and cathedral. **Framwellgate Bridge** originally dates from the twelfth century, though it was widened to its present proportions in the mid-nineteenth century. Just along from here, on the riverbank, the university's **Museum of Archeology** (April–Oct daily 11am–4pm; Nov–March Fri–Sun 12.30–3pm; 80p) occupies an old stone fulling mill, its displays a mixture of permanent archeological relics and temporary exhibitions. Eighteenth-century **Prebends Bridge** boasts celebrated views of the cathedral, and the path then continues round to handsome **Elvet Bridge**, again widened far beyond its medieval course, though still retaining traces of both its erstwhile bridge houses and the chapel, St Andrew's, which once stood at its eastern end.

The alternate route from Prebends to Elvet Bridge is along South and North Bailey, a cobbled thoroughfare lined by well-worn Georgian houses, many of them occupied by university college buildings. The church of St Mary-le-Bow, on North Bailey, immediately below the cathedral, now does duty as the **Durham Heritage Centre** (Easter to late May Sat & Sun 2–4.30pm; late May to June & Sept daily 2–4.30pm; July & Aug daily 11.30am–4.30pm; 70p), a pot-pourri of audio-visual displays, dioramas, exhibitions and activities, such as brass rubbing.

Durham has a smattering of other attractions, the most noteworthy being the university's **Oriental Museum** (Mon–Fri 9.30am–1pm & 2–5pm, Sat & Sun 2–5pm; £1), set among college buildings a couple of miles to the south of the city centre on Elvet Hill, whose wide-ranging collection contains an outstanding display of Chinese ceramics. To get there from the bus station, take service #41 to Elvet Hill Road, and follow the signposted footpath. You may as well continue on foot to the nearby **Botanic Gardens** (daily 9am–4pm; free), whose glasshouses, visitor centre and café are set in eighteen wooded acres near Collingwood College; buses run back to the centre from either Elvet Hill Road or South Road. North of the centre, a twenty-minute walk from the train station takes you to the **Durham Light Infantry Museum and Art Gallery** (Tues–Sat 10am–5pm, Sun 2–5pm; 80p), whose military section – consisting of uniforms, weapons and medals – won't be to everyone's taste.

Practicalities

Durham **train station** is about ten minutes' walk from the city centre, either via Millburngate Bridge or via North Road – the site of the **bus station** – then the pedestrianized Framwellgate Bridge; **minibuses** link the cathedral with both stations. The **tourist office** is on Market Place (June & Sept Mon–Sat 9.30am–5pm; July & Aug Mon–Sat 9.30am–6.30pm, Sun 2–5pm; Oct–May Mon–Fri 10am–4.30pm, Sat 9.30am–1pm; ☎0191/384 3720); pick up a copy of *What's on in Durham*, listing local events. If you want to get out onto the river, you can rent **rowing boats** from *Brown's Boathouse*, Elvet Bridge (£2 per hour), or take the one-hour **cruise** aboard the *Prince Bishop* (£2.50), which has regular summer departures, again from Elvet Bridge.

Durham has a long list of **guest houses** and **B&Bs**: convenient choices include *Mrs Cummings*, 99 Gilesgate (☎0191/384 4361; ③); *Bees Cottage Guest House*, Bridge

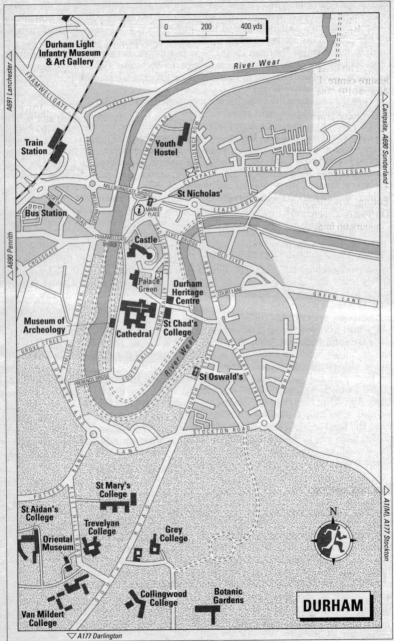

Street, off Sutton Street (☎0191/384 5775; ④); and the *Colebrick Guest House*, 21 Crossgate (☎0191/384 9585; ④). The *Georgian Town House*, 10 Crossgate (☎0191/386 8070; ⑤) is precisely that, and some rooms have cathedral views. Of the city's two best **hotels**, the *Royal County* (☎0191/386 6821; ⑨) is on Old Elvet, just across Elvet Bridge; while its sister hotel, the *Three Tuns* (☎0191/386 4326; ⑨), stands nearby on the New Elvet. The latter is the more attractive choice, and also has access to the *Royal Court*'s leisure centre. Durham **youth hostel** is in the *Durham Sixth Form Centre* (mid-July to Aug; ☎0191/384 2217; advance booking ☎01287/635 831), ten minutes' walk northeast of Millburngate Bridge on Providence Row. During student vacations **Durham University** provides dormitory-style accommodation (£10–12 per person) and private rooms (£35–55 a double, including breakfast) – the best colleges are *University College* (March–April & Dec; ☎0191/374 3863), whose rooms are inside the castle, and *St Chad's College*, behind the cathedral at 18 North Bailey (March–April, June–Sept & Dec–Jan; ☎0191/374 3370). The nearest **campsite**, the *Grange Camping and Caravan Site* (☎0191/384 4778), lies beside the junction of the A1(M) and the A690 (bus #220).

Eating, drinking and nightlife

On Palace Green, to the side of the cathedral, *The Almshouse Café* (daily 9am–5pm) conjours up imaginative **lunches** at the £3–4 mark, almost all of which are vegetarian – and don't forget the excellent *Undercroft*, inside the cathedral itself (Mon–Sat 10am–5pm, Sun 11am–5pm). *Shaheens*, 48 North Bailey (closed Sun), serves the best curry in town, while for Italian food, the honours are shared between *San Lorenzo*, at 96 Elvet Bridge, and *Pizzeria Venezia*, 4 Framwellgate Bridge (closed Sun). Indeed, the latter is the very paradigm of an Italian **restaurant**, but it's reliable and inexpensive. If you're looking to blow serious amounts of money, the very expensive, oak-panelled *Tudor Restaurant* inside the *Three Tuns* hotel on New Elvet serves an international-style menu. For riverside views, eat a **pub** lunch at the *Coach and Eight*, at the foot of Framwellgate Bridge, or the *Swan and Three Cygnets* on the west side of Elvet Bridge.

Durham's central **pubs** include the *Shakespeare* on Saddler Street, and the lively *Brewer and Firkin*, a little further up, with live rock, blues and jazz, and stand-up comedy nights. Another to try is the students' favourite, the *Dun Cow*, a five-minute walk east of the bridge at 37 Old Elvet. Bleary-eyed old Socialists will also want to make time for a quick pint in the *Market Tavern*, on Market Place, where the influential Durham Miners' Association was founded in 1871. With respects duly paid, you can move on to dancing at a couple of **nightclubs**: *Rixy's*, near the bus station on North Road, and *K2 Bar and Klute*, on Elvet Bridge. **Durham Student's Union** (☎0191/374 3310) puts on gigs, with rock, jazz and comedy most regularly performed at Dunelm House, New Elvet. The local **cinema** is *Robins Cinema*, on North Road (☎0191/384 3434), which has a film club as well as showing mainstream releases.

Annual events and **festivals** come thick and fast in the summer. In June the **Durham Regatta** packs the riverbanks and river, and the same month usually sees the start of the university's revamped **arts week**. The **Miners' Gala** in July – when the traditional lodge banners are paraded through the streets – recalls the city's proud industrial past; while sorrows about its demise are drowned at two respected annual **beer festivals**, one in February, one in September.

The rest of County Durham

In the 1910s, **County Durham** produced 41,000,000 tons of coal each year, raised from 300 pits by 170,000 miners. This was the heyday of an industry that since the 1830s had transformed the county's landscape, spawning scores of pit villages which matted the rolling hills from the Pennines to the North Sea, between Newcastle and Stockton-on-

Tees. The miners' union, waging a long struggle against serf-like pay and conditions, achieved a gradual improvement of the miners' lot, but could not prevent the slow decline of the Durham coalfield from the 1920s: just 127 pits were left when the mines were nationalized in 1947, and only 34 in 1969. Today, only a mere handful of pits remain strung out along the coast to exploit the broader seams that run under the sea.

For a taste of the old days, most people troop off to the reconstructed colliery village (and much more) at the open-air **Beamish Museum**, north of Durham. Another piece of industrial heritage, George Stephenson's *Locomotion*, is on permament display in **Darlington**, twenty miles south of Durham. Durham's other obvious tourist attractions are to the west of the coalfield: **Raby Castle**, a stately home near the market town of **Barnard Castle**, itself the setting for the opulent art collection of the Bowes Museum, and further west; the Pennine valleys of **Teesdale** and **Weardale**, whose upper reaches boast some enjoyable moorland scenery, most dramatically at Teesdale's **High Force** waterfall, which adjoins the Pennine Way.

Beamish Museum

Established in 1970, open-air **Beamish Museum** (April–June, Sept & Oct daily 10am–5pm; £6.99; July & Aug daily 10am–6pm; £7.99; Nov–March Tues–Thurs, Sat & Sun 10am–4pm; £2.99), spreading out across the fields beside the A693, ten miles north of Durham, is extremely popular with local people, who come to chew the fat with the costumed guides, most of whom are recruited for their real-life experience. The collier who takes you down the reopened drift mine was once a miner, and the blokes driving the steam engine used to work for British Rail, adding a touch of authenticity and sadness to the proceedings, as those industries continue to deteriorate in tandem with the boom in heritage museums like this one.

The museum divides into four main sections: a pint-sized colliery village as of 1913, complete with cottages, chapel, old stone winding house and mine; a train station and goods yard; a manor and farmstead; and a large-scale re-creation of a 1920s north country town, its High Street lined by three shops, a pub, a dentist's surgery, a printer's workshop, newspaper office, garage and a soliticor's office – all painstakingly kitted out with period furnishings and fittings. There's a great deal to see and most people make a day of it – reckon on around five hours to get round the lot in summer, much less in winter when only the town and train station are open.

Bishop Auckland

Eleven miles southwest of Durham, **BISHOP AUCKLAND** has been the country home of the bishops of Durham since the twelfth century and their official residence for more than a hundred years. Their palace, the gracious **Auckland Castle** (May–Sept Tues 10am–12.30pm, Wed, Thurs & Sun 2–5pm, Aug also Sat 2–5pm; £2), standing in 800-acre grounds, is approached through an imposing gatehouse just off the town's Market Place. The palace has been extensively remodelled since its medieval incarnation, redesigned to satisfy the whims of such occupants as the seventeenth-century Bishop Cosin who refurbished the original banqueting hall to create today's splendid marble and limestone **chapel**. Here, the stained-glass windows relate the stories of early Christian saints familiar throughout the northeast, especially Cuthbert, Bede and Aidan. The other rooms are rather sparse, though there's an outstanding exception in the long dining room, with its thirteen paintings of Jacob and his sons by Zurbarán, commissioned in the 1640s for a monastery in South America.

Bishop Auckland is linked by **train** to Darlington, while **buses** drop you centrally, just a few minutes' west of the town hall, in Market Place, which houses the **tourist office** (Mon–Fri 10am–5pm, Sat 9am–4pm; ☎01388/604 922). **Accommodation** options include the slightly down-at-heel, *Postchaise Hotel*, 36 Market Place (☎01388/ 661 296; ④) or the *Albion Cottage Guest House*, on Albion Terrace (☎01388/602 217; ③). For **food**, the *Postchaise*, 36 Market Place, has a decent bar serving lunches, while *The Bishop's Bistro*, 17 Cockton Hill, has a good lunch and dinner menu (closed Sun).

Barnard Castle and around

Fifteen miles southwest of Bishop Auckland, the skeletal remains of **Barnard Castle** (April–Sept daily 10am–6pm; Oct–March Wed–Sun 10am–4pm; £1.80; EH), poking out from a cliff high above the River Tees, overlook the town which grew up in its shadow. First fortified in the eleventh century, the castle was long a stronghold of the Balliols, an Anglo-Scottish family interminably embroiled in the struggle for the Scottish crown. It was one of this clan, Bernard, who built the circular tower which survives to this day, an impressive thirteenth-century fortification just to the right of the later Round Tower, where a beautiful oriel window carries the emblematic boar of Richard III, one of the subsequent owners. By the seventeenth century the castle had outlived its usefulness and the Vanes quarried its stone to repair their premises at Raby (see below).

The town of Barnard Castle is a modest, well-kept place, though its other attactions are all firmly on the outskirts. Prime among them is the grand French-style chateau that constitutes the **Bowes Museum** (Mon–Sat 10am–5.30pm, Sun 2–5pm; £2.50), a mile or so east of the town centre (bus #X74). Begun in 1869, the chateau was commissioned by John and Josephine Bowes, who spent much of their time in Paris, collecting the ostentatious treasures and antiques of the Second Republic in bulk. They then shipped the whole lot back to Durham, everything from furniture, paintings, tapestries and ceramics to incidental curiosities, notably a late eighteenth-century mechanical silver swan which still performs twice daily. Among the paintings, look out for El Greco's *The Tears of St Peter* and a couple of Goyas.

Back in the town centre, it's a pleasant mile-and-a-half stroll from the castle, south-east along the banks of the Tees, to the glorious shattered ruins of **Egglestone Abbey** (dawn–dusk; free), a minor Premonstratensian foundation dating from 1195. Turner painted here on one of his three visits to Teesdale, and also at nearby **Rokeby Hall** (June to mid-Sept Mon & Tues 2–5pm; £3), a Palladian country house where Walter Scott wrote his ballad *Rokeby*. The house is noted for its extensive collection of eighteenth-century needlework pictures (bus #78 or #79 from Barnard Castle).

Buses stop on central Galgate – once the road out to the town gallows, hence the name. The **tourist office** is in the Council Offices at 43 Galgate (daily 10am–6pm; ☎01833/690 909). There's plenty of accommodation, including several convenient if rather mundane **B&Bs**, such as *Mrs Chesman*, 85 Galgate (☎01833/638 757; ③) and *Mr Kilgarriff*, 98 Galgate (☎01833/637 493; ③). For **food**, the *Hayloft*, in Horsemarket off Galgate (Nov–April closed Sun), has tasty and inexpensive home-baked snacks and meals during the day. The *Golden Lion* in Market Place or the *Old Well Inn*, 21 The Bank, a little further along the street, both do decent bar meals. *Prior's Vegetarian Restaurant*, at 7 The Bank, is open until around 5pm.

Raby Castle and Staindrop

The #8 bus from Barnard Castle provides access to the splendid, sprawling battlements of **Raby Castle** (May & June Wed & Sun 1–5pm; July–Sept daily except Sat 1–5pm; £3.50), seven miles to the northeast. The castle mostly dates from the fourteenth century, reflecting the power of the Neville family, who ruled the local roost until 1569. It was then that Charles Neville helped plan the "Rising of the North", the abortive attempt to replace Elizabeth I with Mary Queen of Scots. The revolt was a dismal failure, and Neville's estates were confiscated, with Raby subsequently passing to the Vanes, now the Lords Barnard, who still live in the castle. Raby's focal point is the first-floor Baron's Hall, still of cathedral-like dimensions in spite of the floor being raised ten feet in 1787 to let carriages pass through the neo-Gothic entrance below. Also of note are the Palladian library and the octagonal drawing room, unchanged since its completion in the 1840s. The whole castle is stuffed with antiques, from the usual family portraits and Meissen porcelain, to paintings by Joshua Reynolds and Luca Giordano.

Outside the castle, in the two-hundred-acre **deer park**, are the walled **gardens** (same days as castle 11am–5.30pm; gardens only, £1), where peach, apricot and pineapple trees once flourished under the careful gaze of forty Victorian gardeners. Heated cavity walls and curtains protected the trees from frost – above the last remaining apricot tree you can still see the hooks for the curtain rail. The castle's stables contain a collection of horse-drawn carriages. One mile south of the castle lies the pretty little village of **STAINDROP**, whose fortunes have always depended on the lords of Raby, and whose church, **St Mary's**, contains their tombs, including the bruised alabaster memorial of Ralph Neville, grandfather of Edward IV and Richard III. The church – a large rambling construction of Saxon origin – also possesses an especially fine thirteenth-century sedilia.

Teesdale

Extending twenty-odd miles northwest from Barnard Castle, **Teesdale** begins calmly enough, though the pastoral landscapes of its lower reaches are soon replaced by wilder Pennine scenery, beyond Newbiggin. The Tees itself becomes more vigorous as the road travels the two miles on to **Bowlees Country Park and Visitor Centre** (April–Sept daily 10.30am–5.30pm; 50p), the stop for the rapids of **Low Force**. Close by is the altogether more impressive **High Force**, a seventy-foot cascade which rumbles over an outcrop of the Whin Sill, a black dolerite ridge that pokes up in various parts of northern England. The waterfall is on private Raby land, and visitors must pay 50p to view the falls. You can avoid the entrance fee by walking up from Low Force on the opposite bank of the river along the **Pennine Way**, but the view isn't as spectacular.

The Pennine Way continues the six miles upstream to **Cauldron Snout**, near the source of the Tees, where the river rolls two hundred feet down a dolerite stairway as it leaves **Cow Green Reservoir**. It's also possible to reach the reservoir by car: turn off the main road at **Langdon Beck** – about a mile north of the stone-built **youth hostel** at Forest-in-Teesdale (Feb–Nov, weekends only in winter; ☎01833/622 228) – and follow the three-mile-long lane to the car park, a mile's walk from the Snout.

Darlington

DARLINGTON hit the big time in 1825, when George Stephenson's *Locomotion* hurtled from here to nearby Stockton-on-Tees, with the inventor at the controls and flag-carrying horsemen riding ahead to warn of the onrushing train, which reached a terrifying fifteen miles per hour. This novel form of transport soon proved popular with passengers, an unlooked-for bonus for Edward Pease, the line's instigator: he had simply wanted a fast and economical way to transport coal from the Durham pits to the docks at Stockton. Subsequently, Darlington grew into a rail engineering centre, and didn't look back till the pruning of the network and the closure of the works in 1966.

Trains still stop at Darlington's North Road station, which was completed in 1842, but the building's primary function is to house the **Darlington Railway Centre and Museum** (daily 9.30am–5pm; £1.70), whose pride and joy is the original *Locomotion*. There are other locally made engines and memorabilia too, but the museum feels strangely lifeless except on one of the half-dozen summer "steam weekends", when an engine hauls visitors up a nearby quarter-mile stretch of track.

As for the rest of Darlington, there's little else of any interest, despite the town's long history as an agricultural centre and staging post on the Great North Road. You could, however, have a look around the Victorian covered market, next to the clock tower, and the nearby church of **St Cuthbert** (Mon, Wed & Sat 11am–3pm), where the needle-like spire and decorative turrets herald the delicate Early English stonework inside. The **Darlington Museum** on Tubwell Row (Mon–Wed & Fri 10am–1pm & 2–6pm, Thurs 10am–1pm, Sat 10am–1pm & 2–5.30pm; free) has more on the town's industrial history, as well as a collection of local minerals.

From the **train station**, walk up Victoria Road to the roundabout and turn right down Feethams for the central Market Place. You'll pass the new town hall on Feethams, behind which is the **bus station**. The town's **tourist office** (Mon–Fri 9am–5.30pm, Sat 10am–4pm; ☎01325/382 698), in part of the Market Hall building at 4 West Row, has a substantial list of **B&Bs** – the *Bluebird Guest House*, 100 Victoria Road (☎01325/467 855; ②) is closest to the train station. There are two **hotels**: the *King's Head* on Priestgate (☎01325/380 222; ⑧) and the more reasonable *Cricketers Hotel* at 53 Parkgate (☎01325/384 444; ⑤–⑥). Cheap and basic board is available at the town's *Arts Centre* (☎01325/483 271; ①), about half a mile west of the centre in Vane Terrace; follow Duke Street from central Skinnergate.

Newcastle and around

At first glance **NEWCASTLE UPON TYNE** – virtual capital of the area between Yorkshire and Scotland – may appear to be just another grimy industrial conurbation, but the banks of the Tyne have been settled for nearly two thousand years and the city consequently has a greater breadth of attractions than many of its northern rivals. The Romans were the first to bridge the river here, and the "new castle" appeared as long ago as 1080. In Elizabethan times a regional monopoly on **coal** export brought wealth and power to Newcastle and engendered its other great industry, shipbuilding. At one time, 25 percent of the world's shipping was built here, and the first steam train and steam turbine also emerged from Newcastle factories. In its Victorian heyday, Newcastle's engineers and builders gave the city an elegance which has survived the ravages of recent development. Hard times and a sense of remoteness from the capital have given Newcastle's inhabitants, known as **Geordies**, a partisan pride in their city, which finds its most evident expression in fanatical support for **Newcastle United** football team. The death of United's most famous goal scorer, Jackie Milburn, brought thousands on to the streets for what was almost a state funeral. His statue – the inscription reads "Footballer and Gentleman" – stands in the city centre.

Arrival, information and city transport

The train station, **Central Station,** is a five-minute walk south of the city centre. *National Express* **coach** services arrive at Gallowgate station opposite St James's Park football ground, while regional bus services use the **Haymarket** bus station, north of the centre close to the university. All other local bus services arrive at and depart from the undergound bus station at **Eldon Square**. Newcastle also has an **airport**, six miles north of the city at Woolsington. It's linked to Central Station by Metro (see below) with departures every 8–15 minutes (6.20am–11pm; 25min; £1). **Ferry arrivals** from Scandanavia or Germany dock at Royal Quays, North Shields, seven miles east of the city. Connecting bus services run you into the centre, stopping at Central Station.

There are **tourist offices** at the **airport** (Mon–Fri 8am–8pm, Sat 8am–1pm, Sun noon–5pm; ☎0191/214 4422), in **Central Station** (June–Sept Mon–Sat 10am–8pm, Sun 10am–5pm; Oct–May Mon–Sat 10am–5pm; ☎0191/230 0030) and in the **Central Library**, behind Northumberland Street (Mon & Thurs 9.30am–8pm, Tues, Wed & Fri 9.30am–5pm, Sat 9am–5pm; ☎0191/261 0691). The best local **listings magazine** is *The*

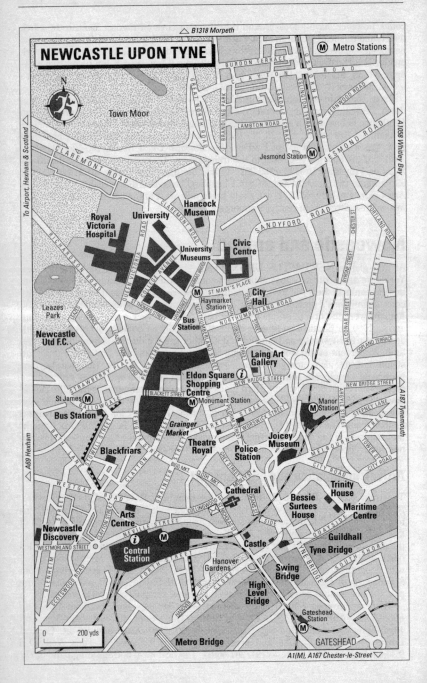

△ *B1318 Morpeth*

NEWCASTLE UPON TYNE

Ⓜ Metro Stations

N

Town Moor

BURDON TERRACE

CLAYTON ROAD

OSBORNE ROAD

BRANDLING PARK

NORTH ROAD

ESKDALE TERRACE

AKENSIDE TERRACE

OSBORNE ROAD

FERNWOOD ROAD

JESMOND ROAD

△ *A1058 Whitley Bay*

LAMBTON ROAD

CLAREMONT ROAD

Jesmond Station Ⓜ

To Airport, Hexham & Scotland △

RICHARDSON ROAD

CLAREMONT ROAD

CLAREMONT ROAD

SANDYFORD

CHESTER ST

PORTLAND ROAD

Hancock Museum

University

Royal Victoria Hospital

QUEEN VICTORIA ROAD

COLLEGE AVENUE

ST THOMAS STREET

University Museums

Civic Centre

BARRAS BRIDGE

CIVIC CENTRE

Leazes Park

LEAZES TERRACE

ST MARY'S PLACE

Haymarket Station

City Hall

NORTHUMBERLAND ROAD

JOHN DOBSON STREET

FALCONAR STREET

SHIELD STREET

COPLAND TERRACE

Ⓜ

Newcastle Utd F.C.

STRAWBERRY PLACE

LEAZES PARK ROAD

Bus Station

NORTHUMBERLAND STREET

Laing Art Gallery

NEW BRIDGE STREET

△ *A167 Tynemouth*

PERCY STREET

Eldon Square Shopping Centre ⓘ

BLACKETT STREET

Monument Station Ⓜ

NEW BRIDGE STREET

Manor Station Ⓜ

STEPNEY LANE

ST James Ⓜ

GALLOWGATE

Bus Station

NEWGATE STREET

GRAINGER STREET

MARKET STREET

WORSWICK STREET

PILGRIM STREET

ARGYLE STREET

MELBOURNE STREET

TOWER STREET

BATH LANE

STOWELL STREET

Blackfriars

Grainger Market

Theatre Royal

GREY STREET

Police Station

Joicey Museum

CITY ROAD

CITY ROAD

CLAYTON STREET

WESTGATE ROAD

BIGG MKT.

CLOTH MKT.

MOSLEY STREET

Cathedral

DEAN STREET

Bessie Surtees House

QUAYSIDE

Trinity House

Maritime Centre

Arts Centre

NEVILLE STREET

COLLINGWOOD ST

ST NICHOLAS STREET

SANDHILL

Guildhall

Tyne Bridge

BLENHEIM STREET

Newcastle Discovery

WESTMORLAND STREET

ⓘ Ⓜ

Central Station

Castle

QUAYSIDE

SOUTH SHORE

FORTH STREET

Hanover Gardens

Swing Bridge

SCOTSWOOD ROAD

HANOVER STREET

THE CLOSE

High Level Bridge

TYNE BRIDGE

Gateshead Station Ⓜ

0   200 yds

Metro Bridge

GATESHEAD

△ *A1(M), A167 Chester-le-Street* ▽

Crack, available (monthly) all over the city; look out, too, for *Paint It Red*, also monthly; while theatre and cinema listings are contained in the *Evening Chronicle*.

You can walk around the whole of central Newcastle easily enough, though if you're staying at the hostel or hotels in Jesmond you'll need to master the public transport system. City and suburban **buses** depart in the main from Eldon Square, although the #33 to Jesmond in fact leaves from Bewick Street, near Central Station. East of Eldon Square, **Monument** marks the city centre and site of the main interchange for the conurbation's efficient rail system, the **Metro** (services every 7–15min, 5.30am– 11.30pm). This runs on two lines: *Greenline*, connecting South Shields, Central Station, Monument and Jesmond with the airport; and the circular *Yellowline* connecting Monument with Jesmond, North Shields and Whitley Bay.

To get out on the Tyne, sign up for one of *River Tyne Cruises*' three-hour **sightseeing cruises**, which depart from the Quayside (June–Aug Sun 2pm; £6; ☎0191/251 5920). The local public transport authority also operates cruises from North and South Shields, at the mouth of the river (Aug only; £5; ☎0191/454 8183).

Accommodation

The biggest concentration of **hotels** and **guest houses** is in Jesmond, along and around Osborne Road, a mile north of the city centre: take the Metro to Jesmond or the #33 bus from Bewick Street, opposite the train station. You shouldn't have difficulty finding a bed at any time of the year, though businesspeople visiting make weekdays busier than weekends for most of the year. Consequently, many hotels offer discounts for Friday- and Saturday-night stays, especially at the upper end of the scale where savings can be considerable. The very cheapest beds are at the **youth hostel** or in one of the **student residences** during the summer: book well in advance for these. The nearest **campsite** is *Newcastle Racecourse Campsite*, High Gosforth Park (☎0191/236 3258), four miles north of the city (bus #42, #43, #44 or #45 from Haymarket).

Hotels and guest houses

Carlton Hotel, 82–86 Osborne Rd (☎0191/281 3361). Recently renovated, this remains excellent value, with tasteful en-suite rooms, bar and restaurant. ⑨.

Copthorne Hotel, The Close, Quayside (☎0191/222 0333). With superb location, bang on the riverside, this modern hotel has Tyne views from most of its rooms. Around £130 a night, though prices drop to well under £100 at the weekend. ⑨.

Da Vinci's Hotel, 73 Osborne Rd (☎0191/281 5284). Light, well-furnished rooms; classy dining room complete with piano and Leonardo prints. ④.

George Hotel, 88 Osborne Rd (☎0191/281 4442). Family-run Victorian town-house hotel with some of the city's cheapest rooms. If you're saving money, ask to share a "single" with a double bed. ③.

Minerva Hotel, 105 Osborne Rd (☎0191/281 0190). Family-run place with pleasant rooms and a cosy bar; serves late breakfasts and inexpensive dinners, and has car parking too. ③.

Portland Guest House, 134 Sandyford Rd (☎0191/232 7868). Simple, spotless rooms in a renovated Georgian house, a 10-min walk from the city centre and close to Jesmond Metro station. ③.

Royal Station Hotel, Neville St (☎0191/232 0781). The city's original Victorian station hotel, built in 1858 and now fully modernized. Great central location and surprisingly low prices. ⑤–⑥.

Tilley's, 105–107 Westgate Rd (☎0191/232 0692). Extremely basic rooms above a noisy city centre pub, with no private facilities, but undeniably bargain-priced. Book in advance. ①–②.

The Waterside, 48–52 Sandhill (☎0191/230 0111). Small, luxury hotel right in the centre of the Quayside night-time action. Very good weekend prices. ⑦.

Hostels and university accommodation

Newcastle University, Leazes Terrace Student House (☎0191/222 8150). Centrally located student accommodation near the football ground, available early July to late Sept. There are lots of single rooms (B&B £16); doubles are a shade under £30.

Newcastle YHA Youth Hostel, 107 Jesmond Rd (☎0191/281 2570). Town-house hostel with 60 beds near Jesmond Metro station. Closed Dec and Jan.
University of Northumbria, Lovaine Hall, Ellison Building, Ellison Place (☎0191/227 4024). Central student hall of residence offering B&B for £17; available April and July–Sept.

The City

Anyone arriving by train from the north will get a sneak preview of the **Castle** (Tues–Sun April–Sept 9.30am–5.30pm; Oct–March 9.30am–4.30pm; £1), as the rail line splits the keep from its gatehouse, the Black Gate, on St Nicholas' Street. A wooden fort was built here by Robert Curthose, illegitimate eldest son of William the Conquerer, but the present keep dates from the twelfth century and is everything a castle should be – thick, square and labyrinthine. Staircases and rooms, including a Norman chapel, lie off a draughty central hall, and there's a great view from the top. Little remains of the outer fortifications except the Black Gate, topped by a seventeenth-century house.

Further along St Nicholas' Street stands the **Cathedral** (Mon–Fri & Sun 7am–6pm, Sat 8.30am–4pm), dating mainly from the fourteenth and fifteenth centuries and remarkable chiefly for its tower, erected in 1470, and topped with a crown-like structure of turrets and arches supporting a lantern. Inside, behind the high altar, is one of the largest funerary brasses in England, commissioned by Roger Thornton, who arrived penniless and died Newcastle's richest merchant in 1430. Much of the interior was given a neo-Gothic remodelling in the late nineteenth century under Sir George Gilbert Scott – the ornate reredos, depicting various Northumbrian saints, is from this period, as is the font canopy with its intricate pinnacles.

From between the castle and the cathedral a road known simply as Side, formerly the main road out of the city, descends to the **Quayside** and the area known as Sandhill, where the first bridges across the Tyne stood. Looming overhead is the symbol of the city, the **Tyne Bridge** of 1929, which became the model for the Sydney Harbour bridge. To the west of it, road and rail lines cross the river on the **High Level Bridge**, built by Robert Stephenson in 1849 – Queen Victoria was one of the first passengers across, promoting the railway revolution. Further west, under the bridge and up to Hanover Street, a section of the old encircling medieval city wall survives; the river views from the adjacent **Hanover Gardens** are magnificent.

This district became the commercial heart of the city in the sixteenth and seventeenth centuries, its half-timbered houses owned by Newcastle's wealthiest merchants. One is **Bessie Surtees' House**, at 41–44 Sandhill (Mon–Fri 10am–5pm; free), the residence of a well-heeled eighteenth-century woman who scandalously eloped to Scotland with a local yokel; all ended well and the groom in question went on to become Lord Eldon, Chancellor of England. The house has been renovated with materials, and even staircases and windows, appropriated from other buildings of the same era.

Opposite is the **Guildhall**, where court sessions were held; John Wesley preached here in 1742 and had to be rescued from a volatile crowd by a hefty fishwife. On Sundays (9am–2.30pm) a busy **market** spreads around the nearby **Swing Bridge**, which was built in 1876 by Lord Armstrong to replace the old Tyne Bridge, so that larger vessels could reach his shipyards upriver. Further east along the quay, up Broad Chare, is the unspoiled ensemble of **Trinity House** (April–Sept Tues–Thurs 2pm–4pm; 50p), built in 1505 for the Mariners' Guild and still run by the Brethren of Master Mariners. Controllers of all shipping on the river, the guild had its own naval school whose alumni included Collingwood and Captain Cook. On show are the entrance hall, with a few leathery old turtles, and the original chapel, a beautiful and intimate place. Next door, the **Trinity Maritime Centre** (April–Oct Tues–Fri 11am–4pm; £1) has a few rooms of maritime mementos and some lovingly detailed model ships.

Grey Street to the city walls

Connecting ancient and modern Newcastle is **Grey Street** – "that descending, subtle curve", as John Betjeman described it. Planned by John Dobson in the 1830s, this elegant thoroughfare is typified by the plush **Theatre Royal**, which hosts the Royal Shakespeare Company every February and March. The street takes its name from the Northumberland dynasty of political heavyweights whose most illustrious member was the second Earl Grey, prime minister from 1830 to 1834. In the middle of his term of office he carried the Reform Bill through parliament, an act commemorated by **Grey's Monument** at the top of the street. Its 164 steps can be climbed on Saturdays and Bank Holidays, Easter to September (11.30am–4.30pm; 40p).

West of here, behind Gallowgate coach station, is the most complete stretch of the old **city walls**, leading down to Westgate Road. Several towers were used by the city guilds as meeting houses and one, the **Morden Tower** behind Stowell Street (Newcastle's Chinatown), gained more recent prestige as the haunt of poets such as Allen Ginsberg, Basil Bunting and Tom Pickard. Poetry readings are still held here (☎0191/286 2129 for details). At the other side of Stowell Street is the tranquil court-yard of **Blackfriars** (Mon–Sat 9am–5.30pm; closed Mon in winter; free), a thirteenth-century stone monastery now restored to house a crafts centre and restaurant.

Further south of here, off Blenheim Street, the **Newcastle Discovery** in Blandford House, Blandford Square (Mon–Sat 10am–5pm; free) attempts to put the city's history into context, with various galleries concentrating on Newcastle's maritime history, its pioneering inventors, armed forces, local costumes and community groups. The hands-on *Science Factory* gets rave reviews from children.

The Laing Gallery and the university museums

Newcastle's – indeed, the Northeast's – premier art collection is the **Laing Gallery** on Higham Place (Mon–Sat 10am–5pm, Sun 2–5pm; free), off John Dobson Street, behind the library. It's a splendidly organized museum, in which local pottery, glassware, costume and sculpture play their part, while on permanent display is a sweep through British art from Reynolds to John Hoyland, with a smattering of Pre-Raphaelites, so admired by English industrial barons. The real treat here, though, is the lashings of **John Martin** (1789–1854), a self-taught local painter with a penchant for massive Biblical and mythical scenes inspired by the dramatic northeastern scenery. The other must-see in the gallery is the **Art on Tyneside** exhibition, which romps through the history of art and applied art in the region since the seventeenth century with consider-able gusto. The exhibition comes up to date with coverage of Sixties' pop artists Richard Hamilton and Victor Pasmore, both of whom taught at the university, and an analysis of the award-winning Byker Wall project, pioneered by Ralph Erskine.

Newcastle University, opposite Haymarket Metro, contains a knot of fine museums and galleries: the **Museum of Antiquities** (Mon–Sat 10am–5pm; free) makes a good place to get to grips with the history of Hadrian's Wall; the small **Greek Museum** (Mon–Fri 9.30am–12.30pm & 2–4.30pm; free) contains a valuable collection of armour, jewellery and pottery; and the **Hatton Gallery** (Mon–Fri 10am–5.30pm, plus Sat in term-time 10am–4.30pm; free) features a collection of African sculpture, the only surviving example of Kurt Schwitters' *Merzbau* (a sort of architectural collage) and a variety of temporary exhibitions, often showcasing work by local students. Also attached to the university is the **Hancock Museum** on adjacent Claremont Road (Mon–Sat 10am–5pm, Sun 2–5pm; £1.80); based on an eighteenth-century natural history collection, it's grown to immense dimensions – with more than 150,000 insect specimens. Beyond the university stretch the 1200 acres of the **Town Moor**, the city's green lung. It's the site of the annual "Hoppings" in June, a huge week-long **fair** of rides, stalls and other attractions which keeps going until well after dark.

Eating, drinking and nightlife

The population's tastes have moved a long way from traditional dishes, such as black pudding or the gargantuan bread rolls called stottie cakes. At the budget end of the market Italian, Indian and Chinese food dominates the scene, while at the top end of the scale the city is beginning to attract some top-class chefs. If you're counting the pennies, aim to eat early – many city-centre restaurants offer **early-bird/happy-hour** deals before 7pm, while others serve **set lunches** at often ludicrous prices.

On a Friday night the entire population seems to be spending like mad in the pubs and clubs. Newcastle's **nightlife** centres on the older parts of town: between Grainger Street and the cathedral in the area called the Bigg Market – spiritual home of Sid the Sexist and the Fat Slags, from the locally based *Viz* magazine – and on the Quayside, where the bars are smaller and more atmospheric. As with restaurants, **happy hour** is a big deal in Newcastle – serial early-doors drinking is positively encouraged.

There's a full **theatrical** life in the city, from the offerings of the splendid Victorian *Theatre Royal* to those of the smaller contemporary theatre companies. **Live music and stand-up comedy** take place most nights, too, either at one of the venues listed below or organized by the **students' unions** at Newcastle University (☎0191/232 8402) and Northumbria University (☎0191/232 8761). Two **festivals** to note are the annual *Newcastle Jazz Festival* every July, and the *Newcastle Free Festival* in August, when anything from flamenco to folk hits the streets.

Snacks and coffee

Blakes Coffee House, 53 Grey St. Near the Theatre Royal, this is the best coffee house in town for sandwiches, mountainous *ciabatta* included. Closed Sun.

Fenwick, Northumberland St. Give the department store a whirl – inside is a good second-floor coffee shop, as well as three restaurants, a wine bar and self-service café.

Heaven Café, 47 Pink Lane and 83 Westgate Rd. Lurking at the back of the *Zone* photograph gallery, the city's bright young things stock up on cappuccino, pitta-bread sandwiches and salads.

Tyneside Coffee Rooms, 2nd floor, *Tyneside Cinema*, 10–12 Pilgrim St. Coffee, snacks and art-house movie talk in the cinema café.

Restaurants

Barn Again, 25 Leazes Park Rd (☎0191/261 7079). Fine Anglo-French bistro cooking, hidden away in a courtyard up an alley close to the football ground. Good wine list, too. Expensive, moderate at lunch.

Café Procope, 35 Side (☎0191/232 3848). As international as they come – from Lithuania to Cuba via goulash and German sausages. Eat here and drink in the *Crown Posada* afterwards (see below). Moderate, but inexpensive at lunch.

Don Vito's, 82–84 Pilgrim St. The cheapest pizzas and pasta in town, especially so if you dig in before 7pm. Inexpensive.

Dragon House, 30–32 Stowell St (☎0191/232 0868). One of the best Cantonese restaurants on this street, where the city's Chinese eateries are concentrated. Moderate.

Fisherman's Lodge, Jesmond Dene (☎0191/281 3281). Classy, formal restaurant in Jesmond Dene park, offering well-received modern British cuisine. Excellent vegetarian choices and the set lunches are a good deal. Closed Sat lunch and Sun. Very expensive.

Gianfranco, 6–10 Leazes Park Rd (☎0191/222 0659). Long-established Italian restautrant with a wide choice of dishes and some attractive lunch and happy-hour deals. Inexpensive to moderate.

Heartbreak Soup, Baltic Chambers, 77 Quayside. Good-value Mexican-Caribbean food in colour-splashed surroundings down by the river. Moderate.

Leela's, 20 Dean St (☎0191/230 1261). High-quality south Indian cuisine, with plenty of vegetarian options. Closed Sun. Moderate to expensive.

Pierre Victoire, 4 Queen St (☎0191/232 2399). Airy, jazzy, rather scatty bistro close to Quayside serving great-value set lunches for £5 and a wider evening menu of brasserie favourites. Moderate.

21 Queen Street, 21 Queen St (☎0191/222 0755). Newcastle's premier restaurant, serving inventive seafood. A good £40 a head, though set lunches are a veritable bargain at under £20. Closed Sat lunch and Sun.

Pubs, bars and clubs

Bigg Market. There's not a great deal of point listing the Bigg Market pubs and bars – everyone swans in and out of each in the biggest (and largely good-natured) cattle market in western Europe.

The Cooperage, 32 The Close. A cosy Quayside pub, just along from the Tyne Bridge, with a good range of beers and, often, live bands.

Crown Posada, 31 Side. Local beers and guest ales in a highly attractive wood-and-glass-panelled pub down by the Quayside.

Forth Hotel, Pink Lane. Trendy *Tetley's* pub that's a current fave, near the *Jazz Café*.

The Mayfair, Newgate St. Converted ballroom with legendary heavy rock nights at the weekend.

Planet Earth, Low Friar Street. One of the latest of the city's dance clubs, with different music policies depending on the night; check the local press for details.

Trent House, 1–2 Leazes Lane. Soul bar with keen student following.

Tuxedo Royale, Tyne Bridge. Floating nightclub, on the south side of the river below the bridge, with a raucous 18–25-year-old crowd rolling back the pop years.

Live music and comedy

Bridge Hotel, Castle Square, St Nicholas Street (☎0191/232 7780). Right opposite the castle, by the High Level Bridge, this has a great view of the Tyne from its beer garden and fine live folk, blues and jazz at the *Jumpin' Hot Club*.

The Comedy Café, Westgate Rd (☎0191/232 0899). Most reliable city venue for stand-up comedy with several gigs a week.

Dog & Parrot, Clayton St West (☎0191/261 6998). Local and touring bands of dubious repute gig here nightly.

Irish Centre, 43 Gallowgate (☎0191/232 9422). Opposite the coach station. Regular Irish folk gigs, jazz and a *ceilidh* every Sunday.

The Riverside, 57–59 Melbourne St (☎0191/261 4386). Best spot in the city for touring live bands and club nights.

The arts and culture

City Hall, Northumberland Rd (☎0191/232 0007). The city's main concert venue; the *Northern Sinfonia* performs from September to May.

The Garage, Peel Lane, off Waterloo Street (☎0191/261 0505). Modern dance productions in a small city venue.

Live Theatre, 27 Broad Chare (☎0191/261 2694). Enterprising youthful theatre company with regular productions promoting local actors and writers; Sunday jazz concerts, too.

Newcastle Arts Centre, Westgate Rd (☎0191/261 5618). Art gallery, exhibition space and concert and drama venue – always worth checking what's on.

Newcastle Playhouse, Barras Bridge (☎0191/230 5151). Modern theatre, home of Newcastle's own *Northern Stage* company.

Theatre Royal, Grey St (☎0191/232 2061). Drama, ballet, opera and dance; and the annual RSC season in February and March.

Tyneside Cinema, Pilgrim St (☎0191/232 8289). The city's premier art-house cinema; hosts an acclaimed annual International Film Festival in November.

Listings

Airport and flight enquiries Call *Newcastle International Airport* (☎0191/286 0966).

Banks Banks are concentrated around Grey and Northumberland streets. There's a *bureau de change* at the airport.

Bus enquiries *National Express* (☎0191/261 6077); *Scot Express* and *Blue Line* (☎0191/232 3377).

Car rental *Avis*, at the airport (☎0191/286 0815); *Eurocar*, airport (☎0191/286 5070); and *Hertz*, airport (☎0191/286 6748). The best local rates are offered by *Auto Hire*, 79–81 Blenheim St (☎0191/232 7774).

Ferry information North Shields ferry terminal at Royal Quays, 7 miles east of the city, has sailings to Scandinavia and Germany. Contact *Color Line* (for Bergen and Stavanger; ☎0191/296 1313) or *Scandinavian Seaways* (Gothenberg, Esbjerg, Hamburg; ☎0191/296 0101). Buses leave from Central Station to the terminal before each sailing; nearest metro station is Percy Main, from where it's a 20-min walk to the ferry terminal.

Football You've got virtually no chance of getting tickets for regular league matches at Newcastle United's St James' Park, Barrack Road (☎0191/232 8361), but if you want to make the pilgrimage, then at least visit the club museum (Mon–Fri 10am–4pm, Sat 2–4pm; £1).

Hospital *Royal Victoria Infirmary*, Queen Victoria Rd, behind the university (☎0191/232 5131).

Laundry *Clayton Road Launderette*, 4 Clayton Rd, off Osborne Road, a short walk from Jesmond Metro.

Police Corner of Market and Pilgrim streets (☎091/232 3451).

Post office Main office is on Blackett Street, inside the Eldon Square shopping centre.

Shopping Mall junkies should make the trip out to Gateshead *MetroCentre*, Europe's largest shopping and lesiure centre, with three miles of malls and 50 restaurants and cafés.

Train enquiries *British Rail*, Central Station (☎0191/232 6262).

Around Newcastle

The Metro network connects most of the day-trip destinations around Newcastle, and a **Day Rover** ticket, costing £3 from booths at Monument and Haymarket, enables you to get the best out of the local transport systems. In addition to the Metro, it's valid for most buses in the county of Tyne and Wear, the BR train to Sunderland and the ferry between North and South Shields.

Seaton Delaval Hall

One of Vanbrugh's great Baroque houses, **Seaton Delaval Hall** (May–Sept Wed & Sun 2–6pm; £2), lies eleven miles northeast of Newcastle (bus #364 from Haymarket), its gloomy north facade looking over the bleak terrain towards the port of Blyth. Fire badly damaged the hall in 1822, a century after it was built, but subsequent restorations have done ample justice to the sombre grandeur of a building that exemplifies the architect's desire to create country houses with "something of the castle air".

THE JARROW CRUSADE

Jarrow provides the perfect example of what happens to a company town when its company closes. It owed its growth in the last century to the success of the steelworks and shipyard owned by local MP Charles Palmer. Producer of the world's first oil tanker, the Jarrow production line was a phenomenal organization, employing at its zenith some 10,000 men. However, demand for steel and ships went into decline after World War I, and eighty percent of the workforce had been laid off by 1934, the year Palmer's was sold off and broken up.

On October 5, 1936, led by the town's radical MP Ellen Wilkinson, two hundred men left Jarrow to walk the 290 miles to London under the "Jarrow Crusade" banner. Supported by all the town's politicians, the protesters gathered sympathy and support all along the road to the capital, becoming the most potent image of the hardships of 1930s Britain. In the end, the real recovery only came about through the rearmament of Britain in the build-up to World War II. Palmers was resurrected at nearby Hebburn, and struggled through a series of takeovers into the 1970s, by which time the local economy was on the brink of a state nearly as bad as that of the 1930s. In 1986, with unemployment on Tyneside reaching 32 percent, the fiftieth anniversary of the Jarrow Crusade was marked by another march on the seat of government. The hardships of the 1930s were instrumental in the creation of the Welfare State; the hardships of the 1980s were all but ignored.

Belsay and Wallington

Belsay Hall, Castle and Gardens (April–Sept daily 10am–6pm; Oct–March Tues–Sun 10am–4pm; £2.60; EH), fourteen miles northwest of Newcastle, were inherited in 1795 by Sir Charles Monck, who eleven years later decided to build a brand new hall here after his return from a honeymoon-cum-grand-tour of Europe. Inspired by the Neoclassical buildings of Berlin and the Classical architecture of Athens, Sir Charles planned a majestic Doric house, an austere one-hundred-foot-square sandstone block raised on a podium of three steps. Built between 1807 and 1817, the **hall** has now been impressively restored, though the equally severe interior, with the bedrooms and state rooms surrounding a multi-columned hall, is devoid of furnishings and fittings.

To the west lie the **gardens**, where a footpath threads through the trim formality of the winter gardens to reach the **Quarry Gardens**. Here, in the quarry used for the building of the hall, lush vegetation cascades over exposed rock faces, planned by Sir Charles as a Romantic antidote to the severity of the hall. The track also leads to the substantial remains of the medieval **castle**, its battlements punctuated by four formidable corner turrets. **Belsay village**, on the main road about a mile from the hall, is readily reached by **bus** from Newcastle (#506 or #508 from Percy Street).

Eight miles northwest of Belsay lies the tiny village of **Cambo**; occasional local bus services connect the two. Just outside Cambo stands **Wallington House** (April–Oct daily except Tues 1–5.30pm; £4.60; NT), an ostentatious mansion rebuilt by Sir Walter Blackett, the coal- and lead-mine owner, in the 1740s. The interior's highlight is the Rococo plasterwork, though William Bell Scott's Pre-Raphaelite decorations in the central hall are good fun too.

Washington

Five miles south of Newcastle, **WASHINGTON** was the ancestral home of the family which spawned the first US president. The Washingtons lived in the **Old Hall**, on The Avenue, until 1613; there's not a great deal to see in the house now, but it has fine eighteenth-century panelling and plenty of George Washington memorabilia (April–Oct Mon–Thurs & Sun 11am–5pm; £2.30). **Buses** from Newcastle run regularly to Washington station, from where there's a connecting service out to the Old Hall. There are several other museums and attractions in the Washington area – mining relics at the Washington "F" Pit Museum, North East Aircraft Museum, Bowes Railway steam-train rides – but all are difficult to reach without your own transport. Easiest to get to, and in many ways the nicest, is the **Washington Wildfowl and Wetlands Centre** (daily June–Sept 9.30am–5.30pm; Oct–May 9.30am–4.30pm; £3.50), east of town (bus #168) and close to the River Wear, its one hundred acres designed by Sir Peter Scott and home to swans, geese, ducks and flamingoes. Its trails, hides, play areas, visitor information centre and children's activities make for an enjoyable day out.

Hadrian's Wall and Hexham

In 55 and 54 BC, Julius Caesar launched two swift invasions of southeast England from his base in Gaul, his success proving that Britain lay within the Roman grasp. The full-scale assault began under Claudius in 43 AD and, within forty years, Roman troops had reached the Firth of Tay. In 83 AD, the Roman governor Agricola ventured further north, but Rome subsequently transferred part of his army to the Danube, and the remaining legions withdrew to the frontier which was marked by the **Stanegate**, a military roadway linking Carlisle and Corbridge.

The **Emperor Hadrian**, who toured Roman Britain in 122 AD, found this informal arrangement unsatisfactory. His imperial policy was quite straightforward – he wanted the empire to live at peace within stable frontiers, most of which were defined by geographical features. In northern Britain, however, there was no natural barrier and so Hadrian decided to create his own by constructing a 76-mile **wall** from the Tyne to the Solway Firth. It was not intended to be an impenetrable fortification, but rather as a base for patrols that could push out into hostile territory and as a barrier to inhibit movement. It was to be punctuated by **milecastles**, which were to serve as gates, depots and mini-barracks, and by observation **turrets**, two of which were to stand between each pair of milecastles. Before the wall was even completed, major modifications were made: the bulk of the garrison had initially been stationed along the Stanegate, but they were now moved into the wall, occupying a chain of new **forts**, which straddled the wall at six- to nine-mile intervals. These new arrangements concentrated the wall's garrison into a handful of key points and brought them nearer the enemy, making it possible to respond quickly in force to any threat. Simultaneously, a military zone was defined by the digging of a broad ditch, or **vallum**, on the south side of the wall, crossed by causeways to each of the forts, turning them into the main points of access and rendering the milecastles, in this respect, largely redundant. The revised structure remained in operation until the last Roman soldiers left in 411 AD.

Most of Hadrian's Wall disappeared centuries ago, yet travelling its length remains a popular pastime. Approached from Newcastle along the Tyne valley, via the Roman museum and site at **Corbridge**, the prosperous-looking market town of **Hexham**, with its fine eleventh-century Abbey, makes an ideal base. Most visitors stick to the best-preserved portions of the wall, which are concentrated between the hamlet of **Chollerford**, three miles north of Hexham, and **Haltwhistle**, sixteen miles to the west. It's here, especially between **Housesteads** and **Steel Rigg**, that the wall is at its most beautiful, as it clings to the edge of the Whin Sill, a precipitous line of dolerite crags towering above the austere Northumberland National Park moorland. Walking this part of the wall couldn't be easier: a footpath runs along the top of the ridge, incorporating a short stretch of the **Pennine Way**, which meets the wall at Greenhead and leaves at Housesteads, where it cuts off north for Bellingham. Scattered along this section are a variety of key archeological sites and museums, notably **Chesters Roman Fort and Museum**, near Chollerford; the remains of **Housesteads Fort** and that of **Vindolanda**; and the milecastle remains at **Cawfields**, north of Haltwhistle.

VISITING THE WALL

Using **Hexham** as your base, you can see most of the Northumbrian section of the wall by bus or car, with the B6318 Miltary Road following the line of the wall from Chollerford to Greenhead. In summer, bus #890 (mid-July to early Sept Mon–Sat 4 daily, 2 on Sun; early May to mid-July & last 3 weeks of Sept Sat & Sun only) links Hexham bus and train stations with Chesters, Housesteads, Once Brewed Visitor Centre, Vindolanda, the Milecastle Inn (for Cawfields), Haltwhistle town and train station, the Roman Army Museum and Greenhead; timetables from Hexham tourist office or the Once Brewed Visitor Centre.

All the sites from Greenhead to Once Brewed/Vindolanda are also connected by **bus** #682 (☎01228/812 812 for information), which originates in **Carlisle** (p.470) and calls first at Birdoswald; this service complements the #890 and only runs Mondays to Fridays, twice a day, from late April to late October. There's also an hourly service (every 2hr on Sun), the #685, which runs along the A69 between Carlisle, Greenhead, Haltwhistle and Newcastle (Eldon Square).

Throughout the rest of the year, the only public transport links are the **train** stations on the Newcastle–Carlisle line at Hexham, Bardon Mill and Haltwhistle, leaving you a fair walk to Chesters, Vindolanda and Cawfields/Greenhead respectively. Finally, the **#880 or #882 bus** from Hexham to Bellingham (Mon–Sat 4–6 daily; ☎01434/602 217), runs via Chollerford, from where Chesters is just half a mile's walk along the road to the west; during May to mid-September, some of these services divert to Chesters itself.

Corbridge

Buses from Newcastle and trains on the Newcastle–Hexham–Carlisle train line all stop at **CORBRIDGE**, a quiet and well-heeled town overlooking the River Tyne from the top of a steep ridge. This spur of land was first settled by the Saxons, and their handiwork survives in parts of the church of **St Andrew**, on the central Market Place, but it's the adjacent **Vicar's Pele** that catches the eye, an unusually well-preserved fortified towerhouse dating to the fourteenth century. Other buildings are less striking but form a handsome ensemble, with tawny-coloured stone houses alternating with some surprisingly upmarket shops and eating places.

One mile to the west of the Market Place, accessible either by road or along the riverside footpath – take the street opposite the *Watling Coffee House* – lies **Corbridge Roman Site** (April–Oct daily 10am–6pm; Nov–March Wed–Sun 10am–4pm; £2.20; EH), the location of the garrison town of Corstopitum. Most of the archeological remains date from the third century, when the town, the most northerly in the Empire, served as the nerve centre of Hadrian's Wall, guarding the bridge at the intersection of Stanegate and Dere Street. Clearly labelled, the ruins provide a pleasurable insight into the lay-out of the civilian town, including the best-preserved Roman granaries in Britain as well as the foundations of temples, workshops and houses. The site **museum** boasts a good selection of Roman artefacts, including the *Lion and Stag* fountainhead – the so-called "Corbridge Lion".

The **train station** is half a mile outside the town, across the river; **buses** stop at the *Angel Inn* on Main Street or near the post office on Hill Street, around the corner. Corbridge **tourist office** is also on Hill Street, underneath the library (Easter–Oct Mon–Sat 10am–1pm & 2–5pm, June–Aug until 6pm, Sun 1–5pm; ☎01434/632 815). There are plenty of convenient **B&Bs** near the train station on Station Road – try *Fellcroft* (☎01434/632 384; ③) or *Holmlea* (☎01434/632 486; ③) – and, more centrally, on Main Street – the *Riverside Guest House* (☎01434/632 942; ③–④). You'll need to book in advance for the ivy-covered *Angel Inn* on Main Street (☎01434/632 119; ⑤), which has just five en-suite rooms, or at the *Lion of Corbridge Hotel*, Bridge End (☎01434/632 504; ⑤), which is right by the bridge on the way in from the train station.

The *Watling Coffee House*, on Hill Street just off the main square, serves light **meals** throughout the day, and further down Hill Street, more intriguing is the *Valley* (☎01434/633 434; closed Sun), an Indian restaurant housed in the Old Station House right by the train station. Further up the same road, the *Ramblers Country House Restaurant* (☎01434/632 424) at Farnley (closed Mon, & Sun dinner) is a comfortable place with gardens and set dinners for around £17. Back in town, for bar meals and beer, visit the *Wheatsheaf* on Watling Street or – in the other direction – you could try the stone-built *Black Bull* on Middle Street. Otherwise, the *Dyvels*, very close to the train station, is a nice, small local pub with a beer garden.

Hexham and around

In 671, on a bluff above the Tyne, four miles west of Corbridge, Saint Wilfrid founded a Benedictine monastery whose church was, according to contemporary accounts, the finest to be seen north of the Alps. Unfortunately, its gold and silver proved irresistible to the Vikings, who savaged the place in 876, but the church was rebuilt in the eleventh century as part of an Augustinian priory, and the town of **HEXHAM**, governed by the Archbishop of York, grew up in its shadow. It's a handsome market town of some interest and however keen you are to reach the wall, you'd do well to give Hexham a night or even make it your base.

The stately exterior of **Hexham Abbey** (daily May–Sept 9am–7pm; Oct–April 9am–5pm; free), still dominates the west side of the Market Place. Entry is through the south transept, where there's a bruised but impressive first-century tombstone honouring Flavinus, a standard-bearer in the Roman cavalry, who's shown riding down his bearded enemy. The memorial lies at the foot of the broad, well-worn steps of the canons' **night stair**, one of the few such staircases – providing access from the monastery to the church – to have survived the Dissolution. From the heavily restored high-arched nave beyond, you gain access to the **crypt**, a Saxon structure made out of old Roman stones, where pilgrims once viewed the abbey's reliquaries. The nave's architect also used Roman stonework, sticking various sculptural fragments in the walls, many of which he had unearthed during the rebuilding. At the end of the nave is the splendid sixteenth-century **rood screen**, whose complex tracery envelopes the portraits of local bishops. Behind the screen, the chancel displays the inconsequential-looking **Frith Stool**, an eighth-century stone chair that was once believed to have been used by Saint Wilfrid, rendering it holy enough to serve as the medieval sanctuary stool. Nearby, close to the high altar, there are four panels from a fifteenth-century **Dance of Death**, a grim, darkly varnished painting.

The rest of Hexham's large and irregularly shaped Market Place is peppered with remains of its medieval past. The massive walls of the fourteenth-century **Moot Hall** were built to serve as the gatehouse to "The Hall", a well-protected enclosure that was garrisoned against the Scots. Nearby, the archbishops also built their own prison, a formidable fortified tower (1330), constructed using stones plundered from the Roman ruins at Corbridge. Now, as the **Old Gaol**, this accommodates the tourist office (see below) and the **Border History Museum** (Feb–Easter & Nov Mon, Tues, Sat & Sun 10am–4.30pm; Easter–Oct Mon–Sat 10am–4.30pm; £1.30), which provides information and displays concerning the border-raiding reivers (see p.550), as well as covering the building's use as a prison – a function it abandoned in 1824.

Hexham **train station** is ten minutes' walk east of the town centre and the **tourist office** on Hallgate (Easter to mid-May & Oct Mon–Sat 9am–5pm, Sun 10am–5pm; mid-May to Sept Mon–Sat closes 6pm; Nov–Easter Mon–Sat only; ☎01434/605 225). The **bus station** is situated off Priestpopple, a few minutes'stroll south of the tourist office. The most convenient **B&B** is *Middlemarch*, on Hencotes (☎01434/605 003; ④), just down Beaumont Street from the abbey; otherwise try the secluded *West Close House*, on Hextol Terrace off Allendale Road (☎01434/603 307; ③–④), or *Topsy Turvy*, 9 Leazes Lane (☎01434/603 152; ③). The town's **hotels** include the *County Hotel* on Priestpopple (☎01434/602 030; ⑤), and the *Beaumont Hotel*, overlooking the abbey from Beaumont Street (☎01434/602 331; ⑧). The **youth hostel** (☎01434/602 864) occupies converted stable buildings in the village of Acomb, two miles away (bus #880 or #882). **Bar meals** are served at the *Heart of All England* on Market Street, with more elaborate (and expensive) offerings in the *County*. For full-blown **dinners**, there's Italian at *Fortinis* and Indian at *Diwan-e-Am*, both on Priestpopple. The best option, though, is *Harlequin's*, the licensed café-restaurant in the *Queen's Hall Arts Centre* on Beaumont Street, which puts on a year-round programme of theatre, dance, music and art exhibitions.

Chollerford and Chesters Roman Fort

At **CHOLLERFORD**, around four miles north of Hexham, a bridge crosses the North Tyne river, looked over by the swanky *George Hotel* (☎01434/681 611; ⑨), with its renowned restaurant. Two thousand years ago, the main river crossing was a little way downstream, half a mile west of present-day Chollerford, where **Chesters Roman Fort** (daily April–Sept 10am–6pm; Oct–March 10am–4pm; £2.20; EH), otherwise *Cilurnum*, was built to guard the erstwhile Roman bridge over the river, its six-acre plot accommodating a cavalry regiment roughly five hundred strong. Enough remains of the original structure to pick out the design of the fort, and each section has been clearly labelled, but the highlight is down by the river where the vestibule, changing room and steam range of the garrison's **bathhouse** are still visible, along with the furnace and the latrines. Back at the entrance, the **museum** has an excellent collection of Roman stonework, including a sculpture of Mars from Housesteads, a relief depicting three water nymphs, and an incised representation of a strange phallus-like fish.

Housesteads to Vindolanda

Overlooking the bleak and bare Northumbrian moors from the top of the Whin Sill, **Housesteads Roman Fort** (daily April–Sept 10am–6pm; Oct–March 10am–4pm; £2.30; EH & NT), eight miles west of Chester, has long been the most popular site on the wall. The fort was built in the second phase of the Hadrianic construction and is of standard design but for one enforced modification – forts were supposed to straddle the line of the wall, but here the original stonework tracked along the very edge of the cliff, so Housesteads was built on the steeply sloping ridge to the south. Access is via the tiny **museum**, from where you stroll across to the south gate, beside which there are a few remains of the civilian settlement that was dependent on the one thousand infantrymen stationed within. Inside the perimeter, look out for the distinctive cubicles of the barrack blocks, the courtyard plan of the commanding officer's house, and the tooth-like stone supports of the granaries.

You don't need to pay for entrance to Housesteads if you simply intend to walk west along the wall from here. The three-mile hike past the lovely wooded **Crag Lough** to **Steel Rigg** (car park) offers the most fantastic views, especially when you spy the course of the wall as it threads over the crags ahead. Leaving the wall at Steel Rigg, it's roughly half a mile south to the main road and the very informative **Once Brewed National Park Visitor Centre** (March & April daily 10am–5pm; May–Oct daily 10am–6pm; Nov Sat & Sun 10am–3pm; ☎01434/344 396), which has exhibitions and information on both the wall and the national park. The popular Once Brewed **youth hostel** (closed Jan; ☎01434/344 360) is next to the visitor centre, and the side road beyond the centre continues for half a mile down to Vindolanda (see below). There are a couple of other local accommodation choices, too, the most obvious being the *Twice Brewed Inn* (☎01434/344 534; ③), west down the main road from the visitor centre. Drivers could cut the three miles southeast across the back roads to the *Bowes Hotel* (☎01434/344 237; ③–④) in the one-shop-one-pub village of **Bardon Mill** (also a stop on the Hexham–Carlisle train line).

The excavated garrison fort of **Vindolanda** (March & Oct 10am–5pm; April & Sept 10am–5.30pm; May–Aug 10am–6pm; Nov–Feb 10am–4pm; £3.50) actually predates the wall itself – as do several of the forts hereabouts – though most of what you see today dates from the second to third century AD, when the fort was a thriving metropolis of 500 soldiers with its own civilian settlement attached. The **excavations** at Vindolanda are spread over a wide area, with civilian houses, inn, guest quarters, administrative building, commander's house and main gates all clearly visible; a full-scale re-created section of the wall gives an idea of what a mile-tower would have looked like. The path through the excavations then descends to the café, shop and **museum** (same hours as site, though closed late Nov to early Feb), the latter housing the largest collection of Roman leather items ever discovered on a single site – dozens of shoes, belts, even a pair of baby boots. More intriguing are the excavated hoard of around 200 **writing tablets**, dealing with subjects as diverse as clerical filing systems and children's schoolwork, plus several recent finds graphically depicting the realities of military life in Northumberland: soldiers' requests for more beer, birthday party invitations, even letters from home containing gifts of underwear for freezing frontline grunts.

Haltwhistle to Greenhead

There's not much to **HALTWHISTLE**, three miles west of Once Brewed/Steel Rig and a mile south of the wall, but there is a selection of **B&Bs**, including the attractive, stone *Hall Meadows*, right at the top of Main Street (☎01434/321 021; ③). Two or three pubs also offer accommodation, including the *Manor House Hotel* (☎01434/322 588; ③–④) on Main Street. The *Haltwhistle Camping Site* (March–Oct; ☎01434/320 106) is in Burnfoot Park, beside the Tyne on the southeast edge of town. For beer and **bar meals**, the *Spotted Cow Inn*, down on Castle Hill, the eastern extension of Main Street, is an agreeable spot. **Market day** in Haltwhistle is Thursday. The **train station**, incidentally, is right at the western edge of town, close to the A69 – walk up to West Gate, which becomes Main Street.

A further four-mile trek west along the wall from Haltwhistle takes you past the remains of **Great Chesters Fort** before reaching a spectacular section of the wall, known as the **Walltown Crags**, where a turret from a signal system predating the wall still survives. The views from here are marvellous. Adjacent to the crags, at Carvoran, the **Roman Army Museum** (daily 2nd half Feb & 1st half Nov 10am–4pm; March, April, Sept & Oct 10am–5pm; May–Aug 10am–6pm; £3.50) does its best to inject some interest into its rather tame dioramas, reconstructions and exhibits.

Push on just a mile southwest, and you're soon in minuscule **GREENHEAD**, where the *Greenhead Hotel* (☎016977/47411; ④), which serves reasonable food, sits opposite the **youth hostel** (March–Dec; ☎016977/47401), located in a converted Methodist chapel. If neither of these appeal, *Holmhead Guest House* (☎016977/47402; ④) probably will, an old stone farmhouse with exposed beams, partly built with stones taken from the wall itself. The hamlet is where the **Pennine Way** cuts **east**, following the wall as far as Housesteads before bearing north again. Both the eastbound #890 (to Hexham) and #682 (Haltwhistle) buses stop in Greenhead. Heading **west**, the next section of Hadrian's Wall worth exploring is at Birdoswald, a four-mile walk or ten-minute ride on the westbound #682, which then continues on to Carlisle.

Northumberland National Park

Northwest Northumberland, the great triangular chunk of land between Hadrian's Wall and the coastal plain, is dominated by the wide-skied landscapes of the **Northumberland National Park**, whose four hundred windswept square miles rise to the **Cheviot Hills** on the Scottish border. These uplands are interrupted by great slabs of forest, mostly the conifer plantations of the Forestry Commission, and a string of river valleys, of which Coquetdale, Tynedale and Redesdale are the longest.

Remote from lowland law and order, these dales were once the hangout of the **Border reivers**, turbulent clans who ruled the local roost from the thirteenth to the sixteenth centuries. The reivers took advantage of the struggles between England and Scotland to engage in endless cross-border rustling and general brigandage, activities recalled by the ruined **bastles** (fortified farmhouses) and **peels** (defensive tower houses) that lie dotted across the landscape.

Good walking country can be found right across the National Park and it's this activity that attracts thousands of visitors every year. The most popular trail is the **Pennine Way**, which, entering the National Park at Hadrian's Wall, cuts up through Bellingham on its way to The Cheviot, the park's highest peak at 2674ft, finishing at Kirk Yetholm, over the border in Scotland. This part of the Pennine Way is 64 miles long in total, but it's easy to break the hike up into manageable portions as the footpath passes through a variety of tiny settlements, several of which have youth hostels, B&B accommodation and campsites. As an introduction, it's hard to beat the lovely moorland scenery of the fifteen-mile stretch from Housesteads/Hadrian's Wall to **Bellingham**, a pleasant town on the North Tyne. Bellingham is also on the road to **Kielder Water**, a massive pine-surrounded reservoir which has been vigorously promoted as a water-sports centre and nature reserve since its creation in 1982. Further north, **Rothbury**, in Coquetdale, is close to both the Simonside Hills and **Cragside**, the nineteenth-century country home of Lord Armstrong.

Bellingham

The stone terraces of **BELLINGHAM** (pronounced Bellin*jum*) slope up from the banks of the Tyne on the eastern edge of the Northumberland National Park. There's nothing outstanding about the place, but it is a restful spot set in splendid rural surroundings, and it does contain the much modified medieval church of **St Cuthbert**, which has an unusual stone-vaulted roof – designed (successfully) to prevent raiding Border reivers from burning the church to the ground. The volunteer-run **Heritage Centre** on Front Street (mid-April to Sept Mon & Fri–Sun 10.30am–5.30pm; 50p) has more on this turbulent period and also offers changing exhibitions about traditional local life.

Buses from Hexham stop in the centre, while the Pennine Way passes right through the village. The **tourist office** on Main Street (Easter–Oct Mon–Sat 10am–1pm & 2–6pm, Sun 1–5pm; Nov–Easter Tues–Sat 2–5pm; ☎01434/220 616) is housed in Bellingham's former Poor House building. You may want to book **accommodation** ahead in summer, particularly if you're coinciding with the last Saturday in August, when the Bellingham Show, the big agricultural event of the year, is staged. The **youth hostel** (March–Oct; ☎01434/220 313) is in a primitive-looking green hut above the village on Woodburn Road (signposted from Main Street). Less spartan lodgings are available at the **B&B** of *Mrs Batey*, Lynview, opposite the tourist office (☎01434/220 334; ③) on Fountain Terrace; the *Lyndale Guest House* (☎01434/220 361; ④), just past the *Rose & Crown* pub, has cheaper rates in winter. The local **campsite** is at *Demesne Farm* (March–Oct; ☎01434/220 258), right in the centre near the police station. For **food**, you're dependent on the bar meals served at the pubs.

Kielder Water

From Bellingham, the road heads west, skirting the forested edge of **Kielder Water**, passing the assorted visitor centres, waterside parks and anchorages that fringe its southern shore. First stop is the Visitor Centre at **Tower Knowe** (daily April & Oct 10am–5pm; May–Sept 10am–6pm; Nov–March 10am–4pm; ☎01434/240 398), eight miles from Bellingham, with a café and an exhibition on the history of the valley and lake (£1). Another four miles west, at **Leaplish**, the waterside park (April–Sept daily 10am–6pm; ☎01434/250 312), lodge and restaurant are the focus of most of Kielder's outdoor activities – watersports, bike rental, pony trekking and fishing.

Eighteen miles from Bellingham, at the top of the reservoir, just three miles from the Scottish border, stands **Kielder Castle** (Easter–Sept daily 10am–5pm, until 6pm in Aug; Oct–Easter Sat & Sun 10am–5pm; ☎01434/250 209), built in 1775 as the hunting lodge of the Duke of Northumberland, and now an information centre and exhibition area praising the work of the Forestry Commission. The castle is surrounded by the **Border Forest Park**, several million spruce trees subdivided into a number of approximately defined forest areas: Wark and Kielder are broadly to the south of the reservoir, Falstone and Redesdale to the north. Several easy and clearly marked **footpaths** lead from the castle into the forest – try the *Duke's Trail* through Ravenshill Wood, a slice of ancient and semi-natural woodland. There's mountain **bike rental** available from *Kielder Bikes* (☎01434/220 392) at the castle, too.

If you want to **stay** in the area, options are limited. On the road in from Bellingham, a couple of miles before the water, the early seventeenth-century *Pheasant Inn* (☎01434/240 382; ⑤–⑥) at **STANNERSBURN** has eight comfortable rooms. **FALSTONE**, a mile or so to the north, boasts the smaller *Blackcock Inn* (☎01434/240 200; ⑤) as well as B&B in two rooms at *High Yarrow Farm* (May–Oct; ☎01434/240 264; ③) – which, incidentally, maintains the only herd of free-ranging **reindeer** in

England (visits April to mid-Sept daily except Fri 10.30am–5pm; £2). Both *Pheasant* and *Blackcock* inns also serve bar meals at lunch and dinner. Otherwise, there are a couple of B&Bs in **KIELDER** village itself, close to the castle, and the possibility of renting rural cottages in the locality for longer stays – ask at Bellingham tourist office. *Kielder Campsite* (Easter–Sept; ☎01434/250 291) is by the banks of the Tyne, about half a mile north of the castle.

Redesdale

From Bellingham, it's a fifteen-mile trek north along the Pennine Way to **BYRNESS** in **Redesdale**, which can also be reached direct from Kielder Castle via a rough, eleven-mile forestry road that snakes through the pine-clad hills of the northeast portion of the Border Forest Park. Set beside the main road, Byrness is a tiny place, but it does have a simple **youth hostel** (March–Sept; ☎01830/520 519) at 7 Otterburn Green, a **campsite** (Easter–Oct; ☎01830/520 259) and a **hotel**, the *Byrness* (☎01830/520 231; ③).

Redesdale has only one settlement of any size, **OTTERBURN**, ten miles southeast of Byrness down the A68. It's an undistinguished place today, surrounded by heather-clad, sheep-laden countryside, with little except the name of the local pub, the *Lord Percy Arms*, to recall its most notable hour. It was at Otterburn in August 1388 that an English army led by Sir Henry Percy "Hotspur" was defeated by the Scots under James, Earl of Douglas. Douglas was killed in battle, as were 1800 English troops, while Percy Hotspur was taken prisoner – a chain of events later made the subject of the medieval ballad of *Chevy Chase*. The supposed battle site is about a mile northwest of the village, off the A68, marked by a stone cross set in a little pinewood – though you may as well pick virtually any large field in the vicinity, since historians not only dispute its exact location, but also argue about the site of the Scottish base camp and even the exact date of the battle itself.

There are several places **to stay**, including *The Butterchurn Guest House*, opposite the church on Main Street (☎01830/520 585; ④), and the comfortable *Lord Percy Arms* itself (☎01830/520 261; ⑧), further down the road. B&B accommodation is available on a couple of local farms: there are four rooms at *Blakehope Farm* (☎01830/520 266; ③), for example. The *Border Reiver* (☎01830/520 682) is a strange sort of place, part village shop, part coffee house-restaurant, with just about every other service you could think of – from lottery tickets to dry cleaning – thrown in to boot. *The Butterchurn* has a café attached to it and at the *Lord Percy Arms* you can get coffee, bar meals and full **dinners**, too. After Byrness comes Northumberland's longest uninterrupted stretch of the Pennine Way, the 27-mile haul to the end of the hike at Kirk Yetholm.

Rothbury and Cragside

ROTHBURY, straddling the River Coquet some eighteen miles northeast of Otterburn, prospered as a late Victorian resort because it gave ready access to the forests, burns and ridges of the Simonside Hills. In the centre, where the High Street widens to form a broad triangle, there are hints of past pretensions in the assertive facades overlooking the **Rothbury Cross**, erected in 1902. Rothbury remains a popular spot for walkers, and the Northumberland National Park **Visitor Centre**, near the Cross on Church Street (mid-March to Sept daily 10am–5pm; ☎01669/620 887) offers advice on local trails, several of which begin in the Simonside Hills car park, a couple of miles southwest of town. The most appealing of these trails is the five-mile round trip along the Simonside ridge, with panoramic views out over Coquetdale.

Victorian Rothbury was dominated by the first Lord Armstrong, the immensely wealthy engineer and arms manufacturer, who built his country home at **Cragside** (April–Oct Tues–Sun 1–5.30pm; £5.50, gardens only £3.50; NT), on the steep, forested slopes of Debdon Burn, a mile to the east of the village. At first, Armstrong was satisfied with his modest house, but in 1869 he decided to build something more substantial, and hired Norman Shaw, one of the period's top architects, to do the job. Work continued until the mid-1880s, the final version being a grandiose Tudor-style mansion, whose black and white timber-framed gables and upper storeys are entirely out of place in the Northumbrian countryside. The overly spick and span interior is stuffed with Armstrong's furnishings and fittings, heavy dark pieces enlivened by the William Morris stained glass in the library. The most extraordinary feature is, however, the spectacularly hideous Renaissance-style marble chimneypiece of the drawing room.

Armstrong was an avid innovator, fascinated by hydraulic engineering and hydro-electric power. At Cragside he could indulge himself, damming the Debdon Burn to power several domestic appliances, like the spit and the dumb waiter in the kitchen. In 1880, after several false starts, he also managed to supply Cragside with electricity, making this the first house in the world to be lit by hydroelectric power. The remains of the original system – including the powerhouse – are still visible in the grounds, which, together with the splendid **gardens**, have longer opening hours (same days, 10.30am–7pm).

Rothbury is well-connected by **bus** to Newcastle; you can get local tourist **information** from the National Park Visitor Centre (see above). There are several convenient **B&Bs** – the *Orchard Guest House*, at the top of the High Street (☎01669/620 684; ⑥) includes dinner, bed and breakfast in the price, though during winter you should be able to negotiate a cheaper rate. The *Queen's Head Hotel* (☎01669/ 620 470; ④), at the other end of the High Street, has a good-value carvery and restaurant; it also has a few cheaper rooms without shower. The *Vale Milk Bar*, across from the large *Newcastle Hotel* in the centre, serves all-day breakfasts and café **meals**; while *Pizzeria Katerina*, on the High Street, is open for dinner (April–Oct).

The Northumberland coast

The low-lying **Northumberland coast**, stretching 64 miles north from Newcastle to the Scottish border, boasts many of the region's principal attractions, but first you have to clear the disfigured landscape of the old Northumbrian coalfield, which extends as far north as the port of Amble. In its heyday at the beginning of the twentieth century this area employed a quarter of Britain's colliers, but most of the mines closed years ago and the district is a real eyesore.

Beyond Amble, you emerge into a pastoral, gently wooded landscape that spreads over the thirty-odd miles to Berwick-upon-Tweed. On the way there's a succession of mighty fortresses, beginning with **Warkworth Castle** and **Alnwick Castle**, the strong-hold-cum-stately-home of the Percys, the county's biggest landowners. Further along, there's the formidable fastness of **Bamburgh** and then, last of all, the magnificent Elizabethan ramparts surrounding **Berwick-upon-Tweed**. In between you'll find splen-did sandy beaches – notably at Bamburgh and the tiny seaside resort of **Alnmouth** – as well as the site of the Lindisfarne monastery on **Holy Island** and the seabird and nature reserve of the **Farne Islands**, reached by boat from Seahouses.

Warkworth

WARKWORTH, a coastal hamlet set in a loop of the River Coquet a couple of miles from Amble, is best seen from the north, from where the grey stone terraces of the long main street slope up towards the commanding remains of **Warkworth Castle** (daily April–Oct 10am–6pm; Nov–March 10am–4pm; £1.80; EH), which perch on top of an immense grassy mound at the far end of the village. Enough remains of the outer wall to give a clear impression of the layout of the medieval bailey, but – apart from the well-preserved gatehouse through which the site is entered – nothing catches your attention as much as the **keep**. Mostly built in the fourteenth century, this three-storeyed structure, with its polygonal turrets and high central tower, has a honeycomb-like interior, a fine example of the designs developed by the castle builders of Plantagenet England. It was here that most of the Percy family, Earls of Northumberland, chose to live throughout the fourteenth and fifteenth centuries.

The main Castle Street sweeps down into the village, flattening out at the church of **St Laurence**, which preserves many Norman features, most impressively the fine ribbed vaulting of the chancel. Just beyond here, there's also an enjoyable half-mile stroll along the right bank of the Coquet to the little boat that shuttles visitors across to **Warkworth Hermitage** (April–Sept Wed & Sun 11am–5pm; £1; EH), a series of simple rooms and a claustrophobic chapel that were hewn out of the cliff above the river some time in the fourteenth century. If you're interested in getting out on the river itself, there's a **rowing boat rental** outlet, signposted down the alley to the side of *Topsey Turvey's* (see below) on Castle Street.

Warkworth is on the route of the #X18 **bus service** linking Alnwick, Alnmouth and Newcastle; Alnmouth (see below) has the nearest **train station**, and is much better placed for the beach, so you probably won't want to stay in Warkworth. However the village does possess a handful of inexpensive **B&Bs**, including *Roxbro House*, 5 Castle Terrace (☎01665/711 416; ③), perfectly sited immediately below the castle walls. Set back on the same terrace at no. 6 is the splendid *Sun Hotel* (☎01665/711 259; ⑦), whose conservatory is a fine place for meals and teas with views of the castle and coast. If **meals** at the *Sun* are out of your league – French-inspired table d'hôte dinners from around £15 – you'll need to eat down in the village itself. Superior lunches and teas are available at *The Greenhouse*, near the church, while *Topsey Turvey's*, over the way at 2 Dial Place, is open for lunch and dinner (closed Sun & Mon evening). Next door, the *Mason's Arms* has more traditional **pub food** and a beer garden.

Alnmouth

It's just three miles north from Warkworth to the seaside resort of **ALNMOUTH**, a strange little place whose narrow, mostly nineteenth-century centre is strikingly situated on a steep spur of land between the sea and the estuary of the Aln. It's a lovely setting, and there's a wide sandy beach and rolling dunes, but even on the sunniest of days the place seems quite forlorn. Alnmouth was a busy and prosperous port up until 1806, when the sea, driven by a freakish gale, broke through to the river and changed its course, moving the estuary from the south to the north side of Church Hill and rendering the original harbour useless. Alnmouth never really recovered, though it has been a low-key holiday spot since Victorian times, as attested by the elegant seaside villas at the south end of town.

The Newcastle to Alnwick **bus** calls at Alnmouth **train station** at Hipsburn, a mile and a half west of the centre. The resort is well equipped with **B&Bs** – in summer, you'd do best to book ahead, particularly during Alnwick Fair in June (see below), when all local accommodation is scarce. Halfway down the main Northumberland Street, at no. 56, the *Copper Beach* (☎01665/830 443; ③) has en-suite rooms in a period stone cottage. At the end of Northumberland Street, the *Blue Dolphins*, at 11 Riverside Rd (☎01665/830 893; ③) boasts sea and beach views. A string of **pubs** along Northumberland Street also offers accommodation, the best the *Saddle Hotel*, at no. 25 (☎01665/830 476; ④), whose top-floor rooms enjoy (partial) sea views. There are a couple of coffee houses along the main street, while **lunches and dinners** are served in the bar lounges and dining rooms of the pubs: the *Saddle Hotel* has a large bar menu and £10 set dinners; the *Red Lion*'s restaurant is better, more adventurous and more expensive, serving fresh fish and other meals, often with a Chinese twist.

Alnwick

The unassuming town of **ALNWICK** (pronounced "Annick"), some thirty miles north of Newcastle and four miles inland from Alnmouth, is renowned for its castle – seat of the dukes of Nothumberland – which overlooks the River Aln immediately to the north of the town centre. The castle buildings and walls receive plaudits from all who see them, but Alnwick itself deserves time, too. It's an appealing market town of cobbled streets and Georgian houses, centred on the old cross in Market Place, site of a weekly **market** (Sat) since the thirteenth century. Other than catching the market in full swing, the best time to visit is during the boisterous week-long **Alnwick Fair**, a medieval re-enactment which starts on the last Sunday in June. There's a costumed procession on that day, preceded by street entertainment, with stalls doing a roaring trade in roast ox sandwiches. During the week that follows, the *Playhouse* stages special concerts, pubs lure in punters with Yard-of-Ale contests and the like, while the Market Place is given over to a craft fair (daily 10am–5pm), various entertainments and a "Pie Court", where unfortunates suffer duckings and a spell in the stocks. For those determined to enter into the spirit of the thing, costumes are available for rent during the fair – ask at the tourist office.

The Percys – who were raised to the dukedom of Northumberland in 1750 – have owned the **Castle** (Easter to mid-Oct daily 11am–5pm; £4.50) since 1309, when Henry de Percy reinforced the original Norman keep and remodelled its curtain wall. His successor, another Henry, built the imposing barbican and connecting gatehouse. In the eighteenth century, the castle was badly in need of a refit, so the first duke had the interior refurbished by Robert Adam in an extravagant Gothic style – which in turn was supplanted by the gaudy Italianate decoration preferred by the fourth duke in the 1850s. Nowadays, the castle is part of a business empire based on the duke's extensive Northumbrian estates. Your stiff entry fee contributes to the company's coffers, which would be better justified if more of the castle were open to the public: most of Capability Brown's grounds remain out of bounds and so do the bulk of the rooms – only six can be visited out of around one hundred and sixty. The most lavish decoration is in the **red drawing room**, where the rich polygonal panels of the ceiling bear down on damask-covered walls and some magnificent ebony cabinets rescued from Versailles during the French Revolution. Each room carries part of the duke's extensive collection of paintings, including pieces by Canaletto, Titian, Tintoretto, Van Dyck and Turner.

From outside the castle, it's a few minutes' walk north along Bailiffgate and then Ratten Row to the gates of **Hulne Park**, a tract of hilly woodland to the northwest of Alnwick. Deep inside the park, three miles from the entrance, are the remains of **Hulne Priory**, a thirteenth-century Carmelite monastery built above the north bank of the River Aln. It's a lovely, peaceful spot and, although the grey-stone ruins are slight, they are enlivened by several whimsically carved stone monks, modern sculptures which have the place pretty much to themselves. The duke owns the park, and access is controlled – pedestrians and cyclists only, from 11am to sunset in summer.

The tiny town of Alnwick has a trim and tidy cobbled Market Place, but there's not much to see, except for the **gatehouses** on Pottergate and Bondgate, the principal remains of the medieval town walls, and the grandiose **Percy Tenantry Column** just to the southeast of the centre along Bondgate. This 75-foot-high column, surmounted by the Percy lion, was built by the tenants of the second duke in 1816 after he had reduced their rents by 25 percent. As it turned out, their humble gratitude was somewhat premature. The third duke promptly bumped the rents up again and locals wryly renamed their monument the "Farmers' Folly".

Practicalities

Alnwick **bus station** is on Clayport Street, a couple of minutes' walk west of the Market Place, where you'll find the **tourist office** on the Shambles (April–Sept Mon–

Sat 9am–5pm, Sun 11am–5pm; Oct–March Mon–Fri 9am–5pm, Sat 9am–4.30pm; ☎01665/510 665). An inexpensive and convenient **B&B** is the *Oronsay Guest House*, a Victorian villa at 18 Bondgate Without (☎01665/603 559; ③), just beyond the gatehouse at the end of the street. Alnwick's main **hotel**, *The White Swan*, on Bondgate Within (☎01665/602 109; ⑦), is a little overpriced, though you might want to pop in to the hotel's fine panelled lounge, swiped from an old ocean liner. Many prefer the more intimate *Bondgate House Hotel*, at 20 Bondgate Without (☎01665/602 025; ④). You can **camp** at *Alnwick Rugby Club* in Greensfield Park (April–Oct; ☎01665/602 987), a little way south of the centre but walkable. For **food**, the *Market Tavern Hotel*, Fenkle Street, offers filling **bar** meals, as does the *Oddfellows Arms*, on Narrowgate. Just off Narrowgate, in Dorothy Foster Court, *John Blackmore's* (dinner only; ☎01665/604 465; Mon, Sun & Jan closed) stands out as one of the best (and most expensive) **restaurants** in the region, a friendly place with imaginative cooking using local ingredients. The other **pubs** along Narrowgate – *Ye Olde Cross* and the *Black Swan* – are crowded and boisterous at the weekend.

The Farne Islands and Bamburgh

Heading northeast out of Alnwick along the B1340, it's eighteen miles to **SEAHOUSES**, a desultory fishing-port-cum-resort that's the embarkation point for **boat trips** to the windswept and treeless **Farne Islands**, a rocky archipelago lying a few miles offshore. Owned by the National Trust and maintained as a nature reserve, the Farnes are the summer home of many species of migrating seabirds, especially puffins, guillemots, terns and kittiwakes. To protect the birds, only two of the islands are open to visitors: **Inner Farne** (April, Aug & Sept daily 10.30am–6pm; £2.80; May–July daily 1.30–5pm; £3.50) and **Staple Island** (same times & prices except May–July 10.30am–1pm). The crossing can be rough, but the islands have a wild beauty that makes it all worthwhile, and on Inner Farne you can also visit a tiny chapel built in honour of Saint Cuthbert, who spent much of his life here. Weather permitting, several boat owners operate daily excursions: *Billy Shiels* (☎01665/720 308), the best of the bunch, runs a varied programme (Easter–Oct), from two-and-a-half-hour **cruises** round either island (£5), to five-hour trips landing at both (£10); all trips also visit the grey-seal colonies off the islands.

It's unlikely you'd choose to stay the night in Seahouses, and there are regular **buses** to both Alnwick and Berwick-upon-Tweed, but, if you've returned from the Farnes late in the day, you may not want to go any further. Seahouses has a range of reasonably priced **B&Bs** – details from the **tourist office** (daily April & Oct 10am–4pm; May–Sept 10am–6pm; ☎01665/720 884), in the car park above the harbour. The *Olde Ship*, at 9 Main St (☎01665/720 200; ⑥), quite apart from its pleasant rooms, is a great place to drink, full of nautical bits and pieces and serving good **food**. If you want to take some of the local catch home, the *Fisherman's Kitchen* at 2 South St (May–Sept Mon–Fri 9am–5pm, Sat 9am–4pm; winter reduced hours) sells smoked kippers and salmon from its traditional **smokehouse**.

Flanking a triangular green in the lee of its castle, three miles north of Seahouses, the tiny village of **BAMBURGH** is only a five-minute walk from two splendid sandy beaches, backed by rolling, tufted dunes. From the sands – in fact from everywhere – **Bamburgh Castle** (April–Oct daily 11am–5pm; £2.50) is a spectacular sight, its elongated battlements crowning a formidable basalt crag high above the beach. This beautiful spot was first fortified by the Celts, but its heyday was as an Anglo-Saxon stronghold, one-time capital of Northumbria and the protector of the preserved head and hand of Saint Oswald, the seventh-century king who invited Saint Aidan over from Iona to convert his subjects. To the Normans, however, Bamburgh was just one of many border fortresses administered by second-rank vassals: as an eleventh-century monastic chronicler expressed it, "[Bamburgh], renowned formerly for the magnifi-cent splendour of her high estate, has been burdened with tribute and reduced to the condition of a handmaiden." Nonetheless, rotted by sea spray and buffeted by winter storms, Bamburgh Castle struggled on until 1894, when the new owner, Lord Armstrong (see p.552), demolished most of the structure to replace it with a cumber-some castle-mansion. The focal point of the new building was the Great Hall, a soulless teak-ceilinged affair of colossal dimensions, whose main redeeming feature is an exqui-site collection of Fabergé stone animal carvings. In the adjacent Faire Chamber there's also a pastoral miniature by Jan Brueghel the Younger. In the basement of the keep, the stone-vaulted ceiling maintains its Norman appearance, making a suitable arena for a display of suits of armour and other antique militaria.

The village is also the home of the **Grace Darling Museum** (April to mid-Oct Mon–Sat 11am–7pm, Sun 2–6pm; £1), which celebrates the daring sea rescue accom-plished by Grace and her lighthouseman father, William, in September 1838. It began when a gale dashed the steamship *Forfarshire* against the rocks of the Farne Islands. Nine passengers struggled onto a reef, where they were subsequently saved by the Darlings, who left the safety of the lighthouse to row out to them. *The Times* trumpeted Grace's bravery, offers of marriage and requests for locks of her hair were sent to the Darlings, and for the rest of her brief life Grace was plagued by unwanted visitors – she died of tuberculosis aged 26 in 1842. The museum details the rescue and displays the fragile boat the Darlings used; in the churchyard of thirteenth-century **St Aidan's** opposite is the pompous Gothic Revival memorial that covers Grace's body.

A regular **bus** service links Alnwick and Berwick-upon-Tweed with Bamburgh; you'll be dropped by the green. There are several places to **stay**, including the *Lord Crewe Arms Hotel*, Front Street (March–Oct; ☎01668/214 243; ⑥), very close to the castle, a comfortable old inn with oak beams, open fires (and cheaper rates) in winter, and a moderately priced **restaurant**. Have a drink at least in the inn. The *Glenander Guest House*, 27 Lucker Rd (☎01668/214 336; ④) is one of two or three places on the same road offering B&B. For budget **meals**, the *Victoria Hotel*, also on Front Street, has a reasonably priced restaurant, and serves substantial meals in its back-room bar.

Holy Island

There's something rather menacing about the barnacle-encrusted marker poles that line the causeway over to **Holy Island**, and the danger of drowning is real enough if you ignore the safe crossing times posted at the start of the three-mile trip across the tidal flats. (The island is cut off for about five hours every day, so to avoid a tedious delay it's best to consult the tide timetables at one of the region's tourist offices.) Once you've got over there, however, first impressions are disappointing. Just one and a half miles by one, the island is sandy, flat and bare, its historic remains are scant, and the sole village is plain in the extreme. But give the place time – it has a distinctive and isolated atmosphere, especially out of season.

Once known as **Lindisfarne**, Holy Island has an illustrious history. It was here that Saint Aidan of Iona founded a monastery at the invitation of King Oswald of Northumbria in 634. The monks quickly evangelized the northeast and established a reputation for scholarship and artistry, the latter exemplified by the **Lindisfarne Gospels**, the apotheosis of Celtic religious art, now kept in the British Museum. The monastery had sixteen bishops in all, the most celebrated being **Saint Cuthbert**, who only accepted the job after Ecgfrith, another Northumbrian king, pleaded with him. But Cuthbert never settled here and, within two years, he was back in his hermetic cell on the Farne Islands, where he died in 687. His colleagues rowed the body back to Lindisfarne, which became a place of pilgrimage until 875, when the monks abandoned the island in fear of marauding Vikings, taking Cuthbert's remains with them – the first part of the saint's long posthumous journey to Durham (see p.530). In 1082 Lindisfarne, renamed Holy Island, was colonized by Benedictines from Durham, but the monastery was a shadow of its former self, a minor religious house with only a handful of attendant monks, the last of whom was evicted in the Dissolution.

Situated near the centre of the village, the pinkish sandstone ruins of the church of **Lindisfarne Priory** (April–Sept daily 10am–6pm; Oct–March Tues–Sun 10am–4pm; £2.30; EH) are from the Benedictine foundation. Enough survives to provide a clear impression of the original structure, notably the tight Romanesque arches of the nave and the gravity-defying stonework of the central tower's last remaining arch. Behind lie the scant remains of the monastic buildings and next door is the mostly thirteenth-century church of **St Mary the Virgin**. The adjacent **museum** features a collection of incised stones that constitute all that remains of the first monastery. The finest of them is a round-headed tombstone showing armed Northumbrians on one side, and kneeling figures before the Cross on the other – presumably a propagandist's view of the beneficial effects of Christianity.

Stuck on a small pyramid of rock half a mile away from the village, past the dock and along the seashore, **Lindisfarne Castle** (April–Oct daily except Fri 1–5.30pm; £3.60; NT) was built in the middle of the sixteenth century to protect the island's harbour from the Scots. It was, however, merely a decaying shell when Edward Hudson, the founder of *Country Life* magazine, stumbled across it in 1901. Hudson bought the castle and turned it into a holiday home to designs by Edwin Lutyens, who used the irregular levels of the building to create the L-shaped living quarters that survive today. Lutyens kept the austere spirit of the castle alive in the great fireplaces, stone walls, columns and rounded arches which dominate the main rooms.

The **bus** service from Berwick-upon-Tweed to Holy Island runs twice daily, except on Sundays, during the summer, but only once a week between October and March. Departure times vary with the tides, and the journey takes thirty minutes. The island is short on places to **stay** and consequently it's advisable to make an advance booking through any of the region's tourist offices. Alternatively, you can try direct at the *North View Guest House*, on Marygate (☎01289/389 222; ④–⑤), which offers comfortable rooms in a sixteenth-century listed building; *Britannia House* (March–Oct; ☎01289/389 218; ③); or the *Crown & Anchor Hotel*, Fenkle Street (☎01289/389 215; ③), a likeable old-fashioned inn with just a few rooms, opposite the priory. The **food** at the latter's restaurant and bar is good too – try the oysters, a local speciality.

Berwick-upon-Tweed

Before the union of England and Scotland in 1603, **BERWICK-UPON-TWEED**, some twelve miles north of Holy Island, was the quintessential frontier town, changing hands no fewer than fourteen times between 1174 and 1482, when the Scots finally ceded the stronghold to the English. Interminable cross-border warfare ruined Berwick's economy, turning the prosperous Scottish port of the thirteenth century into an impoverished garrison town, which the English forcibly cut off from its natural trading hinterland up the River Tweed. By the late sixteenth century, Berwick's fortifications were in a dreadful state of repair and Elizabeth I, apprehensive of the resurgent alliance between France and Scotland, had the place reinvested in line with the latest principles of military architecture.

The new design recognized the technological development of artillery, which had rendered the traditional high stone wall obsolete. Consequently, Berwick's **ramparts** – one and a half miles long and still in pristine condition – are no more than twenty feet high but incredibly thick: a facing of ashlar protects ten to twelve feet of rubble which, in turn, backs up against a vast quantity of earth. Further protected by ditches on three sides and the Tweed on the fourth, the walls are strengthened by immense bastions, whose arrowhead-shape ensured that every part of the wall could be covered by fire. Begun in 1558, the defences were completed after eleven years at a cost of £128,000, more than Elizabeth paid for all her other fortifications put together. As it turned out, it was all a waste of time and money: the French didn't attack and, once England and Scotland were united, Berwick was stuck with a white elephant.

The Town

Today, the easy stroll along the top of the ramparts offers a succession of fine views out to sea, across the Tweed and over the orange-tiled rooftops of a town that's distinguished by its elegant Georgian mansions. These, dating from Berwick's resurgence as a seaport between 1750 and 1820, are the town's most attractive feature, with the tapering **Lions' House**, on Windmill Hill, and the daintily decorated facades of **Quay Walls**, beside the river, of particular note. The three bridges spanning the Tweed are worth a second look too: the huge arches of the **Royal Border Railway Bridge**, built in the manner of a Roman aqueduct by Robert Stephenson in the 1840s, contrasting with the desultory concrete of the **Royal Tweed**, completed in 1928, and the modest seventeenth-century **Berwick Bridge**. This last was opened in 1624 and cost £15,000 to build, an enormous sum partly financed by James VI of Scotland, who is said to have been none-too-impressed with its rickety wooden predecessor which he crossed on his way to be crowned James I of England in 1603.

Within the ramparts, the Berwick skyline is punctured by the stumpy spire of the eighteenth-century **Town Hall** at the bottom of Marygate, right at the heart of the compact centre. This retains its original jailhouse, now housing the **Cell Block Museum** (May–Sept 2 daily tours; £1) with its tales of crime and punishment in Berwick. From here, it's a couple of minutes' walk along Church Street to **Holy Trinity church** (1648), one of the few churches built during the Commonwealth, the absence of a tower supposedly reflecting the wishes of Cromwell, who found them irreligious.

Opposite the church, the elongated **Barracks** (April–Sept daily 10am–6pm; Oct–March Wed–Sun 10am–4pm; £2.20; EH) date from the early eighteenth century and were in use until 1964, when the King's Own Scottish Borderers regiment decamped. Inside, there's a predictable regimental museum, as well as a pedestrian English Heritage exhibition, *By Beat of Drum*, which in a series of pictureboards traces the life of the British infantryman from the sixteenth to the nineteenth century. If all this sounds worthy but dull, it is – rescued only by the fine proportions of the barracks buildings themselves, and by a superior **Borough Museum and Art Gallery**, sited in the so-called Clock Block. Geared up for school parties, the museum features imaginative dioramas, recordings and displays of local traditional life, even a model of a local clergyman haranguing visitors from his pulpit. Upstairs is the kernel of the gallery's fine and applied art collection, the gift of the shipping magnate William Burrell. Highlights include a charcoal sketch by Degas, on show in a little Eastern pavilion; ceramic Oriental jars displayed under glass-floor panels in a sinuous, walk-in dragon; and Roman glassware, church sculpture and several Chinese bronzes.

Practicalities

It's about ten minutes' walk downhill from Berwick **train station** to the town centre via Castlegate, where – off to the left in Castlegate Car Park, near the ramparts – you'll find the **tourist office** (Easter–Oct daily 10am–6pm; Nov–Easter Mon–Sat 10am–1pm & 2–4pm; ☎01289/330 733); the **bus station** is a little further down the hill. The town has plenty of **accommodation** or you could try the tourist office, which offers a room-booking service. The best-value **B&B** in the centre is at *3 Scott's Place* (☎01289/305 323; ③–④), a Georgian town house one block up Castlegate from the tourist office. Other options include the *Arisaig Guest House*, 49 Church St (☎01289/330 412; ③), near the town hall and the *Riverview Guest House*, 11 Quaywalls (March–Dec; ☎01289/

306 295; ④–⑤), with its obvious, namesake attraction. The best central **hotel** is the white-fronted *King's Arms* on Hide Hill (☎01289/307 454; ⑥), one of the myriad English coaching inns that Charles Dickens is supposed to have slept and lectured in. Across Berwick Bridge in Tweedmouth, you can't beat the delightful *Old Vicarage Guest House* (☎01289/306 909; ⑤), a spacious Victorian villa at 24 Church Rd. The only **campsite** with tent space is the *Beachcomber House* (April–Sept; ☎01289/381 217), five miles south of town, off the A1 on the coast at Goswick (no public transport).

Berwick is not that well served by its **restaurants**. Choices include the vegetarian *Humble Pie Café* at 83b Marygate, or the financially hazardous *Funnyway t'mekalivin* (closed Mon, Tues evening & Sun; ☎01289/308 827), 41 Bridge Street, which serves sensational four-course French-Northumbrian dinners at under £25 a head. Similarly priced dinners are available at the *Rob Roy* (☎01289/306 428), ten minutes' walk south of Berwick Bridge on Dock Road in Tweedmouth, a converted pub specializing in fine local seafood and steaks. In 1799, there were 59 **pubs** and three coaching inns in Berwick; strange, then, that today there's barely one worth drinking in; the *Barrels Inn*, on Bridge Street at the foot of the Berwick Bridge, has guest beers, a pool table and a youngish crowd. For more cerebral pastimes, the *Maltings* is Berwick's **arts centre**, on Eastern Lane (☎01289/330 999), with a year-round programme of music, theatre and dance, and river views from its licensed café.

travel details

Trains

Darlington to: Bishop Auckland (every 1–2hr; 30min).

Durham to: Darlington (every 30min; 20min); London (hourly; 3hr); Newcastle (every 30min; 20min).

Hexham to: Carlisle (approx hourly; 1hr); Haltwhistle (approx hourly; 20min); Newcastle (approx hourly; 40min);

Middlesbrough to: Durham (hourly; 50min); Newcastle (hourly; 1hr 10min); Saltburn (hourly; 40min).

Newcastle to: Alnmouth (Mon–Sat 5 daily, Sun 3; 30min); Berwick-upon-Tweed (hourly; 45min); Corbridge (Mon–Sat approx hourly, Sun 4); Durham (every 30min; 20min); Haltwhistle (approx hourly; 1hr); Hexham (approx hourly; 40min); London (hourly; 3hr 15min).

Buses

Alnwick to: Bamburgh (4–6 daily; 1hr 5min); Berwick-upon-Tweed (3 daily; 2hr).

Bamburgh to: Alnwick (4–6 daily; 1hr 5min); Seahouses (Mon–Sat 9 daily, Sun 4; 10min).

Barnard Castle to: Bishop Auckland (Mon–Sat 9 daily, Sun 6; 50min); Darlington (hourly; 35–45min); Middleton-in-Teesdale (hourly; 25–

35min); Raby Castle (9 daily; 15min); Staindrop (Mon–Sat 9 daily, Sun 6; 15min).

Berwick-upon-Tweed to: Holy Island (2 daily; 30min); Newcastle (3–6 daily; 2hr 20min–3hr 10min).

Bishop Auckland to: Barnard Castle (Mon–Sat 9 daily, Sun 6; 50min); Cowshill (Mon–Sat 7 daily, Sun 4; 1hr 10min); Darlington (Mon–Sat hourly; 35min); Hexham (1 weekly; 1hr 50min); Newcastle (hourly; 1hr 15min); Stanhope (Mon–Sat 7 daily, Sun 4; 45min).

Blanchland to: Consett (Mon–Sat 4 daily; 40min), Hexham (1 weekly; 45min).

Darlington to: Barnard Castle (hourly; 35–45min); Bishop Auckland (every 20min; 45min); Carlisle (1 daily; 3hr 15min); Middleton-in-Teesdale (Mon–Sat 9 daily; Sun 3; 1hr 20min).

Durham to: Barnard Castle (1 daily; 1hr); Beamish (May–Sept 1–3 daily; 25min); Bishop Auckland (every 30min; 30min); Consett (hourly; 40min); Darlington (every 30min; 1hr); Newcastle (hourly; 1hr); Stanhope (June–Sept 1–2 weekly; 45min).

Hexham to: Allendale (Mon–Sat 4–6 daily; 25min); Bellingham (Mon–Sat 5 daily; 40min); Bishop Auckland (1 weekly; 1hr 50min); Byrness (1 weekly; 1hr 15min); Chesters (mid-July to early Sept 1–4 daily; 15min); Haltwhistle (hourly;

40min); Housesteads (mid-July to early Sept Mon–Sat 4 daily, Sun 1; 30min); Once Brewed (mid-July to early Sept Mon–Sat 4 daily, Sun 1; 35min); Otterburn (1 weekly; 1hr); Vindolanda (mid-July to early Sept Mon–Sat 4 daily, Sun 1; 40min).

Haltwhistle to: Alston (Mon–Sat 4–5 daily; 45min); Greenhead (mid-July to early Sept Mon–Sat 4 daily, Sun 1; 5min); Hexham (hourly; 40min).

Middlesbrough to: Newcastle (hourly; 1hr); Redcar (hourly; 25min); Saltburn (hourly; 40min).

Middleton-in-Teesdale to: High Force (Tues, Wed, Fri, Sat & Sun 2–3; 12min); Langdon Beck (Tues, Wed, Fri, Sat & Sun 2–3; 18min).

Newcastle to: Alnmouth (hourly; 1hr 30min); Alnwick (3–6 daily; 1hr 10min–1hr 45min); Bamburgh (3 daily; 2hr 30min); Barnard Castle (1 daily; 1hr 25min); Berwick-upon-Tweed (3–6 daily; 2hr 20min–3hr 10min); Corbridge (Mon–Sat every 30min, Sun every 2hr; 1hr); Durham (hourly; 1hr); Hexham (Mon–Sat every 30min, Sun every 2hr; 1hr 15min); Otterburn (2 daily; 2hr); Rothbury (2–7 daily; 1hr 15min); Seahouses (3 daily; 2hr 10min); Stanhope (1–2 weekly; 1hr 10min); Warkworth (hourly; 1hr 20min).

PART THREE

WALES

CHAPTER 16
NORTH COAST

CHAPTER 15
**DEE VALLEY &
SNOWDONIA**

N

CHAPTER 13
POWYS

CHAPTER 14
**CAMBRIAN
COAST**

CHAPTER 12
**SOUTHWEST
WALES**

CHAPTER 11
**SOUTHEAST
WALES**

CHAPTER ELEVEN

SOUTHEAST WALES

Home to almost 1.8 million people, sixty percent of the country's population, the southeastern corner of Wales, the counties of Gwent and Glamorgan, is also one of Britain's most industrialized regions. Both population and industry here are most heavily concentrated in the seaports and former coal mining valleys where rivers slice through mountainous terrain.

Monmouthshire is the easternmost county in Wales, starting at the English border in a beguilingly rural way, the **River Wye** criss-crossing between the two countries from its mouth at the fortress town of **Chepstow**; here, you'll find one of the most impressive castles in a land where few towns are without one. In the Wye's beautiful valley lie the spectacularly placed ruins of **Tintern Abbey**, downstream of the old county town of **Monmouth**. To the north, the foothills of the Black Mountains rise up out of the fertile river plains, making market towns such as **Abergavenny**, and the quieter valleys to its north, popular walking and outdoor pursuits centres.

Monmouthshire becomes increasingly industrialized as you travel west towards **Newport**, Wales' third largest conurbation. Although it is hardly likely to feature on a swift tour of Wales, the town has an excellent museum and the remains of an extensive Roman settlement at **Caerleon**, a northern suburb of the town. Western Monmouthshire and northern Glamorgan constitute the world-famous **valleys**, once the coal- and iron-rich powerhouse of the nation. This is the Wales of popular imagination: hemmed-in valley floors packed with lines of blank, grey houses, slanted almost impossibly towards the pithead. Although nearly all of the mines have since closed, the area is still one of tight-knit towns, with a rich working-class heritage that displays itself in some excellent museums and colliery tours, such as the **Big Pit** at Blaenafon and the **Rhondda Heritage Park** in Trehafod. The valleys follow rivers coursing down towards the coast, where great ports stood to ship their products all over the world. The greatest of them all was **Cardiff**, long past its heyday as the world's busiest coal port, but bouncing back in its comparatively new status as Wales' upbeat capital. Excellent museums, a massive castle, exciting rejuvenation projects around the stolid Victorian docks and Wales' best cultural pursuits make the city an essential stop.

The west of Glamorgan is dominated by Wales' second city, **Swansea**, rougher, tougher and less anglicized than the capital. Like Cardiff, Swansea grew principally on the strength of its docks, and sits on an impressive arc of coast that shelves round from the belching steel works of Port Talbot in the east to **Mumbles** and **Oystermouth**, holiday towns of amusement arcades, copious pubs and chip shops, on the jaw of the delightful **Gower Peninsula** in the west. The Gower – one of the country's favourite playgrounds – juts out into the sea, a mini-Wales of grand beaches, rocky headlands, bracken heaths and ruined castles.

The Wye valley

Perhaps the most anglicized corner of Wales, the **Wye Valley** – along with the rest of Monmouthshire – was only finally recognized as part of Wales in the local government reorganization of 1974, before which the county was officially included as part of neither England nor Wales, so that maps were frequently headlined "Wales and

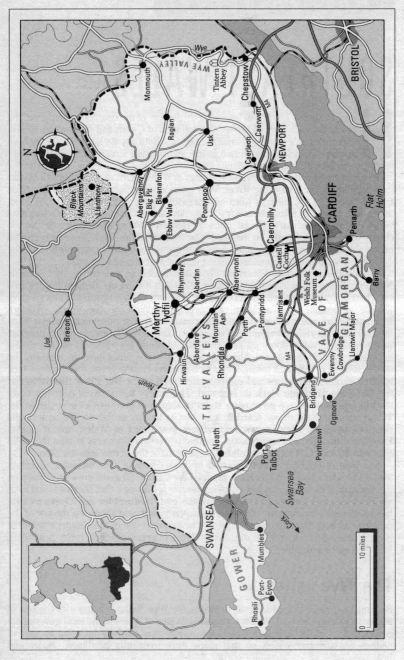

Monmouthshire". Most of the rest of Monmouthshire is firmly and redoubtably Welsh, but the woodlands and hills by the meandering River Wye share more similarities with the landscape over the border. The two main centres are **Chepstow**, with its massive castle radiating an awesome strength, high above the muddy flats and waters of the river estuary; and the spruce, old-fashioned town of **Monmouth**, sixteen miles upstream. Six miles north of Chepstow lie the inspirational ruins of the Cistercian **Tintern Abbey**, worth catching first thing in the morning or into the evening when the crowds of coach-trippers have evaporated.

Chepstow and Tintern Abbey

Of all the places that call themselves "the gateway to Wales", **CHEPSTOW** (Cas-Gwent) has probably the greatest claim, situated on the western bank of the River Wye, the current border, just over a mile from where its tidal waters flow out into the muddy Severn estuary. Chepstow is a sturdy place robbed of the immediate charm of many other Welsh market towns by the soulless modern developments that have combined to overwhelm the identifiably medieval street plan.

Chepstow's position as a former port is evident in the thirteenth-century **Port Wall**, encasing a tight loop of the River Wye centred on the strategically sited **Chepstow Castle** (April–Oct daily 9.30am–6.30pm; Nov–March Mon–Sat 9.30am–4pm, Sun 11am–4pm; CADW; £2.50), guarding one of the most important routes into Wales. Chepstow was the first stone castle to be built in Britain, the Great Tower keep rising in 1067 to help subdue the restless Welsh. The Lower Ward is the largest of the three enclosures and dates mainly from the thirteenth century. Here you'll find the **Great Hall**, the home of a wide-ranging exhibition on the history of the castle, with particular emphasis on the English Civil War years, when Royalist Chepstow was twice beseiged. Twelfth-century defences separate the Lower Ward from the Middle Ward, which is dominated by the still imposing ruins of the **Great Tower**. Beyond the Great Tower is the far narrower Upper Ward which leads up to the Barbican **watch-tower**, from which there are superlative views looking down the cliff to the river estuary.

Opposite is the **Chepstow Museum** (Mon–Sat 11am–1pm & 2–5pm, Sun 2–5pm; £1) containing nostalgic photographs and paintings of the trades supported in the past by the River Wye, and recording Chepstow's brief life in the early part of this century as a shipbuilding centre.

Practicalities

Chepstow's **train station** is five minutes' walk to the south of the High Street. Buses depart from the small **bus station** at the back of the shops on the other side of the Town (West) Gate from the High Street. The **tourist office** is located in the castle car park, off Bridge Street (daily Easter–Oct 10am–6pm; Nov–Easter 10am–4pm; ☎01291/623772). Inexpensive B&B **accommodation** can be found off Welsh Street, north from the Town Gate: try *Mrs Langdale's*, 71 St Kingsmark Ave (☎01291/625569; ③), and *Mrs Batchelor's*, 7 Lancaster Way (☎01291/626344; ③). A mile east of town, over the Wye in Sedbury Lane, is a wonderful B&B in an old converted jail house at *Upper Sedbury House* (☎01291/627173; ③). For pricier accommodation, head for stately *George Hotel* in Moor St, next to the West Gate (☎01291/625363; ④).

The town is blessed with some good **pubs**. The cosy *Coach and Horses*, up near the Town Gate on Welsh Street, has a regular diet of evening live folk and rock, and real ale. In the High Street, the grimy but friendly *White Lion* boasts a bowling alley, and at the bottom of the cobbled Hawker Hill Street is the cheery *Five Alls*. Of the pubs, the *Coach and Horses*, near the Town Gate on Welsh Street, is the best for **food**, or try the moderately priced *Afon Gwy*, down by the river on Bridge Street (☎01291/620158), great for local and Welsh speciality dishes, as well as cheaper snacks.

Tintern Abbey

Six miles north of Chepstow alongside some of the River Wye's most spectacular stretches, **Tintern Abbey** (April–Oct daily 9.30am–6.30pm; Nov–March Mon–Sat 9.30am–4pm, Sun 11am–4pm; £2.20; CADW) has inspired writers and painters – Wordsworth and Turner amongst them – for over two hundred years. Such is the place's enormous popularity, however, that it's advisable to go out of season or at the beginning or end of the day when the hordes have thinned out. The abbey was founded in 1131 by Cistercian monks brought wholesale from Normandy. Most of the remaining buildings, however, date from the massive rebuilding and expansion plan in the fourteenth century, when Tintern was at its mightiest. Its survival after the destructions of the Dissolution is largely thanks to its remoteness, as there were no nearby villages ready to use the abbey stone for rebuilding.

The centrepiece of the complex is the magnificent Gothic **church**, whose remarkable tracery and intricate stonework remains firmly intact. Around the church are the less substantial ruins of the monks' domestic quarters and cloister, mostly reduced to one-storey rubble. The course of the abbey's waste disposal system can be seen in the **Great Drain**, an irregular channel that links kitchens, toilets and the Infirmary with the nearby Wye. The **Novices' Hall** lies handily close to the Warming House, which together with the kitchen and Infirmary, would have been the only heated parts of the abbey, suggesting that novices might have gained a falsely favourable impression of monastic life before taking their final vows.

Monmouth and Raglan

Enclosed on three sides by the rivers Wye and Monnow, **MONMOUTH** (Trefynwy) retains some of its quiet charm as an important border post and the old county town. The centre of the town is **Agincourt Square**, a handsome open space at the top of the wide, shop-lined Monnow Street, gently descending to the thirteenth-century bridge over the River Monnow. The cobbled square is dominated by the arched Georgian **Shire Hall**, in which is embedded an eighteenth-century statue of the Monmouth-born King Henry V, victor at the 1415 Battle of Agincourt. In front is the pompous statue of another local, the Honourable Charles Stewart Rolls – the co-founder of Rolls-Royce, and the first man, in 1910, to pilot a double-flight over the English Channel. Almost opposite Shire Hall is **Castle Hill**, which you can walk up to glimpse some of the scant ruins of the **castle**, founded in 1068.

Priory Street leads north from Agincourt Square to the town's **Museum** (Mon–Sat 10am–1pm & 2–5pm, Sun 2–5pm; £1), located in the market hall complex, and housing their **Nelson Collection**, which attempts to portray the life of one of the most success-ful sea-going Britons through use of the Admiral's personal artefacts. At the very bottom of Monnow Street, the road narrows to squeeze into the confines of the seven-hundred-year-old **Monnow bridge**, crowned with its hulking stone gate of 1262, that served both as a means of defence for the town and a toll-collection point.

Buses operate from the **bus station** behind *Kwik Save* at the bottom of Monnow Street, and the **tourist office** is in the Shire Hall, Agincourt Square (Easter–Oct daily 9.30am–5.30pm; ☎01600/713899). You'll find **accommodation** at the intimate *Riverside Hotel* on Cinderhill Street, over the Monnow bridge (☎01600/715577; ⑤), or in B&Bs at *Red Lion House*, 16 Draybridge St (☎01600/713633; ③), and the welcoming *Old Gaol* on Hereford Rd (☎01600/712463; ③). The **youth hostel** is located right in the heart of town in a converted fifteenth-century priory on Priory Street (March–Oct; ☎01600/715116). Slightly pricey lunchtime and evening **food** is available at the *Punch House* in Agincourt Square; cheaper lunches can be had at the *Green Dragon* in St Thomas Square, down by the Monnow Bridge.

Raglan

RAGLAN (Rhaglan), seven miles west of Monmouth by bus, is an unassuming village worth visiting for its glorious **Castle** (April–Oct daily 9am–6.30pm; Nov–March Mon–Sat 9.30am–4pm, Sun 11am–4pm; CADW; £2.20), whose fussy and comparatively intact style make it stand out from so many other crumbling Welsh fortresses. The last medieval fortification built in Britain, Raglan was begun on the site of a Norman motte in 1435 by Sir William ap Thomas, whose design combines practical strength with ostentatious style. The **gatehouse**, still used as the main entrance, houses the best examples of the castle's showy decoration in its heraldic shields, intricate stonework edging and gargoyles. Ap Thomas' grandson, William Herbert II, was responsible in the mid-fifteenth century for the two inner courts, built around his grandfather's original gatehouse, hall and keep. The first court is the cobbled **Pitched Stone Court**, designed to house the functional rooms like the kitchen (with two vast double-flued chimneys) and the servants' quarters. To the left is **Fountain Court**, a well-proportioned grassy space surrounded by opulent residences that included grand apartments and state rooms. Separating the two are the original 1435 **Hall**, the **Buttery**, the remains of the **chapel** and the dank, cold **cellars** below.

Abergavenny and North Monmouthshire

Of all the towns in Monmouthshire, **Abergavenny** is the best base for a holiday. As well as a fine range of places to eat, drink and stay, the lively market town has a delightfully whimsical Museum of Childhood and a town museum in the ugly castle keep. Abergavenny is surrounded by commanding hills, a magnet for walkers, of which the **Sugar Loaf** and the legend-infused **Skirrid** are deservedly the most popular. The town is also a good base for the pastoral border country to the east, most commonly visited to see White, Skenfrith and Grosmont castles, known collectively, if unimaginatively, as the **Three Castles**. A pointing finger of the north of the county stretches from Abergavenny along the **Vale of Ewyas** and the Honddu River at the bottom of the stark **Black Mountains**. Lost in rural isolation are the astounding churches at **Partrishow** and **Cwmyoy**, a couple of miles below **Llanthony Priory**, which has many features in common with Tintern Abbey, although with a fraction of the crowds.

Abergavenny

Although only a couple of miles and a few hills from the iron and coal towns of Gwent's northern valleys, **ABERGAVENNY** (Y Fenni) grew because of its weaving and tanning trades, giving it an entirely different feel. These industries prospered alongside its flourishing market, still the focal point for a wide area, drawing many people up from the valleys every Tuesday. In World War II, Hitler's deputy, Rudolf Hess, was kept in the town's mental asylum as a prisoner after his plane crash-landed in Scotland in 1941. He was allowed a weekly walk in the nearby hills, growing, it is said, to love the Welsh countryside. From the train station, Monmouth Road rises gently, eventually becoming High Street, off which Market Street runs down past the sites of the markets to the **Museum of Childhood and the Home** (Mon–Sat 10am–5pm, Sun 1–5pm; £2), an unashamed wallow in nostalgia, from Victorian dolls (and an Edwardian one saved from the *Titanic*) and a reputedly haunted doll's house to cigarette cards, rocking horses and clockwork toys.

Abergavenny's **train station** (☎01873/852393) lies on the well-used line between Newport and Hereford and buses depart from Swan Meadow **bus station** in all directions. The **tourist office** (Easter–Oct daily 10am–6pm; ☎01873/857588) and **Brecon Beacons National Park office** (daily Easter–Oct 9.30am–5.30pm; Nov–Easter 10am–1pm & 2–4pm) are in the same building in the Swan Meadow car park. *Brook Bikes*, 9 Brecon Rd (☎01873/857066), **rents cycles**. **Accommodation** comes in the form of B&Bs, many on the Monmouth Road, between the town centre and the station: *Maes Glas*, Raglan Terrace, Monmouth Road (☎01873/857855; ③) is the best; nearby, the Georgian *Park Guest House*, 36 Hereford Rd (☎01873/853715; ③) is also very good.

There are places to **eat** everywhere in Abergavenny including the moderately priced *Greyhound Vaults*, Market Street, opposite the Museum of Childhood (☎01873/858549), great for a wide range of tasty Welsh and English specialities, including the best vegetarian dishes in town; and the *Greco*, 40 Cross St, a huge place, great for cheap piles of cholesterol. The *Walnut Tree Inn*, on the B4521 at Llanddewi Sgyrrid, two miles north of town (☎01873/852797) is a legendary foodies' paradise, drawing diners from all over Britain, just for the evening. Of Abergavenny's **pubs**, the best is the staunchly traditional *Hen and Chickens*, Flannel St, off the High St, with the best beer in town and a separate dining room for inexpensive food.

The Three Castles

The fertile, low-lying land between the Monnow and Usk rivers was important as an easy access route into the agricultural lands of south Wales, and the Norman invaders built a trio of strongholds here to protect their interests. Skenfrith, Grosmont and White castles were founded in the eleventh century, and lie within an eight-mile radius of each other. In 1201, the three were presented as a unit by King John to Hubert de Burgh, who fought extensively on the continent and brought back sophisticated new ideas on castle design to replace earlier castles with square keeps. He rebuilt Skenfrith and Grosmont, and his successor as overlord, Walerund Teutonicus ("the German"), worked on White Castle. In 1260, the advancing army of Llywelyn ap Gruffydd began to threaten the king's supremacy in south Wales, and the three castles were refortified in readiness. The only return to military usage came in 1404–5, when Owain Glyndŵr's army pressed down to Grosmont, only to be defeated by the future King Henry V. The castles slipped into disrepair, and were finally sold separately in 1902, the first time since 1138 that the three had fallen out of single ownership.

White Castle (Castell Gwyn; April–Sept daily 10am–6pm; £1.70; Oct–March daily; free), six miles east of Abergavenny, is the most awesome of the three, sited in rolling countryside with some superb views over to the hills surrounding the River Monnow. A few patches of the white rendering that gave the castle its name can be seen on the exterior walls. Entering the grassy Outer Ward, enclosed by a curtain wall with four towers, gives an excellent view over to the brooding mass of the castle, situated neatly in a moat on the Inner Ward. A bridge leads over the moat into the dual-towered Inner Gatehouse, where the western tower, on the right, can be climbed for its sublime vantage point. Here, you can appreciate the scale of the tall twelfth-century curtain walls in the Inner Ward. Of the domestic buildings within the walls, only the foundations and a few inches of wall remain. At the back of the ward, there are massive foundations of the Norman keep, demolished in about 1260 and unearthed once more in the early part of this century.

Seven miles northeast of White Castle is the thirteenth-century **castle** (open all year; free) in the the attractive border village of **SKENFRITH** (Ynysgynwraidd), dominated by the circular keep that replaced an earlier Norman incarnation. Whilst not as impressive as White Castle, Skenfrith is in a pretty riverside setting, its castle walls built of a sturdy red sandstone in an irregular rectangle. In the centre of the ward is the 21-foot-high round keep, raised slightly on an earth mound to give archers a greater firing range, and containing the vestiges of the private apartments of the castle's lord on the upper floors; most notable are the huge fireplace and private latrine.

Five miles upstream of Skenfrith, right on the English border, the most dilapidated of the Three Castles, **Grosmont Castle** (Castell y Grysmwnt; open all year; free), sits on a small hill above the village. Entering over the wooden bridge above the dry moat, brings you into the small central courtyard, dominated on the right-hand side by the ruins of a large Great Hall, dating from the first decade of the thirteenth century.

The Vale of Ewyas

In total contrast to the urban blights in the north valleys just a handful of miles away, the northern finger of Monmouthshire, stretching along the English border, is one of the most enchanting and reclusive parts of Wales. The main A465 Hereford road leads six miles north out of Abergavenny to Llanfihangel Crucorney, where the B4423 diverges off to the north into the beautiful **Vale of Ewyas**, along the banks of the Honddu River.

After a mile, a lane heads west towards the enchanting valley of the **Gwyrne Fawr**, and the delightful **church** and **well of St Issui** in the hamlet of **PARTRISHOW**. First founded in the eleventh century, the tiny church was refashioned in the thirteenth and fourteenth centuries, in the next century gaining the lacy rood screen carved out of solid Irish oak, and adorned with crude symbols of good and evil – most notably in the corner, where an evil dragon consumes a vine, a symbol of hope and well-being. The rest of the whitewashed church breathes simplicity by comparison. Of special note are the wall texts painted over the doom picture of a skeleton and scythe – before the Reformation, such pictures were widely used in the hope of teaching an illiterate population about the scriptures, until King James I ordered that such "Popish devices" should be whitewashed over and repainted with scripture texts.

Back on the main B4423, the road winds its way on the valley's western side, past the fork at the *Queen's Head* inn (☎01873/890241; ②), excellent for B&B and pony trekking, as well as a place to **camp**. In the adjacent village of **CWMYOY** the parish **church of St Martin** has substantially subsided due to geological twists in the underlying rock. Nothing squares up: the tower leans at a severe angle from the bulging body of the church, and the view inside from the back of the nave towards the sloping altar, askew roof and straining windows is unforgettable.

Four miles further up this most remote of valleys is the hamlet of **LLANTHONY**, nothing more than a small cluster of houses, an inn and a few outlying farms around the wide open ruins of **Llanthony Priory** – a grander setting, and certainly a quieter one than Tintern, though the buildings are far more modest in scale. It was founded around 1100 by the Norman knight, William de Lacy, who, it is said, was so captivated by the spiritual beauty of the site that he renounced worldly living and founded a hermitage, attracting like-minded recluses and forming Wales' first Augustine priory. The roofless church with its pointed transitional arches and squat tower were constructed in the latter half of the twelfth century and retain a real sense of spirituality and peace. The *Abbey Hotel* here, fashioned out of part of the tumbledown priory, was built in the eighteenth century as a hunting lodge. Along the road from the priory is the *Half Moon Inn* (☎01873/890611; ②), home of superb beer, good-value food and accommodation.

Newport and around

Dominating the once industrious valley towns of southern Monmouthshire, **NEWPORT** (Casnewydd-ar-Wysg), Wales' third largest town, is a downbeat, working-class place that grew up around the docks at the mouth of the River Usk. Its rich history has been largely swept away by the twentieth century, but isolated nuggets remain, most notably at Roman **Caerleon** – the "old port" on the River Usk – now a northern suburb of Newport, but predating the town by about a thousand years.

The Town

The pathetic remains of Newport's **castle** stand on a sheer cliff above the foul and muddy River Usk, along which stands Peter Fink's giant red 1990 sculpture, **Steel Wave**, a nod to one of Newport's great industries. The High Street leads to Newport and Westgate squares, and the **Westgate Hotel**, an ornate Victorian successor to the hotel where soldiers sprayed a crowd of Chartist protesters (see box) with gunfire in 1839, killing at least a dozen – the hotel's original pillars still show bullet marks.

A hundred yards along **Commercial Street**, in John Frost Square, the quirky **Newport clock** shudders, shakes, spits smoke, and comes near to apparent collapse every hour, usually drawing an appreciative crowd. In front of the clock is the town's library, tourist office and imaginative civic **Museum** (Mon–Thurs 9.30am–5pm, Fri 9.30am–4.30pm, Sat 9.30am–4pm; free). Starting with the origins of Gwent, the displays look at the county's original occupations and early lifestyles, and include a section on mining with a roll-call of those killed in local pit accidents – 3,508 men between 1837 and 1927. Newport's spectacular growth from 1000 in 1801 to a grimy port town of 70,000 people by the turn of this century is well charted, but the two most interesting sections deal with the Chartist uprising and the Roman remains excavated at Caerwent.

Dominating the Newport skyline with its comical, spidery legs is the 1906 **Transporter Bridge** (Tues–Sun 8am–6pm; free), built to enable cars and people to cross the river without disturbing the shipping channel, as they had to be hoisted high above the Usk on a dangling platform.

Caerleon

Half-hourly buses wind their way along the three-mile journey north to the compact town centre of **CAERLEON** (Caerllion), peppered with the remnants of the Roman

---

THE CHARTISTS

During an era when wealthy landowners bought votes from the enfranchised few, the struggles of the Chartists were a historical inevitability. Thousands gathered around the 1838 People's Charter that called for universal male franchise, a secret (and annual) ballot for Parliament and the abolition of property qualifications for the vote. Demonstrations in support of these principles were held all over the country, with some of the most vociferous and bloodiest taking place in the radical heartlands of industrial south Wales. On November 4, 1839, Chartists from all over Monmouthshire marched on Newport and descended Stow Hill, whereupon they were gunned at by soldiers hiding in the Westgate Hotel, who killed 22 protesters. The leaders of the rebellion were sentenced to death, which was commuted to transportation, by the self-righteous and wealthy leaders of the town. Queen Victoria even knighted the mayor who ordered the random execution.

town. It was the River Usk (Wysg) that gave Caerleon its old Roman name of Isca, a major administrative and legionary centre (on a par with York and Chester) built to provide ancillary and military services for the smaller, outlying camps in the rest of south Wales. Although the town fell gradually into decay after the Romans had left, there were still some massive remains standing when, in 1188, episcopal envoy Giraldus Cambrensis noted with evident relish the "immense palaces, which, with the gilded gables of their roofs, once rivalled the magnificence of ancient Rome".

Although time has had an inevitable corrosive effect on the remains since Giraldus' time, there's a powerful sense of history running through the Roman **fortress baths** (April–Oct daily 9.30am–6.30pm; Nov–March Mon–Sat 9.30am–4pm, Sun 2–4pm; £1.70; CADW). The bathing houses, cold hall and communal pool area are remarkably intact and beautifully presented, with highly imaginative uses of audio-visual equipment, sound commentary and models. On the High Street, the Victorian Neoclassical portico is the sole survivor of the original **Legionary Museum** (April–Sept Mon–Sat 10am–6pm, Sun 2–6pm; Oct–March Mon–Sat 10am–4.30pm, Sun 2–4.30pm; £1.70), now housed in a modern building behind and laden with artefacts unearthed here.

Opposite the Legionary Museum, Fosse Lane leads down to the hugely atmospheric Roman **amphitheatre** (same times as the baths; free), the only one of its kind preserved in Britain. Hidden under a grassy mound until the 1920s, the amphitheatre was built around 80 AD, the same time as the Colosseum in Rome; legions of up to six thousand would take seats to watch the gory combat of gladiators, animal baiting or military exercises.

Practicalities

Newport's **tourist office** is in the museum complex on John Frost Square (Mon–Wed & Fri 9.30am–6pm, Thurs & Sat 9.30am–5pm; ☎01633/842962), a hundred yards from Kingsway **bus station**, and a quarter-mile from the **train station**. Caerleon has an informal **tourist office** (April–Oct daily 10am–1pm & 2–5pm; ☎01633/430777) in the Ffwrrwm shopping arcade. Staying in Caerleon is a more amenable option than nearby Newport. You can follow in the footsteps of Lord Tennyson by staying at the comfortable *Hanbury Arms* (☎01633/420361; ④), at the bottom of the High Street. Alternatively, there's **B&B** at *Blairgowrie* on White Hart Lane (☎01633/421788; ②). If you stay in Newport, try the informal *Queen's Hotel*, 19 Bridge St (☎01633/262992; ③), or the genteel *St Etienne*, 162 Stow Hill (☎01633/262341; ③), or *Kepe Lodge* (☎01633/262351; ③), 46a Caerau Rd, at the western end of Bridge Street. There is a **campsite** at *Tredegar House* (☎01633/815880); bus #15A or 15C from the town centre. For **food**, make for the *Scrum Half* café, Commerecial St, excellent for cheap and filling breakfasts and lunches, or the *Ristorante Vittorio*, 113 Stow Hill (☎01633/840261), a popular and traditional Italian trattoria. The best place in Caerleon is *Tabards* on the High Street, a hospitable bistro, where you can also **drink** without eating.

The Valleys

No other part of Wales is as instantly recognizable as **The Valleys**, a generic name for the string of settlements packed into the narrow cracks in the mountainous terrain to the north of Newport and Cardiff. Arriving from England, the change from rolling countryside to sharp contours and a post-industrial landscape is almost instantaneous. Each of the valleys depended almost solely on coal mining which, although nearly defunct as an industry, has left its mark in the staunchly working-class towns, where row upon row of brightly painted terraced housing, tipped along the slopes at some incredible angles, are broken only by austere chapels, the occasional remaining pithead or the miners' old institutes and drinking clubs.

This is not traditional tourist country, and yet is doubtless one of the most interesting and distinctive corners of Wales dripping with sociological and human interest. Some of the former mines have reopened as gutsy and hard-hitting museums – **Big Pit** at Blaenafon and the **Rhondda Heritage Park** at Trehafod being the best. Other civic museums, at **Pontypool**, **Pontypridd** and **Merthyr Tydfil**, have grown up over decades, chronicling the lives (and, all too frequently, the deaths) of miners and their families. A few older sites, such as vast **Caerphilly Castle** and the sixteenth-century manor house of **Llancaiach Fawr**, have been attracting visitors for hundreds of years. But it is beyond the mainstream sights that the visitor can gain a more rounded impression of Valleys life: the roundhouses at **Nantyglo**, fortified against an anticipated workers' uprising, the iron gravestones of **Blaenafon**, and the dignified memorials found in almost every community to those who died underground.

Pontypool

The easternmost identifiable Valleys town – although never a coal-mining centre – is **PONTYPOOL**, a sprawling, hilly town that isn't likely to keep you busy for long. It's worth a short stop at the **Valley Inheritance Museum** (Feb–Dec Mon–Sat 10am–5pm, Sun 2–5pm; £1.50), housed in a Georgian stable block at the western entrance of Pontypool Park. The building once served as a mansion and is now a school, belonging to the Hanbury family, local landowners and the pioneers of the town's staple tin-plate industry. The exhibition inside the museum casts a wide net over the town's history and trades, all of which seems to have sprung from one family. A rare surviving feature of Valleys towns can be found in Pontypool, in the shape of the steamy *Mario's Café* at the bottom of Broad Street, opened by Italian emigrants who flocked to south Wales in the nineteenth century. The **train station** is inconveniently sited over a mile east of the town centre, making **buses**, which stop by the handsome Victorian Town Hall, a far easier option.

WORKING THE BLACK SEAM

The land beneath the inhospitable south Wales valleys had some of the most abundant and accessible natural seams of coal and iron ore to be found, readily milked in the boom years of the nineteenth and early twentieth centuries. Wealthy, predominantly English, capitalists came to Wales and ruthlessly stripped the land of its natural assets, while simultaneously exploiting those who risked life and limb underground. The mine owners were in a formidably strong position – thousands flocked to the Valleys in search of work and some sort of sustainable life. By the turn of the twentieth century the Valleys – virtually unpopulated a century earlier – became blackened, packed with pits, chapels and Welsh peasants, bolstered by their Irish, Scottish and Italian peers.

In 1920, there were 256,000 men working in the 620 mines of the south Wales coalfield, providing one third of the world's coal. Vast Miners' Institutes jostled for position with the Nonconformist chapels, whose fervent brand of Christianity was matched by the zeal of the region's politics, trade-union-led and avowedly left-wing. Great socialist orators rose to national prominence, cementing the Valleys' reputation as a world apart from the rest of Britain, let alone Wales. Even Britain's pioneering National Health Service, founded by a radical Labour government in the years following World War II, was based on a Valleys' community scheme by locally born Aneurin Bevan.

Over half of the original pits closed in the harsh economic climate of the 1930s as coal seams became exhausted and the political climate changed, and the number of men employed in the industry has dipped down into four figures, precipitated by the aftermath of the 1984–85 miners' strike. No coalfield was as solidly behind the strike as south Wales but, a decade on, all of the south Wales pits, bar one temporarily reprieved in April 1994, have closed.

Blaenafon and the Big Pit

Road and river continue six miles north from Pontypool to the airy iron and coal town of **BLAENAFON**, whose population has shrunk to five thousand, a quarter of its nineteenth-century size. The town's boom kicked off at the Blaenafon **ironworks**, just off the Brynmawr Road (May–Sept Mon–Sat 11am–5pm, Sun 2–5pm; £1.20; CADW; ☎014955/52036), founded in 1788. Limestone, coal and iron ore – ingredients for successful iron smelting – were abundant locally, and the Blaenafon works grew to become one of the largest in Britain in the early nineteenth century, finally closing in 1900. The site remains and the museum in the workers' cottages offers a thorough picture both of the process and the lifestyle that went with it.

Just as it is now possible to visit the scene of Blaenafon's iron industry, the town's defunct coal trade has also been transformed smoothly into the site which most clearly evokes the experience of a miner's work and life. At the **Big Pit** (March–Nov daily 9.30am–5pm, last underground tour 3.30pm; £4.75, surface tour only £1.75), a mile west of the town and reached by a half-hourly shuttle bus from Blaenafon, you are lowered three hundred feet, kitted out with lamp, helmet and very heavy battery pack, into the labyrinth of shafts and coal faces for a guided tour. The guides – most of whom are ex-miners – lead you through explanations and examples of the different types of coal mining, from the dodgy old stack-and-pillar operation, to modern mechanically worked seams. Constant streams of rust-coloured water flow by, adding to the dank and chilly atmosphere that must have terrified the small children who were once paid twopence for a six-day week (of which one penny was taken out for the cost of their candles) pulling the coal wagons along the tracks. Back on the surface, the old pithead baths, blacksmiths, miners' canteen and winding engine house have all been preserved and filled with some fascinating displays about the local and south Wales mining industries, including a series of characteristically feisty testimonies from the miners made redundant here in 1980.

Caerphilly

A few miles west, **CAERPHILLY** (Caerffili), seven miles north of Cardiff, is a flattened and colourless town, notable only for its **Castle** (April–Oct daily 9.30am–6.30pm; Nov–March Mon–Sat 9.30am–4pm, Sun 11am–4pm; £2.20; CADW), the first in Britain built concentrically, with an inner system of defences overlooking the outer ring. Looming out of its vast surrounding moat, the medieval fortress with its cock-eyed tower occupies over thirty acres, presenting an awesome promise not entirely fulfilled inside. The castle was begun in 1268 by Gilbert de Clare as a defence against Llewelyn the Last. Two years later, Llywelyn largely destroyed the castle, which was swiftly rebuilt, but for the next few hundred years Caerphilly was little more than a decaying toy, given at whim by kings to their favourites. By the turn of the twentieth century, Caerphilly Castle was in a sorry state, sitting amidst a growing industrial town that saw fit to build in the now dry moat and the castle precincts. Houses and shops were demolished in order to allow the moat to be reflooded in 1958.

You enter the castle through a great **gatehouse** that punctuates the barbican wall by a lake, much restored and now housing an exhibition about the castle's history. A platform behind the barbican wall exhibits medieval war and siege engines, pointing ominously across the lake. On the left is the southeastern tower, outleaning its rival in Pisa. Of the rest of the castle, the most interesting section is the massive eastern gatehouse, which includes an impressive upper hall and oratory and, to its left, the wholly restored and reroofed **Great Hall**.

The Taff and Cynon valleys

The River Taff flows out into the Bristol Channel at Cardiff, after passing through a condensed couple of dozen miles of industry and population. The first town in the Taff vale is **Pontypridd**, one of the most cheerful in the Valleys, and about the best base. Continuing north, the river splits again at **Abercynon**, where the Cynon River flows in from Aberdare, site of Wales' only remaining deep mine. Just outside Abercynon is the enjoyable sixteenth-century **Llancaiach Fawr** manor house. To the north, the Taff is packed into one of the tightest of all the Valleys, passing **Aberfan** five miles short of the imposing valley head town of **Merthyr Tydfil**.

Pontypridd

PONTYPRIDD's quirky arched **bridge** of 1775 was once the largest single-span stone bridge in the world and was built by local amateur stonemason, William Edwards, whose previous attempts had crumbled into the river below. Across the river is **Ynysangharad Park**, where Sir W. Goscombe John's gooey statue honours Pontypridd weaver Evan James who composed the stirringly nationalistic *Mae Hen wlad fy nhadau* (*Land of My Fathers*) that has become the Welsh national anthem. By the bridge at the end of Taff Street, the **Pontypridd Historical and Cultural Centre** (Mon–Sat 10am–5pm; 25p) is one of the best museums in the Valleys – a real treasure trove of photographs, video, models and exhibits that succeed in painting a warm and human picture of the town and its outlying valleys. The interior of the old *tabernacl* itself has been lovingly restored and also pays homage to the town's famous sons, crooner Tom Jones and opera star and actor Sir Geraint Evans.

Pontypridd is well connected to bus, train and road networks. The **tourist office** (Mon–Sat 10am–5pm; ☎01443/409512) is in the Historical and Cultural Centre on Bridge Street. **Accommodation** is rather scarce: in the town centre, try the lively *Millfield Hotel* on Mill Street, near the station (☎01443/480111; ④), or, right in the thick of the action, the bustling *Market Tavern* on Market Street (☎01443/485331; ③). The **youth hostel** at Llwynypia is only four short stops up the valley rail line.

Llancaiach Fawr

The river divides at **ABERCYNON**, a stark, typical valley town of punishingly steep streets lined with blank, grey houses, fading out into a coniferous hillside. Two miles east, just north of the village of Nelson, is the sixteenth-century **Llancaiach Fawr** (April–Sept Mon–Fri 10am–5pm, Sat & Sun 10am–6pm; Oct–March times same except Sun 2–6pm; £3.65), a Tudor house, built around 1530, that has been transformed into a living history museum set in 1645, the time of the Civil War, with all of the guides dressed as house servants, speaking the language of seventeenth-century Britain. Although potentially tacky, it is quite deftly done, with well-researched period authenticity and numerous fascinating anecdotes from the staff; visitors are even encouraged to try on the master of the household's armour. Regular buses from Pontypridd, Cardiff and Ystrad Mynach station pass the entrance.

Merthyr Tydfil

MERTHYR TYDFIL sits at the top of the Taff valley, on the cusp of the industrial Valleys to the south and the grand, windy heights of the Brecon Beacons to the north. In the seventeenth century, the village became a focal point for Dissenters and Radicals, movements which, through poverty and crass inequality, gained momentum in the eighteenth century as the town's four massive ironworks were founded to exploit the abundant seams of iron ore and limestone. Merthyr became the largest iron-producing town in the world, as well as by far the most populous town in Wales.

ABERFAN

North of Abercynon, the Taff valley contains one sight that is hard to forget: the two neat lines of distant arches that mark the graves of the 144 people killed in October 1966 by an unsecured slag heap sliding down a hill and on to the Pantglas primary school in the village of **ABERFAN**. Thousands of people still make the pilgrimage to the village graveyard, to stand silent and bemused by the enormity of the cost of coal, while the human cost – including 116 children that died huddled in panic at the beginning of their school day – is beyond comprehension. Amongst the gravestones that strive so hard to rationalize the tragedy, one of the most humbling and beautiful valedictions to be seen is to a ten-year-old boy, who, it simply records, "loved light, freedom and animals". Official enquiries all told the sorry tale that this disaster was an almost inevitable eventuality, given the cavalier approach to safety so often displayed by the coal bosses. Gwynfor Evans, then the newly elected first *Plaid Cymru* MP in Westminster, spoke with well-founded bitterness when he said, "Let us suppose that such a monstrous mountain had been built above Hampstead or Eton, where the children of the men of power and wealth are at school . . .". That, of course, could never have happened.

Merthyr's radicalism bubbled furiously, breaking out into occasional riots and prompting the election of Britain's first socialist MP, Keir Hardie, in 1900.

The sights listed here are all around the Taff to the immediate northwest of the town centre. The **Ynysfach Engine House** (Mon–Fri 10am–5pm; Easter–Oct also Sat & Sun 2–5pm; £1.15) contains a gritty look at the social conditions in the urban chaos of the nineteenth century. Half a mile further up the River Taff, just off Nant-y-Gwenith Street, the lower end of the Neath Road, is **Chapel Row**, a line of skilled ironworkers' cottages built in the 1820s, one of which holds composer **Joseph Parry's Birthplace** (April–Oct daily 2–5pm; 60p): Parry wrote the national favourite *Myfanwy* which is piped between rooms, some given over to a display of his life and music.

Back across the other side of the river, just beyond the Brecon Road, is a home in absolute contrast to Parry's humble and cramped birthplace: **Cyfartha Castle** (April–Sept Mon–Sat 10am–6pm, Sun noon–5pm; Oct–March closes 5pm; £1), built in 1825 as an ostentatious mock-Gothic castle for William Crawshay II, boss of the town's original ironworks. The castle is set within a vast, attractive parkland which slopes down to the river and afforded Crawshay a permanent view over his iron empire. The old wine cellars contain a varied and enjoyable walk through the history of Merthyr, with the political turmoil and massive exploitation of the past couple of centuries picked over in gory detail. The museum's modern art **gallery** houses an impressive collection of Welsh pieces, including offerings by Augustus John, Cedric Morris, Vanessa Bell, Jack Yeats, Vanessa Bell and Kyffin Williams.

The **train station** is a minute's walk from the High Street. North up the High Street from here is Glebeland Street with the bus station and the **tourist office**, 14a Glebeland St (Mon–Sat 9.30am–5.30pm; ☎01685/379884). **Accommodation** includes the unpretentious *Tregenna Hotel* in Park Terrace, next to Penydarren Park (☎01685/723627; ③); there are humbler surroundings at the *Hanover Guest House*, 31 Hanover St (☎01685/379303; ③). There is a **campsite** four miles north of town in the beautiful surroundings of *Glawen Farm*, Cwmtaff, near Cefn-Coed (☎01685/723740).

The Rhondda

The most famous of all the Welsh valleys and heart of the massive south Wales coal industry, **The Rhondda Fawr** – sixteen miles long and never as much as a mile wide – for many immediately conjures up Richard Llewellyn's 1939 book *How Green Was My Valley*, which was based on the author's life in Ton Pentre, Rhondda Fawr. Beween

MALE VOICE CHOIRS

Fiercely protective of its reputation as a land of song, the voice of Wales is most commonly heard amongst the ranks of male voice choirs. Although found all over the country, it is in the southern, industrial heartland that they are loudest and strongest. Their roots lie in the Nonconformist religious traditions of the seventeenth and eighteenth centuries, when Methodism in particular swept the country, and singing was a free and potent way of cherishing the frequently persecuted faith. Classic hymns like *Cwm Rhondda* and the Welsh national anthem, *Mae Hen Wlad Fy Nhadau* (*Land of My Fathers*), are synonymous with the choirs, whose full-blooded interpretation of them continues to render all others insipid. Each valleys town still has its own (often depleted) choir, most of whom happily accept visitors to sit in on rehearsals. A leaflet, available from tourist offices, gives contact phone numbers for each choir's secretary. Contact them directly, and take the chance to hear one of the world's most distinctive choral traditions in full, roof-raising splendour.

1860 and 1910 the Rhondda's population grew from 3000 to nearly 160,000 squeezed into ranks of houses grouped around sixty or so pitheads. The Rhondda, more than any other of the Valleys, became a self-reliant, hard-drinking, chapel-going, deeply poor and terrifically spirited breeding ground for radical religion and firebrand politics. The Communist Party ran the town of Maerdy (nicknamed "Little Moscow" by Fleet Street in the 1930s) for decades. But the last pit in the Rhondda closed in 1990, leaving behind not some dispiriting ragbag of depressing towns, but a range of new attractions, cleaned-up hillsides and some of the friendliest pubs and working men's clubs to be found anywhere in Britain.

Specific attractions though are few. The only one which really stands out is the colliery museum of the **Rhondda Heritage Park** (daily 10am–6pm, last admission 4.30pm; £4.45), at Trehafod, formed by locals when the Lewis Merthyr pit closed in 1983. You can explore the engine-winding houses, lamp room, fan house and a new trip underground, with stunning visuals and sound effects, re-creating 1950s and late nineteenth-century life (and death) through the eyes of colliers. A chilling roll-call of pit deaths and a final narration by Neil Kinnock about the human cost – especially for the valley women – of mining are stirringly moving.

A **train** line, punctuated with stops every mile or so, runs the entire length of the Rhondda. Buses also cover the route, continuing up into the mountains and the Brecon Beacons. The Llwynypia **youth hostel**, in the Glynocornel Centre opposite the station (mid-Feb to Oct; ☎01443/430859), is well placed for residential environmental studies and walking. Other **accommodation** includes the *Village Inn* (☎01443/688204; ③), opposite the Rhondda Heritage Park, and the scruffy but friendly *G&T's*, 64–66 Pontypridd Rd, Porth (☎01443/685775; ③), which also serves winning **food**.

Cardiff and around

Official capital of Wales since only 1955, the buoyant city of **CARDIFF** (Caerdydd) has swiftly grown into its new status, and although the country is still without any directly elected government or assembly of its own, the increasing number of Welsh Office subsections in Cardiff, together with new, progressive developments, are beginning to give the city the true feel of an international capital. The "not very Welsh" charge frequently levelled at the city is, in some ways, justified – if compared with Swansea, Cardiff is very anglicized – you'll rarely hear *Cymraeg* on the city's streets.

The second Marquis of Bute built Cardiff's first dock in 1839, opening others in swift succession. The Butes, who owned massive swathes of the rapidly industrializing south Wales valleys, insisted that all coal and iron exports used the family docks in Cardiff, and it became one of the busiest ports in the world. In the hundred years up to the turn of the twentieth century, Cardiff's population had soared from almost nothing to 170,000, and the spacious and ambitious new civic centre in Cathays Park was well under way. The twentieth century has seen swinging fortunes: the dock trade slumped in the 1930s, and the city suffered heavy bombing in World War II, but with the creation of Cardiff as capital in 1955 optimism and confidence in the city have blossomed. Many large governmental and media institutions have moved here from London, and the development of the dock areas has given a positive boost to a flagging cityscape. Unlike so many British cities, there is an almost tangible feeling here of optimism.

Arrival, information and accommodation

The city **bus station** is on the southwestern side of the city centre. Across the fore-court is Cardiff Central **train station** (☎01222/228000), for all *InterCity* services, as well as many suburban and *Valley Line* services. **Queen Street station**, at the eastern edge of the centre, is for local services only. The **tourist office**, in the forecourt of **Cardiff Central station** (April–Sept Mon–Sat 9am–6.30pm, Sun 10am–4pm; Oct–March Mon–Sat 9am–5.30pm, Sun 10am–4pm; ☎01222/227281), will provide good free maps of the city and a copy of *The Buzz!*, a free monthly guide to arts in the city.

Cardiff is compact enough to walk around, as even the bay area is within twenty minutes' stroll of Central station. Once you're out of the centre, however, it's best to fall back on the extensive **bus network**, most reliably operated by the garish orange *Cardiff Bus* (*Bws Caerdydd*) company – information at the bus station in Wood Street (Mon & Fri 8am–5.30pm, Tues–Thurs & Sat 8.30am–5.30pm). The city is divided into four colour-coded **fare zones**, and prices depend on the number of zones crossed, from 30p off-peak in one zone to £1 in the rush hour across all four. A **Capital ticket** (£3), bought from a sales office or on the bus, gives unlimited travel around Cardiff and Penarth for a day.

Accommodation

The main belt of **guesthouses** and **hotels** lies along the genteel and leafy Cathedral Road, easily reached by foot from the city centre. The other main area for accommoda-tion is around the Newport Road, heading northeast out of the city centre through Roath, about fifteen minutes' walk from the centre. Cardiff's **youth hostel**, 2 Wedal Rd, Roath Park (☎01222/462303) is a large, purpose-built building, situated just underneath the A48 Eastern Avenue flyover at the top of Roath Park, almost two miles from the city centre. Buses #78, #80 or #82 go from the central bus station. *Pontcanna Fields* **camp-site**, off Cathedral Road (☎01222/398362) has limited tent spaces, so book ahead.

Angel Hotel, Castle St (☎01222/232633). Cardiff's grandest hotel, opposite the castle. ⑧.

Arosa House, 24 Plasturton Gardens, Pontcanna (☎01222/395342). Lying next to the city centre, the *Arosa* is very friendly and reasonably priced. ③.

Cardiff Bay, Schooner Way, Atlantic Wharf, Cardiff Bay (☎01222/465888). Grand Victorian build-ing transformed into a smart hotel in an area that is slowly coming together as part of the great plan for the old docks. ⑦.

Churchills Hotel, Cardiff Rd, Llandaff (☎01222/562372). Mock-Edwardian hotel in a quiet part of the city near the cathedral of Llandaff. ⑥.

Courtfield Hotel, 101 Cathedral Rd, Pontcanna (☎01222/227701). Popular and lively hotel with a large gay clientele. Good restaurant. ④.

Ferriers, 130 Cathedral Rd, Pontcanna (☎01222/383413). Best-value B&B in Cardiff – welcoming, inexpensive and with excellent service. ③.

Lincoln Hotel, 118 Cathedral Rd, Pontcanna (☎01222/395558). One of the nicest hotels along Cathedral Road, housed in two comfortable Victorian houses.⑤.

CARDIFF

△ M4 Junction 29a, Bristol & London   △ Newport

WATERLOO ROAD

RAILWAY STREET

CARLISLE STREET

CONSTELLATION ST

BROADWAY

CLIFTON STREET

Royal
Infirmary

College
of Art

CITY ROAD

MARLBOROUGH ROAD

ALBANY ROAD

PEN-Y-LAN RD

PEN-Y-LAN ROAD

ROATH COURT ROAD

RICHMOND ROAD

NINIAN ROAD

Roath Park

TY-DRAW ROAD

EASTERN AVENUE

MACKINTOSH PLACE

SHIRLEY ROAD

COBURN ST

SALISBURY ROAD

Cathays
Station

STUTTGART STRASSE

WEDAL ROAD

△ M4 Junction 32

FAIROAK ROAD

ALLENSBANK ROAD

WHITCHURCH ROAD

CRWYS ROAD

WOODVILLE ROAD

WYEVERNE ROAD

SENGHENNYDD ROAD

PARK PLACE

Nat. Mus.
of Wales

MUSEUM AVE

BLVD DE NANTES

City Hall

Youth
Hostel

CATHAYS TERRACE

University
College
of Wales

King George VII AVE

County Hall

Welsh
Office

COLUM ROAD

COLUM ROAD

MAENDY ROAD

NORTH ROAD

Bute Park

Welsh Institute
of Sport

CATHEDRAL ROAD

Glamorgan
Cricket
Ground

River Taff

△ Llandaff

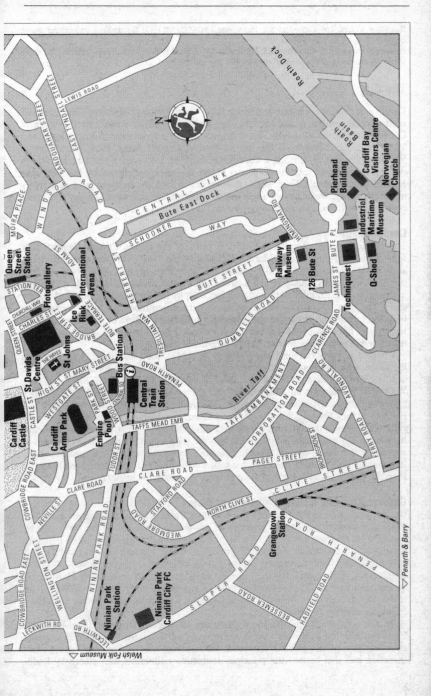

Rambler Court, 188 Cathedral Rd, Pontcanna (☎01222/221187). Good-value, welcoming guest house with a few en-suite rooms. ③.
Rosanna House, 175 Cathedral Rd, Pontcanna (☎01222/229780). Very cheap, reflected, to some extent, in the decor of the place. Handy for the city and the river. ②.

The City

Cardiff's sights are clustered around fairly small, distinct districts. The compact **commercial centre** is bounded by the River Taff which flows past the walls of Cardiff's extraordinary **castle**, an amalgam of Roman remains, Norman keep and Victorian fantasy. Nearby is the the the fat bowl of **Cardiff Arms Park**, the mecca of Welsh rugby and as obvious a Cardiff landmark as any, even if the national team's performance slipped into the doldrums before the unexpectedly successful 1994 Five Nations Championship. Even so, the atmosphere in the Park, or in the pubs and streets of the city, when Wales have a home match – particularly against old enemy England – is charged with good-natured beery fervour.

Cardiff Castle

The political, geographical and historical heart of the city is **Cardiff Castle** (daily May–Sept 10am–6pm; March–April & Oct 10am–5pm; Nov–Feb 10am–4pm with tours at 10.30am, 11.45am, 2pm & 3.15pm; £3.70), an intriguing, appealing hotch-potch of remnants of the city's history. The fortress hides inside a vast walled yard corresponding roughly to the outline of the original fort built by the Romans, Cardiff's first inhabitants. The neat Norman motte, crowned with its eleventh-century **keep**, looks down onto the turrets and towers of the **domestic buildings**, dating in part from the fourteenth and fifteenth centuries, but much extended in Tudor times, when residential needs began to overtake military safety in terms of priority.

Ultimately, it was the third Marquis of Bute (1847–1900), one of the richest men on the globe, who lavished a fortune on upgrading his pile – lived in for only six weeks a year – commissioning architect and decorator William Burges (1827–81) to aid him. With their passion for the religious art and the symbolism of the Middle Ages, they systematically overhauled the buildings, adding a spire to the octagonal tower and erecting a clock tower; but it was inside that their imaginations ran free, and they radically transformed the crumbling interiors into palaces of vivid colour and intricate, high-camp design. These buildings can only be seen as part of the guided tour covering the winter and summer Smoking Rooms, the nursery, the Arab room and the Banquating Hall, making the extra fee well worthwhile. On the **Animal Wall**, visible from the Castle Street outside, stone creatures are frozen in cheeky poses.

Cathays Park and National Museum of Wales

On the north side of the city centre is **Cathays Park**, a large rectangle of grass that forms the centrepiece for the impressive Edwardian buildings of the **civic centre**. Dating from the first couple of decades of this century, the gleaming white buildings arranged with pompous Edwardian precision speak volumes about Cardiff's self-assertion, even half a century before it was officially declared capital of Wales. Centrepiece of the complex is the magnificent dragon-topped domed **City Hall** (1905), an exercise in every cliché about ostentatious civic self-glory, with a roll-call of (all male) Welsh heroes – Welsh Princes, Giraldus Cambrensis and Owain Glyndŵr – frozen for eternity as statues.

To the right stands the **National Museum of Wales** (Tues–Sat 10am–5pm, Sun 2.30–5pm; £3), one of Britain's finest, attempting both to tell the story of Wales, as well as reflect the nation's place in the wider, international sphere. You enter directly into the main hall that houses the principal **sculpture collection** with pieces by Rodin,

Henry Moore, the prolific nineteenth-century Welsh sculptor W. Goscombe John, notably his spirited evocation of *David Lloyd George*, and rival John Evan Thomas, represented by his masterpiece *Death of Tewdric, King of Gwent*. Amongst the predictable dinosaur gallery, science collection and zoology section, the **botany collection** stands out. **Archeology** is strong, too, with prehistoric finds, the comparatively sophisticated Bronze Age **Caergwrle Bowl**, a delicate, gold-leafed ornament that's 3000 years old, and the developing styles of the stone crosses into recognizable Celtic designs.

The bulk of the East Wing is given over to fine art, with ten galleries on the first floor containing the majority of the museum's extraordinary art collection. The oldest part of the collection starts with a gathering from the fifteenth- and sixteenth-century **Italian schools**, pushing on to **seventeenth-century** galleries rich in Flemish and Dutch work, including Rembrandt's coolly aloof portrait of *Catrina Hooghsaet* and Jacob van Ruisdael's mesmerizing *Waterfall*. The most famous, or perhaps infamous, pieces here are the **Cardiff Cartoons**, four monumental tapestries bought at great expense in 1979 and, at the time, presumed to be the work of Rubens. The first of the great Welsh artists is shown to maximum effect in the **eighteenth-century** galleries where landscapes by Richard Wilson (1714–82) include *Caernarfon Castle* and *Dolbadarn Castle*. The **nineteenth-century** galleries include a round-up of some of the century's greatest painters, such as J.M.W. Turner, whose *Thames Backwater, with Windsor Castle* is gently diffused with a characteristic wash of colour and light.

The artistic pride of the National Museum, however, is the Davies collection of **Impressionist paintings**. Cezanne figures predominantly among Corot's legendary *Distant view of Corbeil, Morning*, Pissaro's classic views of Rouen and Paris, Renoir's chirpy portrait of *La Parisienne*, and numerous paintings by Monet and Degas. The **contemporary galleries** contain the work of some of Wales' greatest twentieth-century artists: Augustus and Gwen John's delicate portraits, vivid still lifes and gentle landscapes, especially Augustus' captivating portrait of a belligerent, but fragile, *Dylan Thomas*. Ceri Richards' meaty, almost cubist portrayals of industrial and rural Welsh life are amongst the most arresting pictures in the entire gallery.

Cardiff Bay

A thirty-minute walk from the city centre (or a short ride on half-hourly bus #8) is the area known as **Cardiff Bay**, the spicier tag of Tiger Bay (immortalized by Cardiff-born Shirley Bassey) being rarely used these days. The first impression is one of immense and rapid change. Cardiff Bay has become one of the world's biggest regeneration projects, aiming to transform the seedy dereliction of the old docks into a designer heaven. Central to the whole project is the controversial **Cardiff Bay Barrage**, due to be built right across the Ely and Taff estuaries, transforming a vast mud flat into a freshwater lake. You are unlikely to be in Cardiff long before hearing one side or other of the long-running argument between opponents fearing for the wading bird population and supporters behind urban rejuvenation at all costs. The most tangible results so far are the four excellent sites of the **Welsh Industrial and Maritime Museum** (WIMM) (Tues–Sun 10–5pm; £1.50), the architectural highlights of the whole area, detailed in a free leaflet, *Butetown Walkabout*, which can be picked up in the tourist office or any of the local museums.

The first stop is at the **Railway Gallery** housing display boards and photographs of the history of Welsh railways, together with working models of trains and locomotive works. Bang opposite is **126 Bute Street**, whose old pub and house interiors mingle with a well-documented display that focuses on the people who lived in Tiger Bay, having come from all over the world, and created a multiracial community in the first half of this century. At the bottom of Bute Street you'll find the main site of the **Welsh Industrial and Maritime Museum**, mainly made up of a series of modern buildings purpose-built around the giant engines and boats that form a major part of the exhibition. Alongside expositions on Wales' coal and iron industries, Cardiff's nautical heritage is represented in exhibits like the transplanted bridge of an ocean-going steamship and buxom figureheads that once ruled the waves. Outside in the yard are numerous railway locomotives, including an impressive replica of Richard Trevithick's engine that made the world's first train journey in 1804 up the Taff valley. The museum's temporary exhibition space, **Q-shed**, was converted out of a Victorian shipping warehouse facing the bay; behind it is Stuart Street and **Techniquest** (Mon–Fri 9.30am–4.30pm, Sat & Sun 10.30am–5pm; £4.50), a fun, "hands-on" science gallery perfect for kids.

East of the main WIMM site is the modern tubular **Cardiff Bay Visitor Centre** (Mon–Fri 9.30am–4.30pm, Sat & Sun 10.30am–5pm; free), looking like a giant eye out on to the bay. Although it's a thinly disguised PR job for the controversial developments in the bay, the centre contains a fabulous scale model of the entire docks area.

Llandaff Cathedral

Llandaff is a small, quiet ecclesiastical village two miles northwest of the city centre along Cathedral Road. The church that has now grown up into the city's **Cathedral** is believed to have been founded in the sixth century by Saint Teilo, but was rebuilt in Norman style from 1120 and well into the thirteenth century. From the late fourteenth century, the cathedral fell into an advanced state of disrepair, one of the twin towers and the nave roof eventually collapsing. Restoration only began in earnest in the early 1840s, and Pre-Raphaelite artists such as Edward Burne-Jones, Dante Gabriel Rossetti and the firm of William Morris were commissioned for colourful new windows and decorative panels.

The fusion of different styles and ages is evident from outside, especially in the mismatched western towers. Inside, Jacob Epstein's overwhelming *Christ in Majesty* sculpture, a concrete parabola topped with a soaring Christ figure, was the only entirely new feature added in the postwar reconstruction, and dominates the nave today. At the west end of the north aisle, the **St Illtyd Chapel** features Rossetti's cloying triptych *The Seed of David*. Most of the windows along the south aisle came from similar sources, namely William Morris' stained-glass company and Edward Burne-Jones. Along a little further, in the south presbytery, is the tenth-century Celtic cross that is the cathedral's only pre-Norman survivor.

Eating, drinking and nightlife

The city's long-standing internationalism has paid handsome dividends in the range of **restaurants**, notably the Italian influence, still evident in the range of cafés, bistros and restaurants. Most places are within easy walking distance of the city centre, although a few of the better cafés and restaurants are in the cheaper corners of Cathays and Roath (particularly the curry houses along Crwys, Albany and City roads), a stone's throw from the centre beyond the University. Cardiff's **pub** life has expanded exponentially over recent years, and includes some wonderful Edwardian palaces of etched smoky glass and deep red wood. Don't forget Cardiff's own beer, Brains.

Top-flight **concert venues** such as *St David's Hall* and the *Cardiff International Arena* have brought internationally acclaimed orchestras and performers to the city, although these sterile environments are no match for the sweatier gigs and traditional rock found in some of Cardiff's earthier pubs and clubs. The burgeoning Welsh rock scene, both English and Welsh language, breaks out regularly in the capital. Cardiff also has a modest **gay scene**. The best source for current information and advice is **Friend** (Tues–Sat 8–10pm; ☎01222/340101) or **Lesbian Line** (Tues 8–10pm; ☎01222/374051). A couple of venues are listed below.

Theatre in Cardiff encompasses everything from the radical and alternative at the *Sherman* and the *Chapter* to big, blowzy productions at the *New Theatre*, home of the *Welsh National Opera*. **Classical music** is best heard at *St David's Hall*, although the newly opened *Cardiff International Arena* is likely to siphon off some of the more prestigious shows.

Cafés and restaurants

Babs' Bistro, 14 West Bute St, Cardiff Bay. Legendary licensed café, serving great piles of Italian and British food until 7.30pm in the week and right through the small hours between Thursday and Saturday. Popular after-club haunt at the weekend. Inexpensive.

Blas ar Gymru, 48 Crwys Rd, Cathays (☎01222/382132). Meaning "taste of Wales", this is a comfortable restaurant with a highly imaginative menu culled from delicious traditional recipes of every corner of Wales. Closed Sun. Moderate.

Bombay Brasserie, 175 City Rd, Roath (☎01222/494779). One of the better Indian restaurants amongst the many in the area. Inexpensive.

Celtic Cauldron, Castle Arcade. Right opposite the castle's main entrance is this friendly daytime café, dedicated to bringing a range of simple Welsh food – soups, stews, laver bread, cakes – to an appreciative audience. Inexpensive.

Da Giovanni Ciao Ciao, The Hayes (☎01222/220077). One of Cardiff's best-reputed Italian restaurants, Giovanni's is lively and enormously friendly, with a wide menu of old favourites and some unusual house specialities. Closed Sun. Moderate.

La Brasserie, 60 St Mary St (☎01222/372164). Extremely loud and lively, with beautifully prepared French food and a speciality of sublime charcoal grills. Moderate.

Louis Restaurant, 32 St Mary St. Wonderful old-fashioned tea rooms with an eclectic mix of genteel old ladies and bargain-hungry students. Food is basic, cheap, lavish in quantity and superb in quality. Last orders 7.45pm Mon–Sat; closed Sun. Inexpensive.

Noble House, 9–10 St David's House, Wood St (☎01222/388317). The best Chinese restaurant in town, with an excellent range of Peking and Szechuan dishes. Moderate.

Bars, pubs and clubs

Chapter, Market Rd, Canton. Three bars in the arts complex, far better than the traditional rather downmarket arts centre bar. Good choice of real ale and whisky.

Clwb Ifor Bach, Womanby St (☎01222/232199). A sweaty and massively fun live music club with nightly gigs and sessions, many by Welsh language bands.

Duke of Wellington, corner of Caroline St and The Hayes. Over-restored Edwardian city pub, serving excellent beer, piped all the way from the brewery next door.

Exit Bar, 48 Charles St. Opposite *Club X*, this is where most people have their pre-club drinks. Late-opening (until midnight) disco bar, with loud music and frantic atmosphere.

Gassey Jacks, 39–41 Salisbury Rd, Cathays (☎01222/239388). Loud, boisterous and enjoyable pub and club, with nightly live R & B, blues, soul and jazz in a studenty environment.

Golden Cross, 283 Hayes Bridge Rd. A few hundred yards from the Duke of Wellington, but a better bet for an unhurried pint in a more laid-back restored Victorian atmosphere.

King's Cross, Hayes Bridge Rd/Caroline St. Large and long-established gay pub, with few frills but a friendly atmosphere.

Theatre, cinema and classical music

Chapter Arts Centre, Market Rd, Canton (☎01222/399666). Home of fine British and touring theatre and dance companies in a multi-use arts complex including Cardiff's main art-house and alternative cinema.

New Theatre, Park Place (☎01222/394844). Splendid Edwardian city centre theatre that plays host to big London shows. Currently the home of the *Welsh National Opera*, at least until their shiny new opera house is built in Cardiff Bay.

Sherman Theatre, Senghenydd Rd, Cathays (☎01222/230451). An excellent two-auditorium repertory theatre hosting a mixed bag of new and translated classic Welsh-language pieces, stand-up comedy, children's entertainment, drama classics, music and dance.

St David's Hall, The Hayes (☎01222/371236). Part of the massive St David's shopping centre, this large and glamorous venue is possibly the most architecturally exciting building in town. Home to visiting orchestras and musicians from jazz to opera, it's frequently used by the excellent *BBC Welsh Symphony Orchestra and Chorus*.

Listings

Bike rental *Taff Trail Cycle Hire*, Forest Farm Country Park, Whitchurch (Easter–Oct daily 10am–6pm; ☎01222/751235). Located on the other side of the river from Radyr station.

Bus enquiries *Cardiff Bus* (☎01222/396521); *National Express* (☎01222/344751).

Car rental *Avis*, 4 Saunders Rd, Station Approach (☎01222/342111); *Crwys Auto Service*, 59 Crwys Rd (☎01222/225789); *Hertz*, 9 Central Square (☎01222/224548).

Exchange *American Express*, 3 Queen St (☎01222/665843); *Thomas Cook*, 56 Queen St (☎01222/343044).

Hospital *Cardiff Royal Infirmary*, Newport Rd (☎01222/492233).

Laundries *Drift Inn*, 104 Salisbury Rd, Cathays Park; *GP*, 244 Cowbridge Rd, Canton; *Launderama*, 60 Lower Cathedral Rd.

Left luggage At Central station (Mon–Fri 10am–9pm, Sat 10am–8.30pm).

Pharmacy *Boots*, 5 Wood St (Mon–Sat 8am–8pm, Sun 6–7pm; ☎01222/234043).

Police *Cardiff Central Police Station*, King Edward VII Ave, Cathays Park (☎01222/222111).

Post office The Hayes (Mon–Fri 9am–5.30pm, Sat 9am–12.30pm; ☎01222/227363).

Travel agencies *Campus Travel* in the YHA shop, 13 Castle St (☎01222/220744); *John Cory Travel*, Park Place (☎01222/371878); *Welsh Travel Centre*, 240 Whitchurch Rd, Cathays (☎01222/621479).

Around Cardiff

On the edge of the Cardiff suburbs, the thirteenth-century fairy-tale castle of **Castell Coch** stands on a hillside in woods. West of the city, the massively popular **Welsh Folk Museum** tells the country's history with bricks and mortar, with a sundry collection of buildings salvaged from all over Wales; the museum lies in the grounds of the rambling Elizabethan country house of **St Fagans Castle**.

Castell Coch

Four miles north of Llandaff, the turreted **Castell Coch** (April–Nov daily 9.30am–6.30pm; Nov–March Mon–Sat 9.30am–4pm, Sun 11am–4pm; CADW; £2.20) was a ruined thirteenth-century fortress that was rebuilt and transformed into a fantasy castle in the late 1870s by William Burges for the third Marquess of Bute. With its working portcullis and drawbridge, Castell Coch is the ultimate wealthy man's medieval fantasy, isolated on its almost Alpine hillside, yet only a few hundred yards from the motorway and Cardiff suburbs. Many similarities with their joint work on Cardiff Castle can be seen here, notably the outrageously lavish decor, culled from religious and moral fables, that dazzle in each room. Bus #136 from Central station turns round at the castle gates, or the #26 drops in Tongwynlais village, ten minutes' away.

The Museum of Welsh Life and St Fagans Castle

ST FAGANS (Sain Ffagan), four miles west of the city centre, has a rural feel that is only partially disturbed by the bus loads of tourists that roll in regularly to visit the excellent **Museum of Welsh Life** (daily July–Sept 10am–6pm; Oct–June 10am–5pm; £4–5), built around **St Fagans Castle**, a country house built in 1580 and furnished in early nineteenth-century style. The most impressive part of the museum is the fifty-acre outdoor collection, buildings saved from extinction in all corners of Wales which have been carefully dismantled and rebuilt on this site since the museum's inception in 1946. There are particular highlights, like the diminutive whitewashed 1777 Pen-Rhiw Chapel from Dyfed, the pristine and evocative Victorian St Mary's Board School from Lampeter and the ordered mini-fortress of a 1772 tollhouse that once guarded the southern approach to Aberystwyth. The best demonstration of how life changed over the years for a section of the Welsh population comes in the superlative Rhyd-y-car ironworkers' cottages from Merthyr Tydfil. Built originally around 1800, each of the six houses, with their accompanying strip of garden, has been furnished in the style of a different era – stretching from 1805 to 1985. Even the frontages and roofs are true to their age, offering a wade through working-class Welsh life over the past century. Hourly bus #32 (and the irregular #C1) leaves Central station for the village.

Swansea

Dylan Thomas called his birthplace an "ugly, lovely town" a description still true today. Large, sprawling and boisterous, **SWANSEA** (Abertawe), with around 200,000 people, is the second city of Wales. It has great aspirations to be the first, and is certainly far more of a Welsh town than Cardiff. A jumble of tower blocks dot the horizons, while the city centre was massively rebuilt after devastating bomb attacks in World War II. But Swansea's multifarious charms appear on closer inspection: some intact old corners of the city centre, the spacious and graceful suburb of Uplands, a wide seafront overlooking Swansea Bay and a bold marina development around the old docks. Spread throughout are some of the best funded museums in Wales.

The city's Welsh name, Abertawe, refers to the settlement at the mouth of the River Tawe, a grimy ditch that is slowly being teased back to life after centuries of usage as a sewer for Swansea's metal trades. The first reliable origins of Swansea came in 1099, when a Norman castle was built here as an outpost of William the Conqueror's empire. A small settlement grew near the coalfields and the sea, developing into a mining and shipbuilding centre that, by 1700, was the largest coal port in Wales. Copper smelting became the area's dominant industry in the eighteenth century, soon attracting other metal trades to pack out the lower Tawe valley, making it one of the world's most prolific metal-bashing centres. Over the years it became a five-mile stretch of rusting, stagnant land and water that has only recently begun to be re-landscaped.

Arrival, information and accommodation

The **train station** (☎01792/467777) is at the top end of the High Street, a ten-minute hike from the **bus station**. Nearby on Singleton Street, you'll find the municipal **tourist office** (Mon–Sat 9.30am–5.30pm; ☎01792/468321). **Getting around** Swansea is easy: most of the sights are within walking distance of each other. Popular suburbs, such as Uplands and Sketty, near the University, are a bracing half-hour walk from the centre, although SWT buses cover the suburbs extremely thoroughly.

As a lively city on the edge of some of Wales' most popular and inspirational coast and rural scenery, Swansea makes a logical base. Transport is good out into the surrounding areas and **beds** tend to be less expensive in the city than in the more picturesque parts of the Gower. There are dozens of dirt-cheap hotels and B&Bs stretched out along the seafront Oystermouth Road, whose trade is particularly pitched at those catching the Swansea–Cork ferry. There are no campsites or hostels in the city itself, although nearby Gower places are easily reached.

Crescent, 132 Eaton Crescent, Uplands (☎01792/466814). Large and pleasant well-converted Edwardian guest house with sublime views over the city and the bay. ②.

Oystercatcher, 386 Oystermouth Rd (☎01792/456574). Cheap and cheerful seafront hotel with a slightly wider range of facilities than many others in this price band. ②.

Parkway, 253 Gower Rd, Sketty (☎01792/201632). Quiet and extremely comfortable hotel in a comparatively salubrious area. ③.

St James, 76B Walter Rd, Uplands (☎01792/649984). Small and friendly hotel in airy Victorian house. ③.

Uplands Court, 134 Eaton Crescent, Uplands (☎01792/473046). Welcoming and enjoyable guest house within a gracious Victorian villa in a pleasant area. ②.

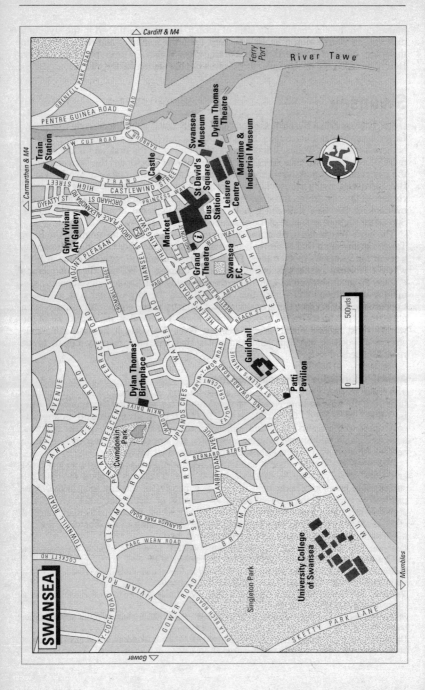

The City

Alexandra Road forks right off the High Street immediately south of the train station, leading down to the **Glynn Vivian Art Gallery** (Tues–Sun 10.30am–5.30pm; free) a delightful Edwardian showcase of inspiring Welsh art including the huge, frantic canvases of Ceri Richards, Wales' most respected twentieth-century painter, and works by Gwen John and her brother, Augustus, whose mesmerizing portrait of *Caitlin Thomas*, Dylan's wife, is a real highlight. In the early nineteenth century, Swansea was a noted centre of fine porcelain production, of which the gallery houses a large collection, together with pieces of contemporary works from Nantgarw, near Cardiff.

The main shopping streets lie to the south, notably underneath the Quadrant Centre where the curving-roofed **market** makes a lively sight, with traditional and long-standing stalls selling local delicacies such as laver bread, a delicious savoury made from seaweed, as well as cockles trawled from the nearby Loughor estuary, typical Welsh cakes, fish and cheeses.

Hourly buses leave the Quadrant depot for Uplands, a half-hour walk from the city centre. North of the main road, leafy avenues rise up the slopes past the sharp terraces of **Cwmdonkin Park**, at the centre of which is a memorial to Dylan Thomas inscribed with lines from *Fern Hill*, one of his best-known poems. On the eastern side of Cwmdonkin Park is Cwmdonkin Drive, a sharply rising set of solid Victorian semis, notable only for the blue plaque on no. 5, birthplace in 1914 of Dylan Thomas.

The spit of land between the Oystermouth Road, sea and the Tawe estuary has been christened the **Maritime Quarter** – tourist board-speak for the old docks – built around a vast marina surrounded by legions of unsold modern flats. The city's old South Dock, now cleaned and spruced up, features the **Swansea Museum** (Tues–Sun 10.30am–5.30pm; free), Wales' oldest public museum, founded in 1835, and is still enticingly old-fashioned. A small grid of nineteenth-century streets around the museum has been thoughtfully cleaned up and now houses some enjoyable cafés, pubs and restaurants.

Behind the museum, Burrows Place leads down to the marina and the superb new **Maritime and Industrial Museum** (Tues–Sun 10.30am–5.30pm; free). Taking Swansea's seaside position as its starting point, the museum presents a lively history of the city, with an especially compulsive section on the horrors of the Blitz. A large number of vehicles include an old tram that once rattled along the seafront to Mumbles, and a rare example of Gilbern cars, Wales' principal (and long-dead) contribution to the motor industry.

Eating, drinking and nightlife

Swansea's metamorphosis from a working-class, industrial city into a would-be tourist centre is well demonstrated in the **pubs**, **restaurants** and **entertainment** venues of the city. For nightlife, the city is well placed as a major centre in Wales, with most passing theatre, opera and music of all sorts being obliged to make a stop here. The *BBC Welsh Symphony Orchestra* appears at the *Brangwyn Hall* in the Art Deco Civic Centre. Thomas' classics get a regular airing at the *Dylan Thomas Theatre* by the marina, while the *Taliesin Arts Centre*, in the University, is the city's more offbeat venue.

Adam and Eve, 207 High St. Traditional pub, with a great atmosphere and varied clientele. Well known for the excellence of its beer.

Bengal Brasserie, 47 Walter Rd (☎01792/643747). Best of the many Indian restaurants in Swansea, well worth the 10-min hike from the city centre. Moderate.

Bizzie Lizzie's, 55 Walter Rd (☎01792/473379). Relaxed and informal cellar bar bistro, with a good range of cheapish Welsh, international and vegetarian dishes. Inexpensive.

Cardiff Arms, 53 The Strand. Boisterous and packed live rock pub, with visiting bands and a laid-back atmosphere. Sat afternoon blues sessions.

Duke of York, Princess Way. Swansea's best venue for jazz and blues music, as their *Ellington's* club (small fee payable) hosts nightly gigs.

DV8 at the *Palace*, High St. Spruced-up gay club, open Wed–Sat until 2.30am.

Footlights Coffee Bar, Grand Theatre, Singleton St. Good daytime meeting space with a delicious lunch menu, including some imaginative vegetarian options. Inexpensive.

Hwyrnos, Green Dragon Lane, off Wind Street (☎01792/641437). Fixed Welsh evening menu plus harp-twanging entertainment in an extremely convivial, bordering on boozy, atmosphere. More sedate lunchtime menu also available. Moderate.

New Capriccio, 89 St Helen's Rd (☎01792/648804). Popular Italian restaurant, with bargain lunch menu. Closed Mon and Sun evening. Inexpensive.

Queen's Hotel, Gloucester Place, near the marina. Large old seafaring hotel and pub, with good snack lunches and Sunday roasts. Regular evening live music and quizzes.

The Schooner, 4 Prospect Place (☎01792/649321). Excellent international restaurant, with a speciality of locally caught dishes. Closed Sun evening. Moderate.

The Gower

A fifteen-mile-long peninsula of undulating limestone, the **GOWER** (Gwyr) points down into the Bristol Channel to the west of Swansea. The area is fringed by sweeping yellow bays and precipitous cliffs, caves and blowholes to the south, and wide, flat marshes and cockle beds to the north; brackened heaths with prehistoric remains and tiny villages lie between, and castle ruins and curious churches are spread evenly around. Out of season, the winding Gower lanes afford opportunities for exploration; but in the height of the summer, they are congested with caravans shuffling between one overpriced car park and the next.

The Gower can be said to start in Swansea's western suburbs, along the coast of Swansea Bay that curves round to a point in the pleasantly old-fashioned resort of **Mumbles**, and finish with **Rhossili Bay**, a spectacular four-mile yawn of sand backed by the village of Rhossili, and occupying the entire western end of the peninsula. The southern coast is punctuated by sites exploited for their defensive capacity, best seen in the eerie isolation of the sand-bound **Pennard Castle**, high above **Three Cliffs Bay**. West, the wide sands of **Oxwich Bay** sit next to inland reedy marshes, beyond which is the village of **Port Eynon**, home to an excellent youth hostel (mid-Feb to Nov; ☎01792/390706) and a beautiful beach. West of Port Eynon, the coast becomes a wild, frilly series of inlets and cliffs, topped by a five-mile path that stretches all the way to the peninsula's glorious westernmost point, **Worms Head**. The northern coast merges into the tidal flats of the estuary, running past the salted marsh of **Llanrhidian**, overlooked by the gaunt ruins of **Weobley Castle**, and on to the famous cockle beds at **Pen-clawdd**.

The Mumbles and Oystermouth

At the far westernmost end of Swansea Bay, **The Mumbles** (Mwmbwls) derives its name from the French *mamelles*, or breasts, a reference to the twin islets off the end of Mumbles Head, and is now used as the name for all of the loose sprawl around **OYSTERMOUTH** (Ystumllwynarth). Here, the seafront is an unbroken curve of budget hotels, breezy pubs and cafés leading down to the old-fashioned pier and funfair towards the rocky plug of Mumbles Head. Around the headland, reached either by the longer barren coast road or a short walk over the hill, is the district of **Langland Bay**, with a sandy beach, fairly popular with surfers. The small seasonal **tourist office** on the seafront lies opposite Newton Road, which leads up to the hilltop ruins of **Oystermouth Castle** (April–Oct daily 11am–5pm; £1). Founded as a Norman watch-tower, the castle was strengthened to withstand attacks by the Welsh, before being converted for more amenable residential purposes during the fourteenth century. Today you can see the remains of a late thirteenth-century keep next to a more ornate three-storey ruin incorporating an impressive banqueting hall and state rooms.

The Mumbles is a lively and enjoyable base for the southern Gower coast, with a good clutch of typically tacky seaside entertainment on offer. **Accommodation** is plentiful: try the shorefront *Tides Reach*, 388 Mumbles Rd (☎01792/404877; ②), or the *Jarvis Osborne Hotel*, on a clifftop in Rotherslade Road, Langland Bay (☎01792/366274; ③). Of the dozens of **eating places**, the most notable are *Easterbrooks*, 590 Mumbles Rd (closed Sun eve & Mon; ☎01792/362338), for Welsh specialities, and the cosy Italian atmosphere of *Quo Vadis*, 614–616 Mumbles Rd (☎01792/360706). Scores of seafront pubs constitute the **Mumbles Mile**, one of Wales' most notorious pub crawls. Of them all, *The Antelope*, the *Oystercatcher* and the *White Rose* are the most enjoyable, if most touristy alternatives. Most tourists feel that they have to have a pint in *Dylan's Tavern*, which, when it was known as the *Mermaid*, was the young writer's most regular haunt. Unsurprisingly, it's now packed full of Dylan Thomas kitsch and memorabilia.

Rhossili and Worms Head

The village of **RHOSSILI** (Rhosili), at the western end of the Gower, is a centre for walkers and beach loungers alike. Dylan Thomas described the terrain to the west of the village as "rubbery, gull-limed grass, the sheep-pilled stones, the pieces of bones and feathers", and you can tread in his footsteps to **Worms Head**, an isolated string of rocks, accessible for only five hours at low tide. At the head of the road, near the village, is a well-stocked **National Trust information centre** (April–Oct daily 10.30am–5.30pm; Nov–Dec Sat & Sun 11am–4pm; ☎01792/390707). They post the tide times outside for those heading for Worms Head, and hold details of local companies renting surfing and hang-gliding equipment.

Below the village, a great curve of white sand stretches away into the distance, a dazzling coastline vast enough to absorb the crowds, especially if you are prepared to head north along it towards **Burry Holms**, an islet that is cut off at high tide. The northern end of the beach can also be reached along the small lane from Reynoldston, in the middle of the peninsula, to Llangennith, on the other side of the towering sandstone **Rhossili Down**, rising up to 633 feet. **Surf instruction** and rental are available from *PJ's* at Llangennith (☎01792/386669).

In Rhossili village, there's reasonable **B&B** in *Broadpark* (☎01792/390515; ②). **Campsites** can be found at *Pitton Cross Park* (☎01792/390593), a mile short of Rhossili off the B4247 and, at the foot of the northern slopes of Rhossili Down, *Hillend* (☎01792/386204), at the end of the southern lane from Llangennith, behind the dunes that bump down to the glorious beach. Evening **drinking** and **food** in Rhossili is largely down to the bar of the rather dingy, but friendly, hotel in the middle of the village.

travel details

Trains

Cardiff to: Abergavenny (hourly; 40min); Bristol (every 30min; 45min); Caerphilly (every 30min; 20min); Chepstow (hourly; 30min); London (hourly; 2hr); Merthyr Tydfil (hourly; 1hr); Newport (every 15–30min; 12min); Swansea (hourly; 50min); Ystrad Rhondda (every 30min; 50min).

Newport to: Abergavenny (hourly; 25min); Cardiff (every 15–30min; 12min); Chepstow (hourly; 20min).

Buses

Abergavenny to: Cardiff (hourly; 2hr); Merthyr Tydfil (hourly; 1hr 20min); Newport (hourly; 1hr 10min).

Cardiff to: Abergavenny (hourly; 2hr); Blaenafon (hourly Mon–Sat; 1hr 40min); Caerphilly (every 30min; 40min); London (6 daily; 3hr 10min); Merthyr Tydfil (every 30min; 45min); Newport (every 20min; 45min); Swansea (hourly; 1hr).

Chepstow to: Monmouth (11 daily Mon–Sat; 55min); Newport (hourly; 1hr); Tintern (8 daily Mon–Sat; 20min); Usk (every 2hr Mon–Sat; 45min).

Merthyr Tydfil to: Abergavenny (hourly Mon–Sat; 1hr 20min); Cardiff (every 30min; 45min).

Monmouth to: Chepstow (11 daily Mon–Sat; 55min); Tintern (9 daily Mon–Sat; 30min); Usk (every 2hr Mon–Sat; 30min).

Newport to: Abergavenny (hourly; 1hr 10min); Blaenafon (every 30min; 1hr 10min); Cardiff (every 20min; 45min); Chepstow (hourly; 1hr).

Swansea to: Cardiff (hourly; 1hr); Mumbles (every 10min; 15min); Rhossili (every 2hr; 1hr 15min); Uplands (hourly; 10min).

CHAPTER TWELVE

SOUTHWEST WALES

The most westerly outposts of Wales, the counties of **Carmarthenshire** and, in particular, **Pembrokeshire** attract thousands of visitors. The principal draw is the glorious coastline, sweeping and flat around **Carmarthen Bay** and rocky, indented and spectacular around the **Pembrokeshire Coast National Park** walk. Of all the routes that converge on the county town of **Carmarthen**, the most glorious is the winding road along the Tywi Valley, past ruined hilltop forts on the way to **Llandeilo** and Wales' most impressively sited castle at **Carreg Cennen**, high up on the dizzy plug of rock of the Black Mountain. Burrowing further into the sparsely populated countryside, broken only by endearing small market towns such as **Llandovery**, leads to remote hills and tiny valleys, home to the Roman gold mines at **Dolaucothi**.

The wide sands of southern Carmarthenshire, just beyond Dylan Thomas' adopted home town of **Laugharne**, merge into the popular south Pembrokeshire bucket-and-spade seaside resort of **Tenby**. Tenby sits at the entrance to the south Pembrokeshire peninsula, its turbulent, rocky coast ruptured by some remote historical sites, including the Norman baronial castle at **Manorbier** and **St Govan's chapel**, a minute place of worship wedged into the rocks of a sea cliff near Bosherston. At the top of the peninsula is the old county town of **Pembroke**, dominated by its fearsome castle, and the market town and transport interchange of **Haverfordwest**, dull but seemingly difficult to avoid. **St Bride's Bay**'s rutted coastline is the most glorious part of the coastal walk, leading north to brush past the impeccable village of **St David's**, whose exquisite cathedral shelters from the town in its own protective hollow. St David's, founded by Wales' patron saint in the sixth century, is a magnet for visitors; aside from its own charms, there are opportunities locally for spectacular coast and hill walks, hair-raising dinghy crossings to local islands and numerous other outdoor activities.

The coast turns towards the north at St David's, becoming the southern stretch of Cardigan Bay. Sixteen miles away by road, and well over thirty by rugged nips and tucks of the coastal walk, is the pretty port of **Fishguard**, terminus for ferries to Rosslare in Ireland.

South Carmarthenshire

Frequently overlooked in the stampede towards the resorts of Pembrokeshire, **southern Carmarthenshire** is a quiet part of the world, with few of the problems of mass tourism suffered by more popular parts of Wales. The coastline is broken by the triple estuary of the Tywi, Taf and Gwendreath rivers; between the Tywi and Taf is a knotted landscape of hills and tiny, winding lanes. **Kidwelly**, with its dramatically sited castle is the only reason to stop before **Carmarthen**, the unquestioned capital of its region but one which fails to live up to the promise of its status. It's a useful transport interchange and lively market town, but there's little of real interest. On the western side of the Taf Estuary, the village of **Laugharne** is the area's sole big tourist attraction, on the strength of its position as a place of pilgrimage for Dylan Thomas devotees.

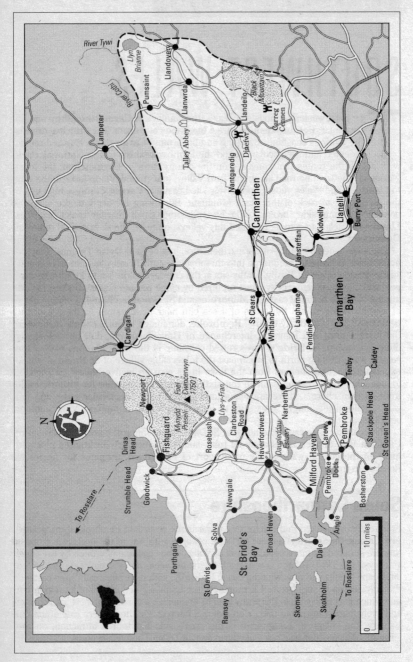

Kidwelly

The sleepy little town of **KIDWELLY** (Cydweli) is dominated by its imposing **Castle** (April–Oct daily 9.30am–6.30pm; Nov–March Mon–Sat 9.30am–4pm, Sun 2–4pm; £1.50; CADW) sited over the River Gwendraeth. The castle was established around 1106 by the Bishop of Salisbury as a satellite of Sherborne Abbey in Dorset at a strategic point overlooking vast tracts of coast. On entering through the massive fourteenth-century gatehouse, you can still see portcullis slats and murder holes, through which noxious substances could be tipped onto unwelcome visitors. The **gatehouse** forms the centrepiece of the impressively intact semicircular outer ward walls, which can be climbed for some great views over the grassy courtyard and rectangular inner ward above the river. This is the oldest surviving part of the castle, dating from around 1275, with the upper stories added in the fourteenth century by warlord Edward I's nephew.

The small-scale **Industrial Museum** on Priory Street, on the northwest edge of the town (Easter–Sept Mon–Fri 10am–5pm, Sat & Sun 2–5pm; £1) is housed in an old tin-plate works with many of the original features preserved, including the rolling mills where long lines of tin were rolled and spun into wafer-thin slices. There's decent pub **accommodation** at the *Old Malthouse*, by the castle (☎01554/891091; ③), and B&B at 21 Ferry Rd (☎01554/891368; ②), off the main street towards the Carmarthen Bay **campsite** at *Tanylan Farm* (☎01267/267306). Good **food** and drink are available at the cosy *Boot and Shoe*, 2 Castle St.

Carmarthen and around

Dull architecture and shabby streets make **CARMARTHEN** (Caerfyrddin) a less than enticing place to stay for long, but it is the first major town in west Wales, where the native language is heard at all times, and was once – in the early eighteenth century – the largest town in the principality. Founded as a Roman fort, Carmarthen's most popular moment of mythological history dates from the Dark Ages and the supposed birth of the wizard Merlin (Myrddin in Welsh gives the town its name).

The most picturesque eighteenth- and nineteenth-century part of town lies spread out at the base of Edward I's **castle**, around King Street and Nott Square, the town's main shopping hub. Lying just off Nott Square is the town's handsome eighteenth-century **Guildhall**, the other side of which leads you out on to Darkgate and Lammas Street, a wide Georgian thoroughfare flanked by coaching inns. From Nott Square, King Street heads northeast towards the undistinguished **St Peter's church** and the Victorian School of Art, which has now metamorphosed into the **Oriel Myrddin** (Mon–Sat 10.30am–4.45pm; free), a craft centre and excellent art gallery that acts as an imaginative showcase for many local artists.

The severe grey Bishop's Palace at **Abergwili**, two miles east of Carmarthen, was the seat of the Bishop of St David's between 1542 and 1974, and now houses the **Carmarthen County Museum** (Mon–Sat 10am–4.30pm; 50p), a spirited amble

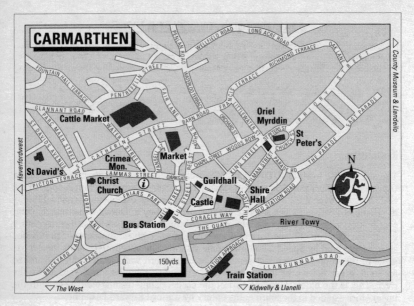

through the history of the area. This surprisingly interesting exhibition covers the history of Welsh translations of the New Testament and Book of Common Prayer – both translated for the first time here in 1567. Local pottery, archeological finds, wooden dressers and a lively history of local castles are presented in well-annotated displays. The upstairs section looks at local police and crime, geology, the origins of Wales' first eisteddfod in Carmarthen in 1450, the local coracle industry and education.

The **train station** (☎01267/235803) lies over the Carmarthen Bridge on the south side of the river. All **buses** terminate at the bus station on Blue Street, and many connect with trains at the station. The town's **tourist office** is located on Lammas Street, close to the Crimea Monument (daily Easter–Oct 9.30am–5.30pm; Nov–Easter 10.30am–4.30pm; ☎01267/231557). There's lots of **accommodation** in town, especially on Lammas Street, where you'll find the *Boar's Head* (☎01267/222789; ④), one of the town's grandest old coaching inns, and the *Drovers Arms* (☎01267/237646; ③). **B&B** accommodation is best at *Y Dderwen Fach*, 98 Priory St (☎01267/234193; ②), and the *Old Priory* guesthouse, 20 Priory St (☎01267/237471; ②), both out along the main road to Lampeter and Llandeilo. For **food**, daytime snacks are great at the old-fashioned *Morris Tea Rooms*, almost opposite the Lyric Theatre in King Street, and the vegetarian café in the *Waverley Stores* health food shop, 23 Lammas St. For evening food, try the smartish but inexpensive *Hamilton's Wine Bar*, 11–12 Queen St (☎01267/235631), or, right next door, *The Queens*, a friendly, oak-panelled pub.

Laugharne

The village of **LAUGHARNE**, on the western side of the Taf Estuary, is being increasingly taken over by the legend of Dylan Thomas, the nearest thing that Wales has to a national poet. Along an excruciatingly narrow lane bumping along the estuary, you'll stumble across the **Dylan Thomas Boathouse** (Easter–Oct daily 10am–6pm; Nov–

DYLAN THOMAS

Dylan Thomas (1914–53) was the quintessential Celt – fiery, verbose, richly talented and habitually drunk. Born into a snugly middle-class family in Swansea's Uplands district, Dylan's first glimmers of literary greatness came when he was posted, as a young reporter, on the *South Wales Evening Post* in Swansea, from which some of his most popular tales in the *Portrait of the Artist as a Young Dog* were inspired.

Rejecting the coarse provincialism of Swansea and Welsh life, Thomas arrived in London as a broke twenty-year-old in 1934, weeks before the appearance of his first volume of poetry, which was published as the first prize in a *Sunday Referee* competition. Another volume followed shortly afterwards, cementing the engaging young Welshman's reputation in the British literary establishment. He married in 1937, and the newlyweds returned to Wales, settling in the hushed, provincial backwater of Laugharne. Short stories – crackling with rich and melancholy humour – tumbled out as swiftly as poems, further widening his base of admirers, though, like so many other writers, Thomas has only gained star status posthumously. Perhaps better than anyone, he writes in an identifiably Celtic, rhythmic wallow in the language. Although Thomas knew little Welsh – he was educated during the time when the native language was stridently discouraged – his English usage is definitively Welsh in its cadence and bold use of words.

Thomas, especially in public, liked to adopt the persona of what he perceived to be an archetypal stage Welshman: sonorous tones, loquacious, romantic and inclined towards a stiff tipple. Playing this role was particularly popular in the United States, where he journeyed on lucrative lecture tours. It was on one of these, in 1953, that he died, poisoned by a massive whisky overdose. Just one month earlier, he had put the finishing touches to what many regard as his masterpiece: *Under Milk Wood*, the "play for voices". Describing the dreams, thoughts and lives of a straggling Welsh seaside community of Llareggub (mis-spelt Llaregyb by the po-faced BBC, who couldn't sanction the usage of the expression "bugger all" backwards) it is loosely based on Laugharne, New Quay in Cardiganshire and a vast dose of Thomas' own imagination.

Easter daily except Sat 10.30am–3.30pm; £1.75), the simple home of Dylan, his wife Caitlin and their three children from 1949 until his death in 1953. It's an enchanting museum with a feeling of inspirational peace above the ever-changing water and light of the estuary and its "heron-priested shore". The family's living room has been preserved intact, with the rich tones of the man himself reading his work via a period wireless set. Contemporary newspaper reports of his demise show how he was, while alive, a fairly minor literary figure. Back along the narrow lane, you can peer into the blue garage where he wrote: a gas stove, curling photographs of literary heroes, pen collection and numerous scrunched-up balls of paper on the cheap desk suggest quite effectively that he is about to return at any minute. The poet is buried in the graveyard of the parish church in the village centre, marked by a simple white cross.

Laugharne has numerous Thomas connections and plays them with curiously disgruntled aplomb – none more so than the great alcoholic's old boozing hole, **Brown's Hotel** on the main street where, in the nicotine-crusted front bar, Dylan's cast-iron table still sits in a window alcove. At the bottom of the main street, the gloomy hulk of **Laugharne Castle** (may–Sept 10am–5pm; £1.70; CADW) broods over the estuary. Two of the early medieval towers survive, although most of the ruins are those of the Tudor mansion built over the original for Sir John Perrot.

Surprisingly, Laugharne has very little B&B **accommodation**; try the very comfortable *New Three Mariners* pub on Victoria Street (☎01994/427426; ③). Alternatively, there are numerous cheap places down the road in Pendine, or a **campsite** at *Waunygroes* in Llanybri (☎01267/241250). For **eating**, the choice is a little wider, although not a great deal better.

The Tywi Valley

The **River Tywi** curves and darts its way east from Carmarthen through some of the most magical scenery in south Wales. The thirty-mile trip to Llandovery is punctuated by gentle, impossibly green hills topped with ruined castles. It's not hard to see why the Merlin legend has taken such a hold in these parts – the landscape does seem infused with some kind of eerie splendour.

Llandeilo and Carreg Cennen Castle

Fifteen miles east of Carmarthen, the main street – Rhosmaen Street – of the handsome small market town of **LLANDEILO** climbs up from the Tywi bridge, behind which are the **tourist office** (Easter week & May–Sept Mon–Sat 10am–5pm) and the **train station**. Although there is little in the way of actual sights in the town, Llandeilo is brilliantly situated in a bowl of hills, a quiet, rustic place, whose few streets cluster around the main thoroughfare. You can **stay** in the relatively plush *Cawdor Arms* on Rhosmaen Street (☎01558/823500; ④). Rhosmaen Street and New Road are home to numerous small **cafés** and **pubs**, the best of which are the *Farmers Arms* and the old coaching inn, the *White Horse*.

Isolated in the rural hinterland four miles southeast of Llandeilo is one of the most magnificently sited castles in the whole of Wales: **Carreg Cennen Castle** (daily May–Sept 9.30am–7.30pm; Oct–April 9.30am–4.30pm; £2.20), just beyond the tiny hamlet of Trapp. It was first constructed on its fearsome rocky outcrop in 1248, although Sir Urien, one of King Arthur's knights, is said to have built his fortress here. Carreg Cennen fell to the English in 1277 during Edward I's initial invasion of Wales, and was finally abandoned after being partially destroyed in 1462 by the Earl of Pembroke, who believed it to be the base of a group of lawless rebels. The most astounding aspect of the castle is its commanding position, three hundred feet above a sheer drop down into the green valley of the small Cennen River. The highlights of a visit are the views down the sheer drop into the river valley and the long descent down into a watery, pitch-black cave that is said to have served as a well. Torches are essential (50p rental from the excellent tea room near the car park), although it is worth continuing as far as possible and then turning them off to experience absolute darkness.

Llandovery

Twelve miles beyond Llandeilo, the town of **LLANDOVERY** (Llanymddyfri) has architecture and a layout that have changed little for centuries. Like so many other mid-Wales settlements, an influx of New Agers from the 1960s has had discernible effect on the town: there's a thriving independent theatre, and bookshops and wholefood stores abound. Alongside this more alternative flavour, Llandovery is still a major centre for cattle markets every other Tuesday.

On the south side of the main Broad Street, a grassy mound holds the scant remains of the town's **castle**. Broad Street has been the main through route for years, as can be seen from the solid early nineteenth-century town houses and earlier inns that line it; the road widens up towards the cobbled, rectangular Market Square. Stone Street heads north from the square, to the redoubtable **Llandovery Theatre**, home of part of the theatre bookselling operation of Hay-on-Wye's Richard Booth, as well as a coffee shop – an excellent place in which to pick up an update on events in the area.

Llandovery **train station** sits on the main A40 just before Broad Street, and **buses** leave from Broad Street and Market Square. The **tourist office** in Broad Street (Easter–Sept daily 9.30am–5.30pm; ☎01550/720693) is combined with an excellent Brecon Beacons National Park office. The best **accommodation** is at the *King's Head*

Inn in the Market Square (☎01550/720393; ③), a friendly, popular pub-cum-restaurant. Slightly more expensive is the colonnaded *Castle Hotel*, Broad Street (☎01550/720343; ④). Cheap B&Bs include *Mrs Billingham's*, Pencerrig New Road (☎01550/721259; ②), and *Ashgrove*, Llangadog Road (☎01550/720136; ②). The nearest **campsite**, a mile east of Llandovery off the A40, is the *Erwlon* (☎01550/203321). The *King's Head* in the Market Square offers delicious lunchtime and evening **food**, as do the *Castle Hotel* on Broad Street (slightly more expensive) and the *White Swan* on the High Street. For **drinking**, the eccentric and bizarrely old-fashioned *Red Lion*, tucked away in an easy-to-miss corner at 2 Market Square, can't be beaten.

The Dolaucothi Gold Mine

The countryside to the west of Llandovery is blissfully quiet, with just a handful of main roads and lanes rarely containing traffic of any volume. The principal route off the A40 between Llandeilo and Llandovery, the A482 heads towards the straggling village of **PUMSAINT** (Five Saints), whose etymology is explained in the stone seen near the entrance of the **Dolaucothi Gold Mine** (site daily April–Sept 10am–5pm; £1.50; underground tours mid-May to Sept; £.3.50; NT), half a mile off the main road: the indentations in the rock are said to be the marks left by five sleeping saints, who rested here one night. Pumsaint is the only place in Britain where the Romans definitely mined gold, laying complicated and astoundingly advanced systems to extract the precious metal from the rock, and remains of Roman workings – a few water channels and an open cast mine – can still be seen from the self-guided walk around the site. Today, the underground tour goes deep into the mine workings and usually allows visitors to prospect for gold themselves.

Tenby and Caldey Island

On a natural promontory of great strategic importance, the beguilingly old-fashioned resort of **TENBY** (Dynbych-y-Pysgod) has a long pedigree. First mentioned in a ninth-century bardic poem, the town grew under the twelfth-century Normans, who erected a castle on the headland in their attempt to colonize south Pembrokeshire and create a "Little England beyond Wales" – an appellation by which the area is still known today. Three times in the twelfth and thirteenth centuries the town was ransacked by the Welsh. In response, the castle was refortified and the stout town walls which largely still exist were built. Tenby prospered as a major port for a wide variety of foodstuffs and fine goods between the fourteenth and sixteenth centuries, but decline followed, and, with the arrival of the train, the town became a fashionable resort. Lines of neat, prosperous hotels and expensive shops still stand haughtily along the seafront.

Although the town is extremely conservative, with a large population of retired people, there is plenty of entertainment and a huge number of pubs and restaurants. In the middle of summer, it can seem full to bursting point, with heavy traffic restrictions and a considerable rush on decent accommodation. Tenby is also one of the major stopping-off points along the **Pembrokeshire Coast Path**, a welcome burst of glitter and excitement amidst mile upon mile of undulating cliff scenery. The **National Park** boundary skirts around the edge of the town. A couple of miles offshore from Tenby, the old monastic ruins of **Caldey Island** make for a pleasant day trip.

The Town

Tenby is shaped like a triangle, with two sides formed by the coast meeting at Castle Hill. The third side is formed by the remaining twenty-foot-high town **walls**, first built in the late thirteenth century and massively strengthened by Jasper Tudor, Earl of Pembroke and uncle of the future king, Henry VII, in 1457. Further refortification came in the 1580s, when Tenby was considered to be in the frontline against a possible attack by the Spanish Armada. In the middle of the remaining stretch is the only town gate still standing at **Five Arches**, a semicircular barbican that combined practical day-to-day usage with hidden look-outs and angles acute enough to surprise invaders.

The centrepiece, and most notable landmark, of the town centre is the 152-foot spire of the largely fifteenth-century **St Mary's church**, between St George's Street and Tudor Square. A pleasantly light interior shows the elaborate ceiling bosses in the chancel to good effect, and fifteenth-century tombs of local barons demonstrate Tenby's important mercantile tradition.

Wedged between the town walls and the two bays, the **old town** is a great place to wander, with many of the original medieval lanes still intact in the immediate area around the parish church. **Sun Alley** is a tiny crack between overhanging white-washed stone houses that connects Crackwell and High streets. Due east, on the other side of the church, **Quay Hill** runs parallel, a narrow set of steps and cobbles tumbling down past some of the town's oldest houses to the top of the harbour. Wedged in a corner of Quay Hill is the **Tudor Merchant's House** (April–Sept Mon–Fri 10am–5pm, Sun 1–5pm; Oct Mon–Fri 10am–3pm, Sun noon–3pm; £1.60; NT), built in the late fifteenth century for a wealthy local merchant at the time when Tenby was second only to Bristol as an important west coast port. The rambling house is on three floors, packed with period furniture from the sixteenth century, although more notable are the examples of a prominent local weakness, tapering Flemish-style chimney pieces.

During the day, the **harbour** is the scene of considerable activity as the departure point for numerous excursion boats, the most popular being the short trip over to Caldey Island (see below). Above the harbour is the headland and **Castle Hill**, where paths and flower beds have been planted around the sparse ruins of the Norman **Castle**. Here, the town **Museum** (Easter–Oct daily 10am–6pm; Nov–Easter Mon–Fri 10am–noon & 2–4pm; £1) doubles as a small art gallery and is typical of Tenby: slightly ponderous and municipally minded, but still interesting.

Caldey Island

Looming large over Tenby's seascape is **Caldey Island** (Ynys Pyr), a couple of miles offshore. Celtic monks first settled here in the sixth century, perhaps establishing an offshoot of St Illtud's monastery at Llantwit Major. Little is then known of the island until 1136 when it was given to the Benedictine monks of St Dogmael's at Cardigan, who founded their priory here. Upon the Dissolution of the monasteries in 1536, the Benedictine monks left the island and a fanciful succession of owners bought and sold it on a whim, until it was, once again, sold to a Benedictine monastic order in 1906 and subsequently to an order of Reformed Cistercians. The island has been a monastic home almost constantly ever since.

Boats leave Tenby Harbour every fifteen minutes in season (mid-May to mid-Sept Mon–Fri 9.45am–4pm; Easter to mid-May & mid-Sept to early Oct occasional sailings; school summer holidays also Sat 1–4pm; ☎01834/842402; £5). Tickets (not tied to any specific sailing) are sold at the kiosk in Castle Square, directly above the harbour. On landing at Caldey's jetty, a short walk leads through the woods to the island's main settlement. Just before the village is reached, a fuchsia-soaked lane cuts up to the right in the direction of a tiny **chapel**, built out of an original watchtower constructed by the first Benedictines in the early part of the twelfth century.

The village itself is the main hub of Caldey life. As well as a tiny post office and popular tea room, there's a **perfume shop** selling the herbal fragrances distilled by the monks from Caldey's abundant flora. The narrow road going to the left leads down to the heavily restored **chapel of St David**, whose most impressive feature is the round-arched Norman door. Opposite is the gathering point for daily (men only) tours of the garish twentieth-century **monastery**, a white, turreted heap that resembles a Disney castle. In peak season, tours take place every couple of hours. A lane leads south from the village to the old **priory**, abandoned at the Dissolution and restored at the turn of this century. Centrepiece of the complex is the remarkable twelfth-century **St Illtud's church**, which houses one of the most significant pre-Norman finds in Wales, the sandstone **Ogham Cross**, carved with an inscription from the sixth century and added to, in Latin, during the ninth, found under the stained-glass window on the south side of the nave. The lane continues south from the site, climbing up to the gleaming white island **lighthouse**, built in 1828. Views from here are memorable.

Practicalities

The **train station** is at the western end of the town centre, at the bottom of Warren Street. Some **buses** stop at South Parade, at the end of Warren Street, although most call at the bus station on Upper Park Road. The **tourist office** faces the North Beach on The Croft (daily July & Aug 10am–9pm; Easter–June, Sept & Oct 10am–6pm; Nov–March 10am–4pm; ☎01834/842402).

As a major resort, there are dozens of **hotels** and **B&Bs** near the South Beach: try *Ashby House*, 24 Victoria St (☎01834/842867; ③), or the nearby *Atlantic*, on the Esplanade (☎01834/842881; ④), with a small indoor pool. *Castle View*, the Norton (☎01834/842666; ③), is well located, staring out over Castle Hill and the harbour, while *Lyndale Guest House*, Warren St (☎01834/842836; ②), is a welcoming B&B near the station, happy to cater for vegetarians. There are a couple of **YHA hostels** nearby: *Pentlepoir* (☎01834/812333), four miles north near Saundersfoot station (bus #350), and the bright and modern *Skrinkle Haven* (☎01834/871803), near Manorbier Bright four miles west of Tenby overlooking the cliffs. You can **camp** here or at *Red House Farm*, New Hedges (April–Sept; ☎01834/813918), a pleasant and cheap campsite midway between Tenby and Saundersfoot, just off the A478.

There are dozens of **cafés** and **restaurants** around the town. For sixty varieties of ice-cream and Italian snacks, there's *Fecci and Sons*, Upper Frog St. *Charney's*, High St (☎01834/842024), is a popular café, with some imaginative menu choices, while *La Cave*, Upper Frog St (☎01834/843038), and *Plantagenate*, Quay Hill (☎01834/842350) are slightly pricier places, offering well-cooked local specialities. As for **pubs**, the local youth head for the *Lifeboat Tavern*, Tudor Square, or the *Coach and Horses*, Upper Frog St, while the *Three Mariners*, St George's St, has good beer and live music.

Southern Pembrokeshire

The southern zigzag of coast that darts west from Tenby is a strange mix of caravan parks and Ministry of Defence shooting ranges, above some spectacularly beautiful bays and gull-covered cliffs. From Tenby, the A4139 passes through **Penally**, little more than an extended suburb of the town, before delving down past the **Lydstep Haven** beach. A road dips south, past **Skrinkle Haven** and into the winding streets of **Manorbier**, whose ghostly castle sits above a small bay. The coast nips and tucks in past some excellent, and comparatively quiet, beaches before rising up to some impressive cliffs en route to the beautiful **Barafundle Bay** and the National Trust's **Stackpole Head**. Behind Stackpole, and the neighbouring **Broad Haven** beach, is the picturesque village of **Bosherston** and its lily lakes. Between Bosherston and the coast is the first MoD artillery range, which has to be crossed if you want to see the remarkable and ancient **St Govan's chapel**, squeezed into a rock cleft above the crashing waves. The ancient castle town of **Pembroke** really only warrants time spent at its impressive castle before pressing on to the neighbouring **Lamphey**, with its fine Bishop's Palace. To the north, the chief town of the region, **Haverfordwest**, makes an important market and transport centre that, despite some handsome architecture, remains rather soulless.

THE PEMBROKESHIRE NATIONAL PARK AND COAST PATH

The **Pembrokeshire Coast** is Britain's only predominantly sea-based national park, hugging the rippled coast around the entire western section of Wales. Established in 1952, the park is not one easily identifiable mass, rather a series of occasionally unconnected patches of coast and inland scenery.

Crawling around almost every wriggle of the coast, the **Pembrokeshire Coast Path** winds 186 miles from St Dogmaels near Cardigan in the north to its southern point at Amroth. For the vast majority of the time, the path clings precariously to clifftop routes, overlooking seal-basking rocks, craggy offshore islands, unexpected gashes of sand and shrieking clouds of sea birds. The most popular, and ruggedly inspiring, segments of the coast path are around St David's Head and the Marloes Peninsula, either side of St Bride's Bay; the stretch from the castle at Manorbier to the tiny cliff chapel at Bosherston along the southern coast; and, generally quieter, the undulating contours, massive cliffs, bays and old ports along the northern coast, either side of Fishguard.

Few walkers appreciate the danger of the path, on which there is a grim annual death toll, mainly through those falling over the cliffs. Of all the seasons, perhaps spring is the finest for walking as the crowds are yet to arrive and the clifftop flora is at its most vivid. There are numerous publications available about the coast path, of which the best is Brian John's *National Trail Guide*, which includes section 1:25,000 maps of the route. The National Park publishes a handy *Coast Path Accommodation* guide, detailing B&Bs and campsites the entire length of the route.

Penally to Bosherton

Just over a mile down the A4139 from Tenby, the dormitory village of **PENALLY** is unremarkable save for the vast beach. The coastal path hugs the clifftop from the viewpoint at Giltar Point, just below Penally, reaching the glorious privately owned beach at the 54-acre headland of **Lydstep Haven** after two miles (a fee being charged for the sands). A mile further west is the cove of **Skrinkle Haven**, and above it an excellent **youth hostel** (☎01834/871803).

The next part of the coast path heads inland to avoid the artillery range that occupies the beautiful outcrop of **Old Castle Head**, then leads straight into the quaint village of **MANORBIER**, pronounced "Manner-beer" (Maenorbŷr), birthplace in 1146 of Giraldus Cambrensis. Founded in the early twelfth century as an impressive baronial residence, the **Castle** (April–Sept daily 10.30am–5.30pm; £2) sits above the village and its beach on a hill of wild gorse. The Norman walls are in a very decent state of repair, surrounding an inner grass courtyard in which the extensive remains of the castle's chapel and state rooms jostle for position with the nineteenth-century domestic residence, whose TV aerial strikes a note of contemporary discord. In the walls and buildings are a warren of dark passageways to explore, occasionally opening out into little cells with lacklustre wax figures, purporting to illustrate the castle's history.

The rocky little harbour at **Stackpole Quay**, reached via the small lane from Freshwater East through East Trewent, is a good starting point for walks along the breathtaking cliffs to the north, or half a mile south to the finest beach in Pembrokeshire: **Barafundle Bay**, with its idyllically clear water and a soft beach fringed by wooded cliffs at either end. The path continues around the coast, through the dunes of **Stackpole Warren**, to **BROAD HAVEN**, where a pleasant small beach overlooks several rocky islets, now managed by the National Trust. Basing yourself here gives good access inland to the nearby **Bosherston Lakes**, three fingers of water artificially created in the late eighteenth century, but beautifully landscaped. The westernmost lake is the most scenic, especially in late spring and early summer when the lilies that form a carpet across its surface are in full bloom.

Another lane dips south from the village of **BOSHERSTON**, across the MoD train-ing grounds, to a spot overlooking the cliffs where **St Govan's chapel** is wedged: it's a remarkable tiny, grey chapel, known to be at least eight hundred years old. Steps descend straight into the sandy-floored chapel, now devoid of any furnishings, save for the simple stone altar.

Pembroke and around

The old county town of **PEMBROKE** (Penfro) and its fearsome castle sit on the south-ern side of the Pembroke River, a continuation of the massive Milford Haven waterway, described by Nelson as the greatest natural harbour in the world. Despite its location, Pembroke is surprisingly dull, with one long main street of attractive Georgian and Victorian houses, some intact stretches of medieval town wall but little else to catch the eye. The town grew up solely to serve the castle, the mightiest link in the chain of Norman strongholds built across southern Wales. The walled town, drawn out along a hilltop ridge, flourished as a port for Pembrokeshire goods to be exported throughout Britain and to Ireland, France and Spain. The castle was ruined by Cromwell during the Civil War, and though the town developed as a centre of leather making, weaving, dyeing and tailoring, it never really regained its former importance.

Pembroke's history is inextricably bound up with that of the impregnable **Castle** (daily April–Sept 9.30am–6pm; Oct–March 10am–5pm; Nov–Feb 10am–4pm; £2.50), founded by the Normans, but rebuilt between 1189 and 1245. During the Civil War, Pembroke was a Parliamentarian stronghold until the town's military governor suddenly switched allegiance to the King. Cromwell's troops sacked the castle after besieging it for 48 days. Yet despite Cromwell's incessant battering and centuries of subsequent neglect, Pembroke still inspires feelings of awe at its sheer, bloody-minded bulk, even if it is largely due to extensive restoration over the last century. You enter through the soaring gatehouse into the large, grassy courtyard around the vast, round Norman **keep**, 75ft high and with walls 18ft thick, crowned by a dome. Apart from a dungeon tower there's a Norman Hall, where the period arch has been disappointingly over-restored and reinforced, next to the Oriel or Northern Hall, a Tudor re-creation of an earlier antechamber. The intact towers and battlements contain many heavily restored communal rooms, now empty of furniture, and to a large extent, atmosphere too, although some of the rooms, mainly in the gatehouse, are used to house some excellent displays on the history of the castle and the Tudor empire.

Opposite the castle walls at 7 Westgate Hill (the continuation north of the Main Street) is the delightfully eccentric **Museum of the Home** (May–Sept Mon–Thurs 11am–5pm; £1.20), an all-encompassing name for the thousands of objects packed into a steep town house. It's a collection of utterly ordinary items from the eighteenth to the twentieth centuries, loosely gathered into themes – the dairy, toiletries, personal and smoking accessories, kitchen equipment, bedroom accessories and children's games – all demonstrated with great enthusiasm.

Pembroke's **train station** is east of the town centre on Station Road. The **tourist office** is on Commons Road (Feb–Easter Tues, Thurs & Sat 10am–5pm; Easter–Sept daily 10am–5.30pm; ☎01646/622388), parallel to Main Street, and provides a useful free town booklet guide. At the entrance to the castle is a small **National Park informa-tion centre** (Easter–Sept Mon–Sat 9.30am–1pm & 2–5.30pm; ☎01646/682148). **Accommodation** ranges from cheap B&Bs such as the *Connaught*, 123 Main St (☎01646/684655; ②), to slightly plusher hotels like the *King's Arms*, near the castle on the Main Street (☎01646/683611; ④). For **food**, try the excellent *Woodhouse* restau-rant (☎01646/687140), which specializes in a limited, but beautifully cooked, menu of local produce, or the bar food at the *King's Arms Hotel*, also on Main Street.

Carew and Lamphey

A tiny village that can become unbearably packed in high season, **CAREW**, four miles east of Pembroke by the Carew River, is a pretty place. Just south of the river crossing, by the main road, is the village's **Celtic cross**, the graceful, remarkably intact taper of the shaft covered in fine tracery of ancient Welsh designs. A small hut beyond the cross serves as the ticket office for **Carew Castle** and **Mill** (Easter–Oct daily 10am–5pm; £1.40 castle only, £2 castle and mill). The castle, a hybrid of Elizabethan fancy and earlier defensive necessity, is reached across a field. A few hundred yards west of the castle is the **Carew French Mill**, the only mill powered by the shifting tides in Wales. The impressive eighteenth-century exterior belies the pedestrian exhibitions and self-guided audio-visual displays of the milling process at different stages.

The humdrum village of **LAMPHEY**, two miles southeast of Pembroke, is best known for the ruined **Bishop's Palace** (May–Sept daily 10am–5pm; £1.70; Oct–April free entry at all times; CADW), off a quiet lane to the north of the village. This was a country retreat for the bishops of St David's, dating from at least the thirteenth century and abandoned at the Reformation in the mid-sixteenth century. Stout walls surround the palace ruins, scattered over a large area, with many of the palace buildings having long been lost under the grassy banks. Most impressive are the remains of the Great Hall across the entire eastern end of the complex, with fourteenth-century Bishop Gower's hallmark arcaded parapets on its top, similar to those that he built in the Bishop's Palace of St David's.

Haverfordwest to Fishguard

The most western point of Wales – and the very furthest you can get from England – is one of the country's most enchanting areas. The coast around **St Bride's Bay** is broken into rocky crops, islands and broad, sweeping beaches curving around between two headlands that sit like giant crab pincers facing out into the warm Gulf Stream amidst the crashing Atlantic. The southernmost headland winds around every conceivable angle, offering calm, east-facing sands at **Dale** and sunny expanses of south-facing beach at **Marloes**. Near **Martin's Haven**, boats depart for the offshore islands of **Skomer**, **Skokholm** and **Grassholm**. To the north, the spectacularly lacerated coast veers to the left and the **St David's peninsula**, along stunning cliffs interrupted only by occasional gashes of sand. Just north of **St Non's Bay**, the tiny cathedral city of **St David's**, founded in the sixth century by Wales' patron saint, is a justified highlight. Rooks and crows circle above the impressive ruins of the huge **Bishop's Palace**, sitting beneath the delicate bulk of the **cathedral**, the most impressive in Wales.

The north-facing coast that forms the very southern tip of Cardigan Bay is noticeably less commercialized and far more Welsh than the touristy coasts of south and mid-Pembrokeshire. From the crags and cairns above St David's Head, the coast path perches precariously on the cliffs, where only the thousands of seabirds have access. There are only the modest charms of small bays and desolate coves to detain you en route to **Fishguard**, and the ferries to Ireland. Bus transport to most corners of the peninsula radiates out from **Haverfordwest**.

Haverfordwest

In the seventeenth and eighteenth centuries, the town of **HAVERFORDWEST** (Hwlffordd), ten miles north of Pembroke, prospered as a port and trading centre, but despite its natural advantages, it is scarcely a place to linger. A cursory loook at the dingy shell of the thirteenth-century **castle** and the less-than-exciting **district museum** (April–Sept Mon–Sat 10am–5.15pm; Oct–March Mon–Sat 11am–4pm; 50p) is enough, though as the main transport hub and shopping centre for western Pembrokeshire you are likely to pass through. The **tourist office** is next to the bus terminus at the end of the Old Bridge (Mon–Sat May–Sept 10am–5.30pm; Oct until 5pm; Nov–April until 4.30pm; ☎01437/763110), and there is also an excellent **National Park office** at 48 High St. Haverfordwest offers **accommodation** at the solidly Georgian *Castle Hotel* in Castle Square (☎01437/769322; ⑤), or, a little cheaper, the *College Guest House*, 93 Hill St (☎01437/763710; ③). There's a **campsite** two miles northwest on the A487, at the *Rising Sun Inn* in Pelcomb Bridge (☎01437/765171).

Marloes and Dale peninsula

DALE, fourteen miles from Haverfordwest, is not an especially attractive village, and can be unbearably crowded in peak season, but its east-facing shore makes it excellent for watersports in the lighter seas. Equipment and instruction for windsurfing, sailing, surfing and even mountain biking are available on the seafront from *West Wales Windsurfing & Sailing* (☎01646/636642). The calm waters of Dale are deceptive, and as soon as you head further south towards **St Ann's Head**, one of the most invigoratingly desolate places in the county, the wind speed whips up, with waves and tides to match. The coast path sticks tight to the undulating coastline, passing tiny bays en route to the St Ann's lighthouse.

The coast turns and heads north from St Ann's Head to the broad sands of **MARLOES**, a mile from the village, a safe place to swim looking out towards the island of Skokholm. From here, the coast path continues for two miles to the National Trust-owned deer-free **Deer Park**, the name given to the far tip of the southern peninsula of St Bride's Bay. Alternatively, take the narrow lane across the wind-battered heights from Marloes to the Deer Park car park at **MARTINS HAVEN**, from where you can make crossings out to the islands of Skomer, Skokholm and Grassholm.

Skomer, Stokholm and Grassholm islands

Skomer Island (boats April–Oct Tues–Sun 10am, 11am & noon; £6) is a 722-acre flat-topped island rich in seabirds and spectacular carpets of wild flowers, perfect for bird-watching and walking. You can also cross to **Skokholm Island** from Martins Haven (boats June–Aug Mon 10am; £15.50; ☎01437/781412), a couple of miles south of Skomer and far smaller, more rugged and remote, noted for its warm red cliffs of sandstone. Britain's first bird observatory was founded here as far back as the seventeenth century, and there is still a huge number of petrels, gulls, puffins, oystercatchers and rare Manx shearwaters. The trip includes a guided tour by the island's warden. The final boat trips head out even further, to the tiny oupost of **Grassholm Island**, over five miles west of Skomer (boats June–Sept landing trip Mon, round trip Fri, evening trip Thurs; £20 to land, £16 otherwise; ☎01646/601636), an unforgettable experience, largely due to the 60,000 or so screaming gannets who call it home. No booking is required for Skomer trips, Stokholm Monday trips and Grassholm Thursday trips, although this can be done via National Park centres.

Practicalities

For **accommodation**, there's the *Post House Hotel* in the middle of Dale (☎01646/636201; ④). Marloes village is well stocked for B&Bs: pick from the *East End* guest house (☎01646/636365; ②), or *Greenacre* (☎01646/636400; ②). The **youth hostel** at Runwayskiln (April–Sept; ☎01646/636667) consists of a series of converted farm buildings overlooking the northern end of Marloes Sands. **Camping** is possible at *Greenacre* (see above), near the youth hostel at Runwayskiln (☎01646/636257), or at *West Hook Farm* (☎01646/636424) near Martins Haven. **Food** and **drink** are available at the *Post House Hotel* in Dale, and at the *Foxes Inn* in Marloes.

St David's

ST DAVID'S (Tyddewi) is one of the most enchanting spots in Britain. This miniature city clusters around the foot of its purple- and gold-flecked cathedral at the very western point of Wales in bleak, treeless countryside; spiritually, it is the centre of Welsh ecclesiasticism, totally independent from Canterbury. Traditionally founded by the Welsh patron saint himself in 550 AD, the see of St David's has drawn pilgrims for a millennium and a half – William the Conqueror included – and by 1120, Pope Calixtus II decreed that two journeys to St David's were the spiritual equivalent of one to Rome. The surrounding city – in reality, never much more than a large village – grew up in the shadow cast by the cathedral, and St David's today still relies on the imported wealth of newcomers to the area, attracted by its savage beauty, together with the spending power of numerous visitors.

The Town

The main road from Haverfordwest enters St David's inauspiciously, passing a **Celtic cross**, and continuing under the thirteenth-century **Tower Gate**, which forms the entrance to the serene **Cathedral Close**, backed by a windswept landscape treeless heathland. The cathedral lies down to the right, hidden in a hollow by the River Alun. This apparent modesty is explained by reasons of defence, as a towering cathedral, visible from the sea on all sides, would have been vulnerable. On the other side of the babbling Alun lie the ruins of the Bishop's Palace. New Street heads north past the enjoyable **Oceanarium** (daily 10am–6pm; Oct–March 10am–4pm; £3), complete with a shark tank overlooked by a viewing gallery.

Approached down the Thirty-nine Articles (or steps) that run from beyond the powerfully solid Tower Gate, the gold and purple stone **Cathedral**'s 125-foot tower has clocks on only three sides (the people of the northern part of the parish couldn't raise enough money for one to be constructed facing them), and is topped by pert golden pinnacles. You enter through the south side of the low twelfth-century nave in full view of its most striking feature, the intricate latticed oak **roof**, built to hide sixteenth-century emergency restoration work, when the nave was in danger of collapse. The nave floor still has a discernible slope and the support buttresses inserted in the northern aisle of the nave look incongruously new and temporary. At the end of the nave, an elaborate **rood screen** was constructed under the orders of fourteenth-century Bishop Gower, who envisaged it as his own tomb. Behind the rood screen and the organ, the choir sits directly under the magnificently bold and bright lantern ceiling of the tower, another addition by Gower. At the back of the right-hand choir stalls is a unique **monarch's stall**, complete with royal crest, for, unlike any other British cathedral, the Queen is an automatic member of the St David's Cathedral Chapter.

Separating the choir and the presbytery is a finely traced, rare **Parclose screen**. The back wall of the **presbytery** was once the eastern extremity of the cathedral, as can be seen from the two lines of windows. The upper row has been left intact, while the lower three were blocked up and filled with delicate gold mosaics in the nineteenth century. The colourful fifteenth-century roof, a deceptively simple repeating medieval pattern, was extensively restored by Gilbert Scott in the mid-nineteenth century. At the back of the presbytery, around the altar, the **sanctuary** has a few fragmented fifteenth-century tiles still in place. On the south side is a beautifully carved sedilla, a seat for the priest and deacon celebrating mass. To its right are thirteenth-century tombs of two bishops, Iorwerth (1215–31) and Anselm de la Grace (1231–47), and on the other side of the sanctuary is the disappointingly plain thirteenth-century tomb of St David, largely destroyed in the Reformation.

From the cathedral, a path leads to the splendid **Bishops' Palace** (April–Oct daily 9.30am–6.30pm; Nov–March Mon–Sat 9.30am–4pm, Sun 2–4pm; £1.70; CADW), built by Bishops Beck and Gower around the turn of the fourteenth century. The huge central quadrangle is fringed by a neat jigsaw of ruined buildings in extraordinarily rich colours: the distinctive green, red, purple and grey tints of volcanic ash, sandstone and many other types of stone. The **arched parapets** that run along the top of most of the walls were a favourite feature of Gower, who did more than any of his predecessors or successors to transform the palace into an architectural and political powerhouse. Two ruined but still impressive halls – the **Bishops' Hall** and the enormous **Great Hall**, with its glorious rose window – lie off the main quadrangle, above and around a myriad of rooms adorned by some eerily eroded corbels. Underneath the Great Hall are dank vaults containing an interesting exhibition about the palace and the indulgent lifestyles of its occupants. The destruction of the palace is largely due to Bishop Barlow (1536–48), who supposedly stripped the buildings of their lead roofs to provide dowries for his five daughters' marriages to bishops.

Practicalities

From the bus terminus situated in New Street, the friendly and efficient **tourist office** (Easter–Oct daily 9.30am–5.30pm; ☎01437/720392) is just a short walk away in City Hall on the High Street. **Bike rental** is available from *St David's Cycle Hire* (☎01437/721611 or 721802); reservations from the *Coastal Trader* office in the High Street.

There are numerous **places to stay** in St David's. The cheapest option in town is *Y Glennydd*, 51 Nun St (☎01437/720576; ③), followed by *Pen Albro*, 18 Goat St (☎01437/721865; ③) next to the *Farmers Arms. Old Cross*, Cross Square (March–Oct; ☎01437/720387; ④), is a comfortable, creaky hotel with a good restaurant, while *Ramsey House*, Lower Moor (☎01437/720321; ③), is an excellent small hotel on the road to Porth Clais, with superb Welsh cuisine. The nearest **YHA hostel** is *Llaethdy* (☎01437/720345), a large and popular place, two miles northwest of St David's near Whitesands Bay; and there's decent hostel accommodation at *Twr-y-Felin*, Caerfai Road, St David's (☎01437/720391). St David's best **camping** is at *Caerfai Farm*, Caerfai Bay (May–Sept; ☎01437/720548), a fifteen-minute walk from the city.

Fosters Bistro, 51 Nun St (April–Oct), is a moderately priced **restaurant** with a menu of local dishes and international favourites. Similarly priced, *Cartref*, Cross Square (March–Dec), has a menu of well-cooked local dishes. Cheaper home-cooked Indian delicacies can be had at the hotel bar of the *City Inn*, New St. **Nightlife** boils down to the lively *Farmers Arms*, Goat St, the city's only pub, with a terrace overlooking the cathedral, and the *Cawl a Chan* evenings at St David's rugby club, out on the road to Whitesands Bay. Here there are weekly summer (Thurs) nights of raucous singing, beer and Welsh broth – snacks and entertainment for £4; details from the tourist office.

St David's Peninsula

Surrounded on three sides by inlets, coves and rocky stacks, St David's is an easy base for some excellent walking around the headland of the same name. A mile due south, accessed along the signposted lane from the main Haverfordwest road just near the school, popular **Caerfai Bay** provides a sandy gash in the purple sandstone cliffs, rock from which was used in the construction of the cathedral. To the immediate west is the craggy indentation of **St Non's Bay**, reached from St David's down the tiny rhododendron-flooded lane, signposted to the *Warpool Court Hotel* that leads off Goat Street. Saint Non reputedly gave birth to Saint David at this spot during a tumultuous storm around 500 AD, when a spring opened up between Non's feet, and despite the crashing thunder all around, an eerily calm light filtered down on to the scene. St Non has received pilgrims for centuries, resulting in the foundation of a tiny chapel in the pre-Norman age, whose successor's thirteenth-century ruins now lie in a field to the right of the car park, beyond the sadly dingy well and coy shrine where the nation's patron saint is said to have been born.

The road from St David's to St Non's branches at the *St Non's Hotel*, where Catherine Street becomes a winding lane that leads a mile down the tiny valley of the River Alun to its mouth at **PORTH CLAIS**. Supposedly the place at which Saint David was baptized, Porth Clais was the city's main harbour, the spruced-up remains of which can still be seen at the bottom of the turquoise river creek. Today, commercial traffic has long gone, replaced by a boaties' haven.

Running due west out of St David's, Goat Street ducks past the ruins of the Bishop's Palace and over the rocky plateau for two miles to the harbour at **ST JUSTINIANS**, little more than a lifeboat station, car park and ticket hut for the boats over to Ramsey Island, which leave here at great regularity during the summer (*Ramsey Island Pleasure Cruises;* April–Oct; ☎01437/720285 or 721423). Under the extremely able stewardship of the RSPB since 1992, **Ramsey Island** itself, a dual-humped plateau less than two miles long, is quite enchanting. Birds of prey circle the skies, and on the beaches seals laze sloppily below the deer paths beaten out by a herd of red deer.

Fishguard

From St David's, the coast road runs northeast parallel to numerous small and less-commercialised bays to **Strumble Head**, which protects the harbour at **FISHGUARD** (Abergwaun), an attractive, hilltop town seldom seen as anything more than a brief stop-off place to the ferries, which leave regularly for Rosslare in Ireland from the suburb of **GOODWICK** (Wdig).

Near the town hall is the **Royal Oak Inn**, where the bizarre Franco-Irish attempt to conquer Britain in 1797 at nearby Carregwastad Point is remembered. The hapless forces arrived to negotiate a cease-fire, which was turned by the assembled British into an unconditional surrender. Part of the invaders' low morale – apart from the drunken farces in which they'd become embroiled – is said to have been sparked off by the sight of a hundred local women marching towards them. The troops mistook their stovepipe hats and red flannel dresses for the outfit of a British Infantry troop and instantly capitulated. Even if this is not true, it is an undisputed fact that 47-year-old cobbler Jemima Nicholas, the "Welsh Heroine", single-handedly captured fourteen French soldiers. Her grave can be seen next to the uninspiring Victorian **parish church**, St Mary's, behind the pub.

Fishguard's main **tourist office** (daily: April–July 10am–5.30pm; Aug 10am–5.30pm; Sept & Oct 10am–5pm; Nov–March 10am–4pm; ☎01348/873484) is in the old town, at the bottom of Hamilton Street on Main Street; there's another branch (same times; ☎01348/872037) by the ferry terminal. **Buses** stop by the town hall in the central Market Square. The road arrives in the unprepossessing surroundings of Goodwick, where the **ferries** leave daily for Rosslare in Ireland (☎01348/872881). The **train station** is next to the ferry terminal on Quay Road. **Accommodation** is plentiful and cheap, with most places well used to visitors coming and going at odd times for the ferries. Next to the port is the faded elegance of the *Fishguard Bay Hotel* on Quay Road (☎01348/873571; ③). Down in Lower Fishguard is the *Hotel Plas Glyn-y-Mel* (☎01348/872296; ④).

travel details

Trains

Carmarthen to: Fishguard Harbour (1 daily; 55min); Haverfordwest (10 daily; 40min); Kidwelly (10 daily; 15min); Pembroke (8 daily; 1hr 10min); Tenby (8 daily; 45min).

Haverfordwest to: Carmarthen (12 daily; 40min); Swansea (10 daily; 1hr 30min).

Tenby to: Carmarthen (8 daily; 45min); Pembroke (8 daily; 20 & 25min); Swansea (8 daily; 1hr 35min).

Buses

Carmarthen to: Haverfordwest (7 daily Mon–Sat; 55min); Kidwelly (4 daily Mon–Sat; 25min); Laugharne (hourly Mon–Sat; 35min); Manorbier (4 daily Mon–Sat; 1hr 25min); Pembroke (5 daily Mon–Sat; 1hr 40min); Swansea (hourly Mon–Sat; 1hr 30min); Tenby (5 daily Mon–Sat; 1hr).

Fishguard to: Cardigan (hourly Mon–Sat; 50min); Haverfordwest (hourly Mon–Sat; 45min); St David's (7 daily Mon–Sat; 50min).

Haverfordwest to: Broad Haven (5 daily Mon–Sat; 15min); Carmarthen (7 daily Mon–Sat; 55min); Dale (2 buses Tues & Fri; 35min); Fishguard (hourly Mon–Sat; 45min); Manorbier (hourly Mon–Sat; 1hr 10min); Marloes (Tues & Fri 1 bus; 35min); Pembroke (hourly Mon–Sat; 50min); St David's (hourly Mon–Sat; 50min); Tenby (hourly Mon–Sat; 1hr 25min).

Llandeilo to: Carmarthen (hourly Mon–Sat; 35min); Llandovery (8 daily Mon–Sat; 35min).

Pembroke to: Bosherston (3 daily Mon–Fri; 1hr); Haverfordwest (hourly Mon–Sat; 50min); Manorbier (hourly Mon–Sat; 20min); Tenby (hourly Mon–Sat; 40min).

Tenby to: Carmarthen (5 daily Mon–Sat; 1hr); Haverfordwest (hourly Mon–Sat; 1hr 25min); Manorbier (hourly Mon–Sat; 20min); Pembroke (hourly Mon–Sat; 40min).

CHAPTER THIRTEEN

POWYS

T he only county in Wales with no coastline, **Powys** occupies a quarter of the country from the fringes of the Glamorgan valleys south of the Brecon Beacons, through the sparsely populated lakelands of Radnorshire and up to the open moorland of the Berwyn Mountains. Powys has only been a county since local government reorganization in 1974, but its name harks back to a fifth-century Welsh kingdom.

By far the most popular attraction in the county is **Brecon Beacons National Park** at the southern end of Powys, stretching from the moody heights of the Black Mountain in the west, through the gentler Beacons themselves, and out to the English border beyond the confusingly named Black Mountains. The main centres within the Beacons are Abergavenny (see p.569), in the far southeast, and the small city of **Brecon**, a curious mix of traditional market town, army garrison and often very pretty tourist centre. The bleaker part of the Beacons lies to the west, around the raw peaks of the **Black Mountain** and **Fforest Fawr**. A few roads cut through the glowering countryside, connecting popular attractions such as the immense **Dan-yr-ogof caves**, opera prima donna Adelina Patti's gilded home and theatre at nearby **Craig-y-nos** and the caves and waterfalls around the popular walking centre of **Ystradfellte**. Walkers are equally well catered for in settlements like **Crickhowell** and **Talgarth**, small towns set in quiet river valleys.

At the northern corner of the National Park, the border town of **Hay-on-Wye** draws in thousands to see the town's dozens of bookshops, housed in warehouses, the old castle and outdoor yards. West of Hay, the peaks of the **Mynydd Eppynt** now form a vast training ground for the British army, on the other side of which lie the old spa towns of Radnorshire, among them earthy **Llanwrtyd Wells** and twee **Llandrindod Wells**. The countryside to the north, crossed by spectacular mountain roads such as the **Abergwesyn Pass** from Llanwrtyd, is barely populated and beautiful – quiet, occasionally harsh country, dotted with ancient churches and introspective villages, from the border town of **Knighton**, home of the flourishing **Offa's Dyke path** industry, to inland centres like **Rhayader**, the nearest centre of population for the grandiose reservoirs of the **Elan Valley**.

Montgomeryshire is the northern portion of Powys, similarly underpopulated and as remote as its two southern siblings. In common with most of mid-Wales, country

---

ACCOMMODATION PRICE CODES

Throughout this guide, hotel and B&B accommodation is priced on a scale of ① to ⑨, the number indicating the **lowest price** you could expect to pay per night in that establishment for a **double room** in high season. The prices indicated by the codes are as follows:

① under £20/$30	④ £40–50/$60–75	⑦ £70–80/$105–120
② £20–30/$31–45	⑤ £50–60/$75–90	⑧ £80–100/$120–150
③ £30–40/$45–60	⑥ £60–70/$90–105	⑨ over £100/$150

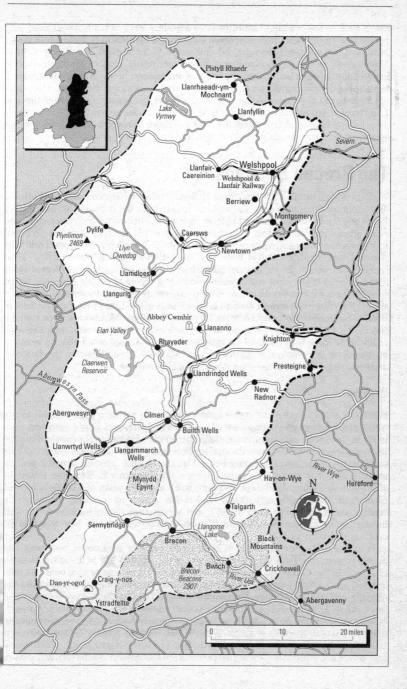

towns such as the beautiful **Llanidloes** has a healthy stock of old hippies amongst its population. To the west, the inhospitable mountain of **Plynlimon** is flecked with boggy heathland and gloomy reservoirs, beyond which is the popular and hearty town of Machynlleth, stranded out on a limb of Powys (see p.634). Eastern Montgomeryshire is home to the anglicized old county town, **Montgomery**, between the robust town of **Welshpool** on the English border, and the charmless centre of Newtown. The northern segment of the county is even quieter, with regional centres like **Llanfyllin** and **Llanrhaeadr-ym-mochnant** that are little more than villages, leaving the few crowds seen around here to cluster along the banks of **Lake Vyrnwy**, a flooded-valley reservoir which has harmoniously moulded itself into the landscape around it.

The Brecon Beacons

With the lowest profile of Wales' three National Parks, the **Brecon Beacons** are the destination of thousands of urban walkers largely from the industrial areas of south Wales and the West Midlands of England. Spongy hills of heather and rock tumble and climb around river valleys that lie between sandstone and limestone uplands, peppered with glass-like lakes and villages that seem to have been hewn from one rock. The National Park straddles Powys from west to east, covering 520 square miles. Most remote is the area at the far western side, where the vast, open terrain of **Fforest Fawr** forms miles of tufted moorland tumbling down to a region of porous limestone in the south. Here is a rocky terrain of rivers, deep caves and spluttering waterfalls, especially around the village of **Ystradfellte** and in the chasms of the **Dan-yr-ogof caves**. East of Brecon, the series of interlocked peaks known as the **Black Mountains** stretch all the way to the English border, offering the region's most varied scenery, with the wide valley of the River Usk, home to the main settlement of **Crickhowell** and the beautiful double castle at **Tretower**, alongside almost impossibly green hills. On the Beacons' northern fringe lies the bibliophiles' paradise of **Hay-on-Wye**.

Brecon

BRECON (Aberhonddu) is a sturdy county town at the northern edge of the Beacons with a proliferation of well-proportioned Georgian buildings which, while bearing testimony to the town's past importance, have little to offer visitors to the nearby National Park. Fairweather walkers base themselves here and explore the well-waymarked hills to the south of the town, including Pen y Fan, the highest, most challenging peak in south Wales. For sedentary tourists, there's the **Brecknock Museum** (Mon–Sat 10am–1pm & 2–5pm; April–Sept also Sun; free), at the junction of The Bulwark and Glamorgan Street, with agricultural implements unique to the area; a nineteenth-century assize court, last used in 1971; and a collection, dating back as far as four hundred years, of painstakingly carved Welsh love spoons that were betrothal gifts for courting Welsh lovers.

From the town-centre crossroads, High Street Superior goes north, becoming The Struet, running alongside the rushing waters of the Honddu. Off to the left, a footpath climbs up to the **Cathedral**. The building's dumpy external appearance belies its lofty interior, graced with a few Norman features (includinga hulking font) intact from the eleventh-century. The **Games Monument** (1555), in the southern aisle, is made up of three oak beds and depicts an unknown woman whose hands remain intact in prayer, but whose arms and nose have been unceremoniously hacked off. The consummate finish to a day in the hills is a visit to the **Welsh Whisky Visitor Centre** (Mon–Fri 10am–5pm; May–Sept also Sat 10am–5pm, Sun 11.30am–3.30pm; £2.50), where you'll find Welsh gin, whisky and even *Taffski* vodka – a little-known commodity and considerably better than you might think – all thrown in with the entry fee. The centre is located off the bypass roundabout to the east of town.

Practicalities

The **tourist office** (Easter–Oct daily 10am–6pm; Nov–Easter Tues–Sun 9.15am–5.15pm; ☎01874/622485) and **National Park office** (Easter–Oct daily 9.30am–5.30pm) share the same building in the Lion Yard car park off Lion Street, next to the cattle market, the former providing details of the town's annual **jazz festival** over a long weekend in mid-August. Brecon, and adjacent Llanfaes, is bulging with **accommodation** to suit all pockets, except during the jazz festival. Best bets are the small and pleasant *Tir Bach Guest House*, 13 Alexandra Rd (☎01874/624551; ②) behind the cattle market; *Beacons Guest House*, 16 Bridge St, Llanfaes (☎01874/623339; ③); and *Castle Hotel*, Castle Square (☎01874/624611; ⑤), a sumptuous hotel built into the castle ruins, overlooking the Usk. *Llanfaes Guest House*, Llanfaes (☎01874/611115; ④) is an exclusively lesbian and gay retreat in a pleasant Georgian town house; and there are a couple of **YHA hostels**, the closest of which is *Ty'n-y-Caeau*, Groesfford (☎01874/665270; ①), two miles east of the town and reached via the path (Slwch Lane) from Cerrigcochion Road in Brecon or a mile walk from bus stops at either Cefn Brynich lock (Brecon–Abergavenny buses) or Troedyrharn Farm (Brecon–Hereford buses). *The Brynich Caravan and Camping Park*, Brynich (☎01874/623325) is situated a mile east of town, just off the A40, overlooking the town and the river.

Brecon is a lively and cosmopolitan town always well served for **food** and **drink**. The *Coracle Café*, High St Inferior, provides a solid and inexpensive daytime menu of snacks and hearty meals; *Castle Hotel*, Castle Square (☎01874/624611) is worth investigating for the moderately priced fixed-dinner menu in this enjoyable and smart restaurant; and the *Beacons Guest House*, 16 Bridge St, Llanfaes (☎01874/623339) is open to non-residents for excellent and inexpensive lunches, teas and evening meals, many inspired by local produce and traditional Welsh recipes. Of the town's pubs, the *Bull's Head*, The Struet, is a small and cheery locals' pub, with views over the Honddu River and towards the cathedral and good-value food; the *Wellington Hotel*, The Bulwark, is a surprisingly unstuffy hotel bar, a frequent venue for live music, especially jazz.

The Fforest Fawr

Covering a vast expanse of hilly landscape west of the central Beacon Beacons, **Fforest Fawr** (Great Forest) seems something of a misnomer for an area of largely unforested sandstone hills dropping down to a porous limestone belt in the south. The hills rise up to the south of the A40 west of Brecon, with the A4067 piercing the western side of the range and the A470 defining the Fforest's eastern limit. Between the two, a twisting mountain road crosses a bleak plateau and decends into the one of Britain's classic limestone landscapes, around the tiny hamlet of **YSTRADFELLTE**. With a dazzling countryside of lush, deep ravines on its doorstep it has become a phenomenally popular centre for walking over great pavements of bone-white rock next to cradling potholes, disappearing rivers and crashing waterfalls.

A mile to the south, the River Mellte tumbles into the dark mouth of the **Porth-yr-ogof** (White Horse Cave), emerging into daylight a few hundred yards further south. A signposted path heads south from the Porth-yr-ogof car park and into the green gorge of the River Mellte. After little more than a mile, the first of three waterfalls is reached at **Sgwd Clun-Gwyn** (White Meadow Fall), where the river crashes fifty feet over two huge, angular steps of rock before hurtling down course for a few hundred yards to the other two falls – the impressive **Sgwd Isaf Clun-Gwyn** (Lower White Meadow Fall) and, around the wooded corner, the **Sgwd y Pannwr** (Fall of the Fuller). The path continues to the confluence of the rivers Mellte and Hepste, half a mile further on. A quarter of a mile along the Hepste is the most popular of the area's falls – the **Sgwd yr Eira** (Fall of Snow), whose rock below the main tumble has eroded back six feet, allowing people to walk directly behind a dramatic twenty-foot curtain of water. A shorter two-mile walk to Sgwd yr Eira leads from the village of **PENDERYN**, off the A4059 three miles north of Hirwaun, through which regular buses from Aberdare pass. There's a cosy **youth hostel** (☎01639/720301; ①) at **TAI'R HEOL**, half a mile south of Ystradfellte and just a short walk from Porth-yr-ogof.

Dan-yr-ogof Showcaves and Craig-y-nos

Six miles of upland forest and squelchy moor lie between Ystradfellte and the **Dan-yr-ogof Showcaves** (April–Oct daily 10am–4pm; Nov–March phone for details; ☎01639/730284; £5.95), off the A4067 to the west. Only discovered in 1912, they claim to form the largest system of subterranean caverns in Western Europe, and, although relentless marketing has turned them into something of an overdone theme park, the caverns are truly awe-inspiring in their size. A path to the first series of caves, reached around the hideously kitsch park of plastic dinosaurs, leads through a warren of caverns, framed by eerie stalactites and frothy limestone deposits spewing, frozen, over the crags and walls. Highlight of the bewildering subterranean trip is the **Dan-yr-ogof** cave itself, the longest showcave in Britain. Even better is the trip along the path through the downbeat re-created Iron Age "village", which leads to the opening of a series of spookily lit caverns that culminate in the 150-foot-long, 70-foot-high **Cathedral Cave**. The **Bone Cave** is reached along a fearful path behind the dinosaur park, and was known to be inhabited by prehistoric tribes, so the owners have fenced off an assortment of dressed-up mannequins in the cave for an accompanying *son-et-lumière* show that makes Iron Age woman look like a reject from *Miss Selfridge*.

By the main car park for the complex is the Dan-yr-ogof **trekking centre**, which arranges horse rides, and also has a **hotel** (☎01639/730284 or 730693; ③) and **campsite**.

The central Beacons

Far more popular for walking and pony trekking than the Fforest Fawr, the **central Beacons**, grouped around the two highest peaks in the National Park, are easily accessible from Brecon, just six miles to the north. This is classic old red sandstone country: sweeping peaks rising up out of glacial scoops of land. Although the peaks never reach 3000 feet, the terrain is unmistakably, and dramatically, mountainous. The panorama fans out the **Brecon Beacons Mountain Centre** (daily March–June, Sept & Oct 10.30am–5pm; July & Aug 10am–6pm; Nov–Feb 10.30am–4.30pm; ☎01874/623366) on a windy ridge, amongst gorse heathland just off the A470 (turn off at Libanus), five miles southwest of Brecon. As well as an excellent café, there are interesting displays on the flora, fauna, geology and history of the area, together with a well-stocked shop of maps, books and walking gear.

Pen y Fan (2907ft) is the highest peak in the Beacons, indeed in all south Wales. Together with **Corn Du** (2863ft), half a mile to the west, they form the most popular ascents in the park, particularly along the well-trampled muddy red path that starts from Pont ar Daf, half a mile south of Storey Arms on the A470 midway between Brecon and Merthyr Tydfil. This is the most direct route from a road, where a comparatively easy five-mile round trip gradually climbs up the southern flank of the two peaks. A longer and generally quieter route leads up to the two peaks from the "Gap" route, the ancient main road that winds its way north from the Neuadd reservoirs (immediately south of Brecon), through the only natural break in the sandstone ridge of the central Beacons to the bottom of the lane that eventually joins the main street in Llanfaes, Brecon, as Bailihelig Road. Although the old road is no longer accessible for cars, car parks at either end open out onto the track for an eight-mile round-trip ascent up Pen y Fan and Corn Du from the east.

The Black Mountains

The easternmost section of the National Park centres on the **Black Mountains**, far quieter than the central belt of the Brecon Beacons and skirted by the wide valley of the River Usk. The only exception to the Black Mountains' unremitting sandstone is an isolated outcrop of limestone, long divorced from the southern belt, that peaks due north of Crickhowell at Pen Cerrig-calch (2302ft). The Black Mountains have the feeling of a landscape only partly tamed by human habitation: tiny villages, isolated churches and delightful lanes are folded into the undulating green landscape

In the very south of this region and only three miles north of urban Merthyr Tydfil (p.576), the hamlet of **PONTSTICILL** neighbours the tiny **Brecon Mountain Railway** (Easter–Oct mostly daily; ☎01685/722988) which shuttles passengers along a two-mile section of track on the eastern bank of the Pontsticill Reservoir and down to Pant, just north of Merthyr.

Tretower

Rising out of the valley floor, dominating the view from both the A40 and A479 mountain road, the solid round tower of the **Castle and Court** (April–Oct daily 9.30am–6pm; Nov–March Mon–Sat 9.30am–4pm, Sun 2–4pm; £2.20; CADW) at **TRETOWER** (Tre-tŵr), was built to guard the valley pass. The bleak thirteenth-century round tower replaced an earlier Norman fortification, and in the late fourteenth century, was supplemented by a comparatively luxurious manor house, itself gradually being expanded over the ensuing years. In the summer, Shakespeare and contemporary plays are acted out in the inspirational surroundings of the court (details on ☎01874/730279) which has been fully restored, with its ostentatious beam-ceilinged Great Hall facing in on the central cobbled courtyard and square sandstone gatehouse. An enjoyable self-guided Walkman tour takes you around an open-air gallery and wall walk, and demonstrates late medieval building methods through the exposed plaster and beams where work is still underway.

Crickhowell

Compact **CRICKHOWELL** (Crucywel), on the northern bank of the wide and shallow Usk, makes for a lively base from which to explore the surrounding area, but there really isn't much to see in town apart from a grand seventeenth-century **bridge** with thirteen arches visible from the eastern end and only twelve from the west, spawning many a local myth. **Table Mountain** (1481ft) provides a spectacular northern backdrop topped by the remains of the 2500-year-old hill fort (*crug*) of Hywel accessed on a path past The Wern off Llanbedr Road. Many walkers follow the route to the north from Table Mountain, climbing two miles up to the plateau-topped limestone hump of **Pen Cerrig-calch** (2302ft).

The **tourist office** (April–Oct daily 9am–1pm & 2–5pm; ☎01837/812105) is in Beaufort Chambers on Beaufort Street. The *Crickhowell Mountain Gear* shop, 1 High St (☎01873/810020), **rents bikes**. **Accommodation** is abundant, with the grandiose coaching inn, the *Bear Hotel* on Beaufort Street (☎01873/810408; ④), and the *Dragon* on the High Street (☎01873/810362; ③); for cheaper B&B, try *Greenhill Villa*, Beaufort St (☎01873/811177; ③). There's also the town-centre *Riverside Park* **campsite** on New Road (☎01873/810397), and in the delightful, nearby village of Llanbedr, *Perth-y-pia* (☎01873/810050), an outdoor centre offering excellent **hostel** accommodation (①), together with **B&B** (②) and home-cooked evening meals, and it's handily close to the *Red Lion* pub. **Eating** is best in the town's pubs: the *Bear Hotel* (see above) wins legions of awards for its delectable, pricier-than-average bar and restaurant food; the local delicacies on offer in the *White Hart* on Brecon Road are cheaper.

Hay-on-Wye

The sleepy border town of **HAY-ON-WYE** (Y Gelli), at the northern tip of the Brecon Beacons, is synonymous with books. One Richard Booth opened Hay's first second-hand bookshop in 1961 and has since become a bibliophile's paradise and the greatest market of used books in the world, with just about every spare inch given over to the trade, including the old cinema, houses, shops and even the ramshackle stone castle. The minuscule town now boasts over twenty bookshops, the largest – Booth's own flag-ship – containing around half a million tomes.

Success in the face of declining rural populations and minimal job prospects little helped by the machinations of hefty bureaucracy led Booth to declare Hay independent of the UK in 1977, with himself, naturally as king. It carries no weight officially, but King Richard continues to take his self-appointed role seriously, pumping out a series of tracts and pamphlets on subjects dear to his heart, from the predictable rallying cries against supermarket developments to criticism of the town's annual high-profile bash founded on the basis of Hay's bibliophilic reputation. In the last week of May, all fashionable London literary life decamps to Hay for the **Hay Literary Festival**, held in venues around the town. The atmosphere during the festival is superb, bursting with riverside parties, travelling fairs and a vast shifting population. Outside this season, Hay's creaky little streets maintain an unhurried charm.

The best bookshop to start sampling the spirit of the town is up the gated track towards the castle opposite the Oxford Road car park, where you'll find Richard Booth's self-styled **independent tourist information centre** and **Five Star book-shop**, with racks of overspill books under canopied covers outside, together with honesty boxes for payment. The shop itself specializes in an unlikely mix of sci-fi, horror, leisure and tourism, including many a tract containing the Thoughts of King Richard. Here – or from the official tourist office – you can pick up the invaluable free *Hay-on-Wye Booksellers & Printsellers* leaflet, detailing all of the town's literary concerns. Just beyond the *Five Star* bookshop is the **castle**, a fire-damaged Jacobean mansion built into the walls of a thirteenth-century fortress, and owned – like just about everything in Hay – by Richard Booth. The ruling monarch lives in part of the castle, affected by fires in 1939 and 1978, and his wife runs the *Castle Bookshop*, a collection of fine art, antiquarian and photography books in another part of the mansion.

A bookshop-lined alleyway leads from the gated track to Castle Street, where **H.R. Grant and Son** at no. 6 and **Castle Street Books** at no. 23 are the best in town for contemporary and historical guides and maps. Beyond the colonnaded **Buttermarket** at the top end of Castle Street, **Richard Booth's Bookshop**, 44 Lion St, is the largest shop in Hay, a huge, draughty warehouse of almost unlimited browsing potential. Lion Street dips down to Broad Street at the clock tower near **Y Gelli Auctions** (☎01497/821179), with regular sales of books, maps and prints. Further along tree-lined Broad Street is **West House Books**, best for Celtic and women's works.

Practicalities

Buses stop off Oxford Road next to the cheery official **tourist office** (daily Easter–Oct 10am–1pm & 2–5pm; Nov–Easter 11am–1pm & 2–4pm; ☎01497/820144), housed in a grim craft centre. They can advise on **accommodation**, best sought at the classy *Belmont House*, Belmont Rd (☎01497/820718; ②), on the continuation of Broad Street; the excellent, thirteenth-century *Old Black Lion*, Lion St (☎01497/820841; ③) which favours candlelight in the evenings; or the *Old Post Office*, Llanigon (☎01497/820008; ②), a wonderful seventeenth-century vegetarian B&B two miles south of Hay, well placed for local walks, including the Offa's Dyke path. **Bike** and **canoe rental** is available from *Paddles and Pedals* on Castle Street (☎01497/820604).

Of a number of good **eating** places, the ones to head for are *Granary*, Broad St (☎01497/820790), an unpretentious bistro serving excellent vegetarian food and local produce; *Pinnochio's*, Broad St (☎01497/821166), a relaxed and popular Italian restaurant, with a delightfully convivial atmsophere on a warm summer's evening; and the cheaper bar meals at the *Blue Boar*, Castle St, with a tasteful wood-panelled bar and excellent beer. The *Old Black Lion*, Lion St, has won numerous awards for its excellent food. There's more good **drinking** at the *Three Tuns*, Broad St, a time-warped pub with a dusty, flagstoned bar filled with disorganized mounds of memorabilia. Go easy on the lethal draught local cider.

The Wells towns

Up until the eighteenth century, the four spa towns of mid-Wales, strung out along the Heart of Wales rail line, were all obscure villages, but then came the great craze for spas, and anywhere with a decent supply of apparently healing water joined in on the act. Royalty and nobility spearheaded the fashion, but come the railways, they became the domain of everyone, each with its own clientele. The westernmost, **Llanwrtyd Wells**, was a popular haunt of the Welsh middle classes, some of whom arrived over the bleak moors by the **Abergwesyn Pass**, still a narrow road connecting the area to the Cambrian Coast. Far prettier – although considerably more twee and anglicized – is **Llandrindod Wells** to the north, whose spa is the only one of the four in any state of decent repair. In between, the larger town of Builth Wells was very much the spa of the Welsh working classes and is best known nowadays as the home of the huge Royal Welsh Showground. There's no reason to stop other than to change buses. The fourth spa town, Llangammarch Wells warrants, even less attention.

Llanwrtyd Wells

Of the four spa towns, **LLANWRTYD WELLS** is the most appealing. It's friendlier, more Welsh, more unspoiled and in more beautiful surroundings than the other three. This was the spa to which the Welsh – farmers of Dyfed alongside the Nonconformist middle classes from Glamorgan – came to great *eisteddfodau* in the valley of the Irfon.

South of where the Main Street crosses the turbulent Irfon, a lane winds for half a mile along the river to the *Dolecoed Hotel*, built near the original sulphurous spring. Although the distinctive aroma had been noted in the area for centuries, it was truly "discovered" in 1732 by the local priest, Theophilus Evans, who drank from an evil-smelling spring after seeing a rudely healthy frog pop out of it. The spring, named **Ffynon Droellwyd** (Stinking Well), can still be sniffed out in the fields beyond the hotel, now erupting around a dome-shaped extension behind the neat red-and-white spa buildings, in the process of restoration. The **Neuadd Arms** pub is the base for a wide range of bizarre and entertaining annual events, including a Man versus Horse race, a Drovers' Walk, a town festival in the first week of August, a snorkelling competition in a local bog, a beer festival in November and a New Year's Eve torchlight procession through the town.

Llanwrtyd's **tourist office** is on the Square (Easter–Oct daily 10am–5pm; ☎01591/610236). **Accommodation** includes the *Neuadd Arms* on the main square (☎01591/610236; ③), which also rents out **bikes**; the solidly Victorian *Belle Vue Hotel* a few yards away (☎01591/610237; ③); and the cheaper *Cerdyn Villa*, Station Rd (☎01591/610635; ②). Both the *Neuadd Arms* and the *Belle Vue* provide cheap, hearty **food**. The *Drovers' Rest* café, by the bridge, serves wholesome traditional Welsh dishes during the day.

Abergwesyn and the Pass

A lane from Llanwrtyd meets up with another road from Beulah at the riverside hamlet of **ABERGWESYN**. From here, a quite magnificent winding thread of an ancient cattle drovers' road – the **Abergwesyn Pass** – climbs the perilous **Devil's Staircase** and pushes up through dense conifer forests to miles of wide, desolate valleys where sheep graze unhurriedly by – and on – the road. At the little bridge over the tiny Tywi River, a track heads south past an isolated, gaslit **youth hostel** (March to mid-Sept; ☎01974/298680) at **DOLGOCH**. This is as remote a walking holiday as can be had in Wales – paths lead from Dolgoch, through the forests and hillsides to the tiny chapel at **SOAR-Y-MYNYDD** and beyond, over the mountains to the next hostel at Tŷ'n-y-cornel (Feb to mid-Sept; ☎01222/222122), five miles from Dolgoch. Although the entire Llanwrtyd–Tregaron route is less than twenty miles in length, it takes a good hour to negotiate the twisting, narrow road safely. The old drovers, driving their cattle to Shrewsbury or Hereford, would have taken a good day or two over the same stretch.

Llandrindod Wells and around

If anything can sum up a town so succinctly, it is the plaque at **LLANDRINDOD WELLS** train station, commemorating the 1990 "Revictorianization of Llandrindod station". The town has not been slow to follow suit, peddling itself as Wales' most upmarket Victorian inland resort despite its one-time reputation for licentiousness. It was the railway that made Llandrindod, arriving in 1864 and bringing carriages full of well-to-do Victorians to the fledgling spa. Llandrindod blossomed, new hotels were built, neat parks were laid out and the town came to rival many of the more fashionable spas and resorts over the border. Even now, the town can seem like a salty breath of fresh air with its finer buildings swabbed and sandblasted, ornate cast-iron railings restored, and the spa brought back to some kind of life.

Llandrindod's Victorian opulence is still very much in evidence in the town's grandiose public buildings, especially the lavishly restored **spa pavilion** inside the pleasant **Rock Park**, with its trickling streams and well-manicured glens. EU regulations prohibit the use of the Llandrindod spa taps in the café inside, and if you're desperate to taste the waters, you'll have to settle for a chalybeate fountain outside that spouts the stuff. The architecture around the park entrance is Llandrindod at its most confidently Victorian, with elaborately carved terracotta frontages and expansive gabling. The **High Street** runs from here to the centre, containing antiques, books and junk shops. Behind the tourist office on Temple Street, you'll find the small town **Museum** (April–Sept daily except Wed 10am–12.30pm & 2–4.30pm; Oct–March Mon–Fri 10am–12.30pm & 2–4.30pm, Sat 10–12.30pm; free), where the exhibition is largely dedicated to excavated remains from the Roman fort at Castellcollen, a mile northwest of Llandrindod; kitsch Victoriana makes up the bulk of the rest of the collection, including a large group of dolls.

Buses pull in at the **train station** in the heart of town, between the High Street and Station Crescent. The **tourist office** is on Temple Street (April–Oct Mon–Fri 9am–6pm, Sat & Sun 10am–1pm & 2–6pm; Nov–March Mon–Fri 9am–1pm & 2–5pm; ☎01597/822600). **Bike rental** is from the *Greenstiles Bike Shed* (☎01597/824594), behind the station on the High Street. As the major tourist centre for the past 130 years in all of mid-Wales, Llandrindod is well served for **accommodation**. For something smart and reasonable close to the station, try *Greylands*, High St (☎01597/822253; ③), or nearby *Rhydithon*, Dyffryn Rd (☎01597/822624; ②). The *Kincoed Hotel*, Temple St (☎01597/822656; ③) is well appointed but not a patch on the *Metropole Hotel*, Temple St (☎01597/822881; ⑤), an elegant and large old spa hotel, the centrepiece of the town. It has a refined dining room, open to non-residents; but for more reasonably priced **eating**, head for *The Herb Garden*, Spa Rd, a welcoming veggie and whole-food restaurant, or the *Llanerch Inn*, Llanerch Lane, central Llandrindod's only **pub**, and an excel lent one at that – it's a cosy sixteenth-century inn that predates most of the surrounding town, with a solid menu of good-value, well-cooked classics.

North and East Radnorshire

Before the reorganization of British counties in 1974, Radnorshire was the most sparsely populated one in England and Wales, and it's still a remote area, especially in the north and east. In the northwest, **Rhayader** is the only settlement of any size, a gateway to the four interlocking reservoirs of the **Elan Valley** and the surrounding wild, spartan countryside of waterfalls, bogland and bare peaks. The countryside to the northeast of Rhayader is slightly tamer, and lanes and bridle paths delve in and around the woods and farms, occasionally brushing through minute settlements like the village of **Abbeycwmhir**, whose name is taken from the deserted Cistercian abbey that sits below in the dank, eerie valley of the Clywedog Brook. The hills roll eastwards towards the English border and some of the most intact parts of **Offa's Dyke** (see box overpage) by the handsome town of **Knighton**, perched right on the border.

Elan Valley and around

The poet Shelley spent his honeymoon in buildings now submerged by the waters of the **Elan Valley** reservoirs, a nine-mile-long string of four lakes built between 1892 and 1903 to supply water to the rapidly growing industrial city of Birmingham, 75 miles away. Although the lakes enhance an already beautiful and idyllic part of the world, the colonialist way in which Welsh valleys, villages and farmsteads were seized and flooded to provide water for England is something the tourist boards prefer to gloss over in favour of the wildlife, in particular the profusion of rare plants and birds – red kites especially.

From Rhayader, the B4518 heads southwest four miles to **ELAN** village, a curious collection of stone houses built in 1909 to replace the reservoir constructors' village that had grown up on the site. Just below the dam of the first reservoir, **Caban Coch**, the **Elan Valley Visitor Centre** (mid-March to Oct daily 10am–6pm; free), incorporates a tourist office (☎01597/810898), and a permanent exhibition stressing just how awful conditions were in nineteenth-century Birmingham, how rich the wildlife and flora around the lakes is and even how some of the water is now drunk in Wales. Frequent guided **walks** and even **Land Rover safaris** head off from the centre. From the visitor centre, a road tucks in along the bank of Caban Coch to the **Garreg Ddu** viaduct, where a road winds along the bank for four spectacular miles to the vast, rather chilling 1952 dam on **Claerwen Reservoir**. More remote and less popular than the Elan lakes, Claerwen is a good base for a **serious walk** from the far end of the dam across eight or so harsh but beautiful miles to the monastery of Strata Florida (p.631). Alternatively, the path that skirts around the northern shore of Claerwen leads across to the lonely **Teifi Pools**, glacial lakes from which the Teifi River springs.

Back at the Garreg Ddu viaduct, a more popular road continues north along the long, glassy finger of **Garreg Ddu** reservoir, before doubling back on itself just below the awesome **Pen-y-garreg** dam and reservoir; if the dam is overflowing, the vast wall of foaming water is mesmerizing. Situated just off the road, above the hairpin bend, is the friendly *Flickering Lamp* **hotel** (☎01597/810827; ③) and **restaurant**, which does good food. At the top of Pen-y-garreg lake, it's possible to drive over the final dam on the system, at **Craig Goch**; the most photographed of all the dams, thanks to its gracious curve, elegant Edwardian arches and neat little green cupola.

ABBEYCWMHIR (Abaty Cwm Hir) seven miles northeast of Rhayader, takes its name from the abbey whose sombre ruins lie behind the village. Cistercian monks founded the abbey in 1146, planning one of the largest churches in Britain, whose 242-foot nave has only ever been exceeded in length by the cathedrals of Durham, York and Winchester. Destruction by Henry III's troops in 1231 scuppered plans to continue the building, but the sparse ruins – a rocky outline of the floor plan – lie in a conifer-carpeted valley alongside a gloomy green lake, lending weight to the site's melancholic associations. Llywelyn ap Gruffydd's body was rumoured to have been buried here, and a new granite slab carved with a Celtic sword, lies on the altar to commemorate this last native prince of Wales.

Practicalities

If the very limited accommodation in the Elan Valley doesn't appeal, you may want to make use of **RHYADER** where buses stop opposite the **tourist office** (April–Oct daily 10am–6pm; Nov–March Fri & Sat 10am–5pm; ☎01597/810591). Eighteenth-century coaching inns still line the main streets, and there's more modern **accommodation** at the *Bryncoed* B&B on Dark Lane (☎01597/811082; ②), opposite the tourist office; the *Elan Hotel*, West St (☎01597/810373; ③); or *The Mount*, East St (☎01597/810585; ②), a friendly B&B and the base for *Clive Powell Mountain Bikes*, from whom you can either rent **bikes** or join one of his organized trips around the tracks of mid-Wales. There's a municipal **campsite** (☎01597/810183) at Wyeside, north of the town off the A44.

Knighton

A town that straddles King Offa's eighth-century border as well as the modern Wales–England divide, **KNIGHTON** (Tref-y-clawdd, "the town on the dyke") has come into its own as the most obvious centre for those walking the **Offa's Dyke Path**. Located almost exactly halfway along the route, Knighton, although without any specific sights, is a lively, attractive place that easily warrants a stop-off. So close is Knighton to the border that the town's **train station** and its accompanying hotel (ironically called *Central Wales)* are actually in England. From here, Station Road crosses the River Teme into Wales and climbs a couple of hundred yards to Brookside Square. Further up the hill is the town's Victorian alpine-looking clock tower, where Broad Street becomes West Street and the steep High Street soars off up to the left, past rickety Tudor buildings and up to the mound of the old **castle**.

In West Street, the excellent **Offa's Dyke Centre** also houses the **tourist office** (April–Oct daily 9am–5.30pm; Nov, Feb & March Mon–Fri 9am–5pm, Sat & Sun 10am–3.30pm; Dec & Jan closed Sat & Sun; ☎01547/528753). **Accommodation** is plentiful:

OFFA'S DYKE

George Borrow, in his classic *Wild Wales*, notes that once "it was customary for the English to cut off the ears of every Welshman who was found to the east of the dyke, and for the Welsh to hang every Englishman whom they found to the west of it". Certainly, **Offa's Dyke** has provided a potent symbol of Welsh–English antipathy ever since it was created in the eighth century as a demarcation line by King Offa of Mercia, ruler of central England.

The earthwork – up to 20ft high and 60ft wide – made use of natural boundaries like rivers in its run north to south, and is best seen in the sections near Knighton. Today's England–Wales border crosses the dyke many times, although the basic boundary has changed little since Offa's day. The glorious **long-distance footpath**, opened in 1971, runs from Prestatyn in the north for 177 miles to Chepstow (see p.567), and is one of the most rewarding walks in Britain. The path is maintained by the *Offa's Dyke Association*, whose headquarters are in the Offa's Dyke centre in Knighton (see above).

there's *Fleece House*, Market St (☎01547/520168; ③), the basic but cheerful *Red Lion* on West Street (☎01547/528231; ②) and the *Plough Hotel* on Market Street (☎01547/528041; ③), which also has a **backpacker's caravan** for overnight stays in dorm-style accommodation. For **eating and drinking**, it's hard to beat the comfortable *Horse and Jockey* at the town end of Station Road, though there's folk and jazz in the *Plough*.

Montgomeryshire

The northern part of Powys is made up of the old county of **Montgomeryshire** (Maldwyn), an area of enormously varying landscapes and few inhabitants. The best base for the spartan and mountainous southwest of the county is the solid little town of **Llanidloes**, less than ten miles north of Rhayader, a base for ageing hippies on the River Severn (Afon Hafren). Gentle, green contours characterize the east of the county, where the muted old county town of **Montgomery**, with its fine Georgian architecture, perches above the border and Offa's Dyke. The Severn runs a few miles to the west, near the impeccable village of **Berriew**, home of the bizarre **Andrew Logan Museum of Sculpture**. In the north of the county, **Welshpool** forms the only major settlement, packed in above the wide flood plain of the Severn. An excellent local museum, the impossibly cute toy rail line that runs to **Llanfair Caereinion**, good pubs and reasonable hotels make the town a fair stop for a day or two. On the southern side of Welshpool is Montgomeryshire's one unmissable sight, the sumptuous **Powis Castle** and its exquisite terraced gardens. The very north of the county is pastoral, deserted and beautiful. The few visitors that there are throng **Lake Vyrnwy** and make their way down the dead-end lane to the **Pistyll Rhaedr** waterfall.

Llanidloes and around

Thriving when so many other small market towns seem in danger of atrophying, the secret of success for **LLANIDLOES** seems to be in its adaptability, from rural village to weaving town and, latterly, a centre for artists, craftsfolk and assorted alternative life-stylers. One of mid-Wales' prettiest towns, the four main streets meet at the black and white **market hall**, built on timber stilts in 1600, allowing the market to take place on the cobbles beneath. The market has long since moved, as has the town's wonderfully eclectic **museum** that is in the tourist office (Easter–Sept daily 11am–5pm; Oct–Easter Tues–Sat 11am–5pm). Off Longbridge Street is Church Street, which opens out into a yard surrounding the dumpy parish **church of St Idloes**, whose impressive fifteenth-century hammerbeam roof is said to have been poached from Abbeycwmhir.

From the market hall, the broad, architecturally unified Great Oak Street heads west to the **Town Hall**, home of the tourist office, originally built as a temperance hotel to challenge the boozy **Trewythen Arms** opposite. A plaque on the hotel commemorates Llanidloes as an unlikely-seeming place of industrial and political unrest, when, in April 1839 Chartists stormed the hotel, dragging out and beating up special constables who had been despatched to the town as a futile attempt to suppress the political fervour for change amongst the town's flannel weavers.

China Street curves down to the car park from where all **bus** services operate. The **tourist office** (daily 9.30am–5pm; Oct–Easter closed Sun; ☎01686/412605), One alternative happening worth investigating is the annual **Fancy Dress Night**, on the first Friday of July, when the pubs open late, the streets are cordoned off and, apparently, virtually the whole town gets kitted out. **Accommodation** spans the *Red Lion Hotel*, Longbridge St (☎01686/412270; ④), the genteel *Unicorn*, also on Longbridge Street (☎01686/413167; ③), and for B&B, the *Severn View*, China St (☎01686/412 207; ②). There's B&B and **camping** at *Esgair-maen farmhouse* (☎0155 16/272; ②), a couple of miles north near the old mines at Y Fan. Among the many options for **food**, there's the *Piccola Italia* pizzeria on the Llangurig road, the cheap and hearty *Traveller's Rest* on Longbridge Street or, for a bit of a treat, the *Orchard House* on China Street (☎01686/413700). The lively *Red Lion* **pub** on Longbridge Street does good food.

Montgomery and around

Tiny **MONTGOMERY** (Trefaldwyn), at the base of a **castle** on the Welsh side of Offa's Dyke, is Montgomeryshire at its most anglicized. From the castle mound there are wonderful views over the lofty church tower and the handsome Georgian streets, notably the impressively symmetrical main street – well-named Broad Street – which swoops up to the perfect little redbrick **Town Hall**, crowned by a pert clock tower. The rebuilt tower of Montgomery's parish **Church of St Nicholas** dominates the snug proportions of the buildings around it. Largely thirteenth-century, the highlights of its spacious interior include the 1600 monument to local landowner, Sir Richard Herbert, and his wife whose eight children have been carved in beatific kneeling positions behind them; and the elaborately carved double screen and accompanying loft.

Montgomery is near one of the best-preserved sections of **Offa's Dyke**, which the long distance footpath shadows either side of the B4386 a mile east of the town. Ditches almost twenty feet high give one of the best indications of the dyke's original look and, to the south of the main road, the England–Wales border still exactly splices the dyke, twelve hundred years after it was built. If you want to **stay** here, *Little Brompton Farm*, (☎01686/668371; ③), two miles north on the B4385, is handily close to the Offa's Dyke Path. For **food** and **drink** there's *Chequers*, on Broad Street.

Berriew

North of Montgomery, just five miles southwest of Welshpool, the neat village of **BERRIEW** is more redolent of the black and white settlements over the English border than anywhere in Wales, its Tudor houses grouped picturesquely around a small church, the shallow waters of the Rhiw River and the slightly twee *Lion Hotel* (☎01686/640452; ④). Just over the river bridge, the **Andrew Logan Museum of Sculpture** (May–Sept Wed–Sun noon–6pm; £2) makes for an incongruous attraction in such a setting, with a good selection of the notable British modern sculptor's work. Andrew Logan is the man who inaugurated the great drag-and-grunge ball known as the *Alternative Miss World Contest* in the 1970s, launch pad of the formidable Divine's career, from which astounding costumes and memorabilia form a large chunk of the exhibits at the museum. There's also Logan's oversized horticultural sculpture, including giant lilies encrusted with shattered mirrors and vast metal irises that rise to scrape the roof, as well as his smaller-scale jewellery and model goddesses that only add to the sublime camp of the exhibition.

Welshpool

Three miles from the English border, eastern Montgomeryshire's chief town of **WELSHPOOL** (Y Trallwng) was formerly known as just Pool, its prefix added in 1835 to distinguish it from the English seaside town of Poole in Dorset. It's not a very Welsh place, lying in the anglicized valley of the River Severn (Afon Hafren), and with a history that depended largely upon the patronage of English landlords and kings, but it has a number of Tudor and many good Georgian and Victorian buildings, and neighbours the sumptuous **Powis Castle** (see below).

Along Severn Street from the **train station**, a hump-backed bridge over the much restored **Montgomery Canal** hides the canal **wharf**, from where gaudily painted boats will chug you up the navigable section for a few miles and a couple of hours (☎01938/

553271); and a carefully restored warehouse containing the **Powysland Museum** (Mon, Tues, Thurs & Fri 11am–1pm & 2–5pm, Sat & Sun 2–5pm; May–Sept also Sat & Sun 10am–1pm; free). The impressive local history collection has a display about the impact of the Black Death here, when half the town's population died, and Roman remains from the now obliterated local Cistercian abbey of Strata Marcella.

From the **Royal Oak Hotel**, at the centre of town, follow Broad Street which changes name five times as it rises up the hill towards the tiny Raven Square terminus station of the **Welshpool and Llanfair Light Railway**. The eight-mile narrow gauge rail line (April–Sept daily 10am–4pm; ☎01938/810441) was open for less than thirty years to passengers until its closure in 1931, but now scaled-down engines once more chuff their way along to the almost eerily quiet village of **LLANFAIR CAEREINION**, a good daytime base for walks and pub food at the *Goat Hotel*. The post office, opposite the church, stocks free leaflets of some good local circular walks.

Powis Castle

In a land of ruined castles, the sheer scale and beauty of **Powis Castle** (April–June, Sept & Oct Wed–Sun 11am–5pm; July & Aug Tues–Sun 11am–5pm; gardens and museum £4; castle, gardens and museum £6; NT), a mile from Welshpool up Park Lane, is reason enough for coming to the town. On the site of an earlier Norman fort, the castle was started in the reign of Edward I by the Gwenwynwyn family; to qualify for the site and the barony of De la Pole, they had to renounce all claims to Welsh princedom. In 1587, Sir Edward Herbert bought the castle and began to transform it into the Elizabethan palace we see today. Inside, the **Clive Museum** – named after Edward Clive, son of Clive of India, who married into the family in 1784 – forms a lively account of the British in India, through diaries, letters, paintings, tapestries, weapons and jewels, although it is the sumptuous period rooms that impress most, from the vast and kitsch frescoes by Lanscroon above the balustraded staircase to the mahogany bed, brass and enamel toilets and decorative wall hangings of the state bedroom. The elegant Long Gallery has a rich sixteenth-century plasterwork ceiling overlooking winsome busts and marble statuettes of the four elements, placed in between the glowering family portraits. The **gardens**, designed by Welsh architect William Winde, are spectacular. Dropping down from the castle in four huge stepped terraces, the design has barely changed since the seventeenth century, with a charmingly precise orangery and topiary that looks as if it is shaved daily. Summertime outdoor concerts, frequently with firework finales, take place in the gardens.

Practicalities

The pompous neo-Gothic turrets of the old Victorian **train station**, behind which its less appealing modern counterpart sits, is at the top of Severn Street, which leads down into the town centre. The **tourist office** is at the northern edge of the town in the *Flash Leisure Centre*, on Salop Road (daily 9.30am–5.30pm; ☎01938/552043), twenty minutes' walk from the central town crossroads. There is plenty of B&B **accommodation** in town, with a dozen or so along the Salop Road between the town centre and the *Flash Centre*; of them all, Mrs Kaye's *Montgomery House* (☎01938/552693; ②) is the surest bet. Other places include *Severn Farm* on Leighton Road (☎01938/553098; ③), just beyond the Industrial Estate to the east of the station, which will also let you pitch a tent; and *Dysserth Hall* (☎01938/552153; ③), opposite Powis Castle along a small lane running off Berriew Road. Welshpool's four main streets are home to most of the town's **eating** and **drinking** establishments. Many of the town's pubs do lunchtime food with some, notably the *Talbot* on the High Street, serving excellent evening meals as well. Cheap and filling breakfasts, lunches and teas are served in the *Buttery*, opposite the town hall on the High Street.

Llanfyllin and around

The hills and plains of northern Montgomeryshire conceal a maze of deserted lanes and farm outposts along the contours that swell up towards the north and the foothills of the Berwyn Mountains. The only real settlement of any size is **LLANFYLLIN**, a peaceful but friendly hillside town with a Thursday market, ten miles northwest of Welshpool, that's the best-equipped place in the area to **stay**. Try the old coaching inn, the *Cain Valley* on the main High Street (☎01691/648366; ③), or *The Chestnuts* B&B, High St (☎01691/648179; ②). Just west of the town is the splendid *Bodfach Hall* (Easter–Sept; ☎01691/648272; ④), set in luscious grounds. There's an excellent **restaurant** on the High Street, *Seeds* (☎01691/648604), which does a wonderful three-course set dinner menu.

Llanrhaeadr-ym-mochnant and Pistyll Rhaeadr

For a place so near the English border, **LLANRHAEADR-YM-MOCHNANT** is surprisingly Welsh in its language and appearance. The small, low-roofed village, six miles north of Llanfyllin, is best remembered as the serving parish of Bishop William Morgan, who translated the Bible into Welsh in 1588. The village has two great **pubs** – the *Three Tuns* and *Wynnstay Arms* – as well as an excellent **B&B** at *Plas-y-Llan* (☎01691/780236; ③). Llanrhaeadr lies at the foot of a lane which courses northwest alongside the Rhaeadr River, through an increasingly rocky valley for four miles to **Pistyll Rhaeadr**, Wales' highest waterfall at 150ft. The river tumbles down the crags in two stages, flowing furiously under a natural stone arch that has been christened the Fairy Bridge. When it's quiet, tame chaffinches swoop and settle all around this enchanting spot, although, with the added attraction of a tacky tea room, the charms are a little hard to appreciate amid the tourists on a warm summer Sunday.

Lake Vyrnwy

A monument to the self-aggrandizement of the Victorian age, **Lake Vyrnwy** (Llyn Efyrnwy) combines its functional role as a water supply for Liverpool with a touch of architectural genius, in the shape of the huge nineteenth-century dam at its southern end and the Disneyesque turreted straining tower which edges out into the icy waters. It's a magnificent spot, and a popular centre for walking and birdwatching, with nature trails. The village of Llanwddyn was flattened and rebuilt at the eastern end, people receiving compensation of just £5 for losing their homes. The story is told, somewhat apologetically, in the **Vyrnwy Visitor Centre** (April–Sept daily 11am–6pm; Oct–March Sat & Sun 11am–6pm), which combines with the **tourist office** (same times; ☎01691/870346) and a Royal Society for the Protection of Birds centre, in the cluster of buildings on the western side of the dam. **Bike rental** is available from *Mandy's Tea Shop*, next door.

If you want to **stay** near the lake, there's the grand *Lake Vyrnwy Hotel* (☎0169 173/692; ⑤), overlooking the waters above the southeastern shore. It's a mite pricey, but if you just want a look, it serves a full afternoon tea in a chintzy lounge overlooking the lake, while *The Tavern*, part of the hotel, does excellent bar meals, as well as being the local pub for the area. You'll find cheaper B&B at *Tyn-y-maes* (☎01691/870216; ③), a couple of miles east of the new village of Llanwddyn on the B4393.

travel details

Trains

Knighton to: Llandovery (4 daily; 1hr 40min); Llandrindod Wells (6 daily; 40min).

Llandrindod Wells to: Knighton (6 daily; 40min); Llanwrtyd Wells (4 daily; 30min); Swansea (4 daily; 2hr 20min).

Welshpool to: Aberystwyth (6 daily; 1hr 30min); Shrewsbury (8 daily; 30min).

Buses

Brecon to: Aberdulais (3 daily; 1hr 5min); Abergavenny (6 daily; 55min); 40min); Dan-yr-ogof (4 daily; 30min); Crickhowell (6 daily Mon–Sat; 25min); Hay-on-Wye (6 daily Mon–Sat; 45min); Llandrindod Wells (3 daily Mon–Sat; 1hr); Swansea (5 daily; 1hr 25min).

Knighton to: Ludlow (5 daily Mon–Sat; 45min); Newtown (3 on Tues & Thurs; 1hr).

Llandrindod Wells to: Abbeycwmhir (1 postbus daily Mon–Fri; 2hr); Aberystwyth (1 on Tues, Thurs & Sat; 1hr 45min); Brecon (3 daily Mon–Sat; 1hr); Elan Village (1 postbus daily Mon–Fri; 35min); Hay-on-Wye (1 daily Mon–Sat; 1hr 10min).

Llanfyllin to: Llanwddyn for Lake Vyrnwy (school bus; 20min); Oswestry (4 daily Mon–Sat; 45min).

Llanidloes to: Aberystwyth (1 daily; 1hr 20min); Welshpool (5 daily Mon–Sat; 1hr 15min).

Llanwrtyd Wells to: Abergwesyn (postbus Mon–Sat; 15min).

Shrewsbury (Shropshire) to: Llanidloes (4 daily Mon–Sat; 2hr); Montgomery (3 daily Mon–Sat; 50min); Welshpool (7 daily; 45min).

Welshpool to: Berriew (7 daily Mon–Sat; 15min); Llanidloes (3 daily Mon–Sat; 1hr 15min); Montgomery (school bus; 25min).

CHAPTER FOURTEEN

THE CAMBRIAN COAST

C ardigan Bay (Bae Ceredigion) takes a huge bite out of the west Wales coast, leaving behind the Pembrokeshire peninsula in the south and the Llŷn peninsula in the north. Between them lies the **Cambrian Coast**, a loosely defined mountain-backed strip stretching from Cardigan in the south to Pwllheli in the north. Before the railway, the Cambrian coast was isolated from the rest of Wales, the Cambrian Mountains presenting an awkward barrier only breached by narrow passes – cattle-droving routes to the markets in England. Today large sand-fringed sections are peppered with low-key coastal resorts packed in summer with English Midland families, although the presence of English-dominated resorts can still create local antipathy in this staunchly nationalistic part of the country.

The Cardigan coast starts where the rugged seashore of Pembrokeshire ends, continuing in much the same vein of great cliffs, isolated beaches and swirling seabirds around the spirited former county town of **Cardigan**. The coast breaks at some popular seaside resorts and the robust and cosmopolitan "capital" of mid-Wales, **Aberystwyth**. Inland, the best sights are grouped around two river valleys: the lush and quiet **Teifi** and the dramatic ravines around the **Rheidol**. Along the Teifi, which flows out into the sea at Cardigan, the best base is **Lampeter**, home also of a branch of the University of Wales. The Rheidol is great walking country, accessed on the narrow-gauge railway that climbs out of Aberystwyth to the popular tourist honey pot of **Devil's Bridge**, where three bridges, one on top of the other, span a turbulent chasm of waterfalls. **Machynlleth** lies to the north, a magical place, the seat of Owain Glyndŵr's putative fifteenth-century Welsh parliament and still a thriving market centre and base for the **Centre for Alternative Technology**, an impressive showpiece for community living and renewable energy resources.

Due north from **Machynlleth**, the southern reaches of **Snowdonia National Park** are dominated by the mountain massif of **Cadair Idris**, its southern crag-fringed faces best explored on the narrow-gauge Talyllyn railway. Cadair Idris' northern flank slopes down to the scenic Mawddach Estuary flanked by the market town of **Dolgellau** and the likeable resort of **Barmouth**. High on its rocky promontory stands the castle at **Harlech**, the southernmost link in Edward I's chain of thirteenth-century castles, overlooking the coast as it sweeps north to the Italianate dream village of **Portmeirion** and the coastal terminus of the wonderful Ffestiniog railway at **Porthmadog**, before turning west along the Llŷn. The Welsh castle at **Criccieth** and the museum devoted to Lloyd George a couple of miles away are the only reasons to pause before Wales ends in a flourish of small coves around **Abersoch** and **Aberdaron**.

Cardigan and around

An ancient borough and fomer port at the lowest bridging point of the Teifi Estuary, **CARDIGAN** (Aberteifi) was founded by the Norman lord Roger de Montgomery around its castle in 1093. From the castle mound by the bridge, Bridge Street sweeps through High Street to the turreted oddity of the **Guildhall**, with the Welsh flag skewered adamantly to its grey frontage. Through the Guildhall courtyard is the town's **covered market**, a typically eclectic mix of fresh food, local craft and secondhand

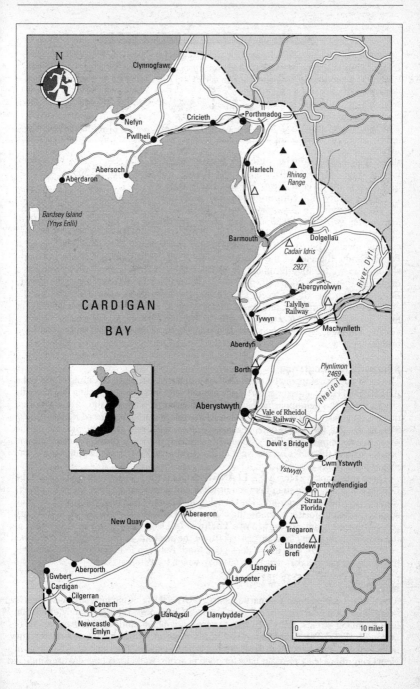

stalls. The helpful **tourist office** (Easter fortnight & May–Sept daily 10am–6pm; Easter–May Mon–Sat 10am–5pm; Oct–Easter Mon–Sat 10am–5.30pm; ☎01239/613230) is in the foyer of *Theatr Mwldan*, Bath House Rd.

There's plenty of **accommodation**, with numerous B&Bs along the Gwbert Road, off North Road: the *Brynhyfryd* (☎01239/612861; ②), at the town end, and the *Maes-a-Mor* (☎01239/614929; ②), just up in Park Place, are the best. On the High Street, the old-fashioned *Black Lion* pub (☎01239/612532; ③) does good B&B and evening meals. There's a YHA **youth hostel** (☎01239/612936), four miles away at Poppit Sands, the end of the Pembrokeshire Coast Path. Summer buses go there, although in winter they terminate at St Dogmaels, two miles short. For **eating** and **drinking**, there are a couple of wholefood cafés in Black Lion Mews, a lane behind the *Black Lion* on the High Street. The *Theatr Mwldan* café is open daily and for the evenings of performances, and has a cheap range of local dishes and specialities. For more substantial food, *Jackets*, 58 North Rd (☎01239/615206), serve pizzas, potatoes, kebabs and pies. The best pub food is at the *Eagle*, at the southern end of the town bridge.

Aberporth to Llangranog

The most popular stopping-off point on the stretch of coast north of Cardigan has to be **ABERPORTH**, an elderly resort built around two less than appealing bays, easily shown up by the neighbouring hamlet of **TRE-SAITH**, a mile to the east, staggering down a tiny valley to the compact beach. Here, the non-smoking *Iscoed* B&B(☎01239/810030; ②) and the wholesome, seafood *Skippers* restaurant (☎01239/810113) on the shore are recommended. Every Sunday in summer, there are **dinghy races** from the beach. Around the rocks on the right of the beach, the River Saith plummets over the mossy black rocks in a waterfall.

Three miles north of the A487, **LLANGRANOG** is the most attractive village on the Ceredigion coast, wedged in between bracken and gorse-beaten hills, the main streets winding to the tiny seafront. The beach can become horribly congested in midsummer, when it's better to follow the cliff path to **Cilborth Beach**, and on to the glorious NT-owned headland, up to **Ynys Lochtyn**. In Llangranog, you can **stay** either at the excellent *Ship Inn* (☎01239/654423; ③) on the seafront, or the earthier *Pentre Arms* (☎01239/654345; ②), which also does good **food**. Between Penbryn and Llangranog is the *Maesglas* caravan park (☎01239/654268), which takes tents.

New Quay

Along with Laugharne in Carmarthenshire, **NEW QUAY** (Cei Newydd) lays claim to being the original Llareggub in Dylan Thomas' *Under Milk Wood*. Certainly, it has the little tumbling streets, prim Victorian terraces, a cobbled stone harbour and an air of dreamy isolation that Thomas invoked in his play but, in the height of summer, the quiet isolation can be hard to find. Although there is a singular lack of excitement in New Quay, it is a truly pleasant base for good beaches, walking, eating and drinking.

Buses arrive at Uplands Square from where it's a walk down any of the steep streets to the pretty **harbour** and a small curving beach backed by a higgledy-piggledy line of multi-coloured shops and houses. The beachfront streets comprise the **lower town**, the more traditionally seaside part of New Quay, full of cafés, pubs and beach shops. Acutely inclined streets lead to the upper town, more residential and with some delightful views over the sweeping shoreline below. By the fork is the **tourist office** (April–Sept daily 10am–6pm; ☎01545/560865). The northern beach soon gives way to a rocky headland, **New Quay Head**, where an invigorating path steers along the top of the sheer drops to the aptly named **Bird Rock**.

Accommodation includes cheap B&Bs at *Elvor* on George Street (☎01545/560554; ②), the main road to Llanarth, in the upper town; *The Moorings* on Glanmor Terrace (☎01545/560375; ②); and the wonderful *Seahorse Inn* on Margaret Street (☎01545/560736; ③), a little further into town. There's a **campsite** a mile down the B4342 at *Wern Mill* (☎01545/580699), just outside the grim village of **Gilfachreda**. New Quay contains innumerable cheap, stodgy **cafés**, and the *Mariner's Café*, by the harbour wall, is a sure bet. Most of the **pubs** serve food, the best being the *Black Lion*, tucked up above the harbour and a regular haunt of folk and traditional music.

Aberaeron

ABERAERON, six miles down the coast, seems marginally more exciting than New Quay but is almost unique amongst the Ceredigion resorts for being on an unappealing stretch of coastline. Nonetheless, the town, with its pastel-shaded houses encasing a large harbour inlet, has a rare unity of design, the result of a complete nineteenth-century rebuilding by the Reverend Alban Gwynne. He spent his way through his wife's inheritance by dredging the Aeron Estuary and constructing a formally planned town around it as a new port for mid-Wales.

The A487 runs straight through the heart of Aberaeron, down Bridge Street and past the large **Alban Square**, named after the rich rector. On the north side of the town bridge, the grid of streets stretches down to a neat line of ordered, colourful houses on the seafront. Right on the harbour, the **Hive on the Quay** (summer daily 9am–5.30pm; winter closed Sun; ☎01545/570445) combines an exhibition of bees with chances to sample honey products, including delicious ice cream. Quay Parade runs down the side of the seafront past some of the old fisherman's houses and pubs to the fairly interesting **Sea Aquarium** (Easter–Oct 11am–5pm; £3) and the **tourist office** (Easter, Whitsun & July–Sept daily 10am–6pm; Oct–Easter Mon–Sat 10am–5pm; ☎01545/570602).

For **accommodation**, there are town-centre B&Bs at the genteel *Pier Cottage* on Ship Street (☎01545/570132; ③), near the tourist office, and, overlooking the harbour, *Fairview* on Cadwgan Place (☎01545/571472; ②). Along the northern shore, there's a **campsite** at the *Aeron Coast Caravan Park* (☎01545/570349), reached by car off North Road. For **food**, the *Siop Te* on Cadwgan Place is a good all-round day and early-evening café, or there's good pub food at the *Feathers Royal*, on Alban Square.

The Teifi Valley

The Teifi is one of Wales' most eulogized rivers – for its rich spawn of fresh fish, its meandering rural charm and the coracles that were a regular feature from pre-Roman times – and flows through some gloriously green and undulating countryside to its estuary at Cardigan. It passes the massive ramparts of **Cilgerran Castle**, and winds its way over the falls at **Cenarth**, before flowing around three sides of another fortress at **Newcastle Emlyn**, and also takes in the proudly Cymric university town of **Lampeter**. The river's infancy can be seen near the ruins of **Strata Florida Abbey**, beyond which the river emerges from the dark and remote **Teifi Pools**.

Cilgerran Castle

Just a couple of miles up the Teifi River from Cardigan, the attractive village of **CILGERRAN** clusters around its wide main street. Behind are the massive ramparts of the **Castle** (April–Oct daily 9.30am–6pm; Nov–March Mon–Sat 9.30am–4pm, Sun 2–4pm; if closed, get the key from the adjoining Castle House; £1.70; CADW), founded in 1100 at a commanding vantage point on a high wooded bluff above the river, then still navigable for sea-going ships. This is the legendary site of the 1109 abduction of Nest (the "Welsh Helen of Troy") by a love-struck Prince Owain of Powys. Her husband, Gerald of Pembroke, escaped by slithering down a toilet waste chute through the castle walls. The massive dual-entry towers still dominate the castle, and the outer walls, some four feet thicker than those facing the inner courtyard, are traced by deleriously high walkways. The outer ward, over which a modern path now runs from the entrance, is a good example of the keepless castle evolving throughout the thirteenth century. Another ditch and drawbridge pit protect the inner ward underneath the two entry towers. The views over the forested valley towards the pink and grey Georgian fantasy castle of **Coedmore**, on the opposite bank, are inspiring.

A footpath runs down from the castle to the river's edge and the River Teifi **information centre** (April–Sept daily 10am–5pm). Display boards tell the story of the emigrants to America, for whom Cardigan was the last sight of home, and the history of the Teifi valley industries, particularly quarrying, brick making and coracle fishing.

Cenarth and Newcastle Emlyn

A tourist magnet since it was swooped on by nineteenth-century Romantics and artists, **CENARTH**, five miles east of Cilgerran, is a pleasant spot, but hardly merits the mass interest that it receives. The village's main asset, its **waterfalls**, are close to the main road, ideal for lazy visitors. The path to the falls runs from opposite the *White Hart* pub and past the **National Coracle Centre** (Easter–Oct daily except Sat 10.30am–5.30pm; £1.50), a small museum with displays of original coracles from all over the world, before continuing to a restored seventeenth-century flour mill by the falls' edge.

An ancient farming and droving centre, **NEWCASTLE EMLYN**, four miles beyond, is the only town of any size nearby, but warrants little attention. Only a few stone stacks and an archway survive of the "new" castle, but there is a **tourist office** (Easter–Oct daily 10am–6pm; ☎01239/711333) located in the miniature town hall on Bridge Street and **accommodation** at the *Plough* on Emlyn Square (☎01239/710994; ②).

The area's prolific past as a weaving centre is best seen at the **Museum of the Welsh Woollen Industry** (April–Sept Mon–Sat 10am–5pm; Oct–March closed Sat; £2), in the village of **DRE-FACH FELINDRE**, five miles southeast, which once had 43 working mills.

Lampeter

Eighteen miles from Newcastle Emlyn, **LAMPETER** (Llanbedr Pont Steffan) is the home of possibly the most remote university in Britain. The St David's University College, now a constituent of the University of Wales, was the country's first university college, founded in 1822 by the Bishop of St David's to aid Welsh students who couldn't afford the trip to England to receive a full education. With a healthy student population together with large numbers of resident hippies, the small town is well geared up for young people and visitors.

There's not a great deal to see in Lampeter, and what you are able to visit is fairly low-key. **Harford Square** forms the hub of the town around the corner from **Y Galeri**, a showcase for local artists' work, at the back of the *Mulberry Bush* health-food shop at 2 Bridge St, which has a good bulletin board. The main buildings of the **University College** lie off College Street, and include a quadrangle modelled on an Oxbridge college and the motte of Lampeter's long-vanished castle looking incongruous amidst such order. The **High Street** is the most architecturally distinguished part of town, its eighteenth-century coaching inn, the *Black Lion*, dominating the streetscape; you can see its old stables and coach house through an archway.

There is a **tourist office** (Mon–Thurs 9am–1pm & 1.45–4.30pm) of sorts in the Town Hall. *Haul Fan*, 6 Station Terrace, behind University College (☎01570/422718; ②) is the best **B&B**, and there's the *Black Lion* on the High Street (☎01570/422172; ④). The nearest **campsite** is five miles northeast at *Moorlands*, near Llangybi (☎01570/493543). Just off the B4343, running up the Teifi valley towards Llanddewi Brefi, is one of the area's best farmhouse B&Bs at *Pentre Farm* (☎01570/493313; ③), near Llanfair Clydogau, five miles from Lampeter. There are plenty of fine places to **eat** in town. *Peppers*, 14 High St, does a wonderful Welsh vegetarian lunch menu, while *Lloyds* is an upmarket fish-and-chip shop and restaurant in Bridge Street. *Cottage Garden* restaurant, opposite the University on College Street, is cheap and popular with students, as is the *King's Arms* on Bridge Street, a small stone pub with well-kept beer.

Strata Florida Abbey

Twenty miles northeast of Lampeter, the mighty **Strata Florida Abbey** (April–Sept 9.30am–6.30pm; £1.75; CADW; Oct–April open all times) dominates the bucolic *Ystrad Fflur*, the valley of the flowers. This Cistercian abbey was founded in 1164, swiftly growing into a centre for milling, farming and weaving, and becoming an important political centre for Wales. In 1238, Llywelyn the Great, whose conquering exploits throughout the rest of Wales had brought him to the peak of the Welsh feudal pyramid, summoned the lesser Welsh princes here. He was near death, and worried that his work of unifying Wales under one ruler would disintegrate, so he commanded the assembled princes to pay homage not just to him but also to his son, Dafydd, so sealing the succession. The church here was vast – larger than the cathedral at St David's and, although very little survived Henry VIII's Dissolution of the monasteries, the huge Norman west doorway gives some idea of its dimensions. Fragments of one-time side chapels include beautifully tiled medieval floors, and there's also a serene cemetery, but it's really the abbey's position that impresses most, in glorious rural solitude amongst wide open skies and fringed with a scoop of sheep-spattered hills. A sinewy yew tree reputedly shades the spot where Dafydd ap Gwilym, fourteenth-century bard and contemporary of Chaucer, is buried.

Aberystwyth and around

The liveliest seaside resort in Wales, **ABERYSTWYTH** is an essential stop along the Ceredigion coast and, rooted in all aspects of Welsh culture, is possibly the most enjoyable and relaxed place to gain an insight into the nation's psyche. It is the capital of sparsely populated mid-Wales, and with one of the most prestigious colleges of the University of Wales in the town, there are plenty of cultural and entertainment diversions here, as well as an array of Victorian and Edwardian seaside trappings. The *Cymdeithas yr Iaith* (Welsh Language Society) was founded in 1963 and is still located here, and the National Library was begun here in 1907. It was no surprise that, after decades of Liberal domination, this constituency finally plumped for a Plaid Cymru MP in the 1992 election, thus turning the whole west coast – from Anglesey to the bottom of Cardigan Bay – Plaid green on the political map.

The Town

With two long, gentle bays curving around between two rocky heads, Aberystwyth's position is hard to beat. **Constitution Hill** (430ft), at the north end of the long Promenade, rises sharply away from the rocky beach. It is a favourite jaunt, crowned

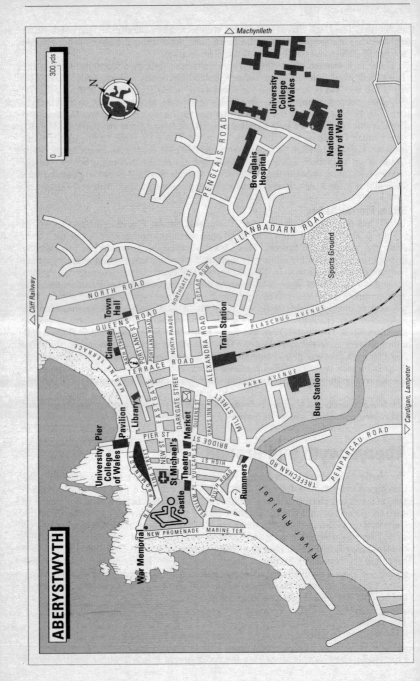

with a tatty jumble of amenities – café, picnic area, telescopes and an octagonal **camera obscura** (Easter–Oct daily 10am–5.30pm; free) – reached on foot or by the clanking 1896 **cliff railway** (Easter–Oct daily 10am–6pm; 50p) from the grand terminus building at the top of Queen Street, behind the Promenade. South along the **Promenade** – officially Marine Terrace – the **Ceredigion Museum** (Easter–June, Sept & Oct Mon–Sat 10am–6pm; July & Aug daily 10am–6pm; Nov–Easter Mon–Sat 10am–5pm; free), houses cosy reconstructed cottages, dairies and a nineteenth-century pharmacy in the atmospherically ornate Edwardian *Coliseum* music hall.

Marine Terrace continues past the spindly **pier**, to the John Nash-designed 1790 **villa**, later converted to a hotel to soak up the anticipated masses arriving on the new rail line, but when the venture failed, the building was sold to the fledgling university, which is still here. The Promenade cuts around the front of the building to the ruins of Edward I's thirteenth-century **Castle** (free access), notable more for its breezy position than for the buildings themselves. Penglais Road climbs the hill northwards towards the **University**'s main campus, and the **National Library of Wales** (Mon–Fri 9.30am–6pm, Sat 9.30am–5pm; free) with excellent temporary exhibitions and **A Nation's Heritage**, giving a well-rounded introduction to the history of the written word and printing in Wales, shown in the absorbing range of old texts, maps, photos, and the first Bible in Welsh from 1588.

Practicalities

Aberystwyth's BR and Vale of Rheidol **train stations** are adjacent on Alexandra Road, a ten-minute walk from the seafront on the southern side of the town centre. **Local buses** stop outside the station, with **long-distance** ones using the bus depot around the corner on Park Avenue. The busy **tourist office** (daily June–Aug 10am–6pm; Sept–May 10am–5pm; ☎01970/612125) is a ten-minute stroll from the station, straight down Terrace Road towards the seafront. *Red Dragon*, Llanbadarn Rd, just up from the *Y Cŵps* pub (☎01970/880397) does **bike rental**.

Aberystwyth has hundreds of **places to stay**, so beds are generally easy to find, mostly in the streets around the station and along South Marine Terrace, where you'll find *Yr Hafod*, at no. 1 (☎01970/617579; ②). The intimate *Sinclair* guest house, 43 Portland St (☎01970/615158; ③) is another good choice. *Four Seasons*, 50–54 Parkland St (☎01970/612120; ④) is an upmarket Victorian town house behind the seafront. **B&B** is available during the student vacations on the Penglais site of the *University College of Wales*, Penglais (☎01970/623757; ②) and also down by the seafront. The best of the local caravan parks is *Glan-y-mor Leisure Park* (☎01970/828900), in Clarach Bay, on the other side of Constitution Hill.

Aberystwyth's cultural and gastronomic life is an ebullient, all-year-round affair, thriving on students in term-time, visitors in the summer. *Gannets Bistro*, 7 St James Square (closed Tues), manages imaginative, inexpensive dishes from local farm and sea produce. *Y Graig*, 34 Pier St (☎01970/611606), is a trendy wholefood **café** with a great atmosphere, serving as a focal point for a wide-ranging clientele. Pricier *Little Italy*, 51 North Parade (☎01970/625707), has an animated cellar bar and inventive upstairs **restaurant**. The *Castle Hotel*, South Rd, is also a harbourside **pub**, built in the style of an ornate Victorian gin palace, with vegetarian specialities; *Y Cŵps*, Llanbadarn Rd, is fun and friendly, with regular Welsh folk and jazz nights. For a slice of Edwardian gentility, take afternoon tea in any of the seafront hotels along the Promenade, and visit the *Aberystwyth Arts Centre*, the University, Penglais (☎01970/623232) for art-house cinema, touring theatre and wide-ranging temporary exhibitions.

The Vale of Rheidol

Inland from Aberystwyth, the Rheidol River winds its way up to a secluded, wooded valley, where occasional old industrial workings have moulded themselves into the contours, rising up past waterfalls and minute villages to Devil's Bridge. It's a glorious route, and by far the best way to see this part of the world is on board one of the trains of the **Vale of Rheidol railway** (April–Oct; ☎01970/625819; £10), a narrow-gauge steam train that wheezes its way along sheer rock faces from the terminus in Aberystwyth. It was built in 1902, ostensibly for the valley's lead mines but with a canny eye on its tourist potential as well, and has run ever since. Part way along, a punishing path on the north side of the river from the **Rhiwfron** stop scrambles up over the mines for a mile and into the sombre little village of **YSTUMTUEN**, a former lead-mining community whose school has been converted into a basic **youth hostel** (☎01970/890693). From here it's also a couple of miles walk to Devil's Bridge.

Folk legend, idyllic beauty and travellers' lore combine at **DEVIL'S BRIDGE** (Pontarfynach), a tiny settlement built solely for the growing visitor trade of the last few hundred years, twelve miles east of Aberystwyth. Be warned, however, that Devil's Bridge has been a seriously popular day excursion for centuries with no sign of its attraction waning. In order to escape some of the inevitable congestion, it is wisest to come here at the beginning or end of the day, or out of season.

The main attraction here is the **Devil's Bridge** itself, which is actually three stacked bridges spanning the chasm of the churning River Mynach yards above its confluence with the Rheidol. The road bridge in front of the striking, but distinctly antiquated, *Hafod Arms* hotel (☎01970/890693; ③) is the most modern of the three, dating from 1901. Immediately below it, wedged between the rock faces, are the stone bridge from 1753 and, at the bottom, the original bridge, dating from the eleventh century and reputedly built by the monks of Strata Florida Abbey (p.631). For a remarkable view of the bridges, you have to enter the turnstiles (50p) on either side of the modern road bridge: east down slippery steps to the scooped rock Punch Bowl, a deep cleft in the rock, where the water pounds and hurtles through the gap crowned by the bridges; or west on a path that tumbles down into the valley below the bridges, descending ultimately to the crashing **Mynach Falls**. The scenery here is magnificent: sharp, wooded slopes rising away from the frothing river, with distant mountain peaks surfacing on the horizon. A platform overlooks the series of falls, from where a set of steep steps takes you further down to a footbridge dramatically spanning the river at the bottom of the falls. For **camping**, there's a site by the petrol station, just beyond the bridges. In the other direction, the road towards Aberystwyth runs past the *Hafod Arms* and the Devil's Bridge post office to the terminus **station** of the Vale of Rheidol railway.

Machynlleth and around

The flat river plain and rolling hills of **Dyfi Valley** lay justifiable claims to being "one of the greenest corners of Europe", an area rife with B&Bs and other businesses started up by idealistic New Agers who have flocked to this corner of Wales since the late 1960s. The focal point is the genial town of **MACHYNLLETH** (pronounced Mah-hun-cthleth), a candidate for the Welsh capital in the 1950s and site of Owain Glyndŵr's embryonic fifteenth-century Welsh parliament. In the hills to the north, the renowned, self-contained **Centre for Alternative Technology** runs on co-operative lines and makes for one of the most interesting days out in Wales.

It is difficult to imagine what could have been the nation's capital, consisting essentially of just two streets, the wide main street, **Heol Maengwyn**, busiest on Wednesdays when a lively **market** springs up out of nowhere, and Heol Penallt, intersecting at an over-fussy **clock tower**. Glyndŵr's partly fifteenth-century **Parliament House** (Easter–Sept daily 10am–5pm, otherwise by arrangement; free; ☎01654/702827; free) sits halfway along Heol Maengwyn, a modest looking black-and-white fronted building, concealing a large interior. Displays chart the course of Glyndŵr's life (see box), his military campaign, his downfall and the 1404 parliament in the town, when he controlled almost all of what we now know as Wales and even negotiated international recognition of the sovereign state. The sorriest tales are from 1405 onwards when tactical errors and the sheer brute force of the English forced a swift retreat and an ignominious end to the greatest Welsh uprising.

On the Aberystwyth road, at Y Plas, the brand new **Celtica** exhibition (daily 10am–6pm; £4.65) combines audio-visual trickery with tales of the Celtic peoples in a fascinating romp through history. Around the corner on Heol Penallt is **Y Tabernacl** (Mon–Sat 10am–4pm; free; ☎01654/703355), a beautifully serene old chapel that has been converted into a cultural centre, including the small collection of the **Wales Museum of Modern Art**. It also hosts films, theatre and the annual **Gŵyl Machynlleth** festival in mid to late August, with a combination of classical music, debate, theatre and some folk music.

The old Victorian **train station** and **bus stop** are both a five-minute walk up the HeolPenallt/Doll from the clock tower. The **tourist office** (daily Easter–Sept 10am–6pm; Oct–Easter 10am–5pm; ☎01654/702401) is next to the Glyndŵr Parliament House on Heol Maengwyn. **Accommodation** includes the grand *Wynnstay Arms* (☎01654/702941; ④) on Heol Maengwyn, and the earthier *Glyndŵr Hotel* (☎01654/703989; ②) on Heol Doll, towards the station. *Mrs Fleming*, Brooklyn, Heol Powys (☎01654/702662; ②) is a handy B&B, and there's a **campsite** three miles north near the Centre for

---

OWAIN GLYNDŴR

No name is so frequently invoked in Wales as that of **Owain Glyndŵr** (*c.* 1349–1416), a potent figurehead of Welsh nationalism since he rose up against the occupying English in the early fifteenth century. Little is known about the man described in Shakespeare's *Henry IV, Part I* as "not in the roll of common men". There's little doubt that the charismatic Owain fulfilled many of the mystical medieval prophecies about the rising up of the red dragon. He was of aristocratic stock, and had a conventional upbringing, part of it in England studying English in London and becoming a loyal and distinguished soldier of the English king. He returned to Wales to take up his claim as Prince of Wales, being directly descended from the princes of Powys and Cyfeiliog, but became the focus of a rebellion born of discontent simmering since Edward I's stringent policies of subordinating Wales.

Goaded by a parochial land dispute in north Wales in which the courts failed to back him, Glyndŵr garnered four thousand supporters and declared anew that he was Prince of Wales. He attacked Ruthin, and then Denbigh, Rhuddlan, Flint, Hawarden and Oswestry, before encountering an English resistance at Welshpool, but whole swathes of North Wales were his for the taking. The English king, Henry IV, despatched troops and rapidly drew up a range of severely punitive laws against the Welsh, even outlawing Welsh-language bards and singers. Battles continued to rage until, by the end of 1403, Glyndŵr controlled most of Wales.

In 1404, Glyndŵr assembled a parliament at Machynlleth, drawing up mutual recognition treaties with France and Spain, and being crowned king of a free Wales. A second parliament in Harlech took place a year later, with Glyndŵr making plans to carve up England and Wales into three as part of an alliance against the English. The English army, however, concentrated with increased vigour on destroying the Welsh uprising, and the Tripartite Indenture was never realized. From then on, Glyndŵr lost battles, ground, castles and was forced into hiding, dying, it is thought, in Herefordshire. The draconian anti-Welsh laws stayed in place until the accession to the English throne of Henry VII, a Welshman, in 1485. Wales became subsumed into English custom and law, and Glyndŵr's uprising becoming an increasingly powerful symbol of frustrated Welsh independence. Even today, the shadowy organization that surfaced in the early 1980s to burn holiday homes of English people and English estate agents dealing in Welsh property has taken the name *Meibion Glyndŵr*, the Sons of Glyndŵr.

Alternative Technology at *Lleyngwern Farm* (☎01654/702492). There are plenty of **cafés**, **restaurants** and **pubs** in town, including a great wholefood shop and café at *Siop y Chwarel*, opposite the post office on Heol Maengwyn. The *Wynnstay Arms* does reasonable evening meals, and the *Glyndŵr Arms*, on Heol Doll, has live music at the weekend.

Centre for Alternative Technology

Since its foundation in the middle of the oil crisis of 1974, the **Centre for Alternative Technology**, or *Canolfan y Dechnoleg Amgen* (daily April–Sept 10am–5pm; Oct–March 11am–4pm; £3.50–4.95; ☎01654/702400), just over two miles north of Machynlleth off the A487, has become one of the biggest attractions in Wales. A former derelict slate quarry, covering seven acres, the centre has over the last twenty years become an entirely self-sufficient community, generating its own power and water from on-site equipment. It's not a museum, but it is open to the public and is a fascinating place to visit, combining earnest education about renewable resources and practices with flashes of pzazz, such as the water-powered cliff rail line that whisks the visitor 197 feet up from the car park. Whole houses have been constructed to showcase energy-saving ideas and the fifty-strong staff – who all live communally and receive identical (very low) wages – are ebullient and helpful in explaining the ideas. There are also organic gardens, beehives, a water wheel, an adventure playground and numerous hands-on exhibits. The wholefood restaurant and adjoining bookshop are excellent. The CAT also run residential **courses** here, their most popular one being a guide to building your own energy-efficient home.

The Cadair Idris area

The southern coastal reaches of Snowdonia National Park are almost entirely dominated by **Cadair Idris** (2930ft), a five-peaked massif standing in isolation, which has some demanding but very rewarding walks. Tennyson claimed never to have seen "anything more awful than the great veil of rain drawn straight over Cader Idris", but catch it on a good day, and the views are stunning. During the last Ice Age, the heads of glaciers scalloped out two huge cwms from Cadair Idris' distinctive dome, leaving thousand-foot cliffs dropping away on all sides to cool, clear lakes. The largest, the **Chair of Idris** may take its name from the seat-like rock formation on the summit ridge, where anyone spending the night will become a poet, go mad or die.

To the north lies the Mawddach which Wordsworth found to be "a sublime estuary" – romantic hyperbole perhaps, but these broad tidal flats gouging deep into the heart of the mid-Wales mountains create dramatic backdrops from every angle. With the sun low in the sky and the tide ebbing, the constantly changing course of the river trickles silver through the golden sands. But the colour of the sands isn't illusory: they really do contain gold, though not enough for gold-mining company *Rio Tinto Zinc*, who thankfully abandoned their plans to dredge for the stuff in the early Seventies. Spasmodic outbursts of gold fever still occasionally hit the region's main town, **Dolgellau**, but most people are content to come here for some excellent walking up Cadair Idris and along the estuary around **Barmouth**, or to ride the **Talyllyn Railway**, one of Wales' most popular narrow-gauge lines, to the minor pleasures of the Talyllyn and Dysynni valleys.

The Talyllyn and Dysynni valleys

TYWYN is primarily of interest as a base for the Talyllyn and Dysynni valleys, although the town does have miles of sandy beach and the five-foot-high

Ynysmaengwyn or St Cadfan's Stone, within the Norman nave of the **Church of St Cadfan** (daily 9am–5pm, later in summer) bearing the earliest example of written Welsh, dating back to around 650 AD.

The **Talyllyn narrow-gauge railway** (April–Oct daily 2–8 trains; round trip £7.50; ☎01654/710472), belches seven miles inland through the delightful wooded Talyllyn Valley to Nant Gwernol. From 1866 to 1946, the rail line was used to haul slate to Tywyn Wharf station, then just four years after its closure, dedicated trainheads restarted services, making this the world's first volunteer-run railway. At a leisurely 15mph the round trip takes two hours, longer if you get off to take in some fine broadleaf forest walks. The best of these starts at Dôlgogh Falls station, where three trails (maximum 1hr) lead off to the lower, mid and upper falls. At the end of the line, more woodland walks take you around the site of the old slate quarries.

From Tywyn, the road up the **Talyllyn Valley** runs parallel to the Talyllyn Railway, meeting it at Dolgoch Falls, the site of some wooded walks, a couple of miles short of the twin valley's largest settlement, **ABERGYNOLWYN**, comprising a few dozen quarry workers' houses and two pubs. The Dysynni Valley branches northwest here, but Talyllyn Valley continues northeast to **Tal-y-Llyn Lake** and the fifteenth-century **St Mary's Church**, a fine example of a small Welsh parish church, unusual because of its chancel arch painted with an alternating grid of red and white roses, separated by grotesque bosses.

The Dysynni Valley has more to offer in the way of sights, though the lack of public transport makes it difficult to get to. A mile and a half northwest of Abergynolwyn, a side road cuts northeast to the hamlet of **LLANFIHANGEL-Y-PENNANT** and the scant ruins of the native Welsh **Castell-y-Bere** (unrestricted access; CADW), a fortress built by Llywelyn the Great in 1221 to protect the mountain passes. One of the most massive of the Welsh castles, it was besieged twice before being consigned to

---

WALKS AROUND DOLGELLAU

Torrent Walk

Victorians seldom passed up the lowland, beechwood **Torrent Walk** (2 miles; 100ft ascent; 1hr) which follows the course of the Clywedog River as it carves its way through the bedrock to the *Clywedog Tea Garden*, where home-baked scones are served beside the river. Bus #2 takes you the two miles east along the A470 to the start by the junction of the B4416.

Precipice Walk

Nowadays, more people head for the not remotely precipitous **Precipice Walk** (3–4 miles; negligable ascent; 2hr), a circuit around the bracken and heather-covered Foel Cynach, with great views along the Mawddach Estuary and towards the thousand-foot ramparts of Cadair Idris. Best done in the late afternoon, the walk is fairly well signposted from the start, three miles north of Dolgellau along the Llanfachreth road which turns off the A494 by the Big Bridge. Bus #33 runs to the start three times on Tuesdays and Fridays only.

Pony Path

More ambitious Victorians climbed **Cadair Idris** on the since eroded Fox's Path, now widely ignored in favour of the classic and straightforward **Pony Path** (6–7 miles; 2500ft ascent; 4–5hr), starting three miles up Cadair Road in the car park at Ty Nant. As you begin by the sign near the telephone box, the view to the craggy flanks of the massif are tremendous, but they disappear as you climb steeply to the col where a left turn leads to the summit shelter on **Penygadair** (2930ft). Return by the same route or plan your own off the 1:25,000 OS Outsoor Leisure map of "Cadair Idris/Dovey Forest".

seven centuries of obscurity and decay. There's still plenty to poke around, with large slabs of the main towers still standing, but it's primarily a great place just to sit gazing over Cadair Idris, or three miles seaward to **Craig yr Aderyn** (Birds' Rock), a 760-foot-high cliff where there are thirty breeding pairs of cormorants who have remained loyal to the spot as, over the centuries, the sea has receded.

Practicalities

Tywyn's three main roads meet at the joint **train station** and main **bus** stop, a short walk from the **tourist office**, High St (Easter–Oct daily 10am–6pm; ☎01654/710070), and two hundred yards to the south, the Talyllyn narrow-gauge train station (Tywyn Wharf). The Talyllyn Valley is served by the #30 **bus**, running from Tywyn to Abergynolwyn, continuing to Minffordd (where you can catch #2 to Dolgellau) and Machynlleth. Decent **accommodation** can be found at the *Ivy Guest House*, High St (☎01654/711058; ②), opposite the tourist office, or the cheaper, non-smoking *Glenydd Guest House*, 2 Maes Newydd (☎01654/711373; ②), two hundred yards from the beach off Pier Road. The handiest **campsite** is *Ynysmaengwyn Caravan Park* (April–Sept; ☎01654/710684), a mile out on the Dolgellau road. The best **eating** in town is upstairs at moderately priced *The Proper Gander*, High St (☎01654/711270), and at the inexpensive *Y Gegin Fach* (☎01654/710072) on College Green, the eastern extension of High Street.

In the Talyllyn and Dysynni valleys, stay at *Tan-y-Coed-Uchaf* (March–Nov; ☎01654/782228; ②), a superb farmhouse **B&B** close to Dolgoch Falls; the *Riverside Guesthouse and Café*, Cwrt (☎01654/782235; ③) in Abergynolwyn; or the *Minffordd Hotel* (March–Dec; ☎01654/761665; ⑥), an eighteenth-century farmhouse and coaching inn by Tal-y-Llyn Lake, open to non-residents for moderately priced traditional British dinners (Thurs–Sat). There is a basic **campsite** at *Cedris Farm* (☎01654/782280), a mile north-east of Abergynolwyn.

Dolgellau

Its distance from England and its historical position in the heartland of Welsh nationalism should make **DOLGELLAU** (pronounced Dol-gethl-aye) the Welshest of towns, but the town's granite architecture draws more from nineteenth-century England, with a dour series of small neo-Georgian squares all bearing English names. Victorian tourists came to marvel at Cadair Idris and the Mawddach Estuary, still the best policy as the town has little to offer.

The only central diversion is the **Quaker Interpretive Centre**, in the tourist office (see below), detailing the lives of the Society of Friends forced by persecution to seek a better life in Pennsylvania where towns still bear Welsh names: Bangor, Bryn Mawr and others. Dolgellau has a history of short-lived and generally miserable gold rushes, but the hopeful still occasionally open up an ore vein. The most recent enterprise combines the dig with a three-hour-long, overpriced **Gold-Mining Tour** (April–Oct daily 10am–3.50pm; reduced hours in winter; £9.50; ☎01341/423332), which leaves from the **Welsh Gold Visitor Centre** (April–Oct daily 9am–7pm; reduced hours in winter; free) at the far end of the car park by the Big Bridge. On the half-mile walk through the mine you do get to see some of the small workforce operating the milling and separating equipment, but most of the tour is designed with the visitor in mind, with a staged blasting and the opportunity to chip away at the rock for a few minutes.

Dolgellau has no train station but is well served by **buses** which all pull into the central Eldon Square close by the **tourist office** (Easter–Oct daily 10am–6pm; Nov–Easter Mon & Thurs–Sun 10am–5pm; ☎01341/422888). Central **accommodation** is best found at the cheap *Aber Café*, Smithfield St (☎01341/422460; ②), and the good-value *Clifton House Hotel*, Smithfield Square (☎01341/422554; ③), built in an ex-police station and jail with the basement cells used as a restaurant. Other places are liberally

---

> ### WALKS FROM BARMOUTH
>
> The best lowland walk on the Cambrian Coast, the **Barmouth–Fairbourne Loop** (5 miles; 300ft ascent; 2–3hr) is a fine way to spend an afternoon with fine mountain scenery, estuarine and coastal views all the way. The walking component can be reduced dramatically by using both the BR and Fairbourne railways. The route first crosses the estuary rail bridge (small fee) to Morfa Mawddach BR station, follows the lane to the main road, crosses it onto a footpath that loops behind a small wooded hill to Pant Einion Hall, then follows another lane back to the main road near Fairbourne. In Fairbourne, turn north either walking along the beach to the end of the spit, or catching the **Fairbourne Railway** (Easter–Oct 3–6 daily) to the **passenger ferry** (Easter–Oct) across the eastuary mouth back to Barmouth.

scattered round about, notably the eighteenth-century *Tyddynmawr Farmhouse*, Islawrdref (☎01341/422331; ③), on the slopes of Cadair Idris at the foot of the Pony Path, and the superb seventeenth-century *George III Hotel*, Penmaenpool (☎01341/422525; ⑧), right by the Mawddach Estuary two miles west of Dolgellau. The tent-only *Bryn-y-Gwyn* **campsite**, Cader Rd (☎01341/422733) is less than a mile southeast of Dolgellau. There's little choice for **eating** in Dolgellau: the best bets are the creative and moderately priced *Bwyty Dylanwad Da*, Smithfield St (phone ☎01341/422870 for opening hours) and the *Tyn-y-Groes Hotel*, Glanllwyd (☎01341/40275), four miles north of Dolgellau in the Coed y Brenin forest, with good beer, fine bar meals and à la carte dinners.

Barmouth and around

The best approach to **BARMOUTH** (Abermo) is from the south, where the Cambrian coast rail line sweeps from tiny Fairbourne over 113 rickety-looking wooden spans across the Mawddach River. It is still the haunt of English Midlands holidaymakers, who fashioned Barmouth as a sea-bathing resort in the nineteenth-century, but warrants some attention for breezy rambles on the cliffs of **Dinas Oleu** above the town, and a great walk around the mouth of the estuary (see box). Central attractions don't extend beyond the **Tŷ Gwyn Museum** (July–Sept Tues–Sun 10.30am–5pm; free), a medieval tower house (now a Tudor museum) where Henry VII's uncle, Jasper Tudor, is thought to have plotted Richard III's downfall; and the **Tŷ Crwn Roundhouse**, on the hill behind (same times) which once acted as a lockup for drunken sailors.

    Buses from Harlech and Dolgellau stop in the leisure centre car park by the **train station** and just a few yards from the **tourist office** on Station Road (Easter–Oct daily 10am–6pm; ☎01341/280787). **Accommodation** is plentiful, and best at *The Gables*, Mynach Rd (☎01341/280553; ②), ten minutes' walk north of town and particularly welcoming to walkers. The closest of a long string of **campsites** is *Hendre Mynach*, Lanaber Rd (March–Oct; ☎01341/280262), a mile north of town and just off the beach. Basic **cafés** are plentiful, though for not much more money you can get mammoth French sticks and pancakes at the inexpensive *Rowleys Licensed Restaurant*, The Quay, and good pizzas next door. Close to The Quay, *The Last Inn*, in a former cobbler's shop, serves good pub meals.

Harlech

It's hard to dislike **HARLECH**, ten miles north of Barmouth, with its time-worn castle dramatically clinging to its rocky outcrop, and the town cloaking the ridge behind commanding one of Wales' finest views over Cardigan Bay to the Llŷn. There are good beaches nearby, and the town's twisting narrow streets along the ridge harbour places where you can eat and sleep surprisingly well for such a small place.

Harlech's substantially complete **Castle** (April to late Oct daily 9.30am–6.30pm; late Oct to March Mon–Sat 9.30am–4pm, Sun 11am–4pm; £3; CADW) sits on its 200-foot-high bluff, a site chosen by Edward I for one more link in his magnificent chain of fortresses. Begun in 1285, it was built of a hard Cambrian rock, known as Harlech grit, hewn from the moat. One side of the fortress was originally protected by the sea, now receded and leaving the castle dominating a stretch of duned coastline. Harlech with-held a siege in 1295, was taken by Owain Glyndŵr in 1404, and the youthful, future Henry VII – the first Welsh king of England and Wales – withstood a seven-year siege at the hands of the Yorkists until 1468, when the castle was again taken. It fell into ruin, but was put back into service for the king during the Civil War, and in March 1647, it was the last Royalist castle to fall. The first defensive line comprised the three successive pairs of gates and portcullises built between the two massive half-round towers of the **gatehouse**, where an exhibition now outlines the castle's history. Much of the castle's outermost ring has been destroyed, leaving only the twelve-foot-thick curtain walls rising up forty feet to the exposed battlements, and only the towering gatehouse prevents you from walking the full circuit.

Harlech's **train station** is on the main A496 under the castle. Most **buses** call both here and on High Street a few yards from the **tourist office** (Easter–Oct daily 10am–6pm; ☎01766/780658). The pick of the local **places to stay** are the friendly *Aris Guesthouse*, 4 Pen y Bryn (☎01766/780409; ③), just above the village past the Lion Hotel, and the cosy, informal *Castle Cottage* hotel (☎01766/780479; ③), with the trappings of a place charging twice as much and excellent meals. Other possibilities include the *Plas Newydd* **youth hostel**, Plas Newydd (☎01341/241287), three miles south in Llanbedr (buses #38 & #94), and the *Min y Don* **campsite**, Beach Rd (Easter–Sept; ☎01766/780286), three minutes' walk from the beach, taking the first right out of the station. You won't go hungry in Harlech with such wonderful **eating** places as the inexpensive but licensed *Plâs Café*, High St, with a good range of food and fabulous views from the garden and conservatory; the moderately priced bistro-style *Yr Ogof* (☎01766/780888), with a good-value range of inventive vegetarian and meaty dishes; and classy modern dishes at *Castle Cottage*.

Porthmadog and around

Located right at the point where the coast makes a sharp left turn along the south side of the Llŷn, **PORTHMADOG** was once the busiest slate port in north Wales. Nowadays, it's a pleasant enough town to spend a night or two, although it sadly makes little of its situation on the north bank of the vast, mountain-backed estuary. Two things it does make a fuss about are the Italianate folly of Portmeirion, two miles east of the town, and the Ffestiniog Railway that originally carried down slates from Blaenau Ffestiniog through thirteen miles of verdant mountain scenery to Porthmadog-made schooners for export. Porthmadog would never have existed at all without the entrepreneurial ventures of a Lincolnshire MP named William Alexander Madocks, who named the town after both himself and the Welsh Prince Madog, who some say sailed from the nearby Ynys Fadog (Madog's Island) to North America in 1170. Between 1808 and 1812, Madocks fought tides and currents to build the mile-long embankment of The Cob, southeast of present-day Porthmadog, enclosing 7000 acres of the estuary. A wharf was built and with the completion of the Blaenau Ffestiniog railway in 1836, the town spread along a waterfront thick with orderly heaps of slate and the masts of merchant ships.

Without a doubt, the **Ffestiniog Railway** (Easter–Oct 4–10 daily; Nov–Easter mainly weekends) ranks as Wales' finest narrow-gauge rail line, twisting and looping up 650 feet from the wharf at Porthmadog to the slate mines at Blaenau Ffestiniog, thirteen miles away. When the line opened in 1836, it carried slates from the mines down to the port with the help of gravity, horses riding with the goods, then hauling the empty carriages back up again. Steam had to be introduced to cope with the 100,000 tons of slate a year that Blaenau Ffestiniog was churning out in the late nineteenth century, but the slate roofing market collapsed between the wars and passengers were carried instead, until 1946 when the line was finally abandoned. Most of the tracks and sleepers had disappeared by 1954 when a bunch of dedicated volunteers began to reconstruct the line, only completing the entire route in 1982. Leaving Porthmadog, trains cross The Cob then stop at Minffordd, a mile-long walk to Portmeirion (see below), then at Plas Halt from where it is a short stroll to *The Grapes* pub at Maentwrog and to start the Vale of Ffestiniog walk.

Practicalities

Cambrian coast trains pull into the mainline **train station** at the north end of the High Street; the **Ffestiniog station** is located down by the harbour, about half a mile to the south. In between the two, *National Express* **buses** stop on Avenue Road outside *The Royal Sportsman Hotel*; local bus services stop outside *The Australia Inn* on High Street. The helpful **tourist office**, High St (Easter–Oct daily 10am–6pm; Nov–Easter daily except Tues 10am–5pm; ☎01766/512981) is towards the harbour.

While limited budgets are well catered for, there's not much really decent **accommodation** without pressing on to Cricieth or Harlech, unless you're prepared to lash out for a night at the swanky *Portmeirion Hotel* (☎01766/770228; ⑧), for which see below. *Skellerns*, 35 Madog St (☎01766/512843; ②) is the cheapest guest house around, near the Ffestiniog train station. *Camelia*, 12 Church St (☎01766/512201; ②), a non-smoking guest house five minutes' walk from the centre, is another good choice. *Eric's Bunkhouse*, two miles north of Porthmadog on the A498 to Beddgelert, opposite *Eric Jones' Café*, is the cheapest option, with mattresses for around £2 a night. *Tŷ Bricks*, Snowdon St (March–Sept; ☎01766/512597) is showerless but the cheapest of local **campsites**, less than a mile northeast of the centre.

For **food**, there's the *Blue Anchor*, Pen-y-Cei (☎01766/514959), a moderate, harbourside seafood restaurant with a good three-course set menu. Seafood also predominates at the *Harbour Restaurant*, High St (Thurs–Sat only in winter), opposite the tourist office. *Passage to India Tandoori*, 26a Lombard St (☎01766/512144), is a highly rated Indian restaurant, across the park west of the High Street, and cheapest of the lot is *The Ship and Cantonese Restaurant*, a popular pub on Lombard Street, noted for its oriental beer and its bar meals, predominantly Thai and Malaysian with some vegetarian.

Portmeirion

Porthmadog's other main lure is the unique Italianate private village of **PORTMEIRION** (daily 9.30am–5.30pm; £1.60–3.20), set on a small rocky peninsula in Tremadog Bay, three miles east near Minffordd. Both the main-line and Ffestiniog trains, as well as buses #1, #2 and #3 stop in Minffordd, from where it is a 25-minute walk to Portmeirion. Perhaps best known as "The Village" in the Sixties British cult TV series *The Prisoner*, Portmeirion is the brainchild of eccentric architect, Clough Williams-Ellis, and his dream to build an ideal village which enhances rather than blends in with the surroundings, using a "gay, light-opera sort of approach". The result is certainly theatrical: a stage set with a lucky dip of unwanted buildings arranged to distort perspectives and reveal tantalizing glimpses of the seascape behind.

In the 1920s, Ellis bought the site and turned a house already on it into a hotel, the income from it providing funds for Ellis' "Home for Fallen Buildings". Endangered buildings from all over Britain and abroad were broken down, transported and rebuilt, every conceivable style being plundered: a Neoclassical colonnade from Bristol,

Siamese figures, a Jacobean town hall, and the Italianate touches, a Campanile and a Pantheon. Ellis designed his village around a Mediterranean piazza, piecing together a scaled-down nest of loggias, grand porticoes and tiny terracotta-roofed houses and painting them in pastels: turquoise, ochre and buff yellows. Continually surprising, with hidden entrances and cherubs popping out of crevices, the ensemble is eclectic, yet never quite inappropriate.

It is in need of a lick of paint here and there, but even so, more than three thousand visitors a day come to ogle in summer when it can be a delight, fewer in winter when it is just plain bizarre. In the evening, when the village is closed to the public, patrons at the opulent waterside *Hotel Portmeirion* (see "Porthmadog Accommodation") get to see the place at its best: peaceful, even ghostly. Much of your time will be spent walking the grounds except for viewing a film on Portmeirion, popping into the shops selling *Prisoner* memorabilia, and eating.

The Llŷn

The Llŷn takes its name from an Irish word for peninsula, an apt description for this most westerly part of north Wales, which, until the fifth century, had a significant Irish population. The cliff-and-cove-lined finger of land juts out south and west separating Cardigan and Caernarfon bays, its hills tapering away along the ancient route to Aberdaron where pilgrims sailed for Ynys Enlli (Bardsey Island). Today it is the beaches that lure people to the south-coast family resorts of **Cricieth**, **Pwllheli** and **Abersoch**, and unless you want to rent windsurfers or canoes, it's preferable to press on along the narrow roads that dawdle down towards Aberdaron. Not even in Snowdonia does it feel more remote than the tip of the Llŷn, and nowhere in Wales is more staunchly Welsh: road signs are still bilingual but the English is frequently defaced; Stryd Fawr is used instead of High Street, and in most local shops you'll only hear Welsh spoken.

Cricieth and Llanystumdwy

When seabathing became the Victorian fashion, English families descended on the sweeping sand and shingle beach at **CRICIETH**, five miles west of Porthmadog, a quiet amiable resort which curiously abounds with good places to stay and great restaurants, making it a good touring base for the peninsula and Porthmadog. There isn't much here, however, but for the battle-worn remains of **Cricieth Castle** (April–Oct daily 9.30am–6.30pm; Nov–March Mon–Sat 9.30am–4pm, Sun 2–4pm; £2.20; CADW), dominating the coastline with its twin D-towered gatehouse. Started by Llywelyn ap Iorwerth in 1230, it was strengthened by Edward I around 1283, and razed by Owain Glyndŵr in 1404, leaving little besides a plan of broken walls. It is a great spot to sit and look over Cardigan Bay to Harlech in the late afternoon, but leave time for the fairly workaday exhibition on Welsh castles in the ticket office and a wonderful animated cartoon based on the twelfth-century Cambrian travels of Giraldus Cambrensis as he gathered support for the third Crusade.

A mile west, the village of **LLANYSTUMDWY** celebrates its most famous son, the Welsh nationalist, social reformer and British Prime Minister David Lloyd George. He grew up in Highgate House, now part of the **Lloyd George Museum** (Easter–Sept Mon–Fri 11am–5pm, Sat & Sun 2–5pm; Oct Mon–Fri 11am–4pm; £2.50). A fairly dull collection of gifts, awards and caskets honouring Lloyd George with the freedom of various cities illustrates the great man's popularity, and the museum's displays are full of anecdotes and little-known facts about him, with explanatory panels and a couple of short films giving a broad sweep of his life. Lloyd George is buried by the River Dwyfor under a memorial – a boulder and two simple plaques designed by Portmeirion designer Clough Williams-Ellis. Bus #3 runs from Porthmadog and Cricieth, through the village on its way to Pwllheli.

Trains on the Cambrian coastline stop a couple of hundred yards west of Y Maes, the open square at the centre of town; **buses** also stop here. **Accommodation** is plentiful, with *Preswylfa*, 4 Castle Terrace (Feb–Oct; ☎01766/522829; ②), almost opposite the castle and *Trefaes Guesthouse*, Y Maes (☎01766/523204; ③) at the cheaper end. More luxurious places are further afield: *Mynydd Ednyfed*, Caernarfon Rd (☎01766/523269; ⑤), a luxurious country hotel a mile north on the B4411 with classy moderately priced food too, and *Bron Eifion Country House Hotel* (☎01766/522385; ⑦), a beautiful Victorian country house set in five acres a mile west of town. *Mynydd Du* (April–Oct; ☎01766/522533) is a simple **campsite** a mile towards Porthmadog on the A497. For such a small town, good **restaurants** are surprisingly abundant and offer the best range of eating on the peninsula. The two plusher hotels listed above both serve innovative and fairly expensive meals: *Tir-a-Môr*, 1–3 Mona Terrace (closed Sun; ☎01766/523084) isn't strictly Italian, but serves a large range of moderately priced Italian-influenced dishes in airy surroundings, and *Bryn Hir Arms*, 24 Stryd Fawr, has good beer, a pleasant garden and a wide range of bar meals with pizza specials.

Pwllheli

PWLLHELI (pronounced "Poothl-heli") is the market town for the peninsula, a role it has maintained since 1355, when it gained its charter, though there's little to remind of that. The overall tenor is one of low-brow fun-seeking as holidaymakers flood in from the nearby *Butlin's* **Starcoast World**. Pwllheli's one defining feature is its Welshness. Even in the height of summer, you'll hear far more Welsh spoken here than English and perhaps wish you'd made more of an attempt to learn some.

As the terminus for *National Express* **buses** (which stop on Y Maes) and the final stop for Cambrian coast trains, Pwllheli is hard to avoid, but you should push on if possible, only stopping at the **tourist office**, Station Square (daily 10am–6pm; ☎01758/613000) or to rent a mountain bike during the summer at £10 a day from *Llŷn Cycle Hire*, Ala Rd (☎01758/612414). If pushed, **stay** at 26 High St (☎01758/613172; ②), with TVs in all rooms, or four hundred yards away, *Llys Gwyrfai*, 14 West End Parade (☎01758/614877; ③), a comfortable guest house with sea views and home-cooked meals.

Abersoch

After the distinctly Welsh feel of Pwllheli, **ABERSOCH**, seven miles southwest along the coast, comes as a surprise. This former fishing village pitched in the middle of two golden bays has, over the last century, become a thoroughly anglicized resort, with a haughty opinion of itself. Such high self-esteem isn't really justified, but at high tide the harbour is attractive, and the long swathe of the beach hut-backed Town Beach is a fine spot even if it is barely visible under the beach towels at busy times. A short walk along the beach shakes off most of the crowds, but a better bet is to make for three-mile-long **Porth Neigwl** (Hell's Mouth), two miles to the southwest, which ranks as one of the country's best surf beaches; you'll need your own gear, and beware of the undertow if you are swimming. **Rent windsurfers**, surfboards and wetsuits from *Abersoch Watersports*, Lôn Pont Morgan (☎01758/712483) by the harbour.

Buses from Pwllheli make a loop through the middle of Abersoch, passing the **tourist office**, Village Hall, Lôn Gwydryn (Easter to mid-Sept daily 10.30am–5pm; ☎01758/712929). **Stay** at either the bargain *Trewen*, Lôn Hawen, just off Lôn Sarn Bach (☎01758/712755; ②), *Angorfa Guest House*, Lôn Sarn Bach (closed Dec; ☎01758/712967; ③), or the comfortable *Neigwl Hotel*, Lôn Sarn Bach (☎01758/712363; ⑤). **Eating** involves bar food, best sampled at *The Ship* in Llanbedrog near Pwllheli.

Aberdaron and Bardsey Island

The small lime-washed fishing village of **ABERDARON** backs a pebble beach two miles short of the tip of the Llŷn. For a millennium from the sixth century it was the last stop for pilgrims to **Bardsey Island** or Ynys Enlli (The Island of the Currents), just offshore: three visits were proclaimed equivalent to one pilgrimage to Rome. Many pilgrims came to die there, earning Bardsey its epithet "The Isle of Twenty Thousand Saints". The final gathering place before the treacherous crossing is the fourteenth-century stone *Y Gegin Fawr* (Great Kitchen), which now operates as a café. Without your own transport, the only way to get to Aberdaron is to catch the #17 **bus** from Pwllheli, though on Sunday you'll have to hitch. **Accommodation** is fairly limited; *Brynmor* (☎01758/760344; ②), overlooking the bay, a hundred yards up the road to Porth Oer, is the cheapest. The best and quietest **campsite** around is *Mur Melyn* (Easter, Whit, July & Aug; no phone) just above Porth Oer, two miles north of Aberdaron. Take the B4413 west, fork right then left at Pen-y-Bont house.

travel details

Frequencies for trains are for Monday to Saturday services; Sunday averages 1–3 services.

Trains

Aberystwyth to: Machynlleth (9 daily; 30min); Shrewsbury (6 daily; 2hr); Welshpool (6 daily; 1hr 25min).

Barmouth to: Harlech (8 daily; 25min); Machynlleth (9 daily; 55min); Porthmadog (8 daily; 45min).

Cricieth to: Porthmadog (8 daily; 10min).

Harlech to: Barmouth (8 daily; 25min); Birmingham (5 daily; 4hr 15min); Porthmadog (8 daily; 20min).

Machynlleth to: Aberystwyth (9 daily; 30min); Barmouth (6 daily; 55min); Birmingham (5 daily; 2hr 30min); Harlech (5 daily; 1hr 20min).

Porthmadog to: Barmouth (8 daily; 45min); Blaenau Ffestiniog by Ffestiniog Railway (Easter–Oct 4–10 daily; 1hr); Harlech (8 daily; 20min); Pwllheli (8 daily; 25min).

Pwllheli to: Porthmadog (8 daily; 25min).

Buses

Aberaeron to: Aberystwyth (hourly; 40min); Carmarthen (3 daily; 1hr 45min); Lampeter (5 daily; 35min); New Quay (hourly; 20min).

Aberdaron to: Pwllheli (7 daily Mon–Sat; 40min).

Aberystwyth to: Aberaeron (hourly; 40min); Caernarfon (5 daily; 2hr 40min); Cardigan (hourly; 2hr); Devil's Bridge (2 daily; 40min); Lampeter (5 daily; 1hr 25min); Machynlleth (6 daily; 45min); New Quay (hourly; 1hr).

Barmouth to: Bala (6 daily, 2 Sun in summer; 1hr); Blaenau Ffestiniog (4–6 daily Mon–Sat; 1hr); Dolgellau (14 daily, 2 Sun; 20min); Harlech (9 daily Mon–Sat; 25min).

Cardigan to: Aberaeron (hourly; 1hr 20min); Aberystwyth (hourly; 2hr); Fishguard (hourly Mon–Sat; 50min); Newcastle Emlyn (hourly Mon–Sat; 25min); Newport, Dyfed (hourly Mon–Sat; 30min); New Quay (hourly; 1hr).

Cricieth to: Caernarfon (4 daily Mon–Sat; 45min); Porthmadog (every 30min, 3–4 Sun; 10min); Pwllheli (every 30min, 4 Sun; 20min).

Dolgellau to: Aberystwyth (6 daily, 2 Sun; 1hr 15min); Bala (6 daily, 3 Sun in summer; 35min); Barmouth (14 daily, 2 Sun; 20min); Blaenau Ffestiniog (3 daily Mon–Sat; 50min); Caernarfon (7 daily; 1hr 40min); Llangollen (6 daily, 3 Sun in summer; 1hr 30min); Machynlleth (7 daily, 2 Sun; 35min); Porthmadog (6 daily, 2 Sun; 50min).

Harlech to: Barmouth (9 daily Mon–Sat; 25min); Blaenau Ffestiniog (6 daily Mon–Sat; 35min).

Lampeter to: Aberaeron (5 daily; 35min); Aberystwyth (5 daily; 1hr 25min); Machynlleth (1 daily; 2hr 25min).

Machynlleth to: Aberystwyth (6 daily, 2 Sun; 40min); Bala (6 daily, 1 Sun; 1hr 20min); Cardiff (1 daily; 5hr 15min); Dolgellau (7 daily, 2 Sun; 35min); Lampeter (1 daily; 2hr 25min); Llangollen (6 daily, 1 Sun; 2hr 55min); Porthmadog (5 daily, 2 Sun; 1hr 45min).

New Quay to: Aberaeron (hourly; 20min); Aberystwyth (hourly; 1hr); Cardigan (hourly; 1hr).

Porthmadog to: Beddgelert (6 daily, 2 Sun in summer; 30min); Blaenau Ffestiniog (every 30min, 3–4 Sun; 30min); Caernarfon (hourly, 2–3 Sun; 45min); Cardiff (1 daily; 6hr 40min); Cricieth (every 30min, 3–4 Sun; 10min); Dolgellau (6 daily, 2 Sun; 50min); Machynlleth (5 daily, 2 Sun; 1hr 45min); Pwllheli (every 30min, 3 Sun; 40min).

Pwllheli to: Aberdaron (7 daily Mon–Sat; 40min); Abersoch (20 daily Mon–Sat; 15–50min); Cricieth (every 30min, 3 Sun; 20min); Porthmadog (every 30min, 3 Sun; 40min).

CHAPTER FIFTEEN

THE DEE VALLEY AND SNOWDONIA

Trapped between the brash coastal resorts in the north and the thinly inhabited hill tracts of mid-Wales to the south lies a mountainous strip of land stretching up the Dee Valley and into Snowdonia. Its eastern edge forms part of the Marches, a broad swathe of countryside running the full length of the England–Wales border and notable for its profusion of castles. Though **Chirk Castle** is the only significant, extant Marcher fortress, it remains a potent reminder of the centuries after the Norman conquest of England, when powerful barons fought the Welsh princes for control of these fertile lands. Today they remain pastoral, with the exception of the area around the industrial town of **Wrexham**.

The **Dee Valley** has always remained more firmly Welsh than the Marches, despite the annual onslaught of cross-border visitors to **Llangollen**, the valley's main draw, with an international folk music festival each July and a broad selection of ruins, rides and rambles to tempt visitors throughout the rest of the year. There's more to detain you here than anywhere east of what is – for most people – north Wales' crowning glory, **Snowdonia**. This tightly packed bundle of soaring cliff faces, jagged peaks and plunging waterfalls measures little more than ten miles by ten, but packs enough mountain paths to keep even the most jaded walking enthusiast happy for weeks. The last Ice Age left a legacy of peaks ringed by cwms – huge hemispherical bites out of the mountainsides – while the ranges were left separated by steep-sided valleys, a challenge for even the most fly-footed climber. Even if lakeside ambles and rides on antiquated steam trains are more your style, you can't fail to appreciate the natural grandeur of the scenery which occasionally reveals an atmospheric Welsh castle ruin or decaying piece of quarrying equipment.

The Dee Valley

Llangollen, along with the smaller Bala, grew up partly as a market centre, but also served the needs of cattle drovers who used the passage carved by the river through the hills as the easiest route from the fattening grounds of northwest Wales to the

---

ACCOMMODATION PRICE CODES

Throughout this guide, hotel and B&B accommodation is priced on a scale of ① to ⑨, the number indicating the **lowest price** you could expect to pay per night in that establishment for a **double room** in high season. The prices indicated by the codes are as follows:

① under £20/$30	④ £40–50/$60–75	⑦ £70–80/$105–120
② £20–30/$31–45	⑤ £50–60/$75–90	⑧ £80–100/$120–150
③ £30–40/$45–60	⑥ £60–70/$90–105	⑨ over £100/$150

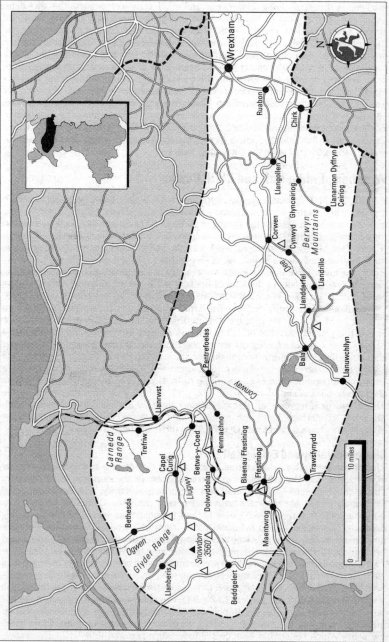

markets in England. Long before rail and road transport pushed the dwindling numbers of drovers out of business at the end of the nineteenth century, they had already been joined by early tourists. Most made straight for Llangollen, where the ruins of both a Welsh castle and a Cistercian abbey lent a gaunt Romantic charm to a dramatic gorge naturally blessed with surging rapids. The arrival of the train, in the middle of the nineteenth century, made Llangollen a firm favourite with tourists from the mill towns of northwest England. The train line closed in the 1960s, but Bala has fought neglect to become one of Wales' top watersports venues, a mecca for windsurfing and white-water kayaking. The final few miles before the River Dee flows into the sea form an arc around the anglicized town of **Wrexham**. Its unappealing light-industrial tenor is only relieved by its proximity to the Marcher fortress of **Chirk Castle**, and a fine country house incongruously lodged in what was briefly north Wales' early industrial core, the **Clywedog Valley**.

Wrexham, Erddig Hall and Chirk Castle

If **WREXHAM** (Wrecsam) is your introduction to Wales, don't be disappointed. It certainly isn't pretty, nor is it characteristically Welsh. There's little reason to stop except to use it as a base for the nearby attractions, which in any case are better visited from Llangollen if you have your own transport. You might call in at **St Giles' Church** (Easter–Oct Mon–Fri 10am–4pm; free) with its Gothic tower gracefully rising above the kernel of small lanes at the end of Hope Street. Topped off with a steeple in the 1520s, the tower's five distinct levels, stepping up to four hexagonal pinnacles, is replicated at Yale University in the USA in homage to the ancestral home of the college's benefactor, Elihu Yale, whose tomb is here at the base.

Wrexham has two **train stations**, half a mile apart, all services stopping at Wrexham General on Mold Road, ten minutes' walk northwest of the centre. Part way along Hope Street, King Street branches off left to the **bus station** where *National Express* buses (tickets from *Key Travel*, King St) arrive, and **local buses** leave frequently to Chester and Llangollen. For information, make for the **tourist office**, Lambpit St (Mon–Sat Easter–Sept 10am–5pm; Oct–Easter 10am–4pm; ☎01978/292015), reached by turning left where Hope Street takes a turn to the right. If you need to **stay**, make for *Monfa Guesthouse*, 65 Ruabon Rd (☎01978/354888; ②), a short walk from the centre on the A5152 towards Llangollen, or *Abbotsfield Priory Hotel*, 29 Rhosddu Rd (☎01978/261211; ④), a very comfortable hotel with en-suite rooms, converted from an old priory: follow Regent Street towards Wrexham General, then turn right into Grosvenor Road.

Clywedog Valley and Erddig Hall

The **Clywedog Valley**, which forms an arc around the western and southern suburbs of Wrexham, was the crucible of industrial success in the northern Welsh borders during the eighteenth century. Iron was the principle activity, but as the Industrial Revolution forged ahead, water power harnessed from the Clywedog became less important, and factories moved closer to their raw materials, leaving the valley barely disturbed. A series of former industrial sites – ironworks, lead mines and the like – are now linked by the seven-mile-long **Clywedog Trail**. It is all a bit heavy on packaged heritage, but if you're interested, pick up a leaflet from the Wrexham tourist office.

Despite the closure of the ironworks, coal continued to be mined in the valley up until 1986. After World War II, coal tunnels were pushed under nearby **Erddig Hall** (April–Sept Mon–Wed, Sat & Sun 11am–5pm; Oct–March "below stairs" and grounds only; full tour £5, "below stairs" and gardens £3.20; NT), two miles south of Wrexham on the #37 bus, adding subsidence to the troubles of an already decaying seventeenth-century building. Ever since the mansion was built, its owners maintained a conservative building policy which resulted in near decrepitude, since restored to its 1922 appearance.

The house itself isn't distinguished, as eighteenth-century architects James Wyatt and Thomas Hopper were tightly reined when suggesting alterations. The State Rooms upstairs have their share of fine furniture and portraits – including one by Gainsborough – but any interest really lies in the quarters of the servants, whose lives were fully documented by their unusually benevolent masters. Portraits of the servants painted in the eighteenth- and early nineteenth-centuries are still on display in the Servants' Hall, and each has a verse written by one of the Yorkes, not noted for their poetic prowess, but whose extraordinary devotion to their servants is touching. You can also see the blacksmith's shop, lime yard, stables, laundry, the still-used bakehouse and kitchen.

Chirk Castle

Seven miles south of Wrexham, the busy Dee valley cuts west to Llangollen, a great contrast to the parallel valley of the River Ceiriog, its entrance guarded by the massive drum-towered **Chirk Castle** (April–June & Sept Tues–Fri & Sun noon–5pm; July & Aug daily except Sat; Oct Sat & Sun only; £4; NT), squatting ominously on a rise half a mile to the west of **CHIRK** (Y Waun). Roger Mortimer began the construction of the castle during the thirteenth century, and it eventually fell to the Myddleton family. The approach to this Marcher fortress, built at the behest of Edward I, is guarded by a magnificent Baroque gate screen, the finest work done by the Davies brothers of Bersham, who wrought it between 1712 and 1719. The ebullient floral designs are capped by the coat of arms of the Myddletons who have lived here for the past four hundred years. A long oak avenue leads up to the austere castle, designed to mimic Beaumaris castle, but lacking Beaumaris' purity and symmetry. The exterior has been extensively remodelled, as have the interiors, leaving a legacy of sumptuous rooms reflecting sixteenth- to nineteenth-century tastes, many returned to their former states after some Victorian meddling by Pugin in the 1840s.

Llangollen and around

LLANGOLLEN, ten miles southwest of Wrexham, is in both setting and character the embodiment of a Welsh town, clasped tightly in the narrow Dee valley between the shoulders of the Berwyn and Eglwyseg mountains. Along the valley's floor, the waters of the River Dee (Afon Dyfrdwy) run down to the town, licking the angled buttresses of the weighty Gothic bridge, which has spanned the river since the fourteenth century. On its south bank, half a dozen streets, their houses harmoniously straggling up the rugged hillsides, are labelled in both Welsh and English, and form the core of the scattered settlement flung out across the low hills which comes alive every July for the **International Music Eisteddfod** (p.650).

As the only river crossing point for miles, Llangollen was an important town long before the early Romantics arrived at the end of the eighteenth century, when they were cut off from their European Grand Tours by the Napoleonic Wars. Turner came to paint the swollen river and the Cistercian ruin of **Valle Crucis**, a couple of miles up the valley; John Ruskin found the town "entirely lovely in its gentle wildness"; and writer George Borrow made Llangollen his base for the early part of his 1854 tour detailed in *Wild Wales*. The rich and famous came not just for the scenery, but to visit the celebrated **Ladies of Llangollen**, an eccentric pair of lesbians who became the toast of society from their house, **Plas Newydd**. But by this stage some of the town's rural charm had been eaten up by the works of one of the century's finest engineers, Thomas Telford, squeezing both his **London–Holyhead trunk road** and the **Llangollen Canal** alongside the river.

The Town

Standing in twelve acres of formal gardens, half a mile up Hill Street from the southern end of Castle Street, the two-storied mock-Tudor **Plas Newydd** (April–Sept daily

THE LLANGOLLEN INTERNATIONAL MUSIC EISTEDDFOD

Llangollen is heaving in summer, but never more so than during the first week of July, when for six days the town explodes into a frenzy of music, dance, poetry and bundles of colour. The **International Music Eisteddfod** comes billed as "the world's greatest folk festival" but unlike the National Eisteddfod, which is a purely Welsh affair, the Llangollen event draws amateur performers from thirty countries, all competing for prizes in their chosen disciplines. Throughout the week, performers present their works at numerous sites around the town, but mainly in the much derided 6000-seat white plastic structure designed to evoke the shape of the traditional marquee which used to be erected on the site each year.

The Eisteddfod has been held in its present form since 1947, when it was started more or less on a whim by one Harold Tudor. Forty choirs from fourteen countries performed at the first event and today more than 12,000 musicians, singers, dancers and choristers from countries around the world descend on this town of 3000 people, further swamped by up to 150,000 visitors. While the whole set-up can seem oppressive, there is an irresistible *joie de vivre* as brightly costumed dancers walk the streets and fill the fish and chip shops.

Unless you are going specifically for the Eisteddfod, the week beginning the first Tuesday of July is probably a good time to stay away. If you come, book early for both accommodation and tickets (☎01978/860236).

9am–5pm; £1.50) was, for almost fifty years, home to the celebrated **Ladies of Llangollen**. Lady Eleanor Butler and Sarah Ponsonby were a lesbian couple from Anglo-Irish aristocratic backgrounds, who tried to elope together at the end of the eighteenth century. After two botched attempts dressed in men's clothes, they were grudgingly allowed to leave in 1778 with an annual allowance of £280, enough to settle in Llangollen, where they became the country's most celebrated lesbians. Despite their desire for a "life of sweet and delicious retirement", they didn't seem to mind the constant stream of gentry who called on them. Walter Scott was well received, though he found them "a couple of hazy or crazy old sailors" in manner, and like "two respectable superannuated clergymen" in their mode of dress. Gifts of sculpted wood panelling formed the basis of the riotous friezes of gloomy woodwork that weigh on your every step around the modest black and white timbered house, and most of the rooms have been left almost empty, so as not to hide the panelling; only one upper room has been devoted to a few of the ladies' possessions and panels covering their life story.

Llangollen takes its name from the **Church of St Collen** on Bridge Street (May–Sept daily until dusk; free tours at 1pm), outside which is a triangular railed-off monument to Mary Carryll erected by her mistresses, the Ladies of Llangollen, who are also buried in the churchyard. On nearby Castle Street is the site of the **European Centre for Traditional and Regional Cultures (ECTARC)** (May–Sept Mon–Fri 10am–5pm, Sat 10am–6pm, Sun 11am–5pm; Oct–April Mon–Sat 10am–5pm, Sun 1–5pm; free), primarily a centre for folk studies. The centre also presents occasional performances and six-monthly displays drawing on each of the fifteen EU countries in turn, focusing on such diverse topics as lesser-used languages, ceramics and, pointedly, the effect of tourism on fragile communities.

Practicalities

Buses stop on Market Street, while the nearest **train station** is five miles away at Ruabon, and passed by frequent buses on the Llangollen–Wrexham run. The **tourist office** (daily Easter–Oct 9am–6pm; Nov–Easter 9.30am–5pm; ☎01978/860828) is fifty yards from the bridge and less than a hundred yards from the bus stop on Market

Street. The energetic can take half-hour open **canoe rides** (☎01978/861444) down the rapids below Mile End Mill, half a mile towards Corwen on the A5.

Finding **rooms** in Llangollen can be a chore in summer, especially during the Eisteddfod. A bargain B&B close to the centre of town is *Mrs Lewis*, 1 Bodwen Villas, Hill St (☎01978/860882; ②); another cheap choice is *Mrs Adams*, 2–3 Aberadda Cottages, Hill St (☎01978/860770). *Gales Wine Bar*, 18 Bridge St (☎01978/861427; ④) is a comfortable guest house above a wonderful restaurant, while *Hillcrest*, Hill St (☎01978/860208; ③) is a good non-smoking guest house. *The Royal Hotel*, Bridge St (☎01978/860331; ⑥), is an excellent nineteenth-century place by the bridge in town. The high standard **Llangollen YHA hostel**, Tyndwr Rd (March–Oct; ☎01978/860330; ①) is a mile and a half from town – go along the A5 towards Shrewsbury, right up Birch Hill, then right again – and *Eirianfa* (☎01978/860919), a mile west of the town on the A5 is the closest **campsite** (they also rent out bikes).

Though not extensive by city standards, Llangollen boasts a fairly good selection of **restaurants** and no shortage of cafés around town. The existence of *Gales*, 18 Bridge St (closed Sun; ☎01978/860089), is a reason in itself to come to Llangollen, with large helpings of delicious homemade bistro-style food. *The Gallery*, 15 Chapel St, serves a good range of pizza and pasta dishes. The *Hand Hotel*, 26 Bridge St, is a straightforward local pub where you can listen to the male voice choir in full song at 7.30pm on Monday and Friday. Another good watering hole is *Jenny Jones*, Abbey Rd, with live country and western music on Wednesday and jazz on Thursday.

North of the River Dee

The hills around Llangollen echo to the shrill cry of steam engines easing along the **Llangollen Steam Railway** (April–Oct daily 9.30am–4.30pm; winter Sat & Sun only 9.30am–4.30pm) shoe-horned into the north side of the valley. From Llangollen's time-warped station it runs along a restored section of the disused Ruabon-Barmouth line, the belching steam engines creeping four miles west along the riverbank, hauling ancient carriages which proudly sport the liveries of their erstwhile owners.

The tiny **Llangollen Wharf Canal Museum** on Wharf Hill near the station (Easter–Oct daily 10am–4pm; £1, free for canal tour passengers) admirably explains the construction in the context of Britain's canal-building mania at the end of the eighteenth century. Thomas Telford avoided using locks for the first fourteen miles of the canal by boldly building the thousand-foot-long **Pontcysyllte Aqueduct** 126ft above the Dee, at **FRONCYSYLLTE**, four miles east. Diesel-driven narrow boats (summer Sat & Sun noon; July & Aug also Tues & Thurs) edge their way across on two-hour trips from Llangollen, or you can drive – or walk the towpath – to Froncysyllte on the A542 and take the short ride (45min) across the aqueduct and back, turning a blind eye to the nearby chemical plant.

The panoramic view, especially at sunset, justifies a 45-minute slog up to **Castell Dinas Brân** (Crow's Fortress Castle), perched on a hill eight hundred feet above the town, and reached by a path near the Canal Museum. The lure certainly isn't the few sad vaulted stumps which stand in poor testament to what was once the district's largest and most important Welsh fortress. Built by the ruler of northern Powys, Prince Madog ap Gruffydd Maelor, in the 1230s, the castle rose on the site of an earlier Iron Age fort. Edward I soon took it as part of his first campaign against Llywelyn ap Gruffydd, and the castle was left to decay; John Leland, Henry VIII's antiquarian, found it "all in ruin" in 1540.

The gaunt ruin of **Valle Crucis Abbey** (April to late Oct daily 9.30am–6pm; late Oct to March Mon–Sat 9.30am–4pm, Sun 2–4pm; £1.70; CADW), mile or so west of Llangollen, greets you with its best side, the largely intact west wall of the church pierced by the frame of a rose window. Though one of the last Cistercian foundations in Wales, and the first Gothic abbey in Britain, it is no match for Tintern Abbey, but stands majestically in a pastoral, and much less visited, setting. Despite a devastating fire in its first century, and a company of far from pious monks, it survived until the Dissolution in 1535. The church fell into disrepair, after which the monastic buildings, in particular the monks' dormitory, were employed as farm buildings. Now they hold displays on monastic life, reached by a detour through the mostly ruined cloister and past the weighty vaulting of the chapter house.

Bala

The little town of **BALA** (Y Bala), at the northern end of Wales' largest natural lake, **Llyn Tegid** (Bala Lake), is a major watersports centre, and if that's of no interest, there's little point in stopping here. The four-mile-long body of water is perfect for **windsurfing** in particular, with buffeting winds whipping up the valley formed by the Bala geological fault line, which slices thirty miles northeast from the coast, up the Talyllyn Valley. Bala's role in Welsh history far outweighs its current status. During the early nineteenth century, the people here became renowned for their piousness and followed the preachings of Nonconformist ministers Thomas Charles who founded the British and Foreign Bible Society

Slalom kayak fans can make for the **Canolfan Tryweryn** white-water course, four miles west up the A4212, which wouldn't exist were it not for a 1960s example of England's long-standing habit of flooding Welsh valleys, so that English cities, in this case Liverpool, can have their drinking water. When water is released (around 200 days a year), it crashes down a mile and a half through the slalom site, the venue for the 1981 World Slalom Championships, frequent summer-weekend competitions, and the only commercial **white-water rafting** trips in Wales (reservations ☎01678/521083). It is a fairly steep £7 a pop for a heart-stopping run down the roughest part, but for £120 a group of up to seven can rent a raft and instructor for two hours, or about five runs.

The only **bus** is the #94, which runs from Llangollen to Dolgellau, stopping on the High Street. The **tourist office** is in the lakeside Penllyn centre, five minutes' walk away on Pensarn road (April–Sept daily 10am–6pm; Oct–March Mon & Fri–Sun 10am–1pm & 2–5pm). Bala has plenty of **places to stay** or you can make the most of the surrounding countryside by staying in the Vale of Edeyrnion, northeast of the town. Centrally, try the *White Lion Royal Hotel*, 61 High St (☎01678/520314; ⑥), the best place in town, favoured in the past by both Queen Victoria and George Borrow. A little further out there's *Abercelyn*, a fine country house half a mile south of Bala on the A494 (☎01678/521109; ③), and the *Plas Rhiwaedog* **YHA hostel**, Plas Rhiwaedog, two miles from Bala (☎01678/520215) – a seventeenth-century manor house reached by taking the B4402 Llandrillo road then third right after crossing the river. *Pen-y-Bont*, on the B4402 Llandrillo road (April–Oct; ☎01678/520549) is the nearest **campsite**.

Snowdonia

What the coal valleys are to the south of the country, the mountains of Snowdonia (Yr Eryri) are to north Wales: the defining feature, not just in their physical form, but in the way they have shaped the communities within them. To Henry VIII's antiquarian, John Leland, the region seemed "horrible with the sight of bare stones"; now it is widely acclaimed as the most dramatic and alluring of all Welsh scenery, a compact, barren land of tortured ridges dividing glacial valleys, whose sheer faces belie the fact that the tallest peaks only just top three thousand feet. It was to this mountain fastness that Llywelyn ap Gruffydd, the last true Prince of Wales, retreated in 1277 after his first war with Edward I; it was also here that Owain Glyndŵr held on most tenaciously to his dream of regaining the title of Prince of Wales for the Welsh. Centuries later, the

English came to remove the mountains; slate barons built huge fortunes from Welsh toil and reshaped the patterns of Snowdonian life forever, as men looking for steady work in the quarries fled the hills and became town dwellers. By the mid-nineteenth century, those with the means began flocking here to marvel at the plunging waterfalls and walk the ever-widening paths to the mountaintops. Numbers have increased rapidly since then and thousands of hikers arrive every weekend for some of the country's best walks over steep, exacting and constantly changing terrain.

Recognizing the region's scientific importance, as well as its scenic and recreational appeal, Snowdonia became the heartland of Wales's first national park, the **Snowdonia National Park** (Parc Cenedlaethol Eryri), an 840-square-mile area which extends south, outside the strict bounds of Snowdonia, to encompass the Rhinogs and Cadair Idris. Not surprisingly the **Snowdon** massif (Eryri) is the focus; several of the widely recognized routes up are superb, and you can always take the cog railway up to the summit café from **Llanberis**. But the other mountains are as good or better, often far less busy and giving unsurpassed views of Snowdon. The **Glyders** and **Tryfan** are particular favourites and best tackled from the **Ogwen Valley**.

If you are serious about doing some **walking** – and some of the walks described here are serious, especially in bad weather (Snowdon gets 200 inches of rain a year) – you need a good map such as the 1:50,000 OS Landranger #115 or the 1:25,000 OS Outdoor Leisure #17; be sure to phone for local weather forecasts (☎01839/500449; premium rate). Weather reports and walking conditions are often posted on the doors or noticeboards of outdoor shops and tourist offices.

Snowdonia isn't all walking. Small settlements are dotted in the valleys, usually coinciding with some enormous mine or quarry. Foremost among these are **Blaenau Ffestiniog**, the "Slate Capital of North Wales", where two mines open their caverns for underground tours, and **Beddgelert** whose former copper mines are also open to the public. The only place of any size not associated with extracting the earth's wealth is **Betws-y-Coed**, a largely Victorian resort away from the higher peaks, but a springboard for the walkers' hamlets of **Capel Curig** and **Pen-y-Pass**.

Betws-y-Coed and around

Sprawled out across a flat plain at the confluence of the Conwy, Llugwy and Lledr valleys, **BETWS-Y-COED** (pronounced Betoos-ah-Coyd) should be the perfect base for exploring Snowdonia. Its riverside setting, overlooked by the conifer-clad slopes of the Gwydir forest, is undeniably appealing, and the town boasts the best selection of hotels and guest houses in the region; but after an hour mooching around the outdoor equipment shops and drinking tea you are left wondering what to do. None of the serious mountain walks start from here, and while there are a couple of easy walks up river gorges leading to the town's two main attractions, the **Conwy Falls** and **Swallow Falls**, these can get depressingly busy in the height of summer. That said, its much touted role as "the gateway to Snowdonia" means it is hard to avoid.

The one-time lead-mining town of Betws-y-Coed remained a backwater until 1815 when, as part of his A5 toll road, Telford completed the graceful **Waterloo Bridge** (Y Bont Haearn), speeding access for the leisured classes already alerted to the town's beauty in landscapes by J.M.W. Turner. The arrival of the train line in 1868 lifted its status from coaching station to genteel resort, an air the town vainly tries to maintain. By the station, the **Conwy Valley Railway Museum** (Easter–Oct daily 10.30am–5.30pm; £1) presents a fairly dull collection of memorabilia and shiny engines, slightly enlivened by the chance of a short ride on a miniature train or tram. The **Motor Museum** (Easter–Oct daily 10am–6pm; 80p), a couple of hundred yards away behind the tourist office, is little better, with a half-dozen classic bikes and fifteen cars such as a 1934 Bugatti Straight 8 and a Model T Ford.

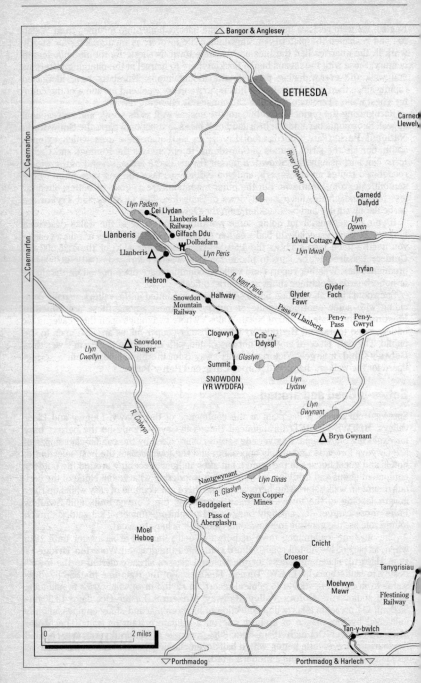

△ Bangor & Anglesey

BETHESDA

Carned
Llewely

Carnedd
Dafydd

River Ogwen

◁ Caernarfon

◁ Caernarfon

Llyn Padarn
Cei Llydan
Llanberis Lake
Railway
Gilfach Ddu
Llanberis · Dolbadarn

Llyn Ogwen

Idwal Cottage △

Llanberis △
Llyn Peris
Llyn Idwal

Hebron

R. *Nant Peris*

Tryfan

Snowdon
Mountain
Railway
Halfway

Glyder
Fawr

Glyder
Fach

Pass of Llanberis

Pen-y-
Pass

Pen-y-
Gwryd

Clogwyn

Crib -y-
Ddysgl

Pen-y-Pass △

*Llyn
Cwellyn*

△ Snowdon
Ranger

Summit
Glaslyn

SNOWDON
(YR WYDDFA)

*Llyn
Llydaw*

*Llyn
Gwynant*

R. Colwyn

△ Bryn Gwynant

Nantgwynant
R. *Glaslyn*

Llyn Dinas

Sygun Copper
Mines

Beddgelert

Pass of
Aberglaslyn

Moel
Hebog

Cnicht

Croesor

Tanygrisiau

Moelwyn
Mawr

Ffestiniog
Railway

Tan-y-bwlch

0   2 miles

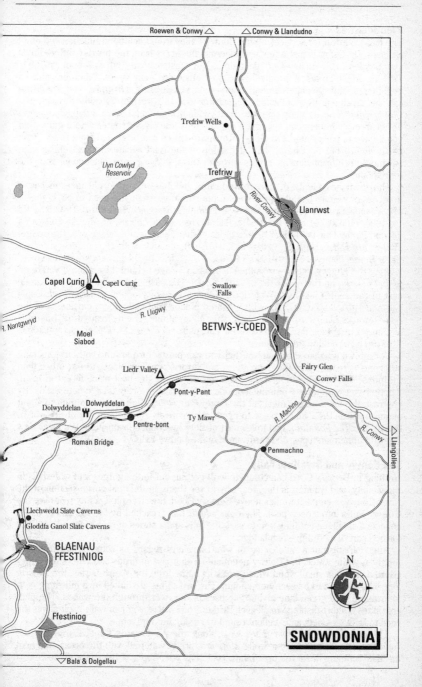

Roewen & Conwy △
△ Conwy & Llandudno

Trefriw Wells

Llyn Cowlyd
Reservoir

Trefriw

River Conwy

Llanrwst

Capel Curig △ Capel Curig

Swallow
Falls

R. Nantgwryd

R. Llugwy

BETWS-Y-COED

Moel
Siabod

Lledr Valley △

Fairy Glen

Conwy Falls

Pont-y-Pant

Dolwyddelan Dolwyddelan

Ty Mawr

R. Machno

△ Llangollen

R. Conwy

Pentre-bont

Roman Bridge

Penmachno

Llechwedd Slate Caverns

Gloddfa Ganol Slate Caverns

BLAENAU
FFESTINIOG

N

Ffestiniog

SNOWDONIA

▽ Bala & Dolgellau

Practicalities

The **train station** for services up the Conwy Valley from Llandudno Junction and on to
Blaenau Ffestiniog is just a few paces across the grass from the **tourist office**, Royal
Oak Stables (daily Easter–Oct 10am–6pm; Nov–Easter 10am–1pm & 2–5pm; ☎01690/
710426). Most **buses** stop outside the post office on Main Street. Whether you're a
beginner or intermediate climber, courses on **scrambling**, **climbing** and **abseiling**
can be arranged by contacting *Snowdonia Guides* (☎01690/710555) through the
Climber and Rambler shop opposite Pont-y-Pair bridge for £15–£25 a day. Competent
but gear-less climbers can also get a day out on some classic routes with a guide, but
you'll have to pay around £75 a day. **Mountain bikes** can be rented from *Beics Betws*
(☎01690/710766) on Church Hill at the top of the road beside the post office, with
permits and information on routes through the Gwydyr Forest obtainable from the
tourist office.

The town has plenty of **accommodation**, but has to cope with an even larger
numbers of visitors pushing prices up in the summer, when you need to book ahead.
The cheapest rooms are above the award-winning *Riverside Restaurant*, Holyhead Rd
(☎01690/710650; ①) near the Pont-y-Pair bridge. *Glan Llugwy*, on the A5 300 yards
beyond Pont-y-Pair (☎01690/710592; ②) is another cheap option, along with the budget
Pont-y-Pair Hotel, High St (☎01690/710407; ②), popular with mountaineers. *Ty'n-y-
Celyn House*, Llanrwst Rd (☎01690/710202; ③), is a friendly Victorian guest house overlooking the Llugwy Valley; cross the suspension bridge behind the station if you're on
foot. *Ty Gwyn*, on the A5 (☎01690/7103383; ④), is a cosy old coaching inn half a mile
east of the centre just over Waterloo Bridge. The luxury option is *Tan-y-Foel*, Capel
Garmon (☎01690/710507; ⑦), with a heated indoor pool and superb cuisine; take the
A470 towards Llanrwst then turn right after about a mile. The nearest **youth hostel** is
at Capel Curig (see p.659); the closest **campsite** is *Riverside* (Easter–Oct; ☎01690/
710310), right behind the station.

For a town so geared to tourism that you can hardly turn around without knocking
someone's cream tea to the floor, there are surprisingly few places to **eat** other than
the pubs. The aforementioned *Ty Gwyn*, on the A5, is the best place to eat in town,
whether you want a tasty pub meal or one of their praiseworthy table d'hôte meals. By
contrast, the low-cost bar meals at the *Pont-y-Pair Hotel*, High St, are nothing to shout
about, but it is the liveliest place to drink. Alternatively (in every sense of the word),
there's the *The Fountain*, two miles east of Betws-y-Coed, a favourite of the local New
Age and bohemian types, 300 yards short of the Conwy Falls.

The Conwy and Swallow Falls

Nothing in Betws-y-Coed can compete with getting out to the gorges and waterfalls in
the vicinity, and walking is the ideal way to see them. In the final gorge section of the
River Conwy, a couple of miles above Betws-y-Coed, the river plunges fifty feet over the
Conwy Falls into a deep pool. The *Conwy Falls Café*, reached by the #49 bus (4 daily)
collects a small fee entitling you to view the falls and a series of rock steps which once
formed part of a primitive fish ladder.

After carving out a mile or so of what kayakers regard as some of north Wales'
toughest white water, the Conwy negotiates a staircase of drops and enters the **Fairy
Glen**, a cleft in a small wood which takes its name from the Welsh fairies, the *Tylwyth
Teg*, who are said to be seen hereabouts. The two sights are linked by a mile-long path
following a cool green lane giving glimpses of the river through the woods. The path
continues a short distance to Beaver Bridge from where you can walk back along the
road to Betws-y-Coed; an excellent round trip using bus and foot.

The **Swallow Falls**, two miles west along the A5 towards Capel Curig, are the
region's most visited sight: a straightforward, pretty waterfall with the occasional mad
kayaker scraping down the precipitous rock. Pay your 30p and you can walk down to a

THE WELSH SLATE INDUSTRY

Slate derives its name from the Old French word *esclater*, meaning to split, an apt reflection of its most highly valued quality. The Romans recognized the potential of the substance, roofing the houses of Segontium with it, and Edward I used it extensively in his Iron Ring of castles around Snowdonia. It wasn't until around 1780 that Britain's Industrial Revolution kicked in, leading to greater urbanization and boosting the demand for Welsh roofing slates. Cities grew; Hamburg was re-roofed with Welsh slate after its fire of 1842, and it is the same material which still gives that rainy-day sheen to interminable rows of English mill town houses.

By 1898, Welsh quarries – run, like the coal and steel industries of the south, by the English – were producing half a million tons of dressed slate a year, almost all of it from Snowdonia. At Penrhyn and Dinorwig, mountains were hacked away in terraces, sometimes rising 2000ft above sea level, with the teams of workers negotiating with the foreman for the choicest piece of rock and the selling price for what they produced. They often slept through the week in damp dormitories on the mountain, and tuberculosis was common, exacerbated by the slate dust. At Blaenau Ffestiniog, the seams required mining underground rather than quarrying, but conditions were no better with miners even having to buy their own candles, the only light they had. In spite of this, thousands left their hillside smallholdings for the burgeoning quarry towns. Few workers were allowed to join Undeb Chwarelwyr Gogledd Cymru (The North Wales Quarrymen's Union), and in 1900 the workers in Lord Penrhyn's quarry at Bethesda went out on strike. For three years they stayed out – Britain's longest ever industrial dispute – but failed to win any concessions. Those who got their jobs back were forced to work for even less money as a recession took hold, and although the two World Wars heralded mini-booms as bombed houses were replaced, the industry never recovered its nineteenth-century prosperity, and most quarries and mines closed in the 1950s.

For the 1862 London Exhibition, one skilled craftsman produced a sheet ten feet long, a foot wide and a sixteenth of an inch thick – so thin it could be flexed – firmly establishing Welsh slate as the finest in the world. Sadly, much of what little is produced today is used for things besides roofing: floor tiles, road aggregate and an astonishing array of nasty ashtrays and coasters etched with mountainscapes.

series of viewing platforms. Better still, leave the car park on the north side of the Pont-y-Pair bridge, in town, and follow the **Llugwy Valley walk** (3 miles; 400ft ascent; 1hr 30min), a forested path following the twisting and plunging river upstream towards Capel Curig. Less than a mile from Pont-y-Pair you first reach the steeply sloping **Miners' Bridge**, which linked miners' homes at Pentre Du on the south side of the river to the lead mines in Llanrwst. The path follows the river on your left for another mile – though path maintenance sometimes means you have to cut up into the pines – to a slightly obscured view of **Swallow Falls**. Detailed maps available from the tourist office show numerous routes back through the Gwydyr Forest or you can continue half a mile to the road bridge from where you can wait for the bus back to Betws-y-Coed.

Blaenau Ffestiniog and around

Every approach to **BLAENAU FFESTINIOG** is dramatic, but none more so than Lledr valley train line from Betws-y-Coed which follows the twists of the river through broad-leaf woods that give way to the smooth, grassy slopes of the Moel Siabod before you bore through over two miles of slate – the longest rail tunnel in Wales – to suddenly emerge right in the town. Blaenau means "head of the valley", in this case the lush Vale of Ffestiniog, a dramatic contrast to this forbidding town, hemmed in by the stark slopes of the Manod and Moelwyn Mountains thickly strewn with discarded heaps of splintered slate that didn't pass muster. When clouds hunker low in this great cwm and rain sheets the grey roofs, grey walls and grey paving slabs, it can be a terrifically gloomy place. Thousands of tons of slate per year were once hewn from the labyrinth of underground caverns here, but these days the town is only kept alive by two mines offering tours, and by tourists who change from the Lledr valley train line onto the wonderful, narrow-gauge **Ffestiniog Railway** which winds up from Porthmadog.

The mines

It is difficult to get a real feeling of what slate means to Blaenau Ffestiniog without a visit to one of the town's two slate mines, a mile or so north of town on the Betws-y-Coed road (bus #140, hourly when the mines are open) both of which present entertaining and informative insights into the rigours of a miner's life.

The **Llechwedd Slate Caverns** (daily March–Sept 10am–5.15pm; Oct–Feb 10am–4.15pm; single tour £5.25, both tours £7.50) are slightly closer to the town and can be visited on one of two tours. The **Miners' Tramway Tour** takes you by a small train a third of a mile along one of the oldest levels to the enormous Cathedral Cave and the open-air Chough's as you are plied with factual stuff about slate mining. The awe-inspiring scale of the place justifies going on the tour even without the tableaux of Victorian miners at work chained high up in the tops of the caverns. On the more dramatic **Deep Mine Tour** you're bundled onto Britain's steepest underground inclined railway and lowered to one of the deepest parts of the mine, a labyrinth of tunnels through which you are guided by an irksome taped spiel of a Victorian miner. The long caverns angling back into the gloom are increasingly impressive, culminating in one filled by a beautiful opalescent pool.

The **Gloddfa Ganol Slate Mine** (Easter–Oct Mon–Fri 10am–5.30pm; July & Aug daily; £4) is slightly further along the same road from Blaenau Ffestiniog and is much less forced, giving a chance to take it all in at your leisure. There are no trains, and the tour is self-gided following taped explanations through fourteen caverns, past mannequins dressed as miners and lamps probing the darker recesses of caverns 240ft deep. Save time to inspect the workings above ground, which still comprise an operational open-cast quarry, and the various museums telling of the changing fortunes of Blaenau Ffestiniog, along with examples of the multifarious uses of slate. And don't miss the excellent **Quarrymen's Cottages**, a faithful reproduction of a three-cottage terrace, each two-up-two-down decorated in a different period: 1885, World War I and World War II. You can also dish out for the hour-long **Land Rover Tour** (reserve at the

---

A WALK FROM BLAENAU FFESTINIOG

One of the most scenic, and easiest, walks around Blaenau Ffestiniog leads down into the **Vale of Ffestiniog** (4–5 miles; descent only; 2–3hr) following the Ffestiniog Railway past its 360° loop, through sessile oak woods and past several cascades all the way to Tan-y-bwlch. From here, you can return to Blaenau Ffestiniog, or continue on the Porthmadog by train; check the times at Tanygrisiau station and buy your ticket to ensure a place on the return train.

The walk can be done from Blaenau Ffestiniog, but involves a fairly dull first mile easily avoided by catching the railway or driving to the reservoir at Tanygrisiau. From the station, turn right past the Tanygrisiau information centre then take the second left, not the road beside the reservoir but the next one following the footpath signs. Cross the train line, then pass a car park on your left before turning left down a track and skirting behind the powerhouse. The path then sticks closely to the train line, occasionally crossing it. Even when there are several paths you can't go far wrong if you keep the train lines in sight. *The Grapes* pub at Maentwrog, half a mile from Tan-y-bwlch, is a great place to while away the time until the next train (or the one after that).

reception; £2.50) which dives into the mountain, climbs up through six levels past the remoter chambers and disgorges you at a wonderful vantage point with views over the vast heaps of discarded slate around Blaenau Ffestiniog.

Practicalities

The **train station** on the High Street serves both the Ffestiniog line from Porthmadog and main-line train services from Betws-y-Coed, and also houses the **tourist office** (April–Oct daily 10am–6pm; ☎01766/830360). **Buses** stop either in the car park around the back or outside *Y Commercial* pub on High Street. A vast number of Blaenau Ffestiniog's visitors ride the train up from Porthmadog, visit a slate mine and leave, and this is reflected in the limited range of **accommodation**. Try the excellent, welcoming cheapie *Afallon*, Manod Rd (☎01766/830468; ②), almost a mile south of the tourist office, and *Fron Heulog Guesthouse* (☎01766/831790; ②), half a mile closer to town; for a few extra pounds, you might want to travel the mile or so south on the A470 to *Cae Du*, Manod Rd (☎01766/830847; ③), in a seventeenth-century farmhouse.

Good **food** isn't especially abundant in Blaenau Ffestiniog. *Caffi Glen*, south of the tourist office on the High Street, does decent all-day breakfasts and snacks, but for something more substantial you're limited to the moderate, broad-ranging menu at *Myfanwys*, 4 Market Place (☎01766/830059), or the hearty, inexpensive Greek and Italian dishes at *The Firefly* (☎01766/830097), opposite *Caffi Glen*. Most locals flock to *Grapes* (☎01766/85208) at Maentwrog, four miles south down the A496, where there's the moderately priced and gamey *Flambard's* restaurant, but the place is lauded for their gargantuan and inexpensive bar meals. Leave room for the desserts if you can.

Capel Curig

Tantalizing glimpses of Wales' highest mountains flash through the forested banks of the Llugwy as you climb west from Betws-y-Coed on the A5. But Snowdon, the mountain which more than any other has become a symbol of north Wales for walkers, mountaineers, botanists and painters alike, eludes you until the final bend before **CAPEL CURIG**, six miles west of Betws-y-Coed, a tiny, scattered village that is a major centre for outdoor enthusiasts. **Plas-y-Brenin: The National Mountaineering Centre**, a quarter of a mile along the A4086 to Llanberis from the town's main road junction, was built around a former coaching inn and hotel, and now runs nationally renowned residential courses in orienteering, canoeing, skiing and climbing. There are daily mountain weather forecasts in reception. Two-hour abseiling, canoeing and dry-slope skiing sessions are held during July and August, there's a state-of-the-art climbing wall open throughout the year (daily 10am–11pm; £2–3), and the opportunity to hear talks or watch slide shows of expeditions (usually Mon–Thurs & Sat 8pm; free).

There are plenty of **places to stay**, though none is especially luxurious. The best is either the *Bron Eryri* (☎01690/720240; ③), a comfortable and welcoming B&B half a mile outside the village towards Betws-y-Coed, or the *Bryn Tyrch Hotel* (☎01690/720223; ③), also on the A5 but closer to the main road junction. The *Llugwy Guesthouse* (☎01690/720218; ②) is on the A4086 towards the adventure centre of **Plas-y-Brenin** (☎01690/720214; ②), which has a limited amount of accommodation. The cheapest option in the village is the **youth hostel** (closed Jan; ☎01690/720225), five hundred yards along the A5 towards Betws-y-Coed. Two and a half miles west down the Ogwen Valley you can stay for a good deal less in the *Williams Barn* bunkhouse and **campsite** (p.660). During the day, walkers patronize the *Pinnacle Café*, grafted onto the post office and general store at the main road junction. In the evening they retire to the warm and lively bar, with great food, at the *Bryn Tyrch Hotel* (see above) to swap tales of the day's exploits, or head for the sociable bar at the Plas-y-Brenin centre.

The Ogwen Valley

Prising apart the Carneddau and Glyder ranges northwest from Capel Curig, the A5 forges through the **Ogwen Valley** to Bethesda, where one of Wales' last surviving slate quarries continues to tear away the end of the Glyders range, only just keeping the tatty town viable. To the north, the frequently mist-shrouded Carneddau range glowers across at the Glyders range and its triple-peaked **Tryfan**, arguably Snowdonia's most demanding mountain, which forms a fractured spur out from the main range and blocks your view down the valley. West of Tryfan the road follows a perfect example of a U-shaped valley, carved and smoothed by rocks frozen into the undersides of the glaciers that creaked down **Nant Ffrancon** ten thousand years ago.

The time-compacted moraine left by the retreating ice formed Llyn Ogwen, and on its shores, **Idwal Cottage**, a settlement so small it isn't named on maps, provides the valleys with a mountain rescue centre, a snack bar and a YHA **youth hostel** clustered around the car park. This is the start of some of Wales' most demanding and rewarding hikes (see box), and the easier half-hour walk to the magnificent classically formed cirque, **Cwm Idwal**. The cwm's scalloped floor traps the beautifully still **Llyn Idwal**, which reflects the precipitous grey cliffs behind, split by the jointed cleft of Twll Du, **The Devil's Kitchen**. Down this, a fine watery haze runs off the flanks of **Glyder Fawr**, soaking the crevices where early botanists found rare arctic-alpine plants, the main reason for designating Cwm Idwal as Wales' first **nature reserve** (NT) in 1954. An easy well-groomed path leads up to the reserve from the car park, where the café (daily 8.30am–5pm; later on summer weekends) will sell you a nature trail booklet for 60p. A five-minute walk down from the car park, the road crosses a bridge over the top of **Rhaeadr Ogwen** (Ogwen Falls), which cascades down this step in the valley floor.

A couple of inconveniently timed **buses** run along the valley daily between Betws-y-Coed and Bangor. **Accommodation** in the valley is limited to a self-catering bunkhouse and **campsite** at _Williams Barn_, Gwern-y-Gof Isaf Farm, two and a half miles west of Capel Curig (☎01690/720276; ①), the smaller _Gwern Gof Uchaf_ campsite, a mile further west, and the _Idwal Cottage_ YHA **youth hostel** (☎01248/600225), at the western end of Llyn Ogwen, five miles from Capel Curig. Residents can get meals at the youth hostel, otherwise the valley is self-catering.

Llanberis and around

Mention **LLANBERIS**, ten miles west of Capel Curig, to any mountain enthusiast and **Snowdon** springs to mind. The two seem inseparable, and it's not just the five-mile-long umbilical of the **Snowdon Mountain Railway**, Britain's only rack and pinion railway, bonding the town to the summit, nor the popular path running parallel to it (see box, p.658). This is the nearest you'll get in Wales to an alpine climbing village, its single main street thronged with weather-beaten walkers and climbers decked out in Gore-Tex and Fibrepile, high fashion for what is otherwise a dowdy town. At the same time Llanberis is very much a Welsh rural community, albeit a depleted one now that slate is no longer being torn from the flanks of Elidir Fawr, the mountain across the towns' twin lakes. The quarries, which for the best part of two centuries employed up to three thousand men to chisel out the precious slabs, closed in 1969, making way for the construction of the Dinorwig Pumped Storage Power Station.

Three of the routes up Snowdon start five miles east of Llanberis at the top of the Llanberis Pass, one of the deepest, narrowest and craggiest in Snowdonia. At the summit, a youth hostel, café and car park comprise the settlement of **PEN-Y-PASS**. Frequent year-round _Sherpa_ **buses** travel up daily to Pen-y-Pass, and from mid-July to

WALKS FROM OGWEN: TRYFAN AND THE GLYDERS

Note: The OS Outdoor Leisure 1:25,000 "Snowdonia"and the 1:50,000 Landranger #115 maps are highly recommended for all these walks.

The sheer number of good walking paths on the Glyders make it almost impossible for us to choose one definitive circular route. The individual sections of the walk have therefore been defined separately in order to allow the greatest flexibility. All times given are for the ascents: expect to take approximately half the time to get back down.

If you've got the head for it, the **North Ridge of Tryfan**, at 3002ft (1 mile; 1hr–1hr 30min; 2000ft ascent), is one of the most rewarding scrambles in the country. It's never as precarious as Snowdon's Crib Goch, but you get a genuine mountaineering feel as the valley floor drops rapidly. The route starts in the lay-by at the head of Idwal Lake and goes left across rising ground, until you strike a path heading straight up following the crest of the ridge to the twin monoliths of **Adam and Eve** on the summit. The courageous, or foolhardy, make the jump between them as a point of honour at the end of every ascent. In theory the leap is trivial, but the consequences of overshooting would be disastrous.

There are two other main routes up Tryfan. The first follows the so-called **Miners' Track** (2 miles; 2hr; 1350ft ascent) from Idwal Cottage, taking the path to Cwm Idwal then, as it bears sharply to the right, keeping straight ahead and making for the gap on the horizon. This is **Bwlch Tryfan**, the col between Tryfan and Glyder Fach, from where the **South Ridge** of Tryfan (800 yards; 30min; 650ft ascent) climbs past the Far South Peak to the summit. This last section is an easy scramble. The second route, which is more often used in descent, follows **Heather Terrace** (1.5 miles; 2hr; 2000ft ascent), which keeps to a fault in the rock running diagonally across the east face.

The assault on **Glyder Fach** (3260ft) begins at Bwlch Tryfan, reached either by the Miners' Track from Idwal Cottage or by the south ridge from Tryfan's summit. The trickier route follows **Bristly Ridge** (1000 yards; 40min; 900ft ascent) which isn't marked on OS maps but runs steeply south from the col up past some daunting-looking towers of rock. In the dry, it isn't that difficult, and saves a long hike southeast along a second section of the **Miners' Track** (1.5 miles; 1hr 30min; 900ft ascent), then west to the summit, a chaotic jumble of huge grey slabs that many people don't bother climbing up, preferring to be photographed on a massive cantilevered rock a few yards away.

From Glyder Fach, it is an easy enough stroll to **Glyder Fawr** (3280ft) (1 mile; 40min; 200ft ascent), reached by skirting round the tortured rock formations of **Castell y Gwynt** (The Castle of the Winds) then following a cairn-marked path to the dramatic summit of frost-shattered slabs angled like ancient headstones. Glyder Fawr is normally approached from Idwal Cottage, following the **Devil's Kitchen Route** (2.5 miles; 3hr; 2300ft ascent) past Idwal Lake, then to the left of the Devil's Kitchen, zigzagging up to a lake-filled plateau. Follow the path to the right of the lake, then where paths cross, turn left for the summit.

August there is also the #96 Pen-y-Pass shuttle from Llanberis, the recommended approach even if you have a car, since the Pen-y-Pass car park is almost always full and is expensive. Use the "Park and Ride" car park at the bottom of the pass.

The Town

Scattered remains are all that is left of thirteenth-century **Dolbadarn Castle** (April to late Oct daily 9.30am–6.30pm; £1, unrestricted access in winter; CADW), on the road to **Parc Padarn** (unrestricted access), where lakeside oak woods are gradually recolonizing the discarded workings of the defunct Dinorwig Slate Quarries. Here, the **Welsh Slate Museum** (Easter–Oct daily 9.30am–5.30pm; £2) occupies the former maintenance workshops of what was one of the largest slate quarries in the world. The line shafts and flapping belts driven by a fifty-foot-diameter water wheel provide a backdrop to workbenches where former quarry workers demonstrate their skills at turning an inch-thick slab of slate into six, even eight, perfectly smooth slivers.To keep everything in working order, the craftsmen here operate an ageing foundry, producing pieces for the scattered branches of the National Museum of Wales, as well as repairing the rolling stock belonging to the nearby **Llanberis Lake Railway** (March to early Oct 4–11 daily except Sat) which formerly transported slate and workers between the Dinorwig quarries and Port Dinorwig on the Menai Straits. It is a tame forty-minute round trip with little to do at the end except come back and explore the old slate workings.

In 1974, five years after the quarry closed, work began hollowing out the vast underground chambers of the **Dinorwig Pumped Storage Hydro Station**, designed to

WALKS ON SNOWDON

The following are justifiably the most popular of the seven accepted routes up Snowdon. *The OS Outdoor Leisure 1:25,000 map of "Snowdonia" is highly recommended for all these walks.*

Llanberis Path
The easiest, longest and most derided route up Snowdon, the **Llanberis Path** (5 miles to summit; 3hr; 3200ft ascent), follows the rail line past the Halfway Station café (March to late Sept daily; winter Sat & Sun only) where the barely believable times of the annual Snowdon Race, which passes on the fourth Saturday in July, are posted inside. Continuing up, the path gets steeper to the "Finger Stone" at **Bwlch Glas** (Green Pass), marking the arrival of the Snowdon Ranger Path (see below), and three routes coming up from Pen-y-Pass to join the Llanberis Path for the final ascent to **Yr Wyddfa**.

The Miners' and Pig tracks
The **Miners' Track** (4 miles to summit; 2hr 30min; 2400ft ascent) is the easiest of the three routes up from Pen-y-Pass, a broad track leading south then west to the dilapidated remains of the former copper mines in Cwm Dyli. Skirting around the right of a lake, the path climbs more steeply to the lake-filled Cwm Glaslyn, then again to Upper Glaslyn, from where the measured steps of those ahead warn of the impending switchback ascent to the junction with the Llanberis Path.

The stonier **Pig Track** (3.5 miles to summit; 2hr 30min; 2400ft ascent) is really just a variation on Miners' Track, leaving from the western end of the Pen-y-Pass car park and climbing up to **Bwlch y Moch** (the Pass of the Pigs) before meeting the Miners' Track prior to the zigzag up to the Llanberis Path.

Snowdon Horseshoe
Some claim that the **Snowdon Horseshoe** (8 miles round; 5–7hr; 3200ft ascent) is one of the finest ridge walks in Europe. The route makes a full anticlockwise circuit around the three glacier-carved cwms of Upper Glaslyn, Glaslyn and Llydaw. Not to be taken lightly, it includes the knife-edge traverse of **Crib Goch**, which requires a minimum of an ice axe and crampons in winter. The path follows the Pig Track to Bwlch y Moch, then pitches right for the moderate scramble up to Crib Goch. If you balk at any of this, turn back: if not, pick your way along the sensational ridge to **Crib-y-ddysgl** (3494ft), and on easier ground to the summit. The return to Llyn Llydaw and the Miners' Track is via **Bwlch-y-Saethau** (Pass of the Arrows) and **Y Lliwedd** (2930ft).

Watkin Path
The most spectacular of the southern routes up Snowdon, the **Watkin Path** (4 miles to summit; 3hr; 3350ft ascent), begins at Bethania Bridge, three miles northeast of Beddgelert in Nantgwynant. The path starts on a broad track through oaks which narrow before heading past a disused tramway to a series of cataracts. A natural amphitheatre contains the ruins of a slate works and **Gladstone Rock**, at which, in 1892, the 83-year-old prime minister and Liberal statesman officially opened the route.

provide power on demand. If you can bear the thinly disguised electricity industry advertisement which comes before it, you can take an hour-long minibus tour around the enormous pipework in the depths. For this, you need to call at **The Power of Wales – Museum of the North** (June to mid-Sept daily 9.30am–6pm; mid-Sept to May 9.30am–6pm; museum £3.50, museum and power station tour £5), by the lake on the A4086 which bypasses the town centre, a museum complex in which the disembodied voice of "Merlin" guides you around some missable tableaux of regional interest.

Snowdon and the Snowdon Mountain Railway

The highest British mountain south of the Scottish Grampians, the **Snowdon** massif (3650ft) forms a star of shattered ridges with three major peaks – Crib Goch, Crib-y-ddysgl and Y Lliwedd – and the summit, **Yr Wyddfa**, crowning the lot. Snowdon sports some of the finest walking and scrambling in the park, and in the winter, the longest season for ice climbers and cramponed walkers. Hardened outdoor enthusiasts dismiss it as overused, and it can certainly be crowded with a thousand visitors a day pressed into the postbox-red carriages of the Snowdon Mountain Railway (see below), while another 1500 pound the well-maintained paths.

Opprobrium is chiefly levelled at the **Snowdon Mountain Railway** (mid-March to Oct 3–18 trains daily; ☎01286/870223) for its mere existence. Completed in 1896, seventy-year-old carriages pushed by equally old steam locos still climb, in just under an hour, from the eastern end of Llanberis opposite the *Royal Victoria Hotel*, to the summit café and bar (open when the trains are running to the top). A "Railway Stamp" (10p) affixed to your letter – along with the usual Royal Mail one – entitles you to use the highest postbox in the UK and enchant your friends with a "Summit of Snowdon – Copa'r Wyddfa" postmark. Times, type of locomotive and final destination vary with demand and ice conditions at the top, but if it is running, the full steam-pushed round trip takes two and a half hours. To avoid disappointment, buy your tickets early on clear summer days. If you walk up by one of the routes detailed in the Walks on Snowdon box (opposite), you can sometimes take the train down if there is space.

Practicalities

All buses stop near the **tourist office**, 41b High Street (April–Sept daily 10am–6pm; Oct–March Wed–Sun 10am–4pm; ☎01286/870765). Adventurous types should contact *Snowdonia Mountaineering* (☎01286/674481) who run specialized courses in scrambling, climbing and canoeing. The **Llanberis Track** (see Snowdon box) is designated a bridleway, making it, the Snowdon Ranger Path and the Pitt's Head Track to Rhyd-Ddu open for **cyclists**. A voluntary agreement exists, restricting access to and from the summit between 10am and 5pm from June to September, but otherwise these paths are open.

There is plenty of low-cost **accommodation** in or close to town: luxurious places are more scarce. Llanberis **youth hostel**, Llwyn Celyn (☎01286/870280), is 700 yards uphill along Capel Goch Road signposted off High Street. A cheaper option is *Nant Peris B&B and Bunkhouse*, three miles east of Llanberis in Gwastadnant (☎01286/870356; ①–②), which also has **camping** facilities. Also consider the *Pen-y-Pass YHA* **youth hostel** (☎01286/870428), four miles east and the *Pen-y-Gwryd Hotel* (March to early Nov daily; winter Sat & Sun only; ☎01286/870211; ④), a mile further west, which is used to muddy boots in the bar. *The Heights*, 74 High St (☎01286/871179; ②–③), also caters to the walking and climbing set, offering B&B and dorm, not to mention a climbing wall, good restaurant and lively bar on site. Also on the High Street, there's *Dolafon Hotel* (☎01286/870933; ③), a comfortable B&B in its own grounds, or the family-run *Mount Pleasant Hotel* (☎01286/870395; ③). The only luxury option is the *Royal Victoria Hotel*, opposite the Mountain Railway (☎01286/870253; ⑥).

For **food** of gut-splitting proportions, climbers and walkers flock to *Pete's Eats*, 40 High St; for real Welsh rarebit, try *Arthur's Café*, next to *Dolafon Hotel*. *Y Bistro*, 43–45

High St (closed Sun; ☎01286/871278) is the best (and most expensive) restaurant for miles around, offering generous two-, three- and four-course set meals from a bilingual menu, all served with canapés on homemade bread. The *Vaynol Arms*, two miles east of Llanberis and the only pub before Pen-y-Gwryd, serves good beer in a convivial atmosphere; it's usually full of campers from across the road.

Beddgelert

Almost all of the prodigious quantity of rain which falls on Snowdon spills down either the Glaslyn or Colwyn rivers which meet at the few dozen hard grey houses which make up **BEDDGELERT**. A sugary and apocryphal tale fabricated by a wily local publican to lure punters tells how the town got its name. **Gelert's Grave** (*bedd* means burial place), an enclosure just south of town, is supposedly the final resting place of Prince Llywelyn ap Iorwerth's faithful dog, Gelert, who was left in charge of the prince's infant son while he went hunting. On his return, the child was gone and the hound's muzzle was soaked in blood. Jumping to conclusions, the impetuous Llywelyn slew the dog, only to find the child safely asleep beneath it's cot and a dead wolf beside him. Llywelyn hurried to his dog, which licked his hand as it died.

Beyond the "grave" the river crashes down the bony and picturesque **Aberglaslyn Gorge** towards Porthmadog. Walk the right bank of the river, past Gelert's Grave, crossing over the bridge onto the disused track bed of the Welsh Highland narrow-gauge rail line. This then hugs the left bank for a mile down to Pont Aberglaslyn, at the bottom of the gorge, an easy path with the more adventurous Fisherman's Path just below it, giving a closer look at the river's course through chutes and channels in sculpted rocks. Return the same way.

A mile in the opposite direction up Nantgwynant, the **Sygun Copper Mine** (Easter–Sept Mon–Fri 10am–5pm, Sat 10am–4pm, Sun 11am–5pm; Oct–Easter daily 11am–4pm; £4), is the delapidated remains of what, until a century ago, had been the valley's prime source of income from Roman times. Restored and made safe, the multiple levels of tunnels and galleries can now be visited on a 45-minute guided tour accompanied by the disembodied voice of a miner telling of his life in the mine.

Buses all stop by the **National Trust shop and information centre** (April–Oct daily 10am–5pm; ☎01766/890293) which is the nearest thing in the village to a tourist office. The best places to **stay** are the *Beddgelert Antiques and Tea Rooms*, Waterloo House, directly opposite the bridge (☎01766/890543; ③), with limited accommodation above the restaurant and tea rooms; *Ael-y-Bryn*, Caernarfon Rd (☎01766/890310; ③), with good views and inexpensive home-cooked evening meals; and *Sygun Fawr Country House*, three quarters of a mile away off the A498 (closed Jan; ☎01766/890258; ④), a partially sixteenth-century house in its own grounds with a sauna and good moderately priced evening meals. The excellent *Beddgelert Forest Campsite* (☎01766/890288) is a mile out on the Caernarfon road, four miles before the highly rated *Snowdon Ranger* **youth hostel** (closed Jan; ☎01286/650391). The *Bryn Gwynant* youth hostel (Jan–Oct; ☎01766/890251) is beautifully sited in Nantgwynant, four miles north-east of Beddgelert on the A498, and has a campsite where you can use the hostel's facilities for half the adult rate.

travel details

Trains

Betws-y-Coed to: Blaenau Ffestiniog (7 daily, 2 buses Sun; 30min); Llandudno Junction (7 daily, 2 buses Sun; 30min).

Blaenau Ffestiniog to: Betws-y-Coed (5 daily, 2 buses Sun; 30min); Llandudno Junction (7 daily, 2 buses Sun; 1hr); Porthmadog by Ffestiniog Railway (April–Oct 4–10 daily; 1hr).

Wrexham to: Chester (every 2hr; 18min); Chirk (every 2hr; 12min).

Buses

Bala to: Dolgellau (6 daily, 2 Sun; 40min); Llangollen (6 daily, 2 Sun; 45min).

Beddgelert to: Caernarfon (5 daily, 1–5 Sun; 30min); Llanberis (5 daily, 1–5 Sun; 55min); Porthmadog (6 daily, 2 Sun in summer; 30min).

Betws-y-Coed to: Capel Curig (7–8 daily, 2–5 Sun; 15min); Conwy (7 daily, 5 Sun; 55min); Llanberis (4–6 daily, 2 Sun; 40min); Ogwen Valley (3 daily except Sun; 25min).

Blaenau Ffestiniog to: Caernarfon (roughly hourly, 4 Sun; 1hr 25min); Porthmadog (every 30min, 4 Sun; 30min).

Capel Curig to: Bangor (2 daily except Sun; 40min); Betws-y-Coed (7–8 daily, 2–5 Sun; 15min); Llanberis (5 daily, 2–5 Sun; 25min); Ogwen (2–3 daily except Sun; 10min).

Llanberis to: Bangor (6 daily except Sun; 40min); Betws-y-Coed (4–6 daily, 2 Sun; 40min); Caernarfon (every 30min, hourly Sun; 25min).

Llangollen to: Bala (6 daily, June–Sept also 2 Sun; 55min); Wrexham (hourly, 6 Sun; 50min).

Ogwen to: Bangor (2 daily except Sun; 30min); Capel Curig (2–3 daily except Sun; 10min).

Wrexham to: Chirk (summer 1 daily; 25min); Llangollen (hourly or better, 7 Sun; 35min).

CHAPTER SIXTEEN

THE NORTH COAST

The **North Coast** encompasses not only the geographical extremities of the country, but takes in an area exhibiting the extremes of the Welsh life. Walking around most of the seaside towns along the eastern section of the coast, only the street signs give any indication that you are in Wales at all: further west, there are places where English is seldom spoken other than to visitors. Those same eastern resorts can be as unashamedly brash as any of their more widely known kin in England, while scattered along the coast, dramatically sited castles work as a superb antidote to low-brow fun-seeking.

In the thirteenth century, the might of English king Edward I all but crushed any aspirations the Welsh princes had, as their armies were forced west towards Anglesey, and Edward set about building the Norman castles which hammered them into subjugation. Walled towns grew up around Edward's castles at **Conwy** and **Caernarfon** that were entirely the preserve of the English, thereby economically and politically marginalizing the Welsh who retreated west where the English wielded less influence. As a response, Edward sited his final castle at **Beaumaris** to protect the entrance to the **Menai Strait**, the treacherous channel that separates the Isle of **Anglesey** from the mainland. The castle's concentric design was militarily more advanced than either Conwy or Caernarfon, but so complete was the English dominance by this stage that Edward never bothered to complete its construction.

The second sweeping change came in the late nineteenth and early twentieth centuries, when the benefits of the Industrial Revolution finally loosened the shackles on English milltown factory workers enough for them to take holidays. Tatty beachfront towns sprang up, epitomized by the stretch of coast from Rhyl to **Colwyn Bay**. In contrast, Victorian **Llandudno**, always the posher place to stay, remains a cut above the rest, lying at the foot of the **Great Orme** limestone peninsula.

A few surprises come embedded into this matrix of bingo halls and caravan sites. The allegedly miraculous waters at **Holywell** have attracted the hopeful since the seventh century, while others come for the National Portrait Gallery's collection at **Bodelwyddan**, and Britain's smallest cathedral at **St Asaph**.

Holywell to Colwyn Bay

Making for the coastal resorts or mountains of Snowdonia, you might be tempted to charge headlong through northern Clwyd, not a bad idea considering the paucity of significant sights. No sooner have you cleared the industrial hinterland that spreads over the border from Cheater than you hit the north Wales coast, a twenty-mile stretch from the end of the Dee Estuary, to Colwyn Bay which constitutes the ugliest piece of Welsh coastline. Its entire length is taken up by unceasing caravan parks with barely an arm's length between neighbouring caravans filled by fun-seekers who descend annually from northern England. Family "amusements" come liberally scattered along the promenades and beachfronts seem designed to keep you off the beaches: a good idea even in the hottest weather since the sea hereabouts is none too clean.

The country flanking the salt marshes of the Dee Estuary was once contested by Marcher lords, but skirmishes were quashed by the construction of the Flint Castle

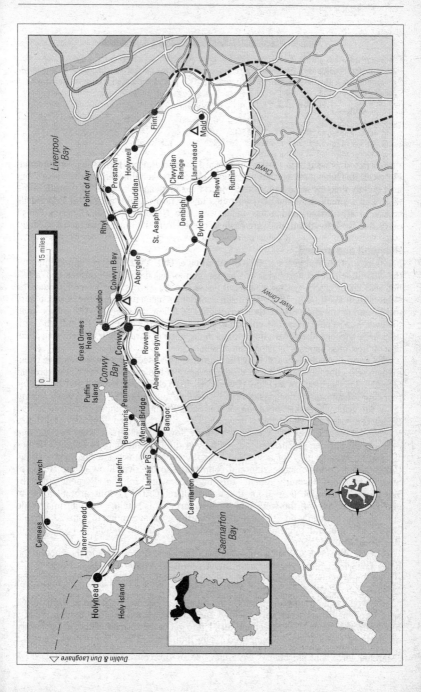

Liverpool Bay

Point of Ayr

Flint

Mold

Holywell

Prestatyn

Clwydian Range

Llanrhaeadr

Rhuddlan

Rhewl

Ruthin

Rhyl

St. Asaph

Denbigh

Bylchau

Clwyd

Colwyn Bay

Abergele

Llandudno

River Conwy

Great Ormes Head

Conwy Bay

Conwy

Rowen

Abergwyngregyn

Puffin Island

Penmaenmawr

Beaumaris

Menai Bridge

Bangor

Amlwch

Llangefni

Llanfair PG

Caernarfon

Cenaes

Llanerchymedd

Caernarfon Bay

Holyhead

Holy Island

N

Dublin & Dun Laoghaire

15 miles

0

(unrestricted access), the earliest of Edward I's Iron Ring of fortresses. Understated Holywell has been an important pilgrimage site for the last thirteen hundred years, but now quietly ticks by almost unvisited. Much the same can be said for **St Asaph**, home to Britain's smallest cathedral. Two miles to the north is the second of Edward I's castles at **Rhuddlan**, and a few miles west, the National Portrait Gallery's Welsh outpost at **Bodelwyddan**; both are easily accessed from the brash resort town of Rhyl.

Holywell and around

For thirteen hundred years a place of pilgrimage, **HOLYWELL** (Treffynnon), just off the A55 fifteen miles northwest of Chester, comes billed as "The Lourdes of Wales", but without the tacky souvenir stalls, it doesn't really warrant such a comparison. **St Winefride's Well** (daily 10am–5pm; 20p donation) – half a mile from the bus station at the far end of the High Street, then turn right and follow the signs – is the source of all the fuss, a calm pool capacious enough to accommodate the dozens of faithful who dutifully wade through the waters three times in the hope of curing their ailments, an adaption of the Celtic baptism by triple immersion.

The spring was first recorded by the Romans, who used the waters to relieve rheumatism and gout, shedding doubt on the veracity of the event that took place around 660 AD. The virtuous Winefride (Gwenfrewi in Welsh) was decapitated here after resisting the amorous advances of Prince Caradoc, and the well is said to have sprung up at the spot where her head fell. When Saint Beuno, her uncle, placed her head beside the body, a combination of prayer and the waters revived her. Richard I and Henry V provided regal patronage, ensuring a steady flow of believers to what became one of the great shrines of Christendom, with even the Catholic king of England, James II, coming here to pray for a son and heir; the eventual answer to his imprecations threatened a Catholic succession and contributed to the overthrow of the House of Stuart. Pilgrims formerly spent the night praying in the Perpendicular **St Winefride's Chapel** (key from the ticket office; CADW), built around 1500 to enclose three sides of the well. The site's importance is waning, but pilgrimages do still take place, mainly on St Winefride's Day, the nearest Sunday to June 22, when a couple of thousand pilgrims are led through the streets behind a relic, part of Winefride's thumb bone.

From St Winefride's Well, a mile-long path runs past the remains of the copper and brass factories which now constitute the **Greenfield Valley Heritage Park**, to the ruined domestic buildings used by the abbot and twelve monks of the Savignac order at **Basingwerk Abbey** (unrestricted access; CADW).

Holywell has no train station, but the bus station, at the southern end of High Street, sees frequent **buses** from here to Rhyl and Chester. From the bus station, head a hundred yards down High Street and turn left to get to the **tourist office**, in the library on North St (Mon 10am–5.30pm, Wed 10am–1pm, Tues, Thurs & Fri 10am–7pm, Sat 9.30am–12.30pm; ☎01352/713157).

St Asaph and around

ST ASAPH (Llanelwy), further west on the A55, ranks as Britain's second smallest city after St David's in Pembrokeshire, and its **cathedral** (open daily 8am–dusk) is the country's most diminutive, no bigger than many village churches. It was founded around 570 AD by Saint Kentigern, the patron saint of Glasgow, and takes its name from the suceeding bishop, Saint Asaph. Both are commemorated in the easternmost window in the north aisle of the cathedral. From 1601 until his death in 1604, the bishopric was held by **William Morgan**, whose grave under the presbytery has gone unmarked since Giles Gilbert Scott's substantial restoration in the 1870s. Morgan was responsible for the translation of the first Welsh-language Bible in 1588, replacing the English ones used up until that time. Over 25 years, he and three other clergymen produced a translation so successful that the Privy Council decreed that a copy should be allocated to every Welsh church, *Y Beibl*, thereby codifying the language and setting a standard for Welsh prose without which, some claim, the language would have died out. One thousand Morgan bibles were printed, of which only nineteen remain, one of them displayed in the north transept along with notable prayer books and psalters.

Buses stop right outside the cathedral. The best central **rooms** are at the *Kentigern Arms* (☎01745/584157; ③), towards the bottom of the High Street, those at the nicely furnished non-smoking *Chalet*, The Roe (☎01745/584025; ③), quarter of a mile away across the river bridge then right, and at the plush *Plas Elwy*, The Roe (☎01745/582263; ⑤), further down the same road. St Asaph's best **food** is served at the moderately priced *Barrow Alms*, High St (☎01745/582260), followed by the bar meals at the *Kentigern Arms*, which is the most alluring pub.

Rhuddlan

RHUDDLAN, two miles north of St Asaph, lies on the banks of a tidal reach of the Clwyd River (Afon Clywedog), which finally meets the sea at Rhyl. The town would be an insignificant suburb of Rhyl but for the diamond-shaped ruin of **Rhuddlan Castle** (May–Sept daily 10am–5pm; £1.70; CADW), built as a garrison and royal residence for Edward I from 1277 to 1282. The still impressive castle commands a canalized section of the river protected by **Gillot's Tower**, seperate from the massive towers behind, the work of James of St George, who was responsible for the concentric plan that allowed archers on both outer and inner walls to fire simultaneously. Important though the castle was, Rhuddlan earns its position in history as the place where Edward I signed the **Statute of Rhuddlan** on March 19, 1284, consigning Wales to centuries of subjugation by the English. A large – and somewhat ironic – plaque in Rhuddlan's main street details the terms of the statute.

Marble Church and Bodelwyddan Castle: the National Portrait Gallery

Barrelling west along the A55 expressway towards the coast, the closest you come to Rhyl is the small village of **BODELWYDDAN**, four miles to the south. The slender 202-foot limestone spire of **Marble Church** heralds the finest art showcase in north Wales, **Bodelwyddan Castle** (Easter–Sept daily 10.30am–5pm; Oct–Easter daily 11am–4pm; £4, gardens £2.50), set amidst landscaped gardens on its hill, half a mile south of Bodelwyddan. The opulent Victorian interiors of what is essentially a nineteenth-century mansion were restored in the 1980s to house one of four provincial outposts of the **National Portrait Gallery**, specializing in works contemporary with the castle.

Most of the two hundred-odd paintings are on the ground floor, approached through the "Watts Hall of Fame", a long corridor specially decorated in William Morris style to accommodate a chair by Morris and 26 portraits of eminent Victorians by G.F. Watts, among them Millais, Rossetti, Browning and Walter Crane. In the Ladies' Drawing Room opposite, a beautiful Biedermeier sofa outshines paintings of little-celebrated nineteenth-century women around the walls. Of the three main rooms, it is the Dining Room that stands out. Two sensitive portraits here highlight the Pre-Raphaelite support for social reform: William Holman Hunt's portrayal of the vociferous opponent of slavery and capital punishment, Stephen Lushington; and Ford Madox Brown's double portrait of Henry Farell, prime mover in the passing of the 1867 Reform Bill, and suffragette Millicent Garrett. Works by John Singer Sargent and Hubert von Herkamer also adorn the room, which like the others, is furnished with pieces from the Victoria and Albert Museum in London. Upstairs, nineteenth-century portraiture, portrait photography and works by female artists get generous coverage along with animal painters, Landseer in particular.

Colwyn Bay

The hilly setting gives **COLWYN BAY** (Bae Colwyn), fourteen miles west of St Asaph, more charm than its neighbours, though there's only one sight, the **Welsh Mountain Zoo** (daily 9.30am–dusk; £4.75), to coax you off the train – and even that is one only really for kids. Perhaps more usefully, there's a good **YHA youth hostel**, Nant-y-Glyn Rd (April–Oct; ☎01492/530627), nearly two miles from the station, up Station Road then left; and a couple of good eating places: the moderately priced Provençal *Café Niçoise*, 124 Abergele Rd (closed all day Sun and Mon lunch; ☎01492/531555) and the inexpensive, vegetarian *Totem*, 2a Erskine Rd (to 6pm; closed Sun).

Llandudno

Almost invariably, the wind funnels between the limestone hummocks of the 680-foot **Great Orme** and its southern cousin the Little Orme, which flank the gently curving Victorian frontage of **LLANDUDNO**; but don't let that put you off visiting this archetype of the genteel British seaside town. Set on a low isthmus, it has an undeniably dignified air, its older set of promenading devotees often huddled in the glassed frontages of once-grand hotels, slowly being replaced by more rumbustious fun-seekers.

Llandudno's early history revolves around the Great Orme, where Saint Tudno, who brought Christianity to the region in the sixth century, built the monastic cell that gives the town its name. When the early Victorian copper mines looked to be worked out in the mid-nineteenth century, local landowner Edward Mostyn exploited the growing craze for seabathing and set about a speculative venture to create a seaside resort for the upper middle classes. Work got under way around 1854 and the resort rapidly gained popularity until the end of the century, when Llandudno had become synonymous with the Victorian ideal of a respectable resort.

No Victorian resort would be complete without its **pier** (open all year; free), and despite the pavilion being destroyed by fire in early 1994, Llandudno's is one of the few remaining in Wales. It juts out into Llandudno Bay, a leisurely ten-minute stroll along The Promenade from Vaughan Street and the region's premier contemporary arts centre, the **Mostyn Art Gallery**, 12 Vaughan St (Mon–Sat 10.30am–5pm; free), which hosts temporary shows featuring works by artists of international renown with a particular leaning towards the current Welsh arts scene.

Kids are better entertained at the **Alice in Wonderland Visitor Centre**, 3–4 Trinity Square (April–Oct daily 10am–5pm; Nov–March closed Sun; £2.50) being guided through the "Rabbit Hole", full of fibre-glass Mad Hatters and March Hares, a headset treating you to readings of *Jabberwocky* and the like, books inspired by Lewis Carroll's meeting with one Alice Liddell, the daughter of friends, here in Llandudno.

The Great Orme

The view from the top of the **Great Orme** (Pen y Gogarth) ranks with those from the far loftier summits in Snowdonia, combining the seascapes east towards Rhyl and west over the sands of the Conwy Estuary with the brooding quarry-chewed northern limit of the Carneddau range where Snowdonia crashes into the sea.

This huge lump of carboniferous limestone was subject to some of the same stresses that folded Snowdonia, producing fissures filled by molten mineral-bearing rock. A Bronze Age settlement developed when people began to smelt the contents of the malachite-rich veins, supplying copper – if current speculation turns out to be true – throughout Europe. The result of their labour is evident at the **Great Orme Copper Mines** (March–Nov daily 10am–5pm; £3.80) acessible by free bus (until end Sept) from Prince Edward Square in town. What were, until recently, considered to be Roman workings have recently revealed 4000-year-old animal bones which had been used as scrapers up to two hundred feet down. Hard hats and miner's lamps are provided for the **guided tour** through just a small portion of the tunnels, enough to get a feel for the cramped working conditions and the dangers of rock fall.

The base of the Great Orme is traditionally circumnavigated on **Marine Drive**, a five-mile anticlockwise circuit from just near Llandudno's pier in your own vehicle. Another road leads up, past the mines, to the **Summit Complex** (Easter–Oct daily; Nov–Easter Sat & Sun only; ☎01492/870610) parallelled by the San Francisco-style **Great Orme Tramway** (April–Oct 10am–6pm; Nov–March 10am–4pm), which creaks up from the bottom of Old Road much as it has done since 1902. From the **Happy Valley** formal gardens, at the base of the pier, a **Cabin Lift** (Easter–Oct daily 10am–12.15pm & 1.45–4.30pm, July & Aug to 5.30pm; £4 return, £3.50 single) carries you up over the Orme to the Summit Complex swinging over *Ski Llandudno* (daily 10am–10pm), where £10 will get you a couple of hours on the dry slopes.

Practicalities

The **train station** at the corner of Augusta and Vaughan streets is five minutes' walk from the **tourist office**, 1 Chapel St (Easter–Sept daily 9.30am–6pm; Oct–Easter Mon–Fri 9.30am–5pm; ☎01492/876413). Chapel Street runs parallel to Mostyn Street, where **local buses** stop. Less than ten minutes' walk south, *National Express* buses pull in to the **coach park** on Mostyn Broadway.

With over seven hundred **hotels**, finding a place to stay is not usually a problem, though in high summer and especially on bank holidays, booking ahead is wise. The greatest concentration of cheaper places is along St David's Road, where you'll find the likes of the non-smoking *Cliffbury Hotel*, 34 St David's Rd (☎01492/877224; ②). *Fernbank*, 9 Chapel St (☎01492/877251; ②), is one of the cheapest and best equipped of a string of low-cost hotels just along from the tourist office. The *Gwesty Leamore Hotel*, 40 Lloyd St (☎01492/875552; ③), is one of the few guest houses in Llandudno actually run by Welsh people. If you've a head for heights, try *The Lighthouse*, Marine Drive (☎01492/876819; ④), three miles from Llandudno, and 370 feet above the Irish Sea. Top-notch accommodation is available at *St Tudno Hotel*, a superb, small seafront hotel on North Parade, just behind the pier (☎01492/874411; ⑦). The closest **camping** is at *Dinarth Hall Farm*, Dinarth Hall Rd, Rhos-on-Sea, three miles east of Llandudno (☎01492/548203), accessible on buses #13, #14 and #15.

Llandudno is blessed with the best choice of **restaurants** in north Wales, ranging from budget cafés to one of the most expensive places in the country. *Richards*, 7 Church Walks, is somewhere in between the two, a basement bistro dishing up imaginative, seafood-based servings. *The Garden Room Restaurant* at the *St Tudno Hotel* is one of Wales' best restaurants producing French-style meals utilizing fresh Welsh produce where possible (moderate to expensive). The *Cottage Loaf*, Market St, is a flag-floored **pub** built from old ships' timbers on top of an old bakehouse, but the oldest pub in town is the *King's Head*, on Old Road, where Edward Mostyn and his surveyor mapped out the town – both are good for substantial, tasty bar meals.

Around the turn of the century, all the best performers clamoured to play Llandudno but today you're lucky to get anything more than faded stars plying the resorts throughout the summer. However, with the new 1500-seat *North Wales Theatre* (Theatr Gogledd Cymru), The Promenade (☎01492/879771) and the **Llandudno October Festival**, things are looking a little rosier.

Conwy and around

Until 1991, traffic ground steadily through **CONWY**, making a visit thoroughly unpleasant, but with the completion of the bypass tunnel under the Conwy River (Afon Conwy), the town has learned to cope with a new tranquillity. A mad scramble is under way to replace tarmac with cobbles, and to prettify the shopfronts, but for the moment, it remains one of the highlights of the north coast with a fine castle, a nearly complete belt of town walls and a wonderful setting on the Conwy Estuary, backed by a forested fold of Snowdonia. Nowhere in the core of medieval and Victorian buildings is more than two hundred yards from the irregular triangle of protective masonry formed by the town walls. This makes it wonderfully easy to potter around and though you'll get to see everything you want to in a day, you may well want to stay longer.

Conwy Castle

Conwy Castle (April to late Oct daily 9.30am–6.30pm; late Oct to March Mon–Sat 9.30am–4pm, Sun 11am–4pm; £3; CADW), now entered through a separate ticket office and over a modern bridge, is the toughest-looking link in Edward I's "Iron Ring"

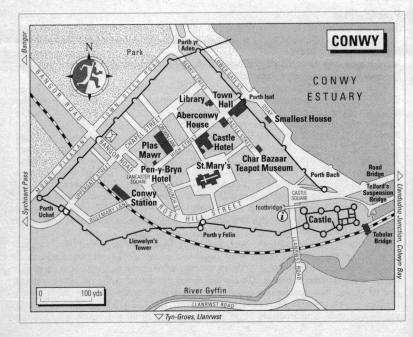

fortresses, and was designed to maintain a bridgehead west of the Conwy River. Once over the river in 1283, Edward set about establishing another of his bastide towns. He chose a strategic knoll at the mouth of the Conwy River and set James of St George to fashion a castle to fit its contours. With the help of 1500 men it took a mere five years.

Richard II stayed at the castle on his return from an ill-timed trip to Ireland in 1399, until lured from safety by Bolingbroke's vassal the Earl of Northumberland. Northumberland swore in the castle's chapel to grant the king safe passage, but Richard was taken and Bolingbroke became Henry IV. Just two years later, on Good Friday when the fifteen-strong castle guard were at church, two cousins of Owain Glyndŵr took the castle and razed the town for Glyndŵr's cause. The castle then fell into disuse, and was bought in 1627 for £100 by Charles I's Secretary of State, Lord Conway of Ragley, who then had the task of refortifying it for the Civil War. At the restoration of the monarchy in 1665, the castle was stripped of all its iron, wood and lead, and was left substantially as it is today.

Being overlooked by a low hill, the castle appears less easily defended than others along the coast, but James constructed eight massive towers in a rectangle around the two wards, the inner one separated from the outer by a drawbridge and portcullis, and further protected by turrets atop the four eastern towers, now the preserve of crows. Strolling along the wall-top gallery, you can look down onto something unique in the Iron Ring fortresses, a roofless but largely intact interior. The outer ward's 130-foot-long Great Hall and the King's Apartments are both well preserved, but the only part of the castle to have kept its roof is the **Chapel Tower**, named for the small room built into the wall whose semicircular apse still shows some heavily worn carving. On the floor below, there's a small exhibition on religious life in medieval castles which won't detain you long from exploring the passages.

The rest of the town

Anchored to the castle walls as though a drawbridge, Telford's narrow **suspension bridge** (March–Oct 10am–5pm; £1; NT) was part of the 1826 road improvement scheme, prompted by the need for better communications to Ireland after the Act of Union and is contemporary with his far greater effort spanning the Menai Strait. The recent restoration has rid the bridge of tarmac, signs and street lighting, returning it to its original structure now operating as a footbridge.

The approach to the modern replacement has created the only breach in the thirty-foot high **town walls** which branch out from the castle into a three-quarter-mile-long circuit, enclosing Conwy's ancient quarter. Inaccessible from the castle they were designed to protect, the walls are punctuated by 21 evenly spaced horseshoe towers, a third of which can be visited on the **wall walk**, starting from Porth Uchaf on Upper Gate Street and running down to a spur into the estuary. Here, you come down off the walls by the brightly rigged trawlers, mussel boats and the *Queen Victoria*, which runs **river trips** (Easter–Oct daily; £2.50 for 30min; ☎01492/592284) from the quay, either upriver or around the estuary, depending on the tide. Porth Isaf, the nearby gate in the town walls, leads up Lower High Street to the fourteenth-century timber and stone **Aberconwy House**, Castle St (April–Oct daily except Tues 10am–5pm; £2; NT), a former merchant's house, its rooms decked out in styles that recall its past. Fans of medieval architecture should continue along the High Street to the Dutch-style **Plas Mawr** at no. 20 (closed for restoration until at least 1997; CADW), a beautifully preserved Elizabethan town house, built in 1576 for one of the first Welsh people to live in the town. Much of the dressed stonework was replaced during renovations in the 1940s and 1950s, but the interior sports more original features, in particular the friezes and superb moulded plaster ceilings depicting fleurs de lis, griffons, owls and rams.

Light relief from all this suffocating history is on hand across the road from Aberconwy House at the **Char Bazaar Teapot Museum**, Castle St (daily April & May

10.30am–5.30pm; June–Aug 10am–6pm; Sept & Oct 10.30am–5pm; £1), which has a thousand mostly pre-1950s pots – Wedgwood and majolica to Bauhaus and Clarice Cliff.

Practicalities

Llandudno Junction, less than a mile across the river to the east, serves as the main **train station**; only slow, regional services stop in Conwy itself. *National Express* **buses** pull up outside the town walls on Town Ditch Road, while local buses use the stops in the centre, mostly on Lancaster Square or Castle Street. The **tourist office** (April to late Oct daily 9.30am–6.30pm; late Oct to March Mon–Sat 9.30am–4pm, Sun 11am–4pm; ☎01492/592248) shares the same building as the castle ticket office.

Accommodation right in the centre of town is a bit thin, so booking ahead is advisable in summer. *Glan Heulog*, Llanrwst Rd, on the outskirts of town half a mile towards Llanrwst on the B5106 (☎01492/593845; ②), is about the best B&B within easy walking distance of Conwy. *Gwynedd Guesthouse*, 10 Upper Gate St (☎01492/596537; ②), is the cheapest central B&B and consequently often full. *Pen-y-Bryn*, 28 High St (☎01492/596445; ③), is another central B&B worth trying; it's housed in a sixteenth-century building above some excellent tea rooms. Further afield, there's *Castle Bank Hotel*, Mount Pleasant (☎01492/593888; ⑤), a licensed, non-smoking hotel with country house atmosphere, ten minutes' walk from the town centre: turn first left outside the town walls on the Bangor road. The nearest **campsite** is *Conwy Touring Park* (April–Oct; ☎01492/592856), a mile or so south along the B5106 (bus #19). There is no **YHA hostel** in town but two in the vicinity: one at Colwyn Bay and a simple but superbly set one at *Roewen* (Easter & May–Aug; ☎01492/650089), a mile up a steep hill above Roewen village, four miles south (hourly bus #19 from Conwy in summer).

Conwy has relatively few **restaurants**, and if you want to sample some really excellent pubs, you've got to get a few miles out of town into the Conwy Valley. In town, you're best off going veggie at *The Wall Place*, Bishop's Yard, Chapel St, which is fast becoming Conwy's trendiest spot; it even has the occasional night of live folk and Welsh music. Otherwise, you can eat Italian at *Alfredo's Restaurant*, Lancaster Square (closed Sun), or Cantonese at *Jade Garden*, 136 Conwy Rd, a mile east of Conwy in Llandudno Junction. For steaming helpings of goulash and paprika schnitzel, head west over Synchnant Pass to the *Austrian Restaurant*, Old Conwy Rd, Capelulo (closed Sun eve & Mon; ☎01492/622170). **Drinking** in town is less rewarding, and nightlife really isn't a feature at all. The best pub in the vicinity is the fifteenth-century *Groes Inn*, in Tyn-y-Groes, two miles south on the B5106 to Llanrwst (☎01492/650545), which serves excellent bar meals and good cask ales.

Around Conwy

The best short walk from Conwy is on to **Conwy Mountain** and the 800-foot peaks behind, all giving great views right along the coast. Follow a sign up Cadnant Park off the Bangor road just outside the town walls, then take the road around until Mountain Road heads off on the right towards a hill fort on the summit. This group is separated from the foothills of the Carneddau range by the narrow cleft of **Sychnant Pass**.

Thousands come to Conwy specifically to see **Bodnant Garden** (mid-March to Oct daily 10am–5pm; £4.20; NT), beside the lower reaches of the Conwy, eight miles to the south. During May and June, the Laburnum Arch flourishes and banks of rhododendrons are in full and glorious bloom all over what ranks as one of the finest formal gardens in Britain. Laid out in 1875 around Bodnant Hall (closed to the public) by its then owner, English industrialist Henry Pochin, the garden spreads out over eighty acres of the east of the Conwy Valley. Facing southwest, the bulk of the gardens – themselves divided into an upper terraced garden and lower Pinetum and Wild Garden – catch the late afternoon sun as it sets over the Carneddau range. Though arranged so that shrubs and plants provide a blaze of colour throughout the opening season, autumn is a perfect time to be here, with hydrangeas still in bloom and fruit trees shedding their leaves. The #25 bus runs here from Llandudno every two hours, calling at Llandudno Junction, or it's a two-mile walk from the Tal-y-Cafn train station on the Conwy Valley line.

Bangor and Penrhyn

After spending a few days travelling through mid-Wales or in the mountains of Snowdonia, **BANGOR** makes a welcome change. It is not big, but as the largest town in Gwynedd and home to **Bangor University**, it passes in these parts for cosmopolitan. The students decamp for the summer, leaving only a trickle of visitors to replace them. The presence of a large non-Welsh student population inflames the passions of the more militant nationalists in what is a staunchly Welsh-speaking area, a dramatic change from the largely English-speaking north coast resorts.

The university takes up much of upper Bangor, straddling the hill that separates the town centre from the Menai Strait. The shape of the college's main building is almost an exact replica of the thirteenth- to fifteenth-century **cathedral** (daily until dusk), which boasts the longest continuous use of any cathedral in Britain, easily predating the town. Pop in if only to see the sixteenth-century wooden **Mostyn Christ**, depicted bound and seated on a rock.

Just over the road, the **Bangor Museum and Art Gallery**, Ffordd Gwynedd (Tues–Fri 12.30–4.30pm, Sat 10.30am–4.30pm; free), offers snippets of local history enlivened by the traditional costume section and the archeology room, containing the most complete Roman sword found in Wales. The art gallery concentrates on predominantly Welsh contemporary works. For a good look down the Menai Strait to Telford's bridge (see below), walk along Garth Road to Bangor's rejuveneated and pristine **Victorian Pier** (20p), which reaches halfway across to Anglesey.

Penrhyn Castle

There can hardly be a more vulgar testament to the Anglo-Welsh landowning gentry's oppression of the rural Welsh than the oddly compelling **Penrhyn Castle** (daily except Tues April–June, Sept & Oct noon–5pm; July & Aug 11am–5pm; £4.50 including 50-min recorded tour, £3 grounds only; NT), two miles east of Bangor, which overlooks Port Penrhyn from its acres of isolating parkland. Built on the backs of slate miners for the benefit of their hated bosses, this monstrous nineteenth-century neo-Norman fancy, with over three hundred rooms dripping with luxurious fittings, was funded by the quarry's huge profits. The sugar and slate fortune built by anti-abolitionist Richard Pennant, First Baron Penrhyn, provide the means for his self-aggrandizing great-great-nephew George Dawkins to hire architect Thomas Hopper, who spent thirteen years from 1827 encasing the neo-Gothic hall in a Norman fortress complete with monumental five-storey keep.

Sour grapes aside, the decoration is glorious, and fairly true to the Romanesque style, with its deeply cut chevrons, billets and double-cone ornamentation. Hopper even looked to Norman architecture for the design of the furniture but abandoned historical authenticity when it came to installing the central heating system, which piped hot air through ornamental brass ducts at the cost of twenty tons of coal a month. Everything is on a massive scale. Three-foot-thick oak doors separate the rooms, ebony is used to dramatic effect and a slate bed was built for, but declined by, Queen Victoria when she visited. The family amassed the Wales' largest private painting collection including a Gainsborough landscape amongst the family likenesses, Canaletto's *The Thames at Westminster* and a Rembrandt portrait.

Gleaming examples of rolling stock from Richard Pennant's slate railway and the country's other private industrial lines are on display in the **Industrial Railway Museum** (same times as castle; entry with castle ticket), including Lord Penrhyn's luxurious coach linked to a quarrymen's car. Buses #5, #6 and #7 run frequently from Bangor to the gates from where it is a mile-long walk to the house.

Practicalities

All trains on the North Coast line stop at Bangor **train station** located on Station Road, at the bottom of Holyhead Road. The **tourist office** (Easter–Sept daily 10am–6pm; ☎01248/352786) is by the Little Chef at the junction of the A5/A55, two miles out of town. Bangor doesn't have a huge choice of **places to stay**, most of the cheaper accommodation bundled at the northern end of Garth Road, about twenty minutes' walk from the train station: try *Dilfan* (☎01248/353030; ③); *Eryl Môr Hotel*, 2 Upper Garth Rd (☎01248/353789; ④), is a quiet and comfortable hotel with views over Bangor's pier and the Menai Strait. The University lets out clean, functional rooms on Ffriddoedd Road (☎01248/372104; ②) in late June and late September and over the Easter vacation. Bangor's **YHA hostel**, Tan-y-Bryn (☎01248/353516) is signposted off the A56, ten minutes' walk east of the centre (bus #6 or #7 along Garth Road). *Tros-y-Waen Farm*, just off B4547 south of Pentir, six miles south of Bangor towards Llanberis (☎01248/364448; ②), is a good-value farmhouse B&B and **campsite**.

With the possible exception of Llandudno, Bangor offers the widest selection of **eating** possibilities in north Wales. Packed out with students and locals, the *Fat Cat Café Bar*, 161 High St, has a menu ranging from massive burgers to salmon and broccoli pasta quills; another good bet is the classy *Greek Taverna Politis*, 12 Holyhead Rd (☎01248/354991). The expensive restaurant of the *Menai Court Hotel*, Craig-y-Don Rd (☎01248/354200) earns plaudits from foodies for its traditional British and European dishes. If you've tried to learn any of the language you can put it to good use at *Tafarn*

Y Glôb, a traditional **pub** on Albert St, where ordering in Welsh is pretty much *de rigueur*. For a pint of beer try "un peint o cwrw, os gwelwch yn dda". *The Victoria Hotel*, Telford St, Menai Bridge, is your best bet for local **live music**, across the water on Menai Bridge.

Caernarfon

It was in **CAERNARFON** in 1969 that Charles, the current heir to the throne, was invested as Prince of Wales, a ceremony which reaffirmed English sovereignty over Wales in this, one of the most nationalist of Welsh-speaking regions. Since 1282, when the English defeated Llywelyn ap Gruffydd, the last Welsh Prince of Wales, the title has been bestowed on heirs to the English throne, but it wasn't until 1911 that the machinations of Lloyd George – MP for Caernarfon, Welsh cabinet minister and future prime minister – brought the ceremony to the centre of his constituency: a paradoxical move for a nationalist considering the symbolic implications. Caernarfon's magnificent

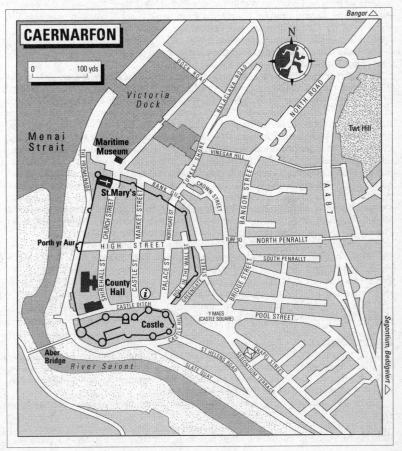

castle and near complete rectangle of town walls make it an appealing place, but apart from the castle, there isn't too much to see: you can only walk a small section of the wall and the rest of the town has been ripped through by a dual carriageway and boxed in by modern buildings. That said, it is well sited on the Menai Strait and has good bus connections to Llanberis and Snowdonia.

The Town

In 1283, Edward I started work on **Caernarfon Castle** (April–late Oct daily 9.30am–6.30pm; late Oct to March Mon–Sat 9.30am–4pm, Sun 11am–4pm; £3.80; CADW), the strongest link in his Iron Ring, a decisive hammer blow to any Welsh aspirations to autonomy and the ultimate symbol of both Anglo-Norman military might and political wrangling. With the Welsh already smarting from the loss of their Prince of Wales, Edward is said to have rubbed salt in their wounds by justifying his own infant son's claim to the title declaring the future Edward II "a prince born in Wales who could speak never a word of English". The story is almost certainly apocryphal. Edward attempted to appease the Welsh in the building of his castle by paying tribute to aspects of local legend. The Welsh had long associated their town with the eastern capital of the Roman Empire: Caernarfon's old name, Caer Cystennin, was also the name used for Constantinople, and Constantine himself was believed to have been born at Segontium. Edward's architect, James of St George, exploited this connection in the distinctive limestone and sandstone banding and polygonal towers, both reminiscent of the Theodosian walls in present-day Istanbul.

In military terms, the castle is supreme. It was taken once, before it was finished, but then withstood two sieges by Owain Glyndŵr with a complement of only 28 men-at-arms. Entering through the **King's Gate**, the castle's strength is immediately apparent. Between the octagonal towers, embrasures and murder holes face in on no fewer than five gates and six portcullises, and that's once you have crossed the moat, now bridged by an incongruous modern structure. Inside, the huge lawn gives a misleading impression since both the wall dividing the two original wards and all the buildings which filled them crumbled away long ago. The towers are in a much better state, and linked by an exhausting honeycomb of wall-walks and tunnels. The most striking and tallest of the towers is the King's Tower at the western end, whose three slender turrets adorned with eagle sculptures give the best views of the town. To the south, the Queen's Tower is entirely taken up by the numbingly thorough **Museum of the Royal Welch Fusiliers** while the Northeast tower houses the **Prince of Wales Exhibition** close to the Dinorwig slate dais used for the Charles' investiture.

A ten-minute walk along the A4085 Beddgelert road brings you to the western end of the Roman road from Chester at **Segontium Roman Fort** (March, April & Oct Mon–Sat 9.30am–5.30pm, Sun 2–5pm; May–Sept Mon–Sat 9.30am–6pm, Sun 2–6pm; Nov–Feb closes 4pm; £1; CADW). The Romans occupied this five-acre site for three centuries from around 78 AD, though most of the remains are from the final rebuilding after 364 AD. The ground plan is seldom more than shin-high and somewhat baffling, making the museum and displays in the ticket office pretty much essential.

Practicalities

With no train station, the hub of Caernarfon's public transport system is Castle Square (Y Maes), right under the walls of the castle, where buses stop. The **tourist office**, Oriel Pendeitsh, Castle St (Easter–Oct daily 10am–6pm; Nov–Easter 9.30am–5pm, closed Wed; ☎01286/672232) is just a few steps away.

There are a number of cheap **accommodation** options close to the centre: try *Isfryn Guesthouse*, 11 Church St (☎01286/675628; ②), or *Wallasea Guesthouse*, 21 Segontium Terrace (☎01286/673564; ②). The characterful *Black Boy Inn*, Northgate St (☎01286/673023; ③), is one of the town's oldest buildings, but for more upmarket accommodation, you'll have to leave the town centre. *Pengwern Farm*, Saron, three miles southwest of Caernarfon (Feb–Nov; ☎01286/830717; ④), has a lovely rural setting, with farm-fresh and inexpensive evening meals. Take the A487 south across the river then turn right towards Saron – Pengwern is just over two miles down on the right. The *Coed Helen* **campsite** (March–Oct; ☎01286/676770) sits right on the Seiont River just across the footbridge from the foot of the castle.

Caernarfon boasts a number of low-key and likeable **restaurants** which may well be the focus of your evening's entertainment: sample the eclectic menu at *Courteney's*, 9 Segontium Terrace (closed Mon, Tues lunch & Sun) or the bistro-style fare at *Stone's*, 4 Hole in the Wall St (closed Sun). The cheapest option is the excellent bar meals at the aforementioned *Black Boy Inn*. For **nightlife**, everyone heads ten miles north to Bangor, though you might catch a Welsh-language band at *Tafarn Yr Albert*, 11 Segontium Terrace, on Saturday nights. Thursday's *Caernarfon Chronicle* has gig information for both Bangor and Caernarfon.

Anglesey

Anglesey (Ynys Môn) welcomes visitors to "Mam Cymru", the Mother of Wales, attesting to the island's former importance as the regional breadbasket. In the twelfth century Giraldus Cambrensis noted that "When crops have failed in other regions, this island, from its soil and its abundant produce, has been able to supply all Wales", and while feeding their less productive kin in Snowdonia is no longer a priority, the land remains predominantly pastoral, with small fields, stone walls and white houses suggestive of England. Linguistically and politically, though, Anglesey is intensely Welsh. One of the four Plaid Cymru MPs represents the islanders, seventy percent of whom are Welsh-speakers. Many people charge straight through to **Holyhead** and the Irish ferries, missing out on the ancient town of Beaumaris, with its fine castle, the Whistler mural at Plas Newydd and some superb coastal scenery; a necklace of fine sandy coves and rocky headlands that's a match for anywhere in the country.

Beaumaris

The original inhabitants of **BEAUMARIS** (Biwmares) were evicted by Edward I to make way for the construction of his new castle and bastide town, dubbed "beautiful marsh" in an attempt to attract English settlers. Today the place can still seem like the small English outpost Edward intended, with its elegant Georgian terrace along the front (designed by Joseph Hansom, of cab fame) and more plummy English accents than you'll have heard for a while. Many of their owners belong with the flotilla of yachts, an echo of the port's fleet of merchant ships, which disappeared with the completion of bridges to the mainland and subsequent growth of Holyhead. While Beaumaris repays an afternoon mooching around and enjoying the views across the Strait, it also boasts more sights than the rest of the island put together, inevitably drawings the crowds in summer.

Beaumaris Castle (April to late Oct daily 9.30am–6.30pm; late Oct to March Mon–Sat 9.30am–4pm, Sun 11am–4pm; £1.70; CADW) may never have been built had Madog ap Llywelyn not captured Caernarfon in 1294. When asked to build the new castle, James of St George abandoned the Caernarfon design in favour of the concentric plan, developing it into a highly evolved symmetrical octagon. Sited on flat land at the edge of town, the castle is denied the domineering majesty of Caernarfon or Harlech, its low outer walls appearing almost welcoming until you begin to appreciate the concentric layout of the defences protected by massive towers, a moat linked to the sea and the Moorish-influenced staggered entries through the two gatehouses. Despite over thirty years' work, the project was never quite finished, leaving most of the inner ward empty and the corbels and fireplaces built into the walls never used. You can explore the internal passages in the walls but, unless the CADW change their policy, the low-parapet wall-walk, from where you get the best idea of the castle's defensive capability, remains off limits. Impressive as they are, none of these defences was able to prevent siege by Owain Glyndŵr, who held the castle for two years from 1403, although they did withhold a Parliamentarian seige during the Civil War.

Almost opposite the castle stands the Jacobean **Beaumaris Courthouse** (Easter & June–Sept Mon–Fri 11am–5.30pm, Sat & Sun 2–5.30pm; May Sat & Sun 2–5.30pm; £1.35, joint ticket for gaol £2.80), built in 1614 and the oldest active court in Britain. It is now used only for the twice-monthly Magistrates Court, but until 1971, when they were moved to Caernarfon, the quarterly Assize Courts were held here. These were traditionally held in English, giving the jury little chance to follow the proceedings and Welsh-speaking defendants no defence against prosecutors renowned for slapping heavy penalties on minor offences. On session days you can watch the trials, but won't be able to take the recorded tour or inspect *The Lawsuit*, a plaque in the magistrates' room depicting two farmers pulling the horns and tail of a cow while a lawyer milks it.

Many citizens were transported from the courthouse to the colonies for their misdemeanours; others only made it a couple of blocks to **Beaumaris Gaol**, Steeple Lane (Easter & June–Sept daily 11am–6pm; £2.30 or joint ticket with courthouse) which, when it opened in 1829, was considered a model prison, with running water and toilets in each cell, an infirmary and eventually heating. Women prisoners did the cooking and were allowed to rock their babies' cradles in the nursery above by means of a pulley system. Advanced perhaps, but nonetheless a gloomy place: witness the windowless punishment cell, the yard for stone-breaking and the treadmill water pump operated by the prisoners. The least fortunate inmates were publicly hanged, the fate of a certain Richard Rowlands, whose disembodied voice leads the recorded tour of the building and various displays on prison life.

Practicalities

With no trains, long-distance coaches or tourist office, Beaumaris seems poorly served, but it does have a regular **bus** service to Bangor (#53 & #57; infrequent on Sun). The best of the **hotels** is the ancient and luxurious *Ye Olde Bull's Head Inn*, 18 Castle St (☎01248/810329; ⑦), used as General Mytton's headquarters during the Civil War. The *Bishopsgate House Hotel*, 54 Castle St (mid-Feb to Dec; ☎01248/810302; ④), is only a stone's throw away and almost of the same standard. The first of the **B&Bs** to head for is the antique-furnished *Swn-y-Don*, 7 Bulkeley Terrace (☎01248/810794; ③). Otherwise, *Bron Menai* (☎01248/810321; ②), opposite the pier above a café, is good, and – as long as you don't smoke and don't object to an 11pm curfew – so is the *Sea View Guesthouse* (☎0248/810384; ②). *Kingsbridge* (☎01248/490636), the nearest **campsite**, is two miles north in Llanfaes. There are plenty of daytime cafés serving snacks, and more substantial **restaurants** are also in good supply, the best being *Ye Olde Bull's Head Inn* and *Bishopsgate House Hotel* (moderate), both of which also do filling bar meals. At the cheaper end of the scale, budget *Bottles Bistro*, 13 Castle St, offers a broad range of bistro perennials.

Llanfair PG and the south coast

In the 1880s a local tailor invented the longest place name in Britain in a successful attempt to draw tourists. However, it is an utter disappointment to arrive at the station bearing the sign Llanfairpwllgwyngyllgogerychwyrndrobwllllantysiliogogogoch, which translates as "St Mary's Church in the hollow of white hazel near a rapid whirlpool and the Church of St Tysilio near the red cave" (commonly known as **LLANFAIR PG**), to find only a tacky wool shop and a **tourist office** (Mon–Sat 9.30am–5.30pm, Sun 10am–5pm; closes 5pm in winter; ☎01248/713177), the only one worth its salt on the island.

The marquesses of Anglesey still live at **Plas Newydd** (April–Sept daily except Sat noon–5pm; Oct Fri & Sun noon–5pm; £4; NT), a mile and a half south of Llanfair PG, a modest three-storey mansion with its incongruous Tudor caps. Inside, architect James Wyatt was given free stylictic rein producing a Gothick Music Room followed by a Neoclassical Staircase Hall with its cantilevered staircase and deceptively solid-looking Doric columns, actually just painted wood. Endure the slog through corridors of oils and period rooms to the highlight, a 58-foot long wall consumed by a *trompe l'œil* painting by Rex Whistler, who spent a couple of years here in the 1930s. Walking along his imaginary seascape, your position appears to shift by over a mile as the mountains of Snowdonia and a whimsical composite of elements, culled from Italy as well as Britain, alter their perspective. Portmeirion (see p.641) is there, as are the Round Tower from Windsor Castle and the steeple from St Martin-in-the-Fields in London. Whistler himself appears as a gondolier, and again as a gardener in one of the two right-angled panels at either end, which appear to extend the room further. The prize exhibit in the **Cavalry Museum** is the world's first articulated leg, all wood, leather and springs, designed for the First Marquess, who lost his leg at Waterloo.

Holyhead and Holy Island

Holy Island (Ynys Gybi) is blessed with Anglesey's best scenery and cursed with its most unattractive town. The spectacular seacliffs around South Stack, and the Stone Age and Roman remains on Holyhead Mountain are just a couple of miles from workaday Holyhead, whose ferry routes to Ireland and good transport links mean you'll probably find your way there at some stage.

The local council's valiant attempts to brighten up **HOLYHEAD** (Caergybi) somehow make this town of dilapidated shopfronts and high unemployment even more depressing. In 1727 Swift found it "scurvy, ill provided and comfortless", and apart from the scurvy, little has changed. Fortunately train and ferry timings are reasonably well integrated, so you shouldn't need to spend much time here. From the combined **train station** and *Stena Sealink* terminal, a pedestrian bridge over London Road, past the A5, leads to the *National Express* bus stop on Victoria Road, at the junction with Market Street, which heads up into the shopping area. The less-than-helpful **tourist office**, Marine Square (Easter–Oct daily 10am–6pm; Nov–Easter Mon–Sat 9.30am–5pm; ☎01407/762622), is in a shed by the docks, half a mile away at the end of Victoria Road; a list of B&Bs that accept late arrivals is posted on the door when the office is closed.

FERRIES TO IRELAND

Since Sealynx **catamarans** were introduced by *Stena Sealink* (☎01407/606606 or 762304 info line) in 1993, it's been possible to get from Holyhead to Dun Laoghaire, six miles south of Dublin, in under two hours. The latest sailing times can be checked with any travel agent but at the time of writing are 7am, noon, 5pm, and – at peak periods – 10pm. High-season passenger fares are around £60 return, £10 more expensive than either the *Stena Sealink* **ferries** to Dun Laoghaire (sailings at 2am, 4am, 2.30pm, and at busy times 4.15pm; 3hr 30min) or the *Irish Ferries* (☎01407/760222) ferries to Dublin (3hr 45min). The latter use a tidal mooring, which occasionally forces changes to their 4am and 3.45pm schedule. There's a shuttle bus from the station to the wharf for foot passengers. *Irish Ferries* generally offer the cheapest **day trips** to Dublin, starting from as little as £8, though this does entail getting the 4am boat. Sealynx day trips are more convenient, shorter and twice as expensive.

Shun the bunch of poor **B&Bs** along the A5 into the town in favour of those around Walthew Avenue, most easily reached by turning left just before the tourist office onto the beachfront Prince of Wales Road then left into Walthew Avenue. *Glan Ifor* at no. 8 (☎01407/764238; ②) and *Orotavia* at no. 66 (☎01407/760259; ②) are both good, as is *Yr Hendre*, Porth-y-Felin (☎01407/762929; ③), a former manse where you can get inexpensive evening meals; turn right after Orotavia. Fast **food** is the staple diet in Holyhead, but you can still eat well; the budget *Omar Khayyam Tandoori*, 8 Newry St (☎01407/760333), serves the tastiest curries for miles around.

Holyhead Mountain and South Stack

The northern half of Holy Island is ranged around the skirts of the 700-foot **Holyhead Mountain** (Mynydd Twr), its summit ringed by the remains of the seventeen-acre Iron Age **Caer y Twr** (unrestricted access; CADW), one of the largest sites in north Wales. The best approach is by car or bus #44 to the car park at **South Stack** (Ynys Lawd), two miles west of Holyhead from where a path (30min) leads to the top of Holyhead Mountain. Most visitors are only walking the few yards to the cliff-top **Ellin's Tower Seabird Centre** (Easter–Sept daily 11am–5pm; free) where, from April until the end of July, binoculars and closed-circuit TV give an unparalleled opportunity to watch up to three thousand birds – razorbills, guillemots and the odd puffin – nesting on the nearby seacliffs while ravens and peregrines wheel outside the tower's windows. When the birds have gone, rock climbers picking their way up the same cliff face replace them as the main interest. A twisting path leads down from the tower to a suspension bridge over the surging waves. Nearby, nineteen low stone circles make up the **Cytiau'r Gwyddelod** or the "huts of the Irish" – a common name for any ancient settlement – in this case late Neolithic or early Bronze Age.

travel details

Trains

Bangor to: Chester (20 daily Mon–Sat, 8 Sun; 1hr 5min); Conwy (9 daily Mon–Sat, 2 Sun; 20min); Holyhead (21 daily Mon–Sat, 10 Sun; 30–40min).

Conwy to: Bangor (7 daily Mon–Sat, 2–3 Sun; 35min).

Holyhead to: Bangor (18 daily Mon–Sat, 6 Sun; 30–40min); Chester (18 daily Mon–Sat, 6 Sun; 1hr 25min–1hr 40min).

Llandudno to: Llandudno Junction (at least hourly Mon–Sat, 2 Sun; 10min).

Llandudno Junction to: Bangor (24 daily Mon–Sat, 12 Sun; 25min); Betws-y-Coed (6 daily Mon–Sat, 2 Sun; 25min); Holyhead (17 daily Mon–Sat, 10 Sun; 45min–1hr).

Llanfair PG to: Bangor (8 daily Mon–Sat; 10min); Holyhead (8 daily Mon–Sat; 30min).

Buses

Bangor to: Beaumaris (roughly hourly Mon–Sat, 2 Sun; 25min); Betws-y-Coed (3 daily Mon–Sat;

55min); Caernarfon (every 30min Mon–Sat, hourly Sun; 40min); Chester (2 daily; 2hr 35min); Holyhead (every 30min Mon–Sat, 4 Sun; 1hr 15min); Llanberis (6 daily Mon–Sat; 40min).

Beaumaris to: Bangor (roughly hourly Mon–Sat, 2 Sun; 25min).

Caernarfon to: Bangor (every 15min Mon–Sat, hourly Sun; 25min); Blaenau Ffestiniog (roughly hourly Mon–Sat; 1hr 25min); Llanberis (every 30min Mon–Sat, hourly Sun; 25min); Llandudno (every 30min Mon–Sat, hourly Sun; 1hr 40min); Porthmadog (23 daily Mon–Sat, 1 Sun; 45min); Pwllheli (23 daily Mon–Sat, 2–3 Sun; 45min).

Conwy to: Bangor (every 30min Mon–Sat, hourly Sun; 45min); Betws-y-Coed (7 daily Mon–Sat, 5 Sun; 55min); Llanberis (4 daily; 1hr 30min).

Holyhead to: Bangor (every 30min Mon–Sat, 4 Sun; 1hr 15min); Chester (1 daily; 3hr 30min); Llandudno (1 daily; 1hr 40min); Llanfair PG (every 30min Mon–Sat; 4 Sun; 1hr).

Llandudno to: Betws-y-Coed (7 daily, 5 Sun; 1hr 15min); Caernarfon (every 30min Mon–Sat, hourly

Sun; 1hr 40min); Llanberis (4–6 daily in summer; 1hr 55min).

Llanfair PG to: Bangor (every 30min Mon–Sat, 4 Sun; 15min); Holyhead (every 30min, 4 Sun; 1hr).

Ferries

Holyhead to: Dublin (2 daily; 3hr 45min); Dun Laoghaire (6–8 daily; catamaran 2hr, ferry 3hr 30min–4hr).

PART FOUR

SCOTLAND

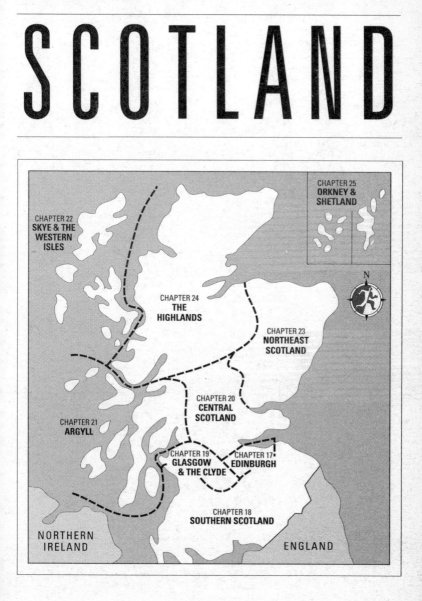

CHAPTER 25
**ORKNEY &
SHETLAND**

CHAPTER 22
**SKYE & THE
WESTERN
ISLES**

CHAPTER 24
**THE
HIGHLANDS**

CHAPTER 23
**NORTHEAST
SCOTLAND**

N

CHAPTER 20
**CENTRAL
SCOTLAND**

CHAPTER 21
ARGYLL

CHAPTER 19
**GLASGOW
& THE CLYDE**

CHAPTER 17
EDINBURGH

CHAPTER 18
SOUTHERN SCOTLAND

NORTHERN
IRELAND

ENGLAND

CHAPTER SEVENTEEN

EDINBURGH

Well-heeled **EDINBURGH**, the showcase capital of Scotland, is a cosmopolitan and cultured city. Its setting is undeniably striking; perched on a series of extinct volcanoes and rocky crags which intrude on the generally flat landscape of the Lothians, with the sheltered shoreline of the Firth of

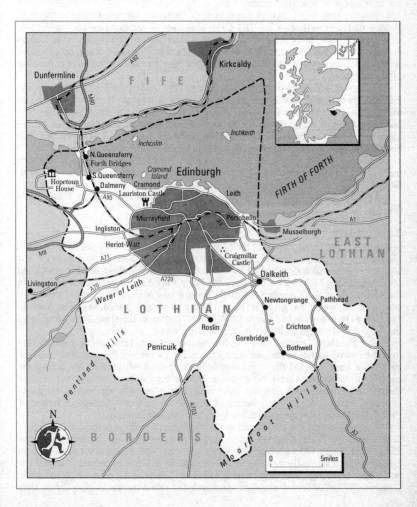

Forth to the north. "My own Romantic town", Sir Walter Scott called it, although it was another native author, Robert Louis Stevenson, who perhaps best captured the feel of his "precipitous city", declaring, "No situation could be more commanding for the head of a kingdom; none better chosen for noble prospects."

The centre has two distinct parts. North of the **Castle Rock**, the dignified, Grecian-style **New Town** was immaculately laid out during the Age of Reason, after the announcement of a plan to improve conditions in the city. The **Old Town**, on the other hand, with its tortuous alleys and tightly packed closes, is unrelentingly medieval, associated in popular imagination with its underworld lore of the schizophrenic Deacon Brodie, inspiration for Stevenson's *Dr Jekyll and Mr Hyde*, and the body snatchers Burke and Hare. Edinburgh earned its nickname of "Auld Reekie" for the smog and smell generated by the Old Town, which for centuries swam in sewage tipped out of the windows of cramped tenements.

Set on the crag which sweeps down from the towering fairytale **Castle** to the royal **Palace of Holyroodhouse**, the Old Town preserves all the key reminders of its role as a capital, while, in contrast, a tantalizing glimpse of the wild beauty of Scotland's scenery can be had immediately beyond the palace in **Holyrood Park**, an extensive area of open countryside dominated by **Arthur's Seat**, the largest and most impressive of the volcanoes.

In August and early September, around a million visitors flock to the city for the **Edinburgh International Festival**, in fact a series of separate festivals that make up the largest arts extravaganza in the world. Among the city's many museums, the **National Gallery of Scotland** boasts as choice an array of Old Masters as can be found anywhere; its offshoot, the **Scottish National Gallery of Modern Art**, has Britain's oldest specialist collection of twentieth-century painting and sculpture.

On a less elevated theme, the city's distinctive howffs (pubs), allied to its brewing and distilling traditions, make it a great **drinking** city. The presence of three **universities**, plus several colleges, means that there is a youthful presence for most of the year – a welcome corrective to the stuffiness which is often regarded as Edinburgh's Achilles' heel.

Some history

It was during the **Dark Ages** that the name of Edinburgh – at least in its early forms of Dunedin or Din Eidyn ("fort of Eidyn") – first appeared. Castle Rock, a strategic fort atop one of the volcanoes, served as the nation's **southernmost border post** until 1018, when King Malcolm I established the River Tweed as the permanent frontier. In the reign of Malcolm Canmore the castle became one of the main seats of the court; and the town, which was given privileged status as a **royal burgh**, began to grow. In 1128 King David established Holyrood Abbey at the foot of the slope, later allowing its monks to found a separate burgh, known as **Canongate**.

Robert the Bruce granted Edinburgh a **new charter** in 1234, giving it jurisdiction over the nearby port of **Leith**, and during the following century the prosperity brought by foreign trade enabled the newly fortified city to establish itself as the permanent **capital of Scotland**. Under King James IV, the city enjoyed a short but brilliant **Renaissance era**, which saw not only the construction of a new palace alongside Holyrood Abbey, but also the granting of a royal charter to the College of Surgeons, the earliest in the city's long line of academic and professional bodies.

This period came to an abrupt end in 1513 with the calamitous defeat by the English at the Battle of Flodden, which led to several decades of political instability. In the 1540s, King Henry VIII's attempt to force a royal union with Scotland led to the sack of Edinburgh, prompting the Scots to turn to France: French troops arrived to defend the city, while the young queen Mary was despatched to Paris as the promised bride of the Dauphin. While the French occupiers succeeded in removing the English threat, they themselves antagonized the locals, who had become increasingly sympathetic to the ideals of the **Reformation**. When the radical preacher John Knox returned from exile in 1555, he quickly won over the city to his Calvinist message.

James VI's rule saw the foundation of the University of Edinburgh in 1582, but following the **Union of the Crowns** in 1603, the city was totally upstaged by London: although James promised to visit every three years, it was not until 1617 that he made his one and only return trip. In 1633 Charles I visited Edinburgh for his coronation, but soon afterwards precipitated a crisis by introducing episcopacy to the Church of Scotland, in the process making Edinburgh a bishopric for the first time. Fifty years of religious turmoil followed, culminating in the triumph of **presbyterianism**. Despite these vicissitudes, Edinburgh expanded throughout the seventeenth century and, constrained by its walls, was forced to build both upwards and inwards.

The **Union of the Parliaments** of 1707 dealt a further blow to Edinburgh's political prestige, though the guaranteed preservation of the national church and the legal and educational systems ensured that it was never relegated to a purely provincial role. On the contrary, it was in the second half of the eighteenth century that Edinburgh achieved the height of its intellectual influence, led by an outstanding group, including David Hume and Adam Smith. At the same time, the city began to expand beyond its medieval boundaries, laying out a **New Town**, a masterpiece of the Neoclassical style. Industrialization affected Edinburgh less than any other major city in the nation, and it never lost its white-collar character. Nevertheless, the city underwent an enormous **urban expansion** in the course of the century, annexing, among many other small burghs, the large port of Leith.

In 1947 Edinburgh was chosen to host the great **International Festival** which served as a symbol of the new peaceful European order; despite some hiccups, it has flourished ever since, in the process helping to make tourism a mainstay of the local economy. In 1979, the inconclusive referendum on Scottish devolution robbed Edinburgh of the chance of reviving its role as a governmental capital; and Glasgow, previously the poor relation, began to overtake the city as a cultural centre. The keen rivalry between the two cities was most recently manifested in a hard-fought campaign, won by Glasgow, for the title of City of Architecture 1999. Despite these blows, however, Edinburgh remains a fascinating and complex place, whose character typifies that of a nation that has maintained its essential autonomy despite nearly three centuries of full political union with England.

Arrival, information and city transport

Edinburgh International Airport (☎0131/333 1000) is at Turnhouse, seven miles west of the city centre, close to the start of the M8 motorway to Glasgow. Regular shuttle buses (£3.20) and taxis (£11) connect to **Waverley Station** (☎0131/556 2451), terminus for all main-line **trains**, conveniently situated at the eastern end of Princes Street. There's a second main-line train stop, **Haymarket Station**, just under two miles west on the lines from Waverley to Glasgow, Fife and the Highlands, although this is only really of use if you're staying nearby. The **bus terminal** for local and inter-city services is on **St Andrew Square**, two minutes' walk from Waverley, on the opposite side of Princes Street. *SMT* (*Scottish Midland Transport*) has a shop (☎0131/558 1616) at the southeastern corner of the station, where timetables are kept and tickets sold for several of the confusing array of private bus operators.

Edinburgh's main **tourist office** is at 3 Princes St beside the northern entrance to the station (July & Aug Mon–Sat 9am–8pm, Sun 11am–8pm; May, June & Sept Mon–Sat 9am–7pm, Sun 11am–7pm; April & Oct Mon–Sat 9am–6pm, Sun 11am–6pm; Nov–March Mon–Sat 9am–6pm; ☎0131/557 1700). Although inevitably flustered at the

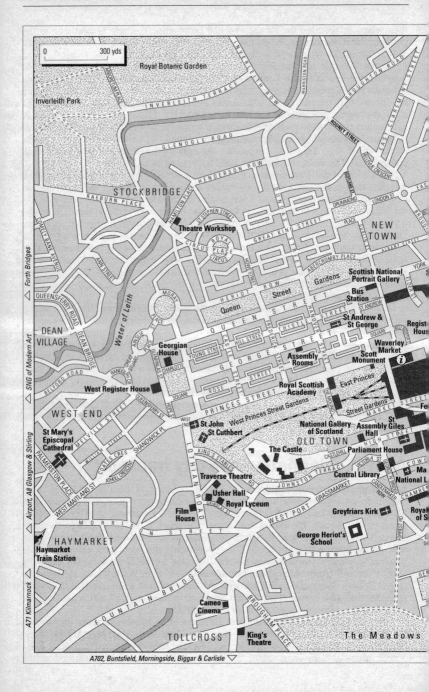

0   300 yds

Royal Botanic Garden

Inverleith Park

INVERLEITH TERRACE

GLENOGLE ROAD

HENDERSON ROW

STOCKBRIDGE

RAEBURN PLACE

RODNEY STREET

NEW TOWN

Theatre Workshop

GREAT KING STREET

ROYAL CIRCUS

ABERCROMBY PLACE

Scottish National Portrait Gallery

Gardens

Bus Station

HERIOT ROW

Queen Street

St Andrew & St George

Waverley Market

DEAN VILLAGE

Georgian House

QUEEN STREET

GEORGE STREET

Assembly Rooms

Scott Monument

West Register House

ROSE STREET

Royal Scottish Academy

East Princes Street Gardens

WEST END

PRINCES STREET

National Gallery of Scotland

West Princes Street Gardens

St Giles

St Mary's Episcopal Cathedral

St John
St Cuthbert

OLD TOWN

Assembly Hall

The Castle

Parliament House

Central Library

National L

Traverse Theatre

JOHNSTON TERRACE

Usher Hall

Royal Lyceum

GRASSMARKET

WEST PORT

Greyfriars Kirk

Royal of S

Film House

HAYMARKET

Haymarket Train Station

George Heriot's School

LAURISTON PLACE

MORRISON STREET

FOUNTAINBRIDGE

Cameo Cinema

BROUGHAM PLACE

The Meadows

TOLLCROSS

King's Theatre

Water of Leith

DEAN BRIDGE

BELFORD ROAD

QUEENSFERRY ROAD

Forth Bridges

SNG of Modern Art

Airport, A8 Glasgow & Stirling

A71 Kilmarnock

A702, Buntsfield, Morningside, Biggar & Carlisle

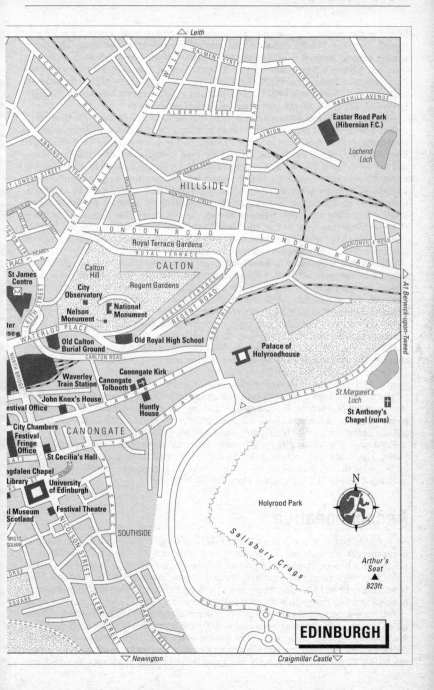

△ *Leith*

DALMENY STREET
ST CLAIR STREET
LEITH WALK
ALBERT STREET
HAWKHILL AVENUE
MCDONALD ROAD
ANNANDALE STREET
EASTER ROAD
ALBION ROAD

Easter Road Park (Hibernian F.C.)

Lochend Loch

ST LONDON STREET
BRUNSWICK ROAD
MONTGOMERY STREET
PICARDY

HILLSIDE

LONDON ROAD
LONDON ROAD
MARIONVILLE ROAD

▷ *A1 Berwick-upon-Tweed*

Royal Terrace Gardens
ROYAL TERRACE

St James Centre

Calton Hill

CALTON

Regent Gardens

REGENT TERRACE
REGENT ROAD

City Observatory

National Monument

Nelson Monument

ABBEYHILL

WATERLOO PLACE

Old Calton Burial Ground

Old Royal High School

Palace of Holyroodhouse

St Margaret's Loch

CARLTON ROAD

NORTH BRIDGE

Waverley Train Station

Canongate Kirk

Canongate Tolbooth

John Knox's House

Huntly House

CANONGATE

QUEEN'S DRIVE

St Anthony's Chapel (ruins)

Festival Office

City Chambers

Festival Fringe Office

St Cecilia's Hall

HOLYROOD ROAD

CANONGATE

agdalen Chapel
Library

University of Edinburgh

Festival Theatre

PLEASANCE

HolyRood Park

N

l Museum
Scotland

NICOLSON STREET

BRISTO SQUARE

SOUTHSIDE

Salisbury Crags

ORGE

SQUARE

CLERK STREET

ST LEONARDS STREET

Arthur's Seat
▲
823ft

QUEEN'S DRIVE

EDINBURGH

▽ *Newington*

Craigmillar Castle ▽

height of the season, it's efficiently run, with scores of free leaflets; when the office is closed, there's a 24-hour computerized information service at the door. The much smaller **airport branch** is in the main concourse, directly opposite Gate 5 (April–Oct Mon–Sat 8.30am–9.30pm, Sun 9.30am–9.30pm; Nov–March Mon–Fri 9am–6pm, Sat 9am–1pm, Sun 10am–2pm; ☎0131/333 2167). For up-to-date maps of the city head for *Map Centre*, 51 York Place (☎0131/557 3011) and to *International Newsagent*, 351 High St (☎0131/225 4827), for the best choice of foreign publications.

Although Edinburgh occupies a large area relative to its population – less than half a million people – most places worth visiting lie within the compact city centre, which is easily explored on foot. This is divided clearly and unequivocally between the maze-like Old Town, which lies on and around the crag linking the Castle and the Palace, and the New Town, laid out in a symmetrical pattern on the undulating ground to the north. It's also worth venturing into the **outskirts**, which range from residential inner suburbs to formerly separate villages that still retain their own distinctive identities. Orientation in Edinburgh is straightforward, particularly as most public transport services terminate on or near **Princes Street**, the city's main thoroughfare, which lies at the extreme southern end of the New Town, with the Old Town on the heights immediately to the rear. If you want to travel out to the suburbs, or are staying outside the centre, the public transport system, although a little confusing, is reliable.

Edinburgh is well served by **buses**, although even locals are confused by the consequences of deregulation, with several companies offering competing services along similar routes. Each bus stop lists the different companies together with the route numbers that stop there. Most useful are the maroon buses operated by *Lothian Regional Transport* (*LRT*); all buses referred to in the text are run by them unless stated otherwise. Timetables and passes are available from the ticket centre at 31 Waverley Bridge (☎0131/225 8616) or their headquarters at 14 Queen St (☎0131/220 4111). You can, of course, buy tickets from the driver, for which you'll need exact change. The green buses run by *Eastern Scottish* and the green and yellow buses of *Lowland Scottish* link the capital with outlying towns and villages. Most services depart from and terminate at the St Andrew Square bus station.

The city is well endowed with taxi ranks, especially around Waverley Bridge. Costs start at about 90p for the first 340 yards and 20p for each additional 240 yards. The phone numbers of the main local cab companies are: *Capital Castle Cabs* (☎0131/228 2555), *Central Taxis* (☎0131/229 2468) and *City Cabs* (☎0131/228 1211).

Edinburgh is a reasonably cycle-friendly city – although hilly – with several **cycle paths**. The local cycling action group, *Spokes* (☎0131/313 2114), publishes an excellent cycle map of the city. For rental, try *Central Cycles*, 13 Lochrin Place (☎0131/228 6333), or *Sandy Gilchrist Cycles*, 1 Cadzow Place (☎0131/652 1760).

Accommodation

As befits its status as a top tourist city, Edinburgh has a larger and wider choice of **accommodation** than any other place in Britain outside London. In addition to Edinburgh's **hotels**, hundreds of **private houses** offer B&B deals at low rates, but in order to protect the guest-house trade from excessive competition, they are only open between Easter and October. There is also a decent choice of both official and private **hostels**, and four **campsites** attached to caravan parks.

Advance reservations are very strongly recommended during the Festival: turning up on spec entails accepting whatever is left (which is unlikely to be good value) or else commuting from the suburbs. The **tourist office** (see p.689) sends out accommodation lists for free, and can reserve any type of accommodation in advance for a non-refundable £3 fee: call in personally when you arrive or write in advance to Edinburgh

Marketing Central Reservations Department, 3 Princes St, Edinburgh EH2 2QP (☎0131/557 9677), stating requirements. In Waverley Station the *Edinburgh Hotel and Guest House Association* runs an agency (Mon–Sat 7am–10pm, Sun 8am–10pm; ☎0131/556 0030) which makes no charge for bookings with any of its members.

Hotels

Although considerably more expensive than the guest houses, Edinburgh's **hotels** are generally of a high standard and cover a wide range of tastes, from the hub of New Town elegance to quieter retreats out of the centre.

NEW TOWN

Ailsa Craig Hotel, 24 Royal Terrace (☎0131/556 6055). One of a clutch of good hotels on this elegant Georgian street overlooking a park. ⑤.

Argus Hotel, 14 Coates Gardens (☎0131/337 6159). Smallish rooms in a low-key hotel close to Haymarket Station. ⑤.

Claymore Hotel, 6 Royal Terrace (☎0131/556 2693). Small, family-run hotel on one of the city's most desirable streets. ⑤.

Clifton Private Hotel, 1 Clifton Terrace (☎0131/337 1002). Another family-run hotel, in roomy Victorian town house directly opposite Haymarket Station. ⑤.

Grosvenor Hotel, Grosvenor St (☎0131/226 6001). Chain hotel retaining its old character; in the West End, just across from Haymarket Station. ⑦.

Halcyon Hotel, 8 Royal Terrace (☎0131/556 1032). A very reasonably priced unpretentious hotel, considering the location. ⑥.

Old Waverley Hotel, 43 Princes St (☎0131/556 4648). Grand hotel in ideal location, right across from Waverley Station and with sweeping city views. Good restaurant, *Cranston's*, serving mainly Scottish dishes, with several vegetarian options. ⑨.

Ritz Hotel, 14–18 Grosvenor St (☎0131/337 4315). Posh five-storey hotel close to Haymarket Station. Some rooms feature antique four-poster beds. ⑦.

Rothesay Hotel, 8 Rothesay Place (☎0131/225 4125). Quiet West End hotel in a Georgian terrace close to St Mary's Cathedral; bright high-ceilinged rooms. ⑤.

Roxburghe Hotel, 38 Charlotte Square (☎0131/225 3921). Characterful traditional hotel, right on the corner of Edinburgh's most beautiful square; food is good but unimaginative. ⑧.

Royal Terrace Hotel, 18 Royal Terrace (☎0131/557 3222). On one of the city's handsomest Georgian streets, part of the eastern extension to the New Town. Has its own landscaped gardens, plus a leisure club with bathing pool. Popular with tour groups. ⑨.

SOUTH OF THE CENTRE

Allison House Hotel, 15–17 Mayfield Gardens (☎0131/667 8049). Popular and well run, with "honesty" bar – guests serve themselves and pay on departure. ⑤.

Arthur's View Hotel, 10 Mayfield Gardens (☎0131/667 3468) Pleasant, friendly hotel in convenient southside location. ⑦.

Braid Hills Hotel, 134 Braid Rd (☎0131/447 8888). Old-fashioned, Baronial-style hotel in a residential area in the hilly outskirts, with fine views (10-min drive from the city). ⑧.

Donmaree Hotel, 21 Mayfield Gardens (☎0131/667 3641). Victorian mansion on the south side of the city, well known for its restaurant specializing in traditional Scottish food. ⑦.

Prestonfield House Hotel, Priestfield Rd (☎0131/668 3346). Edinburgh's most eccentric hotel, a seventeenth-century mansion with opulent interiors set in its own park below Arthur's Seat. Just five rooms, only two of which have private facilities – historical values have not been sacrificed to modern comforts. Must book well in advance. ⑨.

Teviotdale House Hotel, 53 Grange Loan (☎0131/667 4376). Peaceful non-smoking hotel, offering luxurious standards at moderate prices. Particularly renowned for the huge home-cooked Scottish breakfasts. ⑤.

Thrums Private Hotel, 14–15 Minto St (☎0131/667 5545). Excellent hotel in large Georgian house with equally classy restaurant. ⑥.

Guest Houses

Edinburgh's innumerable **guest houses** are excellent value for money and far more personal places to stay than the larger city hotels.

NEW TOWN

Dickie Guest House, 22 E Claremont St (☎0131/556 4032). Friendly B&B in a Victorian town house on the eastern edge of the New Town. ④.

Drummond House, 17 Drummond Place (☎0131/557 9189). Just three rooms in this luxurious guest house in the heart of the New Town, an attractive alternative to the large hotels. ⑦.

Galloway Guest House, 22 Dean Park Crescent (☎0131/332 3672). Friendly, family-run place in elegant Stockbridge, within walking distance of the centre. ④.

Marrakech Guest House, 30 London St (☎0131/556 4444). Small rooms in a residential street just a few minutes' walk south of the bus station. Superb Moroccan restaurant in the basement. ④.

St Bernard's Guest House, 22 St Bernard's Crescent (☎0131/332 2339). Well located in Georgian Stockbridge, with tasteful pink rooms. ⑤.

Sibbet House, 26 Northumberland St (☎0131/556 1078). Small, sumptuous family guest house, where British sangfroid is challenged by a communal breakfast table, an occasion regularly enlivened by the host's bagpipe playing. ⑦.

Six St Mary's Place, Raeburn Place (☎0131/332 8965). Collectively run, "alternative" guest house; has a no-smoking policy, and offers excellent home-cooked vegetarian meals. ⑤.

Stuart House, 12 E Claremont St (☎0131/557 9030). Homely, bright refurbished Georgian house in eastern New Town, a few minutes' walk from the bus station; no smoking. ⑥.

SOUTH OF THE CENTRE

Arrandale House, 28 Mayfield Gardens (☎0131/667 6029). Good-value option among a clutch of guest houses in Mayfield, a residential quarter about a mile from the centre. ④.

International Guest House, 37 Mayfield Gardens (☎0131/667 2511). One of the best of the Mayfield guest houses, with comfortable, well-equipped rooms. ⑤.

Ravensneuk Guest House, 11 Blacket Ave (☎0131/667 5347). Good-value rooms set in a quiet conservation area, close to the Royal Commonwealth Pool and Holyrood Park. ④.

Town House, 65 Gilmore Place (☎0131/229 1985). Small but friendly Victorian guest house close to the King's Theatre; no smoking. ⑤.

LEITH AND INVERLEITH

A-Haven Guest House, 180 Ferry Rd (☎0131/554 6559). Exceptionally friendly place; among the best of a number of guest houses on one of Edinburgh's main east–west arteries. ④.

Ashlyn Guest House, 42 Inverleith Row (☎0131/552 2954). Right by the Botanical Gardens, and within walking distance of the centre. Non-smoking. ④.

Bonnington Guest House, 202 Ferry Rd (☎0131/554 7610). Comfortable, friendly guest house pleasantly sited just by the park. ⑤.

Ravensdown Guest House, 248 Ferry Rd (☎0131/552 5438). Another place on Ferry Road, with fine panoramic views across Inverleith playing fields to the city centre. ④.

Sheridan Guest House, 1 Bonnington Terrace (☎0131/554 4107). Comfortable guest house in elegant Victorian terrace. ④.

EAST OF THE CENTRE

Daisy Park Guest House, 41 Abercorn Terrace (☎0131/669 2503). Relaxed atmosphere in this guest house opposite the Daisy Park and close to the sea. ④.

Devon House Guest House, 2 Pittville St (☎0131/669 6067). Pleasant rooms, 2 minutes from the shore. ③.

Joppa Turrets Guest House, 1 Lower Joppa (☎0131/669 5806). The place to come if you want an Edinburgh holiday by the sea: a quiet establishment right by the beach in Joppa, five miles east of the centre (close to bus routes #15, #26 and #86). ③.

Hostels and campus accommodation

Belford Youth Hostel, 6–8 Douglas Gardens (☎0131/225 6209). Housed in a converted Arts and Crafts church just west of the centre, close to the Dean Village. Open all year; dorm beds and doubles.

Bruntsfield Hostel, 7 Bruntsfield Crescent (☎0131/447 2994; Grade 1). Strictly run SYHA youth hostel, overlooking Bruntsfield Links a mile south of Princes Street; take bus #11, #15 or #16. 2am curfew; closed Jan.

Christian Alliance Female Residence, 14 Coates Crescent (☎0131/225 3608). Clean, women-only hostel in an excellent West End location. No kitchen. Dorm beds and singles. Midnight curfew, extended to 1.30am during the Festival.

Cowgate Tourist Hostel, 112 Cowgate (☎0131/226 2153). Basic, excellent value accommodation, in small apartments with kitchens, in the heart of the Old Town. Laundry facilities. No curfew; July–Sept only.

Edinburgh Central Youth Hostel, College Wynd (Grade 1). Lively SYHA hostel only open July & Aug. Advance bookings through Edinburgh District Office, 161 Warrender Park Rd, Edinburgh EH9 1EQ (☎0131/229 8660).

Eglington Hostel, 18 Eglington Crescent (☎0131/337 1120; Grade 1). SYHA hostel west of the centre, near Haymarket Station; easier-going than its Bruntsfield counterpart. 2am curfew; closed Dec.

High Street Hostel, 8 Blackfriars St (☎0131/557 3984). Privately run venture with room for 130 people, just off the Royal Mile. Slightly cramped, but its lively atmosphere makes up for it. Open 24hr, all year.

Napier University, 219 Colinton Rd (☎0131/445 4621; minimum stay 2 months). Reasonable location in the southern inner suburbs, but open Easter and July to mid-Sept only. ③.

University of Edinburgh Pollock Halls of Residence, 18 Holyrood Park Rd (☎0131/667 1971). Unquestionably the best setting of any of the campuses, right beside the Royal Commonwealth Pool and Holyrood Park. Open Easter and late June to mid-Sept only. ⑤.

Campsites

Little France Caravan Site, 219 Old Dalkeith Rd (☎0131/666 2326). Three miles south of the centre, reached by bus #33, #82 or #89 from Princes Street. April–Sept.

Mortonhall Caravan Park, 38 Mortonhall Gate, Frogston Rd E (☎0131/664 1533). A good site, five miles out, near the Braid Hills; take bus #11 from Princes Street. March–Oct.

Silverknowes Caravan Site, Marine Drive, Silverknowes (☎0131/312 6874). Pleasant campsite, popular with backpackers, close to the shore in the western suburbs, a 20-min ride from the centre by bus #14. April–Sept.

Slatebairns Caravan Club Site, Roslin, Midlothian (☎0131/440 2192). Caravans and tents welcome at this attractive countryside site seven miles from the city centre (bus #87a). Good facilities. Open Easter to October 1.

The Old Town

The **OLD TOWN**, although only about a mile long and three hundred yards wide, represents the total extent of the twin burghs of Edinburgh and Canongate for the first 650 years of their existence, and its general appearance and character remain indubitably medieval. Containing as it does the majority of the city's most famous tourist sights, it's also the best starting point for your explorations. **The Old Town Information**

Centre (late April to May Thurs–Sun 10am–5pm; June–Sept daily 10am–7pm; ☎220 1637) in the Tron Kirk (see p.701) has displays on the history of the Old Town, as well as a wealth of practical information.

In addition to the obvious goals of the **Castle**, the **Palace of Holyroodhouse** and **Holyrood Abbey**, there are scores of historic monuments along the length of the **Royal Mile** linking the two. Inevitably, much of the Old Town is sacrificed to hard-sell tourism – it also gets crowded in the summer, especially during the Festival. A welcome antidote, and a reminder that the Old Town is by no means fossilized for the benefit of tourists, is provided by the area to the south, notably Chambers Street, location of the **Royal Museum of Scotland** and the **University of Edinburgh**. Be sure, too, to spare time for the wonderfully varied scenery and breathtaking vantage points of **Holyrood Park**, an extensive tract of open countryside on its eastern edge.

The Castle

The history of Edinburgh, and indeed of Scotland, is indissolubly bound up with its **Castle** (daily April–Sept 9.30am–6pm; Oct–March 9.30am–5pm; £5.50) that dominates the city from its lofty seat atop an extinct volcanic rock. It requires no great imaginative feat to comprehend the strategic importance that underpinned the Castle's, and hence Edinburgh's, pre-eminence within Scotland: in the dramatic view from Princes Street, the north side rears high above an almost sheer rockface; the southern side is equally formidable, the western, where the rock rises in terraces, only marginally less so. Would-be attackers, like modern tourists, were forced to approach the Castle from the crag to the east on which the Royal Mile runs down to Holyrood.

The oldest surviving part of the castle, St Margaret's Chapel, is from the twelfth century, while the most recent additions date back to the 1920s. Having been lost to (and subsequently recaptured from) the English on several occasions, the defences were dismantled by the Scots themselves in 1313, and only rebuilt in 1356. It last saw action in 1745, when the Young Pretender's forces, fresh from their victory at Prestonpans, made a half-hearted attempt to storm it. Subsequently, advances in weapons technology diminished its importance, but under the influence of the Romantic movement it came to be seen as a great national monument.

The Esplanade and the lower defences

The Castle is entered via the **Esplanade**, a parade ground laid out in the eighteenth century and enclosed a century later by ornamental walls, the southern one of which commands fine views towards the Pentland Hills. Each evening during the Festival (see p.726), the Esplanade is the setting for the city's most shameless and spectacular demonstration of tourist kitsch, the Edinburgh Military Tattoo. An unfortunate side effect of this is that the skyline is disfigured for virtually the entire summer by the grandstands needed to accommodate the spectators.

The **Gatehouse** to the Castle is a Romantic-style addition of the 1880s, complete with the last drawbridge ever built in Scotland. It was later adorned with appropriately heroic-looking statues of Sir William Wallace and Robert the Bruce. Rearing up behind is the most distinctive and impressive feature of the Castle's silhouette, the sixteenth-century **Half Moon Battery**, which marks the outer limit of the actual defences. Continuing uphill, you pass through the **Portcullis Gate**, a handsome Renaissance gateway of the same period, marred by the addition of a nineteenth-century upper storey equipped with anachronistic arrow slits rather than gun holes.

Beyond is the six-gun **Argyle Battery**, built in the eighteenth century by Major-General Wade, whose network of military roads and bridges still forms an essential part of the transport infrastructure of the Highlands. Further west is **Mill's Mount Battery**, setting every weekday for a well-known Edinburgh ritual, the firing of the one o'clock gun – originally designed for the benefit of ships in the Firth of Forth, now used as a time signal by city-centre office workers. Both batteries offer wonderful panoramic views over the city and out to the coastal towns and hills of Fife across the Forth.

Up the tortuously sloping road, the **Governor's House** is a 1740s mansion whose harled masonry and crow-stepped gables are archetypal features of vernacular Scottish architecture. It now serves as the officers' mess for members of the garrison, while the Governor himself lives in the northern side wing. Behind stands the largest single construction in the Castle complex, the **New Barracks**, built in the 1790s in an austere Neoclassical style. The road then snakes round towards the enclosed citadel at the uppermost point of Castle Rock, entered via the seventeenth-century **Foog's Gate**.

St Margaret's Chapel

At the eastern end of the citadel, **St Margaret's Chapel** is the oldest surviving building in the Castle, and probably also in Edinburgh itself. Used as a powder magazine for 300 years, this tiny Norman church was rediscovered in 1845 and was eventually rededicated in 1934, after sympathetic restoration. Externally, it is plain and severe, but the interior preserves an elaborate zigzag archway dividing the nave from the sanctuary. Although once believed to have been built by the saint herself, and mooted as the site of her death in 1093, its architectural style suggests that it actually dates from about thirty years later, and was thus probably built by King David I as a memorial to his mother.

The battlements in front of the chapel offer the best of all the Castle's panoramic views. They are interrupted by the **Lang Stairs**, which provide an alternative means of access from the Argyle Battery via the side of the Portcullis Gate. Just below the battlements there's a small **cemetery**, the last resting place of the **soldiers' pets**: it is kept in immaculate condition, particularly when contrasted with the delapidated state of some of the city's public cemeteries. Continuing eastwards, you skirt the top of the Forewall and Half Moon Batteries, passing the 110-foot-deep **Castle Well** en route to **Crown Square**, the highest and most secure section of the entire complex.

The south side of Crown Square is occupied by the **Great Hall**, built under James IV as a venue for banquets and other ceremonial occasions. Until 1639 the meeting place of the Scottish Parliament, it later underwent the indignity of conversion and subdivision, firstly into a barracks, then a hospital. During this time, its hammer-beam roof – the earliest of three in the Old Town – was hidden from view. It was restored towards the end of last century, when the hall was decked out in the full-blown Romantic manner.

The Palace

The eastern side of Crown Square is occupied by the **Palace**, a surprisingly unassuming edifice built round an octagonal stair turret heightened last century to bear the Castle's main flagpole. Begun in the 1430s, the Palace's present Renaissance appearance is thanks to King James IV, though it was remodelled for Mary, Queen of Scots and her consort Henry, Lord Darnley, whose entwined initials (MAH), together with the date 1566, can be seen above one of the doorways. This gives access to a few historic rooms, the most interesting of which is the tiny panelled bedchamber at the extreme southeastern corner, where Mary gave birth to James VI. Along with the rest of the Palace, the room was remodelled for James' triumphant homecoming in 1617, though this was to be the last time it served as a royal residence.

Another section of the Palace has recently been refurbished with a detailed audiovisual presentation on the **Honours of Scotland**, the originals of which are housed in the Crown Room at the very end of the display. These magnificent crown jewels – the only pre-Restoration set in the United Kingdom – serve as one of the most potent images of Scotland's nationhood. They were last used for the Scottish-only coronation of Charles II in 1651, an event which provoked the wrath of Oliver Cromwell, who made exhaustive attempts to have the jewels melted down. Having narrowly escaped his clutches by being smuggled out of the Castle and hidden in a rural church, the jewels later served as symbols of the absent monarch at sittings of the Scottish parliament before being locked away in a chest following the Union of 1707. For over a century they were out of sight and eventually presumed lost, before being rediscovered in 1818 as a result of a search initiated by Sir Walter Scott. Of the three pieces comprising the Honours, the oldest is the **sceptre**, given to James IV in 1494 by Pope Alexander VI; even finer is the **sword**, a swaggering Italian High Renaissance masterpiece presented to James IV by the great artistic patron Pope Julius II; the jewel-encrusted **crown**, made for James V by the Scottish goldsmith James Mosman, incorporates the gold circlet worn by Robert the Bruce.

The Vaults and the Military Museum

From Crown Square, you can descend to the **Vaults**, a series of cavernous chambers erected by order of James IV to provide an even surface for the showpiece buildings above. They were later used as a prison for captured foreign nationals, who have bequeathed a rich legacy of graffiti. One of the rooms houses the famous fifteenth-century siege gun, **Mons Meg**, which could fire a five-hundred-pound stone nearly two miles. A seventeenth-century visitor, the London poet, John Taylor, commented: "It is so great within, that it was told me that a child was once gotten there". In 1736, Mons Meg was taken to the Tower of London where it stayed till Sir Walter Scott persuaded George IV, on the occasion of his 1822 state visit to Scotland, to return it. Directly opposite the entrance to the Vaults is the **Military Prison**, built in 1842, when the design and function of jails was a major topic of public debate. The cells, though designed for solitary confinement, are less forbidding than might be expected.

The Royal Mile

The **Royal Mile**, the name given to the ridge linking the Castle with Holyrood, was described by Daniel Defoe, in 1724, as "the largest, longest and finest street for Buildings and Number of Inhabitants, not in Britain only, but in the World". Almost exactly a mile in length, it is divided into four separate streets: Castlehill, Lawnmarket, High Street and Canongate. From these, branching out in a herringbone pattern, a series of tightly packed closes and steep lanes are entered via archways known as pends. After the construction of the New Town, the Royal Mile degenerated into a notorious slum, but has since shaken off that reputation, becoming once again a highly desirable place to live, and one that particularly rewards detailed exploration.

Castlehill

The narrow uppermost stretch of the Royal Mile is known as **Castlehill**. On the side facing the Esplanade the pretty Art Nouveau **Witches' Fountain** commemorates the three hundred or more women burned at the spot on charges of sorcery, the last of whom died in 1722. Rising up behind is the picturesque **Ramsay Gardens**, centring on the octagonal **Goose Pie House**, home of the eighteenth-century poet Allan Ramsay, author of *The Gentle Shepherd* and father of the better-known portrait painter of the same name. The rest dates from the 1890s and was the brainchild of Patrick Geddes, a pioneer of the modern town-planning movement, who created these desirable apartments in an attempt to regenerate the Old Town.

At the top of the southern side of Castlehill, the so-called **Cannonball House** takes its name from the cannonball embedded in its masonry, which according to legend was the result of a poorly targeted shot fired by the castle garrison at Bonnie Prince Charlie's encampment at Holyrood. The truth is far more prosaic: the ball marks the gravitation height of the city's first piped water supply. Alongside, the **Scotch Whisky Heritage Centre** (daily 10am–5.30pm; extended opening in high summer; £3.80) is only really worth popping into for its shop, whose stock gives an idea of the sheer range and diversity of the drink, with dozens of different brands on sale.

Across the road, the **Outlook Tower** (April–Oct Mon–Fri 9.30am–6pm, Sat & Sun 10am–6pm; Nov–March until 5pm; £3.20) has been one of Edinburgh's top tourist attractions since 1853, when the original seventeenth-century tenement was equipped with a **camera obscura**. It makes a good introduction to the city: actual moving images are beamed on to a white table, accompanied by live running commentary. For the best views visit when dark, or at noon when there are fewer shadows. The viewing balcony is one of Edinburgh's best vantage points, and there are exhibitions on pinhole photography, holography, Victorian photographs of the city, and topographic paintings made between 1780 and 1860.

A few steps further on is the **Assembly Hall**, meeting place of the annual General Assembly of the Church of Scotland, and, during the Festival, an extraordinarily effective venue for the most ambitious events on the programme. It was built in 1859 for the breakaway Free Church; the established church previously met at the **Tolbooth Kirk** across the road. Stunningly sited at the foot of Castlehill, the Kirk is one of the most distinctive features of the Edinburgh skyline, thanks to its majestic spire, the highest in the city; sadly, it has lain disused since vacated by its Gaelic-speaking congregation in 1981. The church's superb neo-Gothic detailing is due to Augustus Pugin, co-architect of the Houses of Parliament in London.

Lawnmarket

Below the Tolbooth Kirk, the Royal Mile opens out into the much broader expanse of **Lawnmarket**, which, as its name suggests, was once a marketplace. At its northern end is the entry to **Milne's Court**, whose excellently restored tenements now serve as student residences, and immediately beyond, **James Court**, one of Edinburgh's most fashionable addresses prior to the advent of the New Town, with David Hume and James Boswell among those who lived there.

Back on Lawnmarket itself, **Gladstone's Land** (April–Oct Mon–Sat 10am–5pm, Sun 2–5pm; July & Aug Thurs until 8pm; £2.50) takes its name from the merchant Thomas Gledstane (sic), who in 1617 transformed the site into a magnificent six-storey mansion. The Gledstane family are thought to have occupied the third floor, renting out the rest to merchants, in the style of tenement occupation still widespread in the city today. The arcaded ground floor, the only authentic example left of what was once a common feature of Royal Mile houses, has been restored to illustrate its early function as a shopping booth. Several other rooms have been kitted out in authentic period style; the Painted Chamber, with its decorated wooden ceiling and wall friezes, is particularly impressive. You can also stay here.

A few paces further on, steps lead down to Lady Stair's Close, in which stands **Lady Stair's House** (June–Sept Mon–Sat 10am–6pm; Oct–May Mon–Sat 10am–5pm; Sun 2–5pm during the Festival only; free), another fine seventeenth-century residence, albeit one subject to a considerable amount of Victorian refurbishment. It now serves as Edinburgh's literary museum, featuring a collection of personal mementos (among them locks of hair and walking sticks) of the three lions of Scottish literature – Robert Burns, Sir Walter Scott and Robert Louis Stevenson.

The High Kirk of St Giles

Across George IV Bridge, the **High Kirk of St Giles** (Mon–Sat 9am–5pm; extended opening in summer) closes off Parliament Square from High Street. The sole parish church of medieval Edinburgh and where John Knox (see below) launched and directed the Scottish Reformation, the Kirk is almost invariably referred to as a cathedral, although it has only been the seat of a bishop on two brief and unhappy occasions in the seventeenth century. According to one of the city's best-known legends, the attempt in 1637 to introduce the English prayer book, and thus episcopal government, so incensed a humble stallholder named Jenny Geddes that she hurled her stool at the preacher, prompting the rest of the congregation to chase the offending clergy out of the building. A tablet in the north aisle marks the spot from where she let rip.

In the early nineteenth century, St Giles received a much needed but over-drastic restoration, covering most of the Gothic exterior with a smooth stone coating that gives it a certain Georgian dignity while sacrificing its medieval character almost completely. The only part to survive this treatment is the late fifteenth-century tower,

JOHN KNOX

Little is known about **John Knox**'s early years: he was born between 1505 and 1514 in East Lothian, and trained for the priesthood at St Andrews University under John Major (sic), author of a *History of Great Britain* that advocated the union of Scotland and England. Ordained in 1540, Knox then served as a private tutor, in league with the Protestant leader, **George Wishart**; after Wishart was burnt at the stake for heresy in 1546, Knox became involved with the group who carried out the revenge murder of the Scottish Primate, Cardinal David Beaton, subsequently taking over his castle in St Andrews. The following year, this was captured by the French, and Knox was carted off to work as a galley slave.

He was freed in 1548, after the intervention of the English, who invited him to play an evangelizing role in the spread of their own Reformation. Following successful ministries in Berwick-upon-Tweed and Newcastle-upon-Tyne, Knox turned down the bishopric of Rochester to avoid becoming embroiled in the turmoil he guessed would ensue if the Catholic Mary Tudor acceded to the English throne. When this duly happened in 1553, Knox fled to the Continent, ending up as minister to the English-speaking community in Geneva, which was then in the grip of the theocratic government of the Frenchman **Jean Calvin**. Knox was quickly won over to his radical version of Protestantism, declaring Geneva to be "the most perfect school of Christ since the days of the Apostles". In exile, Knox wrote his most infamous treatise, *The First Blast of the Trumpet against the Monstruous Regiment of Women*, a specific attack on the three Catholic women then ruling Scotland, England and France, which has made his name synonymous with misogyny ever since.

Knox was allowed to return to Scotland in 1555, becoming minister of St Giles in Edinburgh, where he established a reputation as a charismatic preacher. However, the establishment of Protestantism as the official religion of Scotland in 1560 was dependent on the forging of an alliance with Elizabeth I, which Knox himself rigorously championed: the swift deployment of English troops against the French garrison in Edinburgh dealt a fatal blow to Franco-Spanish hopes of re-establishing Catholicism in both Scotland and England. Although the return of Mary, Queen of Scots the following year placed a Catholic monarch on the Scottish throne, reputedly Knox was always able to retain the upper hand in his famous disputes with her. Before his death in 1572, Knox began mapping out the organization of the Scots Kirk, sweeping away all vestiges of episcopal control and giving laymen a role of unprecedented importance.

For all his considerable influence, Knox was not responsible for many of the features which have created the popular image of Scottish presbyterianism – and of Knox himself – as austere and joyless. A man of refined cultural tastes, he did not encourage the iconoclasm that destroyed so many of Scotland's churches and works of art: indeed, much of this was carried out by English hands. Nor did he promote the unbending Sabbatarianism, the obsessive work ethic or even the inflexible view of the doctrine of predestination favoured by his far more fanatical successors. Ironically, though, by fostering an irrevocable rift in the "Auld Alliance" with France, he did do more than anyone else to ensure that Scotland's future was to be linked irrevocably with that of England.

whose resplendent crown spire is formed by eight flying buttresses. The **interior** has survived in much better shape. Especially notable are the four massive piers supporting the tower, which date back, at least in part, to the church's Norman predecessor. In the nineteenth century, St Giles was adorned with several Pre-Raphaelite stained-glass windows, the best of which can be seen on the facade wall of the **north aisle**.

At the southeastern corner of St Giles, with its own separate entrance on Parliament Square, the **Thistle Chapel** was built by Sir Robert Lorimer in 1911 as the private chapel of the 16 knights of the Most Noble Order of the Thistle. Self-consciously derivative of St George's Chapel in Windsor, it's an exquisite piece of craftsmanship, with an elaborate ribbed vault, huge drooping bosses, and extravagantly ornate stalls.

Parliament Square

The rest of **Parliament Square** is dominated by the continuous Neoclassical facades of the **Law Courts**, originally planned by Robert Adam, but due to a shortage of funds, eventually built by Robert Reid (1776–1856), who faithfully quoted from Adam's architectural vocabulary without matching his flair. Mentor of William Playfair (see p.719), another architect, William Stark was flamboyant with design, and his **Signet Library**, which occupies the west side of the square, is one of the most beautiful interiors in Edinburgh – its sumptuous colonnaded hall a perfect embodiment of the ideals of the Age of Reason. Unfortunately it can usually only be seen by prior written application.

Around the corner, facing the southern side of St Giles, is **Parliament House**, built in the 1630s for the Scottish Parliament, a role it maintained until the Union, when it passed into the hands of the legal fraternity. Today it is readily accessible during the week, used by lawyers and their clients for hushed conferrals in between court sittings. Inside, the most notable feature is the extravagant hammer-beam roof, and the delicately carved stone corbels from which it springs: in addition to some vicious grotesques, they include accurate depictions of several castles, including Edinburgh.

Outside on the square, an imposing equestrian **monument to King Charles II** depicts him in fetching Roman garb. Set in the pavement beside a bloated memorial to the fifth Duke of Buccleuch, a brickwork pattern known as the **Heart of Midlothian**, immortalized in Scott's novel of the same name, marks the site of the demolished Tolbooth. Passers-by traditionally spit on it for luck. Public proclamations have traditionally been read from the **Mercat Cross** at the back of St Giles. The present structure, adorned with coats of arms and topped by a sculpture of a unicorn, looks venerable enough, but most of it is little more than a hundred years old, a gift to the city from nineteenth-century prime minister, William Ewart Gladstone.

High Street

The third section of the Royal Mile proper is known as **High Street**, and occupies two blocks on either side of the intersection between North Bridge and South Bridge. Directly opposite the Mercat Cross, the U-shaped **City Chambers** were designed by John Adam, brother of Robert, as the Royal Exchange. Local traders never warmed to the exchange, however, so the town council established its headquarters there instead. Beneath the City Chambers lies **Mary King's Close**, one of Edinburgh's most unusual attractions. Built in the early sixteenth century, it was closed off for many years after the devastation of the 1645 plague, before being entirely covered up by the chambers in 1753. Regular tours were successfully held during the 1995 Festival, and it's hoped these will continue (check with the tourist office).

Across the road is the **Tron Kirk**, best known as the favourite rendezvous for hardy Hogmanay revellers. The church was built in the 1630s to accommodate the Presbyterian congregation ejected from St Giles when the latter became the seat of a bishop; the spire is an 1820s replacement for one destroyed by fire. The Tron remained in use as a church until 1952. It was then closed for 40 years before reopening as the **Old Town Information Centre** (see p.695).

Beyond the intersection of North Bridge and South Bridge back on the northern side of High Street, **Trinity Apse**, in Chalmers Close, is a poignant reminder of the fifteenth-century Holy Trinity Collegiate Church, formerly one of Edinburgh's most outstanding buildings, but demolished in 1848 to make way for an extension to Waverley Station. The stones were carefully numbered and stored on Calton Hill so that it could be reassembled at a later date, but many were pilfered before sufficient funds became available, and only the apse could be reconstructed on this new site. A few years ago, it was transformed into a **Brass Rubbing Centre** (June–Sept Mon–Sat 10am–6pm; Oct–May Mon–Sat 10am–5pm; Sun 2–5pm during the Festival only; free), where you can rub your own impressions from Pictish crosses for around 40p.

The noisy **Museum of Childhood** (June–Sept Mon–Sat 10am–6pm; Oct–May Mon–Sat 10am–5pm; Sun 2–5pm during the Festival only; free) was, oddly enough, founded by an eccentric local councillor who disliked children. Although he claimed that the museum was a serious social archive for adults, and dedicated it to King Herod, it has always attracted swarms of kids, who delight in the dolls' houses, teddy bears, train sets, marionettes, and hosts of other paraphernalia.

Almost directly opposite is what's thought to be the city's oldest surviving dwelling, the early sixteenth-century **Moubray House** (closed to the public), a four-storied house which has been, over the years, a tavern, bookshop and temperance hotel, not to mention Daniel Defoe's office during his stay as an English government representative in 1707. Next door lies the picturesque **John Knox's House** (Mon–Sat 10am–4.30pm; £1.30), built some thirty years later. With its outside stairway, Biblical motto, and sundial adorned with a statue of Moses, it gives a good impression of how the Royal Mile must have once looked. Whether or not it was ever really the home of Knox is debatable: he may have moved here for safety at the height of the religious troubles. The rather bare interiors, which give a good idea of the labyrinthine layout of Old Town houses, display explanatory material on Knox's life and career (see p.700).

Canongate

For over seven hundred years, the district through which Canongate runs was a burgh in its own right, officially separate from the capital. In recent decades, it has been the subject of some of the most ambitious restoration programmes in the Old Town, two notable examples of which can be seen at the top of the street. On the south side is the residential **Chessel's Court**, a mid-eighteenth-century development with fanciful Rococo chimneys; formerly the site of the Excise Office, scene of the robbery that led to the arrest and execution of Deacon Brodie. Over the road the **Morocco Land** is a reasonably faithful reproduction of an old tenement, incorporating the original bust of a Moor from which its name derived.

Dominated by a turreted steeple, the late sixteenth-century **Canongate Tolbooth** (June–Sept Mon–Sat 10am–6pm; Oct–May 10am–5pm; Sun 2–5pm during the Festival only; free), a little further down the north side of the street, has served both as the headquarters of the burgh administration and as a prison, and now houses **The People's Story**, a lively museum devoted to the everyday life and work of Edinburgh people down the centuries, with sounds and tableaux on various aspects of city living – including a typical Edinburgh pub. Next door, **Canongate Kirk** was built in the 1680s to house the congregation expelled from Holyrood Abbey when the latter was commandeered by James VII (James II in England) to serve as the chapel for the Order of the Thistle. It's a curiously archaic design, still Renaissance in outline, and built to a cruciform plan wholly at odds with the ideals and requirements of Protestant worship. Among those buried in its churchyard, which commands a superb view across to Calton Hill, are Adam Smith, Mrs Agnes McLehose (better known as Robert

Burns' "Clarinda") and the poet Robert Fergusson, whose headstone was donated by Burns, a fervent admirer, who also wrote the inscription.

Opposite the church, the local history museum in **Huntly House** (June–Sept Mon–Sat 10am–6pm, Oct–May Mon–Sat 10am–5pm, Sun 2–5pm during the Festival only; free) includes a quirky array of old shop signs, some dating back to the eighteenth century, as well as displays on indigenous industries such as glass, silver, pottery and clockmaking, and on the dubious military career of Earl Haig. Also on view is the original version of the National Covenant of 1638; modern science has failed to resolve whether or not some of the signatories signed with their own blood, as tradition has it.

Holyrood

At the foot of Canongate lies **Holyrood**, Edinburgh's royal quarter, the **legend** of whose foundation in 1128 is described in a fifteenth-century manuscript which is still kept there. The story goes that King David I, son of Malcolm Canmore and St Margaret, went out hunting one day and was suddenly confronted by a stag who threw him from his horse and seemed ready to gore him. In desperation, the king tried to protect himself by grasping its antlers, but instead found himself holding a crucifix, whereupon the animal ran off. In a dream that night, he heard a voice commanding him to "make a house for Canons devoted to the Cross"; he duly obeyed, naming the abbey Holyrood (rood being an alternative name for a cross). More likely, however, is that David, the most pious of all Scotland's monarchs, simply acquired a relic of the True Cross and decided to build a suitable home for it.

Holyrood soon became a favoured **royal residence**, its situation in a secluded valley making it far more agreeable than the draughty Castle. At first, monarchs lodged in the monastic guest house, for which a wing for the exclusive use of the court was constructed during the reign of James II. This was transformed into a full-blown palace for James IV, which in turn was replaced by a much larger building for Charles II, although he never actually lived there. Indeed, it was something of a white elephant until Queen Victoria started making regular trips to her northern kingdom, a custom that has been maintained by her successors.

On the north side of **Abbey Strand**, which forms a sort of processional way linking Canongate with Holyrood, Abbey Lairds is a four-storey sixteenth-century mansion which once served as a home for aristocratic debtors and is now occupied by royal flunkeys during the summer seat of the court. Legend has it that Mary, Queen of Scots used to bathe in sweet white wine in the curious little turreted structure nearby known as **Queen Mary's Bath House**; it is more likely, however, that it was either a summer pavilion or a dovecot. Its architecture is mirrored in the **Croft an Righ**, a picturesque L-shaped house in a quiet corner beside the eastern wall of the complex.

The Palace of Holyroodhouse

In its present form, the **Palace of Holyroodhouse** (April–Oct Mon–Sat 9.30am–5.15pm, Sun 10am–4.30pm; Nov–March daily 9.30am–3.45pm; £5) is largely a seven-

---

ADMISSION TO HOLYROOD

Following reorganization, there are no longer guided tours to Holyrood. Visitors are free to move at their own pace and can consult the knowledgeable attendants on hand in each room. It is worth remembering that Holyrood is still a working Palace, so the buildings are closed to the public for long periods during state functions; you won't be able to visit for a fortnight in the middle of May, and during the annual royal visit which takes place in the last two weeks of June and the first in July.

teenth-century creation, planned for Charles II. However, the tower house of the old palace was skilfully incorporated to form the northwestern block, with a virtual mirror image of it erected as a counterbalance at the other end. The three-storey **courtyard** is an early exercise in Palladian style, exhibiting a punctiliously accurate knowledge of the main Classical orders to create a sense of absolute harmony and unity.

Inside, the **State Apartments**, as Charles II's palace is known, are decked out with oak panelling, tapestries, portraits and decorative paintings, all overshadowed by the magnificent white stucco **ceilings**, especially in the Morning Drawing Room. The most eye-catching chamber, however, is the **Great Gallery**, which takes up the entire first floor of the northern wing. During the 1745 sojourn of the Young Pretender this was the setting for a banquet, described in detail in Scott's novel *Waverley*, and it is still used for big ceremonial occasions. Along the walls are 89 portraits commissioned from the seventeenth-century Dutch artist Jacob de Wet to illustrate the royal lineage of Scotland from its mythical origins in the fourth century BC; the result is unintentionally hilarious, as it is clear that the artist's imagination was taxed to bursting point by the need to paint so many different facial types without having an inkling as to what the subjects actually looked like. In the adjacent **King's Closet**, de Wet's *The Finding of Moses* provides a Biblical link to the portraits, the Scottish royal family claiming descent from Scota, the Egyptian pharaoh's daughter who discovered Moses in the bullrushes.

The oldest parts of the palace, the **Historical Apartments**, are mainly of note for their associations with Mary, Queen of Scots and in particular for the brutal murder, organized by her husband, Lord Darnley, of her private secretary, David Rizzio, who was stabbed 56 times and dragged from the small closet, through the Queen's Bedchamber, and into the Outer Chamber. Until a few years ago, visitors were shown apparently indelible bloodstains on the floor of the latter, but these are now admitted to be fakes, and have been covered up. A display cabinet in the same room shows some pieces of **needlework** woven by the deposed queen while in English captivity; another case has an outstanding **miniature portrait** of her by the French court painter, François Clouet.

Holyrood Abbey

In the grounds of the Palace are the wonderfully evocative ruins of **Holyrood Abbey**. Of King David's original Norman church, the only surviving fragment is a doorway in the far southeastern corner. Most of the remainder dates from a late twelfth- and early thirteenth-century rebuilding in the Early Gothic style. The surviving parts of the **west front**, including one of the twin towers and the elaborately carved entrance portal, show how resplendent the abbey must once have been. Unfortunately, its sacking by the English in 1547, followed by the demolition of the transept and chancel during the Reformation, all but destroyed the building. Charles I attempted to restore some semblance of unity by ordering the erection of the great east window and a new stone roof, but the latter collapsed in 1768, causing grievous damage to the rest of the structure. By this time, the Canongate congregation had another place of worship, and schemes to rebuild the abbey were abandoned.

Holyrood Park

Holyrood Park – or **Queen's Park** – a natural wilderness in the very heart of the modern city, is unquestionably one of Edinburgh's main assets, as locals (though relatively few tourists) readily appreciate. Packed into an area no more than five miles in diameter is an amazing variety of landscapes – mountains, crags, moorland, marshes, glens, lochs and fields – representing something of a microcosm of Scotland's scenery.

Opposite the southern gates of the Palace a pathway, nicknamed the Radical Road, traverses the ridge immediately below the **Salisbury Crags**, one of the main features of the Edinburgh skyline. Even though there is no path, you can walk along the top of the basalt crags, from where there are excellent views of the Palace of Holyroodhouse and Holyrood Abbey. Following Queen's Drive in the other direction, you arrive at **St Margaret's Loch**, a nineteenth-century man-made pond, above which stand the scanty ruins of **St Anthony's Chapel**, another fine vantage point. From here, the road's loop is one-way only, ascending to **Dunsapie Loch**, again an artificial stretch of water, which makes an excellent foil to the eponymous crag behind.

This is the usual starting point for the ascent of **Arthur's Seat**, a majestic extinct volcano rising 823ft above sea level. The seat is Edinburgh's single most prominent landmark, resembling a huge crouched lion when seen from the west. The climb from Dunsapie is a fairly straightforward twenty-minute walk, and the views from the top are all you'd expect, covering the entire city and much of the Firth of Forth. The composer, Felix Mendelssohn, climbed Arthur's Seat in July 1829, noting: "It is beautiful here! In the evening a cool breeze is wafted from the sea, and then all objects appear clearly and sharply defined against the gray sky; the lights from the windows glitter brilliantly." As there is little reason to associate it with the British king of the Holy Grail legends, there's no satisfactory story to explain the name.

Queen's Drive circles round to the foot of Salisbury Crags, from where the feline appearance of Arthur's Seat is particularly marked. The road then makes a sharp switchback, passing beneath **Samson's Ribs**, a group of basalt pillars strikingly reminiscent of the Hebridean island of Staffa (see p.825). It continues on to **Duddingston Loch**, the only natural stretch of water in the park, now a bird sanctuary. Perched above it, just outside the park boundary, **Duddingston Kirk** dates back in part to the twelfth century and serves as the focus of one of the most unspoiled old villages within modern Edinburgh.

The rest of the Old Town

Although most visitors to the Old Town understandably concentrate on the Royal Mile, the area has many other intriguing corners, none of which has so much as a hint of commercialism.

Cowgate

Immediately south of, and parallel to, the Royal Mile, **Cowgate** was formerly one of the city's most prestigious addresses. However, the construction of the great **viaducts** linking the Old and New Towns entombed it below street level, condemning it to decay and neglect; and leading the nineteenth-century writer, Alexander Smith, to declare that "the condition of the inhabitants is as little known to respectable Edinburgh as are the habits of moles, earth-worms, and the mining population". In the last decade or so Cowgate has experienced something of a revival, though few tourists venture here.

At the corner with Niddry Street, which runs down from the eastern block of High Street, the unprepossessing **St Cecilia's Hall** (Wed & Sat 2–5pm; £1) was built in the 1760s for the Musical Society of Edinburgh. Inside, Scotland's oldest and most beautiful concert room, oval in shape and set under a shallow dome, makes a perfect venue for concerts of Baroque and early music, held during the Festival and occasionally at other times of the year.

Towards the western end of Cowgate stands the **Magdalen Chapel**, a sixteenth-century almshouse under the jurisdiction of the Incorporation of Hammermen, a guild to which most Edinburgh workers, other than goldsmiths, belonged. The Hammermen added a handsome tower and steeple in the 1620s, and later transformed the chapel into their guild hall, which was suitably adorned with fine ironwork. However, the main feature of the interior is the only significant pre-Reformation stained glass in Scotland, still in its original location. That it escaped the iconoclasts is probably due to the fact that it is purely heraldic.

Grassmarket and George IV Bridge

At its western end, Cowgate opens out into **Grassmarket**, which has played an important role in the murkier aspects of Edinburgh's turbulent history. The public gallows were located here, and it was the scene of numerous riots and other disturbances down the centuries. It was here, in 1736, that Captain Porteous was lynched after he had ordered shots to be fired at the crowd watching a public execution. The notorious duo William Burke and William Hare had their lair in a now-vanished close off the western end of Grassmarket, luring to it victims whom they murdered with the intention of selling their bodies to the eminent physician Robert Knox. Eventually, Hare betrayed his partner, who was duly executed in 1829, and Knox's career was finished as a result. Today, Grassmarket can still be seamy, though the cluster of busy bars and restaurants along its northern side are evidence of a serious attempt to clean up its image.

At the northeastern corner of Grassmarket are five old tenements of the old **West Bow**, which formerly zigzagged up to the Royal Mile. The rest of this was replaced in the 1840s by the curving **Victoria Street**, an unusual two-tier thoroughfare, with arcaded shops below, and a pedestrian terrace above. This sweeps up to **George IV Bridge** and the **National Library of Scotland** which holds a rich collection of illuminated manuscripts, early printed books, historical documents, and the letters and papers of prominent Scottish literary figures, displayed in regularly changing thematic exhibitions (usually Mon–Sat 10am–5pm, Sun 2–5pm; free).

Greyfriars and around

The **statue of Greyfriars Bobby** at the southwestern corner of **George IV Bridge** must rank as Edinburgh's most sentimental tourist attraction. Bobby was a Skye terrier acquired as a working dog by a police constable named John Gray. When the latter died in 1858, Bobby began a vigil on his grave which he maintained until he died fourteen years later. In the process, he became an Edinburgh celebrity, fed and cared for by locals who gave him a special collar (now in the Huntly House Museum; see p.703) to prevent him being impounded as a stray. His statue, originally a fountain, was modelled from life, and erected soon after his death; his story has gained international renown, thanks to a spate of cloying books and tear-jerking movies.

The grave Bobby mourned over is in the **Greyfriars Kirkyard**, which among its clutter of grandiose seventeenth- and eighteenth-century funerary monuments boasts the striking mausoleum of the Adam family of architects. Greyfriars is particularly associated with the long struggle to establish presbyterianism in Scotland: in 1638, it was the setting for the signing of the National Covenant, while in 1679 some 1200 Covenanters were imprisoned in the enclosure at the southwestern end of the yard. Set against the northern wall is the Martyrs' Monument, a defiantly worded memorial commemorating all those who died in pursuit of the eventual victory. The graveyard rather overshadows **Greyfriars Kirk** itself, completed in 1620 as the city's first post-Reformation church. It's a real oddball in both layout and design, built using the anachronistic architectural language of the friary that preceded it, complete with medieval-looking windows, arches and buttresses.

At the western end of Greyfriars Kirkyard is one of the most significant surviving portions of the **Flodden Wall**, the city fortifications erected in the wake of Scotland's disastrous military defeat of 1513. When open, the gateway beyond offers a short cut to **George Heriot's Hospital**, otherwise approached from Lauriston Place to the south. Founded as a home for poor boys by "Jinglin Geordie" Heriot, James VI's goldsmith, it is now one of Edinburgh's most prestigious fee-paying schools; although you can't go inside, you can wander round the quadrangle, whose array of towers, turrets, chimneys, carved doorways and traceried windows is one of the finest achievements of the Scottish Renaissance.

The Royal Museum of Scotland

On the south side of Chambers Street, which runs east from Greyfriars Bobby, stands the **Royal Museum of Scotland** (Mon–Sat 10am–5pm, Sun noon–5pm; free), a dignified Venetian-style palace with a cast-iron interior modelled on that of the Crystal Palace in London. Intended as Scotland's answer to the museum complex in London's South Kensington, it contains an extraordinarily eclectic range of exhibits. The **sculpture** in the lofty entrance hall begins with a superb Assyrian relief from the royal palace at Nimrud, and ranges via Classical Greece, Rome and Nubia to Buddhas from Japan and Burma and a totem pole from British Columbia. Also on the ground floor are collections of stuffed animals and birds, and a hands-on **technology** section featuring classics of the Industrial Revolution, including the *Wylam Dilly* of 1813, twin of the *Puffing Billy,* and the 1896 *Hawk Glider*, the earliest British flying machine. Upstairs there's a fine array of Egyptian mummies, ceramics from ancient Greece to the present day, costumes, jewellery, natural history displays and a splendid selection of European decorative art ranging from early medieval liturgical objects via Limoges enamels and sixteenth-century German woodcarving to stunning **French silverware** from the reign of Louis XIV. Finally, on the top floor, you'll come to a distinguished collection of historic scientific instruments, a small selection of arms and armour, plus sections on geology, fossils, ethnology, and the arts of Islam, Japan and China.

The University of Edinburgh

Immediately alongside the Royal Museum is the earliest surviving part of the **University of Edinburgh**, variously referred to as Old College or Old Quad, although nowadays it houses only a few university departments; the main campus colonizes the streets and squares to the south. The Old College was designed by Robert Adam, but built after his death in a considerably modified form by William Playfair (1789–1857), one of Edinburgh's greatest architects. Playfair built just one of Adam's two quadrangles (the dome was not added until 1879) and his magnificent Upper Library is now mostly used for ceremonial occasions. The **Talbot Rice Art Gallery** (Tues–Sat 10am–5pm; free), housed in the Old College, includes many splendid seventeenth-century works from the Low Countries. There are also some outstanding bronzes, notably the *Anatomical Horse* by an unknown Italian sculptor of the High Renaissance, and *Cain Killing Abel* by the Dutch Mannerist Adrian de Vries.

The New Town

The **NEW TOWN**, itself well over two hundred years old, stands in total contrast to the Old Town: the layout is symmetrical, the streets broad and straight, and most of the buildings are Neoclassical. Originally intended to be residential, the entire area, right down to the names of its streets, is something of a celebration of the Union, which was then generally regarded as a proud development in Scotland's history. Today the New Town is the bustling hub of the city's professional, commercial and business life, dominated by shops, banks and offices.

The existence of the New Town is chiefly due to the vision of **George Drummond**, who made schemes for the expansion of the city soon after becoming Lord Provost in 1725. However, it was not until 1759, when the Nor' Loch below the Castle was drained, that work began. The North Bridge, linking the Old Town with the port of Leith, was built between 1763 and 1772 and, in 1766, following a public competition, a plan for the New Town by a 22-year-old architect, **James Craig**, was chosen. Its gridiron pattern was perfectly matched to the site: the central George Street, flanked by showpiece squares, was laid out along the main ridge, with the parallel Princes Street and Queen Street on either side below, with two smaller streets, Thistle Street and Rose Street in between the three major thoroughfares to provide coach houses, artisans' dwellings and shops. Princes and Queen streets were built up on one side only, so as not to block the spectacular views of the Old Town and Fife. Architects were accordingly afforded a wonderful opportunity to play with vistas and spatial relationships, particularly well exploited by Robert Adam, who contributed extensively to the later phases of the work. The First New Town, as the area covered by Craig's plan came to be known, received a whole series of extensions in the first few decades of the nineteenth century, all carefully in harmony with the Neoclassical idiom.

In many ways, the layout of the New Town is its own most remarkable sight, an extraordinary grouping of squares, circuses, terraces, crescents and parks with a few set-pieces such as Register House, the north frontage of **Charlotte Square** and the assemblage of curiosities on and around Calton Hill. However, it also contains an assortment of Victorian additions, notably the **Scott Monument**, as well as three of the city's most important public collections – the **National Gallery of Scotland**, the combined **Scottish National Portrait Gallery** and **Museum of Antiquities** and the **Scottish National Gallery of Modern Art**.

Princes Street

Although only allocated a subsidiary role in the original plan of the New Town, **Princes Street** had developed into Edinburgh's principal thoroughfare by the middle of the last century, a role it has retained ever since. Its unobstructed views across to the castle and the Old Town are undeniably magnificent. Indeed, without the views, Princes Street would lose much of its appeal: its northern side, dominated by ugly department stores, is almost always crowded with shoppers, and few of the original eighteenth-century buildings remain. It was the coming of the railway, which follows a parallel course to the south, that ensured Princes Street's rise to prominence. The tracks are well concealed at the far end of the sunken **gardens** that replaced the Nor' Loch, which provide ample space to relax or picnic during the summer. Thomas De Quincey (1785–1859), author of *Confessions of an Opium Eater*, spent the last thirty years of his life in Edinburgh and is buried in the graveyard of St Cuthbert's Church, at the western end of the gardens.

The East End

Register House (Mon–Fri 10am–4pm; free), Princes Street's most distinguished building, is at its extreme northeastern corner, framing the perspective down North Bridge, and providing a good visual link between the Old and New Towns. Unfortunately, the majesty of the setting is marred by the **St James Centre** to the rear, a covered shopping arcade now regarded as the city's worst ever planning blunder. Register House was designed in the 1770s by Robert Adam to hold Scotland's historic records, a function it has maintained ever since. Its exterior is a model of restrained Neoclassicism; the interior, centred on a glorious Roman rotunda, has a dome lavishly decorated with plasterwork and antique-style medallions.

Opposite is one of the few buildings on the south side of Princes Street, the **North British Hotel** or "NB" as it is popularly known, despite its re-designation as *The Balmoral* in a gesture of political correctness by its owners: North Britain was an alternative name for Scotland throughout the eighteenth and nineteenth centuries, but has been regarded by Scots as an affront ever since. Among the most luxurious hotels in the city, it has always been associated with the railway, and the timepiece on its bulky clock tower is always kept two minutes fast in order to encourage passengers to hurry to catch their trains. Alongside the hotel, the **Waverley Market** is a sensitive modern redevelopment that carefully avoided repeating the mistakes of the St James Centre. Its roof makes an excellent open-air piazza, a favourite haunt of street-theatre groups and other performing artists during the Festival.

The Scott Monument and the Royal Scottish Academy

Facing the Victorian shopping emporium *Jenners*, within East Princes Street Gardens, the 200-foot-high **Scott Monument** was erected by public subscription within a few years of the writer's death. The world's largest monument to a man of letters, its magisterial, spire-like design is due to George Meikle Kemp, a carpenter and joiner whose only building this is; while it was still under construction, he stumbled into a canal one foggy evening and drowned. The architecture is closely modelled on Scott's beloved Melrose Abbey (see p.736), while the rich sculptural decoration shows sixteen Scottish writers and 64 characters from the *Waverley* novels. Underneath the archway is a **statue** of Scott with his deerhound Maida, carved from a thirty-ton block of Carrara marble.

The Princes Street Gardens are bisected by the **Mound**, which provides a road link between the Old and New Towns. Its name is an accurate description: it was formed in the 1780s by dumping piles of earth brought from the New Town's building plots. At the foot of the mound, Playfair's **Royal Scottish Academy** (Mon–Sat 10am–5pm, Sun 2–5pm; price varies) is a Grecian-style Doric temple used for temporary exhibitions, culminating during the Festival in a big international show, or a display of otherwise unseen Scottish art from the National Galleries. A few years back, the Academy was bequeathed the Borthwick-Norton collection of around thirty Old Masters, but at the time of writing legal complications meant that only four of these had been received – a pair of portraits by Gainsborough and single examples of Rubens and the rare Dutch landscape master Hercules Seghers, much admired by Rembrandt.

The National Gallery of Scotland

To the rear of the Royal Scottish Academy the **National Gallery of Scotland** (Mon–Sat 10am–5pm, Sun 2–5pm; free) is another Playfair construction, built in the 1840s and now housing a choice display of Old Masters, many of which belong to the Duke of Sutherland. The knowledgeable staff now wear tartan trousers, one of a series of innovations introduced by the flamboyant English director, Timothy Clifford. A few years ago, and more controversially, the original Playfair rooms on the ground floor were restored to their 1840s appearance, with the pictures hung closely together, often on two levels, and intermingled with sculptures and *objets d'art* to produce a deliberately cluttered effect (some lesser works, which would otherwise languish in the vaults, are a good 15ft up). Two small late-nineteenth-century works in Room 12 show the gallery as it was, with paintings stacked up even higher than at present.

Though individual works are frequently rearranged, the layout is broadly chronological, starting in the upper rooms above the entrance, and continuing clockwise around the ground floor. The upper part of the rear extension is devoted to smaller panels of the eighteenth and nineteenth centuries, while the basement contains the majority of the Scottish collection.

EARLY NETHERLANDISH AND GERMAN WORKS

Among the gallery's most valuable treasures are the *Trinity Panels*, the remaining parts of the only surviving pre-Reformation altarpiece made for a Scottish church. Painted by **Hugo van der Goes** in the mid-fifteenth century, they were commissioned for the Holy Trinity Collegiate Church by its provost Edward Bonkil, who appears in company of organ-playing angels in the finest and best preserved of the four panels. On the reverse sides are portraits of James III, his son (the future James IV) and Queen Margaret of Denmark. Their feebly characterized heads were modelled from life by an unknown local painter after the altar had been shipped to Edinburgh.

Of the later Netherlandish works, **Gerard David** is represented by the touchingly anecdotal *Three Legends of St Nicholas*, while the *Portrait of a Notary* by **Quentin**

Massys is an excellent early example of Northern European assimilation of the forms and techniques of the Italian Renaissance. Many of his German contemporaries developed their own variations on this style, among them **Cranach**, by whom there is a splendidly erotic *Venus and Cupid*, and **Holbein**, whose *Allegory of the Old and New Testaments* is a Protestant tract painted for an English patron.

ITALIAN RENAISSANCE WORKS

The Italian section includes a wonderful array of **Renaissance** masterpieces. Of these, *The Virgin Adoring the Child* is a beautiful composition set against a ruined architectural background shown in strict perspective: although known to have been painted in the workshop of the great Florentine sculptor **Andrea del Verrocchio**, its authorship remains a mystery. Equally graceful are the three works by **Raphael**, particularly *The Bridgewater Madonna* and the tondo of *The Holy Family with a Palm Tree*, whose striking luminosity has been revealed after recent restoration.

Of the four mythological scenes by **Titian**, the sensuous *Three Ages of Man*, is one of his most accomplished early compositions, while the later *Venus Anadyomene* ranks among the great nudes of Western art. The companion pair of *Diana and Acteon* and *Diana and Calisto*, painted for Philip II of Spain, show the almost impressionistic freedom of his late style. **Bassano**'s truly regal *Adoration of the Kings*, a dramatic altarpiece of *The Descent from the Cross* by **Tintoretto**, and several works by **Veronese** complete the Venetian collection.

SEVENTEENTH-CENTURY SOUTHERN EUROPEAN WORKS

Among the seventeenth-century works is the gallery's most important sculpture, **Bernini**'s *Bust of Monsignor Carlo Antonio dal Pozzo*. El **Greco**'s *The Saviour of the World* is a typically intense, visionary image from his mature years in Spain. Indigenous Spanish art is represented by **Velázquez**'s *An Old Woman Cooking Eggs*, an astonishingly assured work for a lad of nineteen, and by **Zurbarán**'s *The Immaculate Conception*, part of his ambitious decorative scheme of the Carthusian monastery in Jerez. There are two small copper panels by the **Adam Elsheimer**; of these, *Il Contento* is a *tour de force* of technical precision.

The series of *The Seven Sacraments* by **Poussin** are displayed in their own room, whose floor and central octagaonal seat repeat, albeit loosely, some of the motifs in the paintings. Based on the artist's own extensive research into Biblical times, the set marks the first attempt to portray scenes from the life of Jesus and the early Christians in an authentic manner, rather than one overlaid by artistic conventions. Poussin's younger contemporary **Claude**, who likewise left France to live in Rome, is represented by his largest canvas, *Landscape with Apollo, the Muses and a River God*, which radiates his characteristically idealized vision of Classical antiquity.

SEVENTEENTH-CENTURY FLEMISH AND DUTCH WORKS

Rubens' *The Feast of Herod*, an archetypal example of his grand manner, was executed, like all his large works, with extensive studio assistance, whereas the three small *modellos* are all from his own hand. The trio of large upright canvases by **Van Dyck** date from his early Genoese period; of these, *The Lomellini Family* shows his mastery at creating a definitive dynastic image. Among the four canvases by **Rembrandt** is a poignant *Self-Portrait aged 51*, and the ripely suggestive *Woman in Bed*. The largest and probably the earliest of the thirty or so surviving paintings of **Vermeer**, *Christ in the House of Martha and Mary* is here, too, while **Hals** is represented by a typical pair of portraits plus a brilliant caricature, *Verdonck*. There's also an excellent cross section of the specialist Dutch painters of the age, highlights being the mischievous *School for Boys and Girls* by **Jan Steen**, and the strangely haunting *Interior of the Church of St Bavo in Haarlem* by **Pieter Saenredam**.

EUROPEAN WORKS OF THE EIGHTEENTH AND NINETEENTH CENTURIES
Of the large-scale eighteenth-century works, **Tiepolo**'s *The Finding of Moses*, a gloriously bravura fantasy, stands out. Other decorative compositions of the same period are **Goya**'s *The Doctor*, a cartoon for a tapestry design, and the three large upright pastoral scenes by **Boucher**. However, the gems of the French section are the smaller panels, in particular **Watteau**'s *Fêtes Vénitiennes*, an effervescent Rococo idyll, and **Chardin**'s *Vase of Flowers*, a copybook example of still-life painting. One of the gallery's most recent (and most controversial) purchases is Canova's 1817 statue *The Three Graces*. There's also a superb group of Impressionist and Post-Impressionist masterpieces, including a particularly good cross section of the works of **Degas**, three outstanding examples of **Gauguin**, set respectively in Brittany, Martinique and Tahiti, and **Cezanne**'s *The Tall Trees*.

ENGLISH AND AMERICAN WORKS
Surprisingly, the gallery has relatively few English paintings, but those here are impressive. **Hogarth**'s *Sarah Malcolm*, painted in Newgate Prison the day the murderess was executed, once belonged to Horace Walpole, who also commissioned **Reynolds**' *The Ladies Waldegrave*, a group portrait of his three great-nieces. **Gainsborough**'s *The Honourable Mrs Graham* is one of his most memorable society portraits, while **Constable** himself described *Dedham Vale* as being "perhaps my best". There are two prime Roman views by **Turner**, by whom the gallery owns a wonderful array of watercolours. Even more unexpected than the scarcity of English works is the presence of some exceptional American canvases: **Benjamin West**'s Romantic fantasy, *King Alexander III Rescued from a Stag*; **John Singer Sargent**'s virtuosic *Lady Agnew of Lochnaw*; and **Frederic Edwin Church**'s *View of Niagara Falls from the American Side*.

SCOTTISH WORKS
On the face of it, the gallery's Scottish collection, which shows the entire gamut of Scottish painting from seventeenth-century portraiture to the Arts and Crafts movement, is something of an anticlimax. There are, however, some important works displayed within a broad European context; **Gavin Hamilton**'s *Achilles Mourning the Death of Patrocolus*, for example, painted in Rome, is an unquestionably arresting image. **Allan Ramsay**, who became court painter to George III, is represented by his intimate *The Artist's Second Wife* and *Jean-Jacques Rousseau*, in which the philosopher is shown in Armenian costume. Of **Sir Henry Raeburn**'s large portraits note the swaggering masculinity of *Sir John Sinclair* or *Colonel Alistair MacDonell of Glengarry*, both of whom are shown in full Highland dress. Other Scottish painters represented include the versatile **Sir David Wilkie**, with his huge history painting, *Sir David Baird Discovering the Body of Sultaun Tippo Saib*, and **Alexander Nasmyth**, whose tendency to gild the lily can be seen in his *View of Tantallon Castle and the Bass Rock*.

George Street

Just north and parallel to Princes Street is **George Street**, the city's chief financial thoroughfare and the least prepossessing of the main streets of the First New Town, built up on both sides with a preponderance of unsympathetic development. At its eastern end is **St Andrew Square**, in the middle of which is the Melville Monument, a statue of Lord Melville, Pitt the Younger's Navy Treasurer. On the eastern side of the square stands a handsome eighteenth-century town mansion, designed by Sir William Chambers. Headquarters of the Royal Bank of Scotland since 1825, the palatial mid-nineteenth-century banking hall is a symbol of the success of the New Town. On the south side of the street, the oval-shaped church of **St Andrew** (now known as St Andrew and St George) is chiefly famous as the scene of the 1843 Disruption led by Thomas Chalmers, which split the Church of Scotland in two. Famous visitors to

George Street have included Percy Bysshe Shelley, who stayed at no. 60 with the sixteen-year-old Harriet Westbrook during the summer of 1811, and Charles Dickens who gave a number of readings in the Assembly Rooms in the 1840s and 50s.

At the western end of the street, **Charlotte Square** was designed by Robert Adam in 1791, a year before his death. For the most part, his plans were faithfully implemented, an exception being the domed and porticoed church of St George, which was simplified on grounds of expense. Its interior was gutted in the 1960s and refurbished as **West Register House**; like its counterpart at the opposite end of Princes Street, it features changing documentary exhibitions (Mon–Fri 10am–4pm; free).

The **north side** of the square has deservedly become the most exclusive address in the city. No. 6 is the official residence of the Secretary of State for Scotland, while the upper storeys of no. 7 are the home of the Moderator of the General Assembly, the annually elected leader of the Church of Scotland. Restored by the NTS, the lower floors are open to the public under the name of the **Georgian House** (April–Oct Mon–Sat 10am–5pm, Sun 2–5pm; £3.50), whose contents give a good idea of what the house must have looked like during the period of the first owner, the head of the clan Lamont. The rooms are decked out in period furniture, including a working barrel organ which plays a selection of Scottish airs, and hung with fine paintings, including portraits by Ramsay and Raeburn, and a beautiful *Marriage of the Virgin* by El Greco's teacher, the Italian miniaturist Giulio Clovio.

Queen Street

Queen Street, the last of the three main streets of the First New Town, is bordered to the north by gardens, and commands sweeping views across to Fife. Much the best preserved of the area's three main streets, its main attraction is its excellent gallery-cum-museum.

The Scottish National Portrait Gallery and Museum of Antiquities

At the far eastern end of Queen Street is the **Scottish National Portrait Gallery**, which shares its premises with the **Museum of Antiquities** (Mon–Sat 10am–5pm, Sun 2–5pm; free). The gallery building is itself a fascinating period piece, its red sandstone exterior, modelled on the Doge's Palace in Venice, encrusted with statues of famous Scots – a theme taken up in the entrance hall, which has a mosaic-like frieze procession by William Hole of great figures from Scotland's past, with heroic murals of stirring episodes from the nation's history adorning the balcony above.

THE STEWART EXHIBITION

On the ground floor of the western wing an exhibition on the **Stewart dynasty** traces the history of the family from its origins as stewards (hence the name) to medieval royalty, via its zenith under James VI, who engineered the union with England, to its final demise under Bonnie Prince Charlie. From the early periods, look out for two superb artefacts from the reign of Robert the Bruce, the **Kames Brooch** and the **Bute Mazer** (a large wooden bowl). An excellent collection of Mary, Queen of Scots memorabilia includes her **Penicuik Jewels** and a portrait by Rowland Lockey. The reign of Charles I is represented by several outstanding paintings by Flemish artists including **Daniel Mytens** and **Alexander Keirinox**, and there are fine official portraits of the later Stewart monarchs and members of their entourage. Mementos of the Young Pretender include the ornate backsword and silver-mounted shield with which he fought at Culloden, and a Rococo **canteen** he left abandoned on the battlefield.

THE PORTRAIT GALLERY

The floors above the Stewart exhibition are devoted to portraits, accompanied by potted biographies, of famous Scots – a definition stretched to include anyone with the slightest Scottish connection. From the seventeenth century, there's an excellent Van Dyck portrait of Charles Seton, second Earl of Dunfermline, and the tartan-clad Lord Mungo Murray, who died in the disastrous attempt to establish a Scottish colony in Panama. Eighteenth-century highlights include portraits of the philosopher-historian David Hume by Allan Ramsay, and the bard Robert Burns by his friend Alexander Nasmyth, and a varied group by Raeburn: subjects include Sir Walter Scott, the fiddler Niel Gow, and the artist himself. The star portrait from the nineteenth century is that of physician Sir Alexander Morison by his patient, the mad painter **Richard Dadd**. Twentieth-century portraits include a very angular Alec Douglas-Home, briefly prime minister in the 1960s, the stern figure of union leader Mick McGahey, soccer star Danny McGrain (in a kilt) and film-maker Bill Forsyth.

THE MUSEUM OF ANTIQUITIES

Ranged across three levels, objects in the **Museum of Antiquities** are displayed in a splendidly eclectic manner. The ground floor is, in the main, devoted to **Dark Age sculpture**, giving convincing proof of the vitality of artistic life among the tribes who later combined to form the Scottish kingdom: look out for the eighth-century Birsay Stone from Orkney, with its carvings of warriors; the ninth-century Hilton of Cadboll Stone from Easter Ross, whose main scene shows a woman riding side-saddle; and the twelfth-century **walrus ivory chessmen** from the island of Lewis. You can also see the **Deskford Carnyx**, a swine's head in brass which formed part of a Celtic war trumpet, and the so-called **Maiden**, Edinburgh's public guillotine from 1564 to 1710.

On the first floor, the **prehistoric and Viking collection** features excavations from a variety of sites beginning with the Neolithic settlement of Skara Brae in the Orkneys. Most of the artefacts are of specialist appeal only, but the Bronze Age Torrs Chamfrein, a war mask or drinking horn from around 200 BC, and the intricate Viking-period Hunterston Brooch, are eye-catching. Most striking of all is the eighth-century St Ninian's Isle Treasure from the Shetlands, an ornamental set of Pictish silverware. The top floor is devoted to **Roman antiquities**, the most important of which are a mile-stone found near the site of Edinburgh Airport; and the Traprain Treasure, a hoard of fourth- and fifth-century silver buried at Traprain Law near Haddington.

Calton

Of the various extensions to the New Town, the most intriguing is **Calton**, which branches out from the eastern end of Princes Street and encircles a volcanic hill. For years the centre of a thriving **gay** scene (see p.725), it is an area of extraordinary show-piece architecture, all dating from the time of the Napoleonic Wars or just after, and intended as an ostentatious celebration of the British victory. While the predominantly Grecian architecture led to Calton being regarded as a Georgian Acropolis, it is, in fact, more of a shrine to local heroes.

Waterloo Place forms a ceremonial way from Princes Street to Calton Hill. On its southern side is the sombre **Old Calton Burial Ground**, in which you can see Robert Adam's plain, cylindrical memorial to David Hume and a monument, complete with a statue of Abraham Lincoln, to the Scots who died in the American Civil War. Hard up against the eastern wall, above a sheer rockface, is a picturesque castellated building which many visitors arriving at Waverley Station below imagine to be Edinburgh Castle. In fact, it's all that remains of **Calton Gaol**, once Edinburgh's main prison.

Further on, set majestically in a confined site below Calton Hill, is one of Edinburgh's greatest buildings, the Grecian Old **Royal High School**, Edinburgh's oldest school – *alma mater* to, among others, Robert Adam, Walter Scott and Alexander Graham Bell – built by Thomas Hamilton, himself an old boy. Earmarked in the 1970s as the home of the planned Scottish Assembly, the building has remained empty for years, a symbol of the thwarted nationalist aspirations. Across the road, Hamilton also built the **Burns Monument**, a circular Corinthian temple modelled on the Monument to Lysicrates in Athens, as a memorial to the national bard.

Robert Louis Stevenson reckoned that **Calton Hill** was the best place to view Edinburgh; the panoramas from ground level are spectacular enough, but those from the top of the **Nelson Monument** (April–Sept Mon 1–6pm, Tues–Sat 10am–6pm; Oct–March Mon–Sat 10am–3pm; £1) are even better. Begun just two years after Nelson's death at Trafalgar, this is one of Edinburgh's oddest buildings, resembling a gigantic spy-glass. Alongside, Playfair's **National Monument**, had it been completed, would have been a reasonably accurate replica of the Parthenon, but funds ran out with only twelve columns built. At the opposite side of the hill, the grandeur of Playfair's Classical **Monument to Dougald Stewart** seems totally disproportionate to the stature of the man it commemorates: a now forgotten philosophy professor.

Playfair also built the **City Observatory** for his uncle, the mathematician and astronomer John Playfair, whom he honoured in the cenotaph outside. Pollution and the advent of street lighting forced the observatory proper had to be relocated to Blackford Hill, though the equipment here continues to be used by students. The small domed pavilion at the northeastern corner, an addition of the 1890s, now houses the **Edinburgh Experience** (April–June, Sept & Oct Mon–Fri 2–5pm, Sat & Sun 10.30am–5pm; July & Aug daily 10.30am–5pm; £2), a twenty-minute 3-D show on the city's history viewed through special glasses.

Elsewhere in the New Town

The **Northern New Town** was the earliest extension to the First New Town, begun in 1801, and today roughly covers the area north of Queen Street as far as Fettes Row to the north. This has survived in far better shape than its predecessor: with the exception of one street, almost all of it is intact, and it has managed to preserve its predominantly residential character. One of the area's most intriguing buildings is the Neo-Norman **Mansfield Place Church**, on the corner of Broughton and East London streets, designed in the late nineteenth century for the strange, now defunct Catholic Apostolic sect. Having lain redundant and neglected for three decades, it has suddenly acquired cult status, its preservation the current obsession of local conservation groups. The chief reason for this is its cycle of **murals** by the Dublin-born **Phoebe Traquair**, a leading light in the Scottish Arts and Crafts movement. She laboured for eight years on this decorative scheme, which has all the freshness and luminosity of a medieval manuscript, but desperately needs a thorough restoration to avert its already alarming decay.

Dean Village, Stockbridge and the West End

Work began on the western end of the New Town in 1822, in a small area of land north of Charlotte Square and west of George Street. Instead of the straight lines of the earlier sections, there were now the gracious curves of Randolph Crescent, Ainslie Place and the magnificent twelve-sided Moray Place. Round the corner from Randolph Crescent, the four-arched **Dean Bridge**, a bravura feat of 1830s engineering by Thomas Telford, carries the main road high above Edinburgh's placid little river, the **Water of Leith**. Down to the left lies **Dean Village**, an old milling community that is one of central Edinburgh's most picturesque yet oddest corners, its atmosphere of terminal decay arrested by the conversion of some of the mills into designer flats. The riverside path into Stockbridge passes **St Bernard's Well**, a pump room covered by a mock Roman temple, commissioned in 1788 by Lord Gardenstone to draw mineral waters from the Water of Leith.

Stockbridge, which straddles both sides of the Water of Leith on the other side of Dean Bridge, is another old village which has retained its distinctive identity, in spite of its absorption into the Georgian face of the New Town, and is particularly renowned for its antique shops and "alternative" outlets. The residential upper streets on the far side of the river were developed by Sir Henry Raeburn, who named the finest of them **Ann Street**, which after Charlotte Square is the most prestigious address in Edinburgh (writers Thomas de Quincey and J.M. Ballantyne were residents); alone among New Town streets, its houses each have a front garden.

The western extension to the New Town was the last part to be built, deviating from the area's overriding Neoclassicism with a number of Victorian additions. Because of this, the huge **St Mary's Episcopal Cathedral**, an addition of the 1870s, is less intrusive than it would otherwise be, its three spires forming an eminently satifying landmark for the far end of the city centre. The last major work of Sir George Gilbert Scott, the cathedral is built in imitation of the Early English Gothic style and was, at the time of its construction, the most ambitious church built in Britain since the Reformation.

The Scottish National Gallery of Modern Art

Set in spacious wooded grounds at the far northwestern fringe of the New Town, about ten minutes' walk from either the cathedral or Dean Village, the **Scottish National Gallery of Modern Art** (Mon–Sat 10am–5pm, Sun 2–5pm; free) was established in 1959 as the first collection in Britain devoted solely to twentieth-century painting and sculpture. The grounds serve as a sculpture park, featuring works by Jacob Epstein, Henry Moore, Barbara Hepworth and the Constructivist creations of the Edinburgh-born Eduardo Paolozzi. Inside, the display space is divided between temporary loan exhibitions and selections from the gallery's own holdings; the latter are arranged thematically, but are constantly moved around. What you see at any particular time is therefore a matter of chance, though the most important works are usually on view.

French painters are particularly well represented, beginning with Bonnard's *Lane at Vernonnet* and Vuillard's jewel-like *Two Seamstresses*, and by a few examples of the Fauves, notably Matisse's *The Painting Lesson* and Derain's dazzlingly brilliant *Collioure*; there's also a fine group of late canvases by Leger, notably *The Constructors*. Among some striking examples of German Expressionism are Kirchner's *Japanese Theatre*, Feininger's *Gelmeroda III*, and a wonderfully soulful wooden sculpture of a woman by Barlach entitled *The Terrible Year, 1937*. Highlights of the Surrealist section are Magritte's haunting *Black Flag*, Miró's seminal *Composition* and Giacometti's contorted *Woman with her Throat Cut*, while Cubism is represented by Picasso's *Soles* and Braque's *Candlestick*.

Of works by Americans, Roy Lichtenstein's *In the Car* is a fine example of his Pop-Art style, while Duane Hanson's fibre-glass *Tourists* is typically cruel. English artists on show include Sickert, Nicholson, Spencer, Freud and Hockney, but, as you'd expect, considerably more space is allocated to Scottish artists. Of particular note are the so-called Colourists – S.J. Peploe, J.D. Fergusson, Francis Cadell and George Leslie Hunter – whose works are attracting fancy prices on the art market, as well as ever-growing posthumous critical acclaim. Although they did not form a recognizable school, they all worked in France and displayed considerable French influence in their warm, bright palettes. The gallery also shows works by many contemporary Scots, among them portraitist John Bellany, and the poet-artist-gardener Ian Hamilton Finlay.

The Suburbs

Edinburgh's principal sights are by no means confined to the city centre: indeed, at least three of its most popular tourist draws – the **Royal Botanic Garden**, the **Zoo** and the **Royal Observatory** – are out in the suburbs. Other major attractions in the outskirts include **Craigmillar Castle** and the southern hill ranges, the **Braids** and the

Pentlands. Additionally, there are several districts with their own very distinct identity, among them the seaside resort of **Portobello** and the port of **Leith**.

The Royal Botanic Garden

Just beyond the northern boundaries of the New Town, with entrances on Inverleith Row and Arboretum Place, is the seventy-acre site of the **Royal Botanic Garden** (daily March, April, Sept & Oct 10am–6pm; May–Aug 10am–8pm; Nov–Feb 10am–4pm; free), particularly renowned for the rhododendrons, which blaze out in a glorious patchwork of colours in April and May. In the heart of the grounds a group of hothouses designated the **Glasshouse Experience** (daily March–Oct 10am–5pm; Nov–Feb 10am–3.30pm; free, but £1.50 donation requested) display orchids, giant Amazonian water lilies, and a two-hundred-year-old West Indian palm tree. The last named is in the elegant glass-topped Palm House, built in the 1850s. Many of the most exotic plants were brought to Edinburgh by the aptly named George Forrest, who made seven expeditions to southwestern China between 1904 and 1932.

Craigmillar Castle

Craigmillar Castle (April–Sept Mon–Sat 9.30am–6pm, Sun 2–6pm; Oct–March Mon–Wed & Sat 9.30am–4pm, Thurs 9.30am–noon, Sun 2–4pm; £1.50), one of the best-preserved medieval fortresses in Scotland, where the murder of Lord Darnley, second husband of Mary, Queen of Scots was plotted, lies in a green belt five miles southeast of the centre. The oldest part of the complex is the L-shaped **Tower House**, which dates back to the early 1600s: the **Great Hall**, with its resplendent late Gothic chimneypiece, is in good enough shape to be rented out for functions. A few decades after Craigmillar's completion, the tower house was surrounded by a quadrangular wall with cylindrical corner towers. The west range was remodelled as an aristocratic mansion in the mid-seventeenth century, but its owners abandoned the place a hundred years later, leaving it to decay into picturesque ruin.

The Royal Observatory

The **Royal Observatory** (April–Sept daily noon–5.30pm & 7–9pm Oct–March Sat–Thurs 1–5pm & 7–9pm, Fri 1–9pm; £2) stands at the top of Blackford Hill, just a short walk south of Morningside, or by buses #40 or #41 direct from the centre. The visitor centre here seeks to explain the mysteries of the solar system by means of models, videos and space photographs, and you also get to see the two main telescopes, which are put into operation during the winter evenings, the best time for a visit.

Portobello

Among Edinburgh's less expected assets is its **beach**, most of which falls within **PORTOBELLO**, once a lively **seaside resort** but now a folorn kind of place, its funfairs and amusement arcades decidedly down-at-heel. Nonetheless, it retains a certain faded charm, and – on hot summer weekends at least – the promenade and the beach can be a mass of swimmers, sunbathers, surfers and pleasure boats. A walk along the promenade is a pleasure at any time of the year. Portobello is about three miles east of the centre of town, and can be reached on buses #15, #26, #42 or #86 .

Leith

For several hundred years **LEITH** was separate from Edinburgh. As Scotland's major east-coast port, it played a key role in the nation's history, even serving as the seat of government for a time, and in 1833 finally became a burgh in its own right. In 1920, however, it was incorporated into the capital, and in the decades that followed, went into seemingly terminal decline. The 1980s, however, saw an astonishing turnaround. Against all the odds, a couple of waterfront bistros proved enormously successful; competitors followed apace, and by the end of the decade the port had acquired what's arguably the best concentration of restaurants and pubs in Edinburgh. The surviving historic monuments were spruced up, and a host of housing developments built or restored, earning the town the sardonic nickname of "Leith-sur-Mer". To reach Leith from the city centre, take one of the many buses going down Leith Walk (#12).

While you're most likely to come to Leith for the bars and restaurants, the area itself warrants exploration; though the shipbuilding yards have gone, it remains an active port with a rough-edged character. Most of the showpiece Neoclassical buildings lie on or near **The Shore**, the tenement-lined road along the final stretch of the Water of

---

ROBERT LOUIS STEVENSON

Though **Robert Louis Stevenson** (1850–94) is often dismissed in highbrow academic circles for his deceptively simple manner, he was undoubtedly one of the best-loved writers of his generation, and one whose travelogues, novels, short stories and essays remain enormously popular a century after his death.

Born in Edinburgh into a distinguished family of engineers, Stevenson was a sickly child, with a solitary childhood dominated by his governess Alison "Cummie" Cunningham, who regaled him with tales drawn from Calvinist folklore. Sent to the university to study engineering, Stevenson rebelled against his upbringing by spending much of his time in the low-life howffs and brothels of the city, and eventually switching to law. Although called to the bar in 1875, by then he had decided to channel his energies into literature: while still a student, he had already made his mark as an **essayist**, and published in his lifetime over one hundred essays, ranging from lighthearted whimsy to trenchant political analysis. A set of topographical pieces about his native city was later collected together as *Edinburgh: Picturesque Notes,* which conjure up nicely its atmosphere, character and appearance – warts and all.

Stevenson's other early successes were two **travelogues**, *An Inland Voyage* and *Travels with a Donkey in the Cevennes*, kaleidoscopic jottings based on his journeys in France, where he went to escape Scotland's bad weather. It was there that he met Fanny Osbourne, an American ten years his senior, who was estranged from her husband and had two children in tow. His voyage to join her in San Francisco formed the basis for his most important factual work, *The Amateur Emigrant*, a vivid first-hand account of the great nineteenth-century European migration to the United States.

Having married the now divorced Fanny, Stevenson began an elusive search for an agreeable climate that led to Switzerland, the French Riviera and the Scottish Highlands. He belatedly turned to the **novel**, achieving immediate acclaim in 1881 for *Treasure Island*, a highly moralistic adventure yarn that began as an entertainment for his stepson and future collaborator, Lloyd Osbourne. In 1886, his most famous **short story**, *Dr Jekyll and Mr Hyde*, despite its nominal London setting, offered a vivid evocation of Edinburgh's Old Town; an allegory of its dual personality of prosperity and squalour, and an analysis of its Calvinistic preoccupations with guilt and damnation. The same year saw the publication of *Kidnapped*, an adventure novel which exemplified his view that literature should seek above all to entertain.

In 1887 Stevenson left Britain for good, travelling to the United States where he began one of his most ambitious novels, *The Master of Ballantrae*. A year later, he set sail for the South Seas, and eventually settled in Samoa; his last works include a number of stories with a local setting, such as the grimly realistic *The Ebb Tide* and *The Beach of Falesà*. However, Scotland continued to be his main inspiration: he wrote *Catriona* as a sequel to *Kidnapped*, and was at work on two more novels with Scottish settings, *St Ives* and *Weir of Hermiston*, a dark story of father-son confrontation, at the time of his sudden death from a brain haemorrhage in 1894. He was buried on the top of Mount Vaea overlooking the Pacific Ocean.

Leith, just before it disgorges into the Firth of Forth. Note the former **Town Hall**, on the parallel Constitution Street, now the headquarters of the local constabulary, immortalized in the tongue twister, "The Leith police dismisseth us"; the Classical Trinity House on Kirkgate, built in 1816; and the massive Customs House on Commercial Street. To the west, set back from The Shore, is **Lamb's House**, a seventeenth-century mansion, built as the home of the prosperous merchant Andro Lamb.

The Zoo

Edinburgh's **Zoo** (April–Sept Mon–Sat 9am–6pm, Sun 9.30am–6pm; Oct & March Mon–Sat 9am–5pm, Sun 9.30am–5pm; Nov–Feb Mon–Sat 9am–4.30pm, Sun 9.30am–4.30pm; £5.50) lies three miles west of Princes Street on an eighty-acre site on the slopes of Corstorphine Hill (buses from town: #2, #26, #31, #36, #69, #85, #86). Here you can see 1500 animals, including a number of endangered species such as white rhinos, red pandas, pygmy hippos and Madagascar tree boas. However, its chief claim to fame is its crowd of penguins (the largest number in captivity anywhere in the world), a legacy of Leith's whaling trade in the South Atlantic. The penguin parade, which takes place daily at 2pm from April to September, and on sunny March and October days, has gained something of a cult status.

Dalmeny

In 1975, Edinburgh's boundaries were extended to include a number of towns and villages which were formerly part of West Lothian, among them **DALMENY**, nine miles west of the city centre (bus #43 *Scottish Eastern* or train). The main reason for coming out to Dalmeny is to visit **Dalmeny House** (May–Sept Sun 1–5.30pm, Mon & Tues noon–5.30pm; £3.50), the seat of the Earls of Rosebery, two miles northeast of the village on the coast. Built in 1815 by the English architect William Wilkins, it was the first stately home in Scotland in the neo-Gothic style, vividly evoking Tudor architecture in its picturesque turreted roofline, and in its fan vaults and hammer-beam ceilings. The family portraits include one of the fourth Earl (who commissioned the house) by Raeburn, and of the fifth Earl (the last British prime minister to govern from the House of Lords) by Millais; there are also likenesses of other famous society figures by Reynolds, Gainsborough and Lawrence. Among the furnishings are a set of tapestries made from cartoons by Goya, and the Rothschild Collection of eighteenth-century French furniture and *objets d'art*. There's also a fascinating collection of memorabilia of Napoleon Bonaparte – notably some items he used during his exile in St Helena – amassed by the fifth Earl, who wrote a biography of the French dictator.

The Forth Bridges and Inchcolm

Everything in **South Queensferry**, a mile north of Dalmeny, is overshadowed, quite literally, by the two great bridges, each about a mile and a half in length, which traverse the Firth of Forth at its narrowest point. The cantilevered **Forth Rail Bridge**, built from 1883 to 1890 by Sir John Fowler and Benjamin Baker, ranks among the supreme achievements of Victorian engineering. Some 50,000 tons of steel were used in the construction of a design that manages to exude grace as well as might. Derived from American models, the suspension format chosen for the **Forth Road Bridge** makes a perfect complement to the older structure. Erected between 1958 and 1964, it finally killed off the nine-hundred-year-old ferry, and attracts such a heavy volume of traffic that plans are afoot to build yet another bridge. It's well worth walking across its footpath for the tremendous views of the Rail Bridge.

From South Queensferry's Hawes Pier, just west of the Rail Bridge, pleasure boats leave for a variety of cruises on the Forth (Easter, May & June Sat & Sun only; July to mid-Sept daily; £3–7 ☎0131/331 4857). Be sure to check in advance as sailings are always subject to cancellation in bad weather.

The most enticing destination is the island of **Inchcolm**, whose beautiful ruined **Abbey** was founded in 1123 by King Alexander I in gratitude for the hospitality he received from a hermit (whose cell survives at the northwestern corner of the island) when his ship was forced ashore in a storm. The best-preserved medieval monastic complex in Scotland, the abbey's surviving buildings date from the thirteenth to the fifteenth centuries, and include a splendid octagonal chapter house. Although the church is almost totally delapidated, its tower can be ascended for a great aerial view of the island, which is populated by a variety of nesting birds and a colony of grey seals.

Hopetoun House

Immediately beyond the western edge of South Queensferry, just over the West Lothian border, **Hopetoun House** (April–Oct daily 10am–5.30pm; house & grounds £4, grounds only £2) is one of Scotland's grandest stately homes. The original house was built at the turn of the eighteenth century for the first Earl of Hopetoun by Sir William Bruce, the architect of Holyroodhouse. A couple of decades later, William Adam carried out an enormous extension, engulfing the house in a curvaceous main facade and two projecting wings – superb examples of Roman Baroque pomp and swagger. The scale and lavishness of the Adam interiors, most of whose decoration was carried out after the architect's death by his sons, make for a stark contrast with the intimacy of those designed by Bruce. Particularly impressive are the Red and Yellow Drawing Rooms, with their splendid ceilings by the young Robert Adam. Among the house's furnishings are seventeenth-century tapestries, Meissen porcelain, and a distinguished collection of paintings, including portraits by Gainsborough, Ramsay and Raeburn. The grounds of Hopetoun House are also open with magnificent walks along the banks of the Forth and great opportunities for picnics.

Linlithgow Palace

Fifteen miles west of Edinburgh, in the ancient royal burgh of Linlithgow, lies **Linlithgow Palace** (April–Sept Mon–Sat 9.30am–6pm, Sun 2–6pm; Oct–March Mon–Sat 9.30am–12.30pm & 1.30–4pm, Sun 2–4pm; £2), a splendid fifteenth-century ruin romantically set on the edge of Linlithgow Loch and associated with some of Scotland's best-known historical figures – including the ubiquitous Mary, Queen of Scots, who was born here in 1542. A royal manor house is believed to have existed on this site since the time of David I. Fire razed the manor in 1424, after which James I began construction of the present palace, a process that continued through two centuries and the reign of no fewer than eight monarchs. From the top of the northwest tower, Queen Margaret looked out in vain for the return of James IV from the field of Flodden in 1513. The ornate octagonal **fountain** in the inner courtyard, with its wonderfully intricate figures and medallion heads, flowed with wine for the wedding of James V and Mary of Guise. Bonnie Prince Charlie visited during the forty-five, and one year later the palace was burned, probably accidentally, whilst occupied by General Hawley's troops.

This is a great place to take children; the rooflessness of the castle creates unexpected vistas and the elegant rooms with their intriguing spiral staircases seem labyrinthine. The galleried **Great Hall** is magnificent, as is the adjoining kitchen, which has a truly cavernous fireplace. Don't miss the dank downstairs **brewery**, which produced vast quantities of ale; 24 gallons were apparently a good nightly consumption in the sixteenth century. **St Michael's Church,** adjacent to the palace, is one of Scotland's largest pre-Reformation churches, consecrated in the thirteenth century. The present building was completed three hundred years later, with the exception of the hugely incongruous aluminium spire, tacked on in 1946. Inside, decorative woodcarving around the pulpit depicts queens Margaret, Mary and Victoria.

Cafés and restaurants

You can eat well in Edinburgh at almost any price, choosing from a wide range of cuisines. Plenty of places specialize in **traditional Scottish cooking**, using fresh local produce, while the city's ethnic communities, despite their small size, have offered a lot to the **restaurant** scene, including some great **Italian** trattorias, and a host of excellent **Indian** restaurants serving regional dishes. In addition, the adaptation of home-grown ingredients to classic Gallic recipes is something the city does particularly well, resulting in a whole group of fabulous **French** restaurants. **Vegetarians** are well catered for, and there are plenty of **fish** specialists – seafood fans should make some attempt to get out to **Leith**, whose waterside restaurants serve consistently good food. In choosing a place to eat, bear in mind that most **pubs** (which are covered in the following section) serve food, and that many have a restaurant attached.

Budget Food: cafés and diners

Café-Patisserie Florentin, 8–10 St Giles St. French-style café off High St whose extended opening hours make it a popular late-night rendezvous. Open 7am–midnight, 2am at weekends.

Clarinda's, 69 Canongate. Spruce olde-worlde café serving home-cooked breakfasts and light lunches.

Courthouse Café, Brodies Close. Calm retreat just off the Royal Mile, with newspapers to peruse and interesting, well-presented snacks and salads.

Cyberia, 88 Hanover St. Bright internet café in New Town with with a wide range of snacks and 15 computers (£3.50 per hour; e-mail: edinburgh@easynet.co.uk).

Elephant House, 21 George IV Bridge. Attractive new café with a large selection of coffees, teas, sandwiches and cakes. Wonderful views of the castle. Open 8am–10pm.

Elephant's Sufficiency, 170 High St. This bright, lively café near the Fringe Office serves a great selection of sandwiches and baked potatoes.

Laigh Kitchen, 117a Hanover St. Long-established, homely New Town café with flagstone floor and cast-iron stoves. Good salads and soups, but best known for its wonderful home-baked scones and cakes.

Lower Aisle, in the High Kirk of St Giles, High St. Light lunches in the crypt. Popular with lawyers.

Netherbow Café, Netherbow Arts Centre, 43 High St. Excellent wholefood snacks using produce from the café's own allotment.

Scottish National Gallery of Modern Art Café, Belford Rd. Far more than a standard refreshment stop for gallery visitors: many locals come here for lunch or a snack. Changing daily menu of salads, hot food and home baking. Second branch in the National Portrait Gallery building.

Chinese and Southeast Asian

Bamboo Garden, 57a Frederick St. Many of Edinburgh's Chinese community gather in this inexpensive New Town place for great *dim sum* on Sunday lunchtime. Get the waiter to explain the choices rather than rely on the limited English-language menu.

Buntoms, 9–13 Nelson St (☎0131/557 4344). First Thai restaurant in Scotland, located in the New Town, and still as good as any of its competitors.

Loon Fung, 32 Grindlay St (☎0131/229 5757). Across the street from the Lyceum and the Usher Hall with a strong line in fresh fish. Moderately priced.

Singapore Sling, 503 Lawnmarket (☎0131/226 2826). Real fire-in-the-stomach inexpensive Singaporean and Malaysian cuisine in modest surroundings just down from the castle.

French

L'Auberge, 58 St Mary's St (☎0131/556 5888). French nouvelle cuisine in a luxurious setting: a bit of a treat. Splurge on *Le Grand Menu Gourmand* at £30.

Café St Honoré, 34 Thistle St Lane. New Town brasserie serving good, inexpensive traditional French cooking, with fabulous pastries and coffee. Closed Sun.

Chez Jules, 1 Craigs Close (☎0131/225 7007). Classic French food in fine, no-frills establishment. New Town branch at 61 Frederick St (☎0131/225 7983). Closed Sun.

La Cuisine d'Odile, French Institute, 13 Randolph Crescent. Inexpensive and popular French home cooking in a West End basement. Lunch only; closed Sun, Mon & July.

Pierre Victoire, 10 Victoria St (☎0131/225 1721); 38 Grassmarket (☎0131/226 2442); 8 Union St (☎0131/557 8451); 17 Queensferry St (☎0131/226 1890); 5 Dock Place, Leith (☎0131/555 6178). Ever-expanding group offering unmistakably French and affordable meals. Like the service, the food can be erratic, but is normally superb. Very popular so book. Each branch closes either Sun or Mon.

Le Sept, Old Fishmarket Close (☎0131/225 5428). Brasserie upstairs and à la carte restaurant downstairs. Walk in and wait for the brasserie, but book for the restaurant.

The Vintner's Rooms, 87 Giles St, Leith (☎0131/554 6767). Splendid restaurant in a seventeenth-century warehouse. The bar in the cellar has a sombre, candlelit ambience and a coal fire; the ornate Rococo dining room serves expertly prepared food, especially strong on fish and Gallic dishes, using ingredients of the highest quality. Expensive, but well worth it.

Indian

Kalpna, 2 St Patrick Square. Outstanding Southside vegetarian restaurant, popular with students, serving authentic Gujarati dishes. On the southern continuation of Nicholson St. As-much-as-you-want lunchtime buffet for £4. Closed Sun.

Lancers, 5 Hamilton Place. Aficionados rate the curries at this moderately priced Stockbridge restaurant as the best in Scotland. Primarily Bengali and Punjabi.

Shamiana, 14 Brougham Place, Tollcross. Established, first-class North Indian and Kashmiri cuisine in a tasteful environment located midway between the Kings and Lyceum theatres. One of the more expensive restaurants in this category, but well worth it.

Spices, 110 W Bow. A spin-off of the long-established *Kalpna* (in Southside), but geared towards carnivores. Innovative Indian cooking with a few African choices. All-you-can-eat buffet lunches for around a fiver. Closed Sun.

Suruchi, 14a Nicholson St (☎0131/556 6583). Popular establishment introducing genuine South Indian cooking to Scotland for the first time. The emphasis is on rice and vegetables, with a few splendid poultry dishes. Inexpensive; set lunch about £5, and special pre-theatre menu around £12.

Italian

Caprice Pizzerama, 327 Leith Walk. Enormous place, almost exactly halfway between Princes St and Leith. Specializes in giant pizzas baked in a wood-fired oven. Inexpensive.

Cosmo, 58a N Castle St (☎0131/226 6743). Straightforward, delicious Italian cuisine at long-established trattoria. Main courses start at around £10. Closed Sun & Mon.

Giuliano's, 18–19 Union Place (☎0131/556 6590). Raucous trattoria across from the Playhouse, much favoured for family and office nights out. Does its best to conjure the full Italian atmosphere. Closes 2.30am.

Lazio, 95 Lothian Rd (☎0131/229 7788). Pick of the family-run trattorias on this block. Moderately priced and particularly handy for a late-night meal after a show in the nearby theatre district. Closes 2am.

Vito's, 55a Frederick St (☎0131/225 5052). Bustling, quality Italian cooking at mid-range prices with the emphasis on seafood. Closed Sun except during the Festival.

Leith Brasseries

Malmaison Café Bar, 1 Tower Place. Successful attempt to re-create the feel of a French café: not for those on a diet.

Ship on the Shore, 24–26 The Shore (☎0131/555 0409). The homeliest and least expensive of the waterfront brasseries. Changing range of cask ales.

The Shore, 3 The Shore (☎0131/553 5080). Bar-restaurant with good, moderately priced fish and decent wines. Great views at sunset, and live jazz and folk in the adjoining bar. Non-smoking. Closed Sun.

Skippers, 1a Dock Place (☎0131/554 1018). Across the Water of Leith from The Shore, with a vaguely nautical atmosphere and a superb – if expensive – fish-oriented menu that changes according to what's fresh. Closed Sun.

Mexican

Tex Mex, 47 Hanover St (☎0131/225 1796). New Town joint serving authentic, reasonably priced Mexican burritos and steaks.

Viva Mexico, 10 Anchor Close, 50 E Fountainbridge, Tollcross. Two inexpensive restaurants, with plenty of choice for vegetarians, and bargain options at lunchtimes.

Moroccan

Marrakech, 30 London St (☎0131/556 7293). Scotland's only Moroccan restaurant, very reasonably priced, dishing up superb and authentic *couscous*, and *tajine* plus a range of soups, superb fresh bread and pastries. Unlicensed, but you can take your own and there's no corkage charge.

Scottish

The Atrium, Cambridge St (☎0131/228 8882) Award-winning and considered by many the city's best restaurant, with prices to match. Tables made from railway sleepers.

Creelers, 3 Hunter Square (☎0131/220 4447). Excellent seafood restaurant priding itself on fresh produce brought in from a sister restaurant/fish shop on Arran. Lunch £7.50, supper £16.50.

Dubh Prais, 123b High St (☎0131/557 5732). Basement restaurant offering innovative Scottish cuisine at affordable prices. Closed Sun & Mon.

Jacksons, 209 High St (☎0131/225 1793). Upmarket meat restaurant which turns the humble haggis into haute cuisine. Set lunches are among Edinburgh's best bargains at around £6; dinners are nearer £20. Closed Sat & Sun lunch.

Kelly's, 46b W Richmond St (☎0131/668 3847). Southside restaurant with cult status among Edinburgh foodies, serving modern Scottish food and scrumptious desserts. Closed Sun & Mon lunch.

Martin's, 70 Rose St N Lane (☎0131/225 3106). The emphasis is on organic, unfarmed ingredients – salmon, venison, unpasteurized cheeses. Expensive, especially in the evenings, but worth it. Closed Sun & Mon.

Seafood

Café Royal Oyster Bar, 17a W Register St (☎0131/556 4124). Splendidly ornate Victorian interior featured in *Chariots of Fire* – look out for the stained-glass windows showing sportsmen. Classic seafood dishes, including freshly caught oysters, served in a civilized, chatty atmosphere. Expensive – be prepared to pay at least £30 for a full meal.

Harry Ramsden's, 5 Newhaven Place (☎0131/551 5566). Part of the Yorkshire chain, just west of Leith in Newhaven, offering substantial portions of fish and chips in attractive harbourside setting.

Oyster Bar, 10 Burgess St, Leith; 6a Queen St, New Town; 2 Calton Rd, Carlton Hill; 28 W Maitland St, Haymarket. Lively, wood-panelled bars with a superb choice of cask beers and moderately priced fresh oysters.

Spanish

Igg's, 15 Jeffrey St (☎0131/557 8184). A Spanish-owned hybrid, offering tapas snacks and Mediterranean dishes, plus traditional Scottish food. Good lunchtime tapas for around a fiver. Closed Sun & Mon.

Parador, 26 William St (☎0131/225 2973). A convincing West End mock-up of a Spanish bodega, with full restaurant menu as well as tapas. All-you-can-eat lunchtime buffet £6. Bar and tapas 2–6.30pm only.

Swiss

Alp-Horn, 167 Rose St (☎0131/225 4787). Fondues, air-dried meats and wonderful desserts in this handy little restaurant just off Charlotte Square. Good-value two-course lunches. Closed Sun.

Denzlers, 121 Constitution St, Leith (☎0131/554 3268). Although it has moved premises a few times over the years, this has consistently ranked among Scotland's most highly praised restaurants. The ever-innovative menu is constantly changing, and prices are surprisingly reasonable, with most main courses under £10. Closed Sun & Mon.

Vegetarian

Bann's Vegetarian Café, 5 Hunter Square. Inexpensive café, ideally placed half way up the Royal Mile. Reliable, frequently changing menu, with two courses from around £4. Daily 10am–11pm.

Black Bo's, 57 Blackfriars St. Non-meat diner with earthy atmosphere, moderate prices and friendly service. Open after 11pm for drinks only. Closed Sun.

Henderson's, 94 Hanover St. Self-service vegetarian basement restaurant, with adjacent bar. Freshly prepared hot dishes, plus a great choice of salads, soups, sweets and cheeses. An Edinburgh institution, so arrive early for lunch or be prepared to queue. Closed Sun. *Henderson's* also runs the Traverse café, situated in the basement of the Traverse Theatre on Cambridge St in the Old Town. Open till 8pm daily.

Pierre Lapin, 32 W Nicolson St. Drolly named vegetarian offshoot of the *Pierre Victoire* chain, on Southside, offering superb-value set menus. Closed Sun.

Seeds, 51–53 W Nicolson St. Long-standing unlicensed Southside café serving inventive soups, savouries and puddings, and a range of vegan food, to crowds of students.

Pubs and bars

Many of Edinburgh's **pubs**, especially in the Old Town, have histories that stretch back centuries, while others, particularly in the New Town, are unaltered Victorian or Edwardian period pieces that rank among Edinburgh's most outstanding examples of interior design. Add in the plentiful supply of trendy modern bars, and there's a variety of styles and atmospheres to cater for all tastes. Many honest howffs stay open late, and during the Festival especially, it's no problem to find bars open till at least midnight. Currently, Edinburgh has three **breweries**, including the giant Scottish and Newcastle (who produce *McEwan's* and *Younger's*). The small independent Caledonian Brewery uses old techniques and equipment to produce some of the best beers in Britain, and there's also the tiny Rose Street Brewery, which has its own pub.

Edinburgh's main drinking strip is the near-legendary **Rose Street**, a pedestrianized lane of minimal visual appeal tucked between Princes Street and George Street. The ultimate Edinburgh pub crawl is to drink a half-pint in each of its dozen or so establishments – plus the two in West Register Street, its eastern continuation. Most of the **student pubs** are in and around Grassmarket, with a further batch on the Southside, an area overlooked by most tourists. **Leith** has a nicely varied crop of bars, ranging from the roughest type of spit-and-sawdust places to polished pseudo-Victoriana.

The Old Town

Bannermans, 212 Cowgate. The best pub in the street, formerly a vintner's cellar, with a labyrinthine interior and good beer on tap. On weekdays, tasty veggie lunches at rock-bottom prices; breakfasts available at weekends 11am–4pm. Open till 1am Mon–Sat.

Bow Bar, 80 W Bow. Old wood-panelled bar that recently won an award as the best drinkers' pub in Britain. Choose from among nearly 150 whiskies, an almost equally wide range of other spirits, and a changing selection of first-rate Scottish and English cask beers.

Cellar No.1, 2 Chambers St. Lively stone-clad vault that doubles as a restaurant. Excellent wines by bottle or glass. Open until 1am.

Deacon Brodie's Tavern, 435 Lawnmarket. Named after the eighteenth-century city councillor who inspired Stevenson's Jekyll and Hyde, the pub is lined with murals that tell his life story. Busy bars on two floors; good lunches. Open until midnight.

Doric Tavern, 15 Market St. Favoured watering hole of journalists from the nearby *Scotsman* building. The downstairs *McGuffie's Tavern* is a traditional Edinburgh howff, while the upstairs restaurant is more of a brasserie-cum-wine bar.

Fiddlers Arms, 9–11 Grassmarket. Traditional bar serving excellent *McEwan's* 80 shilling. The walls are adorned with forlorn, stringless violins. Open Mon–Thurs till 11.30pm, Fri & Sat 1am.

BREWERY TOURS

If you fancy finding out a bit more about Scottish **beers**, *Scottish and Newcastle*'s *Fountain Brewery*, Fountainbridge (☎0131/229 9377 ext. 3015), run good tours (Mon–Thurs 10.15am & 2.15pm, Fri 10.15am only; £2.95). For the morning tours, you have to book directly with the brewery, for the afternoon tours, with the main tourist office. In summer, the *Caledonian Brewery*, Slateford Rd (☎0131/337 1286), also runs regular tours: phone ahead to reserve a place.

Hebrides Bar, 17 Market St. Home-from-home for Edinburgh's Highland community: ceilidh atmosphere with lots of jigs, strathspeys and reels but no tartan kitsch.

Last Drop, 74–78 Grassmarket. Cheapish pub food, and, like its competitors in the same block, patronized mainly by students.

Malt Shovel, 11–15 Cockburn St. Dimly lit, comfortable bar with an excellent range of cask beers and single malt whiskies. Pub lunches. Open Sun–Wed 11am–midnight, Thurs–Sat 11am–12.30am.

Oddfellows, 14 Forrest Rd. Hip hangout for students and hard-up fashion victims. An amazing clutter of paraphernalia reflects the building's previous incarnation as a flea market.

Sandy Bell's, 25 Forrest Rd. A folk music institution, hosting regular impromptu sessions. Small but busy with an impressive selection of beers and whiskies.

The New Town

Abbotsford, 3 Rose St. Upscale pub whose original Victorian decor, complete with wood panelling and "island bar", is among the finest in the city. Good range of ales, including *Broughton Greenmantle*. Restaurant upstairs serves hearty Scottish food. Closed Sun.

Café Royal, 17 W Register St. The pub part of this stylish Victorian restaurant, the *Circle Bar*, is worth a visit for its decor alone, notably the huge elliptical "island" counter and the tiled portraits of renowned inventors. Open until midnight Thurs–Sat.

Guildford Arms, 1–5 W Register St. Excellent selection of ales, reasonable food and a very mixed clientele in this splendidly Baroque bar.

Kenilworth, 152–154 Rose St. Attractive high-ceilinged pub dating from 1899; has something of a gay tradition, though this is declining. Good Alloa beers, especially the *Arrol*'s 70 shilling.

Milne's Bar, corner Rose St & Hanover St. Cellar bar once beloved of Edinburgh's literati, earning the nickname "The Poets' Pub", courtesy of Hugh MacDiarmid et al. Good range of cask beers, including *McEwan's* 80 shilling. Open Mon–Sat until midnight, Sun 7–11pm.

Rose Street Brewery, 55 Rose St. Edinburgh's only micro-brewery, whose equipment can be inspected in the upstairs restaurant; the two beers made there are also on tap in the ground-floor bar.

Whigham's Wine Cellars, 13 Hope St. Basement wine bar with French wine and fresh oysters amid lots of stone flagging and catacomb-like booths. Closed Sun, otherwise open till midnight.

The Northern New Town and Stockbridge

Baillie Bar, 2 St Stephen St. Basement bar at corner of Edinburgh's most self-consciously bohemian street. English and Scottish ales, including some from the Caledonian Brewery.

Cumberland Bar, 1 Cumberland St. Highly popular bar with no juke box and a wide variety of ales.

Mathers, 25 Broughton St. Relaxed, old-fashioned pub which attracts a mixed crowd. The best place in Edinburgh for stout, with *Guinness* and *Murphy's* on tap, as well as the local *Gillespie's*.

The Southside

Pear Tree House, 36 W Nicolson St. Fine bar in eighteenth-century house with courtyard, one of Edinburgh's very few beer gardens. Decent bar lunches; open until midnight Thurs–Sat.

Southsider, 3–5 W Richmond St. Genuine local pub with a superb range of draught and imported bottled beers.

Stewart's, 14 Drummond St. A Southside institution since the beginning of the century, and seemingly little changed since then; popular with lecturers and students.

Southwest of the Old Town

Bennets Bar, 8 Leven St, Tollcross. Edwardian pub with mahogany-set mirrors and Art Nouveau stained glass. Lunch daily except Sun. Packed in the evening, particularly when there's a show at the King's Theatre next door. Open until midnight Mon–Sat.

Blue Blazer, 2 Spittal St. Traditional Edinburgh howff with oak-clad bar and church pews. Closed Sun.

Braidwood's, 52 W Port. James Braidwood was the city's first firefighter, and this bar is based in an old Victorian fire station. Lunches recommended. Open until 1am.

Canny Man's (Volunteer Arms), 237 Morningside Rd, Morningside. Atmospheric pub-museum adorned with anything that can be hung on the walls or from the ceiling. Open until midnight Mon–Sat.

Leith

Bay Horse, 63 Henderson St. Elegant Edwardian bar with stained-glass windows and walls lined with black and white photographs of old Edinburgh and Leith.

Merman, 42 Bernard St. Intimate pub that dates back to 1775, still preserved in its original state with a blazing log fire. Specializes in high-quality cask beers.

Tattler, 23 Commercial St. Pub-restaurant decked out in plush Victorian style. The award-winning bar meals are wonderful: high-quality Scottish food including fish, meat and poultry.

Nightlife and entertainment

Inevitably, Edinburgh's **nightlife** is at its best during the Festival (see pp.726–27), which can make the other 49 weeks of the year seem like one long anticlimax. However, by any normal standards, rather than by the misleading yardstick of the Festival, the city has a lot to offer, especially in the realm of **performing arts** and **concerts**.

Nightclubs don't offer anything startlingly original, but they serve their purpose, hosting a changing selection of one-nighters. While you can normally hear **live jazz**, **folk** and **rock** every evening in one or other of the city's pubs, for the really big rock events, ad hoc venues – such as the Castle Esplanade, Meadowbank Stadium or the exhibition halls of the Royal Highland Show at Ingliston – are often used.

With an estimated gay and lesbian population of around 15–20,000, Edinburgh has a dynamic **gay** culture, for years centred on the area Calton Hill and the top of Leith Walk (p713). The first gay and lesbian centre appeared in Broughton Street in the 1970s. Since the start of the 1990s, more and more gay enterprises, especially cafés and nightclubs, have moved into this area, now dubbed the "Broughton triangle", and there is a constant stream of new places and old ones changing name. In our listings "mixed" refers to a gay/lesbian crowd.

The best way to find out **what's on** is to pick up a copy of *The List*, a fortnightly listings magazine covering both Edinburgh and Glasgow (£1.50). Alternatively, get hold of the *Edinburgh Evening News*, which appears daily except Sunday: its listings column gives details of performances in the city that day, hotels and bars included. **Tickets** and information on all events are available from the tourist office. Box offices of individual halls and theatres are likewise liberally supplied with promotional leaflets, and some are able to sell tickets for more than one venue.

Nightclubs

La Belle Angèle, 11 Hasties Close (☎0131/225 2774). A rotating selection of Latin, soul, hip-hop and jazz.

THE FESTIVAL

The **Edinburgh Festival**, now the largest arts festival in the world, first took place in August 1947. Driven by a desire for reconciliation and escape from postwar austerity, the Austrian conductor, Rudolf Bing, brought together a host of distinguished musicians from the war-ravaged countries of central Europe. The symbolic centrepiece of his vision was the emotional reunion of Bruno Walter, a Jewish refugee from Nazi tyranny, and the Vienna Philharmonic Orchestra. At the same time, eight theatrical groups, both Scottish and English, turned up in Edinburgh, uninvited, performing in an unlikely variety of local venues, thus establishing the Fringe. Today the festival attracts a million people to the city over three weeks (the last three in August, or the last fortnight and first week in September) and encompasses several separate festivals, each offering a wide variety of artists and events – everything is on show, from the high-brow to the controversial.

The legacy of Rudolf Bing's Glyndebourne connections ensured that, for many years, the official **Edinburgh International Festival** was dominated by opera. Although, in the 1980s, efforts were made to involve locals and provide a broader cultural mix of international theatre, dance and classical music, the official festival is still very much a high-brow event. The **programme** is published in April by the Edinburgh International Festival Society, 21 Market St, EH1 1BW (☎0131/255 5756); bookings begin shortly afterwards.

For many years largely the domain of student revues – notable exceptions include Joan Littlewood's distinguished Theatre Workshop, with their early 1950s production of *The Other Animal*, about life in a concentration camp; and work by the great Spanish playwright, Lorca – the **Festival Fringe** began to really take off in the 1970s. Set up in 1951, the **Fringe Society** has grown from a small group to today's large-scale operation serving an annual influx of more than five hundred acts – national theatre groups to student troupes – using around two hundred venues. In spite of this expansion, the Fringe has remained loyal to the original open policy and there is still no vetting of performers. This means that the shows range from the inspired to the truly diabolical and ensures a highly competitive atmosphere, in which one bad review in a prominent publication means box-office disaster. Many unknowns rely on self-publicity, taking to the streets to perform highlights from their show, or pressing leaflets into the hands of

The Cavendish, W Tollcross. Packed out roots, ragga and reggae night on Fri; "The Mambo" on Sat plays African and Latin rhythms.

Century 2000, 31 Lothian Rd (☎0131/229 7670). Big dance-round-a-hangbag club, converted from a cinema. Open till 3am.

The Citrus, 40-42 Grindlay St (☎0131/229 6697). Eighties indie music along with some funk and disco.

The Cooler, 15 Calton Rd (☎0131/557 3073). Small, intimate sweaty club popular with up-and-coming indie bands. Also used for a variety of hip one-nighters specializing in house, funk and reggae.

Moray House Student Union, Holyrood Rd (☎0131/.556 5184). Popular Saturday club nights ranging from 1970s funk to wistful indie.

The New Calton, 24 Calton Rd (☎0131/228 3252). Popular nightclub with regular gay night on Sat.

Red Hot Pepper Club, 3 Semple St (☎0131/229 7733) Large disco with mainstream music; students free. Open till 2am.

Rocking Horse, Cowgate (☎0131/225 7733). Rock nights from heavy metal to goth-rock and grunge.

The Vaults, 15-17 Niddry St (☎0131/556 0001). Currently the city's most popular nightclub, with the emphasis on the ever-burgeoning dance music scene.

Wide Awake Club, 11 Cowgate (☎0131/226 2151) Popular with students; more mainstream rave than hardcore, plus chart music and soul/funk nights. Open till 4am.

Gay clubs and bars

Blue Moon Café/Over the Moon Brasserie, 1 Barony St/36 Broughton St (☎0131/556 2788) Burgers and salads, coffees and beer. Very mixed crowd. Open 9–1am. Champagne breakfast £4.95.

C.C. Bloom's, 23 Greenside Place (☎0131/556 9331). Big dance floor, stonking rhythms. Mixed friendly crowd.

every passer-by. Performances go on round the clock: if so inclined, you could sit through twenty shows in a day. The full programme is usually available in June from the Festival Fringe Office, 180 High St, EH1 1QS (☎0131/226 5257). Postal and telephone (☎0131/226 5138) bookings can be made almost immediately afterwards.

The **Film Festival** also began at the same time as the main festival, making it the longest running Film Festival in the world. After a period in the doldrums, it has grown to its current position as a respected fixture on the international circuit, incorporating both mainstream and independent new releases and presenting a series of valuable retrospectives from Sam Fuller to Shohei Immamura. It also hosts interviews and discussions with film directors; in recent years visitors have included Kenneth Anger, the Coen brothers, Clint Eastwood and Steve Martin. A particular feature has been the high-profile support given to Scottish film from Bill Douglas's austere and brilliant *Childhood* trilogy, through the lighter style of Bill Forsyth to the recent small budget hit, *Shallow Grave*. Tickets and information are available from the main venue, The Filmhouse, 88 Lothian Rd, EH3 9BZ (☎0131/228 4051). The programme is usually ready by late June, when bookings start.

Meanwhile, other Festivals have emerged: the **Jazz Festival**, which has attracted the likes of Teddy Wilson and Benny Waters and stages a lively parade through the Grassmarket (programme available in July from the office at 116 Canongate, EH8 8DD; ☎0131/557 1624); and the **Book Festival**, which evolved from existing meet-the-author sessions to become a biennial jamboree held in the douce setting of a marquee-covered Charlotte Square. Hundreds of established authors from throughout the English-speaking world come to take part in readings, lectures, panel discussions and audience question-and-answer sessions. For further information, contact the Scottish Book Centre, 137 Dundee St, EH11 1BG (☎0131/228 5444).

Although officially a separate event, the **Edinburgh Military Tattoo**, held in a splendid setting on the Castle Esplanade, is very much part of the Festival scene and an unashamed display of the kilt and bagpipes view of Scottish culture. Pipes and drums form the kernel of the programme, with a lone piper towards the end; performing animals, gymnastic and daredevil displays, plus at least one guest regiment from abroad provide variety. Information and tickets are available from the Tattoo Office, 22 Market St, EH1 1QB (☎0131/225 1188).

Eat Out, 60 Broughton St (☎0131/556 0512). Newly opened café at the Edinburgh *Gay, Lesbian and Bisexual Centre*. Open 11am–1pm.

Kudos, 22 Greenside Place. For the smart young crowd. Mixed clientèle.

New Town Club Bar, 26 Dublin St (☎0131/538 7775). Eclectic male crowd, high number of professionals: raunchy *Jailhouse* bar downstairs.

Picardy's, 2 Picardy Place (☎0131/556 0499). Opened August 1995 with the *LADS* (*Leather and Denim Scotland*) bar in the basement.

Route 66, 6 Baxter's Place. Friendly and relaxed bar located in the heart of the "Broughton Triangle". Mostly male.

Live music pubs and venues

La Belle Angèle, 11 Hasties Close (☎0131/225 2774). A home to both indie bands and Latin divas.

Café Royal, 17 W Register St (☎0131/.556 4124). Regular folk nights upstairs in one of the city's most famous bars.

Cas Rock Café, 104 W Port (☎0131/229 4341). A mixture of sedate folk during the week and raucous punky sounds at the weekends.

The Music Box, 9c Victoria St (☎0131/225 2564). Good size and popular, used by visiting indie and local R & B bands.

Negociants, 45–47 Lothian St (☎0131/225 6313). Upstairs brasserie serves breakfast and lunch, plus Belgian fruit beers alongside more conventional booze. Downstairs bar hosts varied live bands. Popular with students. Open until 1am.

Nobles Bar, 44a Constitution St, Leith (☎0131/553 3873). A standard of the local jazz scene, featuring live sessions six days a week in lovely Victorian pub with leaded glass windows and horseshoe bar. All-day Sunday breakfasts.

Platform 1, Rutland St (☎0131/225 2433). Young, loud and fashionable venue with comfortable downstairs bar. Live music in the basement. Open till 2am.

The Queen's Hall, 37 Clerk St (☎0131/668 3456). Housed in a former Southside church, with some pews still in place, hosting African, funk and rock bands, as well as smaller jazz, folk concerts and comedy nights with well-established comedians.

Tron Ceilidh House, 9 Hunter Square (☎0131/220 1500). Busy huge complex of bars on different levels, with regular jazz and folk nights.

Theatre and comedy

Assembly Rooms, 54 George St (☎0131/220 4348). Varied complex of small and large halls. Used all year, but really comes into its own during the Fringe, with large-scale drama productions and mainstream comedy.

Festival Theatre, Nicholson St (☎0131/529 6000). Everything from the children's show *Singing Kettle* to Engelbert Humperdinck and *La Traviata*.

Gilded Balloon Theatre, 233 Cowgate (☎0131/226 6550). Fringe festival comedy venue, noted for the Late 'n' Live (1–4am) slot which gives you the chance to see top comedians whose main show elsewhere may be booked out.

King's Theatre, 2 Leven St (☎0131/229 1201). Stately Edwardian civic theatre that offers the most eclectic programme in the city: including opera, ballet, Shakespeare, pantomime and comedy.

Netherbow Arts Centre, 43 High St (☎0131/556 9579). Although the centre is run by the Church of Scotland, the emphasis in their adventurous year-round drama productions is more Scottish than religious.

Playhouse Theatre, 18–22 Greenside Place (☎0131/557 2590). The most capacious theatre in Britain, formerly a cinema. Recently refurbished and now used for extended runs of popular musicals and occasional rock concerts.

Pleasance Theatre, 60 The Pleasance (☎0131/556 6550). Fringe festival venue. Cobbled courtyard with stunning views across to Arthur's Seat and an array of auditoria used for a varied programme.

Royal Lyceum Theatre, 30 Grindlay St (☎0131/229 9697). Fine Victorian civic theatre with compact auditorium. The city's leading year-round venue for mainstream drama.

Theatre Workshop, 34 Hamilton Place (☎0131/226 5425). Enticing programmes of international innovative theatre and performance art all year.

Traverse Theatre, 10 Cambridge St (☎0131/228 1404). A byword in experimental theatrical circles, and unquestionably one of Britain's premier venues for new plays. Going from strength to strength in its new custom-built home beside the Usher Hall.

EDINBURGH'S OTHER FESTIVALS

Quite apart from the Edinburgh Festival, the city is now promoting itself as a year-round festival city, beginning with a **Hogmanay Festival** (☎0131/557 3990) which involves street parties, folk and rock concerts and drive-in cinema shows. The **Folk Festival** (☎0131/556 3181) in April draws local and international performers, while the **Science Festival** (☎0131/557 4296) in April incorporates hands-on children's events as well as numerous lectures on a vast array of subjects. There is a **Puppet and Animation Festival** (☎0131/556 9579) in March, and a **Children's Festival** (☎0131/554 6297) in May with readings, magicians et cetera. In the summer, a series of concerts (usually free), ranging from tea dances to World Music, is held in the **Ross Bandstand** in Princes Street Gardens. The *Caledonian Brewery*, 42 Slateford Rd, runs its own German-style **beer festival** in June; the **Edinburgh Traditional Beer Festival**, with real ales from all over Britain, is held at Meadowbank Sports Stadium in October.

The **Open Doors Day**, around mid-September, provides an opportunity to visit a number of noteworthy buildings, otherwise closed to the public. In recent years, these have included private homes in the New Town, disused churches and company offices. Contact the **Cockburn Association** (☎0131/557 8686) for details. The **Filmhouse** (☎0131/228 2688) also has a number of annual seasons of international cinema, notably French (in November) and Italian (April), and a gay season (June).

Concert halls

Queen's Hall, 89 Clerk St (☎0131/668 2019). Converted Georgian church with a capacity of around 800, though many seats have little or no view of the platform. Home base of both the Scottish Chamber Orchestra and Scottish Ensemble, and much favoured by jazz, blues and folk groups. Also hosts established comedians during the Fringe.

Reid Concert Hall, Bristo Square (☎0131/650 4367). Narrow, steeply pitched Victorian hall owned by the university.

St Cecilia's Hall, corner of Cowgate & Niddry St (☎0131/650 2805). A Georgian treasure that is again university-owned and not used as frequently as it deserves.

Usher Hall, corner of Lothian Rd & Grindlay St (☎0131/228 1155). Edinburgh's main civic concert hall, seating over 2500. Excellent for choral and symphony concerts, but less apt for solo vocalists. Avoid the back of the grand tier and the stalls, and head for the cheaper upper circle seats which have the best acoustics.

Art-house Cinemas

Cameo, 38 Home St (☎0131/228 4141). New art-house releases and cult late nighters.

Filmhouse, 88 Lothian Rd (☎0131/228 2688). Eclectic programme of independent, art-house and classic films.

Listings

Airlines *British Airways*, 32 Frederick St (☎0131/0345 222111). Other carriers handled by *Servisair*, Edinburgh Airport (☎0131/344 3111).

American Express, 139 Princes St (☎0131/225 9179).

Books *Bauermeisters*, 19 George IV Bridge (☎0131/226 5561) is a row of separate shops (general and academic, music and stationery, paperbacks). *James Thin*, 53–59 South Bridge (☎0131/556 6743) and 57 George St (☎0131/225 4495): the first is a huge, rambling general and academic shop; the latter is smaller and more genteel, with a good café.

Car rental *Arnold Clark*, Lochrin Place (☎0131/228 4747); *Avis*, 100 Dalry Rd (☎0131/337 6363); *Budget*, 111 Glasgow Rd (☎0131/334 7740); *Carnies*, 46 Westfield Rd (☎0131/346 4155); *Europcar*, 24 E London St (☎0131/557 3456); *Hertz*, Waverley Station (☎0131/557 5272); *Mitchells*, 32 Torphichen St (☎0131/229 5384); *Thrifty Car Rental*, 24 Haymarket Terrace (☎0131/313 1613).

Consulates *Australia*, 25 Bernard St (☎0131/555 4500); *Belgium*, 19 Ainslie Place (☎0131/226 6881); *Denmark*, 4 Royal Terrace (☎0131/556 4043); *Germany*, 16 Eglington Crescent (☎0131/337 2323); *Netherlands*, 53 George St (☎0131/220 3226); *Norway*, 86 George St (☎0131/226 5701); *Sweden*, 6 St John's Place (☎0131/554 6631); Switzerland, 66 Hanover Place (☎0131/226 5660); *USA*, 3 Regent Terrace (☎0131/556 8315).

Exchange *Thomas Cook*, 79a Princes St (Mon–Fri 9am–5.30pm, Sat 9am–5pm; ☎0131/220 4039); currency exchange bureaux in the main tourist office (Mon–Sat 9am–8pm, Sun 10am–8pm) and in the accommodation office in Waverley Station (see "Arrival and Accommodation"). To change money after hours, try one of the swanky hotels – but expect to pay a hefty commission charge.

Football Edinburgh has two Scottish Premier Division teams, who are at home on alternate Saturdays. *Heart of Midlothian* (or *Hearts*) play at *Tynecastle Stadium*, Gorgie Rd, a couple of miles west of the centre; *Hibernian* (or *Hibs*) play at *Easter Road Stadium*, a similar distance east of the centre. Between them, the two clubs dominated Scottish football in the 1950s, but neither has won more than the odd trophy since, though one or the other periodically threatens to make a major breakthrough. Tickets from £10.

Gay and lesbian contacts *Gay Scotland*, 58a Broughton St (☎0131/557 2625); *Gay Switchboard* (☎0131/556 4049); *Lesbian Line* (☎0131/557 0751).

Hospital 24-hr casualty department at the *Royal Infirmary*, 1 Lauriston Place (☎0131/229 2477).

Left luggage Lockers available at Waverley Station and St Andrew Square bus station.

Maps *Carson Clark*, 173 Canongate (☎0131/556 4710) has wonderful antique maps, charts and globes.

Pharmacy *Boots*, 48 Shandwick Place (Mon–Sat 8.45am–9pm, Sun 11am–4pm; ☎0131/225 6757).

Post office 2–4 Waterloo Place (Mon–Fri 9.30am–5.30pm, Sat 9.30am–12.30pm; ☎0131/550 8232).

Travel agents *Campus Travel* (student and youth specialist), 53 Forrest Rd (☎0131/225 6111) and 5 Nicolson Square (☎0131/225 6111); *Edinburgh Travel Centre* (student and youth specialist), 196 Rose St (☎0131/668 3303), 92 South Clerk St (☎0131/667 9488) and 3 Bristo Square (☎0131/668 2221).

travel details

Trains

Edinburgh to: Aberdeen (hourly; 2hr 40min); Aviemore (5 daily; 3hr); Dundee (hourly; 1hr 45min); Fort William (change at Glasgow; 3 daily; 4hr 55min); Glasgow (38 daily; 50min); Inverness (4 daily; 3hr 50min); London (20 daily; 4 hr 30min) Oban (change at Glasgow; 3 daily; 4hr 10min); Perth (6 daily; 1hr 15min); Stirling (every 30min; 45min).

Buses

Edinburgh St Andrew Square bus station to: Aberdeen (13 daily; express 3hr, standard 3hr 50min); Campbeltown (3 daily; 6hr); Dundee (14 daily; express 1hr 25min, standard 2hr); Fort William (3 daily; 5hr); Glasgow (44 daily; 1hr 10min); Inverness (11 daily; express 3hr, standard 4hr); London (2 daily; 7hr 50min); Oban (3 daily; 5hr); Perth (14 daily; 1hr 20min); Pitlochry (11 daily; 2hr).

Flights

Edinburgh to: Birmingham (Mon–Fri 7 daily, Sat & Sun 4; 1hr); Dundee (Mon–Fri 2 daily; 15min); Manchester (Mon–Fri 3 daily; 50min); London (Gatwick Mon–Fri 5 daily, Sat & Sun 3; Heathrow Mon–Fri 20 daily Sat & Sun 15; Stansted Mon–Fri 5 daily, Sat & Sun 2; 1hr 15min).

CHAPTER EIGHTEEN

SOUTHERN SCOTLAND

Although **southern Scotland** doesn't have the high tourist profile of other areas of the country, in many ways the region is at its very heart. Its inhabitants bore the brunt of long wars with the English, its farms have fed Scotland's cities since industrialization, and two of the country's literary icons, **Sir Walter Scott** and **Robbie Burns**, lived and died here. The main roads, the fast routes from northern England to Glasgow and Edinburgh, bypass the best of the region, but if you make an effort to get off the highways, there's plenty to see, from the ruins of medieval castles and abbeys to well-preserved market towns and seaports set within a wild, hilly countryside.

Geographically, southern Scotland is dominated by the **Southern Uplands** – a chain of bulging flat-peaked hills and weather-beaten moorland punctuated by narrow glens, fast-flowing rivers and blue-black lochs – extending south and west from an imaginary line drawn between Peebles and Jedburgh in central southern Scotland over to the Ayrshire coast. They are at their most dramatic in the west in the **Galloway Forest Park**, with peaks soaring over 2000ft, criss-crossed by **walking** trails.

North of the inhospitable Cheviot Hills, which straddle the border with England, a clutch of tiny towns in the **Tweed River Valley** – including delightful **Melrose** – form the nucleus of the Borders, inspiration for countless folkloric ballads telling of bloody battles with the English and clashes between the notorious warring families, the Border Reivers. East of **Kelso**, one of four abbeys founded on the Borders by the medieval Canmore kings, the Tweed Valley widens to form the Merse basin, an area of flat farmland that boasts a series of grand stately homes, principally **Floors Castle** and **Mellerstain House**, both of which feature the work of the Adam family, whose fine skills are also displayed at Ayr's **Culzean Castle**.

North of the Tweed, a narrow band of foothills – the **Pentland**, **Moorfoot** and **Lammermuir** ranges – form the southern edge of the Central Lowlands. These Lowlands spread west beyond Edinburgh, but here they constitute the slender coastal plain of **East Lothian**, which rolls down towards a string of fine sandy beaches. Further east, the coastline becomes more rugged, its cliffs and rocky outcrops harbouring a series of ruined castles, and inland, the flatness of the terrain is interrupted by the occasional extinct volcano, inspiration for all sorts of ancient myths.

The gritty town of **Dumfries** is gateway to **southwest Scotland**, where on the marshy Solway coast you can visit charming **Kirkcudbright** and see the magnificent remains of **Caerlaverock Castle**. The **Ayrshire coast** also rewards a visit for its strong associations with Robert Burns, especially at Ayr and **Alloway**, the poet's birthplace, as well as for its pastoral coastline and sandy beaches.

East Lothian and the coast

East Lothian consists of the coastal strip and hinterland immediately east of Edinburgh. The prosperous market town of **Haddington** serves as a base for exploring the interior, whose bumpy farmland is bordered to the south by the Lammermuir Hills. But most people make a beeline for the fifty miles or so of **coastline** extending right

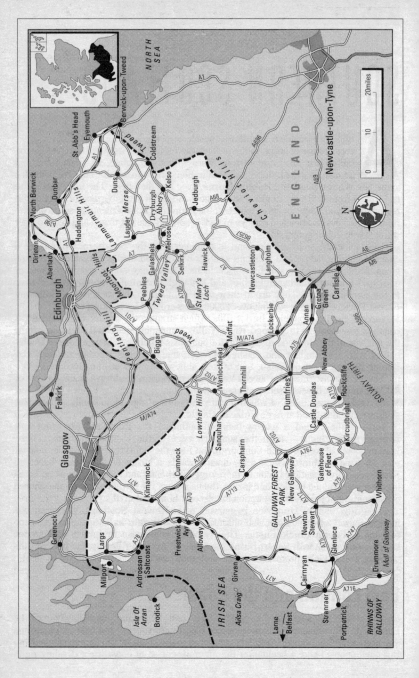

ACCOMMODATION PRICE CODES

Throughout this guide, hotel and B&B accommodation is priced on a scale of ① to ⑨, the number indicating the **lowest price** you could expect to pay per night in that establishment for a **double room** in high season. The prices indicated by the codes are as follows:

① under £20/$30	④ £40–50/$60–75	⑦ £70–80/$105–120
② £20–30/$31–45	⑤ £50–60/$75–90	⑧ £80–100/$120–150
③ £30–40/$45–60	⑥ £60–70/$90–105	⑨ over £100/$150

---

down to England's Berwick-upon-Tweed. There's something for most tastes here, from the sandy beaches and volcanic islets around the resort of **North Berwick** to the ruined medieval stronghold of **Tantallon**.

Haddington

The compact centre of **HADDINGTON**, birthplace of John Knox (see p.700), preserves an intriguing ensemble of seventeenth- to nineteenth-century architectural styles. Yet the town's staid appearance belies an innovative past. During the early 1700s, Haddington became a byword for modernization as its merchants supplied the district's progressive landowners with all sorts of new-fangled equipment, stock and seed, and in only a few decades utterly transformed Lothian agriculture.

Haddington's centre is best approached from the west, where tree-trimmed **Court Street** ends suddenly with the soaring spire, stately stonework and dignified Venetian windows of the **Town House**, designed by William Adam in 1748. Close by, to the right and next door to a fine Italianate facade, the **Jane Welsh Carlyle House** (April–Sept Wed–Sat 2–5pm; £1), was the childhood home of the wife of the essayist and historian Thomas Carlyle. The dining room – the only part of the house open to the public – has been restored to its early nineteenth-century appearance and sports pictures of the influential personalities of the day. The lovely garden is pretty much as Jane would have known it too. Carrying straight on, **High Street** is distinguished by its pastel-painted gables and quaint pends, a tad prettier than those in neighbouring **Market Street**. Keep an eye open, however, for **Mitchell's Close** on Market Street, a recently restored seventeenth-century close with crow-stepped gables, rubble masonry and the narrowest of staircase towers.

Leaving the town centre to the east along High Street, it's a brief walk down Church Street – past the hooped arches of **Nungate Bridge** – to the hulking mass of **St Mary's Church** (daily 10am–4pm). Built close to the reedy River Tyne, the church dates from the fourteenth century, but it's a real hotch-potch of styles, the squat grey tower uneasy above clumsy buttressing and pinkish-ochre stone walls. Inside on the **Lauderdale Aisle** a munificent tomb features the best of Elizabethan alabaster carving, moustachioed knights and their ruffed ladies lying beneath a finely ornamented canopy. In stark contrast, a plain slab nearby is inscribed with Thomas Carlyle's beautiful tribute to his wife, who died on April 21, 1866. Carlyle rounds the inscription off : "Suddenly snatched away from him, and the light of his life as if gone out". They had been married for forty years.

Practicalities

Fast and frequent **buses** connect Haddington with Edinburgh, fifteen miles to the west, and North Berwick on the east coast. All services stop on High Street. There's no **tourist office**, but orientation is easy and *A Walk around Haddington* (£1), detailing every building of any conceivable consequence, is available from local newsagents. If you decide to **stay** the night, there are several central **B&Bs** including *Mrs Richards*, whose well-kept Georgian town house is at 19 Church St (☎01620/825663; ③), and the *Plough Tavern*, 11 Court St (☎01620/823326; ③); alternatively try the more pricy and luxurious *Brown's Hotel*, 1 West Rd (☎01620/822254; ⑧). *Monks' Muir Caravan Park* (all year; ☎01620/860340), on the edge of town by the A1, also takes tents. For daytime **eating**, try *Simply Scrumptious*, next to the Town House. The best place for an evening meal is the *Waterside Bistro*, on the far side of Nungate Bridge; or try the *Brown's Hotel* restaurant, where you'll need to reserve a table.

North Berwick and around

NORTH BERWICK, on the coast northeast of Haddington, has an old-fashioned air, its guest houses and hotels extending along the shore in all their Victorian and Edwardian sobriety. Set within sight of two volcanic heaps – the Bass Rock and North Berwick Law – the resort's pair of wide and sandy **beaches** are the main attraction.

Little now remains of the original medieval town, but the fragmentary ruins of the **Auld Kirk**, next to the harbour, bear witness to one of the most extraordinary events in Scottish history. In 1590, while **King James VI** spent the summer in Denmark wooing his prospective wife, Francis Stuart, **Earl of Bothwell**, summoned the witches of Lothian to meet the Devil in the Auld Kirk. Bothwell turned up disguised as the Devil and instructed his 200 acolytes to raise a storm that would shipwreck the king. To cast the spell, they opened a few graves and engaged in flagellation before kissing the bare buttocks of the "Devil" – reportedly "as cold as ice and as hard as iron" as it hung over the pulpit. Despite these shenanigans, the king returned safely, and since he refused to believe the rumours of Bothwell's treachery, the earl went unpunished.

Resembling a giant molar, the **Bass Rock** rises 350ft above the sea some three miles east of North Berwick. This massive chunk of basalt, formerly a prison, fortress and monastic retreat, is home to millions of nesting seabirds. Weather permitting, there are regular ninety-minute **boat trips** round the island from North Berwick harbour (Easter to early Oct daily; £3.50), but only Fred Marr (☎01620/893863; £10) has landing rights. The other volcanic monolith, 613-foot-high **North Berwick Law**, is about an hour's walk from the beach (take Law Road off High Street and follow the signs). On a clear day, the views out across the Firth of Forth make the effort worthwhile, and at the top you can see the remains of a Napoleonic watchtower and an arch made from the jawbone of a whale.

Practicalities

It's ten minutes' walk east from North Berwick **train station** to the town centre along Abbey Road, Westgate and High Street. **Buses** from Edinburgh stop on High Street and those from Haddington outside the **tourist office**, Quality St (mid-April to May Mon–Sat 9am–6pm; June–Sept Mon–Sat 9am–8pm, Sun 11am–6pm; Oct to mid-April Mon–Fri 9am–5pm; ☎01620/892197).

Several excellent **B&Bs** are open from April to September, including *Mrs Duns*, 20 Marmion Rd (☎01620/892066; ②), and *Mrs McQueen*, 5 West Bay Rd (☎01620/894576; ③). Out of season, try *Mrs Clelland*, 16 Marine Parade (☎01620/892879; ③) or *Mrs Gray*, 12 Marine Parade (☎01620/892884; ③). Alternatively, *Craigview*, 5 Beach Rd (☎01620/892257; ④), is a well-maintained **guest house**, and *Point Garry*, 20 West Bay Rd (April–Oct; ☎01620/892380; ⑦), an upmarket **hotel**. The nearest **campsite**, *Tantallon Rhodes Caravan Park* (April–Oct; ☎01620/893348), occupies a prime clifftop location a couple of miles east of the centre – take the Dunbar bus.

Several little cafés, such as the *Buttercup*, High St, sell cheap **food**, but for an evening meal, head for *Harding's*, 2 Station Rd, next to the train station (Wed–Sat only; ☎01620/894737), which serves good food and wine from a daily menu.

Tantallon Castle

The melodramatic ruins of **Tantallon Castle** (April–Sept Mon–Sat 9.30am–6pm, Sun 2–6pm; Oct–March Mon–Wed & Sat 9.30am–4pm, Thurs 9.30am–noon, Sun 2–4pm; £2) lie three miles east of North Berwick, on the precipitous cliffs facing the Bass Rock. This pinkish sandstone edifice, with its imposing cylindrical towers, protected the powerful "Red" Douglases, Earls of Angus, from their enemies for over 300 years. With a sheer drop down to the sea on three sides and a sequence of moats and ditches on the fourth, the castle's desolate invincibility is daunting, with the wind howling over the remaining battlements and the surf crashing on the rocks far below. In fact, the setting is more striking than the ruins: Cromwell's army savaged the castle in 1651 and only the impressive 50ft-high and 14ft-thick curtain wall has survived relatively intact. To reach Tantallon Castle from North Berwick, a 15-minute trip, take the Dunbar bus.

The Tweed Valley

Rising in the hills far to the west, the **River Tweed** snakes its way across the Borders until it reaches the North Sea at Berwick-upon-Tweed. The eastern reaches of the river, for the most part form the boundary between Scotland and England. For the English, the gentle, rural landscape of the east Borders was the quickest land route to the centre of Scotland and time and again they launched themselves north destroying everything in their way. Indeed, the English turned Berwick-upon-Tweed into one of the most heavily guarded frontier towns in northern Europe, and the massive fortifications survive today (see p.558). The region also witnessed one of the most devastating of medieval battles when the Scots, under James IV, were decimated by the English over the border from Coldstream at **Flodden Field** in 1513.

Nowadays, the Lower Tweed Valley really has only one place of note, **Kelso**, a busy agricultural centre distinguished by the Georgian elegance of its main square and its proximity to Floors Castle and Mellerstein House. **Melrose** makes a great place for exploring the middle reaches of the Tweed Valley, as well as being a beautiful town in its own right. The rich, forested scenery inspired Sir Walter Scott, and the area's most outstanding attractions – the elegaic ruins of **Dryburgh Abbey** and lonely **Snailholm Tower**, not to mention Scott's purpose-built creation, **Abbotsford House** – bear his mark. There's a wide choice of routes on from Melrose; one of the more popular options is to travel 22 miles west along the **Tweed Valley** to the pleasant country town of **Peebles**. On the way, savour the wooded scenery and drop into **Traquair House**, just off the main road at tiny Innerleithen. Perhaps fortunately, Scott died before the textile boom industrialized parts of the Tweed Valley, turning his beloved Selkirk and Galashiels into mill towns.

Kelso and around

Compact **KELSO**, at the confluence of the Tweed and Teviot, grew up in the shadow of its abbey, once the richest and most powerful in Southern Scotland. The abbey was founded in 1128 during the reign of King David, whose policy of encouraging the monastic orders had little to do with spirituality. The bishops and monks David established here, as well as at Melrose, Jedburgh and Dryburgh, were the frontiersmen of his kingdom, helping to advance his authority in areas of doubtful allegiance. This began a long period of relative stability across the region which enabled its abbeys to flourish, until frequent raids by the English, who savaged Kelso three times in the early sixteenth century, brought ruin.

Such was the extent of the devastation – compounded by the Reformation – that the surviving ruins of **Kelso Abbey** (April–Dec Mon–Sat daylight hours, Sun afternoons;

Jan–March ask for key at the tourist office; free) are disappointing: a heavy central tower and supporting buttresses represent a scant memorial to the massive Romanesque original that took over eighty years to build. From the abbey, it's a couple of minutes' walk along Bridge Street to **The Square**, a cobbled expanse where the columns and pediments of the **Town Hall** are flanked by a splendid ensemble of three-storey eighteenth- and nineteenth-century pastel buildings. Beyond the general air of elegance, though, there's little to actually see.

Kelso has one other diversion. Leaving The Square along Roxburgh Street, take the alley down to the **Cobby Riverside Walk**, where a brief stroll leads to Floors Castle (see below). En route is the spot where the Teviot meets the Tweed. This junction has long been famous for its salmon fishing, with permits booked years in advance irrespective of the cost: currently around £5000 per rod per week. Permits for fishing other (less expensive) reaches of the Tweed and Teviot are available from *Tweeside Fishing Tackle*, 36 Bridge St (☎01573/225306).

Kelso **bus station**, Roxburgh St, is a brief walk from The Square where you'll find the **tourist office** (April–June, Sept & Oct Mon–Sat 10am–4.30 or 5pm, Sun 10am–1pm; July & Aug Mon–Sat 9.30am–6.30pm, Sun 10.30am–6pm; ☎01573/223464). The tourist office can provide you with a long list of **B&Bs**, three good choices being the convenient *Wester House*, 155 Roxburgh St (☎01573/224428; ③); the *Charlesfield*, a comfortable Victorian house a few minutes' walk north of The Square on Edenside Rd (☎01573/224583; ③); and, best of all, *Wooden* (May–Sept; 01573/224204; ④), an ivy-clad country house of 1824 half a mile east of Kelso on the B6350. There's also one rather special **hotel**, *Ednam House*, on Bridge St, near The Square (☎01573/224168; ⑧), a splendid Georgian mansion, whose gardens abut the Tweed. For **food**, *Lombardi's Café*, on The Square, sells cheap snacks and meals, as does the *Queen's Head*, Bridge St, though the restaurant of the *Ednam House* hotel stands head and shoulders above the rest.

Floors Castle

There's nothing medieval about **Floors Castle** (May–Aug daily 10.30am–5.30pm; Sept Mon–Thurs & Sun 10.30am–5.30pm; Oct Wed & Sun 10.30am–4.30pm; £3.80), a vast castellated mansion overlooking the Tweed about a mile northwest of Kelso. The bulk of the building was designed by William Adam in the 1720s, and, picking through the Victorian modifications, much of the interior demonstrates his uncluttered style. Not that you'll see much of it: just ten rooms and a basement are open to the public. Highlights include Hendrick Danckerts' splendid panorama of Horse Guards Parade in the entrance hall, paintings by Augustus John and Henri Matisse in the Needle Room, and all sorts of snuff boxes and cigarette cases in the gallery. Floors remains privately owned, the property of the tenth Duke of Roxburghe, whose arrogant features can be seen in a variety of portraits. The duke is a close friend of royalty: it was here, apparently, that Prince Andrew proposed to Sarah Ferguson in 1986.

Melrose and around

Tucked in between the Tweed and the Eildon Hills, minuscule **MELROSE** is the most beguiling of towns, its narrow streets trimmed by a harmonious ensemble of styles, from pretty little cottages and tweedy shops to high-standing Georgian and Victorian facades. At the foot of the town the pink- and ochre-tinted stone ruins of **Melrose Abbey** (April–Sept Mon–Sat 9.30am–6pm, Sun 2–6pm; Oct–March Mon–Sat 9.30am–4pm, Sun 2–4pm; £2.50) soar above their riverside surroundings. The abbey, founded in 1136 by David I, grew rich selling wool and hides to Flanders, but its prosperity was fragile: the English repeatedly razed Melrose, most viciously under Richard II in 1385 and the Earl of Hertford in 1545. Most of the present remains date from the intervening period, when extensive rebuilding abandoned the original austerity for an elaborate, Gothic style inspired by the abbeys of northern England.

The site is dominated by the **Abbey Church**, where the elegant window arches of the nave approach the **monk's choir**, whose grand piers are disfigured by the masonry of a later parish church. The adjacent **presbytery** is better preserved, its dignified lines illuminated by a magnificent Perpendicular window. Legend has it that the heart of Robert the Bruce is buried here beneath the window, although the dying king actually told his friend, James Douglas, to carry his heart on a Crusade to the Holy Land. Douglas tried his best, but was killed fighting the Moors in Spain – and Bruce's heart ended up in Melrose. In the **south transept**, another fine fifteenth-century window sprouts yet more delicate, foliate tracery and the adjacent cornice is enlivened by angels playing musical instruments. Outside, all sorts of **gargoyles** humour the majestic lines of the church from peculiar crouching beasts to a pig playing the bagpipes on the south side of the nave.

The fragmentary ruins of the old monastic buildings edge the church and lead across to the **Commendator's House** (same times as the abbey), which displays a modest collection of ecclesiastical bric-a-brac in the house of the abbey's sixteenth-century lay administrators. Next door to the abbey in the opposite direction is the delightful **Priorwood Garden** (April–Dec Mon–Sat 10am–5.30pm, Sun 1.30–5.30pm; free), whose walled precincts, owned by the NTS, are given over to flowers that are suitable for drying – there's a dried flower shop too. Melrose's other museum, the **Trimontium Exhibition**, just off Market Square (April–Oct daily 10.30am–4.30pm; £1), is a modest affair, with dioramas, models and the odd archeological find outlining the three Roman occupations of the region.

Buses to Melrose stop in Market Square, a brief walk from the **tourist office** (April–Oct Mon–Sat 10am–5pm, Sun 2–5pm; slightly longer hours at the height of summer; ☎01896/822555). Melrose has a clutch of **hotels**, including the smart and tidy *Burts Hotel* on Market Square (☎01896/822285; ⑦), the neat, ten-bedroom *Bon Accord* (☎01896/822645; ⑧) just across the street, and the far less expensive *Station Hotel* (☎01896/822038; ③) up the hill from Market Square. It's among Melrose's **B&Bs**, however, that you'll get the real flavour of the place, most notably at *Braidwood*, Buccleuch St (☎01896/822488; ③), and *Dunfermline House* (☎01896/822148; ③) opposite. The town also has a **youth hostel** (☎01896/822521), occupying a Victorian villa overlooking the abbey from beside the access road into the bypass. The *Gibson Caravan Park* (☎01896/822969), off High Street, is a few minutes' walk west of the square.

Some of the B&Bs serve reasonably priced **dinner** on request, but if you venture forth, *Marmion's Brasserie*, Buccleuch Street, offers well-prepared meals from an imaginative menu. Alternatively, the formal *Melrose Station*, in the old train station above the square, has a good range of daily specials featuring local produce. Back on Market Square, *Pyemont & Company* has good coffee and snacks; while the busy *Burts Hotel* has excellent bar meals, although their attitude to backpackers can be a bit snooty. No such restrictions exist at *Haldane's Fish & Chip Shop* (closed Wed), just off the square, or at the nearby *Ship Inn*, the liveliest pub in town.

Dryburgh Abbey

Hidden away on a bend in the Tweed a few miles east of Melrose, the remains of **Dryburgh Abbey** (April–Sept Mon–Sat 9.30am–6pm, Sun 2–6pm; Oct–March Mon–Sat 9.30am–4pm, Sun 2–4pm; £2) occupy a superb position against a hilly backdrop. The Premonstratensians founded the abbey in the twelfth century, but they were never as successful as their Cistercian neighbours in Melrose. The abbey, demolished and rebuilt on several occasions, incorporates several architectural styles, beginning in the shattered **Church** where the clumsy decoration of the main entrance contrasts with the spirited dog-tooth motif around the east processional doorway. The latter leads through to the **monastic buildings**, a two-storey ensemble that provides an insight into the lives of the monks. Bits and pieces of several rooms have survived, but the real highlight is the barrel-vaulted **Chapter House**, complete with low stone benches, grouped windows and carved arcade. The room was used by the monks for the daily reading of a chapter from either the Bible or their rule book, and was, as they prospered, draped with expensive hangings. Finally, back in the church, the battered north transept contains the grave of **Sir Walter Scott**; close by lies Field Marshal Haig, the World War I commander whose ineptitude cost thousands of soldiers' lives.

SIR WALTER SCOTT

Walter Scott (1771–1832) was born in Edinburgh to a solidly bourgeois family whose roots were in Selkirkshire. As a child he was left lame by polio and his anxious parents sent him to recuperate at his grandfather's farm in Smailholm, where the boy's imagination was fired by his relatives' tales of derring-do, the violent history of the Borders retold amidst a rugged landscape that he spent long summer days exploring. Scott returned to Edinburgh to resume his education and take up a career in law, but his real interests remained elsewhere. Throughout the 1790s he transcribed hundreds of old Border ballads, publishing a three-volume collection entitled *Minstrelsy of the Scottish Borders* in 1802. An instant success, *Minstrelsy* was followed by Scott's own *Lay of the Last Minstrel*, a narrative poem whose strong story and rose-tinted regionalism proved very popular.

More poetry was to come, most successfully *Marmion* (1808) and *The Lady of the Lake* (1810), not to mention an eighteen-volume edition of the works of John Dryden and nineteen volumes of Jonathan Swift. However, despite having two paid jobs, one as the Sheriff-Depute of Selkirkshire, the other as clerk to the Court of Session in Edinburgh, his finances remained shaky. He had become a partner in a printing firm, which put him deeply into debt, not helped by the enormous sums he spent on his mansion, Abbotsford. From 1813, Scott was writing to pay the bills and thumped out a veritable flood of historical novels using his extensive knowledge of Scottish history and folklore. He produced his best work within the space of ten years: *Waverley* (1814), *The Antiquary* (1816), *Rob Roy* and the *The Heart of Midlothian* (both 1818) and, after he had exhausted his own country, two notable novels set in England, *Ivanhoe* (1819) and *Kenilworth* (1821). In 1824 he returned to Scottish tales with *Redgauntlet*, the last of his quality work.

A year later Scott's money problems reached crisis proportions after an economic crash bankrupted his printing business. Attempting to pay his creditors in full, he found the quality of his writing deteriorating with its increased speed and the effort broke his health. His last years were plagued by illness and in 1832 he died at Abbotsford and was buried within the ruins of Dryburgh Abbey.

Although Scott's interests were diverse, his historical novels mostly focused on the Jacobites, whose loyalty to the Stuarts had riven Scotland since the "Glorious Revolution" of 1688. That the nation was prepared to be entertained by such tales was essentially a matter of timing: by the 1760s it was clear the Jacobite cause was lost for good and Scotland, emerging from its isolated medievalism, had been firmly welded into the United Kingdom. Thus its turbulent history and independent spirit was safely in the past, and ripe for romancing – as shown by the arrival of King George IV in Edinburgh during 1822 decked out in Highland dress. Yet, for Sir Walter the romance was tinged with a genuine sense of loss. Loyal to the Hanoverians, he still grieved for Bonnie Prince Charlie; he welcomed a commercial Scotland but lamented the passing of feudal ties; and so his heroes are transitional, fighting men of action superseded by bourgeois figures searching for a clear identity.

Although today many of Scott's works are out of print, Edinburgh University Press has recently begun a long-term project to issue proper critical editions of the Waverley novels for the first time, correcting hitherto heavily corrupted texts and restoring passages and endings that had been altered – often drastically – by the original publishers.

To get to the abbey from Melrose, take the Jedburgh **bus** (Mon–Sat hourly, 5 on Sun; 10min) as far as St Boswells, and walk the last mile; the four-seater **postbus** (Mon–Fri 1 daily; 25min) is direct, but this doesn't make a return trip.

Smailholm Tower

Driving is the only way to reach the fifteenth-century **Smailholm Tower** (April–Sept Mon–Sat 9.30am–6pm, Sun 2–6pm; £1.50) perched on a rocky outcrop a few miles east of Dryburgh. A remote and evocative fastness recalling Reivers' raids and border skirmishes, the tower was designed to withstand sudden attack: the rough rubble walls average six feet thick and both the entrance – once guarded by a heavy door plus an iron yett (gate) – and the windows are disproportionately small. These were necessary precautions. On both sides of the border clans were engaged in endless feuds, a violent history that stirred the imagination of Walter Scott, who was but a "wee, sick laddie" when he was brought here to live in 1773. Inside, ignore the inept costumed models and press on up to the roof, where two narrow **wall-walks**, jammed against the barrel-vaulted roof and the crow-stepped gables, provide panoramic views.

Mellerstain House

Mellerstain House (May, June & Sept Wed, Fri & Sun 12.30–4.30pm; July & Aug daily except Sat 12.30–4.30pm; £3.50), four miles east of Smailholm, represents the very best of the Adams' work: William designed the wings in 1725, and his son Robert the castellated centre fifty years later. Robert's love of columns, roundels and friezes culminates in a stunning sequence of plaster-moulded, plastel-shaded ceilings, from the looping symmetry of the library ceiling, adorned by medallion oil paintings of *Learning* and *Reading* on either side of *Minerva*, to the whimsical griffin and vase pattern in the drawing room. It takes about an hour to tour the house; afterwards you can wander the formal Edwardian gardens, which slope down towards the lake.

Abbotsford House

Abbotsford House (mid-March to Oct Mon–Sat 10am–5pm, Sun 2–5pm; £3), three miles west of Melrose, was designed to satisfy the Romantic inclinations of Sir Walter Scott, who lived here from 1812 until his death twenty years later. Abbotsford took 12 years to evolve with the fanciful turrets and castellations of the Scots Baronial exterior incorporating copies of medieval originals: thus the entrance porch imitates that of Linlithgow Palace and the screen wall in the garden echoes Melrose Abbey's cloister. Inside, visitors start in the wood-panelled study, with its small writing desk made of salvage from the Spanish Armada. The library boasts an extraordinary assortment of Scottish memorabilia, including a lock of Bonnie Prince Charlie's hair, Flora Macdonald's pocket book, the inlaid pearl crucifix that accompanied Mary, Queen of Scots to the scaffold, and even a piece of oatcake found in the pocket of a dead Highlander at Culloden. You can also see Henry Raeburn's famous portrait of Scott hanging in the drawing room and all sorts of weapons, notably Rob Roy's sword, dagger and gun, in the armoury. To get to the house, take the fast and frequent Melrose–Galashiels bus.

Traquair and Peebles

Six miles before you reach Peebles, a mile or so south of the main road near the village of Innerleithen, **Traquair House** (daily mid-April to June & Sept 12.30–5.30pm; July & Aug 10.30am–5.30pm; £3.75) is the oldest continuously inhabited house in Scotland, with the present owners – the Maxwell Stuarts – living here since 1491. Persistently Catholic, the family paid for their principles: Protestant mill workers repeatedly attacked their property, and by 1800 little remained of the family's once enormous estates.

Nevertheless, the house has kept many of its oldest features, including the original vaulted cellars, where locals once hid their cattle from raiders; the twisting main staircase as well as the earlier medieval version, later a secret escape route for persecuted Catholics; and even a **Priest's Room** where a string of resident chaplains lived in hiding until the Catholic Emancipation Act freed things up in 1829. In the **Museum Room** there are several fine examples of Jacobite or **Amen glass**, inscribed with pictures of the Bonnie Prince or verses in his honour; and the cloak worn by the fourth earl during his dramatic escape from the Tower of London. Under sentence of death for his part in the Jacobite Rising of 1715, the earl was saved by his wife, Lady Winifred Herbert, who got his jailers drunk and smuggled him out disguised as a maid. It's worth sparing time for the surrounding gardens where you'll find a maze, several craft workshops and a working brewery, whose products are on sale at the tea room.

Straddling the Tweed, **PEEBLES** has a genteel, relaxing air, its wide High Street bordered by a complementary medley of architectural styles, mostly dating from Victorian times. A stroll around town should include a visit to the **Tweeddale Museum** (April–Sept Mon–Fri 10am–1pm & 2–5pm, Sat & Sun 2–5pm; Oct–March Mon–Fri only; free), housed in the Chambers Institute on High Street. William Chambers, a local worthy, presented the building to the town in 1859, complete with an art gallery dedicated to the enlightenment of his neighbours. He stuffed the place with casts of the world's most famous sculptures, and, although most were lost long ago, today's "Secret Room", once the Museum Room, boasts two handsome friezes: one a copy of the Elgin marbles taken from the Parthenon; the other of the Triumph of Alexander, originally cast in 1812 to honour Napoleon.

Buses to Peebles stop outside the post office, a few doors down the High Street from the well-stocked **tourist office** (April–Oct Mon–Sat 10am–5pm, Sun 10am–2pm; longer hours in peak season; Nov & Dec closed Sun; ☎01721/720138). Of the many **B&Bs**, try *Rowanbrae*, on Northgate, off the High Street (☎01721/721630; ③); the *Minniebank Guest House*, Greenside (☎01721/722093; ④), by the main bridge; or *Viewfield*, 1 Rosetta Rd (☎01721/721232; ②), west of the bridge. The best of the more upmarket **hotels** is *The Park Hotel*, on Innerleithen Road (☎01721/720451; ⑧), followed by the relaxing *Kingsmuir Hotel*, south of the river on Springhill Road (☎01721/720151; ⑦). For **camping**, the *Rosetta Caravan and Camping Park* (April–Oct; ☎01721/720770) is fifteen minutes' walk north of the High Street. For **food**, the *Crown Hotel*, High Street, features good daily specials, and the *Kingsmuir Hotel*, Springhill Road, has more expensive but excellent bar meals.

Jedburgh and Hermitage Castle

JEDBURGH nestles in the valley of the Jed Water near its confluence with the Teviot out on the edge of the wild Cheviot Hills. During the interminable Anglo-Scottish Wars, it was the quintessential frontier town, a heavily garrisoned royal burgh incorporating a mighty castle and abbey. Though the Castle was destroyed by the Scots in 1409, to keep it out of the hands of the English, its memory has been kept alive by local folklore: in 1285, for example, King Alexander III was celebrating his wedding feast in the Great Hall when a ghostly apparition predicted his untimely death and a bloody civil war; sure enough, he died in a hunting accident shortly afterwards and chaos ensued. Today the ruined abbey is the main event, though a stroll round Jedburgh's old town centre is a pleasant way to wile away an hour or two.

The remains of **Jedburgh Abbey** (April–Sept Mon–Sat 9.30am–6pm, Sun 2–6pm; Oct–March Mon–Sat 9.30am–4pm, Sun 2–4pm; £2.50), right in the centre of town, date from the twelfth century. Benefiting from King David's patronage, the monks developed an extravagant complex on a sloping site next to the Jed Water, the monastic buildings standing beneath a huge red sandstone church. All went well until the late thirteenth century, when the power of the Scots kings waned following the death of Alexander III and the prolonged civil war that ensued. The abbey was subsequently burnt and badly damaged on a number of occasions, the worst being inflicted by the English in 1544. The canons gamely repaired their buildings, but were unable to resist the Reformation and the monastery closed in 1560.

Entry to the site is through the **visitor centre**, beside which are the scant remains of the cloister buildings; the **Abbey Church**, which remained a parish kirk for another three centuries after the Dissolution, has survived particularly well preserved. It's best entered from the west through a weathered Norman doorway with gables, arcading and ornamented windows. Behind the doorway lies the splendidly proportioned three-storeyed nave, a fine example of the transition from Norman to Gothic design, with pointed window arches surmounted by the round-headed arches of the triforium, which, in turn, support the lancet windows of the clerestory. This delicacy of form is not matched at the east end, where the squat central tower is underpinned by the monumental circular pillars and truncated arches of the earlier, twelfth-century choir.

It's a couple of minutes' walk from the abbey round to the tiny triangular **Market Place**. Up the hill from here, at the top of Castlegate, **Jedburgh Castle Jail and Museum** (closed for refurbishment until late 1996) will exhibit displays on prison life throughout the ages. Finally, **Mary, Queen of Scots' House** (March to mid-Nov daily 10am–4.30pm; £1.50), situated at the opposite end of the town centre, is something of a misnomer: it's true that Mary stayed here in this bastle house during the assizes of 1566, but she didn't stay long and there's little on show connected with her visit. The attempt to unravel her complex life is cursory, the redeeming features being a copy of Mary's death mask and one of the few surviving portraits of the Earl of Bothwell.

Practicalities

Jedburgh's **bus station** is a few yards from the abbey, and the **tourist office** (April–Oct Mon–Sat 10am–5pm, Sun 12–4pm; longer hours in peak season; Nov–March closed Sat & Sun; ☎01835/863435) lies on Murray's Green. For **accommodation**, try *Kenmore Bank Guest House*, Oxnam Rd (☎01835/862369; ⑥), overlooking the Jed Water south of the abbey; the *Glenbank Country House Hotel*, Castlegate (☎01835/862258; ⑥); or the *Glenfriars Hotel*, The Friars (☎01835/862000; ⑥), a big old house in its own grounds near the north end of High Street. Alternatively, there are several **B&Bs** among the pleasant and antique row houses of Castlegate, notably *Mrs Bathgate*, no. 64 (April–Oct; ☎01835/862466; ②) and *Mrs Poloczek*, no. 48 (☎01835/862504; ④). The *Elliot Park* caravan and **campsite** (March–Sept; ☎01835/863393) is beside the Edinburgh road about a mile north of the centre. Considering its heavy tourist trade, Jedburgh has surprisingly few **restaurants** – stick to the *Castlegate Restaurant*, 26 Castlegate.

JEDBURGH FESTIVALS

Jedburgh is at its busiest during the town's two main **festivals**. The Common Riding, or **Callants' Festival**, takes place in the first two weeks of July, when the young people of the town – especially the lads – mount up and ride out to check the burgh boundaries, a reminder of more troubled days when Jedburgh was subject to English raids. In similar spirit, early February sees the day-long **Jedburgh Hand Ba'** game, an all-male affair between the "uppies" (those born above Market Place) and "downies" (those born below). In theory the aim of the game is to get hay-stuffed leather balls – originally the heads of English men – from one end of town to the other, but there's more at stake than that: macho reputations are made and lost during the two, two-hour games.

Liddesdale

Heading south out of Jedburgh on the A68, it's about a mile to the B6357, a narrow byroad that leads over the moors to the hamlet of Bonchester Bridge. From here, the road cuts south through Wauchope Forest and carries on into **Liddesdale**, whose wild beauty is at its most striking between Saughtree and Newcastleton. In between the two, take the turning to **Hermitage Castle** (April–Sept Mon–Sat 9.30am–6pm, Sun 2–6pm; Oct–March Sat 9.30am–4pm, Sun 2–4pm; £1.20), a bleak and forbidding fastness bedevilled by all sorts of horrifying legends: one owner, William Douglas, starved his prisoners to death, whilst Lord de Soulis, another occupant, engaged the help of demons to fortify the castle in defiance of the king, Robert the Bruce. Not entirely trusting his demonic assistants, Soulis also drilled holes into the shoulders of his vassals, the better to yoke them to sledges of building materials. Bruce became so tired of the complaints that he exclaimed, "Boil him if you please, but let me hear no more of him". Bruce's henchmen took him at his word and ambushed the rebellious baron. Convinced, however, that Soulis would be difficult to kill, they bound him with ropes of sifted sand, wrapped Soulis in lead and boiled him slowly. From the outside, the castle remains an imposing structure, its heavy walls topped by stepped gables and a tidy corbelled parapet. However, the apparent homogeneity is deceptive: certain features were invented during a Victorian restoration, a confusing supplement to the ad hoc alterations that had already transformed the fourteenth-century original. The ruinous interior is a bit of a letdown, but look out for the tight Gothic doorways and gruesome dungeon.

Dumfries and around

With a population of 30,000, bustling **DUMFRIES** crowds the banks of the River Nith a few miles from the Solway Firth, the shallow estuary on the west coast, wedged between Scotland and England. Long known as the "Queen of the South", the town flourished as a medieval seaport and trading centre, its success attracting the attention of many English armies. The invaders managed to polish off most of the early settlement in 1448, 1536 and again in 1570, but Dumfries survived to prosper with its light industries supplying the agricultural hinterland. The town planners of the 1960s badly damaged the town, though it makes a convenient base for exploring the Solway coast, and is at least worth a visit for its associations with Robert Burns.

Hemmed in by the river to the north and west, the snout-shaped centre of Dumfries radiates out from the pedestrianized **High Street**, which runs roughly parallel to the Nith. At its northern edge is the **Burns Statue**, a fanciful piece of Victorian frippery featuring the great man holding a poesy in one hand, whilst the other clutches at his heart. They haven't forgotten his faithful hound either, who lies curled around his feet.

Heading south down High Street, it's a couple of minutes' walk to **Midsteeple**, the old prison-cum-courthouse, and the narrow alley that leads to the smoky, oak-panelled *Globe Inn*, one of Burns' favourite drinking spots, and still a tavern. Continuing down the street, follow the signs to the **Burns' House** (Easter–Sept Mon–Sat 10am–1pm & 2–5pm, Sun 2–5pm; Oct–Easter closed Sun & Mon; 80p), a simple sandstone building where the poet died of rheumatic heart disease in 1796. Inside, there's an incidental collection of Burns' memorabilia – manuscripts, letters and the like – and one of the bedroom windows bears his signature, scratched with his diamond ring.

Burns was buried in a simple grave beside **St Michael's Church**, a monstrous eighteenth-century heap just south of his house. Just twenty years later, though, he was dug up and moved across the graveyard to a purpose-built Neoclassical **Mausoleum**, whose bright white columns hide a statue of Burns being accosted by the Poetic Muse. The subject matter may be mawkish, but the execution is excellent –

notice the hang of the bonnet and the twist of the trousers. All around, in contrasting brownstone, stand the tombstones of the town's bourgeoisie, including many of the poet's friends; a plan indicates exactly where each is interred.

From the mausoleum, saunter back along the Nith and cross Devorguilla Bridge to the tiny **Old Bridge House Museum** (April–Sept Mon–Sat 10am–1pm & 2–5pm, Sun 2–5pm; free) of local bric-a-brac – including a teeth-chattering range of Victorian dental gear – and the **Robert Burns Centre** (April–Sept Mon–Sat 10am–8pm, Sun 2–5pm; Oct–March Tues–Sat 10am–1pm & 2–5pm; free but video 80p), sited in an old water mill, which concentrates on the poet's years in Dumfries. On the hill above, occupying an eighteenth-century windmill, the **Dumfries Museum** (April–Sept Mon–Sat 10am–1pm & 2–5pm, Sun 2–5pm; Oct–March closed Sun & Mon; free) traces the region's natural and human history and features a camera obscura on its top floor (April–Sept only; 80p).

Practicalities

Dumfries **train station**, on the east side of town, is a five-minute walk from the centre. The **bus station** stands beside the River Nith on the west edge of the centre, next to the **tourist office** (April, May & Oct daily 10am–5pm; June–Sept daily 9.30am–6pm; Nov–March Mon–Sat 10am–4.30pm & 2–5pm; ☎01387/253862).

There are lots of **guest houses** and **B&Bs** in the handsome villas clustered round the train station, including *Morton Villa*, 28 Lovers Walk (☎01387/255825; ②), *Lindean*, 50 Rae St (☎01387/251888; ③) and *Redlands Guest House*, 54 Rae St (☎01387/268382; ③). For a more distinctive setting try *The Haven*, 1 Kenmure Terrace (☎10387/251281; ③), overlooking the Nith from beside the footbridge below the Burns Centre. If you're looking for a **hotel**, head for Laurieknowe, west of the bus station, where you'll find the *Edenbank Hotel* (☎01387/252759; ⑤). *Grierson and Graham*, 10 Academy St (☎01387/259483), offer **bike rental**, useful for reaching the nearby Solway coast.

The cheapest **meals** in town are provided by the popular *YMCA* café *Grapevine*, Castle St (Mon–Fri 10am–3pm, Sat 10am–2.30pm), behind and beyond the Burns Statue. The *Hole in the Wa'* **pub**, down an alley opposite *Woolworth's* on High Street, sells reasonable bar food. If you want a pub with more atmosphere, however, you should make your way instead to the earthy *Globe Inn*.

Caerlaverock and Ruthwell

The remote and lichen-stained **Caerlaverock Castle**, eight miles southeast of Dumfries (April–Sept Mon–Sat 9.30am–6pm, Sun 2–6pm; Oct–March Mon–Sat 9.30am–4pm, Sun 2–4pm; £2), forms a dramatic triangle with a mighty gatehouse at the apex. Nowadays, close inspection reveals several phases of construction, which reflect Caerlaverock's turbulent past: time and again, the castle was attacked and slighted, each subsequent rebuilding further modifying the late thirteenth-century original. For instance, the fifteenth-century machicolations of the gatehouse top earlier towers that are themselves studded with wide-mouthed gunports from around 1590. This confusion of styles continues inside, where the gracious Renaissance facade of the **Nithsdale Apartments** was added by the first earl in 1634. Nithsdale didn't get much value for money: just six years later he was forced to surrender his castle to the Covenanters, who proceeded to wreck the place. It was never inhabited again.

From the castle it's about three miles further to the **Caerlaverock Wildfowl and Wetlands Centre** (daily 10am–5pm; £3; ☎01387/770200), 1400 acres of protected salt marsh and mud flat edging the Solway Firth. A National Nature Reserve and a Wildfowl and Wetlands Trust Refuge, the centre is equipped with screened approaches that link the main observatory to a score of well-situated birdwatchers' hides. It's famous for the 12,000 or so Barnacle Geese which return here in winter. Between May and August, when the geese are away, walkers along a wetlands trail may glimpse the rare natterjack toad. Both the castle and the centre are reached along the B725; this is the route the bus takes, mostly terminating at the castle but sometimes continuing to the start of the two-mile lane leading off the B725 to the centre.

From the nature reserve it's about seven miles east along the B725 to both the village of **RUTHWELL** and the B724, the minor Dumfries–Annan road which trims its northern edge. Here you should turn down the short, signposted lane to the modest country church. The keys are kept at one of the houses at the foot of the lane; just look for the notice. Inside the church is the **Ruthwell Cross**, an extraordinary early Christian monument dating from the late seventh century when Galloway was ruled by the Northumbrians. The eighteen-foot-high Cross reveals a striking diversity of influences, with Germanic and Roman Catholic decoration and, running round the edge, a poem written in both runic figures and Northumbrian dialect. But it's the Biblical carvings on the main face that really catch the eye, notably Mary Magdalene washing the feet of Jesus.

Nithsdale

North of Dumfries the A76 strips along the southern reaches of **Nithsdale**, whose gentle slopes and old forests hide one major attraction, the massive, many turreted seventeenth-century mansion of **Drumlanrig Castle**. (house May to mid-June Mon–Wed & Fri 1–5pm, Sat & Sun 11am–5pm; mid-June to Aug daily except Thurs 11am–5pm; park May to mid-Sept daily 11am–6pm; £4), not in fact a castle at all, but the grandiose stately home of the Duke of Buccleuch and Queensberry. Drumlanrig, which has an imperial, pink-sandstone facade, with cupolas, turrets and towers surrounding an interior courtyard, is graced by a charming horseshoe-shaped stairway – a welcome touch of informality to the stateliness of the structure behind.

Inside, a string of luxurious rooms attests to the immense wealth of the family. Among the priceless hoard of antique furnishings and fittings are a trio of famous paintings exhibited in the **staircase hall**. These are Rembrandt's *Old Woman Reading*, a sensual composition dappling the shadow of the subject's hood against her white surplice, Holbein's formal portrait of *Sir Nicholas Carew*, and the *Madonna with the Yarnwinder* by Leonardo da Vinci. Other works are by Breughel, Grossaert and Van Dyck, and there are endless family portraits by Allan Ramsay and Godfrey Kneller. Also look out for John Ainslie's *Joseph Florence the Chef*, a sharply observed and dynamic portrait much liked by Walter Scott. If you're heading here by bus from Dumfries or Ayr, bear in mind it's a one-and-a-half-mile walk from the road to the house.

Sweetheart Abbey

NEW ABBEY, a tidy hamlet eight miles south of Dumfries, is home to the red-sandstone ruins of **Sweetheart Abbey** (April–Sept Mon–Sat 9.30am–6pm, Sun 2–6pm; Oct–March Mon–Wed 9.30am–4pm, Thurs 9.30am–12.30pm, Sat 9.30am–4pm, Sun 2–4pm; £1.50). Founded by Cistercians in 1273, Sweetheart takes its name from the obsessive behaviour of its patron, Devorguilla de Balliol, who carried her husband's embalmed heart around with her for the last sixteen years of her life. The site is dominated by the remains of the Abbey Church, a massive structure that abandons the austere simplicity of earlier Cistercian foundations. The grand, high-pointed window arches of the nave, set beneath the elaborate clerestory, draw the eye to a mighty central tower with a battlemented parapet and flamboyant corbels. The opulent style reflects the monks' wealth, born of their skill in turning the wastes and swamps of Solway into productive farmland. After the abbey, pop into the **Abbey Cottage** tea-rooms next door for a great cup of coffee and a piece of homemade cake.

Along the Solway coast

Edged by tidal marsh and mud bank, much of the **Solway coast** is flat and eerily remote, but there are also some fine rocky bays sheltering beneath wooded hills, most notably at **Rockcliffe**, about twenty miles west of Dumfries. **Kirkcudbright** and **Gatehouse of Fleet**, once bustling ports, were bypassed by the Victorian train network and so slipped into economic decline which in effect preserved their handsome eighteenth- and early nineteenth-century architecture. Both towns are popular with – but not crowded by – tourists, as is **Threave Castle**, a gaunt tower house perched on an islet just outside Castle Douglas. Within striking distance of the coast are the **Galloway Hills**, whose forested knolls and grassy peaks flank lochs and tumbling burns – classic Southern Upland scenery.

Castle Douglas and around

The eighteenth-century streets of **CASTLE DOUGLAS** were designed by the town's owner, William Douglas, a local lad who made a fortune trading in the West Indies. Douglas had ambitious plans to turn his town into a prosperous industrial and commercial centre, but, like his scheme to create an extensive Galloway canal system, it didn't quite work. You'll only need to hang around town long enough to get your bearings as the district's two attractions are well outside the centre. The **bus station** is at the west end of the long main drag, King Street; the **tourist office** (April–Oct daily 9am–5pm; ☎05156/502611) is at the other end; **bike** rental is available at *Ace Cycles*, 11 Church St (☎01556/504542).

It's about a mile's walk west to **Threave Garden** (daily 9.30am–sunset; £3.50), which can also be reached direct from the A75 – the signposted turning is at the roundabout on the west side of town. The garden features a magnificent spread of flowers and woodland, sixty acres sub-divided into over a dozen areas, from the bright, old-fashioned blooms of the Rose Garden to the brilliant banks of rhododendrons in the Woodland Garden and the ranks of primula, astilbe and gentian in the Peat Garden. The **visitor centre** (April to late Oct daily 9.30am–5.30pm) has maps of the garden and the surrounding estate (also NTS property) and a useful restaurant.

To reach **Threave Castle** (April–Sept Mon–Sat 9am–6pm, Sun 2–6pm; £1.50), return to the A75 roundabout and cut straight across, down the mile-long country lane which brings you to the start of the footpath to the River Dee. It's a ten-minute walk down to the river where you ring a brass bell for the boat over to the less stern-looking stronghold, stuck on a flat and grassy islet. Built for a Black Douglas, Archibald the Grim, in around 1370, the fortress was among the first of its kind, a sturdy, rectangular structure completed shortly after the War of Independence when clan feuding spurred a frenzy of castle-building. The bleak lines of the original structure are, however, partly obscured by a ricketty, fifteenth-century curtain wall, thrown up as a desperate – and unsuccessful – attempt to defend the castle against James II. Determined to crush the Black Douglases, the king personally murdered the eighth earl after dinner in Stirling and subsequently appropriated his estate. The Covenanters wrecked the place in the 1640s, but enough remains of the interior to make out its general plan.

Rockcliffe

The **Colvend coast** is a six-mile-long, low-key holiday strip, eleven miles southeast of Castle Douglas. In the middle, nestling round a beautiful cove, is **ROCKCLIFFE**, a beguiling little place from where there are some great walks. At low tide you can waddle out across the mud flats to **Rough Island**, a humpy twenty-acre bird sanctuary owned by the NTS, though it's out of bounds in May and June when the Terns and Oyster Catchers are nesting. Alternatively, you can stroll up the coast along the "Jubilee Path" a mile or so to the **Mote of Mark**, a Celtic hill fort, and continue a few miles to the village of **Kippford**, once a ship-repair centre, and now a cosy holiday spot strung out along an estuary. Rockcliffe has a reasonable range of **accommodation**, but note that reservations are recommended during the summer. The only **hotel**, the grand Victorian *Barons Craig* (April–Oct; ☎01556/660225; ⑧), sits on the hill above the bay; the attractive *Albany* **B&B** (☎01556/630355; ③) is situated right on the seafront.

Kirkcudbright

KIRKCUDBRIGHT (pronounced "Kirkcoobrie"), hugging the muddy banks of the Dee ten miles southwest of Castle Douglas, has a quaint harbour and most beguiling of town centres, a charming medley of simple brick cottages with medieval pends, Georgian villas and Victorian town houses. This is the setting for **MacLellan's Castle** (April–Sept Mon–Sat 9.30am–6pm, Sun 2–6pm; Oct–March Sat 9.30am–4pm, Sun 2–4pm; £1) a sullen pink-flecked hulk towering above the harbourside. Part fortified tower house and part spacious mansion, the castle dates from the late sixteenth century when a degree of law and order permittted the aristocracy to relax its old defensive preoccupations. As a consequence, chimneys have replaced battlements at the wall-heads and windows begin at the ground floor, Keep an eye out for a real curiosity, the laird's lug, or peephole, behind the fireplace of the Great Hall. The castle was built for Sir Thomas MacLellan, who now lies buried in the neighbouring **Greyfriars Church** (daily 9am–5pm; free), where his tomb is an eccentrically crude attempt at Neoclassicism – it even incorporates parts of someone else's gravestone.

Close by, on the L-shaped High Street, **Broughton House** (April to mid-Oct daily 1–5.30pm; £2) was once the home of Edward Hornel, an important member of the late nineteenth-century Scottish art establishment. Hornel and his buddies – The Glasgow Boys – established a self-regarding artists' colony in Kirkcudbright, and some of their work, impressionistic in style, is on display here. It's all pretty modest stuff, but Hornel's paintings of Japan, a country he often visited, are bright and cheery, and the house itself a delight. Hornel had the Georgian manison he bought in 1901 modified to include a studio and a mahogany-panelled gallery decked out with a frieze of the Elgin marbles. He also designed the lovely Japanese garden.

A couple of minutes's walk away is the church-like **Tolbooth**, which once served as court house, prison and town hall. Its clock faces are offset so that they can be viewed down both parts of the High Street. Recently the building has been turned into the **Tolbooth Art Centre** (March–May & Oct Mon–Sat 11am–4pm; June–Sept Mon–Sat 11am–5pm & Sun 2–5pm; Nov–Feb Sat 11am–4pm only; £1.50), featuring more examples of the work of Hornel and his associates, plus a video on the group. Don't miss the **Stewartry Museum** on St Mary St (March, April & Oct daily 11am–4pm; May Mon–Sat 11am–5pm; June–Sept Mon–Sat 11am–5pm, Sun 2–5pm; Nov–Feb Sat only 11am–4pm; £1.50), which houses an extraordinary collection of local exhibits illuminating the life and times of the Solway Coast.

Practicalities

Buses to Kirkcudbright stop by the harbour, next to the **tourist office** (daily April–June, Sept & Oct daily 10am–5pm; July & Aug 10am–6pm; ☎01557/330494). The town has several quality **hotels** – the best among them the Georgian *Gladstone House*, 48 High St (☎01557/331734; ⑤), and the eighteenth-century *Selkirk Arms*, just up the road (☎01557/330402; ⑦). For a convenient **B&B**, walk over to Castle Street where there's the *Castle Guest House*, no. 16 (Feb–Nov; ☎01557/330204; ③), or stick to the High Street for both *Mrs Grant*, no. 82 (☎01557/330197; ③) and *Mrs Durok*, no. 109A

(☎01557/331279; ②). For **camping**, *Silvercraigs Caravan and Camping Site* (Easter to late Oct; ☎01557/330123) is on a bluff overlooking town at the end of St Mary's Place, five to ten minutes' walk from the centre. **Bikes** can be rented from *Tolbooth Crafts*, St Mary St (no phone). Kirkcudbright is light on **restaurants**, though the *Selkirk Arms* serves excellent bar meals. The *Auld Alliance*, 5 Castle St (☎01557/330569), is a superior, if pricy, restaurant offering an imaginative mixture of French and Scottish cuisine.

Gatehouse of Fleet

The quiet streets of **GATEHOUSE OF FLEET**, ten miles east of Kirkcudbright, give no clue that for James Murray, the eighteenth-century laird, this spot was to become the "Glasgow" of the Solway Coast – a centre of the cotton industry whose profits had already made him immeasurably rich. Yorkshire mill owners provided the industrial expertise, imported engineers designed aqueducts to improve the water supply, and dispossessed crofters – and their children – yielded the labour. Between 1760 and 1790, Murray achieved much success, but his custom-built town failed to match its better placed rivals. By 1850 the boom was over, the mills slipped into disrepair, and nowadays tiny Gatehouse is sustained by tourism and forestry.

It's the country setting that appeals rather than any particular sight, but there are some graceful Georgian houses along High Street, which also has an incongruous, granite clock tower and the **Mill on the Fleet Museum** (April–Oct daily 10am–5.30pm; £2.75), gallantly tracing the history of Gatehouse and Galloway from inside an old bobbin mill. The **tourist office** nearby (April–Oct daily 10am–5pm; ☎01557/814212) sells an excellent leaflet on local **walks**. One of them tracks along Old Military Road, passing through deciduous woodland before circling back near the stark remains of **Cardoness Castle** (April–Sept Mon–Sat 9.30am–6pm, Sun 2–6pm; Oct–March Sat 9.30am–4pm, Sun 2–4pm; £1.20). Perched on a hill, this late fifteenth-century stronghold is a classic example of the fortified tower house, with dense walls and tiny windows.

Accommodation in Gatehouse includes the *Murray Arms Hotel* (☎01557/814207; ⑨), close to the clock tower; and some more affordable and convenient **B&Bs**, such as *Mrs Carlisle*, 29 Fleet St (☎01557/814647; ③) and the *Bay Horse B&B*, 9 Ann St (☎01557/814073; ④). The *Angel Hotel* (☎01557/814516) on the main street near the tourist office, provides simple accommodation for ramblers and backpackers from £7.50 per person per night. You can grab a snack at the museum, and the *Murray Arms* offers delicious **meals**, along with advice on local **fishing**, including permits for guests.

Newton Stewart

To the west of Gatehouse, the A75 skirts the mud flats of Wigtown Bay before cutting up to **NEWTON STEWART**, an unassuming market town beside the River Cree, famous for its salmon and trout fishing. The excellent *Creebridge House Hotel* (☎01671/402121; ⑦), in an old hunting lodge near the main bridge, arranges **fishing** permits for around £15 per day, can provide personal gillies (guides) for a further £25 daily, and at a pinch they'll even rent you all the tackle. The season runs from March to mid-October. The hotel serves great bar food too – try the fish or the homemade pies.

The Newton Stewart **tourist office** (April–Oct daily 10am–5pm; ☎01671/402431), just off the main street opposite the bus station, has bags of helpful literature. In town, the cheapest **accommodation** is the convenient Minnigaff **youth hostel** (April–Sept; ☎01671/402211) in an old school house 650 yards from the main street, near the bridge. Alternatively, you could try along Corvisel Road, a quiet street near the tourist office, where there's *Lynwood* (☎01671/402074; ③) and *Kilwarlin* (April–Oct; ☎01671/403047; ②). For **camping**, *Caldons Campsite* (April–Oct; ☎01671/402420) is near the car park at the western tip of Loch Trool.

GALLOWAY FOREST PARK

With its plentiful supply of accommodation and good bus connections along the A75, Newton Stewart has also become a popular base for hikers heading for the nearby **Galloway Hills**, most of which are enclosed within **Galloway Forest Park**. Many hikers aim for the park's **Glen Trool** by following the A714 north for about ten miles to Bargrennan, where a narrow lane twists the five miles over to the glen's **Loch Trool**. From here, there's a choice of magnificent hiking trails, as well as lesser tracks laid out by the forestry commission. Several longer routes curve round the grassy peaks and icy lochs of the Awful Hand and Dungeon ranges, whilst another includes part of the Southern Upland Way, which threads through the Minnigaff hills to Clatteringshaws Loch (see below).

The twenty-mile stretch from Newton Stewart to New Galloway, known as the Queen's Way, cuts through the southern periphery of Galloway Forest Park, a landscape of glassy lochs, wooded hills and bare, rounded peaks. You'll pass all sorts of **hiking trails**, some the gentlest of strolls, others long-distance treks. For a short walk, stop at the *Talnotry Campsite* (April–Oct; ☎01671/402420), about seven miles from Newton Stewart, where the forestry commission has laid out three trails each of which delves into the pine forests beside the road, crossing gorges and burns. The campsite itself occupies an attractive spot among the wooded hills of the park. A few miles further on is **Clatteringshaws Loch**, a reservoir surrounded by pine forest, with a fourteen-mile footpath running right round. If you're serious about doing some hiking, be sure to buy the Ordnance Survey maps and *The Galloway Hills: A Walker's Paradise* by George Brittain.

The Machars

The Machars, the name given to the peninsula of rolling farmland and open landscapes south of Newton Stewart, is a neglected part of the coastline, with a somewhat disconsolate air. From Newton Stewart it's eighteen miles south to **WHITHORN**, with its sloping, airy high street of pastel-painted cottages. This one-horse town occupies an important place in Scottish history, for it was here in 397 AD that **Saint Ninian** founded the first Christian church north of Hadrian's Wall. Ninian daubed his tiny building in white plaster and called it **Candida Casa**, translated as "Hwiterne" (White House), hence Whithorn, by his Pictish neighbours. Ninian's life is shrouded in mystery, but he does seem to have been raised in Galloway and was a key figure in the Christianization of his country. Indeed, his tomb became a popular place of pilgrimage and, in the twelfth century, a priory was built to service the shrine. For generations the rich and the royal made the trek here, but this ended with the Reformation.

Halfway down the main street, the **Whithorn Dig** (early April to Oct daily 10.30am–5pm; £2.70) exploits these ecclesiastical connections. A video gives background details and a handful of archeological finds serve as an introduction for a stroll round the dig. Be sure to take up the complimentary guide service – you won't make much sense of the complex sequence of ruins without one. Beyond the dig the meagre remains of the priory fail to inspire, unlike the adjacent **Whithorn Museum** (April–Sept Mon–Sat 10.30am–5pm, Sun 2–5pm; £1.20), whose impressive assortment of early Christian memorials includes a series of standing crosses and headstones, the earliest being the Latinus Stone of 450 AD. For **lunch**, the *Diner*, near the Dig, offers basic meals.

The pilgrims who crossed the Solway to visit St Ninian's shrine landed at the **ISLE OF WHITHORN**, four miles south of Whithorn. Not an island at all, it's an antique and tiny seaport hiding the minuscule remains of the thirteenth-century **St Ninian's Chapel**. To **stay**, try the unassuming *Steam Packet Inn* (☎01988/500334; ④), right on the quay. This is also the place to eat and find out details of sea angling trips, which leave the harbour on most days throughout the summer.

The Rhinns of Galloway

West of the Machars, the **Rhinns of Galloway** is a hilly, hammer-shaped peninsula at the end of the Solway Coast, encompassing two contrasting towns, the grimy port of Stranraer, from where there are regular ferries over to Northern Ireland, and the beguiling resort of **Portpatrick**, the western terminus of the Southern Upland Way. Between the two, a string of tiny farming villages leads down to the **Mull of Galloway**, the windswept headland at the southwest tip of Scotland.

Stranraer

No one could say **STRANRAER** was beautiful. However, if you're heading to (or coming from) Northern Ireland you may well have to pass through, and at least nearly everything's convenient. The **train station** is close to the *Stena Sealink* **ferry terminal** on the Ross Pier, where boats depart for Larne; a couple of minutes' walk away, on Port Rodie, is the town's **bus station**; and nearby, further round the bay, *Seacat* **catamaran** services leave from the West Pier to Belfast. Less handy, however, is the *P&O* ferry to Larne, which leaves from the port of Cairnryan, some five miles north.

While you're waiting for a Stranraer ferry, a walk along the dishevelled main street, variously Charlotte, George and High streets, takes in the town's one specific attraction, a medieval tower which is all that remains of the **Castle of St John** (April–Sept Mon–Sat 10am–1pm & 2–5pm; 70p). Inside, an exhibition traces the history of the castle down to its use as a police station and prison in the nineteenth century. The old exercise yard is on the roof.

Stranraer has plenty of basic snack bars, but it's well worth paying a little extra to enjoy a **meal** at the *Apéritif*, just up the hill from the bus station along Bellevilla Road. If you're stranded, the **tourist office** (April–Oct daily 9.30am–5pm) will arrange **accommodation**, or you can try *Fernlea*, Lewis St (☎01776/703037; ③). For **camping**, *Aird Donald Camp & Caravan Park* (☎01776/702025) is ten minutes' walk east of the town centre along London Road.

Portpatrick to the Mull

Perched on the west shore of the Rhinns, the pastel houses of **PORTPATRICK** spread over the craggy coast above the slender harbour. Until the mid-nineteenth century, when sailing ships were replaced by steamboats, this was the main embarkation point for Northern Ireland, with coal, cotton and British troops heading in one direction, Ulster cattle and linen in the other. Nowadays, Portpatrick is a quiet, comely resort enjoyed for its rugged scenery and coastal hikes.

Portpatrick has several good **hotels** and **guest houses**, the best of which are the *Portpatrick Hotel* (☎01776/810333; ⑧), a grand turreted Edwardian mansion on the hill above the harbour; the comfortable *Carlton Guest House*, beside the harbour on South Crescent (☎01776/810253; ④), and, close by, the bright, white *Knowe Guest House* (☎01776/810441; ③). For a **meal** and a **drink**, head on down to the *Crown* pub, on the seafront, or the *Auld Acquaintance* coffee shop nearby.

The Rhinns of Galloway, which extend about twenty miles south from Portpatrick, consist of gorse-covered hills and pastureland crossed by narrow country lanes and dotted with farming hamlets. On the sharper, rockier western coastline, near the village of Port Logan, you'll find the **Logan Botanic Garden** (mid-March to Oct daily 10am–6pm; £2), an outpost of Edinburgh's Royal Botanic Garden. There are three main areas, a peat garden, a woodland and a walled garden noted for its tree ferns and cabbage palms. It's a further twelve miles south to the **Mull of Galloway**, a bleak and precipitous headland where wheeling birds and whistling winds circle a bright white-washed lighthouse. On clear days you can see over to Cumbria and Ireland.

The South Ayrshire coast

Fifty miles from top to bottom, the **South Ayrshire Coast** between Stranraer and Ayr is easily seen from the A77 coastal road, which leaves Stranraer to trim thirty miles of low, rocky shore before reaching **Girvan**, a low-key seaside resort where boats depart for **Ailsa Craig**, out in the Firth of Clyde. Back on shore, the A77 presses on through the village of **Turnberry**, home to one of the world's most famous golf courses, where the A719 branches off for eighteenth-century **Culzean Castle** (pronounced "Cullane"). From the castle, it's twelve miles further to **Ayr**. Alternatively, if you keep to the main road, you'll pass by the medieval remains of **Crossraguel Abbey** on the way to the old market town of Maybole, just nine miles from Ayr.

Girvan and Ailsa Craig

Set beneath a ridge of grassy hills, **GIRVAN** is at its prettiest round the harbour, a narrow slit beside the mouth of the Girvan Water. Here, overlooked by old stone houses, the fishing fleet sets about its business, and, for a moment, it's possible to ignore the amusement arcades and seaside tat elsewhere in town. From late May to September boats leave the harbour for the ten-mile excursion west to the **Ailsa Craig**, "Fairy Rock" in Gaelic – though the island looks more like an enormous muffin than a place of enchantment. With its jagged cliffs and summit (1114ft), Ailsa Craig is a privately owned bird sanctuary that's home to thousands of gannets. The best time to make the trip is at the end of May and in June when the fledglings are trying to fly. The best **cruises** are operated by Mark McCrindle (☎01465/713219), whose once- or twice-daily sailings cost £10 per person for six hours, £7 for four.

There are regular **bus** services from Stranraer and Ayr to Girvan, which is also on the Glasgow–Stranraer **train** line. The **tourist office**, on Bridge Street, just up from the harbour (Easter–May Mon–Sat 11am–5pm; June Mon–Fri 11am–5pm, Sat & Sun 10am–5pm; Sept daily 11am–5pm; early Oct daily noon–4pm) has a full list of **accommodation**, or try among the attractive Victorian villas along the seafront, at the neat and tidy *Thistleneuk Guest House*, 19 Louisa Drive (☎01465/712137; ③).

Culzean Castle

Culzean Castle (April to late Oct daily 10.30am–5.30pm; £3.50), designed by Robert Adam, and the surrounding **country park** (April–late Oct daily 10.30m–5.30pm; Nov–March daily 9am–sunset; £3, combined ticket £5.50), whose 565 acres spread out along the seashore, are Ayrshire's premier tourist attractions. At the visitor centre in the modernized Home Farm buildings, you can pick up free maps to help you get your bearings; from here, it's a few minutes' walk over to the castle, whose towers and turrets rise high above the sea cliffs. Nothing remains of the original fifteenth-century structure, since, in 1777, David Kennedy, the tenth Earl of Cassillis, commissioned Robert Adam to remodel the family home. The work took fifteen years to complete, and, although the exterior, with its arrow slits and battlements, preserves a medieval aspect, the interior exemplifies the harmonious Classical designs Adam loved.

On the ground floor, the subtle greens of the old eating room are enlivened by vine-leaf-and-grape plasterwork along the cornice, a motif continued in the adjacent dining room. Nearby, there's the brilliantly conceived oval staircase, where tiers of Corinthian and Ionic columns add height and perspective. All this is a fitting prologue to the impressive circular saloon, whose symmetrical flourishes deliberately contrast with the natural land- and seascapes on view through the windows. Further on, a small exhibition celebrates President Eisenhower's military and civilian career as well as his association with Culzean; Ike stayed here on several occasions and the castle's top floor, was given to him by the old owners, the Kennedys, for his lifetime.

Crossraguel Abbey

The substantial remains of **Crossraguel Abbey** (April–Sept Mon–Sat 9.30am–6pm; Sun 2–6pm; £1.20), a further three miles along the main road, are mostly overlooked – something of a surprise considering their singularity. Founded as a Cluniac monastery in the thirteenth century, Crossraguel benefited from royal patronage with its abbots holding land "for ever in free regality". The abbots took the temporal side of their work seriously and became powerful local lords. By the early sixteenth century, they had constructed an extensive private compound complete with a massive gatehouse and sturdy tower house. Both still stand – behind what remains of the abbey church – recalling the corruption of the monastic ideal that sparked off the Reformation. Behind the gatehouse, you'll also spot the well-preserved dovecot, a funnel-shaped affair that was a crucial part of the abbey's economy; the monks not only ate the doves but also relied on them for eggs.

Ayr and around

With a population of around 50,000, **AYR**, the largest town on the Firth of Clyde coast, was an important seaport and trading centre for many centuries, and rivalled Glasgow in size and significance right up until the late seventeenth century. With the relative decline of its seaborne trade, Ayr developed as a market town, praised by Robert Burns, who was born in the neighbouring village of **Alloway** (see p.753), for its "honest men and bonny lasses". In the nineteenth century, Ayr became a popular resort for middle-class Victorians, with a new town of wide streets and boulevards built behind the beach immediately southwest of the old town. Nowadays, Ayr is both Ayrshire's commercial centre and a holiday resort, its long sandy beach (and prestigious racecourse) attracting hundreds of Scotland's city dwellers.

The Town

The cramped, sometimes seedy streets and alleys of Ayr's **Old Town** occupy a wedge of land between Sandgate and Alloway Place in the west, and the south bank of the treacly River Ayr to the east. Almost all the medieval buildings were knocked down by the Victorians, but the **Auld Brig**, with its cobbles and sturdy breakwaters, has survived from the thirteenth century. The bridge was saved by Robert Burns, or rather his poem *Twa Brigs*, which made it too famous to demolish; an international appeal raised the capital necessary for its refurbishment in 1907.

The bridge connects with High Street where you should turn left and subsequently left again down Kirk Port, a narrow lane leading to the **Auld Kirk** (July & Aug Tues & Thurs only). At the lych gate, a plan of the graveyard shows where some of Burns' friends are buried. Notice also the mort-safe (heavy grating) on the wall of the lych gate. Placed over newly dug graves, these mort-safes were a sort of early nineteenth-century corpse security system meant to deter body snatchers at a time when dead bodies were in great demand by medical schools.

Extending southwest of Sandgate to the Esplanade and the **beach**, the wide, gridiron streets of the Victorian **New Town** contrast with the crowded lanes of old Ayr. It was the opening of the Glasgow to Ayr railway line in 1840 that brought the first major influx of holidaymakers and Ayr remains a busy resort today, with many visitors heading for the plethora of trim guest houses concentrated around **Wellington Square**, whose terraces flank the impressive County Buildings dating from 1820. The new town extends north towards the river, spreading over what remains of the walls of a fort, built by Cromwell. It's here, off Bruce Crescent, that you'll find St John's Tower, all that's left of the parish church used by Cromwell as his armoury.

Practicalities

Ayr **bus station** is at the foot of Sandgate, a ten-minute walk west of both the **train station** and the **tourist office**, on Burns Statue Square (April to early Oct Mon–Sat 9.15am–5pm, Sun 10am–5pm; longer hours in peak season; mid-Oct to March Mon–Sat 9.15am–5pm; ☎01292/288688).

For a place to stay, head straight for the cluster of **hotels** and **guest houses** around Wellington Square, a couple of minutes' walk south of Sandgate along Alloway Place. In particular, try Queen's Terrace where, among others, there's the *Dargil Guest House*, no. 7 (☎01292/261955; ②), *Queens*, no. 10 (☎01292/265618; ③) and the *Daviot*, no. 12 (☎01292/269678; ③). Ayr **youth hostel**, 5 Craigweil Rd (March–Oct; ☎01292/262322; Grade 1), occupies a grand neo-Gothic mansion behind the beach, a twenty-minute walk south of the town centre (it's signposted).

ROBERT BURNS

The first of seven children, **Robert Burns**, the national poet of Scotland, was born in Alloway on January 25, 1759. His father, William, was employed as a gardener until 1766 when he became a tenant farmer at Mount Oliphant, near Alloway, moving to Lochlie farm, Tarbolton, eleven years later. A series of bad harvests and the demands of the landlord's estate manager bankrupted the family, and William died almost penniless in 1784. These events had a profound effect on Robert, leaving him with an antipathy towards political authority and a hatred of the landowning classes.

With the death of his father, Robert became head of the family and they moved again, this time to a farm at Mossgiel, near Mauchline. Burns had already begun writing poetry and prose at Lochlie, recording incidental thoughts in his *First Commonplace Book*, but it was here at Mossgiel that he began to write in earnest, and his first volume, *Poems Chiefly in the Scottish Dialect*, was published in Kilmarnock in 1786. The book proved immensely popular, celebrated by ordinary Scots and Edinburgh literati alike, with the satirical trilogy *Holy Willie's Prayer, The Holy Fair* and *Address to the Deil* attracting particular attention. The object of Burns' poetic scorn was the kirk, whose ministers had obliged him to appear in church to be publicly condemned for fornication – a commonplace punishment in those days.

Burns spent the winter of 1786–87 in the capital, lionized by the literary establishment. Despite his success, however, he felt trapped, unable to make enough money from writing to leave farming. He was also in a political snare, fraternizing with the elite, but with radical views and pseudo-Jacobite nationalism which constantly landed him in trouble. His frequent recourse was to play the part of the unlettered ploughman-poet, the noble savage who might be excused his impetuous outbursts and hectic womanizing.

Burns had, however, made useful contacts in Edinburgh and as a consequence was recruited to collect, write and rearrange two volumes of songs set to traditional Scottish tunes. These volumes, James Johnson's *Scots Musical Museum* and George Thomson's *Select Scottish Airs*, contain the bulk of his songwriting, and it's on them that Burns' international reputation rests with works like *Auld Lang Syne, Scots, wha hae, Coming through the Rye* and *Green Grow the Rushes, O*. At this time too, he produced two excellent poems: *Tam o' Shanter* and a republican tract, *A Man's a Man for a' that*.

In 1788, Burns married Jean Armour and moved to Ellisland Farm, near Dumfries. The following year, he was appointed excise officer, moving to Dumfries in 1791. Burns' years of comfort were short-lived, however. His years of labour on the farm, allied to a rheumatic fever, damaged his heart, and he died in Dumfries on July 21, 1796, aged 37.

Burns' work, inspired by a romantic nationalism and tinged with a wry wit, has made him a potent symbol of "Scottishness". Ignoring the Anglophile preferences of the Edinburgh elite, he wrote in Scots vernacular about the country he loved, an exuberant celebration that filled a need in a nation culturally colonized by England. Today Burns Clubs all over the world mark every anniversary of the poet's birthday with the Burns' Supper, complete with Scottish totems – haggis, piper and whisky bottle.

The best **restaurant** in Ayr is *Fouters*, 2a Academy St, in a cellar off Sandgate (☎01292/261391); steaks and seafood are its specialities. Another good choice, using local produce, is the *Boathouse*, 4 South Harbour St, beside the river at the foot of Fort Street. For filling and more reasonably priced meals, try *Littlejohn's*, 231 High St. The most enjoyable **pub** in town is the *Tam o' Shanter*, High St, whose ancient walls sport quotes from Robert Burns. There are also several lively bars on and around Burns Statue Square, including *O'Briens*, which frequently showcases Irish folk bands.

Alloway

There's little else but Burnsiana in the small village of **ALLOWAY**, a key stop on the Burns Heritage Trail (see p.742) a couple of miles south of Ayr. The first port of call in Alloway is the whitewashed **Burns Cottage and Museum** (April, May, Sept & Oct Mon–Sat 10am–5pm, Sun 1–5pm; June–Aug Mon–Sat 9am–6pm, Sun 10am–6pm; Nov–March Mon–Sat 10am–4pm; £2.50, includes entry to Burns Monument) for a peep at the poet's birthplace, a dark and dank, long thatched cottage where animals and people lived under the same roof. The two-room museum boasts all sorts of memorabilia – the family Bible, letters and manuscripts – plus a potted history of his life.

The modern, faceless **Tam o' Shanter Experience** (daily 9am–6pm), a few minutes further down the road, is for the most part a souvenir shop selling a good selection of books about, and works of, Burns. Across the road from here are the plain, roofless ruins of **Alloway Church**, where Robert's father William is buried. Burns set much of *Tam o' Shanter* here. Tam, having got drunk in Ayr, passes "By Alloway's auld haunted kirk" and stumbles across a witches' dance, from which he's forced to fly for his life over the **Brig o' Doon**, a hump-backed bridge which still curves gracefully over the river below the **Burns Monument** (April–Oct only, same hours & ticket as Cottage), a striking Neoclassical temple in a small carefully manicured garden.

travel details

Trains

Ayr to: Glasgow (3 daily; 50min); Stranraer (5 daily; 1hr 20min).

Dumfries to: Carlisle (5–12 daily; 35min).

Edinburgh to: North Berwick (hourly; 30min).

Glasgow to: Ardrossan Harbour (3–5 daily; 50min); Ayr (every 30min; 50min); Carlisle (2–7 daily; 2hr 15min); Dumfries (2–7 daily; 1hr 40min); Stranraer (3 daily; 2hr 20min).

Stranraer to: Ayr (5 daily; 1hr 20min).

Buses

Ayr to: Castle Douglas (Mon–Sat 2 daily; 2hr); Culzean Castle (hourly; 25min); Girvan (hourly; 1hr); Glasgow (1 express daily; 1hr 15min); Stranraer (3 daily; 2hr).

Dumfries to: Caerlaverock (Mon–Sat 5 daily; 35min); Carlisle (6 daily; 1hr 40min); Castle Douglas (2–4 daily; 45min); Edinburgh (3 weekly; 2hr 20min); Gatehouse of Fleet (2–3 daily; 1hr 30min); Glasgow (express 1–3 daily; 2hr); Kirkcudbright (2–4 daily; 1hr 10min); Newton Stewart (2–3 daily; 2hr); Rockcliffe (2 daily; 1hr 10min); Stranraer (2–3 daily; 3hr).

Edinburgh to: Berwick-upon-Tweed (3–4 daily; 3hr); Carlisle (3–5 daily; 3hr 25min); Haddington (3–6 daily; 1hr 5min); Jedburgh (5 daily; 2hr); Melrose (3–9 daily; 1hr 40min); North Berwick (every 30min; 1hr 20min); Peebles (6–8 daily; 1hr).

Haddington to: North Berwick (4–9 daily; 40min).

Jedburgh to: Kelso (3–6 daily; 30min).

Melrose to: Jedburgh (hourly; 30min); Kelso (6–8 daily; 35min); Peebles (hourly; 1hr 10min); Selkirk (Mon–Sat hourly, Sun 3 daily; 20min).

Newton Stewart to: Ayr (2–5 daily; 2hr 15min); Glentrool (2–5 daily; 25min); Girvan (2–5 daily; 1hr 20min); Stranraer (2–9 daily; 40min);

Whithorn (3–8 daily; 50min); Wigtown (Mon–Sat 10 daily, 3 on Sun; 15min); Isle of Whithorn (3–6 daily; 1hr).

Selkirk to: Carlisle (every 2hr; 2hr).

Stranraer to: Drummore (1–2 daily; 45min); Port Logan (1–2 daily; 35min); Portpatrick (5 daily; 25min).

Ferries

To Arran: Ardrossan–Brodick (up to 5 daily; 55min).

To Larne: Stranraer–Larne (5–10 daily; 2hr 20min); Cairnryan–Larne (3–6 daily; 2hr 15min).

To Belfast: Stranraer–Belfast (hydrofoil 4–5 daily; 1hr 30min).

CHAPTER NINETEEN

GLASGOW AND THE CLYDE

Rejuvenated, upbeat **GLASGOW**, Scotland's largest city, has not enjoyed the best of reputations. Once an industrial giant set on the banks of the mighty River Clyde, today it can initially seem a grey and depressing place, with the M8 motorway screeching through the centre and crumbling slums on its outskirts. However, in recent years Glasgow has undergone a remarkable overhaul, set in motion in the 1980s by a self-promotion campaign featuring a fat yellow creature called Mr Happy, beaming beatifically that "Glasgow's Miles Better". The city proceeded to generate a brisk tourist trade, reaching a climax after beating Paris, Athens and Amsterdam to the title of European City of Culture in 1990.

The epithet is still apt; Glasgow has some of the best-financed and most imaginative museums and galleries in Britain – among them the showcase **Burrell Collection** of art and antiquities – and nearly all of them are free. There's also a robust social scene and nightlife that is remarkably diverse, though somewhat restricted by the Scottish licensing laws. Its **architecture** is some of the most striking in the nation, from the restored eighteenth-century warehouses of the **Merchant City** to the hulking Victorian prosperity of George Square. Most distinctive of all is the work of local luminary Charles Rennie Mackintosh, whose elegantly streamlined Art Nouveau designs appear all over the city, reaching their apotheosis in the **School of Art**.

Despite all the upbeat hype, however, Glasgow's gentrification has passed by deprived inner-city areas such as the **East End**, home of the **Barras market** and some staunchly change-resistant pubs. This area, along with isolated housing schemes such as Castlemilk and Easterhouse, needs more than a facelift to resolve its complex social and economic problems; and has historically been the breeding ground for the city's much-lauded **socialism**. Glasgow has also had a long-standing belief in the power of popular culture. Main attractions include the **People's Palace** – one of Britain's most celebrated social history museums – founded in 1898 to extol ordinary lives and achievements, and the **Citizens' Theatre**, formed in 1942 by playwright James Bridie, whose innovative productions still cost next to nothing to see. In addition, Glasgow's **Mayfest**, with its roots in the traditional working-class spring celebrations, has grown to become Britain's second largest arts bash after the Edinburgh festival.

Quite apart from its own attractions, Glasgow also makes an excellent base from which to explore the **Clyde valley and coast**, made easy by the region's reliable rail service. Of the small communities in the Clyde valley, **Lanark** is probably the best suited for overnight stays, as well as being the home of the remarkable eighteenth-century **New Lanark** mills and workers' village. Beyond that, most of the inland towns (as well as the coastal resorts) are best approached as day trips from Glasgow.

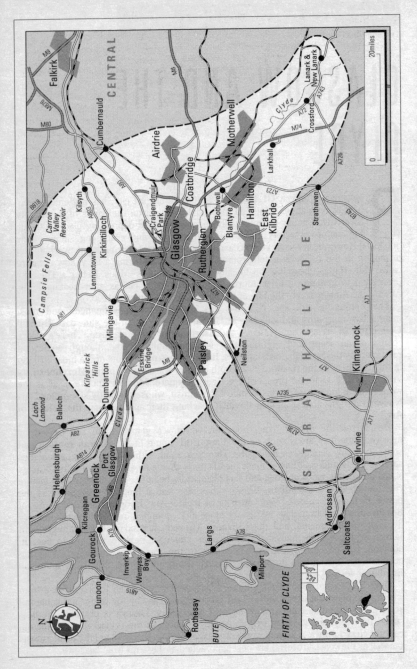

Some history

Glasgow's earliest history, like so much else in this surprisingly romantic city, is obscured in a swirl of myth. The city's name is said to derive from the Celtic *Glas-cu*, which loosely translates as "the dear, green place" – a tag that the tourist board are keen to exploit as an antidote to the sooty images of popular imagination. It is generally agreed that the first settlers arrived in the sixth century to join Christian missionary **Kentigern** – later to become St Mungo – in his newly founded monastery on the banks of the tiny Molendinar Burn.

William the Lionheart gave the town an official charter in 1175, after which it continued to grow in importance, peaking in the mid-fifteenth century when the **University** was founded on Kentigern's site – the second in Scotland after St Andrew's. This led to the establishment of an archbishopric, and hence city status, in 1492, and, due to its situation on a large, navigable river, Glasgow soon expanded into a major **industrial port**. The first cargo of tobacco from Virginia offloaded in Glasgow in 1674, and the 1707 Act of Union between Scotland and England – despite demonstrations against it in Glasgow – led to a boom in trade with the colonies until American independence. Following the **Industrial Revolution** and James Watt's innovations in steam power, coal from the abundant seams of Lanarkshire fuelled the ironworks all around the Clyde, worked by the cheap hands of the Highlanders and, later, those fleeing the Irish potato famine of the 1840s.

The Victorian age transformed Glasgow beyond recognition. The population boomed from 77,000 in 1801 to nearly 800,000 at the end of the century, and new tenement blocks swept into the suburbs in an attempt to cope with the choking influxes of people. Two vast and stately **International Exhibitions** were held in 1888 and 1901 to showcase the city and its industries, necessitating the construction of huge civic monoliths such as the Kelvingrove Art Gallery and the Council Chambers in George Square. At this time Glasgow became known as the **"Second City of the Empire"** – a curious epithet for a place that today rarely acknowledges second place in anything.

By the turn of the **twentieth century**, Glasgow's industries had been honed into one massive shipbuilding culture. Everything from tugboats to transatlantic liners was fashioned out of sheet metal in the yards that straddled the Clyde. In the harsh economic climate of the 1930s, however, unemployment spiralled, and Glasgow could do little to counter its popular image as a city dominated by inebriate violence and, having absorbed vast numbers of Irish emigrants, sectarian tensions. The **Gorbals** area in particular became notorious as one of the worst slums in Europe. The city's image has never been helped by the depth of animosity between its two great rival football teams: the Catholic **Celtic** and Protestant **Rangers**, whose warring armies of fans used to clash with monotonous regularity. Nowadays, the "Old Firm" clashes continue with the same passion on the field, but without the subsequent post-match violence.

In the Eighties the promotion campaign began, snowballing towards the 1988 **Garden Festival** and year-long party as **European City of Culture** in 1990. Today, Glasgow is again preparing for another celebration after beating off Edinburgh and Liverpool to become **City of Architecture and Design in 1999**, expected to be the largest celebration of architecture and design ever held.

Arrival, information and city transport

Glasgow's **airport** (☎0141/887 1111) is out at Abbotsinch, eight miles southwest of the city. To get into town, take *Citylink* bus #500 (£2), which runs to **Buchanan Street** (☎0141/332 7133) bus station, three streets north of George Square, every ten minutes during the day. The main entrance to **Glasgow Central**, where trains from anywhere south of Glasgow arrive, is on Gordon Street, from where a **shuttle bus** (free) sets off every ten minutes to **Queen Street station**, at the corner of George Square, for trains to Edinburgh and the north. The walk between the two takes about ten minutes. All buses arrive at Buchanan Street station, except those run by *Strathclyde Transport* which terminate in depots around the city.

The city's excellent **tourist office**, at 35 St Vincent Place just off George Square (Oct–April Mon–Sat 9am–6pm; rest of the year also Sun 10am–6pm; June & Sept closes 7pm; July & Aug 8pm; ☎0141/204 4400) provides a particularly wide array of maps, leaflets and souvenirs and a free accommodation-booking service. A couple of hundred yards south down Buchanan Street over the St Enoch Underground station sits the neo-Gothic hut of the **Strathclyde Travel Centre** (Mon–Sat 9.30am–5.30pm; ☎0141/226 4826), where you can pick up sheaves of maps, leaflets and timetables. Their comprehensive and colour-coded *Visitors' Transport Guide* is the best free map of the city centre and West End, but if you're staying for longer, or want to explore the city's tiny streets and alleys, it's probably worth investing in a *Bartholomew Glasgow Streetfinder* (£2.99).

Glasgow is a sprawling place, built upon some punishingly steep hills, and with no really obvious centre. However, as most transport services converge on the area around **Argyle Street** and, 200 yards to the north, **George Square**, this pocket of the city is the most obvious candidate for city-centre status. However, with the renovated upmarket **Merchant City** immediately to the east and the main business and commercial areas to the west, the centre, when the term is used, actually refers to a large swathe from **Charing Cross** train station and the M8 in the west through to **Glasgow Green** in the **East End**. Outside the city centre, the **West End** begins just over a mile west of Central station, and covers most of the area west of the M8. In the nineteenth century, as the East End tumbled into poverty, the West End ascended the social scales with great speed, a process crowned by the arrival of the **University**. Today, this is still very much the student quarter of Glasgow, exuding a decorous air, with graceful avenues, parks and cheap, interesting shops and cafés. The suburbs of Govan and the Gorbals, neither of which hold much for visitors, lie south of the Clyde, as does the area known as **South Side**, a relaxed version of the West End.

The best way to get between the city centre, southern suburbs and the West End is to use the city's **Underground**, affectionately known as the "Clockwork Orange" (there's only one, circular route and the trains are a garish bright orange), whose stations are marked with a large U. There's a flat fare of 60p, or you can buy a **day ticket** for £1.80; a **multi-journey ticket** gives ten journeys for £5.40 or twenty for £10.00. Unfortunately, however, trains only begin running from 11am, and stop at 11.30pm between Monday and Saturday and at 6pm on Sunday.

If you're travelling beyond the city centre or the West End, you may need to use the **bus** and **train** networks. Since deregulation, the city has been besieged with a horde of bus companies in hot competition. The biggest are *Strathclyde Transport*, whose buses can be identified by their orange livery, and *Kelvin Central Buses* in cream and red. If it gets too confusing, pick up the *Visitors' Transport Guide* (see above). The suburban train network is swift and convenient. Suburbs south of the Clyde are connected to Glasgow Central main-line station, while trains from Queen Street head into the northeast. The grim but functional **cross-city line**, which runs beneath Argyle Street (and includes a low-level stop below Central station), connects northwestern destinations with southeastern districts as far out as Lanark.

There is no day ticket that combines bus, rail and Underground in Glasgow alone, but if you are in the city for at least a week, it's worth investing in a **Zonecard**, which covers all public transport networks, and is valid for seven days or a month. Costs depend on the number of zones that you want to travel through – ask at the Strathclyde Travel Centre for help to demystify the system.

Should you want to avoid public transport altogether, you can hail black **taxis**, which run all day and night, from the pavement. There are taxi ranks at Central and Queen

Street train stations and Buchanan Street bus station. The fare from Central to Pollok Park and the Burrell Collection, a journey of about three miles, costs £5.

Accommodation

There's a good range of **accommodation** in Glasgow, from an excellent youth hostel in the leafy West End through to some top international hotels in the city centre. Most of the rooms are in the city centre, the West End or down in the southern suburb of Queen's Park. Glasgow's speciality is its profusion of converted Victorian **town houses** in the middle of town, many of which are now privately run B&Bs that offer excellent value for money. During Mayfest or in summer it's worth **booking ahead** to ensure a good room – at any time of year the **tourist office** will do their utmost to secure you somewhere to stay. They also publish a useful brochure of bargain weekend breaks.

City centre

Babbity Bowster, 16–18 Blackfriars St (☎0141/552 5055). A traditional and very lively hotel, bar and restaurant that makes much of its Scottishness, with haggis and neaps and tatties permanently on the menu. ⑤.

Baird Hall, 460 Sauchiehall St (☎0141/553 4148). Lavish Art Deco building that belies the functional, ex-student rooms, near the School of Art and the upper end of Sauchiehall Street. ③.

Central Hotel, Gordon St (☎0141/221 9680). Imposing, comfortable hotel, with its own leisure centre, in the heart of the action near the stations. ⑦.

Copthorne Hotel, George Square (☎0141/332 6711). Large and impressive eighteenth-century hotel on George Square; popular bar in the ground-floor glass verandah. ⑦.

Rab Ha's, 83 Hutcheson St (☎0141/553 1545). Beautiful and highly individual hotel-cum-restaurant in swish Merchant City. They only have a few rooms, so reservations are essential. ⑤.

Town House Hotel, Nelson Mandela Place, 54 W George St (☎0141/332 3320). Sumptuously converted sandstone block with quite a "Scottish" feel. Expensive but original food ⑧.

Victorian House, 212 Renfrew St (☎0141/332 0129). Large and friendly terraced guest house, with some of the cheapest rooms in the city centre. ③.

Willow Hotel, 228 Renfrew St (☎0141/332 2332 or 7075). Well-converted Victorian town house, on the north side of the city centre, offering B&B; clean, spacious rooms. ③.

West End

Alamo Guest House, 46 Gray St (☎0141/339 2395). Good-value, family-run boarding house next to Kelvingrove Park. Small but comfortable rooms. ②.

Ambassador Hotel, 7 Kelvin Drive (☎0141/946 1018). Smallish but comfortable, family-run B&B in lovely surroundings next to the River Kelvin and Botanical Gardens. ④.

Chez Nous, 33 Hillhead St (☎0141/334 2977). Roomy guest house in the heart of the West End. Especially accommodating and good value for single travellers. ②.

Hillhead Hotel, 32 Cecil St (☎0141/339 7733). Quiet, welcoming hotel only a couple of minutes' stroll from Hillhead Underground and the excellent local pubs and restaurants. ④.

ACCOMMODATION PRICE CODES

Throughout this guide, hotel and B&B accommodation is priced on a scale of ① to ⑨, the number indicating the **lowest price** you could expect to pay per night in that establishment for a **double room** in high season. The prices indicated by the codes are as follows:

① under £20/$30	④ £40–50/$60–75	⑦ £70–80/$105–120
② £20–30/$31–45	⑤ £50–60/$75–90	⑧ £80–100/$120–150
③ £30–40/$45–60	⑥ £60–70/$90–105	⑨ over £100/$150

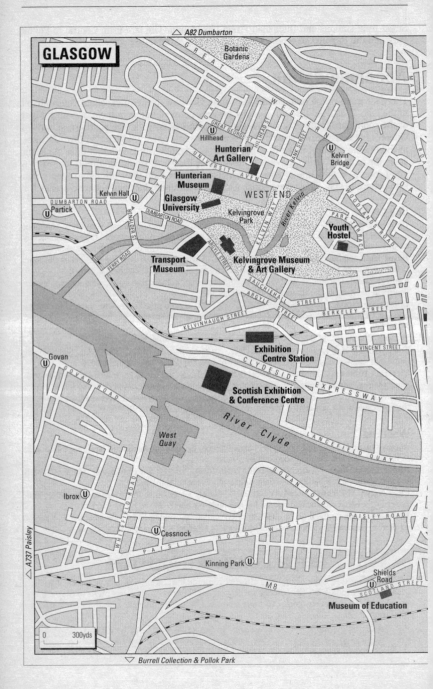

GLASGOW

△ A82 Dumbarton

Botanic
Gardens

GREAT WESTERN ROAD

MARYHILL ROAD

GREAT GEORGE ST

HILLHEAD ST

Hillhead Ⓤ

Hunterian
Art Gallery

Ⓤ Kelvin
Bridge

UNIVERSITY AVENUE

PARK TERRACE

WOODLANDS ROAD

Hunterian
Museum

WEST END

River Kelvin

Kelvin Hall Ⓤ

Glasgow
University

DUMBARTON ROAD

Partick Ⓤ

Kelvingrove
Park

KELVIN WAY

Youth
Hostel

BANKHOUSE ST

DUMBARTON ROAD

BERNARDS ST

FERRY ROAD

ARGYLE STREET

Transport
Museum

Kelvingrove Museum
& Art Gallery

SAUCHIEHALL STREET

ARGYLE STREET

BERKELEY STREET

KELVINHAUGH STREET

ST VINCENT STREET

Exhibition
Centre Station

CLYDESIDE EXPRESSWAY

Scottish Exhibition
& Conference Centre

LANCEFIELD QUAY

Govan Ⓤ

GOVAN ROAD

River Clyde

West
Quay

GOVAN ROAD

PAISLEY ROAD

Ibrox Ⓤ

WHITEFIELD ROAD

PAISLEY ROAD WEST

△ A737 Paisley

Cessnock Ⓤ

Kinning Park Ⓤ

M8

Shields
Road Ⓤ

SCOTLAND STREET

Museum of Education

0 ___ 300yds

▽ Burrell Collection & Pollok Park

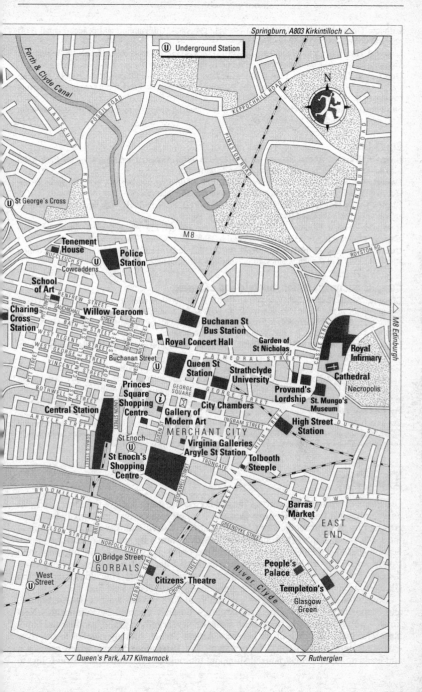

Springburn, A803 Kirkintilloch

N

U Underground Station

Forth & Clyde Canal

GARSCUBE ROAD

POSSIL ROAD

KEPPOCHHILL ROAD

PINKSTON ROAD

SPRINGBURN ROAD

ROYSTON RD

U St George's Cross

M8

M8 Edinburgh

Tenement House

Police Station

BUCCLEUCH ST

U Cowcaddens

School of Art

RENFREW STREET

SAUCHIEHALL STREET

Willow Tearoom

Charing Cross Station

WEST REGENT STREET

BATH STREET

Buchanan St Bus Station

Royal Concert Hall

Garden of St Nicholas

Royal Infirmary

WEST GEORGE STREET

Buchanan Street

Queen St Station

CATHEDRAL STREET

Strathclyde University

CASTLE STREET

Cathedral

Necropolis

ST VINCENT STREET

GEORGE SQUARE

GEORGE STREET

Provand's Lordship

St Mungo's Museum

BOTHWELL STREET

Princes Square Shopping Centre

Central Station

i

Gallery of Modern Art

City Chambers

INGRAM STREET

High Street Station

DUKE ST

ARGYLE STREET

UNION STREET

St Enoch

MERCHANT CITY

HIGH STREET

U

St Enoch's Shopping Centre

Virginia Galleries

Argyle St Station

TRONGATE

Tolbooth Steeple

GALLOWGATE

BROOMIELAW

ST ENOCH SQUARE

SALTMARKET

Barras Market

EAST END

NELSON STREET

BRIDGE ST

NORFOLK STREET

GREENDYKE STREET

U Bridge Street

COOK STREET

GORBALS

West Street

Citizens' Theatre

River Clyde

People's Palace

LONDON ROAD

Templeton's

Glasgow Green

BALLATER STREET

▽ Queen's Park, A77 Kilmarnock

▽ Rutherglen

Hillview Guest House, 18 Hillhead St (☎0141/334 5585). Unassuming and peaceful small B&B near the university and the Byres Road. ③.

Lomond Hotel, 6 Buckingham Terrace (☎0141/339 2339). Discreet B&B in beautifully restored Victorian terrace near the Botanic Gardens and Byres Road. ③.

One Devonshire Gardens, 1 Devonshire Gardens, Great Western Rd (☎0141/339 2001). A 10-min walk up the Great Western Road from the Botanical Gardens, this hotel and its expensive gourmet restaurant are among the city's finest. ⑦.

Sandyford Hotel, 904 Sauchiehall St (☎0141/334 0000). A clean, comfortable B&B, good location for Kelvingrove Park and the SECC. ④.

South Side

Boswell Hotel, 27 Mansionhouse Rd (☎0141/632 9812). Informal, relaxing Queen's Park hotel with a superb real-ale bar, and regular folk and jazz nights. ④.

Ewington Hotel, 132 Queen's Drive (☎0141/422 2030). Comfortable and peaceful hotel facing Queen's Park. Excellent, moderately priced subterranean restaurant. ⑦.

Glades Guest House, 142 Albert Rd (☎0141/423 4911). Friendly B&B, with large rooms, in quiet area near Queen's Park and good transport routes. ③.

Reidholme Guest House, 36 Regent Park Square (☎0141/423 1855). Small and friendly guest house in a quiet side street that was designed by Alexander "Greek" Thomson. ②.

Queen's Park Hotel, 10 Balvicar Drive (☎0141/423 1123). Faintly shabby, but very welcoming and with a crowd of regular visitors. Good views over the hill of Queen's Park. ④.

Campus accommodation, hostels and camping

Glasgow Youth Hostel, 7–8 Park Terrace (☎0141/332 3004), is a luxurious place nuzzled deep in the splendour of the West End. A ten-minute walk south from Kelvinbridge Underground station, or take #11, #44 or #59 *Strathclyde Transport* bus from the city centre, after which it's a short stroll west up Woodlands Road. It's very popular, so book in advance.

University of Glasgow (☎0141/330 5385). Low-priced **self-catering** rooms and flats available from early July to mid-September.

University of Strathclyde (☎0141/553 4148). Various sites, mostly gathered around the cathedral. Vacation lets (③) and self-catering flats for between four and six people (①; minimum 3 people) can be rented near the main campus in Rottenrow for a minimum of three nights. For better rooms, available all year (but pricier than many city hotels), call their *Graduate Business School*, Cathedral St (☎0141/553 6000; ⑦).

Craigendmuir Park, Campsie View, Stepps (☎0141/779 4159). The only **campsite** within a decent distance of Glasgow, four miles northeast of the city centre, a 15-min walk from Stepps train station; adequate facilities with showers, a laundry and a shop, but only ten pitches.

The City

Glasgow's enormous city centre is ranged across the north bank of the River Clyde. At its geographical heart is **George Square**, a nineteenth-century municipal showpiece crowned by the enormous City Chambers at the eastern end. Behind this lies one of the 1980s greatest marketing successes, the **Merchant City**, an area of massive gentrification partially restored to its nineteenth-century glory. The grand buildings and trendy cafés cling to the borders of the run-down **East End**, a strongly working-class district that chooses to ignore its rather showy neighbour. The oldest part of the Glasgow, around the **Cathedral**, lies immediately north of the East End.

Still in the city centre, Glasgow's commercial core spreads west of George Square, and is mostly built on a large grid system – possibly inspired by Edinburgh's New Town – with ruler-straight roads soon rising up severe hills to grand, sandblasted buildings. The main shopping areas here are **Argyle Street**, running parallel to the river east–west underneath Central train station, and **Buchanan Street**, which crosses it and leads up to the pedestrianized shopping thoroughfare, **Sauchiehall Street**. Just to the north of here is Rennie Mackintosh's famous **Glasgow School of Art**. Lying between the commercial bustle of Argyle and Sauchiehall streets, and to the immediate west of Buchanan Street, are the contours of an ice-age drumlin (one of three main drumlins in the area), now known as **Blythswood Hill**. The tightly packed grid of streets piled on its slopes are lined by Georgian buildings filled with offices. In comparison with the bustling shopping parades surrounding it on three sides, this area is remarkably quiet and reserved, crowned by the neat Blythswood Square.

Outside the city centre, the **West End** begins just over a mile west of Central Station, and covers most of the area west of the M8. In the nineteenth century, as the East End tumbled into poverty, the West End ascended the social scales with great speed, a process crowned by the arrival of the **University**. Today, this is still very much the student quarter of Glasgow, exuding a decorously well-healed air, with graceful tree-lined avenues and trendy shops and cafés. Straddling the banks of the cleaned up River Kelvin, the slopes, trees and statues of **Kelvingrove Park** are framed by a backdrop of the Gothic towers and turrets of the university and the **Kelvingrove Museum and Art Gallery**.

Not as genteel as the West End, nor as raffishly downbeat as the East End, the **south side** of the city is nevertheless also worth a visit – though you may want to bypass the scruffy and infamous suburbs of Govan and the Gorbals, immediately south of the Clyde, for the leafy enclaves such as **Pollok Park** and the main attraction south of the river, the **Burrell Collection**.

George Square and the Merchant City

Now hemmed in by speeding traffic, the imposing architecture of **George Square** reflects the confidence of Glasgow's Victorian age. Rising high above the centre of the square is an eighty-foot column topped with Sir Walter Scott, although his links with Glasgow were, at best, sketchy. The florid splendour of the **City Chambers**, opened by Queen Victoria in 1888, occupies the entire eastern end of the square. Built from wealth gained by colonial trade and heavy industry, it epitomizes the aspirations and optimism of late-Victorian city elders. Its intricately detailed facade includes high-minded friezes typical of the era: the four nations (England, Ireland, Scotland, Wales) of the then United Kingdom at the feet of the throned queen, the British colonies and allegorical figures representing Religion, Virtue and Knowledge. It's worth taking a **free guided tour** (Mon–Fri 10.30am & 2.30pm) of the labyrinthine interior to get a look at the intricate gold leaf, Italian marble, Wedgwood ceilings and Rococo trimmings.

Equally opulent is the **Merchant's House** opposite Queen Street station (May–Sept Mon–Fri 2–4pm; free), where the grand Banqueting Hall and silk-lined Directors' Room are highlights. Queen Street leads south to the Royal Exchange Square and the graceful Corinthian **Stirling Library**, built for tobacco lord William Cunninghame in 1780 as the most ostentatious of the Glasgow merchants' homes. Since then it has served as the city's Royal Exchange and central library, and refurbishment is currently under way to give it a new lease of life as the city's Museum of Modern Art.

Merchant City

The grid of streets that lies immediately east of the City Chambers is known as the **Merchant City**, an area of eighteenth-century warehouses and homes once bustling with cotton, tobacco and sugar traders, which in the last decade or so has been sandblasted and swabbed clean with greater enthusiasm and municipal money than any other part of Glasgow in an attempt to bring residents back into the city centre. The cost of living here is prohibitive for most people, however, and many of the gracious warehouses remain smothered with "To let" signs. However, the expensive designer shops with small but immaculate collections sit neatly with bijou bars and cafés to bring some life back into this quiet area.

Look out for the delicate white spire of the National Trust for Scotland's regional headquarters, **Hutcheson's Hall**, at 158 Ingram St (Mon–Fri 9.30am–5pm, Sat 10am–4pm). The NTS have a shop on the ground floor and visitors can see the ornately decorated hall upstairs. Almost opposite, on Glassford Street, the Robert Adam-designed **Trades House** (call ☎0141/552 2418 to arrange a time; free) is easily distinguished by its neat, green copper dome. Built for the purpose in 1794, it still functions as the headquarters of the Glasgow trade guilds. Its history can be traced back to 1605 when fourteen societies of well-to-do city merchants, who were the forerunners of the trade unions, first incorporated. These included a Bakers' Guild, and societies for Hammermen, Gardeners, Bonnet Makers, Wrights and Weavers, although they have since become little more than proto-masonic lodges for men from all sections of Glasgow's business community. The former civic pride and status of the guilds is still evident, however, from the rich assortment of carvings and stained-glass windows, with a lively pictorial representation of the different trades in the silk frieze around the walls of the first-floor banqueting hall.

From Trongate to the East End

Before 1846, **Glasgow Cross** – the junction of **Trongate**, Gallowgate and the High Street – was the city's principal intersection, until the construction of the new train station near George Square shifted the city's emphasis west. The turreted seventeenth-century **Tolbooth Steeple** still stands here, although the rest of the building has long since disappeared, and today the stern tower is little more than a traffic hazard at a busy junction. Further east, down Gallowgate, beyond the train lines, lies the **EAST END**, the district that perhaps most closely corresponds to the old perception of Glasgow. Hemmed in by Glasgow Green to the south, and the old university to the west, this densely packed industrial area essentially created the city's wealth. The Depression caused the closure of many factories, leaving communities stranded in an industrial wasteland. Today isolated pubs, tatty shops and cafés sit amidst this dereliction, in sharp contrast to the gloss of the Merchant City only a few blocks to the west.

Three hundred yards down either London Road or Gallowgate, **The Barras** is Glasgow's largest and most popular weekend market. Red iron gates announce its official entrance, but boundaries are breached as the stalls – selling inexpensive household goods, bric-a-brac, secondhand clothes and records – spill out into the surrounding cobbled streets.

Between London Road and the River Clyde are the wide and tree-lined spaces of **Glasgow Green**. Reputedly the oldest public park in Britain, the Green has been common land since at least 1178, when it was first mentioned in records. Glaswegians hold it very dear, considering it to be an immortal link between themselves and their ancestors, for whom a stroll on the Green was a favourite Sunday afternoon jaunt. It has also been the site of many of the city's major political demonstrations – the Chartists in the 1830s and Scottish republican campaigners in the 1920s – and was the traditional culmination of the May Day marches until the 1950s, when the celebrations were moved to Queens Park. Various memorials (some in bad states of disrepair) are dotted around the lawns: the 146-foot **Nelson Monument**, the ornate – but derelict – terracotta **Doulton Fountain**, rising like a wedding cake to the pinnacle where the forlorn Queen Victoria oversees her crumbling Empire, and the stern monument extolling the evils of drink and the glory of God that was erected by the nineteenth-century Temperance movement – today, quite a meeting place for local drunks.

The People's Palace

On the northern end of Glasgow Green, the **People's Palace** (Mon–Sat 10am–5pm, Sun 11am–5pm; free) is a wonderfully haphazard evocation of the city's history. This squat, red-brick Victorian building, with a vast semicircular glasshouse tacked on the back, was purpose-built as a museum back in 1898 – almost a century before the rest of the country caught on to the fashion for social history collections.

On the ground floor, the medieval city and its first skirmishes with the fiendish English are represented through re-created monastic rooms, pictures and captions, leading into an exhibition of period interiors removed from Stockwell Mansion, the city's last seventeenth-century building, demolished in 1976. The upper floor is more appealing, with exhibits on John Maclean, the most notorious of the Red Clydesiders (members of a radical Independent Labour Party formed in the economic slump post-World War I) who became consul to the Bolshevik government in 1918, on trade unions, suffragettes, the City Council and the products that once made Glasgow the "Workshop of the World". On the top floor, the impressive murals by Scottish artist Ken Currie powerfully evoke the spirit of radical Glasgow, starting from the Carlton weavers strike in 1787 up to the Red Clydesiders of the 1920s.

The glasshouse at the back of the palace is the **Winter Gardens**, whose café, water garden, twittering birds and assorted tropical plants and shrubs make a pleasant place in which to pass an hour or so. A hundred yards across the road from the People's Palace you can see the riotously intricate orange and blue Venetian-style facade of **Templeton's Carpet Factory**, built in 1889. William Leiper, Templeton's architect, is said to have modelled his industrial cathedral on the Doge's Palace in Venice; today it houses a centre for small businesses.

Around the Cathedral

Rising north up the hill from the Tolbooth Steeple at Glasgow Cross is Glasgow's **High Street**. In British cities, the name is commonly associated with the busiest central thoroughfare, and it's a surprise to see how forlorn and dilapidated Glasgow's version is, long superseded by the grander thoroughfares further west. The High Street leads up to the **Cathedral**, on the site of Glasgow's original settlement.

Glasgow Cathedral

Built in 1136, destroyed in 1192 and rebuilt soon after, the stumpy-spired **Glasgow Cathedral** (April–Sept Mon–Sat 9.30am–1pm & 2–6pm, Sun 2–5pm; Oct–March closes 4pm) was not completed until the late fifteenth century, with the final reconstruction of the chapter house and the aisle designed by Robert Blacader, the city's first archbishop. The only Scottish mainland cathedral to have escaped the hands of religious reformers, thanks to the intervention of the city guilds, it is dedicated to the city's patron saint and reputed founder, St Mungo, about whom four popular stories are frequently told – they even make an appearance on the city's coat of arms. These involve a bird that he brought back to life, the bell with which he summoned the faithful to prayer, a tree that he managed to make spontaneously combust and a fish that he caught with a repentant adulterous queen's ring on its tongue.

Because of the sloping ground on which it is built, at its east end the cathedral is effectively on two levels, the crypt actually part of the "lower church". On entering, you arrive in the impressively lofty nave of the **upper church**, completed under the direction of Bishop William de Bondington (1233–58). Either side of the nave, the narrow **aisles** are illuminated by vivid, mostly twentieth-century stained-glass windows. Beyond the nave, the **choir** is hidden from view by the curtained stone pulpit, making the interior feel a great deal smaller than might be expected from the outside. In the choir's northeastern corner, a small door leads into the cathedral's gloomy **sacristy**, in which Glasgow University was first founded over 500 years ago. Wooden boards mounted on the walls detail the alternating Roman Catholic and Protestant clergy of the cathedral, testimony to the turbulence and fluctuations of the Church in Scotland.

Steps from the nave lead down into the **lower church**, where you'll see the dark and musty **chapel** surrounding the tomb of St Mungo. The saint's relics were removed in the late Middle Ages, although the tomb still forms the centrepiece. The chapel itself is one of the most glorious examples of medieval architecture in Scotland, best seen in the delicate fan vaulting rising up from the thicket of cool stone columns. Also in the lower church, is the spaciously light **Blacader Aisle**, whose bright, frequently gory, medieval ceiling bosses stand out superbly against the simple whitewashed vaulting.

Outside, the atmospheric **Necropolis** rises above the cathedral. Inspired by the Pierre Lachaise cemetery in Paris, developer John Strong created a garden of death in 1833, filled with Doric columns, gloomy catacombs and Neoclassical temples reflecting the vanity of the nineteenth-century industrialists buried here. From the summit, next to the column topped with an indignant John Knox, there are superb views over the cathedral and its surrounding area.

Cathedral Square

Back in Cathedral Square, the **St Mungo Museum of Religious Life and Art** (Mon–Sat 10am–5pm, Sun 11am–5pm; free) focuses on objects, beliefs and art from Christianity, Buddhism, Judaism, Islam, Hinduism and Sikhism. Portrayals of Hindu gods are juxtaposed with the stunning Salvador Dali painting *Christ upon the Cross* – moved here from Kelvingrove Art Gallery – that draws the viewer into its morose depths. In addition to the main exhibition is a small collection of photographs, papers and archive material looking at religion in Glasgow, the power and zealotry of the nineteenth-century Temperance movement, Christian missionaries and local boy, David Livingstone, in particular.

Across the square, the oldest house in the city, the **Provand's Lordship** (Mon–Sat 10am–5pm, Sun 11am–5pm; free) dates from 1471, and has been used, among other things, as an ecclesiastical residence and an inn. Many of the rooms have been kitted out with period furniture, including a re-creation of the fifteenth-century chamber of cathedral clerk Cuthbert Simon. As a reminder of the manse's earthier history, the upper floor contains cuttings and pictures telling interesting tales of assorted lowlife characters, such as notorious drunkards, match-sellers and prostitutes of eighteenth- and nineteenth-century Glasgow.

Behind this building lies the small **Garden of St Nicholas**, a herb garden contrasting medieval and Renaissance aesthetics and approaches to medicine; from the muddled clusters of herbs amid stone carvings of the heart and other organs to the controlled arrangement of plants around a small ornate fountain. The garden, bordered by sandstone walkways where you can sit, is an aromatic and peaceful haven away from the High Street.

From Buchanan Street to Sauchiehall Street

The huge grid of streets that runs from Buchanan Street to the M8 a mile to the west, is home to Glasgow's main shopping district as well as its financial and business corporations, piling up the slopes of drumlins shaped by the receding glaciers of the last ice age. At the northern end of Buchanan Street, where it intersects with the eastern end of Sauchiehall Street, lies the £29 million **Royal Concert Hall**, given a prime city perspective but failing miserably to excite much attention. The showpiece hall plays host to world-class musical events (see p.778), while the lobbies are used for temporary art exhibitions.

Sauchiehall Street runs in a straight line west past some unexciting shopping malls, leading to a few of the city's most interesting sights. Charles Rennie Mackintosh fans should head for the **Willow Tea Room**, at 217 Sauchiehall St (daily 9.30am–5pm), a faithful reconstruction (opened in 1980) on the site of the 1904 original, which was created by the architect for Kate Cranston, one of his few contemporary supporters in the city. Everything from the fixtures and fittings right down to the teaspoons and menu cards was designed by Mackintosh. Taking inspiration from the word

CHARLES RENNIE MACKINTOSH

Dark-haired and confident, the figure of **Charles Rennie Mackintosh** (1868–1928) has come to be synonymous with the image of Glasgow. Whether his work was a forerunner of the Modernist movement or merely a sunset of Victorianism, he undoubtedly created buildings of great beauty, idiosyncratically fusing Scots Baronial with Gothic, Art Nouveau and modern design. Though the bulk of his work was conceived at the turn of the century, since the postwar years, Mackintosh's ideas have become particularly fashionable, giving rise to a certain amount of ersatz "Mockintosh" in his home city, with his distinctive lettering and small design features used time and again by shops, pubs and businesses. Fortunately, there are also plenty of examples of the genuine article, making the city something of a pilgrimage centre for art and design students from all over the world.

Although his family did little to encourage his artistic ambitions, as a young child he began to cultivate his interest in drawing from nature during walks in the countryside, taken to improve his health. This talent was to flourish when he joined the **Glasgow School of Art**, in 1884, where the vibrant new director, Francis Newberry, encouraged his pupils to create original and individual work. Here he met Herbert MacNair and the sisters Margaret and Frances MacDonald whose work seemed to be sympathetic with his, fusing the organic forms of nature with a linear, symbolic Art Nouveau style. Nicknamed "The Spook School", the four created a new artistic language, using extended vertical design, stylized abstract organic forms and muted colours, reflecting their interest in Japanese design and the work of Whistler and Beardsley. However, it was architecture that truly challenged Mackintosh, allowing him to use his creative artistic impulse in a three-dimensional and cohesive manner.

His big break came in 1896, when he won the competition to design a new **art school** (see p.768). This is his most famous work, but a number of smaller buildings created during his tenure with the architects Honeyman and Keppie, which began in 1889, document the development of his style. One of his earliest commissions was for a new building to house the **Glasgow Herald headquarters** on Mitchell Street. A massive tower rises up from the corner, giving a dynamism to the enclosed space, dispelling the regularity of the horizontal windows; this use of vertical lines was to play a significant part in his later work.

In the 1890s Glasgow went wild for tea rooms, where the middle classes could play billiards and chess, read in the library or merely chat over some fine dining. The imposing Miss Cranston, who dominated the Glasgow tea shop scene, running the most elegant establishments, gave Mackintosh great freedom of design and in 1896 he started to plan the interiors for her growing business. Over the next twenty years he designed articles from teaspoons to furniture and finally, as in the case of the **Willow Tea Rooms**, the structure itself.

The spectre of limited budgets was to haunt Mackintosh throughout his career, and he never had the chance to design and construct with complete freedom. However, these constraints never managed to dull his creativity, as demonstrated by the **Scotland Street School** of 1904 (near the Burrell Collection; see p.771). Here, the two main stairways that frame the entrance are lit by glass-filled bays that protrude from the building. It is his most symmetrical work, with a whimsical nod to history in the Scots Baronial conical tower roofs and sandstone building material.

Sauchiehall which means "avenue of willow", he chose the willow leaf as a theme to unify the whole structure from the tables to the mirrors and the iron work. The motif is most apparent in the stylized linear panels of the bow window which continues into the intimate dining room as if to surround the sitter, like a willow grove, and is echoed in the distinctively high-backed silver and purple chairs.

A couple of footsteps west are the **McLellan Galleries,** 270 Sauchiehall St (Mon–Sat 10am–5pm, Sun noon–5pm; charges for some exhibitions), recently restored after a severe fire in 1985. Despite its inauspicious frontage, inside the building is as soothing an example of Classical architecture as anywhere in the city. A grand staircase sweeps you up into the main exhibition space, lit naturally by beautiful pedimented windows. There is no permanent display; the McLellan specializes in imaginative touring and temporary exhibitions, many of which have local themes – in recent years, these have ranged from new Glaswegian art to an eccentric display of the city's rubbish, and in 1996 the biggest ever exhibition of Mackintosh's life and work. For relentlessly avant-garde art and culture, stroll down the same side of Sauchiehall Street to no. 350 and the **Centre for Contemporary Arts** (Mon–Sat 11am–6pm; free), with its eclectically internationalist exhibitions and performances, and trendy café and bar that stays open till late (Mon–Wed 11pm, Thurs–Sat midnight).

Glasgow School of Art

Rising above Sauchiehall Street to the north is one of the city centre's steepest hills, where Dalhousie Street and Scott Street veer up to Renfrew Street and, at no. 167, Charles Rennie Mackintosh's **Glasgow School of Art** (guided tours Mon–Fri 11am & 2pm, Sat 10.30am; extra tours April–Sept; £2; booking advised; ☎0141/332 9797). Widely considered to be the pinnacle of Mackintosh's work, the school is a characteristically angular building of warm sandstone which, due to financial constraints, had to be constructed in two sections (1897–99 and 1907–09). There's a clear change in style from the earlier severity of the east wing to the softer lines of the western half. The only way to see the school is by taking one of the student-led daily guided tours, the extent of which are dependent on curricular activities.

All over the school, from the roof to the stairwells, Mackintosh's unique touches – light Oriental reliefs, tall-backed chairs and stylized Celtic illuminations – recur like leitmotifs. Hanging in the main entrance hall stairwell is the artist's highly personal wrought-iron version of the "bird, bell, tree, ring and fish" legend of St Mungo. The stairs lead up to the **Director's Room**, where the rounded lines of the central table and arched window contrast with the starkly angular chairs, cupboard and writing desk. You'll see excellent examples of his early furniture in the tranquil **Mackintosh Room**, flooded with soft, natural light. The **Furniture Gallery**, tucked up in the eaves, shelters an Aladdin's cave of designs that weren't able to be housed elsewhere in the school. Around the room are mounted building designs and a model of the *House for an Art Lover*, which Mackintosh submitted to a German competition in 1901. The building, constructed exactly to Mackintosh's specifications, will house office space for the Glasgow School of Art from spring 1996.

You can peer down from the Furniture Gallery into the school's most spectacular room, the glorious two-storey **Library** below. Here, sombre oak panelling is set against angular lights adorned with primary colours, dangling down in seemingly random clusters. The dark bookcases sit precisely in their fitted alcoves, while of the furniture, the most unusual feature is the central periodical desk, whose oval central strut displays perfect and quite beautiful symmetry.

The Tenement House

Just a few hundred yards northwest of the School of Art – albeit on the other side of the sheer hill that rises and falls down to Buccleuch Street – is the **Tenement House** at no. 145 (March–Oct daily 2–5pm; Nov–Feb by appointment only; NTS; £2.00). This is the perfectly preserved home of the habitually hoarding Agnes Toward, who moved here with her mother in 1911, changing nothing and throwing very little out until she was hospitalized in 1965. On the ground floor, there's a fascinating display on the development of urban Scottish housing, plus relics – ration books, letters, bills, holiday snaps and so forth – from Miss Toward's life. Upstairs you have to ring the doorbell to enter the living quarters, which give every impression of still being inhabited, with a roaring hearth and range, kitchen utensils, framed religious tracts and sewing machine all untouched. The only major change since Miss Toward left has been the reinstallation of the flickering gas lamps she would have used in the early days.

The West End

The urbane veneer of the **West End**, an area which contains many of the city's premier museums, seems a galaxy away from Glasgow's industrial image. In the 1800s, the city's focus moved west as wealthy merchants established huge estates away from the soot and grime of city life, and in 1870 the ancient university was moved from its cramped home near the cathedral to a spacious new site overlooking the River Kelvin. Elegant housing swiftly followed, the Kelvingrove Art Gallery was built to house the 1888 International Exhibition, and in 1896 the Glasgow District Subway – today's Underground – started its circuitous shuffle from here to the city centre.

The hub of life in this part of Glasgow is **Byres Road**, running down from the straight Great Western Road past Hillhead Underground station. Shops, restaurants, cafés, some enticing pubs and hordes of roving young people, including thousands of students, give the area a sense of style. Glowing red sandstone tenements and graceful terraces provide a suitably upmarket backdrop to this cosmopolitan district.

Kelvingrove Museum and Art Gallery

Founded on donations from the city's chief industrialists, the huge, red-brick fantasy castle of **Kelvingrove Museum and Art Gallery** (Mon–Sat 10am–5pm, Sun 11am–5pm; free) is a brash statement of Glasgow's nineteenth-century self-confidence. On the ground floor, a fairly dusty hall contains the Scottish natural history display; directly opposite sits an unremarkable exhibition of European and Scottish weapons. However, it's the art collections, the majority of which are upstairs, that are of most interest. Much of what you see in the Kelvingrove today is largely attributable to Alexander Reid, who shared rooms with Van Gogh in Paris, during which time he bought up works by the burgeoning Impressionists and took them back to Scotland.

The gallery of the **Classical Tradition** takes you from the Florentine and Venetian schools of the fifteenth to the seventeenth century past Sandro Botticelli's delicate *Annunciation* and the rich, vibrant hues of Giorgione's *The Adulteress Brought before Christ*. However, the dark and symbolic portayal of a slaughtered ox, crucified to a stake marks out the work of Rembrandt, next to his quiet portrait *The Man in Armour*. In the **Realist Tradition**, look out for Constable's famous depiction of *Hampstead Heath*, and *Modern Italy – The Pifferari*, a glowing portayal of Italian life by Turner. Boudin, Corot, Millet and Monet are also represented; the presence of these works owes much to the art dealer Alexander Reid, and so it is fitting that his bullish portrait by Van Gogh resides at the end of the gallery, surrounded by the European art that he loved. The gentle and naturalistic *Danai or The Tower of Brass* by pre-Raphaelite Sir Edward Burne-Jones dominates the **Victorian Age** room in an elaborate altar-like frame. The **Modern Period** holds a representative selection of work from Bonnard to Picasso and Matisse. There's also some work by **Glasgow Boys**, George Henry and Edward Hornel, including Henry's *Japanese Lady with a Fan,* its pattern and decoration inspired by the Far East.

The Transport Museum

The twin-towered **Kelvin Hall** is home to the excellent and enormous city **Transport Museum** (Mon–Sat 10am–5pm, Sun 11am–5pm; free), a collection of trains, cars, trams, circus caravans and prams, along with an array of old Glaswegian ephemera, whose entrance is in Bunhouse Road. Near the entrance, "Kelvin Street" is a re-created 1950s cobbled street featuring an old Italian coffee shop, a butcher's, a bakery and an old-time Underground station. A cinema shows fascinating films – mostly on themes based loosely around transport – of old Glasgow life, with crackly footage of Sauchiehall Street packed solid with trams and shoppers and hordes of pasty-faced Glaswegians setting off for their annual jaunts down the coast. Nearby, the Super X simulator (£1.50) rocks the nauseous viewer around in time with videoed skiing, white-water rafting and other stomach-churning activities. The Clyde Room displays intricate models of ships forged in Glasgow's yards – everything from tiny schooners to ostentatious ocean liners such as the *QE2*.

Glasgow University

Dominating the West End skyline, the gloomy turreted tower of Glasgow's **University**, designed by Sir Gilbert Scott in the mid-nineteenth century, overlooks the glades of the River Kelvin. Access to the main buildings and museums is from University Avenue, running east from Byres Road. In the dark neo-Gothic pile under the tower you'll find the **University Visitor Centre** (Mon–Sat 9.30am–5pm), which, as well as giving information for potential students, distributes leaflets about the various university buildings and the statues around the campus.

Next door to the University Visitor Centre, the collection of the **Hunterian Museum** (Mon–Sat 9.30am–5pm; Oct–April Sat closes 1pm; free), Scotland's oldest public museum dating back to 1807, was donated to the university by ex-student William Hunter, a pathologist and anatomist whose eclectic tastes form the basis of a fairly dry, but frequently diverting zoological and archeological museum. Exhibitions include Scotland's only dinosaur, a look at the Romans in Scotland – the chilly furthest outpost of a massive empire – and a vast coin collection.

On the other side of University Avenue is Hunter's more frequently visited bequest: the **Hunterian Art Gallery** (Mon–Sat 9.30am–5pm; free), best known for its works by James Abbott McNeil Whistler – only Washington DC has a larger collection. Whistler's breathy landscapes are less compelling than his portraits of women: look out especially for the trio of full-length portraits, *Pink and Silver – the Pretty Scamp*, *Pink and Gold – the Tulip* and *Red and Black – the Fan*. The gallery's other major collection is of nineteenth- and twentieth-century Scottish art, including the quasi-Impressionist Scottish landscapes of William McTaggart, a forerunner of the Glasgow Boys, represented here by, among others, E.A. Walton – especially in the spirited portrait of his wife – and Edward Hornel's sweeping, extravagantly colourful canvases, that mix Oriental and Scottish styles with bold panache. The selection of French Impressionists includes Corot's soothing *Distant View of Corbeil* and works by Boudin and Pissaro.

A side gallery leads to the **Mackintosh House**, a re-creation of the interior of the now-demolished Glasgow home of Margaret and Charles Rennie Mackintosh. An introductory display contains photographs of the original house sliding irrevocably into terminal decay, from where you are lead into an exquisitely cool interior that contains over sixty pieces of Mackintosh furniture on three floors. Among the highlights are the Studio Drawing Room, whose cream and white furnishings are bathed in expansive pools of natural light, and the Japanese-influenced guest bedroom in dazzling, monochrome geometrics.

The Botanic Gardens

At the top of Byres Road, where it meets the Great Western Road, is the main entrance to the **Botanic Gardens** (gardens daily 7am–dusk; Kibble Palace summer daily 10am–

4.45pm; winter closes 4.15pm; Main Range glasshouses summer Mon–Sat 1pm–4.45pm, Sun noon–4.45pm; winter closes 4.15pm; free). The best-known glasshouse here, the hulking, domed **Kibble Palace** – originally known as the Crystal Palace – was built in 1863 for wealthy landowner John Kibble's estate on the shores of Loch Long, where it stood for ten years, before he decided to transport it into Glasgow, drawing it up the Clyde on a vast raft pulled by a steamer. Today the palace houses a damp, musty collection of swaying palms from around the world. The smell is much sweeter on entering the Main Range glasshouse, home to lurid and blooming flowers and plants – including stunning orchids, cacti, ferns and tropical fruit – luxuriating in the humidity.

South of the Clyde

The southern bank of the Clyde, facing the city centre, is home to the notoriously deprived districts of **Govan**, a community yet to find its niche after the shipbuilding slump, and the **Gorbals**, synonymous with the razor gangs of old. On the southern side of Govan the vast bowl of **Ibrox**, home to the rigidly Protestant Rangers football team, proudly displays the Union flag. This Unionist fortress was totally overhauled following the disaster on January 2, 1971, when 66 fans died after a match against bitter arch-rivals Celtic – a stand collapsed as hundreds of early-leavers stampeded back into the stadium after an unlikely last-minute goal.

Inner-city decay fades into altogether gentler and more salubrious suburbs, commonly referred to as **South Side**. These include Queen's Park, a residential area home to Hampden Park football stadium, and the rural landscape of **Pollok Park**, three miles southwest of the city centre, which contains two of Glasgow's major museums: the **Burrell Collection** and **Pollok House**. Buses #34 and #34A from Govan Underground station set down outside the gate nearest to the Burrell. Slightly further to walk is the route from the Pollokshaws West station (don't confuse with Pollokshields West), served by regular trains from Glasgow Central and nearby bus stops on the Pollokshaws Road: *Strathclyde* buses #45, #48 and #57 from Union Street. However, as Pollok Park is only three miles from the city centre, taking a taxi to the Burrell is an inexpensive option.

The Burrell Collection

The lifetime collection of shipping magnate Sir William Burrell (1861–1958), the outstanding **Burrell Collection** (Mon–Sat 10am–5pm, Sun 11am–5pm; free) is, for some, the principal reason for visiting Glasgow. Unlike many other art collectors, Sir William's only real criterion for buying a piece was whether he liked it or not, enabling him to buy many "unfashionable" works, which cost comparatively little, and subsequently proved their worth. The simplicity and clean lines of the Burrell building, opened in 1983 are its greatest assets, with large picture windows giving sweeping views over woodland and serving as a tranquil backdrop to the objects inside. The sculpture and antiques are on the ground level, arranged in six sections that overlap and occasionally backtrack, while a mezzanine above displays most of the paintings.

On entering the building, the most striking piece, by virtue of sheer size, is the Warwick Vase, a huge bowl containing fragments of a second century AD vase from Hadrian's Villa in Tivoli. Next to it are the first of a series of sinewy and naturalistic bronze casts of Rodin sculptures, among them *The Age of Bronze*, *A Call to Arms* and the infamous *Thinker*. Beyond the entrance hall, on three sides of a courtyard, are a trio of dark and sombre panelled rooms re-erected in faithful detail from the Burrells' Hutton Castle home, their heavy tapestries, antique furniture and fireplaces displaying the same eclectic taste as the rest of the museum.

From the courtyard, leading up to the picture windows, the **Ancient Civilizations** collection – a catch-all title for Greek, Roman and earlier artefacts – includes an exquisite mosaic Roman cockerel from the first century BC and a four-thousand-year-old Mesopotamian lion's head. The bulk of it is Egyptian, however, with rows of inscrutable gods and kings. Nearby, also illuminated by the enormous windows, the **Oriental Art** section forms nearly one quarter of the complete collection, ranging from Neolithic jades through bronze vessels and Tang funerary horses to cloisonné. Near-Eastern art is also represented, in a dazzling array of turquoise- and cobalt-decorated jugs, and a swathe of intricate carpets.

The collection of **Medieval and Post-Medieval European Art**, which encompasses silverware, glass, textiles and sculpture, ranges across a maze of small galleries, whose most impressive sections are the sympathetically lit stained glass – note the homely image of a man warming his toes by the fire – and the hundreds of tapestries. Among the church art and reliquary are simple thirteenth-century Spanish wooden images and cool fifteenth-century English alabaster, while a trio of period interiors, interrupted by an exhibition of fragile, antique lace, cover the Gothic and Elizabethan eras, and seventeenth and eighteenth centuries. In the latter you can see selections from Burrell's vast art collection, the highlight of which is one of Rembrandt's evocative early self-portraits from 1632.

Upstairs, the cramped, and comparatively gloomy mezzanine is probably the least satisfactory section of the gallery, not the best setting for its sparkling array of paintings. The selection incongruously leaps from a small gathering of fifteenth-century religious works to Gericault's darkly dynamic *Prancing Grey Horse* and Degas' thoughtful and perceptive *Portrait of Emile Durant*. Pissarro, Manet, Boudin and Cezanne are also represented along with some exquisite watercolours by Glasgow Boy Joseph Crawhall, revealing his accurate and tender observations of the animal world.

Pollok House and Haggs Castle

A quarter of a mile away down rutted tracks lies the lovely eighteenth-century **Pollok House** (Mon–Sat 10am–5pm, Sun 11am–5pm; free), the manor of the Pollok Park estate and once home of the Maxwell family, local lords and owners of most of southern Glasgow until well into this century. Designed by William Adam in the mid-1700s, the house is typical of its age: graciously light and sturdily built, looking out onto the pristine raked and parterre gardens, whose stylized daintiness contrasts with the heavy Spanish paintings inside, among them works by El Greco, Murillo and Goya. The house itself is, however, like so many stately homes, a little sterile – only the servants' quarters downstairs capture the imagination, a virtually untouched labyrinth of tiled Victorian parlours and corridors that includes a good tea room in the old kitchen.

Close to the eastern entrances to Pollok Park, **Haggs Castle** on St Andrew's Drive (Mon–Sat 10am–5pm, Sun 11am–5pm; free) was built in 1685 as a Maxwell family Baronial hall, the precursor to the far more ornate Pollok House. Today the stark grey turrets and impenetrable stone walls conceal a historical museum aimed squarely at children. Some of the rooms have been decked out with figures and tableaux of the Maxwell family at home, others turned over to interactive exhibitions looking at Scottish history – including an unusually clear explanation of the history and importance of Mary, Queen of Scots.

Cafés and restaurants

Glasgow's renaissance has seen an explosion of fine restaurants and European-style bars and cafés, which, in addition to the imput of its diverse and ethnically mixed population, make eating possibilities pretty wide. Unlike in staid Edinburgh, where a lot of places close on Sunday, most of Glasgow's restaurants are open seven days a week. The city's **restaurants** cover an impressively international spectrum – incorporating cuisines such as Catalan and Irish along with more familiar dishes from France, Italy, India and China. Traditional **Scottish cuisine** has become very trendy in recent years, with an upsurge in the number of outlets, covering most price ranges, that serve local specialities. There are few exclusively **vegetarian** restaurants, but most places – especially around the Merchant City – have good, imaginative vegetarian choices.

Budget food: cafés, bars and diners

Café Gandolfi, 64 Albion St. Trendy Merchant City café-bar that attracts hordes of posing beauties, here to enjoy good-quality soup, salads and fish dishes.

Delifrance, 119–121 Sauchiehall St. French café with takeaway service, serving cheap and authentic food. Open daytime only in winter, until around 8pm during the summer.

Eat Out, 8–19 W George St. The only gay and lesbian café in Glasgow, this colourful and relaxed establishment, under Queen Street train station, is always busy, serving pasta and salads with free coffee refills. Daily food until 10pm, open until 11pm.

Fratelli Sarti, 133 Wellington St & 121 Bath St. Authentic and popular, the deli (Mon–Sat 9am–6pm) on Wellington St also serves delicious pizza and pasta in a frantic café until 10pm; the Bath St restaurant (just next door) is larger with the same quality menu and open Mon–Sat 8am–10pm.

Granary, 82 Howard St. Well situated near the St Enoch Centre, this affordable café serves quiches, lasagne and other vegetarian favourites complemented by a good variety of salads. Open daily till 5pm.

Junkanoo, 111 Hope St, near Central station. Boisterous and inexpensive Latin American bar that successfully, and unusually, combines a pleasant drinking atmosphere with some great food, with tapas and chilli looming large. Mon–Thurs open till 11pm, Fri & Sat till midnight, Sun closes at 5pm.

Kings Café, 71 Elmbank St, off Sauchiehall Street. Good fish-and-chip shop with seating at the back, serving generous helpings of traditional greasy fare and quality pasta to boot.

Tron Theatre, 63 Trongate. Two atmospheres prevail here. The trendy wrought-iron café-bar caters for the quick lunch and coffee crowd, while the old-fashioned Victorian bar is perfect for a laid-back lunch or dinner.

Willow Tea Room, 217 Sauchiehall St. Refined elevenses, lunches and afternoon tea in Mackintosh-designed splendour. Open till 5pm.

Chinese, Japanese, Southeast Asian and Indian

Blossom, 80 Miller St, Merchant City. In a city not terribly well blessed with Chinese restaurants, this is undoubtedly one of the best, with a well-priced and wide-ranging menu that includes an unusually good number of vegetarian options.

Ho Wong, 82 York St, just off Argyle Street west of Central Station. Secluded restaurant offering top-class Cantonese and Szechuan food. Expensive but worth it.

Koh-i-noor, 235 North St, Charing Cross. Good-value range of diverse Indian dishes, especially notable for its highly reasonable Sunday brunches.

Loon Fung, 417 Sauchiehall St. Great *dim sum* and inexpensive vegetarian set meals.

Mata Hari, 17 W Princes St, Charing Cross. Deservedly popular Malaysian restaurant with some unusual, spicy dishes on the moderately priced menu. Closed Sun.

Moshi Moshi, 7 Buccleuch St (☎0141/353 0777). Slip into this small establishment for a taste of downtown Tokyo where tempting sushi, noodle and tempura dishes are served with Japanese beer or sake.

Greek and Middle Eastern

Cafe Serghei, 67 Bridge St. One of the city's few Greek restaurants, serving traditional food in a lively atmosphere, and strictly speaking on the south side of the river.

Prince Armany's, 7 Clyde Place (☎0141/420 6660). Tucked under the railway bridge on the south side of the river near Bridge Street, this restaurant offers Middle Eastern food such as lamb kebabs and delicate vegetable stews served with couscous or deliciously light Arabian bread. The pre-theatre menu (5–7pm) is an excellent bargain.

Icelandic

XO, 28–32 Cathedral Square (☎0141/552 3519). Scotland's only Icelandic restaurant, situated upstairs from the Cathedral House cafe-bar, where you can throw a selection of fish and meat onto a massive slab of oven-heated granite, and watch it fry. Expensive but fun.

Italian and Latin

Cantina Del Rey, 6 Kings Court (☎0141/552 4044). Housed in a converted railway vault, this spacious restaurant serves authentic Mexican cuisine including fajitas, burritos and frozen margaritas at reasonable prices. Open daily 5–10pm, Fri & Sat till 11pm.

Fire Station, 33 Ingram St (☎0141/552 2929). Merchant City restaurant housed in a huge old fire station, dating from 1900, walled with municipal cast-off marble tiling. The excellent menu, especially the pasta and the indulgent puddings, is moderately priced, and they offer a wide choice of beer and wine.

O'Sole Mio, 32 Bath St. A superb, and easily affordable, city-centre restaurant for unusual pasta dishes, as well as pizzas from their log-fired oven.

Scottish

Babbity Bowster, 16–18 Blackfriars St (☎0141/552 5055). Atmospheric and popular Merchant City bar on the ground level serving excellent Scottish food – anything from hearty broths to haggis, salmon and kippers. The restaurant upstairs is pricier, and more sedate, serving venison, fresh fish and the like. Daily till midnight.

City Merchant, 97 Candleriggs (☎0141/553 1577). Intimate restaurant in Merchant City that serves good food using Scottish produce from Dingwall haggis to fresh lobster. Open Mon–Sat till 10.30pm.

Crannog, 28 Cheapside St (☎0141/221 1727). Excellent seafood restaurant tucked away underneath the vast motorway bridge. Much of the food, which is very reasonably priced compared with other city seafood joints, is caught by the restaurant and smoked on the premises. Also has a good vegetarian selection. Closed Sun.

Rogano, 11 Exchange Place, near Buchanan Street (☎0141/248 4055). Although the food here is not solely Scottish, the Rogano is a Glasgow institution, an absolutely superb but shockingly expensive fish restaurant decked out inside as an authentic replica of the 1930s Cunard liner, the *Queen Mary. Café Rogano*, in the basement, is cheaper but not so deliciously ostentatious. Café open till 11.30pm on Sat; both closed Sun.

Vegetarian

Cafe Alba, 61 Otago St. Situated just off Gibson Street, this popular café sells a good selection of vegetarian food. However, it is probably better known for the best home baking in the west.

Granary, 82 Howard St. Well situated near the St Enoch Centre, this affordable café serves quiches, lasagne and other vegetarian favourites complemented by a good variety of salads. Open daily till 5pm.

13th Note, 80 Glassford St. This Merchant City bar stands out for its all vegan menu from vegeburgers to chilli with daily specials that tend to have an international theme. Food served daily until early evening only.

Vegville Diner, 93 St Georges Rd (☎0141/331 2220). Good quality and value for money is the name of the game in this colourful diner. The menu consists of innovative and tasty dishes with several Japanese options.

West End

Predominantly due to the large local student population, the **West End** is best area for cheap, stylish restaurants and cafés, and bars serving food, especially around Hillhead Underground station on Byres Road; nearby, the restaurants along **Ashton Lane** dish out unreservedly good meals. On the other side of Byres Road from the station, **Ruthven Lane** is home to some lively restaurants well known for their happy hours.

Budget food: cafés, bars and diners

Back Alley, 8 Ruthven Lane. This West End burger joint is Glasgow's best, with enormous burgers, smothered in assorted toppings, to be washed down with good beer and finished off with calorific puddings. Moderately priced, with an early-evening happy hour.

California Gourmet, 291 Byres Rd. Daytime American ice-cream and sandwich bar, full of students enjoying the delicious submarines with up to 13 different fillings.

Chimmy Chungas, 499 Great Western Rd. Loud and popular Tex-Mex café-bar that is good for anything from a light snack through to a full blow-out. Sun to Thurs food served until 9.30pm, Fri & Sat until 10.30pm.

Grosvenor Café, 31 Ashton Lane. Small traditional Italo-Scots café tucked behind Hillhead Underground station with a die-hard clientele, addicted to the no-nonsense food (pizzas, fried food, burgers) served at astonishingly low prices. Sun & Mon open till 7pm, Tues–Sat 11pm.

Indian

Ashoka, 19 Ashton Lane (☎0141/357 5904). Moderately priced West End Dhosa house and Indian restaurant, popular with local students.

Mother India, 28 Westminster Terrace (☎0141/221 1633).Good-quality food at affordable prices in the refreshingly laid-back surroundings of this friendly Indian restaurant. It's unlicensed, so bring your own alcohol; small corkage fee.

Shalimar, 23–25 Gibson St, near Glasgow University (☎0141/339 6453). Mix of students and professionals who appreciate the extensive and good-value menu.

Italian and Latin

The Big Blue, 445 Great Western Rd (☎0141/357 1038.) Whitewashed walls and colourful uphol-stery characterize this low-level bar and restaurant that serves simple but tasty pasta dishes. Food served daily until 9pm.

Chimmy Chungas, 499 Great Western Rd (☎0141/334 0884). Looking down into a large bar, this restaurant is deservedly popular with students taking advantage of lunchtime bargains. Food served daily until 10pm.

Di Maggio's, 61 Ruthven Lane (☎0141/334 8560). Inexpensive, extremely popular West End pizze-ria and pasta joint, usually packed solid with bargain-hungry students. Frantic atmosphere with occasional live music.

Salsa, 184 Dumbarton Rd (☎0141/337 1416). A smaller version of the *Cantina Del Rey*, this West End branch serves the same good-quality food in a colourful and laid-back atmosphere. Daily noon–11pm.

Scottish

Ubiquitous Chip, 12 Ashton Lane (☎0141/334 5007). Splendid West End restaurant with a covered patio that resembles an indoor forest. Glasgow's most delicious Scottish food – game, seafood and local cheeses, and occasionally oatmeal ice-cream and venison haggis. Expensive. Open daily till 11pm.

Vegetarian

Bay Tree, 403 Great Western Rd. This small co-operative café offers a decent selection of burgers, salads and soups with good daily specials. Try the sugar-free cakes for a guilt-free pudding.

Pubs and bars

Not so many years ago, Glasgow's rough image was inextricably associated with its **pubs**, widely thought of as no-go areas for any visitor. Although much of this reputa-tion was overexaggerated, there was an element of truth in it. Nowadays, however, you're just as likely to spend an evening in a succession of open and airy café-bars as in a dark, dangerous, nicotine-stained pub. The centre has an admirable range of reliable places to drink; if you tire of the glossy **Merchant City**, head for the **East End**, where a fair number of local spit-and-sawdust establishments make a welcome change. All in all, though, the liveliest area, once again, has to be the **West End**, its good cross section of pubs and bars matching its great restaurants.

City centre

Bar 91, 91 Candleriggs. Well-designed Merchant City bar, using wrought iron to evoke a stylish atmosphere.

Brahms and Liszt, 71 Renfield St. Candlelit cellar bar that takes great pride in its beer selection, some of which is available by the jug. Great atmosphere, but gets very crowded.

Corn Exchange, 88 Gordon St. Slap opposite Central station, this bar has successfully re-created the feel of a traditional Victorian Glaswegian pub.

Horseshoe Bar, 17 Drury St. Traditional old pub, reputedly Glasgow's busiest – loud, frantic and great fun, with a very mixed clientele. Karaoke upstairs, with a downstairs bar for quiet conversation.

Jinty McGinty's, 21–29 Ashton Lane. Wood-panelled and frosted-glassed Irish pub that, as well as serving excellent stout, maintains a small menu of Irish favourites such as bacon and cabbage, steak and Guinness pie or hearty soups.

Nico's, 375–379 Sauchiehall St. Trendy without being painfully so, the ambience in this popular bar strives towards a French flavour – prices are steep.

R.G.'s, 73 Queen St. Nostalgia-soaked bar that serves as a focus for Glasgow's rock music heritage – hence the large portraits of local musical luminaries that adorn the walls. A bit cramped, but a fun atmosphere.

Saracen Head, Gallowgate (opposite the Barras market). Unchanged East End pub that offers an enjoyably beery, sawdust-floored wallow. Look out for the tax demand from Robbie Burns displayed on the wall, from the days when he was the local tax officer.

Scotia Bar, 112 Stockwell St. Laid-back bar popular with writers and other tortured souls. Occasional live folk music – Billy Connolly began his career here, telling jokes in between singing folk songs.

Ten, Mitchell Lane. In a tiny street connecting Buchanan and Mitchell streets, *Ten* was designed by the same crew as Manchester's legendary *Hacienda* club. As you'd expect, it's suitably chic, although with a healthy dose of Glaswegian humour to take off the posey edge.

Variety Bar, 401 Sauchiehall St. Crowded bar with faded Art Nouveau appeal and frequented by local art-school students.

West End

The Aragon, 131 Byres Rd. Old-fashioned bar with mixed crowd. The main attraction here is the vast beer selection, which includes European fruit beers and weekly guest ales.

Bonham's, 194 Byres Rd. Tall, spacious bar with splendid stained-glass windows. Popular, unpretentious and serving reasonable daytime food.

Brewery Tap, 1055 Sauchiehall St. Well known for its excellent selection of real ales and imported lager, this pub caters for students and locals alike with seating outside for those long summer evenings.

The Halt, 106 Woodlands Rd. Great beer and a vast selection of whiskies in this relaxed music pub. Regular live jazz.

Living Room, 5–9 Byres Rd. New hotbed for the young and hip, at the southern end of Byres Road. Wrought iron and candles enhance the pre-club atmosphere.

Mitchell's, 157 North St. Next to the domed Mitchell's Library, a comfortable pub with a scholarly atmosphere. Good beer and an excellent refuge.

Tennent's, 191 Byres Rd. No-nonsense, beery den, a refreshing antidote to all the designer paradises nearby. Large and very popular, especially with real-ale afficianados.

The Western Bar, 80 Dumbarton Rd. A world apart from the student haunts nearby, this genuinely friendly working-class stronghold has walls that read like a city social history treatise, with lots of old photographs and faded memorabilia.

Whistler's Mother, 116–122 Byres Rd. Combines a relaxed restaurant with the more basic bar, which is deservedly popular with students and legions of young people. Great decor that doesn't sacrifice comfort for style.

Nightlife and Entertainment

Glasgow's City of Culture tag resulted in a great liberalization of the city's licensing laws, which transformed the **clubbing** scene almost overnight. Since then, however, many of these laws have been repealed, and a curfew has been passed declaring that no one is to be allowed into a bar or club after 1am (the time has changed twice since being implemented, so check at tourist office first). Considering that many clubs were licensed until 6am during 1990, encouraging club-hopping, the new rules are, in the view of many, absurdly draconian.

Most of Glasgow's nightclubs are in the heart of the main shopping areas off Argyle and Buchanan streets, many of them within walking distance of each other. Establishments are pretty mixed, and although there's still a stack of outdated mega-discos with rigorous dress codes, the last couple of years has seen the arrival of far more stylish haunts. Hours hover from around 9pm to 3am, and cover charges are vari-able – expect to pay around £3 during the week, rising to around £8 at the weekend. Drinks are usually about thirty percent more expensive than in the pubs.

The city's traditional breadth of art, theatre, film and music is impressive, especially during **Mayfest**, Glasgow's most concentrated splurge of cultural activity. The majority of the larger **theatres**, **cinemas** and showpiece **concert halls** are around the shopping streets of the city centre, while the West End is home to student-oriented venues such as the quirky *Grosvenor* cinema. The city's two trendiest theatres, the *Citizens'* and the *Tramway*, are South Side. You can find **details** of the city's events in the *Glasgow Herald* or *Evening Times* newspapers, or the fortnightly listings magazine, *The List* (£1.50), which also covers Edinburgh. To book **tickets** for theatre productions or big concerts, phone the *Ticket Centre* ☎0141/227 5511; or call in at their headquarters at City Hall, Candleriggs, on the Trongate end of Argyle Street (phone bookings Mon–Sat 9am–9pm, Sun noon–5pm; office Mon–Sat 10am–6.30pm, Sun noon–5pm).

Nightclubs

The Arches, Midland St. Deservedly popular weekend club pounding out predominantly dance and rave-orientated music in converted railway arches, literally under central station, off Jamaica Street.

The Cotton Club, 5 Scott St . Friendly club with a variety of one-nighters including "Club Havana", the last Sunday of every month, playing salsa and flamenco and offering free dance lessons. Opposite the art school.

Fury Murray's, 96 Maxwell St, behind the St Enoch Centre. Student-oriented and lively, with music spanning from the 1960s to rave and techno.

Riverside Club, Fox Rd, off Clyde Street. Regular weekend ceilidh that gets absolutely packed out with good-natured, drunken Scottish dancers. Great fun, with a live band and callers involving everyone from seasoned ceilidh dancers to visiting novices. Get there early (8–9pm) to ensure a place.

Sub Club, 22 Jamaica St. Nightclub aimed squarely at the ravier end of the market. Weekend nights are very trendy.

The Tunnel, 84 Mitchell St. Stylish club with arty decor – though now a bit faded; the gents' toilet has cascading waterfall walls. Gay night on Mon.

The Volcano, 15 Benalder St. The major club in the West End, drawing in hordes of students. An eclectic selection of specialist music nights in the week and just a damn good boogie at the weekends.

The Voodoo Room, Cambridge St. Designer club with bleached wood bar, label-conscious clien-tele and distinctive music nights from funk to house and garage.

Gay clubs and bars

Austin's, 183 Hope St. Dingy but lively central cellar bar, with a mainly male — and fairly cruisey – crowd of all ages.

Bennett's, 90 Glassford St, Merchant City. Glasgow's main gay club, predominantly male, fairly old-fashioned but enjoyable nonetheless. Straight nights on Tues.

Club Xchange, Royal Exchange Square, off Queen Street. *Bennett's* biggest rival, this mixed gay club is funkier and more upbeat.

The Court Bar, 69 Hutcheson St. Quiet backstreet pub near George Square, mixed in daytimes and gay in the evenings. Friendlier, and less self-conscious, than most of Glasgow's gay pubs.

Del Monica's, 68 Virginia St. Glasgow's liveliest and most stylish gay bar, very near George Square, with a mixed and hedonistic crowd.

The Waterloo Bar, 306 Argyle St. Very central, garish but enjoyable bar, which gets packed at weekends. Mainly men.

Live music pubs and venues

Barrowlands, 244 Gallowgate (☎0141/226 4679). Legendary East End dance hall, complete with spinning glitter ball, that hosts some of the sweatiest, liveliest gigs you will ever encounter. Has a capacity of a couple of thousand, so tends to attract bands that are just breaking into the big time.

The Garage, 490 Sauchiehall St (☎0141/332 1120). Good-size venue for bands that are just about to make it big.

King Tut's Wah Wah Hut, 272a St Vincent St (☎0141/221 5279). One of the city's best programmes of bands at this splendid city-centre live music pub. Good bar downstairs if you want to sit out the sweaty gig above.

Nice'n'Sleazy, 421 Sauchiehall St (☎0141/333 9637). Alternative bands most nights in the somewhat cramped downstairs bar.

Scotia Bar, 112 Stockwell St, near the St Enoch Centre (☎0141/552 8681). The folkies' favourite, a mellow musical pub that acts as a magnet for folk players and followers. Regular live gigs and frequent jam sessions.

13th Note, 80 Glassford St (☎0141/553 1638). This double-level bar in the Merchant City is a good place to sample local music talent with live bands most nights.

Theatre and comedy

The Arches, 30 Midland St (☎0141/☎0141/221 9736). Trendy base for performances by touring theatre groups.

Blackfriars, 45 Albion Rd (☎0141/552 5924). The city's premier comedy and cabaret venue, renowned for its good-value Saturday night line-ups. Also live music, particularly jazz. In the Merchant City.

Centre for Contemporary Arts, 346 Sauchiehall St (☎0141/332 7521). Radical theatre, dance and art.

Citizens' Theatre, 119 Gorbals St (☎0141/429 0022). Glasgow's infamous theatre that grew from working-class roots to become one of the most respected, and adventurous, theatres in Britain. Three stages, with bargain prices for students and the unemployed, together with free preview nights.

King's Theatre, 297 Bath St (☎0141/227 5511). Mainstream shows and comedy, south of Sauchiehall Street.

Old Athenaeum, 179 Buchanan St (☎0141/332 2333). A smallish base for the *Scottish Youth Theatre*, as well as for visiting companies and stand-up comedians.

Tramway Theatre, 25 Albert Drive, off Pollokshaws Road (☎0141/225 5511). Good venue for experimental theatre, dance, music and regular art exhibitions.

Tron Theatre, 63 Trongate (☎0141/552 4267). Varied repertoire of mainstream and experimental productions from visiting companies, together with one of the city's most laid-back bars.

Concert halls

Royal Concert Hall, 2 Sauchiehall St (☎0141/227 5511). Big-name rock and soul stars, orchestras and opera companies.

Scottish Exhibition & Conference Centre, Finnieston Quay (☎0141/248 3000). Soulless and overpriced huge shed with the acoustics and atmosphere of an aircraft hangar, but, unfortunately, the only venue in Glasgow (often the only venue in Scotland) visited by the megastars on their world tours.

Theatre Royal, Hope St (☎0141/332 9000). Opulent home of the Scottish Opera and regular host to visiting classical orchestras, opera companies, theatre blockbusters and occasional comedy.

Art-house cinemas

Glasgow Film Theatre, 12 Rose St (☎0141/332 8128). The city's main art-house and independent cinema.

Grosvenor, Ashton Lane (☎0141/339 4298). Eclectic mix of repertory, mainstream and art-house movies on two screens in this tiny West End alley. Occasional theme nights and frequent lates for local students.

Listings

Airlines *Aer Lingus*, 19 Dixon St (☎0141/0645/737747); *British Airways*, 66 Gordon St (☎0141/0345/ 222111); *Icelandair* (☎0141/0345/81111); *Loganair*, Glasgow Airport (☎0141/889 1311); *Lufthansa*, 78 St Vincent St (☎0141/0345/737747); *Northwest*, 38 Renfield St (☎0141/226 4175); *Qantas*, 39 St Vincent Place (☎0141/0345/747767).

American Express 115 Hope St (☎0141/221 4366).

Books *John Smith's*, 57 St Vincent St, *Waterstone's*, 132 Union St and *Dillons*, 104–108 Argyle St, all have extensive local studies sections.

Bus enquiries Buchanan Street bus station; for local buses call ☎0141/332 7133, for national buses ☎0141/0990 505050.

Car rental *Arnold Clark*, 16 Vinnicomb St (☎0141/334 9501); *Avis*, 161 North St (☎0141/221 2827); *Budget*, 101 Waterloo St (☎0141/226 4141); *Hertz*, 106 Waterloo St (☎0141/248 7736). Car rental firms at the **airport** include *Avis* (☎0141/887 2261), *Budget* (☎0141/887 0501), *Eurodollar* (☎0141/887 7915), *Europcar* (☎0141/☎0141/887 0414) and *Hertz* (☎0141/887 0414).

Consulates *Germany*, 158 W Regent St (☎0141/221 0304); *Norway*, 80 Oswald St (☎0141/204 1353); *Sweden*, 36 Washington St (☎0141/221 7845).

Exchange Outside banking hours you can change money at *Thomas Cook* in Central station (Mon–Wed, Fri & Sat 8am–7pm, Thurs 8am–8pm, Sun 10am–6pm; ☎0141/204 4496).

Football Of the two big Glasgow teams, you can see Celtic at Celtic Park, 95 Kerrydale St, off A749 London Road (☎0141/556 2611), and bitter opponents Rangers at the mighty Ibrox stadium, Edminston Drive (☎0141/427 8800). Glasgow's other teams include Partick Thistle in Firhill stadium, Firhill Rd (☎0141/945 4811) or, on the South Side, lowly Queen's Park at the national stadium Hampden Park, Mount Florida (☎0141/632 1275). Tickets from £10 depending on the opposing team and match status.

Gay and lesbian contacts *Lesbian and Gay Switchboard* (daily 7–10pm; ☎0141/221 8372), *Lesbian Line* (Weds 7–10pm; ☎0141/552 3355).

Hospital 24-hr casualty department at the *Royal Infirmary*, 84 Castle St (☎0141/552 3535).

Left luggage Staffed office available at Buchanan Street bus station (daily 6.30am–10.30pm) and 24hr lockers at both Central and Queen Street train stations.

Pharmacy *Sinclair's*, 693 Great Western Rd (daily 9am–9pm; ☎0141/339 0012) and at Central station (Mon–Sat 8am–7pm; ☎0141/248 1002).

Police Cranstonhill Police Station, 945 Argyle St (☎0141/532 3200) and Stewart Street station, Cowcaddens (☎0141/532 3000).

Post office George Square (Mon–Fri 8.30am–5.45pm, Sat 9am–7pm; ☎0141/242 4260), with branch offices at 85–89 Bothwell St, 216 Hope St and 533 Sauchiehall St.

Taxis *TOA Taxis* (☎0141/332 7070).

Travel agents *Campus Travel*, The Hub, Hillhead St (☎0141/357 0608) and 90 John St (☎0141/552 2867); *Glasgow Flight Centre*, 143 W Regent St (☎0141/221 8989).

The Clyde

The temptation to speed through the **Clyde valley** is considerable, especially since the raw beauty of the Highlands, the islands and lakes of Argyll and, of course, Edinburgh are all within easy reach of the city. Although many of the towns and villages surrounding Glasgow are decidedly missable, some receive far fewer visitors than they deserve, tarnished with the frequently redundant image of dejected industrial towns. From the city regular trains dip down the southern bank of the Clyde to **Paisley**, where the distinctive cloth pattern gained its name, before heading up to the Firth of Clyde. Heading southeast out of Glasgow, the river's industrial landscape gives way to a far more attractive scenery of gorges and towering castles. Here you can see the stoic town of **Lanark**, where eighteenth-century philanthropists built their model workers' community around the mills of **New Lanark**.

Paisley

Founded in the twelfth century as a monastic settlement around an abbey, **PAISLEY** expanded rapidly after the eighteenth century as a linen-manufacturing town, specializing in the production of highly fashionable imitation Kashmiri shawls. Paisley quickly eclipsed other British centres producing the cloth, eventually lending its name to the swirling pine-cone design. Regular trains from Glasgow Central connect with Paisley's Gilmour Street station in the centre of town. *Strathclyde Transport* **buses** #39, #53, #54 and #55 stop at Paisley Abbey; however, the train is faster and more convenient.

South of the train station, down Gilmour or Smithills streets, lies the bridge over the White Cart Water and the borough's ponderous town hall, home to the **tourist office** (April–May Mon–Fri 9am–1pm & 2–5pm, June–Sept Mon–Sat 9am–6pm; ☎0141/889 0711). Opposite the town hall, the **Abbey** was built on the site of the town's original settlement but was massively overhauled in the Victorian age. The unattractive, fat grey facade of the church does little justice to the renovated interior, which is tall, spacious and elaborately decorated. The elongated choir, rebuilt extensively throughout the last two centuries, is illuminated by jewel-coloured stained glass from a variety of ages and styles. The abbey's oldest monument is the tenth-century Celtic cross of St Barochan, which lurks like a gnarled old bone at the eastern end of the north aisle.

Paisley's tatty High Street leads from the town hall to the west and towards the civic **Museum and Art Gallery** (Mon–Sat 10am–5pm; free), which shelters behind pompous Ionic columns that face the grim buildings of Paisley University. The local history section, nearest the entrance, contains an interesting collection of local artefacts from song sheets and spinning threads to the death warrant and executioner's contract for the last public hanging in Paisley in 1858. The most popular part of the museum, which deals with the growth and development of the Paisley pattern and shawls, shows the familiar pine-cone (or teardrop) pattern from its simplistic beginnings to elaborate later incarnations. Beyond the museum stands the **Thomas Coates Memorial Church** (May–Sept Mon, Wed & Fri 2–4pm), a Victorian masterpiece of hugely overstated grandeur, with huge tower-top buttresses and an interior of seemingly endless marble and alabaster.

The harsh reality of eighteenth-century life is re-created in the **Sma' Shot Cottages** (April–Sept only Wed & Sat 1–5pm; free). These old houses can be found in George Place, off New Street. Each with individual themes, they contain perfect re-creations of eighteenth- and nineteenth- century daily life complete with bone cutlery and ancient looms. The nineteenth-century artisan's home is also filled with artefacts from ceramic hot water bottles to period wallpaper and leads you towards the cosy tea room where you can enjoy some home baking.

Lunchtime and evening bar **meals**, together with reasonably convivial atmospheres, can be found in *Gabriel's Bar* at 33 Gauze St, near the abbey, and the *Bankhouse* on Gilmour Street, almost next to the station. *Chez Jules*, 38 New St (☎0141/848 6611) provides more upmarket French cuisine, while the *Paisley Arts Centre* across the road has a small bar with seating outside.

Blantyre and Bothwell Castle

BLANTYRE, now a colourless suburb of Hamilton, twelve miles southeast of Glasgow, was a remote Clydeside hamlet when explorer and missionary David Livingstone was born there in 1813. From Blantyre station a right turn brings you to a quiet country lane, at the bottom of which, painted a brilliant white, is the **David Livingstone Centre** (Mon–Sat 10am–6pm, Sun 12.30–6pm; £2.50), showing his life from early years as a mill worker up until his death in 1873 searching for the source of the River Nile. In 1813, the building consisted of 24 one-room tenements, each occupied by an entire family. Today the Livingstone family room shows the claustrophobic conditions under which he was brought up; all the others feature slightly defensive exhibitions on the missionary movement with tableaux of scenes from his life in Africa, including the infamous meeting with Stanley. Smaller exhibitions on Blantyre and the Clyde valley area are held inside the main "Africa Pavilion" building.

A mile or so from Blantyre, **Bothwell Castle** (April–Sept Mon–Wed & Sat 9.30am–6pm, Thurs 9.30am–1.30pm, Sun 2–6pm; Oct–March Mon–Wed & Sat 9.30am–4pm, Thurs 9.30am–12.30pm; £1.50) is one of Scotland's most dramatic citadels, a great red sandstone bulk looming high above a loop in the river. The oldest section is the solid *donjon*, or circular tower, at the western end, built by the Moray family in the late 1200s to protect themselves against the English king Edward I during the Scottish wars of independence. Such was the might of the castle, Edward only finally succeeded in capturing it in September 1301 after ordering the construction and deployment of a massive siege engine, wheeled from Glasgow to Bothwell in order to lob huge stones at the castle walls. Over the next two centuries, the castle changed hands numerous times and was added to by each successive owner, with the last section, the Great Hall, in the grassy inner courtyard. **Buses** #55 and #56 from Glasgow to Hamilton will drop you off on the Bothwell Road, near the castle entrance.

Lanark and New Lanark

The neat little market town of **LANARK** is an old and distinguished burgh, sitting in the purple hills high above the River Clyde, its rooftops and spires visible for miles around. Beyond the world's oldest bell, cast in 1130 and visible in the Georgian Church of St Nicholas, there's little to see in town and most people make their way to **NEW LANARK** (daily 11am–5pm; £2.95), a mile below the main town on Braxfield Road.

Although New Lanark is served by an hourly bus from the train station, it's well worth the steep downhill walk to get there. The first sight of the village, hidden away down in the gorge, is unforgettable: large broken curving walls of honeyed warehouses and tenements, built in Palladian style, lined up along the turbulent river's edge. The community was founded by David Dale and Richard Arkwright in 1785 to harness the power of the Clyde waterfalls in their cotton-spinning industry, but it was Dale's son-in-law, Robert Owen, who revolutionized the social side of the experiment in 1798, creating a "village of unity". Believing the welfare of the workers to be crucial to industrial success, Owen built adult educational facilities, the world's first day nursery and playground, and schools in which dancing and music were obligatory and there was no punishment or reward. The Neoclassical **Institute for the Formation of Character** at the very heart of the village was opened by Owen in 1816, and quickly became the main focus of the community, with a library, chapel and dance hall; today, you can see an introductory video about New Lanark and its founders in the spacious congregational hall. Of the three vast old mill buildings open to visitors, one houses the **Annie McLeod Experience**, where a chairlift whisks visitors through a social history of life here from the imaginary perspective of a young mill girl.

The village itself is just as fascinating: everything, from the co-operative store to the workers' tenements and workshops, was built in an attempt to prove that industrialism need not be unaesthetic. Other attractions include **Classic Car Collections** (daily 11am–5pm; £1.95) which houses a selection of cars from the last century to the present; on a similar theme, the **Railway Kingdom** (Mon–Sat 11am–5pm, £1.50) features Scotland's largest model railway on a quarter mile of track. Situated in the Old Dyeworks, **The Scottish Wildlife Trust Visitor Centre** (Feb, March & Oct–Dec Sat & Sun only 1–5pm; April–Sept also Mon–Fri 11am–5pm) provides information about the history and wildlife of the area. Further on, past the visitor centre, a path along the Clyde leads you past the small falls of green water on which the Lanark project was first founded, and the Bonnington hydroelectric station to the major **Falls of The Clyde**, where at the stunning tree-fringed **Cora Linn**, the river plunges 90ft in three tumultuous stages. It is a stunning marker point for the Clyde Walkway, a path that follows the river from Glasgow Green to this valley forest.

Practicalities

By **train**, Lanark is the terminus on the line from Glasgow Central station. The town's **tourist office** (mid-April to Oct Mon–Fri 9am–5pm, Sat 10am–5pm, Sun noon–5pm; Nov & Dec closed Sun; Jan to mid-April also closed Sat; ☎01555/661661) is housed in a circular building one hundred yards west of the station. **Accommodation** varies from the spectacular *Cartland Bridge Hotel* on the town's edge just off the A73 Glasgow Road (☎01555/664426; ⑦), to **B&Bs** such as *Mrs Gray's*, 49 West Port, the continuation of the High Street (☎01555/663663; ②) and *Mrs Gair's*, 10 Park Place (☎01555/664403; ②). The brand new **youth hostel** (☎01555/666710) is beautifully sited amongst the reconstructed buildings of New Lanark itself. *The Cross Café* is a popular old-time Italian-run **café**, with a good atmosphere. There are some more pricey Indian and Italian **restaurants** along Wellgate. The rather posh *Clydesdale Hotel*, at 15 Bloomgate, serves meals in the cellar bar until 9pm, while the far less pretentious *Crown Tavern*, a quiet drinking haunt in Hope Street, serves reasonable food until 9.30pm.

travel details

Trains

Glasgow Central to: Ardrossan (every 30min; 45min); Ayr (every 30min; 50min); Blantyre (every 30min; 20min); Gourock (every 30min; 47min); Greenock (every 30min; 40min); Lanark (Mon–Sat hourly; 50min); Largs (hourly; 1hr); London (8 daily; 5hr 45min); Paisley (every 15min; 10min); Stranraer (3 daily; 2hr 10min); Wemyss Bay (hourly; 55min).

Glasgow Queen Street to: Aberdeen (hourly; 2hr 35min); Aviemore (3 daily; 2hr 40min); Balloch (Mon–Sat every 30min; 45min); Dumbarton (every 20min; 25min); Dundee (hourly; 1hr 20min); Edinburgh (every 30min; 50min); Fort William (3 daily; 3hr 40min); Helensburgh (every 30min; 45min); Inverness (3 daily; 3hr 25min); Mallaig (3 daily; 5hr 15min); Oban (3 daily; 3hr); Perth (hourly; 1hr); Stirling (hourly; 30min).

Buses

Glasgow to: Aberdeen (12 daily; 4hr); Aviemore (hourly; 3hr 30min); Campbeltown (3 daily; 4hr 20min); Dundee (hourly; 2hr 15min); Edinburgh (every 20min; 1hr 15min); Fort William (4 daily; 3hr); Glencoe (4 daily; 2hr 30min); Inverness (hourly; 4–5hr); Kyle of Lochalsh (4 daily; 5hr); Lochgilpead (3 daily; 2hr 40min); Loch Lomond (hourly; 45min); London (5 daily; 7hr 30min); Oban (3 daily; 3hr); Perth (hourly; 1hr 35min); Pitlochry (hourly; 2hr 20min); Portree (4 daily; 6hr); Stirling (hourly; 45min).

Flights

Glasgow to: Birmingham (Mon–Fri 9 daily, 3 on Sat & Sun; 1hr); Manchester (Mon–Fri 8 daily, 1 on Sat, 3 on Sun; 50min); London (Gatwick Mon–Fri 7 daily, 3 on Sat & Sun; 1hr 15min; Heathrow Mon–Fri 20 daily, 8 on Sat & Sun; Stansted Mon–Fri 4 daily, 1 on Sat & Sun).

CHAPTER TWENTY

CENTRAL SCOTLAND

Within easy reach of Edinburgh and Glasgow, **central Scotland** is a much visited area; not least for its spectacular and varied countryside, ranging from the picture-postcard beauty of the Central Lowlands to the wilder more challenging terrain of the Highlands, which officially begin here. The **Highland Boundary Fault**, the dramatic physical divide running southwest to northeast across the region, has rendered central Scotland – from medieval to modern times – the main stage for some of the most important events in Scottish history. Today the landscape is not only littered with remants of the past – well-preserved medieval towns and castles, royal residences and battle sites – but is also coloured by the many romantic myths and legends that have grown up around it.

At the heart of the **Central Lowlands**, above the industrial belt around Falkirk and Grangemouth, is venerable **Stirling**, its imposing castle perched high above the town. Historically one of the most important bridging points across the River Forth it was the site of two of the most famous battles fought under Robert the Bruce during the **Wars of Independence** (1296–1328). To the west and north of Stirling the magnificent scenery centres on the fabled mountains, glens, lochs and forests of the **Trossachs**, a unique and beautiful area of high peaks and steep-sided glens that stretches west from **Callander** to the eastern banks of Loch Lomond. The geography and history of the area caught the imagination of **Sir Walter Scott**, who took so much delight in the tales of local clansman **Rob Roy** MacGregor, the notorious seventeenth-century outlaw, that he set them down in his novel of the same name. Visitors flocked to the Trossachs and according to one contemporaneous account, after Scott's *Lady of the Lake* was published in 1810, the number of carriages passing Loch Katrine rose from fifty the previous year to 270. Thanks to Scott and to William and Dorothy Wordsworth's effusive praise, Queen Victoria decided to visit, placing the area firmly on the tourist map. Today however, the trappings of tourism – evident in twee shops and tea rooms in every small town – don't impinge too much on the experience.

Lying to the east of the Central Lowlands is **Fife**, the only one of Scotland's seven original Pict kingdoms to survive relatively intact. Neither Norse nor Norman influence found its way to this independent corner, and nine and a half centuries later, when the government at Westminster redrew local boundaries in 1975 and again in 1995, the Fifers stuck to their guns and successfully opposed any changes. Here you'll find coastal fishing villages and sandy beaches and the self-assured town of **St Andrews**, inextricably linked in the public consciousness with **golf**.

North of St Andrews on the west bank of the River Tay is the ancient town of **Perth**, surrounded by beautiful rugged country. At nearby **Scone**, Kenneth Macalpine established the capital of the kingdom of the Scots and the Picts in 846. When this settlement was washed away by floods in 1210, William the Lion founded Perth as a royal burgh and it stood as Scotland's capital until 1452. The four great monasteries of Perth were all destroyed during the Reformation after a sermon by John Knox at St John's Church. North of Perth, the Highlands begin in earnest. From **Loch Tay** onwards, beyond the agreeable town of **Aberfeldy**, the countryside becomes more sparsely populated and spectacular, with the **Grampian Mountains** to the east offering

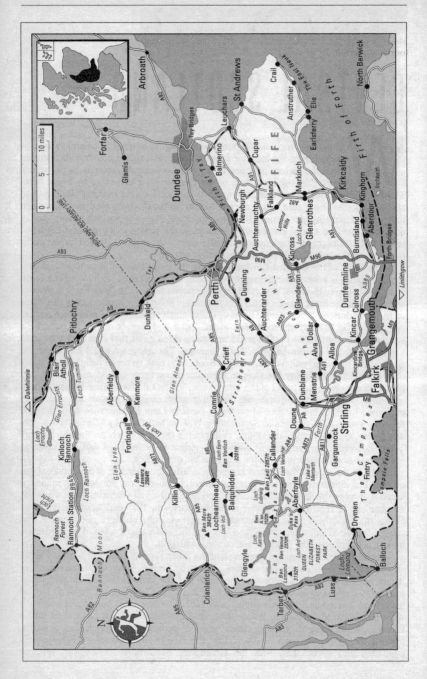

wonderful walks, especially around **Pitlochry**, and the wild expanses of **Rannoch Moor** to the west. This northerly part of the region also boasts Scotland's most popular tourist attraction, **Blair Castle**.

Stirling and around

Straddling the River Forth a few miles upstream from the estuary at Kincardine, at first glance **STIRLING** appears like a smaller version of Edinburgh. With its crag-top castle, steep, cobbled streets and mixed community of locals and students, it's an appealing place, although it does lack the cosmopolitan edge of Edinburgh or Glasgow. It's historic, due to its former importance as a much coveted river crossing, but – geographically trapped between Scotland's two main cities – Stirling remains at heart decidedly provincial.

The town was the scene of some of the most significant developments in the evolution of the Scottish nation. It was here that the Scots under William Wallace defeated the English at the **Battle of Stirling Bridge** in 1297, only to fight – and win again – under Robert the Bruce just a couple of miles away at the **Battle of Bannockburn** in 1314. Stirling enjoyed its golden age in the fifteenth to seventeenth centuries, most notably when its castle was the favoured residence of the Stuart monarchy and the setting for the coronation in 1543 of the young Mary, future Queen of Scots. By the early eighteenth century the town was again besieged, its location of strategic importance during the Jacobite rebellions of 1715 and 1745.

Today Stirling is known instead for its **Castle** – just as beautiful as its Edinburgh counterpart – and the lofty **Wallace Monument**, a mammoth Victorian monolith high on Abbey Craig to the northeast. The **University**, also, has helped to maintain the town's profile. Stirling is at its liveliest during the summer, with buskers and street artists jostling for performing space in the pedestrianized centre. If you get decent weather – which isn't all that uncommon despite the proliferation of surrounding hills – there's very much a holiday air about the place, with kids rushing around the castle ramparts, backpackers struggling up the steep hill to the youth hostel, and students, many of whom choose to stay here over the summer, spilling out of the cafés.

Arrival, information and accommodation

The **train station** is in the centre of town on Station Road; the **bus station** nearby on Goosecroft Road. Stirling's **tourist office** is in the heart of the town centre at 41 Dumbarton Rd (June–Sept Mon–Sat 9am–6pm, Sun 10am–4pm; Oct–May Mon–Sat 9am–5pm; ☎01786/475019). This is the main office for Loch Lomond, Stirling and the Trossachs, with a wide range of books, maps and leaflets.

If you're in Stirling between May and October, you'll need to book a room by lunchtime at the latest, or you're likely to be stranded. The tourist office carries details of **accommodation**; most of the **B&Bs** are concentrated in the residential area nearby, on Causewayhead Road leading to the university, and in the opulent Victorian suburb of King's Park, immediatley south of the tourist office. The *Park Lodge Hotel*, 32 Park Terrace (☎01786/474862; ⑥), is Stirling's finest, overlooking the park and castle, with a *haute-cuisine* restaurant. *The Heritage*, 16 Allan Park (☎01786/473660; ⑤), on the northern edge of King's Park, also has rooms looking up at the castle, and a good Scottish/French restaurant. Two friendly B&Bs to try are *No.10*, 10 Gladstone Place (☎01786/472681; ③), and *Whitegables*, 112 Causewayhead Rd (☎01786/479838; ③).

At the top of the town (a strenuous trek with a backpack), the cheapest option is the **youth hostel** in a recently converted church on St John Street (☎01786/473442). If you prefer to stay out of town, try the **campus accommodation** at Stirling University (June–

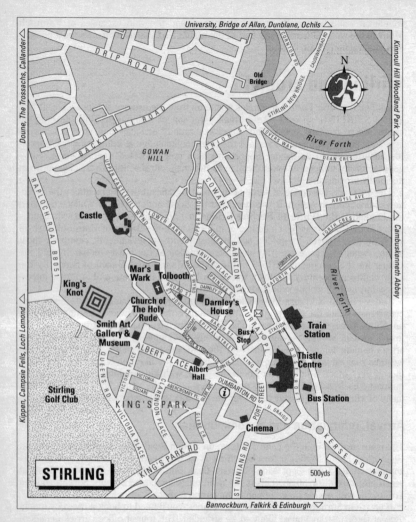

University, Bridge of Allan, Dunblane, Ochils △

Doune, The Trossachs, Callander ◁

Kinnoull Hill Woodland Park ▷

N

Old Bridge

STIRLING NEW BRIDGE

River Forth

DRIP ROAD

BACK O' HILL ROAD

GOWAN HILL

DEAN CRES

RAPLOCH ROAD B8051

UPPER CASTLEHILL WYND

ARGYLL AVE

Cambuskenneth Abbey ▷

Castle

LOWER BARN RD

UNION ST

COWANE ST

BARNTON ST

UPPER BRIDGE ST

QUEEN ST

FORTH CRES

Mar's Wark

Tolbooth

ST MARY'S WYND

IRVINE PLACE

PRINCES ST

DARNLEY ST

River Forth

King's Knot

Church of The Holy Rude

Darnley's House

BROAD ST

ST JOHN ST

SPITTAL STREET

BAKER ST

MURRAY PL

SEAFORTH PL

LOWER PL

Smith Art Gallery & Museum

ALBERT PLACE

STATION RD

Bus Stop

Train Station

Kippen, Campsie Fells, Loch Lomond ◁

QUEENS RD

VICTORIA PLACE

VICTORIA SQUARE

CLARENDON PLACE

ABERCROMBY PL

GLEBE AV

DRIP RD

GOOSECROFT RD

KING ST

Thistle Centre

Albert Hall

Stirling Golf Club

KING'S PARK

VICTORIA PLACE

KING'S PARK RD

GLEBE CR

DUMBARTON RD

PORT STREET

U GRAIGS

Bus Station

i

Cinema

ST NINIANS RD

KERSE RD A90

STIRLING

0   500yds

Bannockburn, Falkirk & Edinburgh ▽

-Aug; ☎01786/467141; ③) a couple of miles north of the town centre (bus #53 or #58 from Murray Place). Also on campus is the new *Stirling Management Centre* (all year; ☎01786/451666; ⑥), as popular with tourists as with the conference guests towards whom it was originally aimed, with rooms looking out at the Wallace Monument. There's a **campsite**, the *Witches Craig* at Blairlogie, three miles east of the town off the A91 road to St Andrews (April–Oct; ☎01786/474947).

The Town

Stirling evolved from the top down, starting with its castle and gradually spreading south and east onto the low-lying flood plain. At the centre of the original **Old Town**,

Broad Street was the main thoroughfare, with St John Street running more or less parallel, and St Mary's Wynd forming part of the original route to Stirling Bridge below. In the eighteenth and nineteenth centuries, as the threat of attack decreased, the centre of commercial life crept down towards the River Forth, with the modern town – commonly called the **Lower Town** – growing on the edge of the plain over which the castle has traditionally stood guard.

Stirling Castle

Stirling Castle (April–Sept Mon–Sat 9.30am–6pm, Sun 10.30am–4.45pm; Oct–March daily 9.30am–5pm; £3.50; HS) must have presented would-be invaders with a formidable challenge. Its impregnability is most daunting when you approach the town from the west, from where the sheer, 250-foot drop down the side of the crag is most obvious. The rock was first fortified during the Iron Age, though what you see now dates largely from the fifteenth and sixteenth centuries. Presently undergoing a massive restoration scheme (due to be completed in 2001), small parts of the castle may be inaccessible.

The **visitor centre** (same times as castle) on the esplanade shows an introductory film giving a potted history of the castle, but the best place to get an impression of its gradual expansion is in the courtyard known as the **Upper Square**. Here you can see the magnificent **Great Hall** (1501–03), with its lofty dimensions and huge fireplaces making it perhaps the finest medieval secular building in Scotland. The exterior of the **Palace** (1540–42) is richly decorated with grotesque carved figures and Renaissance sculpture, including, in the left-hand corner, the glaring bearded figure of James V in the dress of a commoner. Inside in the royal apartments are the **Stirling Heads**, 56 elegantly carved oak medallions, which once comprised the ceiling of the Presence Chamber, where visitors were presented to royalty. Otherwise the royal apartments are bare, their emptiness emphasizing the fine dimensions and wonderful views. The **Chapel Royal** (1594) was built by James VI for the baptism of his son, and replaced an earlier chapel, not deemed sufficiently impressive. The interior is lovely, with a seventeenth-century fresco of elaborate scrolls and patterns.

The castle also houses the Argyll and Sutherland Highlanders **museum**, with its collection of well-polished silver and memorabilia, including a seemingly endless display of Victoria Crosses won by the regiment. The set-up in the recently restored castle **kitchens** re-creates the preparations for the spectacular Renaissance banquet given by Mary, Queen of Scots for the baptism of the future James VI. As well as an audio-visual display describing how delicacies for the feast were procured, and an abundance of stuffed animals in various stages of preparation (who, we are assured, died natural deaths), the kitchens feature *faux* recipe books with such delights as sugar wine glasses, golden steamed custard and dressed peacock.

From the **Douglas Gardens** you can see the surprisingly small window from which the eighth Earl of Douglas, suspected of treachery, was thrown by James II in 1452. There is a bird's-eye view down to the **King's Knot**, a series of grassed octagonal mounds which in the seventeenth century were planted with box trees and ornamental hedges.

The Old Town

Leaving the castle, head downhill into the old centre of Stirling, fortified behind the massive, whinstone boulders of the **town walls**, built in the mid-sixteenth century and intended to ward off the advances of Henry VIII, who had set his sights on the young Mary as a wife for his son, Edward. The walls now constitute some of the best-preserved town defences in Scotland, and can be traced by following the path known as **Back Walk**. This circular walkway was built in the eighteenth century and in the upper reaches encircles the castle, taut along the edge of the crag, offering panoramic views of the surrounding countryside.

The richly decorated facade at the top of Broad Street on Castle Wynd hides the dilapidated **Mar's Wark**, a would-be palace which the first Earl of Mar, Regent of Scotland and hereditary Keeper of Stirling Castle, started in 1570. His dream house was never to be realized, however, for he died two years later and what had been built was left to ruin, its degeneration speeded up by extensive damage during the 1745 Jacobite Rebellion. Behind here is the **Church of the Holy Rude** (May–Sept Mon–Fri 10am–5pm, Sunday service), a fine medieval structure, the oldest parts of which, including the impressive oak hammer-beam roof, date from the early fifteenth century. Go in during the day and imagine the ceremony that was held here in 1567 for the coronation of the infant James VI – later the first monarch of the United Kingdom – and come back in the evening to the atmospheric graveyard, from where you can watch the sun set. Just south of the church on the edge of the crag, the grand E-shaped **Guildhall** was built as a 1649 almshouse for "decayed [unsuccessful] members of the Guild of Merchants". Above the entrance, John Cowane, the wealthy merchant who founded the hospital, is commemorated in a statue which, it is said, comes alive at Hogmanay.

Broad Street was the site of the marketplace and centre of the medieval town. Many of its buildings have been restored in recent years, and preservation work continues. Down here, past the **Mercat Cross** (the unicorn on top is known, inexplicably, as "the puggy"), the **Tolbooth**, sandwiched between Broad and St John streets (with the entrance on Broad Street), was built in 1705 by Sir William Bruce, who designed the Palace of Holyrood House in Edinburgh. It was used as both a courthouse and, after 1809, a prison, from where the unfortunate were led to execution in the street outside. **Darnley's House**, at the bottom of Broad Street, was where Mary Queen of Scots' husband is believed to have lodged while she lorded it up in the castle; it is now a touristy coffee shop.

The Lower Town

The further downhill you go into Stirling's Lower Town, the more recent the buildings become. Follow St John Street into Spittal Street, and then on down into King Street, where austere Victorian facades block the sun from the cobbled road. Stirling's main **shopping** area is down here, along Port Street and Murray Place, while the **Smith Art Gallery and Museum** (April–Oct Tues–Sat 10.30am–5pm, Sun 2–5pm; Nov–March Tues–Fri noon–5pm, Sat 10.30am–5pm, Sun 2–5pm) is a short walk west up Dumbarton Road. Founded in 1874 with a legacy from local painter and collector Thomas Stuart Smith, it houses a permanent exhibition relating the history of Stirling, and a range of changing displays of arts and crafts, contemporary art and photography.

The fifteenth-century **Old Bridge** over the Forth lies on the edge of the town centre (a 20-min walk from Murray Place). Although once the most important river crossing in Scotland – the lowest bridging point on the Forth until the new bridge was built in 1831 – it now stands virtually forgotten, an almost incidental reminder of Stirling's former importance. An earlier, wooden **bridge** nearby was the focus of the Battle of Stirling Bridge in 1297, where William Wallace defeated the English.

Eating, drinking and nightlife

The elegant three-storey *Darnley Coffee House*, on Bow Street, serves reasonably priced lunches and teas, amid an impressive plain barrel-vaulted interior. On Albert Place, the *Café Albert* in the Victorian grandeur of Albert Hall is a good choice for lunch. More upmarket is *Herman's* at 32 St John St (☎01786/450632) with its handsomely austere interior. The downstairs brasserie is open at lunchtime; the Austrian/Scottish evening main courses start at £7. The set lunch at *Pierre Victoire*, 41 Friars St (☎01786/448171), is a great bargain at around £5 per person for three courses. *Italia Nostra*, 25 Baker St (☎01786/473208), serves good well-priced Italian food and is especially lively at weekends. The *East India Club*, 7 Viewfield Place, a five-minute walk from the centre (☎01786/471330), offers fabulous Indian food, Slightly more expensive is the delicious and elegantly served Cantonese food at *The Regent*, 30 Upper Craigs (☎01786/472513).

Nightlife in Stirling revolves around **pubs** and **bars** and is dominated by the student population. The lively *Barnton Bar and Bistro* on Barnton Street, serves a good selection of beers and food, including huge breakfasts. Also popular with students is the beer at Stirling's oldest ale house, the *Settle Inn*, 91 St Mary's Wynd, Near the university, try *The Meadowpark* pub on Kenliworth Road. In July and August there are **ceilidhs** in the Guildhall, near the castle (check with the tourist office; £3.50). The larger Albert Hall is a good venue for classical and pop/rock **concerts**. A very popular Stirling event held on the Esplanade is the annual **Beating of the Retreat**, followed by a firework display (usually in mid-July; seated ticket £5). The main venue for **theatre** and **film** is the excellent *MacRobert Arts Centre* (☎01786/461081) on the university campus (see below), which shows a good selection of drama and art-house films.

Around Stirling

Apart from the visibly prominent **Wallace Monument**, there are several sights within easy striking distance of Stirling: the ruined Abbey at **Cambuskenneth** and the battlefield of **Bannockburn** are almost within the city suburbs, while the cathedral at **Dunblane**, and the castle at **Doune** and above **Dollar**, are full day trips.

The Wallace monument, Cambuskenneth Abbey and Bannockburn

Overlooking the university, two miles north of Stirling, is the prominent **Wallace Monument** (daily March–Oct 10am–5pm; July & Aug 9am–6pm; £2.50), built 1861–69, a rocket-like tribute to Sir William Wallace ("the hammer and scourge of the English"), who has recently been portrayed by Mel Gibson in the film *Braveheart*. It was from the nearby Wallace's Pass that the Scottish hero led his troops down to defeat the English at the Battle of Stirling Bridge in 1297. Exhibits inside the monument include Wallace's long steel sword, swathed in tartan, and the Hall of (Scottish) Heroes, a row of stern white marble busts featuring John Knox and Adam Smith, among others. If you can manage the climb – 246 spiral steps up, well worth it on a clear day – there are superb views across to Fife and Ben Lomond from the top of the 220-foot tower.

A woodland path weaves its way from the monument to the ruins of **Cambuskenneth Abbey**, about a mile east of Stirling (ruin open April–Sept all hours; grounds all year; free; HS). Founded in 1147 by David I on the site of an Augustinian settlement, the abbey is distinguished by its early fourteenth-century bell tower, though there's little else to see there now. Its history, however, makes it worth a brief look: the Scots parliament met here in 1326 to pledge allegiance to Robert the Bruce's son David, and James III (1451–88) and his wife, Queen Margaret of Denmark, are both buried in the grounds, their graves marked by a nineteenth-century monument erected at the insistence of Queen Victoria.

A couple of miles south of Stirling, just north of the village of **BANNOCKBURN**, the **Bannockburn Heritage Centre** (April–Oct daily 10am–5.30pm; £2; NTS) stands close to where Robert the Bruce won his mighty victory over the English at the **Battle of Bannockburn** on June 24, 1314. It was this battle, the climax of the Wars of ˙ Independence, which united the Scots under Bruce and led to independence under the Declaration of Arbroath (1320) and the Treaty of Northampton (1328). Outside, a concrete rotunda encloses a cairn near the spot where Bruce planted his standard after beating Edward II. Of the original bore stone, only a fragment remains, safely on display in the visitor centre. Over-eager visitors used to chip pieces off, and the final straw came when a particularly zealous enthusiast attempted to blast enough of it away to make two curling stones. Pondering the scene is an equestrian statue of Bruce, on the spot from where he is said to have commanded the battle.

Dunblane

Frequent trains, and buses #58 or #258 make the journey four miles north of Stirling to **DUNBLANE**, a small city now indissolubly linked with the massacre that occurred in one of its primary schools in March 1996. Prior to that atrocity, its reputation rested on **Dunblane Cathedral** (April–Sept Mon–Sat 9.30am–12.30pm & 1.30–6pm, Sun 2–6pm; Oct–March Mon–Sat 9.30am–12.30pm & 1.30–4pm, Sun 2–4pm; free; HS), a building dating mainly from the thirteenth century, and restored to its Gothic splendour a century ago. Inside, note the delicate blue-purple stained glass, and the exquisitely carved pews, screen and choir stalls, all crafted in the early twentieth century. Also of interest is the little alcove with its thin stained-glass window, thought to be a hermit's cell; a tenth-century Celtic cross; and a sadly worn thirteenth-century double effigy of the fifth Earl of Strathearn and his countess. The cathedral stands serenely amid a clutch of old-world buildings, among them the seventeenth-century Dean's House, which houses the tiny cathedral **museum** (June–Sept Mon–Sat 10.30am–12.30pm & 1.30–4.30pm; free) with exhibits on local history.

Doune

DOUNE, eight miles northwest of Stirling (bus #59 or #259), is worth a call for its ruined, fourteenth-century **Castle** (April–Sept Mon–Sat 9.30am–6pm, Sun 2–6pm; Oct–March Mon–Wed & Sat 9am–4pm, Sun 2–4pm; £2; HS), a marvellous pile standing on a small hill in a bend of the River Teith. Built by Robert, Duke of Albany, it eventually ended up in the hands of the Earls of Moray (whose descendants still own it), following the execution of the Albany family by James I. In the sixteenth century it belonged to the second earl, James Stewart – son of James V and half-brother of Mary, Queen of Scots – murdered in 1592 and immortalized in the ballad the *Bonnie Earl of Moray*. Today the most prominent features of the castle are its mighty 95-foot gatehouse, with its spacious vaulted rooms, and the kitchens, complete with medieval rubbish chute. The present earl has a fabulous collection of flash vintage cars, which are on show one mile northwest of town in the **Doune Motor Museum** (April–Nov daily 10am–4.30pm; £2.75) off the A84. Among the examples of gleaming paintwork and tanned upholstery you can see legendary models of Bentley, Lagonda, Jaguar, Aston Martin and the second oldest Rolls Royce in the world (built in 1905).

Dollar and Castle Campbell

Above the town of Dollar, twelve miles east of Stirling, the dramatic chasm of Dollar Glen is commanded by **Castle Campbell** (April–Sept Mon–Sat 9.30am–6pm, Sun 2–6pm; Oct–March Mon–Wed & Sat 9.30am–4pm, Thurs 9.30am–noon, Sun 2–4pm; £1.50; NTS & HS), formerly, and still unofficially, known as Castle Gloom – a fine and evocative tag but, prosaically, a derivation of an old Gaelic name. The castle came into the hands of the Campbells in 1481, who changed its name from Castle Gloom in 1489.

John Knox preached here in 1556, although probably from within the castle, rather than from the curious archway in the garden as is traditionally claimed. In 1654 the castle was burned by Cromwell's troops; the remains of a graceful seventeenth-century loggia and a roofless hall bear witness to the destruction. However, the oldest part of the castle, the fine fifteenth-century tower built by Sir Colin Campbell, survived the fire; look out for the claustrophobic pit prison just off the Great Hall and the latrines with their vertiginous views to the ground. You can also walk round the roof of the tower, where there's a wonderful view of the hills behind the castle, and down the glen to Dollar. A mile-long road leads up from the main street to the castle, but it stops short of the castle, with only limited parking at the top. There is also a marked walk through the glen to the castle, past mossy crags and rushing streams.

Loch Lomond

Loch Lomond – the largest stretch of freshwater in Britain – is almost as famous as Loch Ness, thanks to the ballad about its "bonnie, bonnie banks", the Scottish folk song said to be written by a Jacobite prisoner. However, all is not bonnie at the loch nowadays, especially on its overdeveloped west side, fringed by the A82; on the water itself, speedboats tear up and down on summer weekends, destroying the tranquillity which so impressed the likes of Queen Victoria, the Wordsworths and Sir Walter Scott. Nevertheless, the west bank of the loch is an undeniably beautiful stretch of water, and despite the crowds, gives better views than the heavily wooded east side.

LUSS, the setting for the enormously popular Scottish TV soap *Take the High Road*, is the prettiest village, though its picturesque streets can become unbearably crowded in summer. **BALLOCH**, a brash holiday resort at the loch's southern tip, is the place to head for if you want to take a boat trip; various operators offer cruises around the 33 islands scattered near the shore. The tranquil east bank is far better for walking than the west, and can only be traversed in its entirety by the West Highland Way footpath, from where you can head on through Queen Elizabeth Forest Park, or take the hugely rewarding three-hour hike from Rowardennan to the summit of **Ben Lomond**, subject of the Scottish proverb "Leave Ben Lomond where it stands" – just let things be.

Practicalities

The West Highland **train** – the line from Glasgow to Mallaig, with a branch line to Oban – joins Loch Lomond seventeen miles north of Balloch at **TARBET**, and has one other station further on at **ARDLUI**, at the mountain-framed head of the loch. Loch Lomond's **tourist office** (daily April–June, Sept & Oct 10am–5.30pm; July & Aug 9.30am–7.30pm; ☎01389/753533) is above the marina in Balloch. They'll reserve a room for you without charge at one of the many local **hotels** and **B&Bs**, such as the comfortable *Balloch Hotel*, Balloch Rd (☎01389/752579; ⑥), which also has a decent restaurant, or the *Gowanlea Guest House*, Drymen Rd (☎01389/752456; ③). A couple of miles up the west side of the loch at minuscule **ARDEN** is Scotland's most beautiful **youth hostel**: a turreted building complete with ghost (March–Oct; ☎01389/850226). Tents are best pitched at the secluded Forestry Commission **campsite** (April–Oct; ☎01360/870234), two miles south of Rowardennan at Cashel on the east bank.

Passenger ferries cross between Inverbeg and Rowardennan, where there is an eponymous **hotel** (☎01360/870251; ③) and a wonderfully situated **youth hostel** (March–Oct & New Year; ☎01360/870259), which also serves as an activity centre for canoeing, archery and orienteering. On the northeast shore of the loch is the *Inversnaid Lodge* (☎01877/386254; ④), once the hunting lodge of the Duke of Montrose. There is no road from Rowardennnan up the east of the loch to Inversnaid; you have to take the B829 west from Aberfoyle. From Inversnaid you can take the mile-long lochside walk to Rob Roy's cave, a hideout which is said to have given shelter to both Rob Roy and Robert the Bruce.

The Trossachs

The **Trossachs** boast a magnificent diversity of scenery, with dramatic peaks and mysterious, forest-covered slopes that live up to all the images ever produced of Scotland's wild land. This is Rob Roy country, where every waterfall, hidden cave and barely discernible path was once frequented by the seventeenth-century Scottish outlaw who led the Clan MacGregor. Strictly speaking, the name "The Trossachs", normally translated as either "bristly country" or "crossing place", originally referred only to the wooded glen between Loch Katrine and Loch Achray, but today it is usually taken as being the whole area from Callander in the east to Queen Elizabeth Forest Park in the west, right up to the eastern banks of Loch Lomond.

The Trossachs' high tourist profile was largely attributable in the early days to Sir Walter Scott, whose *The Lady of the Lake* and *Rob Roy* were set in and around the area. Since then, neither the popularity – nor beauty – of the region have waned, and in high season the place is jam-packed. Autumn is a better time to come, when the hills are blanketed in rich, rusty colours and the crowds are thinner. In terms of where to stay, **Aberfoyle** has a slightly dowdy air, even at the height of summer, so it is better to opt for the romantic seclusion of the **Lake of Menteith**, or the handsome country town of **Callander**.

Aberfoyle and Lake of Menteith

Like Brigadoon waking once a year from a mist-shrouded slumber, each summer the sleepy little town of **ABERFOYLE**, twenty miles west of Stirling, dusts itself down each summer for the annual influx of tourists. Its position in the heart of the Trossachs is ideal, with Loch Ard Forest and Queen Elizabeth Forest Park stretching across to Ben Lomond and Loch Lomond to the west, the long curve of Loch Katrine and Ben Venue to the northwest, and Ben Ledi to the northeast. Don't come here for lively nightlife or entertainment, but for a good, healthy blast of the outdoors. The town itself is well equipped to lodge and feed visitors (though booking is recommended), and is an excellent base for walking and pony-trekking, or simply wandering the hills.

About four miles east of Aberfoyle towards Doune, the **Lake of Menteith** is a superb fly-fishing centre and Scotland's only lake (as opposed to loch), so named due

---

ROB ROY

"**Rob Roy**, hero or villain?" ponders the tourist literature, in the great spirit of inquiry. Given that Rob Roy's clan, the MacGregors, have the distinction of having invented the term blackmail, and that Rob Roy himself achieved fame through cattle-rustling and thieving, the evidence seems to point to the "villain" thesis. Born in 1671 in Glengyle just north of Loch Katrine, Rob Roy (meaning "Red Robert" in Gaelic) started life as a cattle farmer, supported by the powerful Duke of Montrose. When the Duke withdrew his support, possibly having been robbed of £1000 by Rob Roy, the latter became a bankrupt and a brigand, plundering the rich carse land and revenging himself on the Duke. He was at the Battle of Sherrifmuir in 1715, ostensibly as a Jacobite but probably as an opportunist – the chaos would have made cattle-raiding easier. Eventually captured and sentenced to transportation, Rob Roy was pardoned and returned to Balquhidder, where he remained until his death in 1734. His life has been much romanticized ever since Sir Walter Scott's 1818 version of the story in his novel *Rob Roy*; a process continued in the recent film starring Liam Neeson.

to a historic mix-up with the word *laigh*, the Scots for "low-lying ground", which applied to the whole area. To rent a **fishing boat** contact the Lake of Menteith Fisheries (☎01877/385664). From the northern shore of the lake you can take the little ferry boat (April–Sept Mon–Sat 9.30am–6.30pm, Sun 2–6.30pm, returning 7pm; £2) to the **Island of Inchmahome**, and explore the lovely ruin of the Augustine abbey, perhaps Scotland's most beautiful island monastery. Founded in 1238, the priory's remains rise tall and graceful above the trees. The nave of the church is roofless, but in the choir are preserved the graves of important families from the surrounding area. Most touching is a late thirteenth-century double effigy depicting Walter, the first Stewart Earl of Menteith, and his Countess Mary who, feet resting on lion-like animals, turn towards each other and embrace.

Also buried at Inchmahome is **Robert Bontine Cunninghame Graham** (1852–1936), the adventurer, scholar, socialist and Scottish nationalist, who was Liberal MP for northwest Lanarkshire for 25 years and the first president of the National Party of Scotland. A pal of Buffalo Bill in Mexico as well as an intimate friend of the novelist Joseph Conrad, Cunninghame Graham had a ranch in Argentina, where he was affectionately known as "Don Roberto". Five-year-old **Mary, Queen of Scots** was hidden at Inchamahome in 1547 before being taken to France; there's a knot garden in the west of the island known as Queen Mary's bower, where legend has it the child Queen played. Traces remain of an orchard planted by the monks, but the island is thick now with oak, ash and Spanish chestnut.

Practicalities

Regular **buses** from Stirling to Aberfoyle pull into the car park on Main Street. The **tourist office**, directly next door, has full details of local accommodation, sights and outdoor activities (April–Oct daily 9.30am–7pm; ☎01877/382352). For **accommodation**, try the tartan-carpeted *Covenanter's Inn* (☎01877/382347; ③) at the northern end of town, or the *Inverard Hotel*, Loch Ard Rd (☎018772/382229; ④), with good views over the River Forth. There are scores of B&Bs in the town itself including the Tudor-style *Craigend*, 1 Craiguchty Terrace (☎01877/382716; ③). *The Lake Hotel and Restaurant* (☎01877/385258; ⑦) at Port of Menteith has a lovely lakeside setting, and a classy restaurant. A couple of miles south of Aberfoyle on the edge of Queen Elizabeth Forest Park, *Cobleland Campsite* (☎01877/382392 or 382383) is run by the Forestry Commission; it's open from April to October, and offers **bikes** for rent.

Duke's Pass

Even if you have to walk it, don't miss the trip from Aberfoyle to Callander which for part of the way takes you along the **Duke's Pass** (so called because it once belonged to the Duke of Montrose), as it weaves its way through the Queen Elizabeth Forest Park to just south of Loch Katrine.

The A821 twists up out of Aberfoyle, following the contours of the hills and snaking back on itself in tortuous bends. About half-way up is the excellent **Queen Elizabeth Forest Park visitor centre** (April–Oct daily 10am–6pm; ☎01877/382258), which details the local fauna and flora. From here various marked paths wind through the forests giving splendid views over the lowlands and surrounding hills. A few miles further on, a road branches off to the left, leading to the southern end of **Loch Katrine** at the foot of Ben Venue (2370ft), from where the historic steamer, the SS *Sir Walter Scott*, has been plying the waters since 1900, chugging up the loch to Stronachlachar and the wild Rob Roy country of Glengyle where he was born (April–Sept Sun–Fri 4 daily, 2 on Sat; £3.40). To climb Ben A'an (1520ft), start from the *Trossachs Hotel* on the north bank of Loch Arhray. No longer a hotel, it retains the splendid exterior designed by the outlandishly named Lord Willoughby d'Eresby in 1852.

The final leg of the pass is along the tranquil shores of **Loch Venachar** at the southern foot of Ben Ledi. Look out for the small **Callander Kirk** in a lovely setting at the edge of the loch, where services are still held on the first Sunday of each month at 3pm – presumably because it takes all morning (or month) to get there.

Callander and around

CALLANDER, on the eastern edge of the Trossachs, sits quietly on the banks of the River Teith roughly ten miles north of Doune, at the southern end of the Pass of Leny, one of the key routes into the Highlands. Larger than Aberfoyle, it is an even more popular summer holiday base and a convenient springboard for exploring the surrounding area. Its wide main street recalls the influence of the military architects who designed the town after Bonnie Prince Charlie's Jacobite Rebellion of 1745.

Callander first came to fame during the "Scottish Enlightenment" of the eighteenth and nineteenth centuries, when the glowing reports given by Sir Walter Scott and William Wordsworth prompted the first tourists to venture into the wilds by horse-drawn carriage. Development was given a boost when Queen Victoria chose to visit, and then by the arrival of the train line – long since closed – in the 1860s.

The present community has not been slow to capitalize on its appeal, establishing a plethora of restaurants and tea rooms, antique shops, secondhand book shops, and shops selling local woollens and crafts. The chief formal attraction is the **Rob Roy and Trossachs Visitor Centre** at Ancaster Square on the main street (Jan & Feb Sat & Sun only 10am–5pm; March–May & Oct–Dec daily 10am–5pm; June & Sept daily 9.30am–6pm; July & Aug daily 9am–7pm; £2), an entertaining and partisan account of the life of the diminutive red-head featuring a talking statue of "Soft Southerner" Daniel Defoe. Defoe was sent to Scotland on a government spying mission in 1705, and became fascinated by Rob Roy's exploits.

Callander's **tourist office** is in the Rob Roy and Trossachs Visitor Centre (same times; ☎01877/330342). Good **accommodation** choices include *Arden Guest House*, Bracklinn Rd (☎01877/330235; ③), with views down over the countryside; the *Ben A'an Guest House* (☎01877/330 317; ②) on the main street; and the small, pretty *Highland House Hotel*, South Church St (☎01877/330269; ④). The *Invertrossachs Country House* (☎01877/331126; ⑥) on the southern shores of Loch Venachar is a plush Edwardian mansion offering superior **B&B**. There are few **restaurants** worth recommending in Callander, though the *Murtle Inn* on the eastern edge of town does good pub food.

On to Lochearnhead

On each side of Callander, pleasant and less-than-arduous walks wind through a wooded gorge to the **Falls of Leny** to the north and **Bracklinn Falls** to the south – both distances of only a mile or so. North of town, you can walk or ride the scenic six-mile **Callander to Strathyre Cycleway**, which forms part of the network of cycle ways between the Highlands and Glasgow. The route is based on the old Caledonian train line to Oban, which closed in 1965, and runs along the western side of **Loch Lubnaig**.

To the north, Rob Roy is buried in the small yard behind the ruined church at tiny **BALQUHIDDER**, where he died in 1734. Oddly enough, considering the Rob Roy fever that plagues the region, his grave – marked by a rough stone marked with a sword, cross and a man with a dog – is remarkably underplayed. If you want to **stay** in Balquhidder, go to the award-winning eighteenth-century farmhouse *Monachyle Mhor* hotel (☎01877/384622; ④), which has a terrific restaurant looking out to Loch Voil.

Watersports are the life force of the village of **LOCHEARNHEAD**, at the western end of Loch Earn, a substantial body of water running east into Perthshire and fed by waters off the slopes of **Ben Vorlich** (3201ft) to the south. A more impressive stretch

of water is **Loch Tay**, about fifteen miles north of Callander, which points northeast-
wards like a fourteen-mile finger towards Aberfeldy (see p.810).

The south Fife coast

The ancient Kingdom of **Fife**, designated such by the Picts in the fourth century, is a
small area (barely 50 miles at its widest points), but one which has a definite identity,
inextricably bound with the waters which surround it on three sides – the Tay to the
north, the cold North Sea to the east, and the Forth along the **south coast**. The recent
closure of the coal mines has left local communities floundering to regain a foothold,
and the squeeze on the fishing industry up the coast may well lead to further decline.
In the meantime many of the villages have capitalized on their unpretentious appeal
and welcomed tourism in a way that has enhanced rather than degraded their natural
assets; the perfectly preserved town of Culross is unmissable. East of Culross is
Dunfermline, an overdeveloped town with stunning remains of the first Benedictine
priory in Scotland.

Although the south coast of Fife is predominantly industrial – with everything from
cottage industries to the refitting of nuclear submarines – thankfully only a small part
has been blighted by insensitive development. Even in the old coal-mining areas,
disused pits and left-over slag heaps have either been well camouflaged through landscaping or put to alternative use as recreation areas. If you're driving, it's tempting
once you've crossed the river to beat a path directly north up the M90 motorway;
however, if you do decide to stop off, you'll find the area has much to offer.

It was from **Dunfermline** that Queen Margaret ousted the Celtic Church from
Scotland in the eleventh century; her son, David I, founded an abbey here in the
twelfth century, which acquired vast stretches of land for miles around. Today, even
though the lands no longer belong to the town, Dunfermline remains the chief town
and the focus of the coast. **Culross**, once a lively port, which enjoyed a thriving trade
with Holland, fell into decline for around two hundred years but has been lovingly
restored this century by the NTS.

Fife is linked to Edinburgh by the two **Forth bridges**. You used to be able to take
guided walks across the historic rail bridge, whose boldness of concept was all the
more remarkable for coming so hard on the heels of the Tay Bridge disaster of 1879;
today, however, you'll have to be satisfied with seeing it from a train or a boat (for more
on the Forth bridges see *Edinburgh*).

Culross

Crossing the bridge from the south, with unattractive views of the shipyard at
Inverkeithing and the naval dock at Rosyth, the A985 then heads west along the Forth
before approaching **CULROSS** (pronounced "Cooros"). One of Scotland's most picturesque settlements, the town's development began in the fifth century with the arrival
of St Serf on the northern side of the Forth at "Holly Point", or Culenros, and it is said
to be the birthplace of St Mungo, who travelled west and founded Glasgow cathedral.
The town today is in excellent condition, thanks to the work of the NTS, who have
been restoring its whitewashed, red-tiled buildings since 1932.

Make your first stop the **National Trust Visitor Centre** (Easter–Sept daily 1.30–
5pm; combined ticket for Town House, Palace and Study £3.50), in the **Town House**
on the main road, for an excellent introduction to the burgh's history. Here some of the
four thousand witches executed in Scotland between 1560 and 1707 were tried and
held up in the upper floor of the Town House while awaiting execution in Edinburgh.
Behind the ticket office is a tiny prison with built-in mannacles, where people were

locked up as punishment for minor offences. The focal point of the community is the ochre-coloured **Culross Palace** (Easter–Sept daily 11am–5pm), built by wealthy coal merchant George Bruce in the late sixteenth century. Actually it's not a palace at all – its name comes from the Latin *palatium*, or "hall" – but a grand and impressive house, with lots of small rooms and connecting passageways. The garden is planted with grasses, herbs and vegetables of the period, carefully grown from seed. The café serves homemade food, and is open from 10.30am to 4.30pm.

A cobbled alleyway known as **Back Causeway**, with a raised central aisle used by noblemen to separate them from the commoners, leads up behind the Town House to the **study** (Easter–Sept daily 1.30–5pm), built in 1610, with oak panelling in Dutch Renaissance style. Further up the hill lie the remains of **Culross Abbey**, founded by Cistercian monks in 1217. Although it is difficult to get a sense of what the abbey would have looked like, the overall effect is of grace and grandeur. A ladder leads to a vaulted chamber, which feels as if it is suspended in mid-air. This adjoins the fine seventeenth-century **Manse**, and the choir of the abbey, which became the parish church in 1633. Inside, a tenth-century Celtic cross in the north transept is a reminder of the origins of the abbey – there was a Celtic church here in 450. Recumbent alabaster figures of Sir George Bruce and his lady, with three sons and five daughters kneeling in devotion, decorate the splendid family tomb. The graveyard of the church is fascinating: many of the graves are eighteenth century, with symbols depicting the occupation of the person who is buried; note, too, the Scottish custom, still continued, of marking women's graves with maiden names, even when they are buried with their husband.

Dunfermline

Scotland's capital until the Union of the Crowns in 1603, **DUNFERMLINE** lies seven miles inland east of Culross, north of the Forth bridges. This "auld, grey toun" is built on a hill, dominated by the abbey and ruined palace at the top. Up until the late nineteenth century, Dunfermline was one of Scotland's foremost linen producers, as well as a major coal-mining centre, and today the town is a busy place, its ever-increasing sprawl attesting to its booming economy. At the heart of the town is the imposing abbey, and the dramatic skeleton of the palace.

In the eleventh century, **Malcolm III** (Canmore) offered refuge here to Edgar Atheling, heir to the English throne, and his family, who while fleeing the Norman Conquest were fortuitously shipwrecked in the Forth. Malcolm married Edgar's sister, the Catholic Margaret, in 1067, and in so doing started a process of reformation that ultimately supplanted the Celtic Church. Margaret, an intensely pious woman who was canonized in 1250, began building a Benedictine priory in 1072; her son, **David I**, raised the priory to the rank of abbey in the following century. In 1303, during the first of the **Wars of Independence** (1296–1328), the English king Edward I occupied the castle. He had the church roof stripped of lead to provide ammunition for his army's catapults, and also appears to have ordered the destruction of most of the monastery buildings, with the exception of the church and some of the monks' dwellings. **Robert the Bruce** helped rebuild the abbey, and when he died of leprosy was buried here 25 years later, although his body went undiscovered until building began on a new parish church in 1821. His heart, however, lies in Melrose Abbey (see p.736).

The Town

Dunfermline's **centre**, at the top of the hill around the abbey and palace, holds an appeal of its own, with its narrow, cobbled streets, pedestrianized shopping areas and gargoyle-adorned buildings. One of the best of these, the **City Chambers** on the corner of Bridge and Bruce streets, is a fine example of late nineteenth-century Gothic Revival style. Among the ornate porticoes and grotesques of dragons and winged serpents which adorn the exterior are the sculpted heads of Robert the Bruce, Malcolm Canmore, Queen Margaret and Queen Elizabeth I.

Dunfermline Abbey (April–Sept Mon–Sat 9.30am–6.30pm, Sun 2–6.30pm; Oct–March Mon–Wed & Sat 9.30am–4.30pm, Thurs 9.30am–12.30pm, Sun 2–4.30pm; £1.50) is comprised of the twelfth-century nave of the medieval monastic church, with an early nineteenth-century parish church spliced on. A plaque beneath the pulpit marks the spot where Robert the Bruce's remains were laid to rest, while Malcolm and his queen, Margaret, who died of grief three days after her husband in 1093, have a shrine outside. The nearby pink-harled **Abbot House**, possibly fourteenth century and variously used as an abbot's house, an iron foundry, an art school and a doctor's surgery, is best seen from the outside, since nothing remains of the original interior, The guest house of Margaret's Benedictine monastery, south of the abbey, became the **Palace** (same hours) in the sixteenth century under James VI, who gave both it and the abbey to his consort, Queen Anne of Denmark. Charles I, the last monarch to be born in Scotland, came into the world here in 1600. All that is left of it today is a long, sandstone facade, especially impressive when silhouetted against the evening sky.

Pittencrieff Park, known to locals as "the Glen", covers a huge area in the centre of town. Bordering the ruined palace, the 76-acre park used to be owned by the Lairds of Pittencrieff, whose 1610 estate house, built of stone pillaged from the palace, still stands within the grounds. In 1902, however, the entire plot was purchased by local, rags-to-riches industrialist and philanthropist Andrew Carnegie, who donated it to his home town. Today **Pittencrieff House** (May–Oct daily except Tues 11am–5pm; free) displays exhibits on local history, the glasshouses are filled with exotic blooms, and the Pavilion coffee shop offers refreshment. In the centre of the park are the remains – little more than the foundations – of **Malcolm Canmore's Tower**, which may be the location of Malcolm's residence, known to have been somewhere to the west of the abbey. Dunfermline – meaning "fort by the crooked pool" – takes its name from the tower's location: "Dun" meaning hill or fort, "Fearum" bent or crooked, and "Lin" (or "Lyne/Line") a pool or running water.

Just beyond the southeast corner of the park, the modest little cottage at the bottom of St Margaret Street is **Andrew Carnegie's Birthplace** (April–Oct Mon–Sat 11am–5pm, Sun 2–5pm; Nov–March daily 2–4pm; £1.50). The son of a weaver, the young Carnegie (1835–1919) lived upstairs with his family, while the room below housed his father's loom shop. Following the family's emigration to America in 1848, he worked on the railways before becoming involved with the iron and then the steel industries. From 1873 he began his acquisition of steel-production firms, later to be consolidated into the Carnegie Steel Company; when he retired in 1901 to devote himself to philanthropy, Carnegie was a multi-millionaire. His house, an ordinary two-up two-down, has been preserved as it was at the end of the last century, and the adjacent Memorial Hall details his life and work.

Practicalities

The **train station** is southeast of the centre, halfway down the long hill of St Margaret's Drive, fifteen minutes' walk downhill from the **tourist office**, next to Abbot House, Maygate (April–Sept Mon–Sat 10am–6pm, Sun 11am–3pm; Oct–March Mon–Sat 10am–4pm; ☎01383/720999). From the **bus station**, cut through the shopping centre to High Street. If you do want to **stay**, options include the *Davaar House Hotel*, 126 Grieve St (☎01383/721886; ④). There are some good, well-priced ethnic **restaurants** in Dunfermline: *Blossom's*, 6-8 Chalmers St, for Chinese food; *Khan's*, 33 Carnegie Drive, for Indian cuisine; and *Café Rene*, also on Carnegie Drive, for cheap and cheerful French cooking. *Il Pescatore*, five miles south on the coast at Limekilns is a traditional Italian place, once patronized by Prince Andrew and his naval chums. If you want a drink in town, try the *Watering Hole*, New Row.

Aberdour

ABERDOUR, five miles east of the Forth bridges, clings tight to the walls of its **Castle** (April–Sept Mon–Wed & Sat 9.30am–6.30pm, Sun 2–6.30pm; Oct–March closes 4.30pm; £1.50) at the southern end of the main street. Once a Douglas stronghold, the castle is on a comparatively modest scale, with gently sloping lawns, a large enclosed seventeenth-century garden and terraces. The fourteenth-century tower is the oldest part of the castle, the other buildings having been added in the sixteenth and seventeenth centuries, including the well-preserved dovecote. Worth more perusal is **St Fillan's Church**, also in the castle grounds, which dates from the twelfth century, with a few sixteenth-century additions, such as the porch restored from total dereliction earlier this century. There's little else to see here apart from the town's popular **silver sands** beach, which, along with its watersports, golf and sailing, has earned Aberdour the rather optimistic tourist board soubriquet the "Fife Riviera". From Aberdour you can take a ferry to Inchcolm Island to see its ruined medieval Abbey.

If you want to **stay** you could try the friendly *Aberdour Hotel* on High Street (☎01383/860325; ⑤), which also has an inexpensive **restaurant** downstairs. The real gem though is *Hawkcraig House*, Hawkcraig Point (☎01383/860335; ③), a guest house with a good restaurant in an old ferryman's house overlooking the harbour.

Kirkcaldy and around

The ancient royal burgh of **KIRKCALDY** (pronounced "Kirkcawdy") is familiarly known as "The Lang Toun" for its four-mile-long esplanade, built in 1922–23 – not just to hold back the sea, but also to alleviate unemployment. If you're here in mid-April, you'll see the historic **Links Market**, a week-long funfair that dates back to 1305, and is possibly the largest street fair in Britain. Incidentally, though there's little to show for it today, architect brothers Robert and James Adam were born in Kirkcaldy, as was the eighteenth-century thinker Adam Smith, whose great work *The Wealth of Nations* (1776), established political economy as a separate science.

Kirkcaldy doesn't hold a great deal of interest for the visitor, beyond a stroll along the promenade. The town's history is chronicled in its **Museum and Art Gallery** (Mon–Sat 10.30am–5pm, Sun 2–5pm; free), set in the colourful War Memorial Gardens between the train and bus stations. The gallery, established in 1925, has built up its collection to around three hundred works by some of Scotland's finest painters from the late eighteenth century onwards, including works by the fine portraitist Sir Henry Raeburn, the historical painter Sir David Wilkie, and Scottish "Colourists" S.J. Peploe and William McTaggart. For a town known primarily for linoleum production and whose reputation is firmly rooted in the prosaic, the art gallery is an unexpected boon.

Just beyond the northern end of the waterfront, Ravenscraig Park is the site of the substantial ruin of **Ravenscraig Castle**, a thick-walled, fifteenth-century defence post, which occupies a lovely spot above a beach. The castle looks out over the Forth, and is flanked on either side by a flight of steps – the inspiration, apparently, for the title of John Buchan's novel, *The 39 Steps*. Sir Walter Scott also used it, as a setting for the story of "lovely Rosabella" in *The Lay of the Last Minstrel*.

Beyond Kirkcaldy lies the old suburb of **Dysart**, where tall ships once arrived bringing cargo from the Netherlands, setting off again with coal, beer, salt and fish. Well restored, and retaining historic street names such as Hot Pot Wynd (after the hot pans used for salt evaporation), it's an atmospheric place of narrow alleyways and picturesque old buildings. In Rectory Lane, the birthplace of John McDouall Stuart (who in 1862 became the first man to cross Australia from the south to the north) now holds the **McDouall Stuart Museum** (June–Aug Mon–Sat 2–5pm; free; NTS), giving an account of his emigration to Australia in 1838 and his subsequent adventures.

Practicalities

Kirkcaldy's **train** and **bus stations** are in the upper part of town – keep heading downhill to get to the centre. The **tourist office**, 19 Whytecauseway (April–Sept daily 10am–6pm; Oct–March Mon–Thurs 9am–5pm, Fri 9am–4.30pm; ☎01592/267775), offers an **accommodation**-booking service, useful for getting you into the *Parkway Hotel*, Abbotshall Rd (☎01592/262143; ⑥), or the smaller, more refined *Dunnikier House Hotel*, Dunnikier Park, Dunnikier Way (☎01592/268393; ④). You can get cheaper rooms along the road in neighbouring **Dysart**, at the *Royal Hotel*, Townhead (☎01592/654112; ③), which occupies one of the village's historic buildings. The *Royal Hotel* is a good place for **eating**, as is the *Old Rectory Inn*, West Quality St, also in Dysart. In Kirkcaldy, itself, try *Giovanni's*, 66 Dunnikier Rd for traditional Italian food, or *Maxin*, 5 High St, for Chinese. There's a good **arts cinema** with a restaurant and bar, housed in the *Adam Smith Theatre* on Bennochy Road in the town centre.

The Howe of Fife

Completely different from the industrial landscape of Kirkcaldy and Glenrothes, the **Howe of Fife**, lying north of Glenrothes, is a low-lying stretch of ground ("howe") lying at the foot of the twin peaks of the heather-swathed **Lomond Hills** – West Lomond (1696ft) and East Lomond (1378ft). The area makes an ideal stopping point en route to St Andrews, with **Falkland Palace** and the handsome market town of **Cupar**.

Falkland

Nestling in the lower slopes of East Lomond, the narrow streets of **FALKLAND** are lined with fine and well-preserved seventeenth- and eighteenth-century buildings. The village grew up around **Falkland Palace** (April–Oct Mon–Sat 11am–5.30pm, Sun 1.30–5.30pm; £4, gardens only £2; NTS), home to the Macduffs, the Earls of Fife. James IV began the construction of the present palace in 1500, which was completed and embellished by James V, and became a favoured royal residence. Charles II stayed here in 1650, when he was in Scotland for his coronation, but after the Jacobite rising of 1715 and temporary occupation by Rob Roy, the palace was left to ruin. In the late nineteenth century the third Marquess of Bute acquired the palace and restored it entirely. Today it is a stunning example of Early Renaissance architecture, complete with corbelled parapet, mullioned windows, round towers and massive walls. The gardens are also worth a look, their well-stocked herbaceous borders lining a pristine lawn, and with the oldest tennis court in Britain – built in 1539 for James V and still used.

When not playing tennis, the royal guests at Falkland would hunt deer and wild boar in the forests which then covered the Howe of Fife, stretching towards Cupar, ten miles northeast. There are still deer here today, at the **Scottish Deer Centre** (daily April–Oct 10am–5pm; July & Aug 10am–6pm; £4), three miles west of Cupar on the A91, which specializes in the rearing of red deer, and is also home to species of sika, fallow and reindeer. It's a good place for children, who can pet the tamer animals, and there are play and picnic areas and guided nature trails.

If you want to **stay** in Falkland, there's a **youth hostel**, Back Wynd (March–Sept; ☎01337/857710). Directly opposite the palace is the *Hunting Lodge Hotel*, High St (☎01337/857226; ⑤), and just up the road, the *Covenanter Hotel*. For **B&B** try the attractive *Oakbank Guest House*, The Pleasance (☎01337/857287; ③).

Cupar

Straddling the small River Eden and surrounded by gentle hills, **CUPAR**, the capital of Fife, has retained much of its medieval character – and its self-confident air – from the days when it was a bustling market centre. A livestock auction still takes place here every week. In 1276 Alexander III held an assembly in the town, bringing together the Church, aristocracy and local burgesses in an early form of Scottish parliament. For his troubles he subsequently became the butt of Sir David Lindsay's biting play, *Ane Pleasant Satyre of the Thrie Estaitis* (1535), one of the first great Scottish dramas.

Situated at the centre of Fife's road network, Cupar's main street, part of the main road from Edinburgh to St Andrews, is plagued with thundering traffic. The **Mercat Cross**, stranded in the midst of the lorries and cars which speed through the centre, now consists of salvaged sections of the seventeenth-century original, following its destruction by an errant lorry some years ago.

One of the best reasons for stopping off at Cupar is to visit the **Hill of Tarvit** (daily Easter to mid-Oct 1.30–5.30pm; £3; NTS; gardens open all year daily 10am–sunset; £1), an Edwardian mansion two miles south of town remodelled by Sir Robert Lorimer from a late seventeenth-century building. The estate includes the five-storey, late sixteenth-century **Scotstarvit Tower**, set on a little mound three quarters of a mile west of the present house (keys available from house during season only), and a fine example of Scots tower house, providing both fortification and comfort. The estate was bequeathed to the NTS in 1949, and the house contains an impressive collection of eighteenth-century Chippendale and French furniture, Dutch paintings, Chinese porcelain and a restored Edwardian laundry.

Practicalities

Cupar's **tourist office** (May Mon–Sat 9.30am–5pm; June–Sept Mon–Sat 9.30am–5.30pm, Sun 2–5pm; ☎01334/652874) is based in The Granary Business Centre on Coal Road. The **train station** is immediately south of the centre; **bus** #23 from Stirling to St Andrews stops outside. If you want to **stay**, try the *Eden House Hotel*, 2 Pitscottie Rd (☎01334/652510; ④), which serves good inexpensive Scottish food. There are several good B&Bs in and around Cupar, such as *Mill Cottage*, Cults Mill, just outside town (☎01334/654980; ③). There is no shortage of good **restaurants** in the area; try the excellent *Ostler's Close*, 25 Bonnygate (☎01334/655574); for drinks and bar food try *Watts* next to the tourist office.

St Andrews and around

Confident, poised and well groomed, **ST ANDREWS**, Scotland's oldest university town and a pigrimage centre for golfers from all over the world, is on a wide bay on the northeastern coast of Fife. It's often referred to in tourist literature as "the Oxford or Cambridge of the North", and, like Cambridge, by and large St Andrews *is* its university. According to legend, the town was founded, pretty much by accident, in the fourth century. Saint Rule – or Regulus – a custodian of the bones of Saint Andrew on the Greek island of Patras, had a vision in which an angel ordered him to carry five of the saint's bones to the western edge of the world, where he was to build a city in his honour. The conscientious courier set off, but was shipwrecked on the rocks close to the present harbour. Struggling ashore with his precious burden, he built a shrine to the saint on what subsequently became the site of the cathedral and Saint Andrew became Scotland's patron saint and the town its ecclesiastical capital.

Local residents are proud of their town, with its refined old-fashioned ambience. Thanks to a strong and well-informed local conservation lobby, many of the original

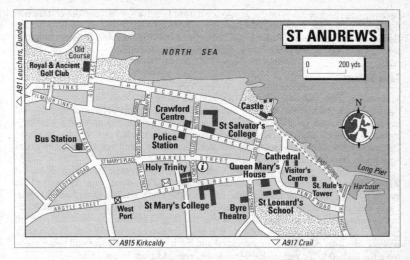

buildings have survived. Almost the entire centre consists of listed buildings, while the ruined castle and cathedral have all but been rebuilt in the efforts to preserve their remains. If you're here in early August, make sure to get to the two-day **Lammas Fair**, Scotland's oldest surviving medieval market, complete with town crier. The other main event in the St Andrews calendar is the **Kate Kennedy Pageant**, usually held on the third Saturday in April, which involves an all-male procession of students taking to the streets dressed as characters associated with the university, from Kate Kennedy herself, niece of one of the university founders, to Mary, Queen of Scots.

There are two main excursion areas from St Andrews. The most popular, with its beaches and little fishing villages is the **East Neuk**, stretching from Fife Ness to Largo Bay; the other is the **Tay coast**, which runs around Fife's northeast headland and along the Tay estuary almost to Perth.

Arrival, information and accommodation

St Andrews is not on the train line. The nearest **train station** is on the Edinburgh–Dundee–Aberdeen line at **Leuchars**, five miles northwest across the River Eden, from where regular (but not always connecting) buses make the trip into town (15min). Frequent **buses** from Edinburgh and Dundee terminate at the bus station on City Road at the west end of Market Street. The **tourist office** is at 70 Market St (Mon–Sat 9.30am–5pm, Sun 2–5pm; ☎01334/472021).

Although rooms in St Andrews cost more than in the surrounding area, they often get reserved in the summer, when booking ahead is strongly recommended. Most of the **guest houses** are around Murray Place and Murray Park between The Scores and North Street. Good ones include *Aedel House*, 72 Murray Place (☎01334/472315; ②) and *Bell Craig Guest House* at 8 Murray Park (☎01334/472962; ②). On North Street, try *Aslar House* at no. 120 (☎01334/473460; ④) or *Cadzow Guest House* at no. 58 (☎01334/476933; ④). Between June and September, the **University** (☎01334/462000; ④) offers about two hundred rooms in various locations, all on a B&B basis with dinner optional. More upmarket are the various **hotels** lining The Scores, beyond the eastern end of the Old (golf) Course, overlooking the bay. The *St Andrews Golf Hotel* at no. 40 (☎01334/472611; ⑨) occupies a three-storey town house, with great views from the bedrooms at the front. As you come into town from Leuchars, you'll see the entrance to the swanky *Rusacks Hotel*, 16 Pilmour Links (☎01334/474321; ⑨) on the left. A little further up the road is the *Tudor Inn*, 129 North St (☎01334/474906; ④) – its uncharacteristic black and white Tudor facade more English than Scottish.

The Town

The centre of St Andrews still follows the medieval layout. Wandering its three main thoroughfares, North Street, South Street and Market Street, which run west to east towards the ruined Gothic cathedral, are several of the original university buildings from the fifteenth century. Narrow alleys connect the cobbled streets, attic windows and gable ends shape the rooftops, and here and there you'll see old wooden doors with heavy knockers and black iron hinges.

The ruin of the great **St Andrews Cathedral** (visitor centre: April–Sept Mon–Sat 9.30am–6pm, Sun 2–6pm; Oct–March Mon–Sat 9.30am–4pm, Sun 2–4pm; £1.50; grounds only Sun am), at the east end of town, gives only an idea of its former importance. The cathedral was founded in 1160, but not finished and consecrated until 1318, in the presence of Robert the Bruce; it was the largest cathedral in Scotland. But on June 5, 1559, the Reformation took its toll, and supporters of John Knox, fresh from a rousing meeting, plundered the cathedral and left it to ruin. Stone was still being taken from the cathedral for various local buildings projects as late as the 1820s.

Standing above the harbour where the land drops to the sea, the cathedral site can be a blustery place, with the wind whistling through the great east window and down the stretch of turf that was once the central aisle. In front of the window a slab is all that remains of the high altar, where the relics of St Andrew were once enshrined. Previously, it is believed that they were kept in **St Rule's Tower**, the austere Romanesque monolith next to the cathedral, which was built as part of an abbey in 1130. From the top of the tower (a climb of 157 steps), there's a good view of the town and surroundings, and of the remains of the monastic buildings which made up the priory. Around the entire complex is a sturdy wall dating from the sixteenth century, over half a mile long and with three gateways.

Southwest of the cathedral enclosure lies **the Pends**, a huge fourteenth-century vaulted gatehouse which marked the main entrance to the priory, and from where the road leads down to the harbour, passing prim **St Leonard's**, one of Scotland's leading private schools for girls. The sixteenth-century, rubble-stonework building on the right as you go through the Pends is **Queen Mary's House**, where she is believed to have stayed in 1563. The house was restored in 1927 and is now used as the school library.

Down at the **harbour**, gulls screech above the fishing boats, keeping an eye on the lobster nets strewn along the quay. If you come here on a Sunday morning, you'll see students parading down the long pier, red gowns billowing in the wind, in a time-honoured after-church walk. The beach, **East Sands**, is a popular stretch, although it's cool in summer, and positively biting in winter. A path leads south from the far end of the beach, climbing up the hill past the caravan site and cutting through the gorse; this makes a pleasant walk on a sunny day, taking in hidden coves and caves.

North of the beach, the rocky coastline curves inland to the ruined **St Andrew's Castle** (April–Sept Mon–Sat 9.30am–6pm, Sun 2–6pm; Oct–March Mon–Sat 9.30am–4.30pm, Sun 2–4.30pm; £2), with a drop to the sea on three sides and a moat on the fourth. It was built around 1200 as part of the palace of the Bishops and Archbishops of St Andrews and was consequently the scene of some fairly grim incidents at the time of the Reformation. There's not a great deal left of the castle, since it fell into ruin in the seventeenth century, and most of what can be seen dates from the sixteenth century, apart from the fourteenth-century Fore Tower. The

Protestant reformer George Wishart was burned at the stake in front of the castle in 1546, as an incumbent Cardinal Beaton looked on. Wishart had been a friend of John Knox's, and it wasn't long before fellow reformers sought vengeance for his death. Less than three months later, Cardinal Beaton was stabbed to death, his body displayed from the battlements before being dropped into the "bottle dungeon", a 24-foot pit hewn out of solid rock visible in the Sea Tower. The perpetrators then held the castle for over a year, and dug a secret passage which can be entered from the ditch in front.

St Andrews University is the oldest in Scotland, founded in 1410 by Bishop Henry Wardlaw. The nominal founder is James I to whom the Bishop was tutor, and the king was certainly a great benefactor of the university. The first building was on the site of the Old University Library and by the end of the Middle Ages three colleges had been built: St Salvator's (1450), St Leonard's (1512) and St Mary's (1538). At the time of the Reformation, St Mary's became a seminary of Protestant theology, and today it houses the university's Faculty of Divinity. The **quad** here has beautiful gardens and some magnificent old trees, perfect for flopping under on a warm day.

If you've got children in tow you may want to visit the huge **Sea Life Centre** on The Scores, at the west end of town close to the golf museum (daily 10am–6pm; July & Aug closes 9pm; £4.25), which examines marine life of all shapes and sizes with displays, live exhibits, observation pools and underwater walkways. Also good for children is the fifty-acre **Craigtoun Country Park** (April–Sept daily 10.30am–6.30pm; £2), a couple of miles southwest of town on the B939. As well as several landscaped gardens there is a miniature train, trampolines, boating, crazy golf and picnic areas, and a country fair each May with craft stalls, wildlife exhibits, and showjumping displays.

GOLF IN ST ANDREWS

St Andrew's **Royal and Ancient Golf Club** (or "R&A") is the governing body for golf the world over, dating back to a meeting of 22 of the local gentry in 1754, who founded the Society of St Andrews Golfers, being "admirers of the ancient and healthful exercise of golf". It acquired its current title after King William IV agreed to be the society's patron in 1834. The game itself has been played here since the fifteenth century. Those early days were instrumental in establishing Scotland as the home of golf, for the rules were distinguished from those in the French game by the fact that participants had to manoeuvre the ball into a hole, rather than hit an above-ground target. (Early French versions were, in fact, more like croquet.) The game developed, acquiring popularity along the way – even Mary, Queen of Scots, was known to have the occasional round. It was not without its opponents, however, particularly James II who, in 1457, banned his subjects from playing since it was distracting them from archery practice.

St Andrews' status as a world-renowned golf centre is particulary obvious as you enter the town from the west, where the approach road runs adjacent to the famous **Old Course**. At the eastern end of the course lies the strictly private clubhouse, a stolid, square building dating from 1854. The first British Open Championship was held here in 1873, having been inaugurated in 1860 at Prestwick in Ayrshire, and since then, the British Open is held here regularly, pulling in enormous crowds. The eighteenth hole of the Old Course is immediately in front of the clubhouse, and has been officially christened the "Tom Morris", after one of the world's most famous golfers. Pictures of Nick Faldo, Jack Nicklaus and other golfing greats, along with clubs and a variety of memorabilia which they donated, are displayed in the admirable **British Golf Museum** on Bruce Embankment, along the waterfront below the clubhouse (April–Oct daily 10am–5.30pm; Nov–March Thurs–Mon 11am–3pm; £3.50). There are also plenty of hands-on exhibits, including computers, video screens and footage of British Open championships, tracing the development of golf through the centuries.

Eating and drinking

St Andrews has no shortage of **restaurants** and **cafés**. In town, *Littlejohns*, at the east end of Market Street, serves hearty burgers and steaks, while *The Vine Leaf Restaurant*, St Mary's Place (☎01334/477497) is known for its good range of seafood. Both *Brambles*, 5 College St and *The Merchant's House*, 49 South St, offer inexpensive home baking, while the licensed *Victoria Café*, 1 St Mary's Place, a popular student haunt, serves baked potatoes and toasted sandwiches. *Ma Belle's*, 40 The Scores, in the basement of the *St Andrews Golf Hotel*, is a lively pub serving cheap food and catering for locals as much as students. In the basement bar of *Rusacks Hotel*, 16 Pilmour Links, you can collapse in large leather armchairs and sofas, or have a game of snooker. For truly great food, head for the *Peat Inn* (☎01334/840206), five miles south of town on the A915 and then one mile west on the B940. This is one of Britain's top restaurants, serving a varied menu of local specialities, and will set you back at least £35 per head.

With its big student population, St Andrews has lots of good **pubs**. Locals and tourists mix with the students at the *Tudor*, 129 North St, which has a late-night licence on Thursdays and Fridays and live bands from time to time. The *Central* on Market Street serves huge pies and a powerful beer brewed by Trappist monks. The *Cellar Bar* on Bell Street has a good range of real ales and malt whiskies, with live music in its upstairs bar.

The East Neuk

South of St Andrews, the **East Neuk** (*Neuk* is Scots for "corner") is a region of quaint fishing villages, all crow-stepped gables and tiled rooves. Perhaps the prettiest of these is **Crail**; with a picturesque pottery near the harbour, but the best beaches are at the resorts of **Elie** and **Earlsferry**, which lie next to each other about twelve miles south of St Andrews. The villages between St Andrews and Elie fall into two distinct types: either scattered higgledy-piggledy up the hillside like **St Monans**, between Pittenweem and Elie, or neatly lined along the harbour like **Anstruther**, between Crail and Pittenweem.

Anstruther and the Isle of May

ANSTRUTHER is home to the wonderfully unpretentious **Scottish Fisheries Museum** (May–Sept Mon–Sat 9.30am–5.30pm, Sun 2–5pm; £2.50), quite in keeping with the no-frills integrity of the area in general. Set in a complex of sixteenth- to nineteenth-century buildings on a total of eighteen different floors, it charts the history of the fishing and whaling industries in ingenious displays. Moored in the harbour outside is the **North Carr Lightship** (Easter–Oct daily 11am–5pm; £1.40), which for almost 45

SCOTLAND'S SECRET BUNKER

Inland between St Andrews and Anstruther on the B940 (bus #61 takes you to within 2 miles of the bunker) is the idiosyncratic **Scotland's Secret Bunker** (April–Oct daily 10am–5pm; Nov–Easter weekends only; £4.75). Opened to the public in 1994, the bunker is just off the secrets list. Entrance is through an innocent-looking farmhouse, then you walk down a vast ramp to the bunker, which is 100ft below ground and encased in 15ft of reinforced concrete. In the event of a nuclear war the bunker would have become Scotland's new administrative centre. From here, government and military commanders would have co-ordinated fire-fighting and medical help for Scotland from a switchboard room with 2800 phone lines. The bunker, which could house 300 people, was due to be equipped with air filters, a vast electricity generator and its own water supply; the best of 1950s technology, today it has a rather kitsch James Bond feel about it. The only concession to entertainment was a couple of cinemas, which now show Fifties newsreel giving painfully inadequate instructions to civilians in the event of nuclear war.

years served off Fife Ness. Have a look around to get a feeling of life on board. A **tourist office** operates from the museum during the summer (times as Museum, above).

The current lighthouse, erected in 1816 by Robert Louis Stevenson's grandfather, is several miles offshore from Anstruther on the rugged **Isle of May**, where you can also see the remains of Scotland's first lighthouse, built in 1636, which burned coals as a beacon. The island is now a nature reserve and bird sanctuary, and can be reached by boat from Anstruther (May–Sept; one sailing per day; £9; ☎01333/310103). Between April and July the dramatic seacliffs are covered with breeding kittiwakes, razorbills, guillemots and shags, while inland there are thousands of puffins and eider duck. Grey seals also make the occasional appearance. Be sure to check up on departure times, and allow between four and five hours for a round trip: an hour each way, and a couple of hours there. Also take plenty of warm, waterproof clothing.

You may choose to **stay** in Anstruther, a pretty and peaceful base for exploring the surrounding area. There are plenty of good **B&Bs**; try the lovely *Hermitage Guest House* (☎01333/310909; ③), Ladywalk; the *Beaumont Lodge Guest House* (☎01333/310315; ②) or *The Spindrift* (☎01333/310573), both on Pittenweem Road; or *The Sheiling* (☎01333/310697; ②) at 32 Glenogil Gardens. There is a **campsite** nearby at Crail, the *Sauchope Links* (☎01337/450460). There is a fine **fish restaurant** in Anstruther, the *Cellar* (☎01333/310378), in one of the village's oldest buildings, once a cooperage and smokehouse.

Perth and around

Surrounded by fertile agricultural land and beautiful scenery, **PERTH** was for several centuries Scotland's capital. Viewed from the hills to the south, Perth still justifies Sir Walter Scott's glowing description of it in the opening pages of his novel *The Fair Maid of Perth* , as "this exquisite landscape". During the reign of James I, Parliament met here on several occasions, but its glory was short-lived; the king was murdered in the town's Dominican priory in 1437 by the traitorous Sir Robert Graham, who was captured in the Highlands and tortured to death in Stirling. During the Reformation, on May 11, 1559, John Knox preached a rousing sermon in St John's Church, which led to the destruction of the town's four monasteries (by those Knox later condemned as "the rascal mulititude") and quickened the pace of reform in Scotland. Despite decline in the seventeenth century, the community has prospered ever since – today it's a finance centre, and still an important and bustling market town. Its long history in **livestock trading** is continued throughout the year, notably with the Aberdeen Angus shows and sales in February and October, and the Perthshire Agricultural Show.

The Town

Perth's compact **centre** occupies a small area, easily explored on foot, on the west bank of the Tay. Two large areas of green parkland, known as the North and South Inch, flank the centre. The **North Inch** was the site of the Battle of the Clans in 1396, in which thirty men from each of the clans Chattan and Quhele (pronounced "Kay") met in a battle, while the **South Inch** was the public meeting place for witch-burning in the seventeenth century. Both are now used for more civilized public recreation, with sports matches to the north, and boating and putting to the south.

A good variety of shops line **High Street** and **South Street**, as well as filling **St John's** shopping centre on King Edward Street. Opposite the entrance to the centre, the imposing **City Hall** is used by Scotland's politicians for party conferences. Behind here lies **St John's Kirk** (daily 10am–noon & 2–4pm; free), founded by David I in 1126, although the present building dates from the fifteenth century and was restored

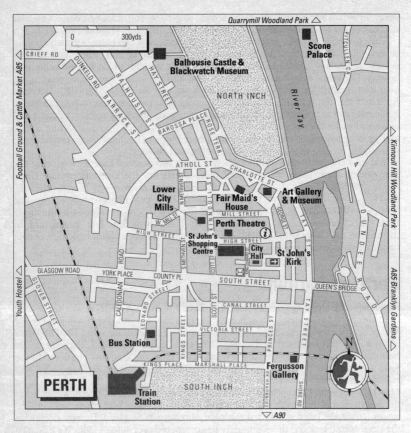

between 1923 and 1928 to house a war memorial chapel designed by Robert Lorimer. It was in St John's that John Knox preached his fiery sermon calling for the "purging of the churches from idolatry" in 1559.

In the north of the centre, the **Fair Maid's House**, on North Port, is arguably the town's best-known attraction, although you can only see it from the outside. Standing on the site of a thirteenth-century monastery, this cottage of weathered stone with small windows and an outside staircase was the setting chosen by Sir Walter Scott as the house of Simon Glover, father of the virginal Catherine Glover, in his novel *The Fair Maid of Perth*. Set in turbulent times at the close of the fourteenth century, the novel tells a traditional story of love, war and revenge, centring on the attempts by various worthies to win the hand of Catherine.

The nearby **Art Gallery and Museum** on George Street (Mon–Sat 10am–5pm; free), gives a good overview of local life through the centuries. In similar vein, at **Lower City Mills**, West Mill St (April–Aug Mon–Sat 10am–5pm; £1.50), a restored oatmeal mill driven by a massive water wheel recalls Victorian Perth. The Round House, a domed circular structure on Marshall Place, used to house the waterworks, and is the unlikely setting for the excellent **Fergusson Gallery**. The gallery holds a collection of the paintings, drawings and sculpture of J.D. Fergusson, the foremost artist of the Scottish

"Colourist" movement. His lifelong companion was the dancer and painter Margaret Morris; her summer schools, held annually for forty years, provided Fergusson with models and inspired his monumental paintings of bathers, in pure bright colours.

North of the town centre, and adjacent to the North Inch, the elegantly restored Georgian terraces beyond the Fair Maid's House give way to newer buildings, which have gradually encroached on the former territory of the fifteenth-century **Balhousie Castle**, off Hay Street (May–Sept Mon–Sat 10am–4.30pm; Oct–April Mon–Fri 10am–3.30pm; free). The castle, restored in Scots Baronial style with turrets and crow-stepped gables, sits incongruously in a peaceful residential area and now houses the headquarters and **Museum of the Black Watch**. This historic regiment – whose name refers to the dark colour of their tartan – was formed in 1739, having been built up by General Wade earlier in the century, who employed groups of Highlanders to keep the peace.

Practicalities

The **bus** and **train stations** are on opposite sides of the road at the west end of town where Kings Place runs into Leonard Street. The **tourist office**, 45 High St (Mon–Sat 9am–5pm; ☎01738/638353), is a ten-minute walk away. Of the numerous **hotels** in Perth's town centre, try the *Station Hotel*, Leonard St (☎01738/624141; ⑤), right by the station, or *Stakis Perth*, West Mill St (☎01783/628281; ⑥). The refurbished *Salutation Hotel*, 34 South St (☎01738/630066; ④), claims to be one of Scotland's oldest hotels, dating back to 1699. There are **B&Bs** all over town, notably on the approach roads from Crieff and Stirling. In the centre, Marshall Place, overlooking the South Inch, is the place to look. Of the many possibilities along here, try *Kinnaird House*, 5 Marshall Place (☎01738/628021; ③), or the *Park Lane Guest House*, 17 Marshall Place (☎01738/637218; ③). The **youth hostel** is housed in an impressive old mansion on Glasgow Road (March–Oct; ☎01738/623658), beyond the west end of York Place.

Within striking distance of the youth hostel is a good basic Indian **restaurant**, the *Café Kamran*, 13 York Place. The *Good Luck Food Palace*, 181 South St, serves well-priced Chinese cuisine. *Pierre Victoire*, 38 South St (☎01738/444222), has cheap and tasteful French food. The best choice for a classier meal is the stylish Art Deco fish restaurant, *Number Thirty Three*, 33 George St (☎01738/633771), with an oyster bar and à la carte restaurant. *Strangeways*, 24 George St, is a popular bar and bistro. A new Irish **pub** in the town centre, *Mucky Mulligans*, 97 Canal St, claims to be the first "Dublin cottage-style" pub in Scotland and serves specialities like Irish stew all day; every night there's live Irish folk music.

Scone Palace

Just a couple of miles north of Perth (along the A93; bus #7 from South St in Perth every 20min, or #26 and #46 every hour) on the eastern side of the Tay, **Scone Palace** (pronounced "Scoon") is worth every penny of the admission charge levied by its owners, the Earl and Countess of Mansfield (mid-April to mid-Oct daily 9.30am–5pm; £4.50). The two-storey palace, restored in the nineteenth century, consists of a sixteenth-century core surrounded by earlier buildings, most built of red sandstone, complete with battlements and the original gateway. The abbey that stood here in the sixteenth century, and where all Scottish kings until James I were crowned, was one of those destroyed following John Knox's sermon in Perth. In the extensive grounds which surround the palace lies the Moot Hill, which was once the site of the famous Coronation **Stone of Destiny** (see box overleaf).

Inside, a good selection of sumptuous rooms is open to visitors, including the library, which has exchanged its books in favour of an outstanding collection of porce-

THE STONE OF DESTINY

Legend has it that the Stone of Destiny (also called the Stone of Scone) was "Jacob's Pillow", on which he dreamed of the ladder of angels from earth to heaven. Its real history is obscure, but it is known that it it was moved from Ireland to Dunadd by missionaries, and thence to Dunstaffnage, from where Kenneth MacAlpine, king of the Dalriada Scots, brought it to the abbey at Scone in 838. There it remained for almost 500 years, used as a coronation throne on which all Kings of Scotland were crowned. In 1296, an over-eager Edward I stole what he believed to be the Stone and installed it at Westminster Abbey. Apart from a brief interlude in 1950, when Scottish nationalists stole it back again and hid it in Arbroath for several months, it has been there ever since.

Speculation surrounds the authenticity of the Stone at Westminster, for the original is said to have been intricately carved, while the one seen today is a plain block of sandstone. Many believe that the canny monks at Scone palmed this off onto the English king and that the real Stone of Destiny lies hidden in an underground chamber, its whereabouts a mystery to all but a chosen few.

lain, one of the foremost in the world, with items by Meissen, Sèvres, Chelsea, Derby and Worcester. Look out too for the beautiful papier-mâché travelling dishes, Marie-Antoinette's writing desk, and John Zoffany's exquisite eighteenth-century portrait of the *Lady Elizabeth Murray* [daughter of the second earl] *with Dido*. You could easily spend at least a morning here, enjoying the gardens with strutting peacocks, a fenced-off area with Highland cattle, picnic spot, donkey park, children's playground and a grand and fragrant pine garden, which was planted in 1848 with exotic conifers.

Strathearn

Strathearn – the valley of the River Earn – stretches west of Perth, across to **Loch Earn** and the watersports centre at **Lochearnhead**. Agricola was here around two thousand years ago, trying to establish a foothold in the Highlands; later the area was frequented by Bonnie Prince Charlie and Rob Roy, both bound up in the north–south struggle between Highlands and Lowlands.

South of Strathearn, the small town of **AUCHTERARDER** sees its fair share of visitors, many of whom come to play golf at the swanky *Gleneagles Hotel* nearby (☎01764/662231; ⑨). There is a **tourist office** on High Street (April–Oct Mon–Sat 9.30am–5.30pm, Sun 11am–4pm; Nov–March Mon–Fri 9.30am–1.30pm; ☎01764/663450). As well as the local bus service, the **Loch Earn Trundler**, a classic 1950s bus, links Callander, Lochearnhead, Comrie and Crieff, and the **Loch Tay Trundler** runs from Callander to Lochearnhead, Kenmore and Aberfeldy (for details call ☎01786/442707).

Dunning

Just southeast of the valley, it is worth taking a detour from the busy A9 to the quiet village of **DUNNING**, five miles east of Auchterarder on the B8062, which has an impressive history. The village was once the capital of the Picts and was the place where Kenneth I, King of the Picts and Scots, died in 860. Dunning was destroyed by the Jacobites and subsequently rebuilt, which accounts for its homogeneous appearance, the houses all being late eighteenth and early nineteenth century. **St Serf's** has survived, a rugged church with a Norman tower and arch. Just west of the village is an extraordinary monument, a pile of stones surmounted by a cross, and scrawled with the words: *Maggie Wall, Burnt here, 1657*. Maggie Wall was burned as a witch, and the rumour is that local women replenish the white writing on the monument every year.

Crieff and around

At the heart of the valley is the old spa town of **CRIEFF**, which lies in a lovely position on a south-facing slope of the Grampian foothills. Cattle traders used to come here in the eighteenth century, since this was a good location – between Highland and Lowland – for buying and selling livestock, but Crieff really came into its own with the arrival of the railway in 1856. Shortly after that, Morrison's Academy, now one of Scotland's most respected schools, took in its first pupils, and in 1868 the grand old *Crieff Hydro* (☎01764/655555; ⑨), then known as the *Strathearn Hydropathic*, opened its doors – still the nicest place to stay in town, despite being dry (of alcohol). Cheaper **B&B** options are *Greenhead House*, 52 Burrell St (☎01764/654603; ②), and *Bank Guest House*, 32 Burrell St (☎01764/653409; ②). There's a pleasing mixture of Edwardian and Victorian houses, with a busy little centre which still retains something of the atmosphere of the former spa town. The **Crieff Visitor Centre** (daily 9.30am–5pm) is a "craftsy" place, crammed with pottery and paperweights. The **tourist office** is in the town hall on High Street (April–Oct Mon–Sat 9.30am–5pm, Sun 11am–4pm; Nov–March Mon–Fri 9.30am–5pm, Sat 9.30am–noon; ☎01764/652578).

From Crieff, it's a short drive or twenty-minute walk to the **Glenturret Distillery** (March–Dec Mon–Sat 9.30am–6pm, Sun noon–6pm, last tour 4.30pm; Jan–Feb Mon–Fri 11.30am–4pm, last tour 2.30pm; free), just off the A85 to Comrie. To get there on public transport, catch any bus going to Crieff, Comrie or St Fillans and ask the driver to drop you at the bottom of the Glenturret Distillery road, from where it's a five-minute walk. This is Scotland's oldest distillery, established in 1775, and a good one to visit, if only for its splendid isolation.

If you enjoy ornate gardens, on no account miss the **Drummond Castle Gardens** near Muthill, two miles south of Crieff on the A822 (bus #17 from Crieff towards Muthill, then a mile-and-a-half-walk up the castle drive). The approach to the garden is extraordinary, up a dark avenue of trees. Crossing the courtyard of the castle to the grand terrace, you can view the garden in all its symmetrical glory. It was laid out by John Drummond, second earl of Perth, in 1630, and shows clear French and Italian influence, although the central structural feature of the parterre is a St Andrews cross. Italian marble statues punctuate the long lines of the cross, and the overall effect is of exceptional harmony and grace. The castle itself (closed to the public) is a wonderful mixture of architectural styles. There is a blunt fifteenth-century keep on a rocky crag, adjoining a much modified Renaissance mansion house.

Northwest Perthshire

A place of magnificent beauty, where the snow-capped peaks of soaring mountains fall away down forested slopes to long, deep lochs on the valley floor, **northwest Perthshire** is dominated by the western Grampian Mountains, a mighty range that controls transport routes, influences the weather and tolerates little development. The **Breadalbane Mountains** run between Loch Tay and Loch Earn; as well as providing walking and watersports, the area is dotted with fine towns and villages, like **Aberfeldy** at the western tip of Loch Tay and **Dunkeld** with its eighteenth-century whitewashed cottages and elegant ruined cathedral. Among the wealth of historical sites in northwest Perthshire is the splendid Baronial **Blair Castle**, north of Pitlochry.

Dunkeld

DUNKELD, fifteen miles up the A9 and the River Tay from Perth, was proclaimed Scotland's ecclesiastical capital by Kenneth MacAlpine in 850. Its position at the southern boundary of the Grampian Mountains made it a favoured meeting place for

Highland and Lowland cultures, but in 1689 it was burned to the ground by the Cameronians – fighting for William of Orange – in an effort to flush out troops of the Stuart monarch, James VII. Subsequent rebuilding, however, has created one of the area's most delightful communities, and it's well worth at least a brief stop to view its whitewashed houses and historic cathedral. The **tourist office** is at The Cross in the town centre (April–Oct Mon–Sat 9.30am–5.30pm, Sun 11am–4pm; longer hours in peak season; Nov & Dec Mon–Sat 9.30am–1.30pm; ☎01350/727688).

Dunkeld's partly ruined **Cathedral** is on the northern side of town, in an idyllic setting amid lawns and trees on the east bank of the Tay. Construction began in the early twelfth century, but the building was more or less ruined at the time of the Reformation. The present structure, in Gothic and Norman style, consists of the fourteenth-century choir and the fifteenth-century nave. The **choir**, restored in 1600 (and several times since), now serves as the parish church, while the **nave** remains roofless apart from the clock tower. Inside, note the leper's peep near the pulpit in the north wall, through which lepers could receive the sacrament without contact with the congregation. Also look out for the great efigy of "The Wolf of Badenoch", Robert II's son born in 1343. The wolf acquired his name and notoriety when, after being excommunicated from the Church for leaving his wife, he took his revenge by burning the towns of Forres and Elgin and sacking Elgin cathedral. He eventually repented, did public penance for his crimes and was absolved by his brother Robert III.

Dunkeld is linked to its sister community, **BIRNAM**, by Thomas Telford's seven-arched bridge of 1809. This little village has a place in history thanks to Shakespeare, for it was on "Dunsinane Hill" to the southeast of the village that Macbeth declared: "I will not be afraid of death and bane/Till Birnam Forest come to Dunsinane", only to be told by a messenger: "As I did stand my watch upon the Hill/I look'd toward Birnam, and anon me thought/The Wood began to move ...". The **Perthshire Visitor Centre** just south of Birnam, down the A9 at Bankfoot (March–Sept daily 9am–6pm; £2), offers "The Macbeth Experience", which encompasses – on film and through talking dummies – bloodshed, ghosts and an untimely death. Several centuries later another literary personality, Beatrix Potter, drew inspiration from the area, recalling her childhood holidays here when penning the *Peter Rabbit* stories.

There are plenty of places to stay in Dunkeld, including some large **hotels**: the *Atholl Arms Hotel* (☎01350/727219; ④), the *Royal Dunkeld* (☎01350/727322; ④) and the Victorian-Gothic *Birnam Hotel* (☎01350/727462; ⑦), all in the village. Just to the north, the luxurious *Stakis Dunkeld* (☎01350/727771; ⑨) is set at the end of a long drive which winds through the hotel's lush estate, where you can fish, shoot, cycle and stroll. For **B&B**, try the pretty *Birnam Bank Cottage* (☎01350/727201; ②), Birnam Glen, Dunkeld, or *The Top Inn* (☎01350/727699;②), Birnam. There are a few mediocre **eating places** on Dunkeld's main street; the best food options are lunch at the *Atholl Arms* or a more expensive dinner at the *Stakis Dunkeld*.

Driving north on the A9 to Pitlochry, you can stop off and walk the mile and a half to **The Hermitage** (also buses from Perth to Pitlochry stop near here), set in the wooded gorge of the River Braan. This pretty eighteenth-century folly, also known as Ossian's Hall, was once mirrored to reflect the water, but the mirrors were smashed by Victorian vandals, and the folly more tamely restored. The hall, appealing yet incongruous in its splendid setting, neatly frames a dramatic waterfall.

Aberfeldy

A largely Victorian town six miles or so further on, **ABERFELDY** makes a good base for exploring the area. The town sits at the point where the Urlar Burn – lined by the silver birch trees celebrated by Robert Burns in his poem *The Birks of Aberfeldy* – flows into the River Tay. The Tay is spanned by **Wade's Bridge**, built by General Wade in

1733 during his efforts to control the trouble in the Highlands, and, with its humpback and four arches, is regarded as one of the general's finest remaining crossing points. Overlooking the bridge from the south end is the **Black Watch Monument**, a pensive, kilted soldier, erected in 1887 to commemorate the peacekeeping troop of Highlanders gathered together by Wade in 1739. The small town centre is a busy mixture of craft and tourist shops, its main attraction the superbly restored early nineteenth-century **Aberfeldy Water Mill** (Easter–Oct Mon–Sat 10am–5.30pm, Sun noon–5.30pm; £1.80), a mill which harnesses the water of the Urlar to turn the wheel that stone-grinds the oatmeal in the traditional Scottish way.

One mile west of Aberfeldy, across Wade's Bridge, **Castle Menzies** (April to mid-Oct Mon–Fri 10.30am–5pm, Sun 2–5pm; £2.50) is an imposing, Z-shaped, sixteenth-century tower house, which until the middle of this century was the chief seat of the Clan Menzies. With the demise of the Menzies line the castle was taken over by the Menzies Clan Society, who have been restoring it for the last 25 years. Now the interior, with its wide stone staircase, is refreshingly free of fixtures and fittings, with structural attributes such as the plasterwork ceilings on show.

The **tourist office** is at The Square (April–Oct Mon–Sat 9.30am–5.30pm, Sun noon–4pm; longer hours in peak season; Nov–March Mon–Fri 9.30am–5pm, Sat 9.30am–1pm; ☎01887/820276). If you want to **stay** in Aberfeldy, *Moness House Hotel and Country Club*, Crieff Rd (☎01887/820446; ⑤) occupies a whitewashed country house and offers fishing, golf and watersports. *Guinach House*, by the Birks (☎01887/820251; ⑦), in pleasant grounds near the famous silver birches, is a tastefully decorated house converted into a small hotel. *Farleyer House* (☎01887/820332; ⑦), a mile out of Aberfeldy on the B846, is highly recommended as a hotel and **restaurant**. For B&B, try *Novar*, 2 Home St (☎01887/820779; ②) or *Marvis Bank*, Taybridge Drive (☎01887/820223; ②), both attractive stone cottages.

Loch Tay

Loch Tay, sits below moody **Ben Lawers** (3984ft), Perthshire's highest mountain; from the top there are incredible views towards both the Atlantic and the North Sea. The ascent – which should not be tackled without all the right equipment (see pp.45–46) – takes around three hours from the NTS **visitor centre** (mid-April to Sept daily 10am–5pm; £1; ☎01567/820397), which is at 1300ft and reached by a track off the A827 along the northern side of the loch. The centre has an audio-visual show, slides of the mountain flowers – including the rare Alpine flora found here – and a nature trail with accompanying descriptive booklet.

The **mountains of Breadalbane** (pronounced "Bread-*al*bane"), named after the Earls of Breadalbane, loom over the southern end of Loch Tay. Glens Lochay and Dochart curve into the north and south respectively from the small town of **KILLIN**, where the River Dochart comes rushing out of the hills and down the frothy **Falls of Dochart**, before disgorging into Loch Tay. There's little to do in Killin itself, but it does make a convenient base for some of the area's best walks. One of the most appealing places to **stay** is the *Dall Lodge Hotel*, Main St (☎01567/820217; ②), which the owner, who lives in the Far East, has filled with all manner of exotic bits and pieces. The dining room serves fine local produce. There is also a **youth hostel** (April–Oct; ☎01567/820546), in a fine old country house north of the village, with views out over the loch.

On the other side of the Breadalbane mountains, north of Loch Tay lies **Glen Lyon** – at 34 miles long the longest enclosed glen in Scotland – where, legend has it, the Celtic warrior Fingal built twelve castles. Access to the glen is usually impossible in winter, but the narrow roads are passable in summer. You can either take the road from Killin up to the **Ben Lawers Visitor Centre**, four miles up Loch Tay, and continue going, or take the road from Fortingall, which is a couple of miles north of the loch's northern end. The two roads join up, making a round trip possible, but bear in mind there is no road through the mountains to Loch Rannoch further north. **FORTINGALL** itself is little more than a handful of thatched cottages, although locals make much of their 3000-year-old yew tree – believed (by them at least) to be the oldest living thing in Europe. The village also lays claim to being the birthplace of Pontius Pilate, reputedly the son of a Roman officer stationed here.

Pitlochry

Surrounded by hills just north of the confluence of the Tummel and Tay rivers at Ballinluig, **PITLOCHRY** spreads gracefully along the eastern shore of the Tummel, on the lower slopes of Ben Vrackie. Even after General Wade built one of his first roads through here in the early eighteenth century, Pitlochry remained little more than a village. Queen Victoria's visit in 1842 helped to put the area on the map, but it wasn't until the end of the century that Pitlochry established itself as a popular holiday centre.

Today the busy main street is a constant flurry of traffic, locals and tourists. Beyond the train bridge at the southern end of the main street (Atholl Rd leading to Perth Rd) is Bells' **Blair Atholl Distillery**, Perth Rd (Easter–Sept Mon–Sat 9am–5pm, Sun noon–4pm; Oct–Easter closed Sat & Sun), where the excellent visitor centre illustrates the process involved in making the Blair Atholl Malt. Whisky has been produced on this site since 1798, in which time production has been stepped up to around two million litres a year, making this only a medium-sized distillery.

A perfect contrast to the Blair Atholl is the **Edradour Distillery** (March–Oct Mon–Sat 9.30am–5pm, Sun 2–5pm; Nov–Feb Mon–Sat 10.30am–4pm), Scotland's smallest, in an idyllic position tucked into the hills a couple of miles east of Pitlochry on the A924. A whistle-stop audio-visual presentation covering more than 250 years of production precedes the tour of the distillery itself.

On the western edge of Pitlochry, just across the river, lies Scotland's renowned "Theatre in the Hills", the **Pitlochry Festival Theatre** (season runs from Easter to early Oct; ☎01796/472680). Set up in 1951, the theatre started in a tent on the site of what is now the town curling rink, before moving to the banks of the river in 1981. Backstage tours, covering all aspects of theatre production (generally Thurs & Fri 2pm; £2.50; booking essential), run through the day, while both mainstream and offbeat productions are staged in the evening.

A short stroll upstream from the theatre is the **Pitlochry Power Station and Dam**, a massive concrete wall which harnesses the water of the man-made Loch Faskally, just north of the town, for hydro-electric power. Although the visitor centre (April–Oct daily 9.40am–5.30pm) explains the ins and outs of it all, the main attraction here, apart from the views up the loch, is the **salmon ladder**, up which the salmon leap on their annual migration – a sight not to be missed.

Practicalities

The **bus** stop and the **train** station are on Station Road, at the north end of town, ten minutes' walk from the centre and the **tourist office** at 22 Atholl Rd (Mon–Fri 9am–1pm & 2–5pm, Sat 9.30am–1.30pm; ☎01796/472215). *Birchwood Hotel*, East Moulin Rd (☎01796/472477; ⑤) has a particularly good restaurant; close by, *Castlebeigh House*, 10 Knockard Rd (☎01796/472925; ④), has good views from the bedrooms. At Tummel Bridge, the *Kynachan Lodge* (☎01882/634214; ⑤) is decorated with oriental *objets d'art* and is a good choice for food. Other possibilities include *McKays Hotel*, 138 Atholl Rd (☎01796/473888; ④), *Craigroyston House*, 2 Lower Oakfield (☎01796/472053; ③) and *Comar House*, Strathview Terrace (☎01796/473531; ③). The **youth hostel** (☎01796/472308) is a fine stone mansion on Knockard Road at the top of town. Pitlochry is the domain of the tea room and pitifully short of **restaurants** and pubs; the best option in town is the very popular *Festival Theatre* or the nearby *Porthacraig Inn & Restaurant*, both of which have beautiful riverside locations.

Killiecrankie and Blair Castle

Four miles north of Pitlochry, the A9 cuts through the **Pass of Killiecrankie**, a breath-taking wooded gorge which falls away to the River Garry below. This dramatic setting was the site of the **Battle of Killicrankie** in 1689, when the Jacobites quashed the forces of General Mackay. Legend has it that one soldier of the Crown, fleeing for his life, made a miraculous jump across the eighteen-feet **Soldier's Leap**, an impossibly wide chasm halfway up the gorge. Exhibits at the slick NTS **visitor centre** (April–Oct daily 10am–5.30pm; £1; ☎01796/473233) recall the battle and examine the gorge in detail.

Before leading the Jacobites into battle, Graham of Claverhouse, Viscount ("Bonnie") Dundee, had seized the whitewashed **Blair Castle** (April–Oct daily 10am–6pm; £5), three miles up the road at Blair Atholl. Seat of the Atholl dukedom, and dating from 1269, the castle presents an impressive sight as you approach up the drive. A piper may be playing in front of the castle: he is one of the Atholl Highlanders, a select group retained by the duke as his private army – a privilege afforded to him by Queen Victoria, who stayed here in 1844. Today the duke is the only British subject allowed to maintain his own force. A total of 32 rooms are open for inspection, and display a selection of paintings, furniture, Brussels tapestries and the like that is sumptous in the extreme, although the vast number of stuffed animals may not be to everyone's liking. The castle has a self-service restaurant, and there's a **riding stable** from where you can take treks and explore the ancient landscaped grounds further.

Loch Tummel and Loch Rannoch

Between Pitlochry and Loch Ericht lies a sparsely populated, ever-changing panorama of mountains, moors, lochs and glens. Venturing into the hills is difficult without a car – unless you're walking – but infrequent local buses do run from Pitlochry to the outlying communities in the surrounding area, and the train to Inverness runs parallel to the A9.

West of Pitlochry, the B8019/B846 twists and turns along the Grampian mountain-sides, overlooking **Loch Tummel** and then **Loch Rannoch**. These two lochs, cele-brated by Harry Lauder in his famous song *The Road to the Isles*, are joined by Dunalastair Water, which narrows to become the River Tummel at the western end of the loch of the same name. **Queen's View** at the eastern end of Loch Tummel is a fabulous vantage point, looking down the loch across the hills to the misty peak of Schiehallion (3520ft), the "Fairy Mountain", whose mass was used in early experi-ments to judge the weight of the Earth. The Forestry Commission's **visitor centre** (April–Oct daily 9.30am–5pm; ☎01350/727284) interprets the fauna and flora of the area, and also has a café.

Beyond Loch Tummel, **KINLOCH RANNOCH** marks the eastern end of Loch Rannoch. This small community is popular with backpackers, who stock up at the local store before taking to the hills again, and you can also stay at *Cuilimore Cottage* (☎01882/632218; ③): the atmosphere is rustic and the food delicious. The road follows the loch to its end and then heads six miles further into the desolation of **Rannoch Moor**, where **Rannoch Station**, a lonely outpost on the Glasgow to Fort William West Highland train, marks the end of the line. The only way back is by the same road as far as Loch Rannoch, where it's possible – but not always advisable, depending on condi-tions – to return on a (very) minor road along the south side of the lochs. The round trip is roughly seventy miles.

travel details

Trains

Kirkcaldy to: Aberdeen (hourly; 2hr); Dundee (hourly; 40min or 1hr); Edinburgh (23 daily; 40min); Perth (7 daily; 40min); Pitlochry (4 direct daily; 1hr 15min; 4 indirect, change at Perth; 1hr 25min).

Perth to: Aberdeen (hourly; 1hr 40min); Dundee (hourly; 25min); Edinburgh (9 daily; 1hr 25min); Glasgow Queen Street (hourly; 1hr 5min); Kirkcaldy (7 daily; 40min); Pitlochry (8 daily; 30min).

Pitlochry to: Edinburgh (5 daily; 2hr); Glasgow Queen Street (3 daily; 1hr 45min); Kirkcaldy (4 direct daily; 1hr 15min; 1 indirect, change at Perth; 1hr 45min); Perth (8 daily; 30min); Stirling (3 daily; 1hr 10min).

Stirling to: Aberdeen (hourly; 2hr 15min); Dundee (hourly; 1hr); Edinburgh (hourly; 1hr); Glasgow Queen Street (hourly; 30min); Perth (hourly; 30min); Pitlochry (5 daily; 1hr 15min).

Buses

Dundee to: Kirkcaldy (7 daily; 1hr 35min); St Andrews (every 30min; 35min); Stirling (9 daily; 1hr 30min).

Dunfermline to: Edinburgh (2 daily; 40min); Kirkcaldy (every 30min; 1hr); St Andrews (11 daily; 2hr).

Kirkcaldy to: Dundee (16 daily; 1hr 10min); Dunfermline (hourly; 1hr); St Andrews (16 daily; 50min).

Perth to: Dunblane (every 30min; 35min); Dunfermline (every 30min; 50min); Edinburgh (12 daily; 1hr 20min); Glasgow (20 daily; 1hr 35min); Gleneagles (12 daily; 25min); Inverness (3 daily; 2hr 30min); London (4 daily; 9hr); Stirling (18 daily; 50min).

St Andrews to: Dundee (every 30min; 40min); Dunfermline (Mon–Sat 13 daily; 1hr 40min); Edinburgh (12 daily; 2hr); Glasgow (6 daily; 2hr 50min); Kirkcaldy (16 daily; 1hr); Stirling (6 daily; 2hr).

Stirling to: Callander (11 daily; 45min); Dollar (13 daily; 35min); Doune (14 daily; 30min); Dunblane (20 daily; 1hr 15min); Dundee (9 daily; 1hr 30min); Dunfermline (13 daily; 50min); Edinburgh (hourly; 1hr 35min); Glasgow (34 daily; 1hr 10min); Gleneagles (16 daily; 30min); Inverness (2 daily; 3hr 30min); Killin (2 daily; 2hr); Lochearnhead (2 daily; 1hr 40min); Perth (15 daily; 50min); Pitlochry (2 daily; 1hr 30min); St Andrews (6 daily; 2hr).

CHAPTER TWENTY ONE

ARGYLL

C ut off for centuries from the rest of Scotland by the mountains and sea lochs that characterize the region, **Argyll** remains remote, its scatter of offshore islands forming part of the Inner Hebridean archipelago (the remaining Hebrides are dealt with in *Skye and the Western Isles*). Geographically, as well as culturally, this is a transitional area between Highland and Lowland, boasting a rich variety of scenery, from lush, subtropical gardens warmed by the Gulf Stream to flat and treeless islands far out in the Atlantic. It's in the folds and twists of the countryside and the views out to the islands, that the strengths and beauties of mainland Argyll lie – the one area of man-made sights you shouldn't miss is the cluster of **Celtic and prehistoric sites** near Kilmartin. The population overall is tiny; even **Oban**, Argyll's main administrative centre and chief ferry port, has barely even a thousand inhabitants, while the prettiest, **Inveraray**, boasts a mere four hundred.

The eastern duo of **Bute** and **Arran** – once a separate county in their own right – are the most popular of Scotland's more southerly islands, the latter justifiably so, with spectacular scenery ranging from the granite peaks of the north to the Lowland pasture of the south. Of the Hebridean islands covered in this chapter, mountainous **Mull** is the most visited, though it is large enough to absorb the crowds, many of whom are only passing through en route to the tiny isle of **Iona**, a centre of Christian culture since the sixth century. **Islay**, best known for its distinctive malt whiskies, is fairly quiet even in the height of summer, as is neighbouring **Jura**, which offers excellent walking opportunities. And for those seeking still more solitude, there are the remote islands of **Tiree** and **Coll**, which, although swept with fierce winds, boast more sunny days than anywhere else in Scotland.

The region's name derives from *Aragàidheal*, which translates as "Boundary of the Gaels", the Irish Celts who settled here in the fifth century AD, and whose **kingdom of Dalriada** embraced much of what is now Argyll. Known to the Romans as *Scotti* – hence Scotland – it was the Irish Celts who promoted Celtic Christianity, and whose Gaelic language eventually became the national tongue. After a brief period of Norse invasion and settlement, the islands (and the peninsula of Kintyre) fell to the immensely powerful Somerled, who became King of the Hebrides and Lord of Argyll in the twelfth century. Somerled's successors, the MacDonalds, established Islay as their headquarters in the 1200s, but were in turn dislodged by Robert the Bruce. Of Bruce's allies, it was the **Campbells** who benefited most from the MacDonalds' demise, and

---

ACCOMMODATION PRICE CODES

Throughout this guide, hotel and B&B accommodation is priced on a scale of ① to ⑨, the number indicating the **lowest price** you could expect to pay per night in that establishment for a **double room** in high season. The prices indicated by the codes are as follows:

① under £20/$30	④ £40–50/$60–75	⑦ £70–80/$105–120
② £20–30/$31–45	⑤ £50–60/$75–90	⑧ £80–100/$120–150
③ £30–40/$45–60	⑥ £60–70/$90–105	⑨ over £100/$150

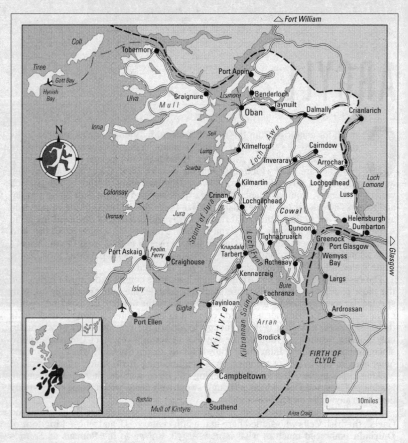

eventually, as the dukes of Argyll, gained control of the entire area – even today they remain one of the largest landowners in the region.

In the aftermath of the Jacobite uprisings, the islands of Argyll, like the rest of the Highlands, were devastated by the **Clearances**, with thousands of crofters evicted from their homes in order to make room for profitable sheep-farming – "the white plague" – and cattle rearing. Today the traditional industries remain under threat, leaving the region ever more dependent on tourism and a steady influx of new settlers to keep things going; while Gaelic, once the language of the majority in Argyll, retains only a tenuous hold on the outlying islands of Islay, Coll and Tiree – all officially part of Scotland's *Gàidhealtachd*, or Gaelic-speaking areas.

Gare Loch and Loch Long

Most people approach Argyll from Glasgow, from where there's a choice of two routes: the most popular is along Loch Lomond (see p.791); a quieter route (and the one which the train takes) is along the shores of **Gare Loch** and **Loch Long** to Arrochar, which marks the beginning of Argyll proper. Apart from Helensburgh, however, there's little to see along the shores of either loch. Both are littered with decaying industrial remains, including the nuclear submarine base at Faslane on Gare Loch and the oil tanks at Finnart on Loch Long. Only occasionally is it possible to glimpse the "unspeakably beautiful" landscape described by eighteenth-century travellers.

Helensburgh

HELENSBURGH, twenty miles or more northwest of Glasgow, is a smart, Georgian grid-plan settlement laid out in an imitation of Edinburgh's New Town. In the eighteenth century it was a well-to-do commuter town for Glasgow and a seaside resort, whose bathing-master, **Henry Bell**, invented one of the first steamboats, the *Comet*, to transport Glaswegians "doon the watter". Today Helensburgh is a stop on the route of the *Waverley,* the last sea-going paddle steamer in the world, which does a zigzag tour of the lochs of Argyll throughout the summer (pick up a timetable from the tourist office).

The inventor of TV, John Logie Baird, was born here, as was Charles Rennie Mackintosh, who in 1902 was commissioned by the Glaswegian publisher Walter Blackie to design **Hill House** (Easter–Dec daily 1.30–5.30pm; £2.80; NTS), on Upper Colquhoun Street. Without doubt the best surviving example of Mackintosh's domestic architecture, the house – right down to light fittings – is stamped with his very personal interpretation of Art Nouveau, characterized by his sparing use of colour and stylized floral patterns. The effect is occasionally overwhelming – it's difficult to imagine actually living in such an environment – yet it is precisely Mackintosh's attention to detail that makes the place so special (for more on Mackintosh see p.767). After exploring the house, head for the kitchen quarters, which have been sensitively transformed into a tearoom.

Hill House is a twenty-minute walk from Helensburgh Central train station, up Sinclair Street, or just five minutes from Helensburgh Upper (where the Oban and Fort William trains stop). The **tourist office** is in the clock tower by Gare Loch (April–Oct Mon–Fri 10am–4.30pm, Sat & Sun 10am–5pm; ☎01436/672642). **Accommodation** options include the luxurious *Commodore*, 112–117 W Clyde St (☎01436/676924; ⑤), or the smaller *Imperial*, at no. 12–14 (☎01436/676924; ③); there are also **B&Bs** such as *Kyra*, at no. 100 (☎01436/675576; ②) and *Ashfield*, 38 William St (☎01436/672259; ②).

Cowal and Bute

West of Helensburgh, the claw-shaped **Cowal peninsula**, formed by Loch Fyne and Loch Long, is the most visited part of Argyll. The landscape here is extremely varied, ranging from the Highland peaks of the Argyll Forest Park in the north, to the gentle low-lying coastline of the southwest, but most visitors confine themselves to the area around **Dunoon** (which has Cowal's only tourist office) in the east, leaving the rest of the countryside relatively undisturbed. The island of **Bute** is in many ways simply an extension of the peninsula, from which it is separated by the merest slither of water; its chief town, **Rothesay**, rivals Dunoon as the major seaside resort on the Clyde.

Argyll Forest Park

The **Argyll Forest Park** stretches from Loch Lomond south as far as Holy Loch, providing the most exhilarating scenery on the peninsula. The park includes the **Arrochar Alps**, north of Glen Croe and Glen Kinglas, whose Munros offer some of the best climbing in Argyll: Ben Ime (3318ft) is the tallest of the range, The Cobbler (2891ft) easily the most distinctive – all are for experienced walkers only. Less threatening are the peaks south of Glen Croe, between Loch Long and Loch Goil (the latter branches off Loch Long), known as **Argyll's Bowling Green** – no ironic nickname but an English corruption of the Gaelic *Baile na Greine* (Sunny Hamlet).

Approaching from Glasgow by road (A83), you enter the park from **ARROCHAR**, at the head of Loch Long. The village itself is ordinary enough, but the setting is dramatic, and it makes a convenient base for exploring the northern section of the park. There's a **train station**, a mile or so up the Tarbert road (A83), and numerous **hotels** and **B&Bs** – try the *Lochside Guest House* (☎01301/702467; ②) or the *Mansefield Hotel* (☎01301/702282; ③). Two miles beyond Arrochar at **ARDGARTAN**, there's a lochside Forestry Commission **campsite** (mid-March to Oct; ☎01301/702293), a **youth hostel** (Feb–Dec; ☎01301/702362) and a **tourist office** (April & Oct Mon–Fri 11am–4pm, Sat & Sun 10am–5pm; May–Sept daily 9am–6pm; ☎01301/702432), which can give you lots of information on the forest park.

Cairndow to Loch Eck

Wherever you're heading in Cowal, if you approach from the east, you're forced to climb **Glen Croe**, a strategic hill pass whose saddle is called for obvious reasons Rest-and-be-Thankful. Here the road forks, with the single-track B828 heading down to Lochgoilhead, beautifully situated at the head of Loch Goil, but otherwise eminently missable. A faster route down into Cowal is to continue along the A83 from the Rest-and-be-Thankful down the grand Highland sweep of **Glen Kinglas** to **CAIRNDOW**, at the head of Loch Fyne. A mile or so around the head of the loch on the A83 is the famous *Loch Fyne Oyster Bar* (☎01499/600264), which sells more oysters than anywhere else in the country, plus lots of other fish and seafood treats.

From Cairndow, the A815 heads southwest to Strachur before heading inland to **Loch Eck**, an exceptionally narrow freshwater loch, squeezed between steeply banked woods, and a favourite for trout fishing. Superior bar food or an **overnight stay** can be had at the *Coylet Inn* (☎01369/840426; ③), halfway down the loch's eastern shores. At the southern tip of Loch Eck are the **Younger Botanic Gardens** (mid-March to Oct daily 10am–6pm; £1.50), an offshoot of Edinburgh's Royal Botanic Gardens, especially striking for its avenue of Great Redwoods, planted in 1863 and now over 100ft high. You could combine a visit here with one of the most popular of the park's forest **walks**, the rocky ravine of **Puck's Glen**; the walk begins from the car park a mile south of the gardens (1hr 30min for the round trip).

Dunoon

In the nineteenth century, Cowal's capital, **DUNOON**, grew from a mere village to a major Clyde seaside resort, a favourite holiday spot for Glaswegians. Nowadays, tourists tend to arrive by ferry from Gourock, and though their numbers are smaller, Dunoon remains by far the largest town in all Argyll, with 13,000 inhabitants. Apart from its practical uses, and its fine pier, there's little to tempt you to linger in Dunoon. It's a good idea, however, to take advantage of Dunoon's **tourist office** (the only one in Cowal) on Alexandra Parade (Easter–Oct Mon–Thurs 9am–5.30pm, Fri 9am–5pm, Sat 10am–5pm, Sun 10am–2pm; Oct–Easter closed Sat & Sun; ☎01369/703785). The shorter, more frequent of the two **ferry crossings** across the Clyde from Gourock to Dunoon is the half-hourly *Western Ferries* service to Hunter's Quay, a mile north of the town centre; *CalMac* have the prime position, however, on the main pier.

If you need to **stay**, try the central *Caledonian* on Argyll Street (☎01369/702176; ③); around Hunter's Quay, go for *Foxbank* on Marine Parade (☎01369/703858; ②). Plusher accommodation can be had at the *Argyll*, Argyll St (☎01369/702059; ④), or the highly reputable *Ardfillayne*, West Bay (☎01369/702267; ⑤). The nearest **campsite** is the lochside *Buthkollidar* (April–Oct; ☎01369/830563), south of Dunoon on Bullwood Road. *Chatters*, 58 John St, is Dunoon's best **restaurant**, offering delicious Loch Fyne seafood and Scottish beef. The town also boasts a two-screen cinema (a rarity in Argyll) on John Street, but by far Dunoon's most famous entertainment is the **Cowal Highland Gathering**, the largest of its kind in the world, held here on the last weekend in August, and culminating in the awesome spectacle of the massed pipes and drums of over 150 bands marching through the streets.

Southwest Cowal

The mellow landscape of **southwest Cowal**, in complete contrast to the bustle of Dunoon or the Highland grandeur of the forest, becomes immediate as soon as you head west to Loch Striven, where, from either side, there are few more beautiful sights than the **Kyles of Bute**, the thin slithers of water that separate the bleak bulk of north Bute from Cowal, and constitute some of the best sailing territory in Scotland.

The most popular spot from which to appreciate the Kyles is the A8003 as it rises dramatically above the sea lochs before descending to the peaceful, lochside village of **TIGHNABRUAICH** on the western Kyle. The **youth hostel** (April–Sept; ☎01700/811622), situated above the village, is well used thanks to the excellent *Tighnabruaich Sailing School*, which offers week-long courses from beginners to advanced. The *Royal Hotel* (☎01700/811239; ⑤), by the waterside, does exceptionally fine bar meals; the *Burnside* café/bistro is also good. In neighbouring **KAMES**, the *Kames Hotel* (☎01700/811489; ⑤) has wonderful views over the Kyles, as does *Piermount* (☎01700/811218; ②) and *Ferguslie* (April–Sept; ☎01700/811414; ②).

Isle of Bute

Thanks to its consistently mild climate and Rothesay's ferry link with Wemyss Bay, the island of **Bute** has been a popular holiday and convalescence spot for Clydesiders – particularly the elderly – for over a century. Even considering the island's small size (15 miles long and 5 miles wide) you can find peace and quiet; most of its inhabitants are centred on the two wide bays on the east coast of the island.

Bute's one and only town, **ROTHESAY**, is a long-established resort, set in a wide sweeping bay, backed by green hills, with a classic promenade and pagoda-style Winter Gardens. It creates a better impression than Dunoon, though it, too, has passed its prime. However, even if you're just passing through, you must pay a visit to the ornate **toilets** (daily 8am–9pm; 10p) on the pier, which were built in 1899 and have since been declared a national treasure (gentlemen have the best time as the porcelain urinals steal the show). Rothesay also boasts the militarily useless, but architecturally impressive, moated ruins of **Rothesay Castle** (April–Sept Mon–Sat 9.30am–6pm, Sun 2–6pm; Oct–March closes 4pm; £1.50), hidden amid the town's backstreets but signposted from the pier. Built in the twelfth century, it was twice captured by the Vikings in the 1400s; such vulnerability was the reasoning behind the unusual, almost circular curtain wall, with its four big drum towers, of which only one remains fully intact.

A very good reason for coming to Bute, is to visit **Mount Stuart** (June–Sept Mon; Wed & Fri–Sun 11am–5pm; £5), three miles south of Rothesay. Seat of the fantastically wealthy Marquesses of Bute, the mansion was built between 1879 and World War II, as an incredible High Gothic fancy, drawing architectural inspiration from all over Europe. The sumptuous interior was decked out by craftsmen who worked with William Burges on the Marquess' earlier medieval concoctions at Cardiff Castle. The gardens, established in the eighteenth century by the third Earl of Bute, who had a hand in London's Kew Gardens, are equally lovely.

For the best overall view of the island, take a walk up **Canada Hill** above the freshwater Loch Fad, which all but divides Bute in two. The northern half of the island is hilly, uninhabited and little visited, while the southern half is made up of Lowland-style farmland. The early monastic history of the island is recalled at **St Blane's Chapel**, a twelfth-century ruin beautifully situated in open countryside on the west coast, close to the very southernmost tip. Bute's finest sandy beach is **Scalpsie Bay**, further up the west coast, beyond which lies **St Ninian's Point**, where the ruins of a sixth-century chapel overlook another fine sandy strand and the deserted island of **Inchmarnock**.

Practicalities

Rothesay's **tourist office** is at 15 Victoria St (April Mon–Fri 9am–5.30pm, Sat 10am–5pm; May–Oct longer hours, also Sun 10am–5pm; Nov–March Mon–Thurs 9am–5.30pm, Fri 9am–5pm; ☎01700/502151). There's no shortage of B&Bs along the seafront from Rothesay to Port Bannatyne, the grandest **place to stay** being the giant, former spa sanatorium *Glenburn Hotel*, Glenburn Rd (☎01700/502500; ⑤). Others like the *Commodore* at 12 Battery Place (☎01700/502178; ③) or the distinctive *Glendale*, at no. 20 (☎01700/502329; ②), both up East Princes Street, are more modest; the *Bute House Hotel* (☎01700/502481; ③), West Princes St, is vegetarian- and even vegan-friendly. Apart from the plush *Queen's Restaurant* in the *Victoria Hotel* on Victoria Street, **food** options are limited to the simple dishes served at the *Winter Gardens* bistro on the prom. Bute holds its own **Highland Games** on the last weekend in August – Prince Charles as Duke of Rothesay occasionally attends – plus a **folk festival** on the last weekend in July, and a mainly trad-**jazz festival** during May Bank Holiday.

Inveraray

A classic example of an eighteenth-century planned town, **INVERARAY** was built on the site of a ruined fishing village in 1745 by the third Duke of Argyll, head of the powerful Campbell clan, in order to distance his newly rebuilt castle from the hoi polloi in the town and to establish a commercial and legal centre for the region. Today Inveraray, an absolute set-piece of Scottish Georgian architecture, has a truly memorable setting, the brilliant white arches of Front Street reflected in the still waters of Loch Fyne, which separate it from the Cowal peninsula.

With a population of just four hundred and squeezed onto a headland some distance from the duke's new castle, there's not much more to Inveraray's "New Town" than its distinctive **Main Street** (running west from Front St), flanked by whitewashed terraces, whose window casements are picked out in black. At the top of the street, the road divides to circumnavigate the town's Neoclassical church, originally built in two parts: the southern half served the Gaelic-speaking community, while the northern half (still in use) served those who spoke English.

East of the church is **Inveraray Jail** (daily April–Oct 9.30am–6pm; Nov–March 10am–5pm; £2.50), whose attractive Georgian courthouse and grim prison blocks ceased to function in the 1930s. The jail is now an imaginative and thoroughly enjoyable museum, which graphically recounts conditions from medieval times up until the nineteenth century. You can also sit in the beautiful semicircular courthouse and listen to the trial of a farmer accused of fraud.

Slightly removed from the New Town, to the north, the neo-Gothic **Inveraray Castle** (April–June Sept & Oct Mon–Thurs & Sat 10am–1pm & 2–5.30pm, Sun 1–5.30pm; July & Aug Mon–Sat 10am–5.30pm, Sun 1–5.30pm; £3) remains the family home of the Duke of Argyll. Built in 1745 by the third duke, it was given a touch of the Loire with the addition of dormer windows and conical roofs in the nineteenth century. Inside, the most startling feature is the armoury hall, whose displays of weaponry – supplied to the Campbells by the British governement to put down the Jacobites – rise through several storeys. Gracing the castle's extensive grounds is one of three elegant bridges built during the relandscaping of Inveraray (the other two are on the road from

Cairndow), while the **Combined Operations Museum** (same times as castle; £1) in the old stables recalls the wartime role of Inveraray as a training centre for the D-Day landings, during which over half a million troops practised secret amphibious manoeuvres around Loch Fyne.

Practicalities

Inverary's **tourist office** is on Front Street (Mon–Fri 10am–4pm, Sat & Sun noon–4pm; longer hours in peak season; ☎01499/302063), as is the town's chief **hotel**, the historic *Great Inn* (April–Oct ☎01499/302466; ⑤), where Dr Johnson and Boswell stayed. There's a **B&B** on Main Street South, *Lorona* (☎01499/302258; ②), and a couple beyond the petrol station on the Campbeltown road (A83): *Arch House* (☎01499/302289; ②) and *Glen Eynord* (☎01499/302031; ②). The **youth hostel** (mid-March to Sept; ☎01499/302454) is just up the Oban road. The **bar** of the *George Hotel* in the middle of town is the liveliest spot. The best place to sample Loch Fyne's delicious fresh fish is the restaurant of the aforementioned *Loch Fyne Oyster Bar* (see p.818), six miles back up the A83 towards Glasgow.

Oban

The solidly Victorian resort of **OBAN** enjoys a superb setting – the island of Kerrera providing its bay with a natural shelter – distinguished by a bizarre granite amphitheatre, dramatically lit at night, on the hilltop above the town. Despite a population of just 7000, it's by far the largest port in northwest Scotland, the second largest town in Argyll, and the main departure point for ferries to the Hebrides. If you arrive late, or are catching an early boat, you may well find yourself staying the night (though there's no real need otherwise); if you're staying elsewhere, it's a useful base for wet-weather activities and shopping, although it does get uncomfortably crowded in the summer.

The only real sight in Oban is the town's landmark, **McCaig's Folly**, a stiff ten-minute climb from the quayside. An imitation of the Coliseum in Rome, it was the brainchild of a local banker a century ago, who had the twin aims of alleviating off-season unemployment among the local stonemasons and creating a family mausoleum. Work never progressed further than the exterior walls before McCaig died, but the folly provides a wonderful seaward panorama, particularly at sunset.

You can pass a few hours admiring the fishing boats in the harbour and looking out for scavanging seals in the bay; or, if the weather's bad, you can take a 45-minute guided tour of the **Oban Distillery** (Mon–Fri 9.30am–4.15pm; Easter–Oct also Sat; £2), in the centre of town off George Street, which ends with a dram of whisky. **The World in Miniature** (Easter–Oct Mon–Sat 10am–5pm, Sun 2–5pm; £1.50), on the north pier, contains an assortment of minute "dolls' house" rooms, with even a couple of mini-Charles Rennie Mackintosh interiors to admire.

Practicalities

The *CalMac* **ferry terminal** for the islands is a stone's throw from the **train station**, itself adjacent to the **bus terminus**. A host of private **boat operators** can be found around the harbour, particularly along its northern side: their excursions – direct to the castles of Mull, to Staffa and the Treshnish Islands – are worth considering. The **tourist office** (Mon–Fri 9am–1pm & 2–5.30pm, Sat & Sun 10am–4pm; longer hours in peak season; ☎01631/563122) is tucked away on Argyll Square just east of the bus station;

There's a whole host of grandiose Victorian **hotels** to choose from on the quayside, ranging from the *Columba* (☎01631/562183; ⑥) on the north pier to the *Palace* (☎01631/562294; ④) on George Street, plus dozens of **B&Bs** on Dunollie Road beyond George Street – try *Glendale* (☎01631/563877; ②) or *Glengorm* (April–Oct; ☎01631/

565361; ②) – and on Ardconnel Road, just below McCaig's Tower. The official **youth hostel** (March–Sept; ☎01631/562025) is north up the Esplanade, plus there are two **independent hostels**: at 21 Airds Crescent (☎01631/565065), and the *Backpackers' Lodge*, Breadalbane St (☎01631/562107). The nearest **campsite** is two miles south of Oban at *Gallanachmore Farm* (April to mid-Oct; ☎01631/566624).

Oban's best **restaurant** is *The Gathering* (☎01631/565421), Breadalbane St, which excels in, among other things, fish and seafood; the *Waterfront* (☎01631/563110), by the train station, does cheaper bar food as well as à la carte meals. The town's **fish-and-chip** shops are also better than average; try *Onorio's* on George Street. Oban's one and only half-decent **pub** is the *Oban Inn* opposite the north pier, with a classic dark-wood-and-brass bar downstairs and food in the lounge upstairs. You might want to make use of the town's **cinema**, confusingly known as *The Highland Theatre* (☎01631/562444), at the north end of George Street.

Isle of Mull

The second largest of the Inner Hebrides, **MULL** is by far the most accessible – just forty minutes from Oban by ferry. First impressions largely depend on the weather: without the sun the large tracts of moorland, particularly around the island's highest peak, Ben More (3196ft), can appear bleak and unwelcoming. There are, however, areas of more gentle pastoral scenery around Dervaig in the north and Salen on the east coast, and the indented west coast varies from the sandy beaches around Calgary to the cliffs of Loch na Keal. The most common mistake is to try and "do" the island in a day or two: Mull is a place that will grow on you only if you have the time and patience to explore.

Historically, crofting, whisky distilling and fishing supported the islanders (*Muileachs*), but the population – which peaked at 10,000 – decreased dramatically in the nineteenth century due to the Clearances and the 1846 potato famine. On Mull, it is a trend that has been reversed, mostly due to the large influx of settlers from elsewhere in the country which has brought the current population up to around 2500. One of the main reasons for this resurgence is, of course, tourism – over half a million visitors come here each year – although oddly enough, there are very few large hotels or campsites. Public transport is limited, and the roads are predominantly single-track, which can cause serious congestion in summer.

Around Craignure

CRAIGNURE is the main entry point to Mull, linked to Oban by several car ferries daily; a faster, less frequent car ferry service crosses from Lochaline on the Morvern peninsula to Fishnish, six miles northwest of Craignure. Fishnish is just a slipway and Craignure itself is little more than a scattering of cottages, though there is a **tourist office** (mid-April to mid-Oct Mon 7.15am–5.30pm, Tues–Fri 8.15am–7.30pm, Sat 6.15am–5.30pm, Sun 10.30am–5.30pm; mid-Oct to mid-April Mon 9.30am–5.30pm, Tues–Fri 8.30am–5.30pm, Sat 6.30am–5.30pm, Sun 4.30–5.30pm; ☎01680/812377), several **guest houses**, a **campsite** by the sea (☎01680/812496), plus the occasional bus connection with Tobermory; and **bike rental** possibilities too (☎01680/812487).

Two castles lie immediately southeast of Craignure. The first, **Torosay Castle** (mid-April to mid-Oct daily 10.30am–6.30pm; £3.50), a full-blown Scottish Baronial creation, is linked to Craignure by the narrow-gauge *Mull Rail* link (mid-April to mid-Oct). The magnificent gardens (daily 9am–7pm; £1.50) with their avenue of eighteenth-century Italianate statues, Japanese section, and views over to neighbouring Duart, are the real highlight. The house itself, in the mid-nineteenth-century style, is stuffed with junk

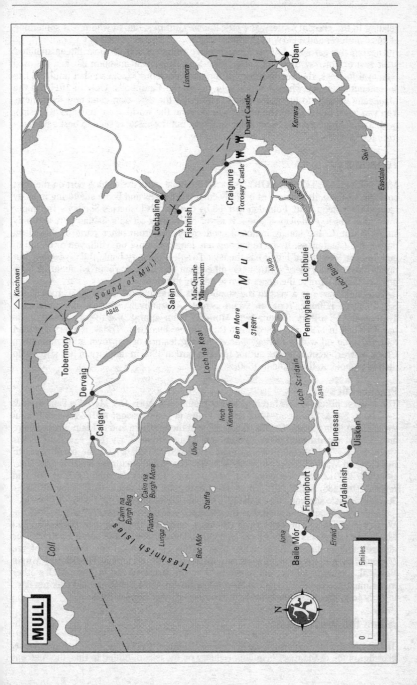

relating to the present owners, the little-known Guthries, one of whom was something of an adventurer and a POW in Colditz.

Lacking the gardens, but on a much more romantic spit of rock, fifteen minutes' walk east of Torosay, **Duart Castle** (May–Sept daily 10.30am–6pm; £3) is a restored medieval fortress, the headquarters of the once powerful MacLean clan until the late seventeenth century when it was left to rot by the Campbells. Only in 1911 did the MacLeans manage to buy it back and restore it – the 27th clan chief now lives there. You can learn more about the MacLean clan (and the world scout movement) inside, peek in the dungeons and ascend the ramparts; but the castle is seen to best advantage from the Oban ferry.

Tobermory

Mull's chief town, **TOBERMORY**, is easily the most attractive fishing port on the west coast of Scotland, its clusters of brightly coloured houses and boats sheltering in a bay backed by a steep bluff. Founded in 1788 by the British Fisheries Society – the upper town is a classic grid-plan village – it never really took off as a fishing port and only survived due to the steady influx of crofters evicted from other parts of the island during the Clearances. If you're staying any length of time on Mull, you're bound to end up here – for one thing, it has the island's sole stationary bank, the *Clydesdale*. But practicalities aside, there's little to do other than watch the harbour go about its business, or take a stroll to the upper town to admire the view.

You could also pay a visit to the small **Mull Museum** (Mon–Fri 10.30am–4.30pm, Sat 10.30am–1.30pm; 70p) on Main Street. Alternatively, there's the minuscule **Tobermory Distillery** (Easter–Sept Mon–Fri 10am–4pm; £2) at the south end of the bay, founded in 1795 but closed down three times since then. Today, it offers a guided tour finishing off with a tasting. One endearing feature of the town is its diminutive **Clock Tower**, erected by the author Isabella Bird in 1905 in memory of her sister who died of typhoid on the island in 1880.

Practicalities

The **tourist office** (Feb–March Mon–Fri 10am–4pm; April–Oct Mon–Fri 9am–1pm & 2–5.30pm, Sat & Sun noon–4pm; longer hours in peak season; ☎01688/302182) is in the same building as the *CalMac* ticket office at the northern end of Main Street. There are several **accommodation** options on Main Street – try the excellent *Fàilte* (☎01688/302495; ④), the *Mishnish Hotel* (☎01688/302009; ⑥), or the friendly **youth hostel** (mid-March to Sept; ☎01688/302481). The grand Victorian *Western Isles Hotel* (☎01688/302012; ⑦) overlooks the bay, as does *Kilmory* (☎01688/302232; ②) and *Ivybank* (☎01688/302250; ②). The nearest **campsite** is *Newdale* (April–Nov; ☎01688/302306), a basic site one and a half miles outside Tobermory on the B8073 to Dervaig.

Tobermory's best **restaurant** is the *Strongarbh House* (☎01688/302328) behind the *Western Isles Hotel*. The *Back Brae* (evenings only), on the corner of Back Brae and Main Street, also serves good local food, and offers a three-course menu for £11.50; for cheaper, filling dishes, head along Main Street to *Gannets*. The lively bar of the *Mishnish Hotel* is the local hangout, and the focus of Mull's annual **Traditional Music Festival**, a feast of Gaelic folk music held on the last weekend in April. Mull's other major musical event is the annual **Mendelssohn on Mull Festival**, held over ten days in early July, which commemorates the composer's visit here in 1829.

Along the west coast

The gently undulating countryside west of Tobermory, beyond the Mishnish lochs, provides some of the most beguiling scenery on the island. Added to this, the road out west, the B8073, is exceptionally dramatic, with fiendish switchbacks much appreciated during the annual Mull Rally, which takes place each October. The only village of any size is **DERVAIG**, which nestles beside a narrow sea loch just eight miles southwest of Tobermory, distinguished by its unusual pencil-shaped church spire and the dinky little cottages on its main street. Dervaig is home to the underfunded *Mull Little Theatre*, one of the smallest professional theatres in the world, which puts on plays adapted for just two resident actors (May–Sept; ☎01688/400245). The theatre lies within the grounds of the *Druimard Country House* (☎01688/400345; ⑥), which offers pricy but excellent pre-theatre dinners. Charles Dickens once stayed at the *Ardbeg House* (☎01688/400254; ④), still one of Dervaig's finest **hotels**; **B&B** options include *Antuim Farm* (April–Oct ☎01688/400230; ③) on the Salen road, or vegetarian-friendly *Glenbellart* (☎01688/400282; ③) on the main street.

A little beyond Dervaig, the **Old Byre Heritage Centre** (Easter–Oct daily 10.30am–6.30pm; £2.50) is better than many of its kind, with a video on the island's history and a passable tea room. The road continues cross-country to **CALGARY**, once a thriving crofting community, now an idyllic holiday spot boasting Mull's finest sandy bay, with wonderful views over to Coll and Tiree. There's just one **hotel**, the lovely *Calgary Farmhouse* (☎01688/400256; ⑥), which has an excellent restaurant, *The Dovecote*, in what was once a dovecote; an unofficial **campsite** by the beach; and a splendid wild hillside **garden** at the House of Treshnish (April–Oct only), overlooking the bay.

Isle of Staffa

Five miles southwest of Ulva, **STAFFA** is the most romantic and dramatic of Scotland's many uninhabited islands. On its south side, the Perpendicular rockface features an imposing series of black basalt columns, known as the Collonade, which have been cut by the sea into cathedralesque caverns, most notably **Fingal's Cave**. The Vikings knew about the island – the name derives from their word for "Island of Pillars" – but it wasn't until 1772 that it was "discovered" by the world. Turner painted it, Wordsworth explored it, but Mendelssohn's *Die Fingalshölle*, inspired by the sounds of the sea-wracked caves he heard on a visit here in 1829, did most to popularize the place – after which Queen Victoria gave her blessing too. The geological explanation for these polygonal basalt organ pipes is that they were created by a massive subterranean explosion some sixty million years ago. A huge mass of molten basalt ejaculated onto land and, as it cooled, solidified into what are, essentially, crystals. Of course, confronted with such artistry, most visitors have found it difficult to believe that their origin is entirely natural – indeed, the various Celtic folk tales, which link the phenomenon with the Giant's Causeway in Ireland, are certainly more appealing. To **get to Staffa**, join one of the many boat trips from Oban, Ulva Ferry, Dervaig and Fionnphort, weather permitting (return trips for around £10–15 per person).

Ben More and the Ross of Mull

Round the coast from Ulva Ferry, the road (A8073) hugs the shores of Loch na Keal, which almost splits Mull in two. South of the loch rise the terraced slopes of **Ben More** (3169ft), a mighty extinct volcano. Beyond Derryguaig, the road carves through the sheer cliffs before heading south past the Gribun rocks which face the tiny island of **Inch Kenneth**, once owned by the Mitford family. There are great views out to Staffa and the Treshnish Isles as the road climbs over the pass to Loch Scribain, where it joins the equally dramatic Glen More road (A848) from Craignure.

Stretching for twenty miles west of the road junction as far as Iona is the rocky peninsula known as the **Ross of Mull**, which, like much of Scotland, appears blissfully tranquil in good weather, and desolate and bleak in bad. Most visitors simply drive through the Ross en route to Iona, but given that accommodation is severely limited on Iona, it's worth considering staying here. The *Pennyghael Hotel* (Easter–Oct; ☎01681/

704205; ⑦), overlooking Loch Scridain, is a luxury option; **BUNESSAN**, roughly two thirds of the way along the Ross, has more choice with the *Assapol Country House* (Easter–Oct; ☎01681/700258; ⑤) and **B&Bs** such as *Ardtun House* (☎01681/700264; ②). **FIONNPHORT**, facing Iona, is the least attractive place to stay; try *Seaview* (☎01681/700235; ②) or *Bruach Mhor* (☎01681/700276; ②), which caters for vegetarians and vegans. The basic *Fidden Farm* **campsite** (☎01681/700427), a mile south along the Knockvologan road by Fidden beach, is the nearest to Iona.

Isle of Iona

Less than a mile off the southwest tip of Mull, **IONA**, although just three miles long and no more than a mile wide, manages to encapsulate all the enchantment and mystique of the Hebrides. It is frequently tagged "the cradle of Christianity": St Columba arrived here from Ireland in 563 and established a monastery which was responsible for the conversion of more or less all of pagan Scotland as well as much of northern England. This history and the island's splendid isolation have lent it a peculiar religiosity; in the words of Dr Johnson, "that man is little to be envied . . . whose piety would not grow warmer among the ruins of Iona". Today, however, the island can

---

A BRIEF HISTORY OF IONA

Legend has it that **St Columba** (Colum), born in Donegal in 521, was a direct descendant of the Irish king, Niall of the Nine Hostages. A scholar and soldier priest, who founded numerous monasteries in Ireland, he became involved in a bloody dispute with the king when he refused to hand over a psalm book copied illegally from the original owned by St Finian of Moville. At the Battle of Cooldrumman, Columba's forces won, though with great loss of life; repenting this bloodshed, he went into exile with twelve other monks, eventually settling on Iona in 563. The Gaelic name for the island is *I-Chaluim-cille* (Island of Columba's Church), often abbreviated simply to *I* (Gaelic for "island"). Columba's miraculous feats included defeating the Loch Ness monster and banishing snakes (and, some say, frogs) from the island.

During his lifetime, Iona enjoyed a great deal of autonomy from Rome, establishing a specifically Celtic Christian tradition. Missionaries were sent out to the rest of Scotland and parts of England, and Iona quickly became a respected seat of learning and artistry; the monks compiled a vast library of intricately illuminated manuscripts – most famously the *Book of Kells* (now on display in Trinity College, Dublin) – while the masons excelled in carving peculiarly intricate crosses. Two factors were instrumental in the demise of the Celtic tradition: relentless pressure from the established Church, and a series of Viking raids which culminated in the massacre of 68 monks on the sands of Martyrs' Bay in 803.

In the eleventh century it was rebuilt as an Augustinian monastery, and by the thirteenth century, Iona had become a more conventional centre for the **Benedictines**, its masons enjoying a second flowering of stone carving. By 1500 Iona had achieved cathedral status, but the complex was ransacked during the Reformation as a bastion of the papal Church, during which nearly all the island's 350 crosses were destroyed. Although plans were drawn up at various times to turn the abbey into a Cathedral of the Isles, nothing came of them until its then owner, the Duke of Argyll, donated the abbey buildings to the **Church of Scotland**, who restored the abbey church for worship by 1910. Iona's modern resurgence began in 1938, when **George MacLeod**, a minister from Glasgow, established a group of priests, students and artisans to begin rebuilding the remainder of the monastic buildings. What began as a male, Gaelic-speaking, strictly Presbyterian community is today mostly a lay, mixed and ecumenical retreat. The entire abbey complex has been successfully restored and the island, apart from the church land and a few crofts, now belongs to the NTS.

barely cope with its thousands of day-trippers, so to appreciate the special atmosphere and to have time to see the whole island, including the often overlooked west coast, you should plan on staying at least one night.

Baile Mór

The frequent passenger ferry from Fionnphort stops at the island's main village, **BAILE MÓR** (literally "large village"), which is in fact little more than a single terrace of cottages facing the red sandstone rocks. Just inland, the ruins of a small **Augustinian nunnery** are built of the same red sandstone. Founded in around 1200, the nunnery fell into disrepair after the Reformation and, if nothing else, gives you an idea of the state of the present-day abbey before it was restored. At a bend in the road just beyond the nunnery stands the fifteenth-century **MacLean's Cross**, a fine example of the distinctive, flowing, three-leaved foliage of the Iona school. To the north the **Iona Heritage Centre** (Mon 10.30am–4.30pm, Tues–Sat 9.30am–4.30pm; £1), in a manse, built, like the nearby parish church, by the ubiquitous Thomas Telford, has displays on the history of the island.

The Abbey

No buildings remain from Columba's time: the present **Abbey** dates from the arrival of the Benedictines in around 1200, was extensively rebuilt in the fifteenth and sixteenth centuries, and restored virtually wholesale in the 1900s. Adjoining the facade is a small steep-roofed chamber, believed to be St Columba's grave, now a small chapel. The three high crosses in front of the abbey date from the eighth to tenth centuries, and are decorated with the Pictish serpent and boss and Celtic spirals for which Iona's early Christian masons were renowned. For reasons of sanitation, the cloisters were placed, contrary to the norm, on the north side of the church (where running water was available to flush away the monks' faeces); entirely reconstructed in the late 1950s, they now shelter a useful historical account of the abbey's development.

South of the abbey, Iona's oldest building, **St Oran's Chapel**, has a Norman door dating from the eleventh century. It stands at the centre of the sacred burial ground, **Reilig Odhráin**, which is said to contain the graves of sixty kings of Norway, Ireland and Scotland, including Shakespeare's Duncan and Macbeth. Archeological evidence has failed to back this up; it's about as likely as the legend that the chapel could only be completed through human sacrifice. Oran, one of the older monks in Columba's entourage, apparently volunteered to be buried alive, and was found to have survived the ordeal when the grave was opened a few days later. Declaring that he had seen hell and it wasn't all bad, he was promptly re-interred for blasphemy. The best of the early Christian gravestones and medieval effigies which once lay in the Reilig Odhráin are now the chief exhibits of the **Abbey Museum**, in the old infirmary behind the abbey.

The grave that most visitors now head for, however, is that of the leader of the Labour Party, **John Smith**, who was buried here, with permission from the local council, despite strong opposition from the islanders. The decision to grant a plot in the cemetery to Smith, a frequent visitor to Iona, but a mainlander born in the town Ardrishaig, appears now to have been an unfortunate mistake. The sheer number of political pilgrims has caused desecration to neighbouring tombstones, and barriers have had to be erected to try and stem the damage. It remains to be seen whether more drastic measures will need to be taken.

Practicalities

There's no **tourist office** on Iona, and, as demand far exceeds supply, you should organize **accommodation** in advance. Of the island's two, fairly pricey, hotels, the *Argyll* (April–Oct; ☎01681/700334; ⑥) is the nicer. B&Bs are cheaper but fill quickly: try

Cruachan (March–Oct; ☎01681/700523; ②), *Finlay Ross* (☎01681/700357; ③) or the vegetarian *Iona Cottage* (☎01681/700579; ③). **Camping** is possible with the crofter's permission. Visitors are not allowed to bring cars onto the island, but **bikes** can be rented from *Finlay Ross* (see above). **Food** options are limited to hotel restaurants (the *Argyll* is particularly good) or the *Martyrs' Bay* restaurant by the pier. The coffee house (daily 11am–4.30pm) run by the Iona Community just west of the abbey serves home-made soup and delicious cakes.

Coll and Tiree

Coll and **Tiree** are among the most isolated of the Inner Hebrides, and if anything have more in common with the outlying Western Isles than with their closest neigh-bour, Mull. Each is roughly twelve miles long and three miles wide, both are low-lying, treeless and exceptionally windy, with white sandy beaches and the highest sunshine records in Scotland. Like most of the Hebrides, they were once ruled by Vikings, and didn't pass into Scottish hands until the thirteenth century. Coll's population peaked at 1440, Tiree's at a staggering 4450, but both were badly affected by the Clearances, which virtually halved the populations in a generation. Coll was MacLean country, but is now two thirds owned by a Dutch millionaire; Tiree has been divided into crofts, though it remains a part of the Duke of Argyll's estate.

The *CalMac* ferry from Oban calls at Coll and Tiree every day throughout the year except Thursdays and Sundays – which means you should plan on staying at least one or two nights. Tiree also has an **airport** with daily flights (Mon–Sat) to and from Glasgow. The majority of visitors stay for at least a week in self-catering accommoda-tion (see p.32), though there are a few B&Bs and hotels on the islands. The only public transport is on Tiree, where the **postbus** calls at all the main settlements.

Isle of Coll

The fish-shaped island of **Coll** (population 150) lies less than seven miles off the coast of Mull. The *CalMac* ferry drops off at Coll's only village, **ARINAGOUR** on the west-ern shore of Loch Eatharna, where half the population now lives. Here, you'll find the island's post office, petrol pump, church, school, two shops, a laundrette and a nine-hole golf course to the northwest.

On the southwest coast there are two edifices – Coll's only formal attractions – both known as **Breachacha Castle**, built by the MacLeans. The oldest, at the head of Loch Breachacha, is a fifteenth-century tower house with an additional curtain wall, recently restored and a training centre for overseas aid volunteers. The "new castle", to the northwest, made up of a central block built around 1750 and two side pavilions added a century later, has been converted into holiday homes. There's little else to see, though you could take a walk over the strip of **giant sand dunes** which link Crossapol, the westernmost tip of Coll, with the rest of the island at low tide; wander along to **Ben Hogh** – at 339ft, Coll's highest point – two miles west of Arinagour; or take a look at the **Cairns of Coll**, a series of prehistoric mounds which rise out of the sea off the northern coastline around the almost abandoned hamlets of Bousd and Sorisdale.

In Arinagour, two **hotels** look over the bay: the *Isle of Coll Hotel* (☎01879/230334; ④), and the more modern *Tigh-na-Mara* (Feb–Nov; ☎01879/230354; ③), which also offers **bike rental**. At **ACHA**, two miles west of Arinagour, there's also *Arinagour Farmhouse* (☎01879/230443; ②), and *Achamore* (☎01879/230430; ③). The island's **campsite** (☎01879/230374), which offers basic facilities, is on Breachacha Bay, in the old walled gardens of the castle; you can also stay in the *Garden House* **B&B** (phone as for campsite; ③). The *Isle of Coll Hotel* doubles as the island's social centre, but for a change from hotel **food**, try the *Coll Bistro* (Easter–Oct) in Arinagour, which serves delicious lobster and Mull salmon, as well as venison and beef.

Isle of Tiree

Tiree, as its Gaelic name *Tir-Iodh* (Land of Corn) suggests, was once known as the breadbasket of the Inner Hebrides, thanks to its acres of rich machair. Nowadays crofting and tourism are the main sources of income for the resident population of more than eight hundred, and every October, the windswept sandy beaches attract large numbers of windsurfers for the International Windsurfers' Championships.

The *CalMac* ferry calls at **SCARINISH**, on a headland to the west of the great sandy beach (*Tràigh Mhór*) of **Gott** Bay. It's just one mile across the island from Gott to Vaul Bay, on the north coast, where the well-preserved remains of a drystone broch, **Dun Mor** – dating from the first century BC – lie hidden in the rocks to the west of the bay. From here it's another two miles west along the coast to the *Clach a'Choire* or **Ringing Stone**, a huge glacial boulder decorated with mysterious prehistoric markings, which when struck with a stone gives out a musical sound. The story goes that should the Ringing Stone ever be broken in two, Tiree will sink beneath the waves. A mile further west you come to the lovely **Balephetrish Bay**.

The most intriguing sights lie in the bulging western half of the island, where Tiree's two landmark hills rise up. The highest of the two, **Ben Hynish** (463ft), is unfortunately occupied by a "golf ball" radar station which tracks incoming transatlantic flights; the views from the top, though, are great. Below Ben Hynish, to the east, is the island's largest village **BALEMARTINE**, a mile or so north of the abandoned **Hynish harbour**, designed by Robert Stevenson in the 1830s, in order to transport building materials for the 140ft **Skerryvore Lighthouse**, which lies on a sea-swept reef some twelve miles southwest of Tiree. The harbour features an ingenious reservoir to prevent silting, and a tall granite signal tower, by the row of lightkeepers' houses, that has been turned into a **museum** telling the history of the Herculean effort required to erect the lighthouse. The best place to get a glimpse of Skerryvore is from the spectacular headland of **Kenavara** (*Ceann a'Mhara*), two miles west of Ben Hynish, across the golden sands of Balephuil Bay. Kenavara's cliffs are home to literally thousands of seabirds; the islands of Barra and South Uist are also visible on the northern horizon.

Practicalities

The only transport around the island is the **postbus**; otherwise, you'll need to make use of the **bike rental** facilities at the *Tiree Lodge* on Gott Bay. Of the two **hotels** in and around Scarinish, the *Tiree Lodge* (☎01879/220353; ④), a mile or so along Gott Bay, has the edge over the *Scarinish* (☎01879/220308; ③), overlooking the old harbour. You could also try the *Kirkapol* **B&B** (☎01879/220729; ③), a converted old kirk by *Tiree Lodge*, or *The Sheiling* (May–Sept; ☎01879/220503; ③), near the airport. Overlooking Balephetrish Bay is the *Balephetrish Guest House* (☎01879/220549; ③) and *Sandy Cove* (April–Oct; ☎01879/220334; ②). There are no official campsites, but **camping** is allowed with the crofter's permission. As for **eating**, just north of Barapol, *The Glassary* (☎01879/220684; ③) serves local lamb, beef and carrageen seaweed pudding, and offers accommodation too.

Isle of Colonsay

Isolated between Mull and Islay, **Colonsay** – eight miles by three at its widest – is nothing like as bleak and windswept as Coll or Tiree. Its craggy hills even support the occasional patch of woodland, plus a bewildering array of plant- and birdlife, wild goats and rabbits, and one of the finest quasi-tropical gardens in Scotland. That said, the population is precariously low at around one hundred, down from a pre-Clearance peak of just under a thousand, and the ferry link with Oban infrequent and incovenient (Mon, Wed & Fri only; 2hr 30min).

The *CalMac* ferry terminal is at **SCALASAIG**, on the east coast, where there's a post office, a petrol pump and a store. Two miles north of Scalasaig, inland, is **Colonsay House** (not open to the public), built in 1722 by Malcolm MacNeil. In 1904, the island and house were bought by the wealthy Lord Strathcona, who made his fortune building the Canadian Pacific Railway. He was also responsible for the house's lovely gardens and woods, which are open to the public, and are slowly being restored to their former glory. Giant breakers roll in from the Atlantic across **Kiloran Bay**, Colonsay's most impressive white sandy beach to the north of Colonsay House, though the shell beach at Balnahard, two miles northeast along a rough track, is even more deserted and backed by rabbit-infested dunes. The island's west coast forms a sharp escarpment, at its most spectacular just west of Kiloran around **Beinn Bhreac** (456ft).

The island's only **hotel**, in **KILORAN**, the other main settlement, two miles north of Scalasaig, is the *Isle of Colonsay* (March–Oct; ☎01951/200316; ⑨), which does dinner, bed and breakfast. There are two **B&Bs**: *Garvard Farmhouse* (☎01951/200343; ④) down by the Strand, and *Seaview* (April–Oct; ☎01951/200315; ④) in Kilchattan. All accommodation for the summer needs to be booked well in advance. The hotel can organize **bike rental**, and there's a **postbus** for those without their own transport.

Isle of Oronsay

Isle of Oronsay (occasionally Oransay), half a mile to the south, is only an island when the tide is in, and, as you can't stay overnight, is basically just a day trip from Colonsay. The two are separated by "The Strand", a mile of tidal mud flats which act as a causeway for two to four hours at low tide; check locally for current timings. Although legends (and etymology) link saints Columba and Oran with both Colonsay and Oronsay, the ruins of the **Oronsay Priory** only date back to the fourteenth century. Abandoned since the Reformation, it still has the original church and cloisters, and the Oronsay Cross, a superb example of late medieval artistry from Iona. Over thirty grave slabs lie within the Prior's House, though you need a torch to inspect them.

Mid-Argyll

Mid-Argyll is a vague term which loosely describes the central wedge of land south of Oban and north of Kintyre, extending west from Loch Fyne to the Atlantic. The highlights of this gently undulating scenery lie along the sharply indented west coast, in particular the rich Celtic remains in the **Kilmartin** valley, one of the most important prehistoric sites in Scotland. Public transport is thin on the ground, with buses to and from Inveraray and Kilmartin, but little else.

LOCHGILPHEAD, on the shores of Loch Fyne, is the chief town in the area, though it has little to offer beyond its practical use – a tourist office, a good supermarket and is the regional transport hub (if that's the right word). It's a planned town in the same vein as Inveraray, but without the pristine whitewashed terraces or the mountainous backdrop. The **tourist office** is at 27 Lochnell St (April–Oct Mon–Fri 10am–1pm & 2–5pm, Sat & Sun noon–4pm; longer hours in peak season; ☎01546/602344). If you're **staying** the night, try the *Argyll,* Lochnell St (☎01546/602221; ③), or *Kilmory House*, Paterson St (☎01546/603658; ②). *The Smiddy*, on Smithy Lane, does the best **home cooking** in town.

Crinan and the Crinan Canal

In 1801 the nine-mile-long **Crinan Canal** opened, linking Loch Fyne with the Sound of Jura across the bottom of the Mòine Mhór, thus cutting out the long and treacherous journey around the Mull of Kintyre. John Rennie's original design, although an impressive engineering feat, had numerous faults and by 1816 Thomas Telford had to be called in to take charge of the renovations.

The largest concentration of locks – there are fifteen in total – is around Cairnbaan, but the best place to view the canal in action is at **CRINAN**, the picturesque fishing port at the western end of the canal. Crinan's tiny harbour is, for the moment at least, still home to a small fishing fleet, though the majority of the traffic on the canal itself is now made up of pleasure boats. Every room in the *Crinan Hotel* (☎01546/830261; ⑨) looks across Loch Crinan to the Sound of Jura – one of the most beautiful views in Scotland, especially at sunset when the myriad islets and the distinctive Paps of Jura are reflected in the still, golden waters of the loch. If the *Crinan* is beyond your means, there are some cheaper but less well-appointed **B&Bs**. Lunch at the *Crinan* is recommended, but may be beyond the reach of some; the bar meals are not correspondingly good and no bargain. Tea and delicious calorific cakes can be had from *Lock 16*, right on the quayside.

Kilmartin and Dunadd

In the tiny village of **KILMARTIN**, eight miles nouth of Lochgilphead, the nineteenth-century **Church** shelters the **Kilmartin Crosses**: one depicts Christ on each side and dates from the tenth century, the other, slightly more recent, is smothered with intricate Celtic knotting. You can also see an interesting collection of medieval grave slabs of the Malcolms of Poltalloch, in a separate enclosure in the graveyard.

The **Kilmartin valley**, fanning out south of the village, is one of the most important prehistoric sites in Scotland. The most significant relic is the **linear cemetery**, where several cairns are aligned for more than two miles, beginning just south of Kilmartin. Whether these represent the successive burials of a ruling family or chieftains, nobody can be sure. The best view of the cemetery's configuration is from the Bronze Age Mid-Cairn, but the Neolithic South Cairn, dating from around 3000 BC, is by far the oldest and the most impressive, with its large chambered tomb roofed by giant slabs.

Close to the Mid-Cairn, in a small copse, the **Templewood** stone circles appear to have been the architectural focus of burials in the area from Neolithic times to the Bronze Age. Visible to the south are the impressively cup-marked **Nether Largie standing stones**, the largest of which looms over 10ft high. **Cup- and ring-marked rocks** are a recurrent feature of prehistoric sites in the Kilmartin valley and elsewhere in Argyll. There are many theories as to their origin: some see them as Pictish symbols, others as African death symbols, primitive solar calendars and so on. The most extensive markings are at **Achnabreck**, off the A816 towards Lochgilphead, but there are other well-preserved rocks in **Slockavullin**, a mile west of Templewood.

The peaty plain of Mòine Mhór (Great Moss), which opens up to the south of Kilmartin, is home to the Iron Age fort of **Dunadd**, one of Scotland's most important Celtic sites, occupying a distinctive 176-foot-high rocky knoll once surrounded by the sea but currently beside the winding River Add. It was here that Fergus, the first King of Dalriada, established his royal seat, having arrived from Ireland around 500 AD. Its strategic position, the craggy defences and the view from the top are all impressive, but it's the **stone carvings** between the twin summits which make Dunadd so remarkable: several lines of inscription in ogam (an ancient alphabet of Irish origin), the faint outline of a boar, a hollowed-out footprint and a small basin. The boar and the inscriptions are probably Pictish, since the fort was clearly occupied long before Fergus got there, but the footprint and basin have been interpreted as being part of the royal coronation rituals of the kings of Dalriada. It is thought that the Stone of Destiny was used at Dunadd before being moved to Scone Palace (see p.808) and eventually to Westminster Abbey in London.

Practicalities

If you don't fancy staying in Lochgilphead (see below), there are several options within a mile radius of Kilmartin. The *Kilmartin Hotel* (☎01546/510250; ④) is in the village itself; *Ri-Cruin* (☎01546/510231; ③) and *Tibertich* (☎01546/510281; ②) are local sheep farms offering **B&B**; and there are further possibilities in the nearby village of Kilmichael Glassary. *The Cairn* (☎01546/510254), opposite the church in Kilmartin, is a great place for lunch, afternoon teas or a moderately expensive evening **meal**, featuring superb Scottish and some Mediterranean dishes.

Kintyre

If it wasn't for the mile-long isthmus between West and the much smaller East Loch Tarbert, **KINTYRE** (from the Gaelic *ceann tire*, "land's end") would be an island. Indeed, in the eleventh century, when the Scottish king, Malcolm Canmore, told Magnus Barefoot, King of Norway, he could lay claim to any island he could navigate his boat round, Magnus succeeded in dragging his boat across the Tarbert isthmus and added the peninsula to his Hebridean kingdom. After the Wars of the Covenant, when the vast majority of the population and property was wiped out by a combination of the 1646 potato blight coupled with the destructive attentions of the Earl of Argyll, Kintyre became a virtual desert until the earl began his policy of transplanting Gaelic-speaking Lowlanders to the region.

Tarbert

A distinctive rocket-like church steeple heralds the fishing village of **TARBERT** (in Gaelic *an tairbeart*, meaning "isthmus"), sheltering an attractive little bay backed by rugged hills. With the local fishing industry under threat from EU quotas, tourism is an increasingly important source of income, as is the money that flows through the town during the last week in May, when the yacht races of the Rover Series take place. Other than shop and watch life go by in the harbour, there's little to do in Tarbert.

The **tourist office** (hours as for Lochgilphead; ☎01880/820429) is on the harbour. If you need to **stay**, there's the *Columba* hotel on the waterfront (☎01880/820808; ③), or *Springside* B&B on Pier Road (☎01880/820413; ②). If you're just looking for a fill-up, the **bar snacks** at the *Islay Frigate Hotel* on the harbour should suffice, but for the best fish and seafood in the whole of Argyll, head for *The Anchorage* nearby (☎01880/820881), unforgettable not least for its eccentric proprietor. You can **rent bikes** from Mr Leitch (☎01880/820287).

One reason you might find yourself staying in Tarbert is its proximity to no fewer than four **ferry terminals**: the nearest is the new *CalMac* service east to Portavadie on the Cowal peninsula; the busiest terminal is eight miles south at **Kennacraig** which runs daily sailings to Islay; further south is the Gigha ferry from Tayinloan, and on the opposite coast the Claonaig ferry to Arran runs from April to October.

Isle of Gigha

Gigha (pronounced "Geeya", with a hard "g") is a low-lying, fertile island, just three miles off the west coast of Kintyre. The island's Ayrshire cattle produce over a quarter of a million gallons of milk a year, some of it used to manufacture the distinctive fruit-shaped cheese which is one of the island's main exports. Like many of the smaller Hebrides, the island was sold by its original lairds, the MacNeils, and has been put on the market twice in less than ten years, causing great uncertainty amongst the 120 or so inhabitants, who have to endure these periods of instability as best they can.

The ferry from Tayinloan, 23 miles south of Tarbert, deposits you at the island's only village, **ARDMINISH**, where you'll find the post office and shop. The only sight as such, is the **Achamore Gardens** (daily 9am–dusk; £2), a mile and a half south of Ardminish. Established by the first postwar owner, Sir James Horlick of hot drink fame, they are best seen in the early summertime, ablaze with rhododendrons and azaleas.

Gigha is so small – six miles by one – that most visitors come here just for the day. However, it is possible to **stay**, either with the McSporrans, at the *Post Office House* (☎01583/505251; ③), or at the *Gigha Hotel* (March–Oct; ☎01583/505254; ⑥), which also runs self-catering flats dotted over the island. Caravans and camping are not allowed on Gigha. Tea, coffee and cakes are best taken by the shore at the *Boathouse* (May–Sept) which overlooks the ferry pier. For something more substantial, the *Gigha Hotel* does really good bar meals. **Bike rental** is available at the McSporrans'.

Campbeltown

There's little to recommend **CAMPBELTOWN** beyond its setting, in a deep bay sheltered by Davaar Island and the surrounding hills. However, with a population of 6500, it is one of the largest towns in Argyll, and if you're staying in the southern half of Kintyre, by far the best place to stock up on supplies. Originally known as Kinlochkilkerran (*Ceann Loch Cill Chiaran*), the town was renamed in the seventeenth century by the Earl of Argyll – a Campbell – when it became one of the main points for immigration from the Lowlands. As is evident from the architecture, Campbeltown's heyday was the Victorian era, when shipbuilding was going strong, coal was shipped by canal from Drumlemble, the fishing fleet was vast and Campbeltown Loch was said to be made of whisky.

Nineteenth-century visitors to Campbeltown frequently found the place engulfed in a thick fog of pungent peat smoke from the town's 34 **whisky distilleries**. Nowadays, only *Glen Scotia* and *Springbank* are left to maintain this regional sub-group of single-malt whiskies, though neither distillery is keen on encouraging visitors. The town's one major sight is the **Campbeltown Cross**, a fourteenth-century blue-green cross with figural scenes and spirals of Celtic knotting, which presides over the main roundabout on the quayside. Back on the harbour is the "**Wee Picture House**", a dinky little Art Deco cinema on Hall Street, built in 1913 and now doubling as a bingo hall (Tues & Fri) and cinema. On the road to Machrihanish, the church known locally as the "Tartan Kirk", partly due its Gaelic associations, but mainly for its stripey bell-cote and pinnacles, has now become the **Campbeltown Heritage Centre** (Mon–Fri noon–5pm, Sat 10am–5pm, Sun 2–5pm; £1), with a mildy diveryting exhibition on the locality.

Practicalities

Campbeltown's **tourist office** on the Old Quay (Feb, March, Nov & Dec Mon–Fri 9am–5.30pm; April–Oct Mon–Fri 9am–5.30pm, Sat & Sun noon–4pm; longer hours in peak season; ☎01586/552056), can help with **accommodation**. The *White Hart Hotel*, Main St (☎01586/552440; ④) is the town's chief hotel; otherwise there's *Westbank Guest House*, Dell Rd (☎01586/553660; ③), or cheaper still, *Barbreck* (☎01586/552173; ②), Kilkerran Rd. There are few **places to eat**, unless you're prepared to fork out for an expensive meal with all the trimmings in the *White Hart Hotel*, or *Seafield Hotel* (☎01586/554385) on Kilkerran Road.

Southend and the Mull of Kintyre

Travelling south from Campbeltown to the bulbous, hilly end of Kintyre takes you through some of the most spectactular scenery on the whole peninsula. Consequently, **SOUTHEND** itself, one of those bleak, blustery spots beloved of fixed caravan sites, comes as something of a disappointment. It does have a sandy beach, but the nicest spot for swimming is **Macharioch Bay**, three miles east, which looks out to distant Ailsa Craig in the Firth of Clyde.

Out to sea, but closer to Southend, is **Dunaverty Rock**, where a force of 300 Royalists were massacred by the Covenanting army of the Earl of Argyll in 1647 despite having surrendered voluntarily. A couple of miles beyond lies **Sanda Island**, which contains the remains of St Ninian's chapel, plus two ancient crosses and a holy well; it's now a holiday retreat (☎01586/553134). Below the cliffs to the west of Southend, a ruined thirteenth-century chapel marks the alleged arrival point of St Columba prior to his trip to Iona, and on a rocky knoll nearby a pair of footprints carved into the rock are known as "Columba's footprints", though only one is actually of ancient origin.

Most people venture south of Campbeltown to make a pilgrimage to the **Mull of Kintyre** – the nearest Britain gets to Ireland, whose coastline, just twelve miles away, is visible on clear days. Although the Mull was made famous by the mawkish number-one hit by one-time local resident, Paul McCartney, with the help of the Campbeltown Pipe Band, there's nothing specifically to see in this godforsaken storm-racked spot but the view. The roads up to the **"Gap"** (1150ft) – where you must leave your car – and down to the lighthouse, itself 300ft above the ocean waves, are terrifyingly precipitous.

There are few places to **stay** in this remote region. Southend's only hotel is currently closed; try instead *Ormsary Farm* (☎01586/830665; ③), *Low Cattadale* (☎01586/830665; ③), or the **campsite** at *Machribeg Farm* (Easter–Sept; ☎01586/830249).

Isle of Arran

Shaped like a kidney bean, **Arran** is the most southerly (and therefore the most accessible) of all the Scottish islands. The Highland–Lowland dividing line passes right through its centre – hence the tourist board's aphorism about "Scotland in miniature" – leaving the northern half underpopulated, mountainous and bleak, while the lush southern half enjoys a milder climate. Despite its immense popularity, the tourists, like the population, tend to stick to the southeastern quarter of the island, leaving the west and the north relatively undisturbed.

Although tourism is now by far its most important industry, at twenty miles in length, Arran is large enough to have a life of its own. While the history of the Clearances on Arran, set in motion by the local lairds, the dukes of Hamilton, is as depressing as elsewhere in the Highlands, in recent years it has not suffered from the depopulation which has plagued other, more remote islands. Once a county in its own right (along with Bute), Arran has been left out of the new Argyll and Bute district in the recent county boundary shake-up, and is now coupled instead with mainland North Ayrshire, with which it enjoys closer transport links, but little else.

Transport is good: daily **buses** circle the island (Brodick tourist office has timetables) and in summer there are two **ferry services**, one from Ardrossan (all year) in Ayrshire to Brodick, and a smaller ferry from Claonaig on the remote Kintyre peninsula to Lochranza in the north (mid-April to mid-Oct).

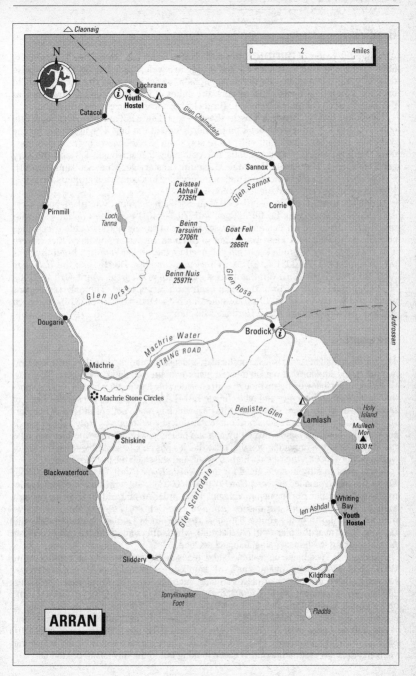

N

△ Claonaig

Lochranza
Youth Hostel
Catacol
Glen Chalmadale

Pirnmill

Loch Tanna

Sannox
Glen Sannox
Corrie

Caisteal Abhail 2735ft

Beinn Tarsuinn 2706ft

Goat Fell 2866ft

Beinn Nuis 2597ft

Glen Iorsa

Glen Rosa

Dougarie

Brodick

△ Ardrossan

Machrie Water

STRING ROAD

Machrie

Machrie Stone Circles

Benlister Glen

Lamlash

Holy Island

Mullach Mor 1030 ft

Shiskine

Blackwaterfoot

Glen Scorrodale

Glen Ashdal

Whiting Bay
Youth Hostel

Sliddery

Kildonan

Torrylinwater Foot

Pladda

ARRAN

Brodick

Although the resort of **BRODICK** (from the Norse *breidr vik*, "broad bay") is a place of little charm, it does at least have a grand setting in a wide, sandy bay set against a backdrop of granite mountains. Its development as a tourist resort on the Clyde was held back for a long time by its elitist owners, the dukes of Hamilton, though nowadays, as the island's main communication hub, Brodick is by far the busiest town on Arran.

The dukes lived at **Brodick Castle** (Easter–Sept daily 11.30am–5pm; Oct Sat & Sun only; £3.50; NTS), on a steep bank on the north side of the bay. The interior is for the dedicated period furniture buff only; more accessible are the views over Brodick Bay, from the flower-filled walled grounds (all year daily 9.30am–dusk; £2) and the very good tea rooms. The **Arran Heritage Museum** (Easter–Oct Mon–Sat 9am–5pm; £1), is a somewhat dry collection of old tools and furniture in a converted crofter's farm halfway between the castle and the town centre.

Brodick's **tourist office** (April–Oct Mon–Sat 9am–7.30pm, Sun 10am–5pm; Oct–April Mon–Sat 9am–5pm, Fri till 7.30pm; ☎01770/302401) is by the *CalMac* pier, with reams of information on bus and ferry services, and the numerous outdoor activities possible on the island. Unless you've got to catch an early-morning ferry, there's very little reason to stay in Brodick. Should you need to, there's old Victorian **hotels** such as the *Douglas* (☎01770/302155; ③) as well as more modest **B&Bs**, like the *Belvedere* Alma Rd (☎01770/302397; ②); the nearest **campsite** is *Glenrosa* (April–Oct; ☎01770/302380), a mile or so north of the town centre, off String Road. The only **restaurant** which really stands out is *Creelers* (mid-March to Oct; ☎01770/302810), a superb seafood restaurant by the Arran Heritage Museum.

The south

The southern half of Arran is less spectacular, and less forbidding than the north; the land is more fertile, and for that reason the vast majority of the population lives here. The tourist industry has followed them, though with considerably less justification. With its distinctive Edwardian architecture and mild climate **LAMLASH** epitomizes the sedate charm of southeast Arran. Its major drawback is its bay, which is made not of sand but of boulder-strewn mud flats. You can take a boat out to the slug-shaped hump of **Holy Island** which shelters the bay, and is now owned by a group of Tibetan Buddhists who have set up a meditation centre – providing you don't dawdle, it's possible to scramble up to the top of Mullach Mòr (1030ft), the island's highest point, and still catch the last ferry back.

If you want to **stay** in style, head for the *Glenisle Hotel* (April–Oct; ☎01770/600 258; ⑥), or the much smaller *Lilybank Hotel* (☎01770/600230; ③), which does superb home-made food; cheaper B&Bs such as *Douglas Villa* (☎01770/600261; ②) are easy enough to find, and *Middleton's* **campsite** (April to mid-Oct; ☎01770/600255) is just five minutes' walk north of the centre. The best **restaurant** in Lamlash is undoubtedly the *Carraig Mhor* near the pier (☎01770/600453), which offers an exclusive and expensive menu featuring fresh local game, fish and seafood.

Although it has been an established Clydeside resort for over a century now, **WHITING BAY**, four miles south of Lamlash, is actually pretty characterless. However, there are plenty of places to stay, among them the *Royal Hotel* (☎01770/700286, ④), *Viewbank* (☎01770/700326; ③) or *Silverhill North* (☎01770/700414; ②), and a **youth hostel** (mid-Feb to Oct; ☎01770/700339). Elsewhere the easiest point of access to the sea is at **KILDONAN**, a small village off the main road, with just one hotel, *Drimla Lodge* (☎01770/820296; ④), the odd B&B like *Dippen House* (☎01770/820223; ②), and a **campsite** (☎01770/820210). There's a nice sandy beach below the village, and, at its east end, a ruined castle looking out to the tiny island of Pladda.

BLACKWATERFOOT, on the western end of String Road that bisects the island, is less a Clyde-style resort than a genuine Hebridean fishing village, and, like Lochranza, a good place to escape the worst of Arran's summer crowds. If you want to **stay**, there's the Victorian *Blackwaterfoot Hotel* (March–Oct; ☎01770/860202; ④) and plenty of cheaper B&Bs: try *Midmar* (☎01770/860413; ③), *Parkhouse* (☎01770/860392; ②), or *Broombrae* (☎01770/860435; ②), a mile or so south of town in Kilpatrick.

The north

The desolate north half of Arran – effectively the Highland part – features bare granite peaks, the occasional golden eagle and miles of unspoilt scenery, within reach only to those prepared to do some serious hiking. Arran's most accessible peak is also the island's highest, **Goat Fell** (2866ft), which can be ascended in just three hours from Brodick (return journey 5hr), though it's a strenuous hike (for the usual safety precautions see p.46). From Goat Fell, experienced walkers can follow the horseshoe of craggy summits and descend either from the saddle below Beinn Tarsuinn (2706ft) or from Beinn Nuis (2597ft).

The ruined castle which occupies the mudflats of the bay, and the gloomy north-facing slopes of the mountains which frame it, make for one of the most spectacular settings on the island – yet **LOCHRANZA**, despite being the only place of any size in this sparsely populated area, attracts far fewer visitors than Arran's southern resorts.

There's a **tourist office** by the *CalMac* pier (mid-May to Sept Mon–Sat 9am–5pm; ☎01770/830320), a **youth hostel** (mid-Feb to Oct; ☎01770/830631) overlooking the castle, and a well-equipped **campsite** (Easter–Oct; ☎01770/830273) on the Brodick Road. Plusher **accommodation** can be had at the *Apple Lodge Hotel* (☎01770/830229; ⑤), the *Lochranza Hotel* (☎01770/830223; ④), or *Belvaren* B&B (☎01770/830647; ②).

An alternative is to continue a mile or so southwest along the coast to **CATACOL**, where the friendly *Catacol Bay Hotel* (☎01770/830231; ③) takes the prize as the island's best pub by far: good, basic pub food (with several veggie options and real chips), great beer on tap, a small adjoining campsite, and seal and shags to view on the nearby shingle. The pub also puts on live music most weeks, and hosts a week-long folk festival in early June.

Isle of Islay

Islay (pronounced "eye-la") is famous for one thing – single-malt **whisky**. The smoky, peaty, pungent quality of Islay whisky is unique, recognizable even to the untutored palette, and five of the six distilleries that still function lay on free guided tours, ending with the customary complimentary tipple. Yet despite the fame of its whiskies, Islay remains relatively undiscovered, much as Skye and Mull were some twenty years ago. Part of the reason, no doubt, is that it takes a pricey, two-hour ferry journey from Kennacraig on Kintyre to reach the island.

In medieval times, Islay was the political centre of the Hebrides, with Finlagan Castle, near Port Askaig, the seat of the MacDonalds, lords of the Isles. The picturesque, whitewashed villages you see on Islay today, however, date from the planned settlements founded by the Campbells in the late eighteenth and early nineteenth centuries. Apart from whisky and solitude, the other great draw is the **birdlife**, in particular, the scores of white-fronted and barnacle geese who winter here. For two weeks in late May/early June, the Islay Festival *Feis Ile* takes place, with whisky-tasting, pipe bands, folk dancing and other events celebrating Islay's Gaelic culture.

Port Ellen and the south

Notwithstanding the ferry from Kennacraig, **PORT ELLEN**, the largest place on **Islay,** is a sleepy little place, laid out as a planned village in 1821 and named after the wife of the founder. The neat terraces along the harbour are pretty enough, but the bay is dominated by the now disused whisky distillery – the smell of malt which wafts across the harbour comes from the modern maltings just off the Bowmore road. As well as the two hotels, the *Trout Fly* restaurant has **rooms** (☎01496/302204; ③), or you could try any of the B&Bs on Frederick Crescent. There's also an **independent hostel**, *Kintra Bunkbarns* (☎01496/302051; ①), with a B&B at *Kintra Farm* (☎01496/302051; ③), which runs an adjacent **campsite** with good facilities (April–Sept), all in **KINTRA**, three miles northwest of Port Ellen, at the southern tip of Laggan Bay.

From Port Ellen, a dead-end road heads off east along the coastline, passing three functioning distilleries in as many miles. First comes **Laphroaig Distillery** (free tours by arrangement only; ☎01496/302418) which produces the most uncompromisingly smoky of the Islay whiskies. As every bottle of Laphroaig tells you, translated from the Gaelic the name means "the beautiful hollow by the broad bay", and, true enough, the whitewashed distillery is indeed in a gorgeous setting by the sea. The **Lagavulin Distillery** (Mon–Fri by appointment; £2; ☎01496/302400), a mile down the road, produces a superb sixteen-year-old single malt, while the **Ardbeg Distillery**, another mile on, sports the traditional pagoda-style roofs of the malting houses – though sadly it's one of the few not to encourage visitors.

There are a handful of **B&Bs** further east along the rapidly deteriorating road – try *Tigh-na-Suil* (☎01496/302483; ③). A mile beyond this, the simple thirteenth-century **Kildalton Chapel** boasts a wonderful eighth-century Celtic cross made from the local "bluestone", which is, in fact, a rich bottle-green. The quality of the scenes matches any to be found on the crosses carved by the monks in Iona: Mary and child are on one side with what look like elephants on the other.

Bowmore and Loch Gruinart

BOWMORE, Islay's administrative capital with a population of around nine hundred, was founded as a planned village in 1768 to replace the village of Kilarrow, which was deemed by the local laird to be too close to his own residence. It's a striking place, laid out in a grid plan rather like Inveraray, with Main Street climbing up the hill in a straight line from the pier on Loch Indaan to the town's crowning landmark, the **Round Church**. A little to the west of Main Street is **Bowmore Distillery** (guided tours Mon–Fri 10.30am & 2pm, Sat 10.30am only; £2; ☎01496/810671), the first of the legal Islay distilleries, founded in 1779 and still occupying its original buildings.

Islay's only official **tourist office** is in Bowmore (Feb, March, Nov & Dec Mon–Sat 9.30am–1pm & 2–5pm; April & Oct Mon–Fri 9.30am–1pm & 2–5.30pm, Sat & Sun noon–4pm; May to mid-June & late Sept Mon–Sat 9.30am–1pm & 2–5.30pm; mid-June to mid-Sept Mon–Sat 9am–5.45pm, Sun 2–5pm; ☎01496/810254), and can help you find accommodation anywhere on Islay or Jura. The nicest of Bowmore's several **hotels** is the *Lochside* on Shore Street (☎01496/810244; ④). Alternatively, there's *Lambeth House*, Jamieson St (☎01496/810597; ②). For **food**, head for the *Harbour Inn*, Main St, where you can sample the local prawns and warm yourself by a peat fire, or settle down to some homely food at *The Cottage*, further up on the same side of the street.

North of Bowmore, the RSPB reserve on the mud flats of **Loch Gruinart** aims to encourage the barnacle geese to winter here rather than on the valuable peat bogs at Duich Moss; in summer this is a good place to spot lapwings, snipes and redshanks. Birdwatchers should hole themselves up in *Loch Gruinart House* (☎01496/850212; ②) by the reserve, or at the rudimentary *Craigens Farm* **campsite** by the loch (April–Oct;

☎01496/850256). Three miles to the west lies the freshwater **Loch Gorm**, occasional winter home of the rare Greenland white-fronted goose.

Port Charlotte and the Rhinns of Islay

PORT CHARLOTTE, named after the founder's mother, is generally agreed to be Islay's prettiest village, the "Queen of the Rhinns" ("rhinns" is derived from the Gaelic word for promontory), its immaculate cottages hugging the sandy shores of Loch Indaal. East of the village, the imaginative **Museum of Islay Life** (April–Sept Mon–Sat 10am–5pm, Sun 2–5pm; Oct–March Mon–Fri 10am–4.30pm; £1.50) has a children's corner, a good library of books about the island. The **Islay Field Centre** (Mon, Wed, Fri & Sun 2–5pm; £2), housed in the former distillery warehouse, is also worth a visit for anyone interested in the island's flora and fauna. As for **accommodation**, there's the *Lochindaal Hotel* (☎01496/850202; ④), plus scores of B&Bs: the wonderful *Taigh-na-Creag*, 7 Shore St (☎01496/850261; ③) and *Craigfad Guest House* (☎01496/850244; ③), as well as a **youth hostel** (mid-Feb to Oct; ☎01496/810385), housed in an old bonded warehouse. The *Croft Kitchen*, near the museum, serves hot meals including several vegetarian dishes.

The coastal road culminates seven miles south of Port Charlotte at **PORTNAHAVEN**, a fishing and crofting community since the early nineteenth century. The familiar Hebridean cottages wrap themselves around the steep banks of a deep bay; in the distance, you can see Portnahaven's twin settlement, **PORT WEMYSS**, a mile south. A short way out to sea are two islands, the largest of which, Orsay, sports the **Rhinns of Islay Lighthouse**, built by Robert Louis Stevenson's father in 1825. There are few amenities in this isolated part of Islay, but you'll get **rooms** at *Glenview House* (☎01496/860303; ②) in Portnahaven.

Port Askaig and around

Islay's other ferry connection with the mainland, and its sole link with Jura, is from **PORT ASKAIG**, a scattering of buildings which tumble down a little cove by the narrowest section of the Sound of Islay. The *Port Askaig Hotel* (☎01496/840245; ⑧) by the pier is the plushest on the island, with views over to the Paps of Jura; there are cheaper B&Bs to choose from, too, such as *Meadowbank* (☎01496/840679; ③). A short walk north along the shore from Port Askaig will bring you to the **Caol Ila Distillery** (guided tours Mon–Fri 10.30am & 2pm; £2; ☎01496/840207), named after the Sound of Islay (*Caol Ila*) which it overlooks. **Bunnahabhainn Distillery** (Mon–Fri free guided tours by appointment; ☎01496/840646) is a couple of miles further up the coast.

Isle of Jura

The long whale-shaped island of **Jura** – or, to be more accurate the distinctive Paps of Jura (so called because of their smooth breast-like shape, though confusingly there are three of them), the tallest of which, Beinn Oír, rises to 2571ft – seems to dominate every view off the coast of Argyll. Twenty-eight miles long and eight miles wide, Jura is one of the wildest and most mountainous of the Inner Hebrides, its entire west coast uninhabited and inaccessible except to the dedicated walker. The island's name derives from the Norse *dyr-oe* (deer island); appropriately enough, the current deer population outnumbers the two hundred humans by 25 to 1.

Anything that happens on Jura happens in **CRAIGHOUSE**. *Western Ferries* run a regular car ferry service all year from Port Askaig to Feolin Ferry, eight miles away. **Craighouse Distillery** (☎01496/820240), which looks out across Small Isles Bay to the mainland of Knapdale, is the island's only industry besides crofting and tourism, and welcomes visitors. The one hotel, the *Jura Hotel* (☎01496/820243; ⑤), is supplemented by a smattering of B&Bs, such as the *Fish Farm House* (☎01496/820304; ③) or *Mrs Woodhouse*, 7 Woodside (☎01496/820379; ②). At **Jura House**, three miles south of Craighouse, you can visit the organic walled garden (daily dawn–dusk; £2) which specializes in Antipodean plants.

In April 1946, Eric Blair (better known by his pen name of **George Orwell**), suffering badly from TB and intending to give himself "six months' quiet" in which to write his novel, *1984*, moved to a remote farmhouse called Barnhill, on the northern tip of Jura. He lived out a spartan existence there for two years but was forced to return to London shortly before his death. The house, 23 miles north of Craighouse up an increasingly poor road, is as remote today as it was in Orwell's day, and sadly there is no access to the interior.

travel details

Trains

Glasgow (Queen St) to: Oban (3 daily; 3hr); Helensburgh Central (every 30min; 44min); Helensburgh Upper (Mon–Sat 4 daily; Sun 3 daily; 45min); Arrochar & Tarbet (Mon–Sat 4 daily; Sun 3 daily; 1hr 15min).

Buses (excluding the postbus)

Brodick to: Lamlash (Mon–Sat 10 daily; 15min); Blackwaterfoot (Mon–Sat 8–9 daily; 25min); Lochranza (Mon–Sat 5 daily; Sun 4 daily; 40min).

Colintraive to: Rothesay (Tues–Thurs at least 2 daily; 30min); Tighnabruaich (Tues–Thurs at least 2 daily; 35min).

Craignure to: Fionnphort (Mon–Sat up to 4 daily; 1hr 15min).

Dunoon to: Colintraive (Mon–Sat at least 2 daily; 45min); Inveraray (Mon–Sat at least 2 daily; 1hr 10min); Rothesay (Mon–Sat at least 1 daily;1hr 30min); Tighnabruaich (at least 2 daily; 1hr 25min)

Glasgow to: Campbeltown (Mon–Sat 3 daily; Sun 2 daily; 4hr 20min); Inveraray (Mon–Sat 6 daily; Sun 4 daily; 1hr 40min); Kennacraig (Mon–Sat 2 daily; Sun 1 daily; 3hr 30min); Lochgilphead (Mon–-Sat 3 daily; Sun 2 daily; 2hr 40min); Oban (Mon–Sat 3 daily; Sun 2 daily; 3hr); Tarbert (Mon–Sat 3 daily; Sun 2 daily; 3hr 15min).

Kennacraig to: Claonaig (1 daily except Wed; 15min).

Lochgilphead to: Kilmartin (Mon–Sat 1 daily; 40min).

Oban to: Kilmartin (Mon–Sat 1 daily; 1hr 5min); Lochgilphead (Mon–Sat 1 daily; 1hr 20min).

Rothesay to: Kilchattan Bay (Mon–Sat 5 daily Sun 3 daily; 25min); Mount Stuart (Mon–Sat up t 9 daily; Sun 5 daily; 12min).

Tarbert to: Claonaig (Mon–Sat 3–4 daily; 30min Kennacraig (Mon–Sat 2–3 daily; 15min).

Tobermory to: Calgary (Mon–Fri 3 daily; Sat daily; 3hr); Craignure (Mon–Sat 5 daily; Sun 2 dail 1hr); Dervaig (Mon–Fri 4 daily; Sat 2 daily; 30min Fishnish (Mon–Sat 5 daily; Sun 2 daily; 50min).

Car ferries (summer timetable)

To Arran: Ardrossan–Brodick (Mon–Sat 5 daily Sun up to 4 daily; 55min); Claonaig–Lochranza (1 daily; 30min); Rothesay–Brodick (Mon & Thurs daily; 1hr 45min).

To Bute: Brodick–Rothesay (Mon & Thurs 1 daily 1hr 45min); Colintraive–Rhubodach (frequently 5min); Wemyss Bay–Rothesay (10 daily; 30min).

To Coll: Oban–Coll (daily except Thurs & Sun 3hr)

To Colonsay: Kennacraig–Colonsay (Wed 1 daily 3hr 35min); Oban–Colonsay (Mon, Wed & Fri up t 2 daily; 2hr 10min).

To Dunoon: Gourock (McInroy's Point)–Dunoor (Hunter's Quay) (every 30min; 20min); Gourock–Dunoon (every 1hr; 15min).

To Gigha: Tayinloan–Gigha (hourly; 20min).

To Iona: Fionnphort–Iona (Mon–Sat frequently Sun hourly; 15min).

To Islay: Kennacraig–Port Askaig (Mon–Sat up t 2 daily; 2hr); Kennacraig–Port Ellen (up to 2 daily 2hr 10min).

To Kintyre: Portavadie–Tarbert (hourly; 30min)

To Mull: Kilchoan–Tobermory (Mon–Sat 6 daily; July & Aug Sun 5 daily; 35min); Lochaline–Fishnish (Mon–Sat every 40–45min; Sun hourly; 15min); Oban–Craignure (Mon–Sat up to 6 daily; Sun up to 5 daily; 40min); Oban–Tobermory – passengers only (Mon, Wed & Sat; 1hr 45min).

To Tiree: Oban–Tiree (daily except Thurs & Sun; 4hr 15min).

Flights

To Campbeltown: Glasgow (Mon–Fri 2 daily; 35min); Islay (Mon–Fri 1 daily 20min).

To Islay: Campbeltown (Mon–Fri 1 daily 20min); Glasgow (Mon–Sat 2 daily; 40min).

To Tiree: Barra (Tues–Thurs 1 daily; 20min); Glasgow (Mon–Sat 1–2 daily; 45min)

CHAPTER TWENTY TWO

SKYE AND THE WESTERN ISLES

A procession of Hebridean islands, islets and reefs off the northwest shore of Scotland, **Skye and the Western Isles** between them boast some of the country's most alluring scenery. It's here that the turbulent seas of the Atlantic smash up against an extravagant shoreline hundreds of miles long, a geologically complex terrain whose rough rocks and mighty seacliffs are interrupted by a thousand sheltered bays and, in the far west, a long line of sweeping sandy beaches. The islands' interiors are equally dramatic, a series of formidable mountain ranges soaring high above great chunks of boggy peat moor, a barren wilderness enclosing a host of tin lakes, or lochans.

Skye and the Western Isles were first settled by Neolithic farming peoples in around 4500 BC. They lived along the coast, where they are remembered by scores of incidental remains, from passage graves through to stone circles – most famously at **Calanais** (Callanish) on Lewis. Viking colonization gathered pace from 700 AD onwards – on Lewis four out of every five place names is of Norse origin – and it was only in 1266 that the islands were returned to the Scottish crown. James VI (and I of England), a Stuart and a Scot, though no Gaelic-speaker, was the first to put forward the idea of clearing the Hebrides, though it wasn't until after the Jacobite uprisings, when many Highland clans disastrously backed the wrong side, that the Clearances began in earnest.

The isolation of the Hebrides exposed them to the whims and fancies of the various merchants and aristocrats who caught "island fever" and bought them up. Time and again, from the mid-eighteenth century onwards, both the land and its people were sold to the highest bidder. Some proprietors were relatively progressive – like **Lord Leverhulme**, who tried to turn Lewis into a centre of the fishing industry in the 1920s – while others were autocratic – such as **Colonel Gordon of Cluny**, who bought Benbecula, South Uist, Eriskay and Barra, and forced the inhabitants onto ships bound for North America at gunpoint – but always the islanders were powerless and almost everywhere they were driven from their ancestral homes. However, their language

ACCOMMODATION PRICE CODES

Throughout this guide, hotel and B&B accommodation is priced on a scale of ① to ⑨, the number indicating the **lowest price** you could expect to pay per night in that establishment for a **double room** in high season. The prices indicated by the codes are as follows:

① under £20/$30	④ £40–50/$60–75	⑦ £70–80/$105–120
② £20–30/$31–45	⑤ £50–60/$75–90	⑧ £80–100/$120–150
③ £30–40/$45–60	⑥ £60–70/$90–105	⑨ over £100/$150

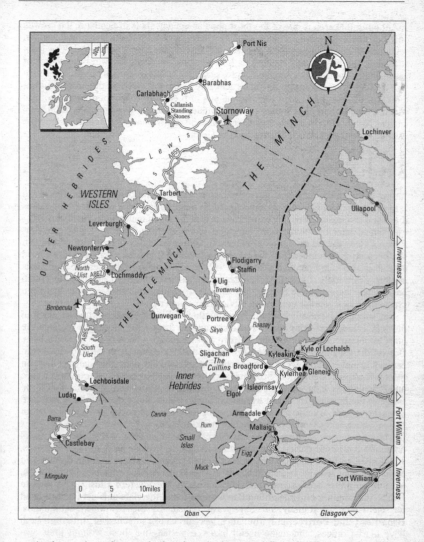

survived, ensuring a degree of cultural continuity, especially in the Western Isles, where even today, the mother tongue of the vast majority is **Gaelic**.

Aficionados of this part of Scotland swear that each island has its own distinct character, which is to some extent true, although you can split the grouping quite neatly into two. **Skye** and the so-called **Small Isles** – the improbably named Canna, Rum, Eigg and Muck – are part of the Inner Hebrides, which also include the islands of Argyll (see the *Argyll* chapter). Beyond Skye, across the unpredictable waters of the Minch, lie the Outer Hebrides or Outer Isles, nowadays known as the **Western Isles**, a 130-mile-long archipelago stretching from **Lewis** in the north to **Barra** in the south.

Although this area is one of the most popular holiday spots in Scotland, the crowds only become oppressive on Skye, and even here, most visitors stick to a well-trodden sequence of roadside sights that leaves the rest of the island unaffected. The main attraction, the spectacular scenery, is best explored on **foot**, following the scores of paths that range from the simplest of cross-country strolls to arduous treks. There are four obvious areas of outstanding natural beauty to aim for: on Skye, the harsh peaks of the **Cuillins** and the bizarre rock formations of the **Trotternish peninsula**, both of which attract hundreds of walkers and mountaineers; on the Western Isles, the mountains of **North Harris**, together with the splendid sandy beaches that string along the Atlantic seaboard of **South Harris** and the **Uists**.

Skye

Jutting out from the mainland like a giant wing, the bare and bony promontories of the **Isle of Skye** (*An t-Eilean Sgiathanach*) fringe a deeply indented coastline that makes the island never more than 25, sometimes as little as seven, miles wide. Justifiably Skye was named after the Norse word for cloud (*skuy*), earning itself the Gaelic moniker, *Eilean a Cheo* (Island of Mist). Yet despite the unpredictability of the weather, tourism has been an important part of the island's economy for almost a hundred years now, ever since the train line pushed through to Kyle of Lochalsh in the western Highlands in 1897. From here, it was the briefest of boat trips across to Skye, and the Edwardian bourgeoisie were soon swarming over to walk its mountains, whose beauty had been proclaimed by an earlier generation of Victorian climbers.

You might not guess it from the large number of English settlers who run much of the tourist industry – the B&Bs, museums and so forth – but Skye also remains the most important centre for **Gaelic culture** and language outside of the Western Isles. Despite the Clearances, which saw an estimated 30,000 emigrate in the mid-nineteenth century, around forty percent of the population is fluent in Gaelic, the Gaelic college on Sleat is the most important in Scotland, and the extreme Sabbatarian Free Church (see p.857) maintains a strong presence. As an English-speaking visitor, it's as well to be aware of the tensions that exist within this idyllic island. For a taste of the resurgence of Gaelic culture, try and get here in time for the Skye and Lochalsh Festival, *Feis an Eilean*, which takes place over two weeks in mid-July.

The most popular destination on Skye is the **Cuillins**, whose jagged peaks dominate the island during clear weather, though to explore them at close quarters, you'll need to be a fairly experienced and determined walker. Equally dramatic in their own way are the rock formations of the **Trotternish** peninsula, in the north, from which there are inspirational views across to the Western Isles. If you want to escape the summer crush, shuffle off to **Glendale** and the cliffs of Neist Point or head for the island of **Raasay**, off Skye's east coast. Of the two main settlements, **Broadford** and **Portree**, only the latter has any charm attached to it, though both have tourist offices, and make useful bases, especially for those without their own transport.

Visiting Skye

Most visitors still reach Skye via **Kyle of Lochalsh**, linked to Inverness by train, or by crossing the new Skye Bridge on one of the frequent buses over to **Kyleakin**, on the western tip of the island. The more scenic approach – and the only way to get to the **Small Isles** – is from the **ferry** port of **Mallaig**, further south to **Armadale**, on the gentle southern slopes of the Sleat peninsula. A third option is the privately operated summer-only car **ferry** which leaves the mainland at Glenelg, south of Kyle of Lochalsh, to arrive at **Kylerhea**, between Armadale and Kyleakin. Most visitors arrive by car, as the **bus** services, while adequate between the villages, peter out in the more remote areas, and virtually close down on Sundays.

The Sleat peninsula

Ferry services (Mon–Sat up to 7 daily; mid-May to mid-Sept also 4 on Sun; 30min) from Mallaig connect with the **Sleat peninsula** (pronounced "Slate"), Skye's southern tip, an uncharacteristically fertile area that has earned it the sobriquet "the Garden of Skye". The *CalMac* ferry terminal is at **ARMADALE** (*Armadal*), an elongated hamlet stetching along the wooded shoreline. Armadale **youth hostel** (mid-March to Sept; ☎01471/844260) is a ten-minute walk up the A851 to Broadford, overlooking the bay; it also rents bikes. There are several B&Bs in neighbouring **ARDVASAR**, to the southwest, plus the *Ardvasar Hotel* (March–Dec; ☎01471/844223; ⑤), which has an excellent restaurant and a lively bar; a cheaper alternative is the *Bistro* café on Armadale pier.

Just past the youth hostel, you'll find the **Clan Donald Visitor Centre** (April–Oct daily 9.30am–5.30pm; gardens open all year; £3.20) whose handsome forty-acre gardens surround the nineteenth-century remains of Armadale Castle. Part of the castle has been turned into a museum that traces the history of the Gaels, concentrating on medieval times when the Donalds were the Lords of the Isles. It's well done, and the sound effects – savage clanging swords and battle songs – just about compensate for the lack of original artefacts. For more substantial information, you'll have to return to the refurbished stable block beside the entrance, where the bookshop carries a wide range of Scottish history books.

Continuing northeast, it's another six miles to **ISLEORNSAY** (*Eilean Iarmain*), a secluded little village of ancient whitewashed cottages that was once Skye's main fishing port. With the mountains of the mainland on the horizon, the views out across the bay are wonderful, overlooking a necklace of seaweed-encrusted rocks and the tidal **Isle of Ornsay** itself, which sports a trim lighthouse, built by Robert Louis Stevenson's father. You can stay at another of Sir Iain Noble's enterprises, the mid-nineteenth-century *Isle Ornsay Hotel* (☎01471/833332; ⑦), a pricey place (also known by its Gaelic name *Hotel Eilean Iarmain*), whose restaurant serves great seafood.

Kyleakin and Kylerhea

The aforementioned Sir Iain Noble is also one of the leading advocates of (and investors in) the privately financed **Skye Bridge**, which nows links the tidy hamlet of **KYLEAKIN** (*Caol Acain*) with the Kyle of Lochalsh (see p.923), just half a mile away on the mainland. The bridge, initially welcomed by the vast majority of islanders, cost the Anglo-German contractors a cool thirty million pounds, which they are aiming to recoup by charging over £5 each way for cars and more than £30 for lorries and coaches, making it the most expensive toll bridge in Europe, and no cheaper than the ferry it replaces. There's nothing much to see or do in Kyleakin, but if you're marooned, the official **youth hostel** (☎01599/534585) is a couple of hundred yards from the ferry dock; close by, there's a *Backpackers' Guesthouse* (☎01599/534510), and a long line of cheap **B&Bs** including *Mrs MacLennan*, 16 Kyleside (☎01599/534468; ③). **Bike rental** is available from *Skye Bikes* (☎01599/534795) on the pier.

You can still have the romance of a trip "over the sea to Skye" at the Mallaig-Armadale crossing, or by taking the ferry service (mid-April to mid-Oct frequently; 15min) from Glenelg to **KYLERHEA**, a peaceful little place, some four miles down the coast from Kyleakin. **Seal trips** (£4.50), organized by *Castle Moil Seal Cruises*, also set off from the ferry pier, taking you to view the seal colony on Eilean Mhal (4 daily; £4.50; ☎01599/534641). Alternatively, you can walk half an hour up the coast to the

Forestry Commission **Otter Hide**, where if you're lucky, you may be able to spot one of these elusive creatures.

Broadford and the Isle of Raasay

Heading west out of Kyleakin or Kylerhea brings you eventually to the island's second largest village, charmless **BROADFORD** (*An t-Ath Leathann*), whose mile-long main street curves round a wide bay. Despite its rather unlovely appearance, Broadford is a useful base for the southern half of Skye, with a **tourist office** (Mon–Sat 9.30am–5.30pm; ☎01471/822361) next door to the *Esso* garage on the main road, and a bank and bakery at the west end of the village. The official **youth hostel** is on the west shore of the bay (June–Oct; ☎01471/822442), or there's the much more beautiful and primitive *Fossil Bothy* (☎01471/822297), a small, independent hostel on the east side of the bay. You can **rent bikes** from the official youth hostel or from *Fairwinds Guest House* (April–Oct; ☎01471/822270; ③).

Travelling west from Broadford, with the Cuillins to your left and the sea to your right, it's thirteen miles to Sconsor, where a car ferry leaves for the **Isle of Raasay** (Mon–Sat 6 daily; 15min) a nature conservancy area, which offers great walks across its bleak and barren hills, and remains well off the tourist trail. The island's ageing population now numbers just 150, most of them members of the Free Presbyterian Church, a Calvinist off-shoot of the already very strict Free Church (see p.857). Strict observance of the Sabbath – no work or play on Sundays – is the most obvious manifestation for visitors, who should respect the islanders' feelings.

The ferry docks at the southern tip of the island, an easy walk (15min) from **INVERARISH**, a tiny village set within thick woods on the island's southwest coast. A further half-mile along the coast, in **CLACHAN**, is the *Raasay Outdoor Centre*, housed in a partially restored Georgian mansion, which offers comfortable **accommodation** in tastefully bohemian rooms (March–Oct; ☎01478/660266; ③), and **camping** in the grounds. Close by, there are comfortable rooms at the likeably old-fashioned *Isle of Raasay Hotel* (☎01478/660222; ⑤), which sits above the seashore looking out over Skye; they also serve delicious traditional Scottish food.

To the north of the *Outdoor Centre*, along the coast, lies the hamlet of **OSKAIG**, from where a rough track cuts up the steep hillside to reach, by turning right at the road, Raasay's isolated put beautifully placed **youth hostel** (mid-May to Sept; ☎01478/660240). Most of the rest of Raasay is starkly barren, a rugged and rocky terrain of sandstone in the south and gneiss in the north, with the most obvious feature being the curiously truncated basalt cap on top of **Dun Caan** (1456ft), where Boswell "danced a Highland dance" on his visit to the island with Dr Johnson in 1773.

The Cuillins and around

For many people the **Cuillins**, whose sharp snow-capped peaks rise mirage-like from the flatness of the surrounding terrain, are Skye's *raison d'être*. When the clouds finally disperse, they are the dominating feature of the island, visible from every other peninsula on Skye. There are basically three approaches to the Cuillins: from the south, by foot or by boat from Elgol; from the *Sligachan Hotel* from the north, or from Glen Brittle to the west of the mountains. Glen Sligachan is by far the most popular route, dividing as it does the granite of the **Red Cuillins** to the east from the dark, coarse-grained gabbro of the **Black Cuillins** to the west. With some twenty Munros between them, these are mountains to be taken seriously, and many routes through the Cuillins are for experienced climbers only (for more on safety see p.46).

Elgol and Glen Sligachan

The only reason to visit the desparate-looking village of **ELGOL**, fourteen miles west of Broadford, is to take the boat trip, which bobs its way across Loch Scavaig (April–Oct 1 or 2 daily), past a seal colony, to the tight entrance of **Loch Coruisk** (*coire uish*, cauldron of water). A wild, glacial loch, this needle-like shaft of water, nearly two miles long but only a couple of hundred yards wide, lies in the shadow of the highest peaks of the Black Cuillins, a wonderfully dramatic landscape. The return trip takes an hour or so and costs around £6 (£5 one-way) – for details of sailing times, ring the skipper, Donald MacKinnon (☎01471/866244). From Loch Coruisk, there are numerous possibilities for walking amidst the Red Cuillins; the most popular route, though, is to head north over the pass into **Glen Sligachan**.

At the northern end of Glen Sligachan, just three miles southwest of Sconser, is the *Sligachan Hotel* (April–Nov; ☎01478/650204; ⑦) and its adjacent **campsite**, strategically placed for hikers. Elgol has a couple of **B&Bs**: try *Mrs MacKinnon*, at 4 Drinen (☎01471/866255; ②), or *Strathaird House* (☎01471/866269; ③), above Kilmarie Bay four miles back towards Broadford; there's also an independent hostel, another two miles further back, *Blaven Bunkhouse* (☎01471/822397). The only public transport along the Elgol road is the **postbus**, which leaves Broadford every weekday morning and returns in the afternoon to connect – in theory at least – with the Loch Coruisk boat; check the times and details at Broadford tourist office.

Glen Brittle and the Black Cuillins

Six miles along the Dunvegan road (A863) from the *Sligachan Hotel*, there's a turning which quickly leads to the entrance to stony **Glen Brittle** (with the settlement, Glenbrittle, at its southern end), edging the western peaks of the Black Cuillins. Climbers and serious walkers tend to congregate at the **youth hostel** (mid-March to Sept; ☎01478/640278) or the **campsite** (April–Sept; ☎01478/640404), a mile or so further south behind the wide sandy beach at the foot of the glen. During the summer, there's one **bus** a day from Portree to the hostel and Glen Brittle; both the youth hostel and the campsite have grocery stores, the only ones for miles.

From the valley a score of difficult and strenuous trails lead into the **Black Cuillins**, a rough semicircle of peaks that, rising to about 3000ft, surround Loch Coruisk. One of the easiest walks is the five-mile round trip from the campsite up **Coire Lagan**, to a crystal-cold lochan squeezed in among the sternest of rockfaces. Above the lochan is Skye's highest peak and the most difficult of the Munros, Sgurr Alasdair (3257ft), while Sgurr na Banachdich is the only other accessible Munro in the Cuillins (for the usual walking safety precautions see p.46).

If the weather's bad and outdoor activities impossible, you could while away an afternoon at **Talisker Whisky Distillery** (April–Oct Mon–Fri 9.30am–4.30pm; July & Aug also Sat; Nov–March Mon–Fri 2–4.30pm; by appointment only; ☎01478/640203), which produces a very smoky, peaty single malt. Talisker is the island's only distillery, situated on the shores of Loch Harport at **CARBOST** (and not, confusingly, at the village of Taliskser itself).

Dunvegan and the Duirnish peninsula

After the Glen Brittle turning, the A863 slips across bare rounded hills to skirt the bony seacliffs and stacks of the west coast twenty miles or so north to **DUNVEGAN** (*Dùn Bheagain*), an unappealing place strung out along the east shore of the sea loch of the same name. From the jetty outside the castle there are regular seal-spotting **boat trips** out along Loch Dunvegan, as well as longer and less frequent sea cruises. Just to the north of the village, **Dunvegan Castle** (April–Oct Mon–Sat 10am–5.30pm & Sun 1–

5.30pm; £4) perches on top of a rocky outcrop, sandwiched between the sea and several acres of beautifully maintained gardens. It's been the seat of the Clan MacLeod since the thirteenth century, but the present greying, rectangular fortress with its uniform battlements and dummy pepper pot dates from the 1840s. The half-dozen rooms open to the public sport all sorts of clannish trinkets, and an intriguing display on the remote archipelago of St Kilda, long the fiefdom of the MacLeods. Most intriguing of all are the battered remnants of the **Fairy Flag**, a yellow silken flag from the Middle East thought to have been the battle standard of the Norwegian king, Harald Hardrada, who was commander of the imperial guard in Constantinople.

The hammerhead **Duirnish peninsula** lies to the west of Dunvegan, much of it inaccessible to all except walkers prepared to scale or skirt the area's twin flat-topped peaks known as **MacLeod's Tables**. The main areas of habitation lie to the north, along the western shores of Loch Dunvegan, and in the broad green sweep of **Glen Dale**, attractively dotted with white farmhouses and dubbed "Little England" by the locals, due to its high percentage of "white settlers", English incomers searching for a better life. Glen Dale's current predicament is doubly ironic given its history, for it was here in 1882 that local crofters staged a rent strike against their landlords, the MacLeods. Five locals – who became known as the "Glen Dale Martyrs" – were given two-month prison sentences, and eventually, in 1904, the crofters became (and remain) the only owner-occupiers in the Highlands.

All this, and much more about crofting, is told through contemporary news cuttings at **Colbost Folk Museum** (daily 10am–6pm; £1), the oldest of Peter MacAskill's three Skye museums, situated in a restored black house, four miles up the road from Dunvegan. Further up the road in **BORRERAIG**, where there was once a famous piping college, is the **MacCrimmon Piping Heritage Centre** (Tues–Sun Easter to late May noon–5.30pm; late May to early Oct 11am–5.30pm; £1.50), on the ancestral holdings of the MacCrimmons, heriditary pipers to the MacLeod chiefs for three centuries, until they were sent packing in the 1770s. The plaintive sounds of the *piobaireachd* of the MacCrimmons, founding family of Scottish piping, fill this illuminating museum.

The west coast of Duirnish is mostly uninhabited now, due to the Clearances of the 1830s, when the villagers were given the choice of emigration or prison. For walkers, though, it's a great area to explore, with blustery but easy footpaths leading to the dramatically sited lighthouse on **Neist Point**, Skye's most westerly spot, which features some fearsome seacliffs, and gives out wonderful views across the sea to the Western Isles.

Practicalities

It's unlikely you'll want to stay in Dunvegan, but there are several reasonably priced **hotels** and **B&Bs** dotted along the main road, including the family-owned *Tables Hotel* (☎01470/521404; ④), and the vegetarian B&B, *Kensalroag House* (April–Nov; ☎01470/521306; ②). Other possibilities include *Janet Kernachan*, 4 Lephin (March–Sept; ☎01470/511376; ②) and *Mrs Hampson* (☎01470/521338; ③), both in Glendale itself. There are two **campsites**, one about half a mile east of the Dunvegan out towards Portree (April–Sept; ☎01470/220206), and a more basic one a short distance west along the head of the Loch Dunvegan. The culinary highlight in the area is a visit to the *Three Chimneys* restaurant (☎01470/511258), located beside Colbost Folk Museum, which serves sublime meals and famously good marmalade pudding.

Portree

PORTREE is the only real town on Skye, and unless you studiously avoid it, you're bound to end up here at some point. In actual fact, it's one of the most attractive fishing ports in northwest Scotland, its deep cliff-edged harbour filled with colourful fishing boats and circled by the restaurants and guest houses. The harbour is bordered by **The Lump**, a steep and stumpy peninsula that was once the site of public hangings on the island, attracting crowds of up to five thousand, the unfortunates dragged from the neighbouring jail-cum-courthouse that now houses the **tourist office**. Up above the harbour is the spick-and-span town centre, centred on **Somerled Square** and built in the late eighteenth century, when it became the island's administrative centre.

The **Royal Hotel** was where Bonnie Prince Charlie took leave of Flora MacDonald (see next page). A mile or so out of town on the Sligachan road, the **Skye Heritage Centre**, also known as *Aros* (daily April–Oct 9am–9pm; Nov–March 9am–6pm; £3.50) displays a collection of dioramas and videos that trace the troubled history of the island. For an alternative and more contemporary view of the island's heritage, head for **An Tuireann Arts Centre**, housed in a converted fever hospital on the Struan road (daily 10am–5pm; free), which puts on exhibitions, stages concerts, and has a fine café with a range of hot meals, including several veggie options.

Buses to Portree arrive in Sommerled Square, from where it's a couple of minutes' walk along Wentworth and Bank streets to the **tourist office** (April–May & mid-Sept to Oct Mon–Sat 9am–5.30pm; June to mid-Sept Mon–Sat 9am–7pm; Nov–March Mon–Fri 9am–5pm; ☎01478/612137); for **bike rental**, go to *Island Cycles* (☎01478/613121) on the Green. Portree has a good range of **hotels**, including the *Caledonian*, Wentworth St (☎01478/612641; ⑤); *The Kings Haven*, overlooking the harbour at 11 Bosville Terrace (☎01478/612290; ④); and the converted fishermen's houses of the *Rosedale Hotel*, on Beaumont Crescent (☎01478/613131; ⑥). There are plenty of **B&Bs** clustered on and around the harbour: try *The Pink Guest House* (☎01478/612263; ④) or, on Bosville Terrace, *Harbour View* (☎01478/612069; ③). The *Portree Backpackers* **hostel** (☎01478/613332) is also on the quayside; Torvaig **campsite** (April–Oct; ☎01478/612209) lies a mile and a half north off the road to Staffin.

The best **food** in town is at the *Ben Tianavaig Bistro*, 5 Bosville Terrace (☎01478/612152), which does vegetarian meals and top-quality fresh seafood. Other good choices are the restaurant in the *Rosedale Hotel* and, for a budget feast, the excellent fish-and-chip shop out towards the pier on Quay Street.

The Trotternish peninsula

Protruding twenty miles north from Portree, the **Trotternish peninsula** boasts some of the island's most bizarre scenery, particularly on the east coast, where volcanic basalt has pressed down on the softer sandstone and limestone underneath, causing massive landslides. These, in turn, have created sheer cliffs, peppered with outcrops of hard, wizened basalt, which run the full length of the coastline. These pinnacles and pillars are at their most eccentric in the Quiraing, above Staffin Bay. The peninsula is best explored with your own transport, but an occasional bus service along the road encircling the peninsula gives access to almost all the coast (ask for times at the Portree tourist office).

The east coast

The first geological eccentricity on Trotternish, six miles north of Portree along the A855, is the **Old Man of Storr**, a distinctive, pear-shaped column of rock, which along with its neighbours is part of a massive land slip, with huge blocks of stone still occasionally breaking off the cliff face of the Storr Mountain (2358ft) above and sliding downhill. At 165ft, the Old Man is a real challenge for climbers – less difficult is the brief and boggy footpath up to the foot of the column from the car park beside the main road, though it's often closed by the forest rangers when it gets too waterlogged. Eight miles further north, there's another car park for the **Kilt Rock**, whose tube-like, basaltic columns rise precipitously from the sea. A mile or two up the minor road which cuts across the peninsula from Staffin Bay, there's a path up to the savage rock formations of the **Quiraing**. a forest of mighty pinnacles including the Needle, the Prison and the Table, where Victorian ramblers used to picnic and play cricket.

For **accommodation** between the Old Man and Kilt Rock, head for the *Glenview Inn* (☎01470/562248; ③), with its very good adjoining restaurant. One of the island's best B&Bs is *Quiraing Lodge* (☎01470/562330; ③), a few minutes' walk from the main road, which serves delicious vegetarian food and also **rents bikes**. There's a **campsite** (mid-April to Sept; ☎01470/562213) at the south end of Staffin; for **food**, head for *The Oystercatcher*, which serves up wonderful seafood platters. Another excellent base for exploring the Quiraing is the exquisite *Flodigarry Country House Hotel* (☎01470/552203; ④), further up the coast between the mountains and a fossil-strewn beach. Behind the hotel is the cottage where local heroine Flora MacDonald and her family lived from 1751 to 1759. The hotel restaurant is superb, if expensive – cheaper food is available at the bar, a favourite haunt of residents from the **independent hostel**, *Dun Flodigarry Backpackers' Hostel* (☎01470/552212), a couple of minutes' walk away.

The west coast

Beyond **Flodigarry**, the road (A855) veers off to the west coast, rounding the tip of the Trotternish ridge before reaching the shattered remains of a headland fortress at

---

BONNIE PRINCE CHARLIE

Prince Charles Edward Stewart – better known as **Bonnie Prince Charlie** or "The Young Pretender " – was born in Rome in 1720, where his father, "The Old Pretender", claimant to the British throne, was living in exile. At the age of 25, with little military experience, no knowledge of Gaelic, an imperfect grasp of English and a strong attachment to the Catholic faith, the Prince set out for Scotland on a French ship, disguised as a seminarist from the Scots College in Paris. He arrived on the island of Eriskay in July 1745, and was immediately implored to return to France by the clan chiefs, who were singularly unimpressed by his lack of army. Charles was unmoved and went on to win the battle of Prestonpans, marching on London and reaching Derby before finally calling a retreat. Back in Scotland, he won one last victory at Falkirk, before the final disaster at Culloden in April 1746.

The prince spent the following five months in hiding, with a price of £30,000 on his head, and literally thousands of government troops searching for him. He certainly endured his fair share of cold and hunger whilst on the run, but the real price was paid by the Highlanders themselves, who risked their lives (and often paid for it with them) by aiding and abetting the Prince. The most famous of these was, of course, 23-year-old **Flora MacDonald**, whom Charles met on South Uist in June 1746. Flora was persuaded – either by his beauty or her relatives, depending on which account you believe – to convey Charles "over the sea to Skye", disguised as an Irish servant girl by the name of Betty Burke. Flora was arrested just seven days after parting with the Prince in Portree, and was held in the Tower of London until her release in July 1747. She went on to marry a local man, had seven children and lived to the age of sixty-eight.

Charles eventually boarded a ship back to France in September 1746, but, despite his promises – "for all that has happened, Madam, I hope we shall meet in St James's yet" – never returned to Scotland, nor did he ever see Flora again. After mistreating a string of mistresses, he eventually got married at the age of 52 to the 19-year-old Princess of Stolberg, in an effort to produce a Stewart heir. They had no children, and she eventually fled from his violent drunkenness; in 1788, a none too "bonnie" Prince Charles died in the arms of his illegitimate daughter in Rome. Bonnie Prince Charlie became a legend in his own lifetime, but it was the Victorians who really milked the myth for all its sentimentality, conveniently overlooking the fact that the real consequence of 1745 was the virtual annihilation of the Highland way of life.

DUNTULM, once a major MacDonald power base, abandoned by the clan in 1732 after a clumsy nurse dropped one of their babies from a window onto the rocks below. The swanky *Duntulm Castle Hotel* (Easter–Oct; ☎01470/552213; ④) is close by, and provides wonderful views across the Minch to the Western Isles. Heading down the west shore of the Trotternish, it's two miles to the cluster of restored thatched houses that make up the **Skye Museum of Island Life** (April–Oct Mon–Sat 9.30am–5.30pm; £1.50), though the emphasis here is strictly on tartan kitsch and the museum shop. Behind the museum up the hill are the graves of **Flora MacDonald** and her husband. Thousands turned out for her funeral in 1790, creating a funeral procession a mile long – her enormous Celtic cross headstone is inscribed with a simple, contemporaneous tribute by Dr Johnson, who visited her in 1773: "Her name will be mentioned in history, if courage and fidelity be virtues, mentioned with honour".

A further four miles south is the ferry port of **UIG** (*Uige*), which curves its way round a dramatic, horseshoe-shaped bay. Uig **campsite** (April–Oct; ☎01470/542360) is by the shore near the dock, while the **youth hostel** (mid-March to Oct; ☎01470/542211) is high up on the south side of the village. Nearby, at the other end of the accommodation spectrum, the *Uig Hotel* (April–Oct; ☎01470/542205; ⑥) serves up great homemade **food**; cheaper B&Bs include *Braeholm* (☎01470/542396; ③) and *Idrigill House* (☎01470/542316; ②). The *Sgitheanach*, at the pier, offers filling pub meals, and the garage by the ferry terminal does great coffee if you're waiting for the ferry to Tarbet (Harris) or Lochmaddy (North Uist).

The Small Isles

The history of the **Small Isles**, which lie to the south of Skye, is typical of the Hebridean islands: early Christianization, followed by a period of Norwegian rule that ended in 1266 when the islands were handed back into Scottish hands. Their support for the Jacobite cause resulted in hard times after the failed rebellion of 1745, but the biggest problems came with the introduction of the **potato**, in the mid-eighteenth century. The consequences were as dramatic as they were unforeseen: the success of the crop and its nutritional value – when grown in conjunction with traditional cereals – eliminated famine at a stroke, prompting a population explosion.

At first, the problem of overcrowding was camouflaged by the **kelp** boom, in which the islanders were employed, and the islands' owners made a fortune, gathering and burning local seaweed to sell for use in the manufacture of gunpowder, soap and glass. But the economic bubble burst with the end of the Napoleonic Wars and, to maintain their profit margins, the owners resorted to drastic action. The first to sell up was Alexander Maclean who sold Rum as grazing land for **sheep**, got quotations for shipping its people to Nova Scotia, and gave them a year's notice to quit. He also cleared Muck to graze cattle, as did the MacNeills on Canna. Only on Eigg was some compassion shown; the new owner, a certain Hugh MacPherson, who bought the island from the Clanranalds in 1827, actually gave some of his tenants extended leases.

Since the Clearances each of the islands has been bought and sold several times, though only Eigg and Muck are now privately owned: **Muck** is owned by the benevolent laird, Lawrence MacEwan, while **Eigg** changed hands in 1995 for £1.5 million, passing to a flame-throwing holistic artist from Stuttgart. The other islands were bequeathed to national agencies: **Rum**, the largest and most visited of the group, possesses a cluster of formidable volcanic peaks and the architecturally remarkable Kinloch Castle, passed to the Nature Conservancy Council (now known as Scottish Natural Heritage) in 1957; **Canna**, by far the prettiest of the Small Isles with its high basalt cliffs, went to the NTS in 1981.

From Mallaig, the round-trip passenger **ferry** crossing to the Small Isles takes around seven hours depending on the route, and far longer in rough weather. The boat bypasses at least one of the islands each weekday, but it drops by each of the four twice on Saturdays, when the sailing times make a day trip to some of them perfectly feasible. Accommodation on the Small Isles is limited and requires forward planning at all times of the year.

Canna

Measuring a mere five miles by one, and with a population of just twenty, **Canna** is run as a single farm by the NTS. The island enjoys the best harbour in the Small Isles, a horn-shaped haven at its southeastern corner protected by the tidal island of Sanday, now linked to Canna by a footbridge. For visitors, the chief pastime is walking: from the dock it's about a mile across a grassy basalt plateau to the bony seacliffs of the north shore, and about the same to the top of Compass Hill (458ft) – so called because its high metal content distorts compasses – from where you get great views across to Rum and Skye. From the buffeted western tip of the island, you can spy the **Heiskeir of Canna**, a curious mass of stone columns sticking up 30ft above the water, some seven miles offshore. There is no accommodation as such (unless you're staying for at least a week), though with permission, you may **camp rough** – remember, however, that there are no shops (bar the post office), so you must bring your own supplies.

Rum

Like Skye, **Rum** is dominated by its Cuillins, which, though they may only reach a height of 2664ft at the summit of Askival, rise up with comparable drama to the south of the island. The island's best beach is at **KILMORY**, to the north, though it is periodically out of bounds to the public, in favour of Rum's red deer population. The majority of the island's forty or so inhabitants, however, live in **KINLOCH**, on the east coast.

Rum's chief attraction is **Kinloch Castle**, a reddish sandstone edifice completed in 1901, whose elongated arcades and squat turrets dominate the village. It's an odd-looking place from the outside, and the interior is even more extraordinary, packed with knick-knacks collected by its creator, self-made millionaire Sir George Bullough. If you're not staying, ask the manager to show you Bullough's orchestrion, an electrically driven barrel organ, which still grinds out an eccentric mixture of pre-dinner tunes. The *pièce de resistance*, though, has to be Bullough's Edwardian **shower**, whose six dials, on the hooded head-piece, fire high-pressure water from every angle imaginable. Outside, but long gone, great glasshouses once sheltered tropical trees, and heated pools were stocked with turtles and alligators, though these were eventually removed at the insistence of the terrified staff. Bullough is buried in an extravagant Neoclassical mausoleum in Harris on the west coast.

Accommodation is limited to the *Kinloch Castle Hotel* (☎01687/462037; ⑨), where rates include a superb dinner and breakfast; the thirty-bed independent **youth hostel** (number as for the hotel) behind the hotel, in the old servants' quarters; and **camping** on the foreshore near the jetty (☎01687/462026). The bistro here dishes up good-value meals, though of course a meal at the castle itself is the ultimate Rum experience. Bear in mind, too, that Rum is the wettest of the generally wet Small Isles, and a haven for midges – come prepared for both.

Eigg

Eigg's main village, **GALMISDALE**, where the ferry drops anchor (again passengers are transferred to the island by a smaller boat), is in the southeast, overlooked by the island's great landmark, **An Sgurr**, a 290ft basalt stump that rises out of the 1000ft hill. The view from the latter out to Rum is spectacular, and around the summit is a large colony of Manx shearwaters. The other special feature of the island – which measures just five miles by three – is the "**Singing Sands**", to the north of the crofting hamlet of **CLEADALE**. Here, the beach is comprised of quartz, which crunches underfoot when dry (hence the name), while above rise the eccentric sandstone clifftops of Camas Sgiotaig. The best of three places **to stay** on Eigg is the refurbished, three-bedroomed croft house, *Lageorna* (☎01687/482405; ②); even cheaper hostel-style accommodation is available at *Laig Farm* (☎01687/482437); there's a shop and post office at Galmisdale.

Muck

Smallest and most southerly of the Small Isles, **Muck** is low-lying, mostly treeless and extremely fertile, and as such shares more characteristics with the likes of Coll and Tiree than its nearest neighbours. Its name derives from *muc*, the Gaelic for "pig" and has long caused much embarassment to generations of lairds who preferred to call it the "Isle of Monk", because it had briefly belonged to the medieval church. **GALLANACH** is the island village, with a fine beach and plenty of opporunities for observing Muck's rich wildlife; **PORT MOR**, on the southeast corner of the island, is where the ferry drops anchor and discharges its passengers onto a smaller vessel. The MacEwan family, who have owned the island since 1879, run the island as a single farm, with around 25 inhabitants. To **stay** here, contact the island Estate Office (☎01687/462365), who may grant permission for **rough camping**.

The Western Isles

The wild and windy **Western Isles** – also known as the Outer Hebrides – vaunt a strikingly hostile mix of landscapes from windswept golden sands to harsh, heather-backed mountains and peat bogs. An elemental beauty pervades each one of the more than two hundred islands that make up the archipelago, only thirteen of which are actually inhabited by a total of just over 30,000 people. The influence of the Atlantic Gulf Stream ensures a mild but moist climate, though you can expect the strong Atlantic winds to blow in rain on two out of every three days even in summer. Weather fronts, however, come and go at such dramatic speed in these parts, there's little chance of mist or fog settling and fewer problems with midges.

The most significant difference between Skye and the Western Isles is that here, tourism is much less important to the islands' fragile economy – still mainly concentrated around crofting, fishing and weaving. The Outer Hebrides also remain the heartland of **Gaelic** culture, with the language spoken by the vast majority of islanders, though its everyday usage remains under constant threat from the national dominance of English. Its survival is, in no small part, due to the all-pervading influence of the Free Church, whose strict Calvinism is the creed of the vast majority of the population, with only South Uist, Barra and parts of Benbecula adhering to the relatively more relaxed demands of Catholicism.

The interior of the northernmost island, **Lewis**, is mostly peat moor, a barren and marshy tract that gives way abruptly to the bare peaks of **North Harris**. Across a narrow isthmus lies **South Harris**, presenting some of the finest scenery in Scotland, with wide sandy beaches trimming the Atlantic in full view of the mountains and a rough boulder-strewn interior lying to the east. Further south still, a string of tiny, flatter islets, mainly **North Uist**, **Benbecula**, **South Uist** and **Barra**, offer breezy beaches, whose fine sands front a narrow band of boggy farmland, which, in turn, is mostly bordered by a lower range of hills to the east.

GAELIC IN THE WESTERN ISLES

Except in Stornoway, and Balivanich on North Uist, **road signs** are now exclusively in **Gaelic**, a difficult language to the English-speaker's eye, with complex pronunciation, though as a (very) general rule, the English names can often provide a rough pronunciation guide. Particularly if you're driving, it's essential to buy the bilingual Western Isles map, produced by the local tourist board, *Bord Turasachd nan Eilean*, and available at most tourist offices. In the text, we've put the English first, with the Gaelic in brackets; thereafter we've stuck to the English names.

In direct contrast to their wonderful landscapes, the Western Isles claim only the scrawniest of villages, unhappy-looking places that straggle out along the elementary road system. Only **Tarbert**, on Harris, and **Lochmaddy**, on North Uist, sustain a modicum of charm; **Stornoway**, Lewis's only town, is eminently unappealing. Many visitors, walkers and nature watchers forsake the settlements altogether and retreat to secluded cottages and B&Bs – though this is difficult without your own transport.

Visiting the Western Isles

British Airways operates fast and frequent **flights** from Glasgow to Stornoway on Lewis, Barra and Benbecula on North Uist. *British Airways Express* (also known as *Loganair*) has small planes flying from Stornoway to Benbecula and Barra. But be warned, the weather conditions on the islands are notoriously changeable, making these flights both prone to delay and sometimes stomach-churningly bumpy. On Barra, the other complication is that you land on the beach, so the timetable is adjusted with the tides. *CalMac* **car ferries** run from Ullapool in the Highlands to Stornoway; from Uig, on Skye, to Tarbert and Lochmaddy; and from Oban to South Uist and Barra. There's also an inter-island ferry from Lochmaddy to Tarbert, and a couple of smaller inter-island routes (for more on ferry services, see "Travel details").

Lewis (Leodhas)

Shaped rather like the top of an ice-cream cone, **Lewis** is the largest and most populous of the Western Isles and the northernmost island in the Hebridean archipelago. After Viking rule ended in 1266, the island was fought over by the MacLeods and MacKenzies, until eventually being sold by the latter in 1844. The new owner, Sir James Matheson, invested heavily in new industries, as **Lord Leverhulme** did with the fishing industry when he aquired the island (along with Harris) in 1918. Though undoubtedly a benevolent despot, Leverhulme's unpopularity with many on Lewis, and his financial difficulties, forced him to give up his grandiose plans in 1923, when he gifted the island to its inhabitants. His departure, however, left a big gap in the economy, and between the wars thousands more emigrated.

Most of the island's 20,000 inhabitants – two thirds of the Western Isles' total population – now live in the crofting and fishing villages strung out along the northwest coast, between Callanish and Port of Ness. On this coast you'll find the islands' best-preserved **prehistoric remains** – at Carloway and Callanish – as well as a smattering of ancient crofters' houses in various stages of abandonment. The landscape is mostly flat peat bog – hence the island's name, derived from the Gaelic *leogach* (marshy) – with a gentle shoreline that only fulfils its dramatic potential around Rubha Robhanais (the Butt of Lewis), a group of rough rocks on the island's northernmost tip, near Port Nis. To the south, where it is physically joined with the Isle of Harris, the land rises to just over 1800ft, providing a more exhilarating backdrop for the excellent beaches, peppered along the isolated coastline to the southwest of Callanish.

Most visitors use Stornoway, on the east coast, as a base for exploring the island, though this presents problems if you're travelling by **bus**. There's a regular service to Port of Ness and Tarbert, and although the most obvious excursion – the 45-mile round trip from Stornoway to Callanish, Carloway, Arnol and back – is almost impossible to complete by public transport, the tourist office's minibus tours make the trip on most days from April to October.

Stornoway (Steornabhagh)

In these parts, **STORNOWAY** is a buzzing metropolis, with some eight thousand inhabitants, a one-way system, pedestrian precinct and all the trappings of a large town. It is a centre for employment, a social hub for the island's youth, and perhaps most importantly of all, home to the **Comhairle nan Eilean** (Western Isles Council), set up in 1974, which has done so much to promote Gaelic language and culture, trying to stem the tide of anglicization. Despite its valiant attempts in that quarter, it is perhaps better known for its supremely incompetent finanicial dealings, which lost the islands £23 million, following the collapse of the *Bank of Credit and Commerce International* (BCCI) in 1991. For the visitor, however, the town is unlikely to win any great praise – aesthetics is not its strong point, and the urban pleasures on offer are limited.

The best thing about Stornoway is the convenience of its services. The island's **airport** is four miles east of the town centre, a £5 taxi ride away, and the **ferry** terminal only a couple of minutes' walk along the harbour front from the **bus station** on South Beach. The **tourist office** is nearby at 26 Cromwell St (mid-Oct to March Mon–Fri 9am–5pm; April to mid-Oct Mon–Fri 9am–6pm, Sat 9am–5pm; ☎01851/703088). For **B&Bs** along Matheson Rd, *Mrs C. Macleod*, at no. 19 (☎01851/704180; ②), and *Mrs A Macleod*, at no. 12 (☎01851/702673; ③), are both good. Other convenient options include *Mrs MacMillan*, 64 Keith St (☎01851/704815; ②), and *Mrs Skinner*, 29 Francis St (☎01851/703482; ③). Stornoway's **independent hostel** is a basic affair about five minutes' walk from the ferry at 47 Keith St (March–Nov; ☎01851/703628). The nearest **campsite**, the *Laxdale Holiday Park* (April–Oct; ☎01851/703234), lies a mile or so along the road to Barabhas, on Laxdale Lane. For **bike rental** go to *Alex Dan's Cycle Centre*, 67 Kenneth St (Mon–Sat 9am–6pm; ☎01851/704025 or 702934).

As for **food**, you can get satisfying snacks and lunches from the *An Lanntair Art Gallery*'s coffee shop, while the *Fisherman Cafeteria* (Mon–Fri 8am–5pm) serves good-value, filling meals in the *National Mission to Deep Sea Fishermen* building on North Beach; the *Crown Hotel*, nearby on Castle Street, serves huge main courses as part of its evening menu – the fish, especially, is delicious; the *Park Guest House*, James St, is another good place to sample the local shellfish; for a more surreal experience, head for *Ali's*, the tandoori place near the bus station on South Beach. The few **pubs** that exist on Lewis are in Stornoway; try either *The Criterion*, Point St, or the *Royal Hotel*, Cromwell St. The most famous watering hole, though, is the bar of the aforementioned *Crown Hotel*, now named after Prince Charles, who drank a cherry brandy here whilst on a school sailing trip (and, more controversially, whilst still under 18).

Barvas (Barabhas) to Port of Ness (Port Nis)

Northwest of Stornoway, the A857 crosses the vast, barren **peat bog** of the interior, an empty wilderness riddled with stretch marks formed by peat cuttings and pockmarked with freshwater lochans. The whole area was once covered by forests, but these disappeared long ago, leaving a smothering deposit of peat that is, on average, 6ft thick, and is still being formed in certain places. For the people of Lewis, peat is a valuable energy resource, with each crofter being assigned a slice of the bog. The islanders spend several very sociable weeks each spring cutting the peat, turning it over and leaving it neatly laid out in the open air to dry, returning in summer to collect the dried sods and stack them outside their houses. Though tempting to take home as souvenirs, these piles are the fruits of hard labour, and remain the island's main source of domestic fuel, its pungent smoke one of the most characteristic smells of the Western Isles.

Twelve miles across the peat bog the road divides, heading southwest towards Callanish (see below), or northeast through **BARVAS** (Barabhas), and a whole string of bleak, fervently Free Church, crofting and weaving villages. Be prepared for the fact that these scattered settlements have none of the photogenic qualities of Skye's white-washed villages. The churches are plain and unadorned; the crofters' houses are fairly modern and smothered in grey, concrete rendering; the stone cottages and enclosures of their forebears often lie half-abandoned in the front garden; while a rusting assort-ment of discarded cars and vans now serves to store peat bags and the like. The main road continues through a string of straggling villages, terminating at the remote village **PORT OF NESS** (Port Nis), nestled round its tiny harbour.

From Port Nis, a minor road heads two miles north to the hamlet of **EOROPIE** (Europaidh) and the **Teampull Mholuaidh** (St Moluag's Church), an austere stone structure dating from the twelfth century. From Europaidh, a narrow road twists north to the bleak and blustery tip of the island, well known to devotees of the BBC shipping forecast as the **Butt of Lewis** (Rubha Robhanais), where a lighthouse sticks up above a series of sheer cliffs and stacks, alive with a cacophany of sea birds, and a great place for seal spotting.

Several **B&Bs** line the main road between Barvas and Port of Ness: one of the most comfortable is *Harbour View* (☎01851/810735; ③), located in an old boatbuilder's house overlooking Port of Nessharbour, and offering good home-cooked food. Other places to stay include the modern Gaelic croft of *Ms Catriona MacLeod* (☎01851/810240; ③) in Coig Peighinnean (Five Penny Borve), four miles northeast of Barvas, and *Mrs Alice MacLeod* (May–Oct; ☎01851/810496; ③) in Lional (Lionel). The luxury option is *Galson Farm* (☎01851/850492; ④), an eighteenth-century farmhouse in South Galson (Gabhsann Bho Dheas), halfway between Barvas and Port of Ness.

Arnol to Callanish (Calanais)

Heading southwest from the crossroads near Barabhas, brings you to the village of **ARNOL**, which meanders down towards the sea. At the far end of the village is the **Black House Museum** (Mon–Sat April–Sept 9.30am–6.30pm; Oct–March 9.30am–4pm; £1.50), which dates from the 1870s and was inhabited right up until 1964. Built low against the wind, the house's thick walls are made up of an inner and outer layer of loose stone on either side of a central core of earth, a traditional type of construction which attracted the soubriquet "black house" around 1850, when buildings with single-thickness walls were introduced to Lewis from the mainland and were commonly called "white houses" (*tigh geal*) by the locals – even though they weren't all white. Thus traditional dwellings came to be called "black houses" (*tigh dubh*).

Returning to the main road, it's about eight miles to the sprawling trio of hamlets that all translate as Carloway. The last of the lot is **DOUNE CARLOWAY** (Dun Charlabhaigh), where **Carloway Broch** perches on top of a conspicuous rocky outcrop overlooking the sea about four hundred yards from the road. Scotland's Atlantic coast is strewn with the remains of over five hundred brochs, or fortified towers, but this is one of the best preserved, its drystone circular walls reaching a height of over 30ft on the seaward side. The broch consists of two concentric walls, the inner one perpendicular, the outer one slanting inwards, originally fastened together by roughly hewn flagstones, which also served as look-out galleries reached via a narrow stairwell. The only entrance to the roofless inner yard is through a low doorway set beside a crude and cramped guard cell. As at Callanish (see below), there have been all sorts of theories about the purpose of the brochs, which date from between 100 BC and 100 AD; the most likely explanation is that they were built to provide protection from Roman slave traders.

RELIGION IN THE WESTERN ISLES

Sharply divided – although with little enmity – between the Catholic southern isles of Barra and South Uist, and the Protestant north of North Uist, Harris and Lewis, it is difficult to underestimate the importance of **religion** in the Western Isles. Most conflicts arise from the very considerable power the ministers of the Protestant Church, or Kirk, wield in secular life in the north, where the creed of **Sabbatarianism** is very strong. Here, Sunday is the Lord's Day, and virtually the whole community (irrespective of their degree of piety) stops work – all shops close, all pubs close, all garages close and there's no public transport, but perhaps most famously of all, even the swings in the children's playgrounds are padlocked.

The other main area of division is, paradoxically, within the Protestant Church itself. Scotland is unusual in that the national church, the **Church of Scotland**, is presbyterian (ruled by the ministers and elders of the church) rather than episcopal (ruled by bishops). At the time of the main split in the Presbyterian Church – the so-called **1843 Disruption** – a third of its ministers left the Church of Scotland, protesting at the law which allowed landlords to impose ministers against parishioners' wishes, and formed the breakaway **Free Church**. Since those days there has been a partial reconciliation; although, in 1893, there was another break, when a minority of the Free Church became the Free Presbyterian Church, while the rest slowly made their way back to the Church of Scotland. The remaining rump of the Free Church – better known as the "Wee Frees" – have their spiritual heartland on Lewis. To confuse matters further, as recently as 1988, the Free Presbyterian Church split over a minister who attended a requiem mass during a Catholic funeral of a friend – he and his supporters have since formed the breakaway Associated Presbyterian Churches.

The various brands and subdivisions of the Presbyterian Church may appear trivial to outsiders, but to the churchgoers of Lewis, Harris and North Uist (as well as much of Skye and Raasay) they are still keenly felt. In part, for social and cultural reasons: Free Church elders helped organize resistance to the Clearances, and the Wee Frees have done the most to help preserve the Gaelic language. A Free Church service is a memorable experience, and in some villages it takes place every evening (and twice on Sundays): there's no set service or prayer book, only Biblical readings, plainchant and a fiery sermon all in Gaelic; the pulpit is the architectural focus of the church, not the altar, and communion is taken only on special occasions.

From Carlabhagh (Carloway), the middle hamlet, you can turn down the mile-long road to the beautifully remote coastal settlement of **GARENIN** (Gearrannan), where several old thatched crofters' houses have been restored, one of which now serves as a primitive **youth hostel** (no phone). The nearest store is back in Carlabhagh.

Five miles south of Doune Carloway lies the village of **CALLANISH** (Calanais), site of the islands' most dramatic prehistoric ruins, the **Callanish Standing Stones**, whose monoliths – nearly fifty of them – occupy a dramatic lochside setting. There's been years of heated debate about the origin and function of the stones – slabs of gnarled and finely grained gneiss up to 15ft high – though almost everyone agrees that they were lugged here by Neolithic peoples between 3000 and 1500 BC. It's also obvious that the planning and construction of the site – as well as several other lesser circles nearby – were spread over many generations. Such an endeavour could, it's been argued, only be prompted by the desire to predict the seasonal cycle upon which these early farmers were entirely dependent, and indeed, many of the stones are aligned with the position of the sun and the stars. This rational explanation, based on clear evidence that this part of Lewis was once a fertile farming area, dismisses as coincidence the ground plan of the site, which resembles a colossal Celtic cross, and explains away the central burial chamber as a later addition of no special significance. These two features have fuelled all sorts of theories ranging from alien intervention to human sacrifice.

You can't actually walk between the stones anymore, only by the fence that surrounds them. An adjacent black house has been refurbished as a **tea shop**, but there's an even bigger **visitor centre** now built on the other side of the stones (thankfully out of view). Nearby, beside the village post office, is the **B&B** of *Mrs Cathy Crossley*, 24 Callanish (March–Oct; ☎01851/621236; ②); there's another, just as good, *Mrs Catherine Morrison*, at no. 27 (March–Oct; ☎01851/621392; ③).

Harris (Na Hearadh)

The "division" between Lewis and **Harris** – they are, in fact, one island – is embedded in a historical split in the MacLeod clan, lost in the mists of time. The border between the two was also a county boundary until 1975, with Harris lying in Inverness-shire, and Lewis belonging to Ross and Cromarty. Nowadays, the dividing line is rarely marked even on maps, though for the record, it comprises Loch Resort in the west, Loch Seaforth in the east, and the six miles in between. Harris itself is more clearly divided by a minuscule isthmus, into the wild, inhospitable mountains of North Harris and the gentler landscape and sandy shores of South Harris.

Along with Lewis, Harris was purchased in 1918 by **Lord Leverhulme**, and after 1923 when he pulled out of Lewis, all his efforts were concentrated here. In contrast to Lewis, though, Leverhulme and his ambitious projects were broadly welcomed by the people of Harris. His most grandiose plans were drawn up for Leverburgh, but he also purchased an old Norwegian whaling station in Bunavoneadar in 1922, built a spinning mill at Geocrab and began the construction of four roads. Financial difficulties, a slump in the tweed industry and the lack of market for whale products meant that none was a whole-hearted success, and when he died in 1925, the plug was pulled on all of them.

Since the Leverhulme era, unemployment has been a constant problem in Harris. Crofting continues on a small scale, supplemented by the Harris Tweed industry, though the main focus of this has shifted to Lewis (see p.854). Fishing continues on Scalpay, while the rest of the population gets by on whatever employment is available: road works, crafts and, of course, tourism.

Tarbert (Tairbeart)

The largest place on Harris is the ferry port of **TARBERT**, sheltered in a green valley on the narrow isthmus that marks the border between North and South Harris. The town's mountainous backdrop is impressive, though there's nothing much to the place – just a few terraces sloping up from the dock. However, it does boast the only **tourist office** (April to mid-Oct Mon–Sat 9am–5pm; summer also Tues, Thurs & Sat 8–9pm; ☎01859/502011) on Harris, close to the ferry terminal. The office can arrange accommodation and has a full set of bus timetables, but its real value is as a source of information on local walks.

If you wish to base yourself in Tarbert, try the easy-going, old-fashioned *Harris Hotel* (☎01859/502154; ⑤), five minutes' walk from the ferry back towards Stornoway. Cheaper, equally convenient places to stay include the *Allan Cottage Guest House* (April–Oct; ☎01859/502146; ④), in the old telephone exchange, and a couple of nearby **B&Bs**, *Rockcliffe* (☎01859/502386; ③) and *Dunard* (☎01859/502340; ③). Excellent, reasonably priced **food** is served at both the *Harris Hotel* and the *Allan Cottage*. The nearest hostels lie to the south of Tarbert: the official **youth hostel** (late March to Sept; ☎01859/530373) is in a converted school in Kyles Stockinish (Caolas Stocinis), six miles to the south; an **independent hostel** (☎01851/511255) lies three miles further south in Drinishader (Drinisiadar).

North Harris (Ceann a Tuath na Hearadh)

The A859 north to Stornoway takes you over a boulder-strewn saddle between mighty **Sgaoth Aird** (1829ft) and **Clisham** (2619ft), the highest peak in the Western Isles.

HARRIS TWEED

Far from being a picturesque cottage industry, as it's sometimes presented, the production of **Harris Tweed** is vital to the local economy with a well-organized and unionized workforce. Traditionally the tweed was made by women, from the wool of their own sheep, to provide clothing for their families. Each woman was responsible for the entire process, from the washing and scouring of the wool through to its dyeing, carding, spinning and warping; finally the cloth was dipped in sheep urine and "waulked" by a group of women, who beat the cloth on a table whilst singing Gaelic waulking songs. Harris Tweed was originally made all over the islands, and was known simply as *clò mór* (big cloth).

In the mid-nineteenth century, the Countess of Dunmore, who owned a large part of Harris, started to sell surplus cloth to her aristocratic friends, thus forming the genesis of the modern industry, which now employs about 400 mill workers and a further 650 weavers – though demand and employment fluctuate wildly as fashions change. To earn the official Harris Tweed Association trademark of the Orb and the Maltese Cross, the fabric has to be hand-woven on the Outer Hebrides from 100 percent pure new Scottish wool, while the other parts of the manufacturing process must take place only in the local mills.

The main centre of production is now Lewis, where the wool is dyed, carded and spun; you can see all these processes by visiting the **Lewis Loom Centre**, on Point Street in Stornoway (Mon–Sat 10am–6pm; £1.50). In recent years, there has been a revival of traditional tweed-making techniques, with several small producers, like *Clo Mór* in Likisto (Liceasto; ☎01859/530364), religiously following old methods. One of the more interesting aspects of the process is the use of indigenous plants and bushes to dye the cloth: yellow comes from rocket and broom, green from heather, grey and black from iris and oak, and, most popular of all, reddish brown from crotal, a flat grey lichen scraped off rocks.

This bitter terrain offers but the barest of vegetation, with the occasional cluster of crofters' houses sitting in the shadow of a host of pointed peaks, anywhere between 1000ft and 2500ft high. These bulging, pyramidical mountains reach their climax around the dramatic shores of the fjord-like **Loch Seaforth**. If you're planning on walking in North Harris, the spectacular *Ardvourlie Castle* (☎01859/502307; ⑧), by the shores of Loch Seaforth, is a wonderful, though pricey launch pad.

A cheaper, but equally idyllic spot is the *Gatliff Trust's* **youth hostel** (no phone) in the lonely coastal hamlet of **RHENIGDALE** (Reinigeadal), until very recently only accessible by foot or boat. To reach the hostel without your own transport, walk east five miles from Tarbert along the road to **KYLES SCALPAY** (Caolas Scalpaigh). After another mile or so, watch for the sign marking the start of the path which threads its way through the peaks of the craggy promontory that lies trapped between Loch Seaforth and East Loch Tarbert. It's a magnificent hike, with superb views out along the coast and over the mountains, but you'll need to be properly equipped and should allow three hours for the one-way trip.

South Harris (Ceann a Deas)
The mountains of **South Harris** are less dramatic than in the north, but the scenery is equally breathtaking. There's a choice of routes from Tarbert to the ferry port of Leverburgh, which connects with North Uist (passengers only); the east coast, known as Bays (Na Baigh), is rugged and seemingly inhospitable, while the west coast is endowed with some of the finest stretches of golden sand in the whole of the archipelago, buffeted by the Atlantic winds. Paradoxically, most people on South Harris live along the harsh eastern coastline rather than the more fertile west side, though not by choice – they were evicted from their original crofts to make way for sheep-grazing.

The main road from Tarbert into South Harris follows the **west coast**, snaking its way west across the lunaresque interior to emerge, after ten miles, at Seilebost, situated above the first of a chain of sweeping sandy **beaches**, backed by rich machair, that stretches for nine miles along the Atlantic coast. In good weather, the scenery is stunning, foaming breakers rolling along the golden sands set against the rounded peaks of the mountains to the north and the islet-studded turquoise sea to the west. Good-value **B&Bs** along the coast include *Moravia* (March–Oct; ☎01859/550262; ③) in Luskentyre (Losgaintir), on the north side of the loch. The swankiest accommodation is three miles further south at *Scarista House* (May–Sept; ☎01859/550238; ⑧), which looks out to sea from above the beach in the village of Scarista (Sgarasta). *Mrs Mary Morrison*'s B&B (April–Sept; ☎01859/520228; ③) is the lee of the sharp headland bordering Harris's last tidal beach in the bayside village of Northton (Taobh Tuath).

From Northton, the road veers to the southeast to trim the island's south shore, eventually reaching the sprawling settlement of **LEVERBURGH** (An t-Ob), named after Lord Leverhulme, who planned to turn the place into the largest fishing port on the west coast of Scotland. From a jetty about a mile south of the main road, a passenger **ferry** leaves for Berneray and North Uist (contact Donald MacAskill on ☎01876/540230), though you need to plan ahead if you're going to the latter as public transport is very limited. There are several **B&Bs** within a two-mile radius of Leverburgh: try *Garryknowe*, Ferry Rd (April–Oct; ☎01859/520246; ③), not too far from the jetty, or *Paula Williams* (☎01859/520319; ③), who offers vegetarian meals.

Three miles southeast of Leverburgh and a mile or so from Renish Point, the southern tip of Harris, is the old port of **RODEL** (Roghadal), where a smattering of ancient stone houses lies among the hillocks surrounding the dilapidated harbour. On top of one of these grassy humps is the castellated tower and thick-walled nave of **St Clement's Church**, burial place of the MacLeods of Harris and Dunvegan in Skye. Dating from the 1520s, the church's gloomy interior is distinguished by its wall-tombs, notably that of the founder, Alasdair Crotach (also known as Alexander MacLeod), whose heavily weathered effigy lies beneath an intriguing cartoon strip of vernacular and religious scenes – elemental representations of, among others, a stag hunt, the Holy Trinity, St Michael, and the Devil weighing the souls of the dead. Look out, too, for the *sheila-na-gig* below a carving of St Clement himself.

North Uist (Uibhist a Tuath)

After the stunning scenery of Harris, the much flatter scenery of **North Uist** – seventeen miles long and thirteen miles wide – cannot help but be something of an anticlimax. Over half the surface area is covered by water, creating a distinctive lochan-studded landscape reminiscent of north Lewis. The main attractions for visitors are its vast sandy beaches, which extend – almost without interruption – along the north and west coast, and the smattering of prehistoric sites on the island.

Despite being situated on the east coast, some distance away from any beach, the ferry port of **LOCHMADDY** (Loch nam Madadh) is easily the best base for exploring the island. The village itself, occupying a narrow, bumpy promontory, is nothing special, though if you've time to kill, take a look round **Taigh Chearsabhagh** (Mon–Sat 10am–5pm; £1.50), a converted eighteenth-century merchant's house, which now harbours the local museum, arts centre and café. Right by the **tourist office** (mid-April to mid-Oct Mon–Sat 9am–5pm; ☎01876/500321) is the spick-and-span *Lochmaddy Hotel* (☎01876/500331; ⑦), whose restaurant serves outstanding seafood and whose bar is the liveliest place on the whole island. There are also a couple of nice Victorian **B&Bs** – the *Old Courthouse* (☎01876/500358; ③), and the *Old Bank House* (☎01876/500275; ③). The SYHA **youth hostel** is *Ostram House* (mid-May to Sept; ☎01876/500368), half a mile from the ferry dock. Not far beyond, the independent hostel in the *Uist Outdoor Centre* (☎01876/500480) offers four-person bunk rooms. The only **bike rental** on the island is at *Morrison Cycle Hire* (☎01876/580211), nine miles away in Carinish (Cairinis), but they will deliver to Lochmaddy if you phone them.

Two prehistoric sights lie within easy cycling distance of Lochmaddy (or even walking distance if you use the postbus for the outward journey). The most significant is the **Barpa Langass**, a large mostly intact chambered cairn seven barren miles to the southwest along the A867; a mile to the southeast is the small stone circle of **Pobull Fhinn**. Three miles northwest of Lochmaddy along the A865 is **Na Fir Bhreige** (The Three False Men), three standing stones which, depending on your legend, mark the graves of three spies buried alive, or three men who deserted their wives and were turned to stone by a proto-feminist witch.

North Uist's other main draw is the **Baranald RSPB Reserve**, in the northwest corner of the island, one of the last breeding grounds of the corncrake, among Europe's most endangered birds. Sightings are rare even here, and you'll only get to hear it if you stay up half the night. The two-mile walk along the headland of the reserve, however, should give ample opportunity for spotting skuas, gannets and Manx shearwaters out to sea – guided walks take place throughout the summer (for more details, contact the warden; ☎01878/602188). A good place for "twitchers" (birders) to **stay** is at *Mrs Joan MacDonald* (☎01876/510279; ②) overlooking the beautiful beach at Hougharry (Hogha Gearraidh), a mile south of Tigh a Ghearraidh.

On leaving North Uist to the south, the main road squeezes along a series of causeways, built by the military in 1960, that trim the west edge of **Grimsay** (Griomasaigh), a peaceful, little visited lobster-fishing island, before heading across to Benbecula.

Berneray (Bearnaraigh)

For those in search of still more seclusion, there's the low-lying island of **Berneray** – eight miles in circumference with a population of just over one hundred – accessible via a short car ferry journey from Newtonferry, eight miles north of Lochmaddy (or passenger ferry from Leverburgh on South Harris). The island's main claim to fame is as the birthplace of Giant MacAskill, and as the favoured holiday hideaway of that other great eccentric, Prince Charles, lover of Gaelic culture, and royal potato picker to local crofter, "Splash" MacKillop. Apart from the sheer peace and isolation of the place, the island's main draw for non-royals is the three-mile long sandy beach on the west coast, two miles across country from the ferry dock. Should you wish to stay, try the **B&Bs** of *Mrs MacLeod* (☎01876/540254; ③) or *Donald MacKillop* (☎01876/540235; ③); or the simple *Gatliff Trust* **youth hostel** (no phone), in a pair of thatched black houses two miles from the dock, on the north side of Bays Loch.

Benbecula (Beinn na Faoghla)

Blink and you could miss the pancake-flat island of **Benbecula** (put the stress on the second syllable), sandwiched between Protestant North Uist and Catholic South Uist. Most visitors simply trundle along the main road that cuts across the middle of the island in less than five miles – not such a bad idea, since nearly half the island's 1200 population are Royal Artillery personnel, working at the missile range on South Uist. Nearly all the military personnel live in the barracks-like housing developments of **BALIVANICH** (Baile a Mhanaich), the grim, grey capital of Benbecula in the northwest. The only reason to come here at all is if you happen to be flying into or out of Balivanich airport (direct flights to Glasgow, Barra and Stornoway), or need to stock up on provisions, best done at the NAAFI "family store", the only one in the UK that's open to the public.

South Uist (Uibhist a Deas)

To the south of Benbecula, the island of **South Uist** is arguably the most appealing of the southern chain of islands. The west coast boasts some of the region's finest beaches – a necklace of gold and grey sand strung twenty miles from one end to the other – while the east coast features a ridge of high mountains rising to 2034ft at the summit of Beinn Mhor. The only blot on the landscape is the Royal Artillery missile range, which occupies the island's northwest, shattering the peace and quiet every so often.

The Reformation never reached South Uist (or Barra), and the island remains Roman Catholic, as is evident from the slender modern statue of *Our Lady of the Isles* that stands by the main road below the small hill of **Rueval**, known to the locals as "Space City" for its forest of aerials and golf balls, which help track the missles heading out into the Atlantic. To the south of Rueval is the freshwater **Loch Druidibeg**, a breeding ground for greylag geese (there's a hide along the road to the north) and a favourite spot for mute swans.

A whole series of country lanes lead west from the island's one main road to the old crofters' villages that straggle along the coast, but – although the paths are rarely more than three miles long – it's surprisingly easy to get lost, tramping round in circles before you stumble upon the shore. This is not the case, however, at **HOWMORE** (Tobha Mor), with its easy mile-long walk from the main road to the gorgeous beach. The village is the prettiest place for miles, the shattered ruins of its medieval chapel and burial ground standing near a cluster of neat little black houses, one of which, the *Gatliff Trust*, operates as a **youth hostel** (no phone).

Six miles south of Tobha Mor, the main road passes the cairn that sits amongst the ruins of **Flora MacDonald's** birthplace (see p.850), before continuing for another seven miles to the ferry terminal of **LOCHBOISDALE** (Loch Baghasdail). Like Lochmaddy in North Uist, Lochboisdale occupies a narrow, bumpy promontory and is the island's chief settlement, though, if anything, it has less to offer than Lochmaddy, with no youth hostel and just the *Lochboisdale Hotel* (☎01878/700332; ⑤) for somewhere to have a drink and a bite to eat. The **tourist office** (Easter to mid-Oct Mon–Sat 9am–1pm & 2–5pm; ☎01878/700286), by the harbour, is also open to meet the night ferry from Oban. There are also several **B&Bs** within comfortable walking distance of the dock: try *Bayview* (March–Oct; ☎01878/700329; ②), or *Lochside Cottage* (☎01878/700472; ②). **Bike rental** is available from *NJ Cycle Hire*.

If you're heading on south to the island of Barra from South Uist, there's an alternative to the *CalMac* ferry from Lochboisdale: the passenger ferry from **Ludag jetty**, ten miles by road from Lochboisdale (buses twice daily), which lands at Eoligarry on the north coast of Barra.

Eriskay (Eiriosgaigh)

Also from Ludag, a frequent car ferry slips across to Haun jetty on the hilly island of **Eriskay**, which lies between South Uist and Barra. For a small island, Eriskay has had more than its fair share of historical headlines. It was on the island's main beach on the west coast on July 23, 1745, that Bonnie Prince Charlie landed on Scottish soil – a big pink convolvulus grows there to this day, said to have sprung from the seeds Charles brought with him from France. Eriskay's other claim to fame came in 1941 when the SS *Politician* sank on its way from Liverpool to Jamaica, along with its cargo of bicycle parts, £3 million in Jamaican currency and 243,000 bottles of whisky, inspiring Compton Mackenzie's book – and the Ealing Comedy (filmed here in 1948) – *Whisky Galore!* (released as *Tight Little Island* in the US). The ship's stern can still be seen to the east of the Isle of Calvey at low tide, and one of the original bottles (and lots of other related memorabilia) is one show in the bar of *The Politician* in the main village of **BALLA** (Baile). As for **accommodation**, there's a self-catering flat (☎01878/720274) but no B&Bs & few amenities – just a shop and a post office.

Barraigh (Barra)

Just four miles wide and eight miles long, **Barra** has a deserved reputation of being the Western Isles in miniature. It has sandy beaches, backed by machair, glacial mountains, prehistoric ruins, Gaelic culture and a laid-back Catholic population of just under 1500. The only settlement of any size is the old herring port of **CASTLEBAY** (Bagh a Chaisteil), which curves around the barren hills of a wide bay on the south side of the island (ferries from Lochboisdale, on South Uist, and Oban stop here). Barra's religious allegiance is immediately apparent thanks to the large Catholic church, Our Lady, Star of the Sea, which overlooks the Castlebay, and the Madonna with Child which stands on the slopes of Heaval (1260ft), the largest peak on Barra.

As its name suggests, Castlebay has a castle in its bay, the medieval islet-fortress of **Kisimul Castle** (opening times subject to tides – check at the tourist office), ancestral home of the MacNeil clan. The MacNeils owned Barra from 1427 to 1838, when they sold it to the infamous Colonel Gordon of Cluny, who offered to clear the island and turn into a state penal colony. The government declined, and in 1937, the 45th chief of the MacNeil clan bought back the castle (and 12,000 acres). It has since been restored to something of its original appearance, making a visit just about worth the effort, though it's best viewed from the ferry. Most people, however, come to Barra for the peace and quiet, walking across the hilly interior or making the twelve-mile excursion right round the island by road.

Barra airport, on the north side of the island, is a sight in itself, with the planes having to land and take off from the shell sands of **Tràigh Mhór** (Cockle Strand); the exact timing of the flights depends on the tides, since at high tide the beach (and therefore the runway) is covered in water. Tràigh Mhór is also famous for its cockles and cockleshells, the latter being used to make harling (the rendering used on most Scottish houses). In 1994, mechanical cockle extraction using tractors was introduced, and quickly began to decimate the cockle stocks and threaten the beach's use as an aiport – as a result it has now been banned, in favour of traditional hand-raking.

A **postbus** does the rounds of the island (Mon–Sat); you can get **bike rental** from *MacDougall Cycles*, 29 St Brendan Rd (☎01871/810284). Near the jetty, the **tourist office** (April to mid-Oct Mon–Sat 9am–1pm & 2–5pm; also open for late ferry arrivals; ☎01871/810336) will advise on walking routes; they also have details of accommodation, including several cheap **B&Bs** clustered in and around Castlebay – try *Tigh-na-*

Mara (April–Oct; ☎01871/810304; ③), or *Grianamul* (April–Oct; ☎01871/810416; ③) – as well as two **hotels**, the *Craigard* (☎01871/810200; ⑥) and the *Castlebay* (☎01871/810223; ⑤). The *Kisimul Gallery* offers a limited selection of **food** and a good bakery. If you're looking for a more isolated spot, the *Isle of Barra Hotel* (April–Oct; ☎01871/810383; ⑥) overlooks the sandy beach of Halaman Bay on the west coast near **TANGASDALE** (Tangasdal). On the other side of the island at **NORTHBAY** (Bagh a Tuath), you've a choice of *Northbay House* (April–Oct; ☎01871/890255; ③) or Compton Mackenzies' former home, *Suidheachan* (May–Sept; ☎01871/890243; ③).

travel details

Trains

Glasgow (Queen Street) to: Mallaig (Mon–Sat 3 daily, 2 on Sun; 5hr 10min); Oban (3 daily; 3hr).

Inverness to: Kyle of Lochalsh (Mon–Sat 3 daily; 2hr 30min).

Buses (excluding the postbus)

Glasgow to: Broadford (2–4 daily; 5hr 30min); Kyleakin (2–4 daily; 5hr 15min); Portree (2–4 daily; 6hr 10min); Sconser (2–4 daily; 5hr 45min); Uig (2–4 daily; 6hr 35min).

Lochboisdale to: Ludag (Mon–Sat 2 daily; 30–45min).

Lochmaddy to: Balivanich (Mon–Sat 1 daily; 1hr); Lochboisdale (Mon–Sat 1 daily; 2hr).

Portree to: Armadale (Mon–Sat 2 daily; 1hr 30min); Broadford (5–15 daily; 45min); Carbost (Mon–Fri 2–3 daily; 35min); Duntulm (Mon–Sat 1–3 daily; 50min); Dunvegan (Mon–Sat 1–2 daily; 50min); Edinburgh (2–3 daily; 6hr 30min); Glen Brittle (Mon–Fri 3 daily; 40min); Inverness (3–4 daily; 3hr 15min); Kyleakin (5–15 daily; 1hr); Sconser (5–15 daily; 20min); Sligachan (5–15 daily; 20min); Staffin (Mon–Sat 1–2 daily; 30min); Uig (Mon–Sat 3 daily; 25min).

Stornoway to: Callanish (Mon–Sat 1 daily; 1hr); Carloway (Mon–Sat 1 daily; 1hr 20min); Port of Ness (1 daily except Wed & Sun; 1hr 20min); Tarbert (Mon–Sat up to 2 daily; 1hr 15min).

Tarbert to: Leverburgh (Mon–Sat 1 daily; 1hr 30min); Rodel (Mon–Sat 2 daily; 1hr 20min); Stockinish (Mon–Sat 1 daily; 30min).

Ferries (summer timetable)

To Barra: Lochboisdale–Castlebay (Tues, Thurs, Fri & Sun; 1hr 45min); Oban–Castlebay (Mon, Wed, Thurs & Sat; 5hr).

To Berneray: Newtonferry–Berneray (car ferry Mon–Sat 6 daily; 10min); Newtonferry–Berneray (passenger ferry Mon–Sat 2 daily; 10min).

To Canna: Eigg–Canna (Mon & Sat; 2hr 45min–3hr); Mallaig–Canna (Mon, Wed, Fri & Sat; 2hr 30min–4hr 15min); Muck–Canna (Sun; 2hr 15min). Rum–Canna (Mon, Wed & Sat; 1hr–1hr 45min).

To Eigg: Canna–Eigg (Fri & Sat; 2hr 15min–3hr); Mallaig–Eigg (Mon, Tues, Thurs & Sat; 1hr 30–50min); Muck–Eigg (Tues, Thurs & Sat; 45–50min); Rum–Eigg (Fri & Sat; 1hr 15min–2hr).

To Harris: Lochmaddy–Tarbert (Mon–Sat 1–2 daily; 1hr 45min–4hr); Newtonferry–Leverburgh (Mon–Sat 2 daily; 30min); Uig–Tarbert (Mon–Sat 1–2 daily; 1hr 45min).

To Lewis: Ullapool–Stornoway (Mon–Sat up to 3 daily; 3hr 30min).

To Muck: Canna–Muck (Sat; 2hr 15min); Eigg–Muck (Tues, Thurs & Sat; 45min); Mallaig–Muck (Tues, Thurs & Sat; 2hr 40min–4hr 45min); Rum–Muck (Sat 1hr 15min).

To North Uist: Leverburgh–Newtonferry (Mon–Sat 2 daily; 30min); Uig–Lochmaddy (1–2 daily; 1hr 45min); Tarbert–Lochmaddy (Mon–Sat 1–2 daily; 2hr).

To Raasay: Sconser–Raasay (Mon–Sat 9 daily; 15min).

To Rum: Canna–Rum (Wed, Fri & Sat; 1hr–1hr 15min); Eigg–Rum (Mon & Sat; 1hr 30min–2hr); Mallaig–Rum (Mon, Wed, Fri & Sat; 1hr 45min–3hr 30min); Muck–Rum (Sat; 1hr 15min).

To Skye: Glenelg–Kylerhea (April–Oct frequently; 15min); Mallaig–Armadale (Mon–Sat up to 7 daily; mid-May to mid-Sept 4 on Sun; 30min).

To South Uist: Castlebay–Lochboisdale (Mon, Wed, Thurs & Sat; 1hr 50min); Oban–Lochboisdale (1 daily except Tues & Sun; 7hr).

Flights

To Barra: Benbecula (Mon–Fri 1 daily; 20min); Glasgow (Mon–Sat 1–2 daily; 1hr 20min); Tiree (Tues–Thurs 1 daily; 20min).

To Benbecula: Barra (Mon–Fri 1 daily; 20min); Glasgow (Mon–Sat 1 daily; 1hr); Stornoway (Mon–Fri 2 daily; 35min).

To Stornoway: Benbecula (Mon–Fri 2 daily; 35min); Glasgow (Mon–Sat 1–2 daily; 1hr); Inverness (Mon–Sat 1–2 daily; 40min).

CHAPTER TWENTY THREE

NORTHEAST SCOTLAND

A large triangle of land thrusting into the North Sea from a line drawn roughly from Perth up to Forres, east of Inverness, the **northeast** of Scotland takes in the county of Angus and the city of Dundee to the south (plus for the purposes of this guide, the part of Perthshire and Kinross around Glen Shee, Meigle and Blairgowrie), and, beyond the **Grampian Mountains**, the counties of Aberdeenshire and Moray and the city of Aberdeen. Geographically diverse, the landscape in the south is made up predominantly of undulating farmland, but, north of the Firth of Tay, this gives way to wooded glens, mountains and increasingly harsh land fringed by a dramatic coast of cliffs and long sandy beaches.

The northeast was the southern kingdom of the **Picts**, reminders of whom are scattered throughout the region in the form of numerous symbolic carved stones found in fields, churchyards and museums – such as the one at **Meigle**. Remote, self-contained and cut off from the centres of major power in the south, the area never grew particularly prosperous, and a few feuding and intermarrying families, such as the Gordons, the Keiths and the Irvines, grew to wield disproportionate influence, building the region's many **castles** and religious buildings and developing and planning its towns.

Although much of the northeast remains economically deprived, parts have, however, been transformed by the discovery of oil in the North Sea in the 1960s, particularly **Aberdeen**, Scotland's third largest city. Aberdeen is the region's most stimulating urban centre, a fast, relatively sophisticated city that continues to ride on the crest of the **oil** boom. In stark contrast, **Dundee**, the next largest metropolis in the northeast, is low-key and rather depressed; although it does boast a splendid site on the banks of the Tay and makes a useful base for visiting nearby **Glamis Castle**, famous from Shakespeare's *Macbeth*. A little way up the Angus coast lie the historically important towns of **Arbroath**, where Robert the Bruce was declared King of Scotland, and **Montrose**, where Edward I was forced to sign over his kingdom. Inland, the **Angus glens** cut picturesquely through the hills, their villages, such as **Blairgowrie** and **Kirriemuir**, perfect centres for hikers and **skiers**.

North of the glens, **Deeside** is a wild, unspoilt tract of land made famous by the royal family, who have favoured **Balmoral** as one of their prime residences since Queen Victoria fell in love with it back in the 1840s. Beyond, the **Don Valley** is less visited, although it does generate something of a tourist season in the winter, when keen skiers head for the **Lecht** area; while **Speyside**, a little way west, is more tranquil and best known as Scotland's premier **whisky**-producing region. Despite the blots of **Peterhead** and **Fraserburgh**, the route further north, around the northeast coast, fringed with mighty oil rigs, offers the best of Aberdeenshire and Moray, with rugged cliffs and remote fishing villages, barely sheltered from the ferocious elements.

Northeast Scotland is well served by an extensive road network, with the A92 following the coast from Dundee to Aberdeen and beyond, and the area north and east of Aberdeen dissected by a series of efficient routes. **Trains** from the south stop at Dundee and Aberdeen, and other towns on the coast. Inland, there is one branch line from Aberdeen northwest to Elgin and on to Inverness. A reasonably comprehensive scheduled **bus service** is complemented by a network of **postbuses**. Only in the most remote and mountainous parts does public tranpsort disappear altogether.

Dundee and around

At first sight, **DUNDEE** can seem a grim place. In the nineteenth century it was Britain's main processor of jute, the world's most important vegetable fibre after cotton. Today, though economically depressed and somewhat overshadowed by its northerly neighbour, Aberdeen, it's still a refreshingly unpretentious and welcoming city, wonderfully located on the banks of the Tay. Even prior to its Victorian heyday, Dundee was a town of considerable importance. It was here in 1309 that Robert the Bruce was proclaimed the lawful King of Scots, and during the Reformation it earned itself a reputation for tolerance, sheltering leading figures such as George Wishart and John Knox. During the Civil War, the town was destroyed by the Royalists and Cromwell's army; later the Stuart Viscount Dundee, who was granted the city for his services to the crown after the Restoration, razed the place to the ground in the Battle of Killiecrankie.

Dundee picked itself up in the 1700s, its train and harbour links making it a major centre for shipbuilding, whaling and the manufacture of jute, although little investment was ploughed back into the city. Despite a burst of prosperity after World War II, there's little left of Dundee's former glory. There's still enough, however, of its Victorian centre, backed by glimpses of the blue Tay, to please. Many of its populace still depend on D.C. Thomson, the local publishing giant that produces the timelessly popular *Beano* and *Dandy* comics, as well as the *Sunday Post*, for their dwindling employment prospects. Dundee was also where marmalade was invented in the nineteenth century by a local housewife determined not to let a cargo of Seville oranges go to waste. Hence the saying that Dundee was built on three Js – jam, jute and journalism.

The City

The best approach to Dundee is across the mile-and-a-half-long **Tay Road Bridge** from Fife. Offering a spectacular panorama of the city spread over its riverbank, the toll bridge, opened in 1966, has a central walkway for pedestrians. This vast man-made construction is home to around a million pairs of starlings – watch them circle at dusk. More impressive as an engineering feat is the neighbouring **Tay Rail Bridge**, opened in 1887 to replace the spindly structure destroyed in a storm only eighteen months after it was built in May 1878. The crew and 75 passengers on a train passing over the bridge at the time died.

Dundee's city centre is focused on the municipal stronghold of **City Square**, a couple of hundred yards north of the Tay. The square and its surrounding streets have been much spruced up in recent years, with fountains, benches and trees making it a far more relaxing environment, though the shops remain the mundane mass of chain stores you see all over Britain. The main thoroughfare, which passes by City Square, starts as Nethergate in the west, becomes High Street in the centre then divides into

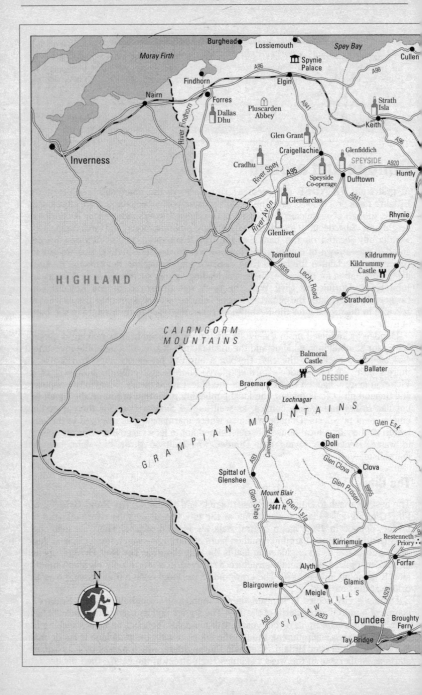

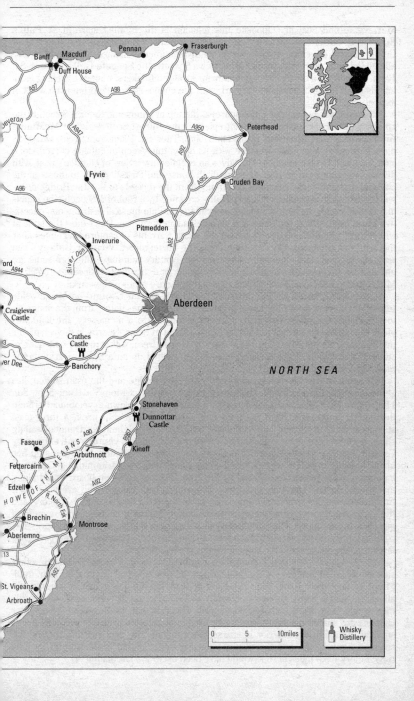

Murraygate and Seagate. Opposite this junction is the mottled spire of **St Paul's Episcopal Cathedral** (Mon–Fri 10am–4pm), a rather gaudy George Gilbert Scott Gothic Revival structure, notable for its vividly sentimental stained glass and the floridly gilded high altar. Fifty yards further down Seagate, the **Seagate Gallery** (Tues–Sat 10am–5pm; free), a centre predominantly for local printmakers, houses travelling exhibitions of all kinds of contemporary art, with the chance to see (and buy) the work of local artists.

A hundred yards north of City Square, at the top of handsome Reform Street, is the attractive **Albert Square**, whose centrepiece is the Gilbert Scott-designed **McManus Art Galleries and Museum** (Mon 11am–5pm, Tues–Sat 10am–5pm; free), Dundee's most impressive Victorian structure with its delightful sweep of outside curved stone staircases and Gothic touches. This gives an excellent overview of Dundee's past, with displays ranging from an Iron Age ring ditch house and Pictish stones to those on the city's industrial history, spanning everything from the three Js to the Tay Bridge disaster. Upstairs, the magnificent **Albert Hall** – crowned by a roof of 480 pitch-pine panels in a Gothic arch – houses stained-glass exhibits, antique musical instruments, decorative glass, gold, silver, sculpture and some exquisite furniture. Don't miss the table at which the Duke of Cumberland signed the death warrants of captured Jacobites after the Battle of Culloden. On the same floor, the barrel-roofed **Victoria Gallery**'s red walls are heaving with nineteenth- and twentieth-century paintings. Although some are undeniably syrupy, the notable Pre-Raphaelite and Scottish collections (William McTaggart's seascapes being a particular highlight) are well worth perusal.

Across Ward Road from the museum, the **Howff Burial Ground** on Meadowside (daily 9am–5pm or dusk) has some great carved tombstones dating from the sixteenth to nineteenth centuries. Originally gardens belonging to a monastery, the land was given to Dundee for burials in 1564 by Mary, Queen of Scots. Nearby is the run-of-the-mill **Barrack Street Museum** (Mon–Sat 10am–5pm; free), with a motley collection of stuffed local wildlife – the skeleton of a whale, washed up on a beach nearby, is the most impressive exhibit.

Just south of the city centre, moored by the Tay Bridge and the train station, lies Dundee's great tourism hope, **Discovery Point** (April–Oct Mon–Sat 10am–5pm, Sun 11am–5pm; Nov–March closes 4pm; £4), a massively overblown development around the hugely impressive royal research ship *Discovery*. The ship itself, a three-mast steam-assisted vessel, was one of the last traditional British-built (in Dundee) sailing ships, berthed here since 1986, and now sitting alongside is a **visitor centre**. Used by Captain Scott in various Antarctic explorations between 1901 and 1929, the ship has been elegantly restored, with polished wood panels and brass trimmings giving scant indication of the privations suffered by the crew. Temperatures on board would plummet to -28° in the Antarctic, and turns at having a bath came round every 47 days. Enthusiastic guides spin some fascinating yarns about the boat's colourful history, and the audio-visual spectacular you experience before boarding is compelling enough, if mercilessly overhyped. The introductory film, *Locked in the Ice*, is certainly impressive, culminating in the screen splitting to release a huge model of the freed ship's bow surging heroically out towards the audience on a carpet of dry ice.

In total contrast, moored behind the Customs House on Victoria Dock (the other side of the road bridge), is the endearingly simple wooden frigate **Unicorn** (mid-March to Sept daily 10am–5pm; £2). Built in 1824, it's the oldest British warship still afloat and was in active service as recently as 1968. During its service years, over 300 men would have lived and worked aboard. The fact that its 46 guns – 18-pounder cannons are still on display – were never fired in aggression probably accounts for its survival. Although the interior is sparse, the cannons, the neck-twisting rooves, the splendid figureheads, and the displays and wonderful model of the ship in its fully rigged glory (23.5 miles of rope would have been used) are fascinating.

Out from the centre

A mile or so north of town, **Dundee Law** is the plug of an extinct volcano, and, at 571ft, the city's highest point. Once the site of a seventh-century defensive hill fort, it is now an impressive lookout, with great views across the whole city and the Tay – although the climb is steep and often windy. It takes thirty minutes to walk to the foot of the law from the city centre, or you can take buses #3 or #4 from Albert Square.

The city's other volcanic plug of rock sits a mile to the west of Dundee Law. **Balgay Hill** is crowned by the wooded **Lochee Park**, at the summit of which sits the **Mills Observatory** (April–Sept Mon–Fri 10am–5pm, Sat 2–5pm; Oct–March Mon–Fri 3–10pm, Sat 2–5pm; free), a unique municipal amenity in Britain. In summer, there's little to be seen through the telescope – winter nights are the best for stellar observation – but well-explained, quirky exhibits and displays chart the history of space exploration and astronomy, and on sunny days, you can play at being a human sundial or a shadow clock and take in the fantastic views over the city through little telescopes. The observatory also has special opening times to coincide with eclipses and other heavenly wonders (details on ☎01382/667138). Buses #2, #36 and #37 drop you in Balgay Road, at the entrance to the park.

Four miles east of Dundee's city centre lies the seaside settlement of **BROUGHTY FERRY,** now engulfed by the city as a reluctant suburb. It's a pleasant enough little resort, and on land at least it's far more unspoilt than Dundee. The level of pollution on the beach itself, however, is pretty dire – all of the city's sewage seems to end up here. If you can't bear the sight of this, **Broughty Castle and Museum**, right by the seashore (July–Sept Mon–Thurs & Sat 10am–1pm & 2–5pm, Sun 2–5pm; Oct–June closed Sun; free), is worth a look. Built in the fifteenth century to protect the estuary, its four floors now house local history exhibits, covering the story of Broughty Ferry as a fishing village and the history of whaling, as well as details of local geology and wildlife.

Just north of Broughty Ferry, at the junction of the A92 and B978, the chunky bricks of **Claypotts Castle** constitute one of Scotland's most complete Z-shaped tower houses. Built from 1569 to 1588, its two round towers have stepped projections to support extra rooms – a sixteenth-century architectural practice that makes Claypotts look like it's about to topple. On going to print the castle was closed, and not expected to reopen until late 1996 or early 1997; call Historic Scotland to check (☎0131/668 8800).

Practicalities

Dundee's **airport** (☎643242) is five minutes' drive west from the city centre; a taxi will only set you back £2. By **train**, Taybridge Station is on South Union Street (☎01382/228046) about 300 yards south of the city centre, near the River Tay. Long-distance **buses** arrive at the Seagate bus station (☎01382/228345), just east of the centre. Dundee's very helpful **tourist office** is at 4 City Square (May, June & Sept Mon–Sat 8.30am–8pm, Sun 11am–8pm; July & Aug Mon–Sat 8.30am–9pm, Sun 11am–9pm; Jan–April & Oct–Dec Mon–Fri 9am–6pm, Sat 10am–noon & 1–4pm; ☎01382/434664); you can pick up the free monthly *What's On* listings magazine here.

In a city that's only just getting used to tourists, **accommodation** is remarkably plentiful. The *Queens Hotel*, 160 Nethergate (☎01382/322515; ⑤), is the city's grandest old hotel with fine views of the Tay and good food. The *Shaftesbury Hotel*, 1 Hyndford St (☎01382/669216; ③), is a converted jute merchant's house very near town, while the *Carlton House Hotel*, 2 Dalgleish Rd (☎01382/462056; ③), is a central, nineteenth-century pile. The *Kemback Guest House*, 8 McGill St (☎01382/461273; ②), is right in the middle of town, with TVs in all rooms. Another possibility is the *Errolbank Guest House*, 9 Dalgleish Rd (☎01382/462118; ②), with good views of the Tay. There are plans to build a youth hostel; until then you'll have to make do with the self-catering and B&B accommodation in the halls of residence of **the University of Dundee** (March, April & July–Sept; ☎01382/344039; ②).

The West End of Dundee, around the principal University and Perth Road, is the best area **eating and drinking**. *Deep Sea*, 81 Nethergate, is the best of Dundee's fish- and-chip restaurants, while *Gunga Din*, 99b–101 Perth Rd, is the choicest of the student-land Indian restaurants. For a warm, friendly and cheap Italian trattoria try *Dellos*, 134a Nethergate, opposite the *Deep Sea*. For gorgeous, fairly pricey Scottish food (and veggie options), go for *Raffles*, 18 Perth Rd (☎01382/201139). The *Royal Oak*, 167 Brook St, serves great pub food until 8.30pm, with Thai and Spanish dishes on the menu. *Laing's*, 8 Roseangle, off Perth Road, does great-value food and offers great views over the Tay. *Lucifer's Mill*, a converted jute mill on Session Street, attracts a mainly student clientele, and is good for up-and-coming indie/blues bands. *Gauger*, Seagate, is a lively, predominantly gay bar opposite the *Seagate Gallery*, while *O'Neill's*, North Lindsay St, is a beery Irish bar, with frequent live Celtic music.

All three of Dundee's **nightclubs** are in South Ward Road, midway between the centre and the University: *Fat Sam's* is the most studenty place, with music tilted towards indie; *De Stihl's* caters for an older, less raucous crowd; and the *Mardi Gras* offers more mainstream dance and chart sounds. Aside from the clubs, the *Dundee Repertory Theatre* (☎01382/223530) on Tay Square, is excellent for contemporary **theatre**, as well as being a focus for many of the city's **festivals**, the best of which are the Jazz and Blues Festival in early June and the Folk Festival in early July. In St Mary Place (off Lochee Rd) the *Dundee Arts Centre* (☎201035) is good for community-based theatre, dance and music. The best venue for **classical** music is *Caird Hall* (☎01382/223141), whose bulky frontage dominates City Square. For slightly more esoteric **cinema** viewing, try the *Steps Film Centre* (☎434037) at the back of the *Wellgate* shopping centre, off Victoria Road.

Around Dundee

There are a handful of sights in the southern corner of Angus within easy reach from Dundee. North of the city, over the Sidlaw Hills, **Meigle** has one of Scotland's foremost collections of Pictish stones, while the splendid **Glamis Castle** was the setting of Shakespeare's *Macbeth*.

Meigle

Hourly buses run from Dundee to the tiny village of **MEIGLE**, fifteen miles northwest in the fertile bed of the Tay Valley. Housed in a modest former school building, the **Meigle Museum** (April–Sept Mon–Sat 9.30am–12.30pm & 1.30–6pm, Sun 2–6pm; £1.20) holds some thirty early Christian and Pictish inscribed stones, dating from the seventh to the tenth centuries, found in and around the nearby churchyard. Most impressive is the seven-foot-tall great cross slab, said to be Guinevere's gravestone, carved on one side with a portrayal of Daniel surrounded by lions, a beautifully executed equestrian group, and mythological creatures including a dragon and a centaur. On the other side various beasts are surmounted by the "ring of glory" – a wheel containing a cross carved and decorated in high relief. The stone is all the more impressive for its deliberate two-tone effect, the slab of sandstone red at the base, merging into grey at the top.

Glamis Castle

Regular buses leave Dundee daily for the pink-sandstone **Glamis Castle** (April–Oct daily 10.30am–5.30pm; castle and grounds £4.50, grounds only £2.20), a wondrously over-the-top, L-shaped five-storey pile, twelve miles to the north. Shakespeare chose

Glamis (pronounced "Glahms") as a central location in Macbeth and its royal connections (as the childhood home of the Queen Mother and birthplace of Princess Margaret) make it one of the essential stops on every bus tour of Scotland. Approaching the castle down the long main drive provides un unforgettable view. The Disneyesque mêlée of turrets, towers and conical rooves appears fantastically at the end of the sweeping avenue of trees, framed by the Grampian Mountains.

Glamis began as a comparatively humble hunting lodge, used in the eleventh century by the kings of Scotland. In 1372, King Robert II gave the property to his son-in-law, Sir John Lyon, who built the core of the present building. His descendants, the Earls of Kinghorne and Strathmore – the fourteenth of which was the Queen Mother's father – have lived here ever since. Most of the castle can only be seen on the guided tours; if you have to wait, you can easily kill some time in the park or in the new underground exhibition in the **Coach House**, which covers everything from the castle's supply of water, electricity and gas, to numerous bits of memorabilia relating to the Queen Mother.

The highlight of the guided tour is the family **Chapel**, completed in 1688. Jacob de Wit was commissioned to produce the frescoes from the family Bible, although his depictions of Christ wearing a hat and St Simon in a pair of glasses have raised eyebrows ever since. The chapel is said to be haunted by the spectre of a grey lady, the ghost of the sixth Lady Glamis who was burnt as a witch under orders of James V. **King Malcolm's Room**, so called because it is believed he died nearby in 1034, is most notable for its carved wooden chimneypiece, on which many of its most decorative panels are, in fact, highly polished leather. From here, the tour passes into the **Royal Apartments**, which are far less grand than might be expected. The Queen Mother's delicate gilt four-poster bed was a wedding present from her mother, who embroidered the names and dates of birth of her ten children into its panels. **Duncan's Hall**, a fifteenth-century guardroom, is the traditional – but inaccurate – setting for Duncan's murder by Macbeth (it actually took place near Elgin). Finally, the tour concludes with a random set of family displays that include the Queen Mother's old doll's house.

Glamis' grounds are worth a few hours in their own right. Highlights include the lead statues of James VI and Charles I at the top of the main drive, the seventeenth-century Baroque sundial, the formal gardens, and the verdant walks out to Earl John's Bridge and through the woodland. In Glamis village the humble **Angus Folk Museum** (Easter–Sept daily 11am–5pm, Oct Sat & Sun 11am–5pm; £2; NTS), housed in six low-slung cottages in Kirk Wynd, has a bewildering array of local ephemera, including bizarrely named agricultural implements, a nineteenth-century horse-drawn hearse and a section on local bothies.

The Angus coast

Two roads link Dundee to Aberdeen and the northeast coast of Scotland. By far the most pleasant option is to take the slightly longer A92 coast road which joins the A94 at Stonehaven, just south of Aberdeen, a route that can also be followed by bus or train. The train line hugging this stretch of coast from Dundee is one of the most picturesque in Scotland, stopping at **Arbroath** and the old seaport of **Montrose**.

Arbroath

Since it was settled in the twelfth century, local fishermen have been landing their catches at **ARBROATH**, where the Angus coast starts to curve in from the North Sea towards the Firth of Tay. The **Arbroath smokie** – a line-caught haddock, smoke-cured over smouldering oak chips and then poached in milk – is probably one of Scotland's best-known dishes. Chiefly due to its harbour, Arbroath had, by the late eighteenth century, become a trading and manufacturing centre, famed for sail-making (the *Cutty Sark*'s sails were made here) and boot-making. It still enjoys a great location, with long sandy beaches and stunning sandstone cliffs on either side of town, but, like Dundee, it has suffered from short-sighted development, its historical associations consumed by pedestrian walkways, a mess of a one-way system and ugly shopping centres.

Arbroath's real glory days came in the thirteenth century with the completion of **Arbroath Abbey** (April–Sept Mon–Sat 9.30am–6pm, Sun 2–6pm; Oct–March Mon–Sat 9.30am–4pm, Sun 2–4pm; £1.20), whose pink-stone ruins, described by Dr Johnson as "fragments of magnificence", stand on Abbey Street, clearly visible from High Street. Founded in 1178 by King William the Lion, and dedicated to his old schoolmate Thomas à Becket, whom he acknowledged as a "sharer of his tribulations" in England, it was completed in 1233, and became an abbey in 1285. One of the most significant events in Scotland's history occured here, when on April 6, 1320, a group of Scottish barons drew up the **Declaration of Arbroath**, asking the Pope to reverse his excommunication and recognize Robert the Bruce as king, asserting Scotland's independence from the English: "For, so long as one hundred remain alive, we will never in any degree be subject to the dominion of the English." It was duly despatched to Pope John XXII in Avignon, who in 1324 agreed to Robert's claim.

The abbey was dissolved during the Reformation, and by the eighteenth century it was little more than a source of red sandstone for local houses. However, there is still enough left to get a good idea of how vast the place must have been: the semicircular west doorway is more or less intact, complete with medieval mouldings, and the south transept has a beautiful round window, once lit with a beacon to guide ships. The **Abbot's House** has also survived, used as a private dwelling long after the complex was abandoned, and now housing a small museum with exhibits that include an ancient headless statue thought to represent the abbey's founder.

Down by the harbour, the elegant Regency **Signal House Museum** (Mon–Sat 10am–5pm; July & Aug also Sun 2–5pm; free) stands sentinel as it has since 1813. The interior is now given over to some excellent local history displays. A school room, fisherman's cottage and lighthouse kitchen have all been carefully re-created, with the addition of realistic smells.

Practicalities

Arbroath's **tourist office** is on the Market Place (Jan–March & Oct–Dec Mon–Fri 9.30am–5pm, Sat 9.30am–12.30pm; April–June & Sept Mon–Sat 9.30am–5.30pm; July & Aug Mon–Sat 9.30am–6pm, Sun 1–5pm; ☎01241/872609). **Buses** stop at the station on Catherine Street, five minutes south of the tourist office, while **trains** arrive at the station, across the road on Keptie Street.

The best part of Arbroath to **stay** in is down by the harbour: try *Harbour House Guest House*, 4 The Shore (☎0241/878047; ②), or the *Sandhutton Guest House*, 16 Addison Place (☎0241/872007; ②). The harbour is also the place for **eating and drinking**: a number of sea-salty pubs along the harbour front offer Arbroath smokies – the *Commercial Bar* on the seafront is a favourite with local fishermen, or check out the *Smugglers Tavern* on The Shore, where you can also try over 180 varieties of rum.

Montrose and around

"Here's the Basin, there's Montrose, shut your een and haud your nose." As the old rhyme indicates, **MONTROSE**, a seaport and market town since the thirteenth century, can sometimes smell a little rich, mostly because of its position on the edge of a virtualy landlocked two-mile-square lagoon of mud known as the Basin. But with the wind in the right direction, Montrose, now an important North Sea oil base, is a great little town to visit, with a pleasant old centre and a good museum. The Basin too is of interest: flooded and emptied twice daily by the tides, it is a rich nature reserve for the host of geese, swans and waders who frequent the ooze to look for food.

Montrose locals are known as Gable Endies, because of the unusual way in which the town's eighteenth- and nineteenth-century merchants, influenced by architectural styles they had seen on the Continent, built their houses gable-end to the street. Most of the gabled houses line the wide **High Street**, which today is split down the middle by banks of flowerbeds and trees. Off either side of the road are numerous tiny alleyways and quiet courtyards, pleasant to explore for an hour or so. The most obvious landmark is the 220-foot **kirk steeple** at the lower end of High Street.

Two blocks behind the steeple, in Panmure Place on the western side of **Mid Links** park, the **Montrose Museum and Art Gallery** (Mon–Sat 10am–5pm; free) is one of Scotland's oldest museums, dating from 1842. For a small-town museum, it has some unusual exhibits, among them the so-called Samson Stone, dating from around 900 AD, which bears a carving of Samson slaying the Philistines. On the upper floor, the maritime history exhibits include a cast of Napoleon's death mask and a model of a British man-of-war, sculpted out of bone by Napoleonic prisoners at Portsmouth.

By the entrance of the museum, a winsome study of a boy by local sculptor William Lamb (1893–1951) is a taster for more of his work, best seen in the **William Lamb Memorial Studio** on Market Street (July & Aug Sun 2–5pm; other times by arrangement; ☎01674/673232; free). Here a variety of his works include bronze heads of the Queen, Princess Margaret and the Queen Mother, the earnings from which enabled him to buy the studio in the 1930s. Lamb's striking work is made the more impressive by the fact that he taught himself to sculpt with his left hand, having suffered a war wound in his right.

Around Montrose: the House of Dun

Across the Basin, four miles west of Montrose, is the Palladian **House of Dun** (late April to late Oct daily 11am–5pm; £3, grounds only free; NTS), reachable by way of the regular Montrose–Brechin bus; alternatively, Bridge of Dun station, the terminus of the Caledonian steam rail line from Brechin, is a fifteen-minute, signposted walk away. Built in 1730 for David Erskine, Laird of Dun, to designs by William Adam, the house was opened to the public in 1989 after extensive restoration, and is crammed full of period furniture and *objets d'art*. Inside, the ornate relief plasterwork is the most impressive feature, extravagantly emblazoned with Jacobite symbolism. You can also see some gorgeous pieces of intricate needlework, stitched by the illegitimate child of King William IV, Lady Augusta, who married into the Dun family in 1827.

Practicalities

The Montrose **tourist office** is in a former public toilet next to the Library, where Bridge Street merges into the High Street (Mon–Sat April, May & Sept 10am–5pm; June–Aug Mon–Sat 9.30am–5.30pm; ☎01674/672000). Most **buses** stop in High Street, while the **train** station lies a block back on Western Road. For B&B **accommodation**, try *Oaklands*, over the river bridge at 10 Rossie Island Rd (☎01674/672018; ②), or the *Murray Lodge Hotel*, 2–8 Murray St (☎01674/678880; ③), the northern continuation of High Street. **Bike** rental is available from *Plan Green*, 33 Ferry St (☎01674/677199).

For **eating**, *Nelson's*, Wharf St (down by the harbour), is popular with visitors for its seafood; however, the liveliest place to eat in Montrose is unquestionably *Roo's Leap*, a newish café-bar in an old golf club off the northern end of Traill Drive near the beach. The food is an unlikely, but excellent, mix of Scottish, American and Australian. If you want a **drink**, High Street has the no-frills *Market Tavern* by the kirk steeple and, further down, the *Cornerhouse Hotel*, which hosts folk nights on Tuesdays. The *Salutation Inn*, 69–71 Bridge St, serves good, cheap food and has a beer garden.

The Angus glens

Lying on the southernmost edges of the Grampian Mountains' heather-covered lower slopes, the **Angus glens** – or "Braes o' Angus" – are tranquil valleys penetrated by few roads that offer some of the most rugged and majestic landscape of northeast Scotland. It's a rain-swept, wind-blown, sparsely populated area, whose links with tourism are fairly new. The first snows nearly always see the roads closed, sometimes as early as October, and in the summer there are ferocious **midges** to contend with. Nevertheless, most of the glens, particularly **Glen Clova**, are now well and truly discovered, and at the height of summer you may find yourself in a traffic jam – unheard of ten years ago. The rolling hills and dales attract hikers, birdwatchers and botanists in the summer, grouse-shooters and deer-hunters in autumn and a growing number of skiers in winter. The most useful road through the glens is the A93, which cuts through **Glen Shee** to Braemar on Deeside (see p.889). It's pretty dramatic stuff, threading its way over Britain's highest main road pass – the **Cairnwell Pass** at 2199ft.

Blairgowrie and Glen Shee

Sprawled over the flanks of four mountains, the **skiing** area at **Glen Shee**, the most visited and best known of the Angus glens, is probably the largest in Scotland. The place comes into its own during the winter season – January to March – when an increasing number of skiers, predominantly from the cities of central Scotland, brave the ridiculously cold temperatures and bitter winds. In summer it's all a bit sad, with lifeless chairlifts, muddy banks, and expanses of woodland cut back for the pistes.

The well-heeled town of **BLAIRGOWRIE** (officially Blairgowrie and Rattray), little more than one main road set among raspberry fields on the glen's southernmost tip, is as good a place as any to base yourself – and is particularly useful in winter if you plan to ski. The **tourist office** is at 26 Wellmeadow (Easter–June & mid–Sept to Oct Mon–Sat 9.30am–5.30pm, Sun 11am–4pm; July to mid-Aug Mon–Sat 9am–7pm, Sun 11am–6pm; Nov–Easter Mon–Fri 9.30am–5pm, Sat 9.30am–1.30pm; ☎01250/872960). You can **rent bikes** from the year-round *Blairgowrie Caravan Park* (☎01250/872941), Rattray's Hatton Rd, where you can also **camp**, and, three hundred yards from the tourist office, from *Mountains and Glens*, Railway Rd (☎01250/874206).

Over the bridge spanning the fast-flowing River Ericht, Blairgowrie melts into its twin community of **Rattray**. On the main street, Boat Brae, is the excellent *Ivy Lodge* B&B (☎01250/873056; ②), offering sweeping views of the river and surrounding hills, as well as free use of a floodlit tennis court. The opulent, ivy-covered *Kinloch House* (☎01250/884237; ⑨), one of the area's most prestigious hotels, is set in its own vast grounds three miles west of town on the A923. There are loads of places to **eat and drink**. Around the main square make for the *Victoria Hotel* for hearty lunches and dinners and, tucked down towards the river bridge, the *Crown Bar*, complete with 116 different malt whiskies.

SKIING IN THE ANGUS GLENS

For **information on skiing** in the Angus glens call the *Glenshee Chairlift Company* (☎013397/41320) or the *Ski Hotline* (☎01891/654656). There are numerous **lift passes**, all of which increase in price in the high season (weekends Feb to mid-April), when adult passes cost around £12.50 for a day, £50 for five days. **Ski rental** starts at around £8 a day. If you need tuition, the *Glenshee Ski School* (☎013397/41216) charges £10 for a day's instruction.

Nearly twenty miles north of Blairgowrie, the **SPITTAL OF GLENSHEE**, though ideally situated for skiing, is little more than a tacky service area, only worth stopping at for a quick drink or bite to eat. It is, however, handily close to one of the nicest places to stay in the area, the *Dalmunzie House* (☎01250/885224; ⑥), a gorgeous, turreted, Highland sporting lodge, evoking the peace and tranquillity that once pervaded this area – to reach it, take the signposted road from just beyond the *Spittal Hotel*. At the other end of the scael, the *Compass Christian Centre*, Glenshee Lodge, just south of Blairgowrie (☎01250/885209; ①), is a good place to meet other hikers.

Kirriemuir

The sandstone town of **KIRRIEMUIR**, known locally as Kirrie, is set on a hill with glens Clova and Prosen as its backdrop. Despite the influx of hunters up for the "season", it's still a pretty special place, a haphazard confection of narrow closes, twisting wynds and steep braes. The main cluster of streets has all the appeal of an old film set, with their old-fashioned bars, tiled butcher's shop, tartan outlets and haberdasheries somehow managing to avoid being contrived and quaint (notwithstanding the twee statue of Peter Pan).

In the nineteenth century a linen-manufacturing centre, it was made famous by a local handloom-weaver's son, J.M. Barrie, with his series of novels about "Thrums", in particular *A Window in Thrums* and his third novel, *The Little Minister*. Barrie's **birthplace**, a plain little whitewashed cottage at 9 Brechin Rd (Easter–Sept Mon–Sat 11am–5.30pm, Sun 2–5.30pm; Oct Sat 11am–5.30pm, Sun 1.30–5.30pm; £1.50; NTS), displays his writing desk, photos and newspaper clippings, as well as copies of his works. The washhouse outside – romantically billed as Barrie's first "theatre" – was apparently the model for the house that the Lost Boys built for Wendy in Never-Never Land. Barrie chose to be buried at the nearby St Mary's Espiscopal Church in Kirrie, despite being offered a more prestigious plot at London's Westminster Abbey.

High above the B957 to Brechin, Kirriemuir Hill is crowned by a sporadically opened camera obscura (call Mr Tucker on ☎01575/572081) in the old cricket pavilion. On the other side of the town centre, a couple of hundred yards down the road to Glamis (A928), is the **Aviation Museum** (April–Sept Mon–Sat 10am–5pm, Sun 11am–5pm; free), the lifetime collection of Richard Moss, who'll invariably be your guide through the jumble of military uniforms, photos, World War II memorabilia (including British and German propaganda leaflets) and *Airfix* models.

Kirrie's helpful **tourist office** (April–May & Sept Mon–Sat 10am–5pm; June–Aug Mon–Sat 9.30am–5.30pm; ☎01575/574097) is in the tacky new development, behind *Visocchi's* on the main square. **Accommodation** can be found at *Crepto*, Kinnordy Place (☎01575/572746; ②), the *Re-Union* bar on the main square (☎01575/572259; ②) or the excellent *Thrums Hotel* (☎01575/572758; ③), Bank St. *Visocchi's* is great for daytime **food**, the *Thrums Hotel* a good bet in the evening. Of the **pubs**, the *Kilt and Clogs*, behind the tourist office, is the current favourite, although live music is more likely at the *Re-Union*, the *Airlie Arms Hotel*, Reform St, or, facing out over the newly cobbled main square, the *Ogilvy Arms*.

Glen Clova

Of all the Angus glens, **Glen Clova** – which in the north becomes Glen Doll – with its stunning cliffs, heather slopes and valley meadows, is the firm favourite of many. Although it can get unpleasantly congested in peak season, the area is still remote enough to be able to leave the crowds with little effort. Wildlife is abundant, with deer on the mountains, wild hares and even grouse and the occasional buzzard. The meadow flowers on the valley floor and arctic plants (including great splashes of white and purple saxifrage) on the rocks also make it something of a botanist's paradise.

The B955 from Dykehead and Kirriemuir divides at the Gella bridge over the swift-coursing River South Esk (unofficially, road traffic is encouraged to use the western branch of the road for travel up the glen, the eastern side down). Six miles north of Gella, the two branches of the road join up once more at the hamlet of **CLOVA**, little more than the hearty *Clova Hotel* (☎01575/550222; ③ or £4 per person per night in their outside bunkhouse accommodation), a car park and a picnic site. In summer, the hotel is a regular venue for barbeques, ceilidhs and even pleasure flights by helicopter or balloon. An excellent, if fairly strenuous, four-hour walk from behind the old school at the back of the hotel leads up into the mountains and around the lip of **Loch Brandy**, which legend predicts will one day flood and drown the valley below.

North from Clova village, the road turns into a rabbit-strewn lane coursing along the riverside for four miles to the car park and informal **camp site** in **Glen Doll**. This is right in the heart of the southern Grampian mountains, as can be seen from the towering humps of Craig Mellon (2841ft) and Cairn Broadlands (2795ft) overlooking the site. It is also a useful starting point for numerous superb walks. From the car park, it's only a few hundred yards further to the **youth hostel** (mid-March to Oct; ☎01575/550236), a restored hunting lodge complete with squash court.

Aberdeen

Some 120 miles from Edinburgh, on the banks of the rivers Dee and Don and smack in the middle of the northeast coast, **ABERDEEN** is commonly known as the Granite City. The third largest city in Scotland, it's a place that people either love or hate, for the beauty of Aberdeen's famous **granite** architecture is definitely in the eye of the beholder. Some extol the many hues and colours of the grandiose designs, while others see only uniform grey and find the city grim, cold and unwelcoming. The weather doesn't help: Aberdeen lies on a latitude north of Moscow and the driving rain (even if it does transform the buildings into sparkling silver) can be tiresome. Since the 1970s, **oil** has made Aberdeen an almost obscenely wealthy and self-confident place. Despite (or perhaps because of) this, it can seem a soulless city: there's a feeling of corporate sterility and sometimes, despite its long history, it seems to exist only as a departure point and service station for the transient population of some ten to fifteen thousand who live on the 130 oil platforms out to sea.

That said, Aberdeen's **architecture** is undeniably striking: a granite cityscape created in the nineteenth century by three fine architects – Archibald Simpson and John Smith in the early years of the century and, subsequently, A. Marshall Mackenzie. Classical inspiration and Gothic-revival styles predominate, giving grace to a material once thought of as only good enough for tombs and paving stones. In addition, in the last few years the city's tourist board has tried to restyle Aberdeen's image from Granite City to **Rose City**. Every spare inch of ground has been turned into a flowerbed, the parks some of the most beautiful in Britain. This positive floral explosion – Aberdeen has been debarred from *Britain in Bloom* competitions because it kept winning – has certainly cheered up the general greyness, but nonetheless the new image, just like the first, is always at the mercy of the weather.

Some history

In the twelfth century, Alexander I noted "Aberdon" as one of his principal towns and by the thirteenth century, it had become a centre for **trade and fishing**, a jumble of timber and wattle houses perched on three small hills, with the castle to the east and St Nicholas' kirk outside the gates to the west. It was here that **Robert the Bruce** sought refuge during the Scottish Wars of Independence, leading to the garrison of the castle by Edward I and Balliol's supporters. During the night in 1306, the townspeople

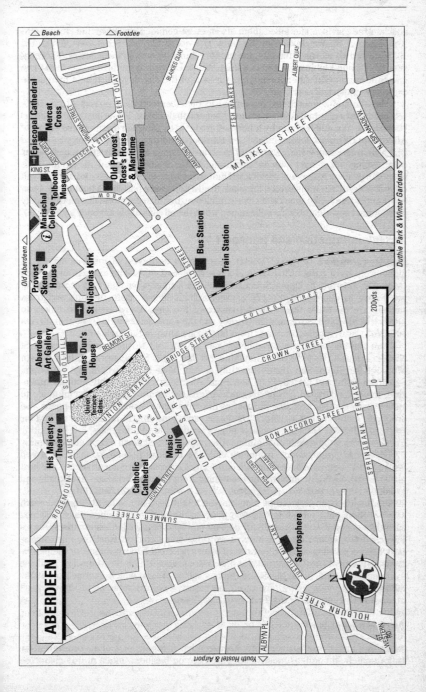

△ Beach   △ Footdee

ABERDEEN

△ Old Aberdeen

† Episcopal Cathedral

■ Mercat Cross

KING ST.

MARISCHAL STREET

CASTLEGATE

■ Marischal College Tolbooth Museum

i ■ Provost Skene's House

■ Old Provost Ross's House & Maritime Museum

SHIPROW

VIRGINIA STREET

REGENT QUAY

BLAIKIES QUAY

JAMIESON'S QUAY

ALBERT QUAY

FISH MARKET

MARKET STREET

△ Duthie Park & Winter Gardens ▷

■ Bus Station

■ Train Station

GUILD STREET

COLLEGE STREET

CROWN STREET

N ESPLANADE W.

BRIDGE STREET

† St Nicholas Kirk

■ Aberdeen Art Gallery

SCHOOLHILL

BELMONT ST.

■ James Dun's House

UNION TERRACE

Union Terrace Gdns.

■ His Majesty's Theatre

ROSEMOUNT VIADUCT

GOLDEN SQUARE

UNION STREET

■ Music Hall

■ Catholic Cathedral

HUNTLY STREET

SUMMER STREET

BON ACCORD STREET

BON ACCORD SQUARE

SPRINGBANK TERRACE

■ Sartrosphere

JUSTICE MILL LANE

ALBYN PL.

HOLBURN STREET

ST WESTERN RD

200yds

0

△ Youth Hostel & Airport

attacked the garrison and killed them all, an event commemorated by the city's motto "Bon Accord", the watchword for the night. The victory was not to last, however, and in 1337 Edward III stormed the city, forcing its rebuilding on a grander scale. A century later the Bishop Elphinstane founded the Catholic **University** in the area north of town known today as **Old Aberdeen**, while the rest of the city developed as a mercantile centre and important port.

Industrial and economic expansion led to the Aberdeen New Streets Act in 1800, setting off a hectic half-century of development that almost led to financial disaster. Luckily, the city was rescued by a boom in trade: in the **shipyards** the construction of **Aberdeen Clippers** revolutionized sea transport, and gave Britain supremacy in the China tea trade, and in 1882, a group of local businessmen acquired a **steam** tugboat for trawl fishing – sail gave way to steam and fisher families flooded in. By the mid-twentieth century Aberdeen's traditional industries were in decline, but the discovery of **oil** in the North Sea transformed the place from a depressed port into a boomtown. Lean times in the late 1980s shook the city's confidence, but Aberdeen remains an extremely prosperous city – though what will happen when the oil runs out is anybody's guess.

Arrival, information and transport

Aberdeen's **airport** (☎01224/722331), seven miles northwest of town, is served by flights from most parts of the UK and a few European cities. The express airport bus (Mon–Fri; £2) runs to Union Street and the bus station; after 6pm and at weekends, you'll have to depend on the #27A (every 90min; 30min). Both the **bus** and **train** stations are on Guild Street, in the centre of the city. Aberdeen is also linked to Lerwick in Shetland, Stromness in Orkney and the Faroe Isles by *P&O* Scottish **ferries** (☎572615), with regular crossings from Jamieson's Quay in the harbour.

From the stations it's a two-minute walk up the hill to the **tourist office** at St Nicholas House, Broad St (Oct–May Mon–Sat 9am–5pm, Sun 10am–2pm; June & Sept Mon–Sat 9am–6pm, Sun 10am–4pm; July & Aug Mon–Fri 9am–8pm, Sat 9am–6pm, Sun 10am–6pm; ☎01224/632727). You'll find Aberdeen's free monthly **listings magazine**, the snappily titled *City of Aberdeen Arts & Recreation Listings*, a useful guide to current events – it's available in most of the pubs and shops. The tourist board also produces a free monthly *What's On* leaflet and runs the 24-hour *What's On Line* (☎01224/636363). *The Vibe*, available at arts venues and trendier bars, is a bi-monthly freesheet with good details on nightlife. Alternatively, track down a copy of the monthly *57° North* magazine, which combines clubbing news with comedy, features, green issues and a comprehensive round-up of the city's extensive live-music scene. The best place for more esoteric information – anything from t'ai chi workshops to festivals and ceilidhs – is the *Lemon Tree Arts Centre*, 5 West North St (☎01224/642230).

Aberdeen is best explored by foot, but you might need to use **local buses** to reach some of the sights, including Old Aberdeen, in the north of the city. Make sure you carry lots of coins: fares (25p–£1.10) depend on distance travelled. Alternatively, buy a **Farecard** (£2, £5 or £10), which saves worrying about change, from the main **transport office**, 395 King St, the City Council offices next to the tourist office, or the permanently busy city-centre kiosk outside *Marks & Spencer*, Union St. **Maps** are available from the tourist office, the kiosk and the bus station. **Taxis**, which operate from ranks throughout the city centre, are rarely necessary, except late at night. If you don't manage to hail one, call *Mairs Taxis* (☎01224/724040).

Accommodation

As befits a high-flying business city, Aberdeen has a large choice of **accommodation**. Unfortunately, though, as most visitors are here on business, much of it is characterless and expensive. Predictably, the best budget options are the **B&Bs** and **guest houses**, most of which are strung along Bon Accord Street and the Great Western Road, linked by buses #17, #18 and #19 to town. If you're really strapped for cash, head for the **youth hostel**, or try the **student halls** left vacant for visitors in the summer months. There's also a **campsite** in the suburbs.

Hotels, B&Bs and guest houses

Albert and Victoria Private Hotel, 1–2 Albert Terrace (☎01224/641717). Listed building at the west end of Union St – convenient for town centre and quiet at night. ②.

Bracklinn Guest House, 348 Great Western Rd (☎01224/317060). Welcoming Victorian house with elegant furnishings – one of the city's best B&Bs. ②.

Caledonian Thistle Hotel, Union Terrace (☎01224/640233). The best of the posh hotels – an impressive Victorian edifice just off Union St. ⑦.

Campbell's Guest House, 444 King St (☎01224/625444). Highly recommended breakfasts. One mile from the city centre and handy for the beach. ②.

Ferryhill House Hotel, 169 Bon Accord St (☎01224/590867). One of the most historic pubs in Aberdeen with colourful rooms and good food. ③.

Fourways Guest House, 435 Great Western Rd (☎01224/310218). A converted manse in the west end of town. ②.

Mannofield Hotel, 447 Great Western Rd (☎01224/315888). Charming old granite building, once a posh private house, one mile west of town. Excellent value three-course dinners. ③.

Queen's Hotel, 51–53 Queen's Rd (☎01224/209999). Cheerful city-centre hotel, recently refurbished, with a good culinary reputation. ④.

Salisbury Guest House, 12 Salisbury Terrace (☎01224/590447). Family-run, comfortable, clean guest house. ②.

Hostels, campsites and campus accommodation

Crombie Johnstone Halls, College Bounds, Old Aberdeen (☎01224/273301). Private rooms in probably the best of the student halls available, in one of the most interesting parts of the city. ①.

Hazelhead (☎01224/321268), five miles west of centre. Grassy campsite with a swimming pool nearby. Follow signs from ring road or take buses #4 or #14. April–Sept. ①.

King George VI Memorial Hostel, 8 Queen's Rd (☎01224/646988). Grade 1 SYHA youth hostel with rooms for four to six, but no café. Closed early Jan to early Feb. Bus #14 and #15 from the train station. Curfew is 2am.

The City

Aberdeen divides neatly into five main areas. The **city centre**, roughly bounded by Broad Street, Union Street, Schoolhill and Union Terrace, features the opulent **Marischal College**, the colonnaded **Art Gallery** with its fine collection, and homes that predate Aberdeen's nineteenth-century town planning and have been preserved as **museums**. Union Street continues west to the comparatively cosmopolitan **West End**, where much of the city's decent nightlife, plus a couple of sights, can be found amid its tall grey town houses. To the south, the **harbour** still heaves with boats serving the fish and oil industries, while north of the centre lies twee **Old Aberdeen**, a village neighbourhood presided over by **King's College** and **St Machar's Cathedral** that is a sanctuary from the rush of the city and harbour. The magnificent **beach** marks the city's entire eastern border.

The City Centre

Any exploration of the city centre should begin at the east end of the mile-long **Union Street**, whose impressive architecture finishes up at **Castlegate**, where Aberdeen's long-gone castle once stood, and which these days holds a somewhat scruffy and uninteresting **market** (Thurs–Sat). The view up gently rising Union Street – a jumble of

OIL AND ABERDEEN

When **oil** was discovered in BP's Forties Field in 1970, Aberdonians rightly viewed it as a massive financial opportunity and, despite fierce competition from other east coast British ports and communities in Scandinavia and Germany, the city succeeded in persuading the oil companies to base their headquarters here. Land was made available for housing and industry, millions invested into the harbour and offshore developments, new schools opened and the airport expanded to include a heliport, which has since become the busiest in the world.

The city's **population** swelled by 60,000, and earnings escalated from fifteen percent below the national average to a figure well above it. Wealthy oil companies built prestigious offices, swish new restaurants, upmarket bars and shops, but as Aberdeen rode on the crest of this new economic wave its other industries were neglected.

At the peak of production in the **mid-1980s**, 2.6 million barrels a day were being turned out, and the price had reached $80 a barrel – from which it plummeted to $10 during the slump of 1986. The effect was devastating – jobs vanished at the rate of a thousand a month, house prices dropped and Aberdeen soon discovered just how dependent on oil it was. The moment oil prices began to rise again, more bad luck struck with the loss of 167 lives in the **Piper Alpha disaster** and the government implemented an array of much needed but very expensive safety measures.

Plans have been put forward to avoid such a crisis happening again, but have been shelved following the recent upturn in oil prices, and while the rest of Britain suffers its worst ever recession, Aberdeen has lower than four percent unemployment and millions have been reinvested into the oil fields. However, the city faces a fierce fight to keep ahead of new **foreign competition** for investment and secure employment for future generations of Aberdonians. Signs are, with the oil boom past its peak, that the city may well have to look beyond such a single-issue economy for the future.

grey spires, turrets and jostling cream buses – is quintessential Aberdeen. City life used to revolve around the late seventeenth-century **Mercat Cross**, now dwarfed by mighty granite buildings such as the Salvation Army Citadel and the Town House (fronted by the *Clydesdale Bank*). It's worth a look, however, carved with a unique portrait gallery of the Stuart sovereigns alongside some fierce gargoyles.

A discreet door on the side of the Town House leads into the **Tolbooth Museum** (April–Sept Tues–Sat 10am–5pm, Thurs till 8pm, Sun 2–5pm; free), quarried out of the seventeenth-century prison lurking behind the steely grey nineteenth-century exterior. The museum takes the theme of law and imprisonment throughout, the claustrophobic staircases giving plenty of opportunity to appreciate the harsh realities of incarceration. At the top of the building, a remarkable audio-visual display, featuring a talking model of a Jacobite prisoner, complete with rattling chains, explains the background and atmosphere of the 1745 Jacobite uprising as well as ensuring that the hairs on the back of your neck bristle nervously. Other displays include some fascinating maps and 3D models charting Aberdeen's development from its old-town beginnings.

Nearby, on King Street, the sandstone **St Andrew's Episcopal Cathedral**, where Samuel Seabury, America's first bishop, was consecrated in 1784, offers a welcome relief to the uniform granite. Inside, its spartan whiteness is broken by impressive and florid gold ceiling bosses of the then 48 states of the USA on one side and, on the other, 48 local families who remained loyal to the Episcopal Church during the eighteenth-century Penal Laws. Even more resplendent is the gilded baldachino canopy over the High Altar. To the right is the Suther Chapel, dominated by the Seabury Centenary window, a light, bright and intensely sentimental splash of primary colours.

West down Union Street brings you to Broad Street, where you'll find Aberdeen's oldest surviving private house, **Provost Skene's House** at 45 Guestrow (Mon–Sat

10am–5pm; free), dating from 1545. Only the intervention of the Queen Mother in 1938 saved the house from being demolished like its neighbours, and its fully restored period rooms with oak panelling, fine plaster and well-preserved furniture now offer a glimpse of how a rich Aberdonian merchant lived in the seventeenth century. Don't miss the Long Gallery, where a series of ornate tempera High Church paintings from 1622 show a spirited defiance against the Protestant dogma of the time.

Nearby, on Broad Street, stands Aberdeen's most imposing edifice and the world's second largest granite building after the Escorial in Madrid – the exuberant **Marischal College**, with its tall, steely grey pinnacled neo-Gothic facade, only completed in 1906. The college itself was founded in 1593 by the fourth Earl Marischal, and co-existed as a separate Protestant university from Catholic King's, just up the road, for over two centuries. Charles I endeavoured to reconcile the two as a single entity, but it wasn't until 1860 that they were united as the University of Aberdeen. The fan-vaulted lobby, once the college's old hall, now houses the wonderful **Anthropological Museum** (Mon–Fri 10am–5pm, Sun 2–5pm; free), two large rooms containing a wealth of weird exhibits, among them Eskimo soapstone carvings, an outrigger canoe carved from a breadfruit tree from Papua New Guinea, a macabre Hawaiian head crafted from basketry and with real dogs' teeth, and a Tibetan prayer wheel. Most bizarre are the high-relief mummy case of an Egyptian five-year-old girl and a stomach-churning foot, unbound and preserved in brine.

On the corner of Schoolhill and Union Street stands the long **St Nicholas Kirk** (Mon–Fri noon–4pm, Sat 1–3pm; free), actually two churches in one with a solid, central bell tower rising from the middle, from where the 48-bell carillon, the largest in Britain, regularly chimes across the city. There's been a church here since at least 1157, but as the largest kirk in Scotland, it was severely damaged during the Reformation and divided into the West and the East Church, separated today by the transepts and crossing; only the north transept, known as Collinson's aisle, survives from the twelfth century. The Renaissance-style **West Church**, formerly the nave of St Nicholas, was designed in the mid-eighteenth century by James Gibbs. Inside, there's a canopied gallery especially for the city councillors – the most grandiose pew is reserved for the Lord Provost. The **East Church** was rebuilt over the groin-vaulted crypt of the restored fifteenth-century St Mary's Chapel (entered from Correction Wynd), which back in the 1600s was a place to imprison witches – you can still see the iron rings to which they were chained. Take time to explore the large peaceful churchyard, which with its green marble tombs and Baroque monuments seems a million miles from the bustling main street. A little further west up Schoolhill, **James Dun's House** (Mon–Sat 10am–5pm; free) is a smallish, two-storey Georgian house built for the rector of Aberdeen's grammar school in 1769 and now housing contemporary art exhibitions and moderately interesting displays on the city's history.

Opposite, Aberdeen's **Art Gallery** (Mon–Wed, Fri & Sat 10am–5pm, Thurs 10am–8pm, Sun 2–5pm; free) was purpose-built in 1884 to a Neoclassical design by Mackenzie. The ground floor features a collection of decorative art that includes Chinese ceramics, Wedgwood pottery and Aberdonian silver, although the first-floor art collection is perhaps more engaging, much of it bequested in 1900 by Alex MacDonald, a local granite merchant who included among his circle the Pre-Raphaelites, Bloomsbury set and a number of Scottish artists. The two room **MacDonald collection** includes a vast number of Victorian landscapes, Pre-Raphaelite works by Rosetti, Burne-Jones and the other usuals, and paintings by "Boys" from the Glasgow school, plus 92 paintings of Victorian artists – mostly self-portraits. The nineteenth-century foreign room houses an Impressionist collection, including works by Boudin, Courbet, Sisley, Monet, Pissaro and Renoir. As for twentieth-century art, there are paintings by Augustus John, Ben Nicholson, Stanley Spencer, Frank Auerbach and David Hockney as well as sculptures by Barbara Hepworth.

West of the gallery, across the rail bridge, the sunken **Union Terrace Gardens** are a welcome relief from the hubbub of heavy traffic on Union Street. Overlooking the scene is a hulking great statue of the "Guardian of Scotland", William Wallace. In summer you'll catch free brass bands and orchestral performances, making it a great place to have a picnic. From here there are views across to the three domes of the Central Library, St Mark's Church and His Majesty's Theatre, traditionally referred to as "Education, Salvation and Damnation".

The West End

Tatty gentility characterizes much of the **West End**, the area around the westernmost part of Union Street, which roughly begins at the great granite columns of the city's **Music Hall**. A block north is **Golden Square**, a misnomer as the trim houses, pubs and restaurants surrounding the statue of the Duke of Gordon are uniformly grey. The city has invested much in gentrifying the area north of Union Street, with the resultant cobbles, old-fashioned lamps and mushrooming designer boutiques. Huntly Street, west of Golden Square, heads off towards the curiously thin spire of **St Mary's Catholic Cathedral** (daily 8am–5pm), a typically foreboding example of Victorian Gothic church architecture.

On the southern side of Union Street, wedged between Bon Accord Street and Bon Accord Terrace, **Bon Accord Square** is a typical, charming Aberdeen square. In the middle, a grassy centre surrounds a great hulk of granite, commemorating **Alexander Sampson**, architect of much of nineteenth-century Aberdeen. West of Bon Accord Terrace is Justice Mill Lane, home to many of the city's favourite bars and nightclubs, and also to the **Sartrosphere** (school terms Mon & Wed–Fri 10am–4pm, Sat 10am–5pm, Sun 1.30–5pm; school holidays Mon–Sat 10am–5pm, Sun 1.30–5pm; £3), Aberdeen's thoroughly entertaining hands-on science exhibition. The Sartrosphere itself – an ingenious illusion of a vast globe surrounded by numerous images of oneself – is created by walking into an open square of four mirrors with a patterned panel head of you. Other exhibits include a superb 3D map of northeast Scotland, and a new biological section in which you can see inside beehives and an anthill.

The harbour

The old cobbled road of Shiprow winds from Castlegate, at the east end of Union Street, down to the north side of the harbour. Just off this steep road, well signposted, is Aberdeen's oldest surviving building, **Old Provost Ross's House** (Mon–Sat 10am–5pm; free), dotted with numerous tiny windows and boasting the original main doorway set into an arched recess. Actually two houses joined together, it was rescued by the NTS in 1954 and became the **Maritime Museum** thirty years later in deference to the eighteenth-century shipping merchant who once lived here. Through the small rooms, low doorways and labyrinthine corridors it tells in detail the many aspects of Aberdeen's nautical history. A wide range of ship models, some used by shipbuilders during construction, others built in painstaking detail by bored sailors, and still more folded into bottles, litter the place, along with numerous paintings and first-hand oral histories. One room focuses on the city's whaling industry between the mid-eighteenth and the mid-nineteenth centuries, while another is devoted to the herring trade. At the top of the house, an exhibition documents Aberdeen's move into the oil industry, with a magnificently detailed scale model of a rig.

At the bottom of Shiprow, the cobbles meet Market Street, which runs the length of the **harbour**. Here brightly painted oil-supply ships, sleek cruise ships and peeling fishing boats jostle for position to an ever-constant clatter and the screech of well-fed seagulls. Follow your nose down the road to the **fish market**, best visited early (7–

8am) when the place is in full swing. The current market building dates from 1982, but fish has been traded here for centuries – the earliest record dating back to 1281 when an envoy of Edward I's was charged for one thousand barrels of sturgeon and five thousand salt fish.

Back at the north end of Market Street, Trinity Quay runs to the shipbuilding yards and down York Street to the east corner of the harbour. Here you'll come to Aberdeen's "fitee" or **Footdee** (bus #14 or #15 from Union St), a nineteenth-century fishermen's village of higgledy-piggledy cottages which back onto the sea, their windows and doors facing inwards to protect from storms but also, so they say, to prevent the Devil from sneaking in the back door. This area, although not dangerous, is now the city's red-light district.

From Market Street it's a twenty-minute bus ride (#6 from Market St or #25 from Union St) to **Duthie Park** on Polmuir Road and Riverside Drive (10am–dusk; free), opened as public gardens in the eighteenth century. The rose garden, known as Rose Mountain due to its profusion of blooms, is great in summer, but the real treat is the Winter Gardens – jokingly held to be a favourite haunt with mean Aberdonians saving on their heating bills. To be fair, the place is most stunning in bad weather, offering a steamy jungle paradise of enormous cacti, exotic plants and even tropical birds.

Old Aberdeen

An independent burgh until 1891, the tranquil district of **Old Aberdeen**, a twenty-minute bus ride north of the city centre, has always maintained a separate village-like identity. Dominated by King's College and St Machar's Cathedral, its medieval cobbled streets, tiny wynds and little lanes are conserved beautifully, with few cars except along St Machar's Drive, and only one bus (#25 from Union St).

The southern half of High Street is overlooked by **King's College Chapel** (Mon–Fri 9am–5pm), the first and finest of the college buildings, completed in 1495 with an imposing Renaissance spire. Named in honour of James IV, the chapel's west door is flanked by his coat of arms and those of his queen. The chapel stands on the quadrangle, whose gracious buildings retain a medieval plan but were built much later; those immediately north were designed by Mackenzie early this century, with the exception of Cromwell Tower at the northeast corner, which was completed in 1658. The first thing you notice inside the chapel is that there is no aisle. Within this unusual plan the screen, the stalls (each unique) and the ribbed arched wooden ceiling are rare and beautiful examples of medieval Scottish woodcarving. The remains of Bishop Elphinstone's tomb and the carved pulpit from nearby St Machars are also here. A spanking new **visitor centre**, in the main college buildings, tells the tempestuous tale of the establishment of the University of Aberdeen, which came about finally in 1860 when Protestant Marischal College and sceptical King's College were merged, well over two hundred years after the first attempt.

From the college, the cobbled High Street leads a short way north to **St Machars Cathedral** on the leafy Chanonry (daily 9am–5pm; free), overlooking Seaton Park and the River Don. The site was reputedly founded in 580 by Machar, a follower of Columba, when he was sent by the latter to find a grassy platform near the sea, overlooking a river shaped like the crook on a bishop's crozier. This setting fitted the bill perfectly, and the cathedral, a huge fifteenth-century fortified building (only half the length of the original after the collapse of the central tower in 1688), is one of the city's first great granite edifices and a well-known Aberdonian landmark. Inside, the stained-glass windows are a dazzling blaze of colour, and above the nave the heraldic oak ceiling from 1520 is illustrated with nearly fifty different coats of arms from Europe's royal houses and Scotland's bishops and nobles.

Next door to the cathedral, the **Cruickshank Botanic Gardens** (Jan–April & Oct–Dec Mon–Fri 9am–4.30pm; May–Sept Mon–Fri 9am–4.30pm, Sat & Sun 2–5pm; free), laid out in 1898, offer lovely glimpses of the cathedral through the trees. In spring and summer its worth checking out the flowerbeds, but don't bother with the dreary zoological museum. A wander through Seaton Park will bring you to the thirteenth-century **Brig' o' Balgownie**, which gracefully spans the River Don, nearly a mile north of the cathedral. Still standing (despite Thomas the Rhymer's prediction that it would fall were it ever to be crossed by an only son riding a mare's only foal), the bridge is best visited at sunset – Byron, who spent much of his childhood in Aberdeen, remembered it as one of his favourite places.

The beach

Among large British cities, Aberdeen could surely claim to have the best **beach**. Less than a mile to the east of Union Street is a great two-mile sweep of clean sand, broken by groynes and lined all along with an esplanade. On a sunny day, most of the city seems to be down there. The southern end of the beach is a cosy collection of arcades, a couple of fairly tatty amusement parks, a vast leisure centre, cafés and bars. As you head further north, most of the beach's hinterland is devoted to successive golf links.

Eating, drinking and nightlife

Aberdeen is certainly not short of good places to **eat**, though you will find it more pricey than elsewhere in northeast Scotland. Union Street and the surrounding area has a glut of attractive **restaurants** and **cafés**. As for **nightlife**, like most ports-of-call Aberdeen caters for a transient population with a lot of disposable income and a desire to get drunk as quickly as possible. Every time a shop closes down in Union Street it seems to reopen as a loud, flashy bar. That said, there are still a number of more traditional old **pubs** which, though usually packed, are well worth digging out.

Restaurants and cafés

Ashvale, 46 Great Western Rd. One of Scotland's finest – and biggest – fish-and-chip shops, with seating for 300. The fish is best, though they also serve inexpensive stovies, meat pies, etc. Open daily until late.

Drummonds, 1 Belmont St. Just off Union St, this is a stylish, café and wine bar during the day and a noisy music venue in the evening.

Elronds Café, *Caledonian Thistle Hotel*, 10–14 Union Terrace. Surprisingly inexpensive lunch and dinner menu, considering its central location in a marble-floored and exclusive hotel.

La Lombarda, Castlegate (☎01224/640916). Smart upstairs trattoria and livelier basement bistro/café in one of the city's oldest established restaurants.

Lemon Tree, 5 W North St (☎01224/642230). Homemade Scottish food. Very reasonably priced, and a buzzing atmosphere with a theatre upstairs.

Owlies, Unit C, Littlejohn St (☎01224/649267). Plain French brasserie food, with plenty of vegetarian options.

Silver Darling Restaurant, Pocra Quay, N Pier (☎01224/576229). Excellent, if pricey, seafood restaurant in the Footdee. Closed Sat lunch.

Wild Boar, 16 Belmont St (☎01224/625357). Upbeat brasserie with well-priced vegetarian food, soups and pastas. A popular evening venue. Closed Sat lunch.

Pubs and bars

Bex Bar, Justice Mill Lane. Studenty and trendy, the place gets packed at the weekend as a pre-club haunt.

Carriages, *Brentwood Hotel*, 101 Crown St. Unusually lively hotel cellar bar with the city's largest range of real ales and ciders. Also serves excellent bar food.

Cocky Hunters, 504 Union St. Small live-music bar, popular with trendies and students.

Ferryhill House, Bon Accord St. Pub with its own garden and very good food.

Glenlivet Bar, 43 Regent Quay. Cheeriest, most cosmopolitan of the harbourside bars.

Ma Cameron's Inn, Little Belmont St. Aberdeen's oldest pub, though only a section remains of the original. Serves food. Closed Sun.

The Prince of Wales, 7 St Nicholas Lane. Aberdeen's most highly regarded pub, with a long bar and flagstone floor. Very central and renowned for its real ales, it's often crowded.

St Machar Bar, 97 High St, Old Aberdeen. The cathedral quarter's sole pub, an old-fashioned bar inevitably full of King's College students.

Triple Kirks, Belmont St. Imaginative church conversion, now an extremely popular drinking hole, with regular live music. Popular with clubbers and theatregoers.

Clubs and live music venues

Franklyn's, Justice Mill Lane. Part of the same complex as the *Bex Bar* and catering for the same studenty crowd. Chart-oriented dance music is the staple.

Joy, 1 Regent Quay. Trendy dance, acid jazz and groove club.

Lemon Tree, 5 W North St. Arts centre with a great buzz at present. The laid-back café-bar is home to regular live music, comedy and folk.

O'Henrys, Adelphi Close. Flash studenty club just off Union Street.

Ministry of Sin, 16 Dee St. The hottest dance club for miles; Sunday nights are legendary.

The Pelican, *Metro Hotel*, Market St. Hot and sweaty club with good bands – mainly indie.

Theatres, art-house cinemas and concert halls

Aberdeen Arts Centre, 33 King St (☎01224/635208). A variety of theatrical productions alongside a programme of lectures, exhibitions and art films.

Capital Theatre, Union St (☎01224/583141). Visiting mainstream rock and pop acts.

Cowdray Hall, Schoolhill (☎01224/646333). Classical music, often with visiting orchestras.

His Majesty's, Rosemount Viaduct (☎01224/641122). Aberdeen's main theatre, in a beautifully restored Edwardian building, with a programme that ranges from highbrow drama and opera to pantomime.

Lemon Tree, 5 W North St (☎01224/642230). Avant-garde events with off-the-wall comedians and plays – many are a spin-off from Edinburgh's festival – plus an art-house cinema.

Music Hall, Union St (☎01224/632080). Big-name comedy and music acts.

Stonehaven and Dunnottar Castle

A busy pebble-dashed town, **STONEHAVEN**, fifteen miles down the coast from Aberdeen, attracts hordes of holidaymakers in the summer because of its sheltered Kincardine coastline. The town itself is split into two parts, the picturesque working harbour area being most likely to detain you. At one end of the harbour, Stonehaven's oldest building, the **Tolbooth** (June–Sept Mon & Thurs–Sat 10am–noon & 2–5pm; Wed & Sun 2–5pm; free), built as a storehouse during the construction of Dunnottar Castle (see below) is now a museum of local history and fishing. **Boat trips** can be arranged with the harbour master (☎01569/762741).

The old High Street – lined with some fine town houses and civic buildings – connects the harbour and its surrounding old town with the late eighteenth-century planned centre on the other side of the River Carron. On New Year's Eve, High Street is the location of the ancient ceremony of **Fireballs**, when people get raging drunk and parade its length, swinging metal cages full of burning debris around their heads. This, it is said, wards off evil spirits for the year ahead. The **new town** focuses on the giant market square, overlooked by the dusky pink granite market hall with its impressive steeple and a wonderfully stern notice warning "No Bills. Commit No Nuisance Here". Evan Street heads inland from the market square before swinging right into Arduthie Road, which climbs up to the train station, a good fifteen-minute walk from the centre.

Two miles outside Stonehaven (the tourist office sells a walking guide for the scenic amble), **Dunnottar Castle** (late March to Oct Mon–Sat 9am–6pm, Sun 2–5pm; £2.50) is a huge ninth-century fortress set on a three-sided sheer cliff jutting into the sea – a spot dramatic enough to be chosen as the setting for Zeffirelli's movie version of *Hamlet*. Once the principal fortress of the northeast, much of Dunnottar now stands in ruins, though the scatter of remains are worth a good root around; don't miss the so-called Marischal's Suite, which gives dramatic views out to the crashing sea. Siege and blood-stained drama splatter the castle's past. In 1297 William Wallace burned the whole English Plantaganet garrison alive here, and one of the more gruesome tales from the castle's history tells of the imprisonment and torture of 122 men and 45 women Covenanters in 1685 – an event, as it says on the Covenanters' Stone in the churchyard, "whose dark shadow is for evermore flung athwart the Castled Rock".

The **tourist office** is at 66 Allardice St, the main street past the square (April–June, Sept & Oct daily 10am–1.15pm & 2–5pm; July & Aug daily 10am–7.30pm; (☎01569/762806). If you want to **stay**, *Arduthie House*, Ann St, is a good B&B (☎01569/762381; ②), as is the *Braemar*, Evan St (☎01569/764841; ②). Down by the harbour, the shabby *Marine Hotel* (☎01569/762155; ③) is a great place for eating and drinking. For **food** in Stonehaven itself, the *Tolbooth Fish Restaurant*, on the harbour, is pricey but worth it, while *Robert's Bakery*, next to the tourist office, has good sandwiches and cakes. Try the *Marine Hotel* or the S*hip Inn* on the harbour for drinking or pub food. In the "new" town, there's regular live **music** at the *Belvedere Hotel* on Evan Street; a folk club at the *St Leonard's Hotel*, Bath St; and generally a lively time at the *Hook and Eye*, Allardice St. Stonehaven's respected **folk festival** takes place in mid-July.

Deeside

More commonly known as Royal **Deeside**, the land stretching west of the coast along the River Dee revels in its connections with the royal family, who have regularly holidayed here, at **Balmoral**, since Queen Victoria bought the estate. Eighty thousand Scots turned out to welcome her on her first visit in 1848, but some weren't so charmed – one local journalist remarked that the area was about to be "desolated by cockneys and other horrible reptiles". Today, however, the locals are fiercely protective of their connections, forever retelling stories of their encounters with blue-bloods.

Considering Victoria had her pick of the country in which to establish a holiday home, it comes as quite a surprise that this windswept, rainy spot should have attracted her so much. Her visitors thought the same: Count von Moltke, then aide-de-camp to Prince Frederick William of Prussia, observed: "It is very astonishing that the Royal Power of England should reside amid this lonesome, desolate, cold mountain scenery", while Tsar Nicholas II whined, "The weather is awful, rain and wind every day and on top of it no luck at all – I haven't killed a stag yet". However, the Queen adored the place, and the woods were said to remind Prince Albert of Thuringia, his homeland.

Deeside is undoubtedly beautiful in a fierce, craggy, Scottish way, and the royal presence has certainly put a stop to any unattractive mass development. Villages strung along the A93, the main route through the area, are as picturesque as you'll find anywhere, and the facilities for visitors, who boost the local economy no end, are first-class, with a couple of youth hostels, some outstanding hotels and plenty of castles and scenic walks.

Ballater and Balmoral

The unassuming little town of **BALLATER**, hemmed in by fir-covered mountains, was dragged from obscurity in the nineteenth century when it was discovered that the local waters were useful in curing scrofula. Scrofula is no longer a problem, but you can still buy Ballater spring water, and the town remains a busy place – these days due to its proximity to Balmoral, which lies eight miles to the west. It was in Ballater that Queen

Victoria first arrived in Deeside by train from Aberdeen back in 1848 – she wouldn't allow a station to be built any closer to Balmoral. Ballater's supremely elegant train station, in the centre of town, is now defunct, but still displays its Victorian timetables. The local shops, having provided the royals with household basics, also flaunt their connections, sporting oversized crests above their doorways. Ballater is a good base for local walks, including a fairly strenuous all-day trek from the Spittal of Glenmuick car park, at the head of the loch, leads up and around Lochnagar (3789ft), the mountain much painted and written about by the current Prince of Wales.

The **tourist office** is opposite the station in Station Square (mid-April to mid-May & Oct daily 10am–1.15pm & 2–5pm; mid-May to late June and Sept daily 9.30am–1.15pm & 2–6.30pm; late June to Aug daily 9.30am–7pm; ☎013397/55306). There are plenty of reasonable **B&Bs**: *Mrs Cowie*, 3 Braemar Rd (☎013397/55699; ②) is the cheapest. Hotels worth trying include the welcoming *Deeside*, Braemar Rd (☎013397/55420; ③) or the nearby *Auld Kirk* (☎013397/55762; ③), complete with spire and an excellent restaurant. For **camping**, the *Anderson Road Caravan Park* (book through the council on ☎01569/762001) down towards the river, has around sixty tent pitches. There are numerous **places to eat**, from smart hotel restaurants to bakers and coffee shops. For non-touristy drinking, try the back bar (entrance down Golf St) of the *Prince of Wales*, which faces the main square. **Bike rental** (as well as canoeing, off-road driving, fishing and gliding) is available from *Making Treks* on Station Square (☎013397/55865).

Balmoral Castle and Crathie Church

Originally a sixteenth-century tower house built for the powerful Gordon family, **Balmoral Castle** (May–July Mon–Sat 10am–5pm; £2.50) has been a royal residence since 1852, when it was converted to the Scottish Baronial mansion that stands today. The royal family traditionally spend their summer holidays here, but despite its fame, it can be something of a disappointment even for a dedicated royalist. For the three months when the doors are nudged open the general riff-raff are permitted to view only the ballroom and the grounds; for the rest of the year it is not even visible to the paparazzi who converge en masse when the royals are in residence here in August.

Opposite the castle's gates on the main road, the otherwise dull granite church of **CRATHIE**, built in 1895 with the proceeds of a bazaar held at Balmoral, is the royals' local church. Princess Anne chose the place as the venue for her second marriage to her former equerry, Commander Tim Laurence. A small **tourist office** operates in the car park by the church on the main road in Crathie (daily April–June & Sept 10am–1.15pm & 2–5.30pm; July–Aug 10am–5.30pm).

Braemar

Continuing for another few miles, the road rises to the upper part of Deeside and the village of **BRAEMAR**, situated where three passes meet and overlooked by a fairly unimposing **Castle** (Easter–Oct daily 10am–6pm; £1.90) of the same name. Everything in Braemar seems to have been prettified to within an inch of its life or have a price tag on it. That said, it's an invigorating, outdoor kind of place, well patronized by committed hikers, although probably best known for its Highland Games, the annual **Braemar Gathering** (1st Sat of Sept). Games were first held here in the eleventh century, when Malcolm Canmore set contests for the local clans in order to pick the bravest and strongest for his army. Attracting "Heavies" – famous Scottish clan members – from around the world, it's an overcrowded, notoriously popular event: Braemar's caber, for the tossing event, is particularly famous, a stripped pine measuring nearly 20ft and weighing 132 pounds. Since Queen Victoria's day it has become customary for successive generations of royals to attend and it is now a huge event. You're unlikely to get in if you just turn up. If you're keen enough to plan that far in advance, tickets are available in about February and March from the Bookings Secretary, BRHS, Coilacriech, Ballater, AB35 5UH (☎013397/55377).

Braemar's **tourist office** is in the modern building known as the Mews in the middle of the village on Mar Road (mid-March to mid-May daily 10am–1.15pm; mid-May to June & Sept daily 10am–7pm; July & Aug daily 10am–8pm; Oct & Nov 10am–1.15pm & 2–6pm; ☎013397/41600). *Clunie Lodge Guest House*, Clunie Bank Rd (☎013397/41330; ①) on the edge of town, is a good **B&B** with lovely views up Clunie Glen, and there's a **youth hostel** at Corrie Feragie, 21 Glenshee Rd (Jan–Oct; ☎013397/41659). Alternatively, the cheery *Braemar Bunkhouse*, 15 Mar Rd (☎013397/41517 or 41242; ①) is right in the thick of the village; they also rent **bikes**. The *Invercauld Caravan Club Park* (☎013397/41373), just south of the village off the Glenshee Rd, has fifteen **camping** pitches. Standard and fairly pricey hotel **food** can be had from the bars of the *Invercauld* or *Moorfield* hotels, or for some cheap stodge try the *Braemar Takeaway* by the river bridge. For **drinking**, the *Invercauld Arms* in the middle of town is a youthful hangout with a pool table. The *Moorfield Hotel* has regular live music, as does the surprisingly informal cocktail bar of the grand *Fife Hotel*, where dances and ceilidhs are frequent.

Dufftown and Speyside

DUFFTOWN lies at the heart of Speyside, and is a far more amenable base for following the malt whisky trail than nearby Keith, a relative ghost town, as is the ancient burgh of Huntly, east of Dufftown. Founded in 1817 by James Duff, the fourth Earl of Fife, Dufftown proudly proclaims itself "Malt Whisky Capital of the World", and indeed it exports more of the stuff than anywhere else in Britain. Dominating the southern approach to the town along the A941 are the gaunt hilltop ruins of **Auchindoun Castle**. Although you can't go inside, it's enjoyable to wander along the track from the main road to this three-storey keep encircled by Pictish earthworks.

Following the A941 through the town brings you past the **Glenfiddich Distillery** (see below) and up to the old Dufftown train station, currently being restored for a steam line through to Keith (they hope to be running diesel trains by summer 1996 and steam by summer 1997). Behind the Distillery, the ruin of the the thirteenth-century **Balvenie Castle** (April–Sept 9.30am–6.30pm; £1.20) sits on a mound overlooking vast piles of whisky barrels. The castle was a Stewart stronghold, later captured by the Jacobites, and finally abandoned after the 1745 uprising, when it was last used as a government garrison.

Practicalities

The four main streets converge on Main Square, surrounded by craft- and book shops and cafés. For maps and information on the **whisky trail**, head straight to the **tourist office** inside the rather handsome clock tower at the centre of the square (April, May & Oct Mon–Sat 10am–5.30pm; June & Sept Mon–Sat 9.30am–6pm, Sun 2–5pm; July Mon–Sat 9.30am–6.30pm, Sun 12.30–6pm; Aug Mon–Sat 9.30am–7pm, Sun 12.30–7pm; ☎01340/820501). Also on the square, the *Morven* offers good, cheap B&B **accommodation** (☎01340/820507; ①), while the *Fife Arms Hotel* (☎01340/820220; ③) is a good-value traditional hotel with large rooms. Alternatively, there's the *Davaar* B&B, Church St (☎01340/204640; ②), which also offers excellent, traditional Scottish meals.

For **eating**, try the *Glenfiddich Café* just beyond the tourist office on Church Street, or, for more substantial meals, the popular *Task of Speyside*, Balverie St, just off the square. Next door, the *Mason Arms* pub has a busy pool room, frequented mainly by a young crowd. The *Grouse Inn* round the corner is quieter, with a good selection of whiskies. **Rent bikes** from *Mini-Cheers* (☎01340/820559), right on the Main Square.

The Coast to Findhorn

The **coastal region** of northeast Scotland from Aberdeen to Inverness is a rugged, often bleak, landscape which is in parts virtually inaccessible. Still, if the weather is good, it's well worth spending a couple of days meandering through the various little at

THE MALT WHISKY TRAIL

Speyside's **Malt Whisky Trail** is a clearly signposted seventy-mile meander around the region via eight distilleries. In this so-called Golden Triangle lies the largest concentration of malt-whisky-making equipment in the world. Unless you're seriously interested in whisky, it's best to just pick out a couple that appeal, although the truly unique claims of each malt make it difficult to choose one over another. Hopefully the list below will help.

All the distilleries offer a guided tour (usually free) with a tasting to round it off – if you're driving you will be offered a miniature to take away with you. Indeed, travelling the route by car is probably the best way to do it, but for those without their own transport, the *Speyside Rambler* offers a connecting service to some of the distilleries during the summer; for more information call ☎01343/544222. Alternatively you could rent a mountain bike for around £10 a day from *Mini-Cheers*, 5 Fife St, Dufftown (☎01340/820559).

Cardhu, B9102 at Knockando (May–Sept Mon–Sat 9.30am–4.30pm; Oct–April closed Sat; £2). This distillery was established over a century ago, when the founder's wife, Helen Cumming, was nice enough to raise a red flag to warn local crofters when the authorities were on the lookout for their illegal stills.

Dallas Dhu, Mannachie Rd, Forres (April–Sept Mon–Sat 9.30am–6.30pm, Sun 2–6.30pm; Oct–March Mon–Wed & Sat 9.30am–4.30pm, Thurs 9.30am–12.30pm, Sun 2–4.30pm; £2). The last distillery of the nineteenth century, preserved in its Victorian splendour. Easily reached by bus or train.

Glenfarclas, Ballindalloch off the A95, 17 miles southwest of Keith (June–Sept Mon–Fri 9am–4.30pm, Sat 10am–4pm, Sun 1–4pm; Oct–May Mon–Fri only; £2). Includes an exhibition in four languages and a gallery for watching the cask-filling. The whisky here has been described as going down "singing hymns".

Glenfiddich, A941 just north of Dufftown (April to mid-Oct Mon–Sat 9.30am–4.30pm, Sun noon–4.30pm; mid-Oct to March closed Sat & Sun; free). Probably the best known of malt whiskies, and the most touristy of the distilleries. Unlike the other distilleries on the trail, Glenfiddich is actually bottled on the premises – prepare yourself for the lethal-smelling bottling plant. The gift shop sells a 50-year-old bottle, a snip at £5000. Right beside the car park you'll see the unspectacular ruins of Balvenie Castle.

Glen Grant, Rothes (May–Sept Mon–Fri 10am–4pm; free). Back in 1840, when it was established, this was Speyside's largest producer, but today this is one of the least interesting stops on the trail. Children under eight not admitted.

Glenlivet, B9008, 10 miles north of Tomintoul (April–Oct Mon–Sat 10am–4pm; free). First licensed distillery in the Highlands, following the 1823 Act of Parliament which aimed to reduce illicit distilling and smuggling. Good display of old whisky tools and artefacts. Children under eight not admitted.

Speyside Cooperage, Craigellachie, 4 miles north of Dufftown (all year Mon–Fri 9.30am–4.30pm; Easter–Sept also Sat 9.30am–4.30pm; £1.70). After all the distilleries, it's a good idea to see the ancient art of cooperage – the painstaking building of the whisky barrels. Buses to Craigellachie from Elgin.

Strathisla, Keith (mid-May to mid-Sept Mon–Fri 9am–4.30pm; £4). A small old-fashioned distillery claiming to be Scotland's oldest (1786) and situated in a highly evocative highland location on the strath of the Isla river. The malt itself is pretty rare, and used as the heart of the better-known Chivas Regal blend.

fishing villages and the miles of deserted, unspoilt beaches. Keen walkers have the best run of the area; some of the cliffs are so steep that you have to hike considerable distances to get the best views of the coast. Most visitors bypass Peterhead and Fraserburgh, the two largest communities, and head instead to smaller places such as the idyllic village of Pennan. The other main attractions are the working abbey at Pluscarden and the infamous spiritual community at Findhorn.

Pennan to Banff

PENNAN, halfway along the coast between Fraserburgh and Macduff, came into the limelight when village scenes from the successful British film *Local Hero* were filmed here in 1982. There's little to do but enjoy the view; if the weather is good you can spot the occasional shoal of porpoise. Pennan's sole place **to stay** is the *Pennan Inn* (☎01346/561201; ④), one in the single row of lovely whitewashed cottages huddled together along the seafront and built right into the cliff face. The inn can arrange fishing and boat trips, and its excellent **restaurant** serves fantastic mussels along with a wide range of whiskies – you'll need to book in advance.

Heading west along the coast from Pennan brings you after ten miles to **MACDUFF**, a famous spa town during the nineteenth century and now with a thriving and pleasant harbour. In late July, it holds the annual **Tarlair Music Festival** (phone Banff tourist office for details), around a vast clifftop swimming pool, where sound resonates around the rocks and cliffs, to the east of town.

Just over the River Devoron via a beautiful seven-arched bridge is the extravagant **Duff House** by the golf course (April–Sept Wed–Mon 10am–5pm, Oct–March Thurs–Sun 10am–5pm; £2.50; HS), an elegant Georgian Baroque house built to William Adam's design in 1730. Originally intended for one of the northeast's richest men, William Braco, who became Earl of Fife in 1759, the house was clearly built to impress, and could have been even more splendid had Adam been allowed to build curving colonnades either side; Braco's refusal to pay for carved Corinthian columns to be shipped in from Queensferry caused such bitter argument that the laird never actually came to live here and even went so far as to pull down his coach curtains whenever he passed by. The house has been painstakingly restored and reopened as an outpost of the **National Gallery of Scotland**'s extensive collection, which includes portraits by Allan Ramsay, paintings by Welsh landscapist, Richard Wilson, and works by El Greco and Raphael.

Duff House is perched on the edge of **BANFF**, the old lodge house near the main car park by the bridge now housing the **tourist office** (daily April–June & Sept to mid-Oct 10am–5pm; July & Aug 10am–6pm; ☎01261/812419). Here, you can pay a £1 deposit for a thoroughly enjoyable **walkman tour** of the town, both the grand Georgian upper town and, down by the harbour, the older, scruffier **Scotstown**. There are lots of good views, interesting buildings and juicy snippets of ancient gossip. For sea swimming, head to the **Links Beach** on the west side of town. The other beach, at the mouth of the Deveron, is susceptible to strong currents and is best avoided.

Taking the A97 Sandyhill Road (signposted Aberchirder) southwest brings you, after a mile, to the excellent **Colleonard Sculpture Park**, otherwise known as the world's only garden of archetypal abstractionism. Sculptor Frank Bruce, usually to be found around the site, began his outdoor collection in 1965. A man of immense talent, he carves figures and scenes of great vitality and intensity from tree trunks, which he then places around the wonderfully peaceful site.

Banff is a pretty good base. **B&Bs** include *Castlehill*, 58 Castle St (an extension of the High St; ☎01261/818372; ③), or, over the river in the heart of Macduff, *Mrs Grieg's*, 11 Gellymill St (☎01261/833314; ②). Four miles south of Macduff, off the A497 Turriff road, the elegant and welcoming Regency *Eden House* (☎01261/821282; ③) is in extensive grounds overlooking the Deveron valley. **Camping** is best near the beach the *Banff Links Caravan Park* (April–Sept; ☎01261/812228). There are plenty of cafés and pubs for **food and drink**, notably the upstanding *Market Arms*, a sixteenth-century town house on High Shore, or the endearingly tatty *Ship Inn* on Deveronside, by the shore.

Cullen

Twelve miles west of Banff, past the quaint village of **Portsoy**, renowned for its green marble once shipped to Versailles, is **CULLEN**, served by bus from Aberdeen. The town, strikingly situated beneath a superb series of snaking rail viaducts, is made up of two sections – Seatown, by the harbour, and the new town on the hillside. There's a lovely stretch of sand, pleasantly sheltered from the winds by the hills behind Seatown, where the colourful houses huddle end-on to the sea – confusingly numbered according to the order in which they were built.

Cullen's lovely old **kirk**, about a twenty-minute walk from the centre, dates back to the 1300s, and is still packed out on a Sunday morning. Inside you'll see an ornate lairds' enclosure for the likes of the Duffs and Ogilvies who worshipped here; Alexander Ogilvie, who expanded the church in 1543, is buried in an ornate tomb, and there are a few lairds' graves in the yard, though the holiday apartments beyond the wall rather ruin the atmosphere.

Most of the **B&Bs** are set back from the seashore on Seafield Place. They're all much of a muchness, but no. 11 is recommended (☎01542/840819; ②). There's little action in the evening; a drink and a fish supper at the local pub is probably your best bet.

Elgin and around

Inland, about fifteen miles southwest of Cullen, the lively market town of **ELGIN** grew up in the thirteenth century around the River Lossie. It's an appealing place, still largely sticking to its medieval street plan, with a busy main street opening out onto an old cobbled marketplace and a tangle of wynds and pends.

On North College Street, just round the corner from the tourist office and clearly signposted, is the still lovely ruin of **Elgin Cathedral** (April–Sept Mon–Sat 9.30am–6pm, Sun 2–6pm; Oct–March Mon–Wed & Sat 9.30am–noon; £1.20, or £2 joint ticket with Spynie Palace). Once considered Scotland's most beautiful cathedral, rivalling St Andrews in importance, today it is little more than a shell, though it does retain its original facade. Founded in 1224, the three-towered cathedral was extensively rebuilt after a fire in 1270, and stood as the region's highest religious house until 1390 when the so-called Wolf of Badenoch (Alexander Stewart, Earl of Buchan and illegitimate son of Robert II) burnt the place down, along with the rest of the town, in retaliation for being excommunicated by the Bishop of Moray when he left his wife. The cathedral survived this onslaught, but went on to suffer even more during the post-Reformation, when all its valuables were stripped and the building was reduced to common quarry for the locals. Unusual features include the Pictish cross slab in the middle of the ruins and the cracked gravestones with their *memento mori* of skulls and cross bones.

At the very top of High Street is one of the UK's oldest museums, the **Elgin Museum** (April–Sept Mon–Fri 10am–5pm, Sat 11am–4pm, Sun 2–5pm; £1), housed in this building since 1843. Along with the usual local exhibits, there's a weird anthropological collection including reptilian skulls, a shrunken head from Ecuador, a head-hunter's basket decorated with monkey skulls, and Indian sculptures. Strangest of all is the grinning mummy from Peru, thought to have been a princess. The "Making of Moray" exhibition includes an informative display of Pictish remains, including two of the Burghead Bull stones and fragments from the assumed Pictish royal court nearby at Kinneddar. A few doors back along High Street is *The Legend*, a shop associated with the Findhorn Foundation (see box below) and a good source of local alternative information.

Just outside the centre on the A941, a converted mill makes a light and airy venue for the **Moray Motor Museum** (April–Oct daily 11am–5pm; £1.50), a collection of some 25 ancient, fully polished vehicles including a 1929 Rolls Royce Phantom, a 1920 Jaguar, a 1914 Renault, a great old Bentley and a selection of motorbikes with their side cars.

Practicalities

Elgin is well served by public transport, with the Aberdeen–Inverness train stopping here several times a day. The **bus station** is at the opposite end of High Street (☎01343/544222), while the **train station** (call Inverness ☎01463/238924 for information) is slightly less convenient on the south side of town on Station Road (turn right out of the station, left at the island and up Moss St to reach the centre).

The **tourist office**, 17 High St (Jan–March, Nov & Dec Mon–Fri 9.30am–5pm; April–May & Oct Mon–Fri 9.30am–5.45pm, Sat 9.30am–1pm & 2–5.45pm; June & Sept Mon–Sat 9.30am–6.15pm, Sun 2–5.15pm; July & Aug Mon–Sat 9.30am–7.15pm, Sun noon–5.45pm; ☎01343/542666), will book **accommodation**. The quiet *Carronvale*, 18 South Guildry St (☎01343/546864; ②), is one of the nicest **B&Bs** in town; for more luxury, the castle-like *Mansion House Hotel* (☎01343/548811; ⑥), one of the most exclusive in the region, offers Scottish and French dishes. For **food and drink**, *Littlejohn's Brasserie*, 199 High St, is part of a popular Scottish chain of TexMex and Cajun theme restaurants. Otherwise, try *Giles Café-bar*, Batchen St, south off the middle of the High Street, or the slightly overdone *Thunderton House* pub, Thunderton Place, off High Street, part of which is rebuilt from the seventeenth-century old Great

---

THE FINDHORN FOUNDATION

Just over thirty years ago, with little money and no employment, Peter and Eileen Caddy, their three children and friend Dorothy Maclean, settled on a caravan site at Findhorn. Dorothy believed she had a special relationship with what she called the "devas", in her own words "the archetypal formative forces of light or energy that underlie all forms in nature – plants, trees, rivers, etc", and from the uncompromising sandy soil they built a garden filled with remarkable plants and vegetables far larger than had ever been seen in the area. Dorothy Maclean has since left the foundation, and the gardens, though beautiful, are not quite as outstanding as they once were.

The Original Caravan – as it is marked on the site's map – still stands, surrounded by a whole host of newer timber buildings and other caravans. The Foundation is now home to a couple of hundred people, with around eight thousand visitors every year. The buildings, employing solar power, earth roofs and other green initiatives, are remarkable in themselves and show the commitment of the Findhorners to a sustainable future. Public amenities such as the arts centre, holistic health centre, café and excellent shop demonstrate their considerable effort to bring in the local community, most of whom are either indifferent or quietly accepting. Spiritual therapies are on offer, as are classes in numerous holistic healing arts. The Foundation also owns Cluny Hill College and Newbold House in nearby Forres and a west coast island retreat.

As can be expected, the Foundation is not without its controversy, a local JP declaring that "behind the benign and apparently religious front lies a hard core of New Agers experimenting with hallucinatory techniques marketed as spirituality", a predictable enough charge from local conservative thought. Findhorn, now a public company, is also accused of being overly well heeled; certainly any mention of the activities on offer is quickly followed by talk of the cost. However, most people here, although honest about the downsides of community living, are extremely positive about its benefits.

Lodge of Scottish kings. Other **pubs** include the *High Spirits* in the Old Kirk on Moss Street, the fusty old *Ionic Bar*, 37 High St or, for **live rock** and **pop**, *The Venue* nearby.

Pluscarden Abbey

About seven miles southwest of Elgin, **Pluscarden Abbey** (daily 5am–10.30pm; free) looms impressively large in a peaceful clearing off an unmarked road. Founded in 1230 for a French order of monks, the abbey remains a working facility, its serene interior wafting with the scent of incense and flooded with red and gold light from stained-glass windows. In 1390 Pluscarden was another of the properties burnt by the Wolf of Badenoch; recovering from this, it became a priory of the Benedictine Abbey of Dunfermline in 1454 and continued as such until monastic life was suppressed in Scotland in 1560. The abbey's revival began in 1897 when the Catholic antiquarian, John, third Marquis of Bute, started to repair the building. His son donated it, in 1948, to a small group of Benedictine monks from Gloucester, who are still in the process of restoring the place, having introduced modern additions such as the splendid stained glass.

The Findhorn Foundation

The **Findhorn Foundation**, ten miles west of Elgin (Mon–Sat 9am–5pm, Sun 2–5pm; free), is a magnet for soul-searchers from around the world. Set up in 1962 by Eileen and Peter Caddy (see below), the foundation has blossomed from its early core of three adults and three children into a full-blown community, with classes and facilities for hundreds of people. Bizarrely enough, despite its enormous growth, the foundation is still situated on the town's caravan and camping park (April–Oct; ☎01309/690203), creating an intriguing combination of people on site. Many of the original caravans have metamorphosed into more permanent structures, including some fascinating houses and community spaces employing the latest in ecological methods. It's an amazing place and, however cynical you might be, well worth at least a flying visit. The Findhorners have also built a magnificent arts centre, **Universal Hall**, complete with irridescent glass frontage. **B&B** (details from the visitor centre on ☎01309/690311) is available on site. **FINDHORN** village, to the immediate northwest of the Foundation, has a magnificent beach, a delightful harbour and a couple of good pubs. It is the third village of the name; the other two succumbed to the shifting sands of the Moray Firth.

travel details

Trains

Aberdeen to: Arbroath (every 30min; 1hr); Dundee (every 30min; 1hr 15min); Edinburgh (1–2 hourly; 2hr 35min); Elgin (hourly; 1hr 40min); Forres (hourly; 1hr 55min); Glasgow (1–2 hourly; 2hr 35min); Montrose (every 30min; 45min); Nairn (hourly; 2hr 5min); Stonehaven (every 30min; 15min).

Dundee to: Aberdeen (every 30min; 1hr 15min); Arbroath (hourly; 20min); Montrose (hourly; 15min).

Elgin to: Forres (hourly; 15min); Nairn (hourly; 25min).

Buses

Aberdeen to: Arbroath (hourly; 1hr 20min); Ballater (hourly; 1hr 45min); Banff (hourly; 1hr 55min); Braemar (4–6 daily; 2hr 10min); Crathie (for Balmoral) (4–6 daily; 1hr 55min); Dufftown (2 weekly; 2hr 10min); Dundee (hourly; 2hr); Elgin (hourly; 2hr 35min–3hr 40min); Forres (5 daily; 2hr 35min); Macduff (hourly; 1hr 50min); Montrose (hourly; 1hr); Nairn (5 daily; 2hr 50min); Stonehaven (every 30min; 25–45min).

Ballater to: Crathie (June–Sept 3 weekly; 15min); Tomintoul (June–Sept 1 daily; 1hr).

Dufftown to: Elgin (7 daily; 1hr).

Dundee to: Aberdeen (hourly; 2hr); Arbroath (every 15min; 40min–1hr); Blairgowrie (every 30min; 50min–1hr); Glamis (2 daily; 40min); Kirriemuir (hourly; 1hr 10min); Meigle (hourly; 40min); Montrose (hourly; 1hr 15min).

Elgin to: Aberdeen (hourly; 3hr 15min); Forres (hourly; 25min); Nairn (4–6 daily; 40min); Tomintoul (June–Sept 1 daily; 1hr 15min).

Forres to: Elgin (hourly; 25min); Findhorn (Mon–Sat 8 daily; 20min).

Ferries

Aberdeen to: Lerwick, Shetland (6 weekly; 14hr); Stromness, Orkney (1 weekly; 10hr); Faroe Islands (1 weekly; 22hr).

Flights

Aberdeen to: Dundee (1 daily; 35min); Edinburgh (4 daily; 40min); Glasgow (3 daily; 45min); Birmingham (Mon–Fri 2 daily; 1hr 30min); Manchester (Mon–Fri 6 daily, 2 on Sat, 1 on Sun; 1hr 20min); London (Gatwick 4 daily, Heathrow 8 daily, Stansted 3 daily, 1hr 30min).

CHAPTER TWENTY FOUR

THE HIGHLANDS

Scotland's **Highlands** cover the northern two thirds of the nation and encompass some of its most fabulous scenery: mountains, glens, lochs and rivers contrast with moorland and fertile farms, and the whole sparsely populated area is surrounded by a magnificent coastline. This varied landscape is without doubt the main attraction of the region, but you may be surprised at just how remote much of it is. The vast peat bogs in the bleak north, for example, are among the most extensive and unspoilt wilderness areas in Europe, while a handful of the west coast's isolated crofting villages can still only be reached by boat.

Exposed to slighty different weather and, to some extent, different historical influences, each of the three coastlines has its own distinct character. Along the fertile **east coast**, green fields and woodland run down to the sweeping sandy beaches of the **Moray**, **Cromarty**, and **Dornoch Firths**, while further northeast, rolling moors give way to peaty wastes and sheep country. Stretching east–west from **John O'Groats** to the wind-lashed **Cape Wrath**, the **north coast** proper, backed by the vast and ecologically unique boglands of the **Flow Country**, is wilder and more rugged, with sheer cliffs and sand-filled bays bearing the brunt of frequently fierce Atlantic storms. Visitors with limited time tend to stick to the more scenic **west coast**, whose jagged shoreline of sea lochs, rocky headlands and white-sand coves is set against some of Scotland's most dramatic mountains, looking across to the Hebrides on the horizon.

Cutting diagonally across the heart of the southern Highlands, the **Great Glen** provides an alternative focus for your travel, linking the long thin sliver of **Loch Ness**, in the centre of the region, with the key towns of Inverness on the east cost, and Fort William in the west. From here it's possible to branch out to some fine scenery, most conveniently the great mass of **Glen Coe**, but also the remote and tranquil **Ardnamurchan peninsula** and the lochs and glens that lead up to **Kyle of Lochalsh** – the most direct route to Skye (see p.844). In the opposite direction, south of the Great Glen, the ski resort of **Aviemore** makes a convenient – if not the most appealing – base for exploring the spectacular **Cairngorm Mountains**.

Of the major urban centres of the Highlands, **Inverness** is an obvious springboard for more remote areas, with its good transport links and facilities, while on the western

---

SAFETY IN THE SCOTTISH HIGHLANDS

The **mountains** of the Scottish Highlands, while not as high or as steep as the Alps, are so far north that weather conditions – including blizzards and icy winds of up to 100mph – can be fatal. In 1993, some 54 climbers died, many of them inexperienced walkers who did not realize the levels of danger involved. It's essential to take proper precautions. *Always* put safety first: never underestimate just how fast the weather can change (or how extreme the changes can be), don't venture off-track if you're inexperienced, and be sure to set out properly equipped, with warm, waterproof clothing, decent footwear, a compass, all the maps you might need, and some food in case you get stuck. Make sure, too, that someone knows roughly where you have gone and when you expect to be back (remember to contact them again on your return).

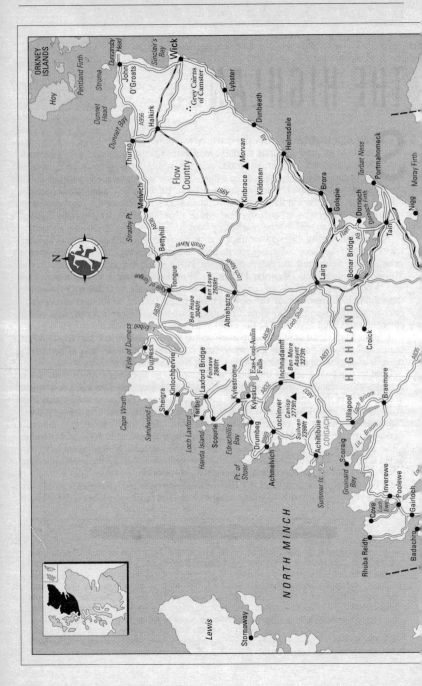

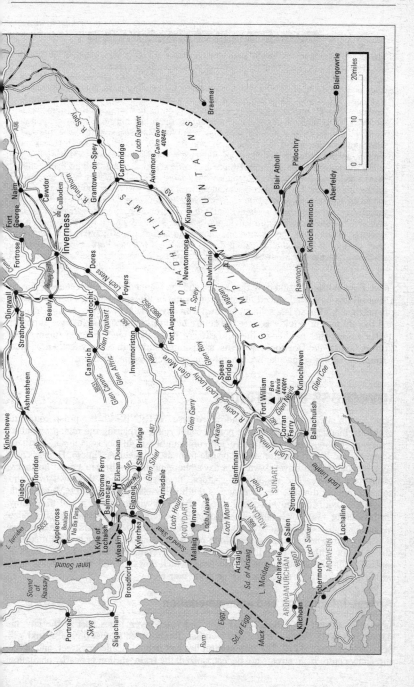

GETTING AROUND THE HIGHLANDS

Unless you're prepared to spend weeks on the road, the Highlands are simply too vast to see in a single trip. Most visitors, therefore, base themselves in one or two areas, exploring the coast on foot, and making longer hops across the empty interior by car, bus or train. **Getting around** the Highlands, particularly the remoter parts, is obviously easiest if you've got your own transport, but with a little forward planning you can see a surprising amount using **buses** and **trains**, especially if you fill in with **postbuses** (timetables are available at most post offices). The infamous A9, a fast but notoriously dangerous road, is a key route into the area, sweeping north from Inverness; in the west, the A82, which follows the line of the Great Glen, and the A835, which leads north across the interior, are the main arteries. However, the most romantic approach to the region has to be via the famous **West Highland Railway**, Scotland's most scenic and brilliantly engineered rail route, which crosses country that can otherwise only be seen from long-distance footpaths. The line has been under threat for the past few years from cut-backs forced by the recent privatization of *British Rail* (now *Scotrail*), but looks safe for the time being. After climbing around Bein Odhar on a unique horseshoe-shaped loop of viaducts, the line traverses desolate Rannoch Moor, where the track had to be laid on a mattress of tree roots, brushwood and thousands of tons of earth and ashes. Skirting Loch Ossian, the train then circumnavigates Ben Nevis to enter Fort William from the northeast, through the Monessie Gorge and the southernmost reach of the Great Glen.

coast, **Fort William**, backed by Ben Nevis, and the planned eighteenth-century port of **Ullapool** are both well placed for exploring some of the spellbinding countryside. In the northeast, **Thurso** is a solid stone town with a regular ferry service to the Orkneys and the old port of **Wick** was once the centre of Europe's herring industry – although its fair to say that neither of these towns are particularly endearing in themselves. Further south lie **Dornoch**, with its sandstone fourteenth-century cathedral, and **Cromarty**, whose vernacular architecture ranks among Scotland's finest.

Inverness and around

Straddling a nexus of major road and rail routes, **INVERNESS** is the prosperous hub of the Highlands, and an inevitable port of call if you're exploring the region by public transport. **Buses** and **trains** leave for communities right across the far north of Scotland, and it isn't uncommon for people from as far afield as Thurso, Durness and Kyle of Lochalsh to travel down for a day's shopping here – Britain's most northerly chain-store centre. The majority of visitors, however, approach the town from the south, dropping down to sea level across the heather-clad plateau of the Monadhliath Mountains, with the snow-streaked slopes of Ben Wyvis to the west and the Moray Firth tapering away northwards. The journey to the centre is less scenic, passing miles of light industry and car showrooms, but once beyond this Inverness is not an unattractive place. Crowned by a pink sandstone **castle**, it has retained much of its medieval street layout (although unsightly concrete blocks overshadow the period buildings in places), while the salmon-packed River Ness, which flows through the centre, is lined with leafy parks and prosperous-looking stone houses.

Arrival, information and accommodation

Inverness **airport** (☎01463/232471) is at Dalcross, seven miles east of the city; an airport bus, #311 (Mon–Fri 11 daily, 7 on Sat; 10min), meets most flights. A **taxi** will set you back around £10. The **bus station** lies just behind Academy Street, one of the three city-centre main streets not pedestrianized; the **train station** is nearby on Station

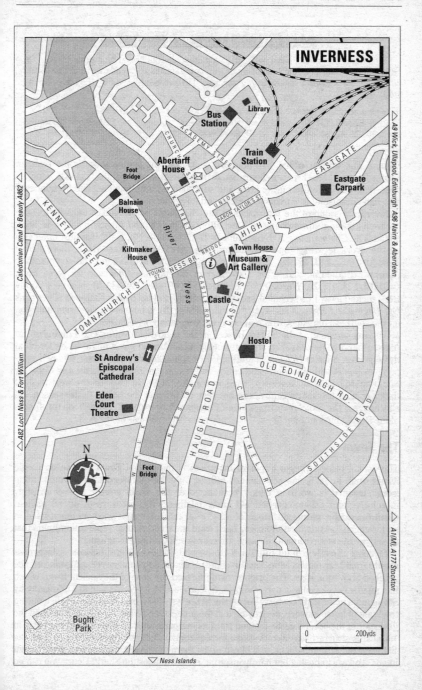

INVERNESS

Square. The **tourist office**, five minutes' walk from the station towards the river on Castle Wynd (Mon–Fri 9am–5pm, Sat & Sun 10am–4pm; ☎01463/234353), stock a wide range of literature on the area, and will book accommodation. The friendly staff also hand out useful free maps of the city and environs.

Inverness is one of the few places in the Highlands where you're unlikely to have problems finding **somewhere to stay**, although in July and August it's wise to book ahead. The *Glenmoriston*, 20 Ness Bank (☎01463/712738; ⑦), is the classiest hotel slap on the riverside with a top-notch Italian restaurant. Also on Ness Bank, there's *Brae Ness*, (☎01463/712266; ④), a homely Georgian hotel overlooking the river and St Andrew's Cathedral, and – for a fraction of the price – *Edenview*, 26 Ness Bank (☎01463/234397; ②). *Heathfield*, 2 Kenneth St (☎01463/230543; ②), is a very comfy B&B tucked away in a secluded backstreet, full of good fall-backs. Kathleen Silver runs *Old Drummond House*, Oak Ave (☎01463/238904; ②), a converted Georgian mansion on the southern outskirts, which offers great vegetarian breakfasts.

The management at the **SYHA hostel**, in the centre of town on Old Edinburgh Rd (closed Jan; ☎01463/231771), are notoriously misanthropic – you might be better off at the *Inverness Student Hotel*, 8 Culduthel Rd (☎01463/236556), a sociable fifty-bed independent hostel with fine views and coffee and tea on tap. *Bught Caravan and Camping Site*, (☎01463/236920), Inverness' main **campsite**, in Bught Park on the west bank of the river near the sports centre, can get very crowded at the height of the season. An alternative is the *Bunchrew Caravan and Camping Park* (☎01463/237802), on the shores of the Beauly Firth in Bunchrew, three miles west of Inverness on the A862.

The Town

The logical place to begin a tour of Inverness is the central **Town House** on Castle Street. Built in 1878, and now council offices, only the old **Mercat Cross** next to the main entrance is worth a look. Presiding over the small square where formerly merchants and traders carried out their business, the cross rests on an ancient **Clachnacuddin stone**, or "stone of tubs" – so called because washerwomen used to rest their buckets on it on their way back from the river. A local superstition holds that as long as the stone remains in place, Inverness will continue to prosper.

Looming directly behind the Town House and dominating the horizon is Inverness **Castle** (mid-May to Sept Mon–Sat 9am–5pm), a nineteenth-century red sandstone edifice perched above the river. The original castle formed the core of the ancient town, which had rapidly developed as a port trading with Europe after its conversion to Christianity by St Columba in the sixth century. Robert the Bruce wrested it back from the English during the Wars of Independence, destroying it in the process, and Mary, Queen of Scots had the governor of the second castle hanged from its ramparts after he had refused her entry in 1562. This structure was also destined for destruction, held by the Jacobites in both the 1715 and the 1745 rebellions, and blown up by them to prevent it falling into government hands. Today's imposing but hardly inspiring edifice houses the Sheriff Court; you can go in, but there's little to see. Around 7.30pm during the summer, a **lone piper** clad in full Highland garb performs for tourists on the esplanade at the south entrance.

The **Inverness Museum and Art Gallery** (Mon–Sat 9am–5pm; free), in the same building as the tourist office, gives a good general overview of the development of the Highlands, but a more enjoyable wet-weather refuge is **Balnain House** (Tues–Sat 10am–5pm; £1.50), over the footbridge that crosses the Ness just below the Old High Church. This immaculately restored, white-painted Georgian mansion, has a modest performance space and an interactive exhibition tracing the development of Highland music from its prehistoric roots to the modern electric folk-rock. CD listening posts and a short video allow you to sample snatches of numerous other musical styles from the region, including clan-gathering and spell-casting songs, complex Shetland fiddle reels and the haunting choral singing of the Hebrides. There's also a café downstairs where ceilidhs, music sessions and recitals take place throughout the summer.

Rising from the west bank directly opposite the castle, **St Andrews Episcopal Cathedral** was intended by its architects to be one the grandest buildings in Scotland. However, funds ran out before the giant twin spires of the original design could be completed, hence Inverness isn't officially a city, but a town. The interior is pretty ordinary, too, though it does claim an unusual octagonal chapter house. From the cathedral, you can wander a mile or so upriver to to the peaceful **Ness Islands**, an attractive public park reached and linked by Edwardian bridges. Laid out with mature trees and

THE TRUTH ABOUT TARTAN

Tartan is big business and an essential part of the tourist industry. Every year, hundreds of visitors return home clutching tartan monsters, foreign-made souvenirs tied with foreign-made tartan ribbon, or lengths of cloth inspiringly named Loch This, Ben That or Glen Something Else, fondly believing that they are bringing authentic history with them. The reality is that tartan is an ancient Highland art form that romantic fiction and commerical interest have enclosed within an almost insurmountable wall of myth.

Real tartan, the kind that long ago was called "Helande", was a fine, hard, and almost showerproof cloth spun in Highland villages from the wool of the native sheep, dyed with preparations of local plants, and with patterns woven by artist-weavers. It was worn as a huge single piece of cloth, which was belted around the waist and draped over the upper body, rather like a knee-length toga. The colours of old tartans were clear but soft, and the broken pattern gave superb camouflage; unlike modern versions, whose colours are either so strong that the pattern is swamped or so dull that it has no impact.

Tartan did not become popular in the Lowlands until the beginning of the eighteenth century, when it was adoped as the anti-Union badge of Jacobitism, and it was not until after '45 that the Lowlands took over it completely. The 1747 ban on wearing tartan put an end to the making of tartan in Highland glens and, instead, whole villages on the Lowland fringes devoted themselves to supplying the needs of the army and emigrant Highlanders in the colonies and, after, those of the home market. Then in 1782, the ban was lifted; Sir Walter Scott set to work, glamorizing the clans; George IV visited Edinburgh in a kilt in 1822, and, finally, Queen Victoria set the royal seal of approval on both the Highlands and tartan.

At about this time, the idea that every clan had, from time immemorial, had its distinguishing tartan also become highly fashionable. To have the "right" to wear tartan, one had to belong, be it ever so remotely, to a clan, and so the way was paved for the what's-my-tartan lists that appear in the tartan picture books and the tartan souvenir shops and, even today, make up the foundation of much wishful genealogy. Great feats of genealogical gymnastics were performed in the concoction of these lists but they could not include every name; for others, there were "district", "national" and "political" tartans, which could be worn for what might be called "sentimental" reasons. As more tartans were wanted, more were invented: myth grew upon myth and the art form suffered.

shrubs, the islands are the favourite haunt of local anglers. Further upstream still, the river runs parallel with the **Caledonian Canal**, designed by Thomas Telford in the early nineteenth century as a link between the east and west coasts, joining Loch Ness, Loch Lochy and Loch Linnhe. Today its main use is recreational, and there are **cruises** through part of it to Loch Ness.

Eating and drinking

Inverness isn't famed for its gastronomy, but there is no shortage of passable **places to eat**. The best food is served in the posh riverside hotels, like the award-winning Scots-French *Dunain Park Hotel Restaurant* (☎01463/224532), set in lovely gardens on the river just southwest of town. *Glen Mhor Hotel Restaurant*, 9 Ness Bank (☎01463/234308), is a more moderately priced brasserie specializing in classy Scottish cuisine. The Eden Court Theatre's *Bishop's Table Restaurant* is an upmarket self-service restaurant with a nice bar and views, or you could try the *River* café and restaurant, 10 Bank St, near the Grieg St footbridge, which serves hot and healthy wholefood dishes. *Lettuce Eat*, Drummond St, doles out seriously filling takeaway sandwiches and soups for under £1.50 during the day, while the *Pizza Gallery*, 1 Bridge St, is a cheerful, family-run pizza parlour that's actively nice to children. The *Brahms and Liszt*, 75 Castle St, is the nearest thing to a wine bar in Inverness, with good-value continental-style snacks and main meals, and even occasional live music.

Nightlife in Inverness revolves around a handful of recently revamped "theme pubs" like the ersatz-Irish *Lafferty's*, Academy St, currently among the most popular of the bunch, along with the *Phoenix* next door and the *Market Bar*, off Church Street. The town's trendiest club has to be the *Railway Club* in a dowdy working mens' club between the back of the train station and a DIY store on Strother's Lane. Finally, the basement café at Balnain House museum, on the east bank of the Ness, opposite Grieg Street footbridge, hosts informal **folk sessions** on Thursday nights that sometimes turn into ceilidhs if enough inebriated tourists make up numbers. **Cinemas** include *La Scala*, Railway Terrace near the bus station, which screens the current mainstream movies; while the *Eden Court Theatre* across the river offers popular and art-house alternatives during the summer, together with plays by touring theatre companies.

Around Inverness

A string of worthwhile sights punctuate the area around Inverness, making it a good base for day trips. The area around the **Moray Firth**, to the east, acts as a commuter belt for Inverness, but it also boasts a lovely coastline and some of the region's best castles and historic sites. Charlie's ill-fated 1745 uprising took place on the outskirts of Inverness at **Culloden**, while the whimsical **Cawdor Castle** features in Shakespeare's *Macbeth*. The low-key holiday resort of **Nairn**, with its championship golf course, is also within easy striking distance of Inverness, as is **Fort George**, one of several impressive Hanoverian bastions erected in the wake of the Jacobite rebellion. To the north of Inverness, the **Black Isle** is littered with dozens of prehistoric sites, but the main incentive here is to visit the picturesque eighteenth-century town of **Cromarty**. A string of villages along the south coast is also worth stopping off for en route, while **Chanonry Point** – is among the best **dolphin-spotting** sites in Europe (see box).

The Moray Firth

East of Inverness lies the fertile, sheltered coastal strip of the **Moray Firth**, its many historic sites and castles accessible as day trips from Inverness, or en route to and from

THE DOLPHINS OF THE MORAY FIRTH

The **Moray Firth**, the great wedge-shaped bay forming the eastern coastline of the Highlands, is one of only three areas in UK waters that supports a resident population of **dolphins**. A little over a hundred of these beautiful, intelligent marine mammals live in the estuary, the most northerly breeding ground for this particular species – the bottle-nosed dolphin (*Tursiops truncatus*) – in Europe, and you stand a good chance of spotting a few, either from the shore, or a boat.

Tursiops truncatus is the largest dolphin in the world, typically growing to a length of around 13ft and weighing between 396 and 660 pounds. The adults sport a tall, sickle-shaped dorsal fin and a distinctive beak-like "nose", and usually live for around 25 years, although a number of fifty-year-old animals have been recorded. During the summer, herds of thirty to forty dolphins have been known to congregate in Moray Firth; no one is exactly sure why, although experts believe the annual gatherings, which take place between late June and August, may be connected to the breeding cycle. Another peculiar trait of the Moray Firth school is their habit of killing porpoises. Several porpoise corpses with serrated tooth marks have been washed ashore in the area, the dolphins tossing dead or dying porpoises around in the waves as if for fun.

Both adults and calves frequently leap out of the water, "bow riding" in front of boats and performing elegant synchronized swimming routines together. This, of course, makes them spectacular animals to watch, and "**dolphin spotting**" has become something of a craze in the Moray Firth area. Arguably the best place in Scotland, if not in Europe, to look for them is **Chanonry Point**, on Black Isle (see p.907) – a spit of sand protruding into a narrow but deep channel, where converging currents bring fish close to the surface, and thus the dolphins close to shore; the hour or so before high tide is the most likely time to see them. **Kessock Bridge**, one mile north of Inverness, is another prime dolphin-spotting location. A team of zoologists from Aberdeen University studying the Moray Firth dolphins have set up a small listening post and **visitor centre** here (daily 10am–5pm; free), where specially installed hydrophones allow you to eavesdrop on the clicks and whistles of underwater conversations.

In addition, several companies run dolphin-spotting **boat trips** around the Moray Firth. However, researchers claim that the increased traffic is causing the dolphins' unneccessary stress, particularly during the all-important breeding period, when passing vessels are thought to force calves underwater for uncomfortably long periods. They have therefore devised a "**code of conduct**" for boat operators, based on the experiences of countries where dolphin-watching has become highly disruptive. So if you decide to go out on a spotting cruise, make sure the operator is a member of the Dolphin Space Programme's Accreditation Scheme; by the summer of 1995, only four outfits in the Moray Firth had made it on to this list: *Dolphin Ecosee* in **Cromarty** (see p.908), *Seaboard Marine* and *J.R .Mackenzie* from **Tain** (on the Dornoch Firth); and *Sea Fair Charters* of **Nairn** (see p.907).

Aberdeen. Both the countryside and the amount of attractions around here make a good contrast to the purely scenic splendours you'll encounter once you head further north into the Highlands. The notoriously dangerous A96 traverses this stretch and is well served by public transport, details of which feature in the accounts below.

Culloden

On April 16, 1746, the windswept moorland of **CULLODEN** (site open all year; visitor centre Feb–Nov 10am–4/5.30pm; £2;NT), five miles east of Inverness, witnessed the last ever battle on British soil. Ill fed and exhausted after a pointless night march, the Jacobites were hopelessly outnumbered by the English. The open, flat ground of Culloden Moor was also totally unsuitable for the Highlanders' style of fighting, which needed steep hills and lots of cover to provide the element of surprise, and they were routed. After the battle, in which 1500 Highlanders were slaughtered, Bonnie Prince

Charlie fled west to the hills and islands and eventually escaped to France (see p.850). Meanwhile, English troops began an orgy of violent reprisals on the Highlanders, raping and pillaging their way across the region; within a century, the Highland way of life had changed out of all recognition. Today you can walk freely around the battle site; flags mark the positions of the two armies; **clan graves** are marked by simple headstones; the **Field of the English**, for many years unmarked, is a mass grave for the fifty or so English soldiers who died; a nearby stone marks the spot where the Duke of Cumberland is said to have watched the proceedings. Thirty Jacobites were burnt alive outside the old cottage next to the **visitor centre**, which has been restored to its eighteenth-century appearance. **Buses** (#12; 14min) leave Inverness eight times daily from the post office to Culloden, the last one returning at 6.30pm from the car park in front of the visitor centre.

The Clava Cairns

If you're visiting Culloden with your own transport, make a short detour to the **CLAVA CAIRNS**, an impressive collection of prehistoric burial chambers grouped around the banks of the Nairn River, a mile southeast of the battlefield. Erected sometime in the fourth or third millennium, the three cairns, which are encircled by **standing stones** in a spiny of mature beech trees, are of two different kinds: one with spoke-like stone lines emanating from them, the other with a narrow passageway cut into its middle. Archeological excavations carried out here in the nineteenth century yielded traces of human remains, suggesting that the structures must originally have been tombs, but little else is known about the nomadic herdsmen who are thought to have built them.

Cawdor Castle

The pretty, if slightly self-satisfied village of **CAWDOR**, eight miles east of Culloden, is the site of the **Cawdor Castle** (May–Sept daily 10am–5pm; £4.50), apocryphally known as the setting for Shakespeare's *Macbeth* (the fulfilment of the witches' prediction that Macbeth was to become Thane of Cawdor sets off his tragic desire to be king). In actual fact, the castle, which dates from the early fourteenth century, could not possibly have witnessed the grizzly historical events on which the Bard's drama was based. However, the immaculately restored monument – a fairy-tale affair of towers, turrets and crenellations whimsically shooting off from the original keep – is still well worth a visit. The Cawdors have lived here for six centuries, and there are plenty of signs of life as you tour the interior, along with the usual stately-home tapestries, pictures and opulent furniture. As you wander around, look out for the **Thorn Tree Room**, a vaulted chamber complete with the remains of an ancient tree, and an ancient pagan fertility symbol believed to ward off fairies and evil spirits. According to Cawdor family legend, the fourteenth-century Thane of Cawdor dreamt he should build on the spot where his donkey lay down to sleep after a day's wandering – the animal chose this tree and building began right away. A good way to wind up a visit to Cawdor is a stroll around the **grounds**, which feature a walled garden and a topiarian **maze**. **Buses** (#12) run direct to the castle from Inverness post office.

Fort George

Eight miles of undulating coastal farmland and estuarine mud flats separate Cawdor Castle from **Fort George** (April–Sept Mon–Sat 10am–6pm, Sun 2pm–6pm; Oct–March Mon–Fri 10am–4.30pm; £2.50), an old Hanoverian bastion considered by military architectural historians to be one of the finest fortifications in Europe. Crowning a sandy spit that juts into the middle of the Moray Firth, it was built (1747–69) as a base for George II's army, in case the Highlanders should attempt to rekindle the Jacobite cause. By the time of its completion, however, the uprising had been firmly quashed and the fort has been used ever since as a barracks; note the armed sentries at the main entrance and the periodic crack of live gunfire from the nearby firing ranges. Apart from the sweeping panoramic views across the Firth from its ramparts, the main incentive to visit Fort George is the **Regimental Museum of the Queen's Own Highlanders**, a predictable array of regimental silver, coins, moth-eaten uniforms and medals.

Walking on the northern, grass-covered casemates, which look out into the estuary, you may be lucky enough to see the school of bottle-nosed dolphins swimming in with the tide. This is also a good spot for birdwatching: a colony of kittiwakes occupies the fort's slate rooftops, while the white-sand beach and mud flats below teem with waders and seabirds. The easiest way to get to Fort George by public transport is by **bus** from Inverness (Mon–Sat 7 daily; 20min), or Nairn (3 or 4 daily; 20min), eight miles east. The nearest **train** station is at **Gollanfield**, three miles southeast, although onward transport from there to the fort can be a problem.

Nairn

Apparently one of the driest and sunniest places in the whole of Scotland, **NAIRN**, about six miles north of Cawdor, began its days as a peaceful community of fishermen and farmers. The former spoke Gaelic, the latter English, allowing James VI to boast that a town in his kingdom was so large that people at one end of the main street could not understand those at the other end. Nairn became popular in Victorian times, when the train line offered a convenient link to its revitalizing sea air and mild climate, and today it still relies on tourism: its windy, coastal golf course, the **Links** (venue for the 1999 Walker Cup), is one of the most popular in Scotland – just as well, as the Moray Firth has become a notorious pollution black spot of late.

Nairn's helpful and well-stocked **tourist office** is at 62 King St (Easter–May, Sept & Oct Mon–Sat 10am–5pm; June–Aug daily 9am–6pm; ☎01667/452753). For **accommodation**, *Greenlawns*, 13 Seafield St (☎01667/452738; ①), is a small **B&B** filled with antiques; although more expensive, the *Golf View Hotel* (☎01667/452301; ④), overlooking the golf course and sea, is also good value. **Bike** rental is available from *Nairn Watersports* (☎01667/455416) down by the harbour.

The Black Isle and around

Sandwiched between the Moray and Cromarty firths, the **Black Isle** is not an island at all, but a fertile peninsula whose rolling hills, prosperous farms, and stands of deciduous woodland make it more reminiscent of Dorset or Sussex than the Highlands. It probably gained its name because of its mild climate: there's rarely frost, which leaves the fields "black" all winter; another explanation is that the name derives from the Gaelic word for black, *dubh* – a possible corruption of Saint Duthac.

Fortrose and Rosemarkie

The most rewarding approach to Cromarty is along the south side of Black Isle, via the A832 from Kessock Bridge. Twelve miles by raod from Inverness, **FORTROSE** is a lacklustre resort dominated by the ruins of a twelfth-century **cathedral**. Founded by King David I, it now languishes on a lovely yew-studded green, hemmed in by redsandstone and colour-washed houses, where a horde of gold coins dating from the time of Robert III was unearthed in 1880. There's also a memorial to the Seaforth family, whose demise the Brahan Seer famously predicted (see below). Jutting into a narrow but deep channel in the Moray Firth (gouged to allow war ships into the estuary during the last war), **Chanonry Point**, reached by a back road from Fortrose, is fringed on one side by a wonderful white sand beach. It's also an excellent place to look for **dolphins** (see p.905). Come here around high tide, and you stand a good chance of spotting a couple leaping through the surf in search of fish brought to the surface by converging currents.

ROSEMARKIE, a one-street village north of Fortrose at the opposite (northeast) end of the beach, is thought to have been evangelized by St Boniface in the early eighth century; indeed, local legend has it that the carved Pictish stone in the churchyard marks his grave. A collection of even better preserved Pictish artefacts is on display at Rosemarkie's **Groam House Museum** (May–Oct Mon–Sat 10am–5pm, Sun 2–4.30pm, Nov–April Sat–Sun 2–4pm; £1.50), at the bottom of the village. In addition to a bumper crop of intricately carved standing stones (among them the famous Rosemarkie Cross Slab), the museum shows films on local topics such as the Picts and Brahan Seer. A lovely mile-and-a-half woodland **walk** along the banks of a sparkling burn to **Fairy Glen** begins at the car park just beyond the village on the road to Cromarty. Inexpensive bar **food** is also available at the wonderfully old fashioned *Plough Inn*, down the lane from the museum.

Cromarty

An ancient legend recalls that the twin headlands flanking the entrance to the Cromarty Firth, known as The Sutor Rocks (from the Gaelic word for shoemaker), were once a pair of giant cobblers who used to protect Black Isle from pirates. Nowadays, however, the only giants in the area are Nigg and Invergordon's colossal oil rigs, marooned in the estuary like metal monsters marching out to sea. Built and serviced here for the Forties North Sea oilfield, they form a surreal counterpoint to the cobbled streets and chocolate-box workers' cottages of **CROMARTY**, the Black Isle's main settlement. Sheltered by the Sutors at the northeast corner of the peninsula, the town is a perfect example of an eighteenth-century Scottish seaport forced out of business by the arrival of the train line.

To get a sense of Cromarty head straight for the award-winning museum house in the old **Courthouse**, Church Street (Easter–Oct 10am–6pm; Nov–Easter noon–4pm; £2), which tells the history of the town using audio-visuals and animated figures (not as dreadful as they sound, and children love them). They also issue you with a personal stereo, a tape and a map for a walking tour around the town. **Hugh Miller**, the nineteenth-century stonemason turned author, geologist, folklorist and Free Church campaigner, was born in Cromarty, and his **birthplace**, a narrow, cramped thatched cottage nearby on Church Street (May–Sept Mon–Sat 10am–1pm & 2–5.30pm, Sun 2–5.30pm; £1.50; NTS), has been restored to look as it did when he lived there, with a small collection of his personal belongings. Once you've seen that you've really seen Cromarty, though before you move on, bear in mind that Bill Fraser will take you out in his boat to see seals, porpoises and bottle-nosed **dolphins** just off the coast (June–Sept every 90min), or killer whales on longer cruises during the winter (4hr); if you're interested, contact him on ☎013817/600323. The tiny two-car Nigg–Cromarty **ferry** (April–Oct 9am–6pm), the smallest in Scotland, also doubles up as a cruiser on summer evenings; you can catch it from the jetty near the lighthouse.

Four **buses** each day run to Cromarty from Inverness (45min), returning from the stop near the playing fields on the western outskirts of town. During summer, **accommodation** is in short supply, so book ahead. The most upmarket is the traditional *Royal Hotel* (☎01381/600217; ⑥), down at the harbour, which has rather small but richly furnished rooms overlooking the Firth, and an excellent bar-restaurant. For **B&B**, try *The Cobbles*, Church St (☎01381/600374; ②), a cosy and immaculate place run by Scotland's most avid dolphin spotters, or *The Old Commercial*, Bank St (☎01381/600540; ②), whose affable Canadian expat owners serve delicious corn-meal muffins for breakfast. The most down-to-earth place in Cromarty to **eat** is the *Cromarty Arms*, which serves basic, inexpensive bar meals, and a good selection of real ales and malts. For something a little more sophisticated, head for the *Thistle Restaurant*, Church St, whose quality cuisine has a distinctly Scottish flavour.

Strathpeffer, Dingwall and the Cromarty Firth

Most traffic nowadays takes the upgraded A9 north from Inverness, bypassing the small provincial town of **DINGWALL** (from the Norse *thing*, "parliament", and *volle*, "place"), a former port that was left high and dry when the river receded during the last century. Today, it's a tidy but dull service and market town with one long main street that's bustling all day and moribund by dinner time. Dingwall's only real claim to fame is that it was the birthplace of Macbeth, whose family occupied the now ruined castle on Castle Street. If you need to **stay**, *Victoria Lodge*, Mill St (☎01349/862494; ②), and *Kirklee* (☎01349/863439; ②) are standard B&Bs, while the posh *Tulloch Castle Hotel*, Castle Drive (☎01349/861325; ⑥), a former Highland clan headquarters, and the two-star *Royal Hotel*, High St (☎01349/862130; ④), are more upmarket options.

STRATHPEFFER, a Victorian spa town seven miles west of Dingwall, is a more congenial place to stop over. During its heyday, this was a renowned European health resort complete with a Pump Room, where visitors could chat while they sipped the water. Today, sadly, several of its fine buildings are in a sorry state, although two or three mammoth faded hotels remain. Activity is concentrated around the main square, where you can sample sulphur-laden water at the Water Sampling Pavilion.

Within striking distance of the bleak Benn Wyvis massif, Strathpeffer is also a popular base for walkers. **Buses** run regularly between Dingwall and Strathpeffer (Mon–Sat), dropping passengers in the square, where you'll find a small **tourist office** (Easter–Nov Mon–Sat 10am–5pm; ☎01997/421415). **Accommodation** can be had at *Holly Lodge Hotel* (☎01997/421254; ⑤), a converted Victorian villa north of the main square, or nearby, at *Inver Lodge* (☎01997/421392; ②) and *Francisville* (☎01997/421345; ②) **B&Bs**, both west of the main square. Alternatively, head for the seventy-bed **youth hostel** (mid-March to Sept; ☎01997/421532), a mile southwest of the square up the hill towards Jameston.

Northeast of Dingwall, the **Cromarty Firth** has always been recognized as a perfect natural harbour. During World War I it was a major **naval base**, and today its sheltered waters are used as a centre for rig repair for the North Sea oilfields. The fifteen-mile stretch of the fast A9 from **Alness** to Tain passes several villages which have boomed with the expansion of the oil industry, notably **Invergordon**, on the coast just west of Nigg Bay. The extraordinary edifice on the hill behind **EVANTON**, ten minutes west along the A9 from Alness, is the **Fyrish Monument**, built by a certain Sir Hector Munro partly to give employment to the area, and partly to commemorate his own capture of the Indian town of Seringapatam in 1781 – hence the design, resembling an Indian gateway. If you want to get a close-up look, it's a tough two-hour walk through pinewoods to the top.

The Great Glen

The **Great Glen**, a huge rift valley formed 400 million years ago by volcanic upheavals, rips through the southern Highlands from Inverness diagonally across to Fort William. Smoothed by glaciers that only retreated around 8000 BC, it's not particularly spectacular by Scottish standards, but provides an obvious and rewarding route from the east to west coast. Of the Great Glen's three long, sliver-thin lochs, the most famous is **Loch Ness**, home to the mythical beast and linked to the other two, Loch Lochy and Loch Linnhe, by the **Caledonian Canal**, surveyed by Thomas Watt in 1773, and completed in the early 1800s by Thomas Telford to enable ships to pass between the North Sea and the Atlantic without having to navigate Scotland's treacherous northern coast. Only 22 miles of it are actually bona fide canal; the other 38 exploit the Glen's natural lochs and rivers, flowing west to reach the Atlantic.

The traditional and most rewarding way to travel through the valley is by **boat**. A flotilla of small vessels takes advantage of the canal and its old wooden locks during the summer, among them *Jacobite Cruises* (☎01463/710188 for details). There's also an excellent Forestry Commission **cycle path** through the Glen, that makes a tranquil alternative to the hazardous A82. In addition, the Great Glen is well served by **buses**, with four or five daily services between Inverness and Fort William, and a couple of extra buses covering the section between Fort William and Invergarry during school terms.

Loch Ness

Loch Ness's fame has little to do with its appearance. It's long and undeniably scenic, with rugged heather-clad mountains sweeping up from a steep, wooded shoreline, but if it weren't for its legendary inhabitant, **Nessie**, the **Loch Ness Monster**, you'd probably drive past without a second glance – especially as the A82, which runs southwest along the west side of the loch to Fort William, gives little opportunity to pull over. The opposite, **eastern side** – skirted by the sinuous single-track B862/852 (originally a military road built to link Fort Augustus and Fort George) affords far more spectacular views. However, buses from Inverness only run as far south as Foyers, so you'll need you own transport to complete the whole loop around the Loch.

Drumnadrochit and around

Situated above a verdant, sheltered bay fifteen miles from Inverness, **DRUMNADROCHIT**, practically the first chance to draw breath as you head down the A82, is the epicentre of Nessie hype, sporting a rash of tacky souvenir shops and two rival monster exhibitions. Of the pair, the **Original Loch Ness Monster Exhibition** (daily April–June 10am–6pm; July & Aug 10am–9pm, Sept–Nov 10am–6pm; £3.50), is the least worthwhile – basically a gift shop with a shoddy audio-visual show tacked on the side. If you're genuinely interested in "Nessie" lore, the **Official Loch Ness Monster Exhibition** (daily April–June 9.30am–5.30pm, July & Aug 9am–8.30pm, Sept & Oct 9.30am–6pm; £4.50), though more expensive (and no more "official" than the other) is a much better bet, offering an in depth rundown of eye-witness accounts through the ages and mock-ups of the various research projects

---

"NESSIE"

The world-famous Loch Ness monster, affectionately known as **"Nessie"** (and by serious aficionados as *Nessiteras rhombopteryx*), has been around a long time. The first mention of her crops up in Saint Adamnan's seventh-century biography of Saint Colomba. While on his way to evangelize the pagan inhabitants of Inverness, the saint allegedly calmed the monster after she attacked one of his monks. Present-day interest, however, is probably greater outside Scotland than in, dating from the 1930s when the A82 was built along the loch's western shore. Recent encounters range from glimpses of ripples by anglers, to the famous occasion in 1961 when thirty hotel guests saw a pair of humps break the water's surface and cruise for about half a mile before submerging.

However, several seemingly conclusive photographic images – including the renowned black-and-white movie footage of Nessie's humps moving across the water, and the photo of her neck and head – have recently been exposed as fakes. Hi-tech sonar surveys carried out over the past two decades have failed to come up with conclusive evidence, but it's hard to dismiss Nessie as pure myth. Too many locals have mysterious tales to tell, which they invariably keep to themselves for fear of ridicule by incredulous outsiders. Loch Ness also has an undeniably enigmatic air; even the most hardened cynics rarely resist the temptation to scan the waters for signs of life, just in case . . ..

carried out in the loch. **Cruises** of the loch can also be booked here; they leave two or three times daily from **Temple Pier**, and last about an hour (£4.50).

Most photographs allegedly showing the monster have been taken a couple of miles further south, around the fourteenth-century ruined lochside **Castle Urquhart** (Sept–June daily 10am–5pm, July–Aug daily 10am–8pm; £3). Built as a strategic base to guard the Great Glen, the castle played an important role in the Wars of Independence. It was taken by Edward I of England and later held by Robert the Bruce against Edward III, only to be blown up in 1692 to prevent it from falling to the Jacobites. It's pretty dilapidated today, though it does look splendid floodlit at night when the crowds have gone.

By far the nicest **hotel** around Drumnadrochit is the *Lewiston Arms* (☎01456/450225; ③) in the adjoining village of **Lewiston**. Otherwise there's the family-run *Benleva Hotel* (☎01456/450288; ③) beside the loch. For **B&B**, you could do a lot worse than *Gilliflowers* (☎01456/450641; ②), a seventeenth-century farmhouse tucked away down a country lane in Lewiston, or the modern *Drumbuie* (☎01456/450634; ②), which has great views, and a resident herd of Highland cattle. Near the latter and signposted from the main road is the *Loch Ness Backpackers Lodge* at Coiltie Farmhouse (☎01456/450807). If you fancy a ride around the Loch on the new cycle path, **mountain bikes**, maps and rain capes may be rented from a stall on Drumnadrochit village green (☎01456/450554). All the hotels in the area serve good **bar food**; in Drumnadrochit the *Glen Restaurant*, and the *Hungry Piper*, two hundred yards down the road, cater mainly for bus parties with basic grills, while *Fiddlers Bistro*, next door to the *Glen*, is more upmarket, offering local steaks, salmon and appetizing home-baked pizza.

Glen Urquhart and Glen Affric

You can head west from Drumnadrochit on the A831 through **Glen Urquhart**, a fairly open valley with farmland giving way to scrubby woodland and heather as you near **CANNICH**. The **youth hostel** here (mid-May to Sept; ☎01456/415244) makes a good base for exploring **Glen Affric**, claimed by many to be Scotland's loveliest valley. It's real calendar stuff, with a rushing river and Caledonian pine and birch woods opening out on to an island-studded loch, that was considerably enlarged after the building of the dam, one of many hydroelectric schemes around here. Hemmed in by a string of Munros, the glen is great for picnics and pottering, particularly on a calm and sunny day, when the loch is still, reflecting the islands and surrounding hills.

The area also offers some tremendous **hiking**. Among the most popular routes is the one winding west through Kintail to Shiel bridge, on the west coast near Kyle of Lochalsh (about 25 miles), which takes at least two full days; a remote but recently revamped **youth hostel** (no phone) makes a convenient night stopover halfway into the walk on the banks of the burn above Loch Affric. The trail is easy to follow, but can get horrendously boggy if there's been a lot of rain, so allow plenty of time and take adequate wet-weather gear.

Invermoriston and Fort Augustus

The south of Loch Ness is far more attractive than its opposite end, and the road skirting the water's edge allows plenty of opportunities to pull over for a little monster watching. **INVERMORISTON**, thirteen miles southwest of Drumnadrochit, is an attractive village, from where you can follow well-marked woodland **trails** past a series of grand waterfalls. Dr Johnson and Boswell spent a couple of nights here planning their journey to the Hebrides; nowadays you can stay at the old-fashioned *Glenmoriston Arms Hotel* (☎01320/351206; ⑤).

FORT AUGUSTUS, at the loch's southwestern tip, was named after George II's son, the chubby lad who later became the "Butcher" Duke of Cumberland of Culloden fame, and was built as a barracks after the 1715 Jacobite rebellion. Today, it's a tiny village, dominated by comings and goings along the Caledonian Canal, which leaves Loch Ness here, and by its large **Benedictine Abbey**, a campus of grey Victorian buildings founded on the site of the original fort in 1876. The abbey housed a Catholic boys' school until 1993, but is now a go-ahead **heritage centre** (daily April–Sept 9am–5pm; Oct–March 10am–4pm; ☎01320/366233; £4), where a walkman tour-cum-sound-and-light-show covers the area's history and sociology. Traditional Highland culture is also the subject of **The Clansmen Centre**'s lively and informative exhibition (Easter to mid-Oct daily 10am–8.30pm: £2), on the banks of the canal. The guides sport sporrans and rough woollen plaids and encourage visitors to do the same; they also wield weapons in the back garden.

Fort Augustus' small **tourist office** (Mon–Sat April–June 10am–5pm; July & Aug 9am–8pm; Sept & Oct 9am–6pm; ☎01320/366367) hands out useful free maps detailing popular **walks** in the area. The best-value **accommodation** has to be the Benedictine Abbey's guest rooms (☎01320/366233; ②); the monks also run a *Backpackers' Lodge*, with some inexpensive doubles (②), and serve great, cheap health-conscious food. The *Bothy Bite Bunk House* (☎01320/366700), in the centre of the village by the canal is even cheaper, and offers a good range of moderately priced fish, steak and pie dishes. Otherwise, try the *Old Pier* (☎01320/366418; ③), a great B&B right on the loch. The small, friendly *Caledonian Hotel* (☎01320/366256; ④) overlooks the Abbey while the good-value *Brae Hotel* (☎01320/366289; ③), just off the main road as you approach the village from the north, lies in wooded surroundings. The *Poachers* on the main road is the liveliest pub, drawing a mixed clientele of locals, yachties and backpackers.

Loch Lochy

The fast A82 runs south from Fort Augustus along the eastern side of **Loch Lochy** towards the junction at Spean Bridge and Fort William beyond, giving fine views across the loch to the steep slopes of Ben Tee on its northern side. At Spean Bridge the minor B8004 branches west towards Gairlochy, at the loch's southern tip, where you once more encounter the **Caledonian Canal** – you can walk easily anywhere along this stretch of the canal, although the best access point is where the B8004 crosses it. The canal debouches into the sea via a series of eleven locks, known as **Neptune's Staircase**, which cover a drop of 80ft and presented Telford with quite an engineering challenge. Meanwhile, the A82 climbs south from Spean Bridge to the famous **Commando Memorial**, erected for the men who trained in the area and later lost their lives during the World War II. The group of guano-splashed bronze soldiers, sculpted in 1952 by Scott Sutherland, stand on a raised promontory that overlooks an awesome sweep of moor and mountain, taking in Lochaber and the Ben Nevis massif.

THE NEVIS RANGE SKI STATION

The Nevis Range Ski Range, seven miles northeast of Fort William on the A82, boasts Scotland's only **cable car** system (daily mid-Dec to June 10am–5pm; July & Aug 10am–8pm; Sept–Nov 10am–5pm; £5.50), in the **AONACH MHOR** ski area – a popular attraction during both winter and the summer off-season period. Built in 1989 with hefty grant aid from the regional council, the one-and-a-half mile gondola ride (15 min) gives an easy approach to some high-level walking, but for most tourists it simply provides an effortless means to rise 2000ft and enjoy the spectacular views from the terrace of the self-service **restaurant** at the top. Return tickets cost £5.50 and can be booked at the Nevis Range gondola station (☎01397/704008). In July and August, you can also ski on the Nevis Range's 246-foot **dry slope** (Mon–Thurs 11am–12.30pm & 2–3.30pm; Sept & Oct; ☎01397/705825 for times). The ticket price for each ninety-minute session (£6) includes ski rental and instruction.

Fort William

Founded in 1655 and named in honour of William III, **FORT WILLIAM** enjoys a beautiful setting on Loch Linnhe, with the snow-streaked bulk of Ben Nevis – at 4406ft Britain's highest peak – rising behind. By rights, "Fort Bill", as it's known by the many walkers and climbers that come here, should be an absolute gem. Sadly, ribbon bungalow development and an ill-advised dual carriageway have wrecked the shore, out-of-place modern buildings mar the outskirts, and the main street is largely given over to tacky tourist gift stores.

Fort William's downturn started in the nineteenth century, when the original fort, which gave the town its name, was demolished to make way for the train line. Today there's very little to detain you in the town centre, although it's worth taking at least a short look at the **West Highland Museum**, on Cameron Square, just off High Street, (July & Aug Mon–Sat 9.30am–5.30pm, Sun 2–5pm; Sept–June Mon–Sat 10am–5pm; £1.50). This splendidly old-fashioned and idiosyncratic collection covers virtually every aspect of Highland life and makes a refreshing change from state-of-the-art museums. There's a good section on Highland clans and tartans, and a secret portrait of Bonnie Prince Charlie, seemingly just a blur of paint that resolves itself into a portrait when viewed against a brass cylinder. Look out, too, for the long Spanish rifle used in the assassination of a local factor (the landowner's tax collector-cum-bailiff) – the murder that subsequently inspired Robert Louis Stevenson's novel, *Kidnapped*.

Practicalities

The **bus** and **train stations** are next door to each other at the east end of High Street. The **tourist office**, on Cameron Square, just off High Street (Mon–Fri 9am–5pm, Sat 9am–4pm; ☎01397/703781), hands out free town maps. **Mountain bikes** are available for rent at *Off Beat Bikes* (☎01397/704008) on Macrae's Lane, behind High Street; and they also have a branch at the Nevis Range gondola station – good for easy access to the area's high ridges. **Excursions** from town include the popular day trip to Mallaig on the **Jacobite Steam Railway** (June–Sept Tues–Fri & Sun depart 10.30am, return 4.05pm). Five **seal cruises** also leave from the town pier every day, offering the chance to spot the marine life of Loch Linnhe, including otters and an array of seabirds.

Fort William's plentiful **accommodation** ranges from the *Alexandra Hotel*, slap in the town centre on The Parade (☎01397/702241; ⑦), to inexpensive, but equally central B&Bs like *Beinn Ard* on Argyll Road (☎01397/704760; ②). If you're looking for something in between, try *The Cruachan*, Achintore Rd (☎01397/702022; ③), a popular and moderately priced hotel overlooking the loch, five minutes' walk from the centre. Fort William and its environs also abound in **hostels**: the *SYHA* hostel (all year except Nov; ☎01397/702336) is at the foot of Glen Nevis, but often full in summer; a more civilized option is the neighbouring *Ben Nevis Bunkhouse*, at Achintee Farm (open all year; ☎01397/702240); in Fort William itself, head for the *Fort William Backpackers*, Alma Rd (open all year; ☎01397/700711), a friendly independent hostel five minutes' walk from the train station.

Most **eating** places in Fort William are pretty basic. The *Good Food Stop* at the *Alexandra Hotel* does inexpensive grills, fish and pasta dishes, and is open all day, but your best bet is the *Crannog Seafood Restaurant* on the pier, where oysters, langoustines, prawns and salmon are cooked with flair in an elegantly converted fish store; the wine list is also excellent, although the prices make it best kept for a treat.

Glen Nevis

A ten-minute drive out of town, **Glen Nevis** is indisputably among the Highlands' most impressive glens: a classic U-shaped glacial valley hemmed in by steep bracken-covered slopes and swathes of blue-grey scree. Herds of shaggy highland cattle also graze the valley floor, where a sparkling river gushes through glades of trees. With the forbidding mass of Ben Nevis rising steeply to the north, it's not surprising this valley was chosen as the location for several scenes in the movie *Rob Roy*. Apart from its natural beauty, Glen Nevis is also the starting point for the ascent of Scotland's highest peak, and you can **rent mountain equipment** and **mountain bikes** at the trailhead. **Buses** run as far as the youth hostel, departing from Middle Street (between High St and the loch in Fort William). Anyone keen to do some serious **planned walking** should contact Donald Watt (☎01397/704340), the leader of the Lochaber Mountain Rescue Team, who organizes half- and whole-day walks.

Glen Coe

Stern and breathtakingly beautiful, **Glen Coe** (literally "Valley of Weeping"), sixteen miles south of Fort William on the A82, is one of the best-known Highland glens: a spectacular mountain valley, bounded on both sides by sheer cliffs and jagged rock summits. In 1692 it was the site of a famous massacre, after Alastair MacDonald, chief of an unruly and cattle-stealing clan, missed the deadline for taking an obligatory oath of allegiance to William III. This gave the authorities the excuse they needed "to root out that damnable sept", and government troops were billeted on the MacDonalds. Entertained by the clan with traditional hospitality – a matter of honour in the Highlands – they waited ten days for orders from Fort William and then turned on their hosts, slaying about 38 and causing more than 300 to flee in a blizzard.

Today, the glen, a honey-pot property of the NTS since the 1930s, is virtually uninhabited, and provides outstanding **climbing** and **walking**. Many famous mountaineers have gained experience on the demanding **Buachaille Etive Mhor** and its neighbour-

---

BEN NEVIS: WALKS AND HIKES

Of all the **walks in and around Glen Nevis**, the ascent of **Ben Nevis**, Britain's highest summit, inevitably attracts the most attention. In high summer, the trail is teeming with hikers, whatever the weather. However, this doesn't mean the mountain should be treated casually. It can snow on top any day of the year and more people perish here annually than on Everest, so take the necessary precautions (see p.897); in winter, of course, the mountain should be left to the experts.

The most obvious **route** to the summit, a Victorian pony path, up the whale-back south side of of the mountain, built to service the observatory that once stood on the top, starts from the Glen Nevis youth hostel, two miles southeast of Fort William (reached by bus #17 from Middle St). This climbs steadily from the trailhead, swinging onto a wide saddle with a small loch before veering right to cross the Red Burn. A series of seemingly endless zigzags rise from here over boulderfields on to a plateau, which you cross to reach the summit, marked by cairns, a shelter and a trig point. Return via the same route or, if the weather is settled and you're confident enough, make the side trip from the saddle mentioned earlier into the **Allt a'Mhuilinn glen** for spectacular views of the great cliffs on Ben Nevis' north face. The Allt a'Mhuilinn may be followed right down to valley level as an alternative route off the mountain, reaching the distillery on the A82 a mile north of Fort William. Allow a full day for the climb.

If you don't fancy a hike up the mountain, a great **low-level walk** runs from the end of the road at the top of the glen. The good but very rocky path leads through a dramatic gorge with impressive falls and rapids, then opens out into a secret hanging valley, carpeted with wild flowers, with a high waterfall at the far end. It's a pretty place for a picnic and if you're really energetic you can walk on over **Rannoch Moor** to **Corrour Station**, where you can pick up one of four daily trains to take you back to Fort William.

WALKS AROUND GLEN COE

Ordnance Survey Landranger Map No.41.

Flanked by sheer-sided Munros, Glen Coe offers some of the Highlands' most challenging hiking routes, with long steep ascents over rough trails and notoriously unpredictable weather conditions that claim lives every year. The **walks** outlined below number among the glen's less ambitious routes, but still require a map. It's essential that you take the proper precautions (see p.897), and **stick to the paths**, both for your own safety and the sake of the soil, which has become badly eroded in places.

A good introduction to the splendours of Glen Coe is the half-day hike over **the Devil's staircase**, which follows part of the old military road that once ran between Fort William and Stirling. The trail, a good option for families and less experienced hikers, starts at the village of **Kinlochleven**, due north across the mountains from Glen Coe at the far eastern tip of Loch Leven (take the B863): head along the single-track road from the British Aluminium Heritage Centre to a wooden bridge, from where a gradual climb on a dirt jeep track winds up to Penstock Farm. The path, a section of the West Highland Way, is marked from here onwards by thistle signs, and is therefore easy to follow uphill to the 1804-foot pass and down the other side into Glen Coe. The Devil's Staircase was named by four hundred soldiers who endured severe hardship to build it in the seventeenth century, but in fine settled weather the trail is safe and affords stunning views of Loch Eilde and Buachaille Etive Mor. A more detailed account of this hike features in *Great Walks: Kinlochleven (No.4)* leaflet, on sale at most tourist offices in the area.

Another leaflet in the *Great Walks* series (*No.5: Glen Coe*) gives a good description of the **Allt Coire Gabhail** hike, another old favourite, but undoubtedly one of the finest walks in the Glen Coe area that does not entail the ascent of a Munro is the **Buachaille Etive Beag (BEB) circuit**, for which we recommend you check out the *Ordnance Survey Pathfinder Guide: Fort William and Glen Coe Walks*. Following the text-book glacial valleys of Lairig Eilde and Lairig Gartain, the route entails a 1968-foot climb in only nine miles of rough trail, and should only be attempted by relatively fit hikers.

ing peaks. An NTS **visitor centre** (April–Oct 10am–5.30pm; 50p), slap in the middle of the glen by the side of the main road, houses a rudimentary audio-visual show about the massacre, along with a gift shop selling the usual books, postcards and Highland kitsch (including cassettes of some positively surreal easy-listening bagpipe music).

Other than a small **youth hostel** (☎01855/811219), **accommodation** in the Glen is limited to the *Clachaig Inn*, on the narrow back road to Glencoe village (☎01855/811252; ③–④), a well-known climbers' haunt with nineteen rather stark rooms, most of which have en-suite facilities. The restaurant specializes in not too pricy Scottish cooking, but its strict dress code and minimum charge make it a lot less relaxing than the two bars, which are warmed by cosy log fires and serve a good range of real ales and malt whiskies.

Strathspey and the Cairngorms

Rising high in the heather-clad hills above Loch Laggan, forty miles due south of Inverness, the **River Spey**, Scotland's second longest river, drains northeast towards the Moray Firth through one of the Highlands' most spellbinding valleys. Famous for its ski slopes, salmon fishing, and ospreys, **Strathspey** forms a broad cleave between the mighty Monadhliath mountains in the north and the craggy large and grey Cairngorm range to the south. Outdoor enthusiasts flock here all year round to take advantage of the superb hiking, abundant water and winter snows, but the valley is also a major transport artery, funnelling traffic along trans-Grampian road and rail routes between Edinburgh and Inverness.

Of Strathspey's scattered settlements, **Aviemore** absorbs the largest number of visitors, particularly in mid-winter when it metamorphoses into the UK's busiest ski resort. The village itself isn't up to much, but the 4000-foot summit plateau of the Cairngorm is often snow-capped, providing stunning mountain scenery on a grand scale. Sedate **Kingussie**, further up the valley, is an older established holiday centre, popular more with anglers and grouse hunters than canoeists and climbers, while the Georgian town of **Grantown-on-Spey**, jumping-off point for the famous **Loch Garten Nature Reserve**, makes another good base for exploring the area. Most of upper Strathspey is privately owned by the **Glen More Forest Park** and **Rothiemurchus Estate**, who provide between them a plethora of year-round outdoor facilities, with masses of **accommodation** of all types. Both bodies actively encourage the recreational use of their land, which gives you the freedom to go virtually anywhere you want.

Aviemore

AVIEMORE was first developed as a resort in the mid-1960s, as the brutal concrete **Aviemore Centre** bears witness: a rundown assortment of cavernous concrete buildings and incongruous high-rise hotels. The village proper, a sprawling jumble of traditional stone houses and tacky tourist shops, isn't much better, but if you can brave all this, Aviemore does make a good springboard for more scenic parts of the valley.

Aviemore's **train station** is just north of the **tourist office** on the main drag, Grampian Road (Mon–Sat 9am–5pm; ☎01479/810363). They offer an accommodation-booking service, free maps and endless leaflets on local attractions. **Accommodation** is not a problem around here. The *Balavoulin Hotel* (☎01479/810672; ③) and *Ver Mont Guest House* (☎01479/810470; ②), both on Grampian Road, are good value. There are also plenty of B&Bs: *Mrs Shaw*, 7 Cairngorm Ave (☎01479/811436; ②), near the war memorial, is the cheapest. Also close to the tourist office is a large **youth hostel** (closed mid-Nov to Dec; ☎01479/810345).

At **GLENMORE**, in the Glen More Forest Park a few miles east of Aviemore, the well-signposted *Badaguish Centre* (☎01479/861285), housed in three log cabins, has dorm beds for sixty people and good facilities for disabled visitors. There are also two more independent youth hostels near the village of **KINCRAIG**, six miles south of Aviemore: the upmarket *Loch Insh Watersports Centre* (☎01540/651272), beautifully sited beside the loch, and *Balaachroick* (☎01540/651323), where the all-in price includes bed linen and as much porridge as you like for breakfast.

All the hotels do run-of-the-mill **bar food**. The *Old Bridge Inn*, down by the river below the bridge on the way to Loch Morlich, has more choice than most, as does the *Gallery Bistro* right in the centre of **INVERDRUIE**, a tiny village a mile southeast of Aviemore on the road to Loch Morlich.

Walks around Aviemore.

Walking is an obvious attraction in the Aviemore area. If you want to walk the **high tops**, it makes sense to take the chairlift up from the *Day Lodge* (see previous page). You should always follow the usual safety rules (see p.897), and you'll need to get hold of *Ordnance Survey Landranger Map No.36*.

In addition to the high mountain trails, there are some lovely **low-level** walks around Aviemore. It'll take you about an hour or so to complete the gentle circular walk around pretty **Loch an Eilean**, beginning at the end of the back road that turns east off the B970 two miles south of Aviemore. The visitor centre at the lochside provides more information on the many woodland trails that criss-cross this area. A longer walk starts at the near end of **Loch Morlich**. Cross the river by the bridge and follow the dirt road, turning off after about twenty minutes to follow the signs to Aviemore. The

WINTER AND SUMMER ACTIVITIES IN AVIEMORE

Winter Sports

By European and North American standards **winter sports in Aviemore** are on a tiny scale, but occasionally snow, sun and lack of crowds coincide and you can have a great day. *Highland Guides* in Inverdruie (☎01479/861276) sell equipment and maps; for a run-down of ski schools and rental facilities in the area, check out the tourist office's *Ski Scotland* brochure. The **Cairngorm Ski Area**, about eight miles southeast of Aviemore, above Loch Morlich in Glen More Forest Park, is well served by **buses** from Aviemore. You can **rent skis** from the *Day Lodge* at the foot of the ski area (☎01479/861261), which also has a shop, a bar and restaurant, and sells tickets for the drag-lifts.

If there's lots of snow, the area around Loch Morlich and into the Rothiemurchus Estate provides enjoyable **cross-country skiing** through lovely woods, beside rushing burns and even over frozen lochs. If you really want to know about survival in a Scottish winter, you could try a week at **Glenmore Lodge** (☎01479/861276) in the heart of the Glen More Forest Park at the east end of Loch Morlich. This superbly equipped and organized centre, run by the Scottish National Sports Council, offers winter courses in hill walking, mountaineering, alpine ski mountaineering, avalanche awareness and much besides. To add to the winter scene, there's a herd of **reindeer** at Loch Morlich, and the **Siberian Husky Club** hold their races in the area.

Summer sports

The chief **summer activities** around Aviemore are **watersports**, and there are two centres that offer sailing, windsurfing and canoeing. The *Loch Morlich Watersports Centre* at Kincraig (☎01479/861221), five miles or so east of Aviemore at the east end of the loch, rents equipment and offers tuition in a lovely setting with a sandy beach, while, up-valley, the *Loch Insh Watersports Centre* (see below) offers the same facilities in a more open and less crowded surroundings. They also rent **mountain bikes**, boats for loch fishing, and give ski instruction on a 164-foot dry slope.

Riding and **pony trekking** are on offer up and down the valley; try the *Ballintean Riding Centre* (☎01540/65132) in Kingussie (see overleaf), or the *Carrbridge Trekking Centre*, Station Rd, Carrbridge, a few miles north of Aviemore (☎01479/84602).

Fishing is very much part of the local scene; you can fish for trout and salmon on the River Spey, and the Rothiemurchus Estate has a stocked trout-fishing loch at Inverdruie, where success is virtually guaranteed. Permits cost around £3.50 per day and are sold at *Speyside Sports* in Aviemore, one mile down the road toward the ski grounds from the tourist office, and at *Loch Morlich Watersports* (see above), who also rent rods and tackle.

path goes through beautiful pine woods and past tumbling burns, and you can branch off to Coylumbridge and Loch an Eilean. Unless you're prepared for a 25-mile hike, don't take the track to the Lairig Ghru, which eventually brings you out near Braemar. The routes are all well marked and easy to follow and depending on what combination you put together can take anything from two to five hours.

Another good halfday walk leads along well-surfaced forestry track from **Glenmore Lodge** up towards the **Ryvoan Pass**, taking in **An Lochan Uaine**, known as the "Green Loch" and living up to its name, with amazing colours that range from turquoise to slate grey depending on the weather. The track narrows once past the loch and leads east towards Deeside, so retrace your steps to avoid a major trek.

Kingussie and Grantown-On-Spey

KINGUSSIE (pronounced King*yoo*sie) lies twelve miles south of Aviemore and is far cosier, stacked around a single main street (also the A9). Beyond its usefulness as a

THE LOCH GARTEN NATURE RESERVE

The **Loch Garten Nature Reserve**, eight miles south of Grantown-on-Spey (or seven miles north of Aviemore), is famous as the nesting site of one of Britain's rarest birds. A little over 50 years ago, the **osprey** (known in North America as the "fish hawk") had completely disappeared from the British Isles. Then, in the mid-1950s, a single pair of these exquisite white-and-grey eagles mysteriously reappeared and built a nest in a tree on the loch. After a gang of egg stealers made off with one year's batch, the RSPB have maintained a high-security operation; and now the birds are present in healthy numbers once more. The **best time to visit** Loch Garten is during the nesting season (late April & Aug), when the RSPB open an observation hide fitted with powerful telescopes. You can also rent binoculars for trips elsewhere in the reserve, where you may catch sight of crossbills, capercaillies, whooper swans and red squirrels. Loch Garten can be difficult to reach without your own transport, although the popular **Strathspey Steam Railway**, which runs between Aviemore and nearby **Boat of Garten**, will get you to within a couple of miles of the reserve.

place to stay, the chief attraction here is the excellent **Highland Folk Museum** (April–Oct Mon–Sat 10am–6pm, Sun 2–6pm; Nov–March Mon–Fri 10am–3pm; £2.50). An absorbing collection of buildings, exhibitions and artefacts covering every aspect of Highland life, the complex includes a farming museum, an old smokehouse, a mill, a Hebridean "black house" (see p.856) and a traditional herb and flower garden; on most days in summer there's a demonstration of various traditional crafts. East across the river on a hillock stand the ruins of **Ruthven Barracks**, the best preserved of the garrisons built to pacify the Highlands after the 1715 Rebellion and stunningly floodlit at night. Taken by the Jacobites in 1744, it was blown up in the wake of Culloden to prevent it from falling into enemy hands.

Kingussie's **tourist office** is on King Street, off the High Street (May–Sept daily 10am–6pm; ☎01540/661297). If you want to base yourself here, try *The Auld Poor House*, Laggan Cottage (☎01540/661558; ②), a congenial **B&B**, ten-minutes' walk northeast of the village on the B9152. If it's full, *Theodore Cottage*, Duke St (☎01540/661886; ③), or *Bhuna Monadh* (☎01540/661186; ③), 85 High St, are good fall-backs. The *Cross Restaurant*, in a converted tweed mill nearby on Tweed Mill Brae (March–Nov & Christmas; ☎01540/661166) is one of the best **restaurants** in the region – expensive, but worth it. *The Tipsy Laird* nearby serves traditional Scottish high teas and filling grills, while the *Café Volante* is the place to head for a cheap-and-cheerful fish-and-chip supper. Finally, the *Royal Hotel* serves standard bar meals, with some vegetarian options, and the cosy *Retro Café* specializes in toasties and home-baked cakes, and offers a choice of eleven kinds of coffee prepared in five different ways.

Buses run from Aviemore and Inverness to the tiny Georgian town of **GRANTOWN-ON-SPEY**, about fifteen miles northwest of Aviemore, which, if you've got your own transport, makes another good base for exploring Strathspey and the Cairngorm area. Activity is concentrated around the attractive central square, where there's a **tourist office** on High Street (May–Sept daily 9am–6pm; ☎01479/872473) and plenty of **accommodation** – *Cumbrae*, South St (☎01479/873216; ②), *Mrs Lawson*, 2 Mossie Rd (☎01479/872076; ②), and *Fearna House*, Old Spey Bridge (☎01479/872016; ②) all do comfortable, good-value B&B. If you're after something more upmarket, head for the large seventeenth-century *Garth Hotel*, Castle Rd (☎01479/872836; ④), or the marginally less expensive *Tyree House Hotel* (☎01479/872615; ③), High Street; both are open all year round and have good restaurants that serve Scottish specialities.

The west coast

For many people, the Highlands' starkly beautiful **west coast** – stretching from the Morven peninsula (opposite Mull) in the south, to wind-lashed Cape Wrath in the far north – is the epitome of "Bonnie Scotland". Serrated by long blue sea lochs, deep glens and rugged green mountains that sweep from the shore line, its myriad islets, occasional white-sand beaches and turquoise bays can, on rare sunny days, look like a picture postcard of the Mediterranean. This also is the least populated part of Britain, with just two small towns, and yawning tracts of moorland and desolate peat bog between crofting settlements.

The **Vikings**, who ruled the region in the ninth century, called it the "South Land" – from which the modern district of Sutherland takes its name – and established a firm clan system, with clansmen holding land owned by their chiefs in return for rent or service. After Culloden, the Clearances emptied most of the inland glens of the far north, however, and left the population clinging to the coastline, where a herring-fishing industry developed. Today, tourism, crofting and salmon farming are the main-stay of the local economy, supplemented by EU construction grants and subsidies for the sheep you'll encounter everywhere.

For visitors, **cycling** and **walking** are the obvious way to make the most of the superb scenery, and countless lochans and crystal-clear rivers offer superlative trout and salmon **fishing**. The shattered cliffs of the far northwest are an ornithologist's dream, harbouring some of Europe's largest and most diverse **seabird colonies**, and the area's craggy mountaintops are the haunt of the elusive golden eagle.

Tempered by the Gulf Stream, the west coast's weather ranges from stupendous to diabolical. Never count on a sunny morning meaning a fine day; it can rain here at any time, and go on raining for days. Beware, too, as always in this part of the world, of the dreaded **midge**, which drives even the hardiest of locals to distraction on warm summer evenings.

Without your own vehicle, **getting around the west coast** can be a problem. Buses and trains are frequent between Inverness and Kyle of Lochalsh, Fort William and Mallaig, and Ullapool is well connected to Inverness by bus. However, services peter out as you venture further afield, and you'll have to rely on **postbuses**, which go just about everywhere, albeit slowly and at odd times of day. **Driving** is a lot less proble-matic: the roads aren't busy, though frequently single-track and scattered with sheep, requiring constant vigilance; and remember to refuel whenever you can, as pumps are few and far between. Finally, **motorcyclists** should avoid breaking down around here at all costs: most recovery policies will only get you as far as the nearest garage, and the only source of spares in the region is Inverness.

Morvern to Morar: the "Rough Bounds"

The remote southwest corner of the Highlands, from the **Morven peninsula** to the busy fishing and ferry port of **Mallaig**, is a dramatic, lonely region: an inhospitable mix of bog, mountain and moorland cleaved by sea lochs and fringed by stunning white beaches that give wonderful views to the Skye and the Western Isles. Its Gaelic name translates as the "**Rough Bounds**", implying a region geographically and spiritually outside current thought and behaviour and, mainly due to its geography, among Scotland's most sparsely populated areas. Even if you haven't got a car, you should spend a few days here exploring by foot – there are so few roads that some determined hiking is almost inevitable.

The southwest Highlands' main road is the A830, which winds in tandem with the rail line across the mountains from Fort William to Mallaig. Along the way, the road passes **Glenfinnan**, the much photographed spot at the head of stunning **Loch Shiel** where Bonnie Prince Charlie gathered the clans to start the doomed Jacobite uprising of 1745. Buses and trains along this main drag are frequent; elsewhere, you'll have to rely on daily post- or school buses. If you have your own transport, the five-minute ferry crossing at **Corran Ferry** (every 15min), a nine-mile drive south of Fort William down Loch Linnhe, provides a more direct point of entry for Morven and the rugged **Ardnamurchan peninsula**.

Morvern, Sunart and Ardgour

Bounded on three sides by sea lochs and, in the north, by desolate Glen Tarbet, the remote southwest part of the Rough Bounds region, known as **Morvern**, is unremittingly bleak and empty. Most visitors only travel through here to get to **LOCHALINE** (pronounced Loch*aa*lin), a remote community on the Sound of Mull, from where a small ferry chugs to **Fishnish**, on the Isle of Mull. If you time to kill, the easy stroll to the nearby fourteenth-century ruins of **Ardtornish Castle**, reached via a track that turns east off off the main road one and a half miles north of Lochaline, makes an enjoyable detour. On the practical front, the tiny *Lochaline Hotel* (☎01967/421657; ③) serves quality bar food, and has a couple of small but comfortable **rooms**.

The predominantly roadless regions of **Sunart** and **Ardgour** make up the country between Loch Shiel, Loch Sunart and Loch Linnhe, north of Morvern: the heart of Jacobite support in the mid-eighteenth century, and a Catholic stronghold to this day. The area's only real village is sleepy **STRONTIAN**, grouped around a green on an inlet of the Loch Sunart. In 1722, lead mines here yielded the first-ever traces of the element strontium, subsequently named after the village. Worked by French POWs, the same mines also furnished shot for the Napoleonic wars. Strontian's other claim to fame is the "**Floating Church**", which was moored nearby in Loch Sunart in 1843. After being refused permission by the local laird to found their own "kirk", or chapel, on the estate, members of the Free Presbyterian Church (see p.857), bought an old boat on the River Clyde, converted it into a church and then had it towed up the west coast to Loch Sunart.

Travelling by public **transport**, you can get to Strontian on the 8am bus from Kilchoan (see below), and on a bus that leaves Corran Ferry at 10.50am. In term-time a direct school bus from Fort William leaves at 3.45pm. Strontian's **tourist office** (Easter–Oct Mon–Fri 9am–5pm, Sat 10am–4pm, Sun 10am–2pm; ☎01967/402131) will book **accommodation** for a small fee. *Loch View* (☎01967/402465; ②) is excellent value, with large rooms in a fine lochside Victorian house. *Sea View* (☎01967/402060; ②) next door, a small cottage swathed in flowers, is a good fall-back, and welcomes dogs. The *Strontian* (☎01967/402029; ③), on the main road, is pretty and comfortable, has an ultra-basic **bothy** in its back yard and is the best place for inexpensive nosh; the posher *Loch Sunart* (☎01967/402471; ⑤) occupies a splendid site right by the water.

The Ardnamurchan peninsula

A tortuous single-track road (the B8007) winds west from Sunart along the northern shore of Loch Sunart to the wild **Ardnamurchan peninsula**, the most westerly point on the British mainland. Comprising a varied landscape of rocky, heather-clad hills, sea loch, woodland, shell-sand beaches and hidden coves, the peninsula, which lost most of its inhabitants during the infamous Clearances, is today virtually deserted apart from the handful of tiny crofting settlements clinging to its jagged coastline. However, Ardnamurchan remains a naturalists' paradise, harbouring a huge variety of birds, animals and wildflowers that are at their best in late May to July, when the machair is carpeted with thrift and wild iris.

An inspiring introduction to the diverse flora, fauna and geology of the unspoilt Ardnamurchan is the **Glenmore Natural History Centre** (April–Oct 10am–5pm;

£2.50), nestled on a seaweed-strewn lochside near the hamlet of **GLENBORRODALE**. Brainchild of local photographer Michael MacGregor (whose stunning work enlivens postcard stands along the west coast), the centre is housed in a sensitively designed timber building, complete with turf roof and wildlife ponds. TV cameras relay live coverage of the comings and goings on feeding tables and underwater pools, and a superb audio-visual show features MacGregor's photographs of the area accompanied by specially composed music. The small café serves good home-baked cakes and snacks.

KILCHOAN, nine miles west of the Glenmore Centre, is Ardnamurchan's main village – a straggling crofting township overlooking the Sound of Mull that still enjoys a marvellous sense of isolation. Between mid-April and mid-October, a **ferry** runs from here to Tobermory and there's a **tourist office** (Easter–Oct Mon–Sat 9am–6.45pm, Sun 10.30am–5.15pm; ☎01972/510222). **Hotels** include the *Meall mo Chridhe Hotel* (☎01972/510328; full board ⑦), a converted eighteenth-century *manse* on the water's edge, or the cheaper *Sonachan Hotel* (☎01972/510211; ④). For **B&B**, try *Doirlinn House* (March–Oct; ☎01972/510209; ③), or *Hillview* (☎01972/510322; ③), just north of the village at Achnaha. The best place to **eat** is the *Meall mlo Chridhe Hotel*, which specializes in west coast seafood and game, served with home-grown vegetables (reservations essential for non-residents; bring your own wine). For down-to-earth bar meals, head for the local pub, *Kilchoan House Hotel*, on the main road. The only direct **bus** to Kilchoan leaves from Corran Ferry at 10.30am, arriving four hours later.

Beyond Kilchoan the road continues to wild and windy **Ardnamurchan Point**, with its unmanned **lighthouse** and spectacular views west to Coll, Tiree and across to the north of Mull. The shell-strewn sandy beach of **Sanna Bay**, about three miles north of the point, offers truly unforgettable vistas of the Small Isles to the north, circled by gulls, terns and guillemots.

Moidart

North of the Ardnamurchan peninsula, the **Moidart** district's largest settlement is **ACHARACLE**, an ancient crofting village lying at the sea end of **Loch Shiel**

THE RAISING OF THE STANDARD

Approaching Moidart from the north by train, or via the fast Fort William–Mallaig road (the A830), you pass a historic site with great resonance for Scots. **Glenfinnan** was where Bonnie Prince Charlie raised his standard to signal the start of the Jacobite uprising of 1745. Surrounded by other loyal clansmen, the young rebel prince waited to see if the Cameron of Loch Shiel would join his army. The drone of this powerful chief's pipers drifting up the glen was eagerly awaited, for without him and the Stuarts' attempt to claim the English throne would have been sheer folly. Despite strong misgivings, however, Cameron did decide to support the uprising, and arrived at Glenfinnan on a sunny August 19 with seven hundred men, thereby encouraging other less convinced clan leaders to follow suit.

Assured of adequate backing, the prince raised his red and white silk colour, proclaimed his father King James III of England, and set off on the long march to London from which only a handful of the soldiers gathered at Glenfinnan would return. The spot is marked by a column, crowned with a clansman in full battle dress, erected as a tribute by Alexander Macdonald of Glenaladale in 1815. Set against a backdrop of grandiose Highland scenery, this atmospheric place inevitably stirs up nationalistic sentiments among Scots, and a certain sympathy for the Jacobite cause among visitors. The **visitor centre** (April–Oct daily 9.30am–6pm; £1), opposite the monument, gives an account of Prince Charlie's ill-fated odyssey around Britain, finishing with the rout at Culloden (see p.905).

Surrounded by gentle hills, it's an attractive place whose scattered houses form a real community, with several shops, a post office, and plenty of **places to stay**. Try the central *Loch Shiel Hotel* (☎01967/431224; ③), where you can get reasonable **bar food**. *Belmont* (☎01967/431266; ②) is a comfortable central B&B, as is *Mrs Cliff's* (☎01967/431318), just across the road. Acharacle's village hall is often used for **ceilidhs**: look out for the notices in the shops.

A mile north of Acharacle, a side road running north off the A861 winds for three miles or so past a secluded estuary lined with rhododendron thickets and fishing platforms to **Loch Moidart**, a calm and sheltered sea loch. Perched atop a rocky promontory in the middle of the loch is **CASTLE TIORAM**, one of Scotland's most atmospheric historic monuments. Reached via a sandy causeway, the thirteenth-century fortress, whose Gaelic name means "dry land", was the seat of the MacDonalds of Clanranald until destroyed by their chief in 1715 to prevent it from falling into Hanoverian hands while he was away fighting for the Jacobites. Today, the surviving walls and tower enclose an inner courtyard and a couple of empty chambers.

Morar
Once beyond the startling turquoise sea loch of Loch Ailort, in the district of **Morar**, getting around is easier, and there are train and bus links to Fort William along the A830. **ARISAIG**, scattered round a sandy bay at the west end of the Morar peninsula, makes a good base for exploring this bit of the coast. There's nothing in the way of specific attractions, but if the weather's fine you can spend hours wandering along the beaches and quiet backroads, and there's a small **seal colony** at nearby Rhumach, reached via the single-track lane leading west out of the village along the headland. A daily boat also leaves from here during the summer for the Small Isles (see p.851); contact Murdo Grant (☎01687/546224). **Accommodation** in the village is plentiful. *Kinloid Farm House* (☎01687/450691; ②) is one of several pleasant B&Bs with sea views, while the more upmarket *Old Library Lodge* (☎01687/450651; ⑥) has a handful of well-appointed but overpriced rooms, some of them in a two-hundred-year-old converted stable overlooking the waterfront. The restaurant downstairs, serving moderately priced lunches and à la carte dinners (reservations recommended), is renowned for adding an exotic twist to fresh local ingredients – try Mallaig cod with Moroccan marinade.

Mallaig
A cluttered, noisy port whose pebble-dashed houses struggle for space with great lumps of granite tumbling down to the sea, **MALLAIG**, 47 miles west of Fort William along the A830 (regular buses and trains run this route), is not a pretty town. But as a ferry stop for Skye and the Western Isles (see p.842), it is always full of visitors. The continuing source of the town's wealth is its thriving fishing industry: on the quayside piles of nets, tackle and ice crates lie scattered around a bustling modern market. When the fleet is in, trawlers encircled by flocks of raucous gulls choke the harbour, and the pubs, among the liveliest on the west coast, host bouts of serious drinking.

If you're waiting for a ferry or train, you could fill in some time at **Mallaig Marine World**, north of the train station near the harbour (daily 9am–7pm; £2.50), where tanks of sea creatures share space with informative exhibits about the port. Two minutes' walk south of the railway bridge, the **Mallaig Heritage Centre** (May–Sept Mon–Sat 9.30am–5pm, Sun 1–5pm; £1.80), displaying old photographs of the town and its environs, is also worth a browse.

Mallaig is a compact place, concentrated around the harbour, where you'll find the **tourist office** (Mon–Sat 9am–8pm, Sun 10am–5pm; ☎01687/462170) and the **bus** and **train stations**. The *CalMac* ticket office (☎01687/462403), serving passengers for Skye and the Small Isles (see p.842), is also nearby, and you can arrange transport to

Knoydart by telephoning Bruce Watt (☎01687/462320), whose three-weekly boat to Inverie (Mon, Wed & Fri) continues east along Loch Nevis to Tarbet; the loch is sheltered, so crossings are rarely cancelled. Mr Watt also operates cruises across to Loch Coruisk on Skye (see p.847) on Tuesdays.

There are plenty of **places to stay**, with budget travellers making a beeline for *Sheena's Backpackers' Lodge* (☎01687/462764), a refreshingly laid-back independent **hostel** overlooking the harbour, with mixed dorms, self-catering facilities, a sitting room and a cosy en-suite double-bedded room with its own coal fire (②). For **B&B**, head around the harbour to East Bay, where you'll find the immaculate *Western Isles Guest House* (☎01687/562320; ③); *Quarterdeck* (☎01687/462604; ③) and *Springbank* (☎01687/462459; ③), nearby are good fall backs. Finally, the *West Highland Hotel* (☎01687/462210; ⑤) is a delightfully old-fashioned place in the centre of town, with splendid views. The only commendable **restaurant** in town is the moderately priced *Cabin*, on the harbour, which specializes in delicious fresh seafood straight off the boat.

Kyle of Lochalsh

KYLE OF LOCHALSH, seven miles northeast of Eileen Donan Castle, is a busy town – a transit point on the route to Skye and an important train terminal. Straggling down the hill towards the pier and train station, it's not particularly attractive – concrete buildings, rail junk and myriad signs of the fishing industry abound – and is ideally somewhere to pass through rather than linger. Since the **Skye road bridge** was opened in 1995, the traffic rumbles freely over the channel a mile north of town, bypassing Kyle completely, leaving its shopkeepers bereft of the passing trade they used to enjoy.

The train station is about five minutes south of the pier; three or four **trains** run daily to Inverness (2hr 30min). **Buses** stop at the pier. Timetables are currently being redrawn because of the new bridge (so check with the companies below), but it seems likely that services will run to Glasgow via Fort William (3 daily; 5hr), and to Inverness via Invermoriston (Mon–Sat 4 daily, 2 on Sun; 2hr). These routes can become very crowded, so book through *Skye-Ways Express Coach Services*, Ferry Pier (☎01599/534328), or *Scottish Citylink* (☎0990/898989).

The **tourist office** (daily 9am–5pm; ☎01599/534276), about five minutes' walk up the hill from the train station towards the pier, opposite the monster car park on the headland, will book **accommodation** for you, which is useful as there are surprisingly few places, particularly in high summer. The *Lochalsh Hotel* (☎01599/534202; ⑧) is wonderfully situated, looking out at Skye, with fabulous seafood and an air of dated luxury, while the *Kyle Hotel*, Main St (☎01599/534204; ⑤), is a traditional mid-range hotel. For **B&B**, try *Mrs Finlayson*, Main St (☎01599/534265; ③), five minutes' walk from the train station; or *Crowlin View* (☎01599/534286; ③), one and a half miles north of Kyle on the Plockton road. The *Seagreen Restaurant*, also on the Plockton road (but closer to the centre) has good, moderately priced, fresh seafood and vegetarian **meals**.

Loch Duich

If you approach the Kyle of Lochalsh by road, you'll skirt the northern shore of **Loch Duich**, the boot-shaped inlet that forms the northern shoreline of the Glenelg peninsula, which features prominently on the tourist trail, with buses from all over Europe thundering down the sixteen miles from **SHIEL BRIDGE** to Kyle of Lochalsh on their way to Skye. The most dramatic approach to the loch, however, is from the east through Glen Shiel, where the mountains known as the **Five Sisters of Kintail**

HIKING IN GLEN SHIEL

The mountains of **Glen Shiel**, sweeping southeast from Loch Duich, offer some of the best hiking routes in Scotland. Rising dramatically from sea level to over 3000ft in less than a couple of miles, they are also exposed to the worst of the west coast's notoriously fickle weather. Don't underestimate either of these two routes. Tracing the paths on a map, they can appear deceptively short and easy to follow; however, unwary walkers die here every year, often because they failed to allow enough time to get off the mountain by nightfall, or because of a sudden change in the weather. Neither of the routes outlined below should be attempted by inexperienced walkers, nor without a map, a compass and a detailed trekking guide – the SMC's *Hill Walks in Northwest Scotland* is recommended.

Taking in a bumper crop of Munros, the **Five Sisters traverse** is deservedly the most popular trek in the area. Allow a full day to complete the whole route, which begins at the first fire break on the left-hand side as you head southeast down the glen on the A87. Strike straight up from here and follow the ridge north along to Scurr na Moraich (2874ft), dropping down the other side to Morvich on the valley floor.

The distinctive chain of mountains across the glen from the Five Sisters is the **Kintail Ridge**, crossed by another famous hiking route that begins at *The Cluanie Inn* on the A87. From here, follow the well-worn path south around the base of the mountain until it meets up with a stalkers' trail, which winds steeply up Creag a' Mhaim (3108ft) and then west along the ridgeway, with breathtaking views south across Knoydart and the Hebridean Sea.

surge up to heights of 3000ft – a familiar sight from countless tourist brochures, but an impressive one nonetheless. With steep-sided hills hemming in both sides of the loch, it's sometimes hard to remember that this is, in fact, the sea. There's a congenial **SYHA youth hostel** just outside Shiel Bridge at **RATAGAN** (March–Oct; ☎01599/511243), popular with walkers newly arrived off the Glen Affric trek from Loch Ness (see p.910).

Eilean Donan Castle

After Edinburgh's hilltop fortress, **Eilean Donan Castle** (April–Oct daily 9am–5pm), ten miles north of Shiel Bridge on the A87, has to be Scotland's most photographed monument. Presiding over the once strategically important confluence of Lochs Aish, Long and Duich, the forbidding crenellated tower rises from the water's edge, joined to the shore by a narrow stone bridge and with sheer mountains as a backdrop.

The original castle was established in 1230 by Alexander II to protect the area from the Vikings. Later, during the Jacobite era, it was occupied by troops dispatched by the King of Spain to help Bonnie Prince Charlie. However, when King George heard of their whereabouts, frigates were sent to weed the Spaniards out, and the castle was blown up with their stocks of gunpowder. Thereafter, it lay in ruins until restored in the 1930s by the Maclean family, still the local lairds, owners and occupants of the castle during the winter months. Eileen Donan has also been the setting of several major movies, including *Highlander*, starring Christopher Lambert (large numbers of film stills are sold at the ticket office). Only two rooms – a banquet hall and the troops' quarters – are open to the public, with displays of various Jacobite and clan relics whose charm is rather hard to detect amid the attentions of the tour parties that file through here in the summer.

Food and limited **accommodation** are available less than a mile away in the hamlet of **DORNIE**, where the *Castle Inn*, Francis St (☎01599/555205; ④) has a handful of comfortable rooms. For a little more luxury, head north out of the village to the *Loch Duich Hotel* (☎01599/555213; ⑤), which has splendid doubles overlooking the loch and a small restaurant serving upmarket bar snacks and evening meals.

Plockton

A ten-minute train ride north of Kyle at the sea end of islet-studded **Loch Carron**, lies **PLOCKTON**: a chocolate-box row of neatly painted fishers' houses ranged around the curve of a tiny harbour. Originally known as *Am Ploc*, the settlement was a minuscule crofting hamlet until the end of the eighteenth-century, when a local laird transformed it into a prosperous fishery, renaming it "Plockton". Today, it's self-consciously twee and touristy, full of yachtsmen, second-home owners and craft shops. The unique brilliance of Plockton's light has also made it something of an artists' hangout, and during the summer the picturesque waterfront, with its row of shaggy palm trees, flower gardens and pleasure boats, is invariably punctuated by painters dabbing at their easels.

If you want **to stay**, the friendly, cosy *Haven Hotel* (☎01599/544223; ⑤) near the seafront is renowned for its excellent food; the family-run *Creag-nan-Daroch Hotel*, Innes St (☎01599/544222; ④) makes a comfortable alternative. The *Plockton Hotel*, Harbour St (☎01599/544274; ⑥) also overlooks the quay and serves good seafood. Of the fifteen or so **B&Bs**, *The Shieling* (☎01599/544282; ③), on a tiny headland at the top of the harbour, is the most attractively placed, with great views on both sides. Excellent-value farmhouse B&B is available at *The Craig Rare Breeds Farm*, midway between Plockton and Stromeferry (☎01599/544205; ②), which does particularly good breakfasts (vegetarian if preferred); you can also check out the ancient breeds of Scottish farm animals rubbing shoulders with llamas and peacocks. The top place to **eat** is the *Haven*'s restaurant, whose gourmet food is in a league of its own. *The Old Schoolhouse* is the next best option, serving reasonably priced steaks, seafood and vegetarian dishes; the *Buttery*, part of the grocer's, on the corner of Main Street by the sea, is also open all day for snacks and inexpensive meals. All the hotels, of course, are happy to feed non-residents.

The Applecross peninsula

The most dramatic approach to the **Applecross peninsula** (the English-sounding name is actually a corruption of the Gaelic *Apor Crosan*, meaning "estuary") is from the south, along the infamous **Bealach na Ba pass** (literally "Cattle Pass"). Crossing the forbidding hills behind **Kishorn** and rising to 2000ft, with a gradient and switch-back bends worthy of the Alps, this route, the highest road in Scotland and a popular cycling *piste*, is hair-raising in places, but the panoramic views across the Minch to Raasay and Skye more than compensate. The other way in is from the north: a beautiful coast road that meanders slowly from **Shieldaig** on Loch Torridon, with tantalizing glimpses of the Cullins to the south.

The sheltered, fertile bay of **APPLECROSS** village, where the Irish missionary monk Maelrhuba founded a monastery in 673 AD, comes as a surprise after the bleakness of the moorland approach. It's an idyllic place; you can wander along lanes banked with wild iris and orchids, and explore beaches and rockpools on the shore. It's also quite an adventure to get here by **public transport**. The nearest railhead is seventeen miles northeast at Strathcarron Station, near Achnasheen, which you have to reach by 9.45am to catch the **postbus** to Shieldaig, on Loch Torridon. From here, a second postie leaves for Applecross at 11.30am (90min). No buses of any kind run over the Bealach na Ba pass. The old *Applecross Inn* (☎01520/744262; ③), right beside the sea, serves real ales, sandwiches and great seafood suppers. Two even more appealing **B&Bs** lie further down the lane towards **Toscaig**, with its pier and inquisitive seals: *Camustiel* (☎01520/744277; ②), a converted manse on the sea shore, and *John Pearson* (☎01520/744272; ③), whose isolated cottage looks over to Skye. There's also **camping** at the *Flowertunnel Restaurant*, off the road to the pass, which sells cakes and freshly baked bread.

Loch Torridon

Loch Torridon marks the northern boundary of the Applecross peninsula, its awe-inspiring setting backed by the menacing mountains of **Liathach** and **Beinn Eighe**, tipped by streaks of white quartzite. The greater part of this area is composed of the reddish Torridonian sandstone, whose 750-million-year-old beds can be seen on the precipices of Liathach; there are also numerous deeply eroded and ice-smoothed corries. Much of Beinn Eighe is forested with Caledonian pinewood, which once covered the whole of the country, and houses pine marten, wildcat, fox and badger – you may even see buzzards and golden eagles. There's also a wide range of flora, with the higher rocky slopes producing spectacular natural alpine rock gardens.

There's an unsightly modern **youth hostel** in the village of **TORRIDON** (Feb–Oct, Christmas & New Year; ☎01445/791284), as well as a couple of **B&Bs** four miles further up the coast at the tiny hamlet of **Inveralligin**: try *Mrs Finan* (☎01445/791325; ③), or *Grianan* (☎01445/791264; ②), which also does evening meals by arrangement. Seven miles west of Torridon, **SHIELDAIG**, an attractive little lochside village below the main road, harbours another batch of B&Bs including *Tigh Fada* (☎01520/755248; ③) and, a little out of the village, *Innis Mhor* (☎01520/755339; ③); both may be booked through the tourist office. For more luxury, the rambling Victorian *Loch Torridon* (☎01445/791242; ⑦), set amid well-tended lochside grounds, is one of the area's top **hotels**.

Loch Maree

About eight miles north of Loch Torridon, **Loch Maree** (pronounced Mu*ree*), dotted with Caledonian pine-covered islands, is one of the west coast's scenic highlights, best viewed from the road (A832) that drops down to its southeastern tip through Glen Docherty. It's also surrounded by some of Scotland's finest deer-stalking country: the remote, privately owned *Letterewe Lodge* on the north shore, accessible only by helicopter or boat, lies at the heart of a famous deer forest. Queen Victoria stayed a few days here at the *Loch Maree Hotel* (☎01445; 791288; ⑥), whose respectable air has altered little since.

WALKING AROUND TORRIDON

There are difficult and unexpected conditions on virtually all hiking routes around Torridon, and the weather can change very rapidly. If you're relatively inexperienced but want to do the magnificent ridge walk along the **Liathach** (pronounced *Lee*-a-gach, or *Lee*-ach) massif, or the strenuous traverse of **Beinn Eighe** (pronounced Ben *Ay*), join a guided hike: contact the long-time NTS ranger, Seamus MacNally on ☎01445/791221, or Cam MacLeay on ☎01445/791216.

For those confident to go it alone, one of many possible routes takes you behind Liathach and down the pass, **Coire Dubh**, to the main road in Glen Torridon. This is a great, straightforward walk if you're properly equipped, covering thirteen miles and taking in superb landscapes. Allow yourself the **whole day**. Start at the stone bridge on the Diabaig road along the north side of Loch Torridon.

A rewarding walk even in rough weather is the seven-mile hike up the coast from **Lower Diabeg**, ten miles northwest of Torridon village, to **Redpoint**. On a clear day, the views across to Raasay and Applecross from this gentle undulating path are superlative, but you'll have to return along the same trail, or else make your way back via Loch Maree on the A832. If you're staying in **Shieldaig**, the road that winds up the peninsula running north from the village, covered by the postbus each morning, makes a pleasant ninety-minute round walk.

The A832 skirts the southern shore of Loch Maree, passing the **Beinn Eighe Nature Reserve**, five miles northwest of Kinlochewe, the UK's oldest wildlife sanctuary. Established to preserve the ancient Caledonian oak forest that still survives on Loch Maree's little islets, the reserve also encompasses a large tract of inhospitable mountain and moorland. The **Aultroy Visitor Centre** (May–Oct daily 10am–5pm) on the A832 gives details of the area's rare plant species, many of which have endured here since the last ice age, and sells pamphlets describing two excellent **walks** in the reserve: a woodland trail through lochside forest, and a more strenuous half-day hike around the base of Beinn Eighe. Both start from the car park a mile north of the visitor centre, where you'll find a vending machine that dispenses the route guides.

Gair Loch

Three buses each week run from Inverness (Mon, Wed & Sat) to **GAIRLOCH**, scattered around the sheltered northeastern shore of the loch of the same name. Lying within easy reach of several tempting sandy beaches and some excellent coastal walks, this former crofting township thrives during the summer as a low-key holiday resort. The **Gairloch Heritage Museum** (Easter–Sept daily 10am–5pm; free) has eclectic, appealing displays covering geology, archeology, fishing and farming, that range from a mock-up of a croft house to an early knitting machine. Probably the most interesting section is the archive, an array of photographs, maps, genealogies, lists of place names and taped recollections, mostly in Gaelic, made by elderly locals.

The area's real attraction, however, is its beautiful coastline. To get to one of the most impressive stretches, head around the north side of the bay and follow the single-track B8021 beyond Big Sand (a cleaner and quieter beach than the one in Gairloch) to the tiny crofting hamlet of **Melvaig** (reachable by the 9.05am Gairloch postbus), from where a narrow surfaced track runs out wind-lashed **Rubha Reidh** (pronounced Roo-a *Ree*) **Point**. The converted **lighthouse** here, which looks straight across the Minch to Harris in the Outer Hebrides, serves slap-up afternoon teas and home-baked cakes (Thurs & Sun noon–5pm). You can also **stay** in their comfortable and relaxed bunkhouse, or double rooms (reserve ahead in high season; ☎01445/771263; ②); they'll drive you out here from Gairloch for £4 return. Around the headland from Rubha Reidh lies secluded **Camas Mór** beach, which has to rank among the most picturesque in Scotland. For a great half-day walk, follow the marked footpath inland (southeast) from here along the base of a sheer scarp slope, and past a string of lochans, ruined crofts and a remote wood to **Midtown** on the east side of the peninsula, five miles north of Poolewe on the B8057. However, unless you leave a car at the end of the trail or arrange to be picked up, you'll have to walk or hitch back to Gairloch as the only transport along this road is an early-morning post van.

A more leisurely way to explore the coast is a **wildlife-spotting cruise**: *Sail Gairloch* departs (10am, 2 & 5pm) from the Shieldaig mooring, five miles south of Gairloch, and head off across the bay in search of dolphins, porpoises, seals and even the odd whale. You can also **rent a boat** for the day through Gairloch's chandlery shop (☎01445/712458) – popular with sea anglers.

Three miles south of Gairloch, a narrow single-track lane (built with the Destitution Funds raised during the nineteenth-century potato famine) peels west off the main A832, past wooded coves and inlets on its way south of the loch to **BADACHRO**, a former fishing village. These days, it's a sleepy place; life revolves around the white-washed *Badachro Inn* (March to late Oct; ☎01445/714255), a characterful pub on the waterfront offering cheap and cheerful bar food. The hospitable landlord and his wife have a couple of **B&B** rooms (③).

Beyond Badachro, the road winds for five more miles along the shore to **Redpoint**, a minuscule hamlet that has no accommodation but marks the trailhead for the wonderful coast walk to **Lower Diabeg** (see p.926). Even if you don't fancy a full-blown hike, follow the path a mile or so to the exquisite beach hidden on the south side of the headland, which you'll probably have all to yourself. Redpoint is served by a Gairloch **postbus** (see below).

Gair Loch practicalities

Without your own transport, you'll have to depend upon **postbuses** to get around Gair Loch. Two services (one for each side of the loch) leave from in front of the post office: one at 9.05am for Melvaig, and the other at 11.20am for Redpoint.

There's a good choice of **accommodation** in Gairloch, most of it mid-range; the central **tourist office** (May–Oct Mon–Sat 9am–7pm, Sun 1–6pm; Nov–April Mon–Sat 9am–5pm; ☎01445/712130) will help if you have problems finding a vacancy. Try the large family-run *Myrtle Bank Hotel* (☎01445/712214; ⑤), on the lochside, which has a decent restaurant; or the *Mountain Lodge*, Strath Square (☎01445/712316; ④), more laid-back, with log fires and a relaxing wood terrace overlooking the loch. Their restaurant is a little overpriced. **B&Bs** are scattered all around Gair Loch from Big Sand to Charleston on the other side of the bay. In the village centre near the bus stop, *Burnbridge House*, Shore St (☎01445/712167; ③), a large traditional stone building, has sea views and plenty of parking. Gaelic-speaking Miss Mackenzie at nearby *Duisary* (☎01445/712252; ②), is another good choice. If you have a car, the best has to be *Little Lodge* (☎01445/712237; ③), at North Erradale, north along the coast towards Rubha Reidh, which has immaculately furnished rooms, a log-burning stove, Cashmere goats and dramatic sea views; their meals are excellent and good value. If you're hostelling, there's a particularly pleasant **youth hostel** (mid-May to Sept; ☎01445/712219), two miles up the Rubha Reidh road at **Carn Deag**, which looks over the bay and is only a short walk from Big Sand.

All of Gairloch's hotels open their restaurants to non-residents, and most of the pubs serve bar **food**. In addition, the *Gairloch Sands Pizza Bar* in the *Gairloch Sands Hotel* (5-min walk round the bay from the tourist office), dishes up burgers and full-on American breakfasts with all the trimmings, as well as home-baked pizza. For authentic inexpensive pasta alongside pricier seafood and meat, try *Gino's* in the *Millcroft Hotel*.

Poolewe

It's a fifteen-minute hop by bus over the headland from Gairloch to the trim little village of **POOLEWE** on the sheltered south side of **Loch Ewe**, at the mouth of the River Ewe as it rushes down from Loch Maree. One of the area's best **walks** begins near here, signposted from the layby-cum-viewpoint on the main A832, a mile south of the village. It takes a couple of hours to follow the easy trail across open craggy moorland to the shores of Loch Maree, and thence to the car park at **Slatterdale**, seven miles southeast of Gairloch. If you don't want to cover the same route twice, start from Slatterdale, leaving your car here, and pick up the *Westerbus* at around 7pm when it passes the lay-by mentioned earlier, which will drop you back at Slatterdale. Also worthwhile is the drive along the small side road running northwest of Poolewe along the south of the loch to **COVE**. Here you'll find an atmospheric cave that was used by the "Wee Frees" as a church into this century; it's quite a perilous scramble up, however, and there's little to see once there. The route is also covered by a Poolewe **postbus** (1.40pm). *Mrs MacDonald* (April–Oct; ☎01445/781354; ③) offers upscale **B&B** here, with fine loch views.

Other accommodation in the area includes *Pool House Hotel* (☎01445/781272; ⑦), right by the sea in Poolewe village, but this is a bit overpriced; try the more old-fashioned *Poolewe Hotel* (☎01445/781241; ⑤), on the Cove road. For B&B in Poolewe, *Fasgadh* (☎01445/781352; ②) is basic but cheap; the marginally posher *Bruach Ard*

(☎01445/781214; ③), four miles north at Inversdale, has mostly en-suite rooms. There's also an excellent NTS **campsite** between the village and Inverewe Gardens (April–Oct; ☎01445/781229). The *Bridge Cottage Café*, at the village crossroads, serves good coffee and home-baked cakes during the summer.

Inverewe Gardens

Half a mile across the bay from Poolewe on the A832, the verdant oasis of **Inverewe Gardens** (daily April–Sept 9.30am–9pm, Oct–March 9am–5pm; £3.50; NTS) forms a vivid contrast with the austere wildness of the rest of the coast. Taking advantage of the area's famously temperate climate, **Osgood Mackenzie**, who inherited the surrounding 12,000-acre estate from his stepfather, the laird of Gairloch, in 1862, collected plants from all over the world for his walled garden, still the nucleus of the complex. By the time Mackenzie died in 1922, his garden sprawled over the whole peninsula, surrounded by a 100 acres of woodland. Around 180,000 visitors each year pour through here, but they are easily absorbed. Interconnected by a labyrinthine network of twisting paths and walkways, more than a dozen gardens feature exotic plant collections from as far afield as Chile, China, Tasmania and the Himalayas. Mid-May to mid-June is the best time to see the **rhododendrons** and **azaleas**, while the **herbaceous garden** reaches its peak in July and August, as does the wonderful Victorian vegetable and flower garden beside the sea. Look out, too, for the grand old **eucalypts** in the Peace Plot, which are the largest in the northern hemisphere, and the nearby **Ghost Tree** (*Davidia involucrata*), which represents the earliest evolutionary stages of flowering trees.

Gruinard Bay and the Scoraig peninsula

Three buses each week (Mon, Wed & Sat) run the twenty-mile stretch along the A832 from Poolewe past **Aultbea**, a small NATO naval base, to the head of **Little Loch Broom**, surrounded by a salt marsh that is covered with flowers in early summer. The road, more or less following the coast, offers fabulous views and passes a string of tiny, anachronistic villages. During World War II, **Gruinard Island**, in the bay, was used as a testing ground for biological warfare, and for years was ringed by huge signs warning the public not to land. The anthrax spores released during the testing can live in the soil for up to a thousand years, but in 1987, after much protest, the Ministry of Defence had the island decontaminated and it was finally declared "safe" in 1990.

The road heads inland before joining the A835 at **Braemore Junction** above the head of **Loch Broom** (3 Inverness–Ullapool buses stop here daily). Just nearby is **CORRIESHALLOCH**, site of the spectacular 164-foot **Falls of Measach**, which plunge through a mile-long gorge. You can overlook the cascades from a special observation platform, or from the impressive suspension bridge that spans the chasm, whose 197-foot vertical sides are draped in a rich array of plant life, with thickets of wych elm, goat-willow and bird cherry miraculously thriving on the cliffs. North from the head of Loch Broom to Ullapool is one of the so-called **Destitution Roads**, built to give employment to local people during the nineteenth-century potato famines.

Hotels along here include the bleak, modern *Ocean View Hotel* at **Laide** (☎01445/731385; ③) which looks pretty tacky, but is good value and in a great position; the *Dundonnell Hotel* (☎01854/612366; ⑤) at the head of Little Loch Broom, is more upmarket – you can stop at either for a meal in the bar. By far the best B&B is *The Old Smiddy* (☎01445/731425; ③) on the main road at Laide. Crammed with travel trophies, family memorabilia, books, and paintings by local artists (some on sale), this former smithy has fine mountain views to the east, and does outstanding food, including *pukka* Indian dishes. The *Sail Mhor Croft* on the lochside at **Dundonnell** is a small independent **youth hostel** (☎01854/633224).

The Scoraig peninsula

The bare and rugged **Scoraig peninsula**, dividing Little Loch Broom and Loch Broom, is one of the most remote places on the British mainland, accessible only by boat from **Badluarach**, two miles off the A832 on the south shore of Little Loch Broom, or on foot. Formerly dotted with crofting townships, it is now deserted apart from tiny **SCORAIG** village, crouched at the isolated western tip of the headland, where an "alternative" New Age community has established itself, complete with windmills, organic vegetable gardens and a Lilliputian primary school. Understandably, Scoraig's inhabitants resent being regarded as tourist curiosities, so only venture out here if you're sympathetic to the community and its aims. A post **boat** leaves Badluarach jetty for the village (Mon, Wed & Fri 10am; 5min); the nearest **bus** stop is south from here at **Badcaul**, on the A832, which you can get to by *Westerbus* from Inverness (Mon, Wed & Sat 5pm; 2hr). Alternatively, **walk** to Scoraig from the hamlet of **Badrallach**, towards the southeastern end of the peninsula, which you can drive to or reach on foot by crossing the pass above the *Aitnaharrie Hotel* opposite Ullapool (see p.931). Once you've arrived, **accommodation** is limited to the pleasant *Samadhan* guest house (☎01854/633260; ② including breakfast and dinner), who also do inexpensive wholefood packed lunches. They prefer an advance deposit of 25 percent for longer stays. This place tends to be reserved for groups during the summer with retreats and workshops, so phone ahead.

Ullapool

ULLAPOOL , the northwest's principal town, was founded at the height of the herring boom in 1788 by the British Fishery Society, on a sheltered arm of land jutting into Loch Broom. The grid-plan town is still an important fishing centre, though its ferry link to Stornoway on Lewis (see p.854) means that in high season the town's personality is practically swamped by visitors. Even so, it's still a hugely appealing place and a good base for exploring the northwest Highlands – especially if you are relying on public transport. Regular buses run from here to Inverness (an easier approach if you are driving than via the sinuous north–south coastal route) and along the coast. Accommodation is plentiful; and Ullapool is an obvious hideaway if the weather is bad, with cosy pubs, a new swimming pool, and the nearest thing on the west coast to an arts centre, *The Ceilidh Place*.

Most of the action in Ullapool centres on the **harbour**, which has an authentic and salty air, especially when the boats are in. During summer, booths advertise **trips** to the Summer Isles – a cluster of uninhabited islets two to three miles offshore – to view seabird colonies, dolphins and porpoises, but if you're lucky you'll spot marine life from the waterfront. Otters occasionally nose around the rocks near the *Ferry Boat Inn*, and on peaceful summer evenings seals swim past begging scraps from the boats moored in the middle of the loch. The majority of these rusting tubs are Russian and Eastern European **factory boats** that come here to buy fish direct from the local trawlers, which they then process and freeze. Their heavily tattooed crews, known as "Klondykers", regularly wander around town weighed down with brand-new audio equipment, crates of fruit and boxes of coffee. You'll even spot Russian notices announcing local events, and the odd sign in Cyrillic scipt.

The only conventional "sight" in town is the **museum**, West Argyle St (April–Oct Mon–Fri 10am–5pm; free), in the old parish church, whose recently revamped exhibition features displays on crofting, fishing, and local religion, and some interesting stuff on emigration. During the Clearances, Ullapool was one of the ports through which evicted crofters left to start new lives in Canada, Australia and New Zealand.

Practicalities

Forming the backbone of its grid plan, Ullapool's two main arteries are the lochside **Shore Street**, and parallel to it, **Argyle Street**, further inland. **Buses** stop at the pier, in the town centre near the ferry dock, with the **tourist office** (Easter–Nov Mon–Fri 9am–6pm, Sat 10am–6pm, Sun 1–6pm; ☎01854/612135), directly opposite.

Ullapool, a popular holiday centre in summer, has all kinds of **accommodation**, ranging from one of Scotland's most expensive hotels, the world-famous *Altnaharrie Hotel* (☎01854/633230; ⑨), across the loch from town – you're collected by launch – to innumerable guest houses and B&Bs. Of the latter, the *Brae Guest House*, Shore St (☎01854/612421; ③), right on the lochside, is one of the nicest. Another good bet is to head for the two traditional inns on Shore Street, right on the waterfront: the *Arch Inn* (☎01854/612454; ④) and the *Ferry Boat Inn* (☎01854/612366; ③). Well out of town, but worth the trip for its wonderful rooms and gourmet veggie/vegan breakfasts, is *Tigh Na Mara*, ten miles away in Ardinrean (☎01854/655282; ③), on the opposite (west) shore of Loch Broom; the restaurant is excellent and open to non-residents. Ullapool's excellent **youth hostel** is on Shore Street (mid-March to Oct; ☎01854/612254), or else there's the *Celidh Place Bunkhouse* (May–Oct; ☎01854/612103; ②), attached to the plush hotel of the same name on West Argyle Street.

Ullapool has a wide array of places to **eat and drink**, ranging from the cheap and cheerful chippies on the harbour to one of Scotland's most expensive gourmet **restaurants**, at the aforementioned *Altnaharrie*. If you're a seafood fan, though, you won't do better than the *Morefield*, Morefield Lane, which serves up some of the best fish dishes on the west coast. *The Ceilidh Place* does filling snacks at the bar, or full meals in the restaurant, with occasional live music. *John MacLean's*, Shore St, is a wholefood shop/deli with a small café upstairs that serves blow-out breakfasts, and grills; they also possess the most northerly *Gaggia* coffee machine in Britain. The two best **pubs** are the *Arch Inn*, home of the Ullapool football team, and the *Ferry Boat Inn*, known locally as the "FBI", with good food at moderate prices, washed down with a pint of real ale at the lochside – midges permitting – plus live folk sessions Wednesdays and Thursdays.

The Coigach peninsula

North of Ullapool, the mountain peaks become more widely spaced and settlements smaller and fewer, linked by twisting single-track roads and shoreside footpaths that make excellent hiking trails. You can easily sidestep the tourist traffic by heading down the peaceful back roads, which, after twisting through idyllic crofts, invariably end up at a deserted beach or windswept headland with superb views west to the Outer Hebrides. Ten miles north of Ullapool, a precariously narrow and twisting single-track road west off the A835 squeezes between the lower slopes of Cul Beag (2523ft) and Stac Pollaidh (2012ft) and the north shore of majestic Loch Lurgainn to reach the **Coigach peninsula**. Dominated by the awesome bulk of Ben More Coigach (2439ft), rising almost vertically up from sea level, this jagged headland is among the most idyllic of Scottish coastal scenery, with a string of sandy beaches and the Summer Isles scattered a couple of miles offshore.

Coigach's main settlement is **ACHILTIBUIE**, an old crofting village strung out above a series of white-sand coves and rocks tapering into the Atlantic, from where a fleet of small fishing boats carries sheep, and tourists, to the island grazing pastures during the summer. The village also attracts large numbers of gardening enthusiasts, thanks to the space-station-like structure overlooking its main beach. Dubbed "The Garden of the Future", the **Hydroponicum** (Easter to early Oct 10am–5pm, 4–7 tours daily) is a kind of glorified greenhouse that maximizes the natural growing power of the feeble Scottish sunshine, while protecting the plants inside from the cold and the acidic soil. The results – tropical plants, fruit, and fragrant flowers and herbs thriving in four separate "climate rooms" – speak for themselves; you can also taste their famous strawberries in the *Lily Pond* café-restaurant, which serves healthy meals, desserts and snacks, in addition to samples of their home-grown produce. Also worth a visit is the **Achiltibuie Smokehouse** (May–Sept Mon–Sat 9.30am–5pm; free), three miles north of the Hydroponicum at **Altandhu**, where you can watch meat, fish and game being cured in the traditional way and buy some afterwards.

If you can afford it, check into the wonderful *Summer Isles Hotel* (April–Oct; ☎01854/622282; ⑥), just up the road from the school, which enjoys a near-perfect setting above a sandy beach with views over the islands, and is virtually self-sufficient. They buy in Hydroponicum fruit and veg, but have their own dairy, poultry, and even run a small smokehouse, so the food in their excellent restaurant (open to non-residents) is about as fresh as it comes. Among Achiltibuie's several **B&Bs**, *Dornie House* (☎01854/622271; ②), is the only one you can book through the tourist office, with a couple of en-suite rooms. There's also a beautifully situated small twenty-bed **SYHA youth hostel** (mid-May to Sept; ☎01854/622254) three miles down the coast at **Achininver**, which is handy for Coigach's many mountain hikes.

Lochinver

The coast road running **north from Coigach** is narrow and rough in places, but unremittingly spectacular, dominated by the forbidding peaks of Cul Beag (2523ft), Cul Mor (2785ft) and the distinctive sugar-loaf Suilven (2398ft), standing like a line of gargantuan sentinels to the east. A scattering of pebble-dashed bungalows on a sheltered sea loch herald your arrival at **LOCHINVER**, the last sizeable village before Thurso. Hemmed in by rocky hillocks that block mountain views, it's a grim little place. However, there's a bank with a cashpoint machine at the south end of the loch – a rarity in these parts – and a better-than-average **tourist office** (April–Oct Mon–Fri 10am–5pm, Sun 10am–4pm; ☎01571/844330), whose new **visitor centre** gives an interesting rundown of the area's geology, wildlife and history; a national park ranger is also on hand upstairs to advise on walks. The majority of Lochinver's visitors are well-heeled fishing enthusiasts, so **accommodation** tends to be upmarket. However, a good mid-range option is the *Albanach Hotel* (☎01571/844407; ④) at Baddaidarach, an attractive nineteenth-century building set in a walled garden that is renowned for its excellent seafood, caught locally and served in a lovely wood-panelled dining room; their lunches are particularly good value, with homemade oat cakes and a couple of vegetarian specialities on offer. Dozens of **B&Bs** advertise through the local tourist office: *Bracklock* (April–Oct; ☎01571/844253; ②) is the cheapest, while *Veyatie* (☎01571/844424; ③), a modern bungalow on the north side of the bay, has marginally more comfortable en-suite rooms and sea views. Finally, if you're on a tight budget, the *Seamen's Mission*, down at the new harbour, is the best place to eat filling basic meals (some vegetarian), and they stay open until 10pm.

Anglers should note that Lochinver is *the* place in the area to stock up on **fishing** gear. *The Fish Selling Co*, next to the pier, has the usual range of rods, reels and bait, while the newsagent in the village, though slightly more pricey, is better for those obscure bits and bobs that can make all the difference.

Inverkirkaig Falls

Approaching Lochinver from the south, the road bends sharply through a wooded valley where a signpost for **Inverkirkaig Falls** marks the start of a long but gentle **walk** to the base of Suilven – the most distinctive mountain in Scotland. Serious hikers use the path to approach the mighty peak, but you can follow it for an easy three-to-four-hour ramble, taking in a waterfall and a tour of a secluded loch. If you're travelling by vehicle, use the car park below the excellent *Achins Bookshop* near the trailhead, which is well stocked with titles on Scotland and the Highlands, and has a café serving cream teas, cakes and good coffee.

East of Lochinver

The area to the **east of Lochinver**, traversed by the A837 and bounded by the gnarled peaks of the Ben More Assynt massif, is a wilderness of mountains, bleak moorland, mist and scree. Dotted with lochs and lochans, it's also an anglers' paradise, home to the only non-migratory fish in northern Scotland, the brown trout, and numerous other sought-after species, including the Atlantic salmon, sea trout, Arctic char and a massive prize strain of cannibal ferox. **Fishing** permits for this area are like gold dust during the summer, snapped up months in advance by exclusive hunting-lodge hotels, but you can sometimes obtain last-minute cancellations (try *The Inver Lodge* on ☎01571/844496).

Although most of the land here is privately owned, 27,000 acres are managed as the **Inverpolly National Nature Reserve**, whose twelve centre (mid-May to mid-Sept daily 10am–5pm; ☎01854/666234) at **Knockan Cliff**, twelve miles north of Ullapool on the A835, gives a thorough overview of the diverse flora and wildlife in the surrounding habitats. The eminent nineteenth-century geologists Horn and Peach also discovered the theory of "fault thrusting" here, and an interpretative **Geological Trail** shows you how to detect the movement of rock plates in the nearby cliffs.

Further north, on the rocky promontory that juts into eastern Loch Assynt, stand the jagged remnants of **Ardveck Castle** (free access), a MacLeod stronghold from 1597 that fell to the Seaforth Mackenzies after a siege in 1691. Previously, the Marquis of Montrose had been imprisoned here after his defeat at Carbisdale in 1650. The rebel duke, whom the local laird had betrayed to the government for £20,000 and 400 bowls of sour meal was eventually led away to be executed in Edinburgh, lashed back to front on his horse.

The *Inchnadamph Hotel* (☎01571/822202; ⑤) on Loch Assynt, is a wonderfully traditional Highland retreat; inside the walls are covered with the stuffed catches of its past guests (worth a look even if you're not planning to stay). The **hotel** offers fine oldfashioned cooking in its moderately priced restaurant and is popular with anglers who get free fishing rights to the Loch Assynt, as well as several hill lochs backing onto Ben More – haunts of the infamous ferox trout.

North from Lochinver: the coast road

Two possible routes lead **north from Lochinver**: the fast A387, along the shore of Loch Assynt, or the narrow coastal road (the B869) that local people love to dub "The Breakdown Zone" because its ups and downs claim so many victims during summer. Hugging the indented shoreline, this route, covered by **postbus** from Lochinver (daily 3.15pm), is the more scenic, offering superb views of the Summer Isles, as well as a number of rewarding side trips to beaches and dramatic cliffs. Unusually, most of the land and lochs around here are owned by local crofters rather than wealthy landlords. Helped by grants and private donations, "The Assynt Crofters Trust" made history in 1993 when it pulled off the first ever community buy-out of estate land in Scotland. The trust now owns the lucrative **fishing** rights to the area, too, selling permits for a mere £3 per day (£15 per week) through local post offices, or the newsagent and tourist information office in Lochinver.

Heading north, the first village worthy of a detour from the road is **ACHMELVICH**, whose tiny bay cradles the whitest beach and most stunning turquoise water you'll encounter this side of the Seychelles. Unfortunately, there's a noisy campsite behind it, so you have to pick your way across the surrounding headlands for total peace and quiet. Achmelvich's forty-bed **youth hostel** (April–Sept; ☎01571/844480) overlooks the beach – with no shower, you'll have to make do with basin baths.

The side road that branches north off the B869 between Stoer and Clashnessie ends abruptly by the automatic lighthouse at **Raffin** – built in 1870 by the Stevenson brothers (one of whom was the author Robert Louis Steveson's dad) – but you can continue for two miles along a well-worn track to **Stoer Point**, named after the colossal rock pillar that stands offshore known as "**The Old Man of Stoer**". Surrounded by sheer cliffs and splashed with guano from the seabird colonies that nest on its 200-foot sides, it was climbed for the first time in 1961.

DRUMBEG, nine miles further on, is a major target for trout anglers, lying within reach of countless lochans linked in a puzzle formation of streams and pools. Permits to fish them are sold at the post office (£3 per day), but you'll need a detailed map and a compass to find your way in and out of this area. *Culkein* (☎01571/833257; ②), an excellent-value **B&B**, is right on the tip of the headland with fabulous views over **Edrachillis Bay**'s dozens of tiny islands. If you turn off the main road at the primary school and follow the signs you'll soon reach *Taigh Druimbeag* (☎01571/833209; ③), an old Edwardian house with period furniture and a large garden, which does superb three-course evening meals for residents.

Kylesku to Kinlochbervie

KYLESKU, 33 miles north of Ullapool and around six miles west of Drumbeg, is the site of the award-winning road bridge spanning the mouth of Lochs Glencoul and Glendhu. It's a pleasant place for a short stay, with plenty of good walks and congenial hotels by the water's edge above a small slipway. The family-run *Kylesku Hotel* (April–Oct; ☎01971/502231; ⑤) has en-suite rooms, a welcoming bar popular with locals, and an excellent restaurant serving imaginative fresh seafood, including lobster, crab, muscles, and local salmon (you can watch the fish being landed on the pier). *Statesman Cruises* runs **boat trips** (daily 11am & 2pm; round trip 2hr; £7.50; ☎01571/844446) from the jetty below the hotel to the 650-foot **Eas-Coul-Aulin**, Britain's highest waterfall, at the head of Loch Glencoul; seals, porpoises and minke whales can occasionally be spotted along the way.

It is also possible to reach Eas-Coul-Aulin on foot: a rough trail (3hr) leaves the A894 three miles south of Kylesku, skirting the south shore of Loch na Gainmhich (known locally as the "sandy loch") to approach the falls from above. Great care should be taken here as the path above the cliffs can get very slippery when wet; the rest of the route is also difficult to follow, particularly in bad weather, and should only be attempted by experienced, properly equipped and compass-literate hikers. However, there are several less demanding **walks around Kylesku** if you just fancy a gentle amble: one of the most popular is the half-day low-level route along the north side of Loch Glendhu, beginning at **Kylestrome**, on the opposite side of the bridge from the hotel. Follow the surfaced jeep track east from the trailhead and turn left on to a footpath that leads through the woods. This eventually emerges on to the open mountainside, dropping down to cross a burn from where it then winds to a boarded-up old house called *Glendhu*, where there's a picturesque pebble beach. Several interesting side trips and variations to this walk may be undertaken with the help of the detailed Ordnance Survey Landranger Map No.15 , but you'll need a compass and wet-weather gear in case of bad weather.

Ten miles north of Kylesku, the widely scattered crofting community of **SCOURIE**, on a bluff above the main road, surrounds a beautiful sandy beach whose safe bathing has made it a popular holiday destination for families, walkers and trout anglers. There's plenty of good **accommodation**; the best by far is the charming *Scourie Lodge*

(☎01971/502248; ③), an old shooting retreat with a lovely garden; the welcoming owners also do great evening meals. **BADCALL** village, three miles south of Scourie and even more remote, has a couple of B&Bs, including Mrs Mackay's *Stoer View* (☎01971/502411; ②), whose clean and comfortable rooms look over Edrachillis Bay to Stoer Point. For a little more luxury, try the nearby old-established *Edrachillis Hotel* (☎01971/5020080; ⑥), which enjoys a spectacular situation on the bay, and serves reasonable food.

Handa Island

Visible just offshore to the north of Scourie is **Handa Island**, a huge chunk of red Torridon sandstone surrounded by sheer cliffs and carpeted with machair and purple-tinged moorland. Teeming with **seabirds**, it's an internationally important wildlife reserve and a real feast for ornithologists, with vast colonies of razorbills and guillemots breeding on its guano-splashed cliffs during summer. From late May to mid-July, large numbers of puffins waddle comically over the turf-covered clifftops where they dig their burrows.

Apart from a solitary warden, Handa is deserted. Until midway through the last century, however, it supported a thriving, if somewhat eccentric, community of crofters. Surviving on a diet of fish, potatoes and seabirds, the islanders, whose ruined cottages still cling to the slopes by the jetty, devised their own system of government, with a "queen" (Handa's oldest widow) and "parliament" (a council of men who met each morning to discuss the day's business). Uprooted by the 1847 potato famine, most of the villagers eventually emigrated to Canada's Cape Breton; today, Handa is private property, administered as a nature sanctuary by the Scottish Wildife Trust.

You'll need about three hours to follow the footpath round the island – an easy and enjoyable walk taking in the north shore's **Great Stack** rock pillar and some fine views across the Minch: a detailed route guide is featured in the SWT's free leaflet available from the warden's office when you arrive. Weather permitting, **boats** leave for Handa throughout the day (until around 4pm) from the tiny settlement of **TARBET**, three miles northwest of the main road and reachable by **postbus** from Scourie (Mon–Sat 1 daily; 3pm), where there's a small car park and jetty. However, if you're travelling south, you may prefer to pick up the *Laxford Cruises* boat that sails from **FANAGMORE** (Easter–Oct daily 10am, noon & 2pm; July & Aug also 4pm; £7.50), a mile further up the coast (reached by the same postbus as above). Camping is not allowed on the island, but the SWT maintains a **bothy** for birdwatchers (reservations essential on ☎0131/312 7765), while in Tarbet, Rex and Liz Norris run a comfortable little **B&B** (☎01971/502098; ②) overlooking the bay. For **food**, Tarbet's excellent *Seafood Restaurant* serves delicious, moderately priced fish and vegetarian dishes, and a good selection of homemade cakes and desserts in its airy waterfront conservatory.

Kinlochbervie and beyond

Beyond Scourie, the road sweeps inland through the starkest part of the Highlands: rocks piled on rocks, bog and water create an almost alien landscape, and the stony coastline looks increasingly inhospitable – there's no public transport at all on the twenty-mile stretch from here to Durness.

Eight miles or so north of Scourie, at **Rhiconich**, you can branch off the main road to **KINLOCHBERVIE**, a major fishing port crouching among the rocks in a dauntingly hostile setting. Trucks from all over Europe pick up cod and shellfish from the trawlers here, crewed mainly by east coast fishermen. The *Old Schoolhouse Restaurant and Guest House* (☎01971/521383; ⑤) provides comfortable **accommodation** and home-cooked meals; while the more upmarket *Kinlochbervie Hotel* (☎01971/521275; ⑧) is well known for its excellent food.

Beyond Kinlochbervie, a single-track road takes you through isolated **Oldmoreshore**, a working crofters' village scattered above a stunning white-sand beach, to **BLAIRMORE**. The road ends a couple of miles further west at **Sheigra**, where you can park for the four-mile walk across peaty moorland to deserted **Sandwood Bay**. Few visitors make this half-day detour north, but the beach at the end of the rough track is possibly the most beautiful in Scotland. Flanked by rolling dunes and lashed by fierce gales for much of the year, the shell-white sands are said to be haunted by a bearded mariner – one of many sailors to have perished on this notoriously dangerous stretch of coast since the Vikings first navigated it over a millennium ago. Around the turn of the last century, the beach, whose treacherous **undercurrents** make it unsuitable for swimming, also witnessed Britian's most recent recorded sighting of a mermaid. Plans are afoot to bulldoze a motorable road up here, so enjoy the tranquillity while you can. Cape Wrath, the most northwesterly point in mainland Britain, lies a day's hike north. However, most people approach the headland from Durness on the north coast (see below).

The North Coast

A constant stream of sponsored walkers, caravans and tour groups make it to John O'Groats, but surprisingly few visitors travel the whole length of the Highlands' wild **north coast**. Those that do, however, rarely return disappointed. Pounded by one of the world's most ferocious seaways, Scotland's rugged northern shore is backed by barren mountains in the west, and in the east by lochs and open rolling grasslands. Between its far ends, mile upon mile of crumbling cliffs and sheer rocky headlands shelter bays whose perfect white beaches are nearly always deserted, even in the height of summer. This is a great area for **birdwatching**, too, with huge seabird colonies clustered in clefts and on remote stacks at regular intervals along the coast; seals also bob around in the surf offshore, and in winter, whales put in the odd appearence in the more sheltered estuaries of the northwest.

Getting around this stretch of coast without your own transport can be a slow and frustrating business: **John O'Groats** and **Thurso**, the area's main town and springboard for the Orkneys, are well connected by **bus** with Inverness, but further west, after the main A836 peters into a single-track road, bus services dry up altogether. The only public transport between Thurso and **Durness**, in the far northwest, is a convoluted series of **postbus** connections via Lairg (see p.947). You can, however, travel direct to Durness on a daily bus from Inverness, calling at the remote and beautiful villages of **Bettyhill** and **Tongue** en route.

Durness and around

Scattered around a string of sheltered coves and grassy clifftops, **DURNESS**, the most northwesterly village on the British mainland, straddles the turning point on the main road as it swings east from the inland peat bogs of the interior to the north coast's fertile strip of limestone machair. First settled by the Picts around 400 BC, the area has been farmed ever since; its crofters being among the few not cleared off estate land during the nineteenth century. Today, Durness is the centre of several crofting communities and a good base for a couple of days, with plenty of accommodation, a couple of decent pubs, and rewarding coast walks. Even if only passing through, it's worth pausing here to see the **Smoo Cave**, a gaping hole in a sheer limestone crag, and to visit beautiful **Balnakiel beach**, to the west. In addition, Durness is the jumping-off place for roadless and rugged **Cape Wrath**, the windswept promontory at the Scotland's northwest tip, which has retained an end-of-the-world mystique lost long ago by John O'Groats.

The Smoo Cave

A short walk south of Durness village centre lies the 200-foot-long **Smoo Cave**, a natural wonder, formed partly by the action of the sea, and partly by the small burn that flows through it. Tucked away at the end of a narrow sheer-sided sea cove, guides will show you the illuminated interior, although the much hyped rock formations are less memorable than the short rubber-dinghy trip you have to make to get to them. In winter to late Spring, this is made even more fun by the waterfall that crashes through the middle of the cavern. However, for a really novel view of the cave, try **abseiling** down its gigantic entrance. Instruction and equipment rental costs between £5 and £10, depending whether you attempt the thirty- or one hundred-foot cliff. Alternatively, hop in the boat that leaves from Smoo Cave for a **wildlife tour** of the coast around Durness. Taking in stretches of the shoreline only accessible by sea, the trip (May–Sept daily; times depend on weather and tide; 90min; £6) takes in seabird colonies at close hand, and sightings of seals, puffins and porpoises are also common.

Balnakiel

A narrow road winds northwest of Durness to the tiny **BALNAKIEL**, whose name derives from the Gaelic *Baile ne Cille* (Village of the Church). The ruined chapel that today overlooks this remote hamlet was built in the seventeenth century, but a church has stood here for at least 1200 years. A skull-and-crossbones stone set in the south wall marks the grave of **Donald MacMurchow**, a seventeenth-century highwayman and contract killer who murdered eighteen people for his clan chief (allegedly by throwing them from the top of the Smoo Cave). The "half-in, half-out" position of his grave was apparently a compromise between his grateful employer and the local clergy, who initially refused to allow such an evil man to be buried on church ground. Balnakiel is also known for its **golf course**, whose ninth and final hole involves a 155-yard drive over the Atlantic; you can rent equipment from the club house. The **Balnakiel Craft Village** (daily 10am–6pm; free), back towards Durness, is worth a visit. Housed in an imaginatively converted 1950s military base, the campus consists of a dozen or so workshops where you can watch painters, potters, leather workers, candle makers, patchwork quilters, horn carvers, soft-toy makers and weavers in action. However, as most of the craftspeople are English or "incomers", you won't see many Scottish crafts here.

The white-sand **beach** on the east side of Balnakiel Bay is a stunning sight in any weather, but most spectacular on sunny days when the water turns to brilliant turquoise. For the best views, head along the path that winds north through the dunes behind it; this eventually leads to **Faraid Head** – from the Gaelic *Fear Ard* (High Fellow) – where you stand a good chance of spotting puffins from late May until mid-July. The fine views over the mouth of Loch Eriboll and west to Cape Wrath make this round **walk** (3–4hr) the best in the Durness area.

Cape Wrath

An excellent day trip from Durness begins three miles south of the village at **Keoldale**, where a foot-passenger ferry (May–Aug hourly 9.30am–4.30pm; Sept 4 daily; no motorcycles; ☎01971/511376) crosses the Kyle of Durness estuary to link up with the minibus (May–Sept; ☎01971/511287) that runs out to **Cape Wrath**, eleven miles further along a dirt track. The UK mainland's most northwesterly point, the headland takes its name not from the stormy seas that crash against it for most of the year, but from the Norse word *parph*, meaning "turning place" – a throw-back to the days when Viking warships used it as a navigation point during raids on the Scottish coast. These days, a lighthouse (another of those built by Robert Louis Stevenson's father) warns ships away from the treacherous rocks. Looking east to the Orkneys and west to the Outer Hebrides, it stands above the famous **Clo Mor cliffs**, the highest seacliffs in Britain and a prime breeding site for **seabirds**. You can **walk** from here to remote Sandwood Bay (see p.936), visible to the south; although the route, which cuts inland across lochan-dotted moorland, is hard to follow in places. Hikers generally continue south from Sandwood to the trail end at Blairmore, six miles west of Kinlochbervie, and hitch from there back to the main road where you can catch buses north to Durness. Don't attempt this route from south to north: if the weather closes in, the Cape Wrath minibus stops running.

As an alternative to the Cape Wrath minibus, you can rent a **mountain bike** from the Durness youth hostel. However, much of the land bordering the headland is a **military firing range**, so check the firing times with the tourist office before you set off.

Durness Practicalities

Durness is connected by regular **bus** services to Inverness, Lochinver and Ullapool, but getting here by public transport from anywhere else on the north coast is very difficult. Amazingly, there are no longer any direct buses between here and Thurso, which you can only reach by postbus – a five-hour journey involving two changes (at Tongue and Bettyhill). Precise timings of these, and other, **postbus** services are displayed in the village shop and at the youth hostel.

Durness has an enthusiastic **tourist office** (March–Oct Mon–Sat 9am–6pm; ☎01971/511259), in the village centre, who can help with accommodation; its small visitor centre also houses some excellent interpretative panels detailing the area's history, geology, flora and fauna. Of the several **hotels** clustered together nearby, the *Parkhill* (☎01971/511209; ③) is best value, while *Rowan House* (☎01971/511252; ③), near the charmless *Smoo Cave Hotel*, is a cosy and immaculately clean B&B overlooking the sea. If neither has any vacancies, try *Puffin Cottage* (☎01971/511208; ③). There's also a friendly **youth hostel** (mid-May to Sept; ☎01971/511244), a mile and a half east of town, and **camping** at *Sango Sands Caravan and Camping Site*, Harbour Rd (☎01971/511262), which has the added advantage of a good **bar** and **restaurant**. The *Cape Wrath Hotel* (☎01971/511212; ⑥), right by the ferry point, is a solidly traditional place popular with anglers; overlooking the estuary, it's the best hotel within easy reach of the village, although the rooms are a little pricey. **Eating** options in Durness are largely confined to bar food: the *Smoo Cave Hotel* is fine for something cheap and cheerful, but for a classier gourmet meal, reserve a table at the *Cape Wrath Hotel*'s restaurant, whose set menus cost around £15 per head.

Loch Eriboll

Ringed by ghost-like limestone mountains, deep and sheltered **Loch Eriboll**, six miles east of Durness, is the north coast's most spectacular sea loch. Servicemen stationed here during World War II to protect passing Russian convoys nicknamed it "Loch 'Orrible", but if you're looking for somewhere wild and unspoilt, you'll find this a perfect spot. Porpoises and otters are a common sight along the rocky shore, and minke whales occasionally swim in from the open sea.

Overlooking its own landing stage at the water's edge, *Port-Na-Con* (mid-March to Oct; ☎01971/511367; ③), seven miles from Durness on the west side of the loch, is a wonderful **B&B**, popular with anglers and divers (it will refill air tanks for £2.50). Top-notch food is served in its small **restaurant** (open all year, including Christmas), with a choice of vegetarian haggis, local kippers, fruit compôte and homemade croissant for breakfast, and adventurous three-course evening meals for around £10; the menu always includes a gourmet vegetarian dish – non-residents are welcome, although you'll need to book. If *Port-Na-Con* is full, a good fall-back is the nearby *Choraidh Croft* (Easter–Nov; ☎01971/511235; ②), a modern lochside B&B on a working croft. This also does good-value lunches and evening meals, and offers plenty of choice for vegetarians/vegans.

Tongue

It's a long slog around Loch Eriboll and east over the top of A Mhòine moor to the pretty crofting township of **TONGUE**. Dominated by the ruins of **Varick Castle**, the village, an eleventh-century Norse stronghold, is strewn over the east shore of the **Kyle of Tongue**, which you can either cross via a new causeway, or by following the longer and more scenic single-track road around its southern side. When the tide recedes, this shallow estuary becomes a mass of golden sand flats, superb on sunny days with the sharp profiles of Ben Hope (3040ft) and Ben Loyal (2509ft) looming to the south.

In 1746, the Kyle of Tongue was the scene of a naval engagement that sealed the fate of Bonnie Prince Charlie's Jacobite rebellion. In response to a plea for help from the Prince, the King of France dispatched a sloop and £13,600 in gold coins to Scotland. However, the Jacobite ship, the *Prince Charles*, was spotted by the English frigate, *Sheerness*, and fled into the Kyle, hoping that the larger enemy vessel would not be able to follow. It did, though, and soon forced the *Prince Charles* aground, its Jacobite crew slipping ashore under cover of darkness in an attempt to smuggle the treasure to Inverness, but they were followed by scouts. The next morning, a large platoon of the local Mackay clan waylaid the rebels, who, hopelessly outnumbered, began throwing the gold into the nearest lochan (most of it was recovered later).

If you want to stay in Tongue, *Rhian Cottage* (☎01847/611257; ②), a pretty white-washed house with an attractive garden, and *Woodend* (☎01847/611332; ②), at the top of the village down a side road, with panoramic views of the estuary, are both pleasant and comfortable **B&Bs**. The *Ben Loyal Hotel* (☎01847/611216; ⑤) and *Tongue Hotel* (☎01847/611206; ③) are more luxurious, and both do **bar food**. There's also a beautifully situated and friendly SYHA **youth hostel** (mid-March to Sept; ☎01847/55301), a mile north of the village centre on the east shore of the kyle.

South from Tongue: the Flow Country

From Tongue, you can head forty miles or so **south** towards Lairg (see p.947) on the A836, skirting the edges of the **Flow Country**. This huge expanse of bogland came into the news a few years ago when ecology experts, responding to plans to transform the area into forest, drew media attention to the threat to this fragile landscape, described by one contemporary commentator as of "unique and of global importance, equivalent to the African Serengeti or Brazil's rain forest". Some forest was planted, but the environmentalists eventually won and the forestry syndicates have had to pull out.

Bettyhill to Dounreay

BETTYHILL, a major crofting village, straggles along the side of a narrow tidal estuary, and down the coast to two splendid beaches. Forming an unbroken arc of pure white sand between the Naver and Borgie Rivers, **Torrisdale beach** is the more impressive of the pair, ending in a smooth white spit that forms part of the **Invernaver Nature Reserve**. During summer, arctic terns nest here on the riverbanks, dotted with clumps of rare Scottish primroses, and you stand a good chance of spotting an otter or two. In the village, the mildy interesting **Strathnaver Museum** (Easter–Sept Mon–Sat 10am–1pm & 2–5pm; £1.50), housed in the old church, is full of locally donated bits and pieces, including a room dealing with the Clearances. You can also see some Pictish stones and a 3800-year-old early Bronze Age beaker. This and other artefacts were found around Strathnaver, the river valley south of the village, whose numerous prehistoric sites are mapped on an excellent pamphlet sold at the entrance desk.

Bettyhill's small **tourist office** (March–Sept Mon–Sat 9am–5pm; ☎016412/521342) can book **accommodation** for you. The central *Bettyhill Hotel* (☎016412/521352; ③) is pretty basic; half a mile away, near the windswept beach, the friendly *Farr Bay Inn*

(☎016412/521230; ④) has a lot more character, and does excellent **bar food**. There are also several good-value **B&Bs**, including *Shenley* (☎016412/521421; ②), a grand detached house on the hillside with four comfortable rooms, and *Hadenrigg* (☎01641/521240; ②), just off the road above the estuary (a mile north of the bridge across the kyle), which has just one double-bedded room and offers wholefood breakfasts with fresh homemade yoghurt.

As you move west from Bettyhill, the north coast changes dramatically; the single-track road widens and sprouts white lines, and the hills on the horizon recede to be replaced by fields fringed with traditional flagstone hedges. At the hamlet of **MELVICH**, twelve miles from Bettyhill, the A897 cuts south through the open valleys of Strath Halladale and the Strath of Kilodonan, both of which offer excellent salmon fishing, to **Helmsdale** on the east coast (see p.944).

Five miles further east, **DOUNREAY** Nuclear Power Station, a surreal collection of stark domes and chimney stacks marooned in the middle of nowhere, is still a fairly major local employer, in spite of the fact that its three fast breeder reactors were decommissioned in April 1994. A permanent exhibition details the processes (and, unsurprisingly, the benefits) of nuclear power, and you can take a **tour** (Easter–Sept daily 10am–5pm; free). Don't, however, expect to hear much about the area's "leukaemia cluster", nor the worryingly high levels of radiation reported over the years on the nearby beaches.

Thurso

Approached from the isolation of the west, **THURSO** looks like a major metropolis. In fact, it's simply a small service town, grey and tidy, with well-planned streets and the higgledy-piggledy remnants of the fishing port it once was strung around a broad bay. The town's name derives from the Norse word *Thorsa*, literally "River of the God Thor", and in Viking times this was a major gateway to the mainland. Later, ships set sail from here for the Baltic and Scandinavian ports loaded with meal, beef, hides and fish. The nearby Dounreay Nuclear Power Station ensured continuing prosperity after World War II; workers from the plant (dubbed "Atomics" by the locals) settled in Thurso in large numbers, and their disappearence following its 1994 closure has hit the local economy hard.

Traill Street is the main drag, turning into the pedestrianized High Street precinct at its northern end. Apart from a handful of mediocre shops, there's not much to see; most visitors who linger are on their way to the Orkney ferry, which leaves from nearby **Scrabster**. If you've got time to fill, however, check out the ruined twelfth-to sixteenth-century **Old St Peter's Kirk**, in the old part of town near the harbour on the way to the **beach** (turn right when you get to the end of High St). You could also visit the average display at the **Thurso Heritage Museum**, High St (Mon–Sat 10am–5pm; 50p), which houses a reconstructed croft house and the prehistoric Pictish "Ulbster Stone", intricately carved with enigmatic symbols.

Practicalities

It's a ten-minute walk from the **train station**, down Princes and Sir George streets, to the **tourist office**, Riverside Rd (April–Oct Mon–Sat 9am–6pm; July & Aug also Sun 10am–6pm; ☎01847/892371). The **bus station**, close by, runs regular buses run to John O'Groats, Wick and Inverness. However, there's no public transport west along the north coast from Thurso; you'll have to travel via Lairg, or else catch an early morning **postbus** to Bettyhill, from where a second postbus leaves later in the day for Durness. **Ferries** operate daily from adjoining Scrabster to Orkney. You can reserve ahead through *P&O Scottish Ferries*, Aberdeen (☎01224/572615) or through any local tourist office. If you just fancy a day trip to Orkney see "John O'Groats", on next page.

Thurso is well stocked with good-value **accommodation**: the tourist office has a full list. On Traill Street, both the *Central Hotel* (☎01847/893100; ③) and the *Royal Hotel* (☎01847/893191; ③) are good value. Of the **B&Bs**, *Mrs Oag*, 9 Couper St (☎01847/894529; ②) is the cheapest, a welcoming place that serves huge breakfasts; also worth a try are *Mrs Budge* (☎01847/893205; ③), 6 Pentland Crescent next to the beachfront. Most of the **restaurants** are in the hotels: the *Pentland Hotel* does upmarket bar meals. For inexpensive Chinese, Indian and seafood dishes, try the *Fountain Restaurant,* Sinclair St; and if you're looking for an enjoyably rowdy local **pub**, check out the *Central*, Traill St. The *Upper Deck*, by the harbour at Scrabster, does well-prepared and moderately priced steaks and wicked puddings. **Nightlife** is as limited as you'd expect, but the *Pentland Hotel*, Princes St, hosts a Highland Night once a week; ask at the tourist office for a copy of the monthly, *What's On in Caithness.*

Dunnet Head to Duncansby Head

Despite the plaudits that John O' Groats customarily receives, Britain's northernmost mainland point is in fact **Dunnet Head** – at the far side of Dunnet Bay, an impressive sweep of sandy beach backed by dunes about six miles east of Thurso. The bay is becoming well known by **surfers**, and even in the winter you can usually spot intrepid figures far out in the Atlantic surf.

For Dunnet Head, turn off at **DUNNET**, at the east end of the bay, onto the B855, which runs for four miles over windy heather and bog to the tip of the headland, crowned with a 350-foot Victorian lighthouse. The red cliffs below it are startling, with weirdly eroded rock stacks and a huge variety of seabirds; on a clear day you can see the whole northern coastline from Cape Wrath to Duncansby Head, and across Pentland Firth to the Orkneys. The *Northern Sands Hotel* (☎01847/851270; ⑥), in Dunnet village, is worth a stop, if only to eat in the restaurant; its Italian owner produces homemade pasta, very popular with the locals.

John O'Groats

Familiar from endless postcards, **JOHN O'GROATS** comes as something of an anticli-max. The views north across the churning waters to the Orkneys are fine enough, but the village itself – neither the most northerly, nor the most easterly point in Britain – turns out to be little more than a windswept grassy slope leading down to the sea, dominated by an enormous car park that is jammed throughout the summer with enor-mous tour buses. Collectors of kitsch seaside souvenirs, however, will have a field day in the many giftshops here. The village gets its name from the Dutchman, Jan de Groot, who obtained the ferry contract for the crossing to the Orkneys in 1496. The eight-sided house he built for his eight quarrelling sons (so that each one could enter by his own door) is echoed in the octagonal tower of the much photographed *John O'Groats Hotel* (☎01955/611203; ③), good as a stop-off for a quick drink and an inex-pensive place to spend the night.

John O'Groats is connected by regular **buses** to Wick (6 or 7 daily; 55min) and Thurso (Mon–Fri 4 daily, 2 on Sat; 40min). *Thomas & Bews* (☎01955/611353) runs a daily passenger ferry across to Burwick in the Orkney Islands (May–Sept 4 daily; 45min; £22 return), the last one at 6pm; officially this is a foot-passenger service, but it will take bicycles and motorbikes if it isn't too busy. The **tourist office** (April–Oct Mon–Sat 9am–5pm; ☎01955/611373) by the car park will help you sort out **accommo-dation**. The *Caber-feidh Guest House* (☎01955/611219; ③), at the junction of the Wick and Thurso roads, has a handful comfortable en-suite rooms and a bar, while *Heaven Gore* (☎01955/611314; ②) is a large and good-value B&B a mile west along the Thurso road. If you're on a tight budget, head for the small **youth hostel** (April–Oct; ☎01955/611424) at Canisbay, one and a half miles west of John O'Groats.

Duncansby Head

If you're disappointed by John O' Groats, press on a couple of miles further east to **Duncansby Head**, which, with its lighthouse, dramatic cliffs and well-worn coastal path, has a lot more to offer. The **birdlife** here is prolific, and south of the headland lie some spectacular 200-foot cliffs, cut by sheer-sided clefts known locally as *geos*. This is also a good place from which to view the Orkneys. Dividing the islands from the mainland is the infamous **Pentland Firth**, one of the world's most treacherous waterways. Only seven miles across, it forms a narrow channel between the Atlantic Ocean and North Sea, and for fourteen hours each day the tide rips through here from west to east at a rate of ten knots or more, flooding back in the opposite direction for the remaining ten hours. Combined with the rocky sea bed and a high wind, this can cause deep whirlpools and terrifying thirty-to-forty-foot towers of water to form when the ebbing tide crashes across the reefs offshore. The latter, known as the **"Bores of Duncansby"**, are the subject of many old mariners' myths from the time of the Vikings onwards.

The East Coast

The **east coast** of the Highlands, between Wick and the Black Isle, is nowhere near as spectacular as the west, with gentle undulating moors, grassland, and low cliffs where you might expect to find sea lochs and mountains. Washed by the cold waters of the North Sea, it's markedly cooler, too, although less prone to spells of perma-drizzle. The fast A9 is the region's main transport artery; winding in tandem with the Inverness–Thurso train line, it never strays far from the coast, which veers sharply northeast exactly parallel with the Great Glen, formed by the same geological fault.

From around the ninth century AD onwards, the **Norse** influence was more keenly felt here than any other part of mainland Britain, and dozens of Scandinavian-sounding names recall the era when this was a Viking kingdom. The clan system the Norsemen left behind, however, did not take root as firmly as it did elsewhere in Scotland. Instead, the northeast evolved more or less separately, avoiding the bloody tribal feuds that wrought such havoc further south and west. Nevertheless, the nineteenth-century **Clearances** hit the region hard, as countless ruined cottages and the empty moorland wastes show. Hundreds of thousands of crofters were evicted, and forced to emigrate to New Zealand, Canada and Australia, or else take up fishing in one of the numerous herring ports established on the coast. The recent oil boom has brought a transient prosperity to many of these over the past two decades, but the area remains one of the country's poorest, reliant on sheep farming, fishing and tourism.

Wick, the east coast's largest town, huddled around a small bay and fishing harbour, turns out to be a lot less appealing than the countryside around it: a treeless, windswept tract of open farmland and bog, dotted peat-black lochans and divided by endless stone walls that converge on whitewashed crofts. South of Wick, the area around the port of **Lybster** is littered with the remains of ancient civilizations, while the award-winning Timespan Heritage Centre further north at **Helmsdale** recounts the human cost of the landlords' greed. Beyond Helmsdale, the ersatz-Loire chateau, **Dunrobin Castle**, is the main tourist attraction, a monument as much to the iniquities of Clearances as to the eccentricity of Victorian taste. South of **Dornoch**, a famous golfing resort renowned for its salubrious climate and sweeping beach, lies the **Black Isle**, an area close to Inverness, covered earlier in this chapter (see p.907).

Wick

Originally a Viking settlement called *Vik*, after the bay on which it stands, **WICK** has been a Royal Burgh since 1140. It's actually two towns: Wick proper, and **Pultneytown**, immediately south across the river, a messy, rather run-down community planned by Thomas Telford in 1806 for the British Fisheries Society to encourage evicted crofters to take up fishing. Wick's heyday was in the mid-nineteenth century, when it was the busiest herring port in Europe, exporting tons of fish to Russia, Scandinavia and the West Indian slave plantations. Robert Louis Stevenson described it as " . . . the meanest of man's towns, situate on the baldest of God's bays", and it's still a pretty grim place, in spite of a bustling shopping centre, and some solid Victorian civic architecture.

Pultneytown, lined with rows of fishermen's cottages, is the area most worth a wander, not least for the **Wick Heritage Centre**, in Bank Row near the harbour (June–Sept Mon–Sat 10am–5pm; £1). Housed in a row of old fishery buildings, this little museum is crammed with lots of good stuff on the herring industry, and a photographic collection covering the town's history from the 1880s. Rising steeply from a needle-thin promontory three miles north of Wick are the dramatic fifteenth- to seventeenth-century ruins of **Sinclair** and **Girnigoe castles**, which functioned as a single stronghold for the Earls of Caithness. In 1570 the fourth earl, suspecting his son of trying to murder him, imprisoned him in the dungeon here until he died of starvation.

The **train** station and **bus** stops are next to each other behind the hospital. Wick also has an **airport** (☎01955/602294), a couple of miles north of the town, with direct flights from Edinburgh, Aberdeen and Orkney and connections further south. From the train station head across the river down Bridge Street to the **tourist office**, just off High Street (Mon–Fri 9am–5pm, Sat 9am–1pm; ☎01955/602596), which gives out a full **accommodation** list. Next door, the *Wellington Guest House*, 41–43 High St (☎01955/603287; ③), is reasonable value, as is the modern *County Guest House*, 101 High St (☎01955/602911; ③). The *Harbour Guest House*, 6 Rose St (☎01955/603276; ②), in a tiny terrace off the Inner Harbour in Pultneytown, offers comfortable rooms in a lovely old building. The best-value **B&B** in Wick is *Leask's* (☎01955/606512; ②), at Holy Terrace on the north side of the harbour, which has a handful of small but inexpensive rooms (with shared bathroom) looking over the rooftops to the port.

As for **eating**, the *Lamplighter Restaurant,* High St, serves large helpings of imaginative food; in the same building, *Houston's* cheerfully churns out good burgers. The *Lorne Restaurant* (open evenings only), near the Heritage Centre, is moderately priced and produces more than adequate servings of meat and two veg. *Gravelli's*, at either end of the High Street, is a real find, trapped in a time-warp and both the cafés serve piles of fish and chips, along with authentic pizza. Of the **pubs**, the *Camps*, at the east end of High Street, is among the liveliest in the evenings, with occasional **live music**.

Between Wick and Helmsdale

The stretch of road south of Wick winds gently along the coast, with great views over the cliffs and out to sea to the oil rigs perched on the horizon. The planned village of **LYBSTER**, established at the height of the nineteenth-century herring boom, once had 200-odd boats working out of its harbour. Today, although still a busy fishing port, it's a grim collection of grey pebble-dashed bungalows centred on a broad main street. Most visitors head straight for the nearby **Grey Cairns of Camster**, seven miles due north and one of the most memorable sights on the northeast coast. Surrounded by bleak moorland, these two enormous prehistoric burial chambers, constructed around 4000 to 5000 years ago, were immaculately designed, with corbelled drystone roofs in their hidden chambers, which you can crawl into through narrow passageways. More extraordinary ancient remains lie at **East Clyth**, two miles north of Lybster on the A9, where a path leads to the "**Hill o' Many Stanes**"; here 200 boulders stand in 22 parallel rows that run north to south; no one has yet worked out what they were used for, although archeological studies have shown there were once 600 stones.

DUNBEATH, hidden at the mouth of a small strath, eight miles southwest of Lybster, was another village founded to provide work in the wake of the Clearances. The local landlord built a harbour here in 1800, at the start of the herring boom, and the settlement flourished briefly. Today, it's a sleepy place, with lobster pots stacked at the quayside and views of windswept **Dunbeath Castle** (closed to the public) on the opposite side of the bay. The novelist **Neill Gunn** was also born here, in one of the terraced houses under the flyover that now swoops above the village; you can find out more about him at the **Dunbeath Heritage Centre** (Easter–Oct Mon–Sat 10am–5pm; £2.25), signposted from the road. The best of the handful of modest **B&Bs** here is *Tormore Farm* (☎01593/731240; ②), a large farmhouse with four comfortable rooms, half a mile north of the harbour on the A9.

Beyond Dunbeath lie miles of treeless green grazing lands, peppered with derelict crofts and latticed by long drystone walls. This whole area was devastated during the Clearances; the ruined village of **BADBEA**, reached via a footpath running east off the main road a short way before the Ord (see below), is a poignant monument of this cruel era. Built by tenants evicted from nearby Ousdale, the settlement now lies deserted, although its ruined hovels show what hardship the crofters had to endure: the cottages stood so near the windy cliff edge that children had to be tethered to prevent them from being blown into the sea. Just before reaching Helmsdale, the A9 begins its long descent from the **Ord of Caithness**. This steep hill used to form a pretty impregnable obstacle, and even now the desolate road gets blocked during winter snowstorms.

Helmsdale

Eleven miles up the A9 from Golspie, **HELMSDALE** is an old herring port, founded in the nineteenth century to house the evicted inhabitants of **Strath Kildonan**, which lies behind it. Today, the sleepy-looking grey village attracts thousands of tourists, most of them to see the **Timespan Heritage Centre**, beside the river (Easter–Oct Mon–Sat 10am–5pm, Sun 2–5pm; £2.75). It's a remarkable venture for a place of this size, telling the local story from prehistoric times to the present through hi-tech displays, sound effects and an audio-visual programme. For a spot of light relief after the exhibition, head across the road to the sugary pink and frilly **Mirage Restaurant**. The proprietor has become something of a Scottish celebrity, modelling herself on the romantic novelist Barbara Cartland, who has a shooting lodge nearby. Photographs proudly displayed on the walls show the paroxide-blond restauranteuse posing with her heroine, while the fittings and furnishings reflect her predeliction for all things pink and kitsch, with fish tanks, fake-straw parasols, and plastic seagulls set off to a tee by the C &W soundtrack. She also dishes up great fish and chips, grills and puddings.

Helmsdale's **tourist office** (April–Sept Mon–Sat 10am–5pm; ☎01431/821640) will book accommodation for you. Most of the **B&Bs** are on the outskirts of town; *Broomhill House*, Navidale Rd (☎01431/821259; ③), is the best of the bunch, with

---

GOLD AT BAILE AN OR

From Helmsdale the single-track A897 runs up the Strath Kildonan to the north coast, following the path of the Helmsdale river, a strictly controlled and extremely exclusive salmon river frequented by the royals. Some eight miles up the Strath at **Baile an Or** (Gaelic for "goldfield"), gold was discovered in the bed of the Kildonan Burn in 1869; a gold rush ensued, hardly on the scale of the Yukon, but quite bizarre in the Scottish Highlands. A tiny amount of gold is still found every year; if you fancy **gold-panning** yourself, pick up a free licence and the relevant equipment from Helmsdale's gift- and fishing-tackle shop, *Strath Ullie*, opposite the Timespan Heritage Centre.

bedrooms in a turret added to the former croft by a miner who struck it lucky in the Kildonan gold rush (see below). If full, try *Torbuie*, in Navidale, on the A9 less than a mile from the village (☎01431/821424; ②), or *Hazelbank*, in Westhelmsdale, half a mile up the river from the tourist office (☎01431/821427; ②); both offer comfortable rooms. There's also a **youth hostel** (mid-May to Sept; ☎01431/821577), about half a mile north of the harbour.

Golspie and around

Ten miles north of Dornoch on the A9 lies the straggling grey town of **GOLSPIE**, whose status as an administrative centre does little to relieve its dullness. It does, however, boast an eighteen-hole golf course and a lovely sandy beach, while half a mile further up the coast, the Big Burn has several rapids and waterfalls that can be seen from an attractive woodland trail (beginning at the *Sutherland Arms Hotel*).

Dunrobin Castle

The main reason to stop in Golspie, though, is to look around **Dunrobin Castle** (May Mon–Sat 10.30am–4.30pm, Sun 1–4.30pm; June–Sept Mon–Sat 10.30am–4.30pm, Sun 1–5.30pm; Oct Mon–Sat 10.30am–4.30pm, Sun 1–4.30pm; £3.70), overlooking the sea a mile north of town. Approached via a long tree-lined drive this fairy-tale confection of turrets and pointed rooves – modelled by the architect Sir Charles Berry (designer of the Houses of Parliament) on a Loire Chateau – is the seat of the infamous Sutherland family, at one time Europe's biggest landowners and the principal driving force behind the Clearances in this area. Staring up at the pile from the midst of its elaborate formal gardens, it's worth remembering that such extravagance was paid for by uprooting literally thousands of crofters from the surrounding glens. Much of the extra income generated by the evictions was squandered on the castle's opulent interior, which is crammed full of fine furniture, paintings (including two Canalettos), tapestries and *objets d'art* displayed in a mausoleum-like gloom.

Set aside at least an hour for Dunrobin's amazing **Museum**, housed in an eighteenth-century building at the edge of the garden. Inside, hundreds of disembodied animals' heads and horns peer down from the walls, alongside other more macabre appendages, from elephants' toes to rhinos' tails. Bagged by the fifth Duke and Duchess of Sutherland, the trophies vie for space with other fascinating family memorabilia, including one of John O'Groat's bones, Chinese opium pipes, and such curiosities as a "picnic gong from the South Pacific". There's also an impressive collection of ethnographic artefacts acquired by the Sutherlands on their frequent hunting jaunts, ranging from an Egyptian sacophagus to more locally found, finely carved Pictish stones.

The Sutherland Moument

You can't miss the one-hundred-foot-high **Monument** to the first Duke of Sutherland, which peers proprietarily down from the summit of the 1293-foot **Beinn a'Bhragaidh**, a mile northeast of Golspie. An inscription cut into its base recalls that the statue was erected in 1834 by "a mourning and grateful tenantry", to "a judicious, kind and liberal landlord . . . (who would) open his hands to the distress of the widow, the sick and the traveller". Unsurprisingly, there's no reference to the fact that the Duke, widely regarded as Scotland's own Josef Stalin, forcibly evicted 15,000 crofters from his one-million-acre estate – a fact which, in the words of one local historian, makes the monument "a grotesque representation of the many forces that destroyed the Highlands". Campaigners are lobbying to have it broken into pieces and scattered over the hillside, so that visitors can walk over the remains to a new, more appropriate memorial; there have even been several attempts to blow the statue up. However, the Sutherland estate and local council have continually resisted moves to replace it.

It's worth the wet, rocky **climb** (round trip 90min) to the top of the hill for the wonderful views south along the coast past Dornoch to the Moray Firth and west towards Lairg and Loch Shin. It's a steep and strenuous walk, however, and there's no view until you're out of the trees, about ten minutes from the top. Take the road opposite *Munro's TV Rentals* in Golspie's main street, which leads up the hill and past the fountain to a farm; from here, follow the Beinn a'Bhragaidh footpath (BBFP) signs along the path into the woods.

Dornoch

DORNOCH, ten miles south of Golspie, lies on a flattish headland overlooking the Dornoch Firth. Surrounded by sand dunes and blessed with an exceptionally sunny climate by Scottish standards, it's something of a middle-class holiday resort, with solid Edwardian hotels, trees and flowers in profusion, and miles of **sandy beaches** giving good views across the estuary to the Tain peninsula. The town is also renowned for its championship **golf course**, ranked eleventh in the world and the most northerly first-class course in the world.

Dating from the twelfth century, Dornoch became a Royal Burgh in 1628. Among its oldest buildings, which are all grouped round the spacious **Square**, the tiny **Cathedral** was founded in 1224 and built of local sandstone. The original building was horribly damaged by marauding Mackays in 1570, and much of what you see today was restored by the Countess of Sutherland in 1835, though her worst Victorian excesses were removed this century, when the interior stonework was returned to its original state. A later addition were the stained-glass windows in the north wall, which were endowed by the expat American-based Andrew Carnegie (see p.797). You can climb the tower (July & Aug Mon–Fri 7.30–8pm). Opposite, the fortified sixteenth-century **Bishop's Palace**, a fine example of vernacular architecture, with stepped gables and towers, is now a hotel. Next door, the **Old Town Jail** (Mon–Sat 10am–5pm; free) has a mock-up of a nineteenth-century cell and a bookshop.

Buses from Tain and Inverness stop in the Square, where you'll also find a **tourist office** (Mon–Sat 9am–1pm & 2–5pm; ☎01862/810400). There's no shortage of **accommodation**: near the golf course on the northeast edge of town, the *Trentham Hotel* (☎01862/810391; ③) is friendly and comfortable if a bit staid. The characterful *Dornoch Castle Hotel* (☎01862/810216; ⑥) in the Bishop's Palace on the Square, has a cosy old-style bar and relaxing tea garden. There are two good-value **B&Bs**: *Fiona MacLean*, 11 Gilchrist Square (☎01862/811024; ②), and *Trevose* (☎01862/810269; ②), on the Square and swathed in roses. For **food**, the stultifyingly floral restaurant in the *Mallin House Hotel*, Church St, north of the Square (☎01862/812335) is terrific, and the *Cathedral Café* serves delicious fare, too.

Bonar Bridge and around

Before the causeway was built across the Dornoch Firth, traffic heading along the coast used to skirt around the estuary, crossing the Kyle of Sutherland at **BONAR BRIDGE**. In the fourteenth and fifteenth centuries, the village harboured a large iron foundry. Ore was brought across the peat moors of the central Highlands from the west coast on sledges, and fuel for smelting came from the oak forest draped over the northern shores of the nearby kyle. However, James IV, passing through here once on his way to Tain, was shocked to find the forest virtually clear-felled and ordered that oak saplings be planted in the gaps. Although now hemmed in by spruce plantations, the beautiful ancient woodland east of Bonar Bridge dates from this era.

Carbisdale Castle

Towering high above the rocky and salmon-packed River Shin, three miles northwest of Bonar Bridge, the daunting neo-Gothic profile of **Carbisdale Castle** (not open to the public) overlooks the Kyle of Sutherland, and the battlefield where the gallant Marquis of Montrose was defeated in 1650, finally forcing Charles II to accede to the Scots demand for presbyterianism. It was erected between 1906 and 1917 for the dowager Duchess of Sutherland, following a protracted family feud. After the death of her husband, the late Duke of Sutherland, the will leaving her the lion's share of the vast estate was contested by his stepchildren from his first marriage. In the course of the ensuing legal battle, the Duchess was found in contempt of court for destroying important documents pertinent to the case, and locked up in Holloway prison for six weeks. However, the Sutherlands' eventually recanted (although there was no personal reconciliation) and, by way of compensation, built their stepmother a castle worthy of her rank. Designed in three distinct styles (to give the impression it was added to over a long period of time), Carbisdale was eventually acquired by a Norwegian shipping magnate in 1933, and finally gifted, along with its entire contents and estate, to the SYHA, who have turned it into what must be one of the most opulent **youth hostels** in the world (March–Sept; ☎0159/421232). Sadly, the interior has been ruined in the process; gutted of its former splendours, it's now overrun by large school parties, who swarm past fake-marble statues and along corridors lined with tacky art prints. The best way to get here by public transport is to take a **train** to nearby **Culrain** station, which lies within easy walking distance of the castle.

Croick Church

A mile or so southwest of Bonar Bridge, the scattered village of **ARDGAY** stands at the mouth of Strath Carron, a wooded river valley winding west into the heart of the Highlands. It's worth heading ten miles up the strath to **Croick Church**, which harbours one of Scotland's most poignant and emotive reminders of the Clearances. Huddled behind a brake of wind-bent trees, the graveyard surrounding the tiny grey chapel sheltered eighteen families (92 individuals) evicted from nearby Glen Calvie during the spring of 1845 to make way for flocks of Cheviot sheep, introduced by the Duke of Sutherland as a quick money earner. A reporter from *The Times* described the "wretched spectacle" as the villagers filed out of the glen " in a body, two or three carts filled with children, many of them infants". An even more evocative written record of the event is preserved on the diamond-shaped panes of the chapel windows, where the villagers scratched graffiti memorials still legible today: "Glen Calvie people was in the churchyard May 24th, 1845", "Glen Calvie people the wicked generation", and "This place needs cleaning".

Lairg

Eleven miles north of Bonar Bridge, the A836 cuts across **Strath Fleet**, with its attractive river, woodlands and farms, to **LAIRG**, a bleak and scattered town at the eastern end of lonely **Loch Shin**. On fine days, the vast wastes of heather and deer grass surrounding the town can be beautiful, but in the rain it can be a deeply depressing landscape. Lairg is predominantly a **transport hub**, and there's nothing to see in town. However, a mile southeast on the A839, there are many signs of early settlement at nearby **Ord Hill**, where archeological digs have recently yielded traces of human habitation dating back to Neolithic times. The **tourist centre** (Mon–Sat 9am–5pm, Sun 1–5pm; ☎01549/402160) hands out leaflets detailing the locations of hut circles and other sites. Every year Lairg hosts an August **lamb sale**, the biggest one-day livestock market in Europe, when sheep from all over the north of Scotland are bought and sold.

Lairg, at the centre of the region's **road system**, is distinctly hard to avoid: the A838, traversing some of the loneliest country in the Highlands, is the quickest route for Cape Wrath; the A836 heads up to Tongue on the north coast; and a few miles south of Lairg. the A837 pushes west through lovely Strath Oykel, to Lochinver on the west coast. For non-drivers, Lairg is on the main **train** line and the nexus of several **postbus** routes around the northwest Highlands. A daily bus from Inverness also passes through en route to Durness. Trains arrive north of the main road along the loch; buses stop right on the loch. Should you need to **stay**, try *Ben Avon*, Station Rd (April–Oct; ☎01549/402428; ②), *Old Coach House* (May–Oct; ☎01549/4023780; ②) at Achany, or *Carnbren,* three hundred yards across the bridge (all year; ☎412259; ②).

travel details

Trains

Aviemore to: Edinburgh (7 daily; 2hr 55min); Inverness (Mon–Sat 8 daily, Sun; 40min).

Dingwall to: Helmsdale (Mon–Sat 3 daily; 2hr); Inverness (Mon–Sat 3 daily; 25min); Kyle of Lochalsh (Mon–Sat 3 daily; 1hr 55min); Lairg (Mon–Sat 3 daily; 1hr 10min); Thurso (Mon–Sat 3 daily; 3hr 20min); Wick (Mon–Sat 3 daily; 3hr 20min).

Fort William to: Arisaig (4 daily; 1hr 10min); Crianlarich (3 daily; 1hr 40min); Glasgow (2–3 daily; 4hr); Glenfinnan (4 daily; 55min); London (1 daily; 11hr 40min); Mallaig (4 daily; 1hr 25min).

Inverness to: Aviemore (Mon–Sat 9 daily, 4 on Sun; 40min); Dingwall (Mon–Sat 3 daily; 25min); Edinburgh (Mon–Sat 7 daily, 2 on Sun; 3hr 30min); Helmsdale (2–3 daily; 2hr 20min); Kyle of Lochalsh (Mon–Sat 3 daily; 2hr 40min); Lairg (Mon–Sat 3 daily; 1hr 40min); London (Mon–Sat 5 daily, 2 on Sun; 8hr 35min); Plockkton (2–3 daily; 2hr 15min); Thurso (Mon–Sat 3 daily; 3hr 45min); Wick (Mon–Sat 3 daily; 3hr 45min).

Kyle of Lochalsh to: Dingwall (Mon–Sat 3 daily; 1hr 55 min); Inverness (Mon–Sat 3 daily; 2hr 30min); Plockton (Mon–Sat 2–3 daily; 20min).

Lairg to: Dingwall (Mon–Sat 3 daily; 1hr 10min); Inverness (Mon–Sat 3 daily; 1hr 40min); Thurso (Mon–Sat 3 daily; 2hr 5min); Wick (Mon–Sat 3 daily; 2hr 5min).

Mallaig to: Arisaig (4 daily; 15min); Edinburgh (2–3 daily; 6hr 20min) Fort William (4 daily; 1hr 25 min); Glasgow (2–3 daily; 5hr 20min); Glenfinnan (4 daily; 35 min).

Thurso to: Dingwall (Mon–Sat 3 daily; 3hr 20min); Inverness (Mon–Sat 3 daily; 3hr 45min); Lairg (Mon–Sat 3 daily; 2hr 5min).

Wick to: Dingwall (Mon–Sat 3 daily; 3hr 20min); Inverness (Mon–Sat 3 daily; 3hr 45min); Lairg (Mon–Sat 3 daily; 2hr 5min).

Buses

Aviemore to: Grantown-on-Spey (5 daily; 40min); Inverness (10 daily; 40 min).

Dornoch to: Inverness (3 daily; 1hr 10min); Thurso with connections for Wick (3 daily; 2hr 20min).

Fort William to: Aracharachle (Mon–Sat 2–3 daily; 1hr 45min); Drumnadrochit (8 daily; 1hr 30min); Fort Augustus (8 daily; 1hr); Inverness (8 daily; 2hr); Mallaig (1 daily; 1 hr 50min).

Gairloch to: Dingwall (3 weekly; 2hr); Inverness (3 weekly; 2hr 20min); Redpoint (1 daily; 1hr 35min).

Inverness to: Aberdeen (hourly; 3hr 30min); Aviemore (Mon–Sat 7 daily, 12 on Sun; 40min); Cromarty (4 daily; 45min); Drumnadrochit (4–5 daily; 25min); Durness (June–Sept 1 daily; 4hr 30min); Fort Augustus (4–5 daily; 1hr); Fort William (4 daily; 2hr); Gairloch (1 daily; 2hr 20min); Glasgow (14 daily; 3hr 35min–4hr 25min); John O'Groats (April–Sept 2 daily; 3hr 40min); Kirkwall (April–Sept 2 daily; 5hr 20min); Kyle of Lochalsh (3–4 daily; 2hr); Lairg (June–Sept Mon–Sat 1 daily; 2hr 10min); Lochinver (1 weekly; 2hr 30min); Nairn (Mon–Sat hourly; 50min); Oban (Mon–Sat 1 daily; 4hr 15min); Thurso (Mon–Sat 3 daily, 1 on Sun; 3hr 30 min); Ullapool (2–4 daily; 1hr 25min); Wick (Mon–Sat 3 daily; 1hr 55min).

Kyle of Lochalsh to: Fort William (3 daily; 1hr 50min); Glasgow (3 daily; 5hr); Inverness (Mon–Sat 2 daily, 1 on Sun; 2hr).

Lochinver to: Inverness (1 weekly; 2hr 15min).

Mallaig to: Aracharachle (1 daily; 1hr 45min); Fort William (1 daily; 2hr).

Thurso to: Bettyhill (1 weekly; 1 hr 20min); Inverness (Mon–Sat 2 daily, 1 on Sun; 2hr 30min); Wick (Mon–Sat 2 daily, 1 on Sun; 35min).

Wick to: Inverness (Mon–Sat 2 daily, 1 on Sun 2hr 55min); Thurso (Mon–Sat 2 daily, 1 on Sun; 35min).

Ferries

To Mull:Kilchoan–Tobermory, see p.824.

To Skye: Mallaig–Armadale; Glenelg–Kylerhea, see p.844.

To the Small Isles: Canna, Mallaig–Eigg, Muck and Rhum, see p.852.

To Lewis: Ullapool–Stornoway (Mon–Sat daily; 2hr 30min).

To Orkney: Scrabster–Orkney.

Flights

Inverness to: Glasgow (Mon–Fri 2 daily; 50min); London (up to 7 daily; 1hr 25min).

CHAPTER TWENTY FIVE

ORKNEY AND SHETLAND

Arching out into the North Sea, in the face of furious tides and bitter winds, the Orkney and Shetland islands gather neatly into two distinct and very different clusters. Often referring to themselves first as Orcadians or Shetlanders, and with unofficial, but widely displayed, flags, their inhabitants regard Scotland as a separate entity. This feeling of detachment arises from their distinctive geography, history and culture, in which they differ not only from Scotland but also from each other.

To the south, just a short step from the Scottish mainland, are the seventy or so **Orkney Islands**. With the major exception of Hoy, which is high and rugged, these islands are low-lying, gently sloping and fertile, and for centuries have provided a reasonably secure living from farming, with some fishing. In spring and summer the days are long, the skies enormous and the meadows thick with wild flowers. There is a peaceful continuity to Orcadian life reflected not only in the well-preserved treasury of **Stone Age settlements**, such as Skara Brae, and **standing stones**, most notably the Stones of Stenness, but also in the rather conservative nature of society here today.

Another sixty miles north, the **Shetland Islands** are in nearly all respects a complete contrast. Higher and more dramatic, here the steep cliffs rise straight out of

ISLAND WILDLIFE

Orkney and Shetland support huge numbers of **seabirds**, particularly during the breeding season, from April to July, when cliffs and coastal banks are alive with thousands of guillemots, razorbills, puffins, fulmars and, particularly in Shetland, gannets. Terns are often to be found on small offshore islets or gravelly spits. On coastal heathland or moorland you should see arctic skuas, great skuas, curlews and occasionally whimbrel or golden plover. Many kinds of wild duck are present, especially in winter, but eiders are particularly common. In autumn and spring, large numbers of migrants drop in on their way north or south and very rare specimens may turn up at any time of year. Fair Isle, in particular, has a long list of rarities; and Shetland's isolation has produced its own distinctive sub-species of wren. Some of the best or most accessible bird sites have been noted in the text.

The separation of the islands from the mainland has also meant that some species of **land mammal** are absent and others have developed sub-species. For instance, Shetland has no voles but Orkney its own distinctive type. However, both groups have considerable populations of seals and otters. Further offshore you may well see porpoises, dolphins and several species of whale including pilot, sperm and killer.

Neither of the island groups support many **trees** and very few of those that are here are native. However, the clifftops, moorlands and meadows of both Orkney and Shetland are rich with beautiful **wild flowers**, including pink thrift, the pale pink heather-spotted orchid, red campion and, in wetter areas, golden marsh marigolds, yellow iris and insect-eating sundew. Notable **smaller plants** include the purple scottish primrose, which grows only in Orkney and the far north of Scotland, and the Shetland (or Edmondston's) mouse-eared chickweed with its delicate white flower streaked with yellow, which grows only on the island of Unst.

the water to form barren heather-coated hills, while ice-sculpted sea inlets cut deep into the land, offering memorable coastal walks in Shetland's endless summer evenings. With a scarcity of fertile ground, Shetlanders have traditionally been crofters rather than farmers, often looking to the sea for an uncertain living in fishing or the naval and merchant services. Perhaps because life has been so hard, islanders have tended to enthusiastically seize new opportunities such as fish farming and computing – Shetland now boasts its own Internet hub. Nevertheless, the past is seldom forgotten; the Norse heritage is clear in every road sign and in the rich archeological sites of **Jarlshof** and the **Broch of Mousa**.

Since people first began to explore the North Atlantic, Orkney and Shetland have been stepping stones on routes between Britain, Ireland and Scandinavia; and both groups have a long history of **settlement**, certainly from around 3500–4000 BC. The **Norse** settlers, who began to arrive from about 800 AD, with substantial migration from around 900 AD, left the islands with a unique cultural character. Orkney was a powerful Norse earldom, and Shetland (at first part of the same earldom) was ruled directly from Norway for nearly 300 years after 1195. The Norse influence is clearly evident today in dialects, accents and place names; and with neither group ever part of the Gaelic-speaking culture of Highland Scotland, the Scottish influence is essentially a Lowland one.

From October to April the **weather** can bring real drama; in late spring and summer, there are often long dry spells with lots of sunshine, but you need to come prepared for wind, rain and, most frustrating of all, the occasional sea fog.

Orkney

Just a short step from John O'Groats, the **Orkney Islands** are a unique and fiercely independent grouping. In spring and summer the meadows and clifftops are a brilliant green, shining with wild flowers, while long days pour light onto the land and sea – a sharp contrast to the bleak enormity of the rugged western Highlands. For an Orcadian "**Mainland**" invariably means the largest island in Orkney, rather than the rest of Scotland, and throughout their history they've been linked to lands much further afield, principally Scandinavia.

Small communities began to settle in the islands around 4000 BC, and the village at **Skara Brae** on the Mainland is one of the best preserved Stone Age settlements in Europe. This and many of the other older archeological sites, including the **Stones of Stenness** and **Maes Howe**, are concentrated in the central and eastern parts of the Mainland. Elsewhere the islands are scattered with chambered tombs and stone circles, a tribute to the sophisticated religious and ceremonial practices taking place here from around 2000 BC. More sophisticated **Iron Age** inhabitants built fortified villages incorporating stone towers known as **brochs**, protected by walls and ramparts, many of which are still in place. Later Pictish culture spread to Orkney and the remains of several of their early Christian settlements can still be seen, the best at the **Brough of Birsay** in the West Mainland, where a group of small houses are gathered around the remains of an early church. Later, around the ninth century, **Norse** settlers from Scandinavia arrived, and the islands became Norse earldoms, forming an outpost of this powerful and expansive culture that was gradually forcing its way south. The last of the Norse earls was killed in 1231, but they had a lasting impact on the islands, leaving behind not only their language but also the great **St Magnus Cathedral** in Kirkwall, one of Scotland's most outstanding pieces of medieval architecture.

After the end of Norse rule, the islands became the preserve of **Scottish earls**, who exploited and abused the islanders, although a steady increase in sea trade did offer

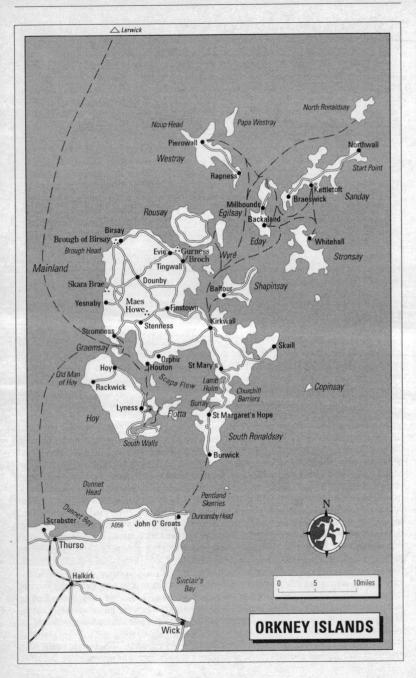

△ Lerwick

North Ronaldsay

Noup Head

Papa Westray

Pierowall

Northwall

Westray

Start Point

Rapness

Kettletoft

Braeswick

Sanday

Rousay

Millbounds

Egilsay I

Backaland

Eday

Birsay

Brough of Birsay

Evie

Gurness

Broch

Wyre

Whitehall

Brough Head

Mainland

Tingwall

Stronsay

Skara Brae

Dounby

Yesnaby

Maes

Howe

Balfour

Shapinsay

Finstown

Stenness

Kirkwall

Stromness

Skaill

Graemsay

Orphir

Houton

St Mary's

Copinsay

Hoy

Old Man

of Hoy

Rackwick

Lamb

Holm

Churchill

Barriers

Lyness

Burray

St Margaret's Hope

Flotta

Hoy

South Ronaldsay

South Walls

Burwick

Dunnet

Head

Pentland

Skerries

Dunnet Bay

Duncansby Head

Scrabster

A956

John O' Groats

Thurso

Halkirk

Sinclair's

Bay

Wick

0   5   10miles

N

ORKNEY ISLANDS

some chance of escape. French and Spanish ships sheltered here in the sixteenth century, and the ships of the **Hudson Bay Company** recruited hundreds of Orcadians to work in the Canadian fur trade. The islands were also an important staging post in the **whaling industry** and the **herring boom**, which brought great numbers of small Dutch, French and Scottish boats. More recently, the naval importance of **Scapa Flow** brought plenty of money and activity during both world wars, and left the seabed scattered with **wrecks**, making for wonderful **diving** opportunities, and the clifftops dotted with gun emplacements. Since the war, things have quietened down somewhat, although in the last two decades the **oil industry**, which now has a large terminal on the island of **Flotta**, and **European Community** funding have brought surprise windfalls, stemming the exodus of young people. Meanwhile, many disenchanted southerners have become "incomers" moving north in search of the peace and simplicity of island life.

Getting Around

On the Orkney Mainland, **scheduled buses** connect Kirkwall to Stromness, Dounby, Houton, Tingwall, Evie, Rendall, Deerness, Burray, South Ronaldsay and, less frequently, Birsay. However, services aren't frequent and many of the most interesting areas are some way from the bus routes. **Cycling** is cheap and effective as there are few steep hills, distances are not too long and in summer, at least, the weather is usually not prohibitive. **Bikes** can be rented in Kirkwall, Stromness and on some of the smaller islands. Bringing a **car** to Orkney is straightforward, if not exactly cheap; alternatively, you can rent one in Kirkwall, Stromness or on several of the islands. Especially if time is limited, it may be worth considering one of the guided **tours** available by bus or minibus operated by *Go-Orkney* or *Wildabout* among others; details are available from the tourist offices.

    Getting to the other islands from Mainland isn't difficult; *Orkney Islands Shipping Company* (☎01856/872044) operates several sailings daily to Hoy, Shapinsay and Rousay and between one and three, depending on route and season, to all the others except **North Ronaldsay**, which has a weekly boat on Fridays. *British Airways Express* flies to **Eday**, **North Ronaldsay**, **Westray**, **Papa Westray**, **Sanday** and **Stronsay**. Travel between individual islands by sea or air isn't so straightforward, but careful study of timetables can reduce the need to come all the way back to Kirkwall.

GETTING TO ORKNEY

Orkney is connected to the mainland by four **ferry** routes. *P&O Scottish Ferries* (☎01856/850655) runs car ferries once a week (June–Aug 2 weekly) from **Aberdeen** (8hr) and daily services on the much shorter crossing (1hr 45min) from **Scrabster**, about two miles northwest of Thurso on the north coast; both arrive at Stromness. *Orcargo* (☎01856/873838) has a service from **Invergordon** (10hr) to Kirkwall. The other mainland connection is a passenger ferry between **John O'Groats** and **Burwick** on South Ronaldsay (May to mid-Sept; 45min); the *Orkney Bus* service from Inverness connects directly with this ferry. A **day trip** is also offered from Inverness or John O'Groats, with a tour of some of the major sights on Mainland; details of both ferry and bus are available from *John O'Groats Ferries* (☎01955/611353). There's also a weekly or, from June to August, twice-weekly *P&O* service from Stromness and to **Lerwick** in Shetland.

    There are direct flights to Orkney from **Wick**, **Inverness**, **Aberdeen**, **Edinburgh** or **Glasgow**, with good connections from **Birmingham, London and Manchester**. There are also flights between Orkney and **Shetland**. All of these services are operated into Kirkwall Airport by *British Airways* (☎01856/872233) or its franchised subsidiary *British Airways Express*, locally still often known by its old name, *Loganair* (☎0345/222111 or ☎01856/872494).

Kirkwall

Sheltered at the south end of its wide bay, the old heart of Orkney's capital, **KIRKWALL**, huddles around the base of the St Magnus Cathedral. The town has two principal focal points: the harbour, which bustles with ferries, cargo ships, yachts and fishing boats, and the main shopping street, Albert Street, which twists back towards the cathedral through a tight knot of paved streets, old stone houses and narrow alleys. By Orkney standards, Kirkwall is a bustling metropolis; a busy market town and home to the island's most important businesses, its more exotic restaurants and better-stocked shops, as well as two distilleries. It hosts several lively **festivals** including the Orkney Folk Festival in May, a celebration of St Magnus in June and of science in September. An interesting place to spend some time, with unusual, quietly impressive architecture and a gentle, unhurried atmosphere, Kirkwall also makes an ideal base from which to explore Mainland or to make day trips out to the northern isles.

The Town

Towering above the town, the **St Magnus Cathedral** (daily 9am–1pm & 2–5pm) is Kirkwall's most intriguing conventional sight, a unique building that employs traditional architectural techniques but gives them a distinctive Orkney twist. The Orkney Earl Kol of Agdir, who began the structure in 1137, decided to make full use of a growing cult surrounding the figure of his uncle Magnus Erlendson. Magnus had shared the earldom of Orkney with his cousin Hakon Paulson from 1103, but Hakon grew jealous of his cousin's popularity and had him killed in 1115. When Magnus's body was buried in Birsay a heavenly light was said to have shone overhead, and his grave soon became a place of pilgrimage attributed with miraculous powers and attracting pilgrims from as far afield as Shetland. When Kol of Agdir finally took over the earldom he built the cathedral in his uncle's honour, moving the centre of religious and secular power from Birsay to Kirkwall.

The first version of the cathedral, which was built using yellow stone from Eday and red stone from Mainland, was somewhat smaller than today's structure, which has been added to over the centuries, with a new east window in the thirteenth century, the extension of the nave in the fifteenth century and a new west window to mark the building's 850th anniversary in 1987. Today the soft sandstone is badly eroded, particularly around the doorways, but it's still an immensely impressive building, its shape and style echoing the great cathedrals of Europe. Inside, the atmosphere is surprisingly intimate, the pink-sandstone columns drawing you up to the exposed brickwork arches, while around the walls a series of gravestones and monuments includes the bones of Magnus himself, a monument to the dead of HMS *Royal Oak* (which was torpedoed in Scapa Flow in 1939 with the loss of 833 men and the tomb of the arctic explorer John Rae, who was born in Stromness. There's also a collection of gravestones from the sixteenth and seventeenth centuries, carved with

---

ACCOMMODATION PRICE CODES

Throughout this guide, hotel and B&B accommodation is priced on a scale of ① to ⑨, the number indicating the **lowest price** you could expect to pay per night in that establishment for a **double room** in high season. The prices indicated by the codes are as follows:

① under £20/$30	④ £40–50/$60–75	⑦ £70–80/$105–120
② £20–30/$31–45	⑤ £50–60/$75–90	⑧ £80–100/$120–150
③ £30–40/$45–60	⑥ £60–70/$90–105	⑨ over £100/$150

chilling inscriptions calling on the reader to "remember death waits us all, the hour none knows".

Alongside the church are the ruined remains of the **Bishop's Palace** (April–Sept Mon–Sat 9.30am–6pm, Sun 2–6pm; £1.20). Built in the twelfth century for Bishop William of Old, the palace consisted of a main hall for ceremonial occasions and a tower which probably served as the bishop's private residence. The palace was rebuilt in the late fifteenth century and restored in the sixteenth, by Bishop Robert Reid, the founder of Edinburgh University. Today the walls and tower still stand, and a narrow spiral staircase takes you to the top for a good view of the cathedral and across Kirkwall's rooftops.

The neighbouring **Earl's Palace**, which dates from 1600, is rather better preserved; it's reckoned to be one of the finest examples of Renaissance architecture in Scotland. With its dank dungeons, massive fireplaces and magnificent central hall, it is a much grander building than the Bishop's Palace and has a confident solidity. Inside, a series of excellent displays analyses the uses of the various rooms, and it's easy enough to imagine the way in which the earl lived here and conducted his ruthless business. The roof is missing, but many domestic details remain, including a set of toilets and the stone shelves used by the clerk to do his filing.

The turreted towers of the Earl's Palace are echoed by those of the Victorian **Town Hall**, opposite the cathedral. Nearby, **Tankerness House** (Mon–Sat 10.30am–12.30pm & 1.30–5pm; May–Sept also Sun 2–5pm; April–Sept £1, otherwise free), a former home for the clergy that has been renovated countless times over the years, first in 1574 and most recently in the 1960s, houses a simple but informative **museum** that takes takes you through Orkney history from the very beginning – well worth a look before you visit the main archeological sites.

Further afield (a mile or so south of the town centre on the Holm road), is the **Highland Park** distillery, billed as "the most northerly legal distillery in Scotland". The distillery has been in operation for more than two hundred years, although it was closed during World War II, when it was used as a military food store and the huge vats served as communal baths. You can decide for yourself whether the taste still lingers by partaking of the regular guided tours of its beautiful old buildings and the customary free dram afterwards (Easter–Oct Mon–Fri 10am–4pm; June–Aug also Sat 10am–4pm; Nov–March Mon–Fri tours at 2pm & 3.30pm only; £2).

Practicalities

Most visitors come to Orkney **by sea** (from either Scrabster or Aberdeen), and arrive at the ferry terminal in Stromness, in the southwest corner of Mainland. Ferries are met by buses to Kirkwall (40min). Arriving **by plane**, the airport is about three miles southeast of Kirkwall on the A960. It's not served by buses, but a taxi into town should only set you back about £6. The **tourist office**, on Broad Street, beside the cathedral graveyard (daily 8am–8pm; ☎018561/872856), books accommodation and gives out an excellent free leaflet, the *Kirkwall Heritage Guide*, which takes you through all the buildings of interest. Most events are advertised in the *Orcadian* (Thurs) and there's a "What's On Diary" on *BBC Radio Orkney* (93.7MHz FM; Mon–Fri 7.30–8am) .

There's an excellent range of **accommodation** in Kirkwall, starting (at the top) with the *Kirkwall* (☎01856/872232; ⑥), the town's most imposing pile, on Harbour Street. Equally central are the *Albert*, on Mounthoolie Lane (☎018561/876000; ⑤), and the slightly shabby, welcoming *West End Hotel*, 14 Main St (☎01856/872368; ④). The *Queen's Hotel*, Shore St (☎01856/872200; ④), is also convenient for the centre. There are several good, central **B&Bs** including *Mrs Bain*, 6 Fraser's Close (☎018561/872862; ②); *Briar Lea*, 10 Dundas Crescent (☎018561/872747; ③); *Mrs Parkins*, 7 Matches Square (☎018561/872440; ②); and *Mrs Forsyth*, 21 Willowburn Rd (☎018561/874020; ②). If you want a basic room, there's the SYHA **youth hostel**

(☎018561/872243) on the road to Orphir, about half a mile southeast of the town centre. **Camping** is available at *Pickaquoy* (mid-May to mid-Sept; ☎873535), on the west side of town; it's well equipped with clothes, washing and drying facilities.

Kirkwall offers a good selection of **cafés** and **restaurants** ranging from the local produce served up in the bar and restaurant of the *Albert Hotel* to Mexican food at *A La Olla*, in The Shore, Anchor Building, 8 Bridge St. There are two Chinese places to choose from, and the *Mumataz Indian Restaurant*, 7 Bridge St. The *Kirkwall Hotel*'s French-tinged menu features local seafood and beef, while the *West End* and *Queen's* hotels both offer good bar snacks. Further afield, the *Foveran Hotel*, two miles out on the A964 to Orphir, is one of the best eating places in Orkney; Last but not least, there's the *Pomona Café*, Albert St, something of a local institution, with simple fare: teas, coffees, cakes, pies, sandwiches and toasties. The liveliest **drinking** hole is the *Bothy Bar* in the *Albert Hotel*, which sometimes has live music and is attached to *Matchmakers* disco, or the public bar in the *Kirkwall* and the cosy lounge bar in the *Queen's*.

West Mainland

The great bulk of the **West Mainland** is Orkney's most fertile, productive ground, fringed by some spectacular coastline and littered with impressive historical sites, ranging from the prehistoric village of **Skara Brae** to the battered concrete huts that mark the remains of Twatt military airfield, a large World War II RAF base. Today this part of the island is still heavily farmed, and there are few real villages. There are still some areas, however, which are too barren to cultivate, and the high ground and wild coastline are protected by several interesting **wildlife reserves**, while a handful of small lochs offer superb **trout fishing**.

Evie and Birsay

Overshadowed by the great wind turbines on Burgar Hill, the little village of **EVIE**, on the north coast, looks out across the turbulent waters of **Eynhallow Sound** towards the island of Rousay. At the western end of the white sands of Evie, the **Broch of Gurness** (April–Sept Mon–Sat 9.30am–6.30pm, Sun 2–6.30pm; £2) is the best preserved of more than five hundred pre-Christian-era villages dotted across the islands – like the others built to a simple pattern, with a compact group of homes clustered around a central tower. The walls and partitions of the houses have survived amazingly well, so has the main tower, which was probably retreated to in times of attack, with its thick, fortified walls and independent water supply.

Northwest from Evie, the parish of **BIRSAY** was the centre of Norse power in Orkney for several centuries, until the earls moved to Kirkwall following the construction of the cathedral. Today a tiny cluster of homes is gathered around the ruins of the **Earl's Palace** at Birsay, which was built in 1574 at the back of a beautiful little bay. The crumbling walls and turrets retain plenty of their grandeur, although there is little remaining evidence of domestic detail. When it was occupied, the palace was surrounded by flower and herb gardens, a bowling green and archery butts. By comparison, the Earl's Palace in Kirkwall seems fairly humble.

Just over half a mile northwest of the palace is the **Brough of Birsay**, a small Pictish settlement on a tidal island that can be reached during the two hours each side of high tide. Don't get stranded, unless you plan to camp, in which case make sure you're well provided for. The focus of the village was the twelfth-century **St Peter's Church**, the shape of which is mapped out by the remains of its walls. Southwest, on the other side of Birsay Bay, is **Marwick Head**, now an RSPB reserve. On it stands the memorial to Lord Kitchener and the crew of the HMS *Hampshire* who died near here when the ship struck a mine in June 1916.

Skara Brae and Maes Howe

About five miles south of Birsay, the beautiful white curve of the **Bay of Skaill** is home to **Skara Brae** (April–Sept Mon–Sat 9.30am–6.30pm, Sun 11.30am–6.30pm; Oct–May Mon–Sat 9.30am–4.30pm, Sun 2–4.30pm; £2), the remains of a small fishing and farming village that was inhabited between 3000 and 2500 BC and rediscovered in 1850 after a fierce storm by the local laird. The village is very well preserved, its houses, many of which still stand, huddled together and connected by narrow passages which would have been covered over with turf. For centuries it was buried in the dunes, which protected a vast array of domestic detail, including dressers, fireplaces, beds and boxes, all carefully put together from slabs of stone. Archeologists have discovered two distinct types of house: an earlier, smaller structure, built around a central hearth, with beds built into the wall; and larger, later homes that have the beds in the main living area with cupboards behind them. Other evidence shows that the inhabitants were settled farmers eating sheep, cattle and grain, as well as fish and shellfish, and using lamps fuelled by the oil from whales, seals and seabirds.

The main road leads back towards Kirkwall via the village of **DOUNBY**, a quiet, former market town, and skirts the shores of Loch Harray (Orkney's most famous trout loch), to reach the great Neolithic burial chamber of **Maes Howe** (April–Sept Mon–Sat 9.30am–6pm, Sun 2–6pm; Oct–May Mon–Sat 9.30am–4pm, Sun 2–4pm; £2). The chamber occupies a central position on Mainland and is proof positive of the ingenuity of prehistoric communities in Orkney. Dating from 2750 BC, its incredible state of preservation is partly due to the massive slabs of sandstone from which it was constructed, the largest of which weighs over three tons. The central chamber is reached down a long stone passage and contains three cells built into the walls, each of which was plugged with an enormous stone. When the tomb was opened in 1861, it was found to be virtually empty, thanks to the work of generations of grave-robbers, who had only left behind a handful of human bones. It is known for certain that the Vikings broke in here in the twelfth century, probably on their way to the crusades, because they left behind large amounts of graffiti on the walls of the main chamber.

The area surrounding Maes Howe was a religious centre for Orkney's Stone Age inhabitants; of the many remains dating back to that era, the closest are the **Stones of Stenness**, just over a mile to the west – a circle of 12 rock slabs, the tallest of which is over 16ft high. Less than half a mile from these, the **Ring of Brodgar** is a nearly complete ring of 27 stones, beautifully sited on a narrow spit of land between two lochs.

West Mainland practicalities

You can easily base yourself in Kirkwall or Stromness, but many good **places to stay** are scattered throughout the West Mainland. There are welcoming **B&Bs** such as *Asgard*, Germiston Rd, Orphir (☎01856/811300; ②) or *Linnadale*, Heddle Rd, Finstown (☎01856/761300; ③). Moving northwards, *Mrs Kirkpatrick* (☎01856/841656; ③) offers comfortable rooms on the loch shore at Sandwick. Other good places include: *Woodwick House* (☎01856/751330; ④) at Evie, *Dounby House* (☎01856/771535; ②) in Dounby, *Primrose Cottage* (☎01856/721384; ②) at Marwick, and *Fiddlers' Green* (formerly *Linkshouse*; ☎01856/721221; ③) in Birsay. The *Smithfield Hotel* (☎01856/771215; ⑤) in the middle of Dounby is a pleasant village inn with good food. Other **hotels** include the *Barony Hotel* (☎01856/721327; ④) on the north shore of the Loch of Boardhouse and the *Merkister Hotel* (☎01856/771515; ⑥) at the north end of the Loch of Harray. Both make a comfortable base and specialize in fishing holidays; the *Merkister* also boasts a bird hide. **Camping** is available at the *Eviedale Centre* (April–Oct; ☎01856/751270).

For **eating**, all the hotels do lunches or bar meals; other places for a snack or something more filling include the *Dale Kitchen* at Evie, the *Northdyke* a mile or so north of Skara Brae, and the top-floor restaurant at *Tormiston Mill*.

Stromness

Orkney's great harbour town, **STROMNESS** is perhaps more than anywhere else the historical heart of the islands. It was here, in the shelter of Hamnavoe, or Haven Bay, on the edge of the great natural harbour of Scapa Flow, that ships from all around the world came and went, sweeping the town into a series of booms, unloading a cargo of sea tales and embarking hundreds of Orcadians on weird and wonderful expeditions.

French and Spanish ships sheltered in Hamnavoe as early as the sixteenth century, and for a long time European conflicts made it safer for ships heading across the Atlantic to travel around the top of Scotland rather than through the English Channel, many of whom called in to Stromness to take on food, water and crew. Crews from Stromness were also hired for herring and whaling expeditions for which the town was an important centre. By 1842, the town was a tough and busy harbour, with some forty or so pubs and reports of "outrageous and turbulent proceedings of seamen and others who frequent the harbour". The herring boom brought large numbers of small boats to the town, along with thousands of young women who gutted and pickled the fish before they were packed in barrels. Today Stromness is still an important harbour town, serving as Orkney's main ferry terminal and as the headquarters of the Northern Lighthouse Board.

The Town

Clustered along the shoreline, Stromness is a tight network of alleyways and slate roofs, crowded onto the lower slopes of **Brinkie's Brae**, which looms up from the harbour front. The single main street, paved with great flagstones and called various names (John St, Victoria St and South End to name but three), winds along behind the waterfront, with narrow alleys meandering off up the hill. Originally all of the waterfront houses had their own piers, from which merchants would trade with passing ships; the **cannon** at the southern end of town (on South End) was fired to announce the arrival of a ship from the *Hudson's Bay Company*. **The Warehouse**, now home to the *P&O* and tourist offices, was originally built in the 1760s to store American rice. At the southern end of town, on the Ness road, **The Doubles** is a large pair of houses on a raised platform that were built as a home by Mrs Christian Robertson with the proceeds of her shipping agency, which sent as many as eight hundred men on whaling expeditions in one year.

The **Stromness Museum**, off the southern end of the main street (Mon–Sat 10.30am–12.30pm & 1.30–5pm; 80p), houses a collection of salty artefacts gathered from shipwrecks and arctic expeditions, including crockery from the German fleet, beaver fur hats, Cree Indian cloth and part of the torpedo that sunk the HMS *Royal Oak*. The **Pier Arts Centre**, right on the waterfront (Tues–Sun 10.30am–12.30pm & 1.30–5pm), gives a more contemporary account of Orkney life; restored to become an important focus of artistic life in the islands, it has regular exhibitions, often featuring painting and sculpture by local artists.

Practicalities

The **tourist office** (Mon–Fri & Sat 8am–8pm, Thurs 8am–6pm, Sun 9am–4pm; ☎01856/850716) is in the ferry terminal building opposite the pier. The town's first **hotel**, the *Stromness* (☎01856/850610; ⑤) is showing its age a bit, but the welcome's warm. The *Braes Hotel* (☎01856/850495; ④), on the hill above the south end of the town has the best views. There are several good and friendly **B&Bs**: close to the ferry terminal are the excellent *Ferry Inn* (☎01856/850280; ③) and *Mrs Hourston* (☎01856/850642; ②), just behind it. At the southern end of town, on the Ness Road, *Stenigar* (☎01856/850438; ③) has lots of character. Stromness has a well-equipped **camping** site (☎01856/873535) in a superb setting at Point of Ness, half a mile along the coast.

Stromness also has a strictly run SYHA **youth hostel** on Helly Hole Road (March–Oct; ☎01856/850589), signposted from the car park outside the *Stromness Hotel*. Alternatively there's *Brown's Hostel*, 45–47 Victoria St (☎01856/850661), an independent youth hostel with bunk beds in shared rooms and kitchen facilities; it's open all day, and there's no curfew.

The *Ferry Inn* on John Street, beside the tourist office, is a popular **restaurant**, serving good, inexpensive meals. *The Coffee Shop*, behind the *Ferry Inn*, is a friendly little café, though it closes at 5pm, as does the *Peedie Coffee Shop* on Victoria Street, the town's oldest establishment. For picnics, *Foodoodles*, also on Victoria Street, is a delicatessen offering cheeses, salamis and made-to-order sandwiches. More expensively, the *Hamnavoe Restaurant* at 35 Graham Place (☎01856/850606) is perhaps Stromness' smartest, making full use of local produce including some delicious vegetarian dishes.

East Mainland

Southeast from Kirkwall, the narrow spur of the **East Mainland** juts out into the North Sea and is joined, thanks to the remarkable Churchill barriers, to the smaller islands of Burray and South Ronaldsay. The land here is densely populated and heavily farmed, but there are several interesting fishing villages and a scattering of unusual historical relics. The northern side of the East Mainland consists of a series of exposed peninsulas, the first of which, **Rerwick Head**, is marked by the remains of World War II gun emplacements. **Mull Head** – the furthest east – is an **RSPB reserve** with a large colony of seabirds, including arctic terns, that swoop on unwanted visitors, screeching threateningly.

On the south coast, just east of the village of **ST MARY'S**, is the **Norwood Museum** (May–Sept Tues–Thurs & Sun 2–5pm & 6–8pm; other times by arrangement; £2; ☎01856/781217), a display of antiques that is the life's work of Norrie Wood,

---

SCAPA FLOW AND THE CHURCHILL BARRIERS

The presence of the huge naval base in **Scapa Flow** during both world wars presented a very tempting target to the Germans, and protecting the fleet was always a nagging problem for the Allies. During World War I, blockships were sunk to guard the eastern approaches, but in October 1939, just weeks after the outbreak of World War II, a German U-boat managed to manoeuvre past the blockships and torpedo the battleship HMS *Royal Oak*, which sank with the loss of 833 lives. The U-boat captain claimed to have acquired local knowledge while fishing in the islands before the war. Today the wreck of the *Royal Oak*, marked by an orange buoy off the Gaitnip Cliffs, is an official war grave.

The sinking of the *Royal Oak* convinced the First Lord of the Admirality, Winston Churchill, that Scapa Flow needed better protection, and in 1940 work began on a series of barriers – known as the **Churchill Barriers** – to seal the waters between the Mainland and the string of islands to the south. Special camps were built to accommodate the 1700 men involved in the project; their numbers were boosted by the surrender of Italy in 1942, when Italian prisoners of war were sent to work here.

Besides the barriers, which are an astonishing feat of engineering when you bear in mind the strength of Orkney tides, the Italians also left behind the beautiful **Italian Chapel** on the first of the islands, Lamb Holm. This, the so-called "miracle of Camp 60", must be one of the greatest adaptations ever, made from two Nissen huts, concrete, barbed wire and parts of a rusting blockship. The chapel deteriorated after the departure of the Italians, but its principal architect, Domenico Chiocchetti, returned in 1960 to restore the building. Today it is beautifully preserved and Mass is said regularly.

a local stonemason who started collecting at the age of thirteen. Only about half of the collection is on display, but it's a fascinating and eccentric selection of bits and pieces from around the world, including pottery, painting, medals, furniture, cutlery, clocks, and even a narwhale's tusk, all housed in a grand Orkney home. If you want to stay, there's **hotel** accommodation at the *Commodore Motel* at St Mary's, which also does satisfying bar meals.

South Ronaldsay

At the southern end of the series of four barriers is the low-lying island of **South Ronaldsay**. The first of the island's old fishing villages, **ST MARGARET'S HOPE**, takes its name either from Margaret, the maid of Norway, who died here in November 1290 while on her way to marry Edward II (then Prince Edward) or less romantically from an ancient chapel in the area. Today St Margaret's Hope is a lovely little gathering of houses at the back of a sheltered bay, and it makes an excellent base from which to explore the area. The village's **Wireless Museum** (June–Sept; check days and times with the tourist office; £1), a small private collection of wartime communications equipment, has some fairly obscure exhibits including a picture of naval women dancing in costumes made from balloon fabric. The village **Smithy** is also a museum (check opening times locally), with a few exhibits relating to this now defunct business.

Despite the fact that it is heavily cultivated, South Ronaldsay also offers some excellent walking, particularly out on the **Howe of Hoxa**, where there is a small broch and a beach at the **Sands O'Right** – the scene of an annual ploughing match in August, in which local boys compete with miniature hand-held ploughs. Further south, seals and their pups can be seen in the autumn in **Wind Wick Bay**, and there is an ancient chambered burial cairn, known as the **Tomb of the Eagles**, at the southeastern corner of the island, where human remains were found alongside eagles' bones. The momument is privately operated and as well as a tour there's hands-on contact with the exhibits (daily 10am–8pm or dusk; £2).

Passenger ferries from John O'Groats arrive at Burwick on the southern tip of the island and are met by buses from Kirkwall; there are also four daily buses between Kirkwall and St Margaret's Hope. The best place **to stay** is the *Creel Restaurant and Rooms* (☎01856/831311; ⑤) in St Margaret's Hope, probably the most enjoyable place to eat in Orkney. Other accommodation includes the *Murray Arms Hotel* (☎01856/831205; ④), with its popular bar, and *The Anchorage* (☎01856/831456; ③), on the seafront. Comfortable **B&Bs** include *Blanster House* (☎01856/831549; ②) and *Bellevue Guest House* (☎01856/831294; ②). For **basic rooms**, head for *Wheems Bothy*, a mile and a half from the War Memorial on the side road leading east (☎01856/831537; £5 per person). Mattresses and ingredients for a wholesome breakfast are provided and organic produce from the croft can be bought. There's a good **café**, the *Coach House*, in St Margaret's Hope, next to the *Murray Arms*.

Hoy

Hoy, Orkney's second largest island, rises sharply out of the sea to the southwest of the Mainland – perhaps the least typical of the islands but certainly the most dramatic, its north and west sides made up of great glacial valleys and mountainous moorland rising to the 1500-foot-high mass of Ward Hill and the enormous seacliffs of St John's Head. This part of the island, though a huge expanse, is virtually uninhabited, with the cluster of houses at Rackwick nestling dramatically in a bay between the cliffs; most of Hoy's four hundred or so residents live on the fertile land in the southeast that is home to the villages of Lyness and Longhope.

Around the island

Much of Hoy's magnificent landscape is embraced by the **RSPB North Hoy Reserve** (which covers most of the northwest end of the island), in which the rough grasses and heather harbour a cluster of arctic plants and a healthy population of mountain hares, as well as merlins, kestrels and peregrine falcons, while the more sheltered valleys are nesting sites for snipe and arctic skua. The best access to the reserve is from the single-track road which follows the **White Glen** across the island to Rackwick. Along the way, the road passes the **Dwarfie Stane**, an unusual solid-stone tomb which dates from 3000 to 2000 BC. A couple of miles further on, the road passes the end of a large open valley which cuts away to the north and along which a footpath runs to the village of **HOY** at the island's northwest tip. On the western side of this valley is the narrow gulley of **Berriedale**, which supports Britain's most northerly native woodland, a huddle of birch, hazel and honeysuckle.

RACKWICK, on the west coast of the island, is a spread of crofts which boldly face the Atlantic weather, flanked by towering sandstone cliffs. Rackwick's crofting community went into a steady decline in the middle of this century and these days many of the houses have been renovated as holiday homes. A small **museum** (open all times), beside the walkers' hostel, tells a little of Rackwick's rough history, and the croft of **Burnmouth Cottage**, just behind the beach, which has been traditionally restored to provide accommodation for walkers (see "Practicalities" below), gives a good idea of how things used to be.

The cliffs at Hoy's northwestern corner are some of the highest in the country, and provide ideal rocky ledges for the nests of thousands of seabirds, including guillemots, kittiwakes, razorbills, puffins and shags. Standing just offshore is the **Old Man of Hoy**, reachable by footpath (4 miles) from Rackwick, a great sandstone column some 450ft high, perched on an old lava flow which protects it from the erosive power of the sea. The Old Man is a popular challenge for rock climbers, and a 1966 ascent was the first televised climb in Britain.

On the opposite side of Hoy, along the sheltered eastern shore, the high moorland gives way to a gentler environment, similar to that of the other islands. At **LYNESS**, which was a main naval base during both world wars, the naval cemetery is surrounded by the scattered remains of what was – incredibly – the largest cinema in Europe, plus the black-and-white concrete facade of the old *Garrison Theatre*, formerly the grand front end of a huge Nissen hut, which disappeared long ago (it's now a private home). The old pump station, which now stands beside the new Lyness ferry terminal, has been turned into the **Scapa Flow Visitor Centre** (Mon–Fri 9am–4pm, Sat & Sun 10.30am–3.30pm; £1), a local museum showing how busy the area was during the wars.

Practicalities

Two **ferry** services run to Hoy: a passenger service from Stromness to the village of Hoy on the northwest edge of the island, and the roll-on, roll-off car ferry from Houton on the Mainland to Lyness and Longhope. If you have time, it's worth staying on Hoy; there are very good, friendly **B&Bs** at *Stonequoy Farm*, Lyness (☎01856/791234; ②), *Burnhouse Farm*, Longhope (☎01856/701263; ②) and the *Old Custom House*, Longhope (☎01856/701358; ②). There are also three hostels providing **basic rooms**: the comfortable *Hoy Outdoor Centre* (☎01856/791261), just up from the pier in Hoy village; the SYHA-affiliated *Rackwick Outdoor Centre* (mid-March to early Aug; ☎01856/791298; no sheets); and the basic *Burnmouth Cottage* (☎01856/791316; no bedding), in a beautiful setting right at the top of the beach. The *Hoy Inn* in Hoy village, down beyond the post office, offers appetizing seafood bar **meals** and snacks. In Lyness the *Anchor Bar*, more prosaic than the name suggests, does typical pub food, with steaks and local fish available in the dining room. A good place for a snack or soup is the *Lyness Visitor Centre* café.

Shapinsay

Just a few miles northwest of Kirkwall, **Shapinsay** is the most accessible of the northern isles. The Balfour family, who had made a small fortune in India, constructed their castle in Baronial style here from 1847 by extending an eighteenth-century farmhouse. They also reformed the island's agricultural system and built **BALFOUR** village, a neat and disciplined cottage development, to house estate workers. **Balfour Castle** (☎01856/711282; full board ⑨; guided tours Wed & Sun afternoon) is a mile or so from the village, hidden by trees, though its towers and turrets are clearly visible from the ferry on the way in. Guided tours must be booked in advance through the Kirkwall tourist office (see p.955).

The Balfour's grandiose efforts in estate management have left some appealingly eccentric relics. Melodramatic fortifications around the harbour include the huge and ornate, if not exactly beautiful, **gatehouse**, now a pub. There's a stone **gasometer** which once supplied castle and village, and, southwest of the pier, the castellated **Dishan Tower**, built as a dovecot but allegedly adapted as a cold-water shower. Elsewhere, the island is heavily cultivated, but within little more than a couple of miles from the ferry terminal there are nice **walks** by the shore to stretches of sand at the **Bay of Furrowend** in the west, with good birdwatching at **Vasa Loch**, and around the sweeping curve of **Veantro Bay** to the north. At the **East Lairo goat farm** (daily except Thurs 12.15–3pm; £2.50; call to arrange transport from ferry; ☎01856/711341) you can meet prizewinning goats and sample their excellent milk, cheese and yoghurt.

Less than thirty minutes from Kirkwall by **ferry**, Shapinsay is an easy day trip, but there's good accommodation on the island if you want to stay. **B&B** is available at comfortable *Girnigoe* (☎01856/711256; ②, full board ③–④), close to the north shore of Veantro Bay. If you're just here for the day, teas and sandwiches from the *Smithy Café* (May–Sept) are your only choice for lunch.

Rousay, Egilsay and Wyre

Just over half a mile away from the Mainland's northern shore, the island of **Rousay** is dominated by high, heather-covered moorland. It's one of the most interesting of the smaller isles, home to a number of intriguing archeological sites, as well as being one of the more accessible. The group of a dozen or so houses above the ferry terminal is the only settlement of any size, but a single road runs around the edge of the island, connecting a string of small farms. The central section of the island is dominated by a cluster of rolling hills, the highest of which is the 750-foot-high **Blotchnie Fiold**. This high ground offers good hill walking, as well as excellent birdwatching: a sizeable section of moorland at the southern end of the island is a protected area in the **RSPB Trumland Reserve**. Here you may well catch a glimpse of merlins, hen harriers, peregrine falcons and red-throated divers. The north and western sides of Rousay are guarded by two sets of steep cliffs, separated by the rocky shores of **Saviskaill Bay**, and again provide spectacular walks and good birdwatching, with puffins, gulls, kittiwakes and arctic terns all nesting here in the summer.

The southwestern side of Rousay is home to the bulk of the island's archeological remains, strung out along the shores of the tide races of **Eynhallow Sound**, which run between the island and the Mainland. Most are on the Westness Walk, a mile-long heritage trail linking Westness Farm, about four miles northwest of the ferry terminal, with **Midhowe Cairn** about a mile further on. Known as "the great ship of death", this well-preserved communal burial chamber dates from about 3500 BC and measures more than 98ft in length. The central chamber, which is like a stone corridor, is partitioned with slabs of rock, with twelve compartments on each side. Archeologists discovered the remains of 25 people inside the tomb, generally in a crouched position with their backs to the wall. This form of burial in stalled tombs dates from the earliest period in the use of chambered burial cairns in Orkney.

A couple of hundred yards south of the Midhowe Cairn is the **Midhowe Broch**, the remains of a fortified Iron Age village which date from the first century AD, and the best preserved of the six brochs that have been found along this shore. It's also thought to be one of the earliest brochs in the Orkneys, with a compact layout that suggests it was a fortified family house rather than a village.

Despite its long history of settlement, Rousay is today home to little more than two hundred people, as this was one of the few parts of Orkney to suffer Highland-style clearances, initially by George William Traill at Quandale in the northwest. His successor, General Traill Burroughs, built the unlovely **Trumland House** (in the trees, near the ferry terminal) in 1873. Continuing to substitute sheep for people, he built a wall to force crofters onto a narrow coastal strip and eventually provoked so much distress and anger that a gunboat had to be sent to restore order.

Sheltering close to the eastern shore of Rousay, the two low-lying smaller islands of Egilsay and Wyre each contain some interesting historical remains. Both are visited by the Rousay ferry as it passes, but in most cases only if someone specifically asks – to arrange this, and to make sure that they come back for you later, call the ferry terminal in Tingwall (☎01856/751360).

The larger of the pair, **Egilsay**, is dominated by the ruins of the St Magnus Church, built on a prominent position in the middle of the island in the twelfth century, probably on the site of a much earlier version. The church, now missing its roof, is the only surviving example of the traditional round-towered churches of Orkney and Shetland and was built as a shrine to the saint who was murdered here in 1115 – a cenotaph marks the spot, about a quarter of a mile southwest of the church.

Over on **Wyre** are the remains of Cubbie Roo's Castle, a twelfth-century Viking stronghold, and the neighbouring St Mary's Chapel, a ruined twelfth-century church, of which only a single wall remains.

Practicalities

Rousay makes a good day trip from the Mainland with regular **ferry sailings** (from Tingwall) and **bus connections** to and from Kirkwall. *Rousay Traveller* (☎01856/821234) runs flexible and very informative minibus tours around the island, or you can rent **bikes** from *Helga's*, behind the *Pier Restaurant* at the ferry terminal (☎01856/821293). Next to the pier is the Trumland Orientation Centre, which is packed with information on every aspect of Rousay past and present. **B&B** is available at *Maybank*, three miles west of the ferry terminal (☎01856/821225; ②); while *Trumland Farm* (☎01856/821252), a mile or so west of the terminal, has a recently built hostel. The only **hotel** on the island is the *Taversoe*, a couple of miles west of the terminal at Frotoft (☎01856/821325; ④), a modern building added onto an old croft. The hotel has a **restaurant** with excellent home cooking, plus a beer garden overlooking the sea. The *Pier Restaurant* (☎01856/821391), right beside the terminal, serves bar-style meals; if you phone in advance, they will pack you a delicious picnic of crab, cheese, fruit and bannock bread. In the evenings, the restaurant functions as a pub.

Eday

Similar in many ways to Rousay and Hoy, the smaller island of **Eday** is dominated by a great block of heather-covered upland, with farmland confined to a narrow strip of coastal ground. Oddly enough, the island is a net exporter of raw materials: peat cut on the high ground is sent to the other northern isles for fuel, and yellow sandstone quarried from the island was used to build the St Magnus Cathedral in Kirkwall.

The island is very sparsely inhabited, and the nearest approximation to a village is the small gathering of houses at **CALFSOUND** in the north, which has the island's only pub. The northern end of the island is also the focus of Eday's archeological heritage. The best way to explore this is to follow the five-mile **Eday Heritage Walk**, which starts at the *Eday Community Enterprise Shop* on the main road in **MILLBOUNDS**, where there's also a display explaining the island's history. Centre stage in the landscape is the **Stone of Setter** – visible from other prehistoric sites and around 15ft high, this eroded, cracked and still enormous standing stone is Orkney's most spectacular. From here, you can climb the Vinquoy Hill to reach the finest of Eday's chambered cairns, the partially restored **Vinquoy Chambered Cairn**. Then you can either head back to the shop or continue north to the dramatic cliffs of **Red Head** and walk around the coast to **Carrick House** (June to mid-Sept Sun afternoon; ☎01857/622260), the grandest home on Eday, originally built by the laird of Eday in 1633. It was once the prison of the pirate John Gow – on whom Sir Walter Scott's novel *The Pirate* is based – whose ship *The Revenge* ran aground here.

Eday's **ferry** terminal is at **Backaland** pier in the south; it's also possible to catch the *British Airways Express* (☎01856/873457) plane from Kirkwall to Eday's London Airport on Wednesdays. You can rent **bikes** from *Millbank* (☎01857/622205) near the post office. B&B **accommodation** is available at *Skaill Farm*, a traditional farmhouse just south of the airport (closed May; ☎01857/6222271; ⑤ including dinner), *Greentoft* on the eastern side of Ward Hill in the south (☎01857/622269; ②) and *Blett* in the north of the island (☎01857/622248; ③). The SYHA-affiliated **hostel** just north of the airport is run by *Eday Community Enterprises* (April–Sept; ☎01857/622248). There's a pub, *The Pirate Gow*, overlooking Calf Sound in the north of the island which does **bar meals** on Friday, Saturday and Sunday evenings, specializing in seafood, vegetarian and vegan dishes.

Stronsay

A three-pronged shape to the southeast of Eday, **Stronsay** is a beautiful, low-lying island that for a long time lived off its herring and kelp industries. Today Stronsay supports a sizeable population of farmers, and boasts some interesting bird and plant life and a scattering of vague archeological remains.

The only village is **WHITEHALL**, made up of a couple of rows of small fishermen's cottages, and blessed with a hotel and pub. Stronsay has few real sights, but like all of these northern isles it offers some fantastic walking. The low-lying central land is almost entirely given over to farming and it's on the coast that you'll see the island at its best, with cliffs home to several seabird colonies and seals basking on exposed rocks at low tide. On the island's western arm there are two broad, arching beaches, the **Bay of Holland** and **St Catherine's Bay**, while over in the east there's a small bird reserve on the shores of **Mill Bay**, just south of Whitehall. Birdwatching is at its best here in September and October, when easterly winds bring migrants such as thrushes, warblers, flycatchers and wrynecks.

Stronsay is served by a twice-daily **ferry** service to Whitehall. The island has one very welcoming **hotel**, *The Stronsay* (☎01857/616213; ②), on the quayside in Whitehall; the bar here serves simple meals. For ornithologists, the *Stronsay Bird Reserve* (☎01857/616363) offers full board (③), bed and breakfast (②) or camping on the shores of Mill Bay. **B&B** is also available at *Airy* (☎01857/616231; ②). You can **rent cars** (*D.S. Peace*; ☎01857/616335) or **boats** (*J. Stevenson*; ☎01857/616341).

Sanday

As its name suggests, **Sanday** is the most insubstantial of the North Isles, a great drifting dune strung out between several rocky points. The island's bays and clean white sands are the finest in Orkney, and in dry, clear weather it's a superb place to spend a day or two. The island has a long history as a shipping hazard, with many wrecks smashed against its shores, although the construction of the Start Point Lighthouse 1802–06, on the island's exposed eastern tip, reduced the risk for seafarers. Today the islanders survive largely from farming and fishing, supplemented by a small knitting business, and a rabbit farm, which specializes in the production of Angora wool.

The shoreline supports a healthy seal and otter population, and behind the beaches are stretches of beautiful open grassland, thick with wild flowers during the spring and summer. The entire coastline presents the opportunity for superb walks, with splendid sandy jaggy protected by jaggy outcrops of rock. Sanday is particularly rich in archeology, with hundreds of sites including cairns, brochs and burnt mounds. The most impressive is the chambered cairn at **Quoyness** (on the peninsula about a mile east of the ferry terminal), which dates from the third millennium BC. The main chamber is 13ft long and holds six small cells, which contained bones and skulls.

Ferries to Sanday arrive in **KETTLETOFT**, a little gathering of houses which is the nearest thing to a village; the **airfield** is just north of here. For **accommodation**, *The Belsair Hotel* (☎01857/600206; ③) in the village is comfortable and does delicious packed lunches as well as offering a varied menu in the restaurant. Car, caravan and trout-fishing boat **rental** are available from Mrs Muir (☎01857/600331).

Westray and Papa Westray

A pair of exposed islands on the western side of the group, Westray and Papa Westray – or "Papey" as Orcadians call it – bear the full brunt of the Atlantic weather. Westray has a fairly stable population of seven hundred or so, producing superb beef, scallops, shellfish and a large catch of whitefish, with its own small fish-processing factory. The main village is **PIEROWALL** in the north, where a handful of impressive ruins, includes the seventeeth-century **Notland Castle**, which stands just inland from the village, and the medieval parish church of **St Mary's** (on the northern side of the village), both of which can be visited at all times.

The spectacular cliffs of **Noup Head**, at the northwestern tip of the island, are packed with nesting seabirds during the summer months. Further south, there's an interesting walk from Tuquoy to Langskaill taking in the **Cross Kirk**, which, although ruined, is still one of the most complete medieval churches in Orkney. Along the shore nearby are the remains of a Norse settlement; on the east side, the ruined walls on the sea stack known as the **Castle of Burrian** reveal the presence of an early Christian settlement. The stack is an excellent place to see puffins in the nesting season.

Across the short Papa Sound, the neighbouring island and former medieval pilgrimage centre of **Papa Westray** is connected to Westray by the world's shortest scheduled flight – two minutes in duration, less with a following wind. Try and stroll out to the **Knap of Howar**, on the western shore, a Neolithic farm building from around 3500 BC that makes a fair claim to being the oldest standing house in Europe, and the remains of **St Boniface's Church**, dating from the twelfth century. On the northern tip of the island there's yet another **RSPB reserve** which plays host to one of the largest arctic tern colonies in Europe, as well as arctic skuas, razor bills and guillemots.

Practicalities

Westray is served by roll-on, roll-off car **ferry** from Kirkwall operated by the *Orkney Islands Shipping Company* (☎01856/872044). There's also a lift-on, lift-off ferry service from Kirkwall to Papa Westray (Tues & Thurs); otherwise you can catch the passenger-only ferry from Westray to Papa Westray, which connects with the Westray service from Kirkwall. It's also possible to **fly** to both islands on *British Airways Express* from Kirkwall to Papa Westray (Mon–Sat) and to Westray (Mon–Sat).

There are two hotels on Westray. The *Pierowall* (☎01857/677208; ②) is a typical North Isle hotel, simple but welcoming with a popular bar and a reputation for fish and chips. Rather more luxurious is the *Cleaton House* (☎01857/677508; ④) about three miles south of Pierowall; with excellent bar and restaurant meals at good prices, it is one of the best eating places in Orkney. B&B accommodation is available at *Sand O' Gill* (☎01857/677374; ②); you can also rent bicycles from them. If you'd like to play the somewhat eccentric golf course on the links north of Notland Castle, clubs can be rented from *Tulloch's* (☎01857/677373) shop. On Papa Westray, the island's *Community Co-operative* (☎01857/644267) runs a hotel (④) restaurant and SYHA-affiliated hostel at Beltane House; they can also fix up B&B (③).

North Ronaldsay

North Ronaldsay, Orkney's most northerly island, has a unique outpost atmosphere, brought about by its extreme isolation. Measuring just three miles by one and rising just 66ft above sea level, the island is almost overwhelmed by the enormity of the sky, the strength of wind, and, of course, the ferocity of the sea – so much so that its very existence seems an act of tenacious defiance. Despite these adverse conditions, North Ronaldsay has been inhabited for centuries. Today the population is mostly over sixty, but the island is still heavily farmed, the land dotted with old-style crofts, their roofs made from huge flagstones. With no natural harbours and precious little farmland, the islanders have been forced to make the most of what they have and seaweed has played an important role in the local economy. The island's sheep, which are a unique breed, tough and goat-like, feed mostly on seaweed, giving their flesh a dark tone and a rich, gamey taste.

The largest buildings on the island are Holland House, which was built by the Traill family who bought the island in 1727, and the lighthouse, which towers over 125ft in height, and is the only feature to interrupt the horizon. Grey and common seals are prevalent on the island, and it serves as an important stopping-off point for migratory birds passing through on their way to and from breeding grounds in Iceland, Greenland and Scandinavia. The peak times of year for migrants are from late March to early June and from mid-August to early November, although there are also many breeding species which spend the spring and summer here, including gulls, terns, waders and cormorants.

There's a once-weekly ferry to North Ronaldsay, usually on Fridays, but sailing may vary depending on the weather so check with the *Orkney Islands Shipping Company* a day before you hope to travel. A more flexible, if more costly option, is to catch a *British Airways Express* plane from Kirkwall (Mon–Sat). The *North Ronaldsay Bird Observatory*, at Twingness Croft on the southwest tip of the island (☎01857/633200; ③–④), runs on wind and solar power. B&B is available at *Garso*, in the northeast (☎01857/633244; ③), or at *Rinarsay Guest House* (☎01857/633221; ③). *Garso* also operates a car-rental and taxi service. Camping is possible, but you must ask the permission of landowners. You can rent bicycles from *Airfield Goods and Services* (☎01857/633220), by the airfield in the west of the island.

Fair Isle

Halfway between Shetland and Orkney and very different from both, Fair Isle supports a vibrant community of around seventy. At one time the population was not far short of four hundred, but clearances forced emigration from the middle of the nineteenth century. By the 1950s, the population had shrunk to just 44, a point at which evacuation and abandonment of the island was seriously considered. George

Waterston, who'd bought the island and set up a bird observatory in 1948, passed it into the care of the NTS in 1954 and rejuvenation began. The island can now boast an advanced electricity system integrating wind and diesel generation; and crafts including boatbuilding, the making of fiddles, felt and stained glass have been developed.

The north end of the island rises like a wall; the **Sheep Rock**, a sculpted stack of rock and grass on the east side is one of the island's most dramatic features. The social and natural history of the island is compellingly told in the **George Waterston Memorial Centre** (☎01595/760244; free), in the village of Stonybreck. The present **Bird Observatory** dates from 1969, just above the North Haven where the ferry from Grutness in Shetland arrives, and is one of the major European centres for ornithology and its work in watching, trapping, recording and ringing birds goes on all year. Fair Isle is a landfall for a huge number and range of migrant birds during the spring and autumn passages. Migration routes converge here and more than 340 species, including many rarities, have been noted.

Fair Isle is even better known for its **knitting** patterns, still produced with as much skill as ever by the local knitwear co-operative, though not in the quantities which you might imagine from a walk around city department stores; there are demonstrations at the Hall from time to time, and the George Waterson Memorial Centre fills in the history. The idea that the islanders borrowed all their patterns from the three hundred shipwrecked Spanish seamen is nowadays regarded as a somewhat patronizing myth.

Practicalities

The **ferry** connects Fair Isle with either Lerwick (alternate Thurs; 4hr 30min) or Sumburgh (Tues, Sat & alternate Thurs; 4hr); for bookings contact *J.W. Stout* (☎01595/760222) in advance. You can also fly from the airport at **Tingwall**, six miles northwest of Lerwick (Mon, Wed, Fri & Sat; a day trip is possible on Wed & Fri).

If you want to **stay**, the *Fair Isle Lodge and Bird Observatory* (April–Oct; ☎01595/760258; ⑤, dorms with full board £20 per person) offers good home cooking and perhaps the opportunity to lend a hand with the observatory's research programme. For good **B&B** accommodation, there's the beautifully restored eighteenth-century *Auld Haa* (☎01595/760264; ③, or ⑤ full-board), where Sir Walter Scott was once entertained, *Schoolton* (☎01595/760250; ④) or *Barkland* (☎01595/760247; ④), all in the south end of the island.

Shetland

Many maps place the **Shetland Islands** in a box somewhere off Aberdeen, but in fact Bergen in Norway is a lot closer than Edinburgh and the Arctic Circle nearer than Manchester. The Shetland **landscape** is a product of the struggle between rock and the forces of water and ice that have, over millennia, tried to break it to pieces. Smoothed by the last glaciation, the surviving land has been exposed to the most violent **weather** experienced in the British Isles. In winter, gales are routine and Shetlanders take even the occasional hurricane in their stride, marking a calm fine day as "a day atween weathers". There are some good spells of dry, sunny weather from June to September, but it's the "simmer dim", the twilight which replaces darkness at this latitude, which makes Shetland summers so memorable; in June especially, the northern sky is an unfinished sunset of blue and burnished copper.

People have lived in Shetland since **prehistoric times**, certainly from about 3500 BC, and the islands display several spectacular remains, including the best-preserved broch anywhere. For six centuries Shetland was part of the **Norse empire** which brought together Sweden, Denmark and Norway. In 1469, Shetland followed Orkney in being mortgaged to Scotland, King Christian of Norway being unable to raise the

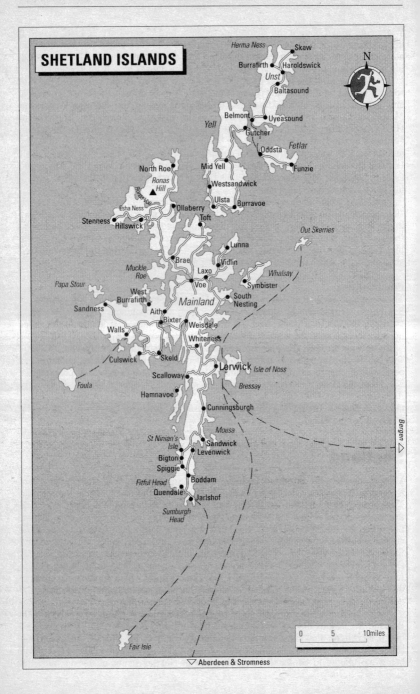

SHETLAND ISLANDS

Herma Ness
Skaw
Burrafirth
Haroldswick
Unst
Baltasound
Belmont
Uyeasound
Yell
Gutcher
Fetlar
Oddsta
Funzie
North Roe
Mid Yell
Ronas Hill
Westsandwick
Ulsta
Burravoe
Esha Ness
Ollaberry
Stenness
Toft
Hillswick
Out Skerries
Lunna
Brae
Vidlin
Muckle Roe
Laxo
Papa Stour
Voe
Symbister
West Burrafirth
South Nesting
Whalsay
Sandness
Aith
Mainland
Bixter
Weisdale
Walls
Whiteness
Culswick
Skeld
Scalloway
Lerwick
Isle of Noss
Foula
Hamnavoe
Bressay
Cunningsburgh
Mousa
St Ninian's Isle
Sandwick
Bigton
Levenwick
Spiggie
Fitful Head
Boddam
Quendale
Jarlshof
Sumburgh Head
Fair Isle

Bergen △

N

0   5   10miles

▽ Aberdeen & Stromness

dowry for the marriage of his daughter Margaret to King James III. The Scottish king annexed Shetland in 1472 and the mortgage was never redeemed. Though Shetland retained links with other North Sea communities, religious and administrative practice gradually become Scottish; and mainland **lairds** set about grabbing what land and power they could. Later, especially in rural Shetland, the economy fell increasingly into the hands of merchant lairds; they controlled the fish trade and the tenants who supplied it through a system of truck, or forced barter.

During the two world wars, Shetland's role as gatekeeper between the North Sea and North Atlantic meant that the defence of the islands and control of the seas around them were critical. With a rebirth of the local economy in the 1960s, Shetland was able to claim, in the following decade, that the **oil industry** needed the islands more than they needed it. Careful negotiation, backed up by pioneering local legislation, produced a substantial income from oil which has been reinvested in the community. Now that income is diminishing, local politicians are having to make some very difficult choices about the way they to spend what's left and the islanders are thinking afresh how to carve out a living in a new century.

Whatever else you do in Shetland you're sure to be based, at least for a day or two, in the lively port of **Lerwick**, the only town of any size and the hub of all transport and communications. Many parts of Shetland can be reached from here in a day trip. South of Lerwick, a narrow finger of land runs some twenty miles to **Sumburgh Head**; this area is particularly rich in archeological remains including the Iron Age **Broch of Mousa** and the ancient settlement of **Jarlshof**. To the north and west, the Mainland is bleaker and more sparsely inhabited, although the landscape, particularly to the north, opens out in scale and grandeur as it comes face to face with the Atlantic. Off the west coast, **Papa Stour** lies just a mile from Sandness and boasts some spectacular caves and stacks; much further out are the distinctive peaks and precipitous cliffs of **Foula**. To the northeast, Shetland ends with the North Isles of **Yell**, **Unst** and **Fetlar**, reaching far up into the North Sea.

Lerwick and around

For Shetlanders, there's only one place to stop, meet and do business and that's "da toon", **LERWICK**. Very much the focus of Shetland's commercial life, Lerwick is home to about 7500 people, roughly a third of the islands' population. All year, its sheltered harbour at the heart of the town is busy with ferries, fishing boats, oil-rig supply vessels and a variety of more specialized craft including seismic survey and naval

---

GETTING TO SHETLAND

There are three **car ferry** routes to Shetland. From **Aberdeen**, *P&O Scottish Ferries* (☎01224/572615 or 01595/694848) operates a direct overnight service four times a week (5 in winter) to **Lerwick** (14hr). There's also a twice-weekly afternoon/overnight indirect service (1 in winter) which calls at Stromness in Orkney (8hr to Stromness, 8hr on to Lerwick). For a very brief taste of Shetland, *P&O* offers short, ship-based mini-cruises to Shetland, some of which take in Orkney.

The main air operators run their services into **Sumburgh Airport**, 25 miles south of Lerwick; there are connecting bus services. *British Airways* (☎0345/222111 or 01950/460345), including its subsidiary *British Airways Express* (☎01595/840246) – still often called *Loganair* – fly from Aberdeen, Edinburgh, Glasgow, Kirkwall and Wick non-stop and also from Birmingham, Inverness, London and Manchester. *Business Air* (☎0500/340146) flies from Aberdeen non-stop and from East Midlands, Edinburgh, Glasgow and Manchester. *Business Air* is usually less expensive, but *BA* has special offers from time to time.

vessels from all round the North Sea. In autumn and winter particularly, the harbour hosts sixty or more **"klondykers"** – fish factory ships from eastern Europe – and the town is thronged with their crews, who stock up on everything from cabbages to old washing machines and ancient Lada cars. In summer, the quaysides in the centre of town come alive with visiting yachts, cruise liners and the occasional tall sailing ship. Behind the old harbour is the compact town centre, solidly stone-built with Commercial Street, the main shopping area, at its heart; from here narrow lanes rise westwards climbing the hill to the late-Victorian "new town".

Lerwick began life as a temporary settlement, catering to the Dutch herring fleet in the seventeenth century, who brought as many as 20,000 men. During the nineteenth century, with the presence of ever-larger Scottish, English and Scandinavian boats, it became a major fishing centre, and whalers called to pick up crews on their way to their northern hunting grounds. In 1839, the visiting Danish governor of Faroe declared that "everything made me feel that I had come to the land of opulence". Business was conducted largely from buildings known as lodberries, each typically having a store, a house and small yard on a private jetty. **Smuggling** was part of the daily routine and there are reputed to be secret tunnels connecting the lodberries to illicit stores. During the late nineteenth century, the construction of the Esplanade along the shore isolated several lodberries from the sea, but further south beyond the *Queen's Hotel* are some that still show their original form. Lerwick expanded considerably at this time and the large houses and grand public buildings established then still dominate, notably the impressive **Town Hall**.

The Town

Commercial Street, universally known to locals as **"da Street"**, is still very much the core of Lerwick. Its narrow, winding form provides shelter from the elements even on the worst days, and is where locals meet, shop, exchange news and gossip and bring in the New Year to the sound of a harbourful of ships' sirens. The Street's northern end is marked by the towering walls of **Fort Charlotte** (daily June–Sept 9am–10pm; Oct–May 9am–4pm; free), originally built for Charles II between 1665 and 1667, during the war with the Dutch, and attacked and burnt down by them in August 1673. In 1782 it was rebuilt and given its name in honour of George III's queen.

Now a desirable place to live in, it's not so long ago that the narrow **lanes**, that connect Commercial Street to the **Hillhead**, were regarded as slumlike dens of iniquity, from which the better-off escaped to the Victorian gridiron "new town" laid out to the west. The stone-flagged lanes run uphill, lined by tall houses with trees, fuschia, flowering currant and honeysuckle pouring over the garden walls. Hillhead is dominated by the splendid **Town Hall** (Mon–Fri 10am–noon & 2–3.30pm; free) a Gothic castle with the stern reverence of a church. Built by public subscription, the many carved stone panels, coats of arms and stained-glass windows celebrate Shetland's history and, in particular, the islands' commercial and cultural links with other parts of Britain and Europe.

On Lower Hillhead, southwest of the town hall, the **Shetland Museum** (Mon, Thurs & Fri 10am–7pm, Tues, Wed & Sat 10am–5pm; free) houses an interesting range of Shetland artefacts relating to the islands' history and prehistory. More unusual exhibits include a stone carving by Adam Christie (1869–1950), a Shetlander who is perhaps best known for his application to patent a submarine invisible to enemies because it would be made of glass.

A mile or so southwest from the town centre on the road leading to Sumburgh, lies the fortified **Clickimin Broch**, began around 700 BC and later enclosed by a defensive wall, whose main tower once rose to around 40ft, though the remains are now around 10ft high. Excavation of the site has unearthed an array of domestic goods that suggest international trade, including a Roman glass bowl thought to have been made in Alexandria around 100 AD.

In earlier times the seasonal nature of the Shetland fishing industry led to the establishment of small stores, known as **böds**, often incorporating sleeping accommodation, beside the beaches where fish were landed and dried. About a mile and a half north of the town centre, right off the A970, stands the beautifully restored **Böd of Gremista** (June–Aug Wed–Sun 10am–1pm & 2pm–5pm; £1), built later than most (at the end of the seventeenth century), and the birthplace of Arthur Anderson (1792–1868), co-founder of the *Peninsular and Oriental Steam Navigation Company (P&O)*. The displays inside explore Anderson's life as naval seaman, businessman, philanthropist, Shetland's first native MP and founder of Shetland's first newspaper.

Practicalities

Arriving by **ferry** you'll come ashore at the *P&O* terminal in the north harbour, about a mile from the town centre. If you arrive by **plane**, almost certainly at Sumburgh Airport (✆01950/460654) at the southern tip of the Mainland, there are regular buses to Lerwick; taxis (around £25) and car rental are also available. **Buses** stop on the Esplanade, very close to the old harbour and Market Cross, or at the **bus station** on Commercial Rd about a quarter of a mile to the north. The **tourist office** at the Market Cross on Commercial St (Mon–Sat 8am–6pm; ✆01595/693434) is a good source of information. For more details of what's on listen in to "Good Evening Shetland" (*BBC Radio Shetland*, 92.7MHz FM; Mon–Fri 5.30pm) or buy the *Shetland Times* (Fri).

Lerwick has lots of good **accommodation**, though in July, August and over the Folk Festival weekend in April, you should reserve in advance. The *Kvelsdro House Hotel*, Greenfield Place (✆01595/692195; ⑨) is Lerwick's luxury option, followed by the beautiful old *Queen's Hotel*, right on the waterfront by the old harbour on Commercial Street (✆01595/692826; ⑧). Two upper-range guest houses are *Glen Orchy House*, 20 Knab

---

UP HELLY-AA

On the last Tuesday in January, whatever the weather, the Victorian "new town" of Lerwick is the setting for the most spectacular part of the **Lerwick Up Helly-Aa**, a huge, fire festival, the largest of several held in Shetland in January and February. Around 900 torch-bearing participants, all male and all in extraordinary costumes, march in procession behind a grand Viking longship. The annually appointed Guizer Jarl and his "squad" appear as Vikings and brandish shields and silver axes; each of the 40 or so other squads is dressed for their part in the subsequent entertainment, perhaps as giant insects, space invaders or ballet dancers. Their circuitous route leads to the King George V Playing Field at which, after due ceremony, all the torches are thrown into the longship, creating an enormous bonfire. A fireworks display follows, then the participants, known as "guizers", set off in their squads to do the rounds of more than a dozen "halls" (which usually includes at least one hotel, the ferry terminal and the Town Hall) from around 8.30pm in the evening until 8am the next morning, performing some kind of act – often a comedy routine – at each.

Up Helly-Aa itself is not that ancient, dating only from Victorian times; but it replaced an older Christmas tradition of burning tar-barrels and other sorts of mischief. Around 1870, perhaps as a result of frustration at the controls increasingly imposed by the Town Council, the tar-barrellers moved their activities into January, coined the name Up-Helly-Aa and introduced both a torchlight procession and an element of disguise; it was some years, though, before the festival took on its Viking associations. Although this is essentially a community event with entry to halls by invitation only, visitors are welcome at the Town Hall, for which tickets are sold in early January; contact the tourist office well in advance. To catch some of the atmosphere of the event check out the **Up Helly-Aa exhibition** (mid-May to Sept Tues & Sat 2–4pm, Thurs & Fri 7–9pm; £1) in the gallery shed on St Sunniva St, where you can see a full-size longship, costumes, shields and photographs.

Rd (☎01595/692031; ⑤) and *Carradale Guest House*, 36 King Harald St (☎01595/695411; ③). For **B&Bs**, try *Mrs Irving*, The Old Manse, 9 Commercial St (☎01595/696301; ③); *Mrs Clark*, 9 Knab Rd (☎01595/693101; ③); *Woosung*, 43 St Olaf St (☎01595/693687; ②); or *Miss Goudie*, 78 King Harald St (☎01595/692384; ③). The Lerwick **youth hostel** (mid-April to Oct; ☎01595/692114) at Islesburgh House on King Harald Street offers unusually comfortable surroundings in a building recently refurbished and extended. **Campers** should head for the *Clickimin Caravan and Camp Site*, Lochside (late April to Sept; ☎01595/694555), a newish site next to a leisure centre with plenty of facilities, including good hot showers.

Lerwick's **eating** options include two good Indian restaurants – *The Golden Bengal*, 33 North Rd and *Raba*, 26 Commercial Rd – and a Chinese, *The Golden Coach*, 17 Hillhead. For something more indigenous, try one of the hotel restaurants: the *Kvelsdro House, Lerwick* and *Queen's* hotels all serve local seafood. *The Candlestick Maker*, 33 Commercial Rd, is a tiny bistro offering simple lunches and a fuller evening menu with vegetarian options. *Solotti's* café, Commercial St, is something of an institution, serving filled rolls, cakes, teas, coffees and great ice cream. Lastly, there's the relaxed, friendly *Havly Centre*, a Norwegian Christian venture on Charlotte Street, much frequented by locals and tourists, with excellent snacks including delicious Norwegian open sandwiches.

At weekends or when the fishing fleet is confined to harbour, Lerwick's **pubs** are great social centres, packed full and brimming with atmosphere; try the downstairs bar in the *Thule* on the Esplanade, an archetypal seaport pub and very much part of Lerwick life; or up Mounthooly St, at the upstairs bar in the *Lounge*. Local musicians usually play Saturday lunchtime and some evenings. Afterwards, the crowd move on to *Posers* in the *Grand Hotel* on Commerical St; the town's longest-established dance venue. **Music** features very strongly in Shetland life and in April, when musicians from all over the world converge on Shetland for the excellent **Folk Festival** (☎01595/694757). In October, there's an **Accordion and Fiddle Festival**: similar format, same mailing address but a different musical focus and separately organized. Throughout the year, there are **traditional dances** in local halls all over Shetland; the whole community turns up and you can watch, or join in. The occasional major concert by visiting groups is almost always staged in the **Clickimin Leisure Centre** beside Clickimin Loch on the west side of the town, although smaller ensembles appear in the town hall.

Bressay and Noss

Shielding Lerwick from the full force of the North Sea is the island of **Bressay**, dominated at its southern end by the conical Ward Hill and accessible on an hourly car and passenger ferry from Lerwick. At the end of the nineteenth century, Bressay had a population of more than a thousand, due mostly to the prosperity brought by the Dutch herring fleet, now about 320 people live here. The island provides interesting cliff and coastal walks, notably to the lighthouse, and huge World War I guns at the northern and southern ends of the island. In the past, Sir Walter Scott and royal visitors have stayed in the laird's Gardie House, one of the largest and, in its Classical detail, finest of the Shetland laird houses. Many visitors head straight for Noss, the smaller but spectacular island to the east, but if you want to **stay** on Bressay, try the *Maryfield House Hotel* (☎01595/820207; ④) by the ferry terminal.

Just off Bressay's western shore **Noss**, which means "a point of rock", was inhabited until World War II but is now given over to sheep farming and is also a National Nature Reserve managed by Scottish Natural Heritage. They operate an inflatable as a ferry from the landing stage below the car park at the east side of Bressay (end May to Aug; on demand except Mon, Thurs and when a red flag is flown on Noss). On the island, the old farmhouse of **Gungstie** contains a small **visitor centre** where you can find out about the island's amazing birdlife and its brief history as a stud farm for Shetland ponies, which were sent to work in the mines of county Durham. The most memorable feature of Noss is its cliffed coastline rising to a peak at the massive 500-foot **Noup,** home to vast colonies of cliff-nesting gannets, puffins, guillemots, shags, razorbills and fulmars, a truly wonderful sight and one of the highlights of Shetland. Be warned: if you stray off the marked path, the great skuas and arctic skuas will do their best to intimidate with dive-bombing raids that may hit you hard.

South Mainland

Shetland's **South Mainland** is a long, thin finger of land, only three or four miles wide, ending in the cliffs of Sumburgh Head and Fitful Head. The main road hugs the eastern side of the Clift Hills which form the peninsula's backbone; on the west side, there's no road between Scalloway and Maywick except for a short spur from Easter to Wester Quarff. It's a beautiful area with wild landscapes but also rich farmland, and has yielded some of Shetland's most impressive archeological treasures.

From Leebitton, halfway to Sumburgh Head, you can take a summer ferry to the small **Isle of Mousa** on which stands the best-preserved broch anywhere. *Tom Jamieson* (☎01950/431367) runs the ferry from the jetty near the impressive laird's house, Sand Lodge. **Mousa Broch** features in both *Egil's Saga* and the *Orkneyinga Saga*, contemporary chronicles of Norse exploration and settlement. In the former, a couple eloping from Norway to Iceland take refuge after being shipwrecked in 900 AD, while in the latter, the broch is besieged by Earl Harald Maddadson when his mother is abducted and brought here from Orkney by Erlend the Young, who wanted to marry her. Rising to more than 40ft and with its curving stonework intact, it has a remarkable presence. The low entrance passage leads through two concentric walls to a central courtyard. Between the walls, there are cells and galleries in which **storm petrels** breed and a rough staircase leads to the top (a torch is useful). Elsewhere on Mousa, there are remains of several buildings, some of which housed the eleven families who lived here in the eighteenth century. Seals can often be seen at the bay on the east side.

Of all the archeological sites in Shetland, **Jarlshof** (April–Sept daily 9.30am–6.30pm, £2; Oct–March, grounds open at all times; free) is the largest and most complex. There's evidence of more than four thousand years of continuous occupation, with buildings dating from the Stone Age to the early seventeenth century. The guide book, available from the small **visitor centre** where you buy tickets, is almost essential in understanding the many layers of human activity laid out before you. As well as Neolithic and medieval buildings these include a **broch, interconnected wheelhouses** and **Norse longhouses**. Sir Walter Scott, rather than any Viking, was responsible for the name; while visiting Shetland in 1814 he decided to use part of the ruins, the Old House of Sumburgh, in his novel, *The Pirate* (see p.964). The **Old House** (only the walls remain) dates from the late sixteenth century, when it was home first to **Robert Stewart**, Lord of the Northern Isles and later to **William Bruce**, first representative in Shetland of another immigrant Scottish family whose landholdings were to become substantial.

The Mainland comes to a dramatic end at **Sumburgh Head**, about two miles from Jarlshof. The **lighthouse**, designed by Robert Stevenson, was built in 1821; although not open to the public its grounds offer great views to Noss in the north and Fair Isle to the south. This is also the easiest place in Shetland to get close to **puffins**. During the nesting season, you simply need to look over the western wall by the lighthouse gate to see them arriving at their burrows with beakfuls of fish or giving flying lessons to their offspring; on no account should you try to climb over the wall. To the west of Sumburgh Head, on the other side of Garths Ness, lies a rusting ship's bow, all that remains of the *Braer*, a Liberian-registered, American-owned oil tanker that ran onto the rocks here on January 5, 1993, a date now etched in the memory of every Shetlander. The thousands of tonnes of spilt **oil** were churned and ultimately cleansed by huge waves built by hurricane-force winds which, unusually even for Shetland, blew for most of January spreading a mist of oil over the South Mainland, Burra and Tondra.

Practicalities

Public transport to the South Mainland is relatively straightforward: there are between three and four **buses** a day between Lerwick and Sumburgh Airport and between four and six buses daily to Sandwick. **Accommodation** includes the *Sumburgh Hotel* (☎01950/460201; ⑤), next to Jarlshof, and a handful of B&Bs in Sandwick: *Mrs M. Leask* at 3 Swinister (☎01950/431302; ②), *Marelda* (☎01950/431379; ②) and *Solbrekke* (☎01950/431410; ②). **Simple accommodation** is available at the *Cunningsburgh Community Club* (☎01950/431321 or 431241); it has dorm beds, good showers and a well-equipped kitchen; or there's the *Levenwick Campsite* (May–Sept; ☎01950/422207), which has adequate facilities and a superb view over the east coast.

Scalloway and the Westside

The village of **SCALLOWAY** was once the capital of Shetland, but its importance waned through the eighteenth century as Lerwick, just six miles to the east, grew in trading success and status. Scalloway's prosperity, always closely linked to the fluctuations of the fishing industry, has recently been given a boost with investment in new fish-processing factories, and in the impressive North Atlantic Fisheries College on the west side of the harbour.

In spite of modern developments nearby, the scene is dominated by the imposing shell of **Scalloway Castle**, built in 1600 for Earl Patrick Stewart using forced labour and thus seen as a powerful symbol of oppression. Stewart eventually upset influential people and was arrested in 1609; his son attempted an insurrection and both were executed in Edinburgh in 1615. On Main Street, a small **museum** (May–Sept Tues–Thurs 2–5pm, Sat 10am–1pm & 2–5pm; free) explains the importance of fishing and tells the story of the **Shetland Bus**, the link between Shetland and Norway which helped to sustain the Norwegian wartime resistance.

Transport in the area is provided by a **bus service** from Lerwick (from the bus stop at the *Thule Bar* on the Esplanade) which runs eight times daily to Scalloway and twice a day to Hamnavoe. **Accommodation** in Scalloway includes *Brylyn Guest House*, Port Arthur (☎01595/880407; ③); and in Upper Scalloway, *Broch Guest House* (☎01595/880767; ③), and *Hildasay Guest House* (☎01595/880822; ③) which specializes in angling holidays. In Hamnavoe there's a friendly **B&B** run by *Mrs J. Marsden*, Setter (☎01595/859688; ②), offering diving and hand-spinning/dyeing tuition. There aren't many **places to eat**, but the *Castle Café* in Scalloway has an excellent reputation for fish and chips, and the *Kiln Bar* does bar food. The *North Atlantic Fisheries College* has a very pleasant restaurant doing teas and snacks as well as meals, with wonderful harbour views.

The Westside

At its heart, **Westside**'s rolling brown and purple moorland is scattered with dozens of small picturesque lochs gleaming blue or silver and patches of bright green, where cultivation and reseeding have taken place. The **coastal scenery**, cut by several deep voes, is very varied; aside from dramatic cliffs, there are intimate coves and some fine beaches. The crossroads for the area is effectively Bixter, southwest of which, at **STANEYDALE**, lies a remarkably large **Neolithic structure** measuring more than 40ft by 20ft internally with immensely thick walls, still around 4ft high, whose roof would have been supported by spruce posts. Called a temple by the archeologist who excavated because it resembled one on Malta, this building, whatever its function, was twice as large as similarly shaped houses and was certainly of great importance, perhaps as some kind of community centre. At nearby Skeld, you can visit the *Shetland Smokehouse*, which smokes salmon and other local produce.

On the west coast the rounded form of **Sandess Hill** (750ft) falls steeply away into the Atlantic. It's an attractive spot; its fertile fields and wide beach come as a contrast to the peat moorland around. The town's modern **spinning mill** (Mon–Fri 8am–5pm; free) produces pure Shetland wool and welcomes visitors; you can watch how they manage to spin the exceptionally fine Shetland wool into yarn.

The only **hotel** in the area is the beautifully situated *Burrastow House* (☎01595/ 809307; ⑨) about three miles west of Walls and dating from 1759; it's also one of the best places to eat in Shetland, and booking is strongly recommended. There are quite a few **B&Bs**, including *Effirth*, just south of Bixter (☎01595/810204; ②); *Reawick House* (☎01595/860273; ③); *Hogan*, Bridge of Walls (☎01595/809375; ②); and *Trouligarth*, west of Walls (☎01595/809373; ②).

Papa Stour

A mile offshore from Sandness is the quintessentially peaceful island of **Papa Stour** ("big island of the priests"); apart from early Christian connections, it was home, in the eighteenth century to people who were mistakenly believed to have been lepers. The sea has eroded its volcanic rocks to produce some of the most impressive coastal scenery in Shetland, with stacks, caves and natural arches. The east side is the most fecund area, partly because much of the soil from the western side was painstakingly transported here. In the nineteenth century, Papa Stour supported around three hundred inhabitants; today the island supports a community of thirty or so. A trail leaflet is available from the tourist office in Lerwick; as well as prehistoric houses and burial cairns. At the **BIGGINGS**, a hamlet halfway along the island's road, are the recently excavated remains of a thirteenth-century **Norse house**, which may have been a royal seat. In summer, the **ferry** runs from West Burrafirth to Papa Stour (Mon, Wed, Fri & Sat mornings, also Fri, Sat & Sun evenings); always book in advance and reconfirm 24 hours before departure (☎01595/873227). There's homely **accommodation** at *North House* (☎01595/873238; ②).

Foula

Southwest of Walls, at "the edge of the world", the island of **Foula** is separated from the nearest point on Mainland Shetland by about fourteen miles of ocean. Seen from the Mainland, its distinctive form changes subtly, depending upon the vantage point, but the outline is unforgettable. Its western cliffs, the second highest in Britain after those of St Kilda, rise at the **Kame** to some 1241ft above sea level; from its highest point at the **Sneug** (1370ft) a clear day offers a magnificent panorama stretching from Unst to Fair Isle and occasionally even the northern isles of Orkney. On a bad day, the exposure is complete and the cliffs generate turbulent blasts of wind known locally as "flans" which tear down the hills with tremendous force. The cliffs and moorland provide a home for a quarter of a million **birds** – the name of the island is based on the Old Norse for "bird island" – and host the largest colony of great skuas in Britain. Foula's human population peaked at around two hundred at the end of the nineteenth century, but has fluctuated wildly over the years, dropping to three in 1720 following an epidemic of "muckle fever". Today, the gentler eastern slopes provide crofting land which, with sheep grazing, helps to support a community numbering about forty. Inhabited since prehistoric times, the people here take pride in their separateness from Shetland, cherishing local traditions such as the observance of the **Julian calendar**, officially dropped in Britain in 1752, where Old Yule is celebrated on January 6 and the New Year arrives on January 13.

Practicalities

A day trip by ferry isn't possible. The summer passenger service to Foula runs from Walls on Tuesdays, Saturdays and alternate Thursdays, with a sailing from Scalloway on remaining Thursdays; it's essential to book and reconfirm (☎01595/753232). There are infrequent **charter flights** to Foula and Papa Stour; check availability with *British Airways Express* at Tingwall Airport (☎01595/840246), five miles or so west of Lerwick.

Choices of **places to stay** on Foula are inevitably limited, and all are on the east side of the island. There's a **B&B** at *Leraback* (☎01595/753226; ④, includes dinner), and the *Ristie Hostel* (☎01595/753233). Self-catering is also possible at *Burns* (☎01595/753232), but remember to take enough **food** for your stay as there's no shop.

North Mainland

The **North Mainland** rises and rolls through a series of grand, virtually uninhabited valleys stretching something like forty miles to the north of Lerwick. The main road crosses open ground occasionally dropping in on small coastal settlements, the first of which is **VOE**, whose tight huddle of homes has a strongly Scandinavian appearance. The village is dominated by the **Sail Loft**, a rich, deep red building, originally used by fisherman and whalers but later for the manufacture of knitwear.

From Voe the main road divides; the northern leg leads to the **Booth of Toft**, the ferry terminal for the island of Yell (see p.977), while the other branch cuts northwest to **BRAE**, a sprawling settlement that still has the feel of a frontier town, expanded in some haste in the 1970s to accommodate the workforce for the huge **Sullom Voe Oil Terminal** to the north. During World War II the deep-water harbour of Sullom Voe was home to the Norwegian Air Force and a base for RAF seaplanes. Although the terminal, built between 1975 and 1982, has passed its production peak, it is still the largest of its kind in Europe.

The peninsula of **Northmaven**, to the north of Brae, is connected by the narrow ithsmus of **Mavis Grind**, at which it's said you can throw a stone from the Atlantic to the North Sea (or at least to Sullum Voe). Northmaven is unquestionably one of the most picturesque areas of Shetland with its often rugged scenery, magnificent coastline and wide open spaces. **HILLSWICK,** the main settlement in the area, was once served by the *North of Scotland, Orkney and Shetland Shipping Company* steamer and in the early 1900s the firm also built a hotel, importing it in the form of a timber kit from Norway; it still stands albeit somewhat altered. Nearer the shore is the much older **Hillswick House** and, attached to it, *Da Böd*, the oldest pub in Shetland, said to have been founded by a German merchant in 1684.

Just outside Hillswick, a side road leads west to **Esha Ness** (*Ay*shaness), celebrated for its splendid coastline views. Spectacular cliffs and stacks are spread out before you as the road climbs away from Hillswick, with stacks called the Drongs in the foreground and distant views to the Westside and Papa Stour. A mile or so back along the road a south turning leads to **Tangwick Haa Museum** (May–Sept, Mon–Fri 1–5pm, Sat & Sun 11am–7pm; free), which through photographs, old documents and fishing gear, tells the often moving story of this remote corner of Shetland and its role in this dangerous trade. The northern branch of the road ends at the **Eshaness Lighthouse**, a great place to view the cliffs, stacks and, in rough weather, blowholes of this stretch of coast. A useful information board at the lighthouse details the dramatic features here, including a partially collapsed cave and a substantial broch, none of which are difficult to reach on foot, and make for a good three-hour walk.

North of Ronas Voe, by the shores of Colla Firth, an unmarked road leads up Collafirth Hill, the easiest place from which to approach the rounded contours of **Ronas Hill**, Shetland's highest point (1516ft). The climb, with no obvious path, is exhausting but rewarding (2hr each way): from the top you can look west to one of the most beautifully sculptured parts of the Shetland coast, as the steep slope of the hill drops down to the arching sand and shingle beach called the **Lang Ayre**. Also at the summit is a Neolithic or Bronze Age **chambered tomb**, one of the best preserved in Shetland and useful as a shelter from the wind.

Practicalities

Just west of Brae is one of the best **hotels** in Shetland, historic *Busta House* (☎01806/522506; ⑥); somewhat less luxurious is the timber-clad *St Magnus Bay Hotel* (☎01806/503371; ⑥) at Hillswick. **Guest houses** include *Greystones* (☎01806/522322; ③) at Brae, or *Valleyfield* (☎01806/522450; ③), just to the south, which also has a small **campsite**. **B&B** options in the Brae area include *Mrs Manson* (☎01806/522362; ②) or *Mrs Brown* (☎01806/522407; ②). For basic accommodation, if you have an airbed or sleeping mat, try the **camping** böds at the *Sail Loft* in Voe, or *Johnnie Notions* at Hamnavoe in Eshaness; book both these through the tourist office in Lerwick. Good pubs and bars to try include *Brae Inn*, in the centre of the village, or *Busta House*, and the *St Magnus Bay Hotel* or *Booth* (more of a bistro) in Hillswick.

The North Isles

Stepping out into the wilds of the North Sea, Shetland's three **North Isles** are all predictably windswept and exposed – north from Unst there's no land until eastern Siberia, beyond the North Pole. Boasting landscapes and seascapes rich in elemental beauty and with a strong sense of defiance, weathered by centuries of fierce storms, the islands offer good walks, much birdlife and archeological sites. They're not difficult to reach either; and at less windy times of year, they make good cycling country, with not too many steep hills. Accommodation in the northern isles isn't abundant, so book ahead especially in summer.

To get to the North Isles, a direct **bus** service to Yell, Unst and Fetlar leaves Lerwick every morning except Sunday, taking around two and a half hours to reach Belmont in Unst or Oddsta in Feltar; there's an afternoon service but the Unst connections only operate on Thursdays and, between April and September, on Saturdays. There are also bus **tours** from Lerwick. Get details of all these services from *Leasks* (☎01595/693162). Taking a car is easy, using the inexpensive and frequent **ferry services** operated by *Shetland Islands Council*, with well-timed ferry connections (Lerwick to Baltasound; 2hr). The Mainland ferry terminal for Yell is at Toft; from there, ferries run to Ulsta about every thirty minutes from early morning to late evening (20min). Ferries leave from Gutcher in north Yell for Belmont on Unst (every 15–30min; 10min) or Oddsta on Fetlar (6 daily; 25min).

Yell

Historically, **Yell**, the largest of the North Isles, hasn't had good write-ups: the Scottish historian Buchanan claimed it was "so uncouth a place that no creature can live therein, except such are born there". Certainly, if you keep to the fast main road, you'll pass a lot of uninspiring peat moorland, but the landscape is relieved by Whale Firth, Mid Yell Voe and Basta Voe, which cut deeply into it, providing superb natural harbours – and used as undetectable hiding places by German submarines during World War II.

The island's largest village, **MID YELL** has a couple of shops, a pub and a leisure centre with a good swimming pool. The road south along the east coast from the village gives access to the ruined broch at **Gossabrough**, to the **"White Lady"** – known locally as the "Widden Wife", a ship's figurehead from the *Bohus* wrecked nearby in 1924 – and to some attractive eastern sections of the coast. In the north of Yell, the area around **CULLIVOE** has relatively gentle, but attractive, coastal scenery. To the west is **GLOUP**, with its secretive, narrow sandy voe, once the largest fishing station in Shetland. This area provides some excellent walking, as does the Atlantic coast further west, where there's an Iron Age fort and field system at **Burgi Geos**. In the southwest, at **BURRAVOE**, is the **Old Haa Museum** (late April to Sept Tues–Thurs, Sat 10am–4pm, Sun 2–5pm; free), housed in a building dating from 1672 and offering an ideal introduction to life on Yell past and present. Just up the road, **St Colman's Church** (1900) is an isolated but delightful example of Arts and Crafts architecture, built in three Gothic-windowed bays with a curved end, surmounted by a tiny, ornate spire.

If you want to **stay** on Yell, there's the modern *Pinewood Guest House* (☎01957/702427; ③) at Aywick. **B&Bs** include *Mrs Johnson* (☎01957/702153; ②) in Mid Yell; *Westerhouse* (☎01957/744203; ②) and *Bayanne House* (☎01957/744219; ②) at Sellafirth; and *Mrs Tulloch* (☎01957/744201; ②) at Gutcher's post office. For more **basic accommodation**, if you've an airbed or mat, you can stay in *Windhouse Lodge*, on the main road near Mid Yell; book through the tourist office in Lerwick. The non-smoking tea room in the *Old Haa Museum* at Burravoe has soup, snacks and delicious home bakes, and there's a simple restaurant and pub in Westsandwick. The *Hilltop Bar* in Mid Yell offers lunches and suppers, while at the Gutcher ferry terminal, the *Seaview Café* has filled rolls, snacks and soup.

Fetlar

Known as "the garden of Shetland", **Fetlar** is the most fertile of the North Isles; much of it lush and green, with masses of summer flowers, though the bulk is covered in heather and grass moorland. Around 900 people once lived here; there might well be more than 100 now were it not for the nineteenth-century clearances. Today Fetlar's population lives on the southern and eastern sides of the island, where the main settlement, **HOUBIE**, has a small but welcoming **interpretative centre** (May–Oct Wed–Sun noon–5pm; free) throwing light on local history and selling crafts and knitwear.

The island has several notable archeological remains, including the **Funzie Girt**, a Neolithic dyke which divides the island into two, a monastic site at Strandibrough, and a ring of stones at Haltadans. The first three of these are within the **RSPB North Fetlar Reserve**, and it's essential to contact the warden at **Baelans** (☎01957/733246) to find out if a visit is possible. The same applies if you want to seek out the birdlife, which has included regular visits by **snowy owls**. Fetlar is also one of very few places you'll see the rare, graceful **red-necked phalarope**; a hide has been provided at the east end of the island near **Funzie** (which incidentally is pronounced *Finn*ie).

Accommodation and places to **eat** on the island are limited to the B&B at *Gord* (☎01957/733227; ②), where you can get an evening meal, and the well-equipped *Garths Campsite* (May–Sept; ☎01957/733269). There's a **café** at the *Fetlar Shop* (Tues, Wed, Fri & Sat 10am–5pm, Thurs & Sun 10am–1pm).

Unst

Unst has a population of around 1000, of whom 300 or 400 are connected to the RAF radar base at Saxa Vord, listening out for any uninvited intruders. The predominantly green landscape features on the eastern side strikingly coloured serpentine rock; though mainly greyish green, this weathers to rusty orange, and in some stone walls there are pieces which are of an extraordinary deep turquoise hue. The serpentine soil also produces unusual vegetation; grass has a bluish-grey cast, and at the **Keen of Hamar National Nature Reserve**, north of Baltasound, numerous rare plants include the unique mouse-eared chickweed.

The island's main settlement is at **BALTASOUND**, where old jetties around the bay testify to a bygone herring industry; there's a hotel with a pub, shop, post office and a leisure centre with a pool. Britain's most northerly post office is over the hill to the north, at **HAROLDSWICK**. Here, down near the shore, is the **Unst Boat Haven** (May–Sept daily 2–5pm; free), an outstanding and beautifully presented display of historic boats with many tools of the trade and information on fishing; most of the boats are from Shetland, with one from Norway. A little to the north, off the main road, is the **Unst Heritage Centre** (May–Sept daily 2–5pm, free) where you can find out about other aspects of Unst life such as crofting and its unique geology. The road ends at **Skaw**, with a beautiful beach and the very last house in Britain.

West of Haroldswick is **Burrafirth**, a north-facing inlet surrounded by cliffs and guarded by the hills of Saxa Vord and Hermaness. **Hermaness National Nature Reserve** is home to more than 100,000 seabirds, the best-known of which has been "Albert Ross", a disorientated black-browed albatross from the South Atlantic. Albert's return to the same ledge year after year, ever hopeful that a mate might turn up, soon became celebrated as a harbinger of spring. A **visitor centre** is located in the former lighthouse keepers' houses; and a marked route into the reserve allows you to look down over the jagged rocks of **Muckle Flugga** and the most northerly bit of Britain, **Out Stack**. There are few more dramatic settings for a lighthouse, and few sites could ever have presented as great a challenge to the builders. The views from here are inevitably marvellous and the walk down the west side of Unst towards Westing is one of the finest in Shetland.

The island's **guest houses** and **hotel** are all in Baltasound; there's historic *Buness House* (✆01957/711315; ④), *Clingera Guest House* (✆01957/711579; ②) and Britain's most northerly **hotel**, the *Baltasound Hotel* (✆01957/711334; ⑤), which provides lunches and dinners to non-residents. **B&Bs** include *Barns* (✆01957/755249; ②) at Westing, *Mrs Ritch* (✆01957/711323; ②) at Haroldswick, *Mrs Nicolson* (✆01957/711503; ②) at Baltasound and *Mrs Firmin* (✆01957/775234; ③) at Uyeasound. For more **basic** accommodation, the independent **youth hostel** at Uyeasound is well equipped (✆01957/755298 or 755311). **Snacks** and teas can be had at the *Nornova Tearoom* just north of Muness Castle or, often on a help-yourself basis, at the *Haroldswick Shop*.

travel details

ORKNEY

Buses

Kirkwall to: Houton (5–6 daily; 30min); St Margaret's Hope (4 daily; 40 min); Stromness (hourly; 40min); Tingwall (3 daily; 25min).

Ferries

Burwick to: John O' Groats (passengers only; 2–4 daily; 45min).

Kirkwall to: Eday, Stronsay, Sanday, Westray and Papa Westray (1–3 daily; 1–2hr); Invergordon (6 weekly, 10hr); North Ronaldsay (1 weekly); Shapinsay (4–6 daily; 45min).

Houton to: Hoy (Lyness) and Flotta (11 daily, 45min).

Stromness to: Aberdeen (once weekly in winter, twice weekly in summer; 10hr/8hr); Hoy (passengers only; 2–3 daily in summer; 30min); Lerwick (once weekly in winter, twice weekly in summer; 8hr); Scrabster/Thurso (1–3 daily except Sun in winter; 1hr 45 min).

Tingwall to: Egilsay, Rousay and Wyre (7 daily; 30min).

Flights

Kirkwall to: Aberdeen (3 daily; 45min); Eday (2 on Wed; 12min); Edinburgh (daily; 1hr 20min); Glasgow (4 daily; 2hr 30min); Inverness (2 daily; 50min); North Ronaldsay (Mon–Sat 1–3 daily; 15min); Papa Westray (Mon–Sat 1–2 daily; 12min); Sanday (Mon–Sat 1–3 daily; 20min);

Stronsay (Mon–Fri 1–2 daily; 25min); Westray (Mon–Sat 1–2 daily; 12min).

SHETLAND

Buses

Cullivoe to: Ulsta (2 daily; 1hr 15min).

Lerwick to: Brae (2–5 daily; 35min); Hamnavoe (Mon–Sat 2 daily; 30min); Hillswick (1–2 daily, 1hr 15min); Laxo (2–3 daily, 30min); Sandwick (Mon–Sat 4–6 daily, 3–4 on Sun; 35min); Scalloway (8 daily Mon–Sat; 15min); Sumburgh (4–6 daily; 45min); Vidlin (Mon–Sat 2–3 daily; 40min); Walls and Sandness (3–4 daily, 50min); Culswick (daily; 1hr 20min); Unst (Mon–Sat 1–2 daily; 2hr 45min); Yell (Mon–Sat 3 daily, 1 on Sun; 1hr 20min).

Unst, Yell and Fetlar: Mon–Sat 1 daily; 2hr 30min to Unst and Fetlar.

Ferries

Mainland

Grutness to: Fair Isle (May–Sept 5 fortnightly; 2hr 40min).

Laxo to: Whalsay (16–18 daily, 30min).

Lerwick to: Aberdeen (6 weekly; direct sailings 14hr overnight, via Orkney 20hr afternoon/overnight); Bressay (21 daily; 5min); Fair Isle (fortnightly, 4hr 30min);

Scalloway to: Foula (May–Sept 1 fortnightly; 3hr).

Toft to: Yell (22–27 daily, 20min).

Vidlin to: Whalsay, when bad weather prevents sailings from Laxo.

Walls to: Foula (May–Sept 5 fortnightly, otherwise weekly, 2hr 30min).

West Burrafirth to: Papa Stour (Mon & Wed–Sun 1–2 daily; 35min).

Other islands

Unst (Belmont) to: Fetlar (direct service 1–2 daily, 25min).

Yell (Gutcher) to: Fetlar (4–7 daily, 25min); Unst (29 daily, 10min).

Flights

Kirkwall to: Aberdeen (Mon–Fri 3 daily; 45min); Eday (2 on Wed; 8min); Glasgow (Mon–Fri 2 daily; 2–2hr 30min); North Ronaldsay (Mon–Fri 2 daily; 15min); Papa Westray (Mon–Fri 2 daily; 12min); Sanday (Mon–Fri 2 daily; 10min); Stronsay (Mon–Fri 2 daily; 8min); Westray (Mon–Sat 2 daily; 12min); Wick (1 on Mon, Wed, Fri & Sat; 15min).

Sumburgh to: Aberdeen (Mon–Fri 7 daily, 5 on Sat & Sun; 1hr); Fair Isle (1 weekly, 15min); Glasgow (Mon–Fri 3 daily, 1 on Sat & Sun; 2hr 25min); Kirkwall (2–3 daily; 35min); Unst (Mon–Fri 1 daily; 35min); Wick (Mon–Sat 1 daily; 50min).

Tingwall to: Fair Isle (1 or 2 on Mon, Wed, Fri & Sat; 25min); Unst (Mon–Fri 1 daily; 25min). Also to Foula, Papa Stour (charter services, seats limited and days and times vary; check with *British Airways Express*).

GETTING TO NORWAY

Thanks to the historical ties and the attraction of a short hop to continental Europe, **Norway** is a popular destination for Shetlanders and Orcadians. Norwegians often think of Shetland and Orkney as their western isles and, particularly in west Norway, wartime bonds with Shetland are strong. Norwegian yachts and sail training vessels are frequent visitors to Lerwick and Kirkwall.

There are weekly **flights** between June and September from Kirkwall, Orkney (1hr 45min) and twice weekly from Sumburgh, Shetland (1hr) to Bergen, and from June to August a weekly **ferry** service from Lerwick (13hr). Short inclusive breaks are available by air from Shetland.

PART FIVE

THE
CONTEXTS

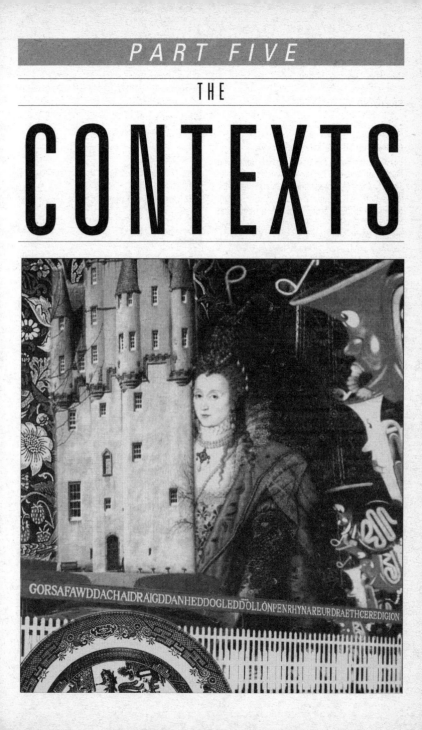

A BRIEF HISTORY OF BRITAIN

THE BEGINNINGS

Off and on, people have lived in Britain for the best part of half a million years, though the earliest evidence of human life dates from about **250,000 BC**. These meagre remains, found near Swanscombe, east of London across the Thames from Tilbury, belong to one of the migrant communities whose comings and goings depended on the fluctuations of the Ice Ages. Renewed glaciation then made the area uninhabitable once more, and the next traces – mainly roughly worked flint implements – were left around 40,000 BC by cave-dwellers at Creswell Crags in Derbyshire, Kent's Cavern near Torquay and Cheddar Cave in Somerset. The last spell of intense cold began about 17,000 years ago, and it was the final thawing of this **last Ice Age** around 5000 BC that caused the British Isles to separate from the European mainland.

The sea barrier did nothing to stop further migrations of nomadic hunting communities, drawn by the rich forests that covered ancient Britain. In about 3500 BC a new wave of colonists arrived from the continent, probably via Ireland, bringing with them a Neolithic culture based on farming and the rearing of livestock. These tribes were the first to make some impact on their environment, clearing forests,

enclosing fields, constructing defensive ditches around their villages and digging mines to obtain flint used for tools and weapons. Fragments of Neolithic pottery have been found near Peterborough and at Windmill Hill, near Avebury in Wiltshire; others – like the well-preserved village of Skara Brae in Orkney – were near the sea, enabling them to supplement their diet by fishing and to develop their skills as boat builders. The most profuse relics of this culture are their graves, usually stone-chambered, turf-covered mounds (called long barrows, cairns or cromlechs), which are scattered throughout the country – the most impressive ones are at Belas Knap in Gloucestershire, Barclodiad y Gawres in Angelsey, and Maes Howe on Orkney.

The transition from the Neolithic to the **Bronze Age** began around 2000 BC, with the immigration from northern Europe of the so-called **Beaker Folk** – named from the distinctive cups found at their burial sites. Originating in the Iberian peninsula and bringing with them bronze-workers from the Rhineland, these newcomers had a well-organized social structure with an established aristocracy, and quickly intermixed with the native tribes. Many of Britain's stone circles were completed at this time, including **Stonehenge** in Wiltshire, and **Callanish** on the Isle of Lewis, while many others belong entirely to the Bronze Age – for example, the Hurlers and the Nine Maidens on Cornwall's Bodmin Moor. Large numbers of earthwork forts were also built in this period, suggesting a high level of tribal warfare, but none of these were able to withstand the waves of Celtic invaders who, spreading from a homeland in central Europe, began settling in Britain around 600 BC.

THE CELTS

Highly skilled in battle, the **Celts** soon displaced the local inhabitants all over Britain, establishing a sophisticated farming economy and a social hierarchy that was headed by **Druids**, a ritual priesthood with attendant poets, seers and warriors. Through a deep knowledge of ritual, legend and the mechanics of the heavens, the Druids maintained their position between the people and a pantheon of over four thousand gods. Familiar with Mediterranean artefacts through their far-flung trade routes, they introduced superior methods of metalworking that favoured iron rather than bronze, from which they forged not just weapons but also coins. Gold was used for ornamental works – the first recognizable British art – heavily influenced by the symbolic, patterned **La Tène** style still thought of as quintessentially Celtic.

The principal Celtic contribution to the landscape was a network of hillforts or brochs, and other defensive works stretching over the entire country, the greatest of them at **Maiden Castle** in Dorset, a site first fortified almost 3500 years earlier, and **Mousa** in the Shetland islands. The original Celtic tongue – the basis of modern Welsh and Scottish Gaelic – was spoken over a wide area, gradually dividing into Goidelic (or Q-Celtic) now spoken in Ireland and Scotland, and Brythonic (P-Celtic) spoken in Wales, Cornwall and later exported to Brittany in France. Great though the Celtic technological and artistic achievements were, the people and their pan-European cousins were unable to maintain an organized civic society to match that of their successors, the Romans.

THE ROMANS

Coming at the end of a lengthy but low-level infusion of Roman ideas into the country, the Roman invasion had begun hesitantly, with small cross-Channel incursions by **Julius Caesar** in 55 and 54 BC. Britain's rumoured mineral wealth was a primary motive behind these raids, but the immediate spur to the eventual conquest nearly a century later was the dangerous collaboration between British Celts and the fiercely anti-Roman tribesmen in France, and the need of the emperor **Claudius**, who owed his power to the army, for a great military triumph. The death of the British king Cunobelin, who ruled all southeast England and was the original of Shakespeare's Cymbeline, offered the opportunity Claudius required, and in **August 43 AD**, a substantial force landed in Kent, from where it fanned out, soon establishing a base along the estuary of the Thames. Joined by Claudius and a menagerie of elephants and camels for the major battle of the campaign, the Romans soon reached Camulodunum (Colchester), and within four years were dug in on the frontier of south Wales.

The Catuvellauni chief, Caratacus, continued to conduct a guerrilla campaign from Wales until his eventual betrayal and capture in about 50 AD. About ten years later, a more serious challenge to the Romans arose when the East Anglian Iceni, under their queen **Boudicca** (or Boadicea), sacked Camulodunum and Verulamium (St Albans), and even reached the undefended port of Londinium, precursor of London. The uprising was soon quashed, and turned out to be an isolated act of resistance, with many of the already Romanized southeastern tribes of England probably welcoming absorption into the empire. However, it was not until 79 AD that Wales and the north of England were subdued.

By 80 AD the Roman governor, Agricola, felt secure enough in the south of Britain to begin an invasion of the north, building a string of forts across the Clyde–Forth line and defeating a large force of Scottish tribes at Mons Graupius. The long-term effect of his campaign, however, was slight. In 123 AD the Emperor Hadrian decided to seal the frontier against the northern tribes and built **Hadrian's Wall**, which stretched from the Solway Firth to the Tyne and was the first formal division of the island of Britain. Twenty years later, the Romans again ventured north and built the **Antonine Wall** between the Clyde and the Forth. This was occupied for about forty years, but thereafter the Romans, frustrated by the inhospitable terrain of the Highlands, largely gave up their attempt to subjugate the north, and instead adopted a policy of containment.

The written history of Britain begins with the Romans, whose rule lasted nearly four centuries. For the first time most of England was absorbed into a unified and peaceful political structure, in which commerce flourished and cities prospered, particularly **Londinium**, which immediately assumed a pivotal role in the commercial and administrative life of the province. Although Latin became the language of the Romano-British ruling elite, local traditions were allowed to co-exist with imported customs, so that Celtic gods were often worshipped at the same time as the Roman, and sometimes merged with them. Perhaps the most important legacy of the Roman occupation, however, was the introduction of **Christianity** from the third century on, becoming firmly entrenched after its official recognition by the emperor Constantine in 313.

THE ANGLO-SAXON PERIOD

As early as the reign of Constantine, Roman England was being raided by Germanic Saxon pirates. As economic life declined and rural areas became depopulated, individual military leaders began to usurp local authority, so that by the start of the fifth century England had become irrevocably detached from what remained of the Roman Empire. Within fifty years the **Saxons** were settling on the island, the start of a gradual conquest that — despite bitter resistance led by such semi-mythical figures as King Arthur, who is alleged to have held court at Caerleon in Wales — culminated in the defeat of the native Britons in 577 at the **Battle of Dyrham** (near Bath), at which three British kings were killed. Driving the few recalcitrant Celtic tribes deep into Cumbria, Wales and England's West Country, the invaders eliminated the Romano-British culture and by the end of the sixth century the rest of England was divided into the Anglo-Saxon kingdoms of Northumbria, Mercia, East Anglia, Kent and Wessex.

Only in Scotland and Wales did the ancient Celtic traditions survive, untouched by the Teutonic invaders as they had been by the Romans. In the fifth century, Irish-Celtic invaders formed distinct colonies in parts of Wales, and in the northwest of Scotland. Between the fifth and the eighth centuries the **Celtic Saints**, ascetic evangelical missionaries, spread the gospel around Ireland and western Britain, promoting the middle-Eastern eremitical tradition of living a reclusive life. In south Wales, Saint David was the most popular (and subsequently Wales' patron saint), while in northwest Scotland, Saint Columba founded several Christian outposts, the most famous of which was on the island of Iona.

The revival of Christianity in England was driven mainly by the arrival of **St Augustine**, who was despatched by Pope Gregory I and landed on the Kent coast in 597, accompanied by forty monks. The missionaries were received by **Ethelbert**, who gave Augustine permission to found a monastery at Canterbury, where the king himself was then baptized, followed by ten thousand of his subjects at a grand Christmas ceremony. Despite some reversals in the years that followed, the Christianization of England proceeded quickly, so that by the middle of the seventh century all of the Anglo-

Saxon kings had at least nominally adopted the faith. Tensions and clashes between the Augustinian missionaries and the more free-booting Celtic monks inevitably arose, to be resolved by the **Synod of Whitby in 663**, when it was settled that the English church should follow the rule of Rome, thereby ensuring a realignment with the European cultural mainstream.

The central English region of **Mercia** became the dominant Anglo-Saxon kingdom in the eighth century under kings Ethelbald and Offa, the latter being responsible for the greatest public work of the Anglo-Saxon period: **Offa's Dyke**, an earthwork stretching from the River Dee to the Severn, marking the border with Wales. After Offa's death **Wessex** gained the upper hand, and by 825 **Egbert** had conquered or taken allegiance from all the other English kingdoms. The supremacy of Wessex coincided with the first large-scale Norse or **Danish** Viking invasions, which began with coastal pirate raids, such as the one that destroyed the great monastery of Lindisfarne in 793, but gradually grew into a migration, chiefly in the Scottish islands Orkney, Shetland and the Hebrides.

In 865 a substantial Danish army landed in East Anglia, and within six years they had conquered Northumbria, Mercia and East Anglia, and were attacking Wessex. At about the same time, the leadership of Wessex was assumed by **Alfred the Great**, a warrior whose dogged resistance and acceptance of the need to co-exist with the Danes ensured the survival of his kingdom. Having established a border demarcating his domain from the northern **Danelaw**, the part of England in which the rule of the now Christianized Danes was accepted (a border roughly coinciding with the Roman Watling Street), Alfred directed his resources into internal reforms and the strengthening of his defences.

Although Danish attacks had recommenced before the end of Alfred's reign in 899, his successor, **Edward the Elder**, established supremacy over the Danelaw and was thus the *de facto* overlord of all England, acknowledged even by Scottish and Welsh chieftains. In 973, **Edgar**, king of Mercia and Northumberland, became the first ruler to be crowned king of England, but the aggression from the Danes was unrelenting, and in 1016 Ethelred the Unready —

having failed to buy off the enemy – fled to Normandy, establishing links there which were to have a far-reaching effect on ensuing events.

The first and best king of the short-lived Danish dynasty was **Canute**, who was followed by his two unexceptional and disreputable sons, after whom the Saxons were restored under Ethelred's son, **Edward the Confessor**. It was said of Edward that he was better suited to have been a priest than a king, and most of his reign was dominated by Godwin, Earl of Wessex, and by Godwin's son Harold. On Edward's death, the Witan – a sort of council of elders – confirmed **Harold** as king, despite the claim of William, Duke of Normandy, that the exiled and childless Edward had sworn himself to be William's vassal, promising him the succession. Harold's brief reign was overshadowed by the events in the last two of its ten months, when he first marched north to fend off an invasion attempt by his brother Tostig (who had been deprived of his earldom of Northumbria) in league with King Harald of Norway. Having defeated their combined forces at Stamford Bridge in Yorkshire, Harold was immediately forced to return south to meet the invading William, who routed his forces at the **Battle of Hastings** in 1066. Harold was killed, and on Christmas Day of that year William the Conqueror was installed as king in Westminster Abbey.

ENGLAND: THE NORMANS AND PLANTAGENETS

Making little attempt to reach any understanding with the indigenous Saxon culture, **William I** imposed a new military aristocracy on his subjects, enforcing his rule with a series of strongholds all over England, the grandest of which was the Tower of London. The sporadic rebellions that broke out during the early years of his reign were ruthlessly suppressed by a scorched earth policy, especially in Yorkshire and its surrounding counties, but perhaps the single most effective controlling measure was the compilation of the **Domesday Book** between 1085 and 1086. Recording land ownership, type of cultivation, the number of inhabitants and their social status, it afforded William an unprecedented body of information about his subjects, providing the framework for the administration of taxation, the judicial structure and feudal obligations.

William was succeeded in 1087 by his son William Rufus, an ineffectual ruler but a notable benefactor of the religious foundations that were springing up throughout the realm. Killed by an arrow while hunting in the New Forest, William was in turn followed by William I's youngest son, Henry I, who spent much of his reign in tussles with the country's barons, but at least was the first Norman king to encourage intermarriage, himself marrying a Saxon princess. On his death in 1135, William I's grandson Stephen of Blois contested the accession of Henry's daughter Mathilda (also called Maud), with the consequence that the nineteen years of his reign were spent in civil war. Mathilda's son was eventually recognized as Stephen's heir, and the reign of **Henry II** (1154–89), the first of the **Plantagenet** branch of the Norman line, provided a welcome respite from baronial brawling. Asserting his authority throughout a domain that reached from the Cheviots to the Pyrenees, Henry presided over immense administrative reforms, including the introduction of trial by jury. His attempts to subordinate ecclesiastical authority to the Crown went terribly awry in 1170, when he sanctioned the murder in Canterbury Cathedral of his erstwhile drinking companion **Thomas à Becket**, whose canonization just three years later created an enduring Europe-wide cult.

The last years of Henry's reign were riven by quarrels with his sons, the eldest of whom, **Richard I** (or Lionheart), spent most of his ten-year reign crusading in the Holy Land. Alienated by the king's rift with the Church in Rome, and by his loss of Henry II's huge legacy of French territory, the barons eventually forced Richard's brother **King John** to consent to a charter guaranteeing their rights and privileges, the **Magna Carta**, which was signed in 1215 at Runnymede, on the Thames. The power struggle with the barons continued into the reign of Henry III, who was defeated by their leader Simon de Montfort at Lewes in 1265, when both Henry and Prince Edward were taken prisoner. Edward escaped, defeated the barons' army at the battle of Evesham in 1265 and killed de Montfort, ascending the throne in 1272 as **Edward I**. A great law-maker in the mould of William I and Henry II, Edward presided over the Model Parliament of 1295, a significant step in the evolution of consensual politics, though he was mostly absorbed in extending his kingdom within the island, annexing Wales and imposing English jurisdiction in Scotland.

THE CONQUEST OF WALES

Though Wales was unable to present a unified opposition to the Norman invaders, William the Conqueror didn't attempt to annex Wales. Instead, he installed a huge retinue of barons, the **Lords Marcher**, along the border to bring as much Welsh territory under their own jurisdiction as possible. Despite generations of squabbling, the barons managed to hold onto their privileges until Henry VIII's Act of Union over four hundred years later.

The status quo between Wales and England changed irrevocably, however, when Edward I succeeded Henry III and began a crusade to unify Britain. The Welsh chief, Llywelyn the Last, had failed to attend Edward's coronation, and refused to pay him homage. With effective use of sea power Edward had little trouble forcing Llywelyn back into Snowdonia. Peace was restored with the **Treaty of Aberconwy** which deprived Llywelyn of almost all his land and stripped him of his financial tributes from the other Welsh princes, but left him with the hollow title of "Prince of Wales". After a relatively cordial four-year period, Llywelyn's brother Dafydd rose against Edward, inevitably dragging Llywelyn along with him. Edward crushed the revolt, captured Llywelyn, and executed him at Cilmeri, after fleeing from the abortive Battle of Builth in 1282. The **Treaty of Rhuddlan** in 1284 set down the terms by which the English monarch was to rule Wales: much of it was given to the Marcher lords who had helped Edward, the rest was divided into administrative and legal districts similar to those in England. Though the treaty is often seen as a symbol of English subjugation, it respected much of Welsh law and provided a basis for civil rights and privileges. Many Welsh were content to accept and exploit Edward's rule for their own benefit, but in 1294 a rebellion led by **Madog ap Llywelyn** gripped Wales and was only halted by Edward's swift and devastating response. Most of the privileges enshrined in the Treaty of Rhuddlan were now rescinded and the Welsh seemed crushed for a century.

Pent-up resentment towards the English sowed seeds of a rebellion led by the tyrannical but charismatic Welsh hero **Owain Glyndŵr**, who declared himself "Prince of Wales" in 1400, and with a crew of local supporters attacked the lands of nearby barons, slaughtering the English. Henry IV misjudged the political climate and imposed restrictions on Welsh land ownership, swelling the general support Glyndŵr needed to take Conwy Castle the following year. In 1404 Glyndŵr summoned a parliament in Machynlleth, and had himself crowned Prince of Wales, with envoys of France, Scotland and Castile in attendance. He then demanded independence for the Welsh Church from Canterbury and set about securing alliances with English noblemen who had grievances with Henry IV. This last ambitious move heralded Glyndŵr's downfall. A succession of defeats saw his allies desert him and by 1408, when the castles at Harlech and Aberystwyth were retaken for the Crown, this last protest against Edward I's English conquest had lost its momentum.

SCOTLAND IN THE MIDDLE AGES

The victory of the Scottish king, **Malcolm III**, known as Canmore ("bighead"), over Macbeth in 1057 marked the beginning of a period of fundamental change in Scottish society. Having avenged his father Duncan, Malcolm III, who had spent the previous seventeen years at the English court, sought to apply to Scotland a range of ideas he had brought back with him. He and his heirs established a secure dynasty based on succession through the male line and introduced **feudalism** into Scotland, a system that was diametrically opposed to the Gaelic system, which rested on blood ties: the followers of a Gaelic king were his kindred, whereas the followers of a feudal king were vassals bought with land. The Canmores successfully feudalized much of southern and eastern Scotland by making grants to their Norman, Breton and Flemish followers, but beyond that, traditional clan-based forms of social relations persisted.

The Canmores, independent of the local nobility, who remained a military threat, also began to reform the **Church**. This development started with the efforts of Margaret, Malcolm III's English wife, who brought Scottish religious practices into line with those of the rest of Europe and was eventually canonized. **David I**

(1124–53) continued the process by importing monks to found a series of monasteries, principally along the border at Kelso, Melrose, Jedburgh and Dryburgh. By 1200 the entire country was covered by a network of eleven bishoprics, although church organization remained weak within the Highlands. Similarly, the dynasty founded a series of **royal burghs**, towns such as Edinburgh, Stirling and Berwick, and bestowed upon them charters recognizing them as centres of trade. The charters usually granted a measure of self-government, vested in the town corporation or guild, and the monarchy hoped this liberality would both encourage loyalty and increase the prosperity of the kingdom. Scotland's Gaelic-speaking clans had little influence within the burghs, and by 1550 Scots – a northern version of Anglo-Saxon – had become the main language throughout the Lowlands.

The policies of the Canmores laid the basis for a cultural rift in Scotland between the Highland and Lowland communities. Before that became an issue, however, the Scots had to face a major threat from the south. In 1286 **Alexander III** died, and a hotly disputed succession gave Edward I, the king of England, an opportunity to subjugate Scotland. In 1291 Edward presided over a conference where the rival claimants to the Scottish throne presented their cases. Edward chose John Balliol, in preference to **Robert the Bruce**, his main rival, and obliged John to pay him homage, thus turning Scotland into a vassal kingdom. Bruce refused to accept the decision, thereby continuing the conflict, and in 1295 Balliol renounced his allegiance to Edward and formed an alliance with France – the beginning of what is known as the "Auld Alliance". In the conflict that followed, the Bruce family sided with the English, Balliol was defeated and imprisoned, and Edward seized control of almost all of Scotland.

Edward had shown little mercy during his conquest of Scotland – he had, for example, had most of the population of Berwick massacred – and his cruelty seems to have provoked a truly national resistance. This focused on **William Wallace**, a man of relatively lowly origins who forged an army of peasants, lesser knights and townsmen that was fundamentally different to the armies raised by the nobility. Figures like Balliol, holding lands in England, France and Scotland, were part of an international aristocracy for whom warfare was merely the means by which they struggled for power. Wallace, by contrast, led proto-nationalist forces determined to expel the English from their country. Probably for that very reason Wallace never received the support of the nobility, and, after a bitter ten-year campaign, he was betrayed and executed in London in 1305.

With Wallace out of the way, feudal intrigue resumed. In 1306 **Robert the Bruce**, the erstwhile ally of the English, defied Edward and had himself crowned king of Scotland. Edward died the following year, but the unrest dragged on until 1314, when Bruce decisively defeated a huge English army under Edward II at the battle of **Bannockburn**. At last Bruce was firmly in control of his kingdom, and in 1320 the Scots asserted their right to independence in a successful petition to the pope, now known as the **Arbroath Declaration**.

FROM BANNOCKBURN TO BOSWORTH

The defeat at Bannockburn added to the unpopularity of **Edward II**, and the king was eventually overthrown by his wife Isabella and her lover Roger Mortimer, by whom he was horribly put to death in Berkeley Castle, Gloucestershire. Although **Edward III** was initially preoccupied by Scottish wars, his reign is chiefly remembered for his claim to the French throne, a feeble pretence – he had earlier recognized the king of France and done homage to him – but one that launched the **Hundred Years War** in 1337. Early English victories such as the Battle of Crécy in 1346, and the capture of Calais the following year, were interrupted by the outbreak of the **Black Death** in 1349, a plague which claimed about a third of the English population. The resulting scarcity of labour produced economic turmoil in the land, and attempts to restrict the rise of wages and to levy a poll tax (a tax on each person irrespective of wealth) provoked widespread riots, which peaked with the **Peasants' Revolt** of 1381. After seizing Rochester Castle and sacking Canterbury, the rebels marched on London, where the boy king **Richard II** met Wat Tyler, the leader of the revolt, at Smithfield. The resulting scuffle led to Tyler's murder and the dispersal of the mob, and soon afterwards the Bishop of Norwich routed the Norfolk rebels, the prelude to a wave of repression and terrible retribution.

Parallel with this social unrest were the clerical reforms demanded by the scholar **John Wycliffe**, whose followers made the first translation of the Bible into English in 1380. Another sign of the elevation of the language was the success enjoyed by **Geoffrey Chaucer** (c.1340–1400), a wine merchant's son, whose *Canterbury Tales* was the first major work written in the vernacular and one of the first English books to be printed.

During the later years of Edward III's reign England had in effect been ruled by his son, **John of Gaunt**, Duke of Lancaster, whose influence remained paramount during the minority of Richard II. In 1399 the vacillating Richard II was overthrown by John of Gaunt's son, who took the title **Henry IV** and founded the **Lancastrian** dynasty. Fourteen years later, he in turn was succeeded by his son, **Henry V**, who promptly renewed the war with France, which had been limping along ingloriously since the victory at Poitiers in 1356. After the much celebrated triumph at **Agincourt**, Henry forced the French king to sign the Treaty of Troyes in 1420, making the English king the heir to the French throne, but on Henry's death just two years later his son was still an infant, which left regents governing the country on behalf of the monarch. Settling their differences, the French rallied under **Joan of Arc** to beat back the English, and by 1454 only Calais was left in English hands.

Meanwhile **Henry VI**, who was temperamentally more inclined to the creation of such architectural coups as King's College Chapel in Cambridge and Eton College Chapel than to warfare, had suffered lapses into insanity. Strongest of the rival contenders for the throne was Richard, Duke of York, by virtue of his direct descent from Edward III. It was no accident that the **Wars of the Roses** – named from the red rose that symbolized the Lancastrian cause and the white Yorkist rose – broke out just a year after the return of the last English garrisons from France, filling the country with footloose knights and archers accustomed to a life of plunder and war. The instability of the time was signalled by **Jack Cade's Rebellion** of 1450, when a disorganized rabble – though with more participation

by dissatisfied gentry than had been the case in the 1381 Peasants' Revolt – challenged the king's authority, winning a battle at Sevenoaks before being scattered. Political disputes within the circle surrounding the mad king were to prove more threatening to the regime. The Duke of York's authority over Henry was challenged by the king's accomplished and ambitious wife, Margaret of Anjou, whose forces defeated and slew Richard at Wakefield in 1460. She and Henry were in turn overwhelmed by Richard's son, who was crowned **Edward IV** in 1461 – the first king of the **Yorkist** line.

The civil strife entered a new stage when Edward attempted to shrug off the overbearing influence of Richard Neville, Earl of Warwick and Salisbury, or "Warwick the Kingmaker", as he became known. Warwick then performed a dramatic volte-face by allying himself with his old enemy Margaret of Anjou, forcing Edward into exile and proclaiming Henry king once more. Henry VI's second term was soon interrupted by Edward's unexpected return in 1471, when Warwick was defeated and killed at the Battle of Barnet and the rest of the Lancastrians were crushed at Tewkesbury three months later. Margaret was captured, Henry's heir was killed and Henry himself was soon afterwards dispatched in the Tower.

Edward IV proved to be a precursor of the great Tudor princes – licentious, cruel and despotic, but also a patron of Renaissance learning. In 1483, his twelve-year-old son succeeded as **Edward V**, but his reign was cut short after only two months, when he and his younger brother were murdered in the Tower of London – probably by their uncle, the Duke of Gloucester, who was crowned **Richard III**. Increasingly unpopular as rumours circulated of his part in the fate of the princes in the Tower, Richard was toppled at Bosworth Field in 1485 by **Henry Tudor**, Earl of Richmond, who took the throne as **Henry VII**.

THE TUDORS

The opening of the Tudor period brought radical transformations. A Lancastrian through his mother's descent from John of Gaunt, Henry VII reconciled the Yorkist faction by marrying Edward IV's daughter Elizabeth, putting an end to the internecine squabbling among the discredited gentry. The growth of the wool and cloth trades and the rise of a powerful merchant class brought a general increase of wealth, while England began to assume the status of a major European power partly as a result of Henry's alliances and political marriages – his daughter to James IV of Scotland and his son to Catherine, daughter of Ferdinand and Isabella of Spain.

The relatively easy suppression of the rebellions of Yorkist pretenders Lambert Simnel and Perkin Warbeck ensured a smooth succession for **Henry VIII** in 1509. Although Henry was himself not a Protestant and even received from the pope the title of "Defender of the Faith" for a book he published criticizing Luther's doctrine, this tumultuous king is chiefly noted for the separation of the English Church from Rome. The schism was triggered not by doctrinal issues but by the failure of his wife Catherine of Aragon – widow of his elder brother – to provide Henry with male offspring. Failing to obtain a decree of nullity from Pope Clement VII, he dismissed his long-time chancellor Thomas Wolsey and followed the advice of Thomas Cromwell, forcing the English Church to recognize him as its head. The most far-reaching consequence of this step was the **Dissolution of the Monasteries**, a decision taken mainly to enjoy the profits of the ensuing land sales. The first phase of the Dissolution in 1536, involving the smaller religious houses, was a factor in the only significant rebellion of the reign, the **Pilgrimage of Grace**, a protest largely in the north of the country, which Henry put down with great cruelty, preparing the ground for the closure of the larger foundations in 1539.

In his later years Henry became a corpulent tyrant, six times married but at last furnished with an heir, **Edward VI**, who was only nine years old when he ascended the throne in 1547. His short reign saw Protestantism established on a firm footing, with churches stripped of their images and Catholic services banned, yet on Edward's death most of the country recognized his half-sister **Mary**, daughter of Catherine of Aragon and a fervent Catholic. She restored England to the papacy and married the future Philip II of Spain, forging an alliance whose immediate consequence was war with France and the loss of Calais, last of England's French possessions. Mary's unpopu-

larity increased when she began a savage persecution of Protestants, executing the leading lights of the English Reformation, Hugh Latimer, Nicholas Ridley and Thomas Cranmer, the archbishop of Canterbury who was largely responsible for the first English Prayer Book, published in 1549.

The accession of the Protestant **Elizabeth I** in 1558 took place in a highly volatile atmosphere, with the country riven between opposing religious loyalties and threatened abroad by Philip II. Heresy and treason were the twin preoccupations of the Elizabethan state, a society in which a sense of English nationhood was evolving on an almost mystical level in the vacuum created by the break with Rome. Aided by a team of exceptionally able ministers, the Virgin Queen provided a focal point for national feeling, enthusiastically supported by a mercantile class which was opposed to foreign entanglements or clerical restrictions, and was represented in a Parliament made stronger by the constitutional decisions of the preceding fifty years.

The forty-five years of Elizabeth's reign saw the efflorescence of a specifically English Renaissance, especially in the field of literature, which reached its pinnacle in the brilliant career of **William Shakespeare** (1564–1616). It was also the age of the **seafarers** Walter Raleigh, Francis Drake, Martin Frobisher and John Hawkins, whose piratical exploits helped to map out the world for English commerce. English navigational skills – as demonstrated by Drake's voyage round the world (1577–80) – and the country's growing naval strength triumphed with the defeat of the **Spanish Armada** in 1588. The commander of the English fleet, Lord Howard of Effingham, was a practising Catholic, a fact that dashed Philip's hope of a Catholic insurrection in England – a hope in part founded on the widespread sympathy for Elizabeth's cousin Mary, Queen of Scots, whose twenty-year imprisonment in England had ended with her beheading in 1587.

WALES UNDER THE TUDORS

Welsh allegiance during the Wars of the Roses lay broadly with the Lancastrians, who had the support of the ascendant north Welsh Tewdwr (or Tudor) family. Welsh expectations of the first Tudor monarch, Henry VII, were high. Henry lived up to some of them, removing many of the restrictions on land ownership imposed at the start of Glyndŵr's uprising, and promoting many Welshmen to high office, but administration remained piecemeal. Control was still shared between the Crown and largely independent Marcher lords until a uniform administrative structure was achieved under Henry VIII.

Wales had been largely controlled by the English monarch since the Treaty of Rhuddlan in 1284, but the **Acts of Union** in 1536 and 1543 fixed English sovereignty over the country. At the same time the Marches were replaced by shires (the equivalent of modern counties), the Welsh laws codified by Hywel Dda were made void and partible inheritance gave way to primogeniture, the eldest son becoming the sole heir. For the first time the Welsh and English enjoyed legal equality, but the break with native traditions wasn't well received. Most of the people remained poor, the gentry became increasingly anglicized, the use of Welsh was proscribed, and legal proceedings were held in English (a language few peasants understood).

Since Christianity had always been a ritual way of life rather than a philosophical code in Wales, Catholicism was easily replaced by Protestantism during the religious upheavals of Henry VIII's reign. What the Reformation did promote was a more studied approach to religion and learning in general. Under the reign of Elizabeth I, Jesus College was founded in Oxford for Welsh scholars, and the Bible was translated into Welsh for the first time by a team led by Bishop **William Morgan**.

With new land ownership laws enshrined in the Acts of Union, the stimulus provided by the Dissolution hastened the emergence of the Anglo-Welsh gentry, a group eager to claim a Welsh pedigree while promoting the English language and the legal system, helping to perpetuate their grasp. Meanwhile, landless peasants continued in poverty, only gaining slightly from the increase in cattle trade with England and the slow development of mining and ore smelting.

THE STEWARTS IN SCOTLAND

In the years following Bruce's death in 1329, the Scottish monarchy gradually declined in influence. The last of the Bruce dynasty died in 1371, to be succeeded by the "Stewards",

hence **Stewarts** (known as Stuarts in England), but thereafter a succession of Scottish rulers, culminating with James VI in 1567, came to the throne when still children. The power vacuum was filled by the nobility, whose key members exercised control as Scotland's regents while carving out territories where they ruled with the power, if not the title, of kings. **James IV** (1488–1513), the most talented of the early Stewarts, might have restored the authority of the crown, but his invasion of England ended in a terrible defeat for the Scots – and his own death – at the battle of Flodden Field.

The reign of **Mary, Queen of Scots** (1542–67) typified the problems of the Scottish monarchy. Mary came to the throne when just one week old, and immediately caught the attention of the English king, Henry VIII, who sought, first by persuasion and then by military might, to secure her hand in marriage for his five-year-old son, Edward. Beginning in 1544, the English launched a series of devastating attacks on Scotland, an episode Sir Walter Scott later called the "Rough Wooing", until, in the face of another English invasion in 1548, the Scots – or at least those not supporting Henry – turned to the "Auld Alliance". The French king proposed marriage between Mary and the Dauphin Francis, promising in return military assistance against the English. The six-year-old queen sailed for France in 1548, leaving her loyal nobles and their French allies in control, and her husband succeeded to the French throne in 1559. When she returned thirteen years later, following the death of Francis, she had to pick her way through the rival ambitions of her nobility and deal with something entirely new – the religious Reformation.

The **Reformation** in Scotland was a complex social process, whose threads are often hard to unravel. Nevertheless, it is quite clear that, by the end of the sixteenth century, the established Church was held in general contempt. Another spur to the Scottish Reformation was the identification of Protestantism with anti-French feeling. In 1554 Mary of Guise, the French mother of the absent Queen Mary, had become regent, and her habit of appointing Frenchmen to high office caused considerable resentment. In 1557, a group of nobles banded together to form the **Lords of the Congregation**, whose dual purpose was to oppose French influence and promote the reformed religion. With English military backing, the Protestant lords succeeded in deposing the French regent in 1560, and, when the Scottish Parliament assembled shortly afterwards, it asserted the primacy of Protestantism by forbidding Mass and abolishing the authority of the pope. The nobility proceeded to confiscate twothirds of Church lands, a huge prize that did much to bolster their new beliefs.

Even without the economic incentives, Protestantism was a highly charged political doctrine. As the Protestant reformer **John Knox** told Queen Mary at their first meeting in 1561, subjects are not bound to obey an ungodly monarch. Mary ducked and weaved, trying to avoid an open breach with her Protestant subjects. Her difficulties were exacerbated by her disastrous second marriage to **Lord Darnley**, a cruel and politically inept character, whose jealousy led to his involvement in the murder of Mary's favourite, David Rizzio, who was dragged from the queen's supper room at Holyrood and stabbed 56 times. The incident caused the Scottish Protestants more than a little unease, but they were entirely scandalized in 1567, when Darnley himself was murdered and Mary promptly married the **Earl of Bothwell**, widely believed to be the murderer. This was too much to bear, and the Scots rose in rebellion, driving Mary into exile in England at the age of just 25. The queen's illegitimate half-brother, the Earl of Moray, became regent and her son, the infant James, was left behind to be raised a Protestant prince. Mary, meanwhile, became perceived as such a threat to the English throne that, after twenty years' imprisonment in England, Queen Elizabeth I had her executed in 1587.

Knox could now concentrate on the organization of the reformed Church, or **Kirk**, which he envisaged as a body empowered to intervene in the daily lives of the people. **Andrew Melville**, another leading reformer, proposed the abolition of all traces of episcopacy – the rule of the bishops in the Church – and that the Kirk should adopt a **presbyterian** structure, administered by a hierarchy of assemblies, part elected and part appointed. At the bottom of the chain, beneath the General Assembly, Synod and Presbytery, would be the Kirk session, responsible for church affairs, the performance of the minister and the morals of the parish. In 1592, the Melvillian party achieved a measure of success when presbyteries and synods were accepted as legal church courts and the office of bishop was suspended.

James VI (1567–1625) disliked presbyterianism because of its quasi-democratic structure – particularly the lack of royally appointed bishops – appeared to threaten his authority. He was, however, unable to resist the reformers until 1610, when, strengthened by his installation as King of England, he restored the Scottish bishops. The argument about the nature of Kirk organization would lead to bloody conflict in the years after James' death.

THE STUARTS AND THE COMMONWEALTH

On Elizabeth's death in 1603, James VI became **James I** of England, thereby uniting the English and Scottish crowns. James quickly moved to end hostilities with Spain – a move resented by the increasingly powerful English Puritans, an extreme Protestant group – but his intention to exercise tolerance towards the country's Catholics was thwarted by the outcry in the wake of the **Gunpowder Plot** of 1605, when Guy Fawkes and a group of Catholic conspirators were discovered preparing to blow up King and Parliament. Puritan fundamentalism and commercial interests converged in the foundation of Virginia in 1608, the first permanent **colony in North America**, followed in 1620 by the landing in New England of the Pilgrim Fathers, the nucleus of a colony that would absorb about 100,000 mainly Puritan immigrants by the middle of the century.

A split was inevitable between James, who clung to the medieval notion of the divine right of kings, and the landed gentry who dominated the increasingly powerful Parliament, a situation exacerbated by the persecution of the Puritans. Recoiling from the demands of the Parliamentarians, the king relied heavily on court favourites, progressing from the skilful Robert Cecil, Earl of Salisbury, and the philosopher Francis Bacon, to the rash and unpopular George Villiers, Duke of Buckingham, who also had a close influence on the second Stuart king, **Charles I** (1625–49).

Raised in Episcopalian England, Charles had little understanding of Scottish reformism, and like his father, he believed in the divine right of kings. In 1637, Charles attempted to impose a new prayer book on the Scottish Kirk, laying down forms of worship in line with those favoured by the High Anglican Church. The reformers denounced these changes as "Popery" and organized the **National Covenant**, a religious pledge that committed the signatories to "Labour by all means lawful to recover the purity and liberty of the Gospel as it was established and professed". Charles declared all the "Covenanters" to be rebels, a proclamation endorsed by his Scottish bishops. Consequently, when the king backed down from military action and called a General Assembly of the Kirk, the assembly promptly abolished the episcopacy. Charles pronounced the proceedings illegal, but lack of finance stopped him from mounting an effective military campaign – whereas the Covenanters, well financed by the Kirk, assembled a proficient army under Alexander Leslie.

In desperation, Charles summoned the English Parliament, the first for eleven years, hoping it would pay for an army. But, like the calling of the General Assembly, the decision was a disaster and Parliament was much keener to criticize his policies than to raise taxes. In 1642, facing the concerted hostility of Parliament, the king withdrew to Nottingham where he raised his standard, the opening military act of the **Civil War**. The Royalist forces were initially successful against the Parliamentarian army, gaining an advantage after the first battle of the war, Edgehill, at which Charles's nephew, the dashing cavalry officer Prince Rupert, displayed the reckless valour which was to distinguish his participation in subsequent engagements. After Edgehill, the Parliamentarian army was completely overhauled by **Oliver Cromwell** as the New Model Army, and won victories at Marston Moor and Naseby. Charles was captured by the Scots at Newark in Nottinghamshire, in 1646 and was finally handed over to the English, by whom, after prolonged negotiations and more fighting, he was executed in January 1649.

The following year, at the invitation of the Earl of Argyll, Charles' son, the future Charles II, came to Scotland. To regain his Scottish kingdom, Charles was obliged to renounce his father and sign the Covenant, two bitter pills

taken to impress the population. In the event, the "presbyterian restoration" was short-lived. Cromwell invaded, defeated the Scots at Dunbar and forced Charles into exile. For the next eleven years the whole country was a **Commonwealth** – at first a true republic, then, after 1653, a Protectorate under Cromwell, who was ultimately as impatient of Parliament and as arbitrary as Charles had been. Cromwell's policies were especially savage in Ireland, where his depredations are remembered to this day. At his death in 1658 his son Richard ruled briefly and ineffectually, and in 1660 Parliament voted to restore the monarchy in the person of **Charles II** (1660–85), the exiled son of the previous king.

THE RESTORATION AND THE GLORIOUS REVOLUTION

The turmoil of the previous twenty years had unleashed a furious debate on every strand of legalistic, theological and political thought, an environment that spawned a host of fringe sects – such as the Levellers, who demanded constitutional reform, and the more radical Ranters, who proposed common ownership of all land. Nonconformist religious groups flourished, prominent among them the pacifist **Quakers**, led by the much persecuted George Fox (1624–91), and the Dissenters, to whom the most famous writers of the day, John Milton (1608–74) and John Bunyan (1628–88), both belonged. With the **Restoration**, however, these philosophical eddies gave way to a new exuberance in the fields of art, literature and the theatre, a remarkable transition from the sombreness of the Puritan era, when secular drama and other such fripperies were banned outright. In the scientific arena, just six months after his accession Charles founded the **Royal Society**, which numbered Isaac Newton (1642–1727) among its first fellows.

The low points of Charles II's reign came with the **Great Plague** of 1665 and the **Great Fire of London** the following year, though the latter had the positive consequence of allowing Christopher Wren (1632–1723) and other great architects to redesign the capital along more contemporary classical lines. Moreover, the political scene was not entirely tranquil: tensions still existed between king and Parliament, where the traditional divisions of court and country began to coalesce into **Whig** and **Tory** parties, respectively representing the low-church gentry and the high-church aristocracy. A measure of vengeance was also wreaked on the regicides and other leading Parliamentarians, though its intensity was nothing like that of the anti-Catholic hysteria sparked off by the Popish Plot of 1678, the fabrication of the trickster Titus Oates.

The succession in 1685 of the Catholic **James II** (James VII of Scotland), brother of Charles II, provoked much opposition, though – as one might expect from a country recently racked by civil war – there was an indifferent response when the **Duke of Monmouth**, favourite of Charles II's illegitimate sons, landed at Lyme Regis to mount a challenge to the new king. His undisciplined forces were routed at Sedgemoor, Somerset, in July 1685; nine days later Monmouth was beheaded at Tower Hill, and in the subsequent **Bloody Assizes** of Judge Jeffreys, hundreds of rebels and suspected sympathizers – mainly in Somerset and Devon – were executed or deported.

When seven bishops protested against James's **Declaration of Indulgence** of 1687, removing anti-Catholic restrictions, the king showed something of his father's obstinacy by having them tried for seditious libel, though he was quickly forced to acquit them. When James's son was born, a child destined to be brought up in the Catholic faith, messengers were dispatched to **William of Orange**, the Dutch husband of Mary, the Protestant daughter of James II. William landed in Brixham in Devon, proceeding to London where he was acclaimed king in the so-called **Glorious Revolution** of 1688, the final postscript to the Civil War.

William and Mary were made joint sovereigns, having agreed to a **Bill of Rights** defining the limitations of the monarch's power and the rights of his or her subjects. This, together with the **Act of Settlement of 1701** – among other things, barring Catholics or anyone married to one from succession to the English throne – made Britain the first country to be governed by a **constitutional monarchy**, in which the roles of legislature and executive were separate and interdependent, a model broadly consistent with that outlined by the philosopher and political thinker John Locke (1632–1704), whose essentially Whig doctrines of toleration and social contract were gradually embraced as the new orthodoxy.

Ruling alone after Mary's death in 1694, William regarded England as a prop in his defence of Holland against France, a stance that defined England's political alignment in Europe for the next sixty years. Mary died without leaving an heir and, on William's death in 1702, the crown passed to her sister **Anne**, who was also childless. In response, the English Parliament secured the Protestant succession by passing the **Act of Settlement** – among other things, barring Catholics or anyone married to one from succession to the English throne – which named the Electress Sophia of Hanover as the next in line to the throne. The Act did not, however, apply in Scotland, and the English feared that the Scots would invite James II's son, James Edward Stuart, back from France to be their king.

Nevertheless, despite the strength of anti-English feeling, the Scottish Parliament passed the **Act of Union** by 110 votes to 69 in 1707. Some historians have explained the vote purely in terms of bribery and corruption, but there were other factors. Scottish politicians were divided between the Cavaliers – Jacobites (supporters of the Stuarts) and Episcopalians – and the Country party, whose presbyterian members dreaded the return of the Stuarts more than they disliked the Hanoverians. There were commercial considerations too. In 1705, the English Parliament had passed the Alien Act, which threatened to impose severe penalties on cross-border trade, whereas the Union gave merchants of both countries free access to each other's markets. The Act of Union also guaranteed the Scottish legal system and the Presbyterian Kirk, though it replaced the two separate parliaments with a new British Parliament based in London.

THE HANOVERIANS

When Anne died in 1714, the succession passed – in accordance with the terms of the Act of Settlement – to a non-English-speaking German, the Duke of Hanover, who became **George I** of England. This prompted the first major **Jacobite uprising** in support of James Edward Stuart, the "Old Pretender" (Pretender in the sense of having pretensions to the throne, Old to distinguish him from his son Charles, the "Young Pretender"). Its timing appeared perfect. Scottish opinion was moving against the Union, which had failed to bring

Scotland any tangible economic benefits. Neither were Jacobite sentiments confined to Scotland. There were many in England who toasted the "King across the water" and showed no enthusiasm for the new German ruler. In September 1715, the fiercely Jacobite John Erskine, Earl of Mar, raised the Stuart standard at Braemar Castle. Just eight days later, he captured Perth, where he gathered an army of over 10,000 men, drawn mostly from the Episcopalians of northeast Scotland and from the Highlands. Mar's rebellion took the government by surprise. They had only 4000 soldiers in Scotland, under the command of the Duke of Argyll, but Mar dithered until he lost the military advantage. There was an indecisive battle at Sheriffmuir in November, but by the time the Old Pretender arrived the following month, 6000 veteran Dutch troops had reinforced Argyll. The rebellion disintegrated rapidly and James slunk back to exile in France in February 1716.

As power leaked away from the monarchy into the hands of the Whig oligarchy – many Tories having been discredited for suspected Jacobite sympathies – the king ceased to attend cabinet meetings, his place being taken by his chief minister. Most prominent of these ministers was **Robert Walpole**, regarded as the Britain's **first prime minister**, who effectively ruled the country in the period 1721–42. This was a tranquil period politically, with the country standing aloof from foreign affrays, but the financial world was prey to a mania for speculation. Of the numerous fraudulent or ill-conceived financial ventures of this time, the greatest was the fiasco of the **South Sea Company**, which in 1720 sold shares in its monopoly of trade in the Pacific and along the east coast of South America. The "bubble" burst when the shareholders took fright at the extent of their own investments and the value of the shares dropped to nothing, reducing many to penury, and almost wrecking the government, which was saved only by the astute intervention of Walpole.

Peace ended in the reign of **George II**, when in 1739 England declared war on Spain, the prelude to the eight-year War of the Austrian Succession. Then in 1745 the country was invaded by the **Young Pretender**, Charles Edward Stuart (Bonnie Prince Charlie), the Old Pretender's dashing son, in the **Jacobite uprising of 1745**. This second rebellion had little chance of success: the Hanoverians had consolidated their hold on the English throne, Lowland society was uniformly loyalist, and even among the Highlanders Charles only attracted just over half of the 20,000 clansmen who could have marched with him. Nevertheless, after a decisive victory over government forces at Prestonpans, Charles made a spectacular advance into England, getting as far as Derby. London was in a state of panic: its shops were closed and the Bank of England, fearing a run on sterling, slowed withdrawals by paying out in sixpences. But Derby was as far south as Charles got. On December 6, threatened by superior forces, the Jacobites decided to retreat to Scotland.

The Duke of Cumberland was sent in pursuit and the two armies met on **Culloden Moor**, near Inverness, in April 1746. Outnumbered and out-gunned, the Jacobites were swept from the field, losing over 1200 men compared to Cumberland's 300 plus. After the battle, many of the wounded Jacobites were slaughtered, an atrocity that earnt Cumberland the nickname "Butcher". Jacobite hopes died at Culloden and the prince lived out the rest of his life in drunken exile. In the aftermath of the uprising, the wearing of tartan, the bearing of arms and the playing of bagpipes were all banned. Rebel chiefs lost their land and the Highlands were placed under military occupation. Most significantly, the government prohibited the private armies of the chiefs, thereby effectively destroying the clan system.

Meanwhile, the **Seven Years War** brought yet more overseas territory, as English armies wrested control of India and Canada from France, then in 1768 **Captain James Cook** departed from Plymouth on his voyage to New Zealand and Australia, further widening the scope of the colonial empire.

In 1760, George II had been succeeded by **George III**, the first native English Hanoverian. The early years of his sixty-year reign saw a revived struggle between King and Parliament, enlivened by the intervention of John Wilkes, first of a long and increasingly vociferous line of parliamentary radicals. The contest was exacerbated by the deteriorating relationship with the thirteen colonies of North America, a situation brought to a head by the American **Declaration of Independence** and Britain's defeat in the Revolutionary War. Chastened by this disaster, Britain chose not to interfere in the momentous events taking place across the Channel, where France, its most consistent foe in the eighteenth century, was convulsed by revolution. Out of the turmoil emerged the country's most daunting enemy yet, Napoleon, whose progress was interrupted by Nelson at Trafalgar in 1805, and finally stopped ten years later by the Duke of Wellington at Waterloo.

THE INDUSTRIAL REVOLUTION

Britain's triumph was largely due to its financial strength, itself largely due to the gradual switch from an agricultural to a manufacturing economy, a process generally referred to as the **Industrial Revolution**. The earliest mechanized production lines were constructed in the Lancashire cotton mills, where cotton-spinning was transformed from a cottage industry into a highly productive factory-based system. Water power became a thing of the past after James Watt patented his **steam engine** in 1781, and the utilization of coal as an engine fuel made it convenient to locate mills and factories near coal mines, a tendency that was accelerated as **ironworkers** took up coal as a smelting fuel, vastly increasing the output from their furnaces. Accordingly there was a shift of population towards the Midlands and north of England, where the great coal reserves were located, resulting in the rapid growth of the industrial towns and the expansion of Liverpool as a commercial port, importing raw materials from India and the Americas and exporting manufactured goods. Commerce and industry were served by steadily improving transport facilities, such as the building of a network of **canals** in the wake of the success of the Bridgewater Canal in 1765, which linked coalmines at Worsley with Manchester and the River Mersey. But the great leap forward occurred with the arrival of the **railway** age, heralded by the opening of the Liverpool–Manchester line in 1830, with power provided by George Stephenson's *Rocket*.

Boosted by influxes of Jewish, Irish, French and Dutch immigrants, many of whom introduced new manufacturing techniques, the country's population rose from about seven and a half million at the beginning of George III's reign to more than fourteen million at its end, an increase whose major cause was the slowing-down of the deathrate owing to improvements in medical science. But while factories and their attendant towns expanded, the rural settlements of England suffered, inspiring the elegiac pastoral yearnings of Samuel Taylor Coleridge and William Wordsworth, the first great names of the **Romantic** movement in English literature. Later Romantic poets such as Percy Bysshe Shelley and Lord Byron took a more socially engaged stance, inveighing against social injustices that were aggravated by the expenses of the Napoleonic Wars and by its aftermath, when many returning soldiers found their jobs had been taken by machines. Discontent emerged in demands for parliamentary reform, and in 1819 demonstrators in Manchester – centre of the cotton industry and most important of the industrial boom towns still unrepresented in Parliament – were mown down by troops in what became known as the **Peterloo Massacre**.

The following year George III, by now weak, old, blind and insane, died and was succeeded by his grandson **George IV**. During his reign religious toleration became a reality, as Catholics and Nonconformists were permitted to enter parliament, workers' associations were legalized, and a civilian police force was created, largely the work of **Robert Peel**, a reforming Tory who outlined the basic ideology of modern Conservatism. More far-reaching changes came under **William IV**, with the passing of the **Reform Act** of 1832, whereby the principle of popular representation was acknowledged (though most adult males still had no vote); two years later, the revised **Poor Law** alleviated the condition of the destitute. Significant sections of the middle classes wanted far swifter democratic reform, as was expressed in public indignation over the **Tolpuddle Martyrs** – the Dorset labourers transported to Australia in 1834 for joining an agricultural trade union – and support for **Chartism**, a working-class movement demanding universal male suffrage. Poverty and injustice were the dominant theme of the novels of **Charles Dickens** (1812–70) and the preoccupation of the paternalistic reform movements that were a feature of the nineteenth century. This social concern had been anticipated in the previous century by the Methodism of John Wesley (1703–91) and the anti-slavery campaign promoted by evangelical Christians such as the Quakers and William

THE HIGHLAND CLEARANCES

Once the clan chief was forbidden his own army, he had no need of the large tenantry that had previously been a vital military asset. Conversely, the second half of the eighteenth century saw the Highland population double after the introduction of the easy-to-grow and nutritious **potato**. The clan chiefs adopted different policies to deal with the new situation. Some encouraged emigration, and as many as six thousand Highlanders left for the Americas between 1800 and 1803 alone. Other landowners developed alternative forms of employment for their tenantry, mainly fishing and kelping. **Kelp** (brown seaweed) was gathered and burnt to produce soda ash, which was used in the manufacture of soap, glass and explosives Other landowners developed **sheep runs** on the Highland pastures, introducing hardy breeds like the black-faced Linton and the Cheviot. But extensive sheep farming proved incompatible with a high peasant population, and many landowners decided to clear their estates of tenants, some of whom were forcibly moved to tiny plots of marginal land, where they were to farm as **crofters**.

The pace of the **Highland Clearances** accelerated after the end of the Napoleonic Wars in 1815, when the market price for kelp, fish and cattle declined, leaving sheep as the only profitable Highland product. As the dispossessed Highlanders scratched a living from the acid soils of some tiny croft, they learnt through bitter experience the limitations of the clan. Famine followed, forcing large-scale emigration to America and Canada and leaving the huge uninhabited areas found in the region today. The crofters eked out a precarious existence, but they hung on throughout the nineteenth century, often by taking seasonal employment away from home.

In the 1880s, however, a sharp downturn in agricultural prices made it difficult for many crofters to pay their rent. This time, inspired by the example of the Irish Land League, they resisted eviction, forming the **Highland Land Reform Association** and the **Crofters' Party**. In 1886, in response to the social unrest, Gladstone's Liberal government passed the **Crofters' Holdings Act**, which conceded three of the crofters' demands: security of tenure, fair rents to be decided independently, and the right to pass on crofts by inheritance. But Gladstone did not attempt to increase the amount of land available for crofting and shortage of land remained a major problem until the **Land Settlement Act** of 1919 made provision for the creation of new crofts. Nevertheless, the population of the Highlands has continued to decline during the twentieth century, with many of the region's young people finding city life more appealing.

Wilberforce. As a result of their efforts, slavery was banned in Britain in 1772 and throughout the colonies in 1833 – putting an end to what had been a major factor in the prosperity of ports such as Bristol and Liverpool.

THE VICTORIAN AGE

In 1837 William IV was succeeded by his niece **Victoria**, who, living through a period in which Britain's international standing reached unprecedented heights, came to be as much a national icon as Elizabeth I had been. Though the intellectual achievements of the Victorian age were immense – as typified by the publication of Charles Darwin's *The Origin of Species* in 1859 – the country saw itself primarily as an imperial power founded on industrial and commercial prowess, its spirit perhaps best embodied by the great engineering feats of Isambard Kingdom Brunel and by the **Great Exhibition** of 1851, a display of manufacturing achievements from all over the world.

With trade at the forefront of the agenda, much of the political debate during this period crystallized into a conflict between the **Free Traders** – represented by an alliance of the Peelites and the Whigs, forming the Liberal Party – and the **Protectionists** under Bentinck and **Disraeli**, guiding light of the Tories. During the last third of the century, Parliament was dominated by the duel between Disraeli and the Liberal leader **Gladstone**. Although it was Disraeli who eventually passed the Second Reform Bill in 1867, further extending the electoral franchise, it was Gladstone who had first proposed it, and it was Gladstone's first ministry of 1868–74 that passed some of the century's most far-reaching legislation, including compulsory education, the full legalization of trade unions and an Irish Land Act.

In 1854 troops were sent to protect the Turkish empire against the Russians in the **Crimea**, an inglorious debacle whose horrors were relayed to the public by the first ever press coverage of a military campaign and by the shocking revelations of Florence Nightingale. The fragility of Britain's empire was further exposed by the Indian Mutiny of 1857, though the country's prestige was not sufficiently dented to prevent Victoria from taking the title Empress of India after 1876. Apart from the Chinese Opium War of 1839–42 and some colonial skirmishes in Asia and Africa, the only other serious conflict to occur in Victoria's reign was the **Boer War** against the Dutch settlers in South Africa (1899–1902), another mishandled affair leading to the establishment of self-government there in 1906 and a military shake-up at home that was to be of significance in the coming European war.

FROM WORLD WAR I TO WORLD WAR II

Victoria died in the first month of 1901, to be succeeded by her son, **Edward VII**, whose leisurely and dissolute life could be seen as the epitome of the complacent era to which he gave his name. The Edwardian era came to an end on August 4, 1914, when the Liberal government, honouring the Entente Cordiale signed with France in 1904, declared war on Germany. World War I was a futile massacre which destroyed millions of lives and eradicated whatever remained of the majority's respect for the ruling classes, whose officers had treated their conscripts as mere cannon fodder.

At the war's end in 1918 the social fabric of the country was changed drastically as the **voting** franchise was extended to all men aged twenty-one or over and to women of thirty or over, subject to certain residential or business qualifications. This tardy liberalization of women's rights – largely due to the radical **Suffragettes** led by Emmeline Pankhurst and her daughters Sylvia and Christabel – was not completed until 1929, a year after Emmeline's death, when women were at last granted the vote at twenty-one, on equal terms with men.

At around this time the progressive wing of British politics, formerly occupied by the Liberal Party, was taken over by the **Labour Party**, the fruit of an alliance between trade-union interests and middle-class radicals. Labour formed its first government in 1923 under Ramsay MacDonald, but following the publication of the **Zinoviev Letter**, a forged document that

seemed to prove Soviet encouragement of British socialist subversion, the Conservatives were returned with a large majority. In 1926, the tensions which had been building up since the end of the war, produced by severe decline in manufacturing and attendant escalating unemployment, erupted with the **General Strike**. Spreading instantly from the coal mines to the railways, the newspapers and the iron and steel industries, the strike lasted nine days and involved half a million workers, provoking the government into draconian action – the army was called in, and the strikers were forced to surrender. The economic situation deteriorated even further after the crash of the New York Stock Exchange in 1929, with unemployment reaching over 2.8 million in 1931, generating a series of mass demonstrations that reached a peak with the **Jarrow March** of 1936. The same year, economist John Maynard Keynes argued in his General Theory of Employment, Interest and Money for a greater degree of state intervention in the management of the economy, though the whole question was soon overshadowed by international events.

Abroad, the structure of the British Empire had undergone profound changes since World War I. The status of Ireland had been partly resolved after the electoral gains of the nationalist Sinn Fein in 1918 led to the establishment of the Irish Free State in 1922, from which the six counties of the mainly Protestant North "contracted out". Four years later, the **Imperial Conference** recognized the autonomy of the British dominions, an agreement formalized in the 1931 Statute of Westminster, whereby each dominion was given an equal footing in a Commonwealth of Nations, though each still recognized the British monarch. The royal family itself was shaken in 1936 by the **abdication of Edward VIII**, following his decision to marry a twice-divorced American, Wallis Simpson. Although the succession passed smoothly to his brother **George VI**, the scandal further reduced the standing of the royals, a process which has gathered pace in recent years.

Non-intervention in the Spanish Civil War and the Sino-Japanese War was paralleled by a policy of appeasement towards **Adolf Hitler**, who had massively rearmed Germany in pursuit of his territorial ambitions. In 1938 Prime

Minister Neville Chamberlain returned from meeting Hitler and Mussolini at Munich with an assurance of good intentions from the two fascist leaders, and when **World War II** broke out in September 1939, Britain was still seriously unprepared. In May 1940 the discredited Chamberlain stepped down in favour of a national coalition government headed by the charismatic **Winston Churchill**, whose bulldog persistence and heroic speeches provided the inspiration needed in the backs-against-the-wall mood of the time. Largely through Churchill's manoeuvrings, the United States, already a supplier of foodstuffs and munitions, entered the war as a combatant, an intervention which, combined with the heroic resistance of the Russian Red Army, swung the balance. In terms of the number of casualties it caused, World War II was not as calamitous as the Great War (as World War I is often known), but its impact upon the civilian population was even more terrible. In its first wave of bombing, the Luftwaffe caused massive damage to industrial and supply centres such as London, Coventry, Manchester, Liverpool, Southampton and Plymouth; in later raids, intended to shatter morale rather than factories and docks, the cathedral cities of Canterbury, Exeter, Bath, Norwich and York were targeted. At the end of the fighting, nearly one in three of all the houses in the nation had been destroyed or damaged, nearly a quarter of a million members of the British armed forces had lost their lives and over 58,000 civilians were dead.

POSTWAR BRITAIN

The end of the war in 1945 was quickly followed by a general election. Hungry for change, the electorate displaced Churchill in favour of the Labour Party under **Clement Attlee**, who, with a large parliamentary majority, set about a radical programme to **nationalize** the coal, gas, electricity, iron and steel industries, as well as the inland transport services. Building on the plans for a social security system presented in Sir William Beveridge's report of 1943, the **National Insurance Act** and the National **Health Service Act** were both passed early in the Labour administration, giving birth to what became known as the **welfare state**. But despite substantial American aid, the huge problems of rebuilding the economy made

austerity the keynote, with the rationing of food and fuel remaining in force long after they had ended in most other European countries.

In April 1949 Britain, the United States, Canada, France and the Benelux countries signed the **North Atlantic Treaty** as a counterbalance to Soviet power in eastern Europe, defining the country's postwar international commitments. Yet confusion regarding Britain's post-imperial role was shown up by the Suez Crisis of 1956, when Anglo-French forces invaded Egypt, only to be hastily recalled following international condemnation. Revealing severe limitations on the country's capacity for independent action, the Suez incident resulted in the resignation of Conservative prime minister Anthony Eden and his replacement by the more pragmatic **Harold Macmillan**. Nonetheless, Macmillan maintained a nuclear policy that suggested a continued desire for an international role, and nuclear testing went on against a background of widespread marches under the auspices of the pacifist Campaign for Nuclear Disarmament.

The 1960s, dominated by the Labour premiership of **Harold Wilson**, saw a revival of consumer spending and a corresponding cultural upswing, with London becoming the hippest city on the planet. The good times lasted barely a decade. Though Tory prime minister Edward Heath led Britain into the brave new world of the European Economic Community, the 1970s were a decade of recession and industrial strife. A succession of public-sector strikes and mistimed decisions by James Callaghan's Labour government handed the 1979 general election to **Margaret Thatcher**, who four years earlier had ousted Heath to become the first woman to lead a major political party in Britain.

THATCHERITE BRITAIN

Thatcher went on to win three general elections, steering the country into a period of ever greater social polarization. While taxation policies and easy credit fuelled a consumer boom for the professional classes, the erosion of manufacturing industry and the weakening of the welfare state created a calamitous number of people trapped in long-term impoverished unemployment. Despite the intense dislike of her regime among a substantial portion of the population, Thatcher won an increased majority in the 1983 election, partly because of the successful outcome of the 1981 war to regain control of the **Falkland Islands**, partly owing to the fragmentation of the Labour opposition, from which the short-lived Social Democratic Party had split in panic at what it perceived as the radicalization of the party. Social tensions surfaced in sporadic urban rioting and the year-long miners' strike (1984–85) against pit closures, an industrial dispute in which the police were given unprecedented powers to restrict the movement of citizens, while the media perpetrated some immensely misleading coverage of events. The violence in Northern Ireland also intensified, and the bombing campaign of the IRA came close to killing the

SCOTTISH AND WELSH NATIONALISM

If any single event can be said to have given birth to Welsh nationalism in the modern sense, it was a meeting amongst Welsh academics at the 1925 eisteddfod in Pwllheli on the Llŷn peninsula. Led by the gifted writer Saunders Lewis, the group metamorphosed into **Plaid Genedlaethol Cymru** (The National Party of Wales). In one of the first modern separatist protests, he joined two other Plaid members and set fire to building materials at an RAF station on the Llŷn, was dismissed from his post and spent his life in literary criticism, becoming one of Wales' greatest modern writers. Similar public displays and powerful nationalist rhetoric won over an intellectual majority, but the masses continued to fuel the Labour ascendency in both local and national politics.

With Plaid Cymru's appeal considered to be restricted to rural areas, Labour was shocked by the 1966 Carmarthen by-election, when **Gwynfor Evans** became the first Plaid MP. It wasn't until 1974 that Plaid also won in the constituencies of Caernarfon and Merioneth, and suddenly the party was a threat, and Labour was forced to address the question of devolution. By 1978 Labour had tabled the **Wales Act**, promising the country an elected assembly to act as a voice for Wales, but with no power to legislate or raise revenue. In the subsequent **referendum** in 1979, eighty percent of voters opposed the proposition, with even the nationalist stronghold of Gwynedd voting against.

The **National Party of Scotland** was formed in 1928, its membership averaging about 7000 people, mostly drawn from the non-industrial parts of the country. Very much a mixture of practical politicians and left-leaning eccentrics, such as poet Hugh MacDiarmid, in 1934 it merged with the right-wing Scottish Party to create the **Scottish National Party**. The SNP, after years in the political wilderness, achieved its electoral breakthrough in 1967 when Winnie Ewing won Hamilton from Labour in a by-election. The following year the SNP won 34 percent of the vote in local government elections and gained control of Cumbernauld; successes that had repercussions within both the Labour and Conservative parties.

Both began to work on schemes to give Scotland a measure of self-government, and the term **"Devolution"** was coined. The objective in both cases was to head off the nationalists.

When the Conservatives came to power in 1970, Edward Heath, the prime minister, shelved plans for devolution because the SNP had only secured a twelve-percent share of the Scottish vote. The situation changed dramatically in 1974, when Labour were returned to power with a wafer-thin majority. The SNP held seven seats, which gave them considerable political leverage. Devolution was back on the agenda. The Labour government put its devolution proposals before the Scottish people in a **referendum** on March 1, 1979. The "yes" vote gained 33 percent, the "no" vote 31 percent; although a majority in favour, it was not by the required 40 percent. Not for the first time, Scottish opinion had shifted away from home rule; the reluctance to embrace it was based on uncertainty about what might follow.

The incoming Conservative government of Margaret Thatcher set its face against any form of devolution. By contrast, proposals for some form of devolution quickly became party policy for Labour and the Liberal Democrats during the 1980s. With the Tories looking increasingly likely to lose the 1997 general election, the prospect of separate **Scottish and Welsh assemblies** looks distinctly possible. However, though the case for devolution has been widely accepted within Scotland, there remain the questions about its consequences for the British parliament and constitution. Simply put, should Scottish MPs continue to have the same amount of influence over the affairs of the rest of Britain once a Scottish parliament has been established? This is an awkward issue for the Labour Party, because any numerical reduction in Scottish representation at Westminster would threaten its ability to form a British government. There has been no enthusiasm in England, and less than might perhaps have been expected in Wales, for the devolved English and Welsh parliaments that would be needed to create directly equivalent structures in those countries.

entire Cabinet when it blew up the Brighton hotel in which the Conservatives were staying for their 1984 annual conference.

The divisive politics of Thatcherism reached their apogee with the introduction of the Poll Tax, a lunatic scheme that led ultimately to Thatcher's overthrow by colleagues who feared annihilation should she lead them into another general election. The uninspiring new Tory leader, **John Major**, won the Conservatives a fourth term in office in 1992, albeit with a much reduced majority in Parliament. Since then, the Conservatives have failed to stop the country's relentless slide down the league table of industrial nations, lift the economy out of recession or resolve their (and the country's) deep divisions on the issue of closer integration within the European Union. Remaining true to Thatcherite principles but appearing not to adopt his predecessor's zealotry, Major has pushed ahead with privatization schemes that are destroying British institutions as diverse as the railways and the health service.

John Major's 1992 electoral victory brought a predictable response from the IRA, who detonated one of their most devastating bombs in the City the very same day, causing billions of pounds worth of damage in the finanical heart of the country. A year later, they struck again in virtually the same place, prompting police roadblocks in the City. The **IRA ceasefire** of 1994–95 brought a brief respite to the mainland bombing campaign. Unfortunately, as the Conservative majority dwindled into single figures, Major was forced to rely increasingly on Unionist support to prop up his government, with the inevitable consequences to the peace process.

Whatever the Tories' electoral problems, they are as nothing to those of the **Royal Family**, whose popularity has plummeted to an all-time low. Such creeping republicanism can be traced back to 1992, which the Queen herself accurately described as an "annus horribilis" ("One's Bum Year" as a *Sun* headline pithily put it). This was the year that saw the marriage break-ups of Charles and Di, and Andrew and Fergie, and the second marriage of divorcee Princess Anne. Matters came to a head, though, when the Conservatives offered millions of pounds of taxpayers' money to pay for the repair of fire-damaged Windsor Castle. After a furore, the Royals agreed that at least some money would be raised from the astronomical admission charges at Buckingham Palace and Windsor Castle – and, in a further development, the Queen herself agreed to pay tax for the first time in her life. If 1992 was a bad year for the Queen, 1995 was even worse, with further damaging revelations about the break-up of Charles and Di's marriage, and the onset of negotiations over their divorce. Still, such is the tourist-pulling potential of the monarchy, that its abolition is very unlikely whatever the outcome of the next general election.

BOOKS

Most of the books listed below are in print and in paperback – those that are out of print (o/p) should be easy to track down in secondhand book shops. Publishers are detailed with the British publisher first, separated by an oblique slash from the US publisher, where both exist. Where books are published in only one of these countries, UK or US precedes the publisher's name; where the book is published by the same company in both countries, the name of the company appears just once.

TRAVEL AND JOURNALS

James Boswell, *The Journal of a Tour to the Hebrides* (Penguin/McGraw Hill). Lively diary account of a journey around the islands taken with Samuel Johnson, written by his biographer and friend.

Bill Bryson, *Notes from a Small Island* (Doubleday). Bryson's best-selling and highly amusing account of his farewell journey round Britain.

Giraldus Cambrensis, *The Journey through Wales* and *The Description of Wales* (Penguin Classics). Two witty and frank books in one volume, written in Latin by the quarter-Welsh clergyman after his 1188 tour around Wales recruiting for the third Crusade with Archbishop Baldwin of Canterbury.

David Craig, *On the Crofter's Trail* (UK Jonathan Cape). Using anecdotes and interviews with descendants, Craig conveys the hardship and tragedy of the Highland Clearances without being mawkish.

Daniel Defoe, *Tour through the Whole Island of Great Britain* (Penguin). Classic travelogue, opening a window onto Britain in the 1720s.

Charles Jennings, *Up North* (Little, Brown). A provocative, but very readable account of a journey round the north of England, by a self-confessed southerner.

Jan Morris, *The Matter of Wales* (Penguin). Prolific half-Welsh travel writer Jan Morris immerses herself in the country that she evidently loves. Highly partisan and fiercely nationalistic, the book combs over the origins of the Welsh character and describes the people and places of Wales with precision and affection. A magnificent introduction to a diverse, and occasionally perverse, nation.

George Orwell, *The Road to Wigan Pier*, *Down and Out in Paris and London* (both Penguin). *Wigan Pier* depicts the effects of the Great Depression on the industrial communities of Lancashire and Yorkshire; *Down and Out* is Orwell's tramp's-eye view of the world, written with first-hand experience – the London section is particularly harrowing.

Samuel Pepys, *The Diary of Samuel Pepys* (HarperCollins/University of California); *The Illustrated Pepys* (Unwin/University of California). Pepys kept a voluminous diary from 1660 until 1669, recording the fall of the Commonwealth, the Restoration, the Great Plague and the Great Fire, as well as describing the daily life of the nation's capital. The unabridged version is published in eleven weighty tomes; Penguin has published an abridged version; Unwin's is made up of just the choicest extracts.

J.B. Priestley, *English Journey* (Mandarin/University of Chicago Press). Account of Bradford-born author's travels around England in the 1930s.

Gilbert White, *Natural History of Selborne* (Penguin//Tuttle). Masterpiece of nature writing, observing the seasons in a Hampshire village.

Dorothy Wordsworth, *Journals* (Oxford University Press). Engaging diaries of Willy's sister, with whom he shared Dove Cottage in the Lake District.

HISTORY, SOCIETY AND POLITICS

Leslie Alcock, *Arthur's Britain* (Penguin). Info-laden assemblage of all archeological and written evidence on the shadowy centuries after the Roman occupation of Britain.

Venerable Bede, *Ecclesiastical History of the English People* (Penguin). First-ever English history, written in seventh-century Northumbria.

Asa Briggs, *Social History of England* (Weidenfeld & Nicolson/Trafalgar Square). Immensely accessible overview of English life from Roman times to the 1980s.

David Daiches, (ed) *A Companion to Scottish Culture* (Polygon/Holmes & Meier). More than 300 articles interpreting Scottish culture in its widest sense, from eating to marriage customs, the Scottish Enlightenment to children's street games.

Friedrich Engels, *The Conditions of the Working Class in England* (Penguin/Oxford University Press). Portrait of life in England's hellish industrial towns, written in 1844 when Engels was only 24.

Geoffrey of Monmouth, *History of the Kings of Britain* (Penguin). First published in 1136 this is the basis of almost all Arthurian legend. Writers throughout Europe and beyond used Geoffrey's unreliable history as the basis of a complex corpus of myth.

Christopher Hill, *The English Revolution* (Lawrence & Wishart/Beekman Publishers o/p); *The World Turned Upside-Down* (Penguin). Britain's foremost Marxist historian, Hill is without doubt the most interesting writer on the Civil War and Commonwealth period.

Philip Jenkins, *A History of Modern Wales 1536–1990* (Longman). Magnificently thorough book, placing Welsh history in its British and European contexts. Unbiased and rational appraisal of events and the struggle to preserve Welsh consciousness, with enough detail to make it of valuable academic interest and sufficient good humour to make it easily readable.

J. Graham Jones, *The History of Wales* (University of Wales). The best step forward from our own entry-level history section, this concise, easy-paced overview of Welsh life comes with a welcome bias towards social history.

Michael Lynch, *Scotland: A New History* (UK Pimlico). Probably the best available overview of Scottish history, going up to 1991 and the bid for a national parliament.

John McLeod, *No Great Mischief If You Fall* (Mainstream/Trafalgar). Gloom and doom on the rape of the Highlands; an enraging, bleak but stimulating book debunking some of the myths upheld by the Highland industry.

E.P. Thompson, *The Making of the English Working Class* (Penguin/Random House). A seminal text – essential reading for anyone who wants to understand the fabric of British society.

Wynford Vaughan-Thomas, *Wales – a History* (Michael Joseph). One of the country's most missed broadcasters and writers, Vaughan-Thomas' masterpiece is this warm and spirited history of Wales. Working chronologically through from the pre-Celtic dawn to the aftermath of the 1979 devolution vote, the book offers perhaps the clearest explanation of the evolution of Welsh culture, with the author's patriotic slant evident throughout.

Jennifer Westwood, *Albion: A Guide to Legendary Britain* (Grafton/Salem House). Highly readable volume on the development of myth in literature, with a section on Scottish legends.

REGIONAL GUIDES

William Condry, *Snowdonia* (David & Charles). A personal guided tour around the Snowdonia National Park dipping into geology, natural history and industrial heritage. The best detailed approach to the region.

Robert M. Cooper, *The Literary Guide and Companion to Northern England* (Ohio University Press). An informative travelogue around Northern England, focusing on the region's literary figures. The author has also written literary guides to Middle England and Southern England.

Joe Fisher, *The Glasgow Encyclopedia* (Mainstream/Trafalgar). The essential Glasgow reference book, covering nearly every facet of this complex urban society.

Christopher Hibbert (ed), *Pimlico County History Guides* (UK Pimlico). An informative series giving a detailed history of selected English counties. Currently available are guides to Bedfordshire, Dorset, Norfolk, Somerset (with Bath and Bristol), Suffolk and Sussex.

Daphne du Maurier, *Vanishing Cornwall* (Penguin/Doubleday o/p). Good overall account of Cornwall from an author who lived most of her life there.

Richard Muir, *The Coastlines of Britain* (UK Macmillan o/p). An exploration of all aspects of Britain's varied coast with chapters on cliffs, beach, dunes, flora and fauna.

Ben Weinreb and Christopher Hibbert, *The London Encyclopaedia* (Papermac/St Martin's Press o/p). More than one thousand pages of concisely presented and well-illustrated information on London past and present – the most fascinating single book on the capital.

ART, ARCHITECTURE AND ARCHEOLOGY

Samantha Hardingham, *England: A Guide to Recent Architecture* (UK Ellipsis). A handy pocket-sized book detailing the best of England's modern buildings.

Andrew Hayes, *Archaeology of the British Isles* (Batsford/St Martin's Press). Useful introductory history from Stone Age caves to early medieval settlements.

Duncan MacMillan *Scottish Art 1460–1990* (Mainstream/Trafalgar). Lavish overview of Scottish painting with good sections on landscape, portraiture and the Glasgow Boys.

Nikolaus Pevsner, *The Englishness of English Art* (UK Penguin). Wide-ranging romp through English art concentrating on Hogarth, Reynolds, Blake and Constable, including a section on the Perpendicular style and landscape gardening.

Nikolaus Pevsner and others, *The Buildings of England & Wales* (UK Penguin). Magisterial series, at least one volume per county, covering just about every inhabitable structure in the country. This project was initially a one-man show, but later authors have revised Pevsner's text, inserting newer buildings but generally respecting the founder's personal tone.

T.W. Potter and Catherine Johns, *Roman Britain* (British Museum Press/Harvard University Press). Generously illustrated account of Roman occupation written by the British Museum's own curators.

LITERATURE CLASSICS

Jane Austen, *Northanger Abbey; Persuasion* (both Penguin). The early *Northanger Abbey* is a parody of the Gothic novel and also a satirical portrait of Bath's spa society, which features prominently too in *Persuasion*, her late masterpiece.

Emily Brontë, *Wuthering Heights* (Penguin). The ultimate bodice-ripper, complete with volcanic passions, craggy landscapes, ghostly presences and gloomy Calvinist villagers.

Charlotte Brontë, *Jane Eyre* (Penguin). Not so many bodices ripped, though still plenty of Calvinism in this quietly feminist story of a much put-upon governess.

R.D. Blackmore, *Lorna Doone* (Penguin/Oxford University Press). Blackmore's swashbuckling, melodramatic romance, set on Exmoor, has done more for West Country tourism than anything else since.

Geoffrey Chaucer, *Canterbury Tales* (Penguin/Bantam). Fourteenth-century collection of bawdy verse tales told during a pilgrimage to Becket's shrine at Canterbury, translated into modern English blank verse.

Charles Dickens, *Bleak House; David Copperfield; Little Dorritt; Oliver Twist; Hard Times* (all Penguin). Many of Dickens's novels are set in London, including *Bleak House, Oliver Twist* and *Little Dorritt*, which contain some of his most trenchant pieces of social analysis; *Hard Times*, however, is set in a Lancashire mill town, while *David Copperfield* draws on Dickens's own unhappy experiences as a boy, with much of the action taking place in Kent and Norfolk.

George Eliot, *Scenes of Clerical Life; Middlemarch* (both Penguin); *Mill on the Floss* (Penguin/Oxford University Press). Eliot (real name Mary Ann Evans) wrote mostly about the county of her birth, Warwickshire, setting for the three depressing tales from her fictional début, *Scenes of Clerical Life. Middlemarch* is a gargantuan portrayal of English provincial life prior to the Reform Act of 1832, while *Mill on the Floss* is based on her own childhood experiences.

Henry Fielding, *Tom Jones* (Penguin). Mock-epic comic novel detailing the exploits of its lusty orphan hero, set in Somerset and London.

Elizabeth Gaskell, *Sylvia's Lovers; Mary Barton* (both Penguin). *Sylvia's Lovers* is set in a Whitby (Monkshaven in the novel) beset by press gangs, while *Mary Barton* takes place in Manchester and has strong Chartist undertones.

Thomas Hardy, *Far from the Madding Crowd*; *The Mayor of Casterbridge*; *Tess of the D'Urbevilles*; *Jude the Obscure* (all Penguin). Hardy's novels contain some famously evocative descriptions of his native Dorset, but at the time of their publication it was Hardy's defiance of conventional pieties that attracted most attention: *Tess*, in which the heroine has a baby out of wedlock and commits murder, shocked his contemporaries, while his bleakest novel, the Oxford-set *Jude the Obscure*, provoked such a violent response that Hardy gave up novel-writing altogether.

Rudyard Kipling, *Stalky & Co* (Oxford University Press). Nine stories about a mischievous trio of schoolboys, drawn from Kipling's experiences of public school in Devon.

The Mabinogion Gwyn and Thomas Jones (transl) (Everyman's). Welsh mythology's classic, these eleven heroic tales were transcribed into the Book of Rhydderch (around 1300–25) and the Red Book of Hergest (1375–1425).

Sir Thomas Malory, *La Morte d'Arthur* (Penguin/Northwestern University Press*)*. Fifteenth-century tales of King Arthur and the Knights of the Round Table, written while the author was in London's Newgate Prison.

Thomas De Quincey, *Confessions of an English Opium Eater* (Penguin/Oxford University Press). Tripping out with the most famous literary drug-taker after Coleridge – *Fear and Loathing in Las Vegas* it isn't, but neither is this a simple cautionary tale.

Sir Walter Scott, *The Waverley Novels* (Penguin). The books that did much to create the romanticized version of Scottish life and history. Recently the first titles in a new series of critical editions have been published by Edinburgh University Press: *Kennilworth; Tale of Old Mortality; Black Dwarf; St Ronan's Well* and *The Antiquary*.

William Shakespeare, *Complete Works* (Oxford University Press/Random House). The entire output at a bargain price. For individual plays, you can't beat the *Arden Shakespeare* series (Routledge), each volume containing illuminating notes and good introductory essays.

Lawrence Sterne, *Tristram Shandy* (Penguin). Anarchic, picaresque eighteenth-century ramblings based on life in a small English village, and full of bizarre textual devices – like an all-black page in mourning for one of the characters.

R.L. Stevenson *Dr Jekyll and Mr Hyde* (Penguin/Vintage); *Kidnapped* (Penguin/Signet); *The Master of Ballantrae* (Penguin/Oxford University Press); *Weir of Hermiston* (UK Penguin). Nineteenth-century tales of intrigue and adventure.

William Makepeace Thackeray, *Vanity Fair* (Penguin). A sceptical but compassionate overview of English capitalist society by one of the leading realists of the mid-nineteenth century.

TWENTIETH-CENTURY WORKS

Peter Ackroyd, *English Music* (UK Penguin). A typical Ackroyd novel, constructing parallels between interwar London and distant epochs to conjure a kaleidoscopic vision of English culture. His other novels, such as *Chatterton*, *Hawksmoor* and *The House of Doctor Dee*, are variations on his preoccupation with the English psyche's darker depths.

Martin Amis, *London Fields* (Penguin/Random House). "Ferociously witty, scabrously scatological and balefully satirical" observation of low-life London, or pretentious drivel from literary London's favourite bad boy, depending on your viewpoint.

Iain Banks, *The Bridge* (UK Sphere); *The Crow Road* (UK Abacus). Banks' work can be funny, pacey, thought-provoking, imaginative and downright disgusting, but never dull.

Arnold Bennett, *Anna of the Five Towns*; *Clayhanger Trilogy* (both Penguin). Bennett's first novel, *Anna*, is the story of a miser's daughter and like the later *Clayhanger* trilogy is set in the Potteries.

George Mackay Brown, *Beside the Ocean of Time* (John Murray). A child's journey through the history of an Orkney island, and an adult's effort to make sense of the place's secrets in the late twentieth century.

John Buchan, *The Complete Richard Hannay* (UK Penguin/Godine). This one volume includes *The 39 Steps, Greenmantle, Mr Standfast, The Three Hostages* and *The Island of Sheep*. Good gung-ho stories with a great feel for Scottish landscape. In the US, both Oxford University Press and Godine publish various editions of the Hannay stories.

Bruce Chatwin, *On the Black Hill* (Picador). This entertaining and finely wrought novel follows the Jones twins' eighty-year tenure of a farm on the Radnorshire border with England. Chatwin casts his sharp eye for detail over both the minutiae of nature and the universal human condition providing a wonderfully gentle angle on Welsh–English antipathy.

Joseph Conrad, *The Secret Agent* (Penguin). Spy story based on the 1906 Anarchist bombing of Greenwich Observatory, exposing the hypocrisies of both the police and Anarchists.

E.M. Forster, *Howard's End* (Penguin/NAL-Dutton). Bourgeois angst in Hertfordshire and Shropshire; the best book by one of the country's best-loved modern novelists.

John Fowles, *The Collector* (Pan/Dell); *The French Lieutenant's Woman*; *Daniel Martin* (both Pan/NAL-Dutton). *The Collector*, Fowles's first, is a psychological thriller in which the heroine is kidnapped by a psychotic poolswinner, the story being told once by each protagonist. *The French Lieutenant's Woman*, set in Lyme Regis on the Dorset coast, is a tricksy neo-Victorian novel with a famous DIY ending. *Daniel Martin* is a dense, realistic novel set in postwar Britain.

Lewis Grassic Gibbon, *A Scots Quair* (Penguin/Schocken o/p). A landmark trilogy, set in northeast Scotland during and after World War I, the events are seen through the eyes of Chris Guthrie, "torn between her love for the land and her desire to escape a peasant culture". Strong, seminal work.

William Golding, *The Spire* (Faber/Harcourt Brace). Atmospheric novel centred on the building of a cathedral spire, taking place in a thinly disguised medieval Salisbury.

Robert Graves, *Goodbye to All That* (Penguin/Hippocrene Books o/p). Horrific and humorous memoirs of public school and World War I trenches, followed by postwar trauma and life in Wales, Oxford and Egypt.

Alasdair Gray, *Lanark* (Canongate/Braziller o/p). A postmodern blend of social realism and labyrinthine fantasy: Gray's extraordinary debut as a novelist, with his own allegorical illustrations, takes invention and comprehension to their limits.

Graham Greene, *Brighton Rock* (Penguin); *The Human Factor* (Penguin/Pocket Books). Two of the best from the prolific Greene: *Brighton Rock* is an action-packed thriller with heavy Catholic overtones, set in the criminal underworld of a seaside resort; *The Human Factor*, written some forty years later, probes the underworld of London's spies.

James Kelman, *The Busconductor Hines* (UK Phoenix). The wildly funny story of a young Glasgow bus conductor with an intensely boring job and a limitless imagination. *How Late It Was, How Late* (Secker & Warburg/Norton) is Kelman's award-winning and controversial look at life from the perspective of a blind Glaswegian drunk. A disturbing study of personal and political violence, with language to match.

D.H. Lawrence, *Sons and Lovers*; *The Rainbow*; *Women in Love* (all Penguin); *Selected Short Stories* (Penguin/Dover). Before he got his funny ideas about sex and became all messianic, Lawrence wrote magnificent prose on daily working-class life in Nottinghamshire's pit villages. His early short stories contain some of his finest writing, as does the early *Sons and Lovers*, a fraught, autobiographical novel.

Laurie Lee, *Cider with Rosie* (Penguin). Reminiscences of adolescent bucolic frolics in the Cotswolds during the 1920s.

Richard Llewellyn, *How Green Was My Valley* (Penguin); *Up into the Singing Mountain* (o/p); *Down Where the Moon is Small* (o/p); *Green, Green My Valley Now* (o/p). Vital tetralogy in eloquent and passionate prose following the life of Huw Morgan from his youth in a south Wales mining valley through emigration to the Welsh community in Patagonia and back to 1970s Wales. A best seller during World War II and still the best introduction to the vast canon of "valleys novels", *How Green was my Valley?* captured a longing for a simple, if tough, life steering clear of cloying sentimentality.

Daphne du Maurier, *Frenchman's Creek* (Arrow/Bentley); *Jamaica Inn*; *Rebecca* (both Arrow/Avon). Nail-biting, swashbuckling romantic novels set in the author's adopted home of Cornwall.

William McIlvanney, *A Gift from Nessus* (UK Mainstream). Moral tale set in 1960s Glasgow that counterposes the outward trappings of materialism with the emptiness of our inner life.

Compton Mackenzie, *Whisky Galore* (UK Penguin). Comic novel based on a true story of the wartime wreck of a cargo of whisky on a Hebridean island. Full of predictable stereotypes but still funny.

Muriel Spark, *The Prime of Miss Jean Brodie* (Penguin/NAL Dutton). Wonderful evocation of middle-class Edinburgh life and aspirations, still apparent in that city today.

Graham Swift, *Waterland* (Picador/Random House). Family saga set in East Anglia's fenlands – excellent on the history and appeal of this superficially drab landscape.

Dylan Thomas, *Under Milk Wood* (Dent Everyman). His most popular play, telling the story of a microcosmic Welsh seaside town over a 24-hour period. *Collected Stories* (Dent Everyman). Far better than buying any of the single editions, this book contains all of Thomas' classic prose pieces: *Quite Early One Morning*, which metamorphosed into *Under Milk Wood*, the magical *A Child's Christmas in Wales* and the compulsive, crackling autobiography of *Portrait of the Artist as a Young Dog*.

Jeff Torrington, *Swing Hammer Swing* (UK Minerva). Gripping contemporary account of working-class Glasgow, centred on a week in the life of Tam Clay.

Evelyn Waugh, *Sword of Honour Trilogy* (Penguin/Knopf); *Brideshead Revisited* (Penguin/Little, Brown). The trilogy is a brilliant satire of the World War I officer class laced with some of Waugh's funniest set-pieces. The best-selling *Brideshead Revisited* is possibly his worst book, rank with snobbery, nostalgia and money-worship.

Irvine Welsh, *Trainspotting; The Acid House* (both UK Minerva); *Marabou Stork Nightmares* (UK Jonathan Cape). Depending on the strength of your stomach, these trawls through the horrors of drug addiction, sexual fantasy, urban decay and hopeless youth will either make you rejoice at an authentic and unapologetic new voice for the dispossessed, or throw up. Thankfully, Welsh's unflinching attention is not without humour.

Virginia Woolf, *Orlando* (Penguin/Harcourt Brace); *Mrs Dalloway* (Flamingo/Harcourt Brace). Woolf's lover, Vita Sackville-West, is the model for the eponym of *Orlando*, whose life spans four centuries and both genders. *Mrs Dalloway*, which relates the thoughts of a London society hostess and a shell-shocked war veteran, sees Woolf's "stream of consciousness" style in full flow.

ANTHOLOGIES

English Mystery Plays (Penguin). These simple Christian tales were produced annually in Chester, York, Wakefield and other great English towns, and are often revived even now.

English Verse, ed. J. Hayward (Penguin). Overview from Sir Thomas Wyatt to Auden, Spender and MacNiece.

Literature of Renaissance England, ed. Hollander & Kermode (Oxford University Press). Spenser's *Faerie Queene*, a bit of Marlowe, Shakespeare's *Sonnets*, Donne, Jonson and Milton.

Medieval English Literature, ed. Trapp (Oxford University Press). Includes *Sir Gawain and the Green Knight*, *Beowulf* and extracts from Chaucer.

Modern British Literature, ed. Hollander & Kermode (Oxford University Press). Weighted towards the classic writers of the earlier part of the century – Hardy, Conrad, Lawrence etc.

The New Poetry, ed. Hulse, Kennedy & Morley (UK Bloodaxe). Over fifty UK poets, all born since World War II.

The Oxford Book of Scottish Verse, ed. John McQueen & Tom Scott (UK Oxford University Press). Claims to be the most comprehensive anthology of Scottish poetry ever published.

Oxford Companion to the Literature of Wales, ed. Meic Stephens (Oxford University Press). A customarily thorough volume of Welsh prose, spanning the centuries from the folk tales of the *Mabinogion* (see p.1005) to modern-day writings.

The Penguin Book of Scottish Verse, ed. Tom Scott. (UK Penguin). Good general selection.

The Restoration and the Eighteenth Century, ed. Price (Oxford University Press). From Dryden, Swift and Pope to Sterne.

Victorian Prose and Poetry, ed. Trilling & Bloom (Oxford University Press). Carlyle, Ruskin, Tennyson, Rossetti and Wilde's *Ballad of Reading Gaol*.

INDEX

HELP US UPDATE

We've endeavoured to make this guide as up-to-date as possible, but it's inevitable that some of the information will become inaccurate between now and the preparation of the next edition. Readers' updates and suggestions are very welcome – please mark letters "Rough Guide Britain Update" and send to:

Rough Guides, 1 Mercer Street, London WC2H 9QJ
  or
Rough Guides, 375 Hudson Street, 9th Floor, New York NY10014
  or
Britain@roughtravl.co.uk

In the UK, Rough Guides are available from all good bookstores, but can be obtained from Penguin by contacting: Penguin Direct, Penguin Books Ltd, Bath Road, Harmondsworth, West Drayton, Middlesex UB7 0DA; or telephone the credit line on 0181-899 4036 (9am–5pm) and ask for Penguin Direct. Visa, Access and Amex accepted. Delivery will normally be within 14 working days. Penguin Direct ordering facilities are only available in the UK and the USA. The availability and published prices quoted are correct at the time of going to press but are subject to alteration without prior

New York	1-85828-171-7	9.99	15.95	21.99
Pacific Northwest	1-85828-092-3	9.99	14.95	19.99
Paris	1-85828-125-3	7.99	13.95	16.99
Poland	1-85828-168-7	10.99	17.95	23.99
Portugal	1-85828-180-6	9.99	16.95	22.99
Prague	1-85828-122-9	8.99	14.95	19.99
Provence	1-85828-127-X	9.99	16.95	22.99
Pyrenees	1-85828-093-1	8.99	15.95	19.99
Romania	1-85828-097-4	9.99	15.95	21.99
San Francisco	1-85828-082-6	8.99	13.95	17.99
Scandinavia	1-85828-039-7	10.99	16.99	21.99
Scotland	1-85828-166-0	9.99	16.95	22.99
Sicily	1-85828-178-4	9.99	16.95	22.99
Singapore	1-85828-135-0	8.99	14.95	19.99
Spain	1-85828-081-8	9.99	16.95	20.99
St Petersburg	1-85828-133-4	8.99	14.95	19.99
Thailand	1-85828-140-7	10.99	17.95	24.99
Tunisia	1-85828-139-3	10.99	17.95	24.99
Turkey	1-85828-088-5	9.99	16.95	20.99
Tuscany & Umbria	1-85828-091-5	8.99	15.95	19.99
USA	1-85828-161-X	14.99	19.95	25.99
Venice	1-85828-170-9	8.99	14.95	19.99
Wales	1-85828-096-6	8.99	14.95	18.99
West Africa	1-85828-101-6	15.99	24.95	34.99
More Women Travel	1-85828-098-2	9.99	14.95	19.99
Zimbabwe & Botswana	1-85828-041-9	10.99	16.95	21.99

Phrasebooks

Czech	1-85828-148-2	3.50	5.00	7.00
French	1-85828-144-X	3.50	5.00	7.00
German	1-85828-146-6	3.50	5.00	7.00
Greek	1-85828-145-8	3.50	5.00	7.00
Italian	1-85828-143-1	3.50	5.00	7.00
Mexican	1-85828-176-8	3.50	5.00	7.00
Portuguese	1-85828-175-X	3.50	5.00	7.00
Polish	1-85828-174-1	3.50	5.00	7.00
Spanish	1-85828-147-4	3.50	5.00	7.00
Thai	1-85828-177-6	3.50	5.00	7.00
Turkish	1-85828-173-3	3.50	5.00	7.00
Vietnamese	1-85828-172-5	3.50	5.00	7.00

Reference

Classical Music	1-85828-113x	12.99	19.95	25.99
Internet	1-85828-198-9	5.00	8.00	10.00
World Music	1-85828-017-6	16.99	22.95	29.99
Jazz	1-85828-137-7	16.99	24.95	34.99

In the USA charge your order by Master Card or Visa (US$15.00 minimum order): call 1-800-253-6476; or send orders, with complete name, address and zip code, and list price, plus $2.00 shipping and handling per order to: Consumer Sales, Penguin USA, PO Box 999 – Dept #17109, Bergenfield, NJ 07621. No COD. Prepay foreign orders by international money order, a cheque drawn on a US bank, or US currency. No postage stamps are accepted. All orders are subject to stock availability at the time they are processed. Refunds will be made for books not available at that time. Please allow a minimum of four weeks for delivery.

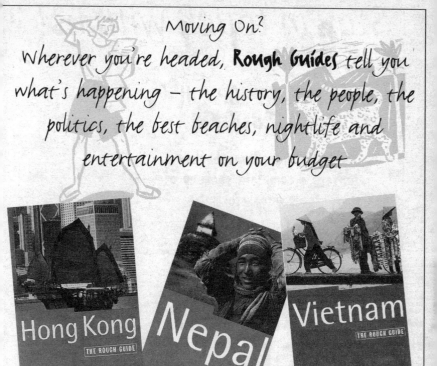

Stay in touch with us!

ROUGH*NEWS* is Rough Guides' free newsletter.
In three issues a year we give you news, travel
issues, music reviews, readers' letters and the
latest dispatches from authors on the road.

THE LOWEST PRICE CAR RENTAL AROUND THE

AND THAT'S A PROMISE†

For convenient, low-price car rental – all around the world – choose Holiday Autos. With a network of over 4,000 locations in 42 countries, when you're off globetrotting you won't have to go out of your way to find us.

What's more, with our lowest price promise, you won't be flying round and round in circles to be sure you're getting the best price.

With Holiday Autos you can be sure of the friendly, efficient service you'd expect from the UK's leading leisure car rental company. After all, we've won the Travel Trade Gazette 'Best Leisure Car Rental Company' award and the Independent Travel Agents' 'Top Leisure Car Rental Company' award time and time again. So, we've quite a reputation to maintain.

With Holiday Autos you simply don't need to search the globe for down-to-earth low prices.

For further information see your local Travel Agent or call us direct on **0990 300 400**

Holiday Autos
WE KNOW YOU HAVE A CHOICE

†Our lowest price promise refers to our pledge to undercut by £5 any other equivalent offer made at the same price or less by an independent UK car rental company for a booking made in the UK prior to departure. Holiday Autos undercut offer is valid unless and until withdrawn by Holiday Autos.

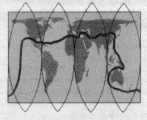